ADVANCES IN WAVELET THEORY AND THEIR APPLICATIONS IN ENGINEERING, PHYSICS AND TECHNOLOGY

Edited by **Dumitru Baleanu**

INTECHOPEN.COM

Advances in Wavelet Theory and Their Applications in Engineering, Physics and Technology
Edited by Dumitru Baleanu

Published by InTech

Janeza Trdine 9, 51000 Rijeka, Croatia

Edition 2014

Publishing Process Manager Vana Persen

Technical Editor Teodora Smiljanic

Cover Designer InTech Design Team

Additional hard copies can be obtained from orders@intechopen.com

Advances in Wavelet Theory and Their Applications in Engineering, Physics and Technology, Edited by Dumitru Baleanu
p. cm.
ISBN 978-953-51-0494-0

INTECH

open science | open minds

Contents

Preface

Wavelets are functions fulfilling certain mathematical requirements and used in representing data or other functions. The basic idea behind wavelets is to analyze according to scale. Wavelets received considerable attention in the last years because they are very appropriate for application in practical problems in areas of Engineering, Physics and Technology.

The book is organized in five main sections denoted as Signal Processing, Electrical Systems, Fault Diagnosis and Monitoring, Image Processing and Applications in Engineering.

The wavelet method is used in this book to extract more information than the standard techniques from a given complex signal and it has capabilities for the deconvolution framework. Applications of wavelet transform to the image processing, audio compression and communication systems are also reported.

The applications of wavelet transform in the field of power system dynamics and stability, in fault diagnosis of analogue electronic circuits as well as for practical condition monitoring issues are covered by this book. In addition the application of wavelet analysis combined with artificial neural networks as automatic rolling bearing fault detection and diagnosis is illustrated. The use of the wavelet transform to the denoising process is an important chapter of this book. The reader can see how the wavelet transform was used as a classification criterion applied to improve the compression of the hyper-spectral images.

The last chapter of the book presents some specific applications of the wavelet transform in engineering, e.g. to robust lossless data hiding by feature-based bit embedding algorithm, for the understanding of vortex-induced vibration, in rotorcraft UAV's integrated navigation system. Also, a constructive design methodology for multi-resolution- scalable mesh compression systems is presented.

The chapters of this book present the problems for which wavelet transform is best well-suited, indicates how to implement the corresponding algorithms efficiently, and finally show how to assign the appropriate wavelets for a specified application.

Researchers, working in the field of the wavelet transform, will find several open problems being mentioned within this book. Both theoretical considerations as well as the corresponding applications are clearly presently in such a way to be understandable by a large variety of readers.

Dumitru Baleanu
Cankaya University, Faculty of Art and Sciences
Department of Mathematics and Computer Sciences, Ankara, Turkey

Institute of Space Sciences, Magurele-Bucharest, Romania

Part 1

Signal Processing

1

Real-Time DSP-Based License Plate Character Segmentation Algorithm Using 2D Haar Wavelet Transform

Zoe Jeffrey[1], Soodamani Ramalingam[1] and Nico Bekooy[2]

[1]*School of Engineering and Technology, University of Hertfordshire,*
[2]*CitySync Ltd., Welwyn Garden City,*
UK

1. Introduction

The potential applications of Wavelet Transform (WT) are limitless including image processing, audio compression and communication systems. In image processing, WT is used in applications such as image compression, denoising, speckle removal, feature analysis, edge detection and object detection. The use of WT algorithms in image processing for real-time custom applications may require dedicated processors such as Digital Signal Processor (DSPs), Field Programmable Gate Arrays (FPGAs) and Graphics Processing Units (GPUs) as reported in (Ma et al., 2000), (Benkrid et al., 2001) and (Wong et al., 2007) respectively.

The interest in this chapter is the use of WT in image objects segmentation, in particular, in the area of Automatic Number Plate Recognition (ANPR) also known as License Plate Recognition (LPR). ANPR algorithm is normally divided into three sections namely LP candidate detection, character segmentation and recognition. The focus of this chapter is on the use of Haar WT algorithms for License Plate (LP) character segmentation on a DSP using Standard Definition (SD) and High Definition (HD) images. This is an extension of the work reported in (Musoromy et al., 2010) by the authors, where Daubechies and Haar WT are used to detect image edges and to enhance features of an image to detect a LP region that contain characters. The work in (Musoromy et al., 2010) demonstrated that 2D Haar WT is favourable in ANPR using DSP due to its ability to operate in real-time. The drive here is the consumer interest in real-time standalone embedded ANPR systems. The next section describes the proposed LP character segmentation algorithm.

The chapter organisation is as follows: Section (2) reviews dedicated hardware for WT-based image processing algorithms. Section (3) gives a review of image processing techniques using WT and in ANPR application. Section (4) presents the proposed LP character segmentation algorithm based on 2D Haar WT edge detector. Section (5) presents experimental setup. Section (6) presents results and analysis. Section (7) gives conclusion and Section (8) gives references.

2. Dedicated hardware for WT review

The objective of this work is to investigate a suitable hardware that is able to perform image processing algorithms using WT in real time. Processing an image with the WT filter is faster in terms of computational cost in applications such as edge detection where a single filter is capable of producing three types of edges in comparison to standard methods where more than one filter masks are required to achieve the same results. In this section we review the special hardware dedicated for WT including DSPs, FPGAs and GPUs.

GPUs provide programmable vertex and pixel engines that accelerates algorithm mapping such as image processing. An example of a cost effective SIMD algorithm that performs the convolution-based DWT completely on a GPU using a normal PC (baseline processor) is reported by Wong (Wong et al., 2007). It is reported, the algorithm unifies forward and inverse WT to an almost identical process for efficient implementation on the GPU through parallel processing (Wong et al., 2007). This demonstrate that GPUs are capable of processing WT algorithms cost effectively, however it is not suitable for our application, which is PC independent.

An example of a scalable FPGA-based architecture for the separable 2-D Biorthogonal Discrete Wavelet Transform (DWT) decomposition is presented by (Benkrid et al., 2001). The architecture is based on the Pyramid Algorithm Analysis, which handles computation along the border efficiently by using the method of symmetric extension using Xilinx Virtex-E (Benkrid et al., 2001). FPGA's are suitable for real-time embedded applications due to their parallel processing abilities.

DSPs are also reported to be powerful and portable for embedded systems. An example system by Desneux and Legat (Desneux & Legat, 2000) show a DSP with an architecture designed specifically for DWT. Their DSP design stops any wait cycles during algorithm execution by using a bi-processor organization. It is able to perform a 3-stage multiresolution transform in real time. Their DSP is fully programmable in terms of filters and picture format as well as being capable of image edge processing.

Using a floating-point DSP, Patil and Abel (Patil & Abel, 2006) used redundant wavelet transform as a tool for the analysis of non-stationary signals as well as the localization and characterization of singularities. Their work focused on producing an optimized method for the implementation of a B-spline based redundant wavelet transform (RWT) using a (DSP) for integer scales leads to an improvement in the execution speed over the standard method.

A DSP-based edge detection comparison is explained in (Abdel-Qader & Maddix, 2005) where three edge detection algorithms performance on DSP are compared using Canny, Prewitt and Haar wavelet-based. The reported outcome is that the Haar wavelet-based edge detector performed best in terms of SNR in noisy images. The authors recommended post-processing of the output edges to make them more optimal.

The review favours DSPs as a suitable choice for our ANPR application. In addition, following successful results in LP detection using a DSP as reported in (Musoromy et al., 2010) using WT, this work extends the use of WT in the LP character segmentation investigation of SD and HD images using a Texas Instrument's C64plus DSP with minimum of 600MHZ clock speed and 1MB of RAM (TI, 2006).

3. Image processing and ANPR using WT

This section gives a review of interesting ANPR algorithms using WT. The use of discrete wavelet transform (DWT) (described in Section 4.2) in ANPR is reported by Wu (Wu et al., 2009) in LP detection process. The methodology works by applying the **"high-low"** subband feature of 2D Haar DWT twice to increase the recognition of vertical edges while decreasing background noise in real world applications. The authors noted an increase in the ease of location and extraction of the license plate by orthogonal projection histogram analysis from the scene image in comparison with the vertical Sobel operator (a single level 2D Haar DWT) used in most License Plate Detection Algorithms. However, due to the down-sampling used in this technique, it is only suitable for use with high-resolution images or cameras in close proximity to the plate (Wu et al., 2009).

An interesting algorithm is proposed by Roomi (Roomi et al., 20011) that consists of two main modules, one for the rough detection of the region of interest (ROI) using vertical gradients and another for the accurate localisation of vertical edges using the vertical subband feature of 2D discrete wavelet transform (DWT). This is followed by the identification of the orthogonal projection histogram for the extraction of the license plate. This method combines the advantage of relatively short runtimes whilst still maintaining accuracy, across a range of vehicle types. The authors reported that the number plates recognition accuracy was reduced where the plates were tilted (Roomi et al., 20011).

WT is also used in the simplification of skew correction in order to reduce computational demands to make the process suitable for real time applications (Paunwala et al., 2010). The method uses two levels WT to extract a skewed feature image of the original LP image, which is then transformed into a binary image from which the feature points can be identified by applying a threshold. These feature points help identify the angle at which the plate is tilted using principal component analysis, from which the correction to the whole plate image can be applied (Paunwala et al., 2010).

To conclude, the use of WT and the advantages are widely reported in the ANPR algorithms and therefore the focus of this chapter is the suitability of WT in HD images and DSPs for real time performance in LP character segmentation but firstly, LP detection process used in this work is summarized in the following section.

3.1 LP detection algorithm

The LP detection is the first part of an ANPR algorithm, which gives the rectangle region that contains characters. The plate detection algorithm used here is divided into four parts. These are input image normalization, edges enhancement using filters, edges finding and linking to rectangles using connected component analysis (CCA) and plate candidate finding (Musoromy et al., 2010). We have used the edge finding method in (Musoromy et al., 2010) to verify the presence of an edge. The edge finding method works by scanning the image and a list of edges is found using contrast comparison between pixel intensities on the edges' boundaries using the original gray scale image. The WT methodologies described by the authors in the literature above are mainly applied to LP detection process and benchmarked on baseline processors. In this chapter, we have expanded the use of Haar based edges in LP character segmentation algorithm. In addition, we have applied these edges in HD images and benchmarked their DSP and baseline processor performance to meet real-time requirement.

4. LP character segmentation algorithm based on 2D Haar WT edge detector

In image processing, edge detection is the key pre-processing step for identifying the presence of objects in images. This is achieved by identifying the boundary regions of an object. There are several robust edge detection techniques widely reported in the literature from early works by Canny (Canny, 1986) and some of the most recent, such as Palacios (Palacios et al., 2011). However, in custom applications, such as embedded ANPR system where both real-time performance and LP recognition success is demanded, a choice of good edge detector that balances these two factors is important.

The proposed algorithm is based on 2D Haar WT edge detector, which is shown to enhance image edges and improve LP region detection in Musoromy (Musoromy et al., 2010). The algorithm used for LP region detection and extraction explained in Section 3.1 is adapted to perform LP character segmentation. The main reasons for adapting the Haar WT for character segmentation are:

- The ability of Haar WT to detect three types of edges using a single filter while traditional methods such as Sobel would require more than one mask for the operation
- Simplicity of the algorithm and its suitability in real-time application

The following sections describe the LP character segmentation algorithm based on a 2D Haar WT edge detector starting with the WT definition.

4.1 Wavelet Transform

In image processing, we can define a function f(x,y) as an image signal and Ψ(x,y) as a wavelet. A wavelet is a function of $\Psi \in L^2(R)$ used to localise a given function such as f(x,y) in both translation (u) and scaling (s). The family of wavelet is obtained by translation and scaling in time (t) using individual wavelet as given in equation (1) and (2) by (Mallat, 1999):

$$\Psi_{(u,s)}(t) = \frac{1}{\sqrt{s}}\Psi\left(\frac{t-u}{s}\right) \tag{1}$$

Wavelets are useful in transforming signals from one domain to another, giving useful information for easier analysis hence the term Wavelet Transform which can be defined as:

$$\mathrm{Wf}(\mathrm{u,s}) = \int_{-\infty}^{+\infty} f(t)\frac{1}{\sqrt{s}}\Psi^*\left(\frac{t-u}{s}\right)dt \tag{2}$$

This represents a Continuous WT (CWT) of a function f at scales s>0 and translated by $u \in R$, which can also be explained as a 1D. When processing an image, we can apply this wavelet in the x direction where $\Psi \in L^2(R)$ as follows:

$$\mathrm{Wf}(\mathrm{u,s}) = \int_{-\infty}^{+\infty} f(x)\frac{1}{\sqrt{s}}\Psi^*\left(\frac{x-u}{s}\right)dx \tag{3}$$

The x and y directions can represent rows and columns of an image f(x,y) ∈ $L^2(R^2)$ and therefore we can also apply the CWT in 2D using wavelet Ψ ∈ $L^2(R^2)$ as (Palacios et al., 2011):

$$W_{(s)}f(u,v) = \int_{-\infty}^{+\infty}\int_{-\infty}^{+\infty} f(x,y)\frac{1}{s}\Psi^*\left(\frac{x-u}{s},\frac{y-v}{s}\right) \tag{4}$$

We can rewrite equation (4) with dilation factor s as

$$\Psi_{(s)}(x,y) = \frac{1}{s}\Psi\left(\frac{x}{s},\frac{y}{s}\right) \tag{5}$$

and $\Psi^{\Theta}(x,y) = \Psi^{\Theta}(-x,-y)$ as a convolution

$$W_{(s)}f(u,v) = f^*\Psi_s^{\Theta}(u,v) \tag{6}$$

The large number of coefficients produced by CWT makes it necessary to discretely sample signals in order to simplify signal analysis process and also for the use in real-time applications such as image processing. This process is technically known as discrete wavelet transform (DWT).

4.2 Discrete Wavelet Transform

Discrete wavelet transform (DWT) or fast wavelet transform (FWT) is a specialised case of sub-band filtering, where DWT is a sampled signal of size N using scale at $s = 2^j$ for j < 0 and time (for scale 1) (Mallat, 1999). Using the wavelet equation:

$$\Psi_j[n] = \frac{1}{\sqrt{s}}\Psi\left(\frac{n}{s}\right) \tag{7}$$

DWT is also a circular convolution where:

$$\Psi^{\Theta}[n] = \Psi_j^*[n] \tag{8}$$

The convolution of signal f and the wavelet is written as follows:

$$Wf[n,s] = \sum_{m=0}^{N-1} f[m]\Psi_j^*[m-n] = f^*\Psi^{\Theta}[n] \tag{9}$$

Calculations of DWT is done using filter bank which can be a series of cascading digital filter. Implementing the DWT using filter banks entails the signal sampled being passed through high-pass and low-pass filters simultaneously to produce detailed and approximated confidents respectively (Qureshi, 2005). The high frequencies DWT are contained similar to equation (9) as follows:

$$W_{High}f[n,s] = \sum_{m=0}^{N-1} f[m]\Psi_j^*[m-n] = f^*\Psi^{\Theta}[n] \tag{10}$$

The low frequencies are contained in equation (12), in the computation of periodic scaling filter where the scaling function in equation (11) is sampled with scale z and integer k (Mallat, 1999). Let $\Phi^{\Theta}[n] = \Phi_k^*[n]$ be a convolution:

$$\Phi_k[n] = \frac{1}{\sqrt{s}}\Phi\left(\frac{n}{s}\right) \tag{11}$$

$$W_{Low}f[n,z] = \sum_{m=0}^{N-1} f[m]\Phi_k^*[m-n] = f*\Phi^{\Theta}[n] \tag{12}$$

The high-pass filter $h_{HP}[n]$ is formed from the low pass filter $h_{LP}[n]$ using the following equation (Qureshi, 2005):

$$h_{HP}[n] = -1^n h_{LP}[N-1-n], \qquad n = 0,\ldots, N-1 \tag{13}$$

where h is the filter and N is the number of taps in the low-pass filter. If the length N of analysis low-pass filter is 4, and

$$h_{LP} = \{h_0, h_1, h_2, h_3\} \tag{14}$$

Applying equation (13), we obtain:

$$h_{HP} = \{h_3, -h_2, h_1, -h_0\} \tag{15}$$

To analyse DWT the input signal $f_{(x,y)}[n]$ is passed through both filters explained in equations (10) and (12) to give filtered output y[n]. The output is then decimated or down sampled by a factor of two (Qureshi, 2005). Decimation means every other sample is taken from an input to form an output such that:

$$y[n] = f_{(x,y)}[2n] \tag{16}$$

The analysis of DWT with the resulting coefficients is shown in figure 1.

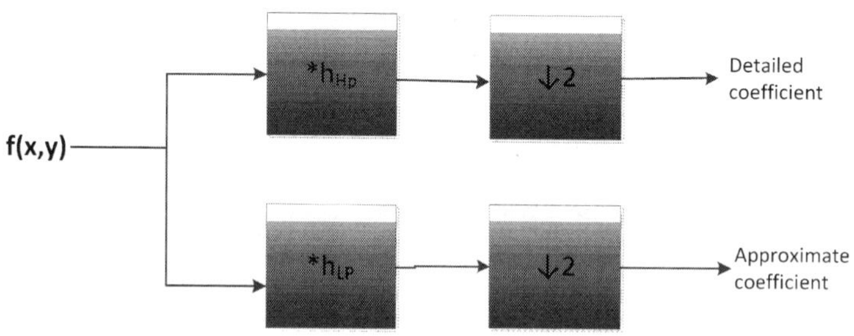

Fig. 1. Single level DWT (analysis stage of $f(x,y)$) (Mallat, 1999)

The 2D DWT of an image function f(x,y) of the size M x N can be written using wavelet functions in equation (17) and (18) (Mallat, 1999)

$$\varphi_{j_0,m,n}(x,y) = 2^{\frac{j_0}{2}}\,\varphi(2^{j_0}x - m, 2^{j_0}y - n) \tag{17}$$

$$\psi_{j,m,n}(x,y) = 2^{\frac{j}{2}}\,\psi(2^{j}x - m, 2^{j}y - n) \tag{18}$$

as follows:

$$W_{\varphi}(j_0, m, n) = \sum_{x=0}^{M}\sum_{y=0}^{N}\frac{1}{\sqrt{MN}}f(x, y)\varphi_{j_0,m,n}(x, y) \tag{19}$$

$$W_{\psi}^{i}(j, m, n) = \sum_{x=0}^{M}\sum_{y=0}^{N}\frac{1}{\sqrt{MN}}f(x, y)\psi_{j,m,n}^{i}(x, y) \tag{20}$$

where i= {1, 2, 3}.

At the end of analysis stage, the transformed image can be reconstructed back to an original image or to a new image using the inverse of DWT (IDWT). The reconstruction is a process of upsampling the wavelet coefficients by a factor of two and passed through reversed low-pass (g_{LP}) and high-pass (g_{HP}) filters simultaneously (Qureshi, 2005). The reconstruction to an original image is demonstrated in figure 2.

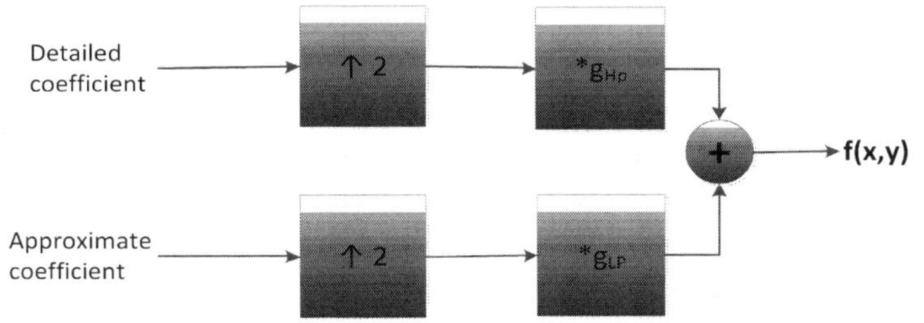

Fig. 2. Single level IDWT (reconstruction of $f(x,y)$) (mallat, 1999)

4.3 2D Haar WT

There is a countless number of wavelets available in the wavelet family with more being reported in the literature of wavelets (Mallat, 1999). For this application, we are interested in the simplest but efficient DWT. The Haar is the first and simplest WT in the family of wavelets (Haar, 1911). Haar WT is derived starting with Haar wavelet function defined as:

$$\Psi(x) = \begin{cases} 1 & 0 \le x < \frac{1}{2} \\ -1 & \frac{1}{2} \le x < 1 \\ 0 & Otherwise \end{cases} \tag{21}$$

and in 1D

$$\psi_{j,k,}(x) = \psi(2^j x - k) \tag{22}$$

Its scaling function $\varphi(x)$ can be defined as:

$$\varphi(x) = \begin{cases} 1 \; 0 \le x < 1 \\ 0 \;\; Otherwise \end{cases} \tag{23}$$

The Haar matrix can be obtained using the wavelets defined in equations (17) to (20) and applying the formula in (10) to form high-pass filter from the low pass filter. The simplest Haar 2x2 matrix when N is 2 is as follows:

$$H_2 = \begin{bmatrix} 1 & 1 \\ 1 & -1 \end{bmatrix} \tag{24}$$

and when N is 4 to give Haar 4x4 matrix as follows:

$$H_4 = \begin{bmatrix} 1 & 1 & 1 & 1 \\ 1 & 1 & -1 & -1 \\ 1 & -1 & 0 & 0 \\ 0 & 0 & 1 & -1 \end{bmatrix} \tag{25}$$

The Haar WT filter can be derived by transformation, for example transforming H_2 to:

$$H_2 = \frac{1}{\sqrt{2}} \begin{bmatrix} 1 & 1 \\ 1 & -1 \end{bmatrix} \tag{26}$$

The 2D Haar WT is computed similarly as shown in equations (14) to (17). The result of applying single level 2D Haar WT in an image is a decomposition of an image into four bands including a low-pass filtered approximation "low-low" (LL) sub image, which is the smaller version of the input image and three high-pass filtered detail subimages, "low-high" (LH), "high-low" (HL) and "high-high" (HH). The subbands and shown in figure 3 and the corresponding resulting images are shown in figure 4. In addition the images can also be discomposed using different levels with a series of cascading filter bank to produce a multi-resolution (Mallat, 1989).

LL	LH
HL	HH

Fig. 3. A Decomposed image into four bands using 2D Haar WT

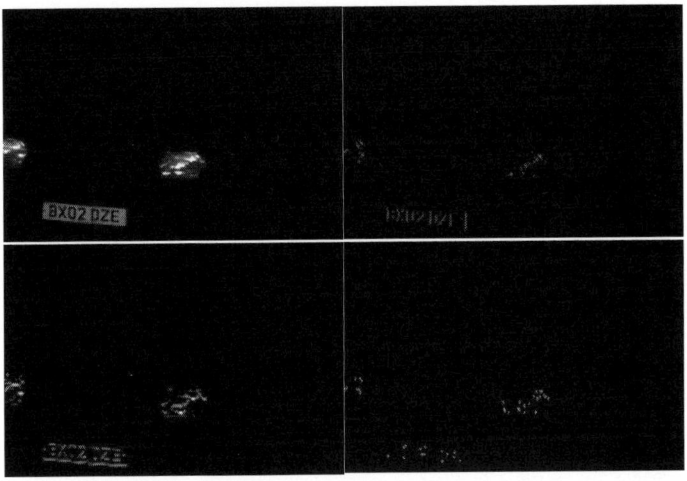

Fig. 4. Single level Haar WT decomposition (enhanced for display), the top left image is the LL, the top right image is LH, the bottom left image is HL and the bottom right image is the HH.

4.4 2D Haar WT based edge detector

The main advantage of applying 2D DWT such as Haar to an image is that it decomposes it to four sub images as seen in figure 4, which is mathematically less intensive operation and more suitable for our application. The suitable edges for our application are obtained by applying a 2D Haar WT (2x2) on an image f(x,y) to obtain high and low frequency subimages as shown by the following equation

$$f(x,y)\underset{DWT}{\rightarrow} a_{LL}(x,y)+ d_{LH}(x,y)+ d_{HL}(x,y)+ d_{HH}(x,y) \tag{27}$$

where d and a are the detailed and approximate components. The low frequency subimage $(a_{LL}(x,y))$ and the "high-high" $(d_{HH}(x,y))$ subimage are then removed from equation (27) to give the vertical $(d_{LH}(x,y))$ and horizontal $(d_{HL}(x,y))$ components $(d_{HV}(x,y))$.

At this stage, the edges can be computed using reconstruction through the use of wavelet transform modulus of $d_{LH}(x,y)$ and $d_{HV}(x,y)$ and then followed by the calculations of edge angles (Mallat, 1999). Alternatively, an estimate of the wavelet transform modulus of the horizontal and vertical components without taking into account the angle of the DWT as reported in (Qureshi, 2005). In this case, the wavelet modulus is compared to the local average. This is the approximation to the wavelet modulus maxima which is then compared to a global threshold dynamically calculated from the coefficients of the estimated modulus of the detail coefficients.

In our application, we choose to perform reconstruction on $d_{HV}(x,y)$ using inverse DWT (IDWT) using 2D Haar WT to obtain horizontal and vertical edges $(E_{HV}(x,y))$. This is computationally efficient on a DSP and it also provides enough edge details for our application. This process is shown in figure 5.

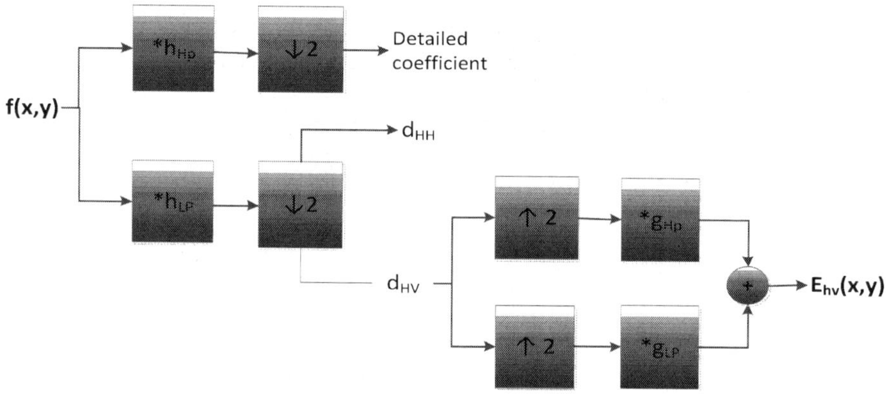

Fig. 5. A reconstruction of $d_{HV}(x,y)$ into $E_{HV}(x,y)$ using 2D IDWT

The absolute edges are then computed where $E_{HV}(x,y) = |E_{HV}(x,y)|$ and then post processing is applied to the edges to make them more prominent and inversion for optimal display is performed using an 8-bit dynamic range. Our application demands more edges and less noise therefore, an automatic thresholding method called autonomous percentile (P-tile) thresholding followed by histogram analysis (Qureshi, 2005).

P-tile histogram thresholding is used here due to the fact that the texts inside the license plate region covers a known region $1/p$ of the total image. The threshold is automatically detected such that $1/p$ of the image area has pixel intensities less than some threshold T knowing that the text is dark and the background is white or the other way around, which is easily determined through inspection. Starting with the normalized histogram is a probability distribution:

$$p(g) = \frac{n_g}{n} \tag{28}$$

That is, the number of pixels n_g having intensity g as a fraction of the total number of pixels n. The intensity level (c) of g is given as,

$$c(g)=\sum_{0}^{g}p(g) \tag{29}$$

Finally the threshold T is set such that

$$c(T)=\frac{1}{p} \tag{30}$$

The results from reconstruction of the vertical and horizontal edges, absolute edges and prominent edges using single level decomposition and reconstruction are shown in figure 6 and figure 7 respectively.

(a) (b)

Fig. 6. The original image is shown in (a) and the resulting image from reconstruction using single level IDWT is shown in (b)

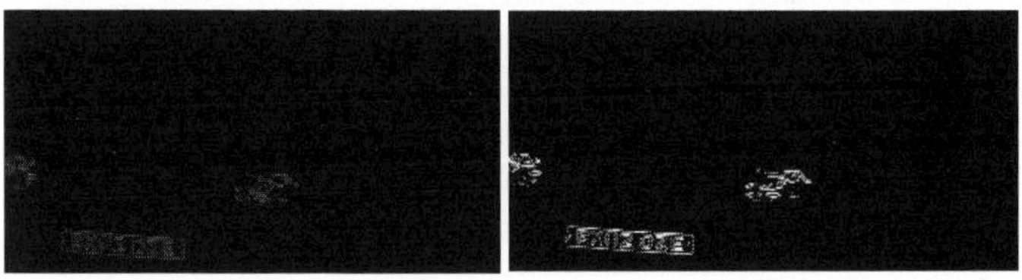

(a) (b)

Fig. 7. Absolute edges are shown on image (a) and image (b) shows prominent edges

(a) (b)

Fig. 8. The original license plate candidate image is shown in (a) and prominent edges in the LP candidate are shown in (b) using single level decomposition

(a) (b)

Fig. 9. The original license plate candidate image is shown in (a) and prominent edges in the LP candidate are shown in (b) two levels decomposition

4.5 LP character segmentation algorithm

The LP character segmentation process follows LP region detection as explained in Section 3.1. In this algorithm shown in figure 10, we segment the characters inside LP rectangle. The procedurals steps following LP detection include:

- Edge detection within the original LP region using 2d Haar WT
- Edge detection through grayscale variation analysis using original image
- Compare Haar edges with the grayscale variation analysis edges to validate the presence of edges as explained in Section 3.1
- Verification of candidate edges if a match is found
- Connecting edges using and drawing a rectangle around object
- Verification of character extraction using histogram analysis
- Compute bounding box

Algorithm listing 1: LP character segmentation based on 2D Haar WT

Let $f(x,y)$ *be an input image*
For each wavelet decomposition level $j = 1 \ldots N$
  Compute DWT coefficients at level j *based on Haar WT*
End
Let $d_{HV}(x,y)$ *be the horizontal and vertical coefficients at final level* N
Compute the reconstruction of $d_{HV}(x,y)$ *using IDWT*
Let $E_{HV}(x,y)$ *be the result from reconstruction*
Compute the absolute value
Let $E_{ABS}(x,y)$ *be the absolute edges*
Compute the prominent edges through optimal threshold T
Let E_{Haar} *be the prominent 2D Haar WT edges*
Compute contrast comparison on $f(x,y)$ *to find edges*
Let E_{CON} *be initial edges by contrast comparison*
Compare E_{CON} *to* E_{Haar} *to confirm edges*
Le E_{FIN} *be the final edges*
Compute connected component analysis on the final edges
Let CCA be the connected components
Compute histogram analysis on CCA to confirm characters
Let HA be the histogram analysis results
Compute bounding box around character

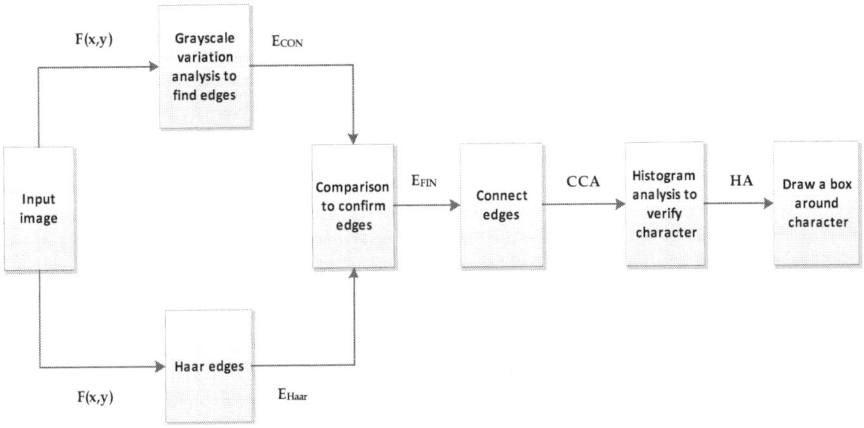

Fig. 10. The LP character segmentation algorithm based on Haar edges

(a) (b)

(c) (d)

Fig. 11. The above figures show input grayscale image (a), the region of interest in red (b), the LP candidate in yellow (b), the 2D Haar WT edges (c) and post - processed 2D Haar WT edges (d)

The Haar edges are used as a reference without further processing of the Haar edges like thinning; we apply the edges comparison algorithm explained in Section 3.1 and compare location where an edge is verified if a match is found. The flow chart is shown in figure 10.

The LP candidate has unique properties where the typical number of edges is between 100 to 2000 edges per plate. There are seven characters in UK LPs, a single character in a LP candidate contains between 30 to 150 edges, the gap of the character is between 2 to 4 pixels, the height of the character is about 20 pixels and width is about 16 pixels. This knowledge is applied to Connected Component Analysis (CCA) (Llorens, 2005) and a window (box) is drawn when a character is found. Finally, histogram analysis is applied to verify the presence of characters in a LP candidate.

5. Experimental setup

The proposed algorithms are optimized using similar experimental setup as reported in (Musoromy etal., 2010) and tested on Standard Definition (SD) and High Definition (HD) images that are a mixture of colour (day) and IR (night) with varying complexity levels such as over exposure, very dark and noisy. The proposed algorithm described in Section 4 forms a unified approach to resolve problems related to the above. The algorithm is implemented in DSP using the following tools:

- A Windows host PC (2.4 GHz clock speed) with Code Composer Studio and a monitor acting as baseline processor
- A Texas Instrument's C64plus DSP (fixed-point DSP based on an enhanced version of the second generation high-performance, advanced Very-Long-Instruction-Word (VLIW)) with minimum of 600MHZ clock speed and 1MB of RAM (TI, 2006)
- DSP host board with a JTAG interface debugger to provide interface between the DSP and the host PC during debugging DSP algorithm
- Testing database of 5000 images of 768X288 resolutions (SD) and 1000 images of 1394X1040 resolutions (HD) provided by CitySync Ltd (CitySync, 2011)

The implementation of Haar WT based edge detector is performed using a TI's DSP. TI provides an image library which has a unique implementation of the DWT through a highly optimised image columns transformation, which provides horizontal and vertical wavelet transform functions (TI, 2006). We apply reconstruction to the vertical and horizontal wavelet transform functions to obtain the edges.

6. Results

The main performance evaluation criteria for the proposed algorithm are average execution time and LP character segmentation rate as shown in Table 1. The results clearly show an improvement when 2D Haar WT is used especially in terms of the character segmentation rate, which is tested on 6000 images combining both image sets of SD and HD. It is also noted that the execution time for character segmentation is close for both SD and HD images due to similar LP candidate size but higher character segmentation rate is observed at higher resolution.

The edges results from 2D Haar WT on an input LP candidate image and segmented characters are shown in figure 12 to figure 14.

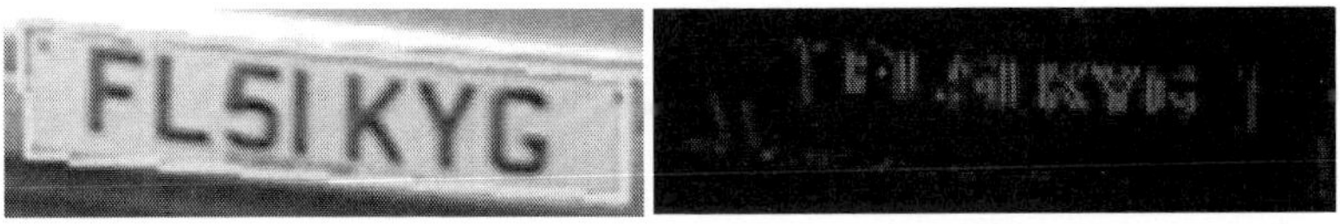

(a) (b)

Fig. 12. (a) The input LP Candidate (f(x,y)) and (b) the detected edges using 2D Haar WT (E(x,y))

(a) (b)

Fig. 13. (a) The post- processed 2D Haar WT edges (E_{Haar}) and (b) the detected edges in green (E_{FIN})

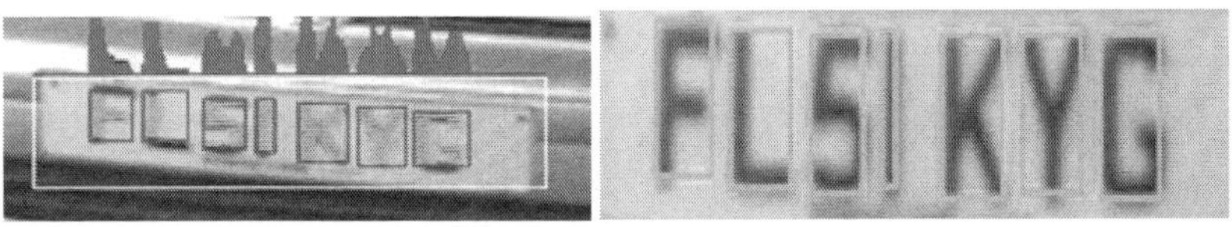

(a) (b)

Fig. 14. (a) Character segmentation using histogram analysis (HA) and CCA, and (b) the segmented characters bounding box

LP character segmentation algorithm	**Overall character segmentation success (6000 images) Percentage**	**Time using PC (ms)**		**Time using DSP (ms)**	
		SD (720x288)	**HD (1394x1040)**	**SD (720x288)**	**HD (1394x1040)**
Without Haar WT	90.4	6.2	6.5	7.6	7.9
Using Haar WT (single level)	95.3	8.8	9.1	10.4	10.6
Using Haar WT (two levels)	96.7	18.2	19.4	22.0	22.6

Table 1. Algorithm profiling results

It is observed that when using high resolution images and reduced number of wavelet decomposition (small scale single level in our case) the result is noisier and more discontinuous edges while at lower resolution and high number of wavelet decomposition have an opposite effect. This was also reported by Qureshi (Qureshi, 2005). In our application, the former effect leads to failed character segmentation due to "bad edges" while the latter improve character segmentation rate at an expense of losing speed for real time application as shown in our results in Table 1. In this case, a good balance between image resolution and wavelet decomposition levels is required.

In conclusion, in Table 1, two levels provide better character segmentation rate compared to a single level. However, the slower times is the downfall, therefore we choose decomposition at a single level that meet real-time requirement, which also gives a good character segmentation rate.

The difference between lower and higher decomposition levels around the LP region are demonstrated in figure 15 for a lower resolution image and similarly, in figure 16 decomposition levels for higher resolution image are shown using similar post processing edge threshold. The results clearly shows images at higher resolution performs better at lower decomposition levels.

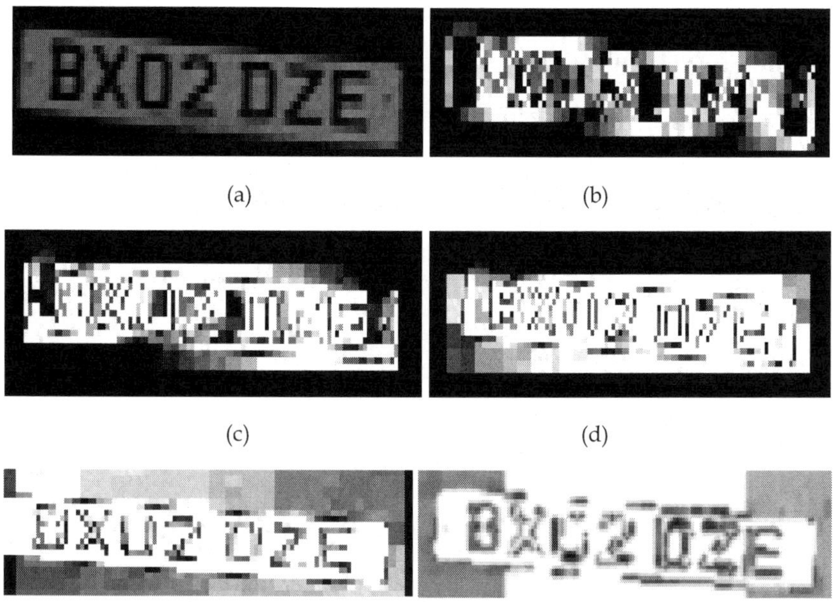

(a) (b)

(c) (d)

(e) (f)

Fig. 15. The original license plate candidate of a lower resolution image 384x144 (a), one level (b), two levels (c), three levels (d), four levels (e) and five levels (f) decomposition of the original image

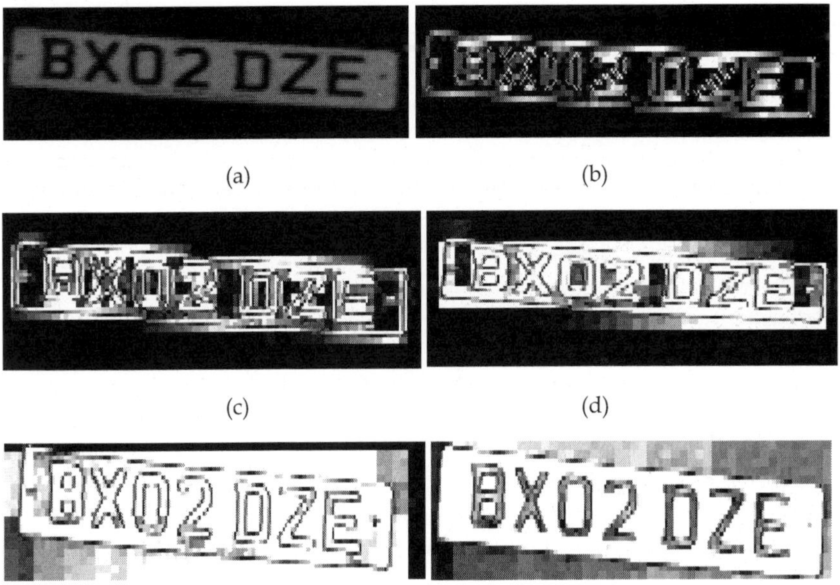

(a) (b) (c) (d) (e) (f)

Fig. 16. The original license plate candidate of a higher resolution image (768x288) (a), one level (b), two levels (c), three levels (d), four levels (e) and five levels (f) decomposition of the original image

The data set is partitioned further into day and night to provide more detailed analysis of test results in Table 2.

LP character segmentation algorithm	Day (3000 images)		Night (Infra-Red) (3000 images)	
	SD (2500 images)	HD (500 images)	SD (2500 images)	HD (500 images)
Without Haar WT	89.2	93.4	90.1	95.4
Using Haar WT (single level)	94.5	96.1	95.4	97.8
Using Haar WT (two levels)	95.6	98.2	97.0	98.9

Table 2. Segmentation success rate for day and night images

It is also noted in Table 2 that there is a small character segmentation success advantage in images taken at night compared to images taken in the day time. This can be explained due to the fact that at night, an Infra-Red (IR) camera is used to capture license plate which provides good images due to license plate's reflectivity to IR camera where the other objects in the background are not captured.

As well as the "bad edges", there are a number of factors that cause license plate character segmentation failure including;

- Dirty due to mud or rain drops
- Broken due to accidents
- Non reflective to IR camera
- Over exposure or uneven lit
- Illegal against known rules such as seven characters per LP in the UK

7. Conclusion

It is demonstrated from the results that Haar based edges can be used not only to enhance image features but also to give an idea on where the objects of interest are located. The major advantages of Haar edges in LP character segmentation application are: ability to detect most edges in image, higher character segmentation rate on HD images, fewer noises (unwanted edges) when using the appropriate decomposition and threshold levels, and speed.

A licence plate algorithm under 40ms is capable of delivering 25 fps, which is in real-time and able to deal with vehicles moving at 70 miles per hour. Therefore, the results suggest that the proposed algorithm will work in real time with SD and HD images in both PC and DSP for embedded systems.

In conclusion, the methodology provides a unified character segmentation process that caters to number plates captured at any time of the day (both day and night), and also different types of noises existing in real World applications, low and high resolution images. It is observed that higher character segmentation rate is at higher decomposition levels; therefore the future work will focus on further DSP optimisation methods for implementing higher level decompositions on both HD and SD images.

8. References

Abdel-Qader, I. M. & Maddix, M. E. (2005). Edge detection: wavelets versus conventional methods on DSP processors. *In MG&V* 14, 1, 83-101.

Benkrid, A., Crookes D. & K. Benkrid. (2001). Design and Implementation of Generic 2-D Biorthogonal Discrete Wavelet Transform on and FPGA, *IEEE Symposium on FieldProgrammable Custom Computing Machines*, pp 1 – 9.

Canny, J. F. (1986). A computational approach to edge detection. IEEE *Trans. on Patt. Anal. And Machine Intell.* Vol. 8, pp. 679-698.

Desneux, P. & Legat J., D. (2000). A dedicated DSP architecture for discrete wavelet transform. *Integr. Comput.-Aided Eng.* 7, 2 (April 2000), 135-153.

Haar, A. (1911). Zur theorie der orthogonalen funktionensysteme, *Mathematische Annalen* 71: 38–53. 10.1007/BF01456927.

Llorens, D., Marzal A., Palazon, V. & Vilar, J. M. (2005). Car License Plates Extraction and Recognition Based on Connected Components Analysis and HMM Decoding, *in Lecture Notes on Computer Science*, vol. 3522, J. S. Marques et al., Eds. New York: Springer-Verlag, pp. 571–578.

Ma, X.D., Zhou C. & Kemp, I.J. (2000) "DSP based partial discharge characterization by wavelet analysis", *IEEE 19th Int. Symp. On Discharge and Electrical Insultaion in Vacuum, Xi'an, China*, pp. 780- 783.

Mallat, S. (1999). *A Wavelet Tour of Signal Processing, Second Edition (Wavelet Analysis & ItsApplications)*, Academic Press.

Mallat, S. (1989). A theory for multiresolution signal decomposition: the wavelet representation, *IEEE Transactions on Pattern Analysis and Machine Intelligence* 11: 674–693.

Musoromy, Z., Bensaali F., Ramalingam S. & Pissanidis G. (2010). "Comparison of Real-Time DSP-Based Edge Detection Techniques for License Plate Detection", *Sixth international Conference on Information Assurance and Security (IAS)*, pp 323-328, Atlanta, USA.

Palacios, G., Beltran, J. R & Lacuesta, R. (2011). Multiresolution Approaches for Edge Detection and Classification Based on Discrete Wavelet Transform, In: *Discrete Wavelet Transforms: Algorithms and Applications*, InTech, ISBN 978-953-307-482-5, Janeza, Croatia .

Patil, S. & Abel, E.W. (2006). Optimization of the Continuous Wavelet Transform for DSP Processor Implementation, *Engineering in Medicine and Biology Society, 2005. IEEE-EMBS 2005. 27th Annual International Conference of the* , vol., no., pp.2787-2789, 17-18.

Paunwala, C.N., Patnaik, S. & Chaudhary, M. (2010). "An efficient skew detection of license plate images based on wavelet transform and principal component analysis," *Signal and Image Processing (ICSIP), 2010 International Conference on* , vol., no., pp.17-22, 15-17.

Qureshi, S. (2005). "*Embedded Image Processing on the TMS320C6000™ DSP*", Springer, ISBN 0-387-25280-3, New York, USA.

Roomi, S.M.M., Anitha, M., & Bhargavi, R. (2011). "Accurate license plate localization," *Computer, communication and Electrical Technology (ICCCET), 2011 International Conference on* , vol., no., pp.92-97, 18-19 .

TI, Texas Instruments. (2006). "*TMS320C64x+ DSP Cache User's Guide*", Literature number: spru862a.

Wong, T.T., Leung, C.S., Heng, P.A. & Wang J. (2007). "Discrete wavelet transform on consumer-level graphics hardware", *IEEE Trans. Multimedia* 9 (3) 668-673.

Wu, M., Wei, J., Shih, H. & Ho, C.C. (2009). "2-Level-Wavelet-Based License Plate Edge Detection," *Information Assurance and Security, 2009. IAS '09. Fifth International Conference on* , vol.2, no., pp.385-388, 18-20.

2

Wavelet Transform Based Motion Estimation and Compensation for Video Coding

Najib Ben Aoun, Maher El'arbi and Chokri Ben Amar
REsearch Groups on Intelligent Machines (REGIM)
University of Sfax, National Engineering School of Sfax (ENIS)
Tunisia

1. Introduction

With the big evolution in the quantity of video data issued from an increased number of video applications over networks such as the videophone, the videoconferencing, and multimedia devices such as the personal digital assistants and the high-definition cameras, it has become crucial to reduce the quantity of video data which will be stored or transmitted. In fact, since the capacity of the storage Medias has become high and sufficient, the data storage problem was resolved but the transmission of the data remains an important problem especially with the limited channel bandwidth.

Actually, the necessity of the development of an efficient video coding method has made video compression a fundamental task for video-based digital communications. Video compression reduces the quantity of video data by eliminating the spatial and the temporal redundancy. Spatial compression is done by transforming video frames and representing them otherwise using the spatial correlation between frames pixels. In the other side, motion estimation and compensation are employed in video coding systems to remove temporal redundancy while keeping a high visual quality. They are the most important parts of the video coding process since they require the most computational power and the biggest consumption in resources and bandwidth. Therefore, many techniques have been developed to estimate motion between successive frames.

Motion estimation and compensation (ME/MC) was conducted in many domains such as spatial domain by applying it directly on images pixels without any transformation, the frequency domain by driving it on the Discrete Cosine Transform (DCT) or the Discrete Fourier Transform (DFT) coefficients. It can be also done in the multiresolution domain by running it on the Discrete Wavelet Transform (DWT) coefficients. However, giving the promising performances of the multiresolution analysis especially the DWT which provides a multiresolution expression of the signal with localization in both space and frequency, many methods have been developed to construct a wavelet based video coding system (Shenolikar, 2009) and the DWT was integrated in new coding standards such as JPEG2000, MPEG-4, and H.264. Furthermore, recently, many motion estimation and compensation systems (BEN AOUN, 2010) have also confirmed that the DWT is the most suitable and the most efficient domain that gives efficient and precise motion estimation.

For this, we have developed a block based ME/MC method in the wavelet domain. Our method exploits the benefits of DWT and the hierarchical relationship between its subbands

(Quadtree) to drive ME/MC on wavelet coefficients, especially in the low frequency subband where we find the most significant visual information. This method is consolidated by several techniques to ameliorate the results. With this method, we have achieved good results in terms of prediction quality, compression performance and computational complexity.

The goal of this chapter is to introduce new motion estimation and compensation system based on the DWT which has given better and superior results compared with others systems conducted in spatial or frequency domains. Our system is also based on the Block Matching Algorithm (BMA) which is the simplest, the most efficient and the most popular technique for motion estimation and compensation. Additional techniques are introduced to accelerate the estimation process and improve the prediction quality. In Section 2, we introduce the multiresolution domains and especially the DWT as a multiresolution description for the image which has proved its efficiency for ME/MC. Section 3 presents the motion estimation principle and methods focusing on the DWT based systems. Section 4 describes our DWT and BMA based proposed method. In Section 5, we will introduce some supplementary techniques which have been developed to improve our method and give the main causes which have made of them crucial parts for an efficient motion estimation system. In Section 6, we evaluate our method and compare it to others conventional methods conducted in different domains. This will prove that our method outperforms conventional method in many terms. Finally, Section 7 summarizes the key findings and suggests future research possibilities. We should mention that, along this chapter, when we say motion estimation, we imply implicitly the motion compensation.

2. Wavelet transform domain

The wavelet transform, as a multiresolution domain that hybrid the frequency and the spatial domain, has proved that it is a very appropriate and reliable domain for a powerful motion estimation and compensation. For this, we have been encouraged to study and exploit it, and more precisely the DWT, in our motion estimation system.

The DWT consists on applying hierarchically low-pass (L) and high-pass (H) filters after decimation (sub-sampling the image on two parts). This procedure is repeated until reaching a prefixed level. Figure.1 shows the decomposition of an image with DWT. In this example there are two levels of DWT decomposition.

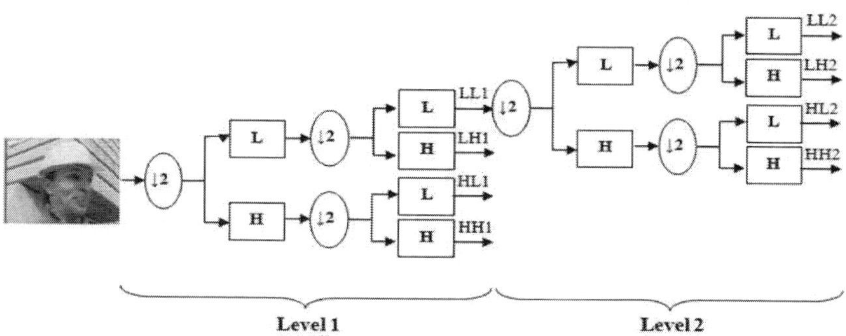

Fig. 1. DWT decomposition (2 levels)

The DWT decomposes the image into different subbands, as shown in Figure.2, aiming to isolate the high frequencies that are not interesting to the human eyes. So, we will have the most important information concentrated in the subband LL of the highest level called also DWT approximation (LL3 in the Fig.2).

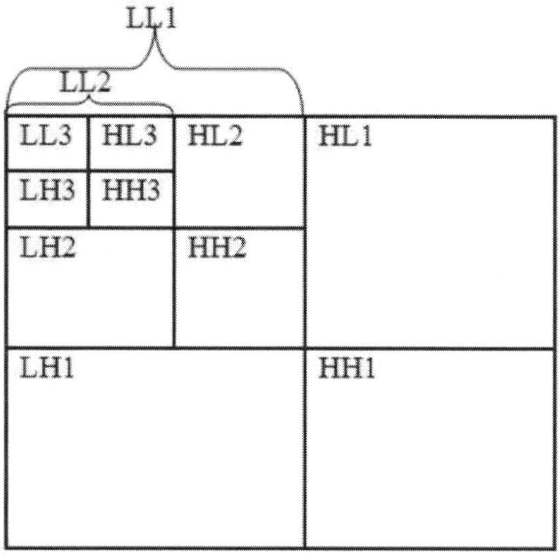

Fig. 2. Different DWT subbands (3 levels)

The Figure.3 bellow shows the decomposition of the Foreman image into three level of DWT. This example illustrates clearly that the DWT approximation presents the most significant information that the human eyes are sensible to. The others subbands (DWT details) give the high frequencies existing in the image along different orientations.

(a) Original image (b) DWT decomposition

Fig. 3. Three levels DWT decomposition applied to Foreman

The fact that the DWT approximation contains the most of the information issued from the original image was encouraging to benefit of this DWT propriety. For this, the motion estimation was conducted principally in this subband which accelerates the motion estimation process.

The discrete wavelet transform (DWT) as a powerful tool for signal processing has found its application in many areas of research. Image compression is still one of the most successful applications in which the DWT has been applied. So, it is natural that researchers are interested in creating a DWT based new technologies for video compression and motion estimation (Kutil, 2003).

3. Motion estimation and compensation

With the continuous growth in the volume of video data in the multimedia databases, it has become crucial to reduce the quantity of the data to be transmitted and stored by video compression and coding. That is why, motion estimation is introduced as a solution to reduce the quantity of data by eliminating the temporal redundancy between adjacent frames in an image sequence. ME/MC are the fundamental parts of video coding systems and form the core of many video processing applications. Motion estimation eliminates temporal redundancy from video by exploiting the temporal correlation between successive frames, so that it reduces the amount of data to be transmitted or stored while maintaining sufficient data quality. However, ME extracts temporal motion information from video sequences, while MC uses this motion information for efficient interframe coding.

Motion estimation process serves to predict motion between two successive frames and produce the motion vectors (MVs) which represent the displacements between these two frames. Consequently, instead of transmitting two frames, we will send only one frame which is the reference frame, the motion vectors and the residue which is the difference between the current frame and the reconstructed frame by motion compensation. So, the MVs and the prediction error are transmitted instead of the frame itself. With this process, the encoder will have sufficient information to faithfully reproduce the frame sequence. The combination of the motion estimation and motion compensation is a key part of the video coding.

There are many methods to achieve ME/MC. In fact, They can be divided into two classes: the statistical methods, the differentials methods as indirect methods (applied to image features) and the optical flow, and the block based method as direct ones (applied to image pixels). Block matching algorithm (Gharavi, 1990) is an effective and popular technique for block based motion estimation. It has been widely adopted in various video coding standards and highly desirable since it maintains an acceptable prediction errors.

Block-based motion estimation is most used method because of its simplicity and performances, which made it the standard approach in the video coding systems. The procedure of BMA is to divide the frames into a block of N×N pixels, to match every block of the current frame (CF) with his most similar block inside a research window in the reference frame (RF) and to generate the motion vector. Consequently, for this method, the most important parameters here are the size of the block N and the size of the search window P. However, the block matching is based on minimizing a criterion like the Mean Absolute Error (MAD) or the Mean Square Error (MSE) which is the most common block distortion measure for matching two blocks and it provides more accurate block matching. The MV will be applicable to every pixels of the same block which reduces the computational requirement.

To identify the best corresponding block, the simplest way is to evaluate every block in the reference frame (exhaustive search, ES). But, although this method finds generally the appropriate block, it consumes a high computation time. Hence, others fast searching strategies (Barjatya, 2004) have been developed where search is done in a particular order. There are the Three Step Search (TSS), the Simple and Efficient Search (SES), the Four Step Search (4SS), the Adaptive Rood Pattern Search (ARPS) and the Diamond Search (DS) which has proved to be the best searching strategies coming close to the ES results. So, the DS was improved in many variants such as the Cross DS (CDS), the Small CDS (SCDS) and the New CDS (NCDS).

In conventional coding systems such as H.261 and MPEG-1/2, BMA is conducted directly on frame which needs a large computing power. That is why many studies have been made and proved that it is better to transform the frame before executing the ME techniques. However, with the development of new video coding standards, wavelets have received an important interest since it has shown good and effective results. The main idea behind wavelet is to generate a space-frequency representation focusing only on the spatial frequencies that are most significant to the human eye. This wavelet decomposition is a reversible procedure which is performed by successive approximations of the initial information (original frame). This process, will improve the coding efficiency since the wavelet coefficients are much correlated and this representation reduces the blocking effects especially in the edges.

Initially, the DWT was used to encode the MVs and the estimation errors after conducting the motion estimation in the spatial or the frequency domains (Figure.4.a). Thereafter, given that the DWT is a spatial-frequency representation for the image that concentrates the most important information in one subband (DWT approximation subband) and since the different DWT subbands are hierarchically correlated, the DWT was used as a domain to conduce the motion estimation and it has shown a great success.

(a) Conventional ME + DWT based MVs and ME errors encoding

(b) Motion estimation in the wavelet domain

Fig. 4. Video coders based on DWT

Exploiting the hierarchical relationship between the wavelet coefficients of the different subbands in different levels, different hierarchical ME methods were developed which are adapted to the wavelet transformation. The hierarchical relationship gives that every wavelet coefficients has four descendants in the lower level of the DWT. The motion estimation is conduced hierarchically so that it is calculated firstly in one of the DWT level and it is corrected with the estimation obtained, thereafter, at the others levels.

In fact, there are two main ME categories of approaches for DWT based: forward and backward approaches. The forward approach consists on conducting the ME in the DWT details subbands of the low level and using it to determine the motion in the higher level subbands (coarse-to-fine). Researchers like Meyer and al (Meyer, 1997) have followed the forward approach to propose a ME method with a new pyramid structure. They have taken the aliasing effect, caused by the BMA used, into consideration and build a ME system given a good perceptual quality after MC. Also, P.Y Cheng and al (Cheng, 1995) has proposed a multiscale forward ME working on the DWT coefficients. They have built a new pyramidal structure overcoming the shift variant problem of the DWT.

Nosratinia and Orchard (Nosratinia, 1995) were the first researchers who developed a ME system based on DWT following a backward approach (coarse-to-fine) where they estimated the motion in the finest DWT resolution (higher level) and then progressively refined the ME by incorporating the finer level. Furthermore, Conklin and Hemami (Conklin, 1997) have proved the superiority of the backward ME approach over the forward one in terms of compression rate and visual quality after compensation. This is what encourages more recent researchers (Lundmark, 2000; Yuan, 2002) to follow this approach in their ME systems.

The effectiveness of the BMA and the suitability of the DWT in the video coding, have led us to develop a block matching based motion estimation method in the wavelet domain.

4. Our proposed method

The motion estimation and compensation are the most important parts in the video coding process. For this, many works have focused on these video coding parts aiming to improve them. But, the results reached still insufficient especially for the real time applications. That is what encourages us to work on these parts and improve them.

The Block Matching Algorithm still one of the most efficient and the most used method for motion estimation since it works directly on image pixels and it accelerates the estimation process by working on pixels blocks. This method suffers like all others methods from some problems such as the Blocking effect (discontinuity across block boundary) in the predicted image. But, we have overcome this problem in our system with several motion estimation improvement techniques.

Thanks to its proprieties and its suitability as a domain to apply motion estimation and compensation, the multiresolution domain has been adopted in our system to conduce the motion estimation directly on its coefficients. Among the method to obtain a multiresolution representation for the image, we have the DWT that has proved its efficiency not only for data compression but also for motion estimation.

The proposed method makes use of the wavelet properties to apply the motion estimation directly in the wavelet coefficients. We have adopted the fine-to-coarse motion estimation strategy which has shown its success by many previous works. After applying the DWT on both CF and RF, the motion is estimated firstly between the DWT approximations of the two images. So, we have provided a better estimation since the approximation contains the most visual information. The motion vectors of the approximation are directly calculated. We have exploited that every DWT coefficient has four descendants in the lower DWT level (Quadtree structure). So, the motion vectors of the details subbands are deducted using the hierarchical relationship that exists between the DWT subbands as shown in Figure 5. We compute the motion vectors of the details subbands following this formula:

$$V_{i,j} = 2^{L-i} V_{L,1}(x,y) + \delta_{i,j} \tag{1}$$

Working on a three level DWT (L=3), we will have i={1, 2, 3} which is the level, j={1, 2, 3, 4} representing the subband number, $V_{i,j}(x, y)$ is the motion vector for the subband "j" at the level "i" and $\delta_{i,j}$ is the refinement factor (equal to 0 if "i" is equal to L). The displacement of every subband block is the double of the displacement of the same subband block in the lower DWT level where we add to it a refinement factor $\delta_{i,j}$ which correct the estimation error as given in the equation and presented in the Figure above.

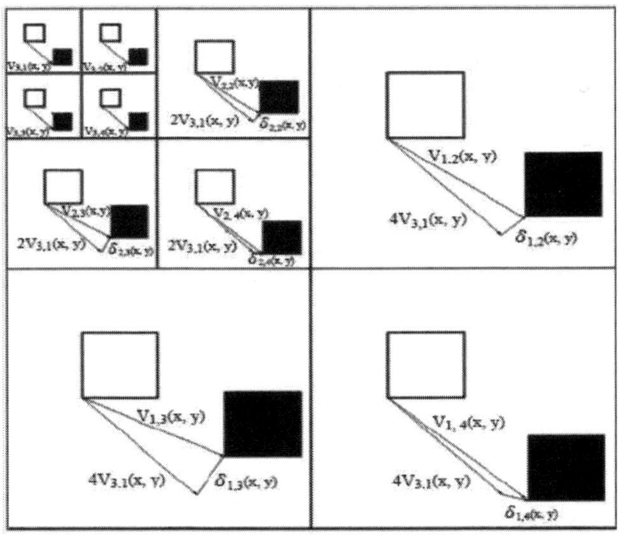

Fig. 5. DWT subbands motion vectors representation (L=3)

Moreover, by predicting the motion only in the approximation which has a small size compared to the original frame and contains the most significant information, not only the computation requirement is highly reduced and the compression ratio is increasing, but also our method maintains a good prediction quality.

The BMA is an efficient method for motion estimation which encourages us to use it in our multiresolution based method. Unfortunately, despite their encouraging proprieties and their promising results, the BMA and DWT suffer from some problems. For this, a several improvement techniques have been implemented to surmount these problems and make our method more robust giving best results.

5. Additional improvement techniques

Despite that it outperforms the conventional motion estimation methods, our proposed DWT based method still having some problems. As we have mentioned before, the DWT representation suffers from the problem of aliasing and the fact that it is a shift variant transformation. Moreover, the block based motion estimation causes the blocking effect which gives a discontinuity in the block boundaries of the predicted image. That is what drives us to develop some additional techniques to overcome these problems.

These techniques make the motion estimation process more precise and more rapid by detecting the moving zones and limiting the estimation operation to it, adding a sub-pixel precision to the motion vector computing, applying the motion estimation to a shifting variants of the original image aiming to make the estimation a shift invariant operation, overlapping the frame blocks to correct the motion vector by their neighbouring vectors and finally, refining the prediction by changing the block size and re-predicting the blocks which are falsely predicted. In this section we will describe these techniques as well as the causes that conduct us to implement them.

5.1 Moving zones detection

To accelerate the ME process, we have focused on the image zones where there are movements so that we will conduct the motion estimation only in them. Many techniques have been developed to detect the moving zones in an image. The simplest method is to subtract the background by comparing every image pixels displacement to a prefixed threshold and assuming that it belongs to the foreground if it is superior to this threshold and it is declared as a background's pixel otherwise (Spagnolo, 2006). Hence, the foreground is considered as moving zones. This method is not very efficient since it depends essentially on the prefixed threshold. For this, recently, more sophisticated methods have been built to overcome this limit. Criminisi and al (Criminisi, 2006) have developed a bilayer segmentation method based on the calculation of a complex energy function.

In our system, we have used the background subtraction technique develop by Zivkovic and van der Heijden (Zivkovic, 2006) which models every image pixel's colour values distribution with a mixture of Gaussians (GMM). The mean and the covariance of each component in the mixture are updated for each new video frame (image) to reflect the change of the pixel values. In the case when the new pixel value is far enough the mixture, the pixel is considered as a foreground. This method has shown its rapidity and its good segmentation results in a big variety of videos (as shown on Figure.5).

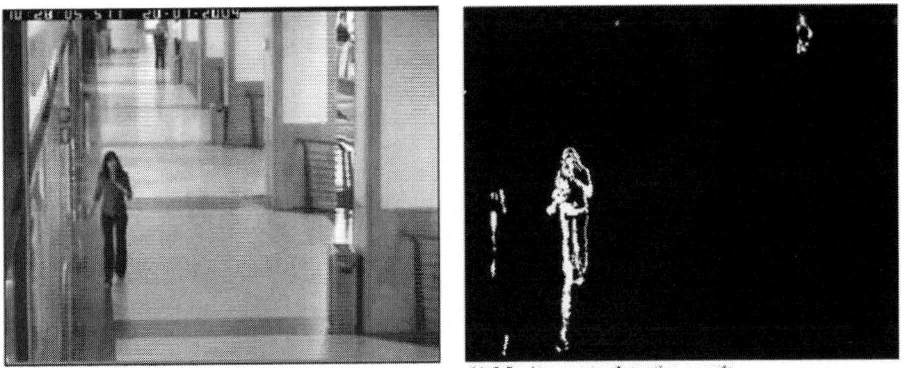

(a) Original video frame (b) Moving zones detection result

Fig. 6. Background subtraction results with the method of Zivkovic

This temporal segmentation based moving zones detection has allowed us to estimate the motion only on limited zones. Thereby, this technique will reduce the computational time of the ME process and gives a more precise estimation with the assumption that the motion vectors of the blocks which are out of the detected zones will have a null value. This gain is increased if the movement is concentrated in very limited zones.

5.2 Sub-pixel precision

Block based motion estimation assumes that every block have an integer pixel displacement which is, in reality, not true. Therefore, to improve the motion estimation and to increase the accuracy of the prediction, we have moved to sub-pixel precision by developing a sub-pixel technique with a bilinear interpolation process. This is done by interposing a line between each two lines of the image I (see Figure.7) and a column between each two columns of the image. Then, ME is applied to the new image O.

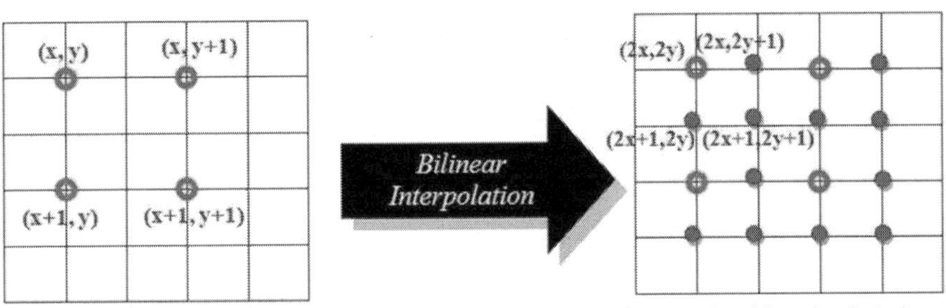

(a) Image I (b) Image O: with a 1/2 of pixel precision

Fig. 7. Bilinear Interpolation for 1/2 pixel precision

The values of the pixels that are in the 1/2 pixel positions are determined relatively to their neighbouring pixels in the integer positions as follows:

$$O(2x, 2y) = I(x, y) \tag{2}$$

$$O(2x+1, 2y) = (I(x, y) + I(x+1, y))/2 \tag{3}$$

$$O(2x, 2y+1) = (I(x, y) + I(x, y+1))/2 \tag{4}$$

$$O(2x+1, 2y+1) = (I(x, y) + I(x+1, y)\ I(x, y+1) + I(x+1, y+1))/4 \tag{5}$$

With this technique, a motion vector can point in a half or quarter of pixel position or even more. In this case, a block which has a real location at a fraction of pixels will be better predicted. The sub-pixel precision can not only increase the accuracy of motion vectors and reduce errors, but also filter the image to eliminate noise and rapid changes. The results of conducting the ME on some standard video sequences shown on the table bellow prove the efficiency of the sub-pixel precision technique.

Precision \ Sequence	Tennis	Susie	Foreman
Integer pixel	31.7586	33.1613	31.2889
1/2 of pixel	34.2206	37.8811	33.6719
1/4 of pixel	34.7099	40.0285	36.6072
1/8 of pixel	31.5650	37.4465	37.7870

Table 1. PSNR of the reconstructed image with different sub-pixel precision

Using the sub-pixel technique as a pre-treatment step for the motion estimation process will improve it. Taken the Tennis sequence results in Table.1, the Peak Signal to Noise Ratio (PSNR), which is a criterion to compare the original frame to the reconstructed frame after motion compensation, is augmented from 31.7586 dB without using the sub-pixel technique to 34.2206 dB with a 1/2 of pixel precision and to 34.7099 dB with a 1/4 of pixel precision. This confirms the need to this technique for motion estimation. It should been noticed here that augmenting the sub-pixel precision level (to 1/8 of pixel precision or more) is not always beneficial since it can, in the most times, perturb the estimation.

That is true that this technique causes a doubling of image size, but is not a big problem since we conduct the motion estimation on the DWT approximation which has a reduced size. Furthermore, this technique saves time since it allows a quick search for the BMA by minimizing the path to find the corresponding block. For all this, in block based ME methods, sub-pixel technique is becoming crucial.

5.3 Shifting technique

The DWT has many advantages of multiresolution domain, which has made this spatial-frequency transformation very useful for the ME. However, the shift-variant property of the DWT caused by the decimation process has made the ME/MC less efficient in the wavelet domain. Otherwise, there is a big difference between the DWT of an image and the DWT of the same image shifted by even one pixel as shown in the Figure.8. This property touches especially the high frequencies in the image's edges, but it has less effect on the low frequencies.

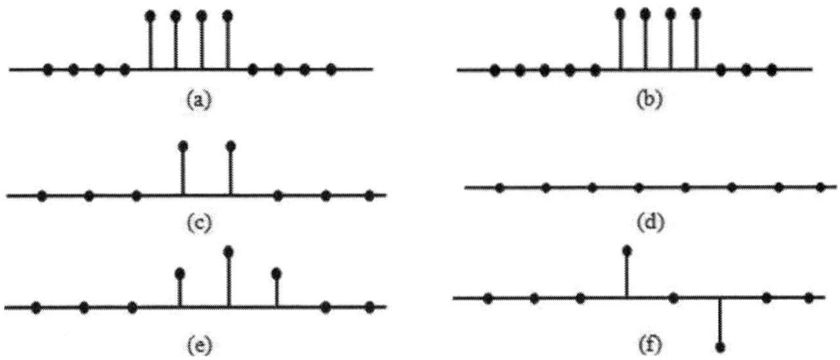

Fig. 8. Example of a DWT coefficients (*Haar* wavelet) for a 1-D signal s(n) and a shifted signal s(n+1) by one pixel. (a) original signal s(n), (b) shifted signal, (c) low-pass frequencies subband s(n), (d) high-pass frequencies subband of s(n), (e) low-pass frequencies subband of s (n+1), (f) high-pass frequencies subband of s(n+1).

In the Figure.8, s(n+1) is a shifted variant by one pixel (shifting to the right) of the 1-D signal s(n). As illustrated in this figure, the difference between the high-pass frequencies subband before and after shifting is much important than the low-pass frequencies subband before and after shifting. This is a simple and a 1-D signal example but it is also the case of the 2-D signal. Hence, this is reinforced more our choice to conduct ME in the approximation (low-pass frequencies subband) of the DWT.

To overcome the shift-variant property of the DWT, a shifting technique is used which increase the prediction quality (Yuan, 2002). Before applying ME, we shift the frame in spatial domain by one pixel in all directions. Then, the shifted frames are transformed to the wavelet domain for motion estimation more precise and more real. After calculating a motion vector for the block in every direction, we generate the final motion vector which is the mean of all calculated vectors.

This technique has increased the estimation results by smoothing the predicted vectors and reducing the aliasing effect. By adding this technique to the ME process, the estimation was remarkably ameliorated as shown in the Table 2. However, this technique has improved the PSNR of the reconstructed image after MC for the Tennis sequence from 31.7586 dB to 32.3164 dB.

Sequence / Precision	Tennis	Susie	Foreman
ME without shifting	31.7586	33.1613	31.2889
ME with shifting	32.3164	35.5236	32.6301

Table 2. PSNR of the reconstructed image without/with the Shifting technique

5.4 Blocks overlapping technique

Supplementary technique for improving the motion estimation is to overlap the neighbouring block to smooth the motions vectors in a way to have a more real prediction (as shown in Figure.9). So, each motion vector will be the average of itself and the direct neighbouring motion vectors with a certain weighting (every MV will have a weight stronger than the weight of the MVs of the neighbouring blocks).

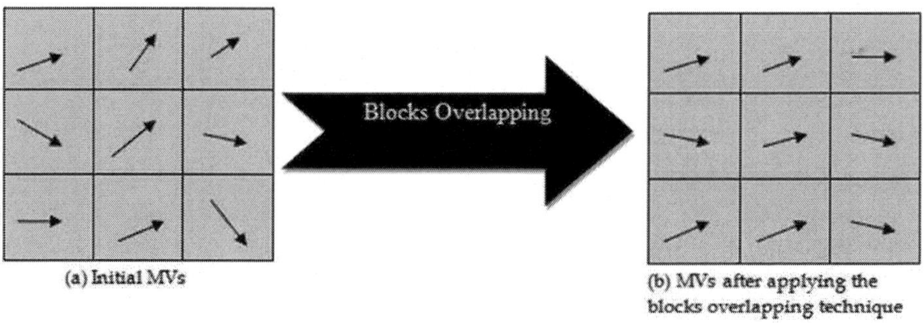

Fig. 9. Correcting the MVs with blocks overlapping technique

This blocks overlapping technique will surmount the false prediction especially the discontinuity at the edges which gives the high frequencies in the estimated image. This is done since the technique is somewhat averaging the possible candidates for each pixel and correcting then a probable false estimation. Hence, this technique will make the visual quality more clear and net.

5.5 Refinement techniques

The basic idea in the BMA is to divide the frame into blocks of a fixed size N×N. This means that all the pixels of the same block have the same displacement. But, this is not true in most cases, since there may be different movements in the same block (movements intra-block).

For this, we have developed two techniques which aim to take into consideration this problem and give each image pixel a MV representing its real movement.

The first technique consists on dividing the blocks which are poorly predicted and conducting a re-estimation on the new sub-blocks. This will fix the blocks size relatively to the movements and we will build then a variable block size ME system (see Figure.10) as develop by Arvanitidou et al (Arvanitidou, 2009).

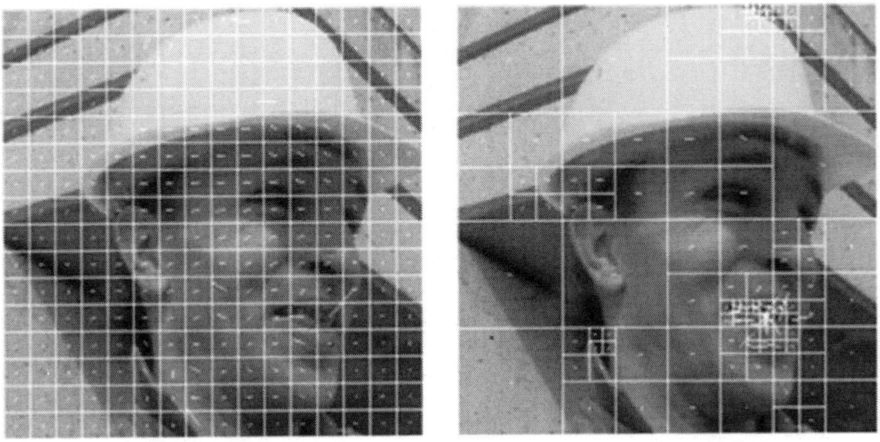

(a) ME with a pre-fixed block size (b) ME with variable block size

Fig. 10. Motion estimation with different block size strategies

This technique is very powerful since it corrects the motion vectors by a hierarchical procedure based on modifying the block sizes. It provides a good estimation and tries to minimize the error by taking into account the intra-block movements.

Another refinement technique is also carried out for our method, which consists on moving the estimation to a lower level (larger resolution) of the DWT. This process is not performed for all blocks, but it runs only on poorly predicted blocks. The refinement will re-estimate the motion of the blocks that has an error greater than certain threshold. This technique has given a more accurate estimation prediction quality.

Sequence / Precision	Tennis	Susie	Foreman
ME without refinement	31.7586	32.5908	17.7091
ME + refinement with changing the block size	32.0609	33.0652	17.6722
ME + refinement by moving to a lower DWT level	32.6278	34.3762	17.9133

Table 3. PSNR of the reconstructed image with different refinement techniques

As presented in the Table above, the second refinement technique has better results, which have encouraged us to use it in our method.

All these techniques have united to improve our methods which make it fast, efficient and accurate. In addition, we can even exploit the human visual system and remove the small variations not recognized by the human eye between the two frames. The motion vectors and the prediction error can be encoded after transformed by DWT using the Embedded Zerotree wavelet algorithm (EZW) developed by Shapiro (Shapiro, 1993) or by the Set Partitioning in Hierarchical Trees Algorithm (SPIHT) developed by Said and Pearlman (Said, 1996) which are algorithms that exploit the wavelet structure for an efficient coding.

6. Experimental results

In our block based method, we have fixed the Diamond Search as a block searching strategy and the MSE as a block matching criterion since it gives better compression performance while not sacrificing image quality. We have also fixed the size of the window to 7 and the size of the block to 2 since we work in the approximation in the third level of the DWT. Furthermore, we have integrated all the techniques mentioned previously with a quarter of pixel precision and a refinement technique by moving to lower DWT level to re-estimate the poorly predicted blocks.

Our method has proved its performance and robustness for several video benchmarks used to test the ME/MC methods such as the "Tennis", “Foreman”, “Susie”, “Claire” sequences and even the “Football” sequence which contains large movements.

Methods \ Sequence	Tennis	Foreman	Susie	Claire
Spatial domain	34.3983	33.5550	36.6450	37.7992
DCT domain	28.2568	31.3646	31.2833	33.0233
Conventional DWT	31.7586	31.2889	33.1613	32.5908
Proposed method	**35.6263**	**34.6025**	**38.3417**	**38.5418**

Table 4. PSNR of the reconstructed image

The reached results showed large performance in terms of quality of reconstructed frame as shown in Table.4 and also in terms of compression ratio. All this, is due to the accuracy of the estimation and the corrections made for the motion vectors.

Our experiments verify the superiority of the proposed ME system, not only versus several other well-known ME systems in the frequency and the multiresolution domains, but also versus the ME systems in the spatial domain. Moreover, it is faster than other methods and the compression ratio is highly increased because it works on the approximation level of the DWT, which is 8 times smaller than the original image.

Furthermore, it is clear from the Figure.11 that there is a big difference between the visual qualities of the reconstructed frames using these different ME/MC systems. We can observe that when the motion estimation is applied on the DCT domain, block effects appeared. On the other hand, using the classical DWT domain, there are also blocks effects, despite its superiority to the DCT domain. Our method gives a better visual quality that resembles to the quality of the reconstructed frame by the spatial domain based ME/MC system.

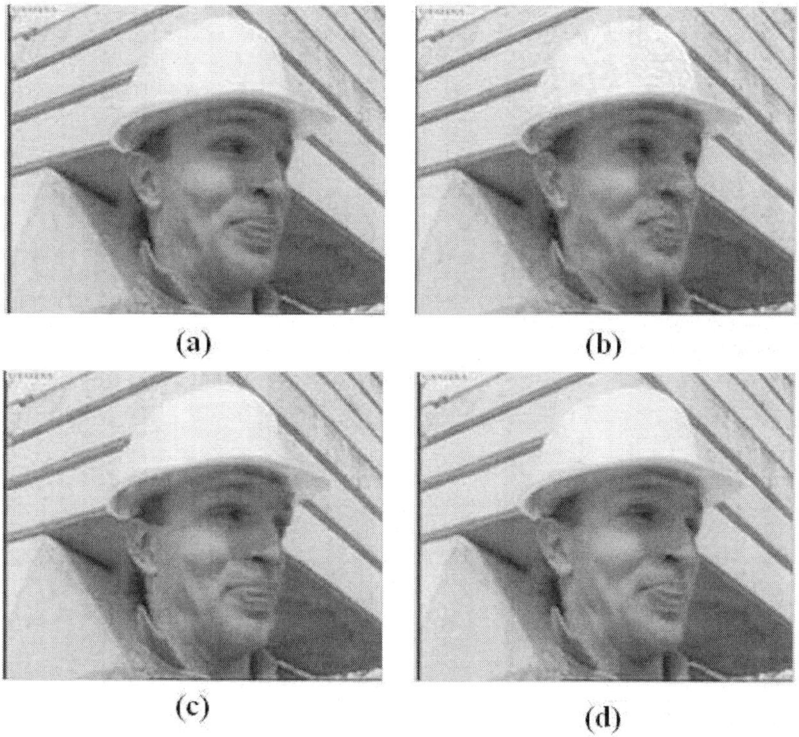

Fig. 11. The ME/MC results on the 129th frame of the "foreman" sequence. (a) The original image. The estimated frame: (b) ME/MC in the DCT domain, (c) ME/MC in the DWT domain, (d) with our method.

The efficiency of our motion estimation method is well confirmed by the results, in the visual qualities of the reconstructed frames, reached by applying the ME/MC on the Tennis sequence conducted in several domains. The results mentored in Figure.12 consolidate the fact that our motion estimation method outperforms other motion estimations methods conducted in different domains.

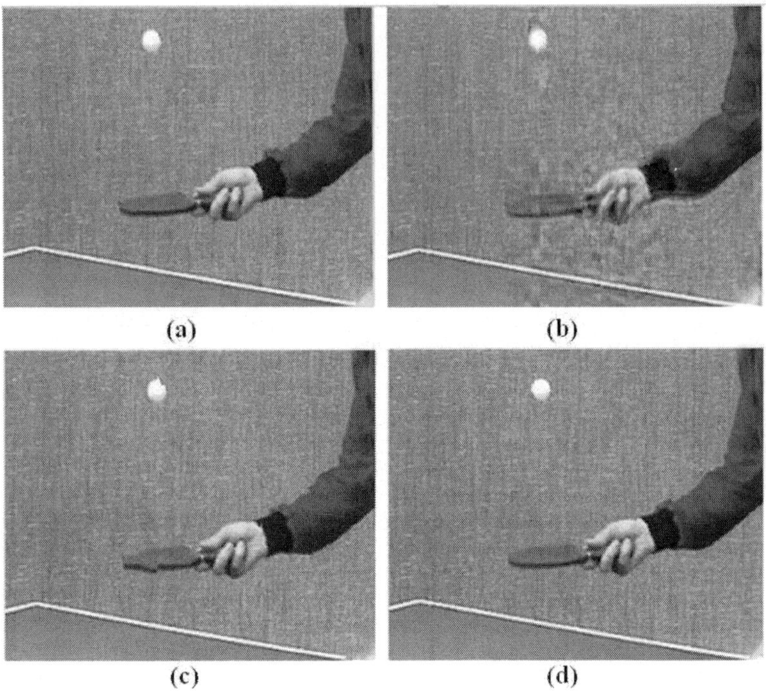

Fig. 12. The ME/MC results on the 17th frame of the "Tennis" sequence. (a) The original image. The estimated image: (b) ME/MC in the DCT domain, (c) ME/MC in the DWT domain, (d) with our method.

7. Conclusion

Video coding has received an increased interest because of the big growth in the quantity of the video data. That is why a big interest has been made for developing an efficient video coding system and improving the motion estimation part which represents the most important part since it consumes most computation time and most resources used for video coding. Making the motion estimation a fast and efficient process was the goal of many researchers. But, unfortunately, that was not reached in the spatial domain. That's why, new ME systems have been conducted in other domain such as the frequency and the multiresolution domain. That is why many studies have been made to improve and simplify the ME methods. In this chapter, we have studied the wavelet as a domain for ME and we have proposed a multiresolution motion estimation and compensation method based on block matching applying in the wavelet coefficients. Because of some problems presented in this chapter, we have integrated some improvements techniques to ameliorate our ME system. As a future works, we will reinforce our method with others techniques such as the spatial segmentation which makes the estimation more accurate by trying to identify real objects in the predicted moving zones.

8. Acknowledgment

The authors would like to acknowledge the financial support of this work by grants from the General Direction of Scientific Research (DGRST), Tunisia, under the ARUB program.

9. References

Arvanitidou, M.G. et al. (2009). Global motion estimation using variable block sizes and its application to object segmentation, 10th *Workshop on Image Analysis for Multimedia Interactive Services*, pp. 173-176, ISBN 978-1-4244-3609-5, London, UK, May 6-8, 2009

Barjatya, A. (2004). Block Matching Algorithms For Motion Estimation, DIP 6620 Spring 2004 Final Project Paper, Available from: http://read.pudn.com/downloads153/sourcecode/graph/texture_mapping/675918/BlockMatchingAlgorithmsForMotionEstimation.PDF

Ben Aoun, N., El'Arbi, M. & Ben Amar, C (2010). Multiresolution motion estimation and compensation for video coding, Proceedings of the 10th International Conference on Signal Processing, Part II, pp.1121-1124, ISBN 978-1-4244-5897-4, Beijing, China, October 24-28, 2010

Cheng, P.Y, Li, J. & Jay Kuo, C.-C. (1995). Multiscale video compression using wavelet transform and motion compensation, *International Conference on Image Processing*, pp. 606–609, Vol.1, ISBN 0-8186-7310-9, Washington D.C., USA, October 23-26, 1995.

Conklin, G.J., Hemami, S.S. (1997). Multi-resolution motion estimation, *International Conference on Acoustics, Speech, and Signal Processing*, pp. 2873–2876, Vol.4, ISBN 0-8186-7919-0, Munich, Bavaria, Germany, April 21-24, 1997

A. Criminisi, A., Cross, G., Blake, A. & Kolmogorov, V. (2006). Bilayer Segmentation of Live Video, *International Conference on Computer Vision and Pattern Recognition*, pp. 53-60, Vol.1 , ISBN 0-7695-2597-0, New York, NY, USA, June 17-22, 2006.

Gharavi, H. & Mills, M. (1990). Block Matching Motion Estimation Algorithms: New Results. *IEEE Transactions on Circuits and Systems for Video Technology*, Vol.37, No.5, (May 1990), pp. 649-651, ISSN 0098-4094

Kutil, R. (2003). Evaluation of wavelet domain block motion compensation (WBMC), *Proceedings of the International Picture Coding Symposium (PCS'03)*, pp. 513-518, Saint Malo, France, April 23-25, 2003

Lundmark, A., Li, H. & Forchheimer, R. (2000). Motion vector certainty reduces bit rate in backward motion estimation video coding, *SPIE Proceedings of Visual Communications and Image Processing*, Vol.4067, pp. 95–104, ISBN 0-8194-3703-4, Perth, AUSTRALIE, June 20-23, 2000

Meyer, F.G, Averbuch A. & Coifman R.R. (1997). Motion compensation of wavelet coefficients for very low bit rate video coding, *Proceedings of IEEE International Conference on Image Processing*, Vol.3, pp. 638-641, ISBN 0-8186-8183-7, Washington, DC, USA, October 26-29, 1997

Nosratinia, A. & Orchard, M.T. (1995). Multi-resolution backward video coding, *International Conference on Image Processing*, pp. 563–566, Vol.2, ISBN 0-8186-7310-9, Washington D.C., USA, October 23-26, 1995.

Park, H. & Kim, H. (2000). Motion estimation using lowband-shift method for wavelet-based moving-picture coding. *IEEE Transactions on Image Processing*, Vol.9, No.4, (April 2000), pp. 577–587, ISSN 1057-7149.

Said, A. & Pearlman, W.A. (1996). A New, Fast, and Efficient Image Codec Based on Set Partitioning in Hierarchical Trees. *IEEE transactions on circuits and systems for video technology*, Vol. 6, No. 3, (June 1996), pp. 243-250, ISSN 1051-8215.

J. M. Shapiro,J.M. (1993). Embedded image coding using zerotrees of wavelet coefficients, *IEEE Transactions on Signal Processing*, Vol.41, No.12, (December 1993), pp. 3445-3463, ISSN 1053-587X.

Shenolikar, P.C. & Narote, S.P. (2009). Motion estimation on DWT based image sequence. *International Journal of Recent Trends in Engineering*, Vol.2, No.4, (November 2009), pp. 168-170, ISSN 1797-9617

Spagnolo, P., Orazio, T.D., Leo, M. & Distante, D. (2006). Moving object segmentation by background subtraction and temporal analysis. *Image and Vision Computing*, Vol.24, No.5, (May 2006), pp. 411–423, ISSN 0262-8856.

Yuan, Y. & Mandal, K.M. (2002). Low-Band-Shifted Hierarchical Backward Motion Estimation and Compensation for Wavelet-Based Video Coding, *Proceedings of the 3rd Indian Conference on Computer Vision, Graphics and Image Processing*, pp. 185-190, Ahmedabad, India, December 16-18, 2002

Zivkovic, Z. & van der Heijden, F. (2006). Efficient adaptive density estimation per image pixel for the task of background subtraction. *Pattern Recognition Letters*, Vol.27, No.7, (May 2006), pp. 773–780, ISNN 0167-8655

3

Speech Scrambling Based on Wavelet Transform

Sattar Sadkhan and Nidaa Abbas
University of Babylon
Iraq

1. Introduction

The increased interest in analog speech scrambling techniques are due to the increased visibility and publicity given to the vulnerability of communication systems to eavesdropping of unauthorized remote access (Gersho & Steele, 1984). In wireless communications, including High Frequency (H.F) and satellite communications, it is almost impossible to prevent unauthorized people from eavesdropping unless speech scramblers may be used to protect privacy. Among speech scramblers, analog scramblers are attractive and wide applicable. The conventional analog scramblers manipulate speech signal in the frequency or time domain or both. A typical frequency domain scrambler is the band splitting scrambler, which breaks the speech signal into several sub bands and permutes them. A typical time domain scrambler is the time division scrambler, which breaks the speech signal into short time segments and permutes them within a block of several segments(Sakurai et al., 1984). These conventional analog scramblers cannot provide sufficient security against cryptanalysis because the number of permutable elements in these scramblers is not large enough to provide an adequate number of different permutations due to hardware limitation and processing delays.

To strengthen security, a two-dimensional scrambler which manipulates the speech signal both in the frequency domain and in the time domain was proposed. Regarding other types of scramblers, which can attain a high degree of security, the transform domain scrambler was proposed.

In 1979, Wyner proposed a method, in which the orthogonal transform called a Prolate Spheroidal transform (PSD) was executed on a set of the sampled speech signal. A mathematical basis for using both band splitting and time division, at the same time was presented by F. Pichler in 1983. He showed how an operation which realizes band splitting and time division can be designed, and pointed out that such an operation can be realized by a fast algorithm. The mathematical background is the theory of group-character for finite Abelian Groups and the theory of the General Fast Fourier Transform (GFFT) (Pichler, 1983). Also in 1984 Lin-Shan et. al., presented frequency domain scrambling algorithm, which is an extension of the Discrete Fourier Transform (DFT) scrambler previously proposed. The use of short-time Fourier analysis and filter bank techniques lead to the special feature that the original speech could be correctly recovered while the frame synchronization is completely unnecessary. In 1990 Sridharan et. Al., presented a comparison among five discrete orthogonal transforms in speech encryption systems. The results of the research showed that the Discrete Cosine Transform (DCT) and the Discrete Prolate Spheroidal Transform (DPST) could be used in narrow band systems. The Karhunen Loeve Transform (KLT) and the Discrete Hadamard Transform (DHT) were more suitable where wider bandwidth was available. The DCT turned out to be the best transform with respect to residual intelligibility of the encryption speech and recovered speech quality. The DFT produced results which were inferior to the DCT. The DCT implementation would also offer speed advantage over the FFT (Sridharan et al., 1990).

Original BSS (Blind Source Separation) - based speech encryption system utilizes BSS to perform decryption, but the complexity of BSS algorithms limits the decryption speed and its real-time applications. In 2010 , fast decryption utilizing calculation for BSS-based speech encryption was proposed. The paper analyzed the correlation of speech signals with key signals, and then utilized the correlation calculation to achieve speech decryption. The experiment results showed that correlation calculation decryption nicely simplifies BSS-bsed speech encryption system, largely speeds up the speech decryption, and slightly improves the quality of decrypted speech signals (Guo & Lin, 2010). While Mermoul and Belouchhrani claimed that the interactability of the under-determined BSS problem has been used for the proposal of BSS-based speech encryption has some weakness from cryptographic point of view. In their paper they proposed new encryption method that bypass these weaknesses. Their proposed approach is based on the subspace concept together with the use of nonlinear function and key signals. An interesting feature of the proposed technique is that only a part of the secret key parameters used during encryption is necessary for decryption (Mermoul & Belouchrani, 2010)

(Mosa, et al., 2010) introduced a new speech cryptosystem, which is based on permutation and masking of speech segments using multiple secret keys in both time and transform domain.

In 2000, an automated method for cryptanalysis of DFT-based analog speech scramblers was presented by Wen-Whei and Heng-Iang, through statistical estimation treatments. In the proposed system, the cipher text only attack was formulated as a combinatorial optimization problem leading to a search for the most likely key estimate. For greater efficiency, they also explored the benefits of Genetic Algorithm to develop the method. Simulation results indicated that the global explorative properties of Genetic Algorithms make them very effective at estimating the most likely permutation and by using this estimate significant amount of the intelligibility could be recovered from the cipher text following the attack on DFT-based speech scramblers (Whei & Iang, 2000)

A time-frequency scrambling algorithm based on wavelet packets was proposed by Ajit S. B. Bopardikar (1995) by using different wavelet packet filter banks, they added an extra level of security since the eavesdropper had to choose the correct analysis filter bank, correctly rearrange the time-frequency segments, and choose the correct synthesis bank to get back the original speech signal. Simulations performed with this algorithm give distance measures comparable to those obtained for the uniform filter bank based algorithm(Bopardikar, 1995). In 2005, an analog speech scrambler which is based on Wavelet Transformation and Permutation was proposed by Sattar B. Sadkhan and evaluating the scrambling efficiency through the calculation of distance measures, and takes the effect of the channel noise into consideration (Sadkhan, et al., 2005). In 2007, A Parallel Structure of different wavelet transforms were applied for speech scrambling. The proposed structure provided a good results in comparison with the system implemented in 2005 (Sadkhan, Falah, 2007)

2. Speech scrambling system

Speech Scrambling seeks to perform a completely reversible operation on a portion of speech, that it is totally unintelligible to unauthorized listener. The most important criteria used to evaluate speech scramblers are:

- The scrambler's ability to produce encrypted speech with low residual intelligibility.
- The extent to which the encryption and decryption processes affect the quality of the speech recovered by intended reception; and
- The scrambler's immunity to cryptanalysis attack.

Cryptographers face the problem of designing scrambling systems which distort the very redundant speech signal to the extent that useful information is unable to be recovered. The encryption process must remain secure when subject to the powerful information processing structures of the human auditory system and knowledge-base automated cryptanalytic processes. There are two fundamentally distinct approaches to achieve voice security in speech communication systems: digital ciphering and analog scrambling. In spite of significant progress in digital speech processing technology, analog speech scramblers continue to be important for achieving privacy in many types of voice communication (Gersho & Steele, 1984), due to the desire for secure communication over existing channels with standard telephone bandwidth at acceptable speech quality and reasonable cost. To make the distinction between analog and digital speech encryption devices, the following definitions can be considered. Analog scramblers produce scrambled speech which is analog signal occupying the same bandwidth as the original speech. Analog or digital signal processing may be used to generate this signal. Digital speech encryption systems digitize and compress the input speech in order to obtain a digital representation at a bit rate suitable for the communications channel to be used. The resulting bit stream is encrypted using well-know data encryption techniques. The ability of a digital encryption schemes to compete with the well-established analog scramblers is depend on the quality of the speech compression algorithms used. The speech quality resulting from contemporary compression schemes is rapidly improving (Sakurai, et al., 1984).

Analog speech scrambling experienced a metamorphosis as a result of the development and release of very high speed signal processing hardware. Analog scrambling algorithms which were impractical due to their complex nature are now being implemented in real time using this technology.

One family of analog scramblers that has shown a great deal of promise is the transform domain scrambler. These scramblers operate on speech which has been sampled and digitized. The sampled speech is portioned into frames of equal length, containing N speech samples. A chosen transformation is then performing on each frame to yield a transform vector with N components. Encryption is achieved by permuting these transform components within the vector before the inverse transform is applied to return the components to the time domain. The encrypted time domain frame is transmitted in place of original speech frame (Pichler, 1983).

2.1 Secure speech communication

There are many reasons that make the user hide the meaning of the transmitted speech. Secure speech communication refers to the masked speech communication. Generally, secure speech communication, shown in Fig. 1 , deals with three parts: -

- The first part is transmitter (T_x) which has the ability to produce encrypted speech with low residual intelligibility;
- The second part is receiver (R_x) which recovers the encrypted speech, which is near as possible to the original speech signal.
- The third part is the eavesdropper that attacks the communication system according to many available methods (Lee, 1985).

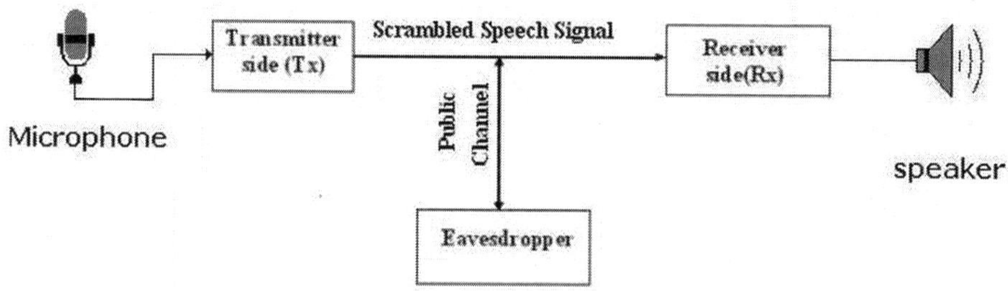

Fig. 1. Block diagram of secure speech communication

The first and second part uses a secure communication channel, while the eavesdropper tries to destroy the security of the communication system. If the system is destroyed, the receiver may lose the ability of getting the transmitted signal. In this case, the first and second parts must try to find another secure algorithm (to be used in the communication system) which is more secure and more difficult to be cryptanalysis by the third part.

The worst case is when the first and second part does not know that the system is destroyed by the third part. The first part wishes to mask or hide the meaning of the transmitted speech where, the second part can recover it without allowing the third part to get any meaningful speech. Almost all speech security systems reduce (at least to some extent) the audio quality of a voice transmission. Security will not be enhanced if the link has been so badly degraded that we have to repeat the same message a number of times.

2.2 Analog speech scrambling

In analog speech scrambling, the only real analog operation is signal transmission, since the signal processing is carried out digitally. Incoming speech signals are digitized using analog to digital converter (ADC) , then processed by a special scrambling algorithm, converted back to analog, and transmitted to a receiver, where they are digitized again, inversely processed (descrambled), and reconverted to analog form for reconstruction, as shown in Fig. 2

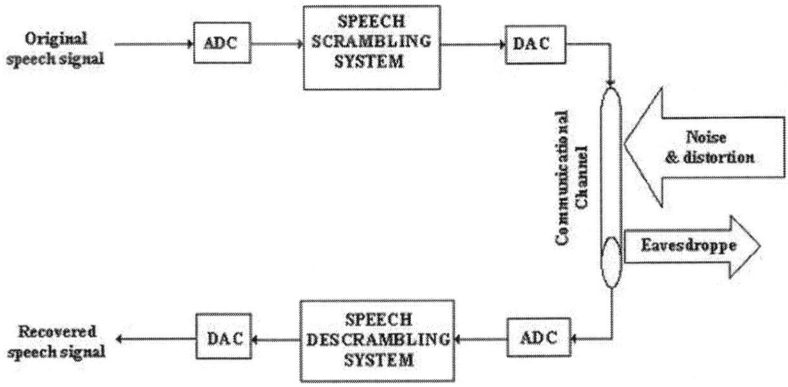

Fig. 2. Block diagram of speech scrambling

There are numerous scrambling methods. The two main processes involve dividing the signal in small time frames and manipulating the frequencies (scrambling in the frequency domain). The descrambler block descrambles the input signal, which must be a scalar or a frame-based column vector. The descrambler block is the inverse of the Scrambler block (Mascarin, 2000). The main attraction of this method arises from the fact that it can be used with the existing analog telephone, H.F., satellite and mobile communication systems, provided the encrypted signal occupies the same bandwidth as the original speech signal (Goldburg, et al., 1991).

3. Wavelet based speech scrambler

The analog scrambling process which employs a transformation of the input speech to facilitate encryption can best be described using matrix algebra. Let us consider the vector x which contains N speech time samples obtained from A/D conversion process, representing a frame of the original speech signal. Let this speech sample vector x be subject to an orthogonal transformation matrix F such that:

$$u = F \cdot x \tag{1}$$

This transformation results in a new vector (u) made up of transform coefficients. A permutation matrix is applied to (u), such that each transform coefficient is moved to a new position within the vector given by:

$$v = P \cdot u \tag{2}$$

A scrambled speech vector y is obtained by returning vector v to the time domain using the inverse transformation F^{-1} where:

$$y = F^{-1} \cdot v \tag{3}$$

Descrambling, or recovery of the original speech vector x' is achieved by first transforming y back to the transform domain .The inverse permutation matrix P^{-1} is then used to return the transform coefficients to their original 'position. Finally, the resulting transform vector is returned to the time domain by multiplying by F^{-1}

$$x' = F^{-1} \cdot P^{-1} \cdot F \cdot y \tag{4}$$

The transform domain scrambling process outlined above requires the transform matrix F to have an inverse. One attempts to insure that the scrambling transformation $T=F^{-1}.P.F$ is orthogonal. The inverse transformation T^{-1} will also be orthogonal. This property is useful since any noise added to the scrambling signal during transmission will not be enhanced by the descrambling process as shown in Fig. 3. The scrambled speech sequence is given by (Goldberg, et al., 1993):

$$y = F^{-1} \cdot P \cdot F \cdot x = T \cdot x \tag{5}$$

At most. N elements are able to be permuted in the transform -based scrambling process. It is important to note that for a given sampling frequency. N will determine the delay introduced by the scrambling device. So a tradeoff between system delay and security .N is usually chosen to be equal to 256. Practically, the number of transform coefficients M! possible coefficient arrangements. this restriction stems from the requirement that the scrambled speech should occupy the same bandwidth as the original speech. If the, and Biorthognal wavelets etc… transform components have a frequency representation. those lying outside the allowable band are set to zero and the reminder are permuted. Methods for generating all M! Possible permutations have been addressed (Bopardikar, 1995) . The permutations must carefully screen to ensure that components will undergo a significant displacement from their original position in the vector. In addition, components which were adjacent in the original vector should be separated in the scrambled vector.

If it is assumed during it's passage over the communications channel, a noise component μ is added to y, then we have

$$y' = y + \mu \tag{6}$$

Where y' is the signal observed by the receiver. The inverse scrambling transformation is then applied to y' in order to descramble and recover the original sequence x.

$$x' = T^{-1} \cdot y' \;\; = x + T^{-1} \cdot \mu \tag{7}$$

Now since T^{-1} is orthogonal, and hence norm preserving $\|\mu\| = \|T^{-1} \cdot \mu\|$ .This implies that the noise energy is not enhanced as a result of the scrambling process.

3.1 Permutation used in the scrambler

The number of possible permutations of ***N*** elements is *N!*. However, all of these permutations cannot be used because some of them do not provide enough security.

Let ***P*** be a set of permutations, and let $\boldsymbol{P^{-1}}$ be the set of inverse permutations corresponding to the permutation in ***P***. The set S has to satisfy the requirement that any permutation in ***P*** must not produce an intelligible scrambled speech. It is difficult to evaluate the intelligibility of the scrambled speech signal and the intelligibility of the descrambled speech signal by a quantitative criterion because intelligibility is substantially a subjective matter, as shown in Fig. 3.

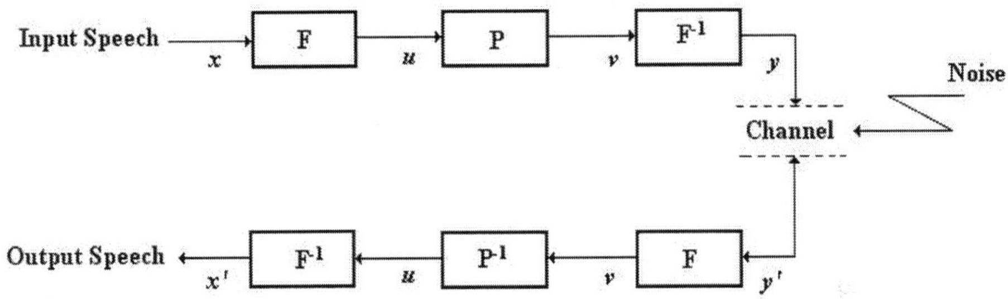

Fig. 3. Block diagram of speech scrambling

A permutation of *N* elements can be expressed as (Rao &Homer, 2001).

$$P = \begin{bmatrix} 1,2,3,............N \\ k_1,k_2,k_3,.....k_N \end{bmatrix} \tag{8}$$

by the permutation P on a set of *N* elements A=(e_1,e_2,e_3,……,e_N), the element of A at the *ith* position is moved to the k_ith position ,namely,

$$P'A = P(e_1,e_2,e_3,.....,e_N) = (d_1,d_2,d_3,.......d_N) \tag{9}$$

Where

$$d_{ki} = e_i \ (i=1,2,3...N) \tag{10}$$

One of the most common and easiest ways of analyzing this is the Hamming distance (HD) between a pair of permutations. The HD of a permutation P is defined as the number of digits which are not coincident in the same position.

3.2 Measures for residual intelligibility and recovered voice quality

Voice quality of the recovered speech and the residual intelligibility of the encrypted speech are usually judged by subjective quality tests. Unfortunately, these tests take much time and labor, and require a large number of trained listeners. Even though intelligibility is a substantially subjective matter, it is possible to use objective tests which are useful, (if not ideal) indicators of intelligibility (Sridharn, et al.; 1991)

The objective measures are useful in indicating the residual intelligibility of encrypted speech and the corresponding quality of recovered speech .

A distance measure is an assignment of a number to an input/output pair of a system. To be useful, a distance measure must posses to a certain degree the following properties :

- It must be subjectively meaningful in the sense that small and large distance must correspond to low and high subjective quality, respectively;
- It must be tractable in the sense that it is possible to mathematically analyze and implement it in some algorithms.

One use of the distance measures is to evaluate the performance of speech scrambling system. The signal-to-noise ratio **(SNR)** and the segmental signal-to-noise Ratio **(SEGSNR)** are the most common time-domain measures (Gray, et al., 1980) · of the difference between original and processed speech signals (scrambled or descrambled speech signals).

3.2.1 Signal-to-Noise Ratio

The signal-to-noise ratio **(SNR)** can be defined as the ratio between the input signal power and the noise power, and is given in decibels **(dB)** as:

$$SNR = 10.\log_{10}\left\{ \sum_{n=1}^{N} X^2(n) \,/\, \sum_{n=1}^{N} \left[X(n) - Y(n)\right]^2 \right\} \text{ (in dB).} \tag{11}$$

Where N is the number of samples, ***X(n)*** is the original speech signal and ***Y(n)*** is the scrambled or descrambled speech signal. The principal benefit of the **SNR** quality measure is its mathematical simplicity. The measure represents an average error over time and frequency for a processed signal. However, **SNR** is a poor estimator for a broad range of speech distortions. The fact that **SNR** is not particularly well related to any subjective attribute of speech quality and that it weights all time domain errors in the speech waveform equality (Gray, Markel 1976) · This can be solved with segmental **SNR**.

3.2.2 Segmental Signal-to-Noise Ratio

An improved version measure can be obtained if **SNR** is measured over short frames and the results are averaged. The frame-based measure is called the segmental **SNR (SEGSNR)** and is defined as:

$$SEGSNR = \overline{SNR(m)} \text{ in (dB).} \tag{12}$$

Where $\overline{SNR(m)}$ is the average of ***SNR(m)*** and ***SNR(m)*** is the **SNR** for segment ***m***. The segmentation of the **SNR** permits the objective measure to assign equal weights to load and soft portions of the speech (Yuan, 2003)

4. Results and discussion

In the proposed Wavelet Transform based Speech Scrambling system, (Arabic) messages have been recorded with sampling frequency of 8 kHz as speech files.

At the transmitter, the sampled speech signal is arranged into frames . Each frame contains 256 samples, and then the Wavelet Transformation is performed on each frame. After that, the transform coefficients are permuted before applying the Inverse Wavelet Transform (IWT). The resulting scrambled speech signal is saved in a wave file.

At the receiver, frame by frame of length 256 samples are descrambled and saved in wave file. The proposed scrambled system investigates four types of wavelets: (Haar, db3, sym2 and sym4), each one with three different levels. Two types of tests have been applied to examine the performance of the simulation, these are:

a. Subjective Test: in which the scrambled speech files have been played back to a number of listeners to measure the residual intelligibility, subjectively. For all cases, the judge was that the files contain noise only, which means that the residual intelligibility is very low. The analog recovered speech files have been tested in a similar way to measure the quality of the recovered speech files, the judge was that the files were exactly the same as the original copies.
b. Objective Test: As mentioned earlier, the objective test is a valuable measure to the residual intelligibility of the scrambled speech, and the quality of the recovered speech.

The distance measures indicate the perceptual similarity of the speech recovered following decryption and the original speech. They are also used to quantify the difference between scrambled speech and original speech.

The signal to noise ratio (SNR) and the segmental signal to noise ratio measure (SEGSNR) have been chosen to test the residual intelligibility of the scrambled speech and the quality of the recovered speech for all files. The segmental signal to noise ratio measure (SEGSNR) is an improved version measure of the (SNR).

Generally, these distance measures for all the scrambled speech files are very low (good negative value) which means that the residual intelligibility is very low, and the distance measures for all the recovered speech files are very high (large positive value) which means that the quality of the recovered speech is very high.

Using the relation between estimated PSD (dB/Hz) in relation with frequency of the used speech signals in two cases, as follows:

- To compare the original and scrambled speech.
- To compare the original and descrambled speech.

The wavelet based speech scrambling system have been tested under two states of the simulation, these are:

4.1 Noise free channel simulation

Simulation results of typical experiments with the Wavelet based scrambler, and descrambler for an Arabic word spoken by women's voice '"evenning" are shown in figures (4) to (8), and Tables (1) to (2), using different wavelets and different levels.

Case Study:

Using (Haar) Wavelet , (db3) wavelet, Sym2 and Sym4 wavelet each one will be considered with three different levels for the **Arabic word'" evening** ".

Figure (4)shows the waveform, spectrum, and spectrogram of a sample original clear speech signal that represents an Arabic word " evening ".

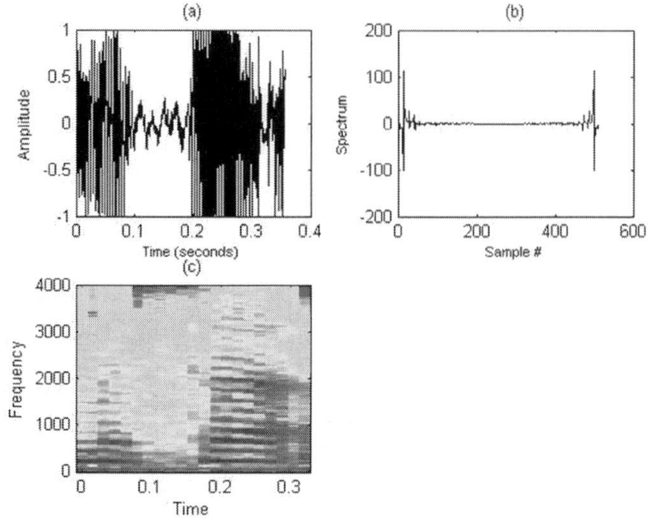

Fig. 4. Original Speech Signal; a) Waveform. (b) Spectrum. (c) Spectrogram.
Using Wavelet Transform (Haar) With Level 1

Figure (5) shows the waveform, spectrum, and spectrogram of the scrambled speech signal, while the comparison of the scrambled speech signal, that resulted from applying a wavelet transform of type (Haar) with a specified level (level 1)is shown in Fig. (6) .

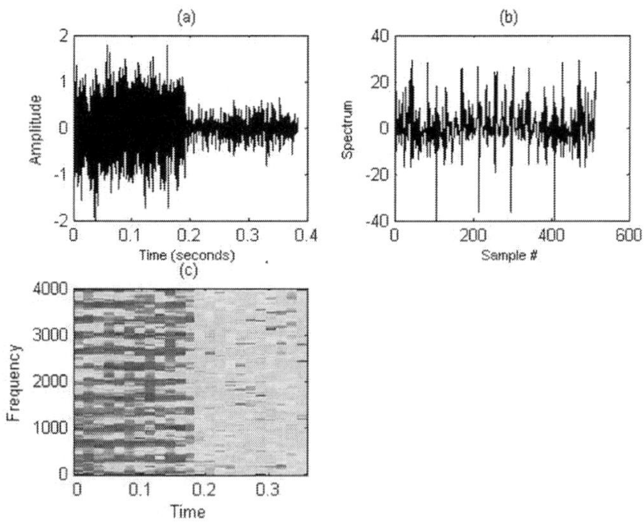

Fig. 5. Scrambled Speech Signal Using Haar Wavelet With Level 1; (a) Waveform. (b)Spectrum. (c) Spectrogram;

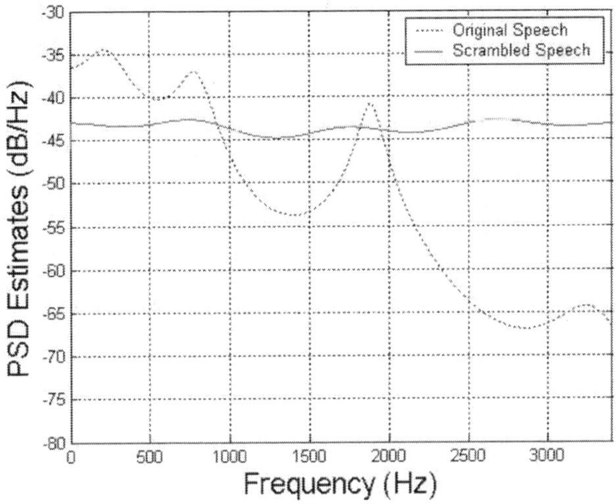

Fig. 6. Comparison between original speech and scrambled Speech using PSD Estimates

Fig. (7) shows the waveform, spectrum , and spectrogram of the resulted descrambled speech signal, while Fig. (8) shows the comparison of the descrambled speech signal and the orignal speech signal.

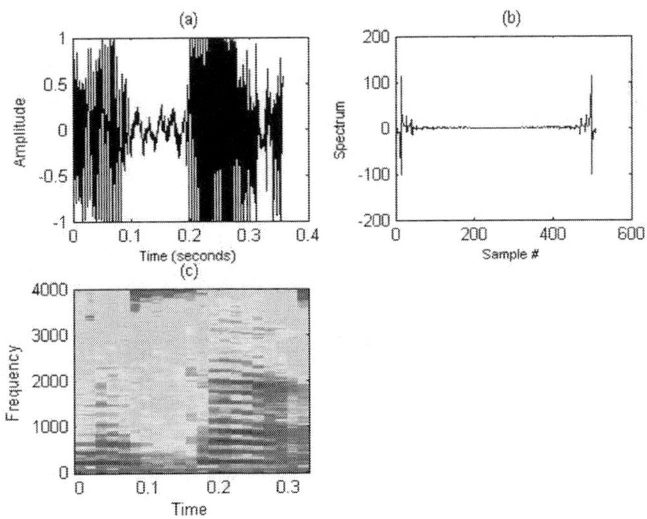

Fig. 7. Descrambled Speech Signal Using Haar Wavelet With Level 1; (a) Waveform. (b) Spectrum. (c) Spectrogram.

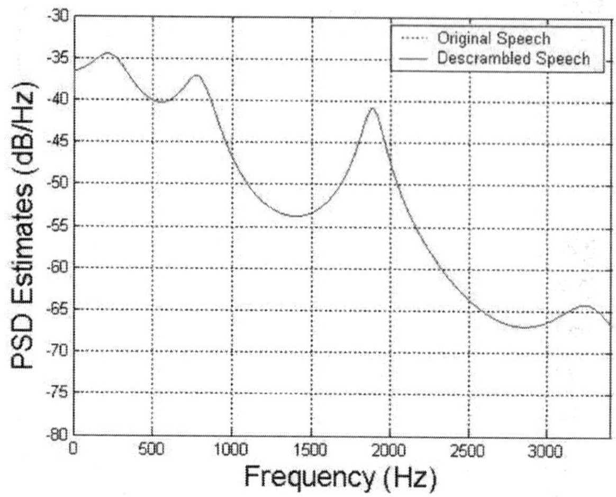

Fig. 8. The Comparison Between Original Speech and Descrambled Speech.

Table (1) shows distance measure (SEGSNRs) for the scrambled speech, while Table (2) shows the (SEGSNRd) distance measure for the descrambled speech for different Wavelets and different decomposition levels.

Level of Decomposition	1	2	3
Haar	-4.8732	-4.0857	-4.0907
Db3	-4.7673	-3.7751	-3.8147
Sym2	-4.8064	-3.7710	-3.6743
Sym4	-4.6620	-3.7125	-3.9071

Table 1. SEGSNRs (dB) for the scrambled speech, for each wavelet with a specific level.

Level of Decomposition	1	2	3
Haar	310.26	305.67	303.12
Db3	15.85	17.46	9.59
Sym2	112.96	18.19	13.91
Sym4	12.88	10.07	13.03

Table 2. SEGSNRd (dB) for the recovered speech, for each wavelet with a specific level.

4.2 Noisy channel simulation

An evaluation of the proposed speech scrambling system with different signal to noise ratios from (5 dB up to 25 dB) was tested.

Case study with **SNR = 15 dB**.

The figures (9) to (11), in each one, figure (a) represents spectrogram comparison between original speech signal and scrambled speech signal, while figure (b) represents the comparison between the spectrogram of the descrambled and original speech signal. Both figures are tested under the same level of the chosen Wavelet Transform-Type: Sym2.

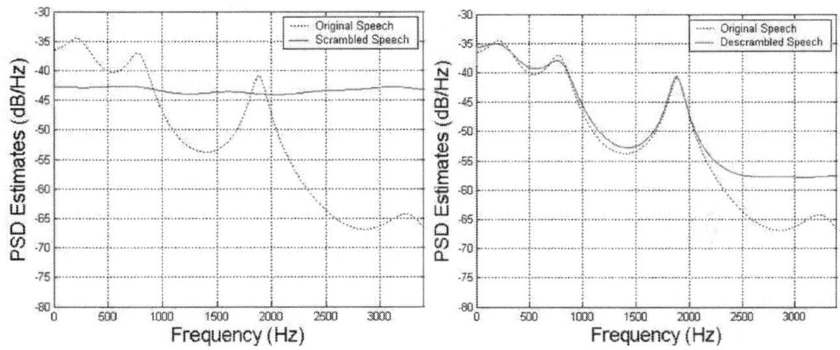

a) b)

Fig. 9. (a) The Comparison between Original Speech and Scrambled Speech Using **sym2 / Level 1**
(b) The Comparison between Original Speech and Descrambled Speech Using **sym2 / Level 1**

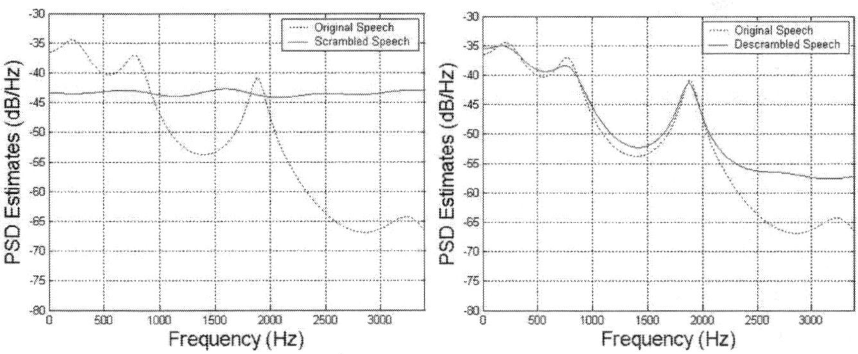

a) b)

Fig. 10. (a) The Comparison between Original Speech and Scrambled Speech Using **sym2 / Level 2**
(b) The Comparison between Original Speech and Descrambled Speech Using **sym2 / Level 2**

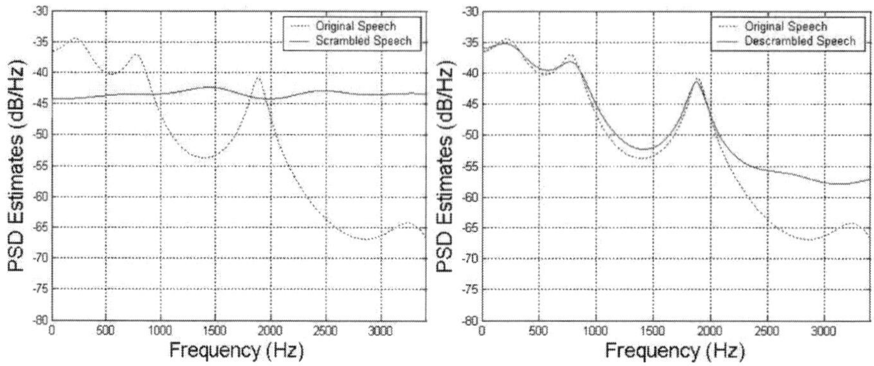

a) b)

Fig. 11. (a) The Comparison between Original Speech and Scrambled Speech Using **sym2/ Level 3**
(b) The Comparison between Original Speech and Descrambled Speech Using **sym2/ Level 3**

The results from such tests are shown in Tables (3) to Table (8). Table (3) shows the SEGSNRs distance measure for the scrambled speech, and Table (4) shows the SEGSNRd distance measure for the descrambled speech, with SNR = 5 dB. Each two tables corresponding to a specific SNR.

Level of Decomposition	1	2	3
Haar	-5.867	-5.383	-5.292
Db3	-5.711	-5.146	-5.293
Sym2	-5.781	-5.094	-5.017
Sym4	-5.723	-5.220	-5.360

Table 3. SEGSNRs (dB) for the scrambled speech, for each wavelet with a specific level, with SNR = 5 dB.

Level of Decomposition	1	2	3
Haar	3.195	2.852	2.993
Db3	2.530	2.015	1.407
Sym2	2.911	2.481	2.151
Sym4	2.262	1.995	1.204

Table 4. SEGSNRd (dB) for the recovered speech, for each wavelet with a specific level, with SNR = 5 dB.

Level of Decomposition	1	2	3
Haar	-5.007	-4.267	-4.249
Db3	-4.863	-3.950	-4.032
Sym2	-4.898	-3.928	-3.625
Sym4	-4.796	-3.932	-4.112

Table 5. SEGSNRs (dB) for the scrambled speech, for each wavelet with a specific level, with SNR = 15 dB

Level of Decomposition	1	2	3
Haar	13.025	12.852	12.993
Db3	10.073	9.218	7.133
Sym2	12.349	11.001	9.438
Sym4	9.472	8.002	7.707

Table 6. SEGSNRd (dB) for the recovered speech, for each wavelet with a specific level, with SNR =1 5 dB.

Level of Decomposition	1	2	3
Haar	-4.892	-4.111	-4.110
Db3	-4.771	-3.793	-3.846
Sym2	-4.805	-3.784	-3.682
Sym4	-4.672	-3.741	-3.932

Table 7. SEGSNRs (dB) for the scrambled speech, for each wavelet with a specific level, with SNR = 25 dB

Level of Decomposition	1	2	3
Haar	23.088	22.852	22.99
Db3	13.933	13.693	9.184
Sym2	20.304	16.255	12.956
Sym4	12.273	9.824	10.641

Table 8. SEGSNRd (dB) for the recovered speech, for each wavelet with a specific level, with SNR =25 dB.

5. Conclusion

The performance of the Wavelet Transform based speech scrambling system was examined on actual " **Arabic Speech Signals** " , and the results showed that there was no residual intelligibility in the scrambled speech signal. The descrambled speech signal at receiver was exactly identical to the original applied speech waveform. Hence it provides the high security scrambled speech signal and the reconstructed signal was perfect . Some interesting points can be mentioned here:

a. It is clear that (SNRs & SEGSNRs) give small values at any decomposition level, while (SNRd & SEGSNRd), give large values. As the level decreases the system performs better. The absolute low values of distance measures does not necessarily mean a perceptually poor assessments. The distance measures (SNR and SEGSNR) for scrambled/descrambled speech, can in some cases, be used for design purposes as a relative number of intelligibility loss or speech quality.
b. The spectrogram is used because it is a powerful tool that allows us to see what's happening in the frequency and time domains all at once. Thus we can easily see the theory at work here by observing the original signal, it's scrambled version, and the descrambled version. Note that on the scrambled plot it is observed that the order of the frequencies has changed. And, as expected the descrambled version has been correctly decoded to its original form.
c. An evaluation of the speech scrambling system with different power levels of the additive white Gaussian noise was tested. The results proved that as the signal to noise ratio increases, the correspondence between original and descrambled speech increases. Hence, it can be concluded that, the WT algorithm can be implemented to scramble and descramble speech with high efficiency.
d. For real time speech scrambling it is recommended to use a wavelet with a small number of order at a reasonable decomposition level (level **3** decomposition or less), because the number of coefficients required to represent a given signal increases with the level of decomposition (higher wavelet decompositions requires more computation time, which should be minimized for real time speech scrambling) and with the large number of order.

6. References

Bopardikar, A. S. (1995). Speech Encryption Using Wavelet Packets. Indian Institute Of Science.

DeelRe, E.; Fantacci, R. & Maffucci, D. (1989). A New Speech Signal Scrambling Method For Secure Communications: Theory, Implementation, And Security Evaluation. IEEE Journal On Selected Areas in Communications, Vol.7, No.4.

Gersho, A. & Steele, R. (1984). Encryption of Analog Signals a Perspective. IEEE Journal on Selected Areas in Communications, Vol. SAC-2, No.3

Goldburg, B.; Dawson, E. & Sridharan, S. (1991). The Automated Cryptanalysis Of Analog Speech Scramblers. Advances in Cryptology: Proceeding of EUROCRYPT'91, New York: Springer Verlag.

Goldburg, B.; Dawson, E. & Sridharan, S. (1993). Design And Cryptanalysis Of Transform-Based Analog Speech Scramblers. IEEE Journal On Selected Areas in Communications, Vol. 11.

Goldburg, B; Sridharan, S. & Dawson, Ed. (1993). Design And Cryptanalysis Of Transform-Based Analog Speech Scramblers. IEEE Journal On Selected Areas in Communications, Vol. 11, No.6.

Graps, A. (2011). An Introduction to Wavelet. IEEE Computational Science and Engineering, http://www.amara.com/IEEEwave/IEEEwavelet.html

Gray, R; Buzo, A. & Matsuyama, Y. (1980). Distortion Measures for Speech Processing. IEEE Trans. Acoustics, Speech and Signal Proc., Vol. ASSP-28, No. 4.

Gray, A. & Markel, J. (1976). Distance Measures for Speech Processing. IEEE Trans. Acoustics, Speech and Signal Proc., Vol. ASSP-24, No. 5.

Guo, Da & Lin Q (2010). Fast Decryption Utilizing Correlation Calculation for BSS-based Speech Encryption System. Sixth International Conference on Neural Computation.

Lee, L. (1985). A Speech Security System Not Requiring Synchronization. IEEE Communications Magazine, Vol.23, no.7.

Mascarin, A. (2000). Wavelet Toolbox-Featured Product. The Math Works Inc. , Natick, MA, http://www.mathworks.com/products/wavelet.

Mermoul, A & Belouchrani, A. (2010). A Subspace – Based Method for Speech Encryption. Int. Conf. On Information Science, signal Processing and their applications (ISSPA 2010).

Mosa, E.; Messiha, N. & Abd El-Samie, F. (2010). Encryption of Speech Signal with multiple secret keys in time and transform domain. Int. J. Speech Technol., 13.

Pichler, F. (1983). Analog Scrambling By The General Fast Fourier Transform. Department of System Science.

Rao, N. & Homer, J. (2001). Speech Compression Using Wavelets. Electrical Engineering Thesis Project.

Sadkhan, S. B, Khaged, N. H., & Al-Saadi, L. H. (2005). A Proposed Speech Scrambling System Based On Wavelet Transform And Permutation. IEEE Communication And Signal Processing, Vol. 3.

Sadkhan, S.; Falah, N. (2007). A Proposed Analog Speech Scrambler Based on Parallel Structure of Wavelet Transform. M.Sc. Thesis, AlNahrain University, IRAQ.

Sakurai, K; Koga, K. & Muratani, T. (1984). A Speech Scrambler Using The Fast Fourier Transform Technique. IEEE Journal on Selected Areas in Communications, Vol. SAC-2, No.3

Sridharan, S.; Dawson, E. & Goldburg, B. (1990). Speech Encryption In The Transform Domain. Electronics Letters, Queensland Univ. of Technol., Vol. 26.

Sridharan, S.; Dawson, E. & Goldburg, B. (1991). Fast Fourier Transform Based Speech Encryption System. IEE Proceedings-I, Vol. 138, No. 3.

Whei, W. & Iang, H. (2000). The Automated Cryptanalysis of DFT-Based Speech Scramblers. IEICE Transactions on Information and Systems, Vol. E83-D, No.12.

Yuan, Z. (2003). The Weighted Sum of The Line Spectrum Pair for Noisy Speech. M.Sc. Thesis, Department of Electrical and Communications Engineering, Helsinki University of Technology.

4

Wavelet Denoising

Guomin Luo and Daming Zhang
Nanyang Technological University
Singapore

1. Introduction

Removing noise from signals is possible only if some prior information is available. The information is employed by different estimators to recover the signal and reduce noise. Most noises in one-dimensional transient signal follow Gaussian distribution. The Bayes estimator minimizes the expected risk to get the optimal estimation. The minimax estimator uses a simple model for estimation. They are the most popular estimators in noise estimation.

No matter which estimator is used, the risk should be as small as possible. Donoho and Johnstone have made a breakthrough by proving that thresholding estimator has a small risk which is close to the lower bound. Thereafter, threshold estimation was studied extensively and has been improved by more and more researchers. Besides the universal threshold, some other thresholds, for example SURE threshold and minimax threshold, are also widely applied.

In wavelet denoising, the thresholding algorithm is usually used in orthogonal decompositions: multi-resolution analysis and wavelet packet transform. Wavelet thresholding faces some questions in its application, for example, the selection of hard or soft threshold, fixed or level-dependent threshold. Proper selection of those items helps generating a better estimation.

Besides the influence of thresholding, the influence of wavelets is also an important factor. In most applications, the wavelet transform uses a few non-zero coefficients to describe a signal or function. Producing only a few non-zero coefficients is crucial in noise removal and reducing computing complexity. Choosing a wavelet with optimum design to produce more wavelet coefficients close to zero is crucial in some applications.

2. Noise estimation

The output acquired by sensing devices, for example transformer and sensor, is a measurement of analogue input signal $\overline{f}(x)$. The output can be modelled as in (1). The output $X[n]$ is composed by a filtered $\overline{f}(x)$ with the sensor responses $\overline{\phi}(x)$ and an added noise $W[n]$. The noise W contains various types of interferences, for instance, the radio frequency interferences from communication systems. It also includes the noises induced by measurement devices, such as electronic noises from oscilloscope and transmission errors. In most cases, the noise W is modelled by a random vector that often follows Gaussian distribution.

$$X[n] = < \bar{f}, \bar{\phi} > + W[n] \tag{1}$$

If the analogue-to-digital data acquisition is stable, the discrete signal can be denoted by $f[n] = < \bar{f}, \bar{\phi} >$. The analogue approximation of $\bar{f}(x)$ can be recovered from $f[n]$. The noisy output in (1) is rewritten as

$$X[n] = f[n] + W[n] \tag{2}$$

The estimation of $f[n]$ calculated from (2) is denoted by $\tilde{F} = DX[n]$, where D is the decision operator. It is designed to minimize the error $f - \tilde{F}$. For one-dimension signal, the mean-square distance is often employed to measure the error $f - \tilde{F}$. The mean-square distance is not a perfect model but it is simple and sufficiently precise in most cases (Mallat, 2009d). The risk of the estimation is calculated by (3):

$$r(D, f) = E\{\| f - \tilde{F} \|^2\} \tag{3}$$

The decision operator D is optimized with the prior information available on the signal (Mallat, 2009d). Two estimation methods: Bayes estimation and minimax estimation are the most commonly used ones. The Bayes estimator minimizes the risk to get optimal estimation. But it is difficult to obtain enough information to model prior probability distribution. The minimax estimator uses simple model. But the risk cannot be calculated. The section 2.1 and section 2.2 introduce the fundamental of Bayes estimator and minimax estimator.

2.1 Bayes estimation

In Bayes estimation, the unknown signal f which is denoted by a random vector F is supposed to have a probability distribution α which is also called prior distribution. The noisy output in (2) can be rewritten as

$$X[n] = F[n] + W[n] \text{ for } 0 \le n < N \tag{4}$$

The noise W is supposed to be independent with F for all n. The distribution of measurement X is the joint distribution of F and W. It is called posterior distribution. Thus, $\tilde{F} = DX$ is an estimator of F from measurement X. Then the risk is the same as in (3). The Bayes risk of $\tilde{F}$ with respect to the prior probability distribution α of the signal is:

$$r(D,\alpha) = E_\alpha\{r(D,F)\} = E\{\| F - \tilde{F} \|^2\} = \sum_0^{N-1} E\{| F[n] - \tilde{F}[n] |^2\} \cdot \tag{5}$$

The estimator $\tilde{F}$ is said to be a Bayes estimator if it minimizes the Bayes risk among all estimators. Equivalently, the estimator which minimizes the posterior expected loss $E_\alpha\{r(D,F) \mid X\}$ for each X also minimizes the Bayes risk and therefore is a Bayes estimator (Lehmann & Casella, 1998).

The risk function is determined by choosing the way to measure the distance between the estimator $\tilde{F}$ and the unknown signal F. In most applications, the mean square error is adopted because of its simplicity. But some alternative estimators are also used such as linear estimation. In this chapter, most estimations use mean square error to measure estimation risk.

2.2 Minimax estimation

It is possible that we have some prior information for a signal, but it is rare to know the probability distribution of complex signals. For example, there is not an appropriate model for the stochastic transient signals in power system or the sound signals from nature environment. In this case, we have to find a "good" estimator whose maximal risk is minimal among all estimators. The prior information forms a signal set Θ . But this set does not specify the probability distribution of signals in Θ . The more prior information, the smaller the set Θ (Mallat, 2009d).

For the signal $f \in \Theta$, the noisy output is as shown in (2). The risk of estimation $\tilde{F} = DX$ is $r(D,f) = E\{\| DX - f \|^2\}$. Since the probability distribution of signal in set Θ is unknown, the precise risk cannot be calculated. Only a possible range is calculated. The maximum risk of this range is (Donoho & Johnstone, 1998):

$$r(D,\Theta) = \sup_{f \in \Theta} E\{\| DX - f \|^2\} \tag{6}$$

In minimax estimation, the minimax risk is the lower bound of risk in (6) with all possible, no matter linear or nonlinear, operators D :

$$r_n(D,\Theta) = \inf_{D \in On} r(D,\Theta) \tag{7}$$

Here, O_n denotes the set of all operators.

3. Threshold estimation in bases

Threshold is the estimated noise level. The values larger than threshold are regarded as signal, and the smaller ones are regarded as noises. When the noisy output is decomposed in a chosen base, the estimator of noises can also be applied because the white noises remain as white noises in all bases. It is proved in section 3.1. Two thresholding functions: hard thresholding and soft thresholding are introduced in section 3.2.

3.1 Estimation in orthogonal basis

When the noisy output is decomposed in an orthogonal basis $B = \{g_m\}_{0 \le m < N}$, the components in (2) is rewritten as $X_B[m] = < X, g_m >$, $f_B[m] = < f, g_m >$, and $W_B[m] = < W, g_m >$. The sum of them gives

$$X_B[m] = f_B[m] + W_B[m]. \tag{8}$$

If the noise W is a zero-mean white noise with variance σ^2, then $E\{W[n]W[k]\} = \sigma^2 \delta[n-k]$. Thus the noise coefficients $W_B[m] = \sum_{n=0}^{N-1} W[n] g_m^*[n]$ also represent a white noise of variance σ^2 . This because,

$$E\{W_B[m]W_B[p]\} = \sum_{n=0}^{N-1}\sum_{k=0}^{N-1} g_m[n]g_p[k]E\{W[n]W[k]\} = \sigma^2 < g_p, g_m >= \sigma^2\delta[p-m]\,. \tag{9}$$

From the analysis above, one can see that the noise remains as white noise in all bases. It is not influenced by the choice of basis (Mallat, 2009d).

3.2 Thresholding estimation

In the orthogonal basis $B = \{g_m\}_{0\le m<N}$, the estimator of f in $X = f + W$ can be written as:

$$\tilde{F} = DX = \sum_{m=0}^{N-1} a_m(X_B[m])X_B[m]g_m\,. \tag{10}$$

Here, a_m is the thresholding function. It could be hard thresholding or soft thresholding.

3.2.1 Hard thresholding

A hard thresholding function is shown as follows (Mallat, 2009d):

$$a_m(x) = \begin{cases} 1 & \text{if} |x| \ge T \\ 0 & \text{if} |x| < T \end{cases}. \tag{11}$$

By substituting $a_m(x)$ into (10), we can obtain the estimator with hard thresholding function

$$\tilde{F} = \sum_{m=0}^{N-1} \rho_T(X_B[m])g_m \quad \text{with} \quad \rho_T(x) = a_m(x) * x = \begin{cases} x & \text{if} |x| \ge T \\ 0 & \text{if} |x| < T \end{cases}. \tag{12}$$

Then the risk of this thresholding is

$$r_{th}(f) = r(D,f) = \sum_{m=0}^{N-1} E\{|f_B[m] - \rho_T(X_B[m])|^2\}\,. \tag{13}$$

3.2.2 Soft thresholding

A soft thresholding function is implemented by (Mallat, 2009d)

$$0 \le a_m(x) = \max(1 - \frac{T}{|x|}, 0) \le 1\,. \tag{14}$$

The resulting estimator $\tilde{F}$ for this case can be written as in (12) with the thresholding function ρ_T replaced by a soft thresholding function as shown in (15).

$$\rho_T(x) = \begin{cases} x - T & \text{if } x \ge T \\ x + T & \text{if } x \le -T \\ 0 & \text{if } |x| \le T \end{cases}. \tag{15}$$

Reducing the magnitude of coefficients X_B that are greater than threshold usually makes the amplitude of the estimated signal $\tilde{F}$ be smaller than the original F. This is intolerable for some applications where precise recovery is required such as noise reduction of partial discharge signal, since the pulse magnitude and shape in such applications are needed for further analysis (Zhang et al., 2007). For other cases where precise recovery of signal magnitude is not required, for example, image noise reduction, the soft thresholding is widely used since it can retain the regularity of signal (Donoho, 1995).

The $\rho_T(x)$ of hard thresholding and soft thresholding are portrayed in Fig.1.

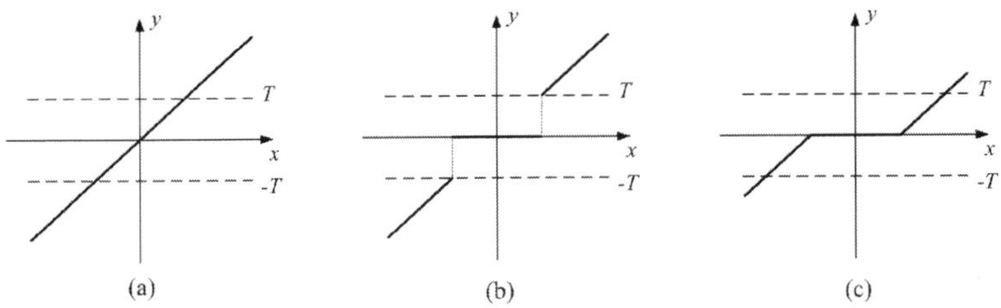

Fig. 1. Thresholding function $\rho_T(x)$, (a) original signal, (b) hard thresholding, (c) soft thresholding

3.3 Threshold estimation and its improvement

As depicted in (13), the risk of thresholding is closely related to the thresholding function ρ_T. The appropriate choice of threshold T is an important factor to reduce the risk of estimation. Several famous thresholds were proposed and proved by different estimation methods.

3.3.1 Universal threshold

Donoho and Johnstone (Donoho & Johnstone, 1994) proposed a universal threshold T. They proved that the risk of thresholding, no matter hard or soft, is small enough to satisfy the requirements of most applications.

If the thresholding function $\rho_T(x) = (x - \lambda sign(x))_{|x|>\lambda}$ is a soft thresholding, for a Gaussian random variable X of mean μ and variance 1, then the estimation risk is

$$r(\lambda, \mu) = E\{|\rho_\lambda(X) - \mu|^2\}. \tag{16}$$

If X has a variance σ^2 and a mean μ, then the following formula can be verified by considering $\tilde{X} = X / \sigma$

$$E\{|\rho_\lambda(X) - \mu|^2\} = \sigma^2 r(\frac{\lambda}{\sigma}, \frac{\mu}{\sigma}). \tag{17}$$

Since the projection $f_B[m]$ in basis $B = \{g_m\}_{0 \le m < N}$ is a constant, the $X_B[m]$ is a Gaussian random variable with mean $f_B[m]$ and variance σ^2. The risk of estimation by soft thresholding with a threshold T is

$$\begin{aligned} r_{th}(f) &= \sigma^2 \sum_{m=0}^{N-1} r(\frac{T}{\sigma}, \frac{f_B[m]}{\sigma}) \\ &\leq N\sigma^2 r(\frac{T}{\sigma}, 0) + \sigma^2 \sum_{m=0}^{N-1} \min(\frac{T^2+\sigma^2}{\sigma^2}, \frac{|f_B[m]|^2}{\sigma^2}) \end{aligned} . \tag{18}$$

Donoho and Johnstone proved that for $T = \sigma\sqrt{2\log_e N}$ and $N \geq 4$, the upper bound of the two parts of risk in (18) are (Donoho &Johnstone, 1994)

$$N\sigma^2 r(\frac{T}{\sigma}, 0) \leq (2\log_e N + 1)\sigma^2 , \tag{19}$$

and

$$\sigma^2 \sum_{m=0}^{N-1} \min(\frac{T^2+\sigma^2}{\sigma^2}, \frac{|f_B[m]|^2}{\sigma^2}) \leq (2\log_e N + 1) \sum_{m=0}^{N-1} \min(\sigma^2, |f_B[m]|^2) . \tag{20}$$

Then, the risk of estimator with threshold $T = \sigma\sqrt{2\log_e N}$ and all $N \geq 4$ is

$$r_{th}(f) \leq (2\log_e N + 1)(\sigma^2 + \sum_{m=0}^{N-1} \min(\sigma^2, |f_B[m]|^2)) \cdot \tag{21}$$

Donoho and Johnstone also mentioned in (Donoho &Johnstone, 1994), the universal threshold is optimal in certain cases defined by (Donoho &Johnstone, 1994).

3.3.2 SURE threshold

The thresholding risk is often reduced by decreasing the value of threshold, for instance, choosing a threshold smaller than universal threshold in section 3.3.1. Sure threshold was proposed by Stein (Stein, 1981) to suit this purpose.

As depicted in (Mallat, 2009d), when $|X_B[m]| < T$, the coefficient is set to zero by soft thresholding. Then the risk of estimation equals $|f_B[m]|^2$. Since $E\{|X_B[m]|^2\} = |f_B[m]|^2 + \sigma^2$, the $|f_B[m]|^2$ can be estimated with $|X_B[m]|^2 - \sigma^2$. But if $|X_B[m]| \geq T$, the soft thresholding substracts T from $|X_B[m]|$. Then the risk is the sum of noise energy and the bias introduced by the reduction of the amplitude of $X_B[m]$ by T. The resulting estimator of $r_{th}(f)$ is

$$Sure(X,T) = \sum_{m=0}^{N-1} C(X_B[m]) , \tag{22}$$

with

$$C(u) = \begin{cases} u^2 - \sigma^2 & \text{if } u \leq T \\ \sigma^2 + T^2 & \text{if } u > T \end{cases} . \tag{23}$$

The $Sure(X,T)$ is called Stein unbiased risk estimator (SURE) and was proved unbiased by (Donoho & Johnstone, 1995). Consider using this estimator of risk to select a threshold:

$$\tilde{T} = \arg\min_{T} Sure(X,T) \tag{24}$$

Arguing heuristically, one expects that, for large dimension N, a sort of statistical regularity will set in, the Law of Large Numbers will ensure that SURE is close to the true risk and that $\tilde{T}$ will be almost the optimal threshold for the case at hand (Donoho & Johnstone, 1995).

Although the SURE threshold is unbiased, its variance will induce errors when the signal energy is smaller than noise energy. In this case, the universal threshold must be imposed to remove all the noises. Since $E\{\| X \|^2\} = \| f \|^2 + N\sigma^2$, $\| f \|^2$ can be estimated by $\| X \|^2 - N\sigma^2$ and compared with a minimum energy level $\varepsilon_N = \sigma^2 N^{1/2} (\log_e N)^{3/2}$. Then the SURE threshold is (Mallat, 2009d)

$$T = \begin{cases} \sigma\sqrt{2\log_e N} & \text{if } \| X \|^2 - N\sigma^2 \le \varepsilon N \\ \tilde{T} & \text{if } \| X \|^2 - N\sigma^2 > \varepsilon N \end{cases}. \tag{25}$$

3.3.3 Minimax threshold

The inequality in (21) shows that the risk can be represented in the form of a multiplication of a constant $2\log_e N + 1$ and the loss for estimation. However, it is natural and more revealing to look for 'optimal' thresholds λ which yield smallest possible constant Λ in place of $2\log_e N + 1$. Thus, the inequality in (21) can be rewritten as

$$r_{th}(f) \le \Lambda(\sigma^2 + \sum_{m=0}^{N-1} \min(\sigma^2, | f_B[m] |^2)) \cdot \tag{26}$$

The minimax estimation introduced in section 2.2 is a possible method to find the appropriate constant Λ that satisfies $\Lambda \le 2\log_e N + 1$, and the threshold $\lambda \le \sqrt{2\log_e N}$.

Donoho and Jonestone (Donoho & Johnstone, 1994) defined the minimax quantities

$$\Lambda \equiv \inf_{\lambda} \sup_{\mu} \frac{\rho_T(\lambda,\mu)}{N^{-1} + \min(\mu^2,1)}, \text{ and } T \equiv \text{the largest } \lambda \text{ attaining } \Lambda \text{ above} \cdot \tag{27}$$

They also proved that Λ attains its maximum Λ^0 at $\mu = 0$. Then T is the largest λ attaining Λ^0. Since $\rho(\lambda,\infty)$ is strictly increasing in λ and $\rho(\lambda,0)$ is strictly decreasing in λ, so that the solution of (27) is

$$(N+1)\rho_T(\lambda,0) = \rho_T(\lambda,\infty). \tag{28}$$

Then with this solution, the minimax threshold T is

$$T \le \sqrt{2\log_e N}, \; T^2 = 2\log_e(N+1) - 4\log_e(\log_e(N+1)) - \log_e 2\pi + o(1) \quad (N \to \infty) \cdot \tag{29}$$

Usually, for the same N, the risk of universal threshold is larger than SURE threshold and minimax threshold. All the three thresholds mentioned in section 3.3.1 to section 3.3.3 are applied to denoise the same noisy data and are evaluated by signal-to-noise ratio (SNR), which is measured in decibels:

$$SNR_{dB} = 10 * \log_{10}\left(\frac{E\{\| F \|^2\}}{E\{\| F - \tilde{F} \|^2\}}\right), \tag{30}$$

where F is the original data without noise and $\tilde{F}$ is the estimation of F.

Fig.2 shows the estimation of a synthesized signal with different thresholds. The noisy data is decomposed in a biorthogonal basis. Since hard thresholding is adopted, setting a wavelet coefficient to zero will induce oscillations near discontinuities in estimation. The estimation with universal threshold in Fig.2(c) shows small oscillations at the smooth parts.

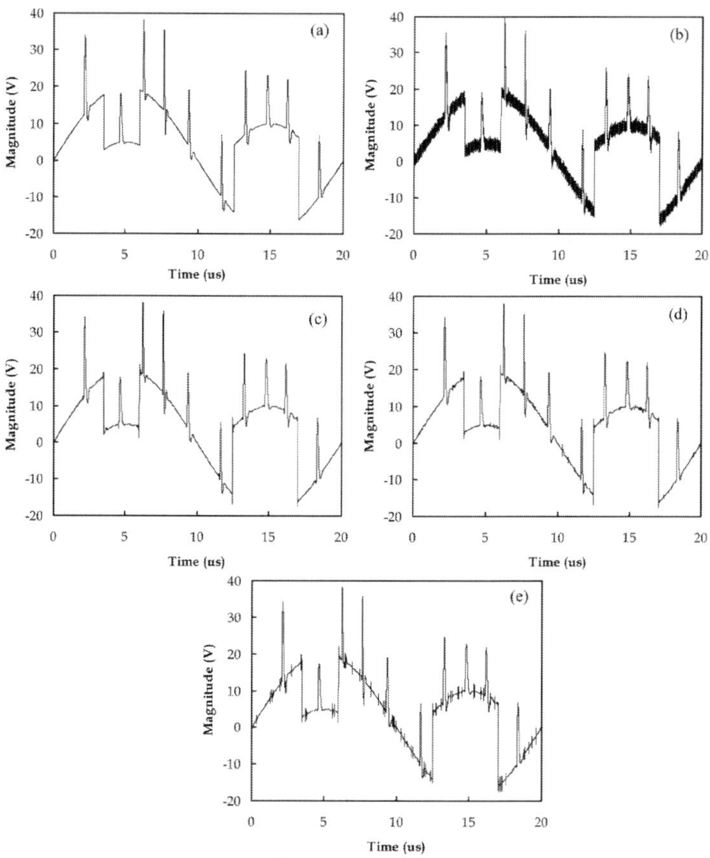

Fig. 2. Estimation with different thresholds. (a) original data, (b) noisy data (SNR=23.59dB), (c) estimation with universal threshold (SNR=31.98dB), (d) estimation with SURE threshold (SNR=34.82dB), (e) estimation with minimax threshold (SNR=33.63dB)

The oscillations result in a smaller SNR (31.98dB). The oscillations are less obvious in estimations in Fig.2(d) and Fig.2(e). But noise with very small magnitude is still found. As mentioned before, universal threshold is usually larger than the other two thresholds. Its risk of estimation $r = E\{\| F - \tilde{F} \|^2\}$ is therefore greater than that of the other two. This can be deduced by values of SNR.

4. Wavelet thresholding

The signals carry a large amount of useful information which is difficult to find. The discovery of orthogonal bases and local time-frequency analysis opens the door to the world of sparse representation of signals. An orthogonal basis is a dictionary of minimum size that can yield a sparse representation if designed to concentrate the signal energy over a set of few vectors (Mallat, 2009a). The smaller amount of wavelet coefficients reveals the information of signal we are looking for. The generation of those vectors is an approximation of original signal by linear combination of wavelets. For all f in $L^2(R)$,

$$P_j f = P_{j+1} f + < f, \psi_{j,k} > \psi_{j,k} , \tag{31}$$

where $< f, \psi_{j,k} >$ stands for the inner product of f and $\psi_{j,k}$, P_j is the orthogonal projection onto V_j. In orthogonal decomposition, V_j is the subspace which satisfies $\cdots V_2 \subset V_1 \subset V_0 \subset V_{-1} \subset V_{-2} \cdots$, $\overline{\bigcup_{j\in\mathbb{Z}} V_j} = L^2(\mathbb{R})$ and $\bigcap_{j\in\mathbb{Z}} V_j = \{0\}$ (Daubechies, 1992).

Thresholding the wavelet coefficients keeps the local regularity of signal. Usually, wavelet thresholding includes three steps (Shim et al., 2001; Zhang et al., 2007):

1. Decomposition. A filter bank of conjugate mirror filters decomposes the discrete signal in a discrete orthogonal basis. The wavelet function $\psi_{j,k}[n]$ and scale function $\phi_{j,k}[n]$ both belong to the orthogonal basis $B = [\{\psi_{j,k}[n]\}_{L<j\le J, 0\le k<2^{-j}}, \{\phi_{J,k}[n]\}_{0\le k<2^{-J}}]$. The scale parameter 2^j varies from $2^L = N^{-1}$ up to $2^J < 1$, where N is the sampling rate of signal X.
2. Thresholding. After decomposition, the threshold is selected. A thresholding estimator in the basis B is written as

$$\tilde{F} = \sum_{j=L+1}^{J} \sum_{k=0}^{2^{-j}} \rho_T(< X, \psi_{j,k} >) \psi_{j,k} + \sum_{k=0}^{2^{-J}} \rho_T(< X, \phi_{J,k} >) \phi_{J,k} , \tag{32}$$

where ρ_T is either a hard threshold or a soft threshold. Normally, the selected threshold is applied on all coefficients except the coefficients contain the lowest frequency energy $< X, \phi_{J,k} >$. This aims to keep the regularity of reconstructed signal. The difference between keeping and not keeping the lowest-frequency approximate coefficients is illustrated by Fig.3. Universal threshold with hard thresholding is used in estimation. The original data in Fig.3(a) has a wide frequency range. It contains both low frequency regular component and high frequency irregular components. Fig.3(c) shows when lowest-frequency part is kept, the regular component is still included in reconstructed signal. But if the lowest-frequency part is removed, only the high-frequency irregular components left as in Fig.3(d).

3. Reconstruction. After thresholding, all the coefficients are reconstructed to form the denoised signal.

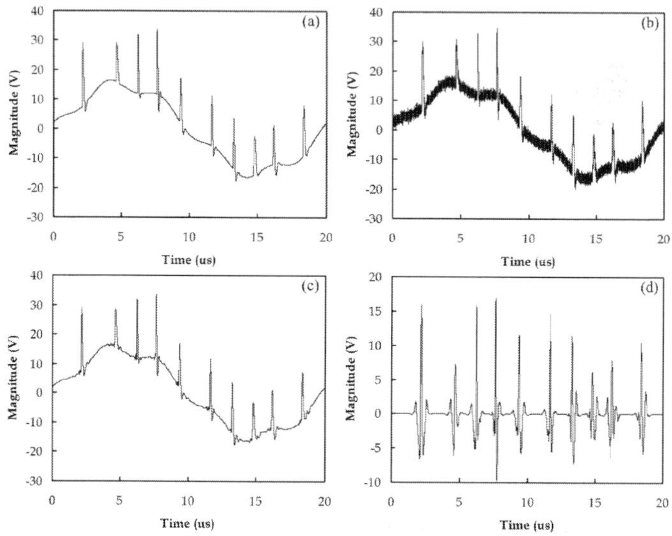

Fig. 3. Difference between keeping lowest-frequency approximates and not keeping it. (a) original data, (b) noisy data (SNR=22.93dB), (c) estimation with $< X,\phi_{J,k} >$ kept (SNR=34.83dB), (d) estimation without $< X,\phi_{J,k} >$ kept (SNR=0.24dB)

Multi-resolution analysis and wavelet packet transform are the most widely employed orthogonal analyses. The wavelet thresholding by using multi-resolution analysis and wavelet packet are introduced in section 4.1 and section 4.2.

4.1 Multi-resolution analysis

Multi-resolution analysis is discrete wavelet transform using series of conjugate mirror filter pairs. The signal f is projected onto a multi-resolution approximation space V_j. This space is then decomposed into a lower resolution space V_{j+1} and a detail space W_{j+1}. The two spaces satisfy $V_{j+1} \perp W_{j+1}$, and $V_{j+1} \oplus W_{j+1} = V_j$ (Daubechies, 1992). The orthogonal basis $\phi_j(t-2^j n)_{n\in\mathbb{Z}}$ of f in V_j is also divided into two new orthogonal bases $\phi_{j+1}(t-2^{j+1}k)_{k\in\mathbb{Z}}$ of V_{j+1}, and $\psi_{j+1}(t-2^{j+1}k)_{k\in\mathbb{Z}}$ of W_{j+1}.

This decomposition process is realized by filtering f by a pair of conjugate mirror filters $h[k]$ and $g[k]=(-1)^{1-k}h[1-k]$. The $h[k]$ and $g[k]$ are also called low pass filter and high pass filter, respectively. They usually denote the filter banks at reconstruction. At decomposition, the wavelet coefficients are calculated with $\bar{h}[k]$ and $\bar{g}[k]$ where $\bar{h}[k]=h[-k]$ and $\bar{g}[k]=g[-k]$. Accordingly, the coefficients generated by low pass filter and high pass filter are called approximates and detail, respectively (Mallat, 2009b)

$$a_{j+1}[p]=\sum_{k=-\infty}^{+\infty} h[k-2p]a_j[n]=a_j*\bar{h}[2p], \text{ and } d_{j+1}[p]=\sum_{k=-\infty}^{+\infty} g[k-2p]a_j[n]=a_j*\bar{g}[2p]. \tag{33}$$

At the reconstruction,

$$\begin{aligned} a_j[p] &= \sum_{k=-\infty}^{+\infty} h[p-2n]a_{j+1}[n]+\sum_{k=-\infty}^{+\infty} g[p-2n]a_j[n] \\ &= \breve{a}_{j+1}*h[p]+\breve{d}_{j+1}*g[p] \end{aligned} . \tag{34}$$

Fig.4 shows the thresholding procedure with multi-resolution analysis.

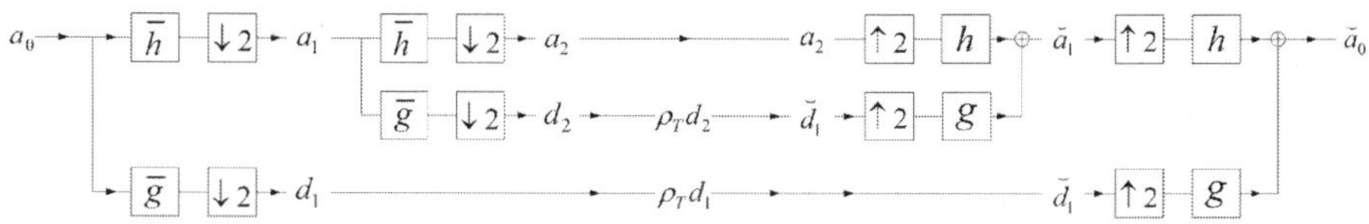

Fig. 4. Thresholding procedure with multi-resolution analysis (the lowest-frequency approximate a_2 is kept)

4.2 Wavelet packet transform

Different time-frequency structures are contained in complex signals. This motivates the exploration of time-frequency representation with adaptive properties. Although similar to multi-resolution analysis, wavelet package can divide the frequency axis in separate interval of various sizes. Its spaces W_j are also divided into two orthogonal spaces. In order to discriminate the detail spaces of wavelet packet from those of multi-resolution analysis, the W_j is represented as W_j^p. Thus, the relation between detail spaces is $W_{j+1}^{2p} \perp W_{j+1}^{2p+1}$, and $W_{j+1}^{2p} \oplus W_{j+1}^{2p+1} = W_j^p$. The orthogonal bases at the children nodes can be represented as $\psi_{j+1}^{2p}(t)=\sum_{k=-\infty}^{+\infty} h[k]\psi_j^p(t-2^jk)$ of W_{j+1}^{2p}, and $\psi_{j+1}^{2p+1}(t)=\sum_{k=-\infty}^{+\infty} g[k]\psi_j^p(t-2^jk)$ of W_{j+1}^{2p+1} (Mallat, 2009c).

Wavelet packet coefficients are computed with a filter bank that is the same as multi-resolution analysis. The wavelet packet transform is an iteration of the two-channel filter bank decomposition presented in section 4.1. At the decomposition, the wavelet coefficients of wavelet packet children d_{j+1}^{2p} and d_{j+1}^{2p+1} are obtained by subsampling the convolutions of d_j^p with low-pass filter $\bar{h}[k]$ and high-pass filter $\bar{g}[k]$:

$$d_{j+1}^{2p}[k] = d_j^p * \bar{h}[2k], \text{ and } d_{j+1}^{2p+1}[k] = d_j^p * \bar{g}[2k]. \quad (35)$$

Iterating the decomposition of coefficients along the branches forms a binary wavelet packet tree with $2^L - 1$ leaves d_L^n $(0 \le n \le 2^L - 1)$ at level L. Then, at the reconstruction,

$$d_j^p[k] = \breve{d}_{j+1}^{2p} * h[k] + \breve{d}_{j+1}^{2p+1} * g[k]. \quad (36)$$

The decomposition and reconstruction of wavelet packet transform are illustrated in Fig.5. The thresholding procedure is added before reconstruction.

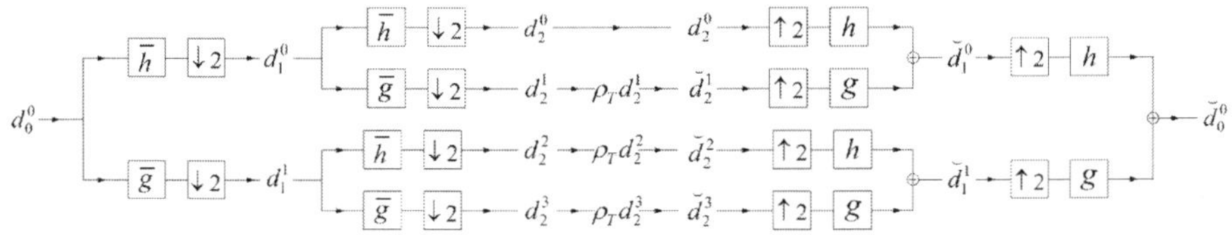

Fig. 5. Thresholding procedure by using wavelet packet transform (the lowest-frequency approximate d_2^0 is kept)

Both multi-resolution analysis and wavelet packet transform are used in estimation of a same noisy signal. The estimations are shown in Fig.6. The coiflet 2 is used to calculate wavelet coefficients and the hard threshold is set as $T = \tilde{\sigma}\sqrt{2\log_e N}$.

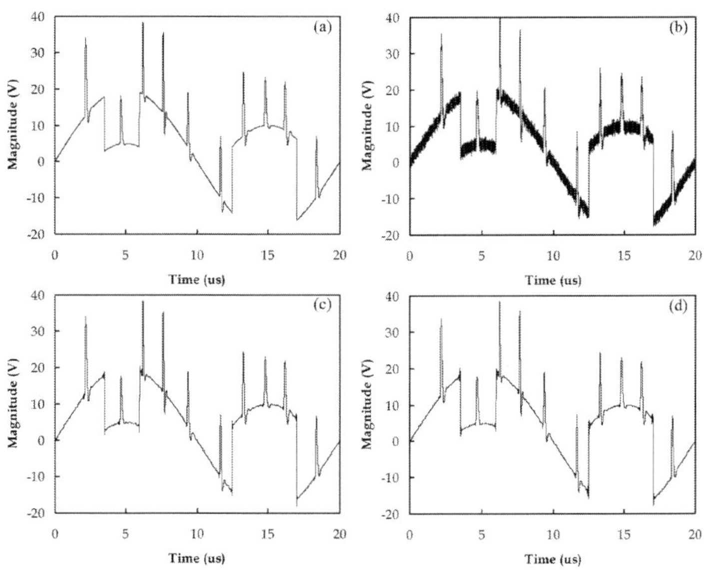

Fig. 6. Estimation with different wavelet transforms, (a) original data, (b) noisy data (SNR=23.56dB), (c) estimation with multi-resolution analysis (SNR=35.3dB), (d) estimation with wavelet packet transform (SNR=33.22dB)

4.3 Noise variance estimation

In threshold estimation discussed in section 3, the variance σ^2 of noise W is an important factor in threshold T. In practical application, the variance is unknown and its estimation is needed. When estimating the variance σ^2 of noise $W[n]$ from the data $X[n] = f[n] + W[n]$, the influence from $f[n]$ must be considered. When f is piecewise regular, a robust estimator of variance can be calculated from the median of the finest-scale wavelet coefficients. Fig.7 depicts the wavelet transforms of three functions: blocks, pulses and heavisine. They are chosen because they often arise in signal processing. It is easy to find the large-magnitude coefficients only occur exclusively near the areas of major spatial activities (Donoho &Johnstone, 1994).

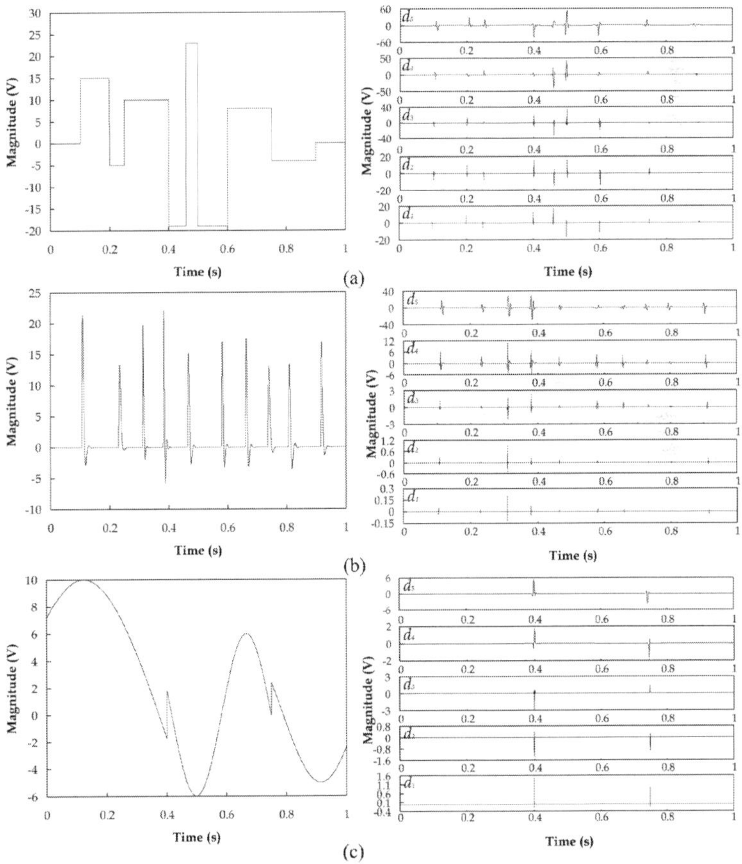

Fig. 7. Three functions and their wavelet transform, (a) blocks (left) and its wavelet coefficients (right), (b) pulses (left) and its wavelet coefficients (right), (c) heavisine (left) and its wavelet coefficients (right)

If f is piecewise smooth, the wavelet coefficients $|< f, \psi_{l,k} >|$ at finest scale l are very small, in which case $< X, \psi_{l,k} > \approx < W, \psi_{l,k} >$. As mentioned in section 3.1, the wavelet coefficients $< W, \psi_{l,k} >$ are still white if W is white. Therefore, most coefficients contribute to noise with variance σ^2 and only a few of them contribute to signal. Then, a robust estimator of σ^2 is calculated from the median of wavelet coefficients $|< W, \psi_{l,k} >|$. Different from mean value, median is independent of the magnitude of those few large-magnitude coefficients related with signal. If M is the median of absolute value of independent Gaussian random variables with zero mean and variance σ_0^2, then one can show that

$$E\{M\} \approx 0.6745\sigma_0 \tag{37}$$

The variance of noise W is estimated from the median M_X of absolute wavelet coefficients $|< W, \psi_{l,k} >|$ by neglecting the influence of f (Mallat, 2009d):

$$\tilde{\sigma} = \frac{M_X}{0.6745} \tag{38}$$

Actually, piecewise smooth signal f is only responsible for a few large-magnitude coefficients, and has little impact on the value of M_X.

4.4 Hard or soft threshold

As mentioned in section 3.2, the estimation can be done with hard and soft thresholding. The estimator $\tilde{F}$ with soft threshold is at least as regular as original signal f since the wavelet coefficients have a smaller magnitude. But this will result in a slight difference in magnitude when comparing estimation with original signal. This is not true if hard threshold is applied. All the coefficients with large-amplitude above threshold T are unchanged. However, because of the error induced by hard-thresholding, oscillations or small ripples are created near irregular points.

Fig.8 shows the wavelet estimation with hard and soft thresholding. The original data consists of a pulse signal and a sinusoidal. It includes both piecewise smooth signal and irregular segments. The wavelet coefficients are calculated with a coiflet 2. The variance σ^2 of white noise is calculated with (38) and the threshold is set to $T = \tilde{\sigma}\sqrt{2\log_e N}$. In Fig.8(c), the hard thresholding removes the noise in the area where the original signal f is regular. But the coefficients near the singularities are still kept. The SNR of estimation with hard thresholding is 36.47dB. Compared with hard thresholding, the magnitude of coefficients with soft thresholding is a little smaller. The soft thresholding estimation attenuates the noise affect at the discontinuities, but it also reduces the magnitude of estimation. The SNR of soft-thresholding estimation reduces to 31.98dB. The lower SNR of soft thresholding doesn't mean poor ability of signal estimation. The two thresholdings are selected in different applications.

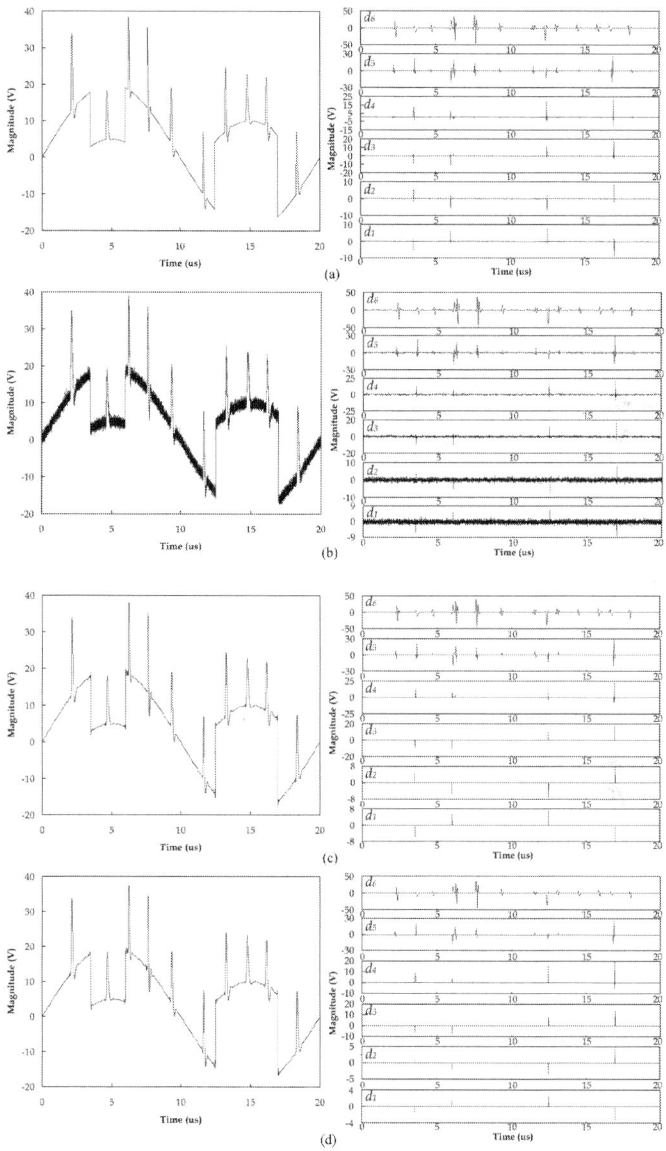

Fig. 8. Wavelet thresholding with hard and soft threshold, (a) original data (left) and its wavelet transform, (b) noisy data (SNR=23.58dB) (left) and its wavelet transform, (c) Estimation with hard thresholding (SNR=36.47dB) (left) and its wavelet coefficients (right), (d) Estimation with soft thresholding (SNR=31.98dB) (left) and its wavelet coefficients (right).

4.5 Fixed or level-dependent variance estimation

If the influence of level is neglected, the estimated variance $\tilde{\sigma}$ of white noise can be set as the estimation of finest scale, or d_1 in Fig.9. As discussed in section 4.3, most wavelet coefficients at finest scale contribute to noise, and only a few of them contributes to signal. The use of fixed estimator $\tilde{\sigma}$ reduces the influence of signal and edge effect in wavelet transform. But when the added noise is no longer white noise, for example, colored Gaussian noises, the noise variance should be estimated level by level (Johnstone & Silverman, 1997). Fig.9 gives the estimation of original signal in Fig.8(a).

In Fig.9, a Gaussian noise is added. Section 4.3 explains how to calculate the threshold value from the wavelet coefficients. Here, the universal threshold $T = \tilde{\sigma}\sqrt{2\log_e N}$ proposed in section 3.3.1 is used. In Fig.9(a), we estimate the noise variance with the median formula in (38) at the finest scale. Only one threshold T is produced. In level-dependent estimation, the estimation of noise variance (38) is done for each scale. That is to say, six scales in Fig.9(b) will generate six estimated variances $\tilde{\sigma}$ and thus six thresholds T. Each threshold is applied on each scale accordingly. The SNR of estimation with level-dependent estimation (36.7dB) is greater than that of fixed estimation (36.4dB).

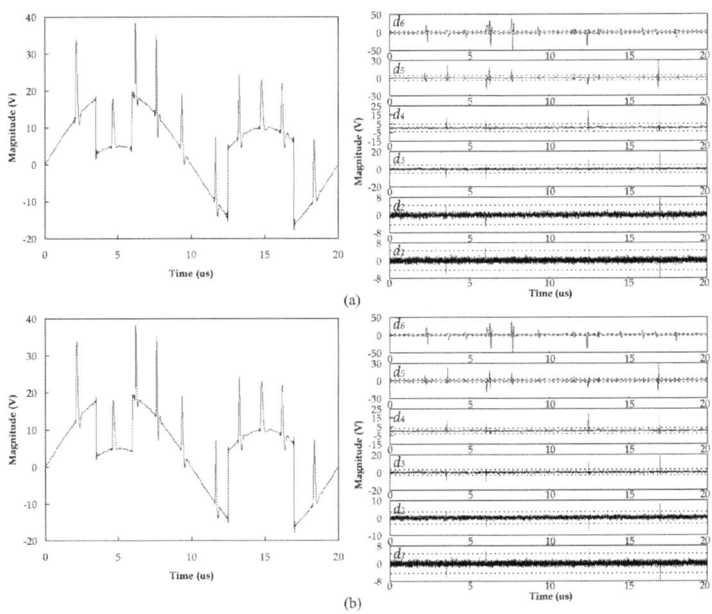

Fig. 9. Wavelet thresholding with fixed and level-dependent variance estimation, (a) Estimation with fixed estimation (SNR=36.4dB) (left) and its wavelet transform (right), (b) Estimation with level-dependent estimation (SNR=36.7dB) (left) and its wavelet transform (right).

5. Selection of optimal wavelet bases

Wavelet thresholding explores the ability of wavelet bases to approximate signal f with only a few non-zero coefficients. Therefore, optimal selection of wavelet bases is an important factor in wavelet thresholding. This depends on the properties of signal and wavelets such as regularity, number of vanishing moments, and size of support.

5.1 Vanishing moments

The number of vanishing moments determines what the wavelet doesn't "see" (Hubbard, 1998). Usually, the wavelet ψ has p vanishing moments if

$$\int_{-\infty}^{+\infty} t^k \psi(t)dt = 0 \quad \text{for } 0 \le k < p . \tag{39}$$

This means that ψ is orthogonal to any polynomial of degree $p-1$. Therefore, the wavelet with two vanishing moments cannot see the linear functions; the wavelet with three vanishing moments will be blind to both linear and quadratic functions; and so on. If f is regular and C^k, which means f is p times continuously differentiable function, when $k < p$ then the wavelet can generate small coefficients at fine scales 2^j (Mallat, 2009b). But it is not the higher the better. Too high vanishing moment may miss the useful information in signal, and leave more useless information such as noise. The proper number of vanishing moments is thus important in optimal wavelet selection.

5.2 Size of support

The size of support is the length of interval in which the wavelet values are non-zero. If f has an isolated singularity at t_0 and if t_0 is inside the support of $\psi_{j,k}(t) = 2^{-j/2}\psi_{j,k}(2^{-j}t-k)$, then $< f, \psi_{j,k} >$ may have a large amplitude. If ψ has a compact support of size N, at each scale 2^j there are N wavelets $\psi_{j,k}$ whose support includes t_0 (Mallat, 2009b). In wavelet thresholding application, the signal f is supposed to be represented by a few non-zero coefficients. The support of wavelet should be in a smaller size.

If an orthogonal wavelet ψ has p vanishing moments, its support size must be at least $2p-1$. The Daubechies wavelets are optimal to have minimum size of support for a given number of vanishing moments. When choosing a wavelet, we have to face a trade-off between number of vanishing moments and size of support. This is dependent on the regularity of signal f.

A polynomial function with degree less than 4 is shown in Fig.10. The noisy data and estimations with Daubechies wavelets are also listed. Here, level-dependent threshold is set as $T = \tilde{\sigma}\sqrt{2\log_e N}$. The estimation with wavelet Daubechies 3 whose vanishing moments p is 3 has larger SNR than others.

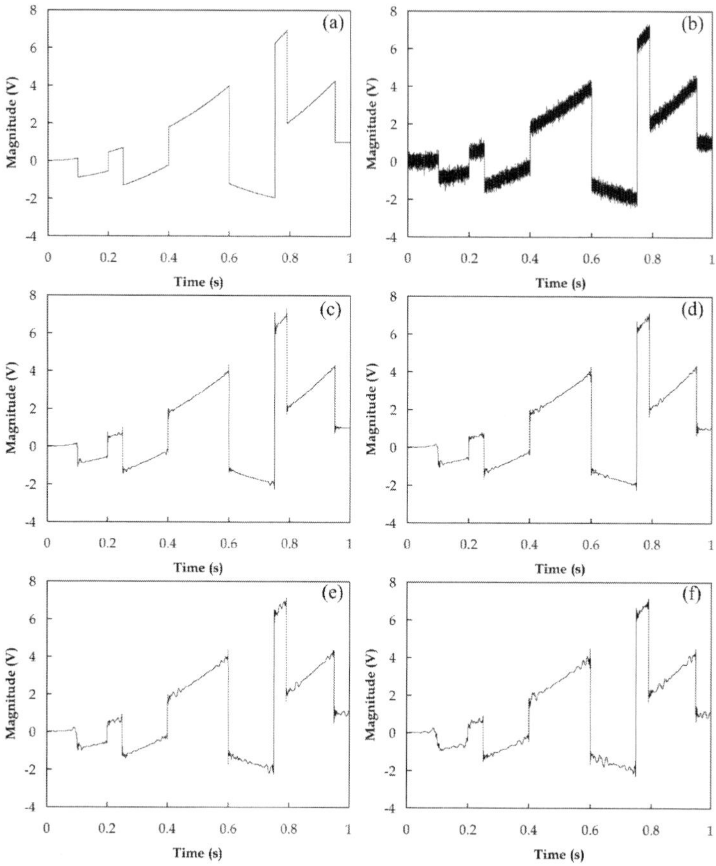

Fig. 10. The estimations by using wavelets with different vanishing moments, (a) original data, (b) noisy data (SNR=22.4dB), (c) estimation with Daubechies 3 (SNR=35.5dB), (d) estimation with Daubechies 7 (SNR=34.6dB), (e) estimation with Daubechies 11 (SNR=33.8dB), (f) estimation with Daubechies 15 (SNR=32.8dB)

5.3 Regularity

The regularity of wavelet induces an obvious influence on wavelet coefficients in thresholding. When reconstructing a signal from its wavelet coefficients $< f, \psi_{j,k} >$, an error ε is added. Then a wavelet component $\varepsilon\psi_{j,k}$ will be added to the reconstructed signal. If ψ is smooth, $\varepsilon\psi_{j,k}$ is a smooth error. For example, in image-denoising, the smooth error is often less visible than irregular errors (Mallat, 2009b). Although the regularity of a function is independent of the number of vanishing moments, the smoothness of some wavelets is related to their vanishing moments such as biorthogonal wavelets.

5.4 Wavelet families

Both orthogonal wavelets and biorthogonal wavelets can be used in orthogonal wavelet transform. Thus, Daubechies wavelets, symlets, coiflets and biorthogonal wavelets are studied in this chapter. Their properties are listed in Table 1 (Mallat, 2009b).

Wavelet name	Order	Number of vanishing moments	Size of support	Orthogonality
Daubechies	$N_{\{1\le N<\infty\}}$	N	$2N-1$	Orthogonal
Symlets	$N_{\{2\le N<\infty\}}$	N	$2N-1$	Orthogonal
Coiflets	$N_{\{1\le N\le 5\}}$	$2N$	$6N-1$	Orthogonal
Biorthogonal wavelets	$N_{d\{1\le N\le 8\}}$ for dec. $N_{r\{1\le N\le 6\}}$ for rec.	N_r	$2N_d+1$ for dec. $2N_r+1$ for rec.	Biorthogonal

Table 1. Information of some wavelet families, 'dec'. is short for decomposition, 'rec'. is short for reconstruction

Choosing the suitable wavelet in wavelet thresholding depends on the features of signal and wavelet properties mentioned in section 5.1, 5.2 and 5.3. For different applications, the optimal wavelets change. For instance, the irregular wavelet Daubechies 2 induces irregular errors in wavelet thresholding of regular signal processing. But it achieves better estimation when applied to estimate transient signal in power system which are often composed by pulses and heavy noises (Ma et al., 2002). As illustrated in Fig.11 and Fig.12, two original datasets are tested with an irregular wavelet Daubechies 2 and a regular wavelet coiflet 3.

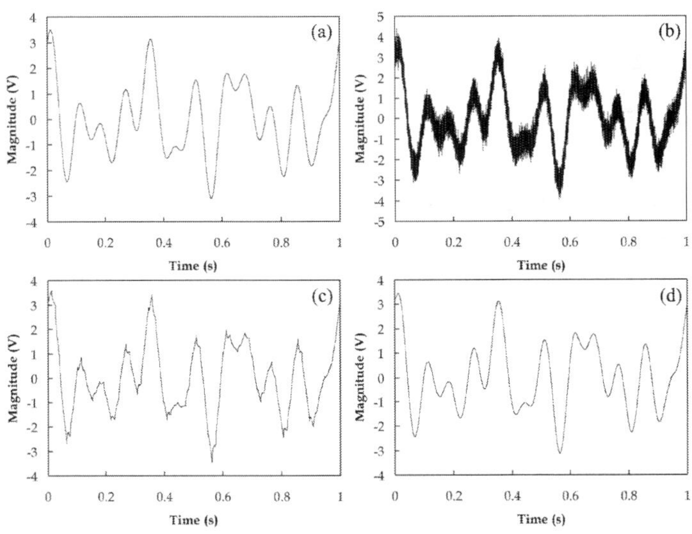

Fig. 11. Estimation of regular data, (a) original data, (b) noisy data (SNR=13.03dB), (c) estimation with 'db2' (SNR=24.75dB), (d) estimation with 'coif3' (SNR=36.96dB)

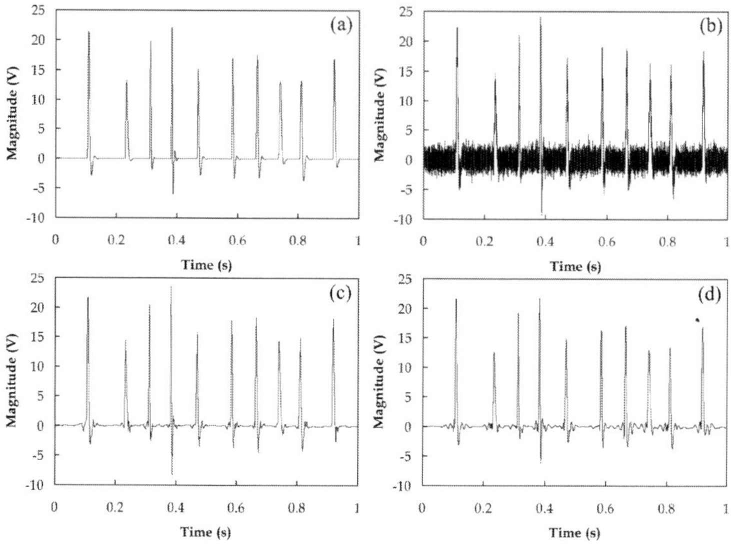

Fig. 12. Estimation of irregular data, (a) original data, (b) noisy data (SNR=10.38dB), (c) estimation with 'db2' (SNR=21.68dB), (d) estimation with 'coif3' (SNR=20.61dB)

6. Conclusion

This chapter focuses on wavelet denoising. It starts with the introduction of two major noise estimation methods: Bayes estimation and Minimax estimation. In orthogonal bases, thresholding is a common method to remove noises. The estimations show that oscillations or ripples will be induced by hard thresholding. Nevertheless, the SNR of estimation with hard thresholding is higher than soft thresholding since the magnitude of coefficients decreases after soft thresholding. Then the thresholds that developed by different noise estimations are proposed. The larger threshold removes more noises but it generates greater estimation risk.

The wavelet denoising methods are usually realized by orthogonal decomposition. The most commonly used orthogonal decompositions are multi-resolution analysis and wavelet packet transform. The influence of wavelet decomposition algorithms, hard or soft thresholdings, and fixed or level-dependent thresholds are studied and compared. For different application, the optimal wavelet thresholding method should be considered carefully.

The wavelet transform is to use a few large magnitude coefficients to represent a signal. The selection of wavelet is another important factor that needs consideration. The properties, for example regularity and degree, of signal should be studied when choosing optimal wavelet that has matching features such as vanishing moments, size of support, and regularity.

7. References

Daubechies, I. (1992). *Ten lectures on wavelets,* Society for Industrial and Applied Mathematics, ISBN 0898712742, Philadelphia, Pa.

Donoho D. L. (1995). De-noising by soft-thresholding. *IEEE transactions on information theory,* Vol.41, No. 3, (May, 1995), pp. 613-627, ISSN 00189448

Donoho D. L. & Johnstone I. M. (1994). Ideal Denoising In an Orthonormal Basis Chosen From A Library of Bases. *Comptes Rendus De L Academie Des Sciences Serie I-Mathematique,* Vol. 319, No. 12, (December 1994), pp. 1317-1322, ISSN 0764-4442

Donoho D. L. & Johnstone I. M. (1995). Adapting to unknown smoothness via wavelet shrinkage. *Journal of the American Statistical Association,* Vol. 90, No. 432, (December 1995), pp. 1200-1224, ISSN 0162-1459

Donoho D. L. & Johnstone I. M. (1998). Minimax estimation via wavelet shrinkage. *Annals of statistics,* Vol. 26, No. 3, (June 1998), pp. 879-921, ISSN 00905364

Hubbard, B. B. (1998). *The world according to wavelets: the story of a mathematical technique in the making,* A. K. Peters, ISBN 1568810725, Wellesley, Mass

Johnstone I. M. & Silverman B. W. (1997). Wavelet threshold estimators for data with correlated noise. *Journal of the royal statistical society: series B (statistical methodology),* Vol. 59, No.2, (May, 1997), pp. 319-351, ISSN 13697412

Lehmann, E. L. & Casella G. (1998). *Theory of point estimation,* Springer, ISBN 0-387-98502-6, New York

Ma, X., Zhou, C. & Kemp, I. J. (2002). Automated wavelet selection and thresholding for PD detection. *IEEE Electrical Insulation Magazine,* Vol. 18, No. 2, (August, 2002), pp. 37-35, ISSN 0883-7554

Mallat, S. G. (2009). Sparse Representations, In: *A wavelet tour of signal processing : the Sparse way,* Mallat, S. G., pp. 1-30, Elsevier/Academic Press, ISBN 13:978-0-12-374370-1, Amsterdam,Boston

Mallat, S. G. (2009). Wavelet Bases, In: *A wavelet tour of signal processing : the Sparse way,* Mallat, S. G., pp. 263-370, Elsevier/Academic Press, ISBN 13:978-0-12-374370-1, Amsterdam,Boston

Mallat, S. G. (2009). Wavelet Packet and Local Cosine Bases, In: *A wavelet tour of signal processing : the Sparse way,* Mallat, S. G., pp. 377-432, Elsevier/Academic Press, ISBN 13:978-0-12-374370-1, Amsterdam,Boston

Mallat, S. G. (2009). Denoising, In: *A wavelet tour of signal processing : the Sparse way,* Mallat, S. G., pp. 535-606, Elsevier/Academic Press, ISBN 13:978-0-12-374370-1, Amsterdam,Boston

Shim I., Soraghan J. J. & Siew W. H. (2001). Detection of PD utilizing digital signal processing methods. Part 3: Open-loop noise reduction. *IEEE Electrical Insulation Magazine,* Vol. 17, No. 1, (February, 2001), pp.6-13, ISSN 0883-7554

Stein C. M. (1981). Estimation of the Mean of a Multivariate Normal-Distribution. *Annals of Statistics,* Vol. 9, No. 6, (November 1981), pp. 1317-1322, ISSN 0090-5364

Zhang H., Blackburn T. R., Phung B. T. & Sen D. (2007). A novel wavelet transform technique for on-line partial discharge measurements. 1. WT de-noising algorithm. *IEEE Transactions on Dielectrics and Electrical Insulation*, Vol. 14, No. 1, (February, 2007), pp. 3-14, ISSN 1070-9878

5

Oesophageal Speech's Formants Measurement Using Wavelet Transform

Begona García Zapirain,
Ibon Ruiz and Amaia Mendez
Deustotech Institute of Technology,
Deustotech-LIFE Unit, University of Deusto, Bilbao,
Spain

1. Introduction

One of the most important concerns for the specialists in otorrinolaringologists and the patients who have suffer a laringectomie is a complex process for their rehabilitation. At the present, it is no available any advanced technique either for the learning or the evaluation of this process.

Esophageal speech is characterized by its low intelligibility, which implies that its objective measurement parameters e.g. pitch, jitter, shimmer or HNR have values outside normal ranges [1]. One of the consequences of this fact is the impossibility of using speech recognizers, speech to text converters or any kind of automatic response device that requires a speech signal.

The here presented paper explains a work which is included in a research whose objective is to adapt speech controlled systems so that they can be used by people with vocal disorders. Esophageal voices are the most grievous among these pathologies.

Our research group has presented many works to the scientific community [2], [3], aimed to the improvement of esophageal speech quality by stabilizing the poles of the system which models the vocal tract with LPC. Nowadays the wavelet transform is being used in order to enhance the Harmonics to noise ratio. For this task, it is crucial to know accurately the frequency values of formants in vowels [7].

In this paper results of a new algorithm are presented, this algorithm uses Wavelets Transform as basis, but proposes a new technique to improve calculation accuracy. In order to evaluate this new technique a comparative between its results and the ones obtained with the LPC will be elaborated. As a reference for the comparative the results of analyzing the FFT transform will be taken [4].

The general objective of the chapter is the enhancement of esophageal speech quality in communications with humans and machines. This aim comes up of the low intelligibility of people who speak with esophageal voice after an operation called laryngectomy which is carry out like treatment of larynx cancer [6].

2. Methods

2.1 Wavelet transform

One of the most important techniques applied in the spectral analysis is the Fourier Transform (STFT), which will allow to recognize the spectral components of speech signal, so it makes possible to distinguish pathological voices and process them.

That transform has a resolution problem which is given by Heisenberg Uncertainty Principle. The Wavelet Transform (WT) was developed to overcome some resolution related problems of the STFT. It is possible to analyze any signal by using an alternative approach called the multiresolution analysis (MRA).

MRA, as implied by its name, analyzes the signal at different frequencies with different resolutions. MRA is designed to give good time resolution and poor frequency resolution at high frequencies and good frequency resolution and poor time resolution at low frequencies. The Continuous Wavelet Transform (CWT) is used for many different applications and it is defined as follows:

$$\Psi_x^{\psi}(\tau,s)=\frac{1}{\sqrt{|s|}}\int x(t)\cdot\psi^*\left(\frac{t-\tau}{s}\right)dt \tag{1}$$

As the here used signals are digital, it is more useful to use Semi-discrete Wavelet Transform (discretized by dyadic grid, described by $s=2^j$ and $t=k\cdot 2^j$) or Discrete Wavelet Transform (DWT). The DWT analyzes the signal at different frequency bands with different resolutions by decomposing the signal into a coarse approximation and detail information [5].

The decomposition of the signal into different frequency bands is simply obtained by successive highpass and lowpass filtering of the time domain signal. The original signal x[n] is first passed through a halfband highpass filter g[n] and a lowpass filter h[n]. This constitutes one level of decomposition and can mathematically be expressed as follows:

$$y_{high}[k]=\sum_n x[n]\cdot g[2k-n] \tag{2}$$

$$y_{low}[k]=\sum_n x[n]\cdot h[2k-n] \tag{3}$$

where $y_{high}[k]$ and $y_{low}[k]$ are the outputs of the highpass and lowpass filters, respectively, after subsampling by 2. This decomposition halves the time resolution since only half the number of samples now characterizes the entire signal.

However, this operation doubles the frequency resolution, since the frequency band of the signal now spans only half the previous frequency band, effectively reducing the uncertainty in the frequency by half. The above procedure, which is also known as the subband coding, can be repeated for further decomposition.

The wavelet packet method is a generalization of wavelet decomposition that offers a richer signal analysis. Wavelet packet atoms are waveforms indexed by three naturally interpreted parameters: position, scale (as in wavelet decomposition), and frequency. It will be then selected the most suitable decomposition of a given signal with respect to an entropy-based criterion.

2.2 Basis of speech analysis

At the present time, many otolaryngologists (ORLs) use the software tools they have available in order to corroborate the diagnosis of vocal cord pathologies by means of objective parameters. These parameters complete the information gathered by the specialist, which usually comprises: the images obtained from a stroboscope and several perceptual tests carried out on the patient.

Special attention needs to be paid to vocal cord cancer, that is to say, to its diagnosis, treatment, rehabilitation and monitoring, as this cancer can cause the death of the patient suffering from it. Once the cancer has been detected, the ORL specialist removes the patient's vocal cords. This means that the patient will no longer be able to produce what is called laryngeal voice and thus loses his/her speech.

After the operation, during rehabilitation, the patient begins the process of learning how to emit oesophageal voice: the voice produced by modulating air coming from the oesophagus. This enables the patient to communicate, albeit experiencing great difficulty to maintain fluent conversations, due to the poor quality of oesophageal voice. However, one of the major problems is that this type of oesophageal voice cannot be evaluated during the rehabilitation process as there is no application available on the market that can automatically obtain the previously mentioned acoustic parameters. The quality of oesophageal voice is so low that the algorithms obtaining the periodicity of the voice do not work properly, and thus measurements obtained by such software packs are not reliable.

Obviously, the accuracy of measurements made by the software pack presented in this work will also be applicable to less severe pathologies, such as polyps, nodules, hypo mobility of the vocal cords, etc. The deterioration of the voice in this type of pathology is also too high for the measurement of objective parameters to be precise. This means that these commercial software packs are not suitable for measuring these parameters in voices suffering from some kind of pathology. Being able to obtain accurate objective parameters is advantageous for the early detection of cancer in cases where the patient's laryngeal voice is of a very poor quality and has high noise levels [1].

The pitch, or fundamental frequency of the speech, is one of the properties of sound or musical tone perceived through frequency. Due to this natural pseudo-periodicity of the voiced voice, there are small variations in the peaks of the voice which change their fi frequency, so that the pitch can be defined as:

$$Pitch(Hz) = \frac{\sum_{i=1}^{N} f_i}{N} \tag{4}$$

N being the number of pitch periods.

Estimating fundamental frequency has been a recurring issue in the area of digital signal processing. This is due to the fact that obtaining the time instants that define voice cycles is a very complex task. These cycles are used to obtain the fi frequency instants. Furthermore, it is vitally important to calculate these instants in the acoustic parameterization, as this is the cornerstone of voice characterizations of this kind.

Jitter [2] is a parameter representing variation of fundamental frequency, that is, the variations of pitch in each voice cycle. On the other hand, specialists also usually employ the shimmer parameter [2], which represents variation in width of voice cycle peaks. The voice produced through larynx modulation is able to almost constantly maintain peak width of voice periods. Therefore, an increase in shimmer value can be a symptom of voice disorder. Tables 1 and 2 present the various mathematical definitions of the jitter and shimmer objective parameters.

As previously mentioned, a number of authors have written several works on the detection of voice cycles [3,4] and there are also many highly detailed techniques to be found in the corresponding literature, such as estimators in the temporary domain (ratio of crosses per zero [5]), estimators of fundamental frequency [6,7], self-correlation methods (Yin estimators [8]), representation of the phase space [9], Cepstrums [10] and statistical methods [11, 12, 13]. Some of these directly define voice cycles [3], whereas others use numerical approximations [8] in order to obtain fundamental frequency values. In that respect, another step must be taken if we are to clearly identify the instants that define voice cycles.

However, none of these works were tried out on oesophageal voices and, what is more, it can be stated without a shadow of a doubt that these algorithms are not suitable for voices of this kind. The software pack presented here is a tool designed for use by specialists in otolaryngology, and is specifically designed to obtain objective voice parameters with excellent precision. The tool contains a basic algorithm to calculate the acoustic parameters related to speech periodicity and serves as an aid for not only diagnosis and rehabilitation but also for monitoring the patient.

It can be concluded that the tool is user-friendly and that ORL specialists can use it for measuring such objective parameters as pitch, jitter and shimmer, as well as for keeping patient records on these parameters.

2.3 Software interface

Speech signal processing plays an important role within the digital processing projects and investigations. Within this field, the esophageal voices are being objective of analysis and transformation [2],[3] but these have the limitation of measuring their quality only with subjective criteria as hearing tests. This is because an evaluation based on the calculation of objective parameters like pitch, jitter, shimmer or the harmonic to noise ratio HNR demands a high precision in the definition of the beginnings and ends of cycle in the voice signal.

The oesophageal voice is generated using the air pass across the oesophagus but without the modulation possibility by the vocal fold because they have been removed due to, generally, a larynx cancer. Because of this their time-spectral characteristics are atypical and include levels of noise, fundamental frequency asymmetry and formant unstructuration. This leads to wrong measures in commercial applications and therefore is impossible to assess the quality of oesophageal voices. The same is applicable to voices with severe pathologies.

In this sense, it is necessary to develop an algorithm for the exact calculation of the marks that correspond to each cycle of the signal of oesophageal or pathological voices so that the calculation of pitch is exact and, with it, the measures of jitter, shimmer or signal to noise ratio. This algorithm has been included in a software interface for allowing users to measure and to plot in a graph the results of the acoustic parameters of the speech signal. This is suitable for evaluating and comparing the results between original oesophageal speech signal and the processed one after applying the wavelet transform.

3. System design

The system design has been divided into two parts: the algorithm for improving the quality of oesophageal speech using wavelet transform and the user interface including the speech signal processing using that algorithm and the acoustic analysis of speech parameters.

3.1 Algorithm using wavelets

As it has been previously mentioned, wavelet packets will be used in order to detect formants location. The reason of the choosing of this technique is their ability to separate the speech signal in different subbands, allowing to separate the formants bands quite exactly.

The here proposed method makes use of a double analysis. Firstly, a general analysis is applied over the whole spectrum, in this step a band in which the formant is located is approximated, and secondly the exact formant location is determined more accurately, the formant location accuracy can be adjusted through introducing more analysis levels inside the formant approximation band.

The main advantage of this method is the possibility of achieving a great frequency resolution, without consuming excessive computational resources, which is crucial when implementing the algorithms in a real-time device, such as a DSP.

3.1.1 Step 1: Band approximation of formants location

The first step consists of a rough analysis of the signal's wavelet packets tree. In order to locate formants frequencies, the energy of each subband is analyzed. The maxima of this energy signal determine formants location. The scheme of the process is shown in Figure 1.

Firstly, the wavelet packets tree is calculated up to the desire level, the chosen level is calculated taking into account the sampling frequency and the resolution required.

After having obtained the wavelet packets, the energy of each last level node is calculated. The Energy is stored in an array and its envelope is estimated. This envelope smoothes the energy signal and thus, the maxima can be easily calculated.

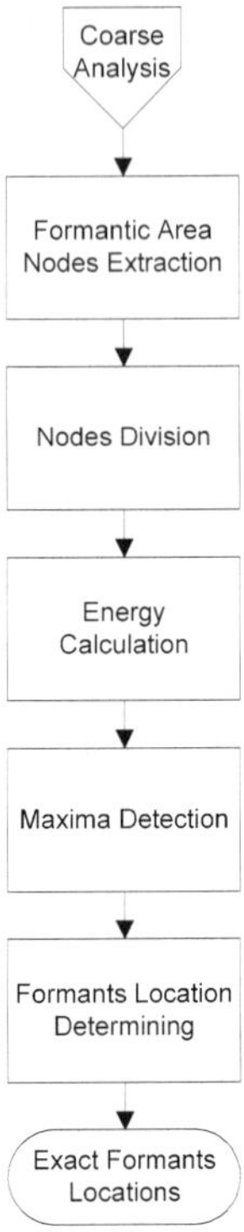

Fig. 1. Adjustable Resolution Analysis Schema

3.1.2 Step 2: Adjustable resolution analysis

In the above explained step, an approximation to the formantic frequencies was obtained. As it will explained in next head, the resolution obtained with this approximation, though it is better than the one obtained with conventional methods, may not be enough for some environments.

In order to achieve a finer resolution, an adjustable resolution analysis was designed. The scheme of this analysis is shown in Figure 1. The core idea of the designed technique is to obtain a higher resolution in the previously detected bands by dividing the selected nodes and their adjacent ones.

The main reason of using narrower bands is that energy in wavelets packet spreads among various adjacent nodes, the solution to this problem is to divide the spectrum in such narrow bands that the energy of the formant locates in only one node.

As it can be seen in Figure 1 the first step of the algorithm consists on splitting the approximated formantic bands and their adjacent as many times as necessary. Secondly, the energy of each node is calculated again and the maximum value located, this value indicates formant location.

The main advantage of this method is that it is possible to save a lot of computational load but preserving a high accuracy level at the same time. For example, if an 8 level basic tree is to be taken and its formantic nodes are expanded two levels, it is possible to obtain a 10 level resolution by consuming an 8 level computational load.

3.2 User interface

Using the advantages of the previously described algorithms, authors have developed a tool called "PAS Voice". The welcome screen will then be displayed:

Fig. 2. Welcome Screen

Once the application has been started up, the main screen will be displayed:

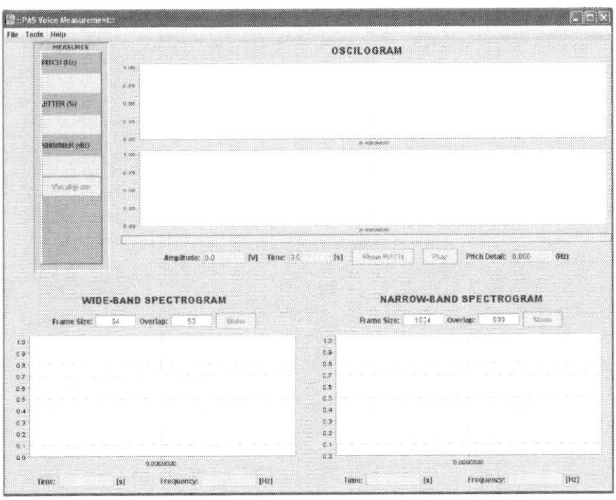

Fig. 3. Main Screen

The following areas can be observed on this screen:

1. Menu: The program's general option menus can be identified in this area:

File.- Menu with the "Open file" option, which allows you to open a voice signal in order to process it. The signal has to be in .WAV, .AU or .AIFF format. Voice processing begins automatically once the file to be analyzed has been chosen.

Save Results - This enables you to save the signal processing results; results from several sessions can be added for the same person or a new profile can be created. Once the results have been correctly saved, a graph will be displayed showing the evolution of the parameters throughout all sessions of analysis. When this graph is closed, an informative message on development since the previous session will be displayed.

Tools.- Tool menu for application configuration.

Language.- This allows the language to be chosen for the program (initially English and Spanish, although personalized translations can be applied). If the language is changed, the application will have to be rebooted.

Octave Path.- The octave.exe file, essential for the running of this program, can be specified using this option.

Help.- By clicking on this, help is provided for running the program.

2. Measurement area: In this area, once the a voice signal has been processed (through the File/Open file option), the numerical measurements of Pitch, Jitter and Shimmer are displayed. If one wishes to observe the measurements in graphic form with the normality threshold, the "Vocaligram" button can be clicked on; this will only be enabled once the processing has been performed to obtain the measurements needed to create the vocaligram. The vocaligram is a graphic representation of a measurement in each axis (in blue) superimposed over the threshold values for each parameter. The measurements are scaled so that abnormal values are always greater than the threshold (a value above the threshold implies that it is abnormal).

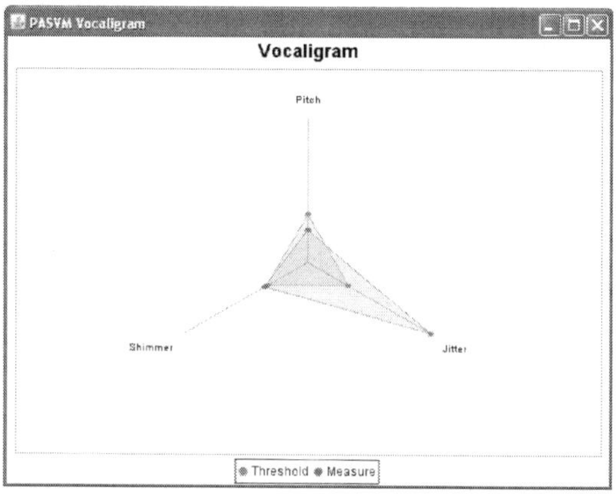

Fig. 4. Sample Vocaligram

3. Graphic Representation Area: In this area, the voice signal graphics and the evolution of pitch over the time are displayed once the voice has been analyzed. Underneath is a progress bar indicating the approximate percentage of analysis completed.
4. Graphic Representation Options Area: Once the voice and pitch evolution have been represented, this area is enabled so as to be able to check other data in greater detail:

Amplitude/Time/Pitch Detail.- When a particular point in the graphics above are clicked on, these frames fill up with information corresponding to the point that has been selected. The Amplitude/Time values (clicking on the upper one) or Pitch Detail values (clicking on the lower) will be displayed in accordance with the graphic function selected. Show Pitch.- Once the pitch of the voice signal has been calculated, when this button is pressed the marks situated in the signal over the relevant points indicating periodicity will be shown.

Play.- By pressing this button, the voice signal will be reproduced through the computer loudspeakers (if applicable).

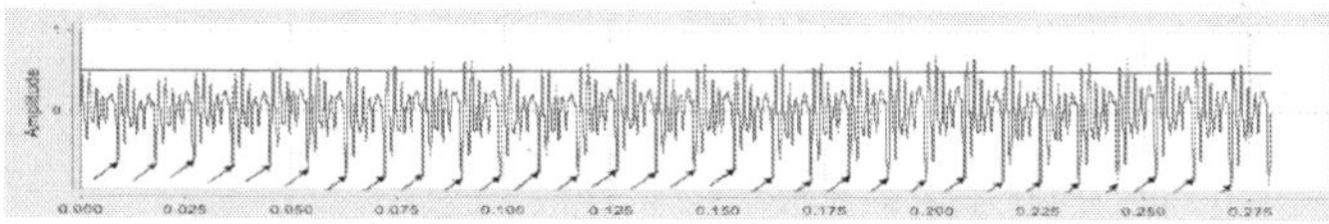

Fig. 5. Example of oscilogram with "Show Pitch" option activated

5. Spectrogram Options Area: By default, the spectrograms are not calculated during the analysis process. If it is wished to do so, this should be done through the following area:

Frame Size/Overlap.- These are the parameters composing the spectrogram. The parameters indicated by default are typical ones for the representation of broad-band and narrow-band spectrograms respectively. Beware! It is not recommended to touch these parameters ... A poor configuration may considerably increase spectrogram calculation time.

Show.- This displays the spectrogram in its area corresponding to the indicated parameters.

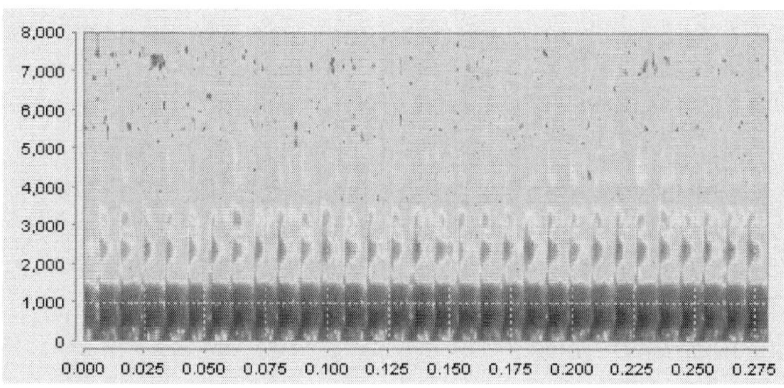

Fig. 6. Example of Broad-Band Spectrogram

6. Spectrogram Area: This shows the spectrograms when the "Show" button is pressed.

4. Results

Tables 1 and 2 show the measurements of the first formant location for healthy (left) and esophageal (right) voices. Tables 3 and 4 show the measurement errors absolutely and relatively, the relative value is calculated comparing the obtained error with the average formant value. As it can be seen in those tables, conventional methods obtain very poor results, achieving an average deviation of about 70 Hz, approximately the value of the pitch in esophageal speech. These deviations could be inappropriate for some applications which require great accuracy, thus a new measurement method is necessary.

A simple wavelet algorithm with approximation to the formant band improves considerably this results reducing the deviation about a 30%. This represents quite an improvement comparing with LPC, but it is possible to obtain higher resolution without increasing substantially computational costs. The results of the adjustable resolution algorithm show that it is possible to reduce the average deviations up to a 50%.

The obtained values prove that it is feasible to locate formants position with minimum errors and effective algorithms. This fact constitutes a fundamental advance in esophageal speech regeneration, because formant location has great importance in many speech processing algorithms. Taking as an example previous works of the research group, for example for such as an algorithm as the one presented in [2], much better results would be obtained with more accurate formant location estimations.

It is important to highlight the great relevance that this results may have in some other speech technologies fields such as speech recognition, etc. So the applications of this analysis is not restricted to esophageal speech processing but can be implemented with many others purposes.

Speech Signal	Original Values (Hz)	F. with LPC (Hz)	F. with B.A (Hz)	F. with R.A. (Hz)
He. 1	851	842	883	848
He. 2	776	633	711	756
He. 3	938	893	969	950
He. 4	960	929	926	966

Table 1. 1st Formant location for **healthy voices** calculated with different methods: LPC, Band Approximation (B.A.) and Resolution Adjustement (R.A.).

Speech Signal	Original Values (Hz)	F. with LPC (Hz)	F. with B.A (Hz)	F. with R.A. (Hz)
Es. 1	894	698	883	890
Es. 2	830	762	754	778
Es. 3	808	774	754	805
Es. 4	776	744	754	756

Table 2. 1st Formant location for **esophageal voices** calculated with different methods: LPC, Band Approximation (B.A.) and Resolution Adjustement (R.A.).

Speech Signal	Deviations obtained with LPC (Hz)			Deviations obtained only wit band approximation (Hz)			Deviations obtained with resolution adjustment (Hz)		
	F1	F2	F3	F1	F2	F3	F1	F2	F3
Healthy 1	10	31	185	31	9	159	4	4	17
Healthy 2	143	12	78	65	31	41	20	9	10
Healthy 3	45	68	157	31	106	30	12	34	16
Healthy 4	31	15	10	34	12	35	6	12	5
Esophageal 1	196	77	72	11	33	35	4	26	75
Esophageal 2	50	193	101	76	77	2	42	48	11
Esophageal 3	34	88	51	54	33	2	3	15	10
Esophageal 4	32	21	60	22	0	13	20	9	21
Average Deviation	65	61	89	41	36	40	18	23	21

Table 3. Deviations obtained in formants location values with different methods.

Speech Signal	Deviations obtained with LPC (%)			Deviations obtained only wit band approximation (%)			Deviations obtained with resolution adjustment (%)		
	F1	F2	F3	F1	F2	F3	F1	F2	F3
Healthy 1	1.135	2.292	7.000	3.518	0.665	6.016	0.454	0.296	0.643
Healthy 2	16.227	0.887	2.951	7.376	2.292	1.551	2.270	0.665	0.378
Healthy 3	5.106	5.028	5.941	3.518	7.837	1.135	1.362	2.514	0.605
Healthy 4	3.518	1.109	0.378	3.858	0.887	1.324	0.681	0.887	0.189
Esophageal 1	23.700	5.487	2.580	1.330	2.352	1.254	0.484	1.853	2.687
Esophageal 2	8.222	13.754	3.619	9.190	5.487	0.072	6.288	3.421	0.394
Esophageal 3	4.111	6.271	1.827	6.530	2.352	0.072	0.363	1.069	0.358
Esophageal 4	3.869	1.497	2.150	2.660	0.000	0.466	2.418	0.641	0.752
Average Deviation	7.964	4.359	3.306	4.747	2.632	1.486	1.790	1.781	0.751

Table 4. Percentual deviations obtained in formants location values with different methods.

After having applied the wavelet transform to the oespphageal speech signal, we can measure the final value of the acoustic parameters. Below is an example describing the basic operation of the software that authors have develop named "PASVoice software pack". It analyses a speech signal in order to obtain objective parameters and graphic representation of values for helping doctors to understand the patient's stage,

When appliying over a healthy voice the results can be as follows:

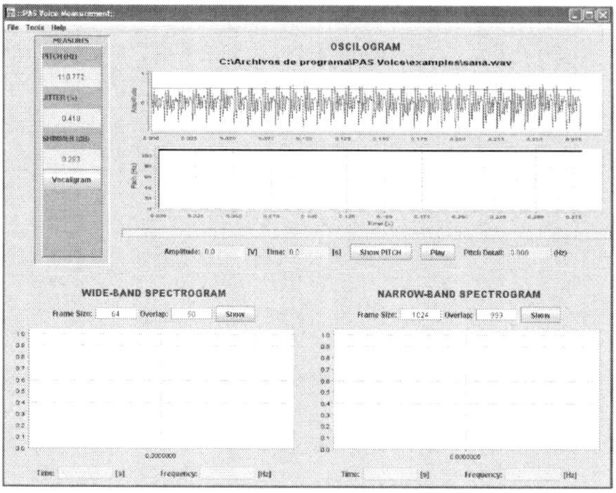

Fig. 7. 'sana.wav' Results

If 'Show Pitch' is pressed/selected, we can observe the marks that have been located as a reference for measuring pitch:

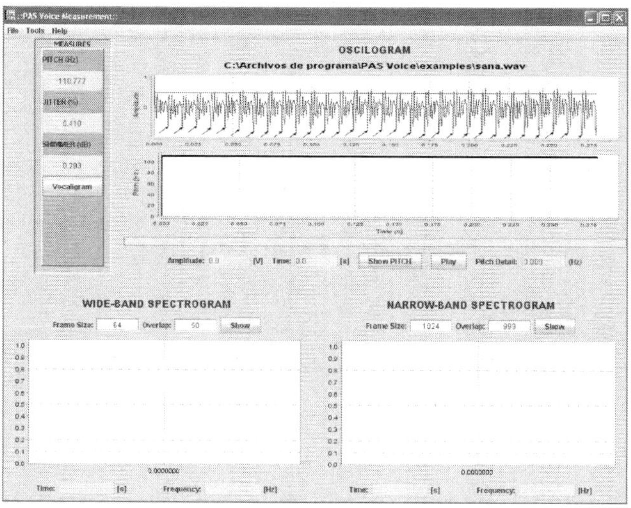

Fig. 8. Details of pitch marks

When the 'Vocaligram' button is clicked on, we can see the same (in this example the results are below the threshold for each parameter, as expected):

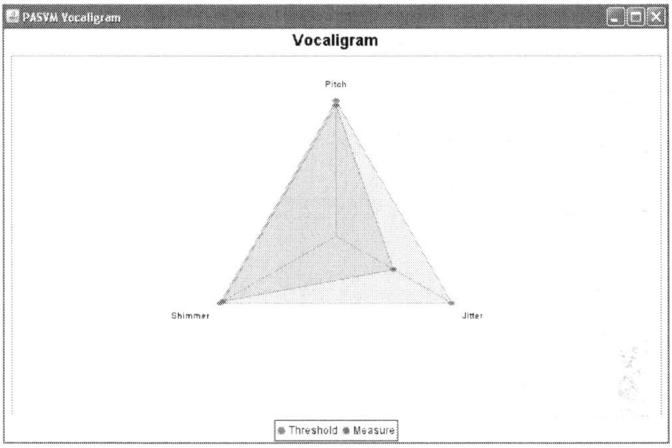

Fig. 9. 'sana.wav' Vocaligram

If any of the spectrogram 'Show' buttons are selected, the corresponding spectrograms are automatically calculated and visualized:

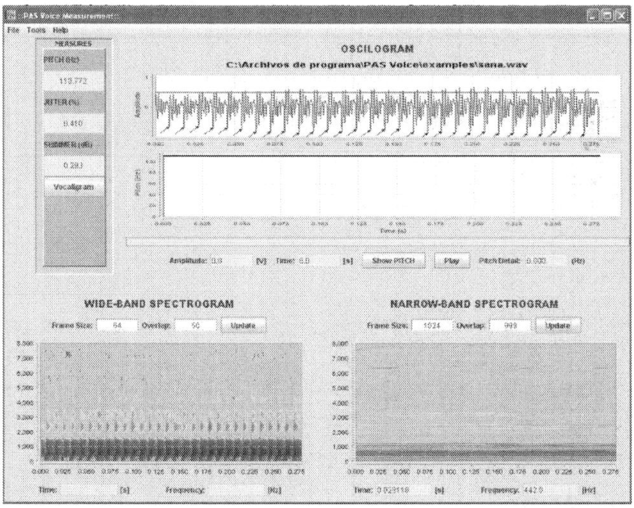

Fig. 10. Details of the application with both spectrograms calculated

Finally, if it is wished to save the numerical results, the File/Save Results option can be chosen, after which the following dialogue appears. As can be seen, it contains data corresponding to other patients:

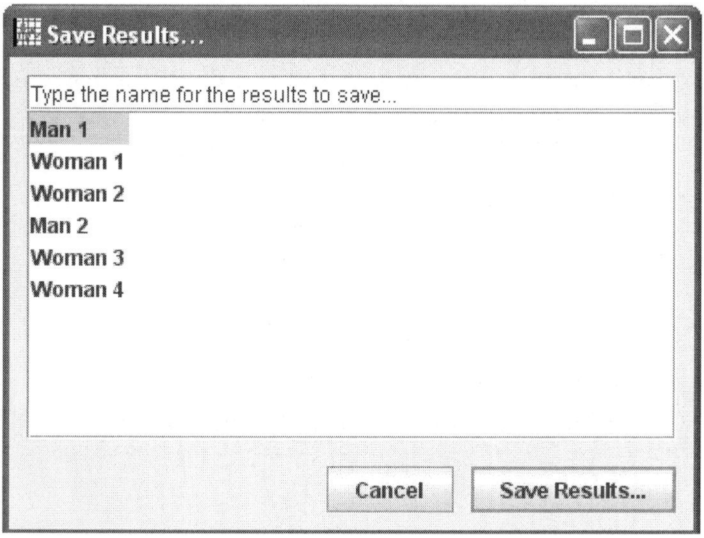

Fig. 11. Dialogue box used to save results

If this is not the first session for the person we are dealing with, his/her name can be searched for by typing the first letters of the name in the box at the top. All concurrences, if there are any, will then be displayed in the main box below.

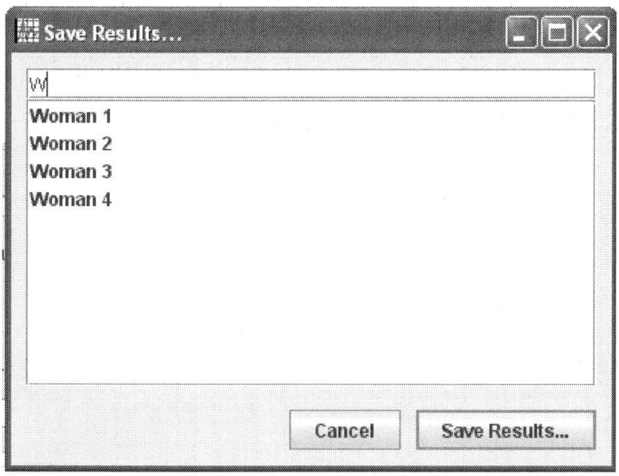

Fig. 12. Search for people whose names begin with 'w'

In our case we are going to create a new profile. As the name "Example" does not exist, by typing it out completely and clicking on "Save Results…", the new name will be created and the data saved. No results will appear as this is the patient's first session:

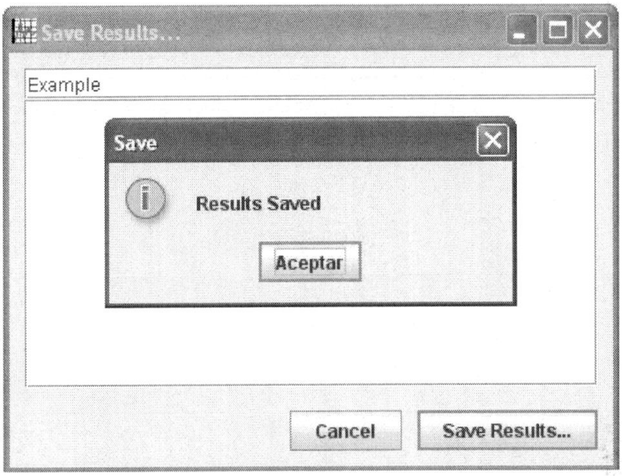

Fig. 13. Message displayed when saving results

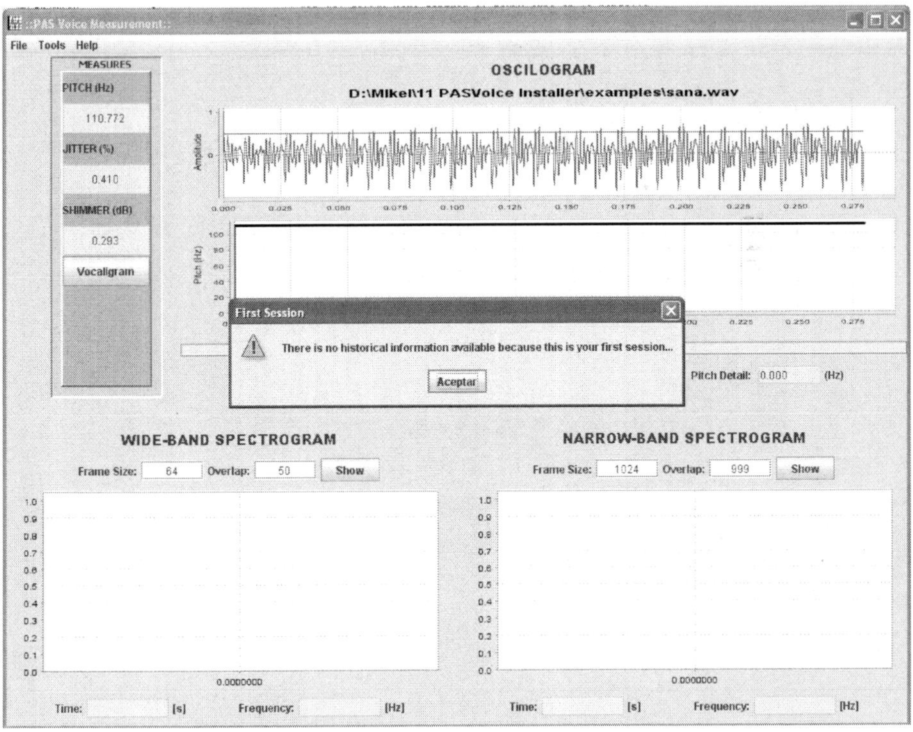

Fig. 14. Message displayed at initial session

We could also have added results as if they were for a patient not coming for the first time. We choose an already existing patient, "Man 1", by choosing from the list and clicking on "Save Results…". A graph showing all the results saved to date from previous sessions is provided (pitch information is separated from that on jitter and shimmer as they are different units):

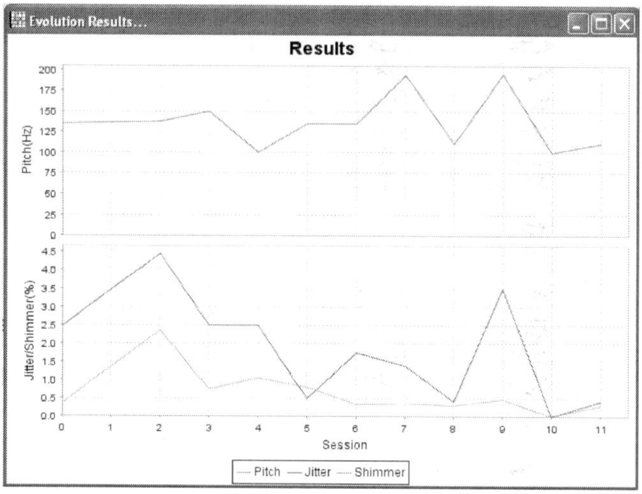

Fig. 15. Evolution of results by session

Finally, when this window is closed (top-right x), we are provided with a message informing us on evolution since the previous session:

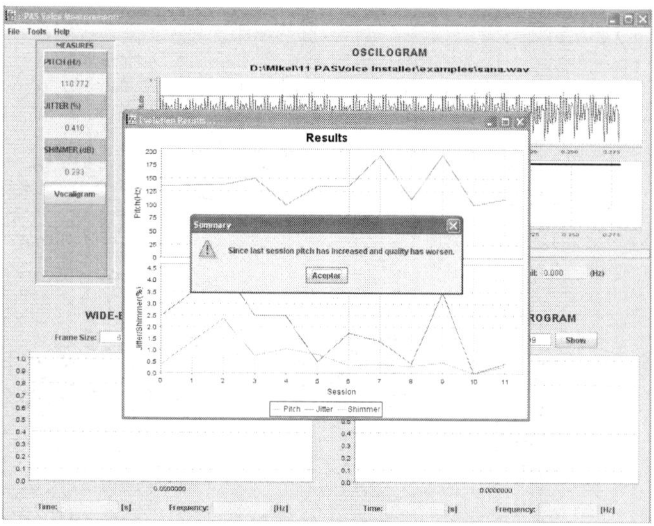

Fig. 16. Message providing information on evolution since last session

Recent scientific progress has made it possible to take great steps forward in such fields of major interest as biomedical engineering. In this area, the application of new technologies becomes essential in order to improve techniques in the diagnosis, treatment and rehabilitation of certain medical pathologies. However, there are also collectives suffering from an illness or treatments that only affect a minority of people. This is a characteristic which usually implies that the level of technological development corresponding to the resources having to be used for these pathologies is way behind that for other more common disorders.

The laryngectomized are people who, for various reasons, have had to undergo surgery to remove their larynx, vocal cords, epiglottis and the cartilages surrounding the larynx. These elements are of vital importance for the generation of speech as they form part of the phoning apparatus. Therefore, the removal of these seriously affects the quality of their speech.

The issue of treating a barely intelligible voice is also of great use from the point of view of the patient's psychology. We have noticed that a high proportion of the laryngectomized feel embarrassed when using this voice, particularly women, who would rather not speak than do so with oesophageal voice, as they consider it unfeminine.

The results obtained from this research work have been useful mainly due to the IT contribution involving the design, development and implementation of a software application specifically intended for the assessment of laryngectomized voices, with a view to performing a correct medical monitoring that will make it possible to measure evolution and prevent relapses. In order to verify improvement in the quality of oesophageal voices, a database containing several phonemes of all kinds of voices was worked with; these voices, both pathological and healthy, were recorded with the help of members from the Asociación Vizcaína de Laringectomizados.

Future work deriving from this research includes, most importantly, the incorporation of functionalities for vocal recognition and synthesis of phrases, as well as implementing the digital signal processing algorithms developed in systems based on cell phones and PDAs; all this with the goal of improving the laryngectomized's quality of life.

5. Conclusions

Due to the great relevance of Wavelet Transform for the analysis and processing of esophageal speech, and assuming that the final goal will be the implementation in a hardware DSP based device, with very strict real-time requirements, a significant computing resources optimization has been achieved, and consequently, a reduction of the code length in order to minimize computational load. Also it is important to highlight that the obtained wavelet calculi can be used in later processing.

These advantages are achieved through a preprocessing algorithm, which, although Wavelets based, includes some improvements. Firstly, an approximation to the formant subband. And secondly, an adjustable resolution applied over the bands among which the formant energy is shared.

On the other hand, the here proposed algorithm allows to optimize previous research works concerning the treatment of the poles of the system which models esophageal speech, according to LPC. Taking into account the obtained accuracy, it is logical to assume an improvement in results if this technique is used as a first stage of the whole algorithm.

6. References

[1] García, B., Vicente, J. & Aramendi, E. "Time-Spectral Technique for Esophageal Speech Regeneration" Biosignal '02, 2002.

[2] García, B., Vicente, J., Ruiz, I., Alonso, A. & Loyo, E. "Esophageal Voices: Glottal flow Restoration" ICASSP 2005.

[3] Baken, R. & Orlikoff, R. "Clinical measurement of speech and voice" Second Edition. San Diego, CA: Singular Publishing Group, ISBN:1565938690, 2000.

[4] Brown, J.C. & Puckette, M.S. "A high resolution fundamental frequency determination based on phase changes of the Fourier transform" J. Acoust. Soc. Amer., vol.94, pp. 662-667, August 1993.

[5] Mallat, S "A Wavelet Tour of Signal Processing" Second Edition.. Academic Press, ISBN: 0-12-466606-X.

[6] Hooper, C.R. "Using evidence-based research in speech-language pathology: a project that changed my thinking"American - Speech - Language - Hearing -Association, January 2003.

[7] Cnockaert, L.; Grenez, F.; Schoentgen, J. "Fundamental Frequency Estimation And Vocal Tremor Analysis By Means Of Morlet wavelet Transforms", ICASSP 2005.

[8] J. K. Maccallum, L. Cai, L. Zhou, Y. Zhang, and J. J. Jiang, "Acoustic analysis of aperiodic voice: perturbation and nonlinear dynamic properties in esophageal phonation.," Journal of Voice, vol. 23, no. 3, pp. 283-90, May 2009.

[9] M. Carello and M. Magnano, "A first comparative study of oesophageal and voice prosthesis speech production," EURASIP Journal on Advances in Signal Processing, vol. 2009, no. 821304, pp. 1-7, 2009.

[10] D. Rudoy and T. Quatieri, "Time-varying autoregressions in speech: detection theory and applications," IEEE Trans. Audio, Speech, and Language Process., vol. 19, no. 4, pp. 977-989, 2011.

[11] S. Aviyente and A. Yener Mutlu, "A time-frequency based approach to phase and phase synchrony estimation," IEEE Transactions on Signal Processing, vol. 59, no. 7, pp. 3086-3098, 2011.

6

The Use of the Wavelet Transform to Extract Additional Information on Surface Quality from Optical Profilometers

Richard L. Lemaster
North Carolina State University
USA

1. Introduction

This chapter investigates the use of advanced signal processing techniques especially wavelet transforms to extract additional information from a two dimensional surface profile. The wavelet transform is able to aid the user in quickly assessing, visually, if the surface profile has a periodic or non-periodic component as well as if the profile signal is stationary or non-stationary. In addition, thresholds could be set at different frequencies of interest to automatically determine for the user if a periodic signal is present and if its magnitude is acceptable or not. The basis of this chapter is a doctoral dissertation by Lemaster (2004). A laser based, non-contact profilometer was used for all the surface profiles presented in this chapter though contact profilometers could also benefit from this type of analysis. The original work was conducted for wood and wood-based composites; however the signal processing techniques discussed in this chapter are applicable to all types of surfaces. In fact, an industry that would also like to determine if a surface profile is stationary or not or has periodic components is the road surface industry. They routinely use laser based optical profilometers very similar to the type used in this study except for the optics used to obtain the desired range and sensitivity. They are interested in detecting and quantifying pot holes, ruts, and washboard which are very similar to the surface characteristics of interest to the wood industry but on a different scale.

Traditional time domain analysis that is commonly used in the analysis of surface quality does not adequately show if a periodicity exits on the surface. While frequency domain analysis can reveal if the surface has a periodicity component it cannot adequately determine if the periodicity continues across the entire surface (stationary) or if it only extends across a portion of the surface (non-stationary). This information is of importance if the user wants to extend the capability of traditional surface quality analysis and not only quantify surface irregularities but classify them to both type and source.

2. Background

2.1 Surface texture

Surface texture, a three-dimensional measurement, has been described as the topography, roughness, or irregularity of the interface between a substance and its surroundings, generally air (Stumbo, 1963). Surface roughness and surface topography are properties of engineering materials that are important to functional performance and can be used as a measure of product quality and process performance. Surface texture can be caused by the nature of the material itself, a manufacturing process applied to the material, or a combination of both. The processing characteristics that affect the surface texture include: inaccuracy in the machine tool, deformation under cutting force, tool or workpiece vibration, geometry of the cutting action, material tearing during chip formation, and heat treatment effects. Wood characteristics that can affect surface texture include: wood species, density, moisture content, and cutting direction. In most instances, however, surface finish has not been fully exploited in the areas of process monitoring, quality and performance prediction. Today, new measurement techniques and signal processing methods make it feasible to take a new look at the ways available for measuring and evaluating surface texture.

The degree of roughness of a surface often affects the way the material itself is used. In general, surface irregularities can cause misalignment and part malfunctions, excessive loading over small areas, friction and lubrication problems, general finish and reflectivity problems, as well as catastrophic failures. Although surface quality for wood products has been a key issue since woodworking first began, the level of precision required does not approach that found in the metal working industry. This has been due, in part, to wood's inherent dimensional instabilities. The other main reason was that many common uses for wood did not require exceptional surface finishes as compared to many metal applications. The monitoring of surface irregularities in wood is, however, important to assure proper fit of machined parts for gluing, acceptable surface finish for furniture, and as a methodology to monitor the accuracy of the manufacturing process. The last reason has become even more important in recent years due to the increased cost of raw materials, the increased production costs, and the higher production speeds available. Any deviation in expected product quality can quickly cause significant economic losses. There has also been a trend toward tighter tolerances for many forest products industries. An example of this would be the lamination of wood or wood-based products with plastic films or ultra-thin veneers. Even the slightest irregularity in the surface will show through the top laminate.

Usually, wood machining processes are heavily influenced by workpiece surface quality considerations. Tool sharpness requirements as well as machine feed and speed decisions are often based on workpiece surface quality. Research in surface measurement technology was aimed at identifying and quantifying defects associated with a variety of machining processes. Surface waviness is often introduced by the machining process or by the vibration of the tool or workpiece, whereas surface roughness is often introduced by the detachment of material from the workpiece. Of particular interest in this research was the use of frequency domain analysis to separate the random from the periodic components of the surface. The optical profilometer surface measurement system discussed in this chapter has been found to be effective for identifying surface defects including surface waviness, torn grain, fuzzy grain, and abrasive (sanding) grit marks.

Though beyond the scope of this chapter, methods of assessment have ranged from entirely subjective methods (simply feeling the wood surface) to modern day computerized three-dimensional (3D scans) assessments of the surface. The very nature of wood has made the quantitative assessment of surface quality difficult. Wood materials exhibit a wide range of defects due to biological as well as machining-related causes. In some cases there is no clear distinction between biological causes of poor surface quality as opposed to machining related causes.

Monitoring the surface quality of a workpiece surface is a good indicator of the state of the machining process regardless of the workpiece material. It is common practice in wood product industries for lumber graders to check the quality of the surface visually, for composite panel manufacturers to use crayons to check for undesirable sanding marks, for planer operators to "feel" the depth and spacing of planer knife marks, and for saw operators to visually check the severity of saw marks. While these procedures are often used to attempt to determine if a process has varied with time, they are very inconsistent from day to day and do not permit the quantification of the defects. Monitoring the surface quality of a machining process is becoming increasingly important as the machining speed, the cost of raw material, and labor, all continue to increase. Any undetected changes in the quality of machining process can cause a significant impact on the economics of the process.

Workpiece quality evaluation during the actual wood machining process (on–line surface evaluation) has been done using cameras, lasers, x-ray, and various combinations of these technologies. These systems are able to provide a relatively rapid scan of the wood material, usually while the sample is moving slowly (or temporarily stopped on a conveyor) prior to or after being sorted or machined. Such systems are in common use in industry and are aimed primarily at detecting biological defects such as rot, discoloration, knots, etc. These types of systems have also been used to detect simple geometry problems, such as gross dimensional variations, etc.

The work that this chapter is based on consisted of using a laser based position sensing device (PSD) to obtain a 2 dimensional surface profile of the surface. The signal processing techniques that are discussed is an attempt to extract more information as to the type and cause of the surface irregularity than simple measuring the magnitude of the irregularity as is normally done based on the U.S. (ASME B461-2009) and international (ISO 4287/1) standards. The utility of simple frequency analysis is demonstrated below, for several idealized (simulated) examples of surface quality issues relevant to wood machining.

As mentioned above, all examples of surfaces analyzed in this chapter were from wood or wood based products. It is beyond the scope of this chapter to go into detail about wood structure. If interested, the reader is referred to "Understanding Wood" by Hoadley, 2000. The surface texture that is generated when machining wood is very complex and has many factors that can contribute to the variations of the surface quality. Surface defects can be either biological or machining based defects. The fact that wood is an anisotropic and hygroscopic material can cause the surfaces generated by a machining process to vary greatly.

Peripheral milling or planing (moulding) may be defined as the removal of wood in the form of single chips by intermittent engagement of the workpiece with knives carried on the periphery of a rotating cutterhead (Koch, 1955). The resulting surface on the workpiece of a peripheral milling operation consists of individual knife traces generated by successive engagements of each knife or cutting edge (Figure 1). In addition to the height of the ridges or scallops (t), the distance between successive ridges or **pitch (Sz)** is also an import feature of surface roughness.

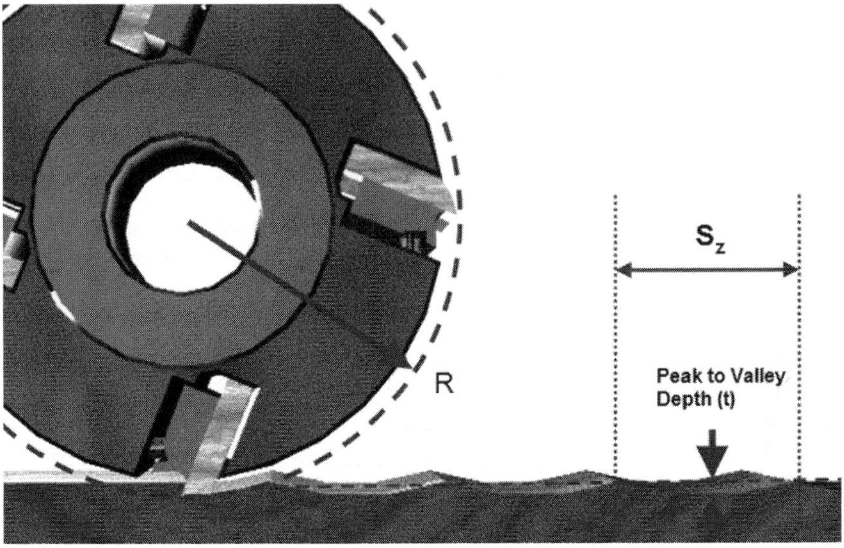

Fig. 1. Definition of pitch and depth of cutter or tool marks (Weinig USA, training manual, www.weinigusa.com).

As the pitch increases the surface appears more "wavy" for a given cutter diameter and depth of cut. Many manufacturers specify the accepted or desirable pitch of a surface while others may specify the "knife marks per inch". The smaller the pitch the "smoother" the resulting surface will be, however, this is sometimes at the expense of quicker tool dulling. Experience (Effner, 1992) has shown that a good surface finish will have a pitch mark of approximately 1.5 - 1.7 mm (0.06 - 0.07 inches). For knife marks per inch this translates to 15-17 marks per inch for a high quality surface. Many moulder manufacturers recommend that the peak-to-valley height of the marks be kept below 0.005 mm (0.02 μin) for fine furniture and between 0.005 and 0.017 mm (0.02 - 0.07 μin.) for average quality building moulding.

Another type of machining of interest is abrasive machining. Abrasive machining includes **abrasive planing** the workpiece to a desired thickness or **sanding** a workpiece to achieve the desired level of smoothness. The surfaces that are generated from this type of machining process is complex in that they often include non-periodic abrasive grit marks running parallel to the feed direction (wide belt sanding) as well as regular periodic "tooling" marks running perpendicular to the feed direction. These "tooling" marks are caused by either the motion of the sanding head, the motion of the workpiece, or a combination of both.

In addition to the surface texture variation that may be caused by machining processes there are other surface defects that are caused by the manufacturing process of wood-based composites. A condition, called **pitting** is where wood fiber or fiber bundles are pulled out of the surface of the wood panel product during panel manufacturing. This can be caused by improper press times, resin content or blending, or the lack of release agents on the platens of the press.

2.2 Conventional surface quality measurement and analysis techniques

Vast amounts of work have been conducted in attempts to develop techniques to measure and evaluate surface texture in materials. These techniques generally fall into two distinct groups. The first is the hardware or method to measure surface texture data. The second is the analysis procedure to evaluate the surface texture. Numerous methods have been developed and researched for both the measurement and evaluation techniques. Measurement techniques normally fall into two distinct categories: contact and non-contact methods. It is beyond the scope of this chapter to discuss the surface measurement techniques that have been investigated in the past. The reader is referred to Lemaster (2004) for an overview of the various works on this topic. A general review of the optical techniques (and surface roughness techniques in general) is provided in several comprehensive reference works (Thomas, 1999; Whitehouse, 2011; Whitehouse, 1994; Thomas and King, 1977; and Riegel, 1993). The work conducted by the author on optical profilometry of wood and wood-based products can also be found in the literature (Lemaster, 2010, Lemaster, 2004; Lemaster 1997a, 1997b; Lemaster and Beall, 1996; Lemaster and DeVries, 1992; Lemaster and Dornfeld, 1983; Jouaneh, Lemaster, and Dornfeld, 1987; and DeVries and Lemaster, 1992).

The heart of any surface quality assessment system is the detector. The optical method used for the detector in this research is a variation of the reflectance method, whereby the positional change of the reflected laser light into the detector is correlated to changes in the test surface height. In this method, a laser spot is projected on the workpiece surface and the reflected light is focused on the surface of a lateral-effect photodiode. The change of the position of the reflected laser spot on the surface of the detector, a′ is correlated to the vertical height change of the workpiece, a. By moving a workpiece beneath the detector and recording the change in the position of the laser spot, a two-dimensional surface profile is obtained that is very similar to that obtained by the traditional stylus system (Figure 2). The resulting surface profile can then be analyzed according to traditional U.S. (ASME B461-2009) and international standards (ISO 4287/1). This method is non-contact and capable of detection at high speed, and since it measures position changes of the reflected light and not spot intensity, it is relatively insensitive to color changes of the workpiece.

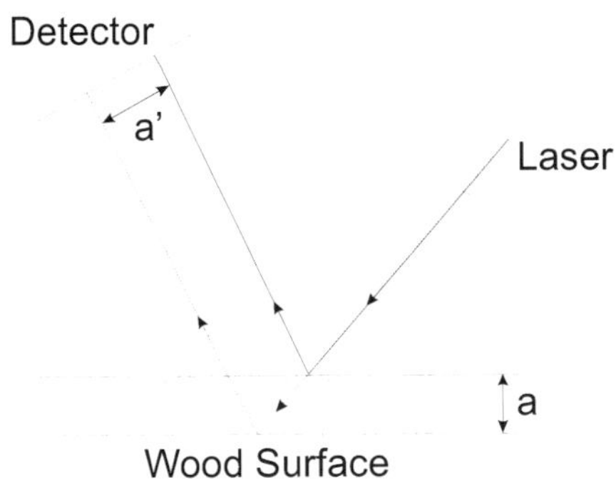

Fig. 2. Schematic of optical profilometer

2.2.1 Time domain characterization

Most surface quality analysis including three-dimensional analysis has been traditionally based upon the surface tracing or surface profile. Most analysis of the surface profile generated by the stylus system has been evaluated using time domain parameters such as height deviations and asperity spacing or wavelength. Whitehouse (1982) gives a brief history of the development of surface quality evaluation techniques and the confusion that has developed due to new developments in measurement technology, lack of coordinated efforts between countries, changes in manufacturing processes resulting in different surface textures for a given part, and economic considerations affecting instrumentation development. King and Spedding (1983) discussed three categories of approaches that have been used to characterize a surface:

- Characterization by process specification (sawing, milling, etc.)
- Characterization according to function (intended use of workpiece)
- Statistical characterization of the surface profile (magnitude of surface irregularities, etc.)

The figure below (figure 3) shows a common example of time domain measurements. The measurements include a measure of the average roughness, R_q (second moment, root mean square), a measure of "extremes" R_{tm}, a measure of whether the surface defects are above or below the average surface, a measure of skewness, R_{sk} (third moment), and a measure of the shape of the surface defects, R_{ku} kurtosis (4th moment).

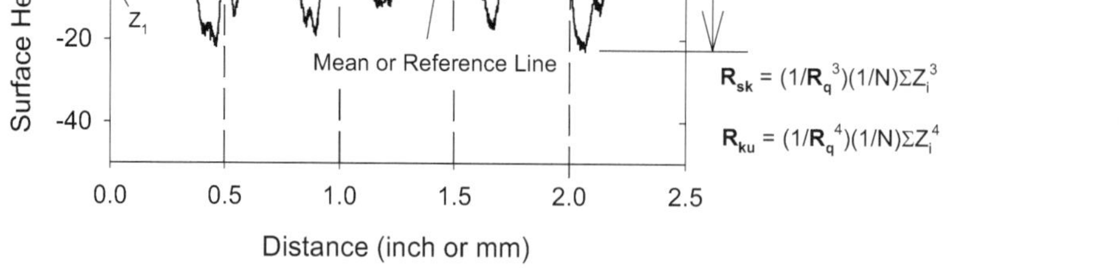

Fig. 3. Definitions of surface descriptors

2.2.2 Frequency domain characterization

Although wood surface description is the main subject here, the potential advantages of frequency analysis has been investigated for metal surface measurement as well as road surface measurement. The use of standard surface descriptors based on time domain analysis is sufficient for some applications; however it does not provide information as to the periodicity of the surface characteristics or the nature or cause of the defects. Frequency is most often expressed as cycles per second known as Hertz (Hz). However, frequency can also be expressed spatially such as cycles per unit length (cycles per inch).

As stated by Brock (1983), in the field of signal processing and analysis as applied to sound and vibration problems, the transformation of the signal from the time domain to the frequency domain is very common due to the ease with which the signal can be analyzed and characterized. Although this approach is not common in the field of surface quality analysis, the same benefits can be realized. The main advantage of frequency analysis is that it can reveal the dominant frequency components contained in the transducer signal. Ber and Braun (1968) showed that the frequency spectra resulting from the measurements on surfaces obtained by turning, grinding, and lapping are dissimilar. Raja and Radhakrishnan (1979) separated the roughness from the waviness component on a surface by using fast Fourier transform techniques. Staufert (1979) also used frequency domain analysis to separate periodic components from random components in the surface. In the literature an industry that has tended to use the power spectrum for surface quality analysis is that of road surface evaluation. In an article by Bruscella, Rouillard, and Sek (1999) a laser based optical profilometer was used to obtain a surface profile of the road. Both the time and frequency domains were analyzed.

Work by Lemaster (1997b) has addressed the use of the frequency spectrum of the surface profile to detect "periodicity" within a surface profile. This approach is suitable because a surface profile is often composed of both random and periodic components. Under ideal cutter conditions, the tool produces evenly spaced cutter marks which occur periodically. In cases where the tool is not concentric, out of balance, or the workpiece is not properly held, the marks are unevenly spaced and vary in depth. More random defects often result from the detachment of material from the workpiece. The utility of simple frequency analysis is demonstrated, for several idealized (simulated) examples of surface quality issues relevant to wood machining is discussed below.

Much work has been conducted on using wavelets in filtering or de-composing the surface profile. The category of interest here is the use of wavelets to separate these surface components. Much of the work discussing wavelets as applied to surface roughness are based on analyzing the gray scales of an image of the surface which is beyond the scope of this chapter and will not be discussed here but the reader is referred to Fricout et. al. (2002) for one discussion of this approach. Other works discussing wavelets and surface texture consists of multi-resolution decomposition of the surfaces including separating the error of form, waviness, roughness, and localized defects. Work by Khawaja (2011) demonstrated the insensitivity of the shape of the wavelet in its ability to decompose the components of a surface trace and obtain a standard roughness descriptor. While these works are very important in the complete understanding of surface texture analysis, it was not the main thrust of the topic in this chapter. In fact, the work by Lemaster (2004) found that this use of wavelets did indeed provide a means of removing the form of the surface texture that, in many cases, yielded superior filtering than the traditional phase correct Gaussian filter.

2.2.3 Shortcomings of simple time and frequency analysis

One of the main objectives of developing a surface quality evaluation system was to be able to detect variations in surface quality from time to time which actually may be viewed as discontinuities. Besides detecting if a random or periodic component exists it is also important to determine if the defect is consistent (stationary) or if it changes with time (non-stationary). This can occur in practice from such things as a failure in the feed system or variation in thicknesses of a board being planed. The problem in defining a non-stationary surface is linked to the time frame being observed. A sanding ridge can be considered non-stationary when only a small sample distance is considered (one board), however, if the ridge occurs over numerous boards and all boards are included in the analysis, then the ridge can be considered stationary as far as the process is concerned. Traditional time and frequency analyses cannot distinguish between stationary and non-stationary surfaces. The following section illustrates this shortcoming and discusses some recent developments in **joint time-frequency analysis (JTFA)** that may overcome these shortcomings in surface quality assessment. Figure 4 illustrates the difficulty or shortcomings of traditional frequency analysis. Two significantly different surface profiles can result in similar frequency spectra.

These two examples show the weakness of traditional frequency analysis in the current descriptions of wood surface applications. Though both signals have a similar frequency spectrum, one signal is non-stationary (top - left) where the other one (lower - left) is stationary. This illustrates a need for a more advanced form of frequency analysis.

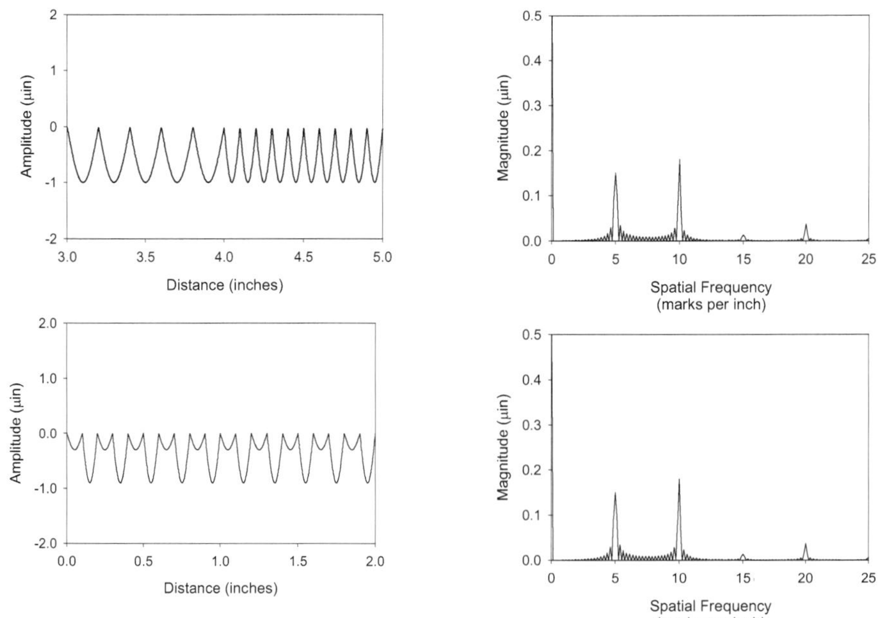

Fig. 4. Two types of signals that have similar frequency spectra

3. Basic joint time / frequency analysis

3.1 The Short Time Fourier Transform (STFT)

The FT is very versatile, but is inadequate when one is interested in the "local" (in time or space) frequency content of the signal. A transform method that can analyze non-stationary signals where the frequency information changes with time is required for this type of analysis.

An obvious method, following on from the FT, is to analyze the time (space) signal over 0-T seconds in a train of shorter intervals such as 0-T/4, T/4-T/2, T/2-3T/4, 3T/4-T, known as windows (Figure 5).

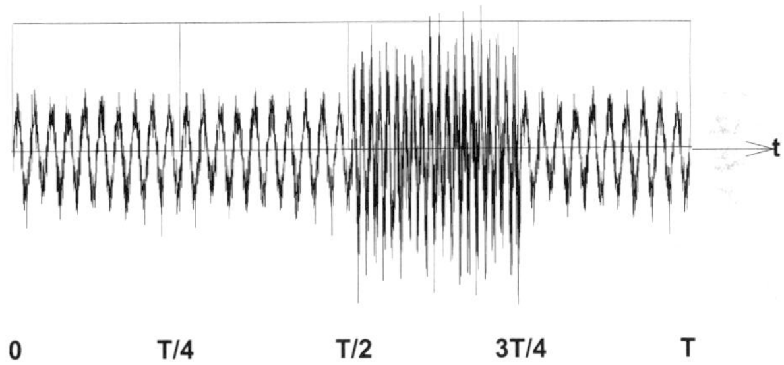

Fig. 5. Short Time Fourier Transform (STFT) with moving non-overlapping rectangular windows.

The individual windows, being only of length T/4 in this case, mean that the lowest frequency f_L will be only one-quarter of the full 0-T window value. This method, first described by Gabor (1956), is known as the **Short Time Fourier Transform** (STFT), (see Goswani and Chan (1999) and Qian (2002) for a full discussion). Today, the individual transforms are usually performed using the FFT algorithm where the window shape can be varied; i.e. rectangular, Hanning, cosine taper, etc.

Note in an STFT, as in the FT, the size of the window is fixed but the frequency of the sinusoids that are compared to the signal varies as does the number of oscillations. A small window is unable to detect low frequencies which are too large for the window. If too large a window is used then information about a brief change will be lost. This implies prior knowledge of the signal's characteristics and will become an important criterion for choosing the analysis method. An additional advantage of the non-overlapping STFT is that perfect reconstruction of the original signal g(t) is still possible.

A more recent, but slower, method known as the **adaptive Gabor spectrogram** was developed by Qian and Chen (1994) where the time and frequency resolutions are defined by one parameter. Unlike the classical Gabor expansion, where the time and frequency resolutions are fixed, the time and frequency resolutions of the adaptive Gabor expansion can be adjusted optimally. This method while, it would be acceptable for "off-line" surface measurements was not investigated further in this research because of the slower computational times and the desire to have an efficient method that could be used on-line in a manufacturing environment.

An improvement to the STFT time-frequency analysis method is to overlap the windows. Figure 6 demonstrates the sliding window principle.

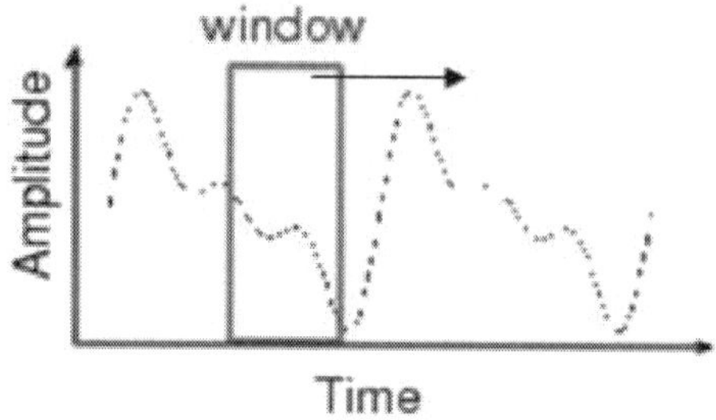

Fig. 6. Example of Sliding Short Time Fourier Transform

With digitized data, the limit to the time resolution is to move the window one sample at a time to yield up to N windows. There is a clear improvement in time resolution and with present day computer speeds so fast, there is little slowdown in the computation.

3.2 The Wavelet Transform

The JTFA methods such as the STFT and Wigner-Ville have been criticized for their failure to resolve both time and frequency simultaneously. This led to a search for other functions, besides sine and cosine waves to overcome this problem. These local basis functions, which have been studied in incredible mathematical detail in recent times, are typically used for analyzing non-stationary signals and are known as **wavelets**. Each wavelet is located at a different position along the time (space) axis which decreases to zero on either side of the center position, (see Figure 7) such that the average value (area under the wavelet) is zero. Wavelets are not necessarily of fixed frequency and can be either compressed or dilated in time, which results in a change of scale (see Figure 8). Much like the FT and STFT, multiplication of the signal g(t) by the wavelet shapes as basis functions yields a set of coefficients which describe the correlation between the signal and the wavelet. In particular, depending on the wavelet shape, discontinuities in the signal can be easily detected.

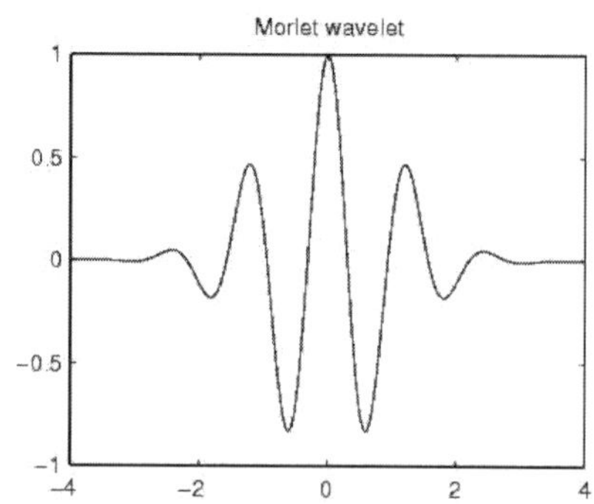

Fig. 7. Morlet mother wavelet function (Hubbard, 1998)

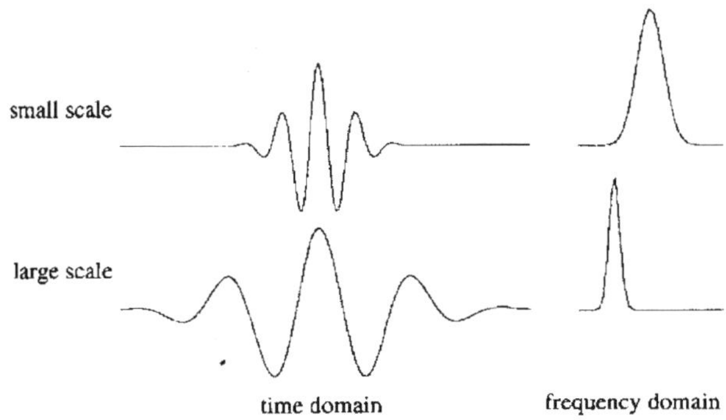

Fig. 8. Example of wavelet compression (top) and dilation (bottom)

Further examination of figure 8 shows that, unlike the STFT (where the size of the windows are fixed, filled with oscillations of the sine and cosine waves of different frequencies) the reverse is now true in that the number of oscillations is fixed (the mother wavelet shape) but the window width or scale is varied. If the window is stretched, the wavelet frequency is decreased to analyze low frequencies (long times). When the window is compressed, analysis of high frequencies (short times) is possible. Hubbard (1998) called this technique a "mathematical microscope". This initial wavelet shape may be viewed as the **mother wavelet** from which all the other wavelets (in this function class or shape) can be derived.

The concept is thus more complicated than the FT in that not only does the multiplying function contain multiple frequencies, but changes its center frequencies as it changes its scale. To overcome the time and resolution uncertainty effect it will be seen that many window (wavelet) widths or resolutions can be written into one algorithm. Although the original idea of the wavelets can be traced back to the **Haar** transform first introduced in 1910 (a German paper published in the Mathematical Annals, Volume 69), wavelets did not become popular until the early 1980's when researchers in geophysics, theoretical physics, and mathematics developed the mathematical foundation (see Qian, 2002). Hubbard (1998) stated that tracing the history of wavelets was almost a job for an archaeologist. Meyer (1989) stated that he had found at least 15 distinct roots of the wavelet theory. Since then considerable work has been conducted by mathematicians and to a lesser degree by engineers. Uses of wavelets were discovered; in particular Mallet (1989) and Meyer (1989) found a close relationship between wavelets and the structure of multi-resolution analysis. Mallat stated that a multi-resolution transform of the signal is equivalent to a set of filters of constant percentage bandwidth in the frequency domain. Work by Mallet and Meyer led to a simple way of calculating the mother wavelet as well as a connection between continuous wavelets and digital filter banks. Following this work, **Daubechies** (1990) further developed a systematic technique of generating finite duration wavelets using sets of discrete difference equations to calculate the wavelet shape. They are designated D4, D20, etc. denoting the number of wavelet describing coefficients, Daubechies (1990).

It is not the intent of this chapter to cover the mathematical details of wavelets. The reader can find a comprehensive treatment of wavelet analysis and descriptions in Burrus (1998), Daubechies (1990), Mallat (2009), Newland (1997), and Strang and Nguyen (1996). For a less intense mathematical treatise of wavelets, the reader is referred to Hubbard (1998).

3.2.1 Description of wavelets

While both STFT (and other JTFA techniques) and wavelets can be used for time-frequency analysis, they each have a distinct set of advantages and disadvantages. The STFT is suited for narrow instantaneous frequency bandwidths (such as chirps), while the wavelet (time-scale) transforms are best suited for signals that have instantaneous peaks or discontinuities (image description, sound generated by engine knocks, etc.) (Qian, 2002).

There are two major categories of wavelet transforms; continuous and discrete (Gaberson, 2002). According to Gaberson, the continuous wavelet transform (CWT) is easier to describe. The CWT is a "short wavy" function that is stretched or compressed and placed at many positions along the signal to be analyzed. The wavelet is then term-by-term multiplied with the signal, each product yielding a wavelet coefficient value. Just as the STFT with its non-overlapping time windows historically came before the (continuous) sliding STFT so have applications of the discrete wavelet transform (DWT) historically come before the CWT. In the DWT there will be a finite number of wavelet comparisons whereas in the CWT there could be an infinite number. Since this chapter is part of a book on applications of wavelets and is companioned with a book on the theory of wavelets the background of wavelets will not be discussed in detail here.

As mentioned above, the original goal of this research was to develop a fast online surface quality technique. While both CWT and DWT were originally investigated only the DWT was considered for much of the research due to the computational speeds of the two types. For an online surface quality evaluation system it was convenient to look at the case of the discrete wavelet transform (DWT), where the number of wavelets is not only finite but also lead to a particularly efficient algorithm. With N samples of the data record taken, the wavelet $\psi(t)$ occupying the time interval 0-T, designated level 0 (see Newland, 1997), is shown in Figure 9.

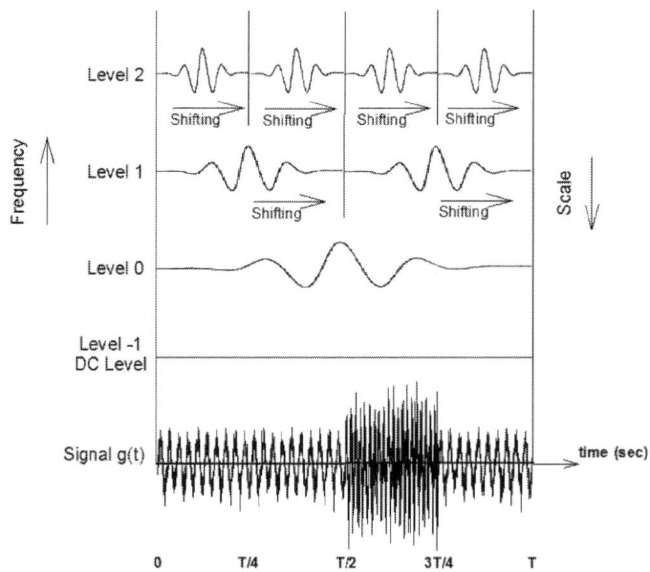

Fig. 9. The scaling and shifting process of the DWT

Next the wavelet is compressed time-wise into two similar shapes of the same amplitude by a factor of one-half to form level 1, then again by another factor of one-half to form 4 wavelets at level 2, etc. Level -1 is the DC level of the signal. These wavelets are compared to the signal by multiplication generating the coefficients $W(s,\tau)$. Plotting the square of these coefficients yields a 3-dimensional time-scale or time-frequency plot similar to the STFT.

As a reminder, each multiplication of a wavelet with a part of the signal is a correlation or comparison of the signal with the wavelet and is called the wavelet transform coefficient $W(s,\tau)$. Note each wavelet waveform contains the **same** number of oscillations unlike the STFT described earlier. Following Newland (1997), with N samples of the data with $N = 2^n$ there will be n+1 levels of wavelet analysis (including the -1 level). There are n sets of wavelet multiplications. If $N = 128 = 2^7$ there will be 1, 2, 4, 8, 16, 32, and 64 wavelet compressions describing the shifts from level 0 through level 7. Note that the total number of multiplications is 127 which is of order (N). Following Hubbard (1998), if each wavelet is described or supported by c samples, the number of multiplications is cN. Thus the DWT is of the same order of computational efficiency as the FFT (where $N\log_2 N$ multiplications are required) for typical values of n.

The alternative filter bank approach (Strang and Nguyen, 1996) looks at data signals conceptually in the frequency domain. Approaching the method via the DWT, each wavelet behaves as a band-pass filter in the frequency domain (see Figure 10).

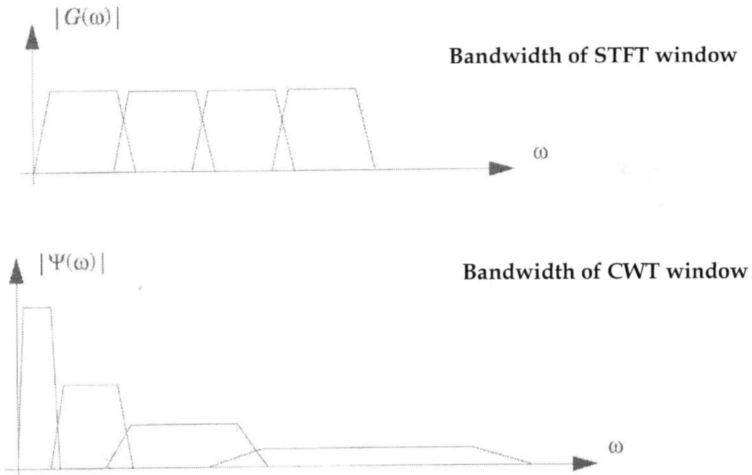

Fig. 10. Bandwidth of data windows for STFT (top) and DWT (bottom)

A third technique proposed by Newland (1993) is based on the fast Fourier transform (FFT) using an **exact** octave-band filter shape defined in the frequency domain (e.g. from frequency ω_1 to ω_2). Fourier coefficients are processed in octave-bands to generate wavelet coefficients by an orthogonal transformation which is implemented by the FFT. Unlike wavelets generated by discrete dilation equations whose shapes cannot be expressed in functional form, **harmonic wavelets** have the simple structure:

$$\psi(t)=\left(e^{(j4\pi t)}-e^{j2\pi t)}\right)/\ j2\pi t \tag{1}$$

This function is concentrated locally around t = 0, and is orthogonal to its own unit translations and octave dilations. Its frequency spectrum is confined exactly to an octave-band so that it is compact in the frequency domain instead of the time domain, see Figure 11, which shows a comparison of the Newland harmonic wavelet with the Daubechies D20 wavelet in the frequency domain (Newland, 1993). The Newland harmonic wavelet, being complex, can incorporate phase like some other wavelets but its amplitude decreases to zero at a slower rate of 1/t than some other wavelets. The Newland harmonic wavelet has been found to be particularly suitable for vibration and acoustic analysis because its harmonic structure is similar to naturally occurring signal structures and, therefore, they correlate well with experimental signals.

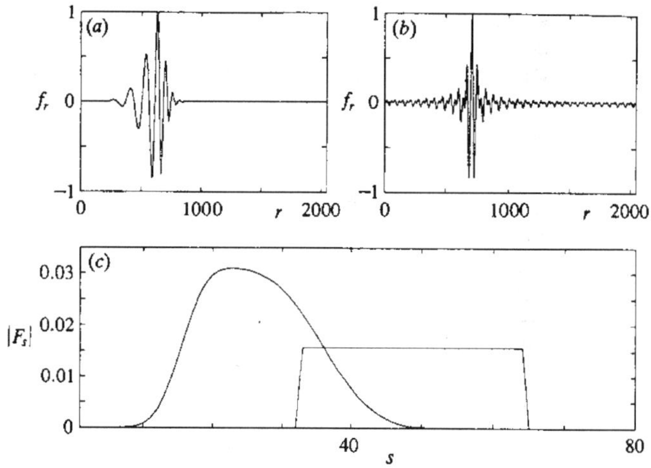

D20 **Harmonic**

Fig. 11. Comparison of the Daubechies - D20 (a) and Newland harmonic wavelets (b) in the time domain as well as the frequency domain (c)

Generally there is no exact simple relationship between the scale (s) and frequency (f), except to say that scale is approximately inversely proportional to the frequency so that high frequencies refer to low scales and vice versa. An advantage of the Newland harmonic wavelet is that he is able to use an **accurate frequency axis** in place of scale and the scale axis may be exactly written as the inverse frequency.

3.2.2 Wavelet selection

A challenge exists in choosing a wavelet best suited for analyzing wood surfaces. Due to the desire to detect small localized defects, a high sample density is needed (i.e. in the range of

8192 samples per inch). Obtaining this level of sampling, on-line and in real-time makes the speed of the analysis process critical. As mentioned before, the literature is full of different wavelet functions but very little advice is presented in the literature on choosing the best wavelet for the task. The advice normally is to choose a wavelet that is "similarly" shaped to the signal to be analyzed and then to try several wavelets. Hubbard (1998) devotes an entire chapter to discussing which wavelet should be used. There are definite differences of opinions on the procedure to follow. One is to use the commonly used wavelets such as the Mexican Hat and Morlet. The other extreme is to develop a new wavelet for a particular purpose. The question, as discussed in Hubbard, then arises as to what are the properties that are desired for the new wavelet. While the desire may be in trying to get fine resolution for **both** time and frequency domain, this is impossible and violates the uncertainty principle.

As mentioned in a previous section, periodic knife marks on a surface are a primary surface defect of interest in wood machining. Usually the higher the frequency of the knife marks, the lower the amplitude and the less objectionable the marks. From a series of field tests conducted as part of this research it was found that objectionable knife marks on moulder and planers as well as sanding "chatter" marks on wide belt sanders often occur in the range of 5 marks per inch.

3.2.3 Comparison of STFT and harmonic wavelet

In the research presented by Lemaster (2004) the various DWT and CWT were compared to the STFT. In addition, direct comparisons between the Harmonic and Daubachies D20 DWT techniques were also conducted. As mentioned previously, the CWT techniques did not provide enough increase in resolution to justify the added computational intensity. Also, a benefit of the Harmonic DWT was that it provided direct frequency information instead of scaling information which is only indirectly proportional to the frequency. So for the remainder of this discussion, a comparison was done between the more established Short Time Fourier Transform (STFT) and the Newland Harmonic DWT.

A series of simulated signals (waves) were generated to compare the ability of the two techniques to detect simulated surface defects including changing frequency and a localized defect (scratch or gouge on wood). The resulting plots were shown in units of length of scan and spatial frequency (marks per inch) to illustrate the plots in terms of spatial frequency for the actual surface scans. The plots consisted of 8192 data points over a 1 inch length of simulated scan. The STFT and DWT plots that were conducted on a reduced data set (every 16th data point for faster calculation speed) missed small defects such as the scratch. As discussed above, for larger defects such as the presence of a periodic component, the reduced data set still yielded a sufficient sampling frequency for the frequency and joint time/frequency analysis while maintaining the high sampling density required for time domain analysis. The first series of comparison was between two sine waves (5 Hz and 20 Hz). These frequencies were chosen because they approximate a single knife and a four knife finish on a typical moulder or planer operation. Two versions of the sine waves can exist, the first is when the two frequencies are superimposed on each other as when there are two sources of machine vibration and the second condition is when the two frequencies are appended to each other as when the feed rate has changed due to an alteration or slippage of the feed system (Figure 12).

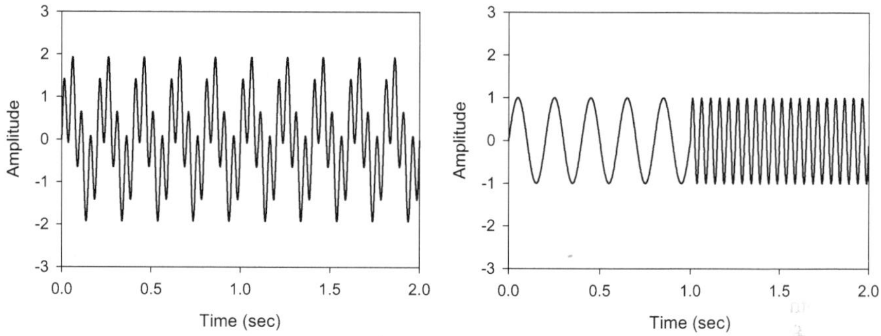

Fig. 12. Time domain signal of two superimposed sine waves (left) and two appended sine waves (5 Hz and 20 Hz)

Figure 13 (left) shows the time-frequency plot of the STFT of the two appended sine waves. From this figure it can be seen that a ridge is detected at 5 Hz extending from 0 to 1.0 second and a second ridge is detected at 20 Hz extending from 1.0 to 2.0 seconds. The edges of the ridges are sloped and not sharp. Similarly in Figure 13 (right), which shows the time-frequency plot of the appended sine waves for the HWT, the two ridges are detected at 5 and 20 Hz and extending only half way across the time axis as they should. The ridge at 5 Hz, however, is not as well defined as the ridge at 20 Hz.

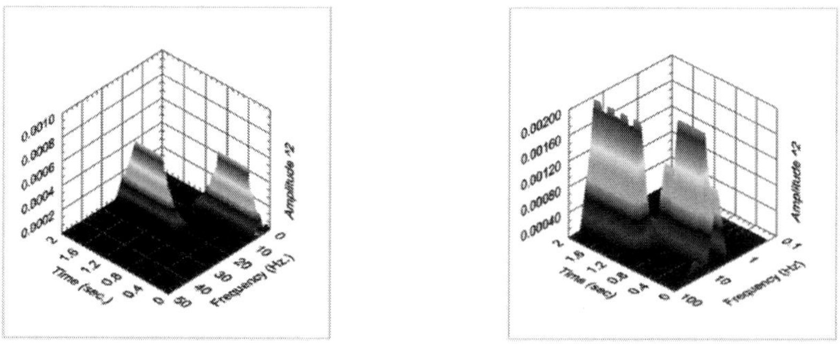

Fig. 13. STFT plot (left) of two appended sine waves (5 Hz and 20 Hz)(used every 16th point of 16384 point data file, 256 point window moved at 2 point intervals and Harmonic wavelet (right)(used every 16th point of 16384 point data file)

From these two figures, it appears that both the STFT and the harmonic wavelet can easily detect the two appended sine waves and provide information regarding where in the time domain the frequency of the sine waves change. The harmonic wavelet appeared to attenuate the lower frequency on the appended sine waves. The STFT attenuated the edges of the ridges at both frequencies.

The next set of simulated surface scans was for a localized defect such as a dent or scratch in the surface while still having knife marks. Since the lower frequencies of knife marks have proven to be more difficult to detect, a surface scan of 5 marks per inch with a small scratch in the surface was simulated. This surface profile is shown in Figure 14. This signal had a 5 Hz sine wave with a peak-to-peak amplitude of 2.0 and a scratch that had an amplitude of 1.5. Figure 15 show the STFT and harmonic wavelet plots respectively. Both the STFT and the harmonic wavelet detected the scratch in the surface. The STFT had to be adjusted so that the length of the analysis window and the amount to advance the window each time was much smaller than previous analyses. This means that a prior knowledge of the type of defect expected is required in order to use the STFT method on-line. Though this configuration of the STFT could detect the scratch, it resulted in a loss of resolution in detecting the 5 Hz sine wave. The harmonic wavelet could detect the scratch with no adjustments to the analysis. Additional tests for both the STFT and the harmonic wavelet showed that the scratch had to be larger than the peak height of the sine wave to be detected. Neither the STFT nor the harmonic wavelet could detect the scratch of a simulated surface scan that had a scratch amplitude of 1.0 with the 5 Hz sine wave having a 2.0 peak to peak amplitude. This means that a scratch would have to be at least of the same magnitude of the knife marks in order to be detected. The Newland HWT has the advantage in that frequency is accurately plotted rather than scale and its use was chosen for the signal analysis of the remainder of this research.

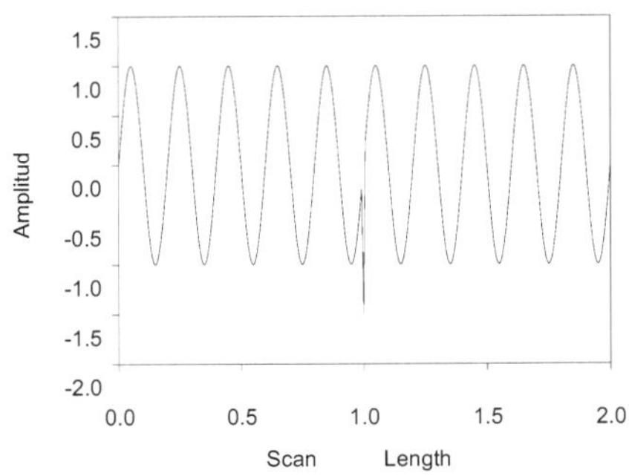

Fig. 14. Simulated surface profile of 5 Hz sine wave (5 marks per inch) with "scratch"

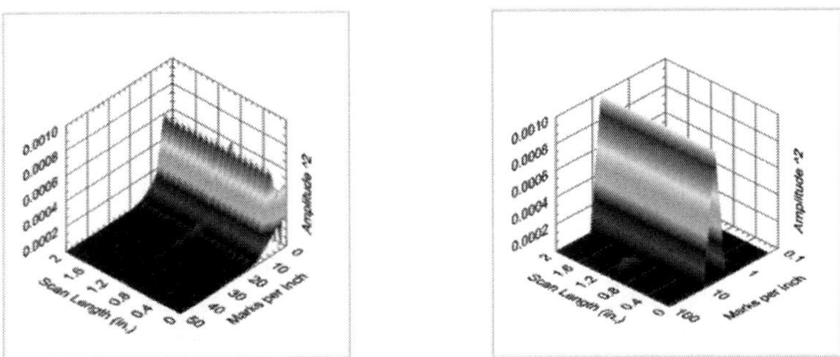

Fig. 15. STFT (left) and HWT (right) of 5 Hz sine wave with "scratch"

4. Results of surface scans

This section will show the results of using the HWT for various surfaces. In review, the surface quality assessment system is being designed to assist wood product manufacturers in monitoring their machining operations and alert them if the operation or the product quality changes during the machining process. To that end, the system must be able to scan the surface, analysis the data and make a decision on the state of the operation in an acceptable time frame. Information in the frequency domain can be limited to below 50 marks per inch since very high spatial frequencies are not of importance to the manufacturer. However, higher frequencies still must be included in order to detect the localized defects in the frequency domain.

4.1 Sanding ridge caused by loss of abrasive

This defect is caused by a portion of the abrasive in an abrasive machining operation separating from the backing of the abrasive belt. This is often caused by the belt striking a foreign object in the surface of the workpiece. The result is a ridge which forms on the surface of the workpiece. Figure 16 shows a photograph of a cabinet door with two sanding ridges on it. This results in a defect that is localized in one location of the surface of the workpiece; but is also considered stationary in that it occurs along the entire length of the surface as well as subsequent workpiece surfaces. This defect is very similar to a machining defect that is caused by a nick in a blade on a moulder, planer, or router. The surface profile for the sanding ridge shows the ridges very clearly (see Figure 17, left). The frequency plot (Figure 17, right) shows very little information or periodicity. The harmonic wavelet plot (see Figure 18) also shows no periodicity but does show the two sanding ridges and the location (in time) where they occur. The wavelet coefficients are negligible over most of the plot; with the two peaks caused by the two sanding ridges clearly shown at both ends of the scan. The advantage of the harmonic wavelet transform is that it shows both time and frequency information together in a single plot. The HWT clearly shows the two peaks and **when** they occurred as well as the fact that no significant periodicity exists on the surface.

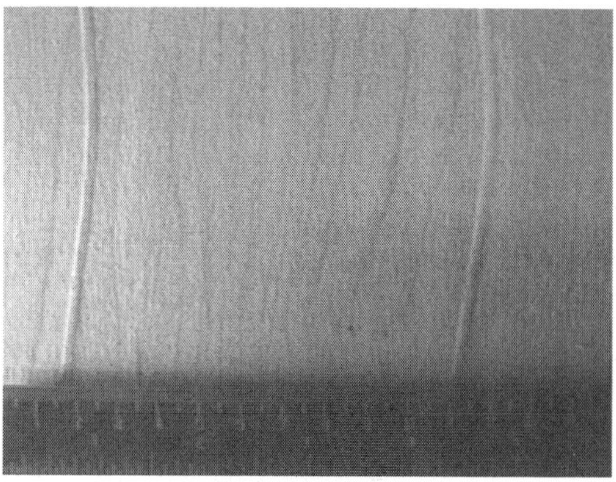

Fig. 16. Photograph of specimen with sanding ridges caused by loss of abrasive

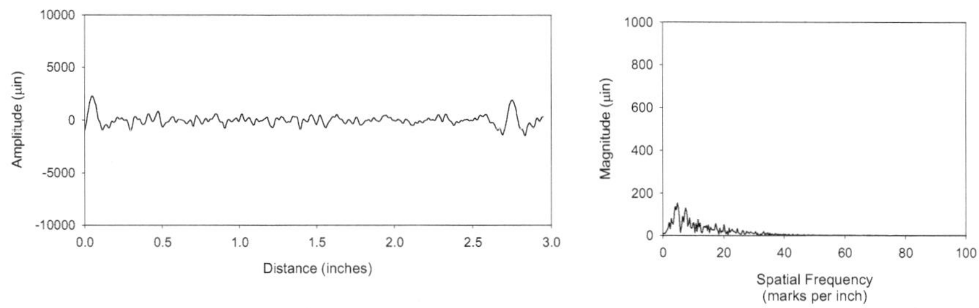

Fig. 17. Profile (left) and frequency spectrum (right) of specimen with sanding ridges caused by loss of abrasive

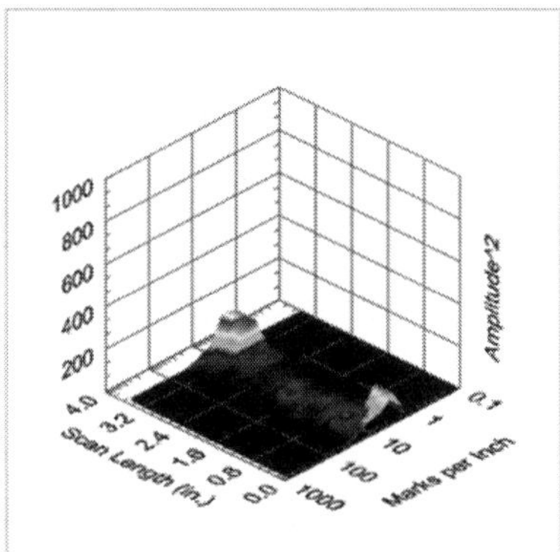

Fig. 18. Harmonic wavelet transform of specimen with sanding ridges

4.2 Surface with varying frequency of knife marks

This section shows a situation in which the knife marks occurring on the surface change in frequency along the length of the surface. This type of surface defect could be due to slippage occurring in the feed works of the machining operation or a slowing of the cutterhead rpm due to motor overload. This type of defect may be both non-stationary (among different workpieces) as well as non-stationary within a workpiece. Figure 19 shows a photograph of this type of surface characteristic. The surface profile (Figure 20, left) shows the varying wavelengths as well as the varying amplitudes on the surface of the workpiece. The frequency spectrum (Figure 20, right) shows the difference in the amplitude of the two frequencies as well as the difference in the spatial frequencies. The harmonic wavelet plot (Figure 21) shows the predominant frequency extending across the majority of the surface scan but changing in amplitude but also with varying frequencies present like a chirp. This plot also shows how the frequency changes along the length of the surface.

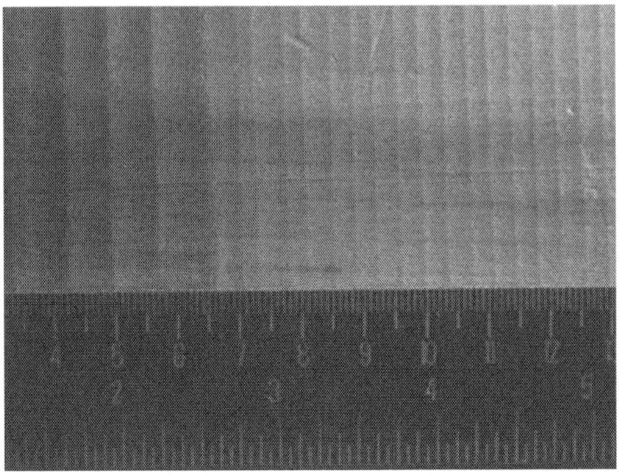

Fig. 19. Photograph of surface with varying frequency of knife marks

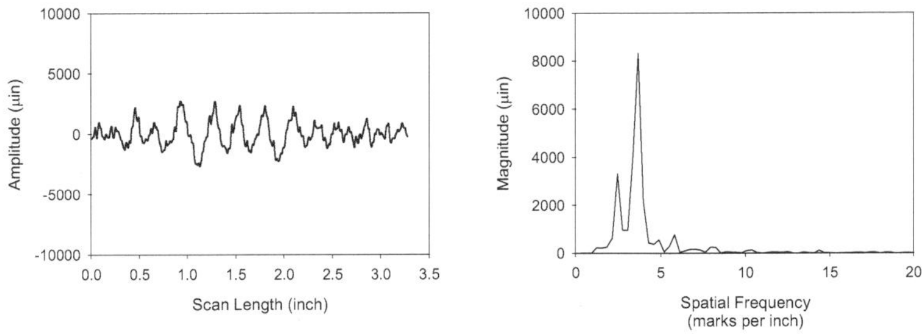

Fig. 20. Profile (left) and HWT (right) of surface with varying frequency of knife marks

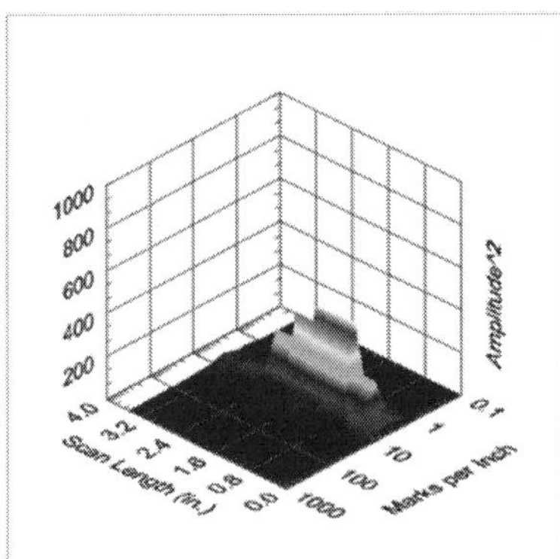

Fig. 21. Harmonic wavelet transform of surface with varying frequency of knife marks

5. Decision making scheme

The final step in developing an on-line surface quality monitoring system was the decision making scheme to determine if an unacceptable condition is present. As mentioned before, one of the objectives was to be able to determine from the data if a surface defect is periodic versus non-periodic and stationary versus non-stationary in nature. This aids the operator in determining the cause of the surface defect and what remedial action to take.

As discussed previously, the time-frequency plots provide information on the magnitude of the surface defect as well as determining if the defect is stationary or non-stationary. There are two approaches to interpreting the time-frequency plots. The first approach is to treat the time-frequency plot as an image and use standard image analysis techniques to determine the magnitude and shape of any "peaks" or "ridges" in the plot. A small diameter "blob" of the color representing a high mean-square value would represent a severe localized defect; whereas a long smear or ridge of the same color would represent a severe periodic condition. Since only the lower periodic frequencies (i.e. less than 50 knife marks per inch) are of interest for machined wood surfaces, the higher frequencies can be combined together for analysis of both non-periodic and localized defects. The second approach is to simply look at the data array representing the time-frequency plot of the harmonic wavelet analysis. For the examples shown, a surface profile generated by 16384 data points resulted in a time-frequency plot array of 15 x 4096 with the 15 columns representing the 15 frequency bandwidths (bins) of the HWT. This second approach was the one used in this research.

The first step in classifying a defect is to determine whether the surface defect is periodic, non-periodic, localized, or a combination of two or more of these categories. One approach is to view the periodic, non-periodic, and localized defects on an x, y, z plot. Since three parameters are required to describe a point in three space, the values of the three surface defect categories would indicate where in space the current specimen falls. A perfectly smooth surface would be at the origin of the plot. As a surface develops greater surface defects (regardless of the type or category of defect), the value on the plot moves further away from the origin. If the value for a periodic defect is higher than the value for the non-periodic defect then the surface in question is more periodic than non-periodic.

There are several methods of determining where along the three-space defect category axes a surface defect falls. One way is to conduct traditional time and frequency analysis and determine the best surface descriptor for the type of defect of interest in each category. The three surface descriptors would then be plotted in three-space with the magnitude of the defect (surface descriptor) being normalized before being plotted.

From the time-frequency plots it can be seen the HWT can differentiate between extreme conditions and can provide the user with comprehensive information about the type of surface that has been scanned. The difference between the periodic and non-periodic situations can be determined by setting a threshold and then counting the number of data excursions above the threshold to indicate that the signal has a periodic component. A single threshold crossing could indicate a scratch or other localized defect. Since only periodic components below 50 marks per inch are typically of interest, only lower frequency bins would need to be monitored for periodic components. The frequency bins representing periodicities (knife marks) greater than 50 marks per inch can be grouped together and used to monitor overall roughness.

By monitoring the amplitudes of the bins of interest (less than 50 marks per inch) and setting an amplitude threshold then a frequency bin that would have, for example, 25 percent of the amplitude values over the amplitude threshold would be considered slightly periodic AND slightly stationary. If 50 percent of the data points in a frequency bin exceeded the threshold value then the signal would be considered slightly periodic and moderately stationary. If the amplitudes exceeded a secondary threshold value then the surface would be considered moderately periodic. An example of the action of the controller is if 5% of data points, at a given frequency, exceed the threshold then the defect was considered a **peak** (representing a localized defect). If 25% of the points at a given frequency exceed the threshold value then the defect is considered a **slight ridge**. If 50% of the points exceed the threshold then the defect is considered a **medium ridge**. This continues for a **long ridge** and a **complete ridge**.

A problem can arise when the surface descriptors get close to the threshold but do not exceed it. An example would be when only slightly less than 25 percent of the amplitude values exceeded the threshold value, which, based on traditional techniques, would be considered non-stationary. The interpretation of the 3-dimensional plots of the results from the time-frequency analysis, while being somewhat easy by a human, is difficult when attempting to have a computer automatically make decisions on the state of the manufacturing process. The approach that was evaluated here was to use fuzzy logic to decide where in three-space the specimen or workpiece of interest belonged. A detailed discussion of using fuzzy logic for surface quality evaluation can be found in Lemaster (2004). Two applications of fuzzy logic were evaluated. The first was to use the standard surface descriptors to determine if a primary surface defect present on a specimen was periodic or not and then the second was to use the results of the HWT to determine if the periodic surface defect was stationary or non-stationary.

6. Conclusion

The overall goal of the research was to be able to detect an unacceptable surface produced during a machining operation and then attempt to provide additional information to the machine operator regarding the type of defect, the degree of the defect, and the possible source of the defect. In manufacturing, a defect that extends above the surface such as a ridge along the surface is usually much easier to deal with (repair) than a defect that extends below the surface such as a gouge or fiber tear-out. It is also desirable to determine if a surface defect is periodic, random-like, or localized in nature. In addition, it is also desirable to determine if the defect is stationary or non-stationary **as referenced to the surface of one specimen** (it has been shown that a wood machining operation in which tool wear occurs is technically a non-stationary process when considering multiple specimens).

As discussed previously an example of a periodic surface are the knife marks from a planer or moulder. An example of a random-like surface would be fuzzy grain. An example of a localized surface defect would be a dent or a ridge caused by a chip in the cutting tool. The difference between a stationary or a non-stationary defect is that a stationary defect would extend along the entire length of the workpiece whereas a non-stationary defect would occur only along a portion of the workpiece.

This research compared various JTFA techniques including the STFT as well as numerous discrete wavelet transforms (DWT) on their ability to detect where in time a periodicity exists on the surface of a wood or wood-based composite product. This research concluded that the Harmonic DWT or HWT worked best from an efficiency in computational time as well as its ability to detect both low frequency periodicity as well as localized defects. From the time-frequency plots it can be seen the HWT can differentiate between extreme conditions and can provide the user with comprehensive information about the type of surface that has been scanned. The difference between the periodic and non-periodic situations can be determined by setting a threshold and counting the number of data excursions above the threshold to indicate whether the signal has a periodic component or not. A single threshold crossing could indicate a scratch or other localized defect. Since only periodic components below 50 marks per inch are typically of interest, only lower frequency bins need to be monitored for periodic components. The frequency bins representing periodicities (knife marks) greater than 50 marks per inch can be grouped together and used to monitor overall roughness. A two tier fuzzy logic scheme was devised to determine if the surface profile had a periodicity or was localized and / or if the surface defect was stationary or non-stationary in nature.

Current and future work includes collecting data on the ability of the system to perform in a variety of manufacturing environments and at a variety of manufacturing speeds.

7. Acknowledgements

The author would like to thank Professor Thomas H. Hodgson for his invaluable help in learning and applying the JTFA techniques discussed in this chapter.

This work was funded by a United States Department of Agriculture: Wood Utilization Research Center Grant.

8. References

American Society of Mechanical Engineers, 2009. *Surface Texture (Surface Roughness, Waviness, and Lay)*. ASME B46.1-2009. ISBN: 9780791832622, ASME New York. United Engineering Center, 345 East 47th Street, New York, NY 10017.

Ber, A., and S. Braun, 1968. Spectral analysis of surface finish. CIRP Annals, Vol. 16, pp. 53-59, ISSN: 0007-8506.

Brock, M., 1983. Fourier analysis of surface roughness. Bruel & Kjaer Technical Review, ISSN: 0007-2621, Marlborough, Mass., No. 3, 48 pages.

Bruscella, B., V. Rouillard, and M. Sek, 1999. Analysis of road surface profiles. Journal of Transportation Engineering, Vol.125(1):55-59, ISSN: 0733-947X.

Burrus, C. S., 1998. *Introduction to Wavelets and Wavelet Transforms – A Primer*. Prentice Hall, ISBN: 0134896009, Upper Saddle River, NJ.

Daubechies, I., 1990. The wavelet transform, time-frequency localization, and signal analysis, IEEE Trans. Information Theory, pp. 961-1005, ISSN: 0018-9448.

DeVries, W.R. and R.L. Lemaster, 1991. Processing methods and potential applications of wood surface roughness analysis. Proceedings of the 10th International Wood Machining Seminar, October 21-23. pp. 276-292.

Effner, J., 2001. How depth of cut affects finish quality. FDM, January: 120-121.

Fricout, G., D. Jeulin, P.-J. Krauth, and T. Jacquot, 2002, Automatic on-line inspection of non-smooth surface, Wear Vol. 264:416-421, ISSN: 0043-1648.

Gaberson, H. A., 2002. The use of wavelets for analyzing transient machinery vibration. Sound and Vibration, Vol. 36(9):12-17 ISSN: 1541-0161.

Hoadley, R. B., 2000, *Understanding Wood: A Craftman's Guide to Wood Technology*, Taunton Press, ISBN: 1-56156-358-8 Newton, CT, 280 pages.

Hubbard, B. B., 1998. *The World According to Wavelets*, second edition, A. K. Peters, LTD., ISBN: 1-56881-072-5, Wellesley, Massachusetts. 330 pages.

ISO Standard 4287/1, "Surface Roughness - Terminology - Part 1: Surface and Its Parameters," 1984.

ISO Standard 4287/2, "Surface Roughness Terminology - Part 2: Measurement of Surface Roughness Parameters," 1984.

Jouaneh, M.K., R.L. Lemaster, and D.A. Dornfeld, 1987. Measuring workpiece dimensions using a non-contact laser detector system. International J. of Advanced Manufacturing Technology, Vol. 2(1):59-74, ISSN: 0268-3768.

Koch, P., 1955. An analysis of the lumber planing process: part I, Forest Products Journal 5:255-264, *ISSN*: 0015-7473.

Khawaja, Z., G. Guillemot, P.-E.Mazeran, M. El Mansori, and M. Bigerelle, 2011, Wavelet theory and belt finishing process, influence of wavelet shape on the surface roughness parameter values, 13th International Conference on Metrology and Properties of Engineering Surfaces, Journal of Physics: Conference Series 311: 012013, pages 1-5.

Lemaster, R.L. and D.A. Dornfeld, 1982. *Measurement of surface quality of sawn and planed surfaces with a laser.* Proceedings of the 7th Wood Machining Seminar, October 1982, University of California Forest Products Laboratory, Richmond, CA, pp. 52-70.

Lemaster, R.L. and W.R. DeVries, 1992. *Non-contact measurement and signal processing methods for surface roughness of wood products.* Proceedings of the 8th International Symposium on Nondestructive Testing of Wood, September 23-25, 1991. Vancouver, WA, pp. 203-218.

Lemaster, R.L., and F.C. Beall, 1996. The use of an optical profilometer to measure surface roughness in medium density fiberboard. Forest Products Journal, Vol. 46(11/12):73-78, *ISSN*: 0015-7473.

Lemaster, R.L., 1997. The use of an optical profilometer to monitor product quality in wood and wood-based products. Proceedings of the National Particleboard Association Sanding and Sawing Seminar, Charlotte, NC, November 1995, published by the Forest Products Society, ISBN: 0-935018-51-4, Madison, Wisconsin, USA, 17 pages.

Lemaster, R.L., 1997. *Hardwood machining R&D: surface quality and process monitoring technologies.* Proceedings of the Eastern Hardwood Resource, Technologies, and Markets Conference. April 21-23, Camp Hill, Pennsylvania. Published by the Forest Products Society, pp. 109-120.

Lemaster, R.L., 2004. *Development of an Optical Profilometer and the Related Advanced Signal Processing Methods for Monitoring Surface Quality of Wood Machining Applications.* Doctoral dissertation, North Carolina State University, ISBN 9780496147298, 254 pages.

Lemaster, R.L., 2010. *The use of frequency and wavelet analysis for monitoring surface quality of wood machining applications.* Scanning, The Journal of Scanning Microscopies: Special Issue on Diverse Applications of Surface Metrology I, July/August 2010, Volume 32, Issue 4, Pages 224 - 232, Issue edited by: Christopher A. Brown. ISSN: 1932-8745

Mallat, S., 2009. A Wavelet Tour of Signal Processing, third edition, Academic Press, ISBN: 13-078-0-12-374370-1, Burlington, Maryland, USA.

Mallat, S., 1989. *Multifrequency channel decompositions of images and wavelet models.* IEEE Trans. Acousitcs, Speech, Signal Processing, Vol.(37):2091-2110, ISSN: 0096-3518.

Newland, D. E., 1993. Harmonic wavelet analysis. Proceedings Royal Society London, A Vol.(43):203-225 ISSN: 0962-8444.

Newland, D. E., 1997. *An Introduction to Random Vibrations, Spectral and Wavelet Analysis,* Third Addition, Addison Wesley Longman Limited, ISBN: 0-582-21584-6 Edinburgh, Harlow. 477 pages.

Qian, S., 2002. Introduction to Time-Frequency and Wavelet Transforms, Prentice Hall PTR, ISBN: 0-13-030360-7, Upper Saddle River, N.J., 280 pages.

Qian, S. and D. Chen, 1996. *Joint Time-Frequency Analysis.* Prentice Hall, ISBN-13: 978-0132543842, Upper Saddle River. New Jersey.

Raja, J. and V. Radhakrishnan, 1979. Filtering of surface profiles using fast Fourier transform. Int. J. Mach. Tool Des. Res. 19:133-141.

Riegel, A., 1993. Quality measurements in surface technologies. International Conference on Woodworking Technologies, Conference at the Ligna 1993, Hannover, Germany. April 20-23. pp. 23.1-23.10.

Staufert, G. 1979. Description of roughness profile by separating the random and periodic components. Wear 57:185-194, ISSN: 0043-1648.

Strang, G. and T. Q. Nguyen, 1996. *Wavelet and Filter Banks,* Prentice Hall, ISBN-13: 978-0961408879, Upper Saddle River, NJ, 484 pages.

Stumbo, D., 1963. Surface texture measurement methods. Forest Prod. J. 13(7):299-304, *ISSN*: 0015-7473.

Thomas, T. R., 1981. Characterization of Surface Roughness. Precision Engineering Vol. 2:97-104, ISSN: 0141-6359.

Thomas, T.R. and M. King, 1977. *Surface topography in engineering - a state of the art review and bibliography.* Cotswold Press LTD, ISBN-13: 978-0900983665.

Thomas, T. R., 1999, *Surface Roughness,* 2nd Edition, Imperial College Press, London, England, ISBN: 1-86094-100-1, 278 pages.

Whitehouse, D. J., 1994. *Handbook of Surface Metrology,* Institute of Physics Publishing, London, England, ISBN: 0-7503-0039-6, , 988 pages.

Whitehouse, D. J., 2011. *Handbook of Surface and Nanometrology*, 2nd Edition, CRC Press, Taylor and Francis Group, Boca Raton, FL, U.S.A, ISBN: 1978-1-4200-8201-2, 976 pages.

7

Multi-Scale Deconvolution of Mass Spectrometry Signals

M'hamed Boulakroune[1] and Djamel Benatia[2]

[1]*Electrical Engineer Department,*
Faculty of Sciences and Technology, Kasdi Merbah Ouargla University, Ouargla
[2]*Electronics Department,*
Faculty of Engineer Sciences, Université Hadj-Lakhdar de Batna, Batna
Algeria

1. Introduction

It has become more important to measure accurate depth profiles in developing more advanced devices. To this aim, Depth profiling in secondary ion mass spectrometry (SIMS) has been extensively used as an informative technique in the semiconductor and electronic devices fields due to its high sensitivity, quantification accuracy and depth resolution (Fujiyama et al, 2011; Seki et al, 2011). However, the depth resolution in SIMS analysis is still limited to provide reliable and precise information in very thin structures such as delta layers, abrupt interfaces, etc. By optimization of the experimental conditions, the depth resolution can be enhanced. In particular, lowering the primary energy seems to be a good solution, but this increases the measurement time and leads to other limitations, owing to the wrong focalization of primary ion beam, such as roughness in the crater bottom, not flat crater, etc. Therefore, the depth resolution remains so far to its perfect limit. It is only by numerical processing like deconvolution that the depth resolution can be improved beyond its experimental limits.

For the past several years, different approaches of deconvolution have been proposed taking into account the different physical phenomena that limit depth resolution, such as collisional mixing, roughness, and segregation (Makarov, 1999; Gautier et al, 1998; Fares et al, 2006; Dowsett et al, 1994; Mancina et al, 2000; Shao et al, 2004; Collins et al, 1992; Allen et al, 1993; Fearn et al, 2005). However, most problems encountered in these deconvolution methods are due to the noise content in the measured profiles. This instrumental phenomenon, which cannot be eliminated by the improvement of operating conditions, strongly influences the depth resolution and therefore the quality of the deconvoluted profiles.

The deconvolution of depth profiling data in SIMS analysis amounts to the solution of an appropriate ill-posed problem in that any random noise in data leads to no unique and no stable solution (oscillatory signal with negative components, which are physically not acceptable in SIMS analysis). Thus, the results must be regularized (Tikhonov, 1963; Barakat et al, 1997; Prost et al, 1984; Burdeau et al, 2000; Herzel et al, 1995; Iqbal, 2003; Varah, 1983;

Essah, 1988; Brianzi, 1994; Stone, 1974; Connolly et al, 1998; Berger et al, 1999; Thompson et al, 1991; Fischer et al, 1998). To this end, the solution is superimposed with certain limitations by introducing some additional limitative operators, whose shape is chosen depending on the formalism used for the solution of the ill-posed problem, into a goal function; usually the goal function is the mismatch between the convoluted solution and the initial data (Makarov, 1999). Indeed, different forms of limitative operator have been used. For example, Collins and Dowssett (Collins et al, 1992) and Allen and Dowssett (Allen et al, 1993) have used the entropy function as a limitative operator. Based on the Tikhonov-Miller regularization, Gautier et al (Gautier et al, 1998) have used a limitative operator that was defined as smoothness of the solution. Mancina et al (Mancina et al, 2000) have introduced *a priori* a pre-deconvoluted signal as a model of solution in an iterative regularized method. Nevertheless, the results of most of these approaches contain artifacts with negative concentrations, which are not physically acceptable. The origin of these artifacts is related to the presence of strong local components of high frequencies in the signal which form part of the noise. To remove the negative components from the deconvoluted profile, some algorithms with non-negativity constraints have been proposed (Makarov, 1999; Gautier et al, 1998; Gautier et al; 1998; Prost et al, 1984). These methods, which constrain the data to be positive everywhere, are sensitive to noise, i.e., a little perturbation in the data can lead to a great difference in the deconvoluted solution. A truncation of the negative data is an arbitrary operation and it is not acceptable, since it results in an artificially steep slope and can lead to the adoption of subjective criteria for profile assessment (Herzel et al, 1995). Moreover, noise in the data increases the distance between the real signal and its estimate, therefore a priori constraint is not enough, and a free-oscillation deconvolution is necessary.

To overcome these limits, it is important to adopt a powerful deconvolution that leads to a smoothed and stable solution without application of any kind of constraints. In this context, multiscale deconvolution (MD), which is never used to recover SIMS profiles, may be the most appropriate technique.

The MD provides a local smoothness property with a high smoothness level in unstructured regions of the spectrum where only background occurs and a low smoothness level where structures arise (Fischer et al, 1998). Based on wavelet transform, the MD seems to be a good solution that can yield information about the location of certain frequencies in the profile on different frequency scales. Therefore, high frequencies, which are related to noise, can be localized and controlled at different levels of wavelet decomposition. The multiscale description of signals has facilitated the development of wavelet theory and its application to numerous fields (Averbuch & Zheludev, 2009; Charles et al, 2004; Fan & Koo, 2002; Neelamani et al, 2004; Zheludev, 1999; Rashed et al, 2007; Garcia-Talavera et al, 2003; Starck et al, 2003; Jammal et al, 2004; Rucka et al, 2006). This chapter is intended to explore capabilities of wavelets for the deconvolution framework. The proposed idea is to introduce a wavelet-based methodology in the Tikhonov-Miller regularization scheme and shrinking the wavelet coefficients of the blurred and the estimated solution at each resolution level allow a local adaptation of limitative operator in the quadratic Tikhonov-Miller regularization. This leads to compensation for high frequencies which are related to noise. As a result, the oscillations which appear in classical regularization methods can be removed. This leads to a smoothed and stable solution.

This work is based on SIMS data, for which reason the results presented here are largely restricted to the conditions of SIMS analysis. The main objective of this work is to show that the MD gives much better deconvolution results than those obtained using monoresolution regularization methods. In particular, the results obtained are compared to those achieved using a regularized monoresolution deconvolution, which is Tikhonov-Miller regularization with a pre-deconvoluted signal as a model of the solution, denoted as TMMS (Mancina et al, 2000).

2. Deconvolution procedure

2.1 Background

Depth profiling in SIMS analysis is mathematically described by the convolution integral which is governed by the depth resolution function (DRF), h(z). If the integral over h(z) is normalized to unity, then the measured (convolved) signal is given by the well-known convolution integral

$$y(z)=\int_{-\infty}^{+\infty} h(z-z')\, x(z')\, dz' + b(z), \tag{1}$$

where x(z) is the compositional depth distribution function and b(z) is the additive noise.

This work deals with the deconvolution of depth profiling SIMS data. Therefore, it is important for further consideration to know the shape of the DRF that is typical of SIMS profiles. We have chosen to describe the DRF analytically in a form initially proposed by Dowsett et al (Dowsett et al, 1994), which is constituted by the convolution of double exponential functions with a Gaussian function. This DRF can be described by three parameters: λ_u (the rising exponential decay), σ_g (the standard deviation of the Gaussian function), and λ_d (the falling exponential decay). The latter characterizes the residual mixing effect, which is considered to be the main mechanism responsible for the degradation of the depth resolution (Boulakroune et al, 2007; Yang et al, 2006). For any possible values of these parameters, the DRF is normalized to unity. The consequences of the fact that the resolution function can be represented in the form of a convolution have been described elsewhere (Gautier et al, 1998; Dowsett et al, 1994; Collins et al, 1992; Allen et al, 1993).

For a discrete system, eq. (1) can be written as

$$y_k = \sum_{i=0}^{N-1} x_i h_{k-i} + b_k, \quad k = 0, \ldots, 2N-2, \tag{2}$$

where N is the number of samples of vectors h, x. Equation (2) can be rewritten as

$$y = Hx + b, \tag{3}$$

where H is a matrix built from h(z). In the case of a linear and shift-invariant system, H is a convolution operator (circular Toeplitz matrix). This means that the multiplication of H with the vector x leads numerically to the same operation as the analytical convolution of h(z) with x(z).

The problem of the recovery of the actual function x from eq. (3) is an ill-posed problem in the sense of Hadamard. (Varah, 1983) Therefore, it is affected by numerical instability, since y contains experimental noise. The term incorrectly posed or ill-posed problem means that the solution x of eq. (3) may not be unique, may not exist, or may not depend continuously on the data. In other words, H is an ill-conditioned matrix, or/and small variations in the data due to noise result in an unbounded perturbation in the solution.

It is well-known that the function H(υ) (the spectrum of the DRF) is a low-pass filter. (Allen, 1993; Barakat, 1997; Berger, 1999; Gautier, 1998) Its components are thus equal or very close to zero for frequencies above a certain cut-off frequency υ_c. Components close to υ_c are very attenuated by the convolution. Furthermore, in the presence of an ill-posed problem, some components below υ_c can be very small, almost null (see Fig. 1). In this case, the inversion of the convolution equation fails for these components, or leads to a very unstable solution.

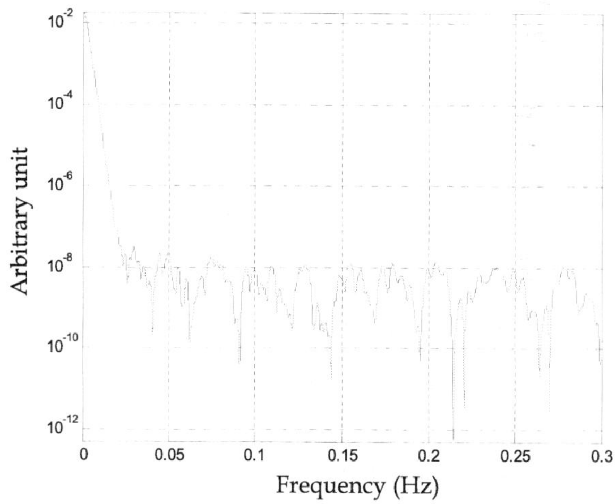

Fig. 1. DFT of the depth resolution function; DRF measured at 8.5 keV/O_2^+.

To solve an ill-posed problem, it is mandatory to find a solution so that the small components of H(υ) do not hinder the deconvolution process, i.e., to stabilize the solution. Moreover, the resolution of an ill-posed problem in the presence of noise leads to an infinite number of solutions, among which it is necessary to choose the unique solution that fits the problem we are trying to solve.

Therefore, in order to solve this problem, a regularization method must be included. This means that the original problem is replaced by an approximate one whose solutions are significantly less sensitive to errors in the data, y. Several regularization methods have been discussed in refs. (Iqbal, 2003; Varah, 1983; Essah, 1988; Brianzi, 1994; Stone, 1974; Connolly et al, 1998; Berger et al, 1999; Thompson et al, 1991). All of these methods are based on the incorporation of a priori knowledge into the restoration process to achieve stability of the solution.

The basic underlying idea in the regularization approaches is formulated as an optimization problem whose general expression is

$$L\{\ \tilde{x}(\alpha,y)\ \} = \{\ L_1(x,\ \tilde{x}_0) + \alpha\, L_2(x,\ \tilde{x}_\infty)\ \}_{x \in X}, \tag{4}$$

where L_1 is a quadratic distance, which provides a maximum fidelity to the data; $\tilde{x}_0$ is the least squares solution, consistent with the data; L_2 is a stabilizing function, which measures the distance between x and an extreme solution $\tilde{x}_\infty$ corresponding to an a priori ultra-smooth solution. The restoration methods, cited in references (Iqbal, 2003; Varah, 1983; Essah, 1988; Brianzi, 1994; Stone, 1974; Connolly et al, 1998; Berger et al, 1999; Thompson et al, 1991), differ from each other in the choice of the distance L_2. The choice leads either to a deterministic or a stochastic regularization. α is the regularization parameter which controls the trade-off between stability (fidelity to the a priori) and accuracy of the solution (fidelity to the data). X represents the set of possible solutions.

2.2 Tikhonov-Miller regularization

As shown in the previous section, the regularization is achieved through a compromise between choosing one solution in the set of solutions that lead to a reconstructed signal close to the measured data (fidelity to the data), and in the set of stable solutions that conform to some prior knowledge of the original signal (fidelity to the a priori). This means that the solution is considered to be close to the data if the reconstruction signal Hx is close to the measured one y, i.e., if $\|y - Hx\|^2$ is reasonably small. Thus, the first task of the deconvolution procedure is to minimize the quadratic distance between y and Hx. Unfortunately, solutions that lead to very small values of $\|y - Hx\|^2$ oscillate and are therefore unacceptable. In order to get a stable solution, one must choose another criterion that checks whether the solution is consistent with the solution of the deconvolution problem: it must be physically acceptable, i.e., a smoothed solution. The smoothness of the solution can be described by its regularity r^2, defined as

$$\|Dx\|^2 \le r^2, \tag{5}$$

where D is a stabilizing operator. The choice of D is based on the processing context and some a priori knowledge about the original signal. D is usually designed to smooth the estimated signal, and then a gradient or a discrete Laplacian is conventionally chosen. In this work, the filter used is a discrete Laplacian: [1 -2 1], its spectrum is a high-pass filter (Gautier et al, 1998; Mancina et al, 2000; Burdeau et al, 2000). This results in the minimization of the quadratic functional proposed by Tikhonov

$$\tilde{x} = \operatorname{argmin}\ [\|y - H\tilde{x}\|^2 + \alpha(\|D\tilde{x}\|^2 - r^2)], \tag{6}$$

where "argmin" denotes the argument that minimizes the expression between the brackets. Perfect fidelity to the data is achieved for α = 0, whereas perfect matching with a priori knowledge is achieved for α = ∞. Therefore, it is necessary to find the optimum α and, hence, a smoothing factor at which the solution of eq. (6) is well-stabilized and still close to a real distribution. This regularization parameter α can be estimated by a variety of techniques (Iqbal, 2003; Varah, 1983; Essah, 1988; Brianzi, 1994; Stone, 1974; Connolly et al, 1998; Berger et al, 1999; Thompson et al, 1991). In a simulation where the regularity of the solution is known, $\alpha = b^2/r^2$, where b^2 is an upper bound for the total power of the noise. Unfortunately, in the real case, there is no knowledge of the regularity of the real profile, but it can be estimated by means of the generalized cross-validation (Thompson et al, 1991) which applies well to Gaussian white noise. The regularized solution takes the following form:

$$\tilde{x} = (H^T H + \alpha D^T D)^{-1} H^T y = (H^+)^{-1} H^T y\,, \tag{7}$$

where $H^+ = H^T H + \alpha D^T D$.

The matrix H characterizing the deconvolution process before regularization is replaced by the generalized matrix $H^+ = (H^T H + \alpha D^T D)$, which is more conditioned. That step is carried out by the modification of the eigenvalues of H; thus the system becomes more stable. Figure 2 shows the spectra of the DRF (H), the filter D and the generalized matrix H^+.

The choice of the regularization operator D should not constitute a difficulty since the rule on the modification of the eigenvalues is respected. The most appropriate choice to be determined for the reconstruction quality is that of the regularization parameter α. Indeed, a poor estimation of this parameter leads to worse conditioning of the matrix H, and as a consequence, the solution is degenerated.

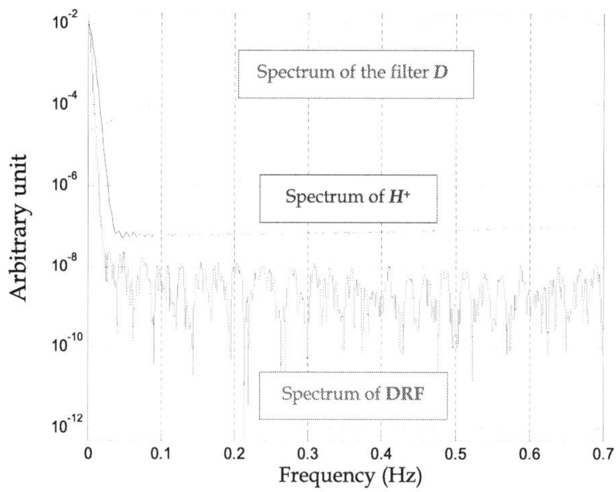

Fig. 2. Spectra of DRF (***H***), filter ***D***, and the generalized matrix $\boldsymbol{H}^+$. Here the regularization parameter α is overestimated, which leads to a well-conditioned $\boldsymbol{H}^+$.

Actually, the regularization can guarantee unicity and stability of the solution but cannot lead to a very satisfactory result. The quantity of information brought is not sufficient to obtain a solution close to the ideal solution because this regularization provides global properties of the signal. Barakat et al (Barakat et al, 1997) have proposed a method based on Tikhonov regularization combined with an a priori model of the solution. The idea of such a model is to introduce local characteristics of the signal. This model may contain discontinuities whose locations and amplitudes are imposed. The new functional to be minimized with respect to x is defined as follows:

$$L = \|y - H\tilde{x}\|^2 + \alpha\|D(\tilde{x} - x_{\mathrm{mod}})\|^2, \tag{8}$$

where x_{mod} is an a priori model of the solution. The solution of eq. (8) is given by:

$$\tilde{x} = (H^T H + \alpha D^T D)^{-1}(H^T y + \alpha D^T D x_{\mathrm{mod}}). \tag{9}$$

The strategy developed in Barakat's algorithm is useful if the a priori information is quite precise and the quality of solution depends on the accuracy of a priori information.

Mancina et al (Mancina et al, 2000) proposed to reiterate the algorithm of Barakat (Barakat et al, 1997) and to use a pre-deconvoluted signal as model of the solution (an intermediate solution between the ideal solution, i.e., the input signal, and the measured one) with sufficient regularization. The mathematical formulation of the Mancina approach in Fourier space is as follows:

$$\begin{cases} \hat{X}_{n+1} = \dfrac{H^* Y + \alpha|D|^2 X_{\mathrm{mod}_n}}{|H|^2 + \alpha|D|^2} \\ X_{\mathrm{mod}_n} = TF[C\hat{x}_n] \\ \hat{x}_n = TF^{-1}[\hat{X}_n] \\ X_{\mathrm{mod}_0} = 0 \end{cases}, \tag{10}$$

where H^* is the conjugate of H, and C represents the constraint operator which must be applied in the time domain after an inverse Fourier transformation.

Actually, in most of the classical monoresolution deconvolution methods, the results obtained are oscillatory Makarov, 1999; Gautier et al, 1998; Fares et al, 2006; Dowsett et al, 1994; Mancina et al, 2000; Yang et al, 2006; Shao et al, 2004. The generated artifacts are mainly due to the strong presence of high-frequency components which are not compensated by the regularization parameter α associated with the regularization operator D, since, in these methods, this parameter is applied in a global manner to all the frequency bands of the signal. This leads to the treatment of the low frequencies, which contain the useful signal, as opposed to the high frequencies, which are mainly noise. Thus, at α = 0, eq. (7) corresponds to the minimum of argmin [eq. (6)] without smoothing of x. The corresponding solution is applicable only in the perfect case, i.e., if there are no errors or noise in the experimental distribution y. Real y always contains errors, and minimization of eq. (6) using α = 0 produces strong fluctuations of the solution (a parameter α that is too weak leads to a solution dominated by the noise within the observed data). With an increase of α, the role of the second term in eq. (6) increases, and the solution stabilizes and becomes increasingly smooth. However, if α is too large, surplus smoothing may noticeably broaden the solution and conceal its important features (a parameter α that is too high leads to a solution that is not very sensitive to noise, but it is very far from the measured data). It is therefore necessary to find the optimum α and, hence, a smoothing factor at which the solution to problem (6) is well-stabilized but still close to the real distribution. Moreover, in the iterative algorithms, if the regularization parameter is not well calculated, the oscillations created at iteration n are amplified at iteration n + 1, which degenerates the final solution. The value of α, the regularization parameter associated with D, is very important in the regularization process, and its value determines the quality of the final solution. This can easily be understood if one analyzes the generalized matrix H^+. As α increases, the matrix $(H^+)^{-1}$ tends toward a diagonal matrix, while the vector H^Ty, which is broadened in comparison to the initial data vector y due to the multiplication by the transposed distortion matrix, remains unchanged. As a result, with an increase of α, the shape of the solution tends to H^Ty, i.e., to the considerably broadened initial data. Figure 3 shows an example of the evolution of the spectrum of the matrix H^+ for various values of the regularization parameter α.

According to Fig. 3, the determination of the classical regularization parameter α_c for the SIMS profile led to a value of 5.9290×10^{-4}. For this value, the spectrum of the generalized matrix H^+ is oscillatory (the matrix is not well-conditioned), leading to an unstable solution. In order to stabilize the system more, Mancina et al (Mancina et al, 2000) proposed multiplying the regularization parameter by a positive factor. The multiplication of this parameter by a factor K (K = 10, 10^2, 10^3) leads to increasingly regularized matrix H^+ (Fig. 2). Nevertheless, this multiplication is arbitrary and it is not based on any physical support

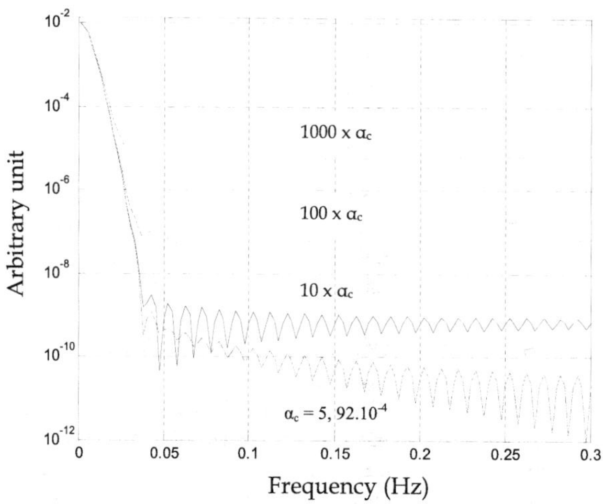

Fig. 3. Evolution of the spectrum of the matrix H^+ according to $k\alpha_c$ (K =1, 10, 10^2, 10^3).

Since the real distribution that is to be deconvoluted is unknown other than in some special cases, the choice of the optimum α requires the use of indirect and sometimes non strict and ambiguous criteria. This causes a clear indeterminacy in the choice of α. One should note that this indeterminacy in ill-posed problems is inherent to any data deconvolution method.

Conventionally, the Tikhonov-Miller approach of searching for the optimum α uses additional information on the level of noise in the initial data. This is often inconvenient, for example, if the data vary over a wide range, and the statistical noise level changes considerably from point to point depending on signal level.

Generally, the choice of optimum smoothing for deconvolution of an arbitrary set of data requires a special study, and this work only outlines the principle for solving this problem. The example in Fig. 3 shows that the regularization parameter must be accurately determined and locally adapted in the differently treated frequency bands in order to ensure a non aberrant result. This allows the deconvolution of signals previously decomposed by projection onto a wavelet basis.

3. Discrete wavelet transform

3.1 Background

Wavelet theory is widely used in many engineering disciplines (Rashed et al, 2007; Garcia-Talavera et al, 2003; Starck et al, 2003; Jammal et al, 2004; Rucka et al, 2006), and it provides a rich source of useful tools for applications in time-scale types of problems. The attention to study of wavelets becomes more attractive when Mallat (Mallat, 1989) established a connection between wavelets and signal processing. Discrete wavelet transform (DWT) is an extremely fast algorithm that transforms data into wavelet coefficients at discrete intervals of time and scale, instead of at all scales. It is based on dyadic scaling and translating, and it is possible if the scale parameter varies only along the dyadic sequence (dyadic scales and positions). It is basically a filtering procedure that separates high and low frequency components of signals with high-pass and low-pass filters by a multiresolution decomposition algorithm (Mallat, 1989). Hence, the DWT is represented by the following equation:

$$W(j,k)=\sum_{j}\sum_{k} y(k)2^{-j/2}\psi(2^{-j}n-k), \tag{11}$$

where y is discretized heights of the original profile measurements, ψ is the discrete wavelet coefficients, and n is the sample number. The translation parameter k determines the location of the wavelet in the time domain, while the dilatation parameter j determines the location in the frequency domain as well as the scale or the extent of the space-frequency localization.

The DWT analysis can be performed using a fast, pyramidal algorithm by iteratively applying low-pass and high-pass filters, and subsequent down-sampling by 2 (Mallat, 1989). Each level of the decomposition algorithm then yields to low-frequency components of the signal (approximations) and high-frequency components (details). This is computed with the following equations:

$$y_{low}[k] = \sum_{n} y[n] f[2k-n], \tag{12}$$

$$y_{high}[k] = \sum_{n} y[n] g[2k-n], \tag{13}$$

where $y_{low}[k]$ and $y_{high}[k]$ are the outputs of the low-pass (f) and high-pass (g) filters, respectively, after down sampling by 2. Due to down-sampling during decomposition, the number of resulting wavelet coefficients at each level is exactly the same as the number of input points for this level. It is sufficient to keep all detail coefficients and the final approximation coefficients (at the roughest level) in order to reconstruct the original data.

The approximation and details at the resolution $2^{-(j+1)}$ are obtained from the approximation signal at resolution 2^{-j}. In the matrix formalism, eqs. (12) and (13) can be written as

$$y_a^{(j+1)} = F\, y_a^{(j)}, \quad y_d^{(j+1)} = G\, y_a^{(j)}, \tag{14}$$

where F and G are Toeplitz matrices constructed from the filters f and g, respectively.

The reconstruction algorithm involves up-sampling, i.e., inserting zeros between data points, and filtering with dual filters. By carefully choosing filters for the decomposition and reconstruction that are closely related, we can achieve perfect reconstruction of the original signal in the inverse orthogonal wavelet transform (Daubechies, 1990). The reconstructed signal is obtained from eq. (14) by

$$\tilde{y} = \tilde{F} y_a^{(J)} + \tilde{G} y_d^{(j)}, \ j = 1, \ldots, J, \tag{15}$$

where $\tilde{F}$ and $\tilde{G}$ are Toeplitz matrices constructed from the reconstruction filters $\tilde{f}$ and $\tilde{g}$, respectively. For a general introduction to discrete wavelet transform and filter banks, the reader is referred to refs. (Mallat, 1989; Daubechies, 1990).

The Mallat algorithm (Mallat, 1989) is a fast linear operation that operates on a data vector whose length is an integer power of two, transforming it into numerically different vectors of the same length. Many wavelet families are available. However, only orthogonal wavelets (such as Haar, Daubichies, Coiflet, and Symmlet wavelets) allow for perfect reconstruction of a signal by inverse discrete wavelet transform, i.e., the inverse transform is simply the transpose of the transform. Indeed, the selection of the most appropriate wavelet is based on the similarity between the derivatives of the signal and the number of wavelet vanishing moments. In practice, wavelets with a higher number of vanishing moments give higher coefficients and more stable performance. In this study, we restrict ourselves to Symlet and Coiflet families; after some experimentation, we chose "Sym4" wavelet with four vanishing moments and "Coif3" wavelet with three vanishing moments. Figure 4 shows the wavelet function, scaling function and the four filters of the wavelets "Sym4" and "Coif3". The decomposition on a wavelet basis (to the level 5) of a SIMS profile containing four delta-layers of boron in silicon to approximation and detail signals is illustrated in Fig. 5.

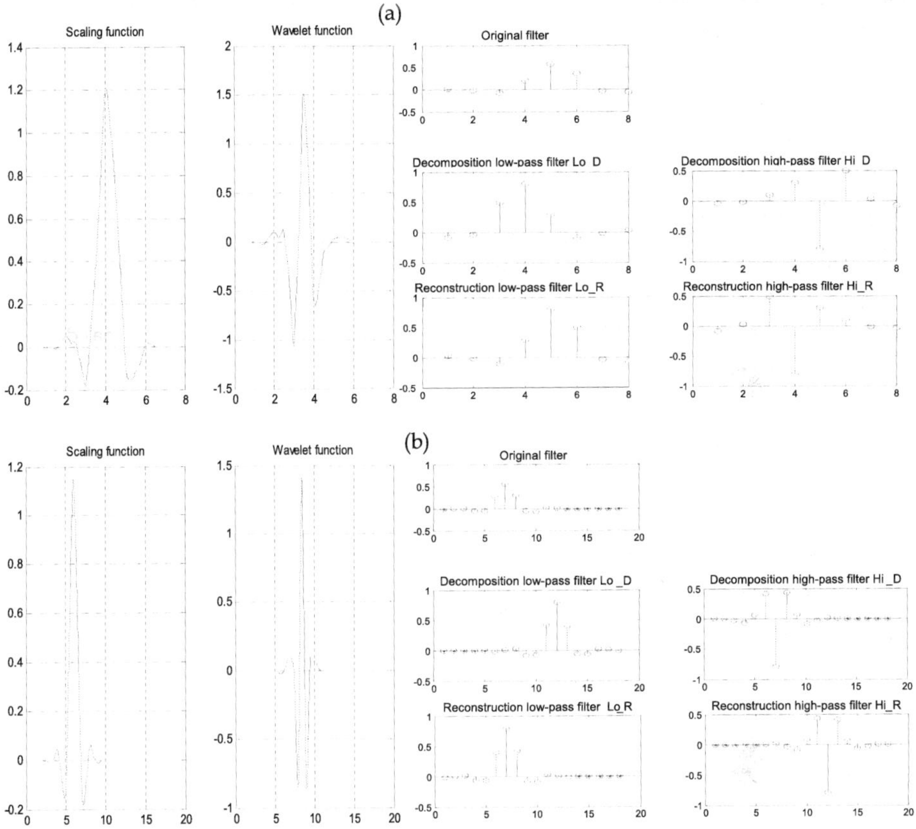

Fig. 4. (a) *Sym4*: scaling function, wavelet function, and the associated filters. (b) *Coif3*: scaling function, wavelet function, and the associated filters.

Due to the compression and dilatation properties of the wavelets in representing a signal, wavelet-based filters can easily follow the sharp edges of the input signal. In other words, they restore any discontinuity in the input signal, or, in terms of the frequency domain interpretation, they pass high frequency components of the input signal. This is a very appealing feature of the wavelet-based methods in many applications, such as finding the location of discontinuities and abrupt changes in a signal. However, this feature may have adverse effects, especially when one wants to get rid of impulsive noise (outliers and gross errors).

We notice that the lower level (high-frequency) wavelet components are similar to a random process, while the higher level (low-frequency) ones are not [Fig. 5(a)]. The noise in SIMS analysis is Gaussian, and one considers that, if there was no signal but the noise alone, the variance of the details would decrease by a factor of 2 at each resolution. Analysis at each level of detail (from small to large) separately on the same signal is shown in Fig. 5(b).

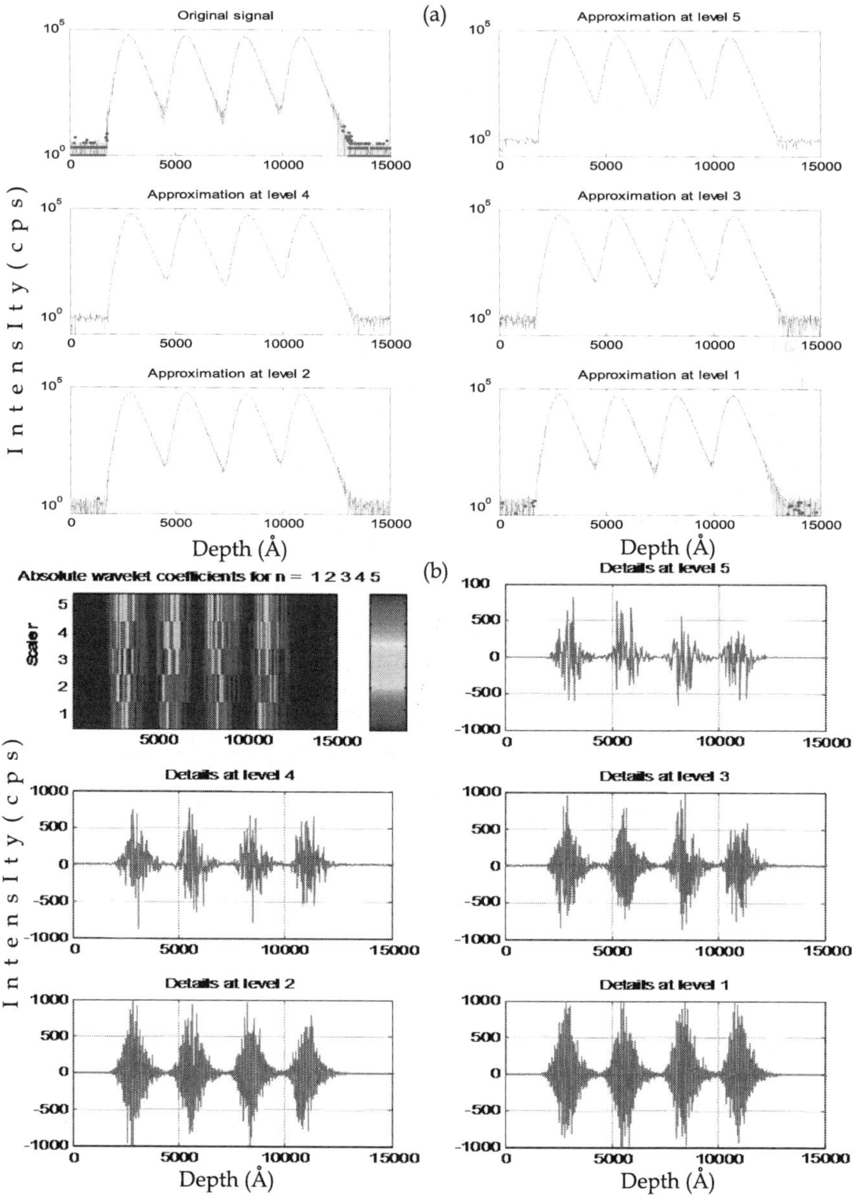

Fig. 5. Wavelet decomposition of SIMS profile measured at 8.5 keV/O_2^+, 38.1 rad.
The wavelet used is *Sym4*; the decomposition level is 5.
(a) The original measured profile with the different approximation signals from level 1 to 5.
(b) Detail signals from level 1 to 5 with absolute wavelet coefficients

Wavelets have multiscale and local properties that make them very effective in analyzing the class of locally varying signals. Together the locality and multiscale properties enable the wavelet transform to efficiently match signals organized into levels or scales of localized variations. Thus DWT transforms the noisy signal in the wavelet domain, and by denoising we obtain a sparse representation with a few large dominating coefficients (Donoho et al, 1994, 1995). A large part of the wavelet coefficients does not carry significant information [see absolute wavelet coefficients for n = 1 to 5 in Fig. 5(b)]. We select the significant ones by a thresholding procedure, which is addressed in the following section.

3.2 Denoising by wavelet coefficients thresholding

Noise is a phenomenon that affects all frequencies. Since the useful signal tends to dominate the low-frequency components, it is expected that the majority of high-frequency components above a certain level are due to noise. In the wavelet decomposition of signals, as has been described, the filter h is an averaging or smoothing filter, while its mirror g produces details. With the exclusion of the last remaining smoothed components, all wavelet coefficients in the final decomposition correspond to details. If the absolute value of a detail component is small (or set to zero), the general signal does not change much. Therefore, thresholding the wavelet coefficients is a good way of removing unimportant or undesired (insignificant) details from a signal. Thresholding techniques are successfully used in numerous data-processing domains, since in most cases a small number of wavelet coefficients with large amplitudes preserve most of the information about the original data set.

A basic wavelet-based denoising procedure is described in the following:

- Decomposition: Select the level N and type of wavelets and then determine the coefficients of SIMS signal by DWT. For wavelet denoising, we must decide from many possible selections, such as the type of mother wavelet, the decomposition levels, and the values of thresholds in the next step. In this study, decomposition at level 5 has been used.
- Thresholding: Estimating threshold values is based upon the analytical and empirical methods. For each level from 1 to 5, we use the estimated threshold values and set the detail coefficients below the threshold values to zero. Based on knowledge of the wavelet analysis in the data set, we use objective criteria to determine threshold values. Basically, the choice of mother wavelet appears not to matter much, while the values of thresholds do. Therefore, setting the values of the threshold is a crucial topic. According to the analysis described, we set threshold values based on the properties of SIMS data sets.
- Reconstruction: We reconstruct the denoised signal using the original approximation coefficients of level N and the modified detail coefficients of levels from 1 to N by the inverse DWT.

Wavelet denoising methods generally use two different approaches: hard thresholding and soft thresholding. The hard thresholding philosophy is simply to cut all the wavelet coefficients below a certain threshold to zero. However, soft thresholding reduces the value (referred to as "shrinkage") of wavelet coefficients towards zero if they are below a certain value. For a certain wavelet coefficient k on scale j, the thresholded details coefficients are given by

$$\hat{y}_d(k) = \text{sign}\left\|y(k)\right| - \lambda\right|, \tag{16}$$

where the function "sign" returns the sign of the wavelet coefficient, and λ is the threshold value. In the case of Gaussian white noise (which is the kind of noise in SIMS analysis), Donoho and Johnstone (Donoho et al, 1994, 1995) modeled this threshold by

$$\lambda = \sigma\sqrt{2\log(N)}, \tag{17}$$

where N is the number of the observed data points, and σ is the standard deviation of noise. This standard deviation, in the case of white and Gaussian noise, is estimated by

$$\hat{\sigma} = \text{median}\left(\left|cd^{(1)}(k)\right|\right/0.6754, \tag{18}$$

where median($cd^{(1)}(k)$) is the median value of detail coefficients at the first level of decomposition which can be attributed to noise. After thresholding, the reconstructed signal of eq. (15) becomes:

$$\tilde{y} = \tilde{F}y_a^{(J)} + \tilde{G}\hat{y}_d^{(j)}, \text{ j} = 1, \ldots, \text{J}. \tag{19}$$

By using this process, high-frequency components above a certain threshold can be removed. A raw SIMS profile and corresponding denoised profile are shown in Fig. 6(a). In particular, the figure shows that low-frequency components, which usually represent the main structure of the signal, are separated from high-frequency components. These preliminary results demonstrate the superior capabilities of the wavelet approach to SIMS profiles analysis over traditional techniques.

In the analysis of SIMS data, we find that most wavelet coefficients at high-frequency levels from 1 to 4 [see Fig. 5(b)], can be mostly ignored. However, we must be very cautious when manipulating the low-frequency components to keep as many true coefficients as possible after thresholding. According to the exploratory data analysis in the beginning of this section, we select a threshold value large enough to ignore most of the wavelet coefficients at levels 1-4, which represent the noise signals, especially in the beginning and the end of the profile. The denoising results show the good performance of wavelet application and exploratory data analysis.

The remaining wavelet coefficients after shrinkage are less than one tenth of those of the original SIMS. These thresholded wavelet coefficients [those "stuttered" 2^n times on level n are concentrated in the zone where the signal is too noisy, see Fig. 6(b)] give us an idea of the remaining details in the approximation (denoised signal) of the original signal, which are higher than the determined threshold (significant details). For example, the estimated threshold of the previous SIMS signal, obtained using soft universal shrinkage [eq. (17)], is λ = 55.7831 cps. The estimated level of noise, using eq. (18), gives a signal-to-noise ratio (SNR) = 40.9212 dB.

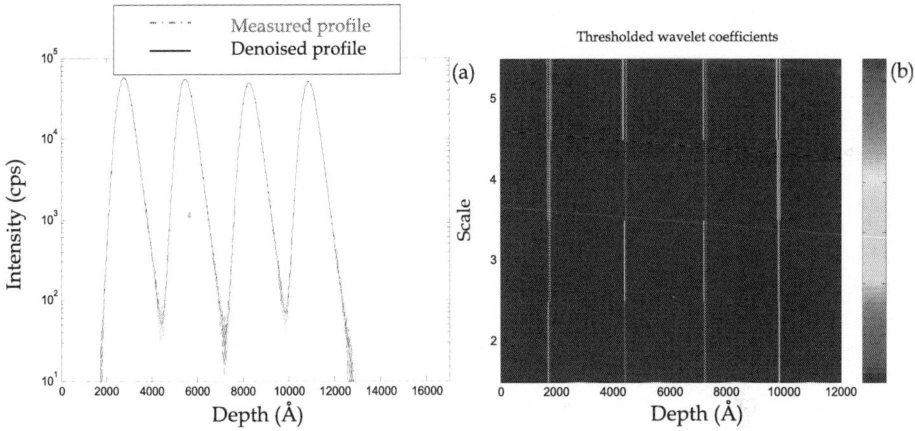

Fig. 6. (a) Original SIMS profile superimposed on the denoised profile. (b) Thresholded wavelet coefficients.

Because the few largest wavelet coefficients preserve almost the entire energy of the signal, shrinkage reduces noise without distorting the signal features. The main results after denoising by wavelet coefficient thresholding are as follows.

- The noise is almost entirely suppressed.
- Sharp features of the original signal remain sharp in the reconstruction.
- It is inferred that progressive wavelet transformations would bring the prediction asymptotically closer towards the true signal.

Finally, we note that the result obtained [Fig. 6(a)] is of both good smoothness and regularity. Thus, we may exploit this advantage in deconvolution procedure without fearing that it will lead to aberrant results.

4. Multiscale deconvolution (MD): The proposed algorithms

4.1 First algorithm: Tikhonov-Miller regularization with a denoisy and deconvoluted signal as model of solution

We have seen in § 2.2 eq. 10 that Mancina (Mancina, 2000) proposed to reiterate the algorithm of Barakat (Barakat et al, 1997) and to use a pre-deconvoluted signal as model of the solution with sufficient regularization. The accuracy of the solution is referred to the accuracy of the model, which suggests a reasonable formulation. It is obvious that a significant lack of precision in the a priori model leads to an error restoration more important than the usual one without the model. Moreover, if the pre-deconvoluted signal is a noisy signal (which is the case for SIMS signals) or contains aberrations, the iterative process worsens these aberrations and the result is an oscillatory signal. For this reason, it is important to remove noise components from the signal (the model of solution). The idea is to introduce a denoisy and deconvoluted signal as model of solution in Barakat's approach, which constitutes our first contribution in this field (Boulakroune, 2008). The first proposed deconvolution scheme is constructed by the following steps:

1. Dyadic wavelet decomposition of the noisy signal at the resolution 2^{-j}.
2. Denoising of this signal by thresholding. One conserves only high-frequency components of details which are above the estimated threshold.
3. Reconstruction of the denoisy signal from the approximations and thersholded details using eq.19.
4. The obtained denoisy signal constitutes the model of solution in iterative Tikhonov-Miller regularization at the first iteration.

The mathematical formulation, in Fourier space, of this algorithm is as follows:

$$\begin{cases} X_{\text{mod}_0} = \tilde{F}y_a^{(j)} + \tilde{G}\hat{y}_d^{(j)} \\ \hat{X}_{n+1} = \dfrac{H^*Y + \alpha|D|^2 X_{\text{mod}_n}}{|H|^2 + \alpha|D|^2} \\ X_{\text{mod}_n} = \hat{X}_{n+1} \end{cases} \quad (20)$$

It can be noted that denoising reduces the noise power in data; the regularization parameter should be evaluated by cross-validation in regards of the denoisy signal.

Since the noise is controlled by multiscale transforms, the regularization parameter does not have the same importance as in standard deconvolution methods. Clearly it will be lower than obtained without denoising.

In order to validate the robustness of the proposed algorithm, the results must be compared with those of the previous Tikhonov-Miller regularization algorithms. In particular, we have chosen to compare our results with those obtained by Mancina algorithm (Mancina, 2000).

The results of deconvolution by Mancina's approach (Mancina, 2000) are given in Figs. 7(a) and 7(b). It is obvious by using this algorithm, that the deconvolution has improved the slope and the regularity of the delta layers which are completely separated. Indeed, their shape is symmetrical for all peaks, indicating that the exponential features caused by the SIMS analysis are removed. The full width at half maximum (FWHM) of the deconvoluted delta-layers is equal to 19.5 nm. This can be considered a very good result if one takes into account that the FWHM of the measured profile is approximately 59.7 nm. This corresponds to an improvement in depth resolution by a factor of 3.06. The dynamic range is enhanced by a factor of 2.03 for all peaks.

At both sides of the deconvoluted peaks, oscillations with negative components [Fig. 7(a)] appear under the level of noise where the reliability of the deconvolution process cannot be guaranteed. These artifacts, which have been produced by the deconvolution algorithm, must not be taken for a real concentration distribution. The negative values of these artifacts are not physically accepted for concentration measurements in SIMS analysis. Although a compromise was made between the iteration number and the quality of the deconvoluted peaks, if one increases the iteration number with a relatively weak regularization parameter (obtained by cross validation, it equals 5.6552×10^{-6}), the number and the level of these oscillations increase more which reinforces the limits of this algorithm. Indeed, these oscillations are directly related to the quantity of noise. Part of this information, in particular in high frequencies, is masked by the noise, and this lack of information is compensated by the generation of artifacts. With an over estimated value of the regularization parameter, which leads to a more conditioned matrix ($\boldsymbol{H}^{+}$) (see Fig. 2), one can reduces the number and the amplitude of these oscillations. The solution can be stable and smooth, but this operation is arbitrary and not based on any physical or mathematical support.

By applying the positivity constraint, one reinforces the positivity of the final deconvolution profile. The solution stays in accordance with physical reality, as is illustrated in Fig. 7(b). However, positiviting the signal is an arbitrary operation; it is only to direct the solution so that it becomes positive, without making sure that it is exact. Furthermore, the measured dose (the number of ions counted) must be identical for all signals (original, measured, deconvoluted) except for the noise. This dose must be preserved in the resolution of convolution equation and must take into account the generated negative components. With the application of the positivity constraint, the dose of the deconvoluted and constrained signal is higher than the initial dose. A variation of a few percent cannot be tolerated in the quantification of SIMS profiles. It is important to note that in the case of SIMS analysis, physical coherence is of paramount importance. The deconvoluted profile must be physically acceptable. Thus, it is important to adopt a method whose result is acceptable; otherwise the result obtained may be mathematically correct but have no connection with physical reality.

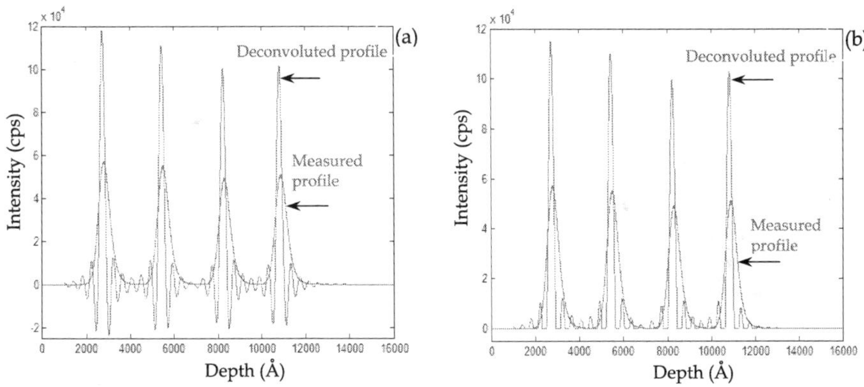

Fig. 7. Results of TMMS algorithm for sample MD4 containing four delta layers of boron in silicon (8.5 keV/O_2^+, 31.8°); $\alpha_c = 5.6552\times10^{-6}$, n= 150 iterations.
(a) Without application of positivity constraint.
(b) With application of positivity constraint.

To completely remove artifacts from the deconvoluted profiles, Gautier et al (Gautier at al, 1997) proposed the application of local confidence level deduced empirically from the reconstruction error in the deconvoluted profiles. The goal of this confidence level is to separate the parts of the signal belonging to the original profile from those generated artificially by the process of deconvolution. According to these authors (Gautier at al, 1997), when the signal falls to the noise level, at which point one cannot be confident in the deconvolution result, one must fix a limiting value of the deconvoluted signal below which one should not take into account the deconvolution result that likely belongs to the original signal. However, a confidence level that authorizes to take into account certain parts of the signal and eliminates the lower parts in which the signal should not be taken into account any more, does not bring any information about the quality of information. One of the advantages of SIMS analysis is the great dynamic range of the signal, and allowing the deconvoluted signal to be restricted to a dynamic range which does not exceed two decades and thus does not reflect the original signal. The parts filtered by the confidence level can provide precious information about the sample. In ref. (Mancina, 2000), Mancina showed that the artifacts are not always aberrations of the deconvolution; they can be structures with low concentrations. The interpretation of the artifacts must be measured, especially if their amount is not negligible, in which case, one cannot eliminate them from the deconvoluted profiles. Therefore, it is important to find another tool which leads to a solution lacking of any non physical features and without any arbitrary operations.

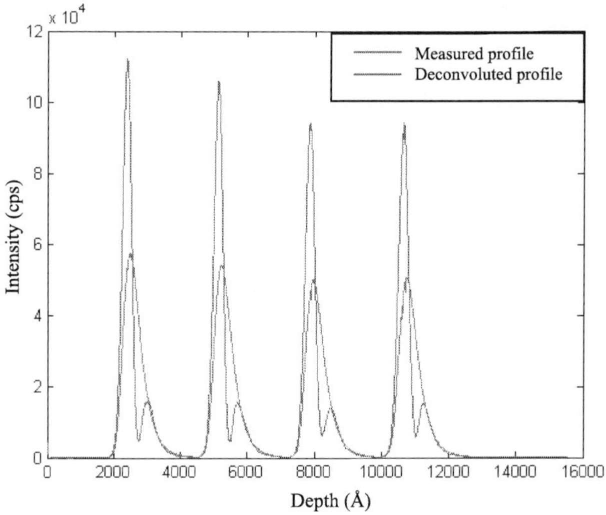

Fig. 8. Result of deconvolution by the first proposed algorithm of SIMS profile containing four delta-layers of boron in silicon (8,5 keV/O_2^+, 38,1°), α = 5,6552.10^{-6}, n = 250 iterations. The level of estimated noise, by using (17) et (18), is of SNR = 40,92 dB. The threshold λ = 55.7831 counts/s. The used wavelet is Sym4.

By using the first proposed algorithm, the results are quite satisfactory suggesting that this approach is indeed self-consistent, see Fig. 8. A significant improvement in the contrast is observed; the delta layers are more separated. The shape of the results is symmetrical for all layers, indicating that the exponential features (in particular the distorted tail shape observed in the boron profile is due to a significantly larger ion mixing effect) caused by SIMS analysis are removed. The same gains that those obtained by Mancina approach of the depth resolution and maximum of picks (dynamic range) are obtained. It can be noted that the width of measured peaks indicates that the δ-layers are not truths deltas - doping, they are close to gaussian more than delta-layers. At the right side of the main deconvoluted peaks some other small peaks appear without any negative component and without application of positivity constraint any more, which validates this approach. The question for the SIMS user is to know whether these peaks are to be considered as physical features or as deconvolution artifacts. The origin of these *positive* oscillations lies in the strong local concentrations of the high frequencies of noise, and which cannot be correctly restored. It should be noted that these small peaks can be eliminated by the support constraint, but we consider that the application of any kind of constraints is a purely arbitrary operation.

In the classical approaches of the regularization (including our first algorithm) the regularization operator applies in a total way to all bands of the signal. This results in treating low frequencies which contain the useful signal like high frequencies mainly constituted by noise. The result is then an oscillating signal, because the regularization parameter is insufficient to compensate all high frequencies. To overcome these limits, it is important to adopt a powerful deconvolution that leads to a smoothed and stable solution. In this context, multiresolution deconvolution, which is never used to recover SIMS profiles, may be the most appropriate technique.

4.2 Second algorithm: Multiresolution deconvolution

Because of the very abrupt concentration gradients in circuits produced by the microelectronics industry the original SIMS depth profiles are likely to contain some very high frequencies (Gautier et al, 1998). SIMS signals can extend over several decades in a very short range of depth. The intention of any SIMS analyst, as well as of any deconvolution user, is to recover completely all the frequencies lost by the measurement process. Unfortunately, considering again the fact that the resolution function is a low-pass filter, the recovery of high frequencies is always limited, and the recovery of the highest frequencies is definitely impossible, particularly when the profile to be recovered is noisy, which is always the case. It is possible to produce some very high frequencies during the deconvolution process, but there are many chances that these high frequencies are only produced by the high-frequency noise or are created during the inversion of eq. (3) from the very small components of $H(\upsilon)$. High frequencies in the results of a deconvolution must be regarded suspiciously, except if we are just trying to recover very sharp spikes with no interesting low frequencies. This is definitely not the case for SIMS signals, which contain an appreciable amount of low frequencies, too. Therefore, the purpose of this work is to solve this problem by separating high frequencies and low frequencies in the signal, and then further recovering correctly the high frequencies which are not attributable to noise and which contain useful information. Using multiresolution deconvolution, the final result of the deconvolution should be reasonably smooth. This arises from the observation that, even though the SIMS profiles are likely to contain very high frequencies, which can be thresholded by wavelet shrinkage.

In classical regularization approaches, in order to limit the noise content, one must give a higher bound to the quantity of high frequencies that are likely to be present in the result of the deconvolution [eq. (5)], which might be invalid. However, by this process one limits the quantity of high frequencies, not the quantity of noise. The best solution is to recover correctly the frequencies in different bands of the signal and to find an objective criterion to separate the high frequencies which contain noise from those containing the useful information. Moreover, in these traditional regularized methods (monoresolution regularized deconvolution), the regularization parameter is applied comprehensively to all signal bands, which results in treating low frequencies which contain the useful signal as high frequencies mainly consisting of noise. The result is then an oscillatory signal, because the regularization parameter is insufficient to compensate high frequencies. Therefore, our idea is to locally adapt the regularization parameter in different frequency bands. This allows us to deconvolute signals previously decomposed by projection onto a wavelet basis.

We have seen in § 3 that the multiscale representation of the signal, or wavelet decomposition allows its associating with an approximation signal at low frequencies (scale coefficients) and a detail signal at high frequencies (wavelet coefficients). Indeed, the approximation signal is very regular (smooth) whereas the detail signal is irregular (rough). This information may be exploited a priori in the deconvolution algorithm. A regular wavelet base will be privileged if one wants to control this regularity, in particular if successive decompositions are used.

It should be noted that the use of a wavelet base with limited support allows preserving a priori knowledge of the signal support in its multiresolution representation. The effectiveness of the constraint of limited support is preserved if the wavelet support is small with respect to that of the signal. In the case of a positive signal, the approximation signal will be positive only if all low-pass filter coefficients are positive. The detail signal always averages to zero; this information can be used like a new soft constraint.

Considering all these advantages, the regularized multiresolution deconvolution can then be performed so that limits of classical monoresolution deconvolution methods are overcome, such as, generating oscillations with negatives components, which limit the depth resolution.

In sharp contrast with the usual multiresolution scheme, it has been established in refs. (Burdeau et al, 2000; Weyrich et al, 1998) that the decimation process is without interest in deconvolution and, in addition, that it incorporates errors in data, if this is the case, then the output of the filters are not decimated.

After wavelet decomposition, the observed noisy data of approximation and details are written under the following mathematical formalism:

$$\begin{aligned} y_a^{(J)} &= H^{(J)} x_a^{(J)} + b_a^{(J)} \\ y_d^{(j)} &= H^{(j)} x_d^{(j)} + b_d^{(j)} \end{aligned} \quad j = 1,\ldots, J. \tag{21}$$

where $b_a^{(J)}$ and $b_d^{(j)}$ represent the approximation and details of the noise at the resolutions 2^{-J} and 2^{-j}, respectively.

We use the Tikhonov regularization method to solve the two parts of eq. (21) separately. The following soft constraints about the solutions $\tilde{x}_a^{(J)}$ and $\tilde{x}_d^{(j)}$ are used:

$$\begin{aligned} \left\| y_a^{(J)} - H^{(J)} \tilde{x}_a^{(J)} \right\|^2 &\le \left\| b_a^{(J)} \right\|^2 \\ \left\| y_d^{(j)} - H^{(j)} \tilde{x}_d^{(j)} \right\|^2 &\le \left\| b_d^{(j)} \right\|^2 \end{aligned} \quad j = 1,\ldots, J, \tag{22}$$

$$\left\|D_a^{(J)}\tilde{x}_a^{(J)}\right\| \le (r_a^{(J)})^2 \quad \text{j= 1,..., J.} \qquad (23)$$
$$\left\|D_d^{(j)}\tilde{x}_d^{(j)}\right\| \le (r_d^{(j)})^2$$

where $d_a^{(J)}$ and $D_d^{(j)}$ are high-pass filters, and $(r_a^{(J)})^2$, $(r_d^{(j)})^2$ are regularities of approximation and detail solutions at resolutions 2^{-J} and 2^{-j}, respectively.

Following the Miller approach, the constraints are quadratically combined. We then have

$$\left\|y_a^{(J)} - H^{(J)}\tilde{x}_a^{(J)}\right\|^2 + \frac{\left\|b_a^{(J)}\right\|^2}{(r_a^{(J)})^2}\left\|D_a^{(J)}\tilde{x}_a^{(J)}\right\| \le 2\left\|b_a^{(J)}\right\|^2 \quad \text{j= 1,..., J.} \qquad (24)$$
$$\left\|y_d^{(j)} - H^{(j)}\tilde{x}_d^{(j)}\right\|^2 + \frac{\left\|b_d^{(j)}\right\|^2}{(r_d^{(j)})^2}\left\|D_d^{(j)}\tilde{x}_d^{(j)}\right\| \le 2\left\|b_d^{(j)}\right\|^2$$

The two deconvolutions are the solutions of the normal equations:

$$\left[(H^{(J)})^T H^{(J)} + \alpha_a^{(J)}(D_a^{(J)})^{(T)}D_a^{(J)}\right]\tilde{x}_a^{(J)} = (H^{(J)})^T y_a^{(J)} \quad \text{j= 1,..., J.} \qquad (25)$$
$$\left[(H^{(j)})^T H^{(j)} + \alpha_d^{(j)}(D_d^{(j)})^T D_d^{(j)}\right]\tilde{x}_d^{(j)} = (H^{(j)})^T y_d^{(j)}$$

with

$$\alpha_a^{(J)} = \frac{\left\|b_a^{(J)}\right\|^2}{(r_a^{(J)})^2} \text{ and } \alpha_d^{(j)} = \frac{\left\|b_d^{(j)}\right\|^2}{(r_d^{(j)})^2} \quad \text{j= 1,..., J.} \qquad (26)$$

In practice, regularity coefficients $(r_a^{(J)})^2$, $(r_d^{(j)})^2$ and noise energies $\left\|b_a^{(J)}\right\|^2$, $\left\|b_d^{(j)}\right\|^2$ are unknown. Fortunately, these parameters can be estimated using generalized cross-validation (Thompson et al, 1991; Weyrich et al, 1998). The mathematical formalisms of these estimations are:

$$V(\alpha_a^{(J)}) = \frac{\frac{1}{N}\left\|y_a^{(J)} - H^{(J)}H^{+(J)}H^{T(J)}y_a^{(J)}\right\|^2}{\left[\frac{1}{N}Trace(I - H^{+(J)})\right]^2}, \; V(\alpha_d^{(j)}) = \frac{\frac{1}{N}\left\|y_d^{(j)} - H^{(j)}H^{+(j)}H^{T(j)}y_d^{(j)}\right\|^2}{\left[\frac{1}{N}Trace(I - H^{+(j)})\right]^2} \qquad (27)$$

To solve eq. (24), we must calculate the reverse of the matrices:

$$H_a^+ = (H^{(J)})^T H^{(J)} + \alpha_a^{(J)}(D_a^{(J)})^{(T)}D_a^{(J)} \quad \text{j= 1,..., J.} \qquad (28)$$
$$H_d^+ = (H^{(j)})^T H^{(j)} + \alpha_d^{(j)}(D_d^{(j)})^T D_d^{(j)}$$

The quality of the solutions $\tilde{x}_a^{(J)}$ and $\tilde{x}_d^{(j)}$ depends on the conditioning of the matrices H_a^+ and H_d^+.

The operators $D_a^{(J)}$ and $D_d^{(j)}$ are selected with important eigenvalues when singular values of $H^{(J)}$ and $H^{(j)}$ are rather weak. Indeed, the choice of the regularization operators is conducted based on the singular values of $H^{(J)}$ and $H^{(j)}$ but not by the considered frequency-band, because it is not useful to choose an operator for each frequency band. We construct $D_a^{(J)}$ and $D_d^{(j)}$ from the same pulse response d(n); this operator is denoted as $D^{(j)}$ at resolution 2^{-j}.

It is important to note that in a multiresolution scheme up to the resolution 2^{-J}, the different filters responses of decomposition and reconstruction should be interpolated by 2^{j-1}-1 zeros at the resolution 2^{-j} in order to contract the filter bandwidth by a factor 2^{j-1}-1. Each matrix should have a size in accordance with the size of the filtered vector that depends on the resolution level.

The different steps in the multiresolution deconvolution algorithm are as follows (Boulakroune, 2009).

1. Dyadic wavelet decomposition of the noisy signal up to the resolution 2^{-j} (j = 1, 2, ...).
2. Denoising of this signal by thresholding. One conserves only high-frequency components of details which are above the estimated threshold. One uses generalized cross-validation for threshold parameter evaluation without prior knowledge of the noise variance.(Weyrich, 1998) It can be noted that the wavelet should be orthogonal, therefore the noise in the approximation and detail remains white and Gaussian if it is, in the blurred signal, white and Gaussian.
3. Solving the two Tikhonov-Miller normal [eq. (22)] at each resolution level.
4. Denoising of the wavelet-decomposed solution of the deconvolution problem by thresholding.
5. Dyadic wavelet undecimated reconstruction of the restored signal up to the full resolution.

By using multiresolution deconvolution, the results are quite satisfactory, suggesting that this approach is indeed self-consistent [Figs. 9(a) and 9(b)]. A significant improvement in contrast is observed; the delta layers are more separated. The shape of the results is symmetrical for all layers, indicating that the exponential features caused by SIMS analysis are removed.

The different regularization parameters obtained using the generalized cross validation [eq. (27)] at different levels necessary for a well regularized system are $\alpha_a^{(1)} = 3.34789\times10^{-4}$, $\alpha_a^{(2)} = 6.7835\times10^{-4}$, $\alpha_a^{(3)} = 0.0013$, $\alpha_a^{(4)} = 0.0026$, $\alpha_a^{(5)} = 0.0048$, $\alpha_d^{(1)} = 1.1012$, $\alpha_d^{(2)} = 2.3287$, $\alpha_d^{(3)} = 4.0211$, $\alpha_d^{(4)} = 9.1654$, $\alpha_d^{(5)} = 16.0773$. The classical regularization parameter is equal to 6.6552×10^{-5}.

The approximation regularization parameter increases proportionally with the decomposition level. This behavior is explained by the decrease of the local regularity of the signal with the scale and inter-scale behavior of wavelet coefficients. The latter determines the visual appearance of the added details information (high frequency contents) in the reconstruction. Therefore, as the degree of accuracy is high, the signal regularity is better; hence, the regularization parameter decreases more.

The detail regularization parameter also decreases according to the decomposition level. This evolution is materialized by the degradation of the precision with the scale, which decreases the regularity from one level to another. As the noise is white and Gaussian and the decomposition is dyadic and regular, this parameter doubles in value from one scale to another.

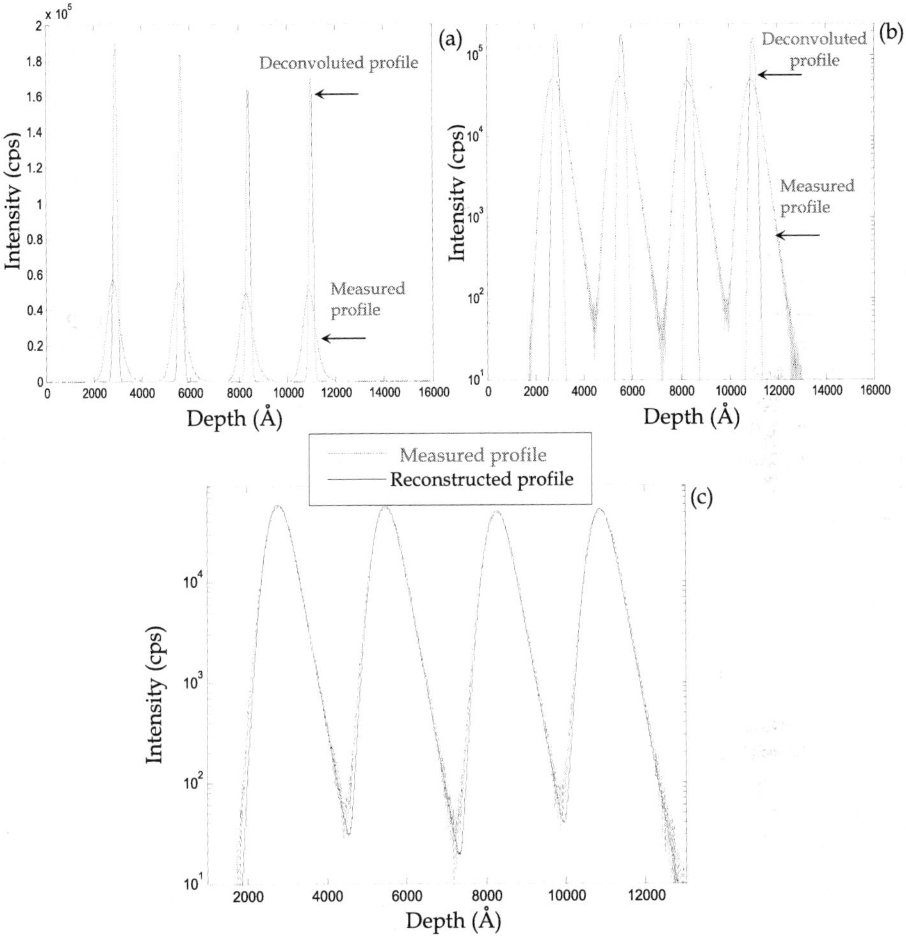

Fig. 9. Results of multiresolution deconvolution of sample MD4 of boron in silicon matrix performed at 8.5 keV/O_2^+, 38.7°. (a) Linear scale plot. (b) Logarithmic scale plot. (c) Reconstruction of the measured profile from the deconvoluted profile and the DRF. The estimated threshold, obtained using soft universal shrinkage [eq. (17)], is $\lambda = 55.7831$ cps. The estimated level of noise, using eq. (18), is SNR = 40.9212 dB. The wavelet used was *Sym4* with four vanishing moments.

The regularization parameter of approximation or detail takes different values according to the decomposition level. This enables it to be adapted in a local manner with the treated frequency bands, either low or high frequencies. This adaptation leads to compensate high frequencies contrary to a classical regularization parameter, which treats low frequencies which contain useful signal as high frequencies mainly consisting of noise.

The FWHM of the deconvoluted peaks is equal to 18.9 nm, which corresponds to an improvement in the depth resolution by a factor of 3.1587 [Figs. 9(a) and 9(b)]. The dynamic range is improved by a factor of 2.13 for all peaks. The width of the measured peaks indicates that the δ-layers are not real deltas - doping (are not very thin layers); they are closer to Gaussian than delta-layers.

The main advantage of MD is the absence of oscillations which appear in TMMS algorithm results due to the noise effect. Actually, these oscillations appear in most of the classical regularization approaches. The question for the SIMS user is to know whether these small peaks (oscillations) are to be considered as physical features or as deconvolution artifacts. In our opinion, the origin of these oscillations is the presence of strong local concentrations of high frequencies of noise in the signal which cannot be correctly restored by a simple classical regularization.

Figure 9(c) represents the reconstructed depth profile, obtained by convolving the deconvoluted profile with the DRF along with the measured profile. It is in perfect agreement with the measured profile over the entire range of the profile depth. This is a figure of merit of the quality of the deconvolution, and it ensures that the deconvoluted profile is undoubtedly a signal which has produced the measured SIMS profile. A good reconstruction is one of the criteria that confirms the quality of the deconvolution and gives credibility to the deconvoluted profile.

Finally, by using the proposed MD, the SIMS profiles are recovered very satisfactorily. The artifacts, which appear in almost all monoresolution deconvolution schemes, have been corrected. Therefore, this new algorithm can push the limits of SIMS measurements towards the ultimate resolution

5. Conclusion

This chapter proposes two robust algorithms for inverse problem to perform deconvolution and particularly restore signals from strongly noised blurred discrete data. These algorithms can be characterized as a regularized wavelet transform. There combine ideas from Tikhonov Miller regularization, wavelet analysis and deconvolution algorithms in order to benefit from the advantages of each. The first algorithm is Tikhonov-Miller deconvolution method, where a priori model of solution, is included. The latter is a denoisy and pre-deconvolved signal obtained firstly by the application of wavelet shrinkage algorithm and after, by the introduction of the obtained denoisy signal in an iterative deconvolution algorithm. The second algorithm is multiresolution deconvolution, based also on Tikhonov-Miller regularization and wavelet transformation. Both local applications of the regularization parameter and shrinking the wavelet coefficients of blurred and estimated solutions at each resolution level in multiresolution deconvolution provide to smoothed results without the risk of generating artifacts related to noise content in the profile. These algorithms were developed and applied to improve the depth resolution of secondary ion mass spectrometry profiles.

The multiscale deconvolution, in particular multiresolution deconvolution (2nd algorithm), shows how the denoising of wavelet coefficients plays an important role in the deconvolution procedure. The purpose of this new approach is to adapt the regularization parameter locally according to the treated frequency band. In particular, the proposed method appears to be very well adapted to the case where the signal-to-noise ratio is poor, because in this case the minimum in the variance of the wavelet coefficients comes out more clearly. Thus, this aspect may be very attractive because it is particularly important to optimize the choice of the regularization parameter, especially at high frequencies. Moreover, the possibility of introducing various *a priori* probabilities at several resolution levels by means of the wavelet analysis has been examined. Indeed, we showed that multiresolution deconvolution can be successfully used for the recovery of data, and hence, for the improvement of depth resolution in SIMS analysis. In particular, deconvolution of delta layers is the most important depth profiling data deconvolution, since it gives not only the shape of the resolution function, but also the optimum data deconvolution conditions for a specific experimental setup.

The comparison between the performance of the proposed algorithms and that of classical monoresolution deconvolution, which is Tikhonov-Miller regularization with model of solution (TMMS), shows that MD results are better than the results of the first proposed algorithm and TMMS algorithm. Because in the classical approaches of the regularization (including our first proposed algorithm), the regularization operator applies in a total way to all bands of the signal. This results in treating low frequencies which contain the useful signal like high frequencies mainly constituted by noise. The result is then an oscillating signal, because the regularization parameter is insufficient to compensate all high frequencies. However, the multiresolution deconvolution (2nd algorithm) helps to suppress the influence of instabilities in the measuring system and noise. Particularly this method works very well and does not deform the deconvolution result. It gives smoothed results without the risk of generating a comprehensive mathematical profile with no connection to the real profile, i.e., free- oscillation deconvoluted profiles are obtained. We can say unambiguously that the MD algorithm is more reliable with regards to the quality of the deconvoluted profiles and the compared gains which show the influence of noise on the TMMS results.

The MD can be used in two-dimension applications and generally in many problems in science and engineering involving the recovery of an object of interest from collected data. SIMS depth profiling is just one example thereof. Nevertheless, the major disadvantage of MD is the longer computing time compared to monoresolution deconvolution methods. However, due to the increase of computer power during recent years, this disadvantage has become progressively less important.

6. References

Allen, P. N., Dowsett, M. G. & Collins, R. (1993). SIMS profile quantification by maximum entropy deconvolution, *Surface and Interface Analysis*, Vol.20, (1993), pp. 696-702, ISSN 1096-9918

Averbuch, A. & Zheludev, V. (2009). Spline-based deconvolution, *Elsevier, Signal Processing*, Vol.89, (2009), pp. 1782–1797, ISSN 0165-1684

Barakat, V., Guilpart, B., Goutte, R. & Prost, R. (1997). Model-based Tikhonov-Miller image restoration, *IEEExplore, Proceedings International conference on Image processing (ICIP '97)*, pp. 310-31, ISBN: 0-8186-8183-7, Washington, DC, USA, October 26- 29, 1997

Berger, T., Stromberg, J. O. & Eltoft, T. (1999). Adaptive regularized constrained least squares image restoration. *IEEE Transactions on Image Processing*, Vol.8, No9, (1999), pp. 1191-1203, ISSN 1057-7149

Boulakroune, M., Benatia, D. & Kezai, T. (2009). Improvement of depth resolution in secondary ion mass spectrometry analysis using the multiresolution deconvolution.

Japanese Journal of applied physics, Vol.48, No6, (2009), pp. 066503- 1,15, ISSN Online 1347-4065 / Print: 0021-4922

Boulakroune, M., Eloualkadi, A., Benatia, D., & Kezai, T. (2007) New approach for improvement of secondary ion mass spectrometry profile analysis, *Japanese Journal of applied physics*, Vol.46 No.11, (2007), pp. 7441-7445, ISSN Online: 1347-4065 / Print: 0021-4922

Boulakroune, M., Slougui, N., Benatia, D. & El Oualkadi, A. (2008). Tikhonov-Miller regularization with a denoisy and deconvolved signal as model of solution for improvement of depth resolution in SIMS analysis, *IEEExplore, 3rd International Conference on Information and Communication Technologies: From Theory to Applications*, pp. 1-6, ISBN 978-1-4244-1751- 3, Damascus, Syria, April 7-11, 2008

Brianzi, P. (1994). A criterion for the choice of a sampling parameter in the problem of laplace transform inversion. *Journal Inverse Problems*, Vol.10, (1994), pp. 55-61, ISSN 0266- 5611

Burdeau, J. –L, Goutte, R. & Prost, R. (2000). Joint nonlinéair-quadratic regularization in wavelet based deconvolution schem. *IEEExplore, Proceedings the 5th International conference on signal processing WCCC-ICSP 2000*, Vol.1, pp. 77-80, ISBN 978-1-4577-0538-0, Beijing, China, August 21 - 25, 2000

Charles, C., Leclerc, G., Louette, P., Rasson, J.-P. & Pireaux, J.-J. (2004). Noise filtering and deconvolution of XPS data by wavelets and Fourier transform, *Surface and Interface Analysis,* Vol.36, (2004), pp. 71–80, ISSN 1096-9918

Collins, R., Dowsett, M. G. & Allen, A. (1992). Deconvolution of concentration profiles from SIMS data using measured response function, *SIMS proceeding, 8th International conference on secondary ion mass spectrometry,* pp. 111-115, ISBN 10 0471930644, Amesterdam, Netherland, September 15-20, 1991

Connolly, T. J. & Lane, R. G. (1998). Constrained regularization methods for superresolution, *Proceedings IEEE 1998 International conference on image processing ICIP 98*, pp. 727 – 731, ISBN 0-8186-8821-1, Chicago Illinois, California, USA, October 4-7, 1998

Daubechies, I. (1990). The wavelet transform, time-frequency localization and signal analysis. *IEEE Transaction on Information theory*, Vol.36, No.5, (1990), pp. 961-1005, ISSN 0018-9448

Donoho, D. L. & Johnstone, I. M. (1994). Ideal spatial Adaptation by wavelet shrinkage, *Biometrika*, Vol.81, No3, (1994), pp. 425-455, ISSN 0006-3444

Donoho, D. L. & Johnstone, I. M. (1995). Adaptating to unknown smoothness via wavelets shrinkage, *American Statistical Association – Journal,* Vol.90, No.432, (1995), pp. 1200-1224, ISSN 0162-1459

Dowsett, M. G., Dowlands, G., Allen, P. N., & Barlow, R. D. (1994). An analytic form for the SIMS response function measured from ultra thin impurity layers, *Surface and Interface Analysis* Vol. 21, (1994), pp. 310-315, ISSN 1096-9918

Essah, W. A. & Delves, L. M. (1988). On the numerical inversion of the Laplace transform). *Journal Inverse Problems*, Vol.4, (1988), pp. 705-724, ISSN 0266-5611

Fan, J. & Koo, J.-Y. (2002). Wavelet deconvolution, *IEEE Transaction on Information Theory,* Vol.48, No.3, (2002), pp. 734–747, ISSN 0018-9448

Fares, B., Gautier, B., Dupuy, J. C., Prudon, G., & Holliger, P. (2006). Deconvolution of very low energy SIMS depth profiles, *Applied Surface Science.* Vol. 252, (2006), pp. 6478-6481, ISSN 0169-4332

Fearn, S. & McPhail, D. S. (2005). High resolution quantitative SIMS analysis of shallow boron implants in silicon using a bevel and image approach. *Applied Surface Science.* Vol.252, No.4, (2005), pp. 893-904, ISSN 0169- 4332

Fischer, R., Mayer, M., Von der Linden, W. & Dose, V. (1998). Energy resolution enhancement in ion beam experiments with Bayesian probability theory. *Nuclear Instruments and Methods in Physics Research Section B,* Vol.136-138, (1998), pp. 1140-1145, ISSN 0168-583X

Fujiyama, N., Hasegawa, T., Suda, T., Yamamoto, T., Miyagi, T., Yamada, K., & Karen, A. (2011). A beneficial application of backside SIMS for the depth profiling characterization of implanted silicon, *SIMS Proceedings Papers, Surface & Interface Analysis, The 12th International Symposium on SIMS and Related Techniques Based on Ion-Solid Interactions,* Vol.43, pp. 654–656, ISSN 1096-9918, Seikei University, Tokyo, Japan, June 10-11, 2010

Garcia-Talavera, M., & Ulicny, B. (2003). *A* genetic algorithm approach for multiplet deconvolution in g-ray spectra. *Nuclear Instruments and Methods in Physics Research A,* Vol. 512, (2003), pp. 585–594, ISSN 0168-9002

Gautier, B., Dupuy, J. C., Prost, R. & Prudon, G. (1997). Effectiveness ans limits of the deconvolution of SIMS depth profiles of boron in silicon. *Journal of Surface & Interface Analysis,* Vol.25, (1997), 464-477, ISSN 1096-9918

Gautier, B., Prudon, G., & Dupuy, J. C. (1998). Toward a better reliability in the deconvolution of SIMS depth profiles, *Surface and Interface Analysis.,* Vol. 26, (1998), pp. 974-983, ISSN 1096-9918

Herzel, F., Ehwald, K. -E., Heinemann, B., Kruger, D., Kurps, R., Ropke, W. &. Zeindl, H.-P. (1995). Deconvolution of narrow boron SIMS depth profiles in Si and SiGe. *Surface & Interface Analysis.* Vol.23, (1995), pp. 764-770, ISSN 1096-9918

Iqbal, M. (2003). Deconvolution and regularization for numerical solutions of incorrectely posed problems. *Journal of computational & Applied Mathematics,* Vol.151, (2003), pp. 463- 476, ISSN: 0377-0427

Jammal, G. & Bijaouib, A. (2004). DeQuant: a flexible multiresolution restoration framework. *Elsevier, Elsevier, Signal Processing,* Vol. 84, (2004), pp. 1049–1069, ISSN: 0165-1684

Makarov, V. V. (1999). Deconvolution of high dynamic range depth profiling data using the Tikhonov method, *Surf. Interface. Anal.,* Vol. 27, (1999), pp. 801-816, ISSN 1096- 9918

Mallat, S. G. (1989). A theory for multiresolution signal decomposition: the wavelet representation. *IEEE Transaction on Pattern Analysis and Machine Intelligence,* Vol.11, No7, (1989), pp. 674-692, ISSN: 0162- 8828

Mancina, G., Prost, R., Prudon, G., Gautier, B., & Dupuy, J.C. (2000). Deconvolution SIMS depth profiles: toward the limits of the resolution by self-deconvolution test, *SIMS Proceedings Papers, the 12th SIMS International Conference,* pp. 497-500 In A. Benninghoven, P. Bertrand, H. N. Migeon, & H. W. Werner, editors, Elsevier, *Proceeding SIMS XII,* ISSN 0169- 4332, Brussels, Belgium, September 5-11, 1999.

Neelamani, R., Choi, H. & Baraniuk, R. (2004). ForWaRD: Fourier-wavelet regularized deconvolutionfor ill-conditioned systems, *IEEE Transaction Signal Processing,* Vol.52, No.2, (2004) pp. 418–433, ISSN 1053-587X

Prost, R. & Goutte, R. (1984). Discrete constrained iterative deconvolution algorithms with optimized rate of convergence. *Elsevier, Signal processing,* Vol.7, No3, pp. 209-230, ISSN 0165-1684

Rashed, E. A., Ismail, I. A. & Zaki, S. I. (2007). Multiresolution mammogram analysis in multilevel decomposition. *Pattern Recognition Letters*, Vol.28, (2007), pp. 286- 292, ISSN 0167-8655

Rucka, M., & Wilde, K. (2006). Application of continuous wavelet transform in vibration based damage detection method for beams and plates. *Elsevier, Journal of Sound and Vibration*, Vol.297, No3-5, (2006), pp. 536-550, ISSN: 0022-460X

Seki, S., Tamura, H., Wada, Y., Tsutsui, K., & Ootomoc, S. (2011). Depth profiling of micrometer-order area by mesa-structure fabrication, *SIMS Proceedings Papers, Surf. Interface Anal., The 12th International Symposium on SIMS and Related Techniques Based on Ion-Solid Interactions,*Vol.43, pp. 154–158, ISSN 1096-9918, Seikei University, Tokyo, Japan, June 10-11, 2010

Shao, L., Liu, J., Wang, C., Ma, K. B., Zhang, J., Chen, J., Tang, D., Patel, S. & Chu, W. -K. (2004). Response Function during Oxygen Sputter Profiling for Deconvolution of Boron Spatial Distribution *Nuclear Instruments and Methods in Physics Research section B*, Vol.219-220, (2004), pp. 303-307, ISSN 0168-583X

Starck, J-L., Nguyen, M. K. & Murtagh F. (2003). Wavelets and curvelets for image deconvolution: a combined approach. *Elsevier, Signal Processing*, Vol.83, (2003), pp. 2279 - 2283, ISSN 0165-1684Stone, M. (1974). Cross-validatory choice and assessment of statistical predictions. *Journal of the Royal Statistical Society: Series B (Statistical Methodology)*, Vol.36, (1974), pp. 111-147, ISSN 1369-7412

Thompson, A. M., Brown, J. C., Kay, J. W. & Titterington, D. M. (1991). A Study of Methods of Choosing the Smoothing Parameter in Image Restoration by Regularization. *IEEE Transactions on Pattern Analysis and Machine Intelligence*, Vol.13, No.4, (1991), pp. 326-339, ISSN 0162-8828

Thompson, A. M., Brown, J. C., Kay, J. W. & Titterington, D. M. (1991). A Study of Methods of Choosing the Smoothing Parameter in Image Restoration by Regularization. *IEEE Transactions on Pattern Analysis and Machine Intelligence*, Vol.13, No.4, (1991), pp. 326-339, ISSN 0162-8828

Tikhonov, A.N. (1963). Solution of incorrectly formulated problems and the regularization method, *Soviet Mathematics Doklady- IAC-CNR*, Vol.4, (1963), pp. 1035-1038, ISSN 0197-6788

Varah, J. M. (1983). Pitfalls in numerical solutions of linear ill-posed problems. *SIAM Journal on Scientific & Statistical Computing*, Vol.4, No.2, (1983), pp. 164- 76, ISSN 0196-5204

Weyrich, N. & Warhola, G. T. (1998). Wavelet shrinkage and generalized cross validation for image denoising, *IEEE Transactions on Image Processing*, Vol.7, (1998) pp. 82-90, ISSN 1057-7149

Yang, M.H. & Goodman, G. G. (2006). Application of deconvolution of boron depth profiling in SiGe heterostructures, *Journal of thin solid films*, Vol.508, (2006), pp. 276-278, ISSN 0040- 6090

Zheludev, V.A. (1998). Wavelet analysis in spaces of slowly growing splines via integral representation, *Real Analysis Exchange*,Vol.24, (1999), pp. 229–261, ISSN 0147-1937

Part 2

Electrical Systems

Wavelet Theory and Applications for Estimation of Active Power Unbalance in Power System

Samir Avdakovic[1], Amir Nuhanovic[2] and Mirza Kusljugic[2]
[1]*EPC Elektroprivreda of Bosnia and Herzegovina, Sarajevo,*
[2]*Faculty of Electrical Engineering, University of Tuzla, Tuzla,*
Bosnia and Herzegovina

1. Introduction

Power system is a complex, dynamic system, composed of a large number of interrelated elements. Its primary mission is to provide a safe and reliable production, transmission and distribution of electrical energy to final consumers, extending over a large geographic area. It comprises of a large number of individual elements which jointly constitute a unique and highly complex dynamic system. Some elements are merely the system's components while others affect the whole system (Machowski, 1997). Securing necessary level of safety is of great importance for economic and reliable operation of modern electric power systems.

Power system is subject to different disturbances which vary in their extent, and it must be capable to maintain stability. Various devices for monitoring, protection and control help ensure reliable, safe and stable operation. The stability of the power system is its unique feature and represents its ability to restore the initial state following a disturbance or move to a new steady state. During transient process, the change of the parameters should remain within the predefined limits. In the case of stability loss, parameters either increase progressively (power angles during angle instability) or decrease (voltage and frequency during voltage and frequency instability) (Kundur, 1994; Pal & Chaudhuri, 2005). Accurate and fast identification of disturbances allows alerting the operator in a proper manner about breakdowns and corrective measures to reduce the disturbance effects.

Several large blackouts occurred worldwide over the past decade. The blackout in Italy (28th Sept. 2003) which left 57 million people in dark is one f the major blackouts in Europe's history ever. The analyses show that the most common causes are cascading propagation of initial disturbance and failures in the power system’s design and operation, for example, lack of equipment maintenance, transmission congestion, an inadequate support by reactive power, system operating at the margin of stability, operators' poor reactions, and low or no coordination by control centres (Madani et al., 2004). It would, therefore, be beneficial to have automatic systems in electric power systems which would prevent propagation of effects of initial disturbance through the system and system's cascade breakdown. In order to prevent the already seen major breakdowns, the focus has been placed on developing algorithms for monitoring, protection and control of power system in real time. Traditionally, power system monitoring and control was based on local measurements of process parameters (voltage, power, frequency). Following major breakdowns from 2003., extensive efforts were made to develop and apply monitoring, protection and control systems based on parameters, the so-called Wide Area Monitoring Protection and Control systems (WAMPC). These systems are based on systems for measuring voltage phasors and currents in those points which are of special importance for power system (PMU devices - Phasor Measurement Unit). This platform enables more real and dynamic view of the power system, more accurate measurement swift data exchange and alert in case of need. Traditional „local" devices cannot achieve optimal control since they lack information about events outside their location (Novosel et al., 2007; Phadke & Thorp, 2008).

On the other hand, wavelet transformation (WT) represents a relatively new mathematical area and efficient tool for signal analysis and signal representation in time-frequency domain. It is a very popular area of mathematics applicable in different areas of science, primarily signal processing. Since the world around us, both nature and society, is constantly subjected to faster or slower, long or short-term changes, wavelets are suitable for mathematical tools to describe and analyse complex process in nature and society. A special problem in studying and analysing these processes are 'non-linear effects' characterised by quick and short changes, thus wavelets are an ideal tool for their analysis.

Historically, the WT development can be tracked to 1980s' and J.B.J. Fourier (Fig. 1a). Namely, in 1988, Belgian mathematician Ingrid Daubechies (Fig. 1b) presented her work to the scientific community, in which she created orthonormal wavelet bases of the space of square integrable functions which consists of compactly supported functions with prescribed degree of smoothness.

a) b)

Fig. 1. a) Jean B. J. Fourier (1768 –1830) (http://en.wikipedia.org) and b) Ingrid Daubechies (August 17, 1954 in Houthalen, Belgium) (http://www.pacm.princeton.edu)

Today, this is considered to be the end of the first phase of WT development. Since it has many advantages, when compared to other signal processing techniques, it is receiving huge attention in the field of electrical engineering. Over the past twenty years, many valuable papers have been published with focus on WT application in analysis of electromagnetic transients, electric power quality, protection, etc., as well as a fewer number of papers focusing on the analysis of electromechanic oscillations/transients in power system. In terms of time and frequency, transients can be divided into electromagnetic and electromechanic. Frequency range for transients phenomena is provided in Table 1.

Electromagnetic transients are usually a consequence of the change in network configuration due to switching or electronic equipment, transient fault, etc. Electromechanical transients are slower (systematic) occurrences due to unbalance of active power (unbalance in production and consumption of active power) and are a consequence of mechanical nature of synchronous machines connected to the network. Such systems have more energy storages, for example, rotational masses of machines which respond with oscillations to a slightest unbalance. (Henschel, 1999).

Frequency range	[Hz]	Phenomena	
Frequency range 1		SF_6 transients	Electromagnetic phenomena
	10^6		
	10^5	Wave propagation, lightning	
	10^4	Switching overvoltages	
	10^3	Transformer saturation	
	10^2		
Frequency range 2	10^1	Steady-state power flow Subsynchronous resonance	Electromechanical phenomena
	10^0	Transient stability: machine rotor dynamics Interarea oscillations	
	10^{-1}		
	10^{-2}	Mid-term and long-term stability:	
	10^{-3}	Automatic generation control	
	10^{-4}		

Table 1. Typical Frequency Ranges for Transients Phenomena in Power System (Henschel, 1999)

If electric power system has an initial disturbance of 'higher intensity', it can lead to a successive action of system elements and cascade propagation of disturbance throughout the system. Usually the tripping of major generators or load busses results in under-voltage or under-frequency protective devices operation. This disturbance scenario usually results in additional unbalance of system power. Moreover, power flow in transmission lines is being re-distributed which can lead to their tripping, further affecting the transmission network structure.

Frequency instability occurs when the system is unable to balance active power which results in frequency collapse. Monitoring *df/dt* (the rate-of-change of frequency) is an immediate indicator of unbalance of active power; however, the oscillatory nature of *df/dt* can lead to unreliable measuring (Madani et al., 2004, 2008).

Given its advantages over other techniques for signal processing, WT enables direct assessment of rate of change of a weighted average frequency (frequency of the centre of inertia), which represents a true indicator of active power unbalance of power system (Avdakovic et al. 2009, 2010, 2011). This approach is an excellent foundation for improving existing systems of under-frequency protection. Namely, synchronised phasor measurements technique provides real time information on conditions and values of key variables in the entire power system. Using synchronised measurements and WT enables high accuracy in assessing of active power unbalance of system and minimal under-frequency shedding, that is, operating of under-frequency protective devices. Furthermore, if a system is compact and we know the total system inertia, it becomes possible to estimate total unbalance of active power in the system using angle or frequency measuring in any system's part by directly assessing of rate of change of a weighted average frequency (frequency of the centre of inertia) using WT. In order to avoid bigger frequency drop and eventual frequency instability, identification of the frequency of the centre of inertia rate of change should be as quick and unbalance estimate as accurate as possible. Given the oscillatory nature of the frequency change following the disturbance, a quick and accurate estimate of medium value is not simple and depends on the system's characteristics, that is, total inertia of the system (Madani et al., 2004, 2008).

This chapter presents possibilities for application of Discrete Wavelet Transformation (DWT) in estimating of the frequency of the centre of inertia rate of change (*df/dt*). In physics terms, low frequency component of signal voltage angle or frequency is very close to the frequency of the centre of inertia rate of change and can be used in estimating *df/dt*, and therefore, can also be used to estimate total unbalance of active power in the system. DWT was used for signal frequency analysis and estimating *df/dt* value, and the results were compared with a common *df/dt* estimate technique, the Method of Least Squares.

2. Basic wavelet theory

Wavelet theory is a natural continuation of Fourier transformation and its modified short-term Fourier transformation. Over the years, wavelets have been being developed independently in different areas, for example, mathematics, quantum physics, electrical engineering and many other areas and the results can be seen in the increasing application in signal and image processing, turbulence modelling, fluid dynamics, earthquake predictions, etc. Over the last few years, WT has received significant attention in electric power sector since it is more suitable for analysis of different types of transient wavelets when compared to other transformations.

2.1 Development of wavelet theory

From a historical point of view, wavelet theory development has many origins. In 1822, Fourier (Jean-Baptiste Joseph) developed a theory known as Fourier analysis. The essence of this theory is that a complicated event can be comprehended through its simple constituents. More precisely, the idea is that a certain function can be represented as a sum of sine and cosine waves of different frequencies and amplitudes. It has been proved that every 2π periodic integrible function is a sum of Fourier series $a_0 + \sum_k (a_k \cos kx + b_k \sin kx)$, for corresponding coefficients a_k i b_k. Today, Fourier analysis is a compulsory course at every technical faculty. Although the contemporary meaning of the term 'wavelet' has been in use only since the 80s', the beginnings of the wavelet theory development go back to the year 1909 and Alfred Haar's dissertation in which he analysed the development of integrable functions in another orthonormal function system. Many papers were published during the 30s'; however, none provided a clear and coherent theory (Daubechies, 1996; Polikar, 1999).

First papers on wavelet theory are the result of research by French geophysicist and engineer, Jean Morlet, whose research focused on different layers of earth, and reflection of acoustic waves from the surface. Without much success, Morlet attempted to resolve the problem using localization technique put forward by Gabor in 1946. This forced him to 'make up' a wavelet. In 1984, Morlet and physicist Alex Grossmann proved stable decomposition and function reconstruction using wavelets coefficients. This is considered to be the first paper in wavelet theory (Teofanov, 2001; Jaffard, 2001).

Grosman made a hypothesis that Morlet's wavelets form a frame for Hilbert's space, and in 1986 this hypothesis was proved accurate by Belgian mathematician Ingrid Daubechies. In 1986, mathematician Ives Meyer construed continuously differentiable wavelet whose only disadvantage was that it did not have a compact support. At the same time, Stephane Mallat, who was dealing with signal processing and who introduced auxiliary function which in a certain way generates wavelet function system, defined the term 'multiresolution analysis' (MRA). Finally, the first stage in the wavelet theory development was concluded with Ingrid Daubechies' spectacular results in 1988 (Graps, 1995).

She created orthonormal wavelet bases of the space of square integrable functions which consists of compactly supported functions with prescribed degree of smoothness. Compact support means that the function is identically equal to zero outside a limited interval, and therefore, for example, corresponding inappropriate integrals come down to certain integrals. Daubechies wavelets reserved their place in special functions family. The most important consequence of wavelet theory development until 1990 was the establishment of a common mathematical language between different disciplines of applied and theoretical mathematics.

2.2 Wavelet Transform

Development of WT overcame one of the major disadvantages of Fourier transformation. Fourier series shows a signal through the sum of sines of different frequencies. Fourier transformation transfers the signal from time into frequency domain and it tells of which frequency components the signal is composed, that is, how frequency resolution is made. Unfortunately, it does not tell in what time period certain frequency component appears in the signal, that is, time resolution is lost. In short, Fourier transformation provides frequency but totally loses time resolution. This disadvantage does not affect stationary signals whose frequency characteristics do not change with time. However, the world around us mainly contains non-stationary signals, for whose analysis Fourier transformation is inapplicable. Attempts have been made to overcome this in that the signal was observed in segments, that is, time intervals short enough to observe non-stationary signal as being stationary. This idea led to the development of short-time Fourier transformation (STFT) in which the signal, prior to transformation, is limited to a time interval and multiplied with window function of limited duration. This limited signal is then transformed into frequency area. Then, the window function is translated on time axis for a certain amount (in the case of continued STFT, infinitesimal amount) and then Fourier transformation is applied (Daubechies, 1992; Vetterli & Kovacevic, 1995; Mallat, 1998; Mertins, 1999).

The process is repeated until the window function goes down the whole signal. It will result in illustration of signals in a time-frequency plane. It provides information about frequency components of which the signal is composed and time intervals in which these components appear. However, this illustration has a certain disadvantage whose cause is in Heisenberg's uncertainty principle which in this case can be stated as: '*We cannot know exactly which frequency component exists at any given time instant. The most we can know is the range of the frequency represented in a certain time interval, which is known as problem of resolution.*'

Generally speaking, resolution is related to the width of window function. The window does not localize the signal in time, so there is no information about the time in frequency area, that is, there is no time resolution. With STFT, the window is of definite duration, which localizes the signal in time, so it is possible to know which frequency components exist in which time interval in a time-frequency plane, that is, we get a certain time resolution. If the window is narrowed, we get even better time localisation of the signal, which improves time resolution; however, this makes frequency resolution worse, because of Heisenberg's principle.

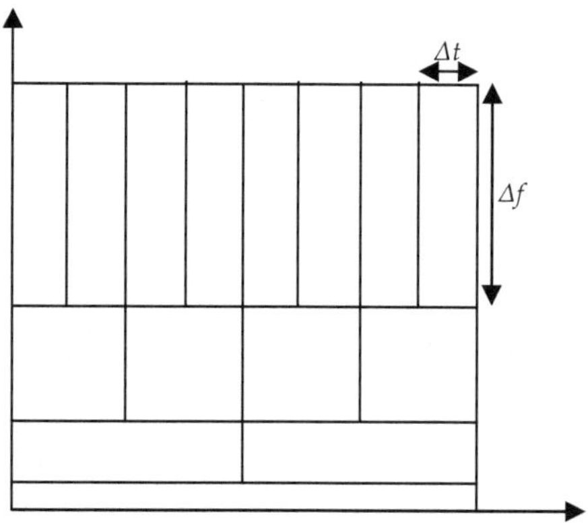

Fig. 2. Relation between time and frequency resolution with multiresolution analysis

Δt i Δf represents time and frequency range. These intervals are resolution: the shorter the intervals, the better the resolution. It should be pointed out that multiplication $\Delta t^*\Delta f$ is always constant for a certain window function. The disadvantage of time-limited Fourier transformation is that by choosing the window width, it defines the resolution as well, which is unchangeable, regardless of whether we observe the signal on low or high frequencies. However, many true signals contain lower frequency components during longer time period, which represent the signal's trend and higher frequency components which appear in short time intervals.

When analysing these signals, it would be beneficial to have a good frequency resolution in low frequencies, and good time resolution in high frequencies (for example, to localise high-frequency noise in the signal). The analysis which meets these requirements is called multiresolution analysis (MRA) and leads directly to WT. Figure 2 illustrates the idea of multiresolution analysis: with the increase of frequency Δt decreases, which improves time resolution, and Δf increases, that is, frequency resolution becomes worse. Heisenberg's principle can also be applied here: surfaces $\Delta t^*\Delta f$ are constant everywhere, only Δt and Δf values change.

WT is based on a rather complex mathematical foundations and it is impossible to describe all details in this chapter of the book. The following chapters will provide basic illustration of Continuous WT (CWT) and Discrete WT (DWT), which have become a standard research tool for engineers processing signals.

In 1946, D. Gabor was the first to define time-frequency functions, the so-called Gabor wavelets (2005/second reference should be Radunovic, 2005). His idea was that a wave, whose mathematical transcript is $\cos(\omega x+\varphi)$ should be divided into segments and should keep just one of them. This wavelet contains three information: start, end and frequency content. Wavelet is a function of wave nature with a compact support. It is called a wave because of its oscillatory nature, and it is small because of the final domain in which it is different from zero (compact support). Scaling and translations of the *mother wavelet* $\psi(x)$ (mother) define wavelet basis,

$$\psi_{a,b}(x)=\frac{1}{\sqrt{a}}\psi\left(\frac{x-b}{a}\right), \qquad a>0., \tag{1}$$

and it represents wave function of limited duration for which the following is applicable:

$$\int_{-\infty}^{\infty}\psi(x)dx=0. \tag{2}$$

The choice of scaling parameter a and translation b makes it possible to represent smaller fragments of complicated form with a higher time resolution (zooming sharp and short-term peaks), while smooth segments can be represented in a smaller resolution, which is wavelet's good trait (basis functions are time limited).

CWT is a tool to break down for mining of data, functions or operators into different components and then each component is analysed with a resolution which fits its scale. It is defined by a scale multiplication of function and wavelet basis:

$$CWT_{\psi}f(a,b)=\frac{1}{\sqrt{|a|}}\int_{-\infty}^{+\infty}f(x)\psi^{*}\left(\frac{x-b}{a}\right)dx \tag{3}$$

where asterix stands for conjugate complex value, a and b $(a,b\in R)$ are scaling parameters (He & Starzyk, 2006; Avdakovic et al. 2010, Omerhodzic et al. 2010).

CWT is function of scale a and position b and it shows how closely correlated are the wavelet and function in time interval which is defined by wavelet's support. WT measures the similarity of frequency content of function and wavelet basis $\psi_{a,b}(x)$ in time-frequency domain. In a=1 and b=0, $\psi(x)$ is called mother wavelet, a - scaling factor, b - translation factor. By choosing values $a>0, b\in R$, mother wavelet provides other wavelets which, when compared to the mother wavelet, are moved on time axis for value b and 'stretched' for scaling factor a (when a>1). Therefore, continued wavelet transformation of signal $f(x)$ is calculated so that the signal is multiplied with wavelet function for certain a and b, followed by integration. Then parameters a and b are infinitesimally increased and the process is repeated. As a result we get wavelet coefficients *CWT (a,b)* which represent the signal in time-scale plane. The value of certain wavelet coefficient *CWT (a,b)* points to the similarity between the observed signal and wavelet generated by shifting on time axis and scaling for values b and a. It can be said that wavelet transformation shows signal as infinite sum of scaled and shifted wavelets, in which wavelet coefficients are weight factors. Using wavelets, time analysis is done by compressed, high-frequency versions of mother wavelet, since it is possible to notice fast changing details on a small scale.

Frequency analysis is done by stretched high-frequency versions of the same wavelet, because a large scale is sufficient for monitoring slower changes. These traits make wavelets an ideal tool for analysis of non-stationary functions. WT provides excellent time resolution of high-frequency components and frequency (scale) resolution of low-frequency components.

CWT is a reversible process when the following condition (admissibility) is met:

$$C_{\psi} = \int_{-\infty}^{\infty} \frac{\left|\Psi(\omega)\right|^2}{\omega} d\omega < \infty \tag{4}$$

where $\Psi(\omega)$ is Fourier transformation of basis function $\psi(x)$. Inverse wavelet transformation is defined by:

$$f(x) = \frac{1}{C_{\psi}} \int_{-\infty}^{\infty} \int_{-\infty}^{\infty} CWT_f(a,b)\psi_{a,b}(x)\frac{da\, db}{a^2} \tag{5}$$

where it is possible to reconstruct the observed signal through CWT coefficient.

CWT is of no major practical use, because correlation of function and continually scaling wavelet is calculated (a and b are continued values). Many of the calculated coefficients are redundant and their number is infinite. This is why there is discretization – time-scale plane is covered by grid and CWT is calculated in nodes of grid. Fast algorithms are construed using discrete wavelets. Discrete wavelets are usually a segment by segment of uninterrupted function which cannot be continually scaled and translated, but merely in discrete steps,

$$\psi_{j,k}(x) = \frac{1}{\sqrt{a_0^j}} \psi\left(\frac{x - kb_0 a_0^j}{a_0^j}\right), \tag{6}$$

where j, k are whole numbers, and $a_0 > 1$ is fixed scaling step. It is usual that $a_0 = 2$, so that the division on frequency axis is dyadic scale. $b_0 = 1$ is usually translation factor, so the division on time axis on a chosen scale is equal,

$$\psi_{j,k}(x) = 2^{-j/2}\psi\left(2^{-j}x - k\right), \text{ i } \psi_{j,k}(x) \neq 0 \text{ } za \text{ } x \in \left[2^j k, 2^j (k+1)\right].$$

Parameter a is duplicated in every level compared to its value at the previous level, which means that wavelet doubles in its width. The number of points in which wavelets are defined are half the size compared to the previous level, that is, resolution becomes smaller. This is how the concept of *multiresolution* is realised. Narrow, densely distributed wavelets are used to describe rapid changing segments of signal, while stretched, sparsely distributed wavelets are used to describe slow changing segments of signal (Mei et al., 2006).

DWT is the most widely used wavelet transformation. It is a recursive filtrating process of input data set with lowpass and highpass filters. Approximations are low-frequency components in large scales, and details are high-frequency function components in small scales. Wavelet function transformation can be interpreted as function passing through the filters bank. Outputs are scaling coefficients $a_{j,k}$ (approximation) and wavelet coefficients $b_{j,k}$ (details). Signal analysis which is done by signal passing through the filters bank is an old idea known as *subband coding*. DTW uses two digital filters: lowpass filter $h(n), n \in Z$, defined by scaling function $\varphi(x)$ and highpass filter $g(n), n \in Z$, defined by wavelet function $\psi(x)$. Filters *h(n) and g(n)* are associated with the scaling function and wavelet function, respectively (He & Starzyk, 2006):

$$\varphi(x) = \sum_{n} h(n)\sqrt{2}\varphi(2x-n) \tag{7}$$

$$\psi(x) = \sum_{n} g(n)\sqrt{2}\varphi(2x-n), \tag{8}$$

and equals to: $\sum_{n} h(n)^2 = 1$ and $\sum_{n} g(n)^2 = 1$, and $\sum_{n} h(n) = \sqrt{2}$ and $\sum_{n} g(n) = 0$.

It is possible to reconstruct any input signal on the basis of output signals if filters are observed in pairs. High frequency filter is associated to low frequency filter and they become Quadrature Mirror Filters (QMF). They serve as a mirror reflection to each other.

DWT is an algorithm used to define wavelet coefficients and scale functions in dyadic scales and dyadic points. The first step in filtering process is splitting approximation and discrete signal details so to get two signals. Both signals have the length of an original signal, so we get double amount of data. The length of output signals is split in half using compression, that is, discarding all other data. The approximation received serves as input signal in the following step. Digital signal *f(n)*, of frequency range 0-$F_s/2$, (F_s – sampling frequency), passes through lowpass *h(n)* and highpass *g(n)* filter. Each filter lets by just one half of the frequency range of the original signal. Filtrated signals are then subsampled so to remove any other sample. We mark $cA_1(k)$ and $cD_1(k)$ as outputs from *h(n)* and *g(n)* filter, respectively. Filtrating process and subsampling of input signal can be represented as:

$$cA_1(k) = \sum_{n} f(n)h(2k-n) \tag{8}$$

$$cD_1(k) = \sum_{n} f(n)g(2k-n) \tag{9}$$

where coefficients $cA_1(k)$ are called approximation of the first level of decomposition and represent input signal in frequency range 0-$F_s/4$ Hz. By analogy, $cD_1(k)$ are coefficients of details and represents signal in range $F_s/4$ - $F_s/2$ Hz. Decomposition continues so that approximation coefficients $cA_1(k)$ are passed through filters *g(n)* and *h(n)* that is, they are split to coefficients $cA_2(k)$ which represent signal in range 0- $F_s/8$ Hz and $cD_2(k)$, range

$F_s/8$ - $F_s/4$ Hz. Since the algorithm is continued, that is, since it goes towards lower frequencies, the number of samples decreases which worsens time resolution, because fewer number of samples stand for the whole signal for a certain frequency range. However, frequency resolution improves, because frequency ranges for which the signal is observed are getting narrower.

Therefore, multiresolution principle is applicable here. Generally speaking, wavelet coefficients of j level can be represented through approximation coefficients of j-1 level as follows:

$$cA_j(k) = \sum_n h(2k-n)cA_{j-1}(n) \tag{10}$$

$$cD_j(k) = \sum_n g(2k-n)cA_{j-1}(n) \tag{11}$$

The result of the algorithm on signals sampled by frequency F_s will be the matrix of wavelet coefficients. At every level, filtrating and compression will lead to frequency layer being cut in half (subsequently, frequency resolution doubles) and reducing the number of sampling in half.

Eventually, if the original signal has the length 2^m, DWT mostly has m steps, so at the end we get approximation as the signal with length one. Figure 3 illustrates three levels of decomposition.

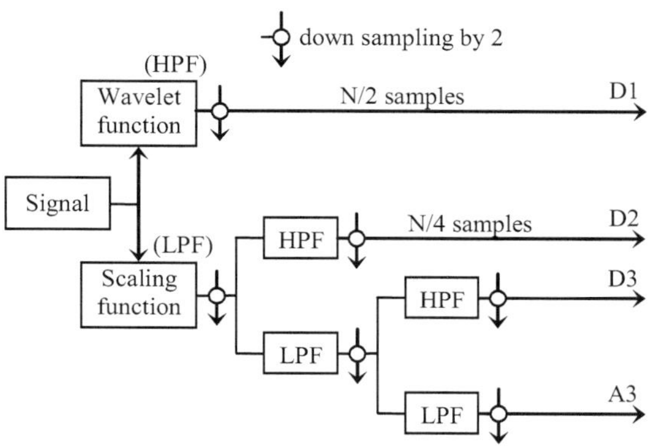

Fig. 3. Wavelet MRA (Avdakovic et al., 2010)

We get DWT of original signal by connecting all coefficients starting from the last level of decomposition, and it represents the vector made of output signals $\left[A_j, D_j, \ldots, D_1\right]$. Assembling components, in order to get the original signal without losing information, is known as reconstruction or synthesis. Mathematical operations for synthesis are called *inverse discrete wavelet transformation* (IDTW). Wavelet analysis includes filtering and compression, and reconstruction process includes decompression and filtering.

3. Frequency stability of power system – An estimation of active power unbalance

Stability of power system refers to its ability to maintain synchronous operation of all connected synchronous generators in stationary state and for the defined initial state after disturbances occur, so that the change of the variables of state in transitional process is limited, and system structure preserved. The system should be restored to initial stationary state unless topology changes take place, that is, if there are topological changes to the system, a new stationary state should be invoked. Although the stability of power system is its unique trait, different forms of instability are easier to comprehend and analysed if stability problems are classified, that is, if "partial" stability classes are defined. Partial stability classes are usually defined for fundamental state parameters: transmission angle, voltage and frequency. Figure 4. shows classification of stability according to (IEEE/CIGRE, 2004). Detailed description of physicality of dynamics and system stability, mathematical models and techniques to resolve equations of state and stability aspect analysis can be found in many books and papers.

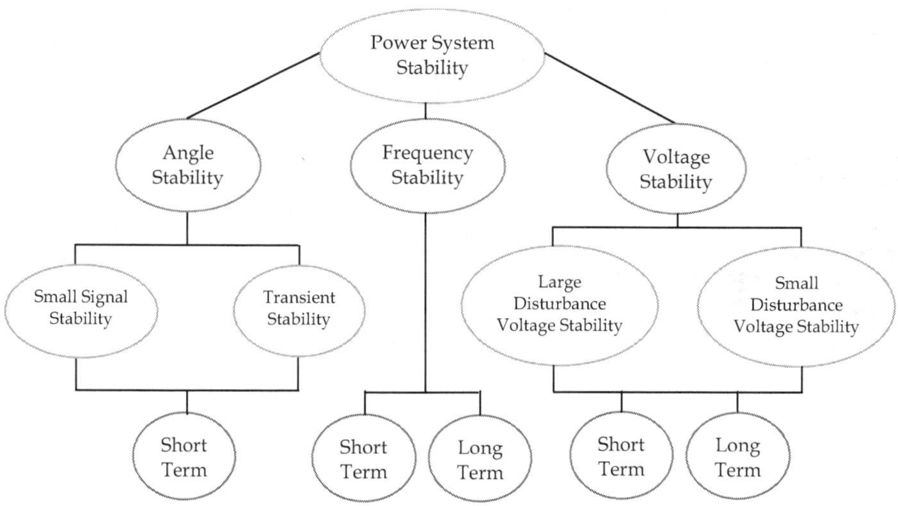

Fig. 4. Classification of „partial" stability of electric power system

Frequency stability is defined as the ability of power system to maintain frequency within standardized limits. Frequency instability occurs in cases when electric power system cannot permanently maintain the balance of active powers in the system, which leads to frequency collapse. In cases of high intensity disturbances or successive interrelated and mutually caused (connected) disturbances, there can be cascading deterioration of frequency stability, which, in the worst case scenario, leads to disjunction of power system to subsystems and eventual total collapse of function of isolated parts of electric power system formed in this way.

In a normal regime, all connected synchronous generators in power system generate voltage of the same (nominal) frequency and the balance of active power is maintained. Then all voltage nods in network have a frequency of nominal value. When the system experiences permanent unbalance of active power (usually due to the breakdown of generator or load bus), power balance is impaired. Generators with less mechanic then electric power due to unbalance redistribution start slowing down. Because inertia of certain generators vary, as well as redistribution of unbalance ratio, generators start operating at different speeds and generate voltage of different frequencies. After transient process, we can assume that the system has a unique frequency again - frequency of the centre of inertia.

During long-term dynamic processes, there is a redistribution of power between generators, and subsequently redistribution of power in transmission lines, which can lead to overload of these elements. In case of the overload of elements over a longer period of time, there are overload protective device which tripping overloaded elements. This leads to cascading deterioration of system stability, and in critical cases (if interconnecting line is tripping), disjunction of system to unconnected elements - islands. In general, this scenario of disturbance propagation causes major problems in systems which have large active power unbalance and small system inertia. Usually, when these critical situations take place, under-frequency protection tripping the generators, additionally worsening the system. In border-line cases, this cascading event can lead to frequency instability, and complete collapse of system function.

3.1 Power system response to active power unbalance

In order to understand the essence of dynamic response of power system, one must be familiar with the physicality of the process, that is, one must do the quality analysis of dynamic response. An example of quality analysis of dynamic response of a coherent group of the effect of a sudden application at $t=0$ of a small load change $P_{k\Delta}$ at node k is analyzed in (Anderson & Fouad, 2002). The analysis was carried out on a linear model of system response to a forced (small) disturbance of active power balance. Although it is an approximatization, the analysis helps understand physicality of the process of dynamic response of power system to active power unbalance . This chapter provides main conclusions of the aforementioned analysis.

Distribution of the forced power unbalance $P_{k\Delta}$ (0^+) between generators during system response is done in accordance with different criteria. When the synchronous operation of generators is maintained (stability of synchronous group is maintained), a new stationary state is established in the system after transient process, namely, new power balance. If criteria for disturbance distribution differ for generators (which is mostly the case), transient process has an oscillatory-muted character. Oscillations of the parameters of state, mostly active power, angles and frequency of generators, reflect transition between certain criteria for unbalance distribution. Generally, three quality criteria for unbalance distribution can be distinguished:

Immediately before unbalance (in $t=0^+$) power balance in the system is maintained on the basis of accumulated electromagnetic energy of generators. Distribution of balance between generators is done according to the criteria of electric distance from the point of unbalance (load at node k). Certain generators take over a part of unbalance $P_{k\Delta}$ (0+) depending on coefficients of their synchronizing powers[1] $P_{Sik}(t)$. Therefore, generators closer to the load bus k (those with lower initial transmission angles and bigger transmission susceptanse) take over a bigger part of unbalance $P_{i\Delta}$(t). Due to a sudden change in power balance, certain generators start to decelerate (Anderson & Fouad, 2002). The change of generators' angle frequency i is defined by a differential equation governing the motion of machine by the swing equation:

$$\frac{2H_i}{\omega_0}\frac{d\omega_{i\Delta}}{dt} + P_{i\Delta} = 0 \tag{12}$$

If unbalance $P_{i\Delta}$ (t) is expressed in the function of total unbalance , then according to (Anderson & Fouad, 2002) the aforementioned equation becomes:

$$\frac{1}{\omega_0}\frac{d\omega_{i\Delta}}{dt} = -\frac{P_{Sik}}{2H_i}\frac{P_{k\Delta}(0^+)}{\sum_{j=1}^{n} P_{Sjk}} \tag{13}$$

Equation (13) provides first criterion for distribution of active power unbalance : *Initial slowing down of generators depends on a.) relative relation of coefficient of synchronising power* $P_{Sik}(t)$ *and total synchronising system power and b.) inertia constant of generator's rotor* H_i.

It is clear that some generators will have different initial slowdowns. Therefore, in transient process, frequencies of different generators vary. Synchronizing powers maintain generators in synchronous operation and if transient stability is maintained, oscillations of frequency and active power for a coherent group of generators have a muted character. When the system retains synchronised operation, it is possible to define system's retarding in general, that is, to define a medium value of frequency of a group of generators. To produce an equation to describe the change of medium frequency, we introduce the term „centre of inertia ". The angle of inertia centre $\overline{\delta}$ and angular frequency $\overline{\omega}$ is defined as follows:

$$\overline{\delta} = \frac{\sum_{i=1}^{n} H_i \delta_i}{\sum_{i=1}^{n} H_i}, \quad \overline{\omega} = \frac{\sum_{i=1}^{n} H_i \omega_i}{\sum_{i=1}^{n} H_i} \tag{14}$$

The equation describing the moving of inertia centre according to (Anderson & Fouad, 2002) is as follows:

[1] Synchronising power of a multi-machine system is defined by: $P_{s_{ij}} = \left.\frac{\partial P_{ij}}{\partial \delta_{ij}}\right|_{\delta_{ij0}} = E_i E_j \left(B_{ij}\cos\delta_{ij0} + G_{ij}\sin\delta_{ij0}\right)$, and it shows the dependance of the change of electric power of i machine with the change of of the difference in angles i and j, provided that the angles of other machines are fixed.

$$\frac{1}{\omega_0}\frac{d\overline{\omega}_\Delta}{dt} = \frac{-P_{k\Delta}(0^+)}{\sum_{i=1}^{n} 2H_i} \tag{15}$$

This equation points out an important trait of power system: *Although some generators retarding at different rates ($d\omega_{i\Delta}/dt$), which change during transient process, the system as a whole retarding at the constant rate* $\left(d\overline{\omega}_\Delta / dt\right)$.

Frequencies of some generators approach the frequency of inertia centre because synchronizing powers in a stable response mute oscillations. After a relatively short time ($t=t_1$), of few seconds, all generators adjust to the frequency of inertia centre, that is, the system has a unique frequency. Distribution of unbalance $P_{k\Delta}(0^+)$ at moment t_1 between generators is defined per criterion (Anderson & Fouad, 2002), which is as follows:

$$P_{i\Delta}(t_1) = \frac{H_i}{\sum_{j=1}^{n} H_j} P_{k\Delta}(0^+) \tag{16}$$

This equation provides second criterion for unbalance distribution: After lapse of time t_1 since the unbalance occurred, the total value of unbalance $P_{k\Delta}(0^+)$ is distributed between generators depending on their relative inertia in relation to the total inertia of a coherent group of generators. Therefore, unbalance distribution according to this criterion does not depend on electric distance of the generator from the point at which the unbalance occurred..

Finally, if the generators' speed regulators are activated, they lead to the change in mechanical power of generator and redistribution of unbalance depending on statistic coefficients of speed regulators. After a certain period of time, an order of ten seconds ($t=t_2$), the system establishes a new stationary state. Frequency in the new stationary state depends on total regulative system constante[2]. This leads to a third criterion for unbalance distribution: *After lapse of time t_2 since the unbalance occurred, the total value of unbalance $P_{k\Delta}(0^+)$ is distributed between generators depending on their constant of statism of speed regulators.*

The previous analysis, although it does not take into account the effects of load characteristics on the amount of power unbalance , credibly illustrates quality processes in power systems with active power unbalance .

3.2 An estimation of active power unbalance – Computer simulation testing

Algorhytam for identification and estimation of unbalance in electric power system presented in Refs. (Avdakovic et all, 2009, 2010) assumes availability of WAMS. Today, these systems are in force in many electric power systems worldwide, and one of their main

---

[2] Relation between arbitraty power change ΔP and its corresponding frequency change Δf, defined as K= $\Delta P/\Delta f$ [MWs] is called regulative energy or regulative constant.

functions is to identify current and potential problems in power system operation in relation to the system's safety and support to operators in control centres when making decisions to prevent disturbance propagations. Phasor Measurement Unit technology (PMU) enabled full implementation of these systems and measurement of dynamic states in wider area. Current control and running of power system is based upon local measurement of statistic values of system parameters of power system (voltage, power, frequency ...). WAMS are based on embedded devices for measuring phasor voltage and current electricity at those points in power system which are of particular importance, that is measuring amplitudes and angles in real time using PMUs. Such implemented platform enables realistic dynamic view of electric power system, more accurate measurement, rapid data exchange and implementation of algorithms which enable coordination and timely alert in case of instability.

Depending on the nature of active power unbalance, the system disturbance can be temporary (short circuit at the transmission line with successful reclosure) or permanent (tripping generators or consumers). Disturbances with permanent power unbalance are of a particular interest. As shown earlier, dominant variables of state which define power system response to a permanent active power unbalance are the change of frequency and generator's active power. Less dominant variables, but not to be ignored, are voltage and reactive power.

In short, algorithm for on-line identification of active power unbalance can be described as:

Analysis of the response of change of generator's frequency $\omega_i(t)$ during the period of first oscillation makes it possible to define transient stability. If transient stability is maintained, then the application of DWT (using low-frequency component of signal) makes it possible to estimate with high precision the change of the frequency of inertia centre. Furthermore, provided that the values of inertia of all generators are known as well as system inertia as a whole, it is possible to define the total forced unbalance $P_{k\Delta}(0^+)$.

To illustrate estimate of active power unbalance in power system, WSCC 9-bus test system has been chosen (Figure 5.). Additional data on this test system can be found in (Anderson & Fouad, 2002). The following example has been analysed in details in (Anderson & Fouad, 2002).

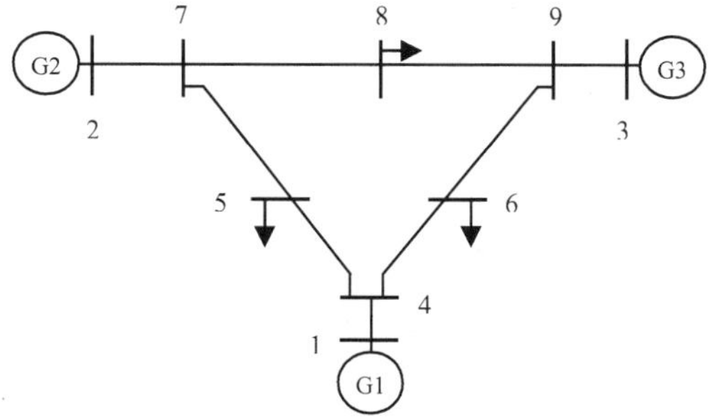

Fig. 5. WSCC 9-bus test system

Connection of nominal 10 MW (0.1 pu) of active power to bus 8 as three phase short circuit circuit with active resistance 10 p.u. is simulated. The change of angle speed or frequency of some generators and centre of inertia (COI) after simulated disturbance are shown in Figure 6. and the show oscillations of machines after the disturbance and slow decrease of frequency in the system. It can be seen that some generators slow down by oscillating around medium frequency of the centre of inertia. The slow down around 0.09 Hz/s is presented as direction (ω_{COI}).

Specialised literature provides many techniques to estimate frequency and the level of frequency change, that is, *df/dt*. One of the methods used with estimating *df/dt* is the Method of Least Squares. It represents one of the most important and most widely used methods for data analysis. Mathematical details which elaborate this method can be found in a number of books and papers.

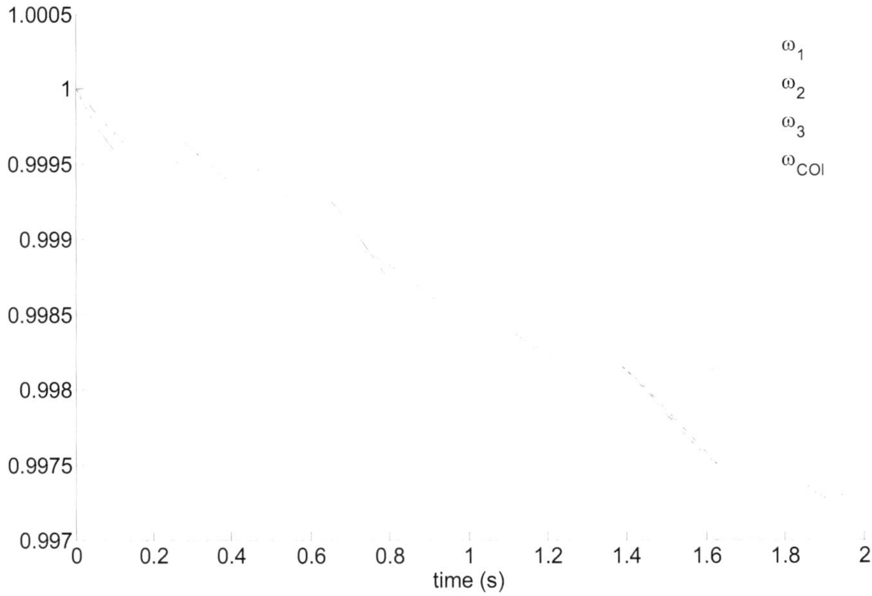

Fig. 6. Speed deviation following application of a 10 MW resistive load at bus 8 (Avdakovic et al., 2011)

Here, the estimation of *df/dt* was done in Matlab using polyfit and polyval functions. Figure 7 shows calculated value of polynomial at given points (yp), using values of angle frequency ω_1 from Figure 6 and polynomials of third degree. The estimate of *df/dt*, that is, *dω/dt* for signals ω_i (i=1,2,3), are provided in Table 2.

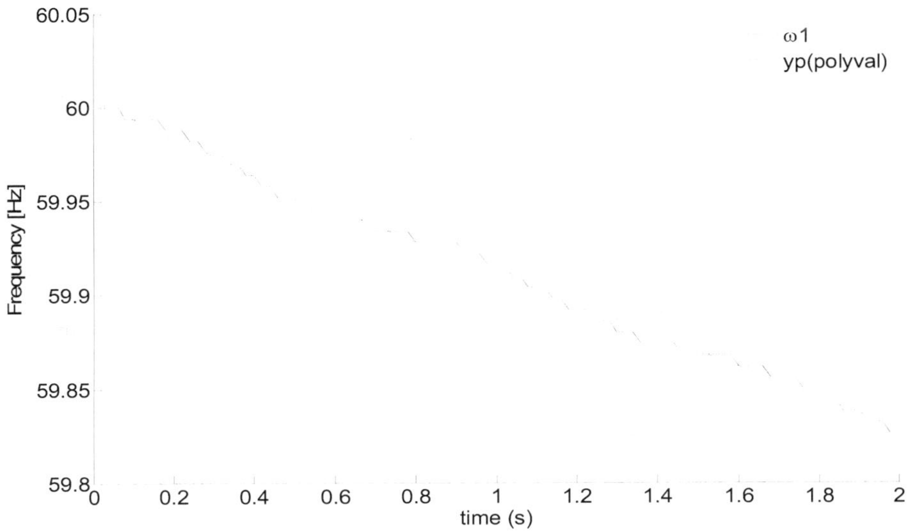

Fig. 7. Curve fitting

The estimate of values *df/dt*, that is, values *dω/dt* for signals ω_i (i=1,2,3) with the DWT application will be provided later on. Frequency range $[F_m/2 : F_m]$ of every level of decomposition of DWT is in direct relation with signal sampling frequency, and is presented as $F_m = F_s/2^{l+1}$, where F_s present sampling frequency and l present the level of decomposition.

The sampling time of 0.02 sec or sampling frequency of analysed signals of 50 Hz were used in order to present this method and simulations,. Based on Nyquist theorem, the highest frequency a signal can have is $F_s/2$ or 25 Hz. Example of the fifth level of ω_1 signal decomposition from Figure 6, using Db4 wavelet function, is given in Figure 8, while frequency range of analysed signals at different levels of decomposition is given in Table 2.

D1	[25.0 – 12.50 Hz]
D2	[12.5 – 6.250 Hz]
D3	[6.25 – 3.120 Hz]
D4	[3.12 – 1.560 Hz]
D5	[1.56 – 0.780 Hz]
A5	[0.00 – 0.780 Hz]

Table 2. Frequency range of analysed signals

Decomposition of signals ω_2 i ω_3 from Figure 6 was done in the same manner. A5 low frequency components of all three signals and centre of inertia are illustrated in Figure 9. It can be seen that the low frequency components of analysed signals are very similar to the calculated value of the centre of inertia, and therefore, suitable for defining values *df/dt*, or in this case, the analysed *dω/dt*. Estimate is given in Table 3. As can be seen, both methods provide rather good results, and estimated values are very similar to the calculated vales.

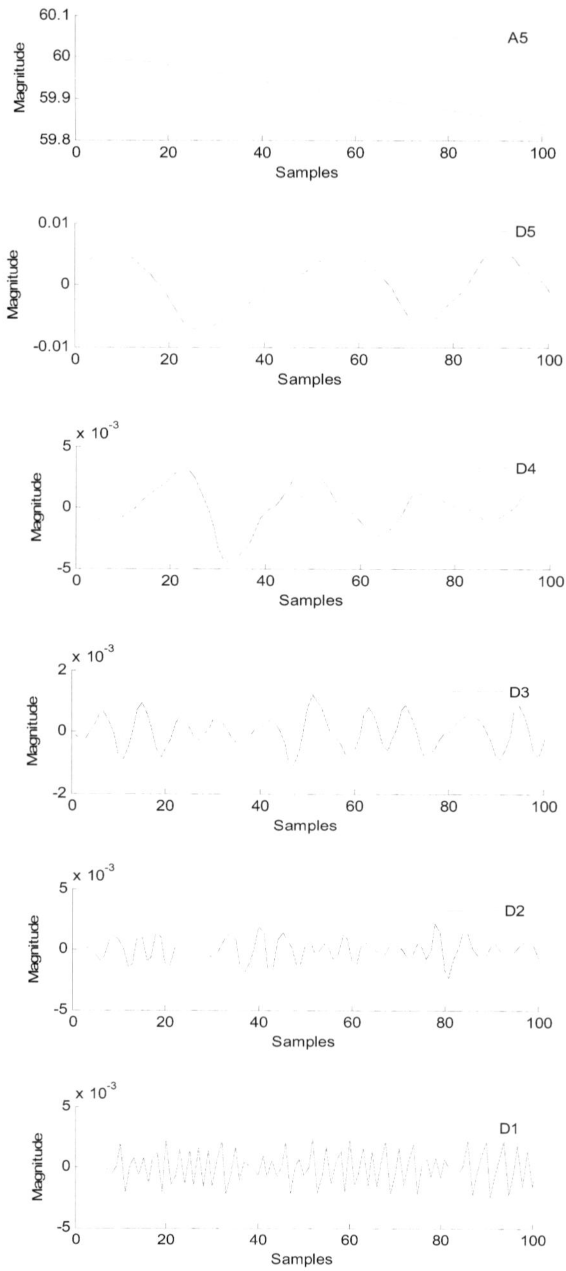

Fig. 8. MRA analysis signal of angular speed ω_1

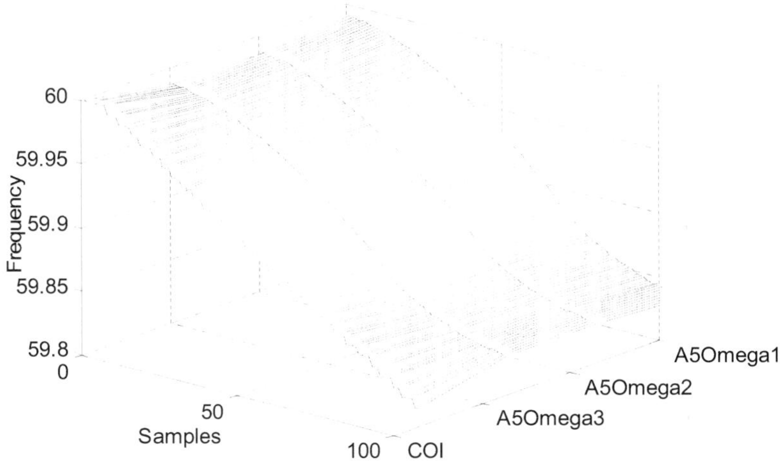

Fig. 9. COI and low frequency (A5) component of signals angular speed ω_1, ω_2 and ω_3

	MLS [Hz/s]	DWT [Hz/s]
$d\omega_1/dt$	-0.0888	-0.0801
$d\omega_2/dt$	-0.0799	-0.0756
$d\omega_3/dt$	-0.0787	-0.0764

Table 3. Comparison of estimates of *df/dt*, and *dω/dt* using the Method of Least Squares and DWT

Inertia of generators for WSCC 9 bus system is H_1=23,64 (sec), H_2=6,4 (sec) and H_3=3,01 (sec), so base on the on the basis of (12), it is easy to determine distribution of unbalance of active power in the system per a generator, and subsequently, the total unbalance of active power in the observed system.

The aforementioned analysed example demonstrates the procedure for estimating *df/dt* value using DWT. It is possible to define (simulate) the value of forced unbalance of active power in more complex power systems in the exact same way. An example of a more detailed analysis and application of this methodology is provided in Ref. (Avdakovic et al., 2010), while simulations and analyses were done on New England 39 bus system. When analysing more complex power systems, the frequency range of low frequency electromechanic occurrences/oscillations is in the range of 5 Hz, so it is a matter of practicality to choose sampling time of 0,1 sec or 10 Hz. With further multiresolution analysis in this chosen frequency range and the availability of WAMS, it becomes possible to obtain some very important information for monitoring and control of power system. This is mostly information related to the very start of some dynamic occurrence in the power system which we obtain from the first level of decomposition of analysed signals. Since electric power systems are mostly widespread across huge geographic area, it is necessary to have information on the location of initial disturbance in the power system, which is easily obtained from DWT signal filters with the frequency range of 1 - 2 Hz. Frequency range of 1 - 2 Hz is the space of local oscillations in power system and by a simple comparison of power values of signals in this frequency range, analysed from multiple geographically distant locations , it is easy to establish the location of disturbance. From the power point of view, power values of local oscillations of signals measured/simulated closer to the disturbance will have higher energy power values compared to those distant from the location of disturbance. Furthermore, as we proceed to the higher levels of decomposition (or lower frequency ranges of filters) of chosen signals with sampling frequency of 0.1 sec, we enter the intra-area and inter-area of oscillations which can represent a real danger for electric power system, and should it be that they are not muted, can lead in a black-out. These signals make it possible to identify intra-area and inter-area oscillations, their character and how to mute them. Furthermore, by comparing these signals it is possible to obtain more information on the system's operation as a whole after disturbance (Avdakovic & Nuhanovic, 2009). In line with what has been demonstrated in the example, low frequency component of signal angle or frequency serves to estimate values *df/dt,* that is, to define total forced unbalance of active power in power system.

4. Conclusion

Power system is a complex dynamic system exposed to constant disturbances of varying intensity. Most of these disturbances are common operator's activities, for example, swich turning on or off system elements, and such disturbances do not have a major influence on the system. However, some disturbances can cause major problems in the system, and the subsequent development of events and cascading tripping of system elements can lead to a system's collapse. One of the most severe disturbances is the outage/failure of one or more major production units, resulting in unbalance of active power in the system, that is, frequency decrease. Many factors influence whether or not the severity of frequency decrease will trigger under-frequency protection. Today, under-frequency protection is based on local measurements of state variables and provides only limited results. Their operation is frequently unselective and affects the whole system.

This chapter illustrated the estimate of unbalance of active power in the power system with DTW application, provided WAMS is available. Estimate of *df/dt* value is a genuine indicator of active power unbalance, and given the oscillatory nature of signal frequency, its estimate is rather difficult. Taking into account its advantages in signal processing when compared to other techniques, WT enables direct estimate of medium value of the change of frequency of the centre of inertia, providing a complete picture about the system's operation as a whole. In this way, and provided with the complete inertia of the system, we obtain very important information about a complete unbalance of active power in the system, in a rather simple manner. In addition to this particularly important piece of information obtained from the low-frequency component of the signal angle or frequency, other levels of signal decomposition in frequency range encompassing low-frequency electromechanic oscillations provide information about the onset of some dynamic occurrence in the system, localize system disturbance, identify and define the character of intra-area and inter-area oscillations and provide insight into the system's operation after the disturbance. All of this points to a possible development of such under-frequency protective measures which will operate locally, that is, whose operation will be at (or in the vicinity of) the disturbance, in order to reduce the effect of disturbance, and adjust the operation of effective measures to identified unbalance of active power.

5. References

Anderson, P. M. & Fouad, A. A. (2002) *Power System Control and Stability, 2nd Edition*, Wiley-IEEE Press, ISBN 0471238627/0-471-23862-7, 2002.

Avdakovic, S. Music, M. Nuhanovic, A. & Kusljugic, M. (2009). An Identification of Active Power Imbalance Using Wavelet Transform, *Proceedings of The Ninth IASTED European Conference on Power and Energy Systems*, Palma de Mallorca, Spain, September 7-9, paper ID 681-019, 2009

Avdakovic, S. Nuhanovic, A. Kusljugic, M. & Music, M. (2010). Wavelet transform applications in power system dynamics. *Electric Power Systems Research, Elsevier*, doi: 10.1016/j.epsr.2010.11.031

Avdakovic, S. Nuhanovic, A. & Kusljugic, M. (2011). An Estimation Rate of Change of Frequency using Wavelet Transform. *International Review of Automatic Control (Theory and Applications)*, Vol. 4, No. 2, pp. 267-272, March 2011.

Daubechies, I. (1992). *Ten Lectures on Wavelets*, Society for Industrial and Applied Mathematics, ISBN 0-89871-274-2, Philadelphia, USA

Daubechies, I. (1996). Where do wavelets come from? A personal point of view. *Proceedings of the IEEE*, Vol. 84, No. 4, pp. 510 - 513, ISSN 0018-9219

Graps, A. (1995). An introduction to wavelets. *IEEE Computational Science & Engineering*, Vol. 2, No. 2, (Summer 1995), pp. 50-61, ISSN 1070-9924

He, H. & Starzyk, J.A. (2006). A Self-Organizing Learning Array System for Power Quality Classification Based on Wavelet Transform. *IEEE Transaction On Power Delivery*, Vol. 21, No. 1, pp. 286-295, ISSN 0885-8977

Henschel, S. (1999). *Analyses of Electromagnetic and Electromechanical Power System Transients With Dynamic Phasors*, PhD Dissertation, The University of British Columbia, Vancouver, Canada

IEEE/CIGRE Joint Task Force on Stability Terms and Definitions, (2004). Definition and Classification of Power System Stability. *IEEE Transaction on Power Systems*, Vol. 19, No. 3, pp. 1387-1399, ISSN 0885-8950

Jaffard S., Meyer Y., Ryan R. D. (2001). *Wavelets - Tools for Science and Technology*, SIAM, Philadeplhia, USA

Kundur, P. (1994) *Power System Stability and Control*, McGraw-Hill, Inc. ISBN 0-07-035958-X, New York, USA

Machowski, J. Bialek, J. W. & Bumby, J. R. (1997). *Power System Dynamics and Stability*, John Wiley & Sons, ISBN 0 471 97174 X, Chichester, England

Madani, V., Novosel, D. Apostolov, A. & Corsi, S. (2004). Innovative Solutions for Preventing Wide Area Cascading Propagation, *Proceedings of Bulk Power System Dynamics and Control -VI*, pp. 729-750, Cortina diAmpezzo, Italy, Aug 22-27, 2004

Madani, V. Novosel, D. & King. R. (2008). Technological Breakthroughs in System Integrity Protection Schemes, *Proceedings of 16th Power Systems Computation Conference*, Glasgow, Scotland, July 14-18, 2008

Mallat, S. (1998). *A Wavelet Tour of Signal Processing*, Academic Press, Inc., ISBN 0-12-466606-X, San Diego, CA, USA

Mei, K. Rovnyak, S. M. & Ong, C-M. (2006). Dynamic Event Detection Using Wavelet Analysis, *Proceedings of IEEE PES General Meeting,* pp. 1-7, ISBN 1-4244-0493-2, Montreal, Canada, June 18-22, 2006

Mertins, A. (1999). *Signal analysis: Wavelets, Filter Banks, Time-Frequency, Transforms and Applications,* John Wiley&Sons Ltd, ISBN 0471986267, New York, USA

Novosel, D. Madani, V. Bhargava, B. Khoi, V. & Cole, J. (2007). Dawn of the grid synchronization, *IEEE Power and Energy Magazine,* Vol. 6, No. 1, pp. 49 - 60 (December 2007), ISSN 1540-7977

Omerhodzic, I. Avdakovic, S. Nuhanovic, A. & Dizdarevic K. (2010). Energy Distribution of EEG Signals: EEG Signal Wavelet-Neural Network Classifier. *International Journal of Biological and Life Sciences,* Vol. 6, No. 4, pp. 210-215, 2010

Pal, B. & Chaudhuri, B. (2005). *Robust Control in Power Systems,* Springer, ISBN 0-387-25949-X, New York, USA

Phadke, A.G. & Thorp, J.S. (2008). *Synchronized Phasor Measurements and Their Applications,* Springer, ISBN 978-0-387-76535-8, New York, USA

Polikar, R. (1999). The Story of Wavelets. *Proceedings of The* IMACS/IEEE CSCC'99, Athens, Greece, July, pp. 5481-5486, 1999

Radunovic, D. (2005). *Talasići,* Akademska misao, ISBN 86-7466-190-4, Beograd, Srbija

Teofanov, N. (2001). Wavelets - a sentimental history, manuscript of the lecture given on 22. XI 2001. , Department of mathematics and informatics, Novi Sad, Serbia

Vetterli, M. & Kovacevic, J. (1995). *Wavelets and subband coding,* Prentice-Hall, Inc., ISBN 0-13-097080-8, New York, USA

9

Application of Wavelet Transform and Artificial Neural Network to Extract Power Quality Information from Voltage Oscillographic Signals in Electric Power Systems

R. N. M. Machado[1], U. H. Bezerra[2],
M. E. L Tostes[2], S. C. F. Freire[1] and L. A. Meneses[1]
[1]Federal Institute of Technological Education, Belém, Pará
[2]Federal University of Pará, Belém, Pará
Brazil

1. Introduction

Post-operation contingencies analysis in electrical power systems is of fundamental importance for the system secure operation, and also to maintain the quality of the electrical energy supplied to consumers. The electrical utilities use equipments as Digital Disturbance Registers (DDR), and Intelligent Electronics Devices (IED) for faults monitoring, and diagnosis about the electrical power systems operation and protection. In general, the DDR and IED are intended to monitor the protection system performance and detect failures in equipments and transmission lines, and also generate analog and digital oscillographic registers that better characterize the disturbing events.

The oscillographic signals often analyzed in the post-operation centers are those generated by events that typically cause the opening of transmission lines due to the action of protective relays. So, these records are analyzed in detail to determine the causes and consequences of these occurrences within the electrical system. Although the software used in the post-operation centers presents numerous features for the evaluation of the recorded signals, the selection of the signals to be analyzed is done in a manual way, which leads to an analysis in an individual basis, and many of the oscillographic records that could help analyzing the occurrences are not evaluated due to the long time that would be spent to select them manually.

Another aspect to be noted is that the oscillographic records remain stored in the post-operation centers for time periods ranging from months to years. These records contain signals acquired in different parts of the electrical system, and the vast majority of them are no longer being considered in the analysis. These data, however, may contain important information about the behavior and performance of the electrical system that may precisely characterize the power quality problem due to a failure or disturbance.

One of the main difficulties in using measurements, obtained by DDR, in the evaluation of power quality as compared with those obtained by power quality monitors, is that many of the signal processing stages are not performed automatically by the first. For the oscillographic records to be useful as power quality indicators, it is first necessary to obtain certain parameters to classify the recorded signals according to the event type that has occurred. Considering the case of short duration voltage variations (SDVV), the parameters of interest are the event amplitude and time duration. Obtaining these parameters enables the application of statistical tools as presented in (Bollen, 2000), for results analysis and visualization, which allows having information about the electrical system behavior at certain time intervals, for example, months or years.

Another difficulty, perhaps the most critical, is the large volume of data obtained from oscillographic monitoring. Many of these recorded signals are due to switching maneuvers, or due to spurious signals or noise, without characterizing voltage changes in the electrical system. For this large amount of data to be evaluated, it is necessary that an automatic classification method be used so that only signals with the desired characteristics are used to determine the parameters of interest. This aspect is highlighted in several publications which present new methods for classification and characterization using digital signal processing and computational intelligence tools (Angrisani et al, 1998; Santoso et al, 2000a; Santoso et al, 2000b and Huang et al, 2002; Machado et al, 2009; Rodriguez et al, 2010).

The first use of wavelet transform in power systems is credited to (Ribeiro, 1994). In recent years, wavelet transform - WT, a powerful tool for digital signal processing, has been proposed as a new technique for monitoring and analysis of different disturbances types in power systems (Machado et al, 2009; Mokryani, 2010; A. Rodriguez et al, 2010; Gong Jing, 2010, 2011). Wavelets, along with computational intelligence techniques like artificial neural networks and fuzzy logic, have been used successfully in automatic classification of power quality problems. (Machado et al, 2009; Mokryani, 2010; Rodriguez et al, 2010)

The present work aims to develop an automated system for classifying power quality problems with respect to the fault type that has occurred and the electric phase involved, and quantify SDVV in electrical power systems from the available oscillography in the electrical utilities post-operation centers, to form a parameter database characterizing power quality problems. The proposed methodology uses the wavelet transform to obtain a characteristic pattern to represent the phenomenon and a probabilistic neural network for classification.

2. Wavelet transform

Wavelets are functions that satisfy certain mathematical requirements. The wavelet name comes from the fact that they must be oscillatory (a wave), and be well placed, therefore exhibiting short time duration. There are several wavelet types, usually grouped into families, from which the Daubechies is one of the best known.

Wavelets are used to represent data or other functions in a similar way as the Fourier analysis uses sines and cosines. The signal analysis by wavelet transform has advantages over traditional methods using Fourier analysis when the signals have time discontinuities or present a non-stationary oscillatory behavior.

The mathematics main branch leading to wavelet analysis began with Joseph Fourier (1807) with his frequency analysis theory, known as Fourier analysis. The first wavelet mention appears in the appendix of A. Haar's thesis (1909). Paul Levy a 1930's physicist, investigating the Brownian motion, found that the Haar basis functions are superior to the Fourier basis functions for studying small and complicated details in the Brownian motion. In 1980, Grossman and Morlet, broadly defined wavelets in the context of quantum physics, providing a way of thinking about wavelets based on physical intuition. In 1985, Stephane Mallat gave wavelets an additional advance. Through his work in digital signal processing, he discovered some relationships among quadrature mirror filters - QMF, pyramidal algorithm, and orthogonal wavelet basis. Based partially on these results, Y. Meyer built the first non-trivial wavelets, which unlike the Haar wavelet, the Meyer wavelets are continuously differentiable, but do not have compact support. Years later, Ingrid Daubechies used Mallat's work to build a set of wavelets with orthogonal basis functions that have become the cornerstone of wavelet applications today.

2.1 Wavelet analysis

The wavelet transform is a technique similar to the windowed Fourier transform with the difference that the window width is variable. The wavelet analysis allows the use of large time intervals when it is desired to get low frequency information and shorter time intervals when the interest is to obtain high frequency information. Unlike Fourier analysis that uses sines and cosines, wavelet analysis uses wavelets. Figure 1 shows as an example, the Daubechies wavelet, db8.

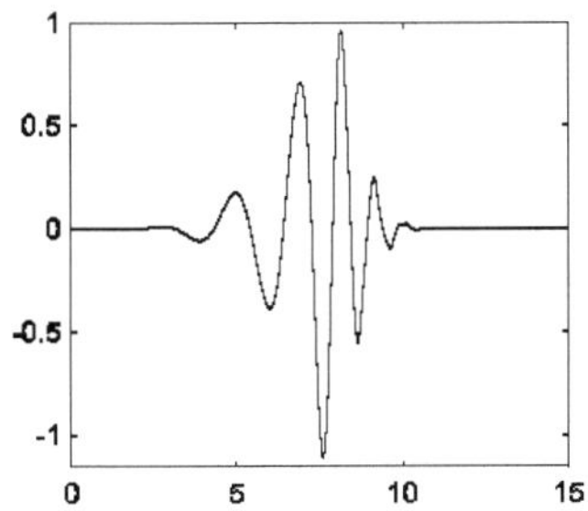

Fig. 1. The Daubechies wavelet, db8.

Wavelets sets are employed to approximate signals, and each set consists of scaled versions (compressed or expanded) and translated (time shifted) from a single wavelet, called mother wavelet.

2.2 Discrete wavelet transform

In the discrete wavelet transform the term "discrete" applies only to the parameters in the transformed domain, that is, scales and translations, and not to the independent variable time, of the function being transformed. The discrete wavelet transform provides a set of coefficients corresponding to points on a grid or two-dimensional lattice of discrete points in the time-scale domain. This grid is indexed by two integers, the first, denoted by m, corresponds to the discrete steps of the scale, while the second, denoted by n, corresponds to the discrete steps of translation (time displacement). The scale a becomes $a = a_0^m$ and translation becomes $b = nb_0a_0^m$, where a_0 and b_0 are the discrete steps of the scale and translation, respectively (Young, 1995). Then the wavelet can be represented by:

$$\psi_{m,n}(t) = a_0^{\frac{-m}{2}} \psi(a_0^{-m}t - nb_0) \tag{1}$$

The discrete wavelet transform is given by:

$$W_f(m,n) = a_0^{\frac{-m}{2}} \int_R f(t)\psi(a_0^{-m}t - nb_0)dt \tag{2}$$

where, $m,n \in Z$, and Z is the set of integer numbers.

The parameter m which is called level, determines the wavelet frequency, while the parameter n indicates its position.

The inverse discrete wavelet transform is given by:

$$f(t) = k\sum_{m=0}^{\infty}\sum_{n=0}^{\infty} W_f(m,n)a_0^{\frac{-m}{2}} \psi(a_0^{-m}t - nb_0) \tag{3}$$

where k is a constant that depends on the redundancy of the combination of the lattice with the used mother wavelet (Young, 1995).

Along with the time-scale plane discretization, the independent variable (time) can also be discretized. The sequence of discrete points of the discretized signal can be represented by a discrete time wavelet series DTWS. The discrete time wavelet series is defined in relation to a discrete mother wavelet, $h(k)$. The discrete wavelet time series maps a discrete finite energy sequence to a discrete grid of coefficients. The discrete time wavelet series is given by (Young, 1995).

$$W_f(m,n) = a_0^{\frac{-m}{2}} \sum f(k)h(a_0^{-m}k - nb_0) \tag{4}$$

2.3 Multiresolution analysis

Multiresolution Analysis - MRA, aims to develop a signal $f(t)$ representation in terms of an orthogonal basis which is composed by the scale and wavelets functions. An efficient algorithm for this representation was developed in 1988 by Mallat (Mallat, 1989) considering a scale factor $a_0 = 2$ and a translation factor $b_0 = 1$. This means that at each decomposition level m, scales are a power of 2 and translations are proportional to powers of 2. Scaling by powers of 2 can be easily implemented by decimation (sub-sampling) and over-sampling of a discrete signal by a factor of 2. Sub-sampling by a factor of 2, involves taking a signal sample from every two available ones, resulting in a signal with half the number of samples than the original one. Over-sampling by a factor of 2, consists of inserting zeros between each two samples resulting in a signal with twice the elements of the original one.

2.3.1 Analysis or decomposition

The structure of the multiresolution analysis is shown in Figure 2. The original signal passes through two filters, a low pass filter $g(k)$, the function scale, and a high pass filter $h(k)$, the mother wavelet. The impulse response of $h(k)$ is related to the impulse response of $g(k)$ by (Mallat, 1989):

$$h(k) = (-1)^{1-k} g(1-k) \tag{5}$$

Filter $h(k)$ is the mirror of filter $g(k)$ and they are called quadrature mirror filters.

In the structure presented in Figure 2, the input signal is convolved with the impulse response of $h(k)$, and $g(k)$, obtaining two output signals. The low pass filter output represents the low frequency content of the input signal or an approximation of it. The high pass filter output represents the high frequency content of the input signal or a detail of it. It should be noted in Figure 2 that the output provided by the filters has together twice the number of samples of the original signal.

This drawback is overcome by the process of decimation performed on each signal, thereby obtaining the signal cD, the wavelet coefficients that are the new signal representation in the wavelet domain, and the signal cA, the approximation coefficients which are used to feed the next stage of the decomposition process in an iterative manner resulting in a multi-level decomposition.

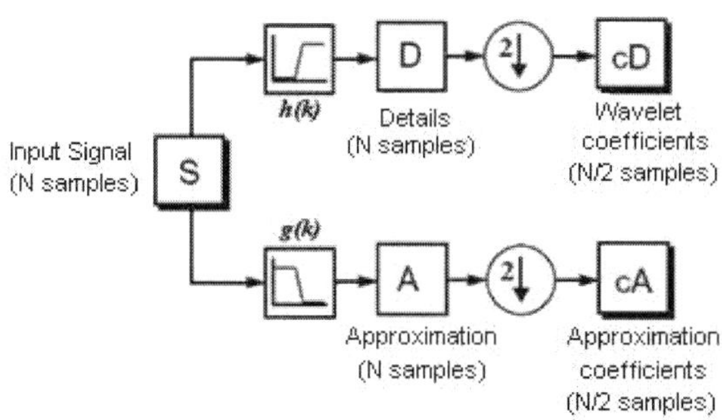

Fig. 2. Structure of the multiresolution analysis

The decomposition process in Figure 2 can be iterated with successive approximations being decomposed, then the signal being divided into several resolution levels. This scheme is called "wavelet decomposition tree" or "pyramidal structure" (Young, 1995 and Misit et al, 2000). Figure 3 shows the schematic representation of a signal being decomposed at multiple levels.

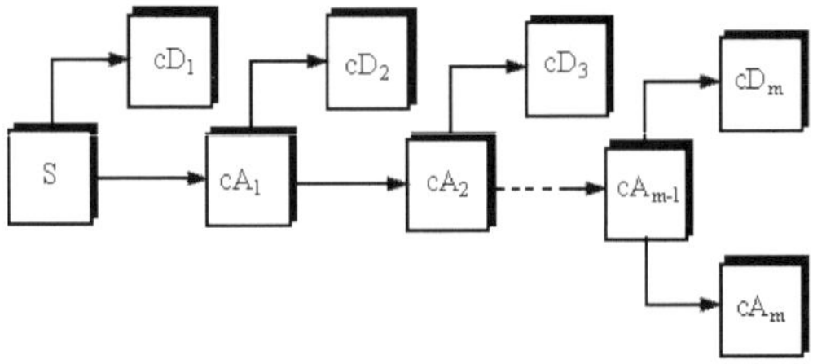

Fig. 3. Schematic representation of a signal being decomposed at multiple levels.

Since the multiresolution analysis process is iterative, it can theoretically be continued indefinitely. In fact, the decomposition can proceed only up to 1 (one) detail, consisting of a single sample. The maximum number of decomposition levels for a signal having N samples is given by $\log_2 N$.

2.3.2 Synthesis or reconstruction

The synthesis process or reconstruction is to obtain the original signal from the wavelet coefficients generated by the analysis or decomposition process. While the analysis process involves filtering and sub-sampling, the synthesis process performs a reverse sequence, over-sampling and filtering. The filters used in the synthesis process are called reconstruction filters, being $g'(k)$ the low pass filter, and $h'(k)$ the high pass filter. Figure 4 shows the reconstruction scheme from a single decomposition stage.

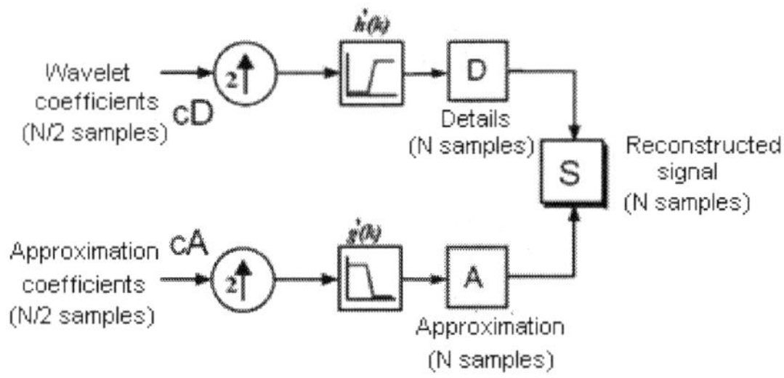

Fig. 4. Reconstruction scheme from a single decomposition stage.

It is observed from Figure 4 that to retrieve the original signal, it is necessary to reconstruct details and approximations. Details could be obtained with over-sampling of the cD coefficients, and a subsequent filtering with $h'(k)$. Approximations are obtained with over-sampling of the coefficients cA , and a subsequent filtering with $g'(k)$ .The original signal is then obtained by:

$$S = A + D \tag{6}$$

The scheme presented in Figure 4 can be extended to a multi-level decomposition.

3. Probabilistic neural network

The structure of a Probabilistic Neural Network (PNN) is similar to a feed forward network. The main difference is that the activation function is no longer the sigmoid; it is replaced by a class of functions which includes, in particular, the exponential function. The main advantage of PNN is that it requires only one step for training and that the decision surfaces are close to the contours of the Bayes optimal decision when the number of training samples increases. Furthermore, the shape of the decision surface can be as complex as necessary, or as simple as desired (Specht, 1990).

The main drawback of PNN is that all samples used for the training process must be stored and used in the classification of new patterns. However, considering the use of high-density memories, problems with storage of training samples should not occur. In addition, the PNN processing speed in the classification of new patterns is quite satisfactory, and even several times faster than using back propagation algorithms as reported by (Maloney et al, 1989).

3.1 The Bayes strategy for pattern classification

One of the traditionally accepted strategies or decision rules used to patterns classification is that they minimize the "expected risk." Such strategies are called Bayes strategies, and can be applied to problems containing any number of categories (Specht, 1988).

To illustrate the Bayes decision rule formalism, it is considered the situation of two categories in which the state of known nature θ , can be θ_A or θ_B. It is desired to decide whether $\theta = \theta_A$ or $\theta = \theta_B$ based on a measurements set represented by a n dimension vector x . Then the Bayes decision rule is given by:

$$\begin{aligned} d(x) &= \theta_A \ if \ h_A l_A f_A(x) > h_B l_B f_B(x) \\ d(x) &= \theta_B \ if \ h_A l_A f_A(x) < h_B l_B f_B(x) \end{aligned} \tag{7}$$

where $f_A(x)$ and $f_B(x)$ are the probability density functions for categories θ_A and θ_B respectively, l_A is the uncertainty function associated with the decision $d(x) = \theta_B$ when $\theta = \theta_A$; l_B is the uncertainty function associated with the decision $d(x) = \theta_A$ when $\theta = \theta_B$, h_A is the a priori probability of category θ_A patterns occurrence, and $h_B = 1 - h_A$ is the a priori probability that $\theta = \theta_B$. Then, the boundary between the regions in which the Bayes decision $d(x) = \theta_A$ and $d(x) = \theta_B$ is given by:

$$f_A(x) = K f_B(x) \tag{8}$$

where:

$$K = \frac{h_B l_B}{h_A l_A} \tag{9}$$

It should be noted that, in general, the decision surfaces of two categories defined by Eq. (8) can be arbitrarily complex, since there are no restrictions on the densities except for those conditions to which all probability density functions must satisfy, namely that they must be always non-negative, and integrable and their integrals over all space be equal to unity.

The ability to estimate the probability density functions, based on training patterns, is fundamental to the use of Eq. (8). Frequently, a priori probabilities can be known or estimated, and the loss functions require subjective evaluation. However, if the probability densities of the categories patterns to be separate are unknown, and all that is known is a set of training patterns, then, these patterns provide the only clue to the estimation of that unknown probability density. A particular estimator that can be used is (Specht, 1990):

$$f_A(x) = \frac{1}{(2\pi)^{\frac{n}{2}}\sigma^n}\frac{1}{m}\sum_{i=1}^{m}\exp\left(-\frac{(x-x_{ai})^T(x-x_{ai})}{2\sigma^2}\right) \tag{10}$$

Where i is the pattern number, m is the total number of training patterns, x_{ai} is the i-th training pattern of category θ_A, and σ is the smoothing factor. It should be noted that $f_A(x)$ is simply the sum of small Gaussian distributions centered at each training sample.

3.2 Structure of the Probabilistic Neural Network

The probabilistic neural network is basically a Bayesian classifier implemented in parallel. The PNN, as described by Specht (Specht, 1988), is based on estimation of probability density functions for the various classes established by the training patterns. A schematic diagram for a PNN is shown in Figure 5. The input layer X is responsible for connecting the input pattern to the radial basis layer. $X = [x_1, x_2, \cdots, x_M]$ is a matrix containing the vectors to be classified.

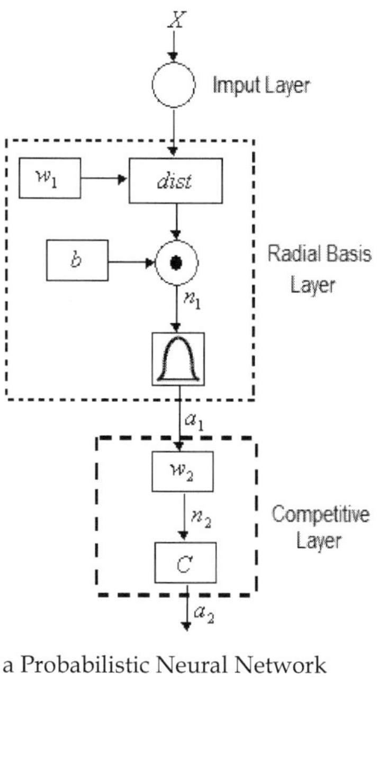

Fig. 5. Schematic diagram of a Probabilistic Neural Network

In the radial basis layer, the training vectors are stored in a weights matrix w_1 . When a new pattern is presented to the input, the block *dist* calculates the Euclidean distance between each input pattern vector for each of the stored weight vectors. The vector in the output block *dist* is multiplied, point by point, by the polarization factor b . The result of this multiplication n_1 is applied to a radial basis function providing as output a_1 , obtained from:

$$a_1 = e^{-n_1^2} \tag{11}$$

This way, a vector in the input pattern close to a training vector is represented by a value close to 1 in the output vector a_1 . The competitive layer of the weight matrix w_2 contains the target vectors representing each class corresponding to each vector in the training pattern. Each vector w_2 has a 1 only in the row associated with a particular class and 0 in other positions. The Multiplication $w_2 a_1$ adds the a_1 elements corresponding to each class, providing the output n_2 . Finally block C provides 1 at output a_2 corresponding to the biggest element of n_2 and 0 for the other values. Thus, the neural network classifies each vector of the input pattern in a specific class, because that class has the highest probability of being correct. The main advantage of PNN is its easy and straightforward project, and not depending on training.

4. Proposed procedure

The proposed procedure is shown schematically in Figure 6. The real data file contains phases A-B-C voltages and currents waveforms, as well as digital signals that indicate the statuses of protective devices, as relays and circuit breakers, acquired by DDR and IED installed in the electrical system substations. These raw data are coded in the COMTRADE format for power systems (IEEE Standard Common Format for Transient Data Exchange), (IEEE Std C37.111, 1999). So, to obtain the voltages and currents signals it is firstly necessary to decode the COMTRADE data, and select the desired waveforms to be analyzed.

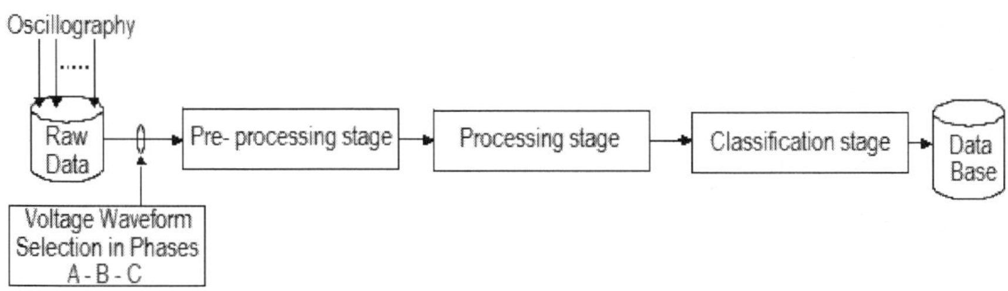

Fig. 6. Schematic diagram representing the proposed processing procedure.

Before inputting the voltages waveforms to the processing stage, a pre-processing routine is accomplished to standardize the raw data due to the different voltage levels that are encountered in the power system topology. In the case study presented here, the power transmission system presents 230 kV and 500 kV voltage levels. The standardization is performed by converting the phase voltages to per unit (p.u.) values considering the voltage peak value as base voltage.

4.1 Processing stage

In the processing stage, the wavelet transform is applied to the voltage waveforms to obtaining signals patterns that characterize short duration voltage variations (SDVV) and transient variations (TV) due to system faults. These obtained patterns are used as inputs to two Probabilistic Neural Networks for SDVV classification (PNN1), as well as to classify the fault type that has occurred (PNN2). The classification results will form a database which can be used to evaluate power quality indices for the electrical system.

4.1.1 Input patterns

Power systems electromagnetic phenomena are characterized by categories according to their spectral content, magnitude and duration (IEEE Std 1250, 1995). These phenomena classification into categories requires an analysis methodology that very frequently must be individualized, which prevents this procedure applicability when the number of signals to be evaluated is very large. Then, procedures to extract signals relevant characteristics have been proposed, so that they can be automatically classified into a specific category. Obtaining parameters for characterizing a given signal usually requires a transformation from the time domain to another domain where the specific characteristics are highlighted.

The use of wavelet transform has proved adequate for obtaining electrical signals characteristics which can be used in classification processes. Studies such those presented in (Lee et al, 1997; Chan et al, 2000; Santoso et al, 2000c; Ramaswamy et al, 2003; Zwe-Lee et al, 2003; Zwe-Lee, 2004 & Machado et al, 2009), use characteristic vectors based on the multiresolution analysis decomposition levels coefficients as input to computational intelligence-based systems to classify different power quality events. The characteristic vectors magnitudes depend on the number of decomposition levels used for the analysis, or the number of coefficients of a given decomposition level. The method proposed here uses the Daubechies wavelet, db4, and the voltage signals are decomposed into three levels. The first signal detail level is used to determine the time instant the disturbance has started and also to characterize the transients in the fault type identification, while the third signal approximation is used to characterize SDVV. The computational algorithms were implemented on MATLAB, and also coded in Java.

Figure 7(a) shows an original voltage waveform in p.u. obtained from a digital disturbance register (DDR) presenting a voltage sag. The original waveform is decomposed into three resolution levels. In Figures 7(b-d) the signal details from level 1 to level 3 are presented and in Figure 7(e) the signal approximation at level 3. Details retain the high-frequency information contained in the signal, divided into frequency bands which are function of the sampling rate used in the acquisition process. In case of Figure 7, the sampling rate is 96 samples per cycle of 60 Hz, or 5,760 samples per second.

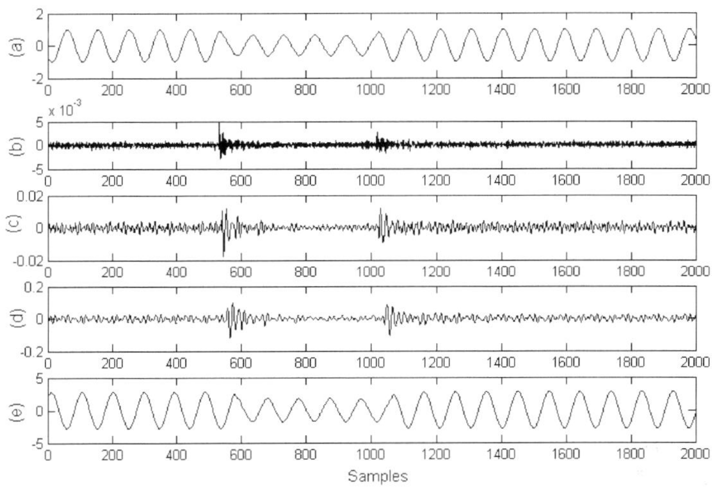

Fig. 7. Signal decomposition in 3 levels. In (a) original signal. From (b) to (d) details from level 1 to level 3, and (e) level 3 approximation.

The wavelet transform performance to detect disturbances in electrical signals is substantially improved if a procedure for reducing noise level is applied to the decomposition level coefficients to be used in the detection process. This feature is highlighted in (Yang et al, 1999; 2000 & 2001). So, to better characterize the disturbance location in the signal, it is applied the following algorithm presented in (Misiti et al, 2000), to the previously selected decomposition level:

$$\hat{d}_s(n) = \begin{cases} d_s(n) - \eta_s & if \ |d_s(n)| \geq \eta_s \ \ and \ \ d_s(n) > 0 \\ d_s(n) + \eta_s & if \ |d_s(n)| \geq \eta_s \ \ and \ \ d_s(n) < 0 \\ 0 & if \ |d_s(n)| < \eta_s \end{cases} \tag{12}$$

Where:

- $n = 1, 2, \cdots, N$ is the number of the decomposition level s, $d_s(n)$, coefficient and N is the number of samples;
- $\hat{d}_s(n)$ is the new value of $d_s(n)$;
- η_s is a threshold based on the maximum absolute value of the decomposition level coefficients s.

The η_s value used was 10% of the maximum absolute value of the decomposition level coefficients considered, as proposed in (Santoso et al, 1997).

A voltage waveform containing voltage sag is shown in Figure 8(a). In (b) it is presented the details level used to detect the disturbance beginning and (c) presents new details values after the noise reduction algorithm is applied. In (c) it can be observed smaller coefficients magnitudes over the entire signal which improves the algorithm performance used to detect the disturbance.

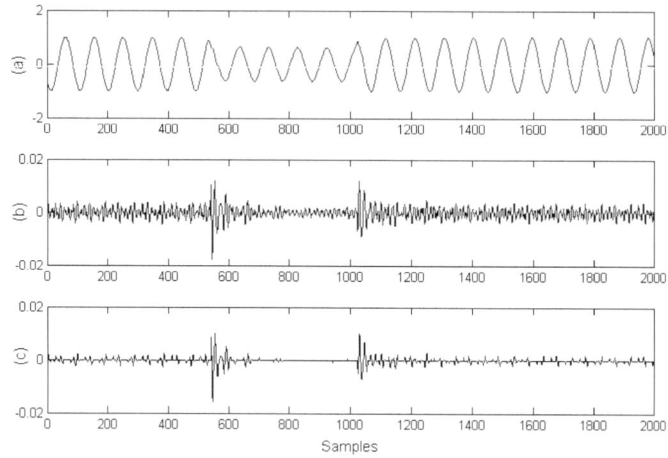

Fig. 8. (a) Original voltage waveform with voltage sag, (b) second details level, and (c) second details level after noise reduction.

The disturbance beginning point is found based on the following algorithm presented in (Gaouda et al, 2002)

$$m(n) = \begin{cases} 0 & [\hat{d}_s(n)]^2 < \sigma \\ 1 & [\hat{d}_s(n)]^2 \geq \sigma \end{cases} \quad (13)$$

where:

- σ is the standard deviation of $[\hat{d}_s(n)]^2$

The algorithm (13) was originally proposed to find the disturbance start and end points. In this particular case, the interest is just the starting point, p_i, which shall be considered as a reference for obtaining the phenomena pattern characterization in the classification stage. For this purpose the following algorithm is proposed:

1. Calculate $[\hat{d}_s(n)]^2$;
2. Calculate σ;
3. Make $n = 0$;
4. Make $n = n + 1$;
5. Compare the value of $\hat{d}_s(n)^2$ with σ:

   If $[\hat{d}_s(n)]^2 < \sigma$, return to step 4;

   If $[\hat{d}_s(n)]^2 \geq \sigma$, $p_i = n$;
6. End

Once the disturbance starting point is obtained, the next step is to determine the signal parameters to input the PNN in order to characterize SDVV and transients.

4.1.1.1 SDVV characterization parameters

As the signal magnitude and duration change during the SDVV occurrence, the norm value (Euclidian distance) will also change if the disturbed signal is considered. So, by monitoring changes in the norm of the third-level signal approximation (the level containing the fundamental frequency) and considering the signal disturbed portion, it can be obtained a standard value characterizing these signal changes. Figure 9 shows the signal norm variation as function of the signal magnitude for the third-level signal approximation of the multiresolution analysis. In this analysis, a 10 cycles signal window was considered and the disturbance magnitude ranging from zero to 1.8 p.u.

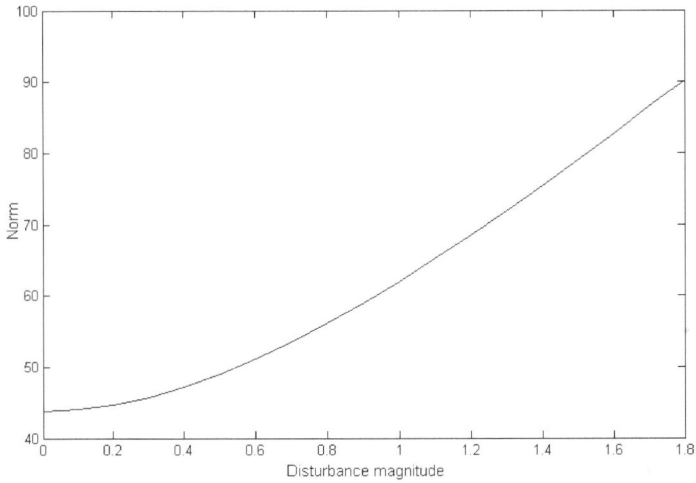

Fig. 9. Signal norm variation as a function of the SDVV magnitude.

So, the SDVV classification pattern is obtained by calculating the signal norm for 10 cycles counting from point p_i , which represents the disturbance starting point. This procedure is applied to the voltage waveforms in phases A-B-C resulting a vector with three elements which is used as input to the PNN for classification purpose.

4.1.1.2 Transients characterization parameters

In the transient analysis case, a two cycles long window is selected from the disturbance starting point which, for real electrical systems, is a time interval within which most of the protective devices operate. This considered signal is then normalized based on the biggest magnitude coefficient, for creating a vector related to each fault type to be analyzed in the classification task.

In three-phase transmission lines, phases are mutually coupled and therefore the high frequency variations generated during a disturbance may also appear in non-faulted phases. Using a modal transformation allows the coupled three-phase system to be treated as a system with three independent single-phase circuits. Each phase values are transformed into three decoupled modes: mode 0 (zero), mode α and mode β, so the three phases are decomposed into nine modes, three for each phase. As mode 0 is the same for all phases, this mode can be calculated only once, reducing to seven the number of signals. Therefore, the three phase voltage signals are decomposed by the multiresolution analysis and the first-level detail 3-dimensioned array is used with the modal matrix to decoupling the original signals.

Mathematically the modal transformation consists of a matrix operation as follows:

$$d_{v0} = W d_{v1} \tag{14}$$

Where d_{v0} d_{v1} are the voltage wavelet coefficients corresponding to the coupled and decoupled phases respectively and W is the decoupling matrix. It is noteworthy that only the voltage signals can be decoupled by the method presented here and the operation described in Eq. (14) should be performed on each signal sample. The matrix W is described by (Silveira; et al, 1999):

$$W = \frac{1}{3}\begin{pmatrix} 1 & 2 & 0 & 1 & -\sqrt{3} & -1 & \sqrt{3} \\ 1 & -1 & \sqrt{3} & 2 & 0 & -1 & -\sqrt{3} \\ 1 & -1 & -\sqrt{3} & -1 & \sqrt{3} & 2 & 0 \end{pmatrix}^{T} \tag{15}$$

This way it is obtained a system that provides seven outputs, being mode α and mode β for each phase and a mode 0 which is common to the three phases. These modes contain the wavelet transform coefficients of the three-phase decoupled input signals. The linearity properties of the wavelet and modal transformations ensure that they can be carried out in a cascading way without causing problems to the classifier algorithm results. So, it is obtained a classification pattern that is represented by a matrix with seven columns and 192 rows.

4.2 Artificial neural networks structures

The ANN used for the SDVV classification, named PNN1, is composed of three classes, namely:

- Class 1 - Voltage sags and interruptions, which are characterized by voltage magnitudes smaller than 0.9 p.u.
- Class 2 - Adequate voltage, which is characterized by magnitudes between 0.9 p.u. and 1.1 p.u.;
- Class 3 – Voltage swell, which is characterized by magnitudes between 1.1 p.u. and 1.8 p.u.

The training values of each class were obtained from points on the curve given in Figure 9, resulting in 19 values stored in the PNN1. As each class covers a different magnitude range, it was established 9 values for class 1, 3 values for Class 2 and 7 values for Class 3. The weight matrix of the competitive layer is a 3x19 matrix, which corresponds to the 19 training values and the three classes considered. The input pattern to be classified consists of a three elements vector, each representing the characteristic of each phase voltage; and the PNN1 output consists of a three elements vector, each one indicating the classification corresponding to each phase.

For transient analysis 11 classes were considered, which correspond to the short circuit types as listed in Table 1.

The PNN2 training matrix has stored seven classification patterns for each class, related to bus voltages. As each pattern has seven vectors derived from the modal transformation, each class is composed of 49 vectors with 192 rows by 49 columns. The output matrix consists of 11 rows, corresponding to the disturbances types classes, and 539 columns corresponding to the training vectors.

Single-Phase Short Circuits	Phase A to Ground
	Phase B to Ground
	Phase C to Ground
Two-Phase and Two-Phase to Ground Short Circuits	Phases AB; Phases AB-to Ground
	Phases AC; Phases AC-to Ground
	Phases BC; Phases BC-to Ground
Three-Phase and Three-Phase to Ground Short Circuits	Phases ABC;Phases ABC-to Ground

Table 1. Short Circuits Types

5. Results

In order to evaluate the performance of the proposed method in classifying SDVV, 311 voltage oscillographic signals obtained from a real power system were used. The oscillographic signals were numbered from 1 to 311 for the purpose of identification. The electrical power system is a 500 kV/230 kV transmission system connecting Tucuruí Hydroelectric Power Plant located in the south of the State of Pará-Brazil, to load centers in the northern region, which is operated by Eletronorte, a generation and transmission utility in the north of Brazil. The oscillography files used are from the 230 kV substation Guamá, located in Belém city, the capital of the state of Pará, and corresponds to a time period within 2004/2005.

Table 2 shows the results corresponding to the PNN1 output. The SDVV parameters represented in Table 2 are the time duration in cycles, and magnitude in p.u. As can be seen, 24 voltage signals were classified as having SDVV.

According to data in Table 2 it may be seen that the PNN1 classification is consistent with the magnitude values calculated for the SDVV. It is observed that in most cases voltage sags were detected in all three phases (classification 1.1.1), and for signals 267 and 268 voltage sags were detected only in phase C, while phase A, and B exhibited adequate voltage magnitudes (classification 2.2.1). It is also worth noting that all these results were compared with the real original voltage waveforms, which proved the results correctness as obtained by the wavelet multiresolution analysis and by the PNN1 classification mechanism.

Voltage Signal Number	PNN 1 Output	Phase A		Phase B		Phase C	
		Time Duration (Cycles)	Magnitude (pu)	Time Duration (Cycles)	Magnitude (pu)	Time Duration (Cycles)	Magnitude (pu)
18	1 1 1	5.5729	0.8331	5.3542	0.8388	5.1979	0.8696
19	1 1 1	5.5729	0.8275	5.3542	0.8556	5.1875	0.8473
58	1 1 1	2.9583	0.4949	2.8646	0.8710	2.8333	0.8449
59	1 1 1	2.9688	0.4929	2.8646	0.8701	2.5313	0.8393
138	1 1 1	5.5729	0.8331	5.3542	0.8388	5.1979	0.8696
139	1 1 1	5.5729	0.8275	5.3542	0.8556	5.1875	0.8473
249	1 1 1	5.5729	0.8275	5.3542	0.8556	5.1875	0.8473
250	1 1 1	5.5729	0.8331	5.3542	0.8388	5.1979	0.8696
251	1 1 1	5.5729	0.8331	5.3542	0.8388	5.1979	0.8696
252	1 1 1	5.5729	0.8275	5.3542	0.8556	5.1875	0.8473
253	1 1 1	2.9583	0.4949	2.8646	0.8710	2.8333	0.8449
254	1 1 1	2.9688	0.4929	2.8646	0.8701	2.5313	0.8393
255	1 1 1	5.5729	0.8331	5.3542	0.8388	5.1979	0.8696
256	1 1 1	5.5729	0.8275	5.3542	0.8556	5.1875	0.8473
257	1 1 1	5.5729	0.8275	5.3542	0.8556	5.1875	0.8473
258	1 1 1	5.5729	0.8331	5.3542	0.8388	5.1979	0.8696
267	2 2 1	5.1667	0.9317	4.5729	0.9153	5.0313	0.6424
268	2 2 1	5.4792	0.9486	4.5729	0.9140	5.0313	0.6393
279	1 1 1	4.9896	0.4158	5.1771	0.8556	4.8854	0.8942
280	1 1 1	4.8750	0.4171	4.5729	0.8523	4.8125	0.8910
287	1 1 1	3.6875	0.8693	3.4479	0.5332	3.2917	0.8789
288	1 1 1	3.6979	0.8699	3.4479	0.5343	3.3542	0.8906
302	1 1 1	5.5729	0.8331	5.3542	0.8388	5.1979	0.8696
303	1 1 1	5.5729	0.8275	5.3542	0.8556	5.1875	0.8473

Table 2. SDVV classification and quantification results for three-phase voltage signals obtained from oscillographic records in a real electrical power system.

For the fault type classification and the faulted phase identification the same 230 kV/500 kV electrical power system was used in which short-circuits were simulated along the transmission lines by varying the incidence angle, and the short-circuit resistance to obtaining a set of voltage waveforms corresponding to the different simulated fault types, using the simulation software ATP.

The simulation studies included 1,029 single-phase to ground short-circuit; 2,058 two-phase and two-phase to ground short-circuits; and 686 three-phase and three-phase to ground short circuits. For the PNN2 training, seven case studies for each fault type as listed in Table 1 were used as input patterns, and the remaining cases were used for testing. Table 3 shows the classification results, noting that misclassification occurred for single-phase and two-phase to ground short circuits, with 6% and 5.4% respectively. Also 58% of the three-phase short circuit were classified as three-phase to ground short circuits, but considering that these two fault types can be considered as a single class there would be no classification error in this case, as presented by the 100% result in Table 3.

Fault Type	Simulated Cases	Results (Correct Classification)
Single-Phase to Ground	1,029	94%
Two-Phase and Two-Phase to Ground	2,058	94,6
Three-Phase and Three-Phase to Ground	686	100%

Table 3. Results for fault type classification

With the purpose of testing the performance of the proposed method in classifying real oscillographic signals, some Eletronorte operational reports in the period 2007/2008 were analyzed which contained 31 labeled transient occurrences, being 17 due to short circuits, and 14 due to lightning discharge. For considering lightning discharges (LD) a new class was added to PNN2, and 7 of the 14 signals were selected for training the PNN2 and the remaining signals were used for testing. The testing signals were applied to the trained PNN2 achieving 100% accuracy for short circuits and 85,7% for lightning discharges.

6. Conclusion

This work presented a methodology for automatic SDVV classification as well as fault type identification using digital signal processing and computational intelligence techniques. Real power system data were used and satisfactory results for both SDVV and fault type classification were obtained. The implementation of the proposed methodology as part of a computational tool and its integration with the post-operational utility analysis routines will enable the automatic analysis of a larger number of signals waveforms, allowing the methodology proposed here to serve as a basis for future applications where automatic analysis procedures are needed.

One should also note that the wavelet used in this work was chosen due to its good performance in determining the disturbance location in the signal waveform. Various wavelets orders from db2 to db16 were tested and the db4 wavelet presented the best performance, and considering also the fact that it has filters with few coefficients, the processing time for the signals decomposition is greatly reduced, which is an important characteristic when a large number of signals are to be analyzed.

7. References

Angrisani, L.; Daponte, P.; D'Apuzzo, M., 1998. A method based on wavelet networks for the detection and classification of transients. *Instrumentation and Measurement Technology Conference. IMTC/98. Conference Proceedings. IEEE* , Volume: 2 , 18-21 May 1998, Page(s): 903-908.

Bollen M.H.J., 2000. *Understanding Power Quality Problems: Voltage Sags and Interruptions*. IEEE Press Series on Power Engineering.

Chan, W.L.; So, A.T.P.; Lai, L.L., 2000. Harmonics load signature recognition by wavelets transforms. *Proceedings International Conference on Electric Utility Deregulation and Restructuring and Power Technologies*, 2000. DRPT 2000., 4-7 April 2000, Page(s): 666 - 671.

Gaouda, A.M.; Kanoun, S.H.; Salama, M.M.A.; Chikhani, A.Y., 2002. Wavelet-based signal processing for disturbance classification and measurement. Generation, *IEE Proceedings - Transmission and Distribution*, Volume: 149 Issue: 3, May 2002, Page(s): 310 -318.

Gong Jing, 2010. The influence study of wavelet properties on transient power disturbance signals detection. *International Conference on Computer, Mechatronics, Control and Electronic Engineering (CMCE)*, 2010 Volume: 5, Page(s): 140 - 143

Gong Jing, 2011. Application of constructed complex wavelet in power quality disturbances detection. *IEEE 2nd International Conference on Computing, Control and Industrial Engineering (CCIE)*, 2011, Volume: 2, Page(s): 155 - 158

Huang, J.S.; Negnevitsky, M.; Nguyen, D.T., 2002. A neural-fuzzy classifier for recognition of power quality disturbances. *IEEE Transactions on Power Delivery*, Volume: 17 Issue: 2 , April 2002, Page(s): 609-616.

IEEE Std 1250, 1995. *IEEE guide for service to equipment sensitive to momentary voltage disturbances*. 28 June 1995

IEEE Std C37.111, 1999. *IEEE Standard Common Format for Transient Data Exchange (COMTRADE) for power systems* ,15 Oct. 1999

Lee, C.H.; Lee, J.S.; Kim, J.O.; Nam, S.W., 1997. Feature vector extraction for the automatic classification of power quality disturbances. *Proceedings of 1997 IEEE International Symposium on Circuits and Systems*, 1997. ISCAS '97., Volume: 4 , 9-12 June 1997; Page(s): 2681 -2684.

Machado, R. N.M.M. ; Bezerra, U. H. ; Tostes, M. E. L. ; Pelaes, E. G. ; Oliveira, R. C. L., 2009. Use of Wavelet Transform and Generalized Regression Neural Network (GRNN) to the Characterization of Short-Duration Voltage Variation in Electric Power System. *IEEE Latin America Transactions*, v. 7, p. 217-222, 2009.

Mallat, S.G., 1989. A theory for multiresolution signal decomposition: the wavelet representation. *IEEE Transactions on Pattern Analysis and Machine Intelligence*, Volume: 11 Issue: 7, July 1989 , Page(s): 674 -693.

Maloney, P.S.; Specht, D.F., 1989. The use of probabilistic neural networks to improve solution times for hull-to-emitter correlation problems. *International Joint Conference on Neural Networks*, 1989. IJCNN., 18-22 June 1989 Page(s):289 - 294 vol.1.

Misiti, M., Misiti, Y., Oppenheim, G., Jean-Michel Poggi, J.-M., 2000. *Wavelet Toolbox For Use with MATLAB®. User's Guide Version 2*, The MathWorks, Inc., 2000.

Mokryani, G.; Haghifam, M.-R.; Latafat, H.; Aliparast, P.; Abdollahy, A.,2010. Detection of inrush current based on wavelettransform and LVQ neural network. *Transmission and Distribution Conference and Exposition, IEEE PES,* 2010 , Page(s): 1 - 5

Ramaswamy, S.; Kiran, B.V.; Kashyap, K.H.; Shenoy, U.J., 2003. Classification of power system transients using wavelet transforms and probabilistic neural networks. *TENCON 2003. Conference on Convergent Technologies for Asia-Pacific Region* Volume 4, 15-17 Oct. 2003 Page(s):1272 - 1276 Vol.4.

Ribeiro, P.F., 1994. Wavelet transform: an advanced tool for analyzing non-stationary harmonic distortions in power systems. *Proceedings of the IEEE International Conference on Harmonics in Power Systems,* Bologna, Italy; September 21-23, 1994, pp. 365-369.

Rodriguez, A.; Ruiz, J.E.; Aguado, J.; Lopez, J.J.; Martin, F.I.; Muñoz, F., 2010. Classification of power quality disturbances using Wavelet and Artificial Neural Networks. *IEEE International Symposium on Industrial Electronics,* 2010, Pages: 1589 - 1594

Santoso, S.; Powers, E.J.; Grady, W.M.; Parsons, A.C., 2000a. Power quality disturbance waveform recognition using wavelet-based neural classifier. I. Theoretical foundation. *IEEE Transactions on Power Delivery,* Volume: 15 Issue: 1, Jan. 2000, Page(s): 222-228.

Santoso, S.; Powers, E.J.; Grady, W.M.; Parsons, A.C., 2000b. Power quality disturbance waveform recognition using wavelet-based neural classifier. II. Application. *IEEE Transactions on Power Delivery,* Volume: 15, Issue: 1, Jan. 2000 Pages:229 – 235.

Santoso, S.; Grady, W.M.; Powers, E.J.; Lamoree, J.; Bhatt, S.C., 2000c. Characterization of distribution power quality events with Fourier and wavelet transforms. *IEEE Transactions on Power Delivery,* Volume: 15 Issue: 1, Jan. 2000, Page(s): 247 –254.

Silveira P.M.; R. Seara and H.H Zurn,1999. An approach using wavelet transform for type identification in digital relayng , IEEE Power Engineering Society Summer Meeting, Conference Proceeding, Volume 2, 1999

Specht, D.F., 1988. Probabilistic neural networks for classification, mapping, or associative memory. *IEEE International Conference on Neural Networks,* 1988. 24-27 July 1988 Page(s): 525 – 532 vol.1

Specht, D.F., 1990. Probabilistic neural networks and the polynomial Adaline as complementary techniques for classification. *IEEE Transactions on Neural Networks,* Volume 1, Issue 1, March 1990 Page(s):111 – 121

Yang, H.-T.; Liao, C.-C.; Yang, P.-C.; Huang, K.-Y., 1999. A wavelet based power quality monitoring system considering noise effects. *International Conference on Electric Power Engineering,* 1999. PowerTech Budapest 99., 29 Aug.-2 Sept. 1999, Page(s): 224

Yang, H.-T; Liao, C.-C., 2000. A correlation-based noise suppression algorithm for power quality monitoring through wavelet transform. *International Conference on Power System Technology,* 2000. Proceedings. PowerCon 2000., Volume: 3, 4-7 Dec. 2000, Page(s): 1311 -1316.

Yang, H.-T.; Liao. C.-C., 2001. A de-noising scheme for enhancing wavelet-based power quality monitoring system. *IEEE Transactions on Power Delivery,* Volume: 16 Issue: 3, July 2001, Page(s): 353 -360.

Young, R.K., *Wavelet Theory and its Applications*. Kluwer Academic Publishers, ISBN 0-7923-9271-X, Norwell, Massachusetts, U.S.E,1995.

Zwe-Lee Gaing; Hou-Sheng Huang, 2003. Wavelet-based neural network for power disturbance classification. *Power Engineering Society General Meeting,* 2003, IEEE, Volume: 3,.13-17 July 2003, Pages: 1628 Vol. 3.

Zwe-Lee Gaing. 2004. Wavelet-based neural network for power disturbance recognition and classification. *IEEE Transactions on Power Delivery,* Volume 19, Issue 4, Oct. 2004 Page(s):1560 - 1568.

10

Wavelet Transform in Fault Diagnosis of Analogue Electronic Circuits

Lukas Chruszczyk
Silesian University of Technology
Poland

1. Introduction

The aim of the chapter is description of a wavelet transform utilisation in fault diagnosis of analogue electronic circuits. The wavelet transform plays a key role in the presented methods and is located in important step of a feature extraction.

The chapter, among wavelet transform, contains also applications of other modern computational technique: evolutionary optimisation on example of a genetic algorithm, which has proven to be robust and effective optimisation tool for this kind of problems (Bernier et al. 1995; Goldberg, 1989; Grefenstette, 1981, 1986; Holland 1968; De Jong, 1975, 1980; Pettey et al., 1987; Suh & Gucht, 1987; Tanese, 1987).

The author's intention is presentation of a practical utilisation of abovementioned methods (and their combination) in field of testing (fault diagnosis) of analogue electronic circuits.

2. Fault diagnosis of analogue electronic circuits

An electrical and electronic circuit testing is an inseparable part of manufacturing process. Depending on circuit type (analogue, digital, mixed), function (amplifier, oscillator, filter, mixer, nonlinear etc.) and implementation (tube or semiconductor, discrete, integrated) there have been proposed variety of testing methods. Together with development of modern electronic circuits, test engineers face more and more difficult problems related with testing procedures. Common problems are constant grow of complexity, density, functionality, speed and precision of circuits. At the same time contradictory factors like time-to-market, manufacturing and testing cost must be minimised while testing speed maximised. Important problem is also limited access to internal nodes of integrated circuits. All these problems are related to any "life epoch" of electronic circuit: from design itself, through design validation, prototype characterisation, manufacturing, post-production test (quality control) and finally board/field testing (Huertas, 1993). It must be noted: the later a fault is detected, the faster grows related cost. While final functional testing is unavoidable, there is still an effort in finding fast and simple methods detecting at least the most probable faults in early life stage of a circuit.

The proposed description of testing methods is limited to fault diagnosis of analogue electronic circuits (AEC). Testing of such circuits meets specific problems (i.e. components tolerance, fault masking, measurement inaccuracy) not presented in testing other circuits types (e.g. digital). Utilisation of a wavelet transform can greatly improve efficiency of selected fault diagnosis and, in some cases, makes the diagnosis feasible at all. The wavelet transform is used here as a feature extraction procedure. It must be noted that despite of dominant role of a digital and microprocessor electronic devices, there will never be escape from analogue circuits. Growing complexity of analogue and mixed-level electronic systems (e.g. system-on-chip - SoC) still rises the bar for testing methods (Baker et al., 1996; Balivada et al., 1996; Chruszczyk et al. 2006, 2007; Chruszczyk & Rutkowski 2008, 2009, 2011; Chruszczyk 2011; Dali & Souders 1989; Kilic & Zwolinski, 1999; Milne et al., 1997; Milor & Sangiovanni-Vincentelli, 1994; Pecenka et al., 2008; Saab et al. 2001; Savir & Guo, 2003; Somayajula et al., 1996).

2.1 Test environment

There have been taken following assumptions on the test procedure:

1. the only available test nodes of a circuit under test (CUT) are the external nodes,
2. CUT is excited by aperiodic excitation and its shape is optimised for given circuit,
3. the only available information about CUT state is read from measurement of four quantities (fig. 1):
   a. output voltage $y_1(t)$,
   b. input current $y_2(t)$,
   c. supply currents $y_3(t)$ and $y_4(t)$.

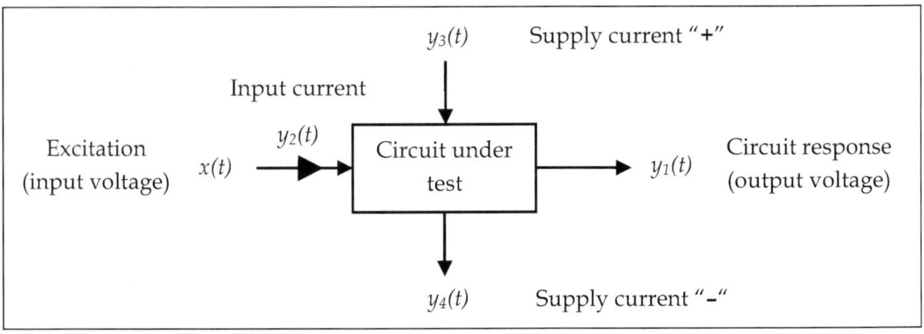

Fig. 1. Assumed test procedure

There are only measured output voltage $y_1(t)$ and input current $y_2(t)$ in case of a passive circuits.

The optimisation goal is the best shape of input excitation voltage (in time-domain). Generally, it can be described as a continuous time function x(t) (fig. 2):

$$x(t) \in \mathbb{R}; \quad t \in [0, t_{max}] \tag{1}$$

Due to practical reasons, there has been assumed discrete form of excitation x(n) described by sequence of N_P samples x_n with constant sampling period T_s. The sampling period always conforms Whittaker-Nyquist-Kotelnikov-Shannon sampling theorem for excitation x(t) and all measured CUT responses. Additionally, value of T_s is set to be 10 times smaller than the smallest time constant of a linear CUT. This ensures good approximation of a continuous excitation x(t) by its discrete equivalent. Maximal time length t_{max} of excitation x(t) (so its discrete approximation x(n) as well) is set to be 5 times greater than the longest time constant of a linear CUT. Value of each sample x_n is quantised to *K* levels (fig. 3):

$$\{x(t_1), x(t_2), x(t_3), \dots\} \in x(t) \tag{2}$$

$$x_n = x(t_n)$$
$$t_{n+1} - t_n = T_s = const\,; \quad n = 1, 2, \dots, N_p \tag{3}$$

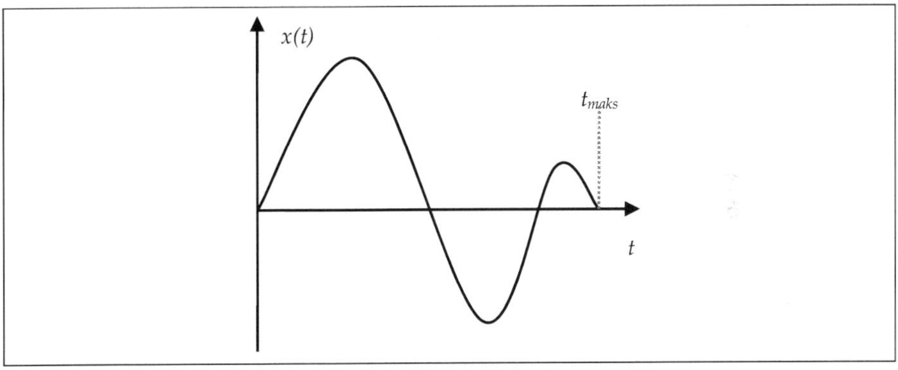

Fig. 2. General form of an input excitation

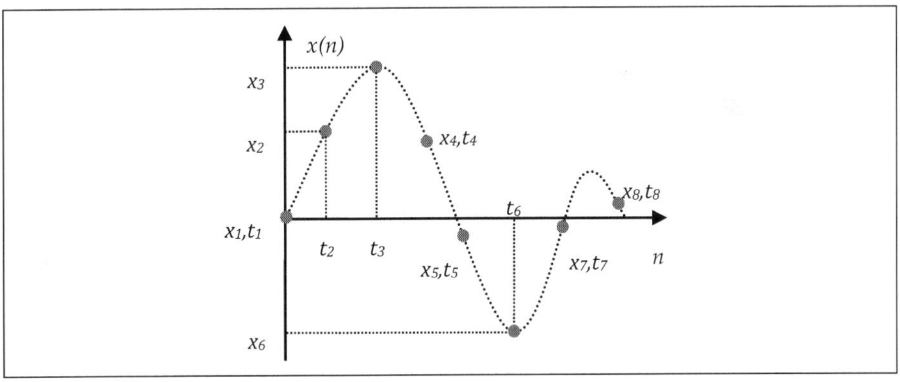

Fig. 3. Input excitation sampling

In order to consider influence of real digital-to-analogue (A/D) converters, there have been used two types of x(n) approximations:

1. "step-shape" (0th-order polynomial), fig. 4,
2. piece-wise linear (1st-order polynomial), fig. 5.

There have been analysed only single catastrophic (hard) and parametric (soft) circuit faults, because such faults are the most probable.

2.2 General tester structure

Fig. 6 presents general tester structure. The tester generates excitation signal and makes decision about CUT state (fault) based on analysis of measured CUT responses.

According to different goals of performed fault diagnosis (detection, location or identification) structure of a diagnostic system is shown on fig. 7. The D-Tester (fault detector) returns on of the following decisions:

- GO – meaning "non-faulty - healthy circuit",
- NO GO – means "faulty circuit" or
- "unknown" if, for any reason, classification cannot be performed.

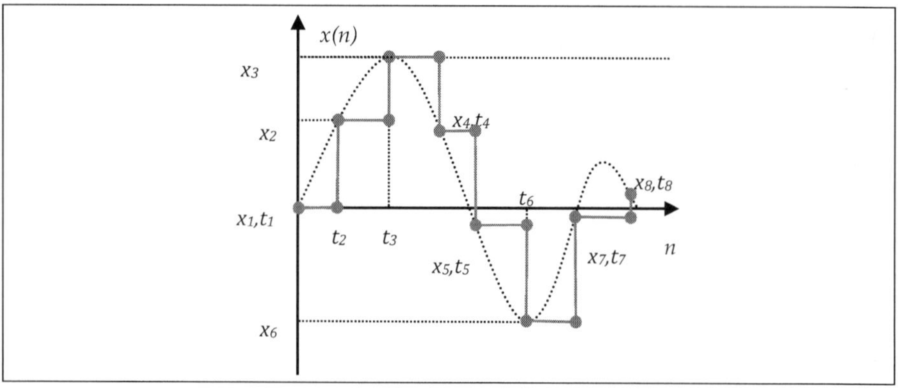

Fig. 4. "Step-shape" (0th-order polynomial) approximation of input excitation

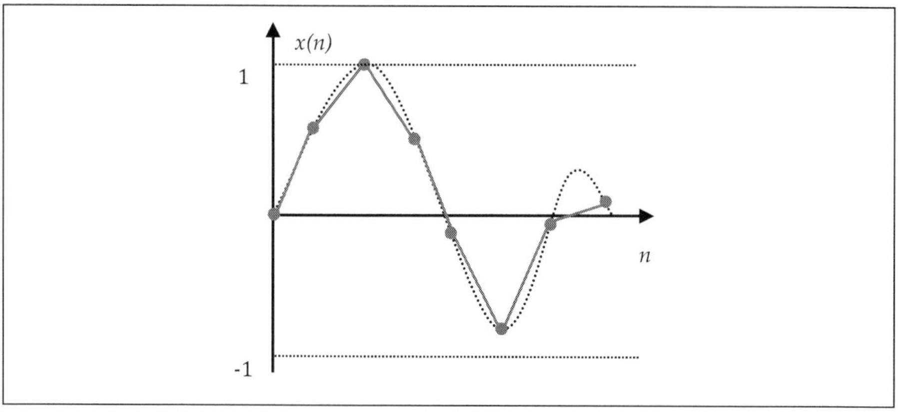

Fig. 5. Piece-wise linear (1st-order polynomial) approximation of input excitation

If fault detection is the only performed diagnosis type, the "unknown" decision can be replaced by NO GO decision (the worst case). This obviously reduces test yield, but does not deteriorates diagnosis trust level.

The L-Tester (fault location) points which circuit element is faulty or decision "?", if proper classification cannot be performed.

The deepest level: fault identification (information about faulty element value or at least its shift - represented by I-Tester) has not been analysed in this work.

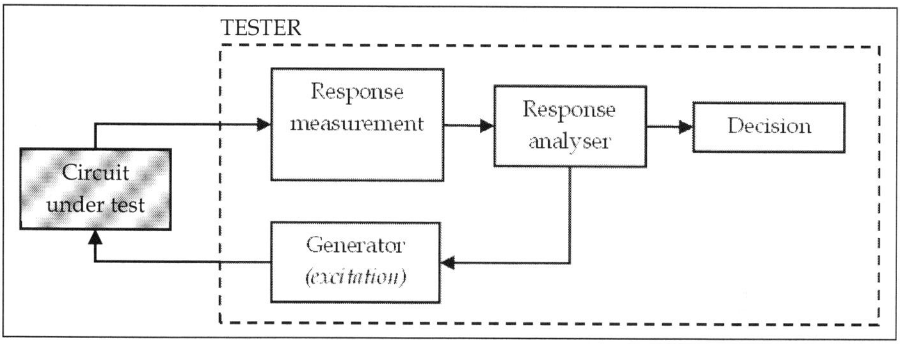

Fig. 6. General tester structure

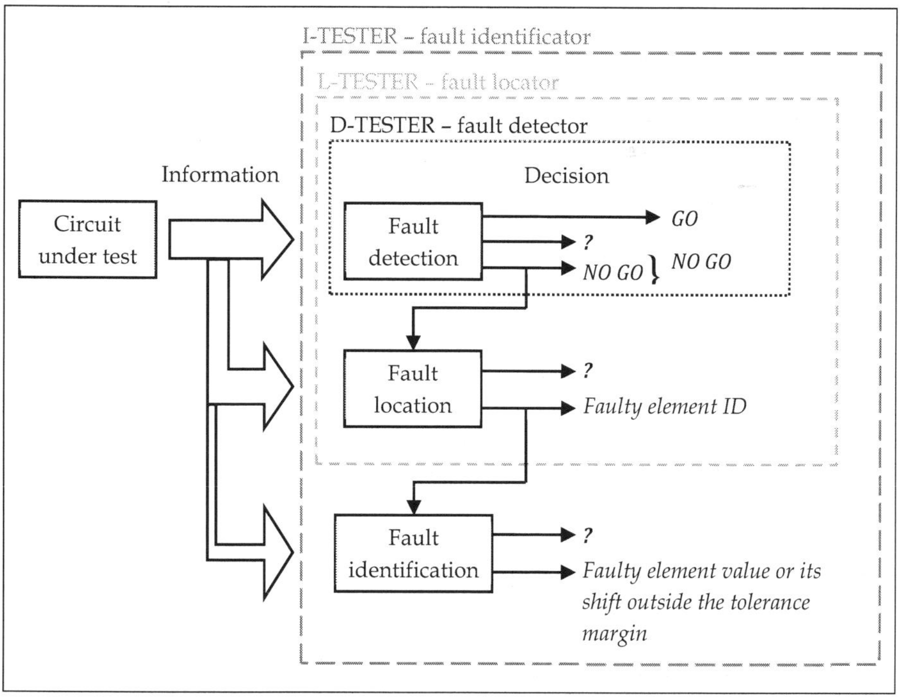

Fig. 7. Fault diagnosis levels

2.3 Fault detection: D-Tester design

Presented fault diagnosis method belongs to class SBT (Simulate-Before-Test) with *fault dictionary*. The dictionary contains information related to selected faults that are simulated *before* circuit measurements. There is defined set **F** containing selected N_F faults F_k, k = 1, 2, …, N_F. Fault numbered 0 (F_0) is used to code healthy (non-faulty) circuit:

$$\boldsymbol{F} = \{F_0, F_1, F_2, \dots, F_{NF}\} \tag{4}$$

Figure below presents structure of the D-Tester (fault detector).

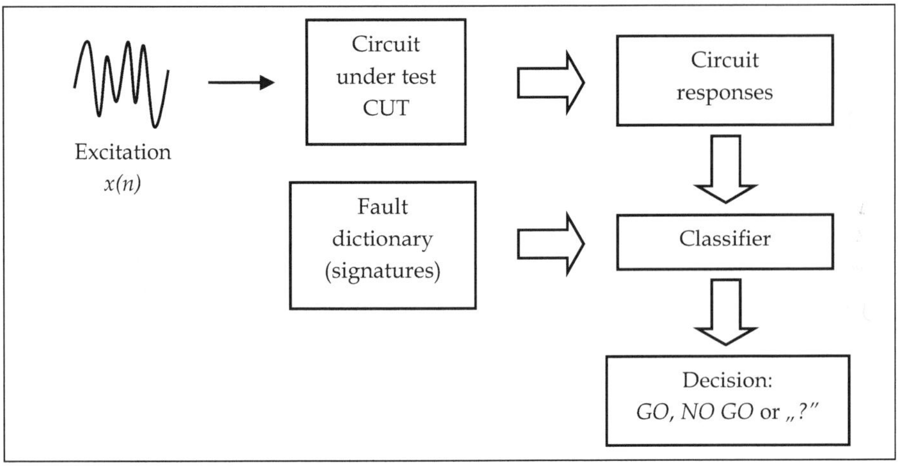

Fig. 8. D-Tester (fault detector) structure

The fault dictionary **S** is built from simulated CUT responses (for all analysed faults). The dictionary contains N_F + 1 fault signatures S_k, k = 0, 1, 2…, N_F, where each signature S_k corresponds to fault F_k (fig. 9).

The example of the fault dictionary for single response y(n) is placed below:

$$\mathbb{S} = \{S_0, S_1, \dots, S_{NF}\} = \begin{bmatrix} S_0 \\ S_1 \\ \dots \\ S_{NF} \end{bmatrix} \tag{5}$$

Each particular signature S_k is vector containing samples of response y(n) = { y_1, y_2, …, y_{Np} }:

$$\mathbb{S} = \begin{bmatrix} S_0 \\ S_1 \\ \dots \\ S_{NF} \end{bmatrix} = \begin{bmatrix} y^{S_0}(n) \\ y^{S_1}(n) \\ \dots \\ y^{S_{NF}}(n) \end{bmatrix} = \begin{bmatrix} y_1^{S_0} & y_2^{S_0} & \dots & y_{N_P}^{S_0} \\ y_1^{S_1} & y_2^{S_1} & \dots & y_{N_P}^{S_1} \\ \dots & \dots & \dots & \dots \\ y_1^{S_{NF}} & y_2^{S_{NF}} & \dots & y_{N_P}^{S_{NF}} \end{bmatrix} \tag{6}$$

so, each signature can represented by discrete series of samples:

$$S_k = y^{S_k}(n) = s_k(n) = \left\{s_1, s_2, \dots, s_{N_p}\right\}_k; \quad k = 0, 1, \dots, N_F \tag{7}$$

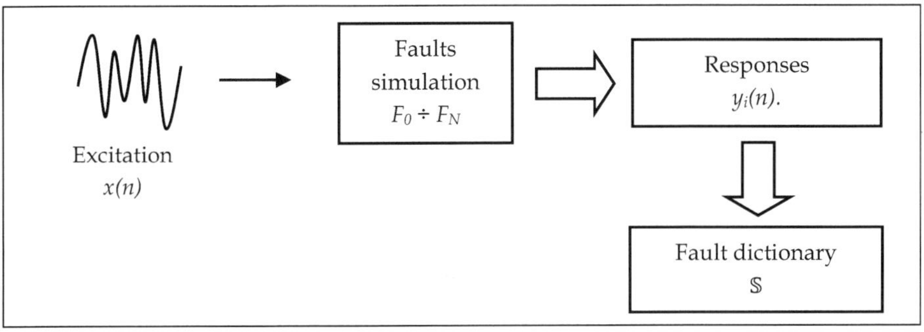

Fig. 9. Schema of fault dictionary creation

According to the test and measurement assumptions, excited passive CUT returns two responses: output voltage $y_1(n)$ and input current $y_2(n)$, where excited active CUT returns four responses - additionally positive $y_3(n)$ and negative supply current $y_4(n)$. The dictionary **S** contains fault signatures $S_{i,k}$, $k = 0, 1, 2\dots, N_F$ for particular CUT responses $y_i(n)$. Example for passive CUT is presented on fig. 10 ($i = 1, 2$):

$$\mathbb{S} = \begin{bmatrix} \mathbb{S}\{y_1(n)\} \\ \mathbb{S}\{y_2(n)\} \end{bmatrix} = \begin{bmatrix} S_{y_1(n),0} \\ S_{y_1(n),1} \\ \dots \\ S_{y_1(n),NF} \\ S_{y_2(n),0} \\ S_{y_2(n),1} \\ \dots \\ S_{y_2(n),NF} \end{bmatrix} = \begin{bmatrix} y_1^{S_0}(n) \\ y_1^{S_1}(n) \\ \dots \\ y_1^{S_{NF}}(n) \\ y_2^{S_0}(n) \\ y_2^{S_1}(n) \\ \dots \\ y_2^{S_{NF}}(n) \end{bmatrix} \tag{8}$$

Tolerances of circuit elements must be taken into consideration when building fault dictionary. There has been used Monte-Carlo (MC) function of a PSpice simulator. Values of non-faulty elements are uniformly random within their tolerance interval. The result is multiplication of CUT responses, thus fault signatures, by factor $N_{MC} + 1$, where N_{MC} is number of performed Monte-Carlo analyses (without nominal circuit). The example below is a fault dictionary for passive CUT ($i = 1, 2$) and two Monte-Carlo analyses ($m = 0, 1, 2$), where $m = 0 =$ „nom" denotes circuit with nominal values of elements:

$$\mathbb{S} = \begin{bmatrix} \mathbb{S}\{y_1(n)\} \\ \mathbb{S}\{y_2(n)\} \end{bmatrix} \xrightarrow{MC\ analysis} \mathbb{S}' = \begin{bmatrix} \mathbb{S}\{y_1(n)\}_{MC="nom"} \\ \mathbb{S}\{y_1(n)\}_{MC=1} \\ \mathbb{S}\{y_1(n)\}_{MC=2} \\ \mathbb{S}\{y_2(n)\}_{MC="nom"} \\ \mathbb{S}\{y_2(n)\}_{MC=1} \\ \mathbb{S}\{y_2(n)\}_{MC=2} \end{bmatrix} \tag{9}$$

$\mathbf{S_{i,k}}$ means set of signatures of k-th fault for i-th response $y_i(n)$, obtained from N_{MC} Monte-Carlo simulation, where $k = 0, 1, 2, \ldots, N_F$ and $i = 1, 2$ for passive or $i = 1, 2, 3, 4$ for active circuit:

$$\boldsymbol{S_{i,k}} = \begin{bmatrix} S_{k,MC=\text{"nom"}} \\ S_{k,MC=1} \\ S_{k,MC=2} \end{bmatrix}; \quad k = 0, 1, \ldots, N_F \tag{10}$$

Totally, the fault dictionary for passive CUT contains $2{\cdot}(N_{MC}+1){\cdot}(N_F+1)$ signatures and for active CUT: $4{\cdot}(N_{MC}+1){\cdot}(N_F+1)$ signatures.

Figure 10 contains exemplary signatures for single CUT response and two selected faults F_1 and F_2. Number of Monte-Carlo analyses is $N_{MC} = 4$. There has been assumed that location of particular signature is distance from signature S_0^{nom} (healthy nominal circuit). If there are no Monte-Carlo analysis performed (all circuits are nominal), the horizontal axis contains only S_i^m signatures. The Monte-Carlo analysis introduces spread around nominal values and single signatures turn into a group of signatures $S_{i,k}^m$, where $m = 1, 2, \ldots, N_{MC}$ for i-th CUT response $y_i(n)$ and k-th fault F_k. This enables finding border values of the signature sets (groups) - fig. 10.

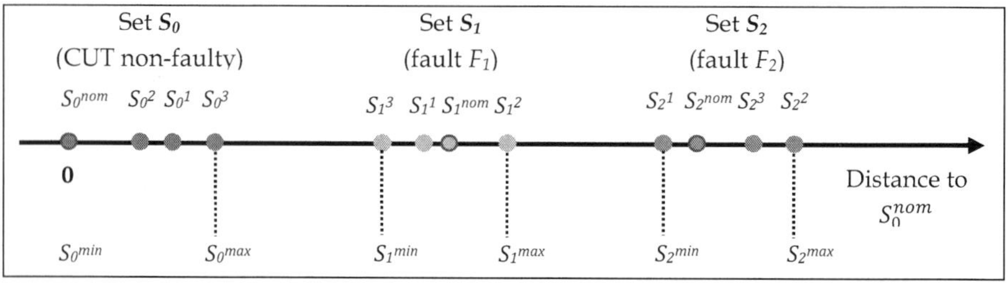

Fig. 10. Example of signature sets (groups) for single response and $N_F = 2$, $N_{MC} = 4$

Distance of each circuit response $y_i(n) = \{y_1, y_2, \ldots y_n, \ldots, y_{N_P}\}_i$ from appropriate fault signature $\boldsymbol{S_{i,k}} = S_{i,k}^m = s_{i,k}^m(n) = \{s_1, s_2, \ldots, s_n, \ldots, s_{N_p}\}_{i,k}^m$ has been calculated in two alternative ways:

1. one-dimensional Euclidean distance d:

$$d^i(k,m) = \sqrt{\sum_{n=1}^{N_p} \left[y_n^i - s_{i,k,n}^m\right]^2} \qquad \begin{matrix} k = 0, 1, \ldots, N_F \\ m = 0, 1, \ldots, N_{MC} \end{matrix} \tag{11}$$

where: $i = 1, 2$ for passive CUT or $i = 1, 2, 3, 4$ for active one,

2. absolute difference d and selected threshold U_{min}:

$$r^i(k,m) = \begin{cases} 1 & if \quad \left|y_n^i - s_{i,k,n}^m\right| > U_{min} \\ 0 & elsewhere \end{cases}; \qquad \begin{matrix} k = 0, 1, \ldots, N_F \\ m = 0, 1, \ldots, N_{MC} \end{matrix} \tag{12}$$

$$d^i(k,m) = \sum_{m=0}^{N_{MC}} \sum_{k=0}^{N_F} r^i(k,m) \tag{13}$$

where: i = 1, 2 for passive CUT or i = 1, 2, 3, 4 for active CUT. Level of the threshold U_{min} is related to measurement accuracy and is chosen arbitrarily by test engineer.

2.4 Fault location: L-Tester design

According to fig. 7, step of the fault location is performed only, if fault detector returns decision NO GO. Then, fault locator tries to find which element is responsible for circuit fault or returns decision "?" ("unknown"). The structure, design and work of L-Tester is similar to the D-Tester, except missing state F_0 (healthy circuit) in set **F** of analysed circuit faults. It must be noted that, despite of one CUT state less to classify from (F_0), the diagnosis goal of fault location is much more difficult than fault detection.

Totally, the fault dictionary contains $2 \cdot (N_{MC}+1) \cdot N_F$ signatures for passive circuit or $4 \cdot (N_{MC}+1) \cdot N_F$ signatures for active CUT.

3. Utilisation of a wavelet transform

One of alternative methods for simultaneous time-frequency analysis is a wavelet transform (Daubechies, 1992). The most important differences comparing to popular Fourier transform are:

- use of base function with limited (or approximately limited) time domain. This implies that base function must be *aperiodic*,
- base function is *scaled* and *shifted* simultaneously.

Conceptually wavelet transform is equivalent to constant percentage bandwidth frequency analysis: $\Delta f/f0$=const, used. e.g. in acoustics, but differently implemented.

The formula below defines continuous real wavelet transform (Daubechies, 1992):

$$X(a,b) = \frac{1}{\sqrt{|a|}} \int_{-\infty}^{\infty} x(t)\, \psi\left(\frac{t-b}{a}\right) dt \ ; \qquad a \neq 0; \ \ a, b \in \mathbb{R} \tag{14}$$

The function $\psi(t)$ is called base wavelet (or mother wavelet) and its stretched and shifted form $\psi_{a,b}(t)$ called just a wavelet:

$$\psi_{a,b}(t) = \psi\left(\frac{t-b}{a}\right); \qquad a \neq 0; \ \ a, b \in \mathbb{R} \tag{15}$$

The parameter a (called *scale* parameter) is responsible for analysis "resolution". Small value corresponds to high detail level which can be analysed in function x(t). This is analogue to high frequency harmonics in Fourier transform. The parameter b (*shift*) is responsible for location on the time axis (fig. 11).

The inverse transform is defined as (Daubechies, 1992):

$$x(t) = \int_{0}^{\infty} \int_{-\infty}^{\infty} \frac{1}{a^2} X(a,b) \frac{1}{\sqrt{|a|}} \varphi\left(\frac{t-b}{a}\right) db \, da \tag{16}$$

where φ is a synthesising function, dual to the analysing wavelet function ψ and satisfying condition:

$$\int_0^\infty \int_{-\infty}^\infty \frac{1}{|a^3|} \varphi\left(\frac{t_1-b}{a}\right) \varphi\left(\frac{t-b}{a}\right) db\, da = \delta(t_1 - t) \tag{17}$$

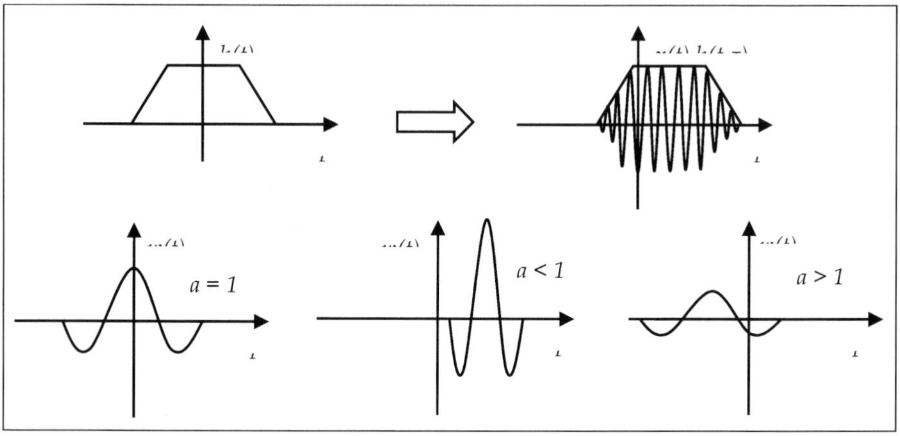

Fig. 11. Scaling and shifting of the base functions in short-time Fourier transform (STFT) and in wavelet transform

3.1 Discrete wavelet transform

In case of a discrete function x(n), the parameters of scale *a* and shift *b* are discrete as well and equation (14) is modified:

$$X(m,n) = a_0^{-\frac{m}{2}} \int_{-\infty}^{\infty} x(t)\, \psi(a_0^{-m}\, t - n\, b_0)\, dt \tag{18}$$

In order to completely, but non redundantly cover domain of analysed function x(n), the parameters *a* and *b* must be calculated as follows (Daubechies, 1992):

$$a = a_0^m; \qquad b = nb_0a_0^m\,; \qquad m, n \in \mathbb{C};\ a_0 > 1;\ b_0 > 0 \tag{19}$$

Unfortunately, in case of a discrete wavelet transform, there is no guarantee of reconstruction of x(n) based only on values of X(m,n) coefficients (Daubechies, 1992).

3.2 Applied modifications of a wavelet transform

Utilisation of a wavelet transform as a feature extractor is based on a continuous transform. Numerical calculations (performed in Matlab environment) lead to following assumptions:

- domain of a function x(n) is limited:

$$\text{supp}[\,x(n)] \in [0; t_{max}] \tag{20}$$

- continuous function x(t) is approximated by discrete x(n) (0th order polynomial, fig. 4),

- values of scale parameter a are limited to natural numbers and value of a_{max} is selected by test engineer:

$$a = 1, 2, \dots, a_{max} \tag{21}$$

- values of shift parameter b are limited to natural numbers including 0:

$$b = 0, 1, \dots, N_P - 1 \tag{22}$$

This allows following transformations of formula (14):

$$X(a,b) = \frac{1}{\sqrt{a}} \sum_{n=-\infty}^{\infty} \int_{n}^{n+1} x(t)\, \psi\left(\frac{t-b}{a}\right) dt \tag{23}$$

$$X(a,b) = \frac{1}{\sqrt{a}} \sum_{n=-\infty}^{\infty} x(n) \int_{n}^{n+1} \psi\left(\frac{t-b}{a}\right) dt \tag{24}$$

$$X(a,b) = \frac{1}{\sqrt{a}} \sum_{n=1}^{N_P} x(n) \left(\int_{-\infty}^{n+1} \psi\left(\frac{t-b}{a}\right) dt - \int_{-\infty}^{n} \psi\left(\frac{t-b}{a}\right) dt \right) \tag{25}$$

where expression:

$$\int_{-\infty}^{n} \psi(t) dt \tag{26}$$

is calculated numerically, dependent on selected base wavelet (Daubechies, 1992). In simplified case, when mother wavelet $\psi(t)$ exists in analytical form, equation (25) can be expressed directly in discrete form:

$$X(a,b) = \frac{1}{\sqrt{a}} \sum_{n=1}^{N_P} x(n)\, \psi\left(\frac{n-b}{a}\right); \quad \begin{matrix} a = 1, 2, \dots, a_{max} \\ b = 0, 1, \dots, N_P - 1 \end{matrix} \tag{27}$$

The above formula clearly shows, that there must performed N_P operations of convolution of sequence x(n) with discrete wavelet $\psi(n)$ for each value of scale parameter a. This allows easy evaluation of a numerical complexity of such transformation.

3.3 Fault detection with wavelet fault dictionary: DW-Tester

CUT returns discrete responses $y_i(n)$ for applied excitation x(n). According to eq. (25) or (27) there is calculated set of wavelet coefficients $Y_i(a,b)$ for each response $y_i(n)$:

$$Y_i(a,b) = TF[y_i(n)] \tag{28}$$

where i = 1, 2 for passive CUT or i = 1, 2, 3, 4 for active CUT and TF is a transform with selected base wavelet function, according to (25) or (27).

$$\mathbb{Y} = \begin{bmatrix} Y_{11} & Y_{12} & \dots & Y_{1,N_P-1} \\ Y_{21} & Y_{22} & \dots & Y_{2,N_P-1} \\ \dots & \dots & \dots & \dots \\ Y_{a_{max},1} & Y_{a_{max},2} & \dots & Y_{a_{max},N_P-1} \end{bmatrix}_{a_{max} \times N_P - 1} \tag{29}$$

Distance of a single CUT response $y_i(n)$ (represented by matrix of wavelet coefficients Y_i) to appropriate fault signature (also in form of a wavelet coefficients $S_k^{F,i,j}$) is calculated as:

1. two-dimensional Euclidean distance:

$$d^i(j,k) = \sqrt{\sum_{a=1}^{a_{max}} \sum_{b=0}^{N_p-1} \left[Y^i(a,b) - S_k^{F,i,j}(a,b)\right]^2} \qquad \begin{matrix} k = 0,1,\dots,N_F \\ j = 1,2,\dots,N_{MC} \end{matrix} \tag{30}$$

where $i = 1, 2$ for passive CUT or $i = 1, 2, 3, 4$ for active CUT;

2. two-dimensional linear Pearson correlation:

$$d_P^i = \frac{\sum_{a=1}^{a_{max}} \sum_{b=0}^{N_P-1} \left[Y^i(a,b) - \overline{Y^i}\right]\left[S_k^{F,i,j}(a,b) - \overline{S_k^{F,i,j}}\right]}{\sqrt{\sum_{a=1}^{a_{max}} \sum_{b=0}^{N_P-1} \left[Y^i(a,b) - \overline{Y^i}\right]^2} \sqrt{\sum_{a=1}^{a_{max}} \sum_{b=0}^{N_P-1} \left[S_k^{F,i,j}(a,b) - \overline{S_k^{F,i,j}}\right]^2}} \tag{31}$$

where:

$$\overline{Y^i} = \frac{1}{a_{maks} \cdot (N_P - 1)} \sum_{a=1}^{a_{maks}} \sum_{b=0}^{N_P-1} Y^i(a,b) \tag{32}$$

and:

$$\overline{S_k^{F,i,j}} = \frac{1}{a_{maks} \cdot (N_P - 1)} \sum_{a=1}^{a_{maks}} \sum_{b=0}^{N_P-1} S_k^{F,i,j}(a,b) \tag{33}$$

for:

$$k = 0,1,\dots,N_F \qquad j = 1,2,\dots,N_{MC}$$

where:
$i = 1, 2$ for passive CUT or $i = 1, 2, 3, 4$ for active CUT,
$\bar{Y}$ and $\bar{S}$ are mean values of elements of respectively matrixes Y and S,
$S_k^{F,i,j}$ denotes wavelet signature (matrix of wavelet coefficients) of i-th response $y_i(n)$, for k-th fault F_k and j-th Monte-Carlo analysis.

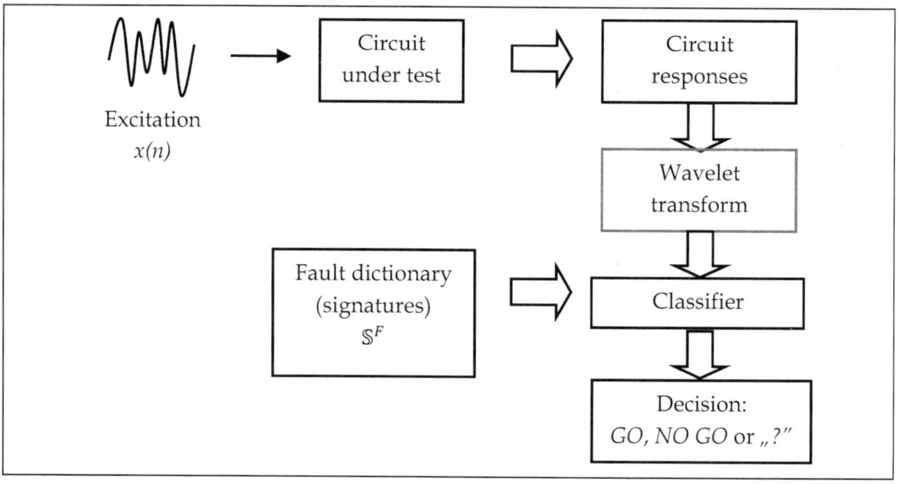

Fig. 12. Schematic of a DW-Tester

3.4 Fault location with wavelet fault dictionary (LW-Tester)

According to fig. 7, the fault location is performed only, if fault detector returns decision NO GO. Then, the fault locator points damaged element or returns decision: "?" ("unknown"). The structure, design and work of LW-Tester is similar to the DW-Tester, except missing state F_0 (healthy circuit) in set **F** of analysed circuit faults.

Distance of a single CUT response $y_i(n)$ (represented by matrix of wavelet coefficients Y_i) from appropriate fault signature (also in form of a wavelet coefficients $S_k^{F,i,j}$) is calculated as follows:

1. two-dimensional Euclid distance:

$$d^i(j,k) = \sqrt{\sum_{a=1}^{a_{max}} \sum_{b=0}^{N_p-1} \left[Y^i(a,b) - S_k^{F,i,j}(a,b)\right]^2} \qquad \begin{array}{l} k = 1,2,\ldots,N_F \\ j = 1,2,\ldots,N_{MC} \end{array} \tag{34}$$

where i = 1, 2 for passive CUT or i = 1, 2, 3, 4 for active CUT;

2. two-dimensional linear Pearson correlation:

$$d_P^i = \frac{\sum_{a=1}^{a_{max}} \sum_{b=0}^{N_P-1} \left[Y^i(a,b) - \overline{Y^i}\right]\left[S_k^{F,i,j}(a,b) - \overline{S_k^{F,i,j}}\right]}{\sqrt{\sum_{a=1}^{a_{max}} \sum_{b=0}^{N_P-1} \left[Y^i(a,b) - \overline{Y^i}\right]^2} \sqrt{\sum_{a=1}^{a_{max}} \sum_{b=0}^{N_P-1} \left[S_k^{F,i,j}(a,b) - \overline{S_k^{F,i,j}}\right]^2}} \tag{35}$$

where:

$$\overline{Y^i} = \frac{1}{a_{max} \cdot (N_P - 1)} \sum_{a=1}^{a_{max}} \sum_{b=0}^{N_P-1} Y^i(a,b) \tag{36}$$

and:

$$\overline{S_k^{F,i,j}} = \frac{1}{a_{max} \cdot (N_P - 1)} \sum_{a=1}^{a_{max}} \sum_{b=0}^{N_P-1} S_k^{F,i,j}(a,b) \tag{37}$$

for:

$$k = 1,2,\ldots,N_F \qquad j = 1,2,\ldots,N_{MC}$$

where:
i = 1, 2 for passive CUT or i = 1, 2, 3, 4 for active CUT,
$\bar{Y}$ and $\bar{S}$ are mean values of elements of respectively matrixes Y and S,
$S_k^{F,i,j}$ denotes wavelet signature (matrix of wavelet coefficients) of i-th response $y_i(n)$, for k-th fault F_k and j-th Monte-Carlo analysis.

4. Examples

4.1 Example 1: Biquadrate active low-pass filter

Fig. 13 presents biquadrate active low-pass filter [Bali96]. Specialised excitation has been found by means of a genetic algorithm and diagnosis efficiency has been compared to case of testing using simple excitation: input voltage step. There have been selected 8 parametric faults among 4 discrete elements: C_1, C_2, R_2 and R_4: ±10% above and below nominal values. Tolerances of non-faulty elements were equal 2% for resistors and 5% for capacitors. Sampling time of discrete excitation and CUT response was equal to T_s = 50 ns.

There have been investigated three cases, different by method of comparison of CUT responses with appropriate fault signatures and utilisation of wavelet transform.

1. The distance between CUT responses and fault signatures is calculated by means of one-dimensional Euclidean distance (11) and wavelet transform is not used. The excitation x(n) and CUT responses $y_i(n)$ were discretised by $N_P = 200$ samples.
2. Fitness value *fit* of a particular solution in a genetic algorithm was modified by energy density in found excitation frequency spectrum. This introduced positive selection "pressure" on solutions (excitations) with lower high frequency components. The first step was calculation of discrete frequency spectrum F(m) of a excitation x(n) [Lyon99]:

$$F(m) = \sum_{n=0}^{N_P-1} x(n) \cdot e^{-j2\pi m \frac{n}{N}} \qquad m = 0, 1, 2, \dots, N_P - 1 \tag{38}$$

Then, obtained spectrum was divided into two equal intervals: $\left[0, \frac{1}{4T_s}\right)$ and $\left[\frac{1}{4T_s}, \frac{1}{2T_s}\right)$, or equivalently $\left[0, \frac{N_P}{2} - 1\right]$ and $\left[\frac{N_P}{2}, N_P - 1\right]$. In last step, total energy E_i in each *i*-th interval was calculated:

$$E_1 = \sum_{m=0}^{\frac{N_P}{2}-1} |F(m)|^2 \quad oraz \quad E_2 = \sum_{m=\frac{N_P}{2}}^{N_P-1} |F(m)|^2 \tag{39}$$

Finally, value of fitness function *fit* was modified as follows:

$$\begin{aligned} &je\acute{s}li\ E_1 > E_2\ to\ fit \rightarrow 2 \cdot fit \\ &je\acute{s}li\ E_1 \le E_2\ to\ fit \rightarrow \tfrac{1}{2} \cdot fit \end{aligned} \tag{40}$$

3. There has been used wavelet transform to build fault dictionary. The excitation x(n) and CUT responses $y_i(n)$ were approximated by $N_P = 100$ samples.

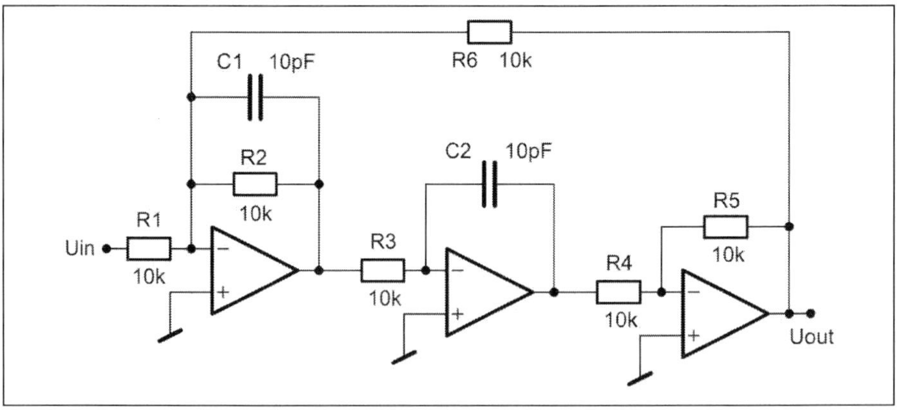

Fig. 13. Biquadrate active low-pass filter [Bali96].

Ad. 1

Figure 14 presents found excitation in time domain and its normalised amplitude spectrum can be found in figure 15. Table 1 shows efficiency of fault detection for step and specialised excitation (probabilities of a healthy circuit correct detection - true positive H_H; healthy circuit incorrect detection – false negative H_F; faulty circuit correct detection - true negative F_F and faulty circuit incorrect detection - false positive F_H). Similar data, but for case of fault location (probabilities of fault F_x classified as D_x, with correct decisions in main diagonal) can be found in table 2 for found excitation and in table 3 for diagnosis with step excitation.

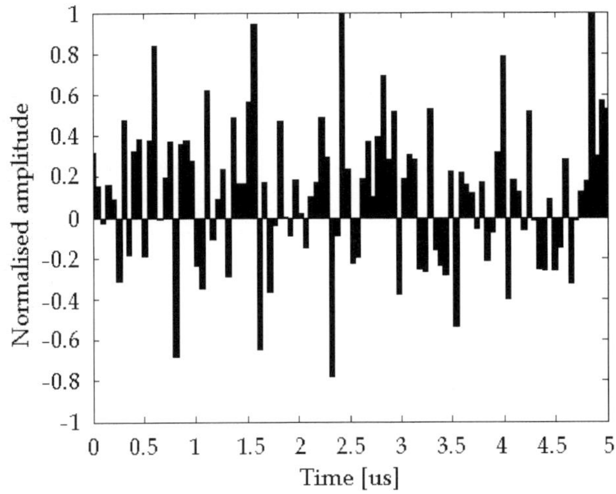

Fig. 14. Found specialised excitation $x_1(n)$

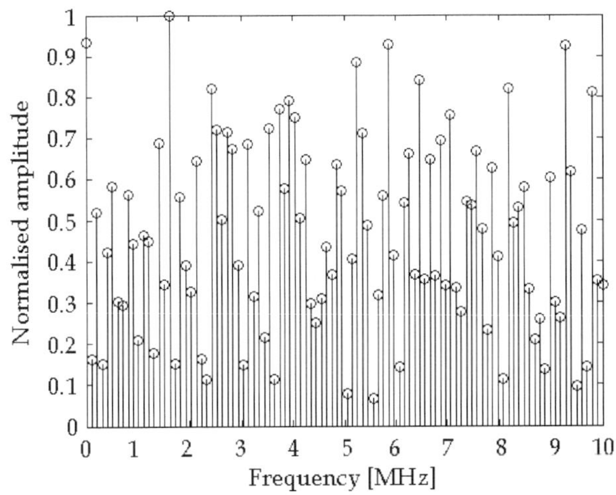

Fig. 15. Normalised frequency (amplitude) spectrum of found excitation $x_1(n)$

Excitation	H_H	H_F	F_F	F_H
$x_1(n)$	0.25	0.75	0.93	0.07
Step	0.03	0.97	0.96	0.04

Table 1. Fault detection efficiency (ad. 1)

	D_1	D_2	D_3	D_4	D_5	D_6	D_7	D_8
F_1	0.32	0.02	0.03	0.29	0.03	0	0.27	0
F_2	0.04	0.36	0.10	0.01	0	0.05	0	0.17
F_3	0.05	0.23	0.47	0	0.04	0	0	0.14
F_4	0.14	0.04	0	0.43	0	0.18	0.08	0
F_5	0.01	0	0.14	0	0.73	0	0.12	0
F_6	0	0.01	0	0.08	0	0.71	0	0.18
F_7	0.17	0	0	0.03	0	0	0.80	0
F_8	0	0.19	0.02	0	0	0.05	0	0.72

Table 2. Fault location efficiency for specialised excitation (ad. 1)

	D_1	D_2	D_3	D_4	D_5	D_6	D_7	D_8
F_1	0.14	0.01	0	0.19	0.29	0.01	0.12	0.22
F_2	0	0.13	0.03	0.03	0.37	0.02	0	0.34
F_3	0	0.11	0.12	0.04	0.35	0	0	0.34
F_4	0.15	0.02	0	0.28	0.20	0.03	0.03	0.21
F_5	0	0	0.06	0.14	0.41	0	0.02	0.37
F_6	0.04	0.06	0	0.05	0.21	0.15	0	0.37
F_7	0.10	0	0	0.20	0.27	0	0.27	0.16
F_8	0	0.21	0.04	0	0.23	0.01	0	0.49

Table 3. Fault location efficiency for step excitation (ad. 1)

It can observed that found specialised excitation $x_1(n)$ increased test yield in case of fault detection (tab. 1) and efficiency proper fault location was 1.5 ÷ 5 times greater (tab. 2 and 3 main diagonals, better values marked red).

Ad. 2

Figure 16 presents found excitation in time domain and its normalised amplitude spectrum in figure 17. Table 4 shows efficiency of fault detection for step and specialised excitation (probabilities of a healthy circuit correct detection - true positive H_H; healthy circuit incorrect detection – false negative H_F; faulty circuit correct detection - true negative F_F and faulty circuit incorrect detection - false positive F_H). Similar data, but for case of fault location (probabilities of fault F_x classified as D_x, with correct decisions in main diagonal) can be found in table 5 for designed excitation and in table 6 for diagnosis with step excitation.

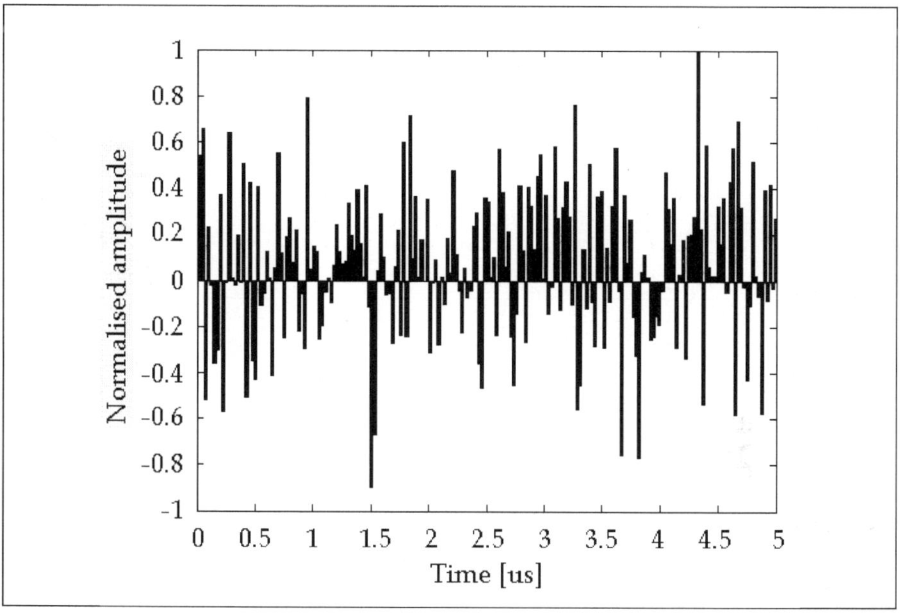

Fig. 16. Found specialised excitation $x_2(n)$

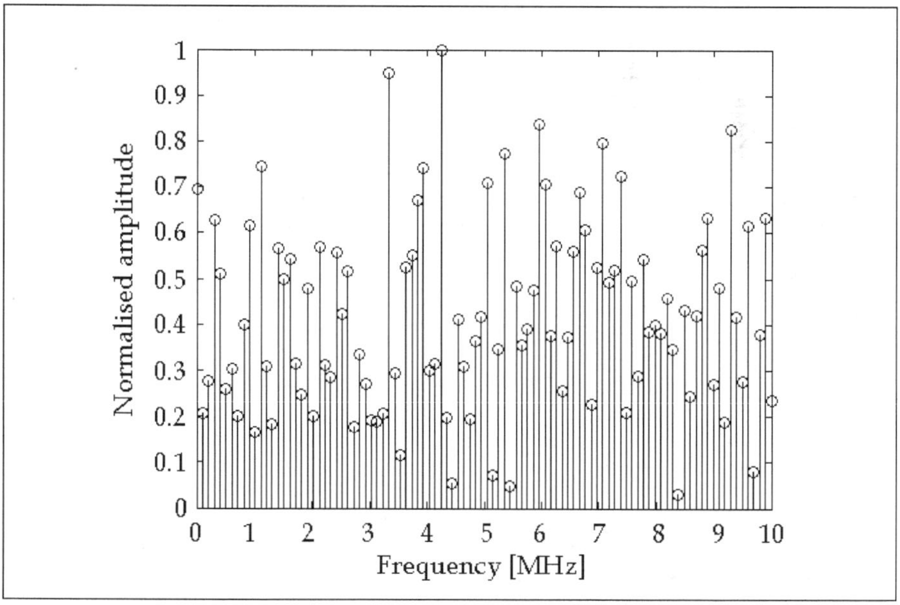

Fig. 17. Normalised frequency (amplitude) spectrum of found excitation $x_2(n)$

Excitation	H_H	H_F	F_F	F_H
$x_1(n)$	0.25	0.75	0.93	0.07
Step	0.03	0.97	0.96	0.04

Table 4. Fault detection efficiency (ad. 2)

	D_1	D_2	D_3	D_4	D_5	D_6	D_7	D_8
F_1	0.32	0.02	0.03	0.29	0.03	0	0.27	0
F_2	0.04	0.36	0.10	0.01	0	0.05	0	0.17
F_3	0.05	0.23	0.47	0	0.04	0	0	0.14
F_4	0.14	0.04	0	0.43	0	0.18	0.08	0
F_5	0.01	0	0.14	0	0.73	0	0.12	0
F_6	0	0.01	0	0.08	0	0.71	0	0.18
F_7	0.17	0	0	0.03	0	0	0.80	0
F_8	0	0.19	0.02	0	0	0.05	0	0.72

Table 5. Fault location efficiency for specialised excitation (ad. 2)

	D_1	D_2	D_3	D_4	D_5	D_6	D_7	D_8
F_1	0.14	0.01	0	0.19	0.29	0.01	0.12	0.22
F_2	0	0.13	0.03	0.03	0.37	0.02	0	0.34
F_3	0	0.11	0.12	0.04	0.35	0	0	0.34
F_4	0.15	0.02	0	0.28	0.20	0.03	0.03	0.21
F_5	0	0	0.06	0.14	0.41	0	0.02	0.37
F_6	0.04	0.06	0	0.05	0.21	0.15	0	0.37
F_7	0.10	0	0	0.20	0.27	0	0.27	0.16
F_8	0	0.21	0.04	0	0.23	0.01	0	0.49

Table 6. Fault location efficiency for step excitation (ad. 2)

Found specialised excitation $x_2(n)$ increased test yield in case of fault detection (tab. 4) and, in most cases, increased efficiency of a proper fault location (tab. 5 and 6).

Ad. 3

Figure 18 presents found excitation in time domain and its normalised amplitude spectrum in figure 19. Table 7 shows efficiency of fault detection for step and specialised excitation (probabilities of a healthy circuit correct detection - true positive H_H; healthy circuit incorrect detection – false negative H_F; faulty circuit correct detection - true negative F_F and faulty circuit incorrect detection - false positive F_H). Similar data, but for case of fault location (probabilities of fault F_x classified as D_x, with correct decisions in main diagonal) can be found in tab. 8 for found excitation and tab. 9 for diagnosis with step excitation.

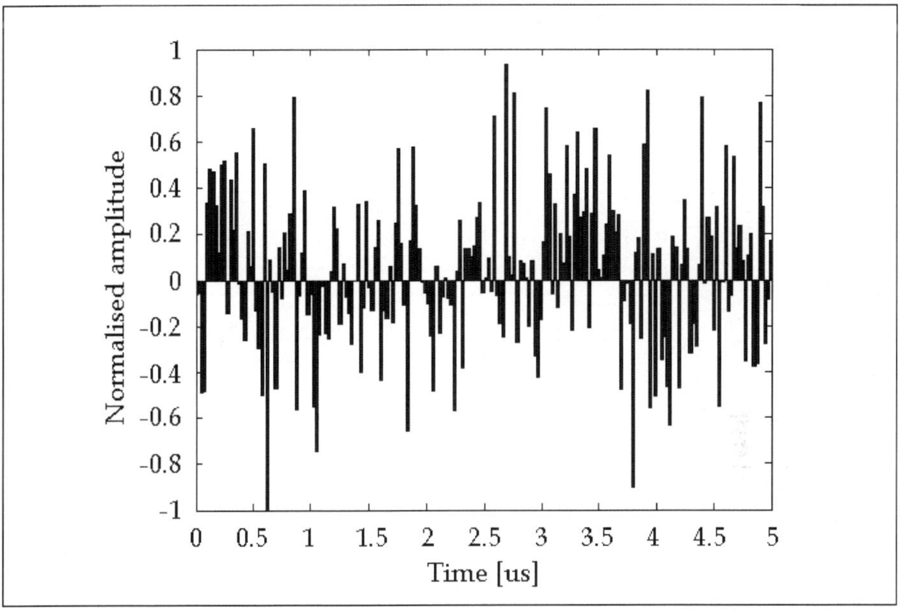

Fig. 18. Found specialised excitation $x_3(n)$

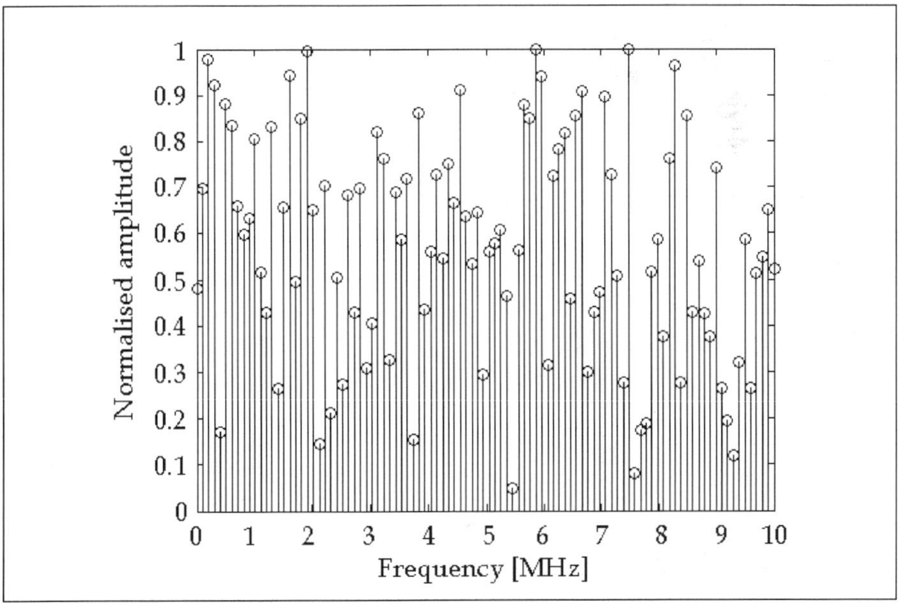

Fig. 19. Normalised frequency (amplitude) spectrum of found excitation $x_3(n)$

Excitation	H_H	H_F	F_F	F_H
$x_3(n)$	**0.17**	0.83	0.90	0.10
Step	**0.16**	0.84	0.91	0.09

Table 7. Fault detection efficiency (ad. 3)

	D_1	D_2	D_3	D_4	D_5	D_6	D_7	D_8
F_1	0.35	0	0.10	0.14	0.07	0	0.30	0
F_2	0.01	0.24	0.16	0.07	0.01	0.07	0	0.28
F_3	0.04	0.19	0.20	0.14	0.02	0.06	0	0.07
F_4	0.33	0.02	0.17	0.15	0.05	0.01	0.18	0
F_5	0.32	0	0.18	0.23	0.11	0	0.12	0
F_6	0.01	0.15	0.16	0.13	0.03	**0.06**	0	0.31
F_7	0.08	0	0	0	0	0	0.92	0
F_8	0	0.17	0	0	0	0.13	0	0.67

Table 8. Fault location efficiency for specialised excitation (ad. 3)

	D_1	D_2	D_3	D_4	D_5	D_6	D_7	D_8
F_1	0.16	0.02	0.10	0.36	0.04	0.07	0.04	0.10
F_2	0.10	0	0.15	0.09	0.02	0.05	0.05	0.45
F_3	0.07	0.02	0.28	0.08	0	0.04	0.01	0.40
F_4	0.12	0.01	0.11	0.37	0.04	0.02	0.05	0.16
F_5	0.12	0.06	0.19	0.14	0	0.06	0.05	0.26
F_6	0.11	0.02	0.25	0.08	0.06	**0.06**	0.02	0.30
F_7	0.24	0.03	0.04	0.52	0.01	0.01	0.09	0.01
F_8	0.05	0.03	0.23	0	0.01	0.03	0	0.57

Table 9. Fault location efficiency for step excitation (ad. 3)

Designed specialised excitation $x_3(n)$ together with utilisation of wavelet transform has increased efficiency of a proper fault location (tab. 8 and 9), with exception of faults F_3 and F_4. However, it must be noted that specialised excitation together with wavelet transform enabled proper location of faults F_2 and F_5 (tab. 9, marked blue), which cannot be localised at all using simple step excitation.

4.2 Example 2: Active low-pass filter

Figure 20 presents active low-pass filter (Kaminska et al., 1997). Designed excitation x(n) has been approximated by a 0th order polynomial (fig. 4). Amplitude of each sample x_n is binary coded by N_B = 3 bits. Width t_w of each interval is changed in range 1 do 8 μs and its resolution is M_B = 2 bits coded by Gray code. Non-faulty tolerances were equal 2% for resistors and 5% for capacitors. There were selected 8 parametric (soft) faults of discrete elements (R_1, R_2, R_3 and C): ±10% shift above and below nominal values.

There have been analysed four active CUT responses (fig. 1). Assumed observation windows was T_{max} = 50 μs after last falling edge of the excitation. This value is also equal to time when circuit reaches steady state after step excitation.

There have been investigated two cases:

1. D-Tester (without wavelet transform) and one-dimensional Euclidean distance metrics (11).
2. DW-Tester with *Meyer* base wavelet and two-dimensional Euclidean distance metrics (30).

Fig. 21 and 22 present found excitations for case 1 and 2 respectively. Tab. 10 presents diagnosis efficiency for defined faults and excitations.

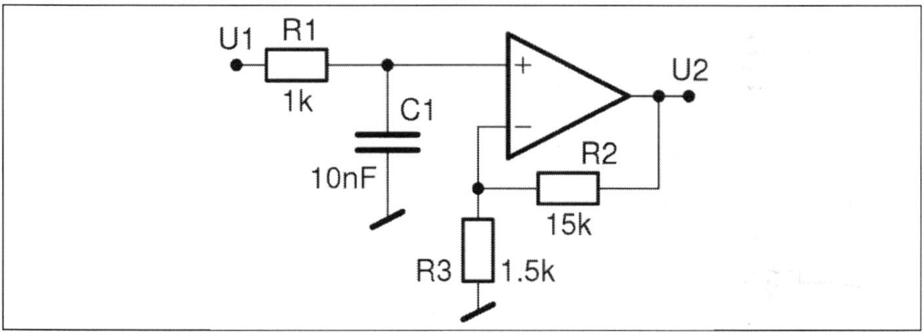

Fig. 20. Active low-pass filter (Kaminska et al., 1997)

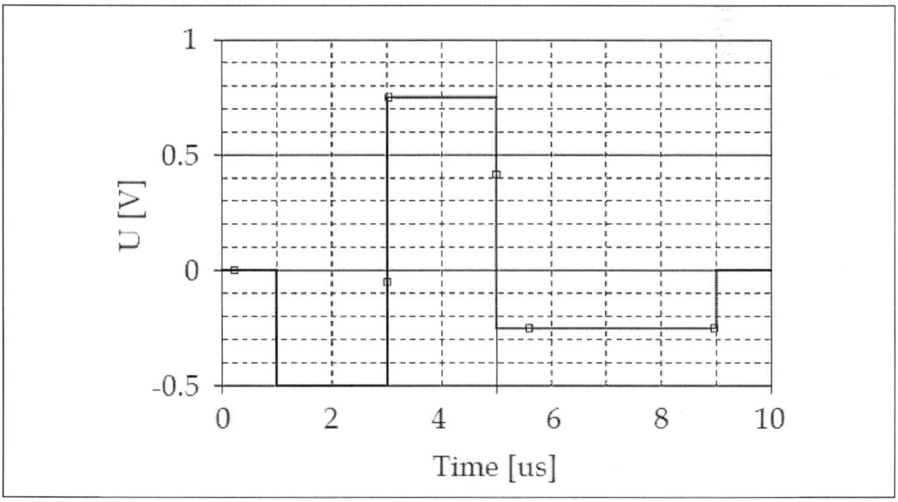

Fig. 21. Found specialised excitation for case 1

Case	Excitation	F_1	F_2	F_3	F_4	F_5	F_6	F_7	F_8
1	$x_1(n)$	0.68	0.63	0.58	0.63	0.74	0.68	1.00	1.00
	Step	0.47	0.42	0.79	0.63	0.37	0.47	0.74	0.89
2	$x_2(n)$	0.58	0.63	0.68	0.47	0.89	0.74	1.00	1.00
	Step	0.58	0.63	0.53	0.63	0.21	0.53	1.00	1.00

Table 10. Fault location efficiency

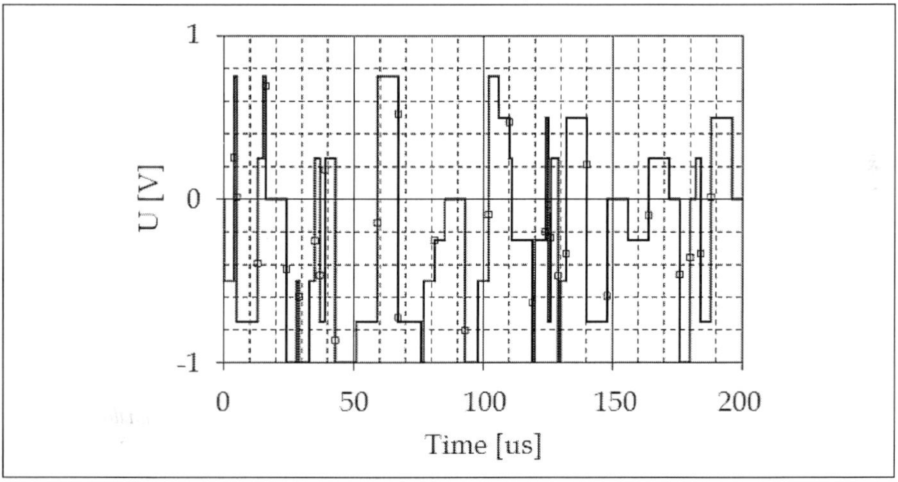

Fig. 22. Found specialised excitation for case 2

Found specialised excitation improved efficiency of analysed single parametric (soft) faults. Utilisation of wavelet transform brought further improvements: i.a. there has been reached 100% proper location of faults F_7 and F_8. Improvement of fault diagnosis was also obtained in testing using simple step excitation (tab. 10, case 2).

5. Conclusions

Utilisation of a wavelet transform as a feature extraction from CUT responses and in building fault dictionary resulted in general improvement of diagnosis efficiency. There have been investigated single catastrophic (hard) and parametric (soft) faults of passive and active analogue electronic circuits. It must be emphasized that the last faults are much more difficult to diagnose, because their influence on circuit behaviour (e.g. transfer function) is much weaker than catastrophic ones. It must be also noted that fault location is more difficult diagnostic goal than fault detection ("just" a differentiation between healthy and faulty circuits). Wavelet transform has been found useful tool in diagnosis of analogue electronic circuits, both in reference cases of simple excitations (step function, real Dirac pulse, linear function) and in cases when excitation has been designed by genetic algorithm. In every case, combination of specialised excitation and wavelet transform resulted in highest efficiency of fault diagnosis.

It has been also found that in some cases (example 2) utilisation of wavelet transform allowed 100% location of a selected faults. Merging genetic algorithm and wavelet transform in example 1 allowed design of test excitation which enabled location of faults completely hidden for diagnosis using step excitation.

It must be also added that abovementioned results have been achieved for simple, non-optimised classifiers based on simple, the closest neighbourhood metrics.

6. References

Baker K., Richardson A. M., Dorey A. P., *Mixed signal test techniques, applications and demands*, IEEE Circuits, Devices, Systems, 1996, vol. 146, pp. 358-365

Balivada A., Chen J., Abraham J. A., *Analog testing with time response parameters*, IEEE Design and Test of Computers, 1996, vol. 13, pp. 18-25

Bernier J. L., Merelo J. J., Ortega J., Prieto A., *Test Pattern Generation for Analog Circuits Using Neural Networks and Evolutive Algorithms*, International Workshop on Artificial Neural Networks, 1995, vol. s. 838–844

Chruszczyk L., Rutkowski J., Grzechca D., *Finding of optimal excitation signal for testing of analog electronic circuits*, International Conference on Signals and Electronic Systems, 2006, Łódź, Poland, pp. 613–616

Chruszczyk L., Grzechca D., Rutkowski J., „Finding of optimal excitation signal for testing of analog electronic circuits", Bulletin of Polish Academy of Sciences, September 2007, pp. 273–280

Chruszczyk L., Rutkowski J., *Excitation optimization in fault diagnosis of analog electronic circuits*, 11th IEEE Workshop on Design and Diagnostics of Electronic Circuits and Systems, 2008, Bratislava, Slovak Republic, pp. 1–4

Chruszczyk L., Rutkowski J., *Optimal excitation in fault diagnosis of analog electronic circuits*, IEEE International Conference on Electronics, Circuits and Systems, 2008, Malta

Chruszczyk L., Rutkowski J., *Specialised excitation and wavelet transform in fault diagnosis of analogue electronic circuits*, IInd International Interdisciplinary Technical Conference of Young Scientists, 2009, Poznan, Poland

Chruszczyk L., *Fault diagnosis of analog electronic circuits with tolerances in mind*, 18th International Conference Mixed Design of Integrated Circuits and Systems, 2011, Gliwice, Poland, *book of abstracts* p. 126. Reprinted in Elektronika № 11/2011 (*in press*), monthly magazine of Association of Polish Electrical Engineers (SEP)

Chruszczyk L., *Tolerance Maximisation in Fault Diagnosis of Analogue Electronic Circuits*, 20th European Conference on Circuit Theory and Design, 2011, Linkoping, Sweden, pp. 914–917

Chruszczyk L., Rutkowski J., *Tolerance Maximisation in Fault Diagnosis of Analogue Electronic Circuits*, Electrical Review № 10/2011 (The Magazine of Polish Electricians), Poland, p. 159

Dai H., Souders M., *Time domain testing strategies and fault diagnosis for analog systems*, 1989, IEEE Instrumentation and Measurement Technology Conference, pp. 293–298

Daubechies I., „Ten lectures on wavelets", CBMS, SIAM, 1992

De Jong K. A., „An analysis of the behavior of a class of genetic adaptive systems", (PhD thesis), 1975, University of Michigan, USA

De Jong K. A., „Adaptive system design. A genetic approach.", IEEE Transactions on Systems, Man and Cybernetics, SMC-10(9), 1980, pp. 566–574

Goldberg D. E., „Genetic Algorithms in Search, Optimization & Machine Learning", Addison-Wesley, 1989

Grefenstette J. J., „Parallel adaptive algorithms for function optimization", 1981, Vanderbilt Univ., Nashville, USA

Grefenstette J., J., *Optimization of Control Parameters for Genetic Algorithms,* IEEE Transactions on Systems, Man and Cybernetics, 1986, vol. 16, pp. 122–128

Holland J. H., „A new kind of turnpike theorem", Bulletin of the American Mathematical Society, 1968, 75, 1311–1317

Huertas J. L., *Test and design for testability of analog and mixed-signal IC: theoretical basic and pragmatical approaches,* European Conference On Circuit Theory And Design, Davos, Switzerland, 1993, pp. 75–156

Kaminska, B. et al., *Analog and mixed-signal benchmark circuits - first release,* IEEE International Test Conference, Washington, USA, 1997

Kilic Y., Zwolinski M., *Testing analog circuits by supply voltage variation and supply current monitoring,* IEEE Custom Integrated Circuits, 1999, pp. 155–158

Milne A., Taylor D., Naylor K., *Assesing and comparing fault coverage when testing analogue circuits,* 1997, IEE Circuits Devices Systems, vol. 144

Milor L., Sangiovanni-Vincentelli A. L., *Minimizing production test time to detect faults in analog circuits,* IEEE CAD of Integrated CAS, 1994, vol. 13, pp. 796–813

Pecenka T., Sekanina L., Kotasek Z., *Evolution of synthetic RTL benchmark circuits with predefined testability,* ACM Transactions on Design Automation of Electronic Systems (TODAES), 2008, vol. 13, ed. 3, art. No. 54

Pettey C. B., Leuze M. R., Grefenstette J. J., *A parallel genetic algorithm,* IInd International Conference on Genetic Algorithms, 1987, pp. 155–161

Saab K., Hamida N.B., Kamińska B., *Closing the Gap Between Analog and Digital Testing,* IEEE Trans. Computer-Aided Design, vol. 20, No. 2, pp. 307-314, 2001

Savir J., Guo Z., *Test Limitations of Parametric Faults In Analog Circuits,* IEEE Trans. on Instrumentation and Measurement, vol. 52, no. 5, October 2003

Somayajula S. S., Sanchez-Sinecio E., Pineda de Gyvez J., *Analog Fault Diagnosis Based on Ramping Power Supply Current Signature Clusters,* 1996, IEEE Circuits and Systems, vol. 43, No. 10, pp. 703

Suh J. Y., Van Gucht D., *Incorporating heuristic information into genetic search,* IInd International Conference on Genetic Algorithms, 1987, pp. 100–107

Tanese R., *Parallel genetic algorithms for a hypercube,* IInd International Conference on Genetic Algorithms, 1987, pp. 177–183

11

Application of Wavelet Analysis in Power Systems

Reza Shariatinasab[1] and Mohsen Akbari[2] and Bijan Rahmani[2]
[1]*Electrical and Computer Engineering Department, University of Birjand*
[2]*Electrical and Computer Engineering Department, K.N. Toosi University of Technology*
Iran

1. Introduction

When you capture and plot a signal, you get only a graph of amplitude versus time. Sometimes, you need frequency and phase information, too. However, you need to know whenever in a waveform the certain characteristics occur. Signal processing could help, but you need to know which type of processing to apply to solve your data-analysis problem.

Many books and papers have been written that explain WT of signals and can be read for further understanding of the basics of wavelet theory. The first recorded mention of what we now call a "wavelet" seems to be in 1909, in a thesis by A. Haar. The concept of wavelets in its present theoretical form was first proposed by J. Morlet, a Geophisicist, and the team at the Marseille Theoretical Physics Center working under A. Grossmann, a theoretical phisicist, in France. They provided a way of thinking for wavelets based on physical intuition. They also proved that with nearly any wave shape they could recover the signal exactly from its transform (Graps, 1995). In other words, the transform of a signal does not change the information content presented in the signal.

The wavelet functions are created from a single charasteristic shape, known as the mother wavelet function, by dialating and shifting the window. Wavelets are oscillating transforms of short duration amplitude decaying to zero at both ends. Like the sine wave in Fourier transform (FT), the mother wavelet $\psi(t)$ is the basic block to represent a signal in WT. However, unlike the FT whose applications are fixed as either sine or cosine functions, the mother wavelet, $\psi(t)$, has many possible functions. Fig. 1 shows some of the popular wavelets including Daubechies, Harr, Coiflet, and Symlet. Dilation involves the stretching and compressing the mother wavelet in time. The wavelet can be expanded to a coarse scale to analyze low frequency, long duration features in the signal. On the other hand, it can be shrunk to a fine scale to analyze high frequency, short duration features of a signal. It is this ability of wavelets to change the scale of observation to study different scale features is its hallmark.

The WT of a signal is generated by finding linear combinations of wavelet functions to represent a signal. The weights of these linear combinations are termed as wavelet coefficients. Reconstruction of a signal from these wavelet coefficients arises from a much older theory known as Calderon's reproducing activity (Grossmann & Morlet, 1984).

The attention of the signal processing community was caught when Mallat (Mallat, 1989) and Daubechies (Daubechies, 1988) established WT connections to discrete signal processing. To date various theories have been developed on various aspects of wavelets and it has been successfully applied in the areas of signal processing, medical imaging, data compression, image compression, sub-band coding, computer vision, and sound synthesis.

There is a plan in this chapter to study the WT applications in power systems. The content of the chapter is organized as follows:

The first part explains a brief definition of wavelet analysis, benefits and difficulties. The second part discusses wavelet applications in power systems. This section is consisted of the modeling guidelines of each application whose the goal is to introduce how to implement the wavelet analysis for different applications in power systems. Also there will be a literature review and one example for each application, separately. In the last part, the detailed analysis for two important applications of wavelet analysis, i.e. detection of the islanding state and fault location, will be illustrated by the authors.

Although, there have been a great effort in references to prove that one wavelet is more suitable than another, there have not been a comprehensive analysis involving a number of wavelets to prove the point of view suggested. Also, the method of comparison among them is not unified, such that a general conclusion is reached. In this chapter, algorithms are also presented to choose a suitable mother wavelet for power system studies.

In general, the properties of orthogonality, compactness support, and number of vanishing moments are required when analyzing electric power system waveforms for computing the power components. All these properties are well described in (Ibrahim, 2009).

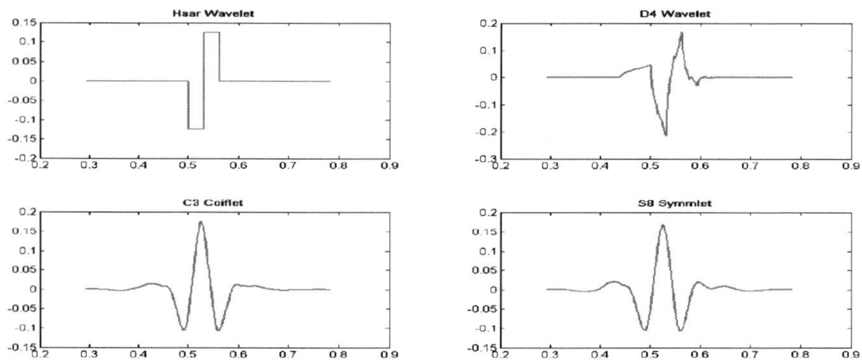

Fig. 1. Some of the popular wavelets used for analysis

2. Wavelet transform

There are several types of WTs and depending on the application, one method is preferred over the others. For a continuous input signal, the time and scale parameters are usually continuous, and hence the obvious choice is continuous wavelet transform (CWT). On the other hand, the discrete WT can be defined for discrete-time signals, leading to discrete wavelet transform (DWT).

2.1 Continuous wavelet transform (CWT)

The CWT is defined as:

$$CWT(a,b)=\int_{-\infty}^{+\infty}x(t)\psi^{*}{}_{a,b}(t)dt \qquad a>0 \tag{1}$$

where $x(t)$ is the signal to be analyzed, $\psi_{a,b}(t)$ is the mother wavelet shifted by a factor (b), scaled by a factor (a), large and low scales are respectively correspondence with low and high frequencies, and * stands for complex conjugation.

$$\psi_{a,b}(t)=\frac{1}{\sqrt{a}}\psi\left(\frac{t-b}{a}\right) \qquad a>0 \quad and \quad -\infty<b<+\infty \tag{2}$$

2.2 Discrete wavelet transform (DWT)

CWT generates a huge amount of data in the form of wavelet coefficients with respect to change in scale and position. This leads to large computational burden. To overcome this limitation, DWT is used. In other words, in practice, application of the WT is achieved in digital computers by applying DWT on discretized samples. The DWT uses scale and position values based on powers of two, called dyadic dilations and translations. To do this, the scaling and translation parameters are discreted as $a=a_0^m$ and $b=nb_0a_0^m$, where $a_0>1$, $b_0>0$, and m, n are integers, then the DWT is defined as:

$$DWT(m,n)=\int_{-\infty}^{+\infty}x(t)\psi^{*}{}_{m,n}(t)dt \tag{3}$$

where $\psi_{m,n}(t)=a_0^{-m/2}\psi\left(\left(t-na_0^{m}b_0\right)/a_0^{m}\right)$ is the discretized mother wavelet. The DWT, based only on subsamples of the CWT, makes the analysis much more efficient, easy to implement and has fast computation time, at the same time, with the DWT, the original signal can be recovered fully from its DWT with no loss of data. Note a continuous-time signal can be represented in a discrete form as long as the sampling frequency is chosen properly. This is done by using the sampling theorem, termed the Nyquist theorem: the sampling frequency used to turn the continuous signal into a discrete signal must be twice as large as the highest frequency present in the signal (Oppenheim & Schafer, 1989).

To implement the DWT, (Mallat, 1989) developed an approach called the Mallat algorithm or Mallat's Multi-Resolution Analysis (MRA). In this approach the signal to be analyzed (decomposed) is passed through finite impulse response (FIR) high-pass filters (HPF) and low-pass filters (LPF) with different cutoff frequencies at different levels. In wavelet analysis the low frequency content is called the approximation (A) and the high frequency content is called the details (D). This procedure can be repeated to decompose the approximation obtained at each level until the desired level is reached as shown in Fig. 2.

2.3 Wavelet Packet Transform (WPT)

The WPT is a generalization of wavelet decomposition that offers a richer range of possibilities for signal analysis. In WPT, the details as well as the approximation can be split as shown in Fig. 3.

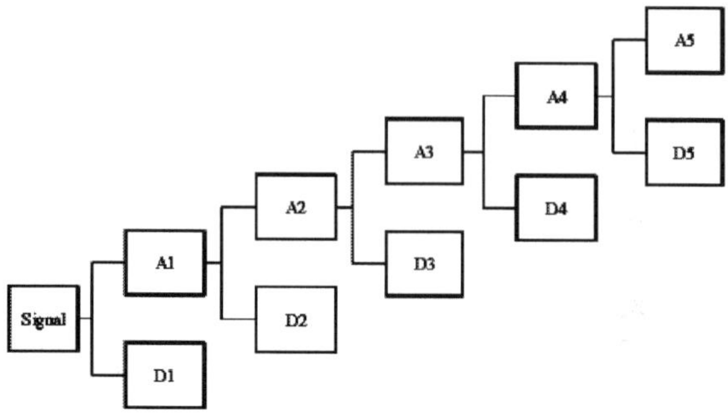

Fig. 2. Decomposition tree for DWT

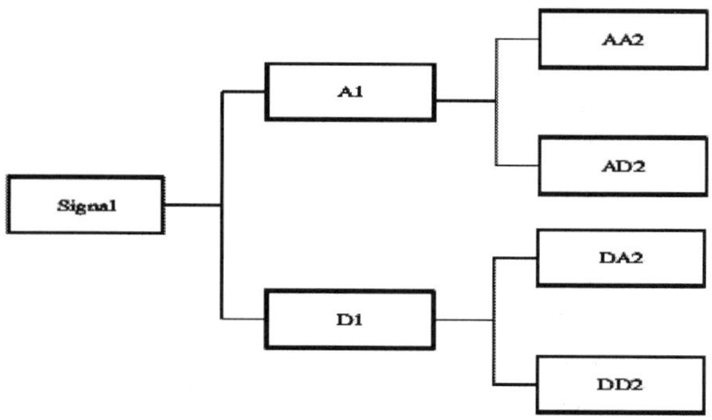

Fig. 3. Decomposition tree for WPT

In view of the fact that WPT generates large number of nodes it increases the computational burden. In DWT only approximations are further decomposed thus reducing the level of decomposition and thereby computational attempts.

3. WT applications in power systems

In the main stream literature, wavelets were first applied to power system in 1994 by Robertson (Robertson et al., 1994) and Ribeiro (Ribeiro, 1994). From this year, the number of publications in this area has increased. The most popular wavelet analysis applications in power systems are as following:

- Power quality
- Partial discharges
- Forecasting in power systems
- Power system measurement
- Power system protection

- Power system transients

Fig. 4 shows the percentage of 196 IEEE papers based in each area (Source: search on IEEE Explore). One can conclude that most research are carried in the field of power quality and power system protection.

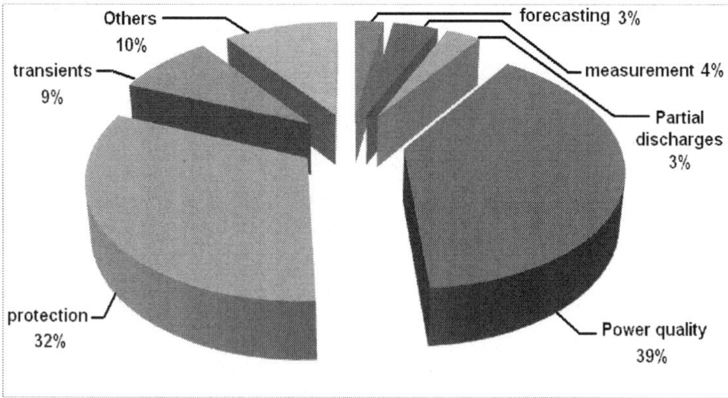

Fig. 4. Percentage of wavelet articles in different areas of power system

Next sections present a general description of wavelet applications in the selected areas of power systems.

3.1 Power quality (PQ)

In the area of PQ, several studies have been carried out to detect and locate disturbances using the WT as a useful tool to analyze sag, swell, interruption, etc. of non-stationary signals. These disturbances are "slow changing" disturbances. Therefore, it contains only the spectral contents in the low frequency range. Therefore, examining WT coefficients (WTCs) in very high decomposition levels would help to determine the occurrence of the disturbance events as well as their occurring time. Counting on this, the DWT techniques have been widely used to analyze the disturbance events in power systems.

Theoretically, all scales of the WTCs may include all the features of the original signal. However, if all levels of the WTCs were taken as features, it would be difficult to classify diverse PQ events accurately within reasonable time, since it has the drawbacks of taking a longer time and too much memory for the recognition system to reach a proper recognition rate. Moreover, if only the first level of the WTCs were used, some significant features in the other levels of the WTCs may be ignored. Beside, with the advancement of PQ monitoring equipment, the amount of data over the past decade gathered by such monitoring systems has become huge in size. The large amount of data imposes practical problems in storage and communication from local monitors to the central processing computers. Data compression has hence become an essential and important issue in PQ area. A compression technique involves a transform to extract the feature contained in the data and a logic for removal of redundancy present in extracted features. For example, in (Liao, 2010) to effectively reduce the number of features representing PQ events, spectrum energies of the

WTCs in different levels calculated by the Parseval's Theorem are proposed. It is well known, in the digital signal processing community, that wavelets revolutionized data compression applications by offering compression rates which other methods could not achieve (Donoho, 1995).

The choice of the mother wavelet is crucial in wavelet analysis of PQ events and it can affect the analysis results. For recognizing the PQ events, maximum number of vanishing moments is the main required property. Beside, per IEEE standards, Daubechies wavelet family is very accurate for analyzing PQ disturbances among all the wavelet families. Nothing that going higher than db43 may lead to instability in the algorithm used to compute the db$N$ scaling filter which affects the filter's frequency response. This is due to the fact that computing the scaling filter requires the extraction of the roots of a polynomial of order 4N (Misiti et al., 2007). Moreover, higher Daubechies means that more filter coefficients will be processed which could influence the required memory size and the computational effort.

Although the WT exhibits its great power in the detection and localization of the PQ events, its ability is often degraded, in actual applications, due to the noises, particularly the white noise with a flat spectrum, riding on the signal. Therefore, to overcome the difficulties of capturing the disturbances out of the background noises in a low-SNR environment, a noise-suppression algorithm should be integrated with the WT. The noise-suppression methods for the noising-riding disturbances have been paid much attention in recent years, with different performances exhibited. However, the threshold is difficult to give in detecting the existence of PQ events.

To do a case study the technique proposed in (Liao, 2010) is studied. First the noise-suppression algorithm based on Brownian bridge stochastic process is applied to signals. After the noise-suppression procedure, the pure WTCs are employed in the feature extraction of the PQ event recognition system. The energy spectrum E_H of each level of the WTCs can be obtained with a distorted signal described by Parseval's theorem and the WTCs. The formula is shown as follows (Oppenheim et al., 1999):

$$E_H = \sum_{l=-\infty}^{\infty} \left|c_0(l)\right|^2 + \sum_{j=0}^{\infty} \sum_{i=-\infty}^{\infty} \left|d_j(i)\right|^2 \tag{4}$$

To enhance the features of PQ events, the energy of the baseband is subtracted from the energy of the distorted signals caused by PQ events, which will derive the energy difference ΔE. Hence, using the differences of energy ΔE as the features of power distorted signals can easily distinguish different PQ events.

Further, in there a genetic k-means algorithm (GKA) based radial basis function (RBF) classification system is used for PQ event recognition. The detailed description of this system can be found in (Liao, 2010).

Four wavelets from Daubechies family db4, db8, db10, and db40 as mother wavelets were used to train and test the proposed PQ recognition system. The corresponding identification rates of PQ events reached 93%, 98%, 99%, and 99% on the average, respectively, for the testing cases. Since fewer coefficients of the mother wavelet can reduce calculation time and make classifying PQ events faster, db8 as the mother wavelet has been good enough to acquire reasonable accuracy and efficient calculation in the recognition system. Hence, db8 was chosen as the mother wavelet in there. Also, the sampling rate of the input signals was set at 61440points/s, with 1024 sampling points for each cycle on the average. The level of noises, included random process of the stationary white Gaussian distribution, with the SNR value was set to be between 25 and 40dB.

Before establishing the recognition system, the features of training samples after the noise-suppression algorithm had to be obtained. Analyzing the energy spectrum of various signals, the dominant features of voltage sag and swell events were obtained as ΔEd_7 to ΔEd_9 mapped to the 7th to 9th energy spectrums of the WTCs.

Then, the normal signal and signals included voltage sag and swell together with their energy spectrum, with and without noise suppression, are obtained and shown in Fig. 5.

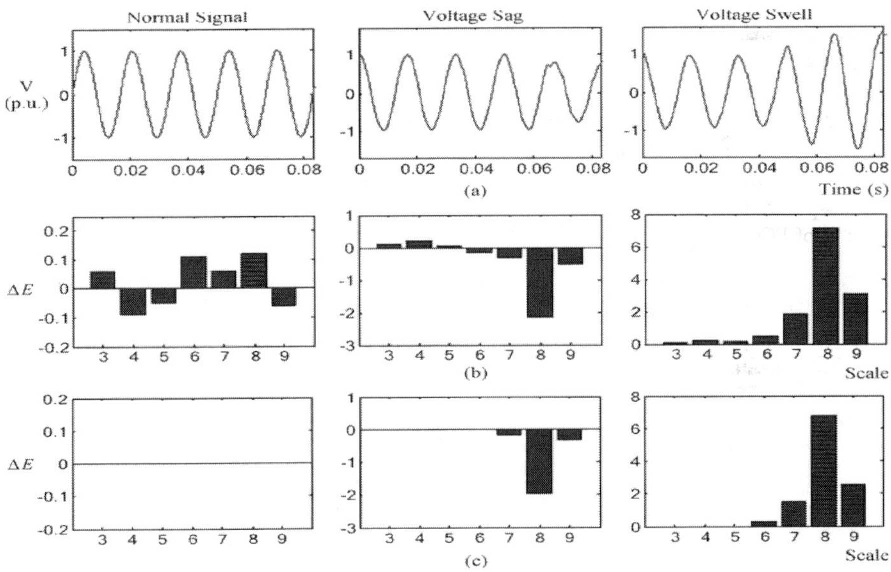

Fig. 5. (a) Actual field data of normal signal, voltage sag, and voltage swell (b) Energy spectrum of the actual signals without noise suppression (c) Energy spectrum of the actual signals with noise suppression

3.2 Partial discharges (PDs)

The PDs are difficult to detect due to their short duration, high frequency and low amplitude signals, but the capacity of the WT to zoom in time the signals with discontinuities unlike the FT, allows identifying local variations of the signal. Almost, DWT technique, among all the WT techniques, is almost proposed and used for detection, measurement and location of PDs.

Beside, PD monitoring has the major problem of electromagnetic interference (EMI). This noise often subsumes completely the very low level PD signals picked up by the sensors. This makes PD detection difficult, particularly for monitoring low level PDs. In addition, there are additional radio frequencies related to mobile phone traffic and so on.

For on-line PD measurement, these excessive interferences cause very low SNR, which means most of the WTCs have to be discarded, as they are noise associated. However, using modified coefficients, especially for on-line PDs measurement where most of the coefficients have to be modified, the IDWT is no longer a perfect reconstruction.

Under such circumstance a wavelet family having the linear phase characteristic is recommended. Linear phase characteristic is necessary as the phase delay and group delay of linear phase FIR filters are equal and constant over the frequency band. This characteristic ensures adjacent signals will not be overlapped together after reconstruction. But, filters with nonlinear phase characteristics will cause signal distortion in the time domain when the signal is filtered.

Also, to some extent, the WT is a measure of similarity. The more similar between the original signal and mother wavelet, the higher the coefficients produce (Zhang et al., 2004). For de-noising and reconstruction considerations, the optimal wavelet suitable for a given signal is the one that is capable of generating as many coefficients with maximal values as possible throughout the time scale domain (Misiti et al, 1996). Based on the above analysis, Bior wavelet family is almost obtained as the most suitable wavelet family to on-line analysis of the PDs.

Also, the number H of decomposition levels, dependent on sampling frequency, can be selected based on trial and error until PD-associated coefficients can be distinguished from noise at a certain WT level (Zhang et al., 2004). Then, coefficients associated with PDs are retained and coefficients corresponding to noise are discarded.

3.3 Forecasting in power systems

Demand forecasting is a key to the efficient management of electrical power systems. The works have been developed for short term electrical load forecasting by combining the WT and neural networks (NNs). As electrical load at any particular time is usually assumed to be a linear combination of different components, from the signal analysis point of view, load can be also considered as a linear combination of different frequencies. Every component of load can be represented by one or several frequencies. The process decomposes the historical load into an approximation part associated with low frequencies and several details parts associated with high frequencies through the WT. Then, the forecast of the part of future load is develop by means of a neural network (Yao et al., 2000) or adjusting the load by a regression method (Yu et al., 2000).

Beside, the increased integration of wind power into the electric grid, as it today occurs in some countries, poses new challenges due to its intermittency and volatility. Wind power forecasting plays a key role in tackling these challenges. (Wang et al., 2009) brings WT into the time series of wind power and verifies that the decomposed series all have chaotic characteristic, so a method of wind power prediction in short-term with WT-based NN model is presented. The obtained results show that the new model is a more effective method in the short-term prediction of wind power than the no WT NN model and ARMA model.

Moreover, price forecasting in a real electricity market is essential for risk management in deregulated electricity markets. Price series is highly volatile and non-stationary in nature. In (Aggarwal et al., 2008) a WT-based price forecasting is proposed. In this work, initially complete price series has been decomposed and then these series have been categorized into different segments for price forecasting. For some segments, WT based multiple linear regression (MLR) has been applied and for the other segments, simple MLR model has been applied.

Daubechies wavelets are most appropriate for treating a non-stationary series (Reis & Silva, 2005). For these families of wavelets, the regularity increases as the order of the functions does. The regularity is useful in getting smoothness of the reconstructed signal. However, with the increase in the order, the support intervals also increase, which leads to poor local analysis and hence may cause the prediction to deteriorate. Therefore, low order wavelet functions are generally advisable. The Daubechies wavelet of order 1 (db1) is the Haar wavelet and is the only wavelet in this family that is discontinuous in nature, and therefore may not be suitable for load, wind or price signal analysis. However, in order to find out the appropriate order of the Daubechies wavelets, effect of the order of Daubechies wavelets, from order 2 to next, should be evaluated on the performance of prediction during the test period. It is necessary to say that according to the authors' research, Db4 mother wavelet have been the most of the applications in forecasting of power systems. Beside, the more levels the original signal is decomposed, the better stationary the decomposed signals are, but great errors will be brought about at the same time (Wang et al., 2009). So the number of decomposition levels should be determined as low as possible.

In (Saha et al., 2006) for forecasting of hourly load demand, Autoregressive (AR) model of coefficients obtained from WT is used. The forecast made by the model of the transformed data appears to be quite satisfactory. Hourly load demand data of past 51 weeks has been utilized for forecasting the demand of 52nd week.

Wavelet coefficients for each of the past 51 weeks demand data are calculated and modeling of time series is done.

The transfer function of AR process in order to transform the non-stationary time series into a stationary series is given by,

$$y_k = \frac{1}{1 - u_1 Z^{-1} - u_2 Z^{-2}} a_k \tag{5}$$

In other words the AR process of order 2 or AR(2) process is represented by

$$y_k = u_1 y_{k-1} + u_2 y_{k-2} + a_k \text{ for } k=3, 4, 5, \ldots, N.$$

where N is number of data points in the series, y_k is the kth observation or data point, u_1 and u_2 are the AR(2) model parameters and a_k is the error term (assumed zero mean random variables or white noise). Therefore, the error term is as: $a_k = y_k - u_1 y_{k-1} + u_2 y_{k-2}$. The error is minimized using least square algorithm and an obtained result by db2 mother wavelet is shown in Fig. 6. The accuracy of forecast is found to be within a satisfactory range.

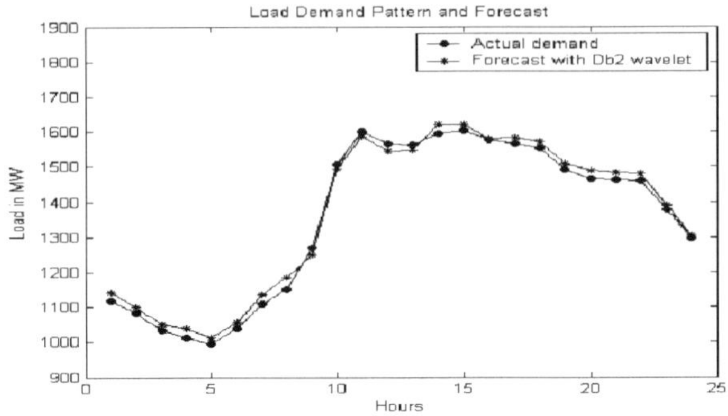

Fig. 6. Load demand pattern and forecast

3.4 Power system measurements

The advantage of using the WT for the application of power/energy and RMS measurements is that it provides the distribution of the power and energy with respect to the individual frequency bands associated with each level of the wavelet analysis.

There are two main approaches to the harmonics field. The first one, carries out an MRA using wavelet filter banks in a first step and usually the application of the CWT to the sub-bands in a second step (Pham & Wong, 1999); the second one, uses a complex wavelet transform analysis or continuous wavelet (Zhen et al., 2000).

There has not been much work on applying DWT for power and RMS measurements. It is important to say that in MRA implemented by DWT filter banks, a signal is decomposed into time-domain non-uniform frequency sub-band components to extract detailed information. For harmonic identification purposes however, it is more useful if the signal is decomposed into uniform frequency sub-bands. This can be achieved using WPT filter banks. The use of the WPT permits decomposing a power system waveform into uniform frequency bands. With an adequate selection of the sampling frequency and the wavelet decomposition tree, the harmonic frequencies can be selected to be in the center of each band in order to avoid the spectral leakage associated with the imperfect frequency response of the filter bank employed. In (Morsi & El-Hawary, 2009) a WPT application is developed for calculating PQ indices in balanced and unbalanced three-phase systems under stationary or non-stationary operating conditions. In order to handle the unbalanced three-phase case, the concept of equivalent voltage and current is used to calculate those indices.

In general, wavelet functions with a large number of coefficients have less distortion and smaller levels of spectral leakage in each output band than wavelets with fewer coefficients. Daubechies wavelet function with 20 coefficients (db20) (Parameswariah & Cox, 2002), and Vaidyanathan wavelet function with 24 coefficients (v24) (Hamid & Kawasaki, 2001; 2002) are proposed as the best solutions for harmonic analysis.

While the WPT provides uniform frequency bands, the main disadvantage is that the computational effort and required memory size increase much more in comparison with the

DWT as the number of levels increase. In (Morsi & El-Hawary, 2007) definitions of power components contained in the (IEEE Std. 1459–2000) are represented by DWT for unbalanced three-phase systems. Also in order to study system unbalance, the concept of symmetrical components is defined in the wavelet domain. The main disadvantage of DWT is the issue of spectral leakage (Barros & Diego, 2006). The errors due to spectral leakage depend on the choice of the wavelet family and the mother wavelet involved in the analysis. In (Morsi & El-Hawary, 2008) a wavelet energy evaluation-based approach is proposed to select the most suitable mother wavelet that can be achieved by evaluating the percentage energy of the wavelet coefficients at each level H

$$\%E_H = \frac{E_H}{E} \times 100 \tag{6}$$

where E is the energy of the original signal and E_H is the energy of the coefficients at each level

$$E_H = \int_R c_H^2(t)dt \ \ or \ \ E_H = \sum_{n\in Z} c_H^2(n) \tag{7}$$

Hence, the most suitable mother wavelet is that which satisfies minimum energy deviations for all decomposition levels.

In (Barros & Diego; 2008) a WPT-based algorithm is proposed to calculating harmonics. By selecting a sampling frequency of 1.6 kHz and using a three-level decomposition tree, the frequency range of the output is divided into eight bands with a uniform 100-Hz interval. The selected sampling window width is ten cycles of the fundamental frequency (200 *ms* in a 50 *Hz* system) as in the IEC Standard 61000-4-7. In each output band, the odd-harmonic frequencies are in the center of the band, this way avoiding the edges of the band where the spectral leakage is higher. Using the decomposition tree of WPT, the fundamental component and the odd-harmonic components from the third to the 15th order, from coefficients d_1 to d_8, can be investigated in the input signal. The RMS value of each harmonic component is exactly considered equal to the RMS value of each of the coefficients of the eight output levels. Also, based on the text above v24 and db20 were selected as the wavelet functions to implement the filter bank.

The distorted signal with 1% white Gaussian noise has been considered in order to study the performance of the algorithm proposed and to compare the results with the IEC approach.

To reduce the spectral leakage caused by the filtering characteristics of the method proposed, a double-stage process is used: First, the fundamental component of the input signal is estimated, and then, this component is filtered out; second, the proposed algorithm is applied to the resultant signal to compute the rest of the harmonic components without the interference of the spectral leakage due to the fundamental component.

Table I shows the results obtained, in the estimation of harmonic distortion of the waveform, using the proposed and IEC methods.

As can be seen, the effect of noise is not the same in the measurement of the different harmonic groups; the algorithm with the v24 wavelet function shows a better performance than using db20 and a similar noise immunity as in the IEC method.

Input signal		IEC method magnitude (%)	db20 magnitude (%)	v24 magnitude (%)
Harmonic order	Magnitude (%)			
1	100	100.01	100.01	100.01
3	1	0.98	1.12	1.03
5	2.5	2.53	2.46	2.50
7	1.1	1.08	0.97	1.05
9	0.2	0.19	0.52	0.31
11	0.3	0.30	0.31	0.31
13	0.1	0.12	0.15	0.16
15	0.1	0.24	0.16	0.15

Table 1. Noise immunity of the IEC and wavelet-packet methods

3.5 Power system protection

The potential benefits of applying WT for improving the performance of protection relays have been also recognized. In (Chaari et al., 1996) wavelets are introduced for the power distribution relaying domain to analyze transient earth faults signals in a 20 kV resonant grounded network as generated by EMTP.

There are two main criteria for the selection of the mother wavelet in power system relay protection. At first, the shape and the mathematical expression of the wavelet must be set such that the physical interpretation of wavelet coefficients is easy. Secondly, the chosen wavelet must allow a fast computation of wavelet coefficients.

In (Osman-Ahmed, 2003) the selection procedure of more suitable mother wavelet is shown for fault location. The most suitable mother wavelet is that which satisfies maximum energy for details coefficients at the first decomposition level based on (7), when fault is occurred. Also, if this energy value of each phase exceeds a predetermined threshold value, the disturbance is identified as a fault in that phase.

In (Bhalja & Maheshwari, 2008) another method is proposed to select an optimal mother wavelet for fault location. In this method, the ratio of the norm of details coefficients to approximation coefficients (RDA) is calculated. Then the mother wavelet having the highest RDA value is selected as the optimal mother wavelet.

The WT is also applied for islanding detection (Hsieh et al., 2008), the bars (Mohammed, 2005), motors (Aktas & Turkmenoglu, 2010), generators and transformers (Saleh & Rahman, 2010) protection. For these cases, entropy and minimum description data length (MDL) criteria are used to determine the optimal mother wavelet and the optimal number of levels of decomposition.

The MDL criterion selects the best wavelet filter and the optimal number of wavelet coefficients to be retained for signal reconstruction. The MDL criterion for indexes K (number of coefficients to be retained) and g (number of wavelet filters) is defined as:

$$MDL(K,g) = \min\left\{\frac{3}{2}K\log N + \frac{N}{2}\log\left\|\tilde{\alpha}_g - \alpha_g^{(K)}\right\|^2\right\},\quad 0 \le K < N;\quad 1 \le g \le M \tag{8}$$

where $\tilde{\alpha}_g = W_g * x$ denotes a vector of the wavelet-transformed coefficients of the signal x using wavelet filters (g) and $\tilde{\alpha}_g^{(K)} = \Theta^K \tilde{\alpha}_g = \Theta^K\left(W_g * x\right)$ denotes a vector that contains K nonzero elements. The thresholding parameter Θ^K keeps a K number of largest elements of the vector $\tilde{\alpha}_g$ constant and sets all other elements to zero. Letters N and M denote the length of the signal and the total number of wavelet filters, respectively. Number of coefficients K, for which the MDL function reaches its minimum value, is considered as the optimal one. With this criterion, the wavelet filters can also be optimized as well.

The entropy $En(x)$ of a signal $x(n)$ of length N is defined as:

$$En(x) = -\sum_{n=0}^{N-1}\left|x(n)\right|^2 \log\left|x(n)\right|^2 \tag{9}$$

To determine the optimal levels of decomposition, the entropy is evaluated at each level. If there is a new level H such that

$$En(x)_H \ge En(x)_{H-1} \tag{10}$$

Then level H is redundant and can be omitted.

3.6 Power system transients

Voltage disturbances shorter than sags or swells are classified as transients and are caused by the sudden changes in the power system. On the basis of the duration, transient over voltages can be divided into switching surge (duration in the range of milliseconds) and impulse spike (duration in the range of microseconds). Surges are high energy pulses arising from power system switching disturbances either directly or as a result of resonating circuits associated with switching devices, particularly capacitor switching. Impulses on the other hand result from direct or indirect lightning strokes, arcing, insulation breakdown, etc.

The selection of appropriate mother wavelet without knowing the types of transients is a challenging task. For short and fast transient disturbances in power systems, the wavelet must be localized in time and oscillate rapidly within a very short period of time. This means short length of LPF and HPF filters. However, a very short filter length leads to a blockness problem (Akansu & Haddad, 2001).

For dyadic MRA, the minimum filter order is equal to two coefficients. However, for more freedom and to eliminate the blockness problem, the filter length must be greater than or equal to 4 coefficients (Akansu & Haddad, 2001). A literature survey by authors and past experience show that for short and fast transient disturbances, db4 and db6 wavelets are better while for slow transient disturbances db8 and db10 are more suitable.

At the lowest scale i.e. level 1, the mother wavelet is most localized in time and oscillates rapidly within very short period of time. As the wavelet goes to higher scale the analyzing wavelets become more localized and oscillate less due to the dilation nature of the WT analysis. Hence, fast and short transient disturbances will be detected at lower scales whereas slow and long transient disturbances will be detected at higher scales. Thus, both fast and slow transients can be detected with a single type of analyzing wavelets.

Apart from the application of wavelets to introduce new identification, classification and analysis methods such as those presented previously, at the moment is also studied the application of wavelets to develop new components models; for example (Abur et al., 2001) extends the results of previous works (Magnago & Abur, 2000) and describes a transmission line model which is based on WT taking into account frequency dependence of modal transformation matrices into the transients simulation. This allows the use of accurate modal transformation matrices that vary with frequency and yet still remain in the time domain during the simulations.

Although wavelet analysis usually combined with a large number of neural networks provides efficient classification of PQ events, the time-domain featured disturbances, such as sags, swells, etc. may not easily be classified. In addition, some important disturbance frequency component may not be precisely extracted by WT. Therefore, (Reddy & Mohanta, 2004) presents a new transform by incorporating phase correction to WT and is known as S–transform. The S-transform separates the localizing-in-time aspect of the real valued Gaussian window with modulation (selection of frequency) so that the window translates, but does not get modulated. (Reddy & Mohanta, 2010) extends the use of S-transform for detection, localization and classification of impulsive transients. The results obtained from S-transform are compared with those obtained from WT to validate the superiority of S-transform for PQ and transients analysis of complex disturbances. To do a case study the technique proposed in (Liao, 2010) is again studied, but for capacitor switching leading to the oscillatory transient. The results obtained are shown in Fig. 7. The dominant features of capacitor switching event was obtained as ΔEd_3 to ΔEd_5 mapped to the 3th to 5th energy spectrums of the WTCs.

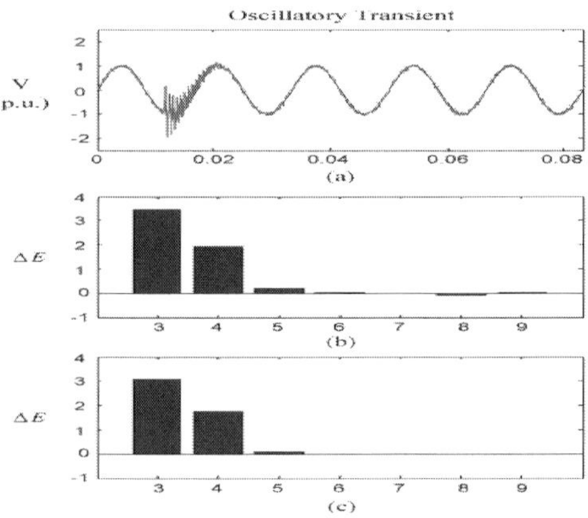

Fig. 7. (a) Simulated data of oscillatory transient with noise. (b) Energy spectrum of the simulated signals without noise suppression. (c) Energy spectrum of the simulated signals with noise suppression.

4. Investigation of WT application on islanding state and fault location

In this section, the detailed analysis of two important application of wavelet analysis, carried on detection of the islanding state and fault location by the authors, will be illustrated.

4.1 Islanding detection

4.1.1 Methodology

The proposed algorithm is based on the study of disturbances existed in the waveform of terminal current of DGs. It should be noted that once the islanding event is occurred, a transient component continues only for a very short time after the switching operation and then it is removed. But in non-islanding events this transient component continues for longer time, so it should be distinguished. In the proposed method, after studies done by the authors, it was found out that third decomposition level with 20 samples as the length of data window and 17 samples as the moving size of data window is accurate leading to detect the islanding state within maximum 54 samples i.e. 5.4 *ms*. In the first step, the ratio of maximum current magnitude in *r*th window to the previous window is calculated as follows:

$$Ratio - I_t(r) = \frac{min\ and\ max\, I_t(r)}{max\, I_t(r-1)} \tag{11}$$

where, the threshold values are:

$$0.98 \le Ratio - I_t(r) \le 1.02 \tag{12}$$

These threshold values are selected according to simulate the different events. If the calculated ratio satisfies (12) then there is no problem and this means that islanding has not been occurred. For values out of range of (12), the following criteria could be used to check whether the islanding event is taken place or not:

$$Ratio - D_3(r) = \frac{maxD_3(r)}{maxD_3(r-2)} \tag{13}$$

Considering different studies done, threshold value chosen for (13) is 0.02. This condition can be expressed by:

$$Ratio\ - D_3(r) \le 0.02 \tag{14}$$

This threshold value is also adopted according to simulate the different events. If value of (14) is less than 0.02, then the islanding event is occurred and trip command should be issued for islanded DGs. The algorithm diagram is shown in (Shariatinasab & Akbari, 2010).

It is worth to point out that moving size of the data window in the proposed algorithm is an important parameter. As decreasing the moving size reduces total time of detection, so the moving size should be decreased as possible.

4.1.2 Case study

The study system consists of two synchronous DGs (DG1 and DG2) operating on PQ mode, and is a part of Iranian distribution network located in Tehran (Fig. 8). The data of the network are available in (Shariatinasab & Akbari, 2010).

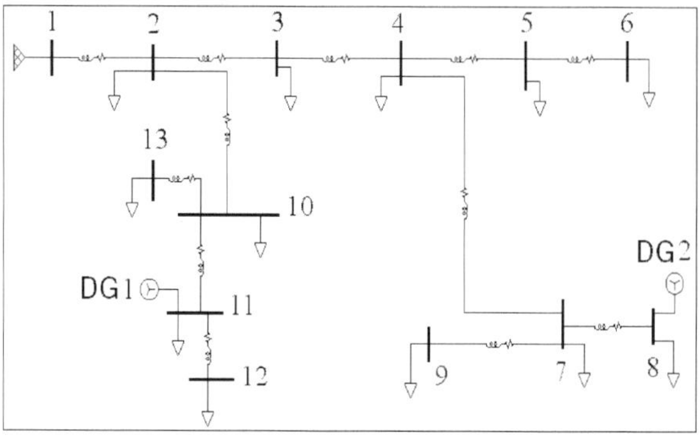

Fig. 8. Test system for islanding detection study

4.1.3 Simulation results

To be ensured of accuracy of the proposed algorithm, all the cases affecting the terminal current of DGs are analyzed. Figs. 9 and 10, show RMS current form and related three decomposition levels using 'Haar' mother wavelet for non-islanded DG1 and islanded DG2, respectively.

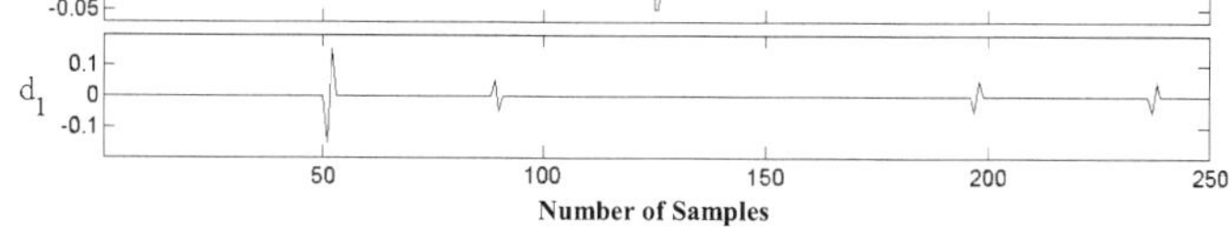

Fig. 9. The waveform of terminal current of DG1, due to breaker opening on line 7-8, d_1-d_3 are detail components of main signal

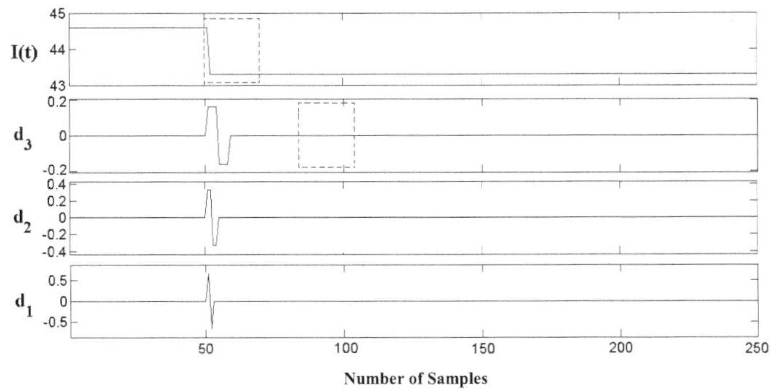

Fig. 10. The waveform of terminal current of DG2, due to breaker opening on line 7-8, d_1-d_3 are detail components of main signal

20 samples length data window is considered. In this window, ratio of the changed current is 1.003 for DG1 which satisfies (12). So as it is expected the algorithm would not issued a trip command for DG1. It is important to point out that in order to get a conservative result; it was assumed that the generated power of DG2 is equal to the customer load at the connected bus. Therefore, DG2 is islanded, the difference between the generated and consumed power in bus 8 will be zero, while the ratio of the changed current in related data window for DG2 is 0.0971 that is less than 0.98 and therefore (12) is not satisfied. Then data window is twice shifted to the right, either one up to 17 samples. In this new window, the obtained value of (13) is nearly zero, in which this value satisfies (14). So the proposed algorithm detects the islanding event in maximum time within 54 samples of 10 *kHz* sampling frequency, i.e. 5.4 *ms,* and issues a trip command for DG2.

The more research is done for various combinations and conditions of islanding for both DG1 and DG2 available in (Shariatinasab & Akbari, 2010).

In order to perform a comprehensive study to check the accuracy of the proposed method, motor starting and capacitor switching are also investigated; as they may cause a similar situation to islanding state and hence should be distinguished correctly. To perform the motor starting study, a 15 *kVA* induction motor starting is studied, and results are shown in Figs. 11-12. For DG1 the value of (11) obtained under this condition is 1.353 that is more than 1.02 and the value of (13) is 0.054 that is more than 0.02. Also, for DG2 the obtained value of (11) is 2.392 and the value of (13) is 0.079, in which both values are more than criteria adopted in the proposed algorithm. Hence, the proposed method distinguishes this situation correctly, i.e. an islanding state is not detected for DGs under motor starting condition.

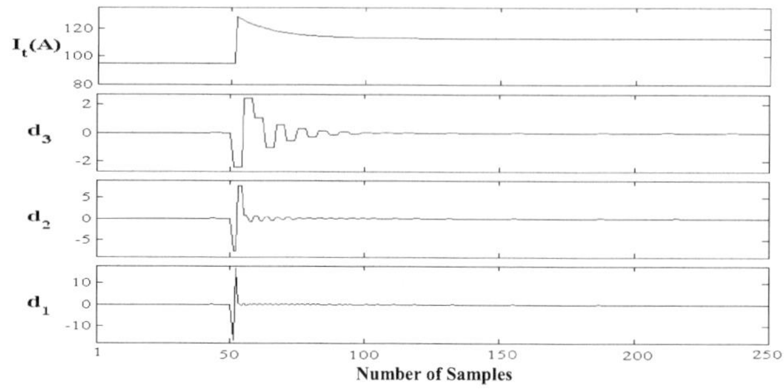

Fig. 11. The waveform of terminal current of DG1, due to motor starting at bus 3, d_1-d_3 are detail components of main signal

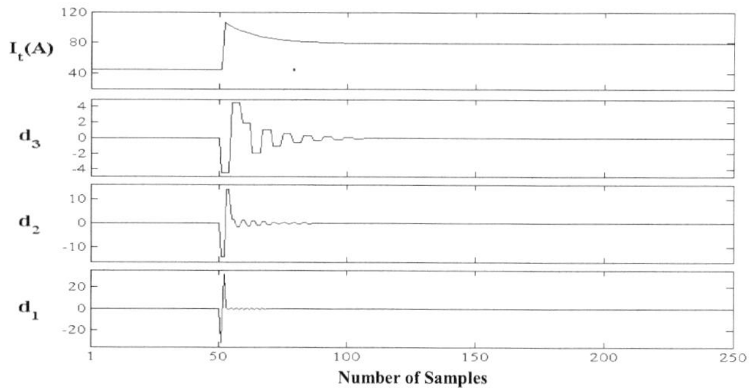

Fig. 12. The waveform of terminal current of DG2, due to motor starting at bus 3, d_1-d_3 are detail components of main signal

Results of the capacitor bank switching are also available in (Shariatinasab & Akbari, 2010).

4.2 Fault location

4.2.1 Methodology and study system

In this section, the fault location by DWT and a trained NN will be discussed. The case study is IEEE 9-bus test system as shown in Fig. 13. This system is a 400 kV transmission system included 3 generators and 6 lines. Each line is divided to 20 points and then a fault is separately applied in each point. Totally 120 faults is applied in 120 points. As the most of faults occurred in transmission systems have low fault impedance, so fault impedance was considered equal to zero in this study. Then the terminal current signal of G1, G2 and G3 during the fault is obtained with sampling rate 10 kHz. The fault signals collected in ETAP software is then transformed to MATLAB software in order to apply the wavelet analysis. Only 46 samples/10 *kHz* sampling rate (equal to 4.6 *ms*) of data are considered after fault time. According to the analyses done, db4 mother wavelet was selected as a suitable solution.

After DWT analysis, it is necessary to extract the characteristics of this transform to provide inputs of NN. To this, 2nd norm (norm2) of signal details was considered as NN inputs. Also, the details of 5 levels were obtained as the optimal solution to train the NN.

To describe the work, norm2 of 3rd level details versus fault distance from a generator (G3) is illustrated in Fig. 14. As shown in Fig. 14, the more fault distance, the lower value of norm2 is reached. In this study, norm2 of details of five levels were used. The NN used in this study was consisted of 3 hidden layers either with 20 neurons. The optimal number of neurons was determined based on the trial and error approach. The transfer functions applied in input, hidden and output layers were considered **tansig**, **tansig** and **purelin**, respectively, and training algorithm was also considered as **trainlm**.

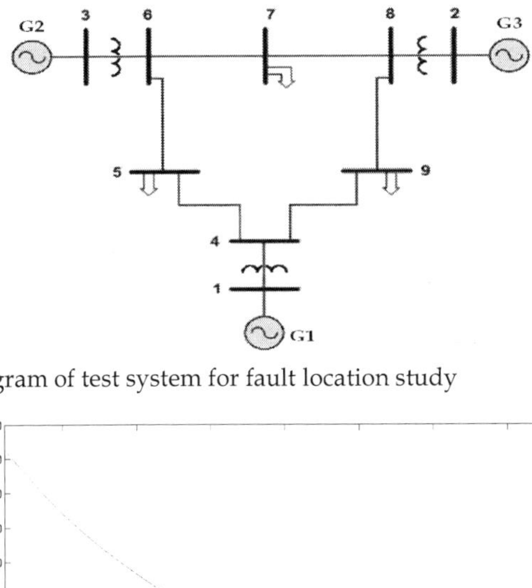

Fig. 13. Schematic diagram of test system for fault location study

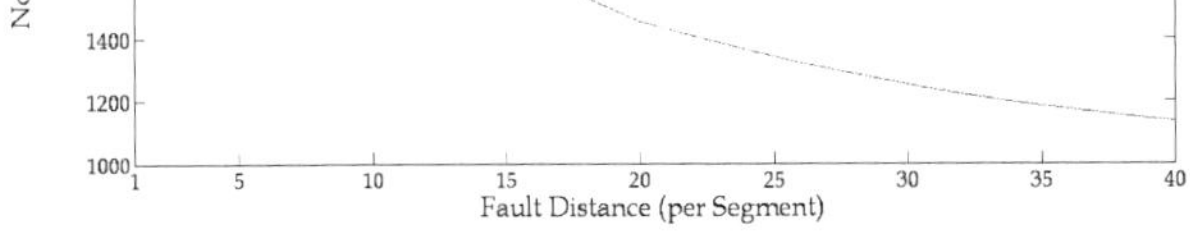

Fig. 14. Norm2 of 3rd level details (d3) for G3

4.2.2 Simulation results

For study system, fault was applied in 120 points which 85 points was considered as training patterns of NN and 35 points was considered for testing.

According to the definition in (IEEE Std. PC37.114, 2004), error percentage of fault location estimation is determined as follows:

$$error\ \% = \frac{error\ \ value}{line\ \ length} \tag{15}$$

Some results obtained from the proposed DWT-NN technique are shown in Table 2. As seen in results, the error values are reasonable values and satisfactory. According to 4.2.1, the time of the fault detection and location is 4.6 *ms* equal to 46 samples per 10 *kHz* sampling rate. Therefore, this technique can be well used to estimate the fault detection and location in a specific transmission system.

Real segment number	Calculated value	Error value	Error %
4	3.8086	-0.1914	-0.96
14	4.0467	0.0467	0.23
29	29.0903	0.0903	0.45
37	37.1833	0.1833	0.92
51	51.1034	0.1034	0.52
66	65.7872	-0.2128	-1.06
74	74.0679	0.0679	0.34
86	86.1994	0.1994	1.00
95	94.8874	-0.1126	-0.56
103	103.2897	0.2897	1.45
112	111.7134	-0.2866	-1.43

Table 2. The results of fault location under db4 mother wavelet and 5 decomposition levels

5. Conclusion

Wavelet transform is a powerful signal processing tool used in power systems analysis. The most of applications of wavelet analysis in power systems include analysis and study of power quality, partial discharges, forecasting, measurement, protection and transients. It transforms a time-domain waveform into time-frequency domain and estimates the signal in the time and frequency domains simultaneously.

The most popular applications of WT are related to CWT, DWT and WPT techniques. CWT generates a huge amount of data in the form of wavelet coefficients with respect to change in scale and position. This leads to large computational burden. To overcome this limitation, DWT is used, as do in digital computers by applying DWT on discretized samples.

According to the done research, DWT is also extensively used to analyze the most of phenomena of power systems. However, an extensive study should be carried on applying DWT for power and RMS measurements. Because in MRA implemented by DWT filter banks, a signal is decomposed into non-uniform frequency sub-bands. However, for harmonic identification purposes, it is more useful if the signal is decomposed into uniform frequency sub-bands. This can be achieved using WPT filter banks.

Further, Although there have been a great effort in references to prove that one wavelet is more suitable than another, there have not been a comprehensive analysis involving a number of wavelets to prove the point of view suggested. Also, the method of comparison among them is not unified, such that a general conclusion is reached.

Therefore, in this chapter for each application in power systems, it was tried to introduce principles and algorithms in order to determine the optimal mother wavelet. According to the literature review, Daubechies family has been the most of applications in power systems analysis. Further, often db4 have been the satisfactory results than the other mother wavelets of Daubechies family. However, it is should be noted that the type of mother wavelet, the number of decomposition levels and etc, may be changed from one application and/or condition to another and therefore not be generalized to all the cases.

6. References

Abur, A.; Ozgun, O. & Magnago, F.H. (2001). Accurate Modeling and Simulation of Transmission Line Transients Using Frequency Dependent Modal Transformations, *IEEE Power Engineering Society Winter Meeting*, Vol.3, pp. 1443-1448, ISBN 0-7803-6672-7, Columbus, USA, January 28/February 01, 2001

Aggarwal, S.K.; Saini, L.M. & Kumar, A. (2008). Price Forecasting Using Wavelet Transform and LSE Based Mixed Model in Australian Electricity Market. *International Journal of Energy Sector Management*, Vol.2, No.4, pp. 521-546, ISSN 1750-6220

Akansu, N., & Haddad, R.A. (2001). *Multi-resolution Signal Decomposition* (2nd Ed.), Academic Press, ISBN 0-12-047141-8, UK

Aktas, M. & Turkmenoglu, V. (2010). Wavelet-Based Switching Faults Detection in Direct Torque Control Induction Motor Drives. *IET Science, Measurement & Technology*, Vol.4, No.6, (November 2010), pp. 303–310, ISSN 1751-8822

Barros, J. & Diego, R.I. (2008). Analysis of Harmonics in Power Systems Using the Wavelet-Packet Transform. *IEEE Transactions on Instrumentation and Measurement*, Vol.57, No.1, (January 2008), pp. 63-69, ISSN 0018-9456

Barros J. & Diego R. (2006). Application of the Wavelet-Packet Transform to the Estimation of Harmonic Groups in Current and Voltage Waveforms. *IEEE Transactions on Power Delivery*, Vol.21, No.1, (January 2006), pp. 533–535, ISSN 0885-8977

Bhalja, B. & Maheshwari, R.P. (2008). New Differential Protection Scheme for Tapped Transmission Line. *IET Generation, Transmission & Distribution*, Vol.2, No.2, (March 2008) pp. 271-279, ISSN 1751-8687

Chaari, O.; Meunier, M. & Brouaye, F. (1996). Wavelets: a New Tool for the Resonant Grounded Power Distribution Systems Relaying. *IEEE Transactions on Power Delivery*, Vol.11, No.3, (July 1996), pp. 1301-1308, ISSN 0885-8977

Daubechies, I. Orthonormal Bases of Compactly Supported Wavelets. (1988). *Communications on Pure and Applied Mathematics,* Vol.41, No.7, (October 1988), pp. 909-996, ISSN 00103640

Donoho, L.D. De-noising by Soft-Thresholding. (1995). *IEEE Transactions on Information Theory*, Vol.41, No.3, (May 1995), pp. 613–627, ISSN 0018-9448

Graps. A. An Introduction to Wavelets. (1995). *IEEE Computational Science & Engineering,* Vol.2, No.2, (Summer 1995), pp. 50-61, ISSN 1070-9924

Grossman A. & Morlet, J. (1984). Decomposition of Hardy Functions into Square Integrable Wavelets of Constant Shape. *SIAM Journal on Mathematical Analysis*, Vol.15, No.4, pp. 723-736, ISSN 0036-1410

Hamid, E.Y. & Kawasaki, Z. (2002). Instrument for the Quality Analysis of Power Systems Based on the Wavelet Packet Transform. *IEEE Power Engineering Review*, Vol.22, No.3, (March 2002), pp. 52-54, ISSN 0272-1724

Hamid, E.Y. & Kawasaki, Z. (2001). Wavelet Packet Transform for RMS Values and Power Measurements. *IEEE Power Engineering Review*, Vol.21, No.9, (September 2001), pp. 49–51, ISSN 0272-1724

Hsieh, C.T., Lin, J.M., & Huang, S.J. (2008). Enhancement of Islanding-Detection of Distributed Generation Systems via Wavelet Transform-Based Approaches. *International Journal of Electrical Power Energy Systems*, Vol.30, No.10, (December 2008), pp. 575–580, ISSN 0142-0615

Ibrahim, W.M. (2009). *Fuzzy Systems and Wavelet Transform Techniques for Evaluating the Quality of the Electric Power System Waveforms*. PHD Thesis, Department of Electrical and Computer Engineering, Dalhousie University, July 2009

IEEE Std. 1459. (2010). *IEEE Standard Definitions for the Measurement of Electric Power Quantities under Sinusoidal, Nonsinusoidal, Balanced, or Unbalanced Conditions*, (March 2010), pp. 1-40, E-ISBN 978-0-7381-6058-0

IEEE Std. PC37.114. (2004). *IEEE Guide for Determining Fault Location on AC Transmission and Distribution Lines*, (June 2005), pp. 1-36, ISBN 0-7381-4653-6.

Liao, C.-C. Enhanced RBF Network for Recognizing Noise-Riding Power Quality Events. (2010). *IEEE Transactions on Instrumentation and Measurement*, Vol.59, No.6, (June 2010), pp. 1550-1561, ISSN 0018-9456

Magnago, F.H. & Abur, A. (2000). Wavelet-Based Simulation of Transients along Transmission Lines with Frequency Dependent Parameters, *IEEE Power Engineering Society Summer Meeting*, pp. 689–694, ISBN 0-7803-6420-1, Seattle, Washington, USA, July 16-20, 2000

Mallat, S.G. (1989). A Theory for Multiresolution Signal Decomposition: the Wavelet Representation. *IEEE Transactions on Pattern Analysis and Machine Intelligence*, Vol.11, No.7, (July 1989), pp 674-693, ISSN 0162-8828

Misiti, M., Misiti Y., & Oppenheim, G. (2007). *Wavelet Toolbox 4 for use with Matlab*. The math works Inc., 2007

Misiti, M., Misiti, Y., Oppenheim, G., & Poggi, J. (1996). *Wavelet Toolbox Manual-User's Guide*, the Math Works Inc., USA

Mohammed, M.E. (2005). High-Speed Differential Busbar Protection Using Wavelet-Packet Transform. *IEE Proceedings- Generation, Transmission and Distribution*, Vol.152, No.6, (November 2005), pp. 927-933, ISSN 1350-2360

Morsi, W.G. & El-Hawary, M.E. (2009). Wavelet Packet Transform-Based Power Quality Indices for Balanced and Unbalanced Three-Phase Systems under Stationary or Nonstationary Operating Conditions. *IEEE Transactions on Power Delivery*, Vol.24, No.4, (October 2009), pp. 2300-2310, ISSN 0885-8977

Morsi, W.G. & El-Hawary, M.E. (2007). Reformulating Three-Phase Power Components Definitions Contained in the IEEE Standard 1459–2000 Using Discrete Wavelet Transform. *IEEE Transactions on Power Delivery*, Vol.22, No.3, (July 2007), pp. 1917-1925, ISSN 0885-8977

Morsi, W.G. & El-Hawary, M.E. (2008). The Most Suitable Mother Wavelet for Steady-State Power System Distorted Waveforms, *Canadian Conference on Electrical and Computer Engineering (CCECE)*, pp.17-22, ISBN 978-1-4244-1642-4, Niagara Falls, Ontario, May 4-7, 2008

Oppenheim, A.V., Schafer, R.W., & Buck, J.R. (1999). *Discrete-Time Signal Processing*, (2nd ed), Prentice-Hall, ISBN 0130834432, 9780130834430, Englewood Cliffs, NJ, USA

Oppenheim, A.V., & Schafer, R.W. (1989). *Discrete-Time Signal Processing Englewood*, Prentice-Hall, ISBN 0132167719, 9780132167710, Englewood Cliffs, NJ, USA

Osman-Ahmed, A. (2003). *Transmission Lines Protection Techniques Based on Wavelet Transform*. PHD Thesis, Department of Electrical and Computer Engineering, Calgary, Alberta, April 2003

Parameswariah, C. & Cox, M. (2002). Frequency Characteristics of Wavelets. *IEEE Transactions on Power Delivery*, Vol.17, No.3, (July 2002), pp. 800–804, ISSN 0885-8977

Pham, V.L. & Wong, K.P. (1999). Wavelet-Transform-Based Algorithm for Harmonic Analysis of Power System Waveforms. *IEE Proceedings- Generation, Transmission and Distribution*, Vol.146, No.3, (May 1999), pp. 249–254, ISSN 1350-2360

Reddy, M.J.B. & Mohanta, D.K. (2010). Detection, Classification and Localization of Power System Impulsive Transients Using S–Transform, *9th International Conference on Environment and Electrical Engineering (EEEIC)*, pp. 373-376, ISBN 978-1-4244-5370-2, Prague, Czech Republic, May 16-19, 2010

Reddy, M.J.B.; Mohanta, D.K. & Karan, B.M. (2004). Power System Disturbance Recognition Using Wavelet and S-Transform Techniques. *International Journal of Emerging Electric Power Systems*, Vol.1, No.2, (November 2004), pp. 1-16, ISSN 1553-779X

Ribeiro, P.F. (1994). Wavelet Transform: an Advanced Tool for Analyzing non-Stationary Harmonic Distortion in Power System, *Proceedings of the IEEE International Conference on Harmonics in Power Systems*, Bologna, Italy, September 21-24, 1994

Robertson, D.; Camps, O. & Mayer, J. (1994). Wavelets and Power System Transients: Feature Detection and Classification, *Proceedings of SPIE international symposium on optical engineering in aerospace sensing*, Vol.2242, pp. 474-487, Orlando, FL, USA, April 5-8, 1994

Rocha, A.J.R. & da Silva, A.P.A. (2005). Feature Extraction via Multiresolution Analysis for Short Term Load Forecasting. *IEEE Transactions on Power Systems*, Vol.20, No.1, (February 2005), pp. 189-98, ISSN 0885-8950

Saha, A.K.; Chowdhury, S.; Chowdhury, S.P.; Song, Y.H. & Taylor, G.A. (2006). Application of Wavelets in Power System Load Forecasting, *IEEE Power Engineering Society General Meeting*, pp. 1-6, ISBN 1-4244-0493-216, October, 2006

Saleh, S.A. & Rahman, M.A. (2010). Testing of a Wavelet-Packet-Transform-Based Differential Protection for Resistance-Grounded Three-Phase Transformers. *IEEE Transactions on Industry Applications*, Vol.46, No.3, (May/June 2010), pp. 1109-1117, ISSN 0093-9994

Shariatinasab, R. & Akbari, M. (2010). New Islanding Detection Technique for DG Using Discrete Wavelet Transform, *IEEE International Power and Energy Conference (PECon 2010)*, pp. 294-299, ISBN 978-1-4244-8947-3, Kuala Lumpur, Malaysia, November 29/ December 01, 2010

Wang, L.; Dong, L.; Hao, Y. & Liao, X. (2009). Wind Power Prediction Using Wavelet Transform and Chaotic Characteristics, *World Non-Grid-Connected Wind Power and Energy Conference (WNWEC)*, pp. 1-5, ISBN 978-1-4244-4702-2, September 24-26, 2009

Yao, S.J.; Song, Y.H.; Zhang, L.Z. & Cheng, X.Y. (2000). Wavelet Transform and Neural Networks for Short-Term Electrical Load Forecasting. *Energy Conversion and Management*, Vol.41, No.18, (December 2000), pp. 1975-1988, ISSN 0196-8904

Yu, I.-K.; Kim, C.-I. & Song, Y.H. (2000). A Novel Short-Term Load Forecasting Technique Using Wavelet Transform Analysis. *Electric Machines and Power Systems*, Vol.28, No.6, pp. 537–549, ISSN 1532-5008

Zhang, H., Blackburn, T.R., Phung, B.T., & Liu, Z. (2004). Signal Processing of On-Line Partial Discharges Measurements in HV Power Cables, *Australasian Universities Power Engineering Conference*, ISBN 1-864-99775-3, Brisbane, Australia, September 26-29, 2004

Zhang, H., Blackburn, T.R., Phung, B.T., & Liu, Z. (2004). Application of Signal Processing Techniques to On-Line Partial Discharge Detection in Cables, *2004 International Conference on Power System Technology*, pp. 1780-1785, ISBN 0-7803-8610-8, Singapore, November 21-24, 2004

Zhen, R.; Qungu, H.; Lin, G. & Wenying, H. (2000). A New Method for Power Systems Frequency Tracking Based on Trapezoid Wavelet Transform, *International Conference on Advances in Power System Control, Operation and Management (APSCOM)*, Vol. 2, pp. 364–369, ISBN 0-85296-791-8, Hong Kong, October 30/November 01, 2000

12

Discrete Wavelet Transform Application to the Protection of Electrical Power System: A Solution Approach for Detecting and Locating Faults in FACTS Environment

Enrique Reyes-Archundia, Edgar L. Moreno-Goytia,
José Antonio Gutiérrez-Gnecchi and Francisco Rivas-Dávalos
Instituto Tecnológico de Morelia, Morelia, Michoacán, México

1. Introduction

The Wavelet Transform has been widely used to process signals in engineering and sciences areas. This acceptance is rooted on its proven capability to analyze fast transients signals which is difficult to perform with the FFT. In the area of electrical engineering, a number of publications have been presented about the analysis of phenomena in electrical grid at medium and high voltage levels. Some solutions have focused on the power quality (Chia-Hung&Chia-Hao, 2006; Tse, 2006), short-term load forecasting (Chen, 2010) and protection of power systems (Kashyap&Shenoy, 2003; Ning&Gao, 2009). However, there are few contributions in the open literature focusing in using WT for implementing relaying protection algorithms in power grids with presence of FACTS. The Thyristor Controlled Series Capacitor (TCSC), the Universal Power Flow Controller (UPFC), the Static Synchronous Series Compensator (SSSC), and the Statcom are some of the power controllers developed under the umbrella name of "Flexible AC Transmission Systems" (FACTS). These devices play a key role in nowadays electrical networks because they have the capability of improving the operation and control of power networks (power transfer, transient stability among others characteristics). Collateral to their many strong points, the FACTS controllers also have secondary effects on the grid that should be taken into account for engineering the next generation of protection schemes.

In power grids, -transmission lines included-, there are three-phase, two-phase and single-phase fault events. At fault occurrence of any type, a fast transient signal, named travelling wave-, is produced and propagates through the power lines. The travelling waves are helpful in determining the fault location in such line, faster than using other methods, if the appropriate tools are used.

This chapter presents the application of the Discrete Wavelet Transform (DWT) for extracting information from the travelling waves in transmission line and separate such waves from the signals associated to the TCSC and SSSC. This signal discrimination is useful to improve protections algorithms.

The chapter also presents a brief description of DWT in section 2 and includes a review of FACTS controllers in section 3. Section 4 presents the procedure to separate the effects of power electronic controller. Finally, sections 5 and 6 present the system under test and the results in locating faults in power lines.

2. Wavelet Transform

The Wavelet Transform (WT) is a tool highly precise for analyzing transient signal. The WT is obtained from the convolution of the signal under analysis, $f(t)$, with a wavelet Ψ, both related to the coefficients C as shown in (1)

$$C(scale, position) = \int_{-\infty}^{\infty} f(t)\Psi(scale, position, t)dt \quad (1)$$

where Ψ is the "mother" wavelet, is so named because it belongs a "family" of special wavelets to compare with $f(t)$. Examples of wavelets families are: Haar, Daubechies, Symlets, Mexican Hat, Meyer, Discrete Meyer. Ψ is selected to analyze a unknown portion of signal using convolution, i.e. the wavelet transform can detect if the analyzed signal is closely correlated with Ψ under a determined scale and position.

The WT produces a time-scale space. In the wavelet context, "scaling" means "stretching" or "compressing" a signal, as shown if fig. 1. In this way, scaling is related to frequency, meaning this that the smaller the scale factor, the more "compressed" the wavelet, i.e. smaller scale factors are corresponding with high frequencies.

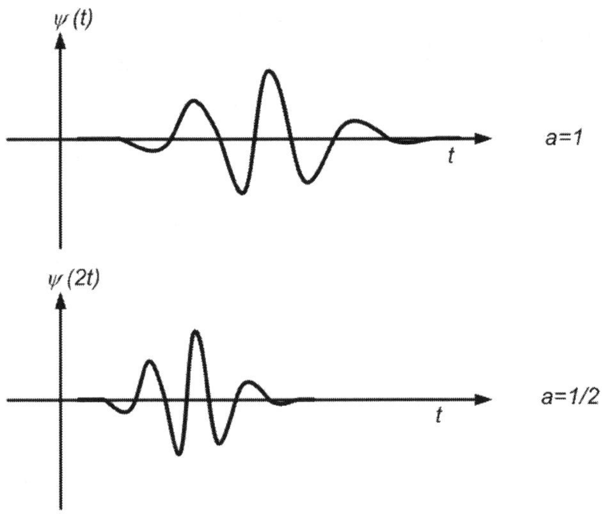

Fig. 1. Scaling the wavelet signal

In the other hand, the term "position" is referred to shifting the wavelet, this is delaying or advancing the signal, as shown if fig 2. $\psi(t-\tau)$ is delayed τ seconds of $\psi(t)$.

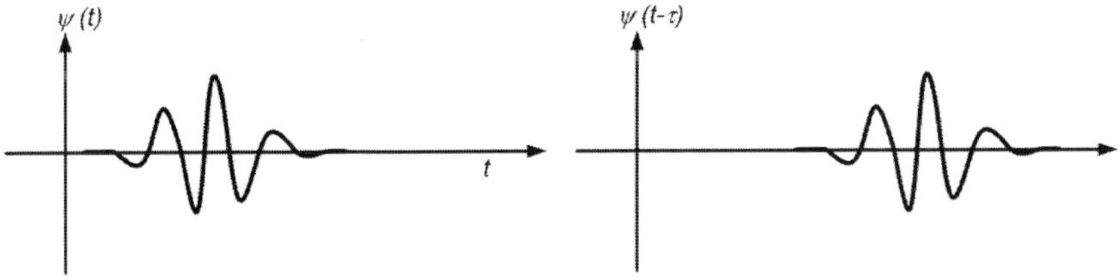

Fig. 2. Shifting the wavelet signal

Due to the easiness to modify the scale-position parameters, the wavelet analysis enables (Misiti, 2001):

1. The use of long time intervals where more precise low-frequency information is needed
2. Shorter regions where high-frequency information is needed.
3. To perform local analysis, that is, to analyze a localized area of a larger signal.

If a subset of scales and positions is taken under consideration instead a large number of coefficients then the analysis can be performed more efficiently. Scales and positions based on power of 2 (known as dyadic) are the common selection. The analysis performed under the aforementioned consideration is named Discrete Wavelet Transform (DWT), because is referred to discrete values.

In the DWT process, the input signal is filtered and sampled down. This processing keeps all valuable information complete but reduces the number of data needed. Two data sequences are obtained once the procedure is perform: Approximations (*cAn*) and Details (*cDn*). The former are the high-scale, low-frequency components of the signal and latter are the low-scale, high-frequency components. Both correspond to DTW coefficients, as shown in fig. 3. After filtering the signal is left down sampled but keeping complete information

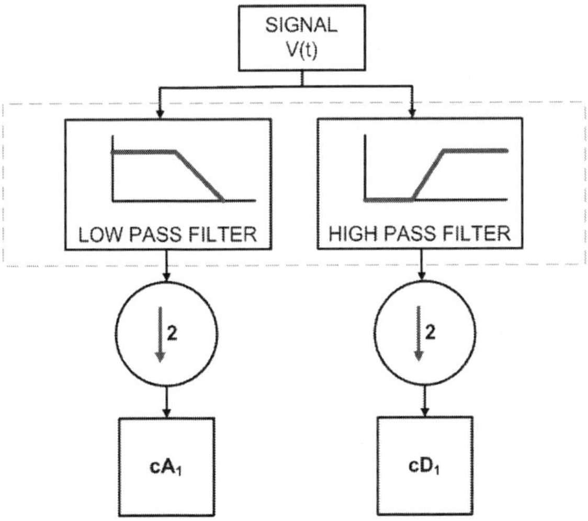

Fig. 3. Discrete Wavelet Transform

cA_1 and cD_1 are obtained by (2) (Misiti et. al. 2001)

$$\begin{aligned} cA_1(t) &= \sum_k f(t).L_d(k-2t) \\ cD_1(t) &= \sum_k f(t).H_d(k-2t) \end{aligned} \tag{2}$$

where cA_1, is the approximation coefficient of level 1, cD_1 is the detail coefficient of level 1. L_d is the low-pass filter and H_d is the high-pass filter. These filters are related to mother wavelet ψ. In this process, signal $f(t)$ is divided in two sequences, cD_1 contains highest frequency components ($f_s/4$ to $f_s/2$ range, where f_s equals sampling frequency of $f(t)$) and cA_1 lower frequencies (lower than $f_s/4$). At this stage, cD_1 extract elements of $f(t)$ in $f_s/4$ to $f_s/2$ range that maintains correlation with ψ.

As aforesaid, the initial decomposition of signal $f(t)$ is the level 1 for Approximations (cA_1) and Details (cD_1). This cA_1 can in turn be divided in two sequences of Approximations and Details and then a new level of decomposition is obtained (cA_2 and cD_2). This procedure is repeated until the required level for the application is reached, as shown in fig. 4.

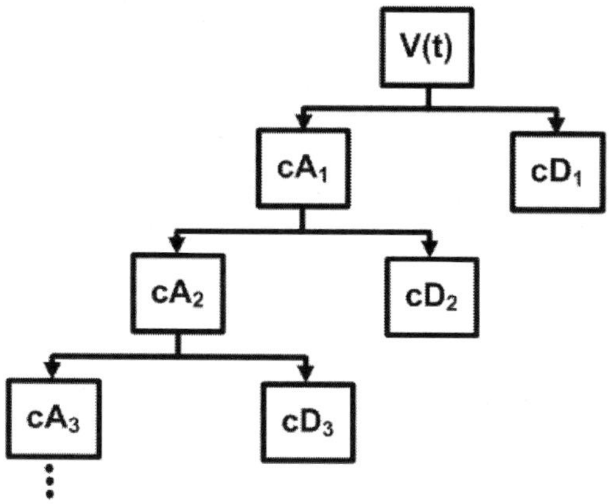

Fig. 4. Wavelet decomposition tree.

Of course, cA_2 and cD_2 are obtained from cA_1 after to pass a filter and sampling down stage. In this way, sequences cD_1, cD_2, ... cD_n relates $f(t)$ to ψ at different scales, i.e. different frequency ranges. (2) can be extended for higher levels cD and cA, as shown in (3)

$$\begin{aligned} cA_{n+1}(t) &= \sum_k cA_n(t).L_d(k-2t) \\ cD_{n+1}(t) &= \sum_k cA_n.H_d(k-2t) \end{aligned} \tag{3}$$

3. Flexible AC Transmission Systems (FACTS)

In this section, a brief description of series and shunt FACTS controllers is presented with emphasis on the TCSC and SSSC.

The FACTS controllers, once installed in the power grid, helps to improve the power transfer capability of long transmission lines and the system performance in general. Some of the benefits of the FACTS controllers on the electric system:

1. Fast voltage regulation,
2. Increased power transfer over long AC lines,
3. Damping of active power oscillations, and
4. Load flow control in meshed systems,

The FACTS controllers are commonly divided in 4 groups (Hingorani&Gyugyi, 2000):

1. Series Controller. These controllers are series connected to a power line. These controllers have an impact on the power flow and voltage profile. Examples of these controllers are the SSSC and TCSC.
2. Shunt Controllers. These controllers are shunt connected and are designed to inject current into the system at the point of connection. An example of these controllers is the Static Synchronous Compensator (STATCOM).
3. Series-shunt controllers. These controllers are a combination of serial and shunt controllers. This combination is capable of injecting current and voltage. An example of these controllers is the Unified Power Flow Controller (UPFC).
4. Series-series controllers. These controllers can be a combination of separate series controllers in a multiline transmission system, or it can be a single controller in a single line. An example of such devices is the Interline Power Flow Controller (IPFC)

The STATCOM, the TCSC and the SSCC are three of the FACTS controllers highlighted by their capacity to provide a wide range of solutions for both normal and abnormal conditions. Figures 5 to 7 illustrates the STATCOM, TCSC and SSSC structures and its network connection.

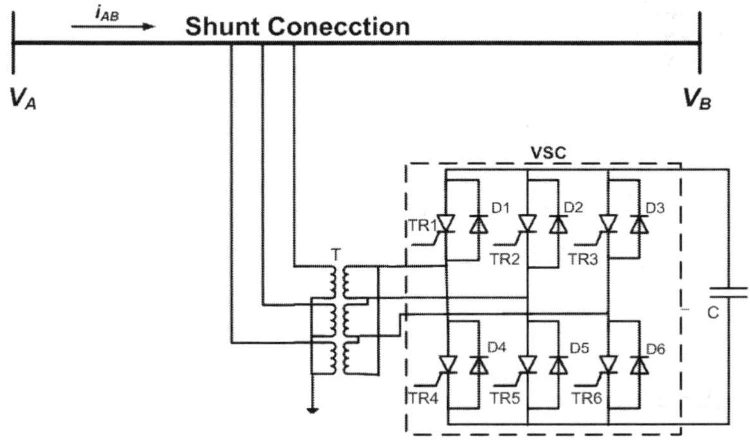

Fig. 5. STATCOM

The STATCOM is a voltage-source converter (VSC) based controller which maintains the bus voltage by injecting an ac current through a transformer.

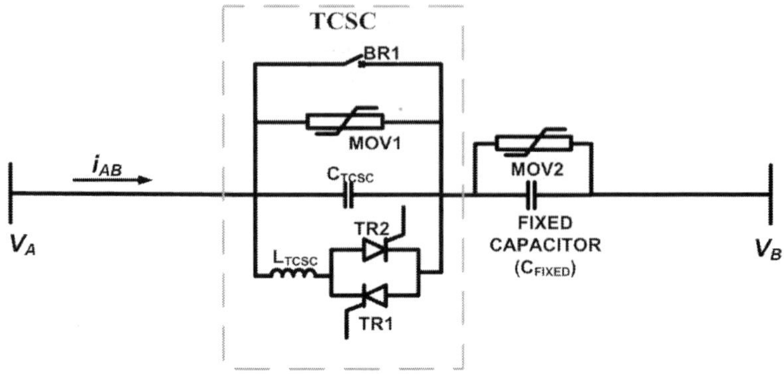

Fig. 6. TCSC

The TCSC is made of a series capacitor (C_{TCSC}) shunted by a thyristor module in series with an inductor (L_{TCSC}). An external fixed capacitor (C_{FIXED}) provides additional series compensating. The structure shown in fig. 4 behaves as variable impedance fully dependable of the firing angle of the thyristors into the range from 180° to 90°. Normally the TCSC operates as a variable capacitor, firing the thyristor between 180° to 150°. The steady state impedance of TCSC (X_{TCSC}) is (4)

$$X_{TCSC}(\alpha) = \frac{X_{CTCSC} X_{LTCSC}(\alpha)}{X_{LTCSC}(\alpha) - X_{CTCSC}} \tag{4}$$

Where

$$X_{LTCSC}(\alpha) = X_{LTCSC} \frac{\pi}{\pi - 2\alpha - \sin\alpha}, X_{LTCSC} < X_{LTCSC}(\alpha) \le \infty$$

where α is the firing angle of thyristor.

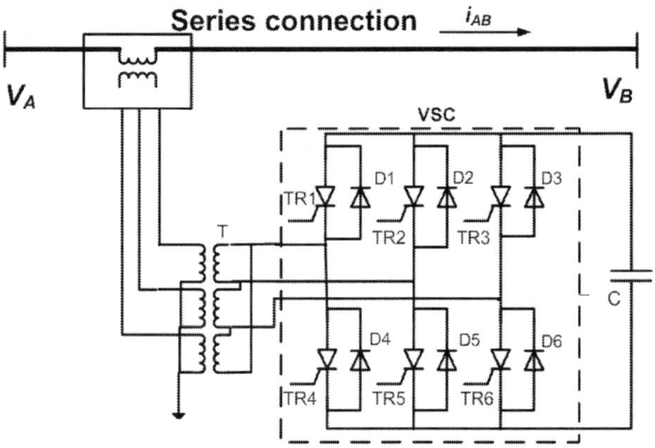

Fig. 7. SSSC

The SSSC injects a voltage in series with the transmission line in quadrature with the line current. The SSSC increases or decreases the voltage across the line, and thereby, for controlling the transmitted power.

3.1 FACTS effects on conventional protection schemes

The transmission lines are commonly protected with a distance protection relay. A key element for this protection is the equivalent impedance measured from the relay to the fault location, as shown on fig. 8. In non-compensated lines, the distance to the fault is lineally related to this impedance.

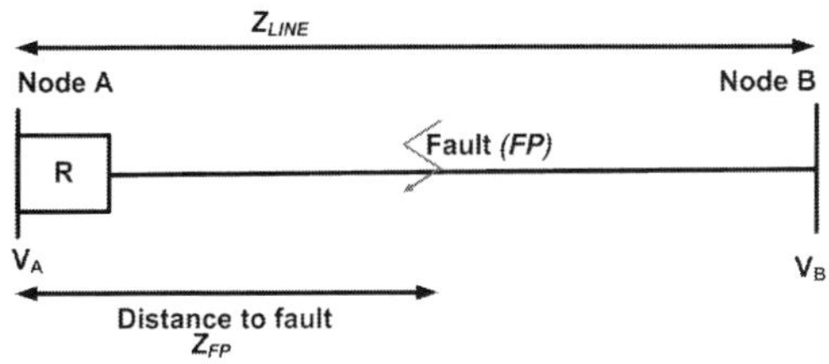

Fig. 8. Distance Relay

Before the fault occurs, the relay (R) measures voltage and current at node A and calculate the total impedance of line (Z_{LINE}). When fault occurs at fault point (*FP*), the impedance measured by R is lower than Z_{LINE} ($Z_{FP} < Z_{LINE}$) and proportional to distance between *FP* and node A.

In transmission lines compensated with series FACTS such impedance, -from measuring point of reference-, presents a nonlinear behavior. The impedance can abruptly change depending on the location of the fault in the line, after or before the FACTS controller. As mentioned above, protection relays for no compensated power lines centers its operation in a linear relationship between the distance to the fault and the equivalent impedance. For instance, the collateral effects of STATCOM on impedance had been presented in some detail (Kazemi et.al., 2005; Zhou et.al., 2005) showing that the shunt controller produces a modification in tripping characteristics for relay of protection. The impedance variation induced by the STATCOM affects the distance protection, meaning this that the fault is not precisely located in the line and the distant to the fault is wrongly determined. In relation with the UPFC, some studies indicate that this controller have significant effects on the grid at the point of common coupling, PCC, greater than those from shunt-connected controller (Khederzadeh, 2008). Similarly, series-connected FACTS controllers tends to reduce the total equivalent impedance a transmission line. As the conventional distance protection relies on the linear equivalent impedance-fault distance relationship, at fault occurrence such protection, -installed at in one end of the line-, faces two scenarios: a) scenario 1: the fault is located between the protection and the series FACTS, and b) scenario 2: the fault is not located between the protection and the series FACTS but after the controller. As example, Figure 9 shows the effect of the TCSC on the equivalent line impedance. It can be notice in Fig. 9 (b) that TCSC reduces the electrical line length, which means a reduction of the total equivalent impedance. In this case, a conventional distance protection can detect and locate a fault for the scenario 1 (a) but wrongly operates for scenario 2 (b).

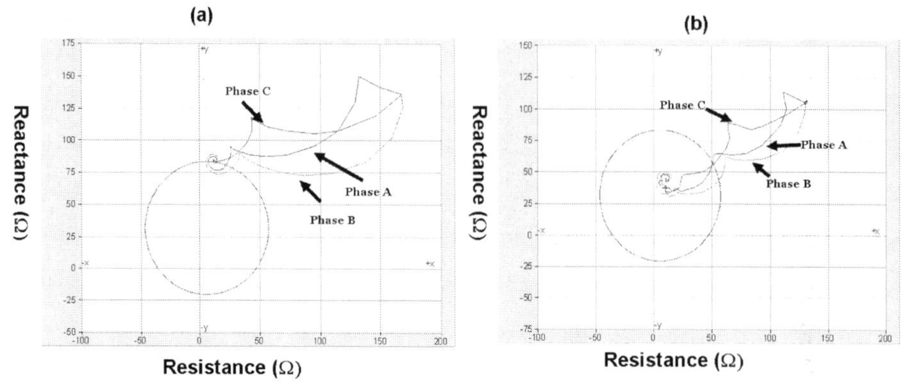

Fig. 9. Impedance of a transmission line after a three-phase fault at the end of line, a) without TCSC, b) with TCSC

The aforementioned nonlinear behavior is caused by the relationship $Z_{LINE\_COMP} = Z_{LINE}-Z_{TCSC}$. In the fault scenario 1 $Z_{LINE\_COMP} = Z_{LINE}$; but in the fault scenario 2 $Z_{LINE\_COMP} = Z_{LINE}-Z_{TCSC}$. Fig. 10 shows the nonlinear relation. The TCSC is situated at the middle of the line.

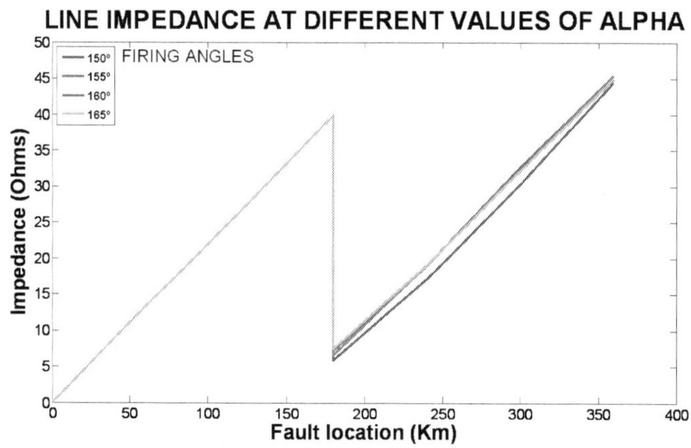

Fig. 10. Line impedance with TCSC after a fault.

As figure 10 shows, if the fault occurs before the TCSC location impedance has a linear relationship with distance to fault, however when fault occurs after the position of FACTS, then the impedance suffers a non linear change, evidenced by reduction of impedance, that cause a malfunction on distance relay.

4. Procedure to detect and locate faults

As shown in section 3, in compensated grid such the conventional distance protection schemes face conditions not taken into account in its original design, therefore the next generation of protection installed should include algorithms with built-in techniques to deal with the particularities of grids in a FACTS context.

Artificial intelligence and digital signal processing techniques, DSP, have both provided a sort of tools to power systems engineers. In particular the combination of wavelets with artificial intelligence and estimation techniques is an attractive option for analyzing electrical grids in the current context.

In order to deal with the impedance nonlinear variation characteristic associated to the series FACTS compensation, various solutions have been proposed in the last decade. One of these proposals uses traveling waves to detect and locate faults in a transmission line (Shehab-Eldin&McLaren, 1988). As is known, after a fault in a transmission line two traveling waves are produced, this is shown if figure 11(a). The traveling wave is used to detect and locate the fault. The latter is achieved determining the time the wave needs to travel from the fault position *(FP)* to the measurement point (M_1). Fig. 11(b), illustrates a lattice diagram of traveling waves. After the fault, the wave needs a time t_1 to travel from *FP* to M_1. When the traveling wave reach a point at which impedance is different to characteristic impedance (Z_0), then the wave is reflected, because of that, the wave is reflected when reach the node *A* and returns to *FP*. Once the wave reaches *FP* is reflected because the impedance at *FP* is different to Z_0 and travels again to node *A* in a time equals to t_2. The fault is detected at time t_1 and time elapsed between t_1 and t_2 is useful to locate the fault position. This is possible because t_2-t_1 has a linear relationship with distance to fault.

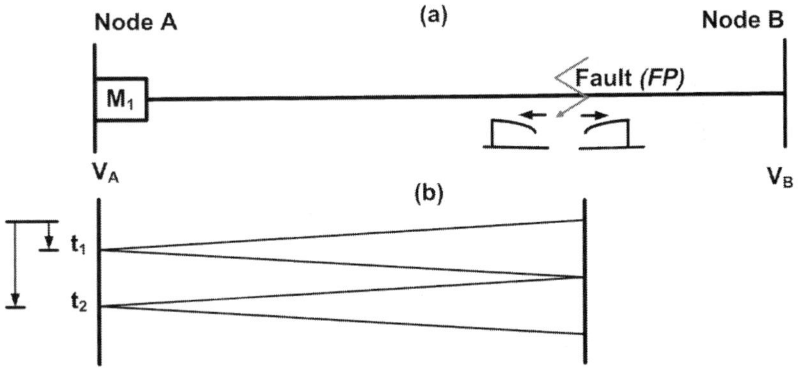

Fig. 11. a) Traveling waves in a faulted line; b) Laticce diagram

It's important to analyze the effects caused by FACTS on traveling wave to determine if this latter can be used to detect and locate faults at FACTS environment. Considering a controller installed at the middle of the line, if fault occurs before the position of FACTS, as illustrated in fig. 12(a), the traveling wave can be analyzed at the same way that without controller, because it don´t encounter points of different impedance to Z_0 between *FP* and M_1. In the other hand, if fault occurs after the position of controller, as shown in Fig. 12(b), the wave encounters the FACTS when traveling from *FP* to M_1.

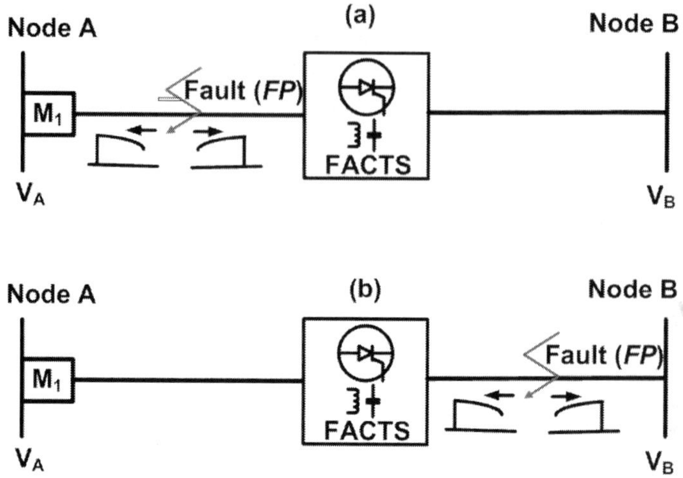

Fig. 12. Travelling waves generated after a fault at FACTS environment

The aim of subsections 4.1 and 4.2 is to show that traveling waves can be used to detect and locate faults when FACTS are installed. To demonstrate the neutrality of some series-connected FACTS on travelling waves, the TCSC and the SSSC are analyzed. Once the wave reaches the FACTS controller, two characteristics are evaluated: a) the effect of FACTS on magnitude of traveling wave, b) the harmonics due to FACTS.

The above are based on two hypotheses: a) the magnitude of traveling wave is not significantly affected when crossing FACTS because this latter doesn't contribute greatly to make different the impedance at location of controller to Z_0 and wave is not reflected at this point; b) the main harmonics of FACTS are the 3th , 5th and 7th (Daneshpooy&Gole, 2001; Sen, 1998), and discrete wavelet transform to analyze traveling wave can be adjusted to separate the harmonics from FACTS of signal due to fault, through proper selection of coefficient of detail.

4.1 Effects on the magnitude of traveling waves

To demonstrate that magnitude of traveling wave is not greatly affected when crossing the FACTS is necessary to analyze the coefficient of reflection (ρ_v) at the FACTS location. ρ_v indicates the energy of traveling wave that is reflected when reach the controller position. If impedance at FACTS location is different to Z_0 then the wave is reflected otherwise there is not reflection.

The voltage equation in any x point along the line for long lines is given by (Pourahmadi-Nakhli&Zafavi, 2011)

$$v_x = (V_- e^{-\gamma x} + V_+ e^{\gamma x}) \tag{5}$$

$$\gamma^2 = \alpha + j\beta = \sqrt{(R + j\omega L)(G + j\omega C)}$$

where α is the attenuation constant , β is phase constant and γ is a propagation constant. $V_{+}e^{+\gamma x}$ represents wave traveling in negative direction and $V_{-}e^{-\gamma x}$ represents wave traveling in positive direction at *x* point (considering *x*=0 at node *A*), as shown in fig. 13.

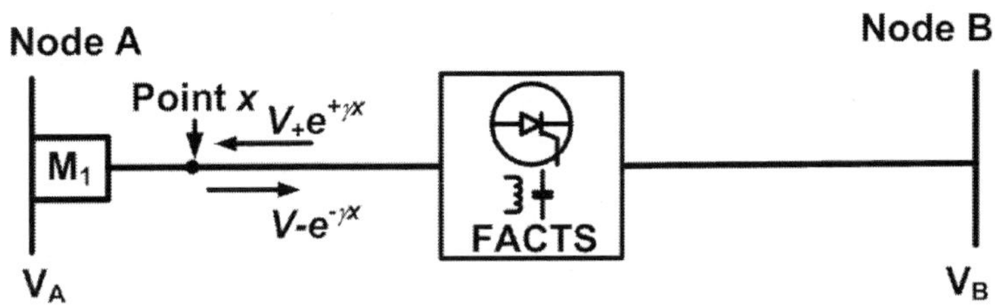

Fig. 13. Voltage in any point along the line

If Z_x (the impedance at *x* point) is different to Z_0, there is a coefficient of reflection (ρ_v) given by (6),

$$\rho_v = \frac{Z_x - Z_0}{Z_x + Z_0} \tag{6}$$

4.1.1 Travelling waves and the TCSC

Considering *x* point matches with FACTS location, then impedance at this point is given by contribution of Z_0 and impedance of TCSC. Fig. 14 illustrates the TCSC scheme under study and table 1 shows its parameters.

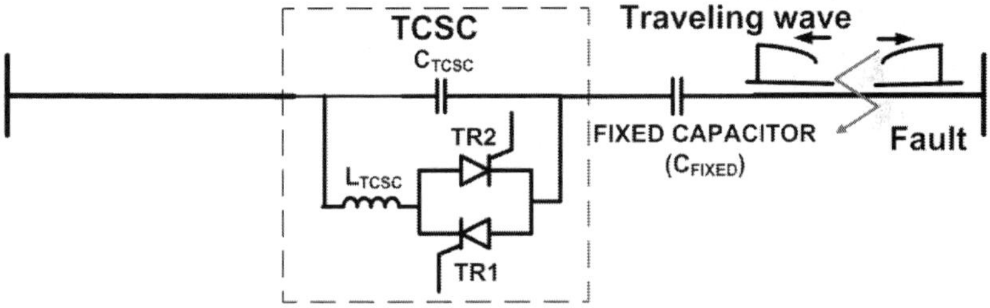

Fig. 14. TCSC controller

Parameter	Value
Line voltage, infinite bus	400 kV
Line length	360 km
C_{TCSC}	95 μF
L_{TCSC}	8.77 mH
Cfixed	98 μF
Z_0 (considering a lossless line)	550 Ω

Table 1. Electric Parameters

When the travelling wave reaches the thyristor, this can be open or closed. If the thyristor is open at the moment when the wave reaches it, the array seen by wave is as shown in fig. 15.

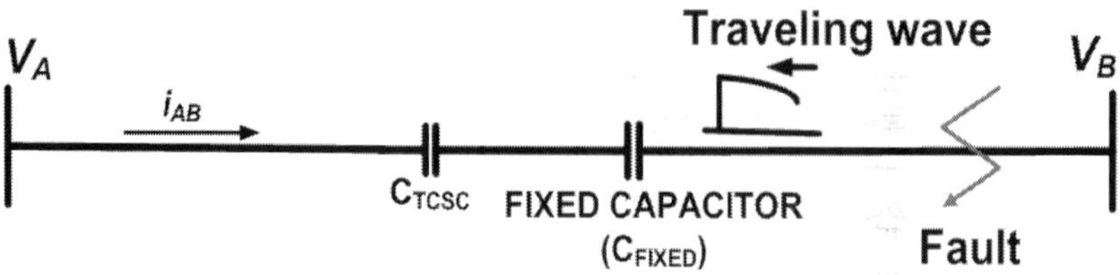

Fig. 15. Traveling wave when Thyristor is open

From fig. 11, the impedance at FACTS location is given by (7)

$$Z_x(s) = Z_0 + \frac{1}{sC_{TCSC}} + \frac{1}{sC_{FIXED}} = Z_0 + \frac{C_{TCSC} + C_{FIXED}}{s(C_{TCSC})(C_{FIXED})} \tag{7}$$

The coefficient of reflection seen at discontinuity is obtained by substituting (7) in (6)

$$\rho_v = \frac{\dfrac{C_{TCSC} + C_{FIXED}}{sC_{TCSC}C_{FIXED}}}{2Z_0 + \dfrac{C_{TCSC} + C_{FIXED}}{sC_{TCSC}C_{FIXED}}} = \frac{\dfrac{1}{sC_{SERIE}}}{2Z_0 + \dfrac{1}{sC_{SERIE}}} = \frac{1}{s2Z_0C_{SERIE} + 1} \tag{8}$$

where $C_{SERIE} = (C_{TCSC})\|(C_{FIXED})$.

Because the capacitor opposes to abrupt changes in voltage, the wave tends to pass through the TCSC without a significant decrement. From (6), the voltage decreases with a constant time given by $\tau = 2Z_0C_{SERIE}$

If C_{TCSC} = 98μF, C_{FIXED} = 95 μF, and Z_0 = 550 Ω, then τ = 53.1 ms. This array needs 212.2 ms to discharge; however, the traveling wave makes the travel in 1.2 ms, so the discontinuity due to TCSC represents only a decrement of 0.6% in magnitude of front of voltage wave.

If thyristor is closed at the moment when the wave reaches it, the array seen by wave is as shown in fig. 16.

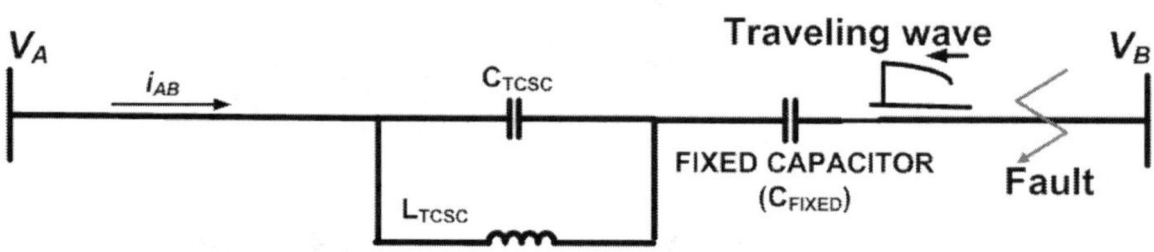

Fig. 16. Traveling wave when Thyristor is closed

From fig. 16, the impedance seen at this point is given by (9)

$$Z_x(s) = Z_0 + \frac{1}{sC_{FIXED}} + \frac{\frac{1}{sC_{TCSC}} sL_{TCSC}}{\frac{1}{sC_{TCSC}} + sL_{TCSC}} \tag{9}$$

ρ_v is obtained by substituting (9) in (6)

$$\rho_v = \frac{\frac{1}{sC_{FIXED}} + \frac{\frac{1}{sC_{TCSC}} sL_{TCSC}}{\frac{1}{sC_{TCSC}} + sL_{TCSC}}}{2Z_0 + \frac{1}{sC_{FIXED}} + \frac{\frac{1}{sC_{TCSC}} sL_{TCSC}}{\frac{1}{sC_{TCSC}} + sL_{TCSC}}} = \frac{\frac{1}{sC_{FIXED}} + \frac{sL_{TCSC}}{1 + s^2 L_{TCSC} C_{TCSC}}}{2Z_0 + \frac{1}{sC_{FIXED}} + \frac{sL_{TCSC}}{1 + s^2 L_{TCSC} C_{TCSC}}}$$

$$\rho_v = \frac{1 + s^2 L_{TCSC} C_{TCSC} + s^2 L_{TCSC} C_{FIXED}}{2Z_0 (1 + s^2 L_{TCSC} C_{TCSC}) s C_{FIXED} + 1 + s^2 L_{TCSC} C_{TCSC} + s^2 L_{TCSC} C_{FIXED}} \tag{10}$$

$$\rho_v = \frac{s^2 (L_{TCSC} C_{TCSC} + L_{TCSC} C_{FIXED}) + 1}{s^3 2 Z_0 L_{TCSC} C_{TCSC} C_{FIXED} + s^2 (L_{TCSC} C_{TCSC} + L_{TCSC} C_{FIXED}) + s 2 Z_0 C_{FIXED} + 1}$$

In this case, L_{TCSC}= 8.8 mH, so the constant time of decrease is τ = 107.5 ms, and 430.1ms are needed to reflect the wave. As the wave need 1.2 ms. to travel along the line, no significant decrease is done.

4.1.2 Travelling waves and the SSSC

An SSSC can emulate a series-connected compensating reactance and is represented by a voltage source (Vq) in series with reactance of coupling transformer (X_L) (Sen, 1998). The Fig. 17 pictures the SSSC equivalent circuit.

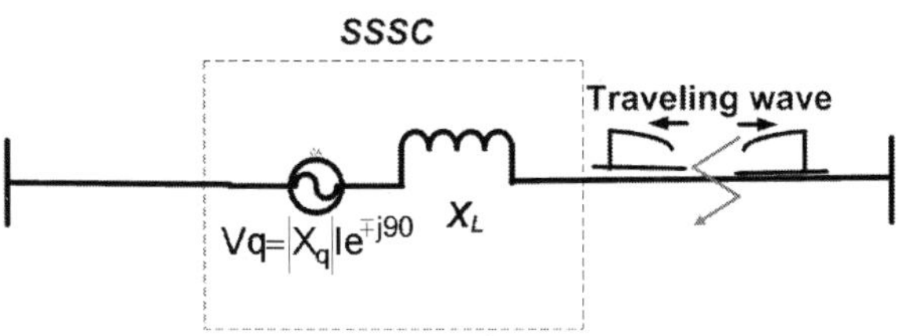

Fig. 17. SSSC Controller

Once the wave reaches the SSSC, the impedance seen by wave is (11)

$$Z_x(s) = Z_0 + jX_L \tag{11}$$

ρ_v is obtained substituting (11) in (6)

$$\rho_v = \frac{jX_L}{jX_L + 2Z_0} \tag{12}$$

Due the transformer was selected to work as a coupling instrument, X_L is enough small to give a ρ_v near to zero. So, the magnitude of incident wave is no significantly affected by SSSC. In the present case $X_L = wL = (2\pi)(60)(0.1\text{mH}) = 0.0377\ \Omega$ and $Z_0 = 550\ \Omega$, then

$$\rho_v = \frac{0.0377j}{0.0377j + 2(550)} \approx \frac{0.0377j}{1100} \approx 0$$

Because of the value of ρ_v is zero and then there is not reflection of wave when reach the position of SSSC, so the magnitude of traveling wave is not affected.

In the case of both controllers, TCSC and SSSC, is evidenced that the magnitude of traveling waves are unaffected when passing through the FACTS controller and they are not an obstacle for the travelling waves to be a good option to detect and locate faults.

4.2 FACTS harmonics effects on WT

Although magnitude of traveling wave is no significantly affected by TCSC, a proper coefficient of detail in wavelet transform is needed to be selected. This is because the wavelet transform can detect the harmonics due to FACTS. This frequency can mix up with the traveling waves at some coefficients of details reason why is important to identify. For instance, the main harmonics of TCSC are 3th and 5th (Daneshpooy&Gole, 2001)

Table 2 shows the frequency ranges of the coefficients of details for the signals under analysis. The above considering a sampling frequency of 10 kHz. It can be seen that cD_5, correspond to 156-312 Hz range, so main harmonics of TCSC are placed in that level.

Level of Coefficient of Detail	Range of frequency
cD1 (level 1)	2500 Hz to 5 kHz
cD2 (level 2)	1250 Hz to 2500 Hz
cD3 (level 3)	625 Hz to 1250 Hz
cD4 (level 4)	312.5 Hz to 625 Hz
cD5 (level 5)	156 Hz to 312 Hz

Table 2. Range of frequency with coefficient of detail

As example to show the above, a three phase to ground fault is simulated at 300 km from M_1, as illustrated in fig. 18. The fault occurs at 0.3 s. Two cases are considered: a) without FACTS and b) with FACTS.

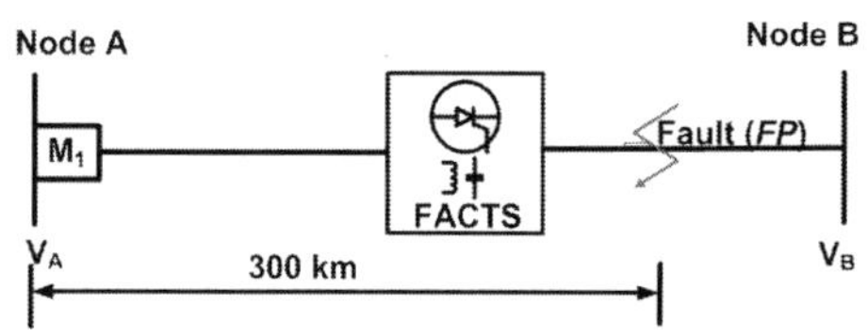

Fig. 18. Three phase to ground fault at 300 km.

Because the fault is simulated after the position of controller, the voltage measurement in M_1, contains harmonics induced by FACTS. To analyze the range of frequency at which fault signal and harmonics of FACTS are present, (3) is used to calculate cD_n of voltage obtained from M_1. Five coefficients of detail are considered because harmonics due to TCSC are present at range 156-312 Hz (see table 2). The results obtained when the fault is simulated with and without FACTS are presented in fig. 19

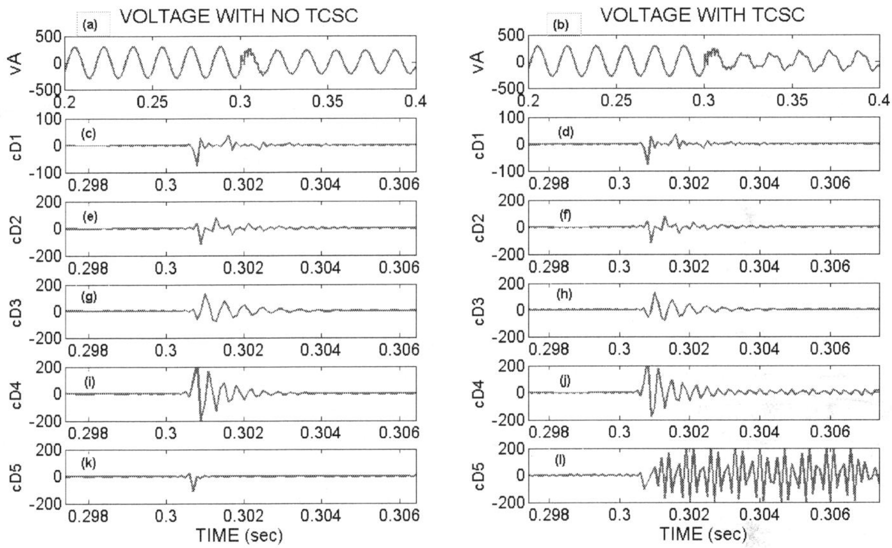

Fig. 19. Detail coefficients obtained in pre-fault and faulted conditions, with and with no TCSC

As can be notice from 19(k) and 19(l), the TCSC effects due the harmonics are detected with cD_5. On the other hand, from 19(c) and (d) the high-frequency traveling waves resulted from the fault are correctly detected with cD_1, regardless of whether or not connected FACTS. Here therefore if lower levels of cDn are used then the harmonics due to TCSC can be discriminated from the mix of signal from the line and fault occurrence.

As a second example, the harmonics injected by the SSSC are also detected with the wavelet transform, because these, it is necessary to separate this signals from those resulted from the fault. In this example, a 6 pulses SSSC is used, so the main harmonic components are 3th, 5th and 7th, which are present at 180 to 420 Hz (Sen, 1998). From table 2, this signal can be analyzed with cD_4 and cD_5, because have a range of 156 to 625 Hz.

To show that harmonics due to SSSC can be discriminated from signals due to fault, a three phase to ground fault is simulated again at 300 km from M_1, as illustrated in fig. 20. The fault occurs at 0.3 s. Two cases are considered: a) without SSSC and b) with SSSC.

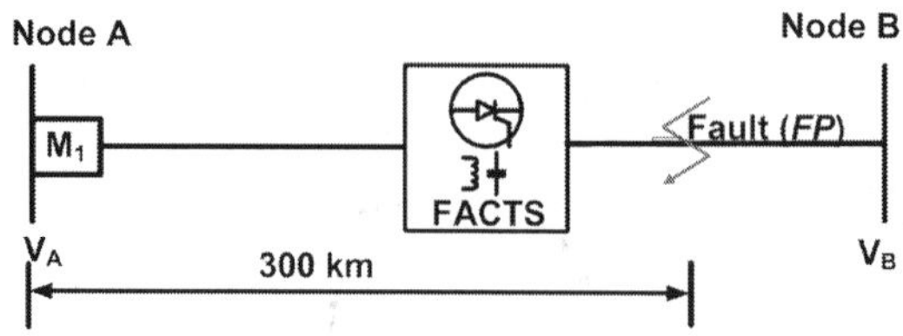

Fig. 20. Three phase to ground fault at 300 km.

As expected, the harmonics due to controller are present with cD_4 and cD_5 as shown in figs. 21(i) to 21 (l). As the same of TCSC case, cD1 can be used to detect the fault signal, with or without the SSSC installed (fig. 21(c) and 21(d)).

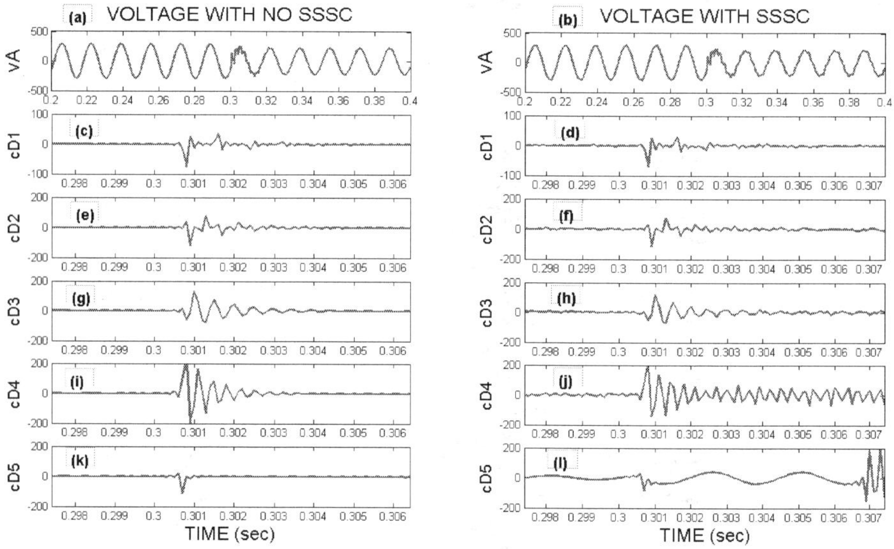

Fig. 21. Coefficients of Detail obtained before and after a fault, with and with no SSSC

As figures 19 and 21 illustrates, the harmonics produced by the FACTS (TCSC and SSSC) are present in levels cD_4 and cD_5. If only lower coefficients of details are considered, then there is no difference between waveforms of voltage/current signals of the faulted line with or without the presence of a FACTS controller. Here therefore cD_1 is a good option for detecting, locating and classifying faults

4.3 Algorithm to detect and locate faults

The algorithm presented in this subsection is based on utilizing traveling waves as mentioned at the beginning of section 4, by means of getting DWT: a) Based on subsection 4.1, the magnitude of traveling wave it's not affected when FACTS lies in its path from fault position (*FP*) to measurement point (M_1); b) Based on subsection 4.2, harmonics due to FACTS don't affect the measurement of traveling wave at M_1, when cD_1 is selected.

Wavelet toolbox from MATLAB is the tool used to calculate detail coefficients and the distance to the fault location. Figure 22 shows the procedure to extract cD_1 obtained of signals from M_1.

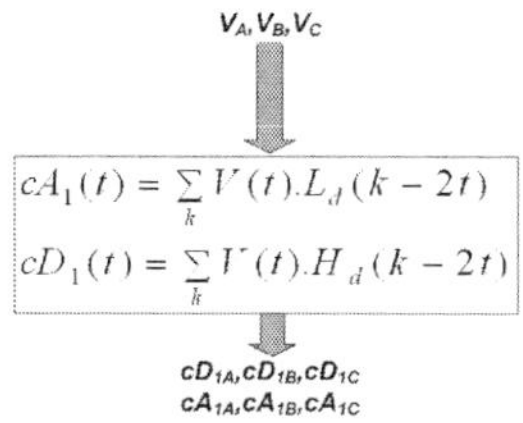

Fig. 22. Procedure to extract the Coefficients of Details

When the voltage signal from M_1 is decomposed in cA_1 and cD_1, cD_1 is used to determinate the instant at which the fault occurs, because of the correspondence with high frequency signals. Figure 23 shows the procedure for analyzing the signals obtained in PSCAD, to detect and locate the fault.

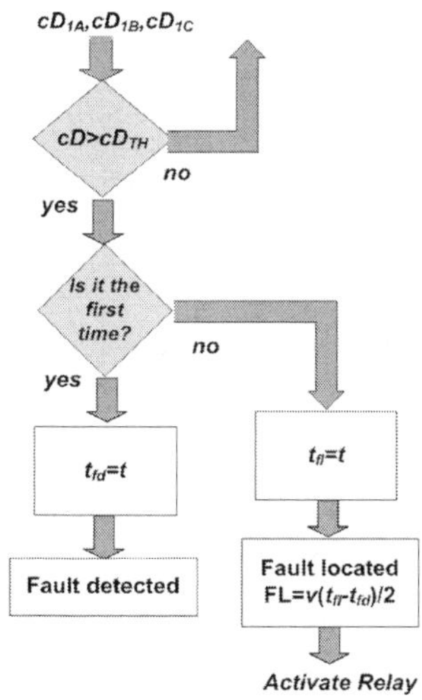

Fig. 23. Procedure to detect and locate fault

Protection relay located at M_1 is continuously monitoring the instant value of voltages V_A, V_B and V_C, in this way, cD_1 is being monitored. If fault is not present, then the only signal monitored by M_1 is the fundamental signal of 60 Hz, as shown in fig. 24 (a). In this case, cD_1 has insignificant values, because there are not signals of frequency determined by this coefficient (2.5 to 5 kHz). Considering a fault occurs in 0.3 seconds at 240 km away from M_1, as illustrated in fig. 24 (b), the transient signal generated by the fault travels across the transmission line and reaches the protection relay, the value of *cD*, exceeds a threshold value (cD_{TH}), because the transitory signal due to fault is situated within the range measured by cD_1, then the system detects the Fault and the value of time of fault is stored ($t_{fd}=t$).

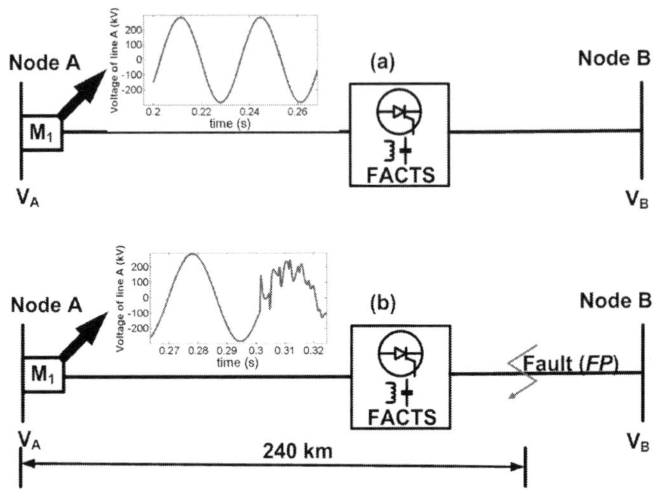

Fig. 24. Signals monitored by M_1, before and after a fault

Once the wave reaches the M_1 position, it is reflected to *FP*, because the impedance at this point is different to Z_0. Because the impedance of *FP* is different to Z_0, the wave is reflected again to M_1, as shown in fig. 25.

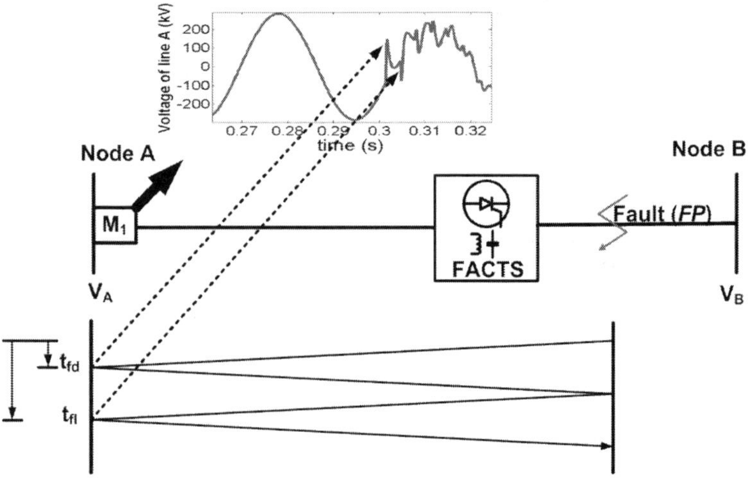

Fig. 25. Path of traveling wave due to fault

When the traveling wave reaches M_1, in a second time, this generates a new peak in cD_1 that uses (13) to locate the distance (*FL*) at which the fault occurs.

$$FL = \frac{v(t_{fl} - t_{fd})}{2} \tag{13}$$

where v=300,000 (km/s) speed of light, t_{fl} = time of second traveling (s) detection and t_{fd} = time of first traveling detection (s)

5. System under study

To demonstrate the correct operation of procedure presented in section 4, an electrical grid was designed in PSCAD. To validate the detection process, several faults are simulated; ten different types of fault are considered.

To corroborate the location process, fault at every 60 km from M_1 are presented. Figure 26 shows the power grid used for the study cases.

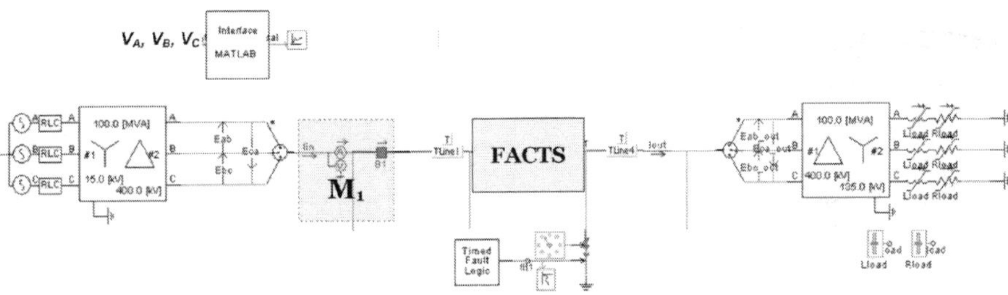

Fig. 26. Electrical grid with series FACTS

cD_1 is used to detect and locate fault. The voltage data (V_A, V_B and V_C) are taken from M_1. These values are fed to MATLAB through an interface. MATLAB performs the tasks presented in subsection 4.3.

After the fault is located a signal of relay activation is sent from MATLAB to PSCAD and protection relay is activated. Protection relay is identified as *B1* in fig. 26 and is located at the same position of M_1.

Electrical parameter of the transmission line are: line voltage: 400 kV; line length: 360 km.; Z_0: 550 Ω, others parameters to adjust TCSC were presented in table 1.

Figures 27 and 28 illustrate the SSSC and TCSC utilized in the case study.

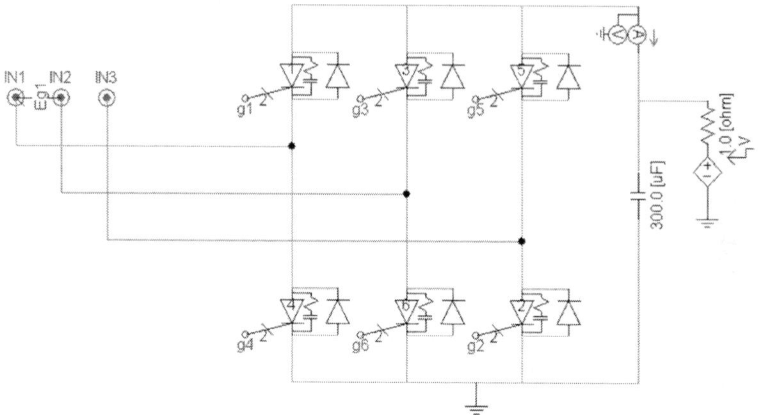

Fig. 27. SSSC configuration for the case study

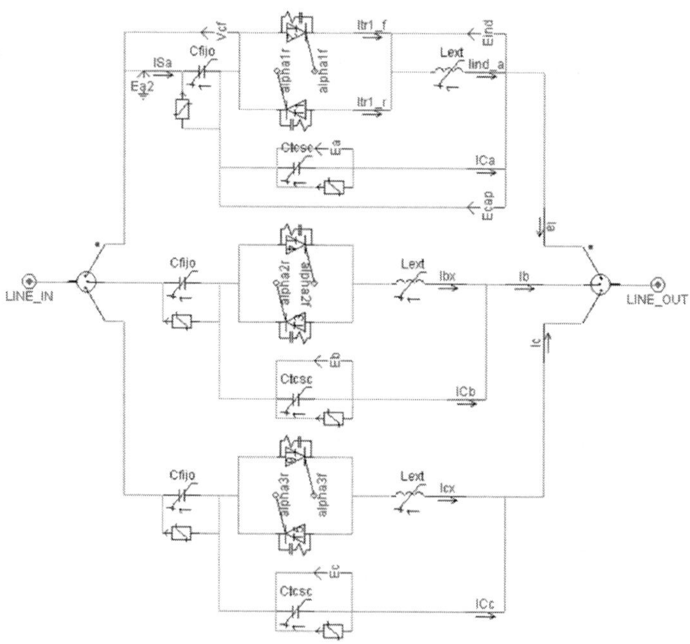

Fig. 28. TCSC configuration for the case study

6. Results

As presented in section 4, traveling waves were no significantly affected by presence of FACTS if cD_1 is selected. Following the procedure showed in section 4, cD_{1A}, cD_{1B}, cD_{1C}, were employed to detect and locate faults. Ten different types of fault were considered to simulation:

1. AG (Phase A to Ground)
2. BG (Phase B to Ground)
3. CG (Phase C to Ground)
4. ABG (Phases A and B to Ground)
5. ACG (Phases A and C to Ground)
6. BCG (Phases B and C to Ground)
7. ABCG (Three Phase Fault to Ground)
8. AB (Phase A to phase B)
9. AC (Phase A to phase B)
10. BC (Phase A to phase B)

Figure 29 shows cD_1 obtained for a fault of type *ABCG* at 240 km from M_1 and t = 0.3 s. As can be notice, cD_{1A}, cD_{1B}, and cD_{1C} appear at 0.3008 s. In this way the fault event can be detected with any cD_1. The magnitude differences among cD_{1A}, cD_{1B}, and cD_{1C} is endorsed to the inception angle of fault, i.e. the value of $V_A(tx)$, $V_B(tx)$ or $V_C(tx)$ (*tx* represents de instant value when fault occurs) at the moment of fault is incepted. It is important to see that wave requires 0.0008 s to travel from *FP* to M_1. This is the reason for the delay of time in which cD_1 appears and fault is detected. This delay time is considered in detecting time and locating distance.

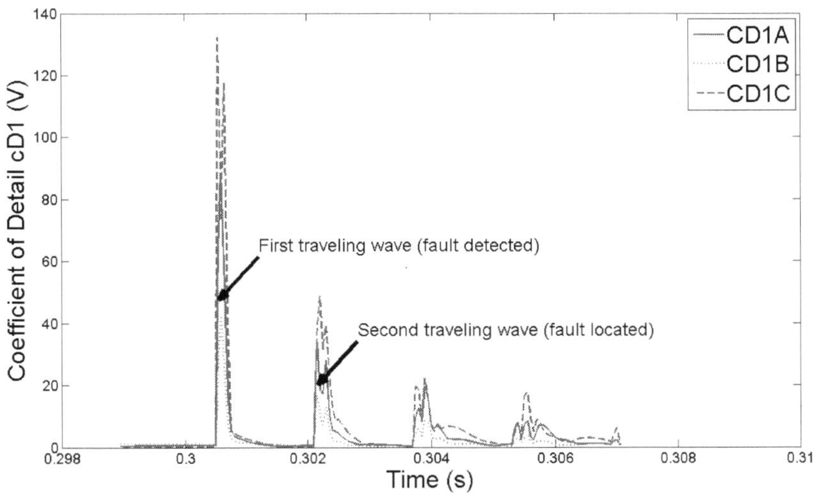

Fig. 29. cD_1 from the three phase fault at t= 0.3 s.

The time elapsed between first and second traveling wave is used by the algorithm to locate the fault. The algorithm developed to detect the fault gives as a result that fault is detected at 0.3 s and is located at 240 km. These is obtained using (13), in this case, time elapsed between the first and second traveling waves is t_{fl}-t_{fd} = 1.6 ms, so

$$FL = \frac{v(t_{fl} - t_{fd})}{2} = \frac{300000km / s(0.0016s)}{2} = 240km$$

To further test the performance of the developed algorithms, the capability for determining the distance to the fault is also evaluated for different distances. Fig. 30 illustrates that transmission line is divided in 60 km segments. In this way, 6 different positions of fault can be analyzed. As example, the fault is simulated in 0.3 s, at 60 km from M_1

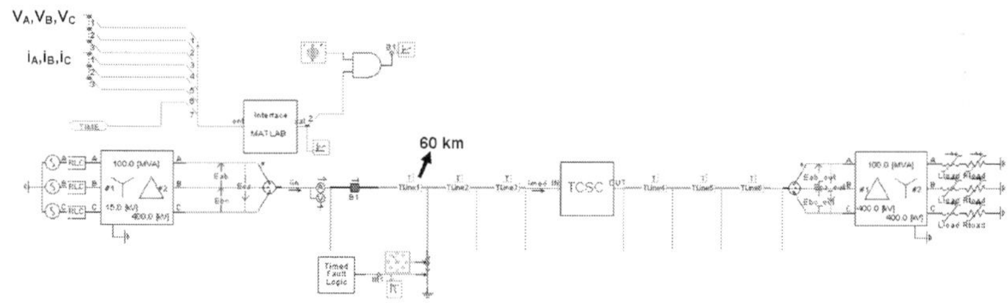

Fig. 30. System used to simulate 6 different locations of faults.

Once the simulation is initiated, voltages values of V_A, V_B and V_C are fed to MATLAB. This latter, develop the algorithm of subsection 4.3 and the result is shown in fig. 31.

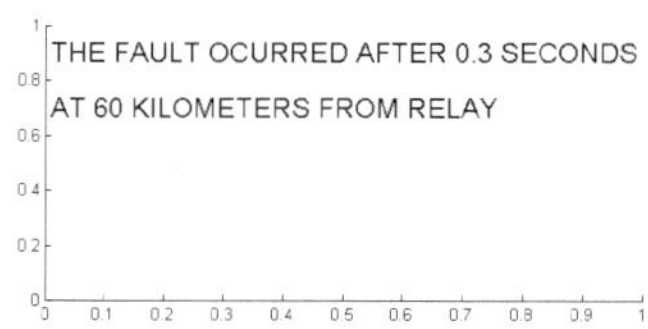

Fig. 31. Result obtained from MATLAB when fault is detected and located

As a resume, the results for 6 different distances to M_1 are shown in tables 3 and 4 for a grid with one FACTS.

	TYPE OF FAULT									
Distance (km) to M1	AG	BG	CG	ABG	BCG	ACG	ABCG	AB	BC	AC
60	60	60	60	60	60	60	60	60	60	60
120	120	120	120	120	120	120	120	120	120	120
180	180	180	180	180	180	180	180	180	180	180
240	240	240	240	240	240	240	240	240	240	240
300	300	300	300	300	300	300	300	292.5	300	300
360	360	360	360	360	360	360	360	360	360	360

Table 3. Distance to the fault for four types of faults in transmission line with TCSC

Distance (km) to M_1	TYPE OF FAULT									
	AG	BG	CG	ABG	BCG	ACG	ABCG	AB	BC	AC
60	60	60	60	60	60	60	60	60	60	60
120	120	120	120	120	120	120	120	120	120	120
180	180	180	180	180	180	180	180	180	180	180
240	240	240	240	240	240	240	240	240	240	240
300	300	300	300	300	300	300	300	292.5	300	300
360	360	360	360	360	360	360	360	360	360	360

Table 4. Distance to the fault for four types of faults in transmission line with SSSC

Tables 3 and 4, show that the algorithm closely determines de distance to the fault. For instance, table 3, illustrates that for faults simulated at 60 km from M_1, the distance at which the fault occurs is correctly identified for all types of faults. This is true for cases when TCSC or SSSC is installed at the middle of the line. The distance to fault is well calculated for 60, 120, 180, 240 and 360 km. The only cases in which the algorithm presents deviations are with AB fault type; these have been linked to those faults with a small inception angle (less than 5 degrees). Fig. 32 shows that transient signal (enclosed in red) generated by fault of type AB at 0.3 s is small, in this condition, it's difficult to calculate efficiently the distance to fault.

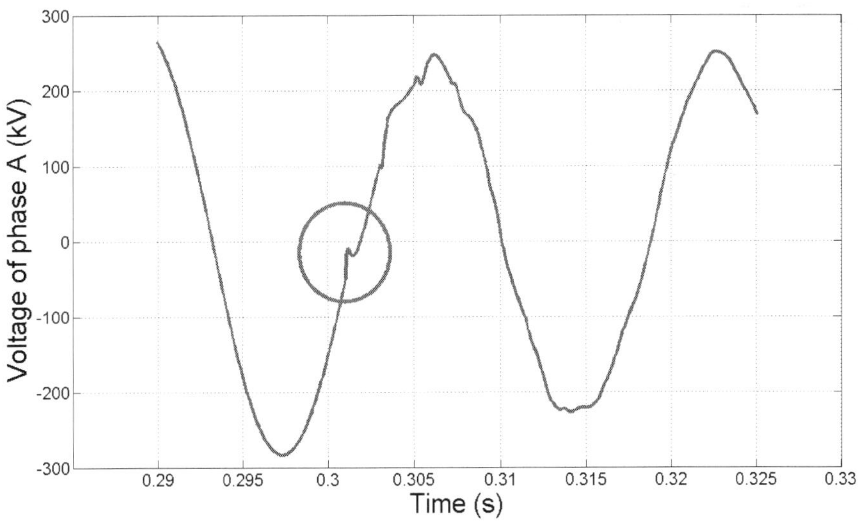

Fig. 32. Voltage of phase A, before and after to AB fault

When the fault is simulated at different time, for example 0.31 s, the fault is correctly detected and located. Fig. 33, shows the screen displayed by MATLAB, after the fault is located.

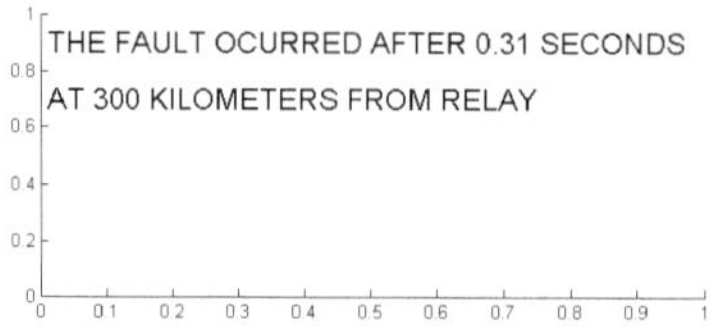

Fig. 33. Screen displayed after *AB* fault, in 0.31 s at 300 km from M_1

The relationship of the time elapsed between first and second traveling waves (t_{elap}=t_{fl}-t_{fd}), has a linear relationship with the distance of fault, this is illustrated in fig 34. This is true when FACTS are or not connected. As this way, the method to calculate de distance to fault using t_{elap} is a better choice compared with distance to fault obtained by measurement of impedance used in conventional schemes. The relationship between distance to fault and impedance are non linear when FACTS is connected (see fig. 10), while using t_{elap}, the distance to fault is easily obtained with (13).

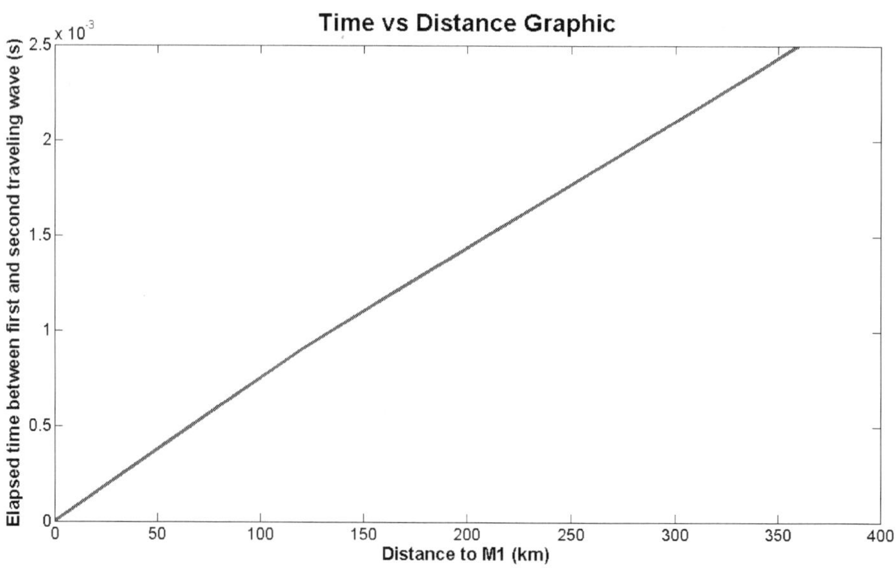

Fig. 34. Relationship between time of traveling waves and distance to fault.

As mentioned earlier, after the detection and location of fault, MATLAB display a screen that includes time of detection and location of fault. After that, MATLAB send an activation signal to protection relay. Fig. 35 shows the line current signals and cD_1, obtained before and after a fault occurs in t=0.3 s at 240 km from M_1

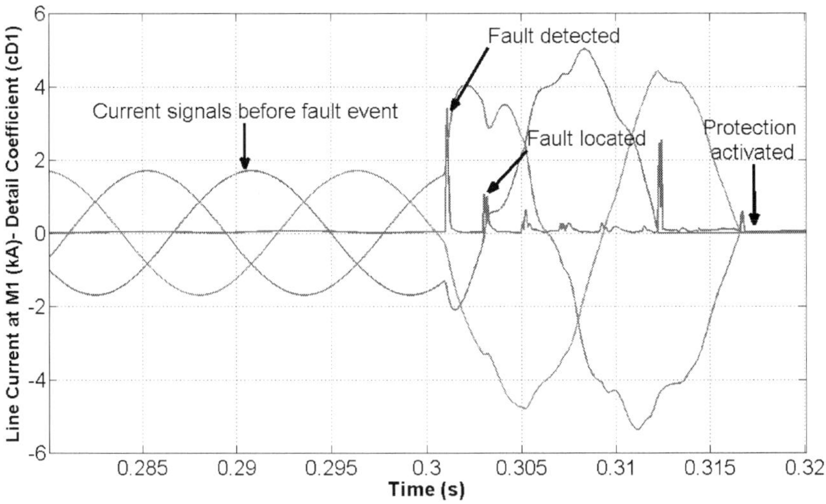

Fig. 35. Protection tripping

As can be seen in fig. 35, before t=0.3 s, the current signals are only the fundamental of 60 Hz. At t=0.3008 s, the algorithm detects the fault event (the wave needs 0.0008 s to reach the M_1 position). The second traveling wave appear at t= 0.3012, at this moment the fault is located. After successful detection and locating of the fault event the protection is activated. The time given to activating relay is sufficiently small (15 ms after detection of fault) to don't compromise coordination with others protection relays.

7. References

Chen Y, et. al. (2010), "Short-Term Load Forecasting: Similar Day-Based Wavelet Neural Networks", *IEEE Transactions on Power Systems, Vol. 25, No. 1*, pp. 322-330, Feb. 2010

Chia-Hung L. & Chia-Hao W. (2006), "Adaptive Wavelet Networks for Power-Quality Detection and Discrimination in a Power System", *IEEE Transactions on Power Delivery, Vol. 21, No. 3*, pp. 1106-111, July 2006

Daneshpooy A.&Gole A.M. (2001), "Frequency Response of the Thyristor Controlled Series Capacitor", *IEEE Transactions on Power Delivery, Vol. 16, No. 1*, pp. 53-58, Jan 2001

Hingorani N. & Gyugyi L. (2000), *Understanding FACTS*, IEEE PRESS, New York USA, 2000

Kashyap K.H. & Shenoy U.J. (2003), "Classification Of Power System Faults Using Wavelet Transforms And Probabilistic Neural Networks", *Proceedings of the 2003 International Symposium on Circuits and Systems*, May 2003, pp 423-426

Kazemi A., Jamali S. & Shateri H. (2005), "Effects of STATCOM on Distance Relay". In *Proc. 2005, IEEE Transmission and Distribution Conference and Exposition*, pp. 1-6

Khederzadeh M. (2008), "UPFC Operating Characteristics Impact on Transmission Line Distance Protection", In *Proc. 2008, IEEE-PES General Meeting - Conversion and Delivery of Electrical Energy in the 21st Century*, pp. 1-6

Misiti M., Oppenheim & Poggi J. M. (2001), "Wavelet Toolbox Users Guide", *The Math Work, Inc.*, 2001

Ning J. & Gao W. (2009), "A wavelet-based method to extract frequency feature for power system fault/event analysis", *Power & Energy Society General Meeting*, IEEE, Calgary, AB, Oct. 2009.

Pourahmadi-Nakhli M. & Safavi A. (2011), "Path Characteristic Frequency-Based Fault Locating in Radial Distribution Systems Using Wavelets and Neural Networks", *IEEE Trans. on Power Delivery*, vol. 26, pp. 772-781, Apr. 2011.

Sen K.K. (1998), "SSSC - Static Synchronous Series Compensator: Theory, Modeling, and Applications", *IEEE Trans. on Power Delivery*, vol. 13, pp. 241-246, Jan. 1998

Shehab-Eldin E.H. & McLaren P.G. (1988), "Travelling wave distance protection - problem areas and solutions", *IEEE Trans. on Power Delivery*, Vol. 3, No. 3, pp. 894-902, Jul. 1988

Tse N.C.F (2006), "Practical application of wavelet to power quality analysis", *Power Engineering Society General Meeting*, IEEE, Montreal, Que, Oct. 2006.

Zhou X.Y, Wang H.F., Aggarwal R.K. & Beaumont P. (2005), "The Impact of STATCOM on Distance Relay", In *Proc. 2005, Power Systems Computation Conference*, pp. 1-7

Part 3

Fault Diagnosis and Monitoring

13

Utilising the Wavelet Transform in Condition-Based Maintenance: A Review with Applications

Theodoros Loutas and Vassilis Kostopoulos
Applied Mechanics Lab, Department of Mechanical Engineering and Aeronautics, University of Patras, Rio, Greece

1. Introduction

Condition monitoring of machinery can be defined as the continuous or periodic measurement and interpretation of data in order to indicate the condition of an machine and determine the need for maintenance. Condition monitoring thus is primarily involved with the diagnostics of faults and failures and aims at an accurate and as early as possible fault detection. It is thus oriented towards an unscheduled preventive maintenance plan with continuous monitoring of the machinery as opposed to scheduled periodic maintenance. The possibility of failures of course cannot be diminished, but confident early diagnosis of incipient failures is extremely useful to avoid machinery breakdown and thus ensure a more cost-effective overall operation reducing equipment down-times. Industrial safety is also enhanced as catastrophic events are avoided when a maintenance-for-cause plan is followed.

When faults occur in machines, phenomena like excessive vibration and/or noise, increased temperatures, increased wear rate, etc. are observed. The concept is to monitor, continuously or periodically, these dynamic phenomena utilizing one or more sensors to capture this behavior. One of the earliest approaches was the sound emission monitoring. An expert human ear played the role of the sensor in the early applications, a sophisticated microphone can play the same role today. The most classic approach -widely used until the present- is the vibration monitoring with few or several accelerometers placed upon the machine. The principle is that when damage occurs, the signature of the vibration response changes in the frequency domain, giving a qualitative indication of fault existence. The Acoustic Emission (AE) technique, famous for its sensitivity in the high frequency domain of micro-damage evolution, has found important applications in gearboxes and bearings as Section 4 presents. Other monitoring techniques include oil condition monitoring (oil debris, oil conductivity or humidity etc.), current and voltage transients monitoring in electric motors as well as temperature measurements/thermography. More than 80% of the applications presented in Section 4 involve vibration monitoring, with AE finding more and more applications the last 15 years and current/voltage measurements being always an option in electric machines. Monitoring generally results in a large number of complex signals with valuable diagnostic information hidden under noise or other irrelevant sources. Over the years and the same time with several breakthroughs in the signal processing field, engineers and researchers realized that the conventional FFT was not suitable to process signals of complex, dynamic nature, often transient and non-stationary, such as the signals from the vibrations of machinery. Among other disadvantages, FFT lacks time localization. To address this problem time-frequency representations were sought and developed. Short-time Fourier Transform (STFT) was introduced as well as non-linear distributions such as the Wigner–Ville distribution (WVD). STFT suffers from the fact that it provides constant resolution for all frequencies since it uses the same window for the analysis of the entire signal. Wigner–Ville distribution and Pseudo-Wigner–Ville distribution are bilinear in nature and artificial cross terms appear in the decomposition results rendering the feature interpretation problematic. Their greatest disadvantage though is that they are generally non-reversible transforms. Wavelet transform (WT) is a relatively recent advancement in the signal processing field. J. Morlet set the first foundations on wavelets back in 1970's but it was not until 1985 when S. Mallat gave wavelets a jump-start through his work in digital signal processing. He discovered some relationships between quadrature mirror filters, pyramid algorithms, and orthonormal wavelet bases. Inspired in part by these results, Y. Meyer constructed the first non-trivial wavelets. A couple of years later, I. Daubechies used Mallat's work to construct a set of wavelet orthonormal basis functions that are perhaps the most elegant, giving a tremendous boost to wavelet applications in numerous scientific fields. The wavelet transform is actually a time-scale method, as it transforms a function from the time domain to the time-scale domain. Scale is indirectly associated with frequency. Furthermore, the wavelet transform is a reversible transform, which makes the reconstruction or evaluation of certain signal components possible, even though the inverse transform may not be orthogonal.

Wavelet transform became very popular in condition monitoring the last 15 years as it is very attractive for the transaction of two major tasks in signals of complex (transient and/or non-stationary) nature: de-noising and feature extraction. De-noising is conducted in order to reduce the fluctuation and pick out hidden or weak diagnostic information. Feature extraction provides usually –though not always- the input to an expert system towards autonomic health degradation monitoring and data-driven prognostics. The generic pattern seen in many studies in the wavelet-based condition monitoring field is summarized in Fig. 1.

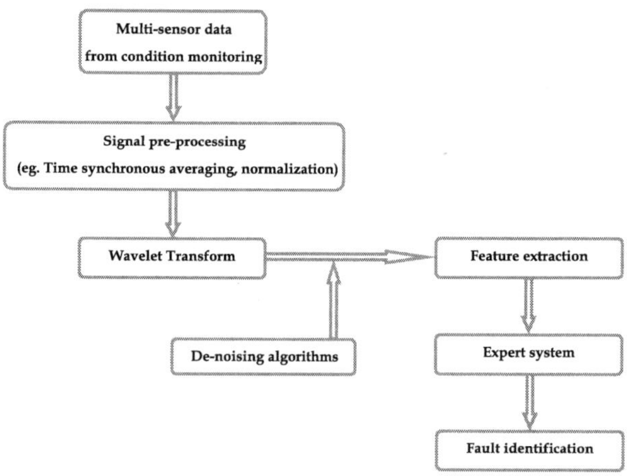

Fig. 1. Schematic representation of wavelet-based condition monitoring philosophy

The current work is organized as follows. Section 2 presents the basic WT versions i.e. DWT, CWT and WPT. Then more recently developed and state-of-the-art wavelet transforms are presented in more detail such as the Dual-Tree Complex Wavelet Transform (DTCWT) as well as Second Generation Wavelet Transforms (SGWT). In section 3 a discussion on the optimum mother wavelet choice issue is conducted and in section 4 a large number of applications -categorized in five application fields- are presented. Section 5 summarizes the main conclusions of this work.

2. Wavelet transforms

2.1 Continuous Wavelet Transform (CWT)

A wavelet is a wave-like oscillation that instead of oscillating forever like harmonic waves drops rather quickly to zero. The continuous wavelet transform breaks up a continuous function *f(t)* into shifted and scaled versions of the mother wavelet ψ. It can be defined as the convolution of the input data sequence with a set of functions generated by the mother wavelet:

$$CW(a,b) = \frac{1}{\sqrt{|a|}} \int_{-\infty}^{\infty} f(t) \cdot \psi^* \left(\frac{t-b}{a}\right) dt \quad (1)$$

with the inverse transform being expressed as:

$$f(t) = \frac{1}{C_\psi} \int_{-\infty}^{\infty} \int_{-\infty}^{\infty} CW(a,b) \cdot \frac{1}{a^2} \cdot \psi\left(\frac{t-b}{a}\right) dadb \quad (2)$$

where a represents scale (or pseudo-frequency) and b represents time shift of the mother wavelet ψ. ψ^* is the complex conjugate of the mother wavelet ψ. The WT's superior time-localization properties result from the finite support of the mother wavelet: as b increases, the analysis wavelet scans the length of the input signal, and a increases or decreases in response to changes in the signal's local time and frequency content. Finite support implies that the effect of each term in the wavelet representation is purely localized. This sets the WT apart from the Fourier Transform, where the effects of adding higher frequency sine waves are spread throughout the frequency axis. CWT can be applied with higher resolution to extract information with higher redundancy, that is, a very narrow range of scales can be used to pull details from a particular frequency band.

2.2 Discrete Wavelet Transform (DWT)

It turned out quite remarkably that instead of using all possible scales only dyadic scales can be utilized without any information loss. Mathematically this procedure is described by the discrete wavelet transform (DWT) which is expressed as:

$$DW(j,k) = \sqrt{2^j} \int_{-\infty}^{+\infty} f(t)\psi^*(2^j t - k)\, dt \quad (3)$$

where DW(j, k) are the wavelet transforms coefficients given by a two-dimensional matrix, j is the scale that represents the frequency domain aspects of the signal and k represents the time shift of the mother wavelet. *f(t)* is the signal that is analyzed and ψ the mother wavelet used for the analysis (ψ^* is the complex conjugate of ψ). The inverse discrete wavelet transform can be expressed as:

$$f(t) = c \sum_j \sum_k DW(j,k)\psi_{j,k}(t) \tag{4}$$

where c is a constant depending only on ψ. Practically DWT is realized by the algorithm known as Mallat's algorithm or sub-band coding algorithm (Mallat, 1989). The DWT of a signal x is calculated by passing it through a series of filters. First the samples are passed through a low pass filter with impulse response h resulting in a convolution of the two. The signal is also decomposed simultaneously using a high-pass filter g. The output from the high-pass filter gives the detail coefficients and the output from the low-pass filter gives the approximation coefficients. The two filters h, g are not arbitrarily chosen but are related to each other and they are known as a quadrature mirror filter. Since half the frequencies of the signal have now been removed, half the samples can be discarded according to Nyquist's rule. The filter outputs are then sub-sampled by 2. This decomposition has halved the time resolution since only half of each filter output characterizes the signal. However, each output has half the frequency band of the input so the frequency resolution has been doubled. The approximation is then itself split into a second-level approximation and detail and the process is repeated as many times as it is desirable. This procedure can be repeated as many times as desirable by the user resulting in N levels of decomposition.

The number of decomposition levels N is related to the sampling frequency of the signal being analyzed (f_s). In order to get an approximation signal containing frequencies below frequency f, the number of decomposition levels that has to be considered is given by (Antonino-Daviu et al., 2007):

$$N = int\left(\frac{log\left(^{f_s}/_{f}\right)}{log(2)}\right) \tag{5}$$

2.3 Wavelet Packet Transform (WPT)

Whereas DWT breaks up only the approximations, WPT simultaneously decomposes approximations and details. In the first resolution, $j = 1$, the signal is decomposed into two packets: A and D. The packet, A, represents the lower frequency component of the signal, while the packet D, represents the higher frequency component of the signal. Then, at the second resolution, $j = 2$, each packet is further decomposed into two sub-packets forming AA, AD, DA, DD. This decomposition process continues and at each subsequent resolution, the number of packets doubles while the number of data points in the packet are reduced by half. The wavelet packets contain the information of the signal in different time windows at different resolution. Each packet corresponds to a specific frequency band.

Both of WPT and DWT operate within the framework of multi-resolution analysis (MRA). Unlike DWT though, WPT has the same frequency bandwidth in every level. Fig. 2 depicts the WPT decomposition tree with A and D corresponding to approximation and detail respectively.

The WPT can thus be seen as a generalization of the wavelet transform and the wavelet packet function is also a time–scale function which can be described as:

$$W_{j,k}^{n}(t) = 2^{j/2}W(2^{j}t - k), \quad j,k \in Z \tag{6}$$

where the integers j and k are the index scale and translation operations.

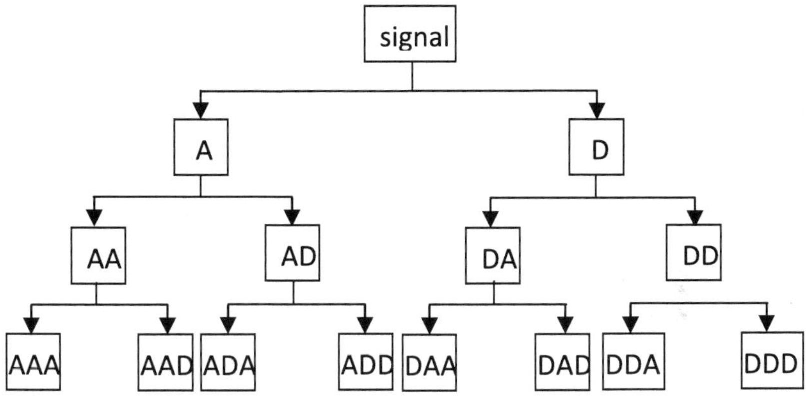

Fig. 2. WPT decomposition tree

The index n is an operation modulation parameter or oscillation parameter. The first two wavelet packets are the scaling function φ(t) and mother wavelet functions ψ(t):

$$W_{0,0}^{0}(t) = \varphi(t) = \sqrt{2}\sum_{k} h(k)\varphi(2t-k) \tag{7}$$

$$W_{0,0}^{1}(t) = \psi(t) = \sqrt{2}\sum_{k} g(k)\varphi(2t-k) \tag{8}$$

When n = 2;3;. . . the function can be defined by the following recursive relationships:

$$W_{0,0}^{2n}(t) = \sqrt{2}\sum_{k} h(k)W_{1,k}^{n}(2t-k) \tag{9}$$

$$W_{0,0}^{2n+1}(t) = \sqrt{2}\sum_{k} g(k)W_{1,k}^{n}(2t-k) \tag{10}$$

where h(k) and g(k) are the quadrature mirror filter associated with the predefined scaling function and mother wavelet function. The wavelet packet coefficients, $w_{j,k}^{n}$ are calculated as:

$$w_{j,k}^{n} = \langle f(t), W_{j,k}^{n}\rangle = \int f(t)\, W_{j,k}^{n} dt\,. \tag{11}$$

The frequency interval of each node is given by $\left(\frac{n-1}{2^{j+1}}S_f, \frac{n-1}{2^{j+1}}S_f\right]$, where S_f is the sampling frequency, j the scale index and n the number of levels n=1,2,...,16.

2.4 Dual Tree Complex Wavelet (DTCWT)

The dual-tree complex wavelet transform (DTCWT) is a relatively recent enhancement to the DWT (Kingsbury, 1998), with important additional properties: reduced aliasing effects, nearly shift-invariance and directionally selective (useful in two and higher dimensions). The frequency aliasing is caused by the overlap of opposing-frequency pass-bands of the wavelet filters. The band-pass filter responses for the DTCWT have nearly all the pass-bands only on one side of zero frequency due to the adopted analytic filters. Thus, DTCWT may possess greatly reduced aliasing effects. Incidentally, this property of analytic filters is also the main reason for the DTCWT to achieve shift-invariance.

In the dual-tree implementation of decomposition and reconstruction, two parallel DWTs with different low-pass and high-pass filters in each scale are used, as can be seen in Fig. 3. The two DWTs use two different sets of filters, with each satisfying the perfect reconstruction condition. Let $\psi_h(t)$ and $\psi_g(t)$ denote the real-valued wavelet used, respectively, in the dual-tree transform. Then a complex-valued wavelet $\psi^C(t)$ can be obtained as:

$$\psi^C(t) = \psi_h(t) + j\psi_g(t) \tag{12}$$

Thus, the two real wavelets constitute a complex analytical wavelet $\psi^C(t)$, which is only supported on the positive of the frequency axis. Fig. 3 shows the frequency response of DTCWT basis and DWT basis functions. It can be seen that all shown basis functions are analytic except for the basis functions corresponding to the scaling coefficients and the first stage wavelet coefficients in comparison with the transfer functions of a real DWT.

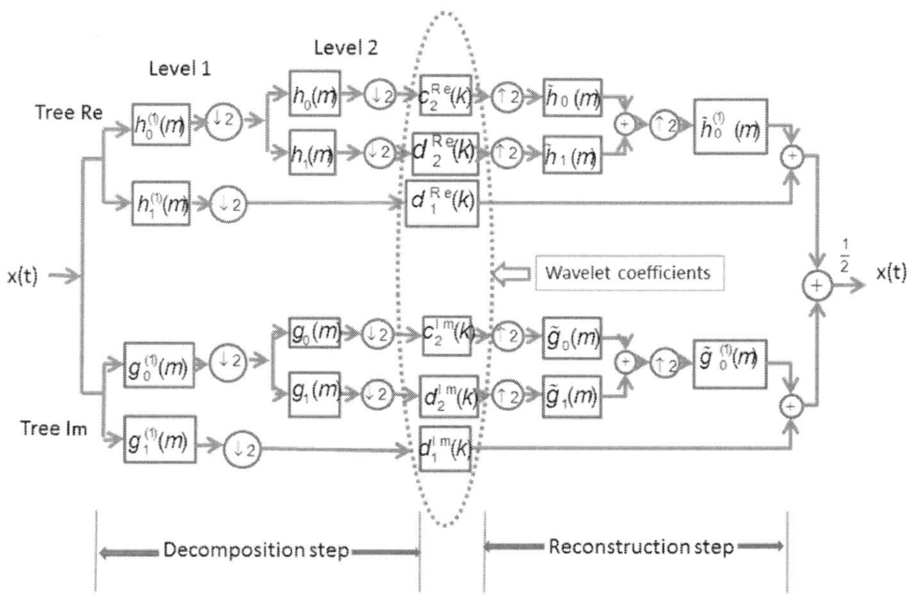

Fig. 3. Decomposition and reconstruction stages of DTCWT

Since DTCWT is composed of two parallel wavelet transforms, according to the wavelet theory, the wavelet coefficients $d_l^{Re}(k)$ and scaling coefficients $c_J^{Re}(k)$ of the upper tree can be computed via inner products (Wang et al., 2010):

$$d_l^{Re}(k) = 2^{l/2} \int_{-\infty}^{\infty} x(t)\psi_h(2^l t - k)dt, \;\; l = 1, \dots, J \tag{13}$$

$$c_J^{Re}(k) = 2^{J/2} \int_{-\infty}^{\infty} x(t)\varphi_h(2^J t - k)dt \tag{14}$$

where l is the scale factor and J is the maximum scale. Similarly, $d_l^{Im}(k)$ and $c_l^{Im}(k)$ coefficients of the lower tree can be computed if $\psi_h(t)$ and $\varphi_h(t)$ are replaced by $\psi_g(t)$ and $\varphi_g(t)$, respectively. The wavelet and scaling of the DTCWT coefficients can then be expressed by combining the output of the dual-tree as follows:

$$d_l^C(k) = d_l^{Re}(k) + jd_l^{Im}(k), \;\; l = 1, \dots, J \tag{15}$$

$$c_J^C(k) = c_J^{Re}(k) + jc_J^{Im}(k) \tag{16}$$

Furthermore, when other coefficients are set to zero, the scaling or wavelet coefficients can be individually reconstructed using the following equations:

$$d_l(t) = 2^{(l-1)/2}\left[\sum_n d_l^{Re}(k)\psi_h(2^l t - k) + \sum_m d_l^{Im}(k)\psi_g(2^l t - m)\right], \;\; l = 1, \dots, J \tag{17}$$

$$c_J(t) = 2^{(J-1)/2}\left[\sum_n c_J^{Re}(k)\varphi_h(2^J t - k) + \sum_m c_J^{Im}(k)\varphi_g(2^J t - m)\right] \tag{18}$$

Coefficients $d_l(t)$ and $c_J(t)$ are real and have equal length with original signal x(t) being different from $d_l^C(t)$ and $c_J^C(t)$. Specifically, for the tree Re, the corresponding decomposed scaling coefficients (approximation) $c_l^{Re}(k)$ and wavelet coefficients (details) $d_l^{Re}(k)$ as well as the inverse transform between the two consecutive resolution levels l and l+1 can be derived by:

$$c_{l+1}^{Re}(k) = \sum_m h_0(m - 2k)c_l^{Re}(m) \tag{19}$$

$$d_{l+1}^{Re}(k) = \sum_m h_1(m - 2k)c_l^{Re}(m) \tag{20}$$

$$c_l^{Re}(k) = \sum_m \tilde{h}_0(k - 2m)c_{l+1}^{Re}(m) + \sum_m \tilde{h}_1(k - 2m)d_{l+1}^{Re}(m) \tag{21}$$

Similarly $c_l^{Im}(k)$, $d_l^{Im}(k)$ for the tree Im can be obtained by:

$$c_{l+1}^{Im}(k) = \sum_n g_0(n - 2k)c_l^{Im}(n) \tag{22}$$

$$d_{l+1}^{Im}(k) = \sum_n g_1(n - 2k)c_l^{Im}(n) \tag{23}$$

$$c_l^{Im}(k) = \sum_n \tilde{g}_0(k - 2n)c_{l+1}^{Im}(n) + \sum_n \tilde{g}_1(k - 2n)d_{l+1}^{Im}(n) \tag{24}$$

Note that a complex transform implemented in this way is no longer critically sampled, because two independent wavelet transforms are required. Thus DTCWT can be implemented using existing DWT software. The computational cost is significantly lower (only 2 times that of the basic DWT). In addition, the transform is naturally parallelized for efficient hardware implementation. Figs. 4 and 5 show the decomposition with DWT and DTCWT respectively of an artificial signal containing four fundamental frequencies: x(t)=2sin(2π·50t)+ 2sin(2π·100t)+ 5sin(2π·150t)+ 2sin(2π·400t).

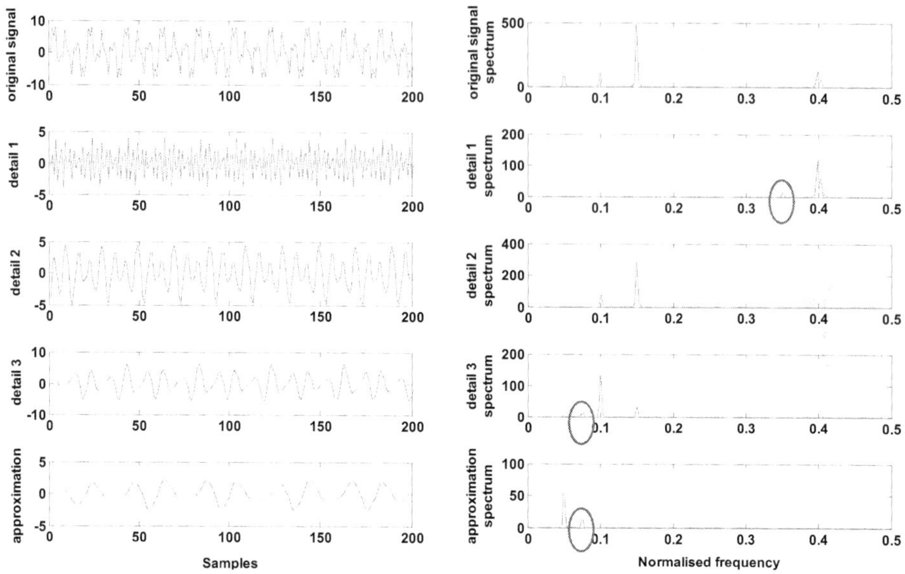

Fig. 4. 3-level decomposition with DWT of x(t)

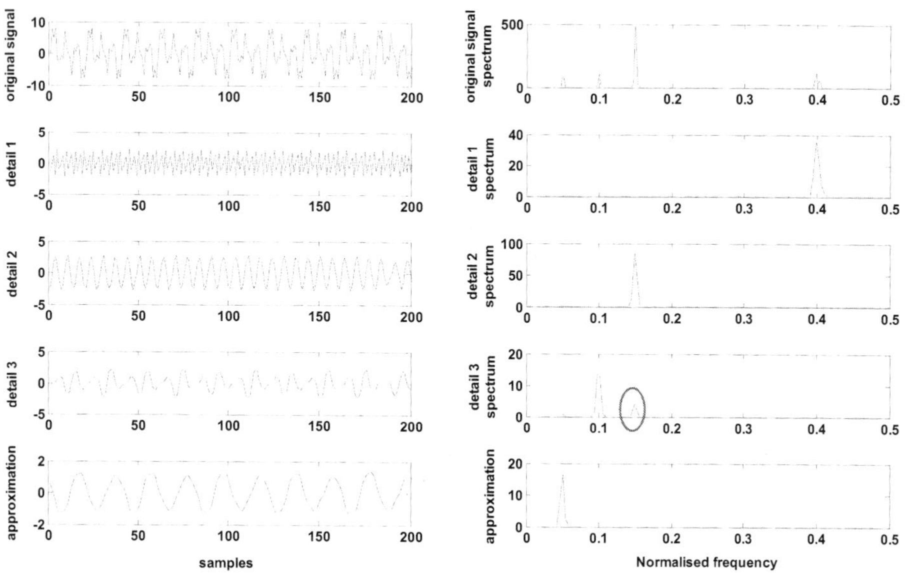

Fig. 5. 3-level decomposition with DTCWT of x(t)

In the DWT decomposition, the highlighted frequencies actually do not exist as the FFT of the original signal confirms. On the contrary artificial peaks do not appear in the DTCWT decomposition as Fig.5 clearly shows proving the reduced frequency aliasing of the DTCWT. A peak highlighted in detail 3 is real though it should appear only in detail 2.

2.5 Second generation wavelet transforms

2.5.1 The Second Generation Wavelet Transform (SGWT)

The classical wavelet techniques (CWT, DWT, WPT) are all dependent on the mother wavelet selection from a library of previously designed wavelet functions, an issue that is discussed in more detail in Section 3. Unfortunately, the standard wavelet functions are independent of a given signal. Towards this direction, the Second Generation Wavelet Transform (SGWT) was developed by (Sweldens, 1998), a new wavelet construction method using the lifting scheme. It is actually an alternative implementation of the classical DWT. The main feature of the SGWT is that it provides an entirely spatial domain interpretation of the transform, as opposed to the traditional frequency domain based constructions. Compared with the classical wavelet transform, the lifting scheme possesses several advantages, including the possibility of adaptive design, in-place calculations, irregular samples and integers-to-integers wavelet transforms. The lifting scheme provides high flexibility, which can be designed according to the properties of the given signal, and thus ensures that the resulting transform is always invertible. It makes good use of similarities between the high and low pass filters to speed up the calculation so that the implementation of the second generation wavelet transform is faster than the first generation wavelet transforms. Additionally, the multi-resolution analysis property is preserved. Consequently, the applications of the SGWT scheme in condition monitoring and fault diagnosis of mechanical equipments have been increasing the last few years (see Section 4). A basic decomposition of the SGWT consists of three main steps (Sweldens, 1998), split, predict, and update. In the split step, an approximate signal a_l at level l is split into even samples and odd samples (Zhou et al., 2010).

$$a_{l+1} = a_l(2i), \quad d_{l+1} = a_l(2i+1) \tag{25}$$

In the prediction step, a prediction operator P is designed and applied on a_{l+1} to predict d_{l+1}. The resultant prediction error d_{l+1} is regarded as the detail coefficients of a_l.

$$d_{l+1}(i) = d_{l+1}(i) - \sum_{r=-M/2+1}^{M/2} p_r a_{l+1}(i+r) \tag{26}$$

where p_r the coefficients of P and M is the length of p_r.

In the update step, a designed update operator U is applied on d_{l+1}. Adding the result to the even samples, the resultant a_{l+1} is regarded as the approximate coefficients of a_l.

$$a_{l+1}(i) = a_{l+1}(i) + \sum_{j=-N/2+1}^{N/2} u_j d_{l+1}(i+j-1) \tag{27}$$

where u_j are the coefficients of U and N is the length of u_j. Iteration of the above three steps on the output a, generates the detail and approximation coefficients at different levels.

The reconstruction stage of SGWT is a reverse procedure of the decomposition stage, which includes inverse update step, inverse prediction step and merging step.

$$a_{l+1}(i) = a_{l+1}(i) - \sum_{j=-N/2+1}^{N/2} u_j d_{l+1}(i+j-1) \tag{28}$$

$$d_{l+1}(i) = d_{l+1}(i) + \sum_{r=-M/2+1}^{M/2} p_r a_{l+1}(i+r) \tag{29}$$

$$a_l(2i) = a_{l+1}, \quad a_l(2i+1) = d_{l+1} \tag{30}$$

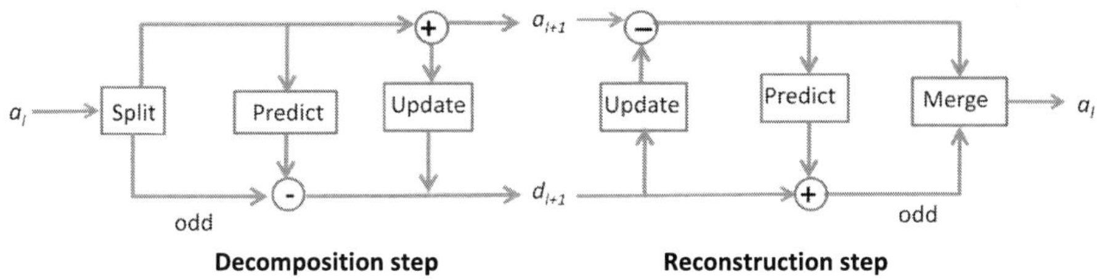

Fig. 6. Decomposition and reconstruction of the signal with SGWT

The operators *P* and *U* are built by means of interpolating subdivision method (ISM) [16]. Choosing different *P* and *U* is equivalent to choosing different biorthogonal wavelet filters. Fig. 6 depicts the structure of SGWT. The computational costs of the forward and inverse transform are exactly the same.

2.5.2 Second Generation Wavelet Packet Transform (SGWPT)

The time-frequency resolution of SGWT varies with the decomposition levels. It gives good time and poor frequency resolution at high frequency sub-band, and good frequency and poor time resolution at low frequency sub-band. In order to obtain a higher resolution in the high frequency sub-band, SGWPT has been constructed and hence the detail coefficients at each level are further decomposed to obtain their approximation and detail components. The decomposition and reconstruction stages of SGWPT are described below.

In the decomposition stage, $X_{l,k}$ is split into even samples $X_{l,ke}$ and odd samples $X_{l,ko}$,

$$X_{l,ke} = X_{l,k}(2i), \quad X_{l,ko} = X_{l,k}(2i+1) \tag{31}$$

where $X_{l,k}$ represents the coefficients of the *k*th node at level *l*. Then calculate each sub-band coefficients at level *l* +1.

$$X_{l+1,2} = X_{l,1o} - P(X_{l,1e}) \tag{32}$$

$$X_{l+1,1} = X_{l,1e} + U(X_{l+1,2}) \tag{33}$$

$$\vdots$$

$$X_{l+1,2^{l+1}} = X_{l,2^l o} - P(X_{l,2^l e}) \tag{34}$$

$$X_{l+1,2^{l+1}-1} = X_{l,2^l e} + U(X_{l+1,2^{l+1}}) \tag{35}$$

In the reconstruction stage, the sub-band coefficients to be reconstructed are reserved, and then other sub-band coefficients are set to be zeroes. Finally, the reconstructed results are obtained by the following formula.

$$X_{l,2^l e} = X_{l+1,2^{l+1}-1} - U(X_{l+1,2^{l+1}}) \tag{36}$$

$$X_{l,2^l o} = X_{l+1,2^{l+1}} + P(X_{l,2^l e}) \tag{37}$$

$$X_{l,2^l}(2i) = X_{l,2^l e} \tag{38}$$

$$X_{l,2^l}(2i+1) = X_{l,2^l o} \tag{39}$$

$$\vdots$$

$$X_{l,1e} = X_{l+1,1} - U(X_{l+1,2}) \tag{40}$$

$$X_{l,1o} = X_{l+1,2} + P(X_{l,1e}) \tag{41}$$

$$X_{l,1}(2i) = X_{l,1e} \tag{42}$$

$$X_{l,1}(2i+1) = X_{l,1o} \tag{43}$$

Overall, the decomposition and reconstruction stages of SGWPT are shown in Figs. 7 and 8.

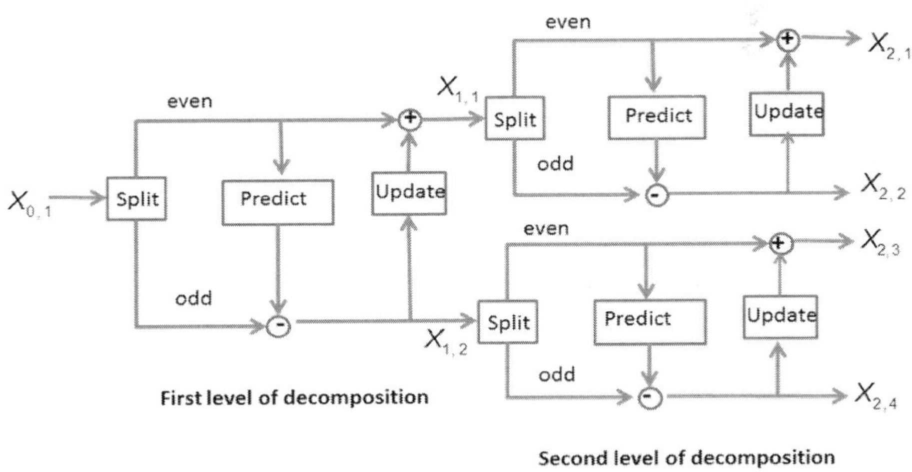

Fig. 7. Decomposition step of SGWPT

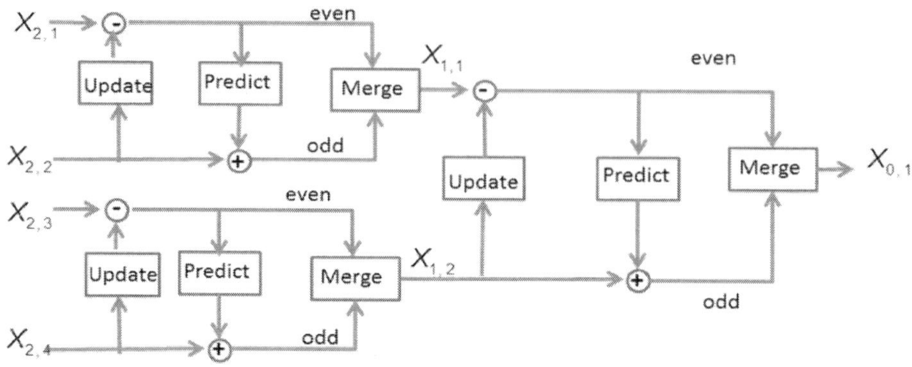

Fig. 8. Reconstruction step of SGWPT

3. Choosing the best wavelet basis

Utilizing the classical WT (DWT, CWT or WPT) brings on the unresolved issue of mother wavelet selection. Different types of wavelets have different time-frequency structures and thus it is always an issue how to choose the best wavelet function for extracting fault features from a given signal. An "inappropriate" wavelet will reduce the accuracy of the fault detection. There is a plethora of options between various wavelet families (with infinite number of members!) or specific wavelets. Haar, Daubechies (db), Symlets, Coiflets, Gaussian, Morlet, complex Morlet, Mexican hat, biorthogonal wavelets, reverse biorthogonal, Meyer, harmonic wavelets, discrete approximation of Meyer, complex Gaussian, Shannon, and frequency B-spline are among the most well established wavelets. In principle, the wavelet decomposition would achieve a better result if the wavelet basis is "similar" to the signal under analysis. The wavelet coefficients reflect the similarity between the signal local and the corresponding wavelet basis. The bigger the coefficient, the more similar the two parts are. Different wavelet basis would lead to quite different results of signal analysis. Currently there are still no generic theoretical guidelines for how to select the optimum wavelet basis, or how to select the corresponding shape parameter and scale level for a particular application. The selection is in many cases done by trial and error. In literature there are some interesting approaches that attempt to address this issue.

(Kankar et al., 2011) presented a methodology for rolling element bearings fault diagnosis using continuous wavelet transform (CWT). Six different base wavelets were considered of which three were real valued and the other three were complex valued. Out of these six wavelets, the base wavelet was selected based on wavelet selection criteria to extract statistical features from wavelet coefficients of raw vibration signals. Two wavelet selection criteria, Maximum Energy to Shannon Entropy ratio and Maximum Relative Wavelet Energy were used and compared to select the appropriate wavelet for feature extraction. The wavelet having Maximum Energy to Shannon Entropy ratio/Maximum Relative Wavelet Energy was considered for fault diagnosis of rolling element bearings. The relative Wavelet Energy is defined as:

$$p_n = {}^{E(n)}/_{E_{total}} \tag{44}$$

Where E(n) the energy at each resolution level,

$$E(n) = \sum_{i=1}^{m} \left|C_{n,i}\right|^2 \tag{45}$$

m is the number of wavelet coefficients and $C_{n,i}$ the ith wavelet coefficient at the nth scale.

The total energy is given by:

$$E(n) = \sum_{n} \left|C_{n,i}\right|^2 \tag{46}$$

whereas the Energy to Shannon Entropy ratio is given by:

$$\zeta(n) = E(n)/S_{entropy}(n) \tag{47}$$

where the entropy of signal wavelet coefficients is defined as:

$$S_{entropy}(n) = -\sum_{i=1}^{m} p_i \cdot log_2 p_i \tag{48}$$

and p_i is the energy distribution of the wavelet coefficients,

$$p_i = \left|C_{n,i}\right|^2/E(n) \tag{49}$$

with $\sum_{i=1}^{m} p_i = 1$.

To find the most suitable mother wavelet, (Rafiee and Tse, 2009), in probably the most thorough study of mother wavelet choice investigation, studied 324 candidate mother wavelet functions from various families including Haar, Daubechies (db), Symlet, Coiflet, Gaussian, Morlet, complex Morlet, Mexican hat, bio-orthogonal, reverse bio-orthogonal, Meyer, discrete approximation of Meyer, complex Gaussian, Shannon, and frequency B-spline. The most similar mother wavelet for analyzing the gear vibration signal was selected based on the following procedure. Raw vibration signals were recorded and synchronized. The feature vector was composed of the variance of CWT coefficients for each of the 2^4 scales calculated by each of the 50 segmented signals in each gearbox condition. The average of the feature vector in the 50 segmented signals was computed for each gearbox condition. Variances of the mentioned average of the four gearbox conditions were determined for each scale (2^4 elements). The five highest values of the calculated vector were selected as the feature because the larger the variance, the greater the ability to properly classify faults. The summation of the five elements, called "SUMVAR" for simplicity, was compared with those obtained from the other 323 candidate mother wavelets (a total of 324 mother wavelets). The one that had the highest SUMVAR was selected as the most similar function to our vibration signals. In a similar work (Rafiee et al., 2010) following a similar procedure found that "Daubechies 44" ("db44") has the most similar shape across both gear and bearing vibration signals. Results also suggested that although "db44" is the most similar mother wavelet function for the studied vibration signals, it is not the proper function for all wavelet-based processing. The research verified that Morlet wavelet has better similarity to both vibration signals in comparison to many other functions such as Daubechies (1–43), Coiflet, Symlet, complex Morlet, Gaussian, complex Gaussian, and Meyer for both experimental set-ups (i.e. gear testing and bearing testing). Among the studied mother wavelets, results also showed that db44 is the most similar function across both gear and bearing vibration signals. The drawback of the db44 function is that the high-order db functions take more CPU time than most others. In another work (Rafiee et al., 2009) utilized genetic algorithms (GAs) to optimize the selection of mother wavelet function (among several members of the Daubechies family), the number of the decomposition levels of the wavelet packet transform (WPT) as well as the number of neurons in the ANNs hidden layers used for the fault classification, resulted in a high-speed, effective two-layer ANN with a small-sized structure. "db11", level 4 and 14 neurons have been selected as the best values for Daubechies order, decomposition level, and the number of nodes in hidden layer, respectively. In (Gketsis et al., 2009) the optimum wavelet choice criterion is the maximization of the cross-correlation between the signal of interest and the wavelet. In an application of condition monitoring in electrical machines, they tested several wavelet functions, namely Haar, Daubechies 2, 4, 8, Symlet 2, 3, 4, 8 and Coiflet 3 and concluded to "db2". (Saravanan and Ramachandran, 2009) found that among the 15 members of Daubechies wavelet, "db1" and "db5" gave the maximum classification efficiency of an expert system (Decision Tree) at around 98.7%.

Other researchers prefer more qualitative explanations. (Xu and Li, 2008) support that in the common family of wavelet bases i.e. Morlet, Haar, Shannon, Symmlets, Coiflets and Daubechies wavelets, etc., the most popular is the Daubechies wavelet, as it bears the shortest compactly supported scaling function in all of orthogonal wavelets when given exponent number of vanishing moment. Moreover, it gives the best overall performance in the respect of both mean squared error between reconstruction signal and original signal, and maximizing the SNR improvement. Therefore, the Daubechies wavelet is applied and others are for comparison in this case. (Jazebi et al., 2011) state that one specific mother wavelet is best suited for a particular application. For this purpose, mother wavelet type and decomposition level have been chosen based on experience and trial and error. The research includes detecting and analyzing low amplitude, short duration, fast decaying, and oscillating type of current signals. For this purpose, Daubechies's mother wavelet seems to be an appropriate choice. In comparison with Haar wavelet, Daubechies are best suited for feature extraction due to their low-pass and high-pass filters. On the other hand because of its inherent orthogonality, it satisfies Parseval theorem, not like biorthogonal wavelets such as Coiflet and Meyer wavelets . db4 mother wavelet over level d4 has been chosen because the maximum energy localization in details (1–4) was obtained using these parameters.

(Daviu et al., 2007) supports that the Daubechies family is well suited for application of DWT in condition monitoring due to its interesting inherent properties. An important fact they observed when using the Daubechies family, was the overlap between the frequency bands (frequency aliasing) associated with the DWT decomposition of their signals. This is due to the non-ideal filtering process performed by the wavelet signals, a fact that makes that the signal components, included within a certain frequency band and placed in the proximity of its limits, overlap partially with the adjacent band. When using a high-order Daubechies wavelet for signal decomposition, this effect is less intense than when using a low-order one. In other words, high-order wavelets behave as more ideal filters. Maximization of statistical features such as kurtosis or crest factor can be utilized as a criterion for the choice of mother wavelet within a family or among various families. In an unpublished study by the authors, an investigation of the optimum parameters for the most effective de-noising with DWT was conducted. The analysis of a representative AE signal from seeded defects in bearings shows how statistical parameters change respectively to the wavelet choice between the 10 first members of the Daubechies family in Fig. 9. Obviously the wavelet that maximizes kurtosis, crest factor and crest value is chosen as optimum, "db2" in this case.

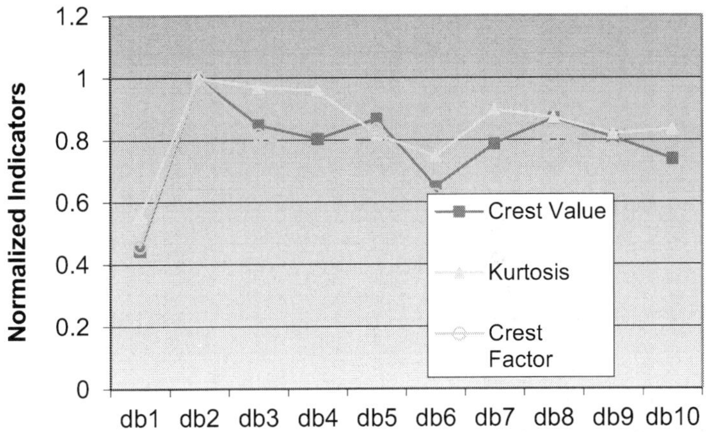

Fig. 9. Kurtosis, crest value and factor features of de-noised AE signal with various "db" wavelets in a DWT de-noising scheme

4. Applications overview of wavelets in condition based maintenance

4.1 Wavelet-based de-noising

Wavelet based de-noising is a very interesting and important application of wavelets in the processing of signals from condition monitoring. It is very widely adopted in many studies as it is ideal to extract hidden diagnostic information and enhance the impulsive components of complex, non-stationary signals with strong background. Wavelet thresholding is based on the idea that the energy of the signal is concentrated in a few wavelet coefficients, while the energy of noise spreads throughout all the resulted wavelet coefficients. Similarity between the mother wavelet and the signal to be analyzed plays a very important role, making it possible for the signal to concentrate on fewer coefficients and thus its choice is critical in the efficiency of the de-noising task. The first foundations in wavelet-based de-noising were set by (Donoho, 1995). Let $x(t)$ be the discrete signal acquired during condition monitoring. The signal series consists of impulses and noise. x(t) can alternatively be expressed as $x(t)=p(t)+n(t)$, where $p(t)$ indicates the impulses to be determined, whereas $n(t)$ indicates equally distributed and independent Gaussian noise with mean zero and standard deviation r. In principle, the wavelet threshold de-noising procedure has the following steps:

1. Transform the signal *x(t)* to the time-scale plane by means of a wavelet transform. The wavelet coefficients on various scales are obtained.
2. Assess the threshold *t* and, in accordance with the established rules, shrink the wavelet coefficients.
3. Use the shrunken coefficients to carry out the inverse wavelet transform. The series recovered is the estimation of impulse p(t).

The second step is probably the most critical and has quite an impact upon the effectiveness of the procedure. There are plenty of thresholding techniques and many different thresholds proposed in the literature. Hard thresholding sets any coefficient less than or equal to the threshold to zero.

$$c_{jk} = \begin{cases} 0, & c_{jk} < t \\ c_{jk}, & c_{jk} \geq t \end{cases} \tag{50}$$

Hard thresholding is the simplest approach but tends to miss useful parts of the signal. In soft thresholding, the threshold is subtracted from any coefficient that is greater than it.

$$c_{jk} = sign(c_{jk}) \cdot (|c_{jk}| - t) \tag{51}$$

t is universal threshold $t = \sigma \cdot \sqrt{2 \cdot logN}$, σ is the standard deviation of the noise and N is the number of data samples in the measured signal. The true value of the noise standard deviation σ is, generally, unknown. It is often estimated by σ = MAD/0.6745, where MAD refers to the median absolute value of the finest scale wavelet coefficients. The combination of the soft thresholding policy and universal threshold is also referred to as "VisuShrink". It ensures a noise-free reconstruction but often the threshold is set too high. (Donoho and Jonestone, 1994) introduced the "minimax" threshold an enhancement of the universal threshold. The "minimax" threshold level can be much lower than the universal threshold level when it comes to small-to-moderate sample sizes. "SureShrink" or "rigsure" approach relies on the minimization of Stein's unbiased estimator of risk (Donoho and Jonestone, 1995). When the wavelet representation is not very sparse, it yields better results. The universal threshold and "minimax" threshold are more effective when it comes to detecting sparse impulses. All the above methods assume that the noise properties are known, which is rarely the case in industrial applications. The maximum likelihood estimation de-noising method is suitable for non-Gaussian noise. A specific threshold rule, which is based on the maximum likelihood estimation method, incorporates a priori information on the impulse probability density function. The probability density function of the impulse to be identified must be known in advance though. The so-called "sparse code shrinkage" method, proposed by (Hyvarinen, 1999), can be utilized for wavelet coefficients shrinkage.

The DTCWT can give a substantial performance enhancement to the conventional DWT-based noise reduction methodologies due to its interesting properties of near shift-invariance and reduced frequency aliasing. (Wang et al., 2010) proposed a scheme based on "NeighCoeff" scheme (Cai and Silverman, 2001). "NeighCoeff" uses lower threshold than "VisuShrink" and outperforms all other shrinkage methods. The de-noising using DTCWT and "NeighCoeff" shrinkage is implemented in the following stages:

1. Transform the data x into the wavelet domain via DTCWT (or any other wavelet transform in general)

2. At each resolution level j, group the noisy wavelet coefficients into disjoint blocks b_{ij} of length $L_0=log(n)/2$; then extend each block bij by an amount of max(1,L_0/2) in each direction to form overlapping larger blocks Bij of length $L=L_0+2L_1$
3. Within each block bij, each noisy wavelet coefficient is processed via "NeighCoeff" shrinkage rule
4. Calculate the de-noised signal using inverse wavelet domain

In Fig. 10 various de-noising algorithms were applied on an AE signal from a bearing with seeded defect. In a) the original signal is depicted. In b) the method of spectral kurtosis (Randall and Antoni, 2011) is utilized. Spectral kurtosis is not a wavelet-based technique and relies on the location of the frequency band where kurtosis is maximized and then the band-pass filtering of the signal in the resulted band. In figure c) the DTCWT wavelet transform is applied in combination with "NeighCoeff" thresholding whilst in d) a parametric procedure was used by the authors to determine the optimum parameters of DWT (wavelet type, number of levels, threshold type, soft or hard application of threshold) that maximize the kurtosis and crest factor of the signal. DTCWT- and DWT-based de-noising proved the most efficient in terms of the resulting signal kurtosis.

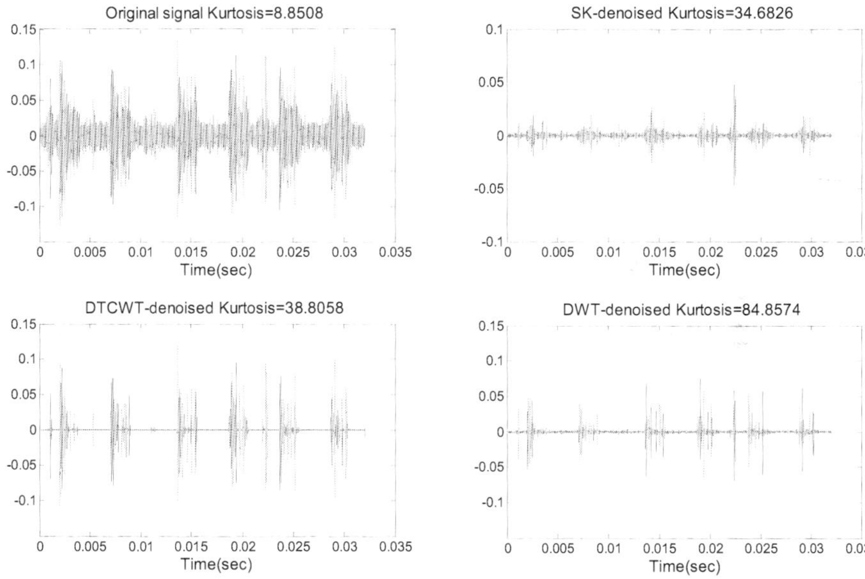

Fig. 10. Effect of various de-noising schemes on an AE signal from defective bearing a) original signal b) de-noised signal via spectral kurtosis technique c) de-noised signal via DTCWT d) de-noised signal via DWT

4.2 Gearboxes

Fault symptoms of running gearboxes must be detected as early as possible to avoid serious accidents. An efficient monitoring plan is needed for any industry because it can optimize the resources management and improve the plant economy, by reducing unnecessary costs and increasing the level of safety. A great percentage of breakdowns in industrial processes as well as in rotorcraft transportation (helicopters etc) are caused by gearbox related failures. Fault symptoms usually begin from early stages, rather long before a destructive failure making the use of effective condition monitoring schemes very attractive. Many high-quality investigations can be found in the recent literature.

(YanPing et al., 2006) explored the statistical characteristics of the continuous wavelet transform scalogram of vibration signals from rotating machinery. Two features, wavelet grey moment (WGM) and first-order wavelet grey moment vector (WGMV), were proposed for condition monitoring of rotating machinery. Wavelet grey moments are defined as:

$$g_k = \frac{1}{m\times n}\sum_{i=1}^{m}\sum_{j=1}^{n} c_{ij}^{k}\sqrt{(i-1)^2+(j-1)^2} \tag{52}$$

Where c_{ij} is the element of matrix $[C]_{mxn}$, $\sqrt{(i-1)^2+(j-1)^2}$ is the Euclidean distance between element c_{ij} and c_{11}, that is corresponding to the geometry length between the point (i,j) and reference point (1,1) in the scalogram. In (Fan and Zuo, 2006) a new fault detection method that combines Hilbert transform and wavelet packet transform was proposed. The wavelet packet node energy method is used as feature. WPT at the 4th decomposition level using "db10" wavelet was utilized. Their results showed that the proposed method is effective to extract modulating signal and help to detect the early gear fault.

(Sanz et al., 2007) proposed a method which combines the capability of DWT to treat transient vibration signals with the ability of auto-associative neural networks (AANNs) for feature extraction. "db6" and 3 levels of decomposition were chosen for real application vibration data from a pump rotor gearset. The detail coefficient vectors of the DWT were taken as input parameters of the AANN. An advantage of the proposed method is that DWT is performed directly on the raw vibration signals not on time-synchronous averaged signals. (Rafiee et al., 2007) presented a new procedure which experimentally recognized gears and bearings faults of a typical gearbox system using a multi-layer perceptron ANN. The feature vector was populated by the standard deviation of wavelet packet coefficients after WPT on the recorded vibration signals. "db4" wavelet and 4 levels of decomposition were used. The gear conditions were considered to be normal gearbox, slight- and medium-worn, broken-teeth gears faults and a general bearing fault. (He et al., 2007) proposed a novel non-linear feature extraction scheme from the time-domain features with wavelet packet preprocessing and frequency-domain features of the vibration signals using the kernel principal component analysis (KPCA) to characterize various gearbox conditions. Experimental analysis on a fatigue test of an automobile transmission gearbox have shown that the KPCA features outperformed PCA features in terms of clustering capability, and both the two KPCA-based subspace methods can be effectively applied to gearbox condition monitoring. The time-domain statistical features with wavelet packet preprocessing and frequency-domain statistical features proved more effective than the conventional time-domain features without WPT preprocessing for extracting the KPCA features. (Li et al., 2007) used the Haar wavelet CWT (HCWT) to diagnose three types of machine faults. To assess its effectiveness, the diagnosis information obtained by HCWT is compared with that by Morlet wavelet CWT (MCWT), which is more popular in machine diagnosis. Their results demonstrate that Haar wavelet is also a feasible wavelet in machine fault diagnosis and HCWT can provide abundant graphic features for diagnosis than MCWT. (Miao and Makis, 2007) have introduced a new feature extraction approach based on wavelet modulus maxima and proposed a Hidden Markov Model (HMM) based two-stage machine condition classification system. The modulus maxima distribution was utilized as the input observation sequence of the system. An adaptive algorithm was proposed and validated by three sets of real gearbox vibration data to classify two conditions: normal and failure. In addition, in condition classification (stage 2), three HMM models were set up to classify three different machine conditions, namely, adjacent tooth failure, distributed tooth failure and normal condition. The validation results showed an excellent performance of the proposed classification system.

(Saravanan et al., 2008) investigated the effectiveness of wavelet-based features for fault diagnosis in a bevel gearbox using support vector machines (SVM) and proximal support vector machines (PSVM). The statistical feature vectors from Morlet wavelet coefficients resulted after CWT at sixty-four scales, were classified using the J48 algorithm and the predominant features were fed as input for training and testing SVM and PSVM. The coefficients of Morlet wavelet were used for feature extraction from the time domain vibration signals. Various statistical features like kurtosis, standard deviation, maximum value, etc. calculated from the wavelet coefficients formed the feature sets. It was concluded that PSVM has an edge over SVM in the classification efficiency of various fault conditions.

(Li et al., 2008) presented a new signal-adapted lifting scheme for rotating machinery fault diagnosis, which allows the construction of a wavelet directly from the statistics of a given signal. The prediction operator based on genetic algorithms was designed to maximize the kurtosis of detail signal produced by the lifting scheme, and the update operator was designed to minimize a reconstruction error. The signal-adapted lifting scheme was applied to analyze bearing and gearbox vibration signals. The conventional diagnosis techniques and non-adaptive lifting scheme were also used to analyze the same signals for comparison. The results demonstrated that the signal-adapted lifting scheme was more effective in extracting inherent fault features from complex vibration signals. (Kar and Mohanty, 2008) conducted an experimental investigation of fault diagnosis in a multistage gearbox under transient loads. The signals studied were vibration measurements, recorded from an accelerometer fitted at the tail-end bearing of the gearbox as well as the current transients monitored at the induction motor. Three defective cases and three transient load conditions were investigated. DWT (with "db8") and a corrected multi-resolution Fourier transform (MFT) were applied to process the vibration and current transients. A statistical feature extraction technique was proposed in search of a trend in detection of defects. A condition monitoring scheme is devised that can facilitate in monitoring vibration and current transients in the gearbox with simultaneous presence of transient loads and defects. (Jafarizadeh et al., 2008) suggested a new noise canceling method, based on time-averaging method for asynchronous input, and CWT with complex Morlet wavelet. The complex Morlet wavelet depends on non-fixed parameters. For the feature extraction from time-domain vibration signals, the optimum values of the Morlet wavelet parameters should be estimated. Wavelet entropy was used towards this optimization. Then CWT was applied and 3-D scalograms were utilized for damage detection. The proposed method was successfully implemented on a simulated signal and real test rig of a Yahama motorcycle gearbox.

(Loutas et al., 2009) reported on the condition monitoring of a lab-scale, single stage, gearbox with cracked gears using different non-destructive inspection methodologies and the processing of the acquired waveforms with advanced signal processing techniques is the aim of the present work. Acoustic emission (AE) and vibration measurements were utilized for this purpose. Emphasis was given on the signal processing of the acquired vibration and acoustic emission signals in order to extract conventional as well as novel parameters-features of potential diagnostic value from the monitored waveforms. Wavelet-based parameters-features were proposed utilizing the DWT and "db10" wavelet. The evolution of selected parameters/features versus test time is provided, evaluated and the parameters with the most interesting diagnostic behavior were highlighted. The differences in the parameters evolution of each NDT technique are discussed and the superiority of AE over vibration recordings for the early diagnosis of natural wear in gear systems was concluded. In (Saravanan and Ramachandran, 2009) the coefficients of Morlet wavelet were used for feature extraction. CWT and sixty four scales were chosen to extract the Morlet wavelet coefficients of the vibration signals. A group of statistical features like kurtosis, standard deviation, maximum value, etc., widely used in fault diagnostics, were extracted from the wavelet coefficients of the time domain signals. For the selection of best features, the decision tree using J48 algorithm was used. The selected features were fed as input to SVM for classification. (Xian and Zeng, 2009) developed a new intelligent method for the fault diagnosis of the rotating machinery based on wavelet packet analysis (WPA) and hybrid support vector machines (hybrid SVM). The faulty vibration signals obtained from a gearbox were decomposed by WPA via Dmeyer wavelet. Shannon entropy was calculated from the coefficients at each subspace of the WPA decomposition and formed the feature vectors that trained/tested the hybrid SVM for estimating the fault type. (Belsak and Flasker, 2009) studied the influence of a fatigue gear crack in a single-stage gear unit on the recorded vibrations. They applied the sparse code shrinkage method to de-noise vibration signals from a faulty gearbox. They discriminated between healthy and cracked gear using scalograms of the resulted CWT coefficients. Gabor wavelet was adopted in their work. (Wu and Chan, 2009) utilized the sound emission from a multi-stage gearbox towards gear fault diagnostics. Continuous wavelet transform with Morlet mother wavelet combined with a feature selection of energy spectrum was proposed for analyzing fault signals and feature extraction. Two artificial neural network (ANN) approaches i.e. the probability neural network and conventional back-propagation network were compared in the recognition of six faulty states and one healthy. (Saravanan and Ramachandran, 2009) recorded vibration signals from a spur bevel gearbox in different lubrication, loading and gear state conditions. They used various members of the Daubechies family (db1-db15) for statistical feature extraction. J48 Decision Tree was used for two reasons, feature selection and classification of the faulty signals. (Rafiee and Tse, 2009) processed vibration signals from a gearbox with three different fault conditions (slight-worn, medium-worn, and broken-tooth) of a spur gear. CWT was used with packet decomposition through the scales. After synchronizing the raw vibration signals, the CWT and autocorrelation function were applied to the synchronized signals and generated continuous wavelet coefficients of synchronized vibration signals. They found that a simple sinusoidal summation function can approximate the waveforms generated by autocorrelation of CWC-SVS for normal gearboxes as well as other defective gears with satisfactory performance. The function achieved proper approximation even though the waveforms were different from one condition to another as they possess different frequency contents of vibration signals. (Rafiee et al., 2009) presented an optimized gear fault identification system using genetic algorithms (GAs) to investigate the type of gear failures of a complex gearbox system using artificial neural networks (ANNs). Slightly-worn, medium-worn, and broken-tooth of a spur gear of the gearbox system were selected as the faults types. GAs were exploited to optimize the selection of mother wavelet function (among several members of the Daubechies family), the number of the decomposition levels of the wavelet packet transform (WPT) as well as the number of neurons in the ANNs hidden layers, resulted in a high-speed, effective two-layer ANN with a small-sized structure. "db11", level 4 and 14 neurons have been selected as the best values for Daubechies order, decomposition level, and the number of nodes in hidden layer, respectively. (Singh and Al Kazzaz, et al., 2009) studied the effect of dry bearing fault on multi-sensor measurements (three line to line voltages, three currents, two vibration signals, four temperatures and one speed signal) in induction machines. Different families of WT have been introduced and implemented with vibration signals covering the dry bearing fault in induction machine. The results of testing various popular types of the WT showed different degree of success in relating the decomposed band with machine condition. It was concluded that the fluctuation in the RMS value of the first and second decomposition level was larger in the case of Mexican hat wavelet and it was thus proposed to investigate the random vibration of all machines in case of dry bearing fault. It was concluded that WT can be used effectively to specify one machine fault at a time, while it cannot treat multiple faults simultaneously. Instead, the combined use of wavelet and Fourier transform proved an effective tool for extracting important information about the machine condition. An intelligent diagnostic methodology for fault gear identification and classification based on vibration signals using DWT and adaptive neuro-fuzzy inference system (ANFIS) is presented in (Wu et al., 2009). After the vibration signal acquisition, 4-level decomposition via the DWT followed resulting in four high frequency details (D1–D4) and one low frequency approximation (A4). Three Daubechies wavelets (db4, db8 and db20) were utilized for the decomposition. The energy distribution of the five subbands was calculated and trained two different ANNs for the successful fault identification. No major differences were observed on the ANNs recognition rates in regard to the different mother wavelets utilized in the DWT. (Wu and Hsu, 2009) described a development of the fault gear identification system using the vibration signal with discrete wavelet transform and fuzzy–logic inference for a gear-set experimental platform. The extraction method of feature vector is based on DWT decomposition followed by level energy calculation. The recognition rate of the classification task using three different Daubechies wavelets ("db4, db8 and db20") coefficients under various working conditions did not show significant discrepancies. The fault recognition rates were in general over 96%.

A diagnostic methodology of artificial defects in a single stage gearbox operating under various load levels and different defect states was proposed by (Loutas et al., 2010) based on vibration recordings as well as advanced signal analysis techniques. Two different wavelet-based signal processing methodologies, using the DWT as well as the CWT, were utilized for the analysis of the recorded vibration signals and useful diagnostic information were extracted out of them.

DWT was applied with "db10" and 10-level decomposition whilst CWT was applied with Morlet wavelet (bandwidth parameter and wavelet center frequency were set at 1 and 1.5 respectively. Averaging across all scales was utilized instead of time synchronous averaging giving very characteristic scalograms for each artificial defect case. A novel method incorporating customized (i.e., signal-based) multiwavelet lifting schemes with sliding window de-noising was proposed in (Yuan et al., 2010). On the basis of Hermite spline interpolation, various vector prediction and update operators with the desirable properties of biorthogonality, symmetry, short support and vanishing moments are constructed. The minimum entropy principle is recommended to determine the optimal vector prediction and update operators in the lifting scheme, by means of measuring the sparsity. Due to the periodic characteristics of gearbox vibration signals, sliding window de-noising favorable to retain valuable information as much as possible is employed to extract and identify the fault features in gearbox signals. Experimental validations including the simulation experiments, gear fault diagnosis and normal gear detection prove the effectiveness of the multi-wavelet lifting schemes as compared to various conventional wavelets. In (Saravanan and Ramachandran, 2010) the vibration signals monitored at a bevel gear box in various conditions and fault conditions were processed with DWT. Wavelet features were extracted for all the wavelet coefficients and for all the signals using the Daubechies wavelets "db1" to "db15". ID3 Decision Tree is used for feature selection and artificial neural network were employed for classification of various faults of the gear box. The features selection of various discrete wavelets was carried out and the wavelet having the highest average efficiency of fault classification was chosen as the most appropriate. In (Rafiee et al., 2010) vibration signals recorded from two experimental set-ups were processed for gears and bearing conditions. Four statistical features were selected: standard deviation, variance, kurtosis, and fourth central moment of continuous wavelet coefficients of synchronized vibration signals (CWC-SVS). An automatic feature extraction algorithm is introduced for gear and bearing defects. It also shows that the fourth central moment of CWC-SVS is a proper feature for both bearing and gear failure diagnosis. Standard deviation and variance of CWC-SVS demonstrated more appropriate outcome for bearings than gears. Kurtosis of CWC-SVS illustrated the acceptable performance for gears only. (Wang et al., 2010) proposed a technique to provide accurate diagnosis of gearboxes under fluctuating load conditions. The residual vibration signal, i.e. the difference of time synchronously averaged signal from the average tooth-meshing vibration, is analyzed as source data due to its lower sensitiveness to the alternating load condition. Complex Morlet continuous wavelet transform was used for the vibration signal processing. A fault growth parameter (FGP) was introduced, based on the continuous wavelet transform amplitudes over all transform scales. FPG actually measures the relative CWT amplitude change. This parameter proved insensitive to varying load and can correctly indicate early gear fault. Other features such as kurtosis, mean, variance, form factor and crest factor, both of residual signal and mean amplitude of continuous wavelet transform waveform, were also checked and proved to be influenced by the changing load. The effectiveness of the proposed fault indicator was demonstrated using a full lifetime vibration data history obtained under sinusoidal varying load.

To overcome the shift-variance deficiency of classical DWT, a novel fault diagnosis method based on the redundant second generation wavelet packet transform was proposed in (Zhou et al., 2010). Initially, the redundant second generation wavelet packet transform (RSGWPT) was constructed on the basis of second generation wavelet transform and redundant lifting scheme. Then, the vibration signals were decomposed by RSGWPT and the faulty features were extracted from the resultant wavelet packet coefficients. In the end, the extracted fault features were given as input to classifiers for identification/classification. The proposed method was applied for the fault diagnosis of gearbox and gasoline engine valve trains. Test results indicate that a better classification performance can be obtained by using the proposed fault diagnosis method in comparison with using conventional second generation wavelet packet transform method. (Wang et al., 2010) employed the dual-tree complex wavelet transform (DTCWT) for the de-noising of vibration signals from gearbox and bearings monitoring. They compared the de-noising via DTCWT with other wavelet-based techniques (DWT and second generation wavelet transform (SGWT)) as well as with fast kurtogram. The results were evaluated through the kurtosis calculated for each signal after the de-noising. NeighCoeff shrinkage scheme was applied in all wavelet-based cases. De-noised results of signals collected from a gearbox with tooth crack showed that the DTCWT-based de-noising approach yielded more promising result than the SGWT- and DWT-based methods, and it can effectively remove the noise and retain valuable information as much as possible. In the case of multiple features detection, diagnosis results of rolling element bearings with combined faults and actual industrial equipment confirmed that the proposed DTCWT-based method is powerful and consistently outperformed the widely used SGWT and fast kurtogram.

(Loutas et al. 2011a) conducted multi-hour tests in healthy gears in a single-stage gearbox. Three on-line monitoring techniques were implemented in the tests. Vibration and acoustic emission recordings in combination with data coming from oil debris monitoring (ODM) of the lubricating oil were utilized in order to assess the condition of the gears. A plethora of parameters/features were extracted from the acquired waveforms via conventional (in time and frequency domain) and non-conventional (wavelet-based) signal processing techniques. DWT was utilized to process vibration and AE signals with "db10" mother wavelet and 10 levels of decomposition. The wavelet levels energy and entropy were used as features. Data fusion was accomplished in the level of integration of the most representative among the extracted features from all three measurement technologies in a single data matrix. Principal component analysis (PCA) was utilized to reduce the dimensionality of the data matrix whereas independent component analysis (ICA) was further applied to identify the independent components among the data and correlate them to different damage modes of the gearbox. (Miao and Makis, 2011) presented an on-line fault classification system with an adaptive model re-estimation algorithm. The machinery condition is identified by selecting the HMM which maximizes the probability of a given observation sequence. The proper selection of the observation sequence is a key step in the development of an HMM-based classification system. In this paper, the classification system is validated using observation sequences based on the wavelet modulus maxima distribution obtained from real vibration signals, which has been proved to be effective in fault detection in previous research. (Li et al., 2011) utilized the Hermitian wavelet to diagnose the gear localized crack fault. The complex Hermitian wavelet is constructed based on the first and the second derivatives of the Gaussian function to detect signal singularities. The Fourier spectrum of Hermitian wavelet is real; therefore, Hermitian wavelet does not affect the phase of a signal in the complex domain. This gives a desirable ability to extract the singularity characteristic of a signal precisely. The proposed method is based on Hermitian wavelet amplitude and phase map of the time-domain vibration signals. Hermitian wavelet amplitude and phase maps are used to evaluate healthy and cracked gears.

4.3 Bearings

The fault diagnosis of rolling element bearings is very important for improving mechanical system reliability and performance in rotating machinery as bearing failures are among the most frequent causes of breakdowns in rotating machinery. When localized fault occurs in a bearing, periodic or non-periodic impulses appear in the time domain of the vibration signal, and the corresponding bearing characteristic frequencies (BCFs) and their harmonics emerge in the frequency domain. However, in the early stage of bearing failures, the BCFs usually carry very little energy and are often suppressed/hidden by noise and higher-level macro-structural vibrations. Consequently an effective signal processing method is of utmost importance in the de-noising of vibration or acoustic emission signals acquired or the extraction of damage sensitive features during the condition monitoring of bearings. Wavelet-based techniques meet this challenge in a variety of applications presented in the following.

(Purushotham et al., 2005) have applied the DWT towards the detection of localized bearing defects. The vibration signals were decomposed up to 4 levels using "db2" mother wavelet. The complex cepstral coefficients for wavelet transformed time windows at Mel-frequency scales constituted the features that trained Hidden Markov Models for the fault detection and classification.

In (Yan and Gao, 2005) the Discrete Harmonic Wavelet Packet Transform (DHWPT) was used to decompose the vibration signals measured from a bearing test bed into a number of frequency sub-bands. Given the harmonic wavelet packet coefficients of a vibration signal x(t), the energy feature in each sub-band was calculated as:

$$Energy(s,i) = \sum_{k=1}^{N} |hwpt(s,i,k)|^2 \tag{53}$$

The key features were then used as inputs to neural network classifiers for assessing the system's health status. Comparing to the conventional approach where statistical parameters from raw vibration signals are used, the presented approach enables higher signal-to-noise ratios and consequently, more effective and intelligent use of the available sensor information, leading to more accurate system health evaluation.

(Qiu et al., 2006) assessed the performance of wavelet decomposition-based de-noising versus wavelet filter-based de-noising methods on signals from mechanical defects. The comparison revealed that wavelet filter is more suitable and reliable to detect a weak signature of mechanical impulse-like defect signals, whereas the wavelet decomposition de-noising method can achieve satisfactory results on smooth signal detection. In order to select optimal parameters for the wavelet filter, a two-step optimization process was proposed. Minimal Shannon entropy was used to optimize the Morlet wavelet shape factor. A periodicity detection method based on singular value decomposition (SVD) was then used to choose the appropriate scale for the wavelet transform. The experimental results verify the effectiveness of the proposed method.

(Abbasion et al., 2007) studied the condition of an electric motor with two rolling bearings (one next to the output shaft and the other next to the fan) with one normal state and three faulty states each. De-noising via the CWT (Meyer wavelet) was conducted and support vector machines (SVMs) were used for the fault classification task. Results have showed 100% accuracy in fault detection. (Ocak et al., 2007) developed a new scheme based on wavelet packet decomposition and hidden Markov modeling (HMM) for the condition monitoring of bearing faults. In this scheme, vibration signals were decomposed into wavelet packets and the node energies of the 3-level decomposition tree were used as features. Based on the features extracted from normal bearing vibration signals, an HMM was trained to model the normal bearing operating condition. The probabilities of this HMM were then used to track the condition of the bearing. In (Zarei and Poshtan, 2007) WPT was used to process stator current signals in order to detect defective bearings at induction motors. The discrete Meyer wavelet was used to decompose the recorded signals in three levels. The defect frequency region was determined, and the coefficient energies in the related nodes were calculated. In comparison with the healthy condition, the energy was found to increase in the nodes related to defect frequency regions, therefore it was used as a diagnostic parameter. (Hu et al., 2007) introduced a methodology for fault diagnosis based on improved wavelet package transform (IWPT), a distance evaluation technique and the support vector machines (SVMs) ensemble. Their method consists of three stages. Firstly, with investigating the feature of impact fault in vibration signals, a biorthogonal wavelet with impact property is constructed via lifting scheme, and the IWPT is carried out for feature extraction from the raw vibration signals. Then, the faulty features can be detected by envelope spectrum analysis of wavelet package coefficients of the most salient frequency band. Secondly, with the distance evaluation technique, the optimal features are selected from the statistical characteristics of raw signals and wavelet package coefficients, and the energy characteristics of decomposition frequency band. Finally, the optimal features are input into the SVMs in order to identify the different abnormal cases. The proposed method was applied to the fault diagnosis of rolling element bearings, and testing results showed that the SVMs ensemble can reliably separate different fault conditions and identify the severity of incipient faults.

(Lei et al., 2009) suggested a method relying on wavelet packets transform (WPT) and empirical mode decomposition (EMD) to preprocess vibration signals and extract fault characteristic information from them. Each of the raw vibration signals is decomposed with "db10" WPT at level 3. From a plethora of features extracted at each sub-band, the most relevant ones were selected via distance evaluation techniques and forwarded into a radial basis function (RBF) network to automatically identify different faults (inner race, outer race, roller) in rolling element bearings. A novel health index called frequency spectrum growth index (FSGI) to detect health condition of gear, based on wavelet decomposition was presented in (Wang et al., 2009). "db9" mother wavelet was chosen for signal decomposition and the maximum wavelet decomposition level is 4. In order to evaluate the performance of the proposed FSGI index various wavelets at various decomposition levels were tested. The results obtained prove that FSGI is insensitive to the selection of wavelet type and decomposition level. Three sets of vibration data collected from a mechanical diagnostics test bed were collected and analyzed in order to validate the method. An anti-aliasing lifting scheme is applied by (Bao et al.,2009) to analyze vibration signals measured from faulty ball bearings and testing results confirm that the proposed method is effective for extracting weak fault feature from a complex background. The simple lifting scheme (or 2nd generation wavelet transform) was altered by discarding the split and merge operations and modifying accordingly the prediction and update operators improving significantly the frequency aliasing issue. Testing results showed that the anti-aliasing lifting scheme performs better than the lifting scheme and the redundant lifting scheme in terms of increasing the accuracy of classification algorithms (ANNs or SVMs) of faulty bearing signals. (Yuan et al., 2009) introduced a new method based on adaptive multi-wavelets via two-scale similarity transforms (TSTs). TSTs are simple methods to construct new biorthogonal multi-wavelets with properties of symmetry, short support and vanishing moments. Based on kurtosis maximization principle, adaptive multi-wavelets were designed to match the transient faults in rotating machinery. Genetic algorithms (GAs) were applied to select the optimal multi-wavelets and the method was used to successfully diagnose bearing outer-race faults. (Zhu et al., 2009) introduced a new method that combines the CWT -through the Morlet wavelet- and the Kolmogorov–Smirnov test to detect transients contained in the vibrations signals from gearbox as well as faulty bearings. CWT initially decomposed the time domain vibration signals into two dimensional time-scale plane. By removing the Gaussian noise coefficients at all scales in the time-scale plane and then applying the inverse CWT to the noise reduced wavelet coefficients, the signal transients in the time domain were evaluated enhancing thus the difficult task of effective and reliable fault identification. A new robust method relying on the improved wavelet packet decomposition (IWPD) and support vector data description (SVDD) is proposed in (Pan et al., 2009). Node energies of IWPD were used to compose feature vectors. Based on feature vectors extracted from normal signals, a SVDD model fitting a tight hypersphere around them is trained, the general distance of test data to this hypersphere being used as the health index. IWPD is based on the second generation wavelet transform (SGWT) realized by lifting scheme. SVDD is an excellent method of one-class classification, with the advantages of robustness and high computation. A methodology developed on the combination of these two methods for bearing performance degradation proved effective and reliable when applied to vibration signals from a bearing accelerated life test. (Feng et al., 2009) introduced the normalized wavelet packets quantifiers as a new feature set for the detection and diagnosis of localized bearing defect and contamination fault. The "Wavelet packets relative energy" measures the normalized energy of the wavelet packets node; the "Total wavelet packets entropy" measures how the normalized energies of the wavelet packets nodes are distributed in the frequency domain; the "Wavelet packets node entropy" describes the uncertainty of the normalized coefficients of the wavelet packets node. Unlike the conventional feature extraction methods, which use the amplitude of wavelet coefficients, these new features were derived from probability distributions and are more robust for diagnostic applications. Acoustic Emission signals from faulty bearings of rotating machines were recorded and the new features were calculated via WPT and Daubechies mother wavelets ("db1-db10"). Their study showed that both localized defects and advanced contamination faults can be successfully detected and diagnosed if the appropriate feature was chosen. The Bayesian classifier was also used to quantitatively analyze and evaluate the performance of the proposed features. They also showed that by reducing the Daubechies wavelet order or the length of the signal segment will generally increase the classification rate probability. (Hao and Chu, 2009) presented a novel morphological undecimated wavelet (MUDW) decomposition scheme for fault diagnostics of rolling element bearings. The MUDW scheme was developed based on the morphological wavelet (MW) theory and was applied for both the extraction of impulse components and de-noising. The efficiency of the MUDW was assessed using simulated data as well as monitored vibration signals from a bearing test rig. (Hong and Liang, 2009) presented a new version of the Lempel–Ziv complexity as a bearing fault (single point) severity measure based on the continuous wavelet transform (CWT). The CWT (realized with the Morlet wavelet) was used to identify the best scale where the fault resides and eliminate the interferences of noise and irrelevant signal components as much as possible. Next, the Lempel–Ziv complexity values were calculated for both the envelope and high-frequency carrier signal obtained from wavelet coefficients at the best scale level. As the noise and other un-related signal components have been removed, the Lempel–Ziv complexity value will be mostly contributed by the bearing system and hence can be reliably used as a bearing fault measure. The applications to the bearing inner- and outer-race fault signals have demonstrated that the proposed methodology can effectively measure the severity of both inner- and outer-race faults.

(Xian, 2010) presented a combined discrete wavelet transform (DWT) and support vector machine (SVM) technique for mechanical failure classification of spherical roller bearing application in high performance hydraulic injection molding machine. The proposed technique consists of preprocessing the mechanical failure vibration signal samples using discrete wavelet transform with 'db2' mother wavelet at the fourth level of decomposition of vibration signal for failure classification. The energy of the approximation and the details was calculated and populated the feature vectors that trained the support vector machine that was built for the classification of mechanical failure types of the spherical roller bearings. In (Yan and Gao, 2010) the generalized harmonic wavelet transform (HWT) was used to enhance the signal-to-noise ratio for effective machine defect identification in rolling bearings that contained different types of structural defects. In harmonic wavelet transform a series of sub-frequency band wavelet coefficients are constructed by choosing different harmonic wavelet parameter pairs. The energy and entropy associated with each sub-frequency band are then calculated. The filtered signal is obtained by choosing the wavelet coefficients whose corresponding sub-frequency band has the highest energy-to- entropy ratio. Experimental studies using rolling bearings that contain different types of structural defects have confirmed that the developed new technique enables high signal-to-noise ratio for effective machine defect identification. (Su et al., 2010) developed a new autocorrelation enhancement algorithm including two aspects of autocorrelation and extended Shannon function. This method does not need to select a threshold and can be implemented in an automatic way and is realized in various stages. First, to eliminate the frequency associated with interferential vibrations, the vibration signal is filtered with a band-pass filter determined by a Morlet wavelet whose parameters are optimized by genetic algorithm. Then, the envelope of the autocorrelation function of the filtered signal is calculated. Finally the enhanced autocorrelation envelope power spectrum is obtained. The method is employed to the simulated signal and the real bearing vibration signals under various conditions, such as normal, inner-race fault and outer-race fault. There are only several single spectrum lines left in the enhanced autocorrelation envelope power spectrum. The single spectrum line with largest amplitude is corresponding to the bearing fault frequency for a defective bearing while it is corresponding to the shaft rotational frequency for a normal bearing. (Huang et al., 2010) utilized the lifting-based second generation wavelet packet transform to process vibration signals from a rolling element bearing test. The wavelet packet energy was calculated by the coefficients at the nth node of the wavelet packet. This corresponds to the energy of the coefficients in a certain frequency band. Normalization is applied to minimize possible bias due to different ranges of the wavelet packet energies. The fuzzy c-means method has been used to assess the bearing performance and classify the faulty and the healthy recordings. In (Pan et al., 2010) a new method based on lifting wavelet packet decomposition and fuzzy c-means for bearing performance degradation assessment is proposed. Vibration signals during run-in tests up to bearing failure were processed with lifting wavelet packet. Feature vectors composed of node energies were constructed and fed in a fuzzy c-means expert system for classification of healthy, degraded and failed bearings. (He et al., 2010) proposed a hybrid method which combines Morlet wavelet filter and sparse code shrinkage (SCS) to extract the impulsive features buried in the vibration signal. Initially, the parameters of a Morlet wavelet filter (center frequency and bandwidth) are optimized by differential evolution (DE) in order to eliminate the interferential vibrations and obtain the fault characteristic signal. Then, to further enhance the impulsive features and suppress residual noise, SCS which is a soft-thresholding method based on maximum likelihood estimation (MLE) is applied to the filtered signal. The results of simulated experiments and real bearing vibration signals verify the effectiveness of the proposed method in extracting impulsive features from noisy signals in condition monitoring.

(Chiementin et al., 2010) studied the effect of wavelet de-noising and other techniques on acoustic emission signals from faulty bearings. They applied DWT and attempted to optimize the various parameters selection involved in a wavelet-based de-noising scheme. They assessed the different de-noising techniques and concluded that the wavelet approach enhanced the signal kurtosis and crest factor more than the other techniques.

4.4 Motors

Electrical, hydraulic motors as well as internal combustion engines are the dominant applications in the related literature. (Chen et al., 2006) worked on fault diagnosis of water hydraulic motors. A modelling of the monitored vibration signals based on the adaptive wavelet transform (AWT) was proposed. The model-based method by AWT was applied for de-noising and feature extraction. Scalograms acquired through the CWT revealed the characteristic signal's energy in time-scale domain and were used as feature values for fault diagnosis of water hydraulic motor. (Wu and Chen, 2006) presented a fault signal diagnosis technique for internal combustion engines based on CWT. The Morlet wavelet was used because in many mechanical dynamic signals, impulses are always the symptoms of faults and the Morlet wavelet is very similar to an impulse component. Different faults have shown different scalograms. A characteristic analysis and experimental comparison of the vibration signal and acoustic emission signal with the proposed algorithm were also presented in their work.

(Daviu et al., 2007) employed wavelet analysis on the stator startup currents in order to detect the presence of dynamic eccentricities in an induction motor. For this purpose, the DWT is applied on the stator startup monitored current signals. The approximation and details were obtained after the DWT decomposition via "db44" wavelet and 8 levels of analysis. The relative increment in the level energy of the wavelet coefficients was used as a quantitative indicator of the degree of severity of the fault. In (Chen et al., 2007) a novel method to process the vibration signals was presented for the fault diagnosis of water hydraulic motors. De-noising was initially conducted by thresholding in the wavelet domain and inversely transforming the de-noised wavelet coefficients. Feature extraction based on the second-generation wavelet of the vibration signals followed next. The statistical probability distributions of the mean, variance and the second-order statistical moment of the scaling coefficients at first, second and third scale were calculated and used to classify the different piston conditions. (Chendong et al., 2007) proposed a new sliding window feature extraction method based on the lifting scheme for extracting transient impacts from signals. A sliding window -designed according to the revolution cycle of rotating machinery- is applied to process the detail signals. By extracting modulus maxima from these windows, fault features and their locations in the original signals were revealed. An incipient impact fault caused by axis misalignment, mass imbalance and a bush broken fault have been successfully detected by using the proposed approach. In (Peng et al., 2007) the wavelet transform modulus maximal (WTMM) method was used to calculate the Lipschitz exponents of the vibration signals with different faults. The Lipschitz exponent can give a quantitative description of the signal's singularity. The proposed singularity based parameters proved a set of excellent diagnostic features, which could separate the four kinds of faults very well. The results showed that, with the fault severity increasing, the vibration signals' singularities and singularity ranges increased as well, and therefore one could evaluate the fault severity through measuring the vibration signals' singularities and singularity ranges.

(Wu and Liu, 2008) instead of WPT utilized a DWT technique combined with a feature selection of energy spectrum and fault classification using ANNs for analyzing fault signals of internal combustion engines. The features of the sound emission signals at different resolution levels were extracted by multi-resolution analysis and Parseval's theorem. (Niu et al., 2008) applied multi-level wavelet decomposition on transient stator current signals for fault diagnosis of induction motors. After the signal preprocessing using smoothing-subtracting and wavelet transform techniques, features were extracted from each level of detail component of decomposed signals using DWT and "db10" mother wavelet. 21 features in total are acquired from each sensor consisting of the time domain (10 features), frequency domain (three features) and regression estimation (eight features). Totally, two $70 \cdot 3 \cdot 21$ features sets are calculated from seven types of signals collected by three current probes at each wavelet decomposition level. The calculated two features sets consisted of the training and test sets respectively and consist of the input in four different classifiers for pattern recognition with quite satisfactory results. (Chen et al., 2008) proposed a methodology based on Wavelet Packet Analysis (WPA) and Kolmogorov-Smirnov (KS) test to analyze monitored vibration signals from the water hydraulic motor to assess the fault degradation of the pistons in water hydraulic motor. The fault detection procedure applied is summarized in the following. First, the time-domain vibration signals were decomposed through the WPT in two levels. The soft-thresholding technique was used in the wavelet and approximation coefficients to get the de-noised coefficients. The reconstructed de-noised vibration signal with improved signal-to-noise ratio (SNR) was obtained by reconstructing the de-noised coefficients in the multi-decomposition of the vibration signal. Then the kurtosis of the de-noised signal was calculated and finally the KS test was used to classify the kurtosis statistical probability distribution (SPD) under seven different piston conditions. Thus the piston condition in water hydraulic motor was successfully assessed. (Widodo and Yang, 2008) introduced an intelligent system for faults detection and classification of induction motor using wavelet support vector machines (W-SVMs). W-SVMs were built by utilizing the kernel function using wavelets. Transient current signals were monitored in various damage conditions of the induction motor. The acquired signals were preprocessed through DWT ("db5", 5 levels) and various statistical features were extracted. Principal component analysis (PCA) and kernel PCA were utilized to reduce the dimension of features and to extract the useful features for classification process. Finally the classification process for diagnosing the faults was carried out using W-SVMs and conventional SVMs based on one against-all multi-class classification.

(Wu and Liu, 2009) proposed a fault diagnosis system for internal combustion engines using wavelet packet transform (WPT) and artificial neural network (ANN) techniques on monitored sound emission signals. In the preprocessing phase, WPT coefficients are used, their entropy is calculated and treated as the input to the ANN in order to distinguish the various fault conditions. ''db4'', ''db8'' and ''db20'' from the Daubechies family were used as mother wavelets with no clear advantage of one of them in the ANN performances.

(Lin et al., 2010) utilized vibration measurements to distinguish effectively between aligned and misaligned motors. The proposed method calculates the difference between the MSE of the original vibration signal and that of the signal after the signal is de-noised by wavelet transform. This study presents a novel use of the multiscale entropy technique by comparing the difference of sample entropy of a signal before and after the signal is de-noised using wavelet transform. De-noising was performed using the Daubechies wavelet transform, which was implemented with Matlab wavelet function with the following parameter settings: threshold type is ''rigrsure''; number of decomposition levels is 4; mother wavelet is ''db4''. (Cusido et al.,2010) have monitored motor current for fault diagnosis in induction machines. The power detail density (PDD) function resulting from a wavelet transformation has proven to be one of the best methods for motor fault estimation under variable load. Power detail density was calculated as the squares of the coefficients of one detail. (Wang and Jiang, 2010) utilized an adaptive wavelet de-noising scheme by combining advantages of both hard and soft thresholding, to de-noise vibration signals from the aircraft engine rotor experimental test rig by block to light rub-impact rotational plate. After the de-noising procedure, the correlation dimension of the vibration signal is computed, and is used as the characteristic feature for identifying the fault deterioration grade.

(Ece and Basaran, 2011) applied wavelet packet decomposition (WPD) in supply-side current signals for the condition monitoring of induction motors with adjustable speed and load levels. In this work, acquired data, sampled at 20 kHz, is analyzed using 11 level WPD. This way, the coefficients of three nodes at the 11th level corresponding to 43.92–48.8 Hz, 48.8–53.68 Hz, and 53.68–58.56 Hz that cover the region of both side-bands as well as the 50 Hz fundamental, are obtained. Using the coefficients of each resulted node, 5 statistical features (i.e. mean, variance, standard deviation, skewness, and kurtosis) are calculated resulting 15 element feature vectors. (Konar and Chattopadhyay, 2011) employed a hybrid CWT–Support Vector Machine approach (CWT-SVM) to analyze the frame vibrations of healthy and faulty induction motors during start-up. Various mother wavelets were utilized in the implementation of CWT. 'Morlet' and 'db10' wavelets were found to be the best choice and used throughout the study. Three statistical features (i.e. root mean square (RMS), crest and kurtosis values) were calculated from the CWT coefficients for each loading condition and consisted of the input in the SVM to classify between healthy and faulty states. In (Anami et al., 2011), a methodology to determine the health condition of motorcycles, based on discrete wavelet transform (DWT) of sound measurements is proposed. The 1-D central contour moments and invariant contour moments, of approximation coefficients of DWT form the feature vectors corresponding to various health states. The sound samples are subjected to wavelet decomposition using Daubechies 'db4' wavelets. The decomposition into approximation and detailed coefficients is carried out for the first 14 levels. The feature vector comprises of four 1D central contour moments (l2;l3; l4 and l5) and their four invariants (F1; F2; F3 and F4) computed on approximation coefficients of a wavelet sub-band. A dynamic time warping (DTW) classifier along with Euclidean distance measure is successfully used for the classification of the feature vectors.

4.5 Tool wear

Tool condition monitoring is a very interesting industrial application. (Velayudham et al., 2005) used wavelet packet transform to study the condition of the drill during drilling of glass/phenolic composite under acoustic emission (AE) monitoring. The energy of the wavelet packet is considered as criterion for the selection of feature packets. Thus, the AE signals were decomposed into four levels, that is, splitting into 16 wavelet packets. Each wavelet packet corresponds to a frequency band ranging from 0–156.25 to 2343.75–2500 kHz. Out of the 16 packets resulted, it is necessary to select the packets (feature packets) that contain useful information. Based on the energy in each packet those with the maximum energy were selected. The monitoring index extracted from wavelet coefficients of highest energy packets could reliably detect the condition of the tool. (Shao et al., 2011) utilized a modified blind sources separation (BSS) technique to separate source signals in milling process. A single-channel BSS method based on wavelet transform and independent component analysis (ICA) was developed, and source signals related to a milling cutter and spindle were separated from a single-channel power signal. The experiments with different tool conditions illustrate that the separation strategy is robust and promising for cutting process monitoring. In (Liao et al., 2007) a wavelet-based methodology for grinding wheel condition monitoring based on acoustic emission (AE) signals was presented. Features were then extracted from each raw AE signal segment using the DWT via "db1" and 12 levels of analysis. An adaptive genetic clustering algorithm was finally applied to the extracted features in order to distinguish between different states of grinding wheel condition. (Li et al., 2005) utilized the DWT to recognize the tool wear states in automatic machining processes. The wavelet coefficients $d(j, k)$ of cutting force signals were calculated after the application of DWT. $d(5,k)$ coefficients proved sensitive and able to identify the different tool wear states and different cutting conditions. (Velayudham et al., 2005) used the WPT in order to characterize the acoustic emission signals released from glass/phenolic polymeric composite during drilling. In their work, the energy of the wavelet packets was taken as criterion for the selection of feature packets, with those having the higher energy to contain the characteristic features of the signal. The results showed that the selected monitoring indices from the wavelet packet coefficients were capable of detecting the drill condition effectively.

4.6 Other applications

(Borghetti et al., 2006) proposed a methodology based on the continuous-wavelet transform (CWT) for the analysis of voltage transients due to line faults, and discussed its application to fault location in power distribution systems. The analysis showed that correlation exists between typical frequencies of the CWT-transformed signals and specific paths in the network covered by the traveling waves originated by the fault. (Belotti et al., 2006) presented a diagnostic tool, based on the DWT, for the detection of wheel-flat defect of a test train at different speeds. DWT was applied on the rail acceleration signals via "db4" wavelet and 10-level decomposition. The results, achieved after an exhaustive experimental campaign, allowed the validation of the effectiveness of the diagnostic tool.

(Xu and Li, 2007) utilized oil spectrometric data from air-compressors. In the first stage de-noising of the original signals through WPT (db4", 3 levels) and "*rigsure*" threshoding strategy was conducted. Then decomposition of the de-noised signal through DWT (with "db1") followed. The variance of approximation coefficients and detail coefficients at level 1 were calculated. In the last stage the improved three-line method was adopted to ascertain decisive criteria for wear condition. The ability of the proposed method for classifying and recognizing wear patterns was verified. (Monsef and Lotfifard, 2007) presented a novel approach for differential protection of power transformers. DWT ("db9, 7 levels) and adaptive network-based fuzzy inference system (ANFIS) were utilized to discriminate internal faults from inrush currents. The proposed method has been designed based on the differences between amplitudes of wavelet transform coefficients in a specific frequency band generated by faults and inrush currents. The ability of the new method was demonstrated by simulating various cases on a typical power system. The algorithm is also tested off-line using data collected from a prototype laboratory three-phase power transformer. The test results confirm the effectiveness and reliability of the proposed algorithm. (Dong and He, 2007) proposed a methodology for the condition monitoring of hydraulic pumps. The collected vibration signals were processed using wavelet packet with "db10" wavelet and five decomposition levels. The wavelet coefficients obtained by the wavelet packet decomposition were used as the inputs to the hidden Markov and semi-Markov models for the classification of the various fault signals. The performance of the two methods was assessed resulting in higher classification rates in the case of hidden semi-Markov models.

(Carneiro et al., 2008) presented an approach for incipient fault detection of motor-operated valves (MOVs) using DWT with "db4" wavelet and six decomposition levels chosen. The motor power signature was acquired through three-phase current and voltage measurements at the motor control center. The results demonstrated the effectiveness of DWT-based methodology on incipient fault detection of motor-operated valves. In the two cases considered, the technique was able to detect incipient faults.

(Gketsis et al., 2009) applied the Wavelet Transform (WT) analysis along with Artificial Neural Networks (ANN) for the diagnosis of electrical machines winding faults. After an optimum wavelet selection procedure they utilized "db2" for the decomposition via DWT of the admittance, current and voltage curves. Level 7 (D7) detail is utilized for feature extraction. The Fourier Transform is employed to derive measures of amplitude and displacement (shift) of D7 details. Motor-operated valves are used in almost all nuclear power plant fluid systems. The purpose of motor-operated valves (MOVs) is to control the fluid flow in a system by opening, closing, or partially obstructing the passage through itself. The readiness of nuclear power plants depends strongly on the operational readiness of valves, especially MOVs. They are applied extensively in control and safety-related systems.

(Tang et al., 2010) employed continuous wavelet transformation (CWT) to filter useless noise in raw vibration signals from gearboxes in wind turbines, and auto terms window (ATW) function was used to suppress the cross terms in Wigner Ville Distribution. In the CWT de-noising process, the Morlet wavelet (similar to the mechanical impulse signal) is chosen to perform CWT on the raw vibration signals. The appropriate scale parameter for CWT is optimized by the cross validation method (CVM). (Niu and Yang, 2010) proposed an intelligent condition monitoring and prognostics system in condition-based maintenance architecture based on data-fusion strategy. They collected vibration signals from a whole test on a methane compressor and trend features were extracted. Then features were normalized and sent into neural network for feature-level fusion. Next, data de-noising was achieved by smoothing with moving average and then wavelet decomposition was applied ('db5', 5 levels of decomposition) to reduce the fluctuation and pick out the trend information. In (Eristi et al.,2010) a novel scheme composed of feature extraction and feature selection procedures for obtaining robust and adequate features of power system disturbances was presented. Firstly, features were obtained by different extraction techniques to the wavelet coefficients of all decomposition levels of the disturbance signal utilizing DWT and 'db4' wavelet. Then, by using sequential forward selection (SFS) technique, robust and adequate features were selected in the feature set resulted from the first stage. The detail coefficients and approximation coefficients were not directly used as the classifier inputs. Reduction of the feature vector dimension was first conducted. In this study, mean, standard deviation, skewness, kurtosis, RMS, form factor, crest-factor, energy, Shannon-entropy, log-energy entropy and interquartile range of the ten level coefficients were used as features. Finally the classification of the power system disturbances using support vector machines (SVMs) was achieved.

(Jiang et al, 2011) introduced a new de-noising method based on adaptive Morlet wavelet and singular value decomposition (SVD) for feature extraction of vibration signals from wind turbine gearbox. Modified Shannon wavelet entropy was utilized to optimize central frequency and bandwidth parameter of the Morlet wavelet so as to achieve optimal match with the impulsive components. The proposed method was applied to extract the outer-race fault in a rolling bearing and the fault diagnosis of a planetary gearbox in a wind turbine. The results show that the proposed method based on adaptive Morlet wavelet and SVD performed much better than the Donoho's "soft-thresholding de-noising", the de-noising method based on CWT and SVD, and the de-noising method based on Morlet wavelet. Thus, it provides an effective tool for fault diagnosis to extract the fault features submerged in the background noise.

5. Conclusions

Tremendous progress has been made the last 15 years in the evolution of WT theory as well as their applications in engineering and especially condition monitoring. WT literally gave a boost to the signal processing of engineering signals opening a wide full-of-options field. WT is now more mature than ever constituting one of the most powerful weapons in the signal analyst's arsenal. In this review, classical as well as second generation wavelet transforms were presented. The issue of mother wavelet choice and a variety of applications in wavelet-based condition monitoring were discussed. Some concepts on the beyond the state-of-the-art in WT were finally discussed. Despite the rapid evolution of WT there are still unresolved theoretical issues such as the optimum mother wavelet choice, the number of decomposition levels in DWT, WPT, SGWT and the number of analyzing scales in CWT. A solution by the mathematicians is expected there in the future. In the engineering field and especially in the condition monitoring, WT is expected to support (directly or indirectly) the developments in the fast evolving field of forecasting and prognostics. Wavelet-based utilization of schemes such as Hidden Markov Models, Particle Filters, Remaining Useful Life PDF, Trend extrapolation etc. are expected to dominate in the literature of condition monitoring the following years.

6. Acknowledgements

The authors would like to thank Mr. Dimitris Roulias for his valuable assistance with many of the figures of this work.

7. References

Abbasion, S.; Rafsanjani, A.; Farshidianfar, A.; Irani, N. (2007). Rolling element bearings multi-fault classification based on the wavelet denoising and support vector machine, *Mechanical Systems and Signal Processing,* Vol.21, No.7, (October 2007), pp. 2933-2945

Anami, B.; Pagi, V.; Magi, S. (2011). Wavelet-based acoustic analysis for determining health condition of motorized two-wheelers. *Applied Acoustics,* Vol.72, No.7, (June 2011), pp. 464-469

Antonino-Daviu, J.; Jover, P. ; Riera, M.; Arkkio, A.; Roger-Folch, J. (2007). DWT analysis of numerical and experimental data for the diagnosis of dynamic eccentricities in induction motors, *Mechanical Systems and Signal Processing,* Vol.21, No.6, (August 2007), pp. 2575-2589

Bao, W.; Zhou, R.; Yang, J.; Yu, D.; Li, N. (2009). Anti-aliasing lifting scheme for mechanical vibration fault feature extraction, *Mechanical Systems and Signal Processing,* Vol.23, No.5, (July 2009), pp. 1458-1473

Belotti, V.; Crenna, F.; Michelini, R.C.; Rossi, G.B. (2006). Wheel-flat diagnostic tool via wavelet transform, *Mechanical Systems and Signal Processing*

Belsak, A.; Flasker, J. (2009). Wavelet analysis for gear crack identification, *Engineering Failure Analysis,* Vol.16, No.6, (September 2009), pp. 1983-1990

Borghetti, A.; Corsi, S.; Nucci, C.A.; Paolone, M.; Peretto, L.; Tinarelli, R. (2006). On the use of continuous-wavelet transform for fault location in distribution power systems, International *Journal of Electrical Power & Energy Systems,* Vol.28, No.9, (November 2006), pp. 608-617

Cai, T.T.; Silverman, B.W. (2001). Incorporating information on Neighboring Coefficients into wavelet estimation, *Sankhya: The Indian Journal of Statistics Series B,* Vol.63, No.2, (2001) pp. 127–148.

Carneiro, A.; da Silva, A.; Upadhyaya, B.R. (2008). Incipient fault detection of motor-operated valves using wavelet transform analysis, *Nuclear Engineering and Design,* Vol.238, No.9, (September 2008), pp. 2453-2459

Chen, H.X.; Chua, P.S.K.; Lim, G.H. (2006). Adaptive wavelet transform for vibration signal modelling and application in fault diagnosis of water hydraulic motor, *Mechanical Systems and Signal Processing,* Vol.20, No.8, (November 2006), pp. 2022-2045

Chen, H.X.; Chua, P.S.K.; Lim, G.H. (2007). Vibration analysis with lifting scheme and generalized cross validation in fault diagnosis of water hydraulic system, *Journal of Sound and Vibration,* Vol.301, No.3-5, (April 2007), pp. 458-480

Chen, H.X.; Chua, P.S.K.; Lim, G.H. (2008). Fault degradation assessment of water hydraulic motor by impulse vibration signal with Wavelet Packet Analysis and Kolmogorov–Smirnov Test, *Mechanical Systems and Signal Processing,* Vol.22, No.7, (October 2008), Pages 1670-1684

Chendong, D.; Zhengjia, H.; Hongkai, J. (2007). A sliding window feature extraction method for rotating machinery based on the lifting scheme, *Journal of Sound and Vibration*, Vol.299, No.4-5, (February 2007), pp. 774-785

Chiementin, X.; Mba, D.; Charnley, B.; Lignon, S.; Dron, J.P. (2010). Effect of the denoising on Acoustic Emission signals, *Journal of Vibration and Acoustics*, Vol.132, No.3, (April 2010), pp. 0310091 1-9

Cusido, J.; Romeral, L.; Ortega, J.A.; Garcia, A.; Riba, J.R. (2010). Wavelet and PDD as fault detection techniques, *Electric Power Systems Research*, Vol.80, No.8, (August 2010), pp. 915-924

Dong, M.; He, D. (2007). A segmental hidden semi-Markov model (HSMM)-based diagnostics and prognostics framework and methodology, *Mechanical Systems and Signal Processing*, Vol.21, No.5, (July 2007), pp. 2248-2266

Donoho ,L.D.; Johnstone IM. (1994). Ideal spatial adaptation by wavelet shrinkage, *Biometrika*, Vol.81, No.3, (September 1994), pp. 425–455

Donoho, L.D. (1995). De-noising by soft-thresholding, *IEEE Transactions on Information Theory*, Vol.41, No.3, (May 1995), pp.613–627

Donoho, D.L.; Johnstone, I.M. (1995). Adapting to unknown smoothness via wavelet shrinkage, *Journal of the American Statistical Association*, Vol.90, (December 1994), pp. 1200–1224

Eristi, H.; Demir, Y. (2010). A new algorithm for automatic classification of power quality events based on wavelet transform and SVM, *Expert Systems with Applications*, Vol.37, No.6, (June 2010), pp. 4094-4102

Eristi, H.; Ucar, A.; Demir, Y. (2010). Wavelet-based feature extraction and selection for classification of power system disturbances using support vector machines, *Electric Power Systems Research*, Vol.80, No.7, (July 2010), pp. 743-752

Fan, X.; Zuo, M.J. (2006). Gearbox fault detection using Hilbert and wavelet packet transform, *Mechanical Systems and Signal Processing*, Vol.20, No.4, (May 2006), pp. 966-982

Feng, Y.; Schlindwein, F. (2009). Normalized wavelet packets quantifiers for condition monitoring, *Mechanical Systems and Signal Processing*, Vol.23, No.3, (April 2009), pp. 712-723

Feng, K.; Jiang, Z.; He, W.; Qin, Q. (2011). Rolling Element Bearing Fault Detection Based on Optimal Antisymmetric Real Laplace Wavelet. *Measurement*, accepted manuscript for publication

Gketsis, Z.; Zervakis, M.; Stavrakakis, G. (2009). Detection and classification of winding faults in windmill generators using Wavelet Transform and ANN, *Electric Power Systems Research* Vol.79, No.11, (November 2009), pp. 1483-1494

Hao, R.; Chu, F. (2009). Morphological undecimated wavelet decomposition for fault diagnostics of rolling element bearings, *Journal of Sound and Vibration*, Vol.320, No.4-5, (March 2009), pp. 1164-1177

He, Q.; Kong, F.; Yan, R. (2007). Subspace-based gearbox condition monitoring by kernel principal component analysis, *Mechanical Systems and Signal Processing*, Vol.21, No.4, (May 2007), pp. 1755-1772

He, W.; Jiang, Z.; Feng, K. (2009). Bearing fault detection based on optimal wavelet filter and sparse code shrinkage, *Measurement*, Vol.42, No.7, (August 2009), pp. 1092-1102

Hong, H.; Liang, M. (2009). Fault severity assessment for rolling element bearings using the Lempel–Ziv complexity and continuous wavelet transform, *Journal of Sound and Vibration*, Vol.320, No.1-2, (February 2009), pp. 452-468

Hu, Q.; He, Z.; Zhang, Z.; Zi, Y. (2007). Fault diagnosis of rotating machinery based on improved wavelet package transform and SVMs ensemble, *Mechanical Systems and Signal Processing*, Vol.21, No.2, (February 2007), pp. 688-705

Huang, Y.; Liu, C.; Zha, X.F.; Li, Y. (2010). A lean model for performance assessment of machinery using second generation wavelet packet transform and Fisher criterion, *Expert Systems with Applications,* Vol.37, No.5, (May 2010), pp. 3815-3822

Hyvarinen, A. (1999). Sparse code shrinkage: denoising of non-gaussian data by maximum likelihood estimation, *Neural Comput,* Vol.11, No.7, (October 1999), pp. 1739–1768

Jafarizadeh, M.A.; Hassannejad, R.; Ettefagh, M.M.; Chitsaz, S. (2008). Asynchronous input gear damage diagnosis using time averaging and wavelet filtering, *Mechanical Systems and Signal Processing,* Vol.22, No.1, (January 2008), pp. 172-201

Jazebi, S.; Vahidi, B.; Jannati, M. (2011). A novel application of wavelet based SVM to transient phenomena identification of power transformers, *Energy Conversion and Management,* Vol. 52, No.2, (February 2011), pp. 1354-1363

Kankar, P.; Sharma, S.; Harsha, S. (2011). Fault diagnosis of ball bearings using continuous wavelet transform, *Applied Soft Computing,* Vol.11, No.2, (March 2011), pp. 2300-2312

Kar, C.; Mohanty, A.R. (2008). Vibration and current transient monitoring for gearbox fault detection using multi-resolution Fourier transform, *Journal of Sound and Vibration,* Vol.311, No.1-2, (March 2008), pp. 109-132

Kingsbury, N.G. (1998). The dual-tree complex wavelet transform: A new technique for shift invariance and directional filters, in *Proceedings of the 8th IEEE DSP Workshop*, Utah, Aug. 9–12, 1998, paper no. 86.

Lei, Y.; He, Z.; Zi, Y. (2009). Application of an intelligent classification method to mechanical fault diagnosis, *Expert Systems with Applications*, Vol.36, No.6, (August 2009), pp. 9941-9948

Lei, Y.; He, Z.; Zi, Y. (2011). EEMD method and WNN for fault diagnosis of locomotive roller bearings, *Expert Systems with Applications,* Vol.38, No.6, (June 2011), pp. 7334-7341

Li, W.; Gong, W.; Obikawa, T.; Shirakashi, T. (2005). A method of recognizing tool-wear states based on a fast algorithm of wavelet transform, Journal of Materials Processing Technology, Vol.170, No.1-2, (December 2005), pp. 374-380

Li, L.; Qu, L.; Liao, X. (2007). Haar wavelet for machine fault diagnosis, *Mechanical Systems and Signal Processing*, Vol.21, No.4, (May 2007), pp. 1773-1786

Li, Z.; He, Z.; Zia, Y.; Jiang, H. (2008). Rotating machinery fault diagnosis using signal-adapted lifting scheme, *Mechanical Systems and Signal Processing*, Vol.22, No.3, (April 2008), pp. 542-556

Li, H.; Zhang, Y.; Zheng, H. (2011). Application of Hermitian wavelet to crack fault detection in gearbox, *Mechanical Systems and Signal Processing*, Vol.25, No.4, (May 2011), pp. 1353-1363

Liao, T. W.; Ting, C.; Qu, J.; Blau, P.J. (2007). A wavelet-based methodology for grinding wheel condition monitoring, *International Journal of Machine Tools and Manufacture,* Vol.47, No.3-4, (March 2007), pp. 580-592

Lin, J.; Liu, J.; Li, C.; Tsai, L.; Chung, H. (2010). Motor shaft misalignment detection using multiscale entropy with wavelet denoising, *Expert Systems with Applications*, Vol.37, No.10, (October 2010), pp. 7200-7204

Loutas, T.H.; Sotiriades, G.; Kalaitzoglou, I.; Kostopoulos, V. (2009). Condition monitoring of a single-stage gearbox utilizing on-line vibration and acoustic emission measurements, *Applied Acoustics*, Vol.70, No.9, (September 2009), pp. 1148-1159

Loutas, T.H.; Kostopoulos, V. (2010). Wavelet-based methodologies for the analysis of vibration recordings for fault diagnosis in gears, *Noise and Vibration Worldwide*, Vol.41, No.7, (July 2010), pp. 10-18

Loutas, T.H.; Roulias, D.; Pauly, E.; Kostopoulos, V. (2011).The combined use of vibration, acoustic emission and oil debris on-line monitoring towards a more effective condition monitoring of rotating machinery, *Mechanical Systems and Signal Processing*, Vol.25, No.4, (May 2011), pp. 1339-1352

Mallat, S. (1989), "A theory for multiresolution signal decomposition: The wavelet representation, *IEEE Transactions on Pattern Analysis and Machine Intelligence*, Vol.11, No.7, (July 1989), pp. 674–693.

Miao, Q.; Makis, V. (2007). Condition monitoring and classification of rotating machinery using wavelets and hidden Markov models, *Mechanical Systems and Signal Processing*, Vol.21, No.2, (February 2007), pp. 840-855 , Vol.20, No.8, (November 2006), pp. 1953-1966

Monsef, H.; Lotfifard, S. (2007). Internal fault current identification based on wavelet transform in power transformers, *Electric Power Systems Research*, Vol.77, No.12, *October 2007*, pp. 1637-1645

Niu, G.; Widodo, A.; Son, J.; Yang, B.; Hwang, D.; Kang, D. (2008). Decision-level fusion based on wavelet decomposition for induction motor fault diagnosis using transient current signal, *Expert Systems with Applications*, Vol.35, No.3, (October 2008), pp. 918-928

Niu, G.; Yang, B. (2010). Intelligent condition monitoring and prognostics system based on data-fusion strategy, *Expert Systems with Applications*, Vol.37, No.12, (December 2010), pp. 8831-8840

Ocak, H.; Loparo, K.A.; Discenzo, F.M. (2007). Online tracking of bearing wear using wavelet packet decomposition and probabilistic modeling: A method for bearing prognostics, *Journal of Sound and Vibration*, Vol.302, No.4-5, (May 2007), pp. 951-961

Pan, Y.; Chen, J.; Guo, L. (2009). Robust bearing performance degradation assessment method based on improved wavelet packet–support vector data description, *Mechanical Systems and Signal Processing*, Vol.23, No.3, (April 2009), pp. 669-681

Pan, Y.; Chen, J.; Li, X. (2010). Bearing performance degradation assessment based on lifting wavelet packet decomposition and fuzzy c-means, *Mechanical Systems and Signal Processing*, Vol.24, No.2, (February 2010), pp. 559-566

Peng, Z.K.; Chu, F.L.; Tse, P.W. (2007). Singularity analysis of the vibration signals by means of wavelet modulus maximal method, *Mechanical Systems and Signal Processing*, Vol.21, No.2, (February 2007), pp. 780-794

Purushotham, V.; Narayanan, S.; Prasad, S.A.N. (2005). Multi-fault diagnosis of rolling bearing elements using wavelet analysis and hidden Markov model based fault recognition, *NDT & E International*, Vol.38, No.8, (December 2005), pp. 654-664

Qiu, H.; Lee, J.; Lin, J.; Yu, G. (2006). Wavelet filter-based weak signature detection method and its application on rolling element bearing prognostics, *Journal of Sound and Vibration*, Vol.289, No.4-5, (February 2006), pp. 1066-1090

Rafiee, J.; Arvani, F.; Harifi, A.; Sadeghi, M.H. (2007). Intelligent condition monitoring of a gearbox using artificial neural network, *Mechanical Systems and Signal Processing*, Vol.21, No.4, (May 2007), pp. 1746-1754

Rafiee, J.; Tse, P.W. (2009). Use of autocorrelation of wavelet coefficients for fault diagnosis, *Mechanical Systems and Signal Processing*, Vol.23, No.5, (July 2009), pp. 1554-1572

Rafiee, J.; Tse, P.W.; Harifi, A.; Sadeghi, M.H. (2009). A novel technique for selecting mother wavelet function using an intelligent fault diagnosis system, *Expert Systems with Applications*, Vol.36, No.3, Part 1, (April 2009), pp. 4862-4875

Rafiee, J.; Rafiee, M.A.; Tse, P.W. (2010). Application of mother wavelet functions for automatic gear and bearing fault diagnosis, *Expert Systems with Applications*, Vol.37, No.6, (June 2010), pp. 4568-4579

Randall, R.; Antoni, J. (2011). Rolling element bearing diagnostics - A tutorial, *Mechanical Systems and Signal Processing*, Vol.25, No.2, (February 2011), pp. 485-520

Sanz, J.; Perera, R.; Huerta, C. (2007). Fault diagnosis of rotating machinery based on auto-associative neural networks and wavelet transforms, *Journal of Sound and Vibration*, Vol.302, No.4-5, (May 2007), pp. 981-999

Saravanan, N.; Siddabattuni, V.N.S.; Ramachandran, K.I. (2008). A comparative study on classification of features by SVM and PSVM extracted using Morlet wavelet for fault diagnosis of spur bevel gear box, *Expert Systems with Applications*, Vol.35, No.3, (October 2008), pp. 1351-1366

Saravanan, N.; Ramachandran, K.I. (2009). Fault diagnosis of spur bevel gear box using discrete wavelet features and Decision Tree classification, *Expert Systems with Applications*,
Vol.36, No.5, (July 2009), pp. 9564-9573

Saravanan, N.; Ramachandran, K.I. (2009). A case study on classification of features by fast single-shot multiclass PSVM using Morlet wavelet for fault diagnosis of spur bevel gear box, *Expert Systems with Applications*, Vol.36, No.8, (October 2009), pp. 10854-10862

Saravanan, N.; Ramachandran, K.I. (2010). Incipient gear box fault diagnosis using discrete wavelet transform (DWT) for feature extraction and classification using artificial neural network (ANN), *Expert Systems with Applications*, Vol.37, No.6, (June 2010), pp. 4168-4181

Sawalhi, N.; Randall, R. (2011). Vibration response of spalled rolling element bearings: Observations, simulations and signal processing techniques to track the spall size, *Mechanical Systems and Signal Processing*, Vol.25, No.3, (April 2011), pp. 846-870

Shao, H.; Shi, X.; Li, L. (2011). Power signal separation in milling process based on wavelet transform and independent component analysis. *International Journal of Machine Tools & Manufacture*, Vol.51, No.9 (September 2011), pp. 701–710

Su, W.; Wang, F.; Zhu, H.; Zhang, Z.; Guo, Z. (2010). Rolling element bearing faults diagnosis based on optimal Morlet wavelet filter and autocorrelation enhancement, *Mechanical Systems and Signal Processing*, Vol.24, No.5, (July 2010), pp. 1458-1472

Singh, G.K.; Kazzaz, S. (2009). Isolation and identification of dry bearing faults in induction machine using wavelet transform, *Tribology International*, Vol.42, No.6, (June 2009), pp. 849-861

Sweldens, W. (1998). The lifting scheme: A construction of second generation wavelets, *SIAM Journal on Mathematical Analysis*, Vol.29, No.2, (March 1998) pp. 511-546

Tang, B.; Liu, W.; Song, T. (2011). Wind turbine fault diagnosis based on Morlet wavelet transformation and Wigner-Ville distribution, *Renewable Energy*, Vol.35, No.12, (December 2010), pp. 2862-2866

Velayudham, A.; Krishnamurthy, R.; Soundarapandian, T. (2005). Acoustic emission based drill condition monitoring during drilling of glass/phenolic polymeric composite using wavelet packet transform, *Materials Science and Engineering: A*, Vol.412, No.1-2, (December 2005), pp. 141-145

Wang, D.; Miao, Q.; Kang, R. (2009). Robust health evaluation of gearbox subject to tooth failure with wavelet decomposition, *Journal of Sound and Vibration*, Vol.324, No.3-5, (July 2009), pp. 1141-1157

Wang, Z.; Jiang, H. (2010). Robust incipient fault identification of aircraft engine rotor based on wavelet and fraction, *Aerospace Science and Technology*, Vol.14, No.4, (June 2010), pp. 221-224

Wang, X.; Makis, V.; Yang, M. (2010). A wavelet approach to fault diagnosis of a gearbox under varying load conditions, *Journal of Sound and Vibration*, Vol.329, No.9, (April 2010), pp. 1570-1585

Wang, W.; Kanneg, D. (2009). An integrated classifier for gear system monitoring, *Mechanical Systems and Signal Processing*, Vol.23, No.4, (May 2009), pp. 1298-1312

Wang, Y.; He, Z.; Zi, Y. (2010). Enhancement of signal denoising and multiple fault signatures detecting in rotating machinery using dual-tree complex wavelet transform, *Mechanical Systems and Signal Processing*, Vol.24, No.1, (January 2010), pp. 119-137

Widodo, A.; Yang, B. (2008). Wavelet support vector machine for induction machine fault diagnosis based on transient current signal, *Expert Systems with Applications*, Vol.35, No.1-2, (July-August 2008), pp. 307-316

Wu, J.; Chen, J. (2006). Continuous wavelet transform technique for fault signal diagnosis of internal combustion engines, *NDT & E International*, Vol.39, No.4, (June 2006), pp. 304-311

Wu, J.; Liu, C. (2008). Investigation of engine fault diagnosis using discrete wavelet transform and neural network, *Expert Systems with Applications*, Vol.35, No.3, (October 2008), pp. 1200-1213

Wu, J.; Hsu, C. (2009). Fault gear identification using vibration signal with discrete wavelet transform technique and fuzzy–logic inference, *Expert Systems with Applications*, Vol.36, No.2, Part 2, (March 2009), pp. 3785-3794

Wu, J.; Chan, J. (2009). Faulted gear identification of a rotating machinery based on wavelet transform and artificial neural network, *Expert Systems with Applications*, Vol.36, No.5, (July 2009), pp. 8862-8875

Wu, J.; Liu, C. (2009). An expert system for fault diagnosis in internal combustion engines using wavelet packet transform and neural network, *Expert Systems with Applications*, Vol.36, No.3, Part 1, (April 2009), pp. 4278-4286

Wu, J.; Hsu, C.; Wu, G. (2009). Fault gear identification and classification using discrete wavelet transform and adaptive neuro-fuzzy inference, *Expert Systems with Applications*, Vol.36, No.3, Part 2, (April 2009), pp. 6244-6255

Xian, G.; Zeng, B. (2009). An intelligent fault diagnosis method based on wavelet packet analysis and hybrid support vector machines, *Expert Systems with Applications*, Vol.36, No.10, (December 2009), pp. 12131-12136

Xian, G. (2010). Mechanical failure classification for spherical roller bearing of hydraulic injection molding machine using DWT–SVM, *Expert Systems with Applications*, Vol.37, No.10, (October 2010), pp. 6742-6747

Xu, Q.; Li, Z. (2007). Recognition of wear mode using multi-variable synthesis approach based on wavelet packet and improved three-line method, *Mechanical Systems and Signal Processing*, Vol.21, No.8, (November 2007), pp. 3146-3166

Yan, R.; Gao, R.X. (2005). An efficient approach to machine health diagnosis based on harmonic wavelet packet transform, *Robotics and Computer-Integrated Manufacturing*, Vol.21, No.4-5, (August-October 2005), pp. 291–301

Yan, R.; Gao, R. (2010). Harmonic wavelet-based data filtering for enhanced machine defect identification, *Journal of Sound and Vibration*, Vol.329, No.15, (July 2010), pp. 3203-3217

YanPing, Z.; ShuHong, H.; JingHong, H.; Tao, S.; Wei, L. (2006). Continuous wavelet grey moment approach for vibration analysis of rotating machinery, *Mechanical Systems and Signal Processing*, Vol.20, No.5, (July 2006), pp. 1202-1220

Yuan, J.; He, Z.; Zi, Y.; Lei, Y.; Li, Z. (2009). Adaptive multi-wavelets via two-scale similarity transforms for rotating machinery fault diagnosis, *Mechanical Systems and Signal Processing*, Vol.23, No.5, (July 2009), pp. 1490-1508

Yuan, J.; He, Z.; Zi, Y. (2010). Gear fault detection using customized multiwavelet lifting schemes, *Mechanical Systems and Signal Processing*, Vol.24, No.5, (July 2010), pp. 1509-1528

Zarei, J.; Poshtan, J. (2007). Bearing fault detection using wavelet packet transform of induction motor stator current, *Tribology International*, Vol.40, Issue 5, (May 2007), pp. 763-769

Zhou, R.; Bao, W.; Li, N.; Huang, X.; Yu, D. (2010). Mechanical equipment fault diagnosis based on redundant second generation wavelet packet transform, *Digital Signal Processing*, Vol.20, No.1, (January 2010), pp. 276-288

Zhu, Z.K.; Yan, R.; Luo, L.; Feng, Z.H.; Kong, F.R. (2009). Detection of signal transients based on wavelet and statistics for machine fault diagnosis, *Mechanical Systems and Signal Processing*, Vol.23, No.4, (May 2009), pp. 1076-1097

14

Wavelet Analysis and Neural Networks for Bearing Fault Diagnosis

Khalid Al-Raheem
Caledonian College of Engineering
Oman

1. Introduction

The manufacturing productivity can be achieved through the availability of the physical resources and improved manufacturing methods and technology. The operational availability of various industrial systems can be increased by adopting efficient maintenance strategies. An ideal maintenance strategy meets the requirements of machine availability and operational safety at minimum cost.

Today, most maintenance actions are carried out by either corrective (run to failure) or preventive (scheduled or predetermined) strategy. In Corrective Maintenance (CM) the components are maintained after obvious faults or actual breakdown has occurred. With this maintenance strategy the associated costs are usually high due to the production losses, fault occurrence damages, restoring equipment until is being used at failure condition, and the safety/health hazards presented by the fault. However, the Preventive Maintenance (PM) approach has been developed to overcome the CM deficiencies. Traditionally, PM is a time driven process which is performed at regular time intervals, commonly termed the maintenance cycle, regardless of the components actual condition, in order to prevent component or systems breakdown. For example, changing the car engine oil at every 5000 KMs traveled distance, where no concern as to the actual condition and performance capability of the replaced oil.

Over recent decades some industries have started to employ a second type of PM actions in a predictive manner, where the actual machinery condition is the key indicator for the maintenance schedule and appropriate maintenance tasks (condition driven), therefore referred to as Condition Based Maintenance (CBM).

In CBM systems, the machinery condition assessment is achieved by acquiring and interpreting the actual machine data continuously with an aim to provide lead-time and required maintenance prior to predicted failure or loss of efficiency (Just-In-Time maintenance). The application of the CBM approach provides the ability to optimize the availability of process machinery, and greatly reduce the cost of maintenance. The CBM system also provides the means to improve product quality, productivity, profitability, safety and overall effectiveness of manufacturing and production plant.

The tools and techniques employed in the field of the CBM systems include: measurement and sensor technology, modeling of failure mechanisms, failure forecasting techniques, diagnostic and prognostic software, communication protocols, maintenance software applications and computer networking technologies.

The concept of condition monitoring consists of a selection of measurable parameters which correlate with the health or condition of a machine, and an interpretation of the collected data to determine the machinery fault existence and identify specific components (e.g. gear set, bearings) in the machine that are degrading, *Detection mode*. Moreover, the condition monitoring activities may include: specify the component failure causes, *Diagnostic mode*, and estimate the remaining life of the monitored component, *Prognostic mode*. For example, the particles content in the lubricant oil is an indicator of the machine's wearing condition. By setting warning limits for the particles content of the lubricant a preventive action can be taken before the catastrophic failure occurs. With more detailed analysis of the measurement the nature of the problem can be identified, and lead to the diagnosis of the problem. The level of automation in assessing the machine condition can vary from human visual inspection to fully automated systems with sensors, data manipulation, condition monitoring, diagnosis, and prognosis.

Various parameters e.g. vibration, temperature, lubricant oil analysis, thermography, electric current, acoustic emission, etc, and different data analysis techniques have been applied and developed to provide significant data analysis for CM, which include:

Time domain methods: using different statistical indicators such as, Root Mean Square (RMS), Peak value, Kurtosis, etc. (Orhan et al. .2006) and (Tandon , 1994).

Frequency domain methods: such as Fourier Transform (FT) spectrum (Reeves, 1994), envelope detection (Weller, 2004), Cepstrum, etc.

Time-Frequency methods: which include Short Time Fourier Transform (STFT) (Thanagasundram and Schlindwein, 2006), Wavelet Analysis (WA) (Peng and Chu, 2004) (Wang and Gao , 2003), (Junsheng *et al.* , 2007) and (Kahaei et al. , 2006), etc.

Adaptive noise cancellation methods: such as Adaptive Noise Canceling (ANC), and Adaptive Line Enhancer (ALE), etc. (Khemili and Chouchane, 2005)

Bearing failures represent a high percentage of the breakdowns in the rotating machinery and result in serious problems, mainly in places where machines are rotating at constant and high speeds, not only because of the large quantity of them installed in rotating machinery, but also due to their role in relation to product quality.

This chapter presents the application of wavelet analysis combined with artificial neural networks as an automatic rolling bearing fault detection and diagnosis, with applied to both simulated (modeling) and real (measured) bearing vibration signals.

The chapter has been divided into two parts, in the first part the application of the wavelet analysis as a bearing fault detection/diagnosis technique is presented. The wavelet fault detection techniques are based on the use of the autocorrelation of the wavelet de-noised vibration signal and the wavelet envelope power spectrums for the identification of bearing fault frequencies.

The second part includes the application of wavelet analysis as a feature extraction method combined with the neural network classifier for automatic detection and diagnosis of the rolling bearing fault.

2. Rolling element bearings

Bearings permit a smooth low friction motion between two surfaces (usually a shaft and housing) loaded against each other. The terms rolling-contact bearing, antifriction bearing, and rolling bearing are all used to describe that class of bearing in which the main load is transferred through elements in rolling contact rather than in sliding contact (sliding bearings).

The basic concept of the rolling element bearing is simple. If loads are to be transmitted between surfaces in relative motion in a machine, the action can be achieved in the most effective way if the rolling elements are interposed between the sliding members. The frictional resistance encountered in sliding is then largely replaced by much smaller resistance associated with rolling, although this arrangement is accompanied with high stresses in the contact regions of effective load transmission.

The standard configuration of a rolling element bearing is an assembly of the outer and inner rings which enclose the rolling elements such as balls (ball bearings), Figure 1a, and cylindrical rollers (roller bearings), Figure 1b, and the cage or separator which assures annular equidistance between the rolling elements and prevents undesired contacts and rubbing friction among them. Some bearings also have seals as integrated components.

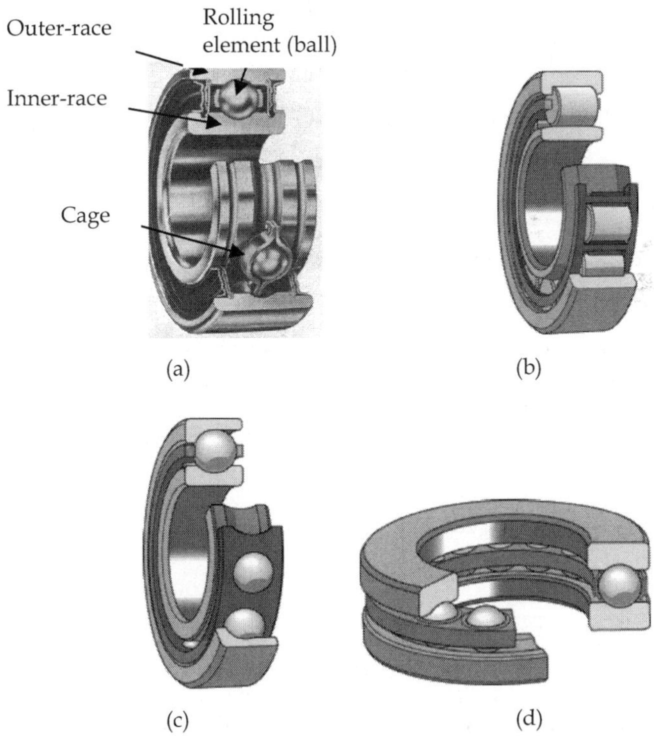

Fig. 1. Rolling element bearing (a) deep groove ball bearing, (b) roller bearing (c) angular contact ball bearing, and (d) thrust bearing (Harris, 2001).

The rolling surfaces on the rings are referred to as raceways. The number of balls is defined as N_b, their diameter as D_b. The pitch diameter or the diameter of the cage is designated D_p. The point of contact between a ball and the raceways is characterized by the contact angle α, Figure 2.

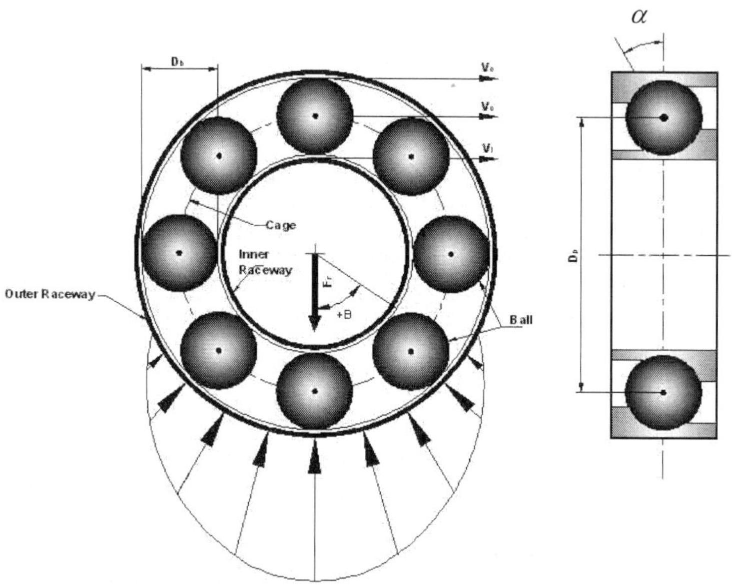

Fig. 2. Rolling element bearing basic geometry and velocities.

The rolling bearings that support loads perpendicular to their axis of rotation are called radial bearing. However, the bearings which support loads parallel to the axis of rotation are termed thrust bearings (the contact angle exceeding 45°), Figure 1d. Angular contact bearings have one ring shoulder removed; this may be from the inner or outer ring, Figure 1c. This allows a larger ball complement than found in comparable deep groove bearings, giving a greater load capacity. Speed capacity of angular contact bearings is also greater than deep groove ball bearing. The normal angular contact bearings have a contact angle which does not exceed 40°. Angular contact bearings support a combination of radial and thrust loads or heavy thrust loads depending on the contact angle. A single angular contact bearing can be loaded in one thrust direction only.

Because roller bearings have a greater rolling surface area in contact with inner and outer races, they generally support a greater load than comparably sized ball bearings. The small contact area (point contact) in the ball bearing compared with the roller bearing (line contact) leads to more stress concentration and is more affected by the fatigue failure during the bearing rotation. Moreover, the angular contact ball bearing can easily separate its components (separable) to introduce the artificial faults. Based on that the angular contact ball bearings have been used in this research for fault detection.

3. Bearing fault diagnosis using wavelet analysis

The Wavelet Transform (WT) coefficients are analyzed in both the time and frequency domains. In the time domain the autocorrelation of the wavelet de-noised signal is applied to evaluate the period of the fault pulses using the impulse wavelet as a wavelet base function. However, in the frequency domain the wavelet envelope power spectrum has been used to identify the fault frequencies with the single sided complex Laplace wavelet as the mother wavelet function.

3.1 Wavelet de-noising method

3.1.1 Impulse wavelet function

The WT is the inner product of a time domain signal with the translated and dilated wavelet-base function. The resulting coefficients reflect the correlation between the signal and the selected wavelet-base function. Therefore, to increase the amplitude of the generated wavelet coefficients related to the fault impulses, and to enhance the fault detection process, the selected wavelet-base function should be similar in characters to the bearing impulse response generated by the presence of a bearing incipient fault. Based on that, the investigated wavelet-base function is denoted as the impulse-response wavelet and given by,

$$\psi(t) = A \; e^{-\frac{\beta}{\sqrt{1-\beta^2}}\omega_c t} \sin(\omega_c t) \tag{1}$$

Where β is the damping factor that controls the decay rate of the exponential envelope in time and hence regulates the resolution of the wavelet, simultaneously it corresponds to the frequency bandwidth of the wavelet in the frequency domain, ω_c determining the number of significant oscillations of the wavelet in the time domain and correspond to the wavelet centre frequency in frequency domain, and A is an arbitrary scaling factor. Figure 3 shows the proposed wavelet and its power spectrum.

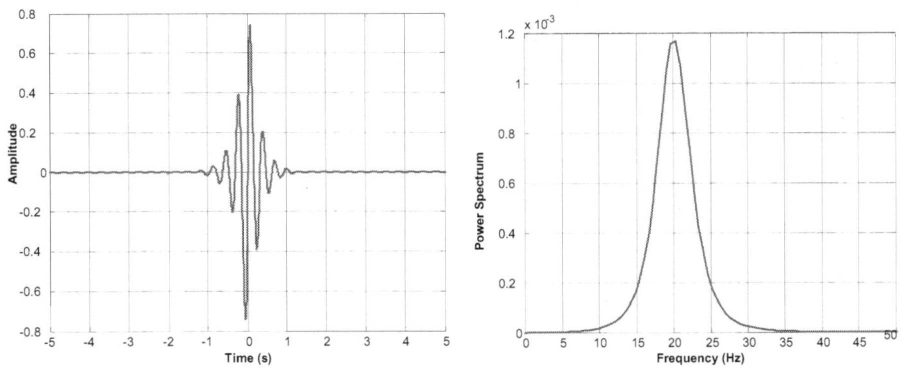

(a) (b)

Fig. 3. (a) the impulse wavelet time waveform, (b) its FFT-spectrum.

3.1.2 The wavelet de-noising autocorrelation technique

The proposed wavelet de-noising technique consists of the following steps:

a. Optimize the wavelet shape parameters (β and ω_c) based on maximization of the kurtosis of the signal- wavelet inner product.

It is possible to find optimal values of β and ω_c for a given vibration signal by adjusting the time-frequency resolution of the impulse wavelet to the decay rate and frequency of the impulses to be extracted.

Kurtosis is an indicator that reflects the "peakiness" of a signal, which is a property of the impulses and also it measures the divergence from a fundamental Gaussian distribution. A high kurtosis value indicates a high impulsive content of the signal with more sharpness in the signal intensity distribution. Figure 4 shows the kurtosis value and the intensity distribution for a white noise signal, pure impulsive signal, and impulsive signal mixed with noise.

The objective of the impulse wavelet shape optimization process is to determine the wavelet shape parameters (β and ω_c) which maximize the kurtosis of the wavelet transform output;

$$Optimal\,(\beta,\omega_c)=\max.\left[\frac{\sum_{n=1}^{N} WT^4(x(t),\psi_{\beta,\omega_c}(t))}{\left[\sum_{n=1}^{N} WT^2(x(t),\psi_{\beta,\omega_c}(t))\right]^2}\right] \tag{2}$$

The genetic algorithm with specifications shown in Table 1 is used to optimize the wavelet shape parameters using Equation 2 as the GA fitness function. A flowchart of the algorithm is shown in Figure 5.

Population size	*10*
Number of generations	*20*
Termination function	*Maximum generation*
Selection function	*Roulette wheel*
Cross-over function	*Arith-crossover*
Mutation function	*Uniform mutation*

Table 1. The applied GA parameters.

b. Apply the wavelet de-noising technique: which consists of:
   1. Perform a wavelet transform for the bearing vibration signal *x(t)* using the optimized wavelet,

$$WT\{x(t),a,b\} = <\psi_{a,b}.x(t)> = \frac{1}{\sqrt{a}}\int x(t)\ \Psi^*_{a,b}(t)\ dt \tag{3}$$

where <. > indicates the inner product, and the superscript asterisk '*' indicates the complex conjugate. The $\psi_{a,b}$ is a family of daughter wavelets derived from the mother wavelet $\psi(t)$ by continuously varying the scale factor a and the translation parameter b. The factor $1/\sqrt{a}$ is used to ensure energy preservation.

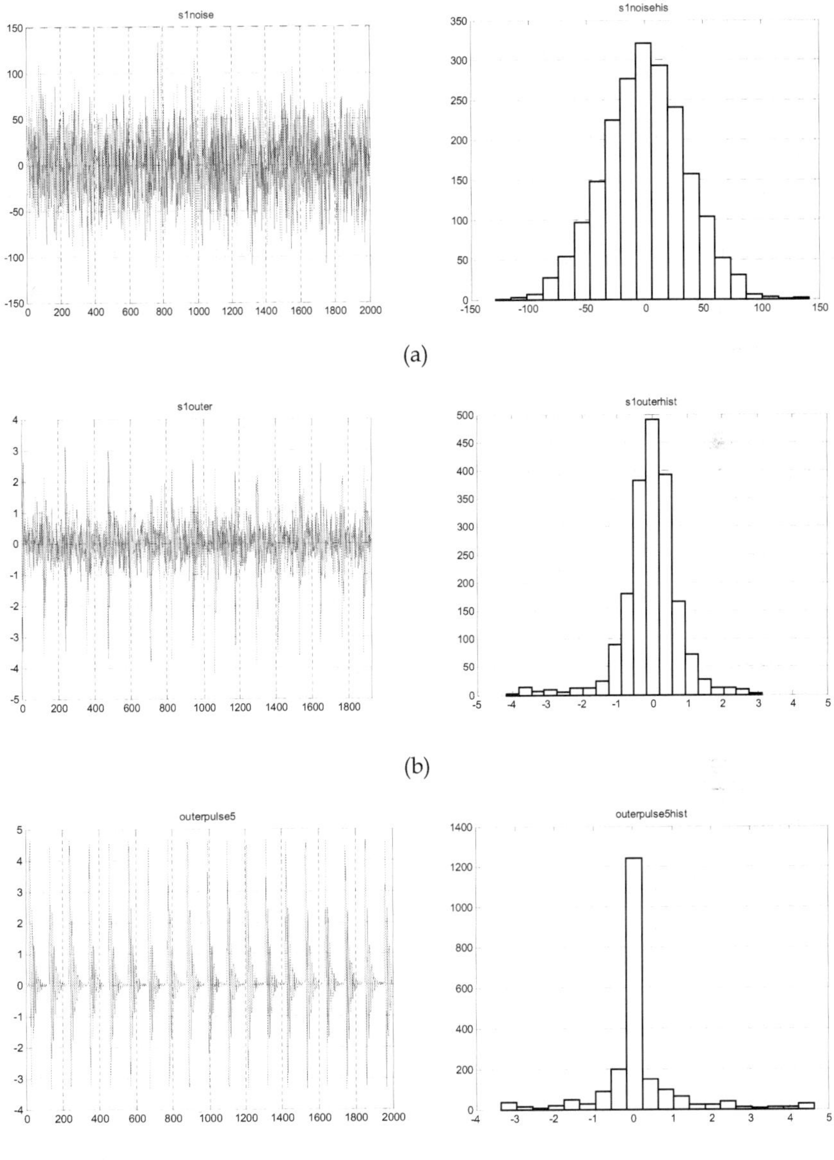

Fig. 4. (a) The noise signal (kurtosis=3.0843), (b) the overall vibration signal (kurtosis=7.7644), and (c) outer-race fault impulses (kurtosis=8.5312), with the corresponding intensity distribution curve.

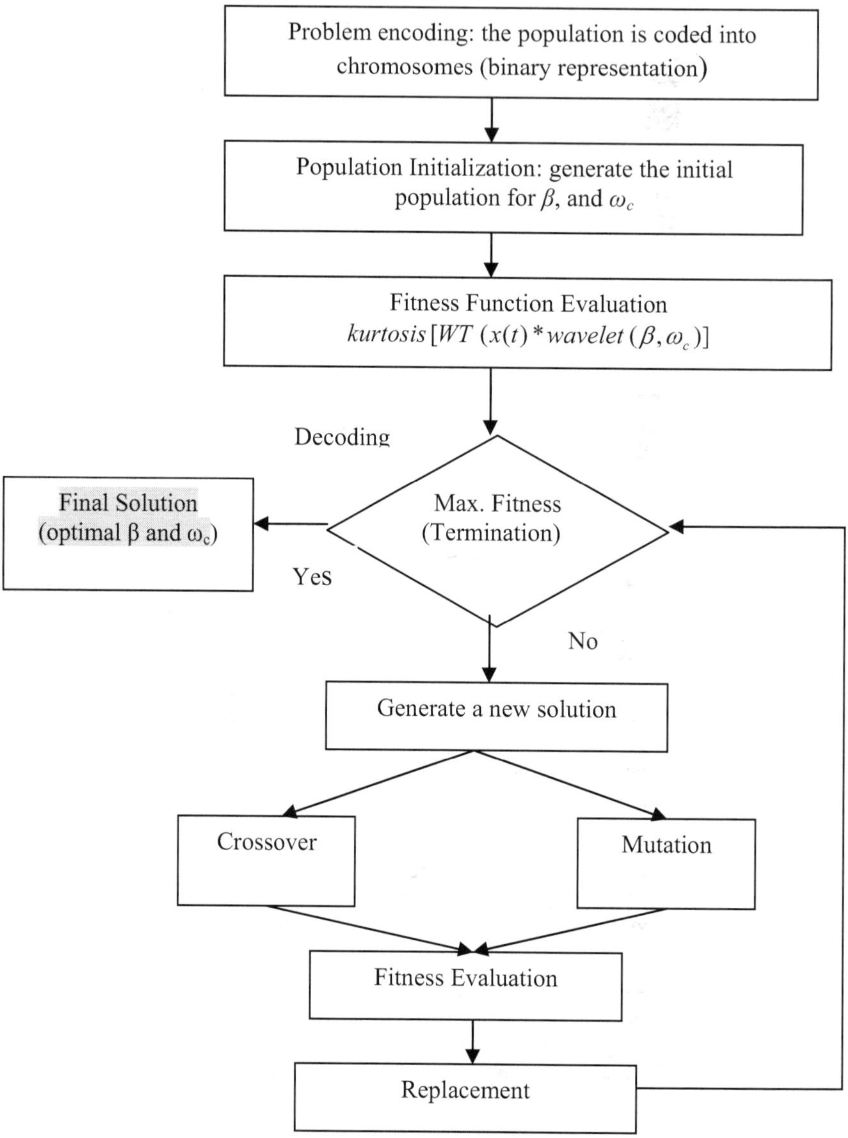

Fig. 5. Wavelet shape parameters optimization process using GA.

2. Shrink the wavelet coefficients expressed in Equation 3 by soft thresholding,

$$WT^{soft} = \begin{cases} 0 & |WT| < thr \\ sign(WT)\,(WT - thr) & |WT| > thr \end{cases} \tag{4}$$

using soft-threshold function (*thr)* proposed by YANG and REN (2004),

$$thr = e^{-[Max(|WT(a,b)|)^{\xi}]} - e^{-[Max(|WT(a,b)|)^{\xi}]} \tag{5}$$

where ξ>0 is parameter governing the shape of the threshold function.

3. Perform the inverse wavelet transform to reconstruct the signal using the shrunken wavelet coefficients.

$$\overset{*}{x}(t) = C_g^{-1} \int_{-\infty}^{\infty} WT^{soft}\ (a,t)\ \frac{da}{a^{3/2}} \tag{6}$$

c. Evaluate the auto-correlation function R_x (τ) for the de-noised signal x*(t) to estimate the periodicity of the extracted impulses

$$R_x(\tau) = E[\ \overset{*}{x}(t).\ \overset{*}{x}(t+\tau)] \tag{7}$$

where τ is the time lag, and *E [ ]* denotes ensemble average value of the quantity in square brackets.

3.1.3 Applications for bearing fault detection

To demonstrate the performance of the proposed approach, this section presents several application examples for the detection of localized bearing defects. In all the examples, the impulse wavelet has been used as the wavelet base-function. The wavelet parameters (damping factor and centre frequency) are optimized based on maximizing the kurtosis value for the wavelet coefficients as shown in Figure 6.

To evaluate the performance of the proposed method, the autocorrelation functions of the optimized impulse wavelet, impulse wavelet with non-optimized parameters, and the widely used Morlet wavelet are carried out and shown in Figure 7. The comparison of Figures 7a, b and c, shows the increased effectiveness of the optimized impulse wavelet over non-optimized impulse and Morlet wavelets for extraction of the bearing fault impulses and corresponding periodicity. Consequently, the performance of the bearing fault diagnosis process has been improved using the proposed technique.

(a) Simulated vibration data

For a rolling element bearing with specifications as given in Table 2, the calculated BCFs (appendix A) for a shaft rotational speed of 1797 rev/min are 107.36 Hz and 162.18 Hz for outer and inner-race faults respectively. Figure 8 (a and d) shows the time domain waveform of the simulated signals for the rolling bearing with outer and inner-race faults based on the bearing vibration mathematical model (Khalid F. Al-Raheem *et al.* 2008). The result of the wavelet de-noising method (wavelet transform, shrink the wavelet coefficients and take the inverse wavelet transform) for the rolling bearing with outer and inner race faults using the optimized impulse wavelet and the corresponding autocorrelation function are displayed in Figure 8 (b, c e and f). The results show that the signal noise has been diminished and the impulses generated by the faulty bearing are easy to identify in the wavelet de-noised signal. The impulse periodicity of 0.00975 sec (F_{BPO}=102.564 Hz) for outer-race fault and 0.006167 sec (F_{BPI}=162.153 Hz) for inner-race fault are effectively extracted through the auto-correlation of the de-noised signal and exactly match the theoretical calculation of the BCF.

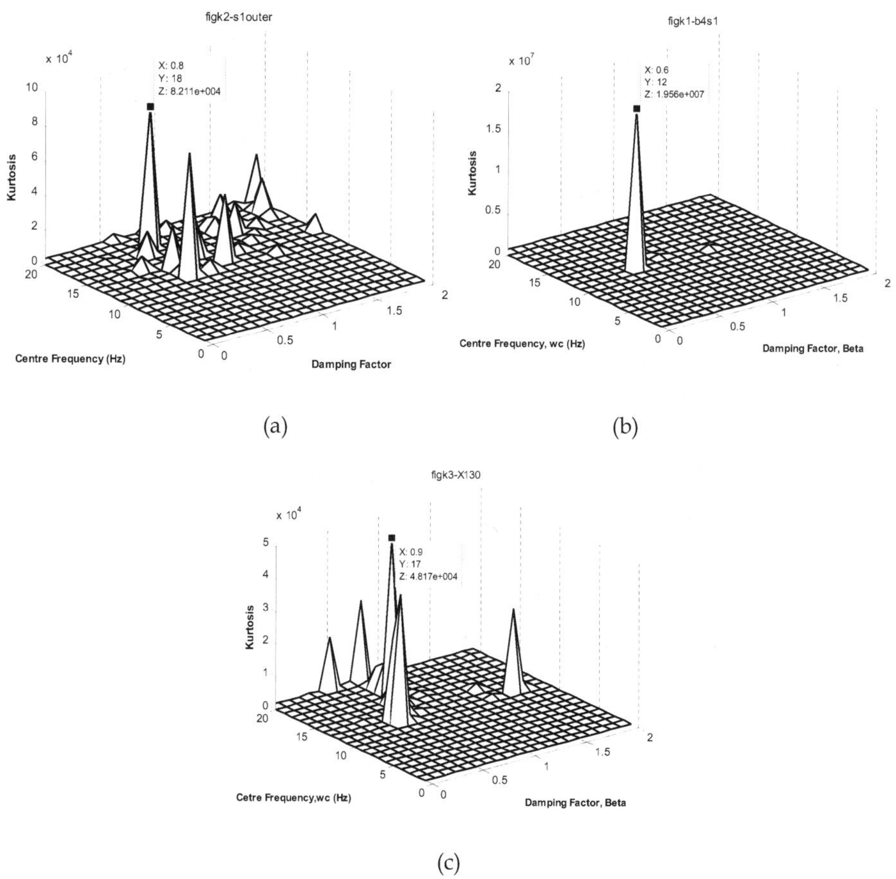

Fig. 6. The optimal values for Laplace wavelet parameters based on maximum kurtosis for,(a) simulated outer-race fault,(b) the measured outer-race fault,(c) the CWRU vibration data.

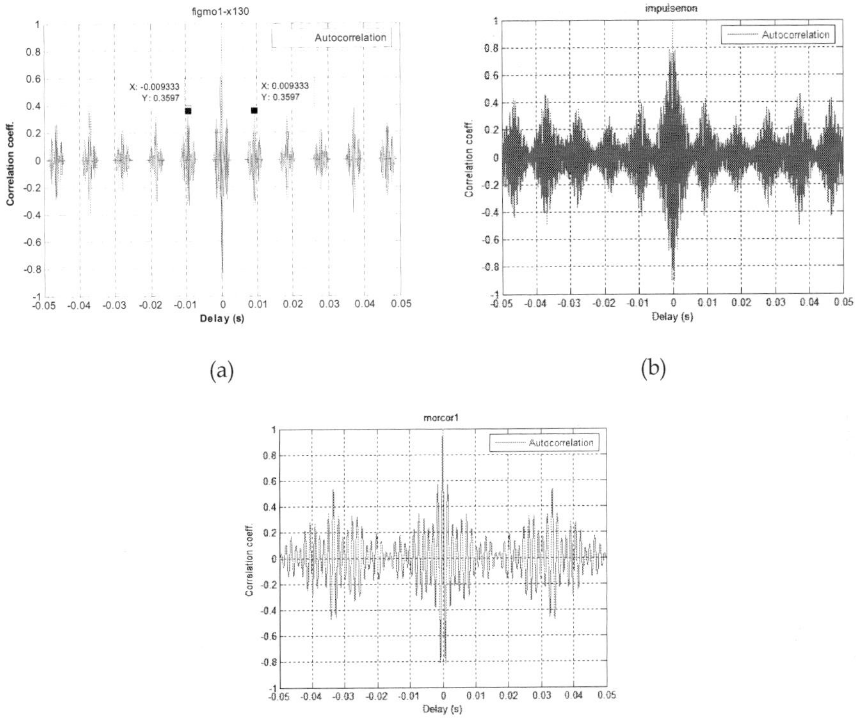

(a) (b)

(c)

Fig. 7. The autocorrelation function of the wavelet de-noised outer-race fault signal using (a) optimized impulse-wavelet, (b) non-optimized impulse-wavelet, and (c) Morlet-wavelet.

(b) Experimental vibration data

Based on the bearing parameters given in Table 2, the calculated outer race fault characteristic frequencies (F_{BPO}) for different shaft speeds are shown in Table 2.

D_p (mm)	D_b (mm)	N_b (ball)	α (degree)	Defect Frequencies (multiple of running speed, Hz)		
				Outer-race	Inner-race	Rolling element
51.16	11.9	8	0	3.069	4.930	4.066

Table 2. Bearing specification: Deep groove ball bearing RHP LJT 1 ¼.

Figures 9 to 11 show the application of the proposed wavelet de-noising technique for the rolling bearing with outer-race fault at different shaft rotational speed. The bearing fault impulses and corresponding periodicity are easily discerned in the wavelet de-noised signal and the de-noised autocorrelation function, respectively. Comparison of Figures 9 to 11 shows the sensitivity of the proposed de-noising technique to the variation of the F_{BPO} as a result of variation in the shaft rotational speed as listed in Table 3.

Shaft Speed (rev/min)	Calculated F_{BPO} (Hz)	Extracted Period (sec)	Extracted F_{BPO} (Hz)
983.887	50.32	0.020310	49.236
2080.28	106.4	0.009297	107.561
3541.11	181.12	0.005391	185.493

Table 3. The calculated and extracted (F_{BPO}) at different shaft rotational speeds.

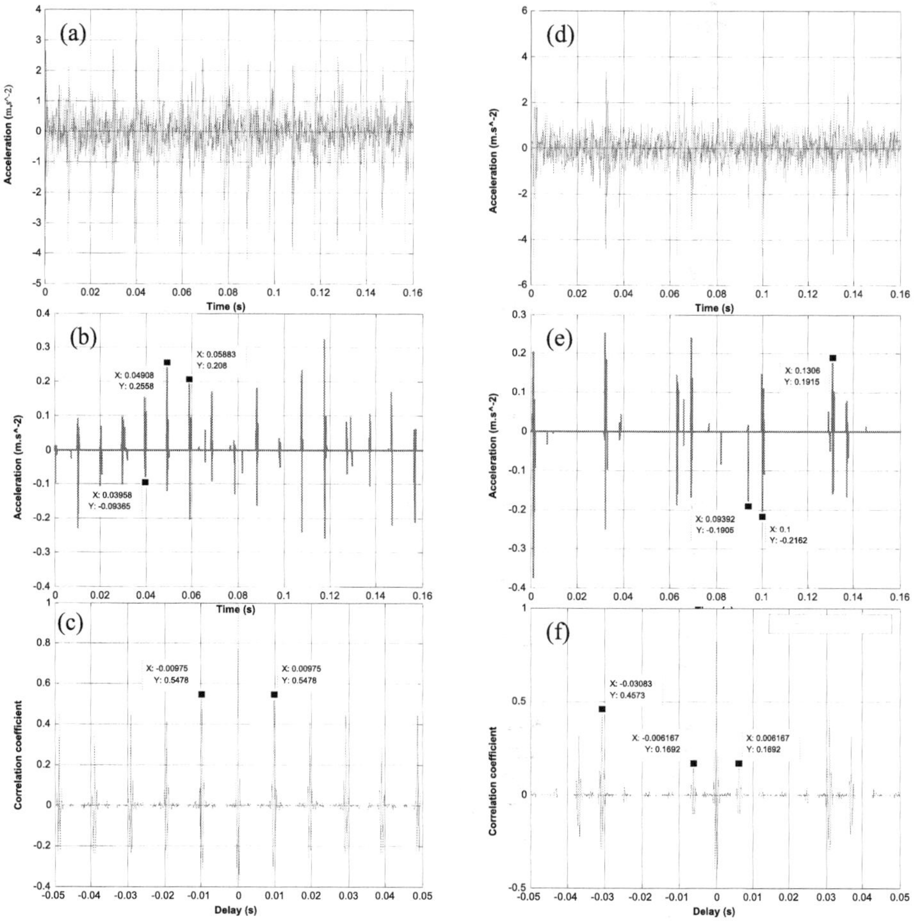

Fig. 8. The simulated vibration signal, the corresponding wavelet de-noised signal and the auto-correlation function $R_x(\tau)$ for bearing with outer-race fault (a, b and c), Inner-race fault (d, e and f) respectively.

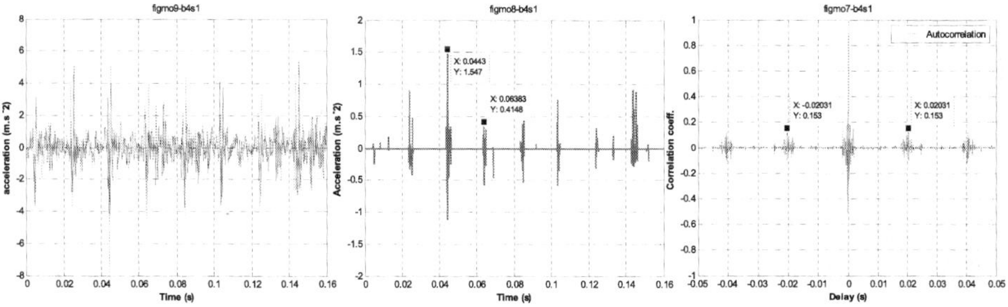

(a) (b) (c)

Fig. 9. (a) the collected vibration signal, (b) the corresponding wavelet de-noised signal, and (c) the auto-correlation function, for bearing with outer-race fault at shaft rotational speed of 983.887 rev/min.

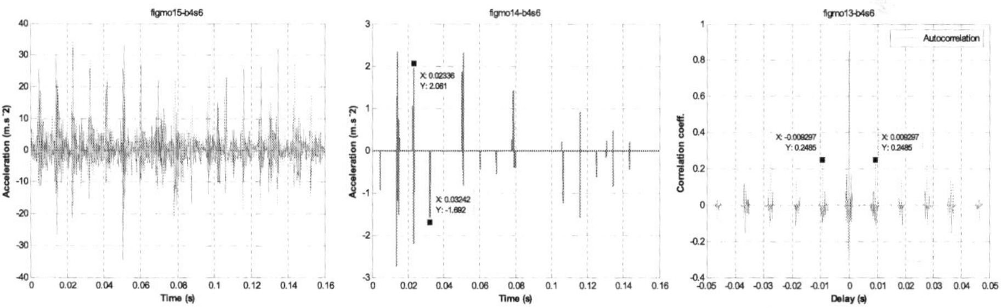

(a) (b) (c)

Fig. 10. (a) the collected vibration signal, (b) corresponding wavelet de-noised signal, and (c) auto-correlation function, for bearing with outer-race fault at shaft rotational speed of 2080.28 rev/min.

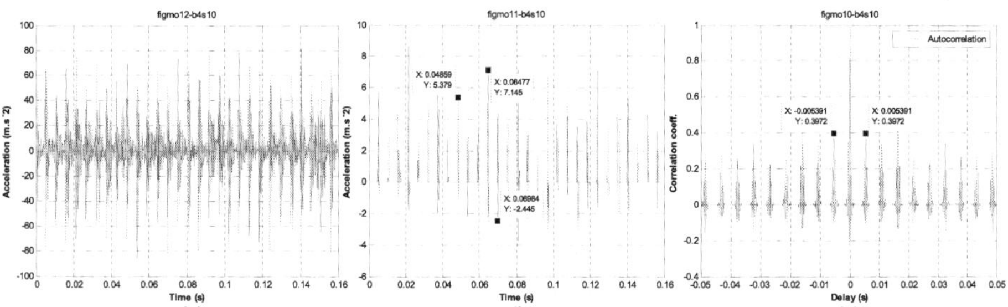

(a) (b) (c)

Fig. 11. (a) the collected vibration signal, (b) corresponding wavelet de-noised signal, and (c) auto-correlation function, for rolling with outer-race fault at shaft rotational speed of 3541.11 rev/min.

(c) CWRU vibration data

The vibration data for deep groove ball bearings (bearing specification shown in Table 4) with different faults were obtained from the Case Western Reserve University (CWRU) website (Bearing Data Center, seeded fault test data, *http://www.eecs.case.edu/*).

D_p (mm)	D_b (mm)	N_b (ball)	α (degree)	Defect Frequencies (multiple of running speed , Hz)		
				Outer-race	Inner-race	Rolling element
39.04	7.94	9	0	3.5858	5.4152	4.7135

Table 4. Bearing specification: Deep groove ball bearing SKF 6205.

At a shaft rotational speed of 1797 rev/min, the calculated BCF for the bearing specifications given in Table 4, are 107.36 Hz for an outer-race fault and, 162.185 Hz for an inner-race fault. The time course of the vibration signals for bearing with outer and inner race faults, the corresponding wavelet de-noised signal and the auto-correlation function are depicted in Figure 12. The autocorrelation functions of the de-noised signal reveal a periodicity of 0.009333 sec (F_{BPO}=107.14 Hz) and 0.006167 sec (F_{BPI}=162.153 Hz) for outer and inner race fault respectively, which are very close to the calculated BCF.

3.2 The wavelet envelope power spectrum

To avoid the wavelet admissibility condition (e.g. double sided wavelet function) which is essential in the inverse wavelet transforms (Mallat, 1999). And to be able to use a single side wavelet function which provides more similarity with the bearing fault pulses. A second approach for bearing fault detection based on the analysis of the wavelet coefficients is developed in this section. The WT coefficients using a single-sided function so called Laplace wavelet have been analyzed in frequency domain using a novel wavelet envelope power spectrum technique.

3.2.1 Laplace wavelet function

The Laplace wavelet is a complex, single side damped exponential function formulated as an impulse response of a single mode system to be similar to data features commonly encountered in health monitoring tasks. It has been applied to the vibration analysis of an aircraft for aerodynamic and structural testing (Lind and Brenner, 1998), and to diagnose the wear of the intake valve of an internal combustion engine (Yanyang *et al.*, 2005).

The Laplace wavelet is a complex, analytical and single-sided damped exponential given by,

$$\begin{aligned} \Psi(t) &= A\, e^{-\left(\frac{\beta}{\sqrt{1-\beta^2}}+j\right)\omega_c t} \qquad \text{if} \qquad t \geq 0 \\ \Psi(t) &= 0 \qquad\qquad\qquad \text{where} \qquad t < 0 \end{aligned} \tag{8}$$

Where β is the damping factor and ω_c is the wavelet centre frequency. Figure 13 shows the Laplace wavelet, its real part, imaginary part, and spectrum. The wavelet shape parameters β *and* ω_c have been optimized using GA based on the maximization of the kurtosis value, Equation 2.

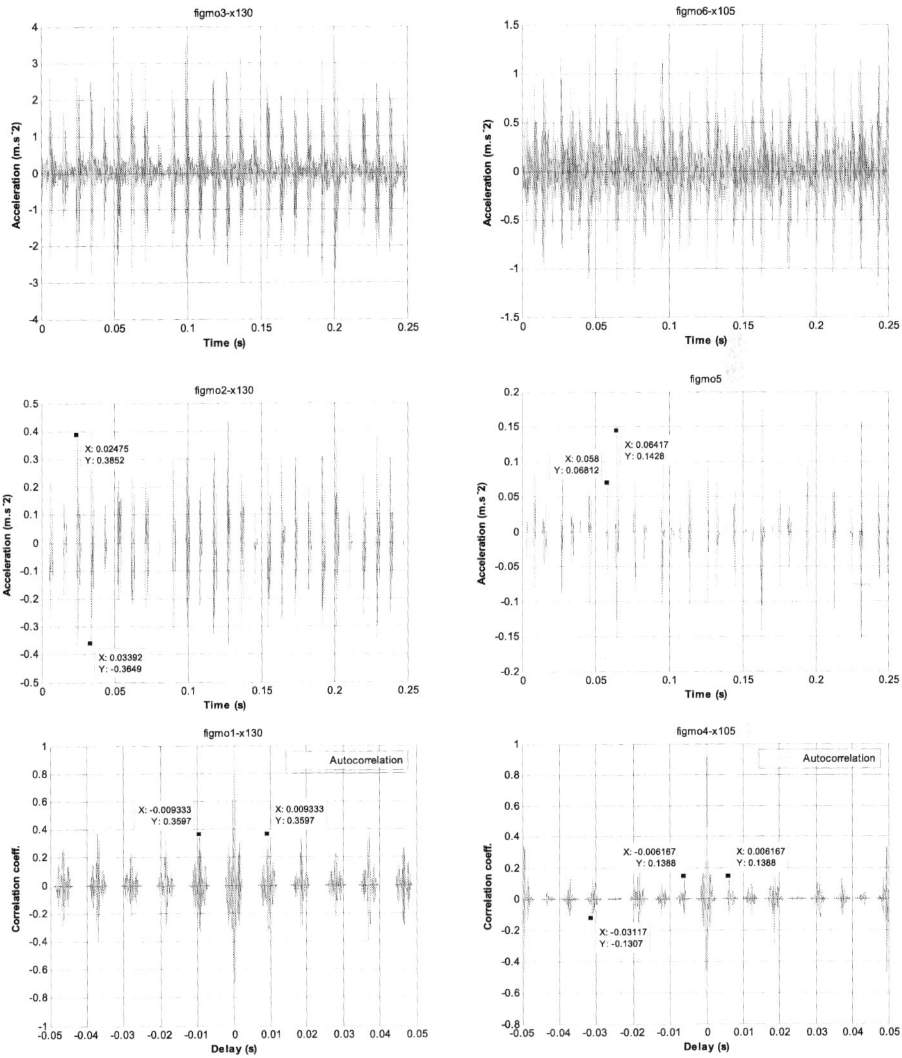

(a) (b)

Fig. 12. The CWRU collected vibration signal, corresponding wavelet de-noised signal and auto-correlation function, respectively for bearing with (a) outer-race fault, and (b) inner-race fault.

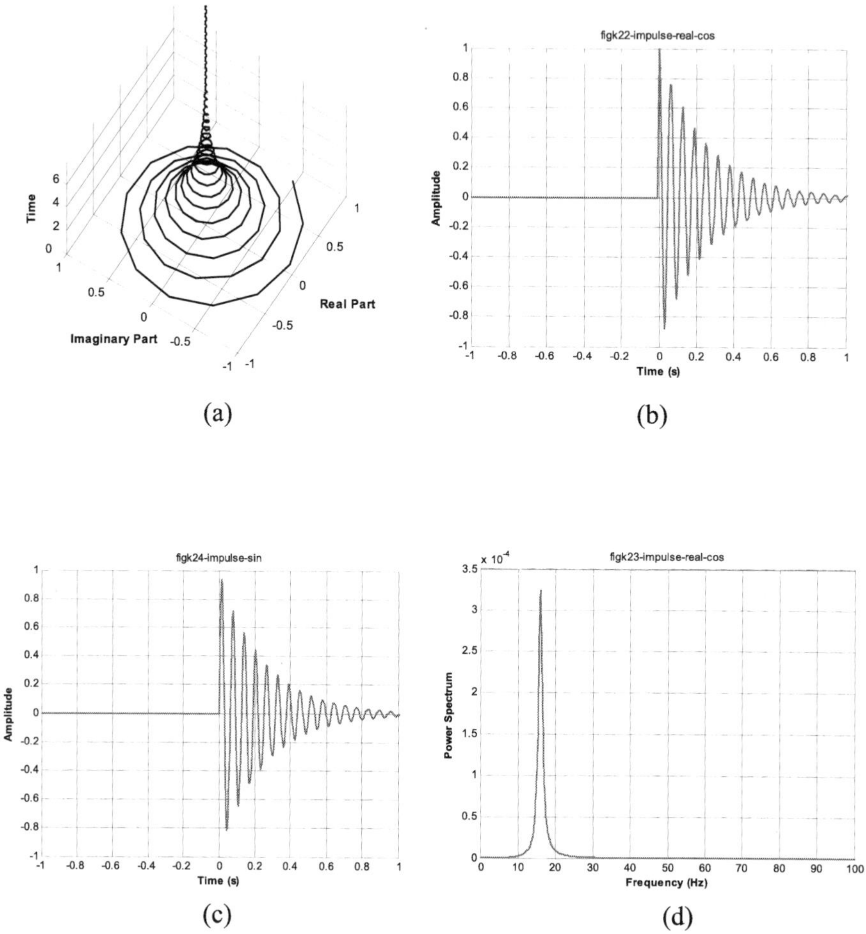

Fig. 13. (a) the Laplace wavelet, (b) the real part, (c) the imaginary part, and (d) wavelet spectrum.

To show the effectiveness of the proposed Laplace wavelet over the widely used Morlet wavelet, Figure 14 shows the scale-kurtosis distribution of the wavelet transform using Morlet and Laplace wavelets respectively, for different bearing conditions. The comparison of the two wavelets indicates the high sensitivity of the Laplace wavelet over the Morlet wavelet for bearing fault diagnosis.

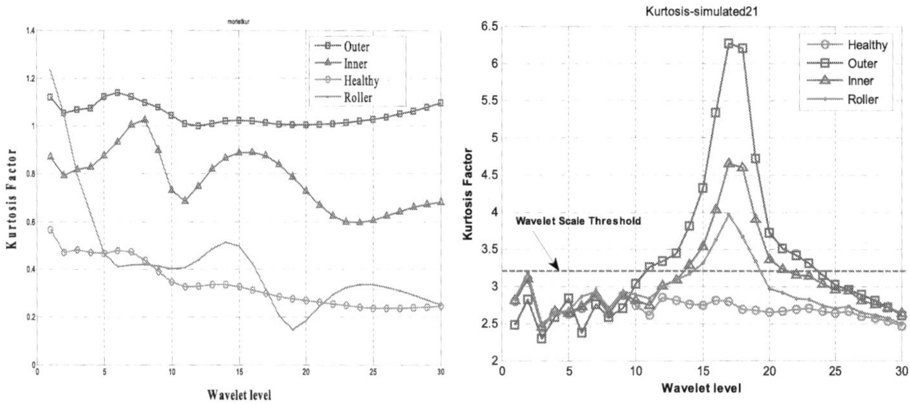

(a) (b)

Fig. 14. The Kurtosis distribution for the wavelet transforms scales using (a) Morlet wavelet, and (b) Laplace wavelet.

3.2.2 Enveloped wavelet power spectrums

The vibration signal of a faulty rolling bearing can be viewed as a carrier signal at a resonant frequency of the bearing housing (high frequency) modulated by a decaying envelope. The frequency of interest in the detection of bearing defects is the modulating frequency (low frequency). The goal of the enveloping approach is to replace the oscillation caused by each impact with a single pulse over the entire period of the impact.

The WT of a finite energy signal $x(t)$, with the mother wavelet $\psi(t)$, is the inner product of $x(t)$ with a scaled and conjugate wavelet $\psi^*_{a,b}$.

Since the analytical and complex wavelet is employed to calculate the wavelets transform, the result of the wavelet transform is also an analytical signal,

$$\begin{aligned} WT\{x(t),a,b\} &= < x(t),\ \psi_{a,b}(t) > = \frac{1}{\sqrt{a}} \int x(t)\ \Psi^*_{a,b}(t)\ dt \\ &= \mathrm{Re}[WT(a,b)] + j\,\mathrm{Im}[\ WT(a,b)] = A(t)\,e^{i\,\theta(t)} \end{aligned} \tag{9}$$

The time-varying function $A(t)$ is the instantaneous Enveloped Wavelet Transform (*EWT*) which extracts the slow time variation of the signal (modulating frequency) is given by,

$$A(t) = EWT(a,b) = \sqrt{\{\mathrm{Re}[WT\ (a,b)]\}^2 + \{\mathrm{Im}[\ WT\ (a,b)]\}^2} \tag{10}$$

To extract the frequency content of the enveloped correlation coefficients, the scale Wavelet Power Spectrum (*WPS*) (energy per unit scale) is given by,

$$WPS(a,\omega) = \int_{-\infty}^{\infty} |SEWT(a,\omega)|^2 \, d\omega \tag{11}$$

where *SEWT (a, ω)* is the Fourier Transform of *EWT(a,b)*.

The total energy of the signal *x(t)*,

$$TWPS = \int |x(t)|^2 \, dt \; = \frac{1}{2\pi} \int WPS(a,\omega) \, da \tag{12}$$

3.2.3 Implementation of WPS for bearing fault detection

To demonstrate the performance of the proposed approach, this section presents several application examples for the detection of localized bearing defects. In all the examples, the Laplace wavelet is used as a WT base-function. The wavelet parameters (damping factor and centre frequency) are optimized based on maximizing the kurtosis value for the wavelet coefficients.

(a) Simulated vibration data

Using a rolling element bearing with specification shown in Table 2, the scale-wavelet power spectrum comparison for the Laplace-wavelet and widely used Morlet wavelet was carried out, Figure 15. It can be found that the amplitude of the power spectrum is greater for the faulty bearing than the normal one, and the power spectrum is concentrated in the scale interval of [15-20] for the Laplace-wavelet compared with the distributed power spectrum over a wide scale range for the Morlet wavelet. That shows the improved effectiveness of the Laplace wavelet over the Morlet wavelet for bearing fault impulses extraction.

The FFT-Spectrum, envelope spectrum using Hilbert Transform and the Laplace wavelet transform envelope spectrum for the simulated outer-race, inner-race and rolling element faults vibration signals at rotational speed of 1797 rev/min, are shown in Figure 16. The results show that the BCFs are unspecified in the FFT-Spectrum and are not clearly defined in the envelope power spectrum but are clearly identified in the Laplace-wavelet power spectrum for both outer, inner race and rolling element faults, Figure 17.

The TWPS effectively extracts the fault frequencies of 105.5 Hz, 164.1 Hz and 141.4 with their harmonics for outer-race, inner-race and rolling element faults, respectively, which are very close to the calculated frequencies (F_{BPO}= 107.364 Hz, F_{BPI}= 162.185 Hz and $2F_B$= 141.169 Hz). The side bands at the rotational speed can be recognized for inner race and rolling element faults as a result of amplitude modulation.

To evaluate the robustness of the proposed technique to extract the BCF for different signal to noise ratio (SNR) , and randomness in the impulses period (τ) as a result of slip variation, Figure 18 shows the *TWPS* for outer-race fault simulated signals for different values of SNR, and τ as a percentage of the pulse period (*T*).

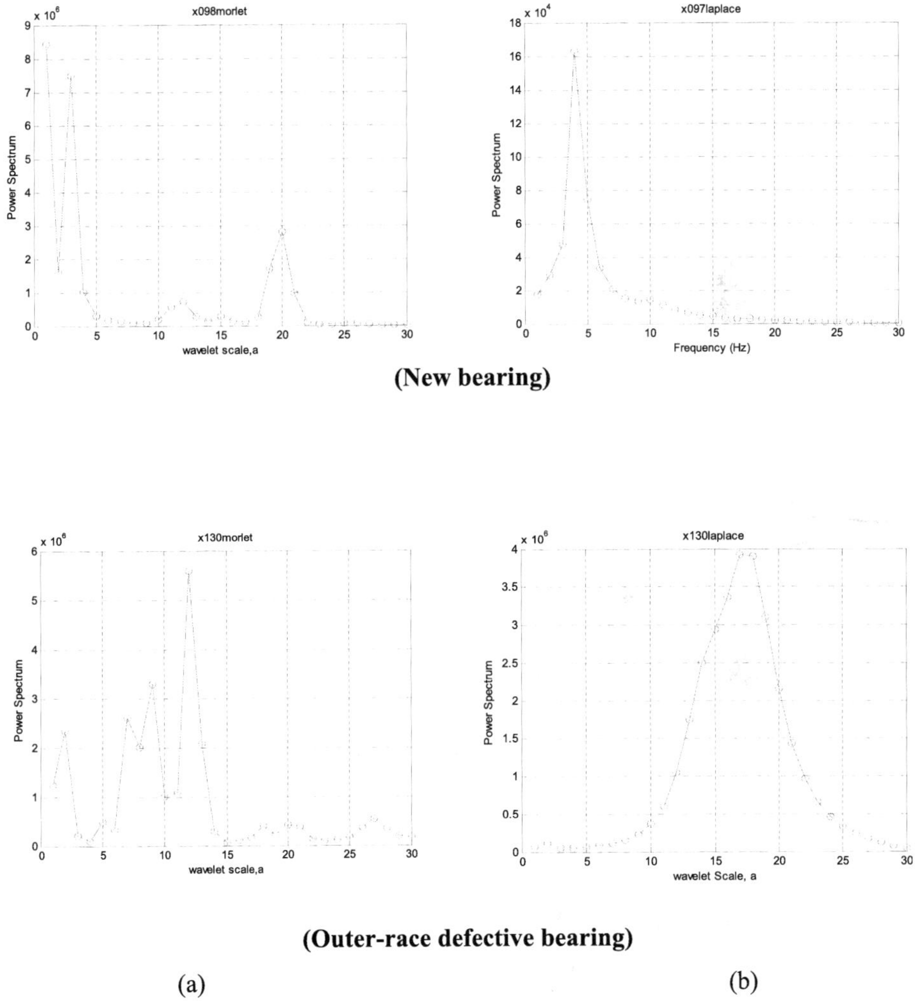

Fig. 15. The wavelet-level power spectrum using (a) Morlet-wavelet, (b) Laplace-wavelet for new and outer-race defective bearing.

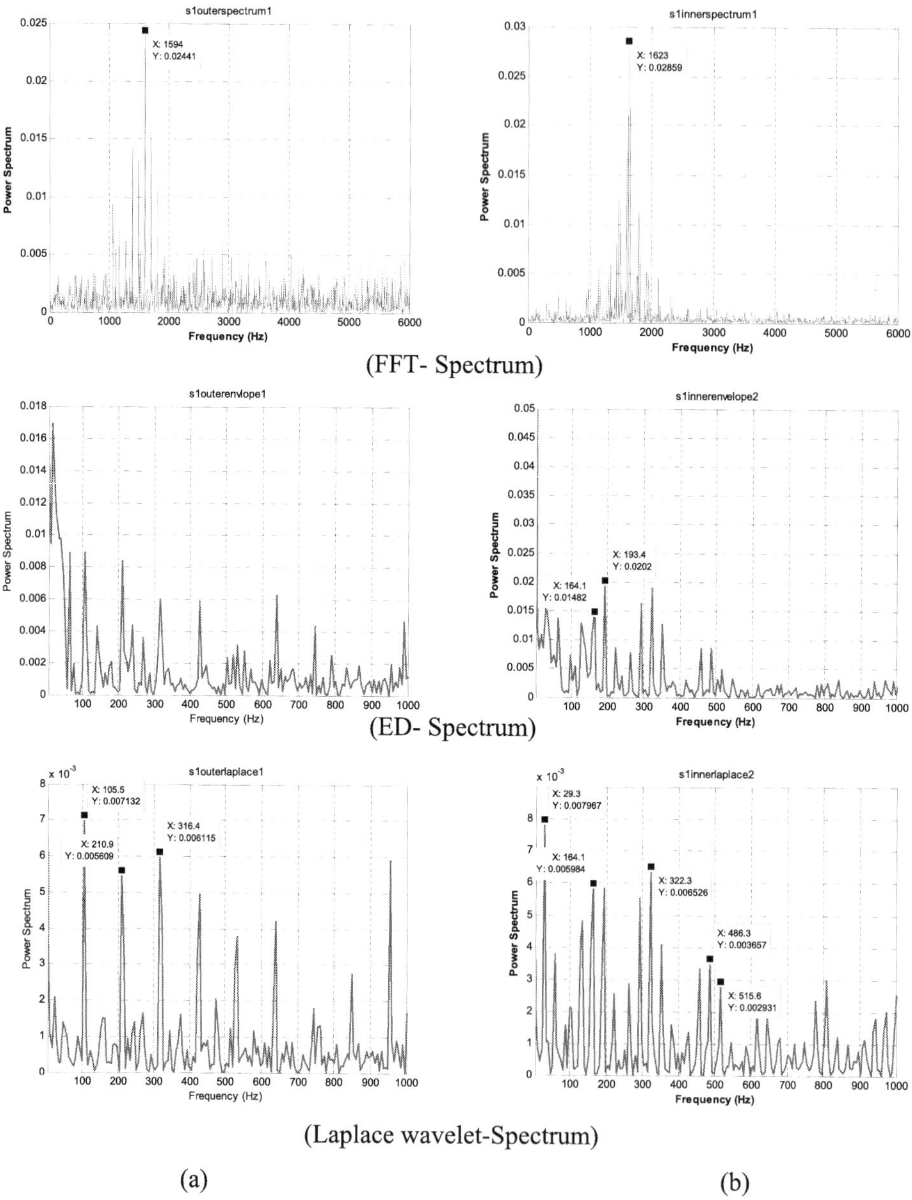

Fig. 16. The simulated vibration signal power spectrum, envelope power spectrum, and Laplace-wavelet transform power spectrum respectively, for rolling bearing with (a) Outer-race fault and, (b) Inner-race fault.

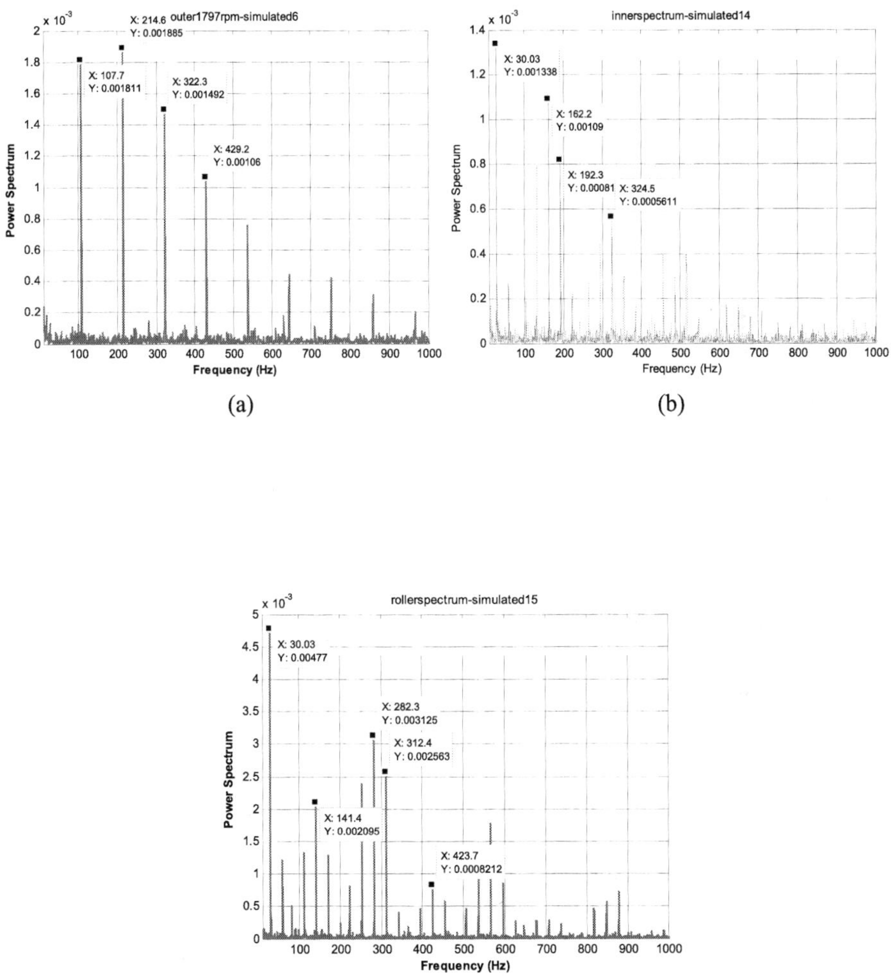

Fig. 17. The Laplace envelope spectrum of the simulated vibration signal for bearing with (a) outer-race fault, (b) inner-race fault, and (c) rolling element fault, at speed of 1797 rev/min.

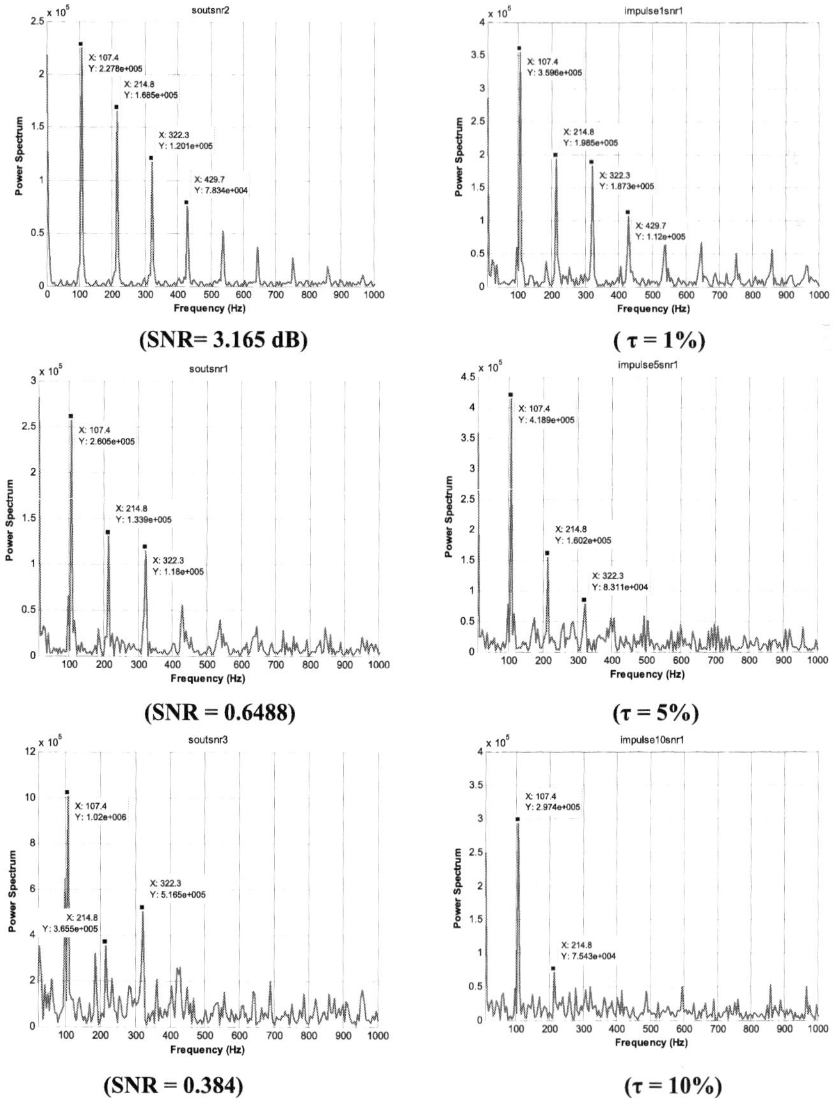

(a) (b)

Fig. 18. The TWPS for Bearing with outer-race fault for different (a) SNR, and (b) slip variation (τ).

(b) Experimental vibration data

For angular contact ball bearings with specifications as given in Table 2, the calculated fault frequencies for different shaft rotational speeds are shown in Table 3.With application of the

TWPS, the power spectrum peak values at the location of the outer-race characteristic frequency and its harmonics are easily defined and match the calculated F_{BPO}, Figure 19. Applied to different shaft rotational speed, Figure 20 shows that the TWPS is sensitive to the variation of the fault frequencies as a result of variation in the shaft rotational speeds, Table 5.

The TWPS for bearings with inner and rolling element faults are shown in Figures 21 and 22, respectively. The fault frequencies are clearly extracted at 126 Hz for inner race fault and 140.1 Hz for rolling element fault which are very close to the calculated fault frequencies.

Outer-Race Fault		
Shaft Speed, rev/min	Calculated F_{BPO}, Hz	TWPS peak , Hz
1000	90.96	91
1250	113.70	112
1500	136.44	135
1750	159.18	166
2000	181.92	182
2500	227.40	226

Table 5. The calculated and extracted (F_{BPO}) at different shaft rotational speeds.

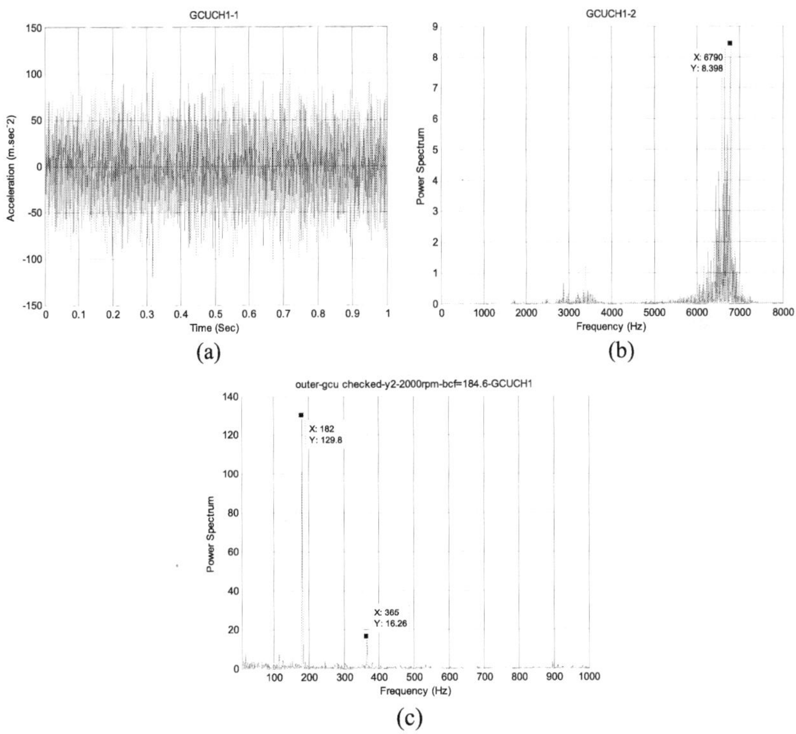

Fig. 19. The measured bearing vibration signal (a) the FFT spectrum (b) and the Laplace wavelet envelope spectrum (c) for bearing with outer race fault at speed of 2000 rev/min (calculated F_{BPO}=181.92 Hz).

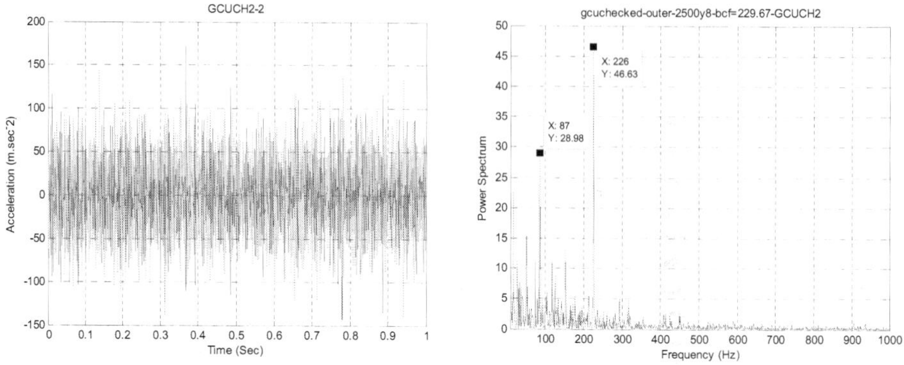

(a) 2500 rev/min

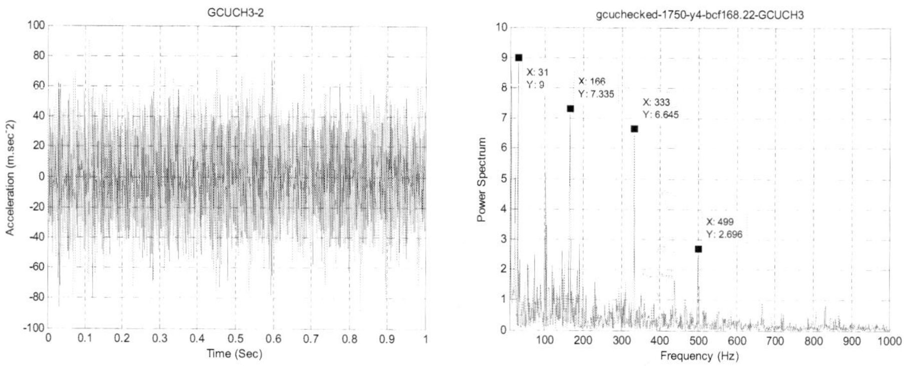

(b) 1750 rev/min

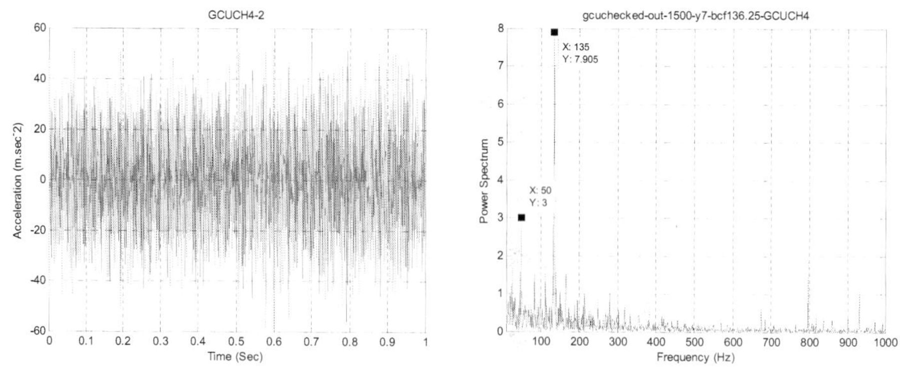

(c) 1500 rev/min

Fig. 20. (a-e) the bearing vibration signals and the corresponding Laplace envelope spectrum column for bearing with outer race fault at different rotational speeds.

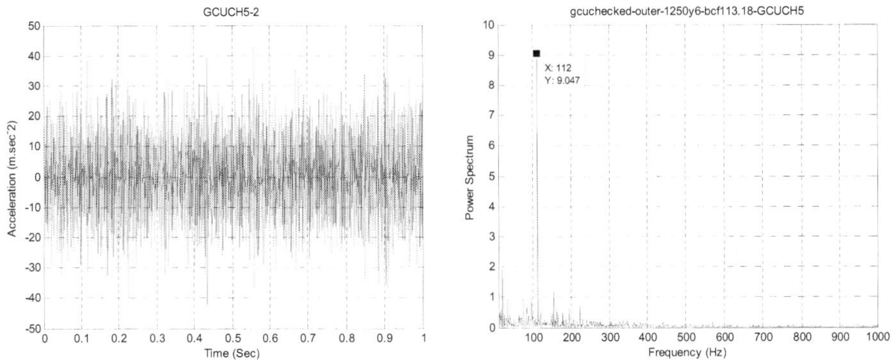

(d) 1250 rev/min

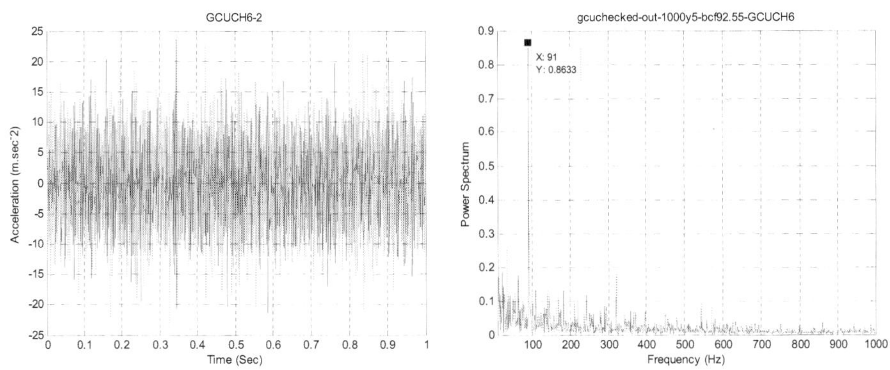

(e) 1000 rev/min

Fig. 20. (cont.) (a-e) the bearing vibration signals and the corresponding Laplace envelope spectrum column for bearing with outer race fault at different rotational speeds.

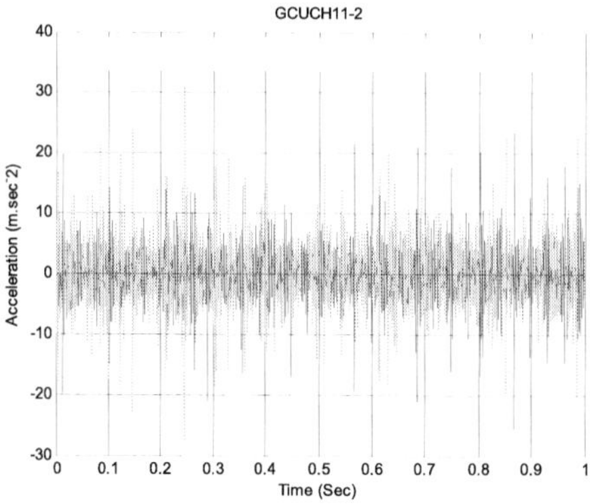

(a)

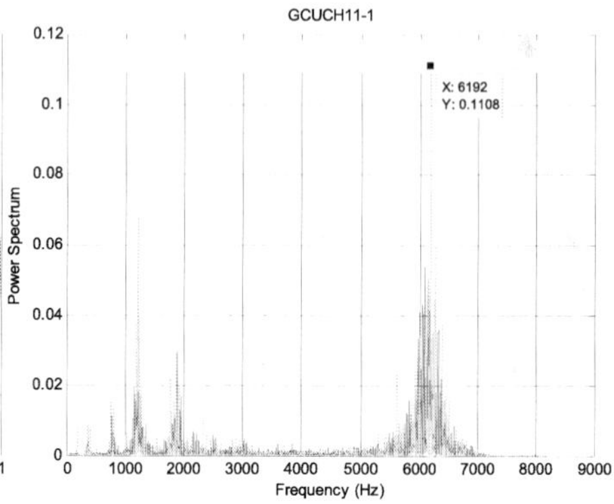

(b)

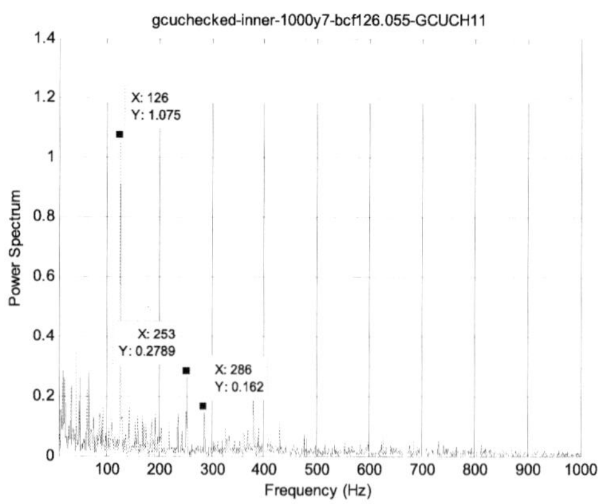

(c)

Fig. 21. The bearing vibration signal (a), the FFT spectrum (b) and the Laplace wavelet envelope spectrum (c) for bearing with inner race fault at speed of 1000 rev/min (the calculated F_{BPI}=125.70 Hz).

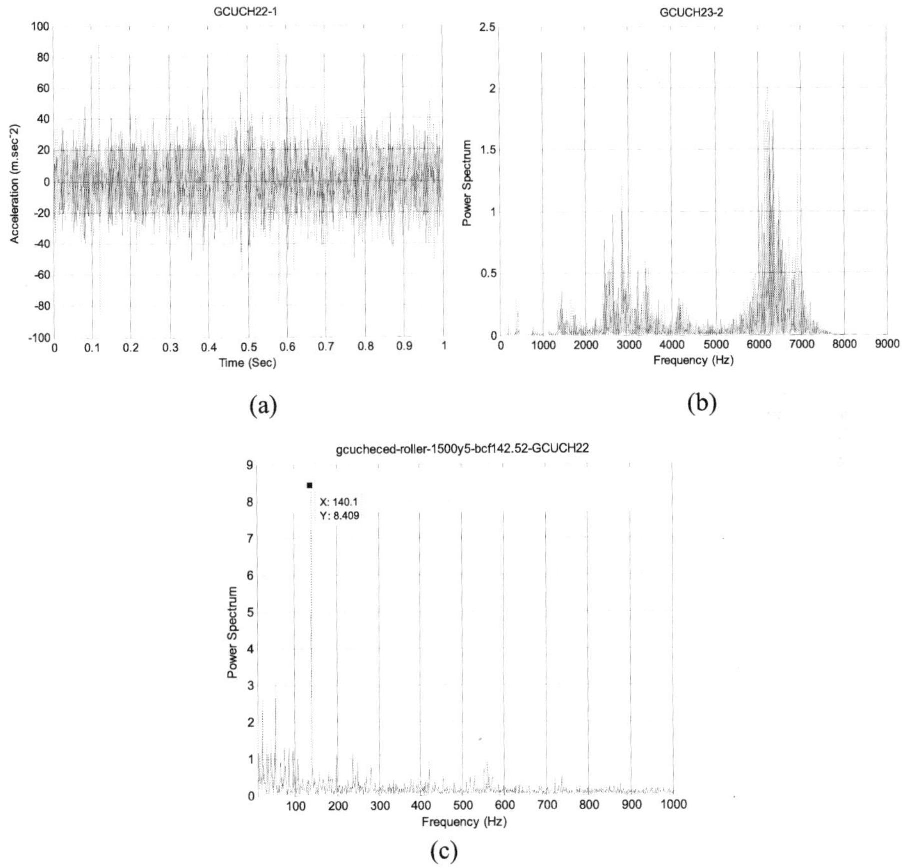

Fig 22. The bearing vibration signal (a), the FFT spectrum (b) and the Laplace wavelet envelope spectrum (c) for bearing with rolling element fault at speed of 1500 rev/min (the calculated, $2F_B$=142.74 Hz).

(c) CWRU vibration data

The time course of the vibration signals for a normal bearing and bearings with outer race, inner race and rolling element faults at a shaft rotational speed of 1797 rev/min with its corresponding TWPS are shown in Figures 23 to 26, respectively.

The TWPS for the vibration data shows spectral peaks at 106.9 Hz, 161.1 Hz and 141.166 Hz and their harmonics for outer race, inner race and rolling element faults, respectively. The sidebands at shaft speed (30 Hz) as a result of amplitude modulation are shown for inner and rolling element faults.

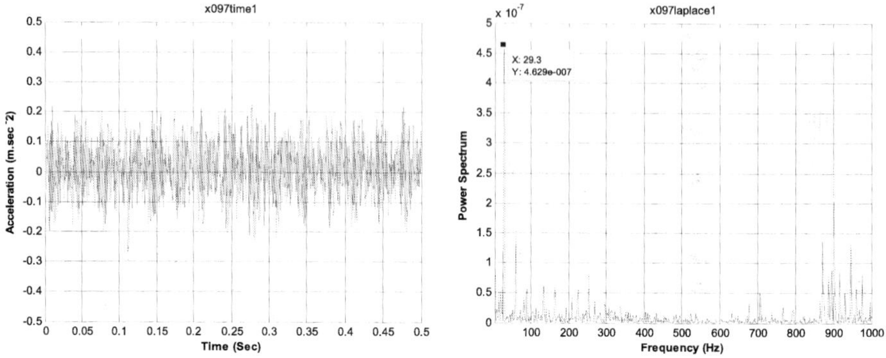

(a) (b)

Fig. 23. The vibration signal (a), and the corresponding TWPS (b) for new rolling bearing (CWRU data).

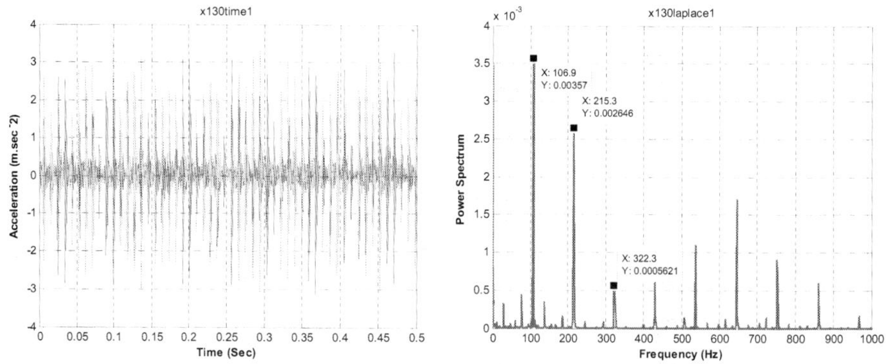

(a) (b)

Fig. 24. The vibration signal (a) and, the corresponding TWPS (b) for rolling bearing with outer-race fault (F_{BPO}= 107.36 Hz).

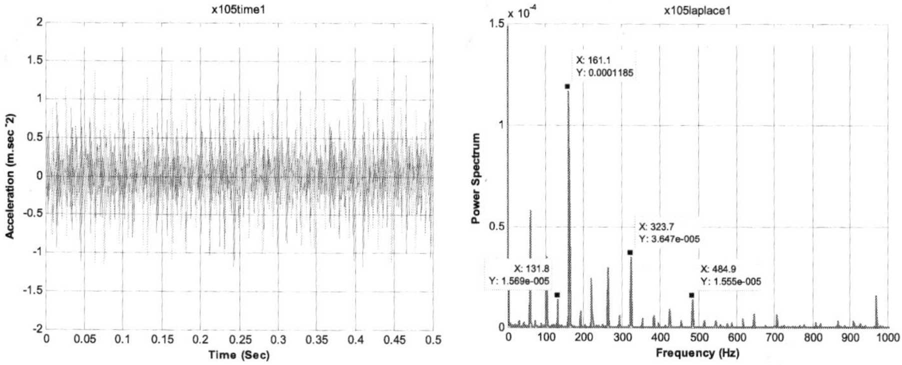

(a) (b)

Fig. 25. The vibration signal (a), and the corresponding TWPS (b) for rolling bearing with inner-race fault (F_{BPI}= 162.185 Hz).

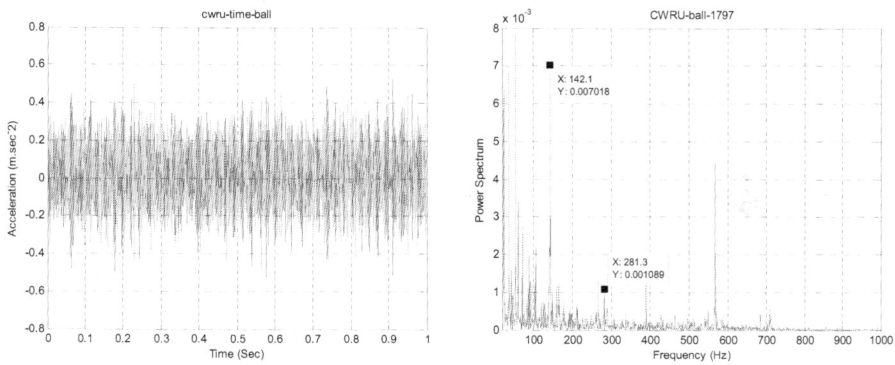

(a) (b)

Fig. 26. The vibration signal (a), and the corresponding TWPS (b) for rolling bearing with rolling element fault ($2F_B$= 141.166 Hz).

4. Automatic rolling bearing fault diagnosis

The interpolation of a CWT can certainly be accomplished by operator visual inspection with some practice and experience. However, computerized inspection is recommended to meet increasing demand for the on-line automated condition monitoring applications.

In this section a new technique for automated detection and diagnosis of rolling bearing conditions is applied. To reduce the number of the ANN inputs and speed up the training process which make the classification procedure suitable for on-line condition monitoring and diagnostics, the most dominant Laplace-wavelet transform scales based on scale-kurtosis level, which represent the most correlated features to the bearing condition, are selected for feature extraction. The extracted features in the time and frequency domains are used as the ANN input vectors for the rolling bearing condition identification. The ANN classifier parameters (learning rate parameter and number of the hidden nodes) are optimized using GA by minimizing the mean square error (MSE).

4.1 Feature extraction using laplace wavelet analysis

The predominant Laplace wavelet transform scales (most informative levels) based on the scale-kurtosis value have been selected for feature extraction. Figure 27 shows the scale-kurtosis distribution for different bearing conditions with the corresponding wavelet scale threshold. By using the maximum kurtosis for a normal bearing as a threshold level (the dotted line in Figure 27) for the wavelet scales, it could be seen that the scales range of 12-22 are the mostly dominant scales which can reveal the rolling bearing condition sufficiently.

The extracted features for the dominant scales are:

1. *Time domain features*: this includes the Root Mean Square (RMS), Standard Deviation (SD), and Kurtosis factor.
2. *Frequency domain features*: this includes the WPS peak frequency (f_{max}) to the shaft rotational frequency (f_{rpm}) ratio, and the WPS maximum amplitude (A_{max}) to the overall amplitude (Sum (A_i)) ratio.

The extracted features were linearly normalized between [0, 1] using the relationship: $x_{nor} = [(x-x_{min})/x_{max})]$, and used as input vectors to the neural network.

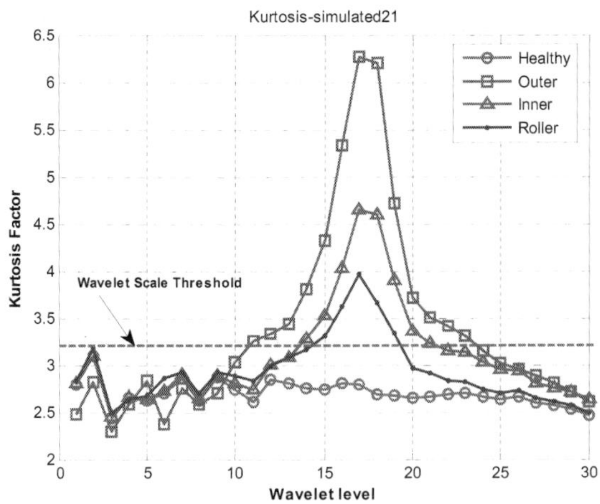

Fig. 27. The Kurtosis distribution for the Laplace wavelet transforms scales using Laplace wavelet.

4.2 Neural networks scheme

A feed-forward multi-layer perceptron (MLP) neural network has been developed, which consists of three layers. The input layer of five source nodes represents the normalized features extracted from the predominant Laplace wavelet transform scales. The hidden layer with four computation nodes has been used. The number of the hidden nodes is optimized using a genetic algorithm by minimization of Mean Square Error (MSE) between the actual network outputs and the corresponding target values. The output layer with four nodes represents the different bearing working conditions to be identified by the neural network.

The four-digit output target nodes that need to be mapped by the ANN are distinguished as: (1, 0, 0, 0) for a new bearing (NB), (0, 1, 0, 0) for a bearing with outer race fault (ORF), (0, 0, 1, 0) for an inner race fault (IRF), and (0, 0, 0, 1) for a rolling element fault (REF). Figure 6-28a depicts the overall architecture of the proposed diagnostic system.

The training sample vector comprises the extracted features and the ideal target outputs expressed by $[x_1, x_2, x_3, x_4, x_5, T]^T$, where x_1-x_5 represent the input extracted features, and T is the four-digit target output.

The input vector is transformed to an intermediate vector of hidden variables h using the activation function f_1, Figure 2-28b. The output h_j of the jth node in the hidden layer is obtained as follows,

$$h_j = f_1 \left(\sum_{i=1}^{N=5} w_{i,j} x_i + b_j\right) \tag{13}$$

Where b_j and $w_{i,j}$ represent the bias and the weight of the connection between the jth node in the hidden layer and the ith input node respectively.

The output vector $O = (o_1\ o_2 \ldots o_M)$ of the network is obtained from the vector of the intermediate variable h through a similar transformation using activation function f_2 at the output layer, Figure 2-28c. For example, the output of neuron k can be expressed as follows:

$$O_k = f_2 \left(\sum_{l=1}^{M=4} w_{l,k}\, h_l + b_k\right) \tag{14}$$

The training of an MLP network is achieved by modifying the connection weights and biases iteratively to optimize a performance criterion. One of the widely used performance criteria is the minimization of the mean square error (MSE) between the actual network output (O_k) and the corresponding target values (T) in the training set. The most commonly used training algorithms for MLP are based on back-propagation (BP). The BP adapts a gradient-descent approach by adjusting the ANN connection weights. The MSE is propagated backward through the network and is used to adjust the connection weights between the layers, thus improving the network classification performance. The process is repeated until the overall MSE value drops below some pre-determined threshold (stopping criterion). After the training process, the ANN weights are fixed and the system is deployed to solve the bearing condition identification problem using unseen vibration data.

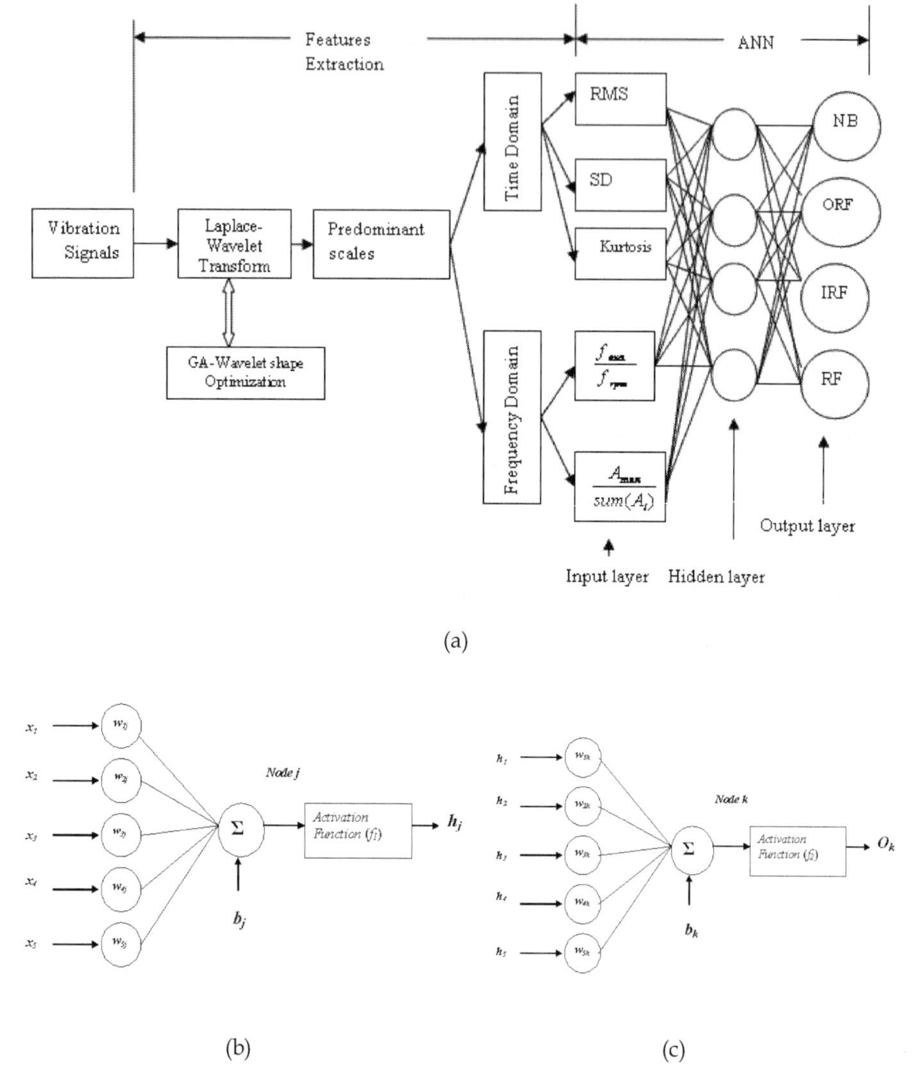

Fig. 28. (a) the applied diagnosis system, (b) the input and hidden layer, and (c) the hidden and output layer.

The ANN was created, trained and tested using MATLAB Neural Network Toolbox with Levenberg-Marquarat Back-propagation (LMBP) training algorithm. In this work, A MSE of 10E-20, a minimum gradient of 10E-10 and maximum iteration (epochs) of 1000 were used. The training process would stop if any of these conditions were met. The initial weights and biases of the network were randomly generated by the program.

4.3 Implementation of WPS –ANN for bearing fault classification

The derived WT-ANN fault classification technique was validated through real and simulated rolling element bearing vibration signals. MATLAB software has been used for the wavelet feature extraction and ANN classification based on the code flowchart shown in Figure 29.

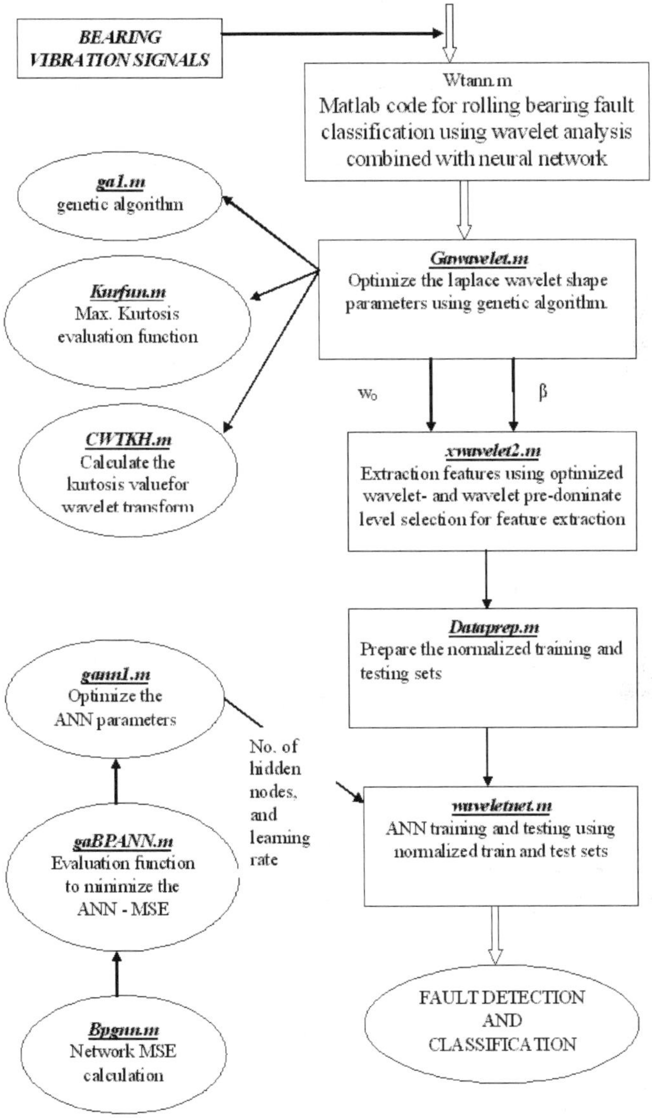

Fig. 29. WT-ANN automatic bearing fault diagnosis MATLAB codes flow chart.

(a) The CWRU vibration data

The smallest fault diameter which introduce smallest fault pulse amplitudes is selected in this study at two different shaft rotational speeds of 1797 rev/min (with no motor load condition) for training data and 1772 rev/min (with 1 HP motor load) for the test data.

The neural network input feature vectors consist of five groups representing the different bearing conditions, a total of 3856 segments of 1000 samples each. The data sets were split between training and test (unseen) sets of size 1928 samples each. The parameters of the applied BP neural network are listed in Table 6.

<table>
<tr><th colspan="5">Neural Network architecture</th></tr>
<tr><td colspan="2">Transfer Function</td><td rowspan="2">No. of input nodes</td><td rowspan="2">Hidden layer nodes</td><td rowspan="2">No. of output nodes</td></tr>
<tr><td>Hidden Layer</td><td>Output Layer</td></tr>
<tr><td>Sigmoid</td><td>Linear</td><td>5</td><td>4</td><td>4</td></tr>
<tr><th colspan="5">NN Training parameters</th></tr>
<tr><td colspan="2">Training Algorithms</td><td>Learning rate</td><td colspan="2">Training Stop Criteria</td></tr>
<tr><td colspan="2" rowspan="2">LM</td><td rowspan="2">0.52</td><td>Max. epoch</td><td>MSE</td></tr>
<tr><td>1000</td><td>10E-20</td></tr>
</table>

Table 6. Applied neural network architecture and training parameters.

The distribution of the extracted features (normalized between 0 and 1), time domain features (RMS and kurtosis) on x-axis and frequency domain features (f_{max}/f_{rpm} and $A_{max}/sum(A)$) on the y-axis , for the most dominant scales of the Laplace wavelet transform for different rolling bearing fault conditions is shown in Figure 30a. It is clear that the normalized feature values for the bearing with outer-race fault are the highest as a result of the high energy fault pulses compared with the less energy pulses generated by inner-race and roller faults as a consequence of amplitude modulation.

The result of the learning process of the developed NN is depicted in Figure 30b, which shows that the training with 300 iterations met the MSE stopping criteria (MSE less than 10E-20). The NN test process for unseen vibration data of the trained ANN combined with the ideal output target values are presented in Figure 30d, which indicates the high success classification rate (≈ 100 %) for rolling bearing fault detection and classification.

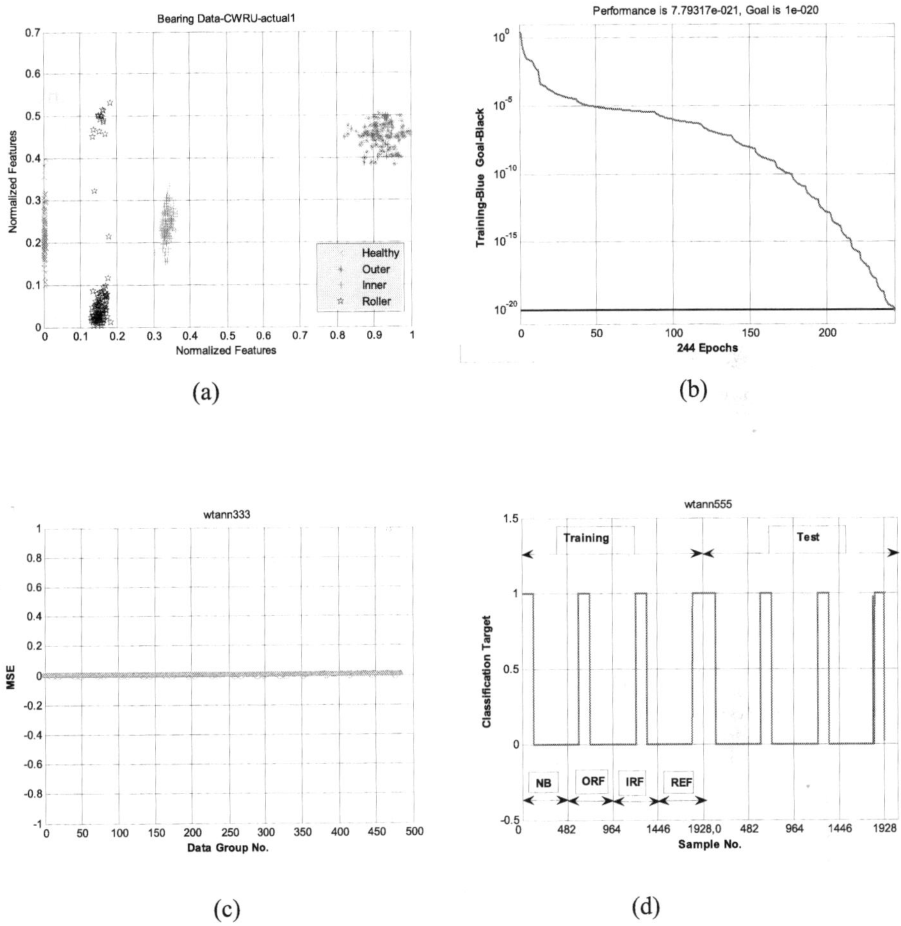

Fig. 30. (a) the extracted features distribution, (b) ANN learning process, (c) ANN classification MSE, (d) ANN Training/Test process, for the CWRU bearing vibration data.

(b) Simulated vibration data

Using the same bearing specifications but CWRU data with 0.6 dB signal to noise ratio and random slip of 10 percent the period T. Figure 31 shows the Wavelet-ANN bearing fault training/classification process for the simulated bearing vibration signal. The results show that the Wavelet-ANN training process reached the specified stopping criteria after 67 epochs, with overall classification MSE less than 6.0E-9, and 100% classification rate.

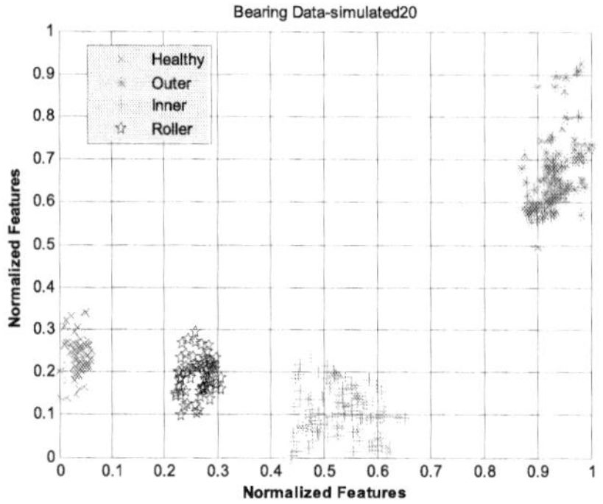

(a)

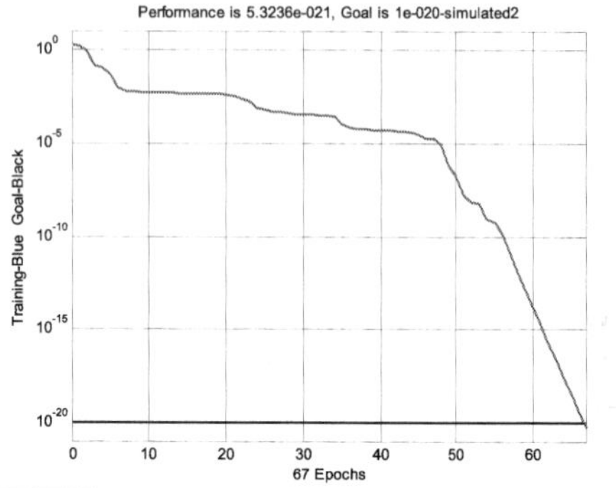

(b)

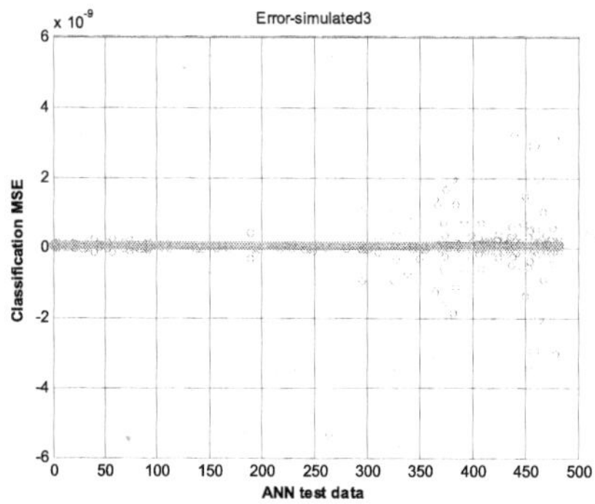

(a)

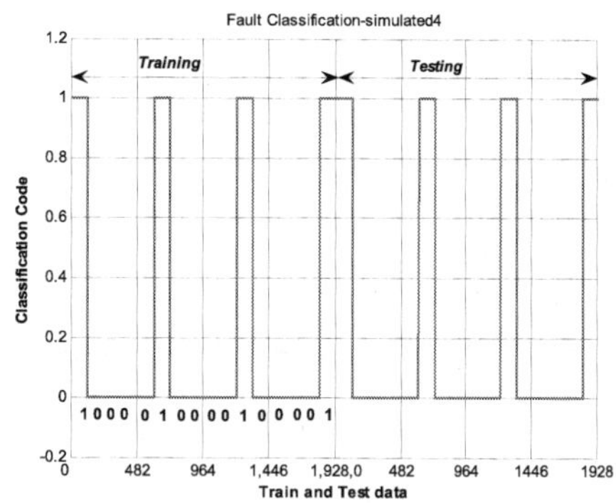

(b)

Fig. 31. (a) the extracted features distribution, (b) ANN learning process, (c) ANN classification MSE, and (d) ANN Training /Test process, for the simulated bearing vibration data.

(c) Experimental vibration data

The ANN training sets have been prepared using an acquired vibration signal at a shaft speed of 1000 rev/min, and the ANN testing set at a shaft speed of 1250 rev/min. Figure 32 shows the Wavelet-ANN bearing fault training/classification process for the measured bearing vibration signals. The results show that the Wavelet-ANN training process achieved the specified stopping criteria after 28 epochs, with overall classification MSE less than 6.0E-5 with 100 % classification rate.

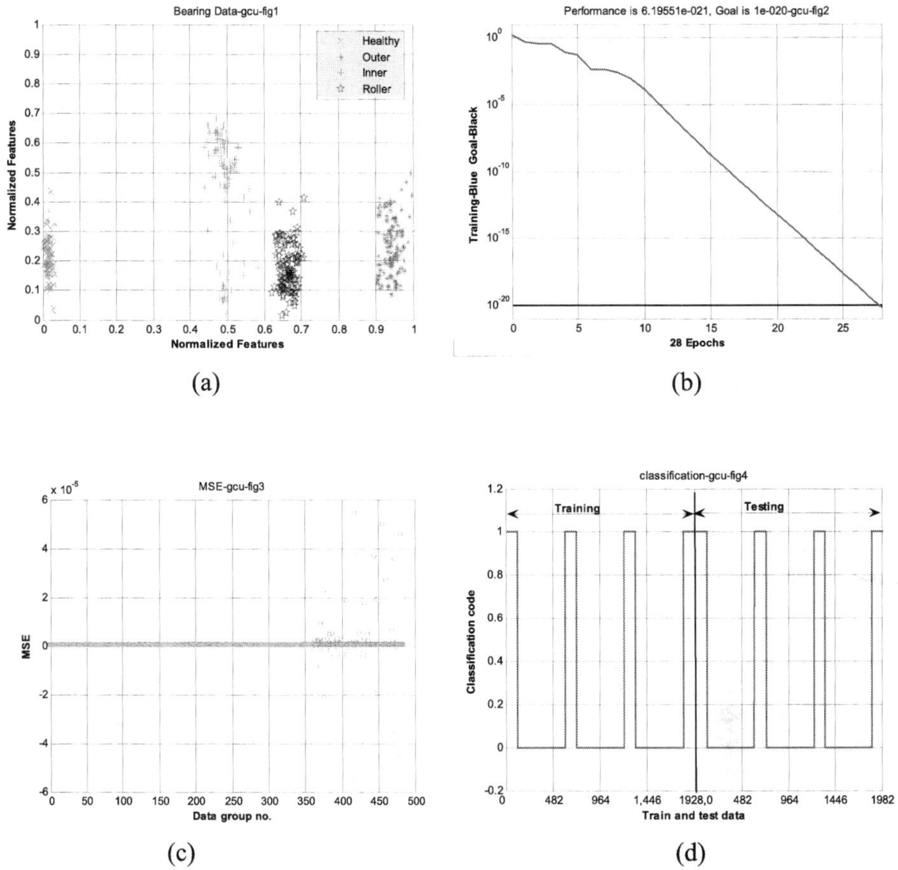

Fig. 32. (a) the extracted features distribution, (b) ANN learning process, (c) ANN classification MSE, and (d) ANN Training / Test process, for the experimental bearing vibration data.

The results for both the simulated and real bearing vibration data show the effectiveness of the combined wavelet-ANN technique for rolling bearing fault pattern detection and classification, and that the Laplace wavelet analysis is an effective approach in fault feature extraction for the NN classifier.

5. Conclusions

The novelty of this chapter is concerned with the applications of the wavelet analysis in two different new approaches:

- Firstly, the impulse wavelet is used as a de-noising technique to extract the fault pulses buried in the noisy signal for fault detection, and by evaluating the periodicity of these pulses through the calculation of the autocorrelation function the location of the fault can be identified.
- Secondly, the implementations of the complex Laplace wavelet for
  - Bearing fault detection through the evaluation of the wavelet envelope power spectrum.
  - Automatic bearing fault detection and diagnosis through the extraction of the input feature vectors to the NN classifier.

From the above wavelet applications the following points can be concluded:

a. The use of the wavelet analysis provides more information related to the bearing fault detection compared with the FFT frequency spectrum which can be used only for a stationary signal. Also the use of a shifted and scaled wavelet window over the analyzed signal produces better detection capabilities than that of the fixed size window used in the STFT.
b. The use of a wavelet base function with more similarity with the fault feature leads to enhance the wavelet analysis and generates wavelet coefficients with more information related to the bearing fault and as a result the efficiency of the fault diagnosis process can be increased. In this project the optimized *Impulse wavelet* and *Laplace wavelet* are used as new wavelet functions for fault detection and feature extraction.
c. The use of more informative features as input vectors to the NN classifier can speed up the classification process and increase its accuracy by reducing the size of the NN through decrease of the input vectors and the hidden layers and nodes.
   Compared with the previously conducted researches that used the normal time and/or frequency domain features as NN input vectors, the use of the wavelet analysis for feature extraction produces a most efficient classifier of the bearing faults with less input features. Furthermore, the use of the optimized wavelet and the most dominant wavelet coefficients in the feature extraction process leads to increase the accuracy and the success rate of the NN classifier.
d. The bearing vibration signals obtained from the bearing simulation model that take into account the effects of the amplitude modulation and the slippage effects which are the main causes of non-stationary bearing signals, can be used to evaluate the performance of the proposed detection techniques with different simulated working conditions.

6. Appendix (A): Bearing rotational frequencies

In general, the bearing inner race is attached to a shaft and therefore has the same rotational frequency as the shaft (F_s) while the outer race can be assumed stationary, since it is generally locked in place by an external casing (i.e. it has a constant rotational frequency of zero). The bearing rotational frequencies can be obtained as follows (Figure 1-7):

6.1 Cage Frequency (F_C)

The rotational frequency of the cage can be expressed in terms of the pitch circle diameter (D_p), the diameter of the rolling element (D_b) and the contact angle (α) as:

$$F_C = \frac{F_s}{2}\left(1 - \frac{D_b}{D_p}\cos\alpha\right) \tag{A-1}$$

6.2 Ball Pass Frequencies (F_{BPI}, F_{BPO})

The rolling element (ball or roller) pass frequencies are the rate at which rolling elements pass a point on the track of the inner or outer race. Given the number of rolling elements (N_b), the theoretical balls (or rolling element) pass frequencies are:

The inner race ball passes frequency (F_{BPI}),

$$F_{BPI} = \frac{F_s}{2}\left(1 + \frac{D_b}{D_p}\cos\alpha\right) N_b \tag{A-2}$$

And the outer race ball passes frequency (F_{BPO}),

$$F_{BPO} = \frac{F_s}{2}\left(1 - \frac{D_b}{D_p}\cos\alpha\right) N_b \tag{A-3}$$

6.3 Ball Spins Frequency (F_B)

The ball (or roller) spin frequency is the frequency at which a point on the rolling element contacts with a given race (inner or outer race), and given by:

$$F_B = \frac{F_s}{2}\frac{D_p}{D_b}\left(1 - (\frac{D_b}{D_p}\cos\alpha)^2\right) \tag{A-4}$$

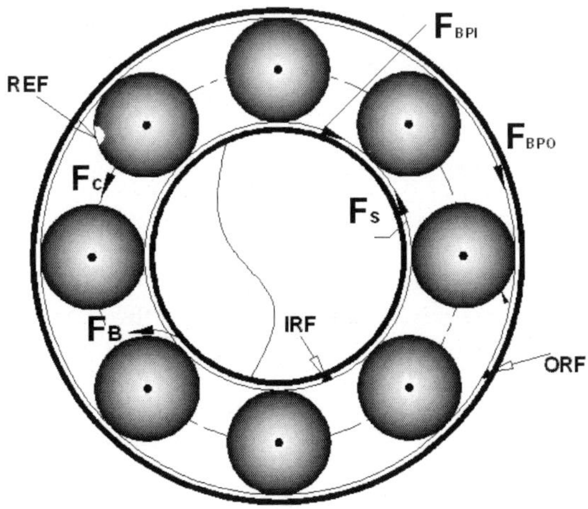

Fig. A1. Basic frequencies and faults in a rolling element bearing.

7. References

Junsheng, C., Dejie, Y. and Yu, Y. (2007): "Application of an impulse response wavelet to fault diagnosis of rolling bearings", *Mechanical systems and signal processing*, vol. 21, pp. 920–929.

Kahaei, M. H., Torbatian, M. and Poshtan, J. (2006): "Detection of Bearing Faults Using Haar Wavelets", *IEICE Transaction fundamentals*, vol.E89a (3), pp.757-763.

Khalid F. Al-Raheem, Roy, A., Ramachandran, K. P., Harrison, D.K. and Grainger, S. (2008):"Application of Laplace Wavelet Combined with Artificial Neural Networks for Rolling Element Bearing Fault Diagnosis", ASME J. of vibration and Acoustics, Vol.130 (5), pp. 051007(1)-051007(9).

Khemili, I. and Chouchane, M. (2005): "Detection of rolling element bearing defects by adaptive filtering", *European Journal of Mechanics and Solids*, vol.24, pp. 293–303.

Lind, R. and Brenner, M. J. (1998): "Correlation filtering of modal dynamics using the Laplace wavelet". NASA Dryden Flight Research center Edwards CA 93523-0273, pp.1-10.

Mallat, S. (1999): *a wavelet tour of signal processing*, 2nd edition, Academic Press.

Orhan, S., Akturk, N. and Celik, V. (2006): "Vibration monitoring for defect diagnosis of rolling element bearings as a predictive maintenance tool: comprehensive case studies", *NDT & E International*, vol.39, pp. 293-298.

Peng, Z.K. and Chu, F.L. (2004): "Application of the wavelet transform in machine condition monitoring and fault diagnostics: a review with bibliography", *Mechanical systems and signal processing, vol.* 18, pp. 199–221.

Reeves T. (1994): "Failure modes of rolling element bearings", *Proceedings of 8th annual meeting vibration inst., pp. 209-217.*

Tandon N. (1994), "A comparison of some vibration parameters for the condition monitoring of rolling element bearings", *Measurements*, vol.12, pp.285-289.

Thanagasundram, S. and Schlindwein, F. S. (2006): "Auto-regression based diagnostics scheme for detection of bearing faults", *Proceeding of ISMA*, pp. 3531-3546.

Wang, C. and Gao, R. X. (2003): "Wavelet transform with spectral post-processing for enhanced feature extraction", *IEEE transactions on instrumentation and measurement*, vol.52 (4), pp. 1296-1301.

Weller, N. (2004): "Acceleration enveloping- higher sensitivity- earlier detection", *Machinery message*.

Yang, W. and Ren, X. (2004): "Detecting Impulses in Mechanical Signals by Wavelets", *EURASIP Journal on Applied Signal Processing*, vol.8, pp.1156–1162.

Yanyang, Z., Xuefeng, C., Zhengjia, H. and Peng, C. (2005): "Vibration based Modal Parameters Identification and wear fault diagnosis using Laplace wavelet", Key Engineering Materials, vol. 293-294, pp.183-190.

15

On the Use of Wavelet Transform for Practical Condition Monitoring Issues

Simone Delvecchio
Engineering Department in Ferrara
Italy

1. Introduction

Condition monitoring is used for extracting information from the vibro-acoustic signature of a machine to detect faults or to define its state of health. A change in the vibration signature not only indicates a change in machine conditions but also points directly to the source of the signal alteration.

Fault diagnosis, condition monitoring and fault detection are different terms which are sometimes used improperly. Condition monitoring and fault detection refer to the evaluation of the state of a machine and the detection of an anomaly. Fault diagnosis could be set apart from other diagnoses since it is more rigorous and requires the type, size, location and time of the detected faults to be determined.

Due to their non-intrusive behaviour and use in diagnosing a wide range of mechanical faults, vibration monitoring techniques are commonly employed by machine manufacturers. Moreover, increases in computing power have helped the development and application of signal processing techniques.

Firstly, the monitoring procedure involves vibration signals to be acquired by means of accelerometers. Due to the selection of acquisition parameters being critical, the data acquisition step is not of minor importance. Sometimes, several steps, such as the correct separation of time histories, averaging and digital filtering is required in order to split the useful part of the signal from noise (electrical and mechanical), which is often present in industrial environments.

Secondly, signal processing techniques have to be implemented by taking into account the characteristics of the signal and the type of machine from which the signal is being measured (i.e. rotating or alternative machine with simple or complex mechanisms). In the final analysis, several features have to be extracted in order to assess the physical state of the machine or to detect any incipient defects and determine their causes.

When the nature of the signal varies over time, repeating the Fourier analysis for consequent time segments could describe the temporal variation of the signal spectrum. This well known technique is called Short Time Fourier Transform (STFT). The principal limitations of this approach are:

- only "average" results being obtained for each analysed time segment, requiring short analysis segments for good time resolution;
- the shorter the analysed time segment is, the coarser the resulting frequency resolution will be.

A more rigorous explanation of the latter is the Uncertainty Principle or Bandwidth-Time product that can be easily proved in [1] using the Parseval theorem and Schwartz inequality. This Principle states that:

$$\Delta f \cdot \Delta t \geq \frac{1}{4\pi} \tag{1}$$

where Δf is the frequency resolution expressed in Hertz and Δt is the time resolution expressed in seconds. It can be easily understood that Eq. 1 points to a limitation in STFT analysis methods: fine resolution in both time and frequency domains cannot be obtained at the same time.

Several techniques have been developed [2][3] to overcome this problem and to analyse different types of non-stationary signals.

As is reported in [2], one can distinguish between three important classes of non-stationary signals:

- Evolutionary Harmonic Signals related to a periodic phenomenon (i.e. rotation) of varying frequency;
- Evolutionary Broadband Signals with a broadband spectrum with spectral content evolving over time (i.e. road noise);
- Transient Signals which show a very short time segment of a wholly evolving nature (i.e. door-slam acoustic response and diesel engine irregularity within one combustion cycle).

Another important class of non-stationary signals is represented by Cyclostationary Signals which are not described here. Since this study deals with Transient signals, Wavelet Transforms (WT) have been proposed as an appropriate analysis tool.

In general, each type of fault produces a different vibration signature which might be detected by means of suitable signal processing techniques. Concerning i.c. engines, fault detection and diagnosis can be carried out using different strategies. One strategy can consist in modelling the whole mechanical system using lumped or finite element methods in order to simulate several faults and compare the results with the experimental data [4][5]. Another strategy is to adopt signal processing techniques in order to obtain features or maps that can be used to detect the presence of the defect [6][7]. Regarding the latter, a decision algorithm is require for a visual or automatic detection procedure. Moreover, maps can also be analysed for diagnostic purposes [8]. This method is used most commonly and is well suited to judgements involving expert technicians.

The latter strategy involves the application of time-frequency distribution techniques which are well suited for the analysis of non-stationary signals and have been widely applied to engine monitoring [9]-[11].

On the one hand, Short-Time Fourier Transforms (STFT), Wigner-Ville Distributions (WVD) and Continuous Wavelet Transforms (CWT) are usually used in order to distinguish faulty conditions for practical fault diagnosis and not to obtain reliable parameters for an automatic procedure led by a data acquisition system [9].

On the other hand, Discrete Wavelet Transforms (DWT) could be applied in order to extract informative features for an automatic pass/fail decision procedure [12]. Moreover, due to their power in identifying de-noising signals, the latter can be used in order to select frequency bands which are mostly characterised by impulsive components.

The aim of this study is to assess the effectiveness of both CWTs and DWTs for machine condition monitoring purposes. In this chapter, WTs are set up specifically for vibration signals captured from real life complex case studies which are poorly dealt with in literature: marine couplings and i.c. engines tested in cold conditions. Both Continuous (CWT) and Discrete Wavelet Transforms (DWT) are applied. The former was used for faulty event identification and impulse event characterization by analysing a three-dimensional representation of the CWT coefficients. The latter was applied for filtering and feature extraction purposes and for detecting impulsive events which were strongly masked by noise.

2. Background theory

This paragràph introduces the theory of fundamental background in order to understand achievements concerning the application of CWT and DWTs on real signals.

2.1 Continuous Wavelet Transforms

When referring to the definition of Fourier Transforms [1], it can be observed that this formulation describes the signal $x(t)$ by means of a set of functions $e^{j\omega t}$ which form the basis for signal expansions. These functions are continuous and of infinite duration. The spectrum in question corresponds to the expansion coefficients. An alternative approach consists of decomposing the data in time-localised waveforms. Such waveforms are usually referred to as wavelets. In recent decades, the theoretical background of wavelet transforms has been extensively reported ([14]-[19]).

The Continuous Wavelet Transform (CWT) of the time signal $x(t)$ is defined as:

$$CWT(a,b) = \frac{1}{\sqrt{a}} \int_{-\infty}^{+\infty} x(t)\psi^*\left(\frac{t-b}{a}\right)dt \tag{3}$$

with $a \in R^+ - \{0\}, b \in R$.

This is a linear transformation which decomposes the original signal into its elementary functions $\psi_{a,b}$:

$$\psi_{a,b}(t) = \frac{1}{\sqrt{a}}\psi\left(\frac{t-b}{a}\right) \tag{4}$$

which are determined by the translation (parameter b) and the dilation (parameter a) of a so called "mother (analyzing) wavelet" $\psi(t)$.

The b translation parameter describes the time localization of the wavelet, while the a dilation determines the width or scale of the wavelet. It is worth noting that, by decreasing the a scale parameter, the oscillation frequency of the wavelet increases, but the duration of the oscillation also decreases, so it can be noted that exactly the same number of cycles is contained within each wavelet.

Therefore, an important difference when compared to the classical Fourier Analysis, in which the time window remains constant, is that the time and frequency resolution now becomes dependent on the a scale factor. For CWTs, in fact, the width of the window in the time domain is proportional to a, while the bandwidth in the frequency domain is proportional to $1/a$. Thus, in the frequency domain, WTs have good resolution for low frequencies and, in the time domain, good resolution for high frequencies; the latter property makes CWTs suitable for the detection of transient signals. More details and applications for CWTs can be found in literature ([20]-[24]).

Two kinds of mother wavelet are known in literature:

- the above defined mother wavelets which can be described by analytical functions;
- mother wavelets obtained by means of an iteration procedure, like orthogonal wavelets, which are well suited for performing Discrete Wavelet Transforms (DWT)[25].

Concerning the former, one of the most interesting is the Morlet wavelet which is defined as:

$$\psi(t)_{morlet} = \frac{1}{\pi^{-1/4}} e^{-t^2/2} e^{i2\pi f_0 t} \tag{5}$$

where f_0 is the central frequency of the mother wavelet. The term $1/\pi^{-1/4}$ is a normalization factor which ensures that the wavelet has unit energy; the Gaussian envelope $e^{-t^2/2}$ modulates the complex sinusoidal waveform. Since the Morlet wavelet is a complex mother wavelet, one can separate the phase and amplitude components within any signal when using it. The CWT result is graphically represented in the time-scale plane, while in this chapter the maps are displayed in the time-frequency domain, using the relationship $f = f_0 / a$ between the central frequency of the analyzing wavelet and the scale. Moreover, when complex analyzing wavelets are used, only the amplitude is considered and represented using a linear scale.

Concerning CWT implementation, the algorithm proposed by Wang and Mc Fadden was applied taking advantage of the FFT algorithm [26].

2.1.1 CWT improvements

Several improvements have been taken into account in this chapter in order to improve CWT power in detecting and localizing transients within a signal. These enhancements concern:

- the choice of mother wavelet;
- the time-frequency map representation;

One experimental investigation was carried out on a marine propulsion package (Fig. 1). The 4-cylinder 4-stroke diesel engine with eight valves was located inboard just forward of the transom. The engine was turbocharged with an exhaust-driven turbo-compressor: the turbo was controlled by a waste-gate valve.

Marine propulsion was assured by a stern-drive unit that contains the transmission and carries the propeller. The boat was steered by pivoting this unit with good characteristics in terms of speed, acceleration, steering and manoeuvring. In fact, the main advantage of stern-drives versus straight inboards is the possibility of changing the drive angle in order to obtain an optimum angle for speed or acceleration. The flexible coupling was mounted between the flywheel of the marine diesel engine and the propeller shaft. The primary side of the coupling was bolted to the flywheel, the secondary side was mounted onto the output shaft; between the two sides there were rubber elements which compensate for all types of misalignment, particularly angular, and dampen vibrations.

The vibration signals were measured from two points (see Fig. 2), which were close to the coupling, in order to analyse the vibration induced by the couplings at different angular positions of the stern drive when gears were repeatedly changed. The two accelerometers were mounted on both sides of the transom, that is, the left and right side. In order to compare the vibration behaviour of the two couplings, all compared vibration signals were picked up under exactly the same operating conditions.

Vibration signals were measured by means of piezoelectric tri-axial accelerometers (frequency range: 1-12000 Hz). All signal records were acquired starting from a crankshaft reference position: a tachometer signal was taken using an inductive proximity probe close to a gear wheel mounted onto the engine crankshaft.

In this context, DWTs were used to analyse the transom right-side signal in order to extract the scaling coefficients $d_{j,k}$. In fact, the signals in time domain obtained during tests, when the gears were repeatedly changed, revealed a train of impulsive components. Fig. 3 shows that the acceleration peaks are unclear in the signal measured from the transom right-side where the noise level was too heavy. In order to indicate which type of coupling provides better vibrational behaviour, the mean value of the acceleration peaks was obtained directly from the original time history from the transom left-side. Concerning the signal measured at the right side, the mean value was obtained for low frequency components at the first level $d_{1,k}$, after DWT application (Fig. 4) with the Symlet analysing wavelet.

Both types of couplings are very sensitive to transient dynamic phenomena due to gear changes. Table 1 shows that the mean value of the acceleration peaks for the Type 1 coupling is higher than the value for Type 2. Thus Type 2 gives better vibrational behaviour than the first type. It can be concluded that the time domain analysis of the coupling acceleration gives good condition monitoring information, if the DWT technique is used for signal denoising purposes.

In order to precisely localise the impulsive phenomena in the time-frequency domain and to validate the previous thesis about Type 2 vibrational behaviour, the Continuous Wavelet Transform for a frame of the transom left-side signal is applied. The impulse with the highest amplitude is isolated for this signal in the time domain, (Fig. 5) and the CWT of this part of the signal is calculated for the two different coupling types. In this work, a Morlet analysing wavelet was used, since its shape is similar to an impulse component.

Fig. 6 reports the wavelet analysis results revealing that the highest amplitude wavelet coefficients for Type 1 (Fig. 6(a)) are in the frequency range of around 1100 Hz. Regarding Type 2 (Fig. 6(b)), the wavelet transform amplitude during the transient phenomena assumes lower values and reveals an appreciatively constant amplitude in the 700-1500 Hz frequency range. The time-frequency plot is able to clearly show the frequency content during the impulse and gives a clearer interpretation of the difference vibrational behaviour of two coupling types.

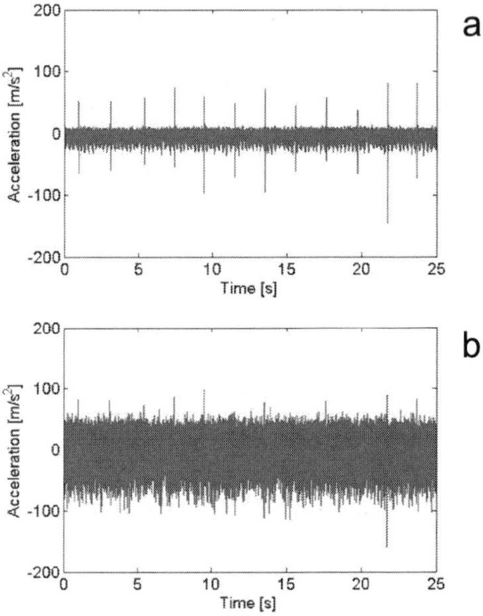

Fig. 3. The vibration signal (TYPE 2) from the transom left-side (a) and the transom right-side (b).

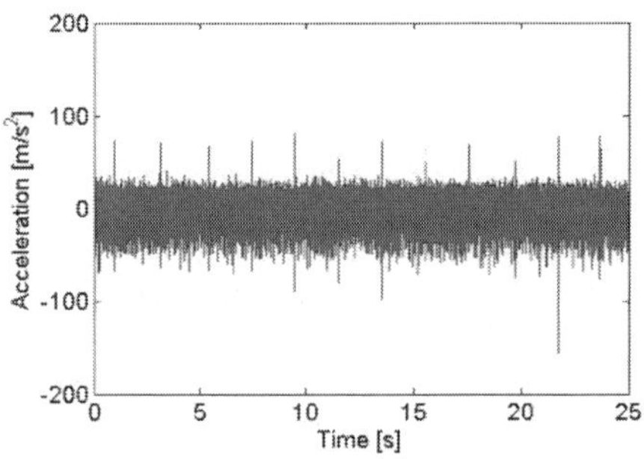

Fig. 4. DWT of the transom right-side signal (TYPE 2).

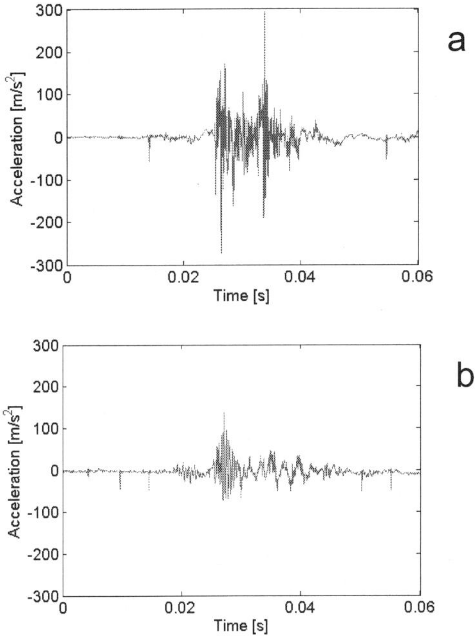

Fig. 5. Highest amplitude impulse for transom left-side acceleration. Coupling: Type 1 (a) and Type 2 (b).

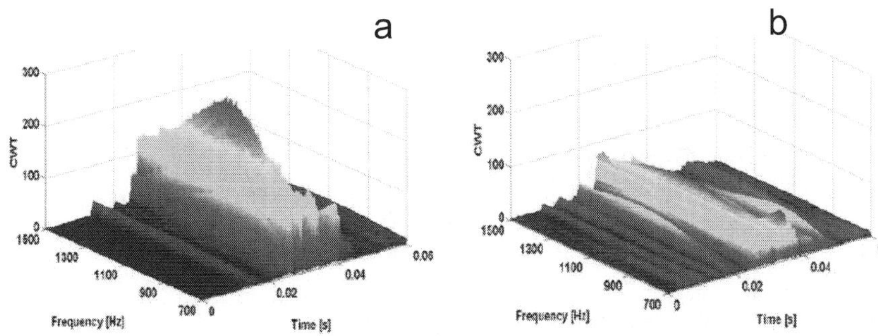

Fig. 6. Continuous wavelet transform (Morlet wavelet) for transom left-side acceleration, 700-1500 Hz frequency range; Coupling: Type 1 (a) and Type 2 (b).

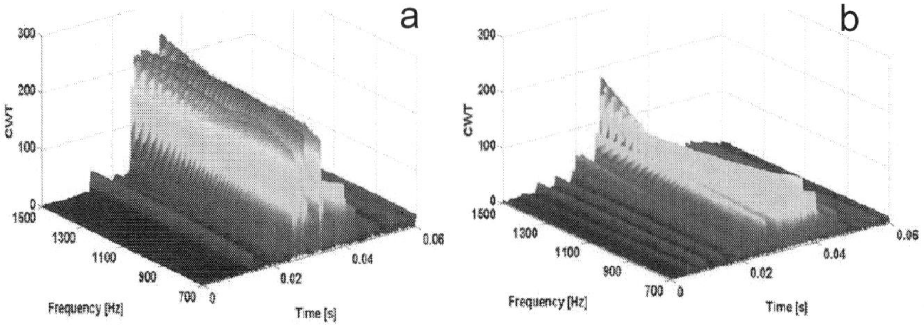

Fig. 7. Continuous wavelet transform (Mexican hat wavelet) for transom left-side acceleration, 700-1500 Hz frequency range; Coupling: Type 1 (a) and Type 2 (b).

Moreover, a comparison between two different Morlet and Mexican hat wavelet functions was evaluated. Undeniably, the Mexican hat wavelet function has a shape which is totally inadequate for analysing the signal impulse components. This is shown by the results in Fig. 7 which indicate that the Mexican hat highlighted the different frequency contempt of two coupling types but was not able to precisely localise the higher frequency components of the impulse signal.

4. Condition monitoring of I.C. engines in cold conditions

This second application addresses the use of CWT and DWTs as a means of quality control for assembly faults in diesel engines using cold test technology. Nowadays, the majority of engine manufacturers test their engines by means of "hot tests", i.e. tests in which the engine is firing. Hot tests are mainly aimed at determining engine performance.

Recently, some companies have introduced "cold tests" which aim to identify assembly anomalies by means of torque, pressure and vibration measurements. Cold tests are more oriented towards identifying the source of anomalies since they are not affected by noise and vibration due to firing. Reciprocating machines, such as IC engines, give non-stationary vibration signals due to changes in pressure and inertial forces and valve operations. Therefore, WTs are an efficient tool for analyzing transient events during the entire engine operation cycle.

Here, CWTs are applied in order to obtain an accurate fault event identification for signals measured from engines with different assembly faults that have not been considered in literature. The analysis takes advantage of cyclostationary modelling developed and tested by Antoni in [8].

Experimental investigations were carried out on a 2.8 dm^3 4-cylinder 4-stroke, four-valve-per-cylinder turbocharged diesel engine with an exhaust-driven turbo-compressor produced by VM Motori. The measurements were carried out in cold conditions (without combustion) while the engine crankshaft was driven by an electric motor via a coupling. The acceleration signal was measured by means of a piezoelectric general purpose accelerometer mounted on the engine block (turbocharger side) close to the bearing support of the crankshaft. A 360 pulse/rev tachometer signal was used to measure the angular position of the crankshaft. During acquisition, the acceleration signal was resampled with a 1 degree angular resolution.

The first faulty condition concerned an engine with a connecting rod with incorrectly tightened screws, that is, screws which were only tightened with a preload of 3 kgm, instead of the correct torque of 9. The second faulty condition concerned an engine with an inverted piston, with incorrectly positioned valve sites. This incorrect assembly hindered the correct correspondence between the valve plates and the valve sites. Since the exhaust valve site area is larger than the intake valve site, the exhaust valves knocked against the non-correspondent intake valve sites.

Fig. 8(a) shows that the CWT map (Impulse wavelet) of the Time Synchronous Average (TSA) detected four cylinder pressurizations and two events related to the faulty condition. Even if a remarkable vertical line at 100 degrees was present in the CWT map of the TSA (Fig. 8 (a)), it is not sufficient to assure the presence of a mechanical fault since its amplitude is comparable to the pressurization peak amplitudes. Therefore, the CWT of the residual signal (i.e. the signal obtained by subtracting the time synchronous average from the raw signal) is an expected step in mechanical fault localization within engine kinematics (Fig. 8(b)). As depicted in Fig. 8(b), the presence of the pre-loaded rod is highlighted by a marked vertical line at about 100°.

As explained in [32] the peak is caused by the absence of controlled bush deformation when the correct tightening torque is not applied. This clearance is abruptly traversed whenever a change in the direction of the resultant force occurs on the rod. In particular, it was demonstrated that the acceleration peak took place at the beginning of the cylinder 3 intake stroke, corresponding to cylinder 2 pressurization (i.e. 'Press 2' in Fig. 8(a)). Hence, fault location can be only achieved by the analysis of the residual signal. It is worth noting that better angular fault localization can be achieved using the Morlet mother wavelet (Fig. 8(c)) which gives lower frequency resolution but higher angular localization of the angle-frequency map. Since the purpose of the proposed approach is to obtain reliable fault diagnostics through accurate angular transient event localization, the Morlet wavelet can be considered the most desirable if compared with the Impulse wavelet.

In order to improve the CWT of the TSA, the purification method was firstly carried out using correlation weighted CWT coefficients, i.e. $\hat{CWT}$, as described in Section 2.1.1.

As previously mentioned, the correlation coefficient $\gamma(a,t)$ used in this method is able to select which coefficient gives the best match between the frequency of the signal and the frequency corresponding to the Impulse wavelet scale.

Fig. 9(a) shows that this method provides a clearer representation in terms of sensitivity to background noise. However, the use of the coefficient correlation method does not improve the angular localization of the main engine events. As noted earlier, this enhancement can be obtained using the Morlet mother wavelet. The Morlet mother wavelet was used to compute the wavelet transform by means of both traditional and TDAS methods. No significant improvements in angular faulty localization can be obtained by using the TDAS method (Fig. 9(b)). Therefore, it can be concluded that a traditional CWT map with a Morlet mother wavelet is sufficient for faulty localization purposes.

It should be noted that CWT is used in order to distinguish faulty conditions from normal ones for practical fault diagnosis and not to obtain reliable parameters for an automatic procedure led by a data acquisition system.

In order to overcome this issue, the DWT technique for the extraction of faulty components from the signal, proposed by Shibata, was evaluated for the second fault which was condition tested, i.e. the inverted piston.

Fig. 10 shows the DWT coefficients ($c_{j,k}$) when Symlet (eight order) is used for the wavelet and the scaling function. Data sampled at 70 μs were used for the DWT.

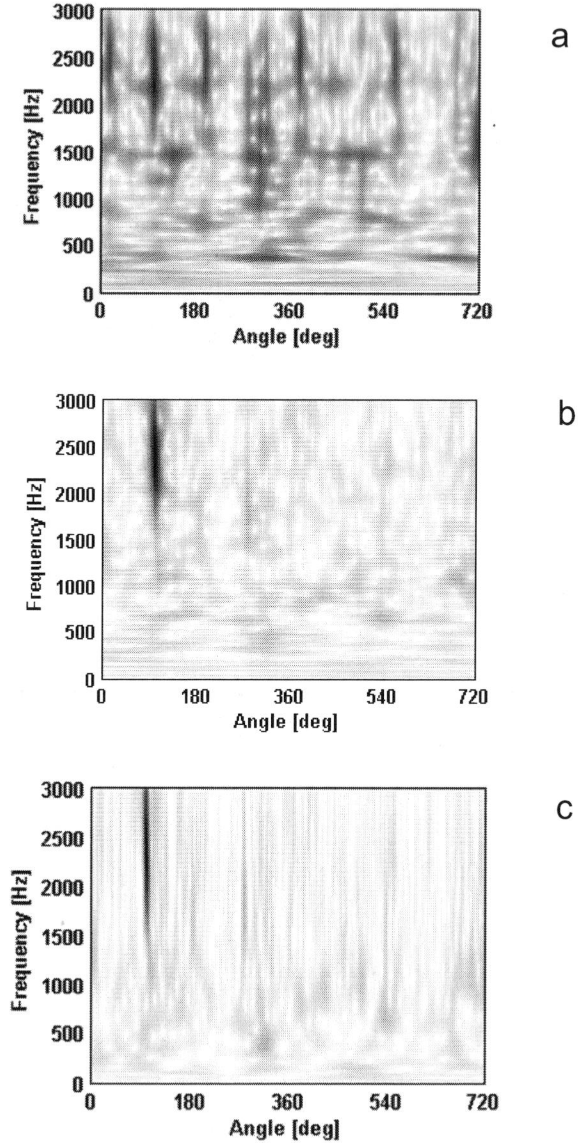

Fig. 8. Faulty engine – (a) CWT (impulse wavelet) of the TSA, (b) residual signal (impulse wavelet); (c) CWT (morlet wavelet) of the residual signal.

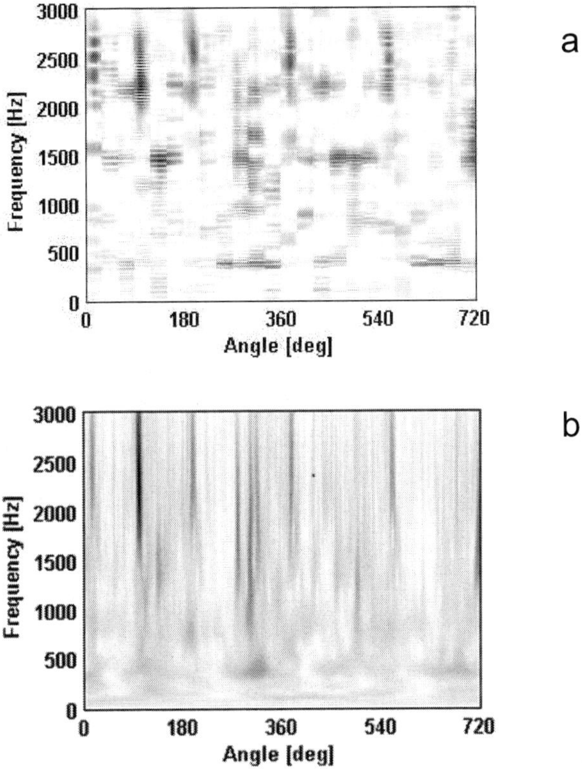

Fig. 9. Faulty engine - (a) CWT of the TSA: purification method (impulse mother wavelet); (b) TDAS method (morlet mother wavelet).

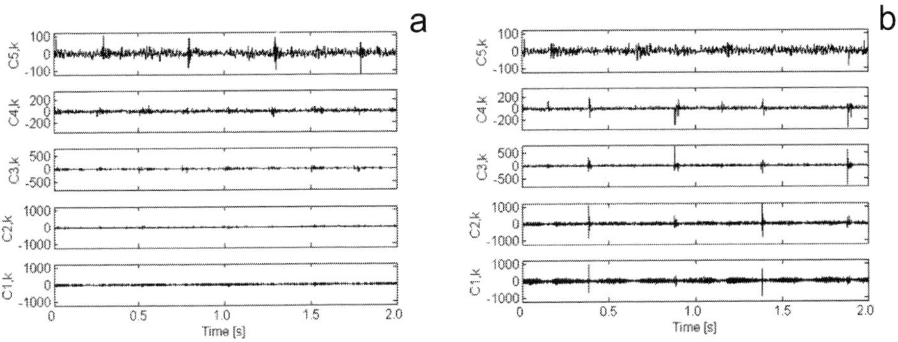

Fig. 10. DWT coefficients for the vibration signals (120 rpm): (a) Normal condition; faulty condition (piston inverted).

Coupling	Original transom left side signal	DWT of the transom right side signal
TYPE 1	102.25	121.13
TYPE 2	58.61	72.87

Table 1. Mean value of the peaks of acceleration (m/s²).

Level $C_{j,k}$	Ratio of RMS F/N Inverted piston
-	1.11
j = 5	1.01
j = 4	1.60
j = 3	2.26
j = 2	3.50
j = 1	**3.76**

Table 2. Comparison with coefficients of DWT: ratio of RMS value between the faulty (F) and normal (N) conditions.

Table 2 shows the comparison between the RMS ratio of the DWT coefficients in faulty (F) and normal (N) conditions with the engine running at 120 rpm. The j = 1 level shows the highest difference between the faulty and normal vibration signals. Thus, the RMS ratio at the first decomposition level may be considered a reliable monitoring feature.

5. Conclusions

This chapter deals with WT applications for practical condition monitoring issues on flexible couplings and i.c. engine. In particular, CWT and DWT capability was assessed. The former was used for faulty event identification and impulse event characterization through the analysis of three-dimensional representations of CWT coefficients. The latter was applied for filtering and feature extraction purposes and for detecting impulsive events which were strongly masked by noise. Several CWT representation improvements were also evaluated.

Comparing the results from both the CWT and DWT analyses, the ability of WTs in satisfying both condition monitoring and fault detection requirements for all tested cases was clearly demonstrated. In particular, traditional CWTs of the residual signal (i.e. the signal obtained by subtracting the time synchronous average from the raw signal) with the Morlet mother wavelet was revealed to be the most powerful tool in angularly localizing the assembly fault within the engine kinematics.

It can be concluded that the application of WTs not only enables changes in the state of the tested machine to be recognized but also the localisation of the source of the alteration.

6. Acknowledgments

This work was developed within the Advanced Mechanics Laboratory (MechLav) of Ferrara Technopole and brought into being with a contribution by the Emilia-Romagna Region – Assessorato Attivita' Produttive, Sviluppo Economico, Piano telematico - POR-FESR 2007-2013, Attività I.1.1.

Information Extraction and Despeckling of SAR Images with Second Generation of Wavelet Transform

Matej Kseneman[1] and Dušan Gleich[2]
[1]Margento R&D d.o.o.,
[2]University of Maribor, Faculty of Electrical Engineering and Computer Science,
Slovenia

1. Introduction

Synthetic Aperture Radar (SAR) technology is mainly used to obtain high-resolution images of ground areas in resolutions even less than meter. SAR is even capable of imaging a wide area of terrain and from two and more images it is possible to reconstruct a 3D digital elevation model of ground terrain. Good thing about SAR is an all whether operation and possibility to capture images under various inclination angles. Because digital images are usually corrupted by noise that arises from an imaging device, there is always a need for a good filtering algorithm to remove all disturbances, thus enabling more information extraction. The SAR images are corrupted by a noise called speckle, which makes the interpretation of SAR images very difficult. The goal of removing speckles from the SAR image is to represent a noise-free image and preserve all important features of the SAR image, as for example edges, textures, region borders, etc.

Many different techniques for SAR image despeckling have been proposed over the past few years. Speckle is a noise-like characteristic of SAR images and it is a multiplicative nature, if the intensity or amplitude image is observed. The despeckling can be performed in the image or in the frequency domain. The well-known despeckling filters are Lee (Lee, 1980), Kuan (Kuan et al., 1985), and Frost (Frost et al., 1982). Lee and Kuan filters can be considered as an adaptive mean filters, meanwhile the Frost filter can be considered as a mean adaptive weighted filter. The Bayesian filters are based on the Bayesian theorem, which defines a posterior probability by using a prior, likelihood and evidence probability density functions (pdf). The solution for noise-free image is found by a maximum a posteriori (MAP) estimate. The MAP estimate of a noise free image was proposed in (Walessa & Datcu, 2000), where the noise free image was approximated by a Gauss-Markov random field prior and the noise was modeled with Gamma pdf. Model based despeckling and information extraction is one of the promising techniques of SAR image denoising and scene interpretation. The wavelet based despeckling algorithms have been proposed in (Dai et al., 2004), (Argenti & Alparone, 2002), and (Foucher et al., 2001). The second generation wavelets Chirplet (Cui & Wong, 2006), Contourlet (Chuna et al., 2006), Bandelet (Le Pennec & Mallat, Apr 2005) have appeared over the past few years.

First transform we used is so called Bandelet transform (Le Pennec & Mallat, Dec 2005), which further divides wavelet subbands into smaller subbands using a rate distortion optimization that enables removing redundancy in wavelet transformation. Bandelets (Le Pennec & Mallat, Dec 2005) contain anisotropic wavelets which combine redundancy in the geometric flow of an image corresponding to local directions of its grey levels. With this geometric flow wavelet warping represents a vector field with indication of regularity along edges. Bandelet decomposition is constructed in much the same way as wavelet with use of dyadic squares containing information about bandelet coefficients (parameterized geometric flow) and segmentation (Le Pennec & Mallat, Apr 2005). These squares summarize geometry by local clustering of similar directional vectors. A Bandelet transform can be viewed as an adaptive wavelet basis transform, which is warped according to local direction.

Bandelet transform is therefore capable to separate two different surface areas with different curvatures, which are then decomposed into optimal estimations of regularity direction (Le Pennec & Mallat, Apr 2005). The geometry itself is obtained with regularity flow estimation. Fig. 1 shows an example of directions acquired with bandelet transform. The computational complexity of this transform is much higher as in the case of the classical dyadic decomposition.

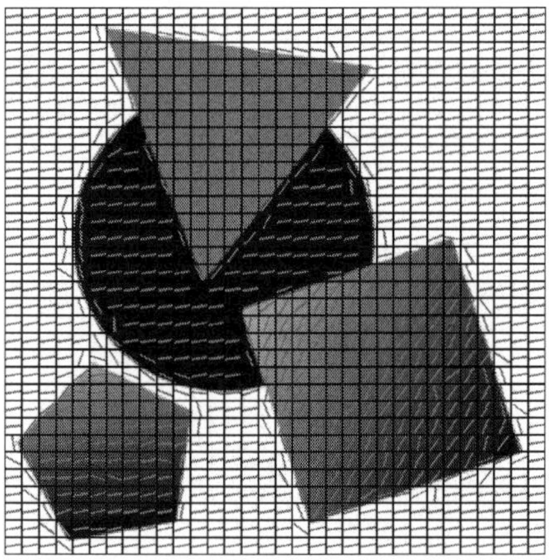

Fig. 1. Directions obtained by bandelet transform

The contourlet transform (Do & Vetterli, 2005) is organized a little bit different, because this transform is directly constructed in a discrete space. Thus, contourlet does not need to be transformed from continuous time-space domain. In order to capture as much as possible directional information a 2D directional filter bank is used in contourlet transform (Do & Vetterli, 2005). Directional filter bank is represented with k-binary tree which decomposes original image into $2k$ bands. These directional filter banks have a flaw mainly because they are designed to capture a direction, which is mainly done in high frequency spectrum of the input image, therefore low frequencies are obstructed. Low frequencies can easily penetrate into several different directional subbands, thus corrupting the transformation subbands. To solve this problem a multiscale decomposition is created with directional decomposition with the help of Laplacian pyramid as a low frequency filter. Laplacian pyramid throughput is a band-pass image which is then led to directional filter bank where a directionality of an image is captured. This scheme can be further applied on a coarser image and thus an iterative scheme can be achieved. It can be concluded that applying iterative contourlet scheme derives to directional subbands in a presence of multiple different scales.

For the despeckling of TerraSAR-X (Wikipedia, 2011) images we used a model based approach, which is supported by first order Bayesian inference. After applying transforms to images a general Gaussian distribution appears in wavelet domain. In this wavelet domain we get subbands different in scales and frequency. The subbands in the wavelet domain have Gaussian distribution and therefore the general Gaussian model is used for a prior density function (pdf). The likelihood pdf is modeled using Gaussian pdf in both, bandelet and contourlet transforms. The despeckling using contourlet (Li et al., 2006) and bandelet (Sveinsson et al., 2008) transforms showed superior despeckling results for SAR images comparing with the wavelet based methods. The model based despeckling mainly depends on chosen models. The image and noise models in the wavelet domain are well defined with presented results in (Argenti & Alparone, 2002), (Gleich & Datcu, 2006) and usually noise-free image is computed using maximum a posteriori estimate.

The despeckling methods were tested using synthetic and real TerraSAR-X data, which were captured in the high resolution spotlight mode. The experimental results showed that the best despeckling method for synthetic images is bandelet transform, because contourlet transform produces artifacts in the homogenous areas. The ratio images between original and despeckled images were examined in order to show estimation of speckle noise, edge and texture preservation using bandelet and contourlet transform. The contourlet transform produces artifacts in form of lines in both homogenous areas and edges.

2. Second generation wavelets

In this section a comparison between bandelets and contourlets is presented. Bandelets and contourlets are presented in great detail, including subbands creation and filter decomposition. These two denoising schemes are a foundation of later proposed model, which builds a denoising scheme on top of these two schemes yielding better denoising results.

2.1 Bandelets

Bandelets (Le Pennec & Mallat, Apr 2005), (Le Pennec & Mallat, Dec 2005) belong to a second generation of wavelet transforms and are composed of anisotropic wavelets, which are in fact a combination of geometric flow of an image corresponding to local directions of its gray levels. This geometric flow represents a regularity of a vector field along edges contained in the image. Typical example of this geometric flow can be seen on Fig. 1, where it can be observed that all directions are aligned to object's edges at the boundary of two different areas.

Edges inside an image are often hard to determine. First generation of bandelet transform uses the vector field (Le Pennec & Mallat, 2001), which determines image regularities and irregularities. Therefore bandelet coefficients represent geometric flow defined by polynomial function. This geometric flow consists of directions of variations in image grey levels, where linear geometric flow is preferred. Bandelet transform image is divided into regions with corresponding vector fields, which describes directions of regularity inside a predefined neighborhood.

If the image intensity is uniformly regular in the neighborhood of a point, then this direction is not uniquely defined, and some form of global regularity is therefore imposed on the flow to specify it uniquely.

In literature it has been proven that the first generation of bandelets has minimum distortion for images whose edges correspond to geometric regularity. However, the first generation of bandelets is composed in continuous space, thus not being able to represent a multi-resolution of the geometric regularity. Thus, the second generation of bandelets (Le Pennec & Mallat, Apr 2005) was introduced, which is an orthogonal multiscale transform constructed directly in discrete domain. The bandelet transform first creates a composition of smaller images representing subbands, and then uses fast subband-filtering algorithms. For applications including speckle-noise removal, the geometric flow is optimized in a way that bandelet transform produces minimum distortion in reconstructed images. The decomposition on a bandelet basis is computed using a wavelet filter bank followed by adaptive geometric orthogonal filters, which require $O((\log_2 N)^3)$ operations.

The key parameters in bandelet transform are: the estimation of basis shapes, the partition of images, and the optimization of geometric flows (Yang et al., 2007). To represent image with as little as possible information, the complex edges must be divided into simpler smaller shapes so that linear geometric flows can represent them sufficiently. The image is commonly divided into smaller square regions that are being divided until there is only one contour inside a square region. It must be noted that the geometric regularity should be discrete, so dyadic decomposition by successive subdivisions of square regions into four smaller sub-squares of twice smaller width can be made. There is a defined maximum and minimum block size (Le Pennec & Mallat, Apr 2005), where the first division produces blocks of maximum size, while later iterations divide those blocks up until minimum size is reached. This partition result can be viewed as a quadtree, where each block is represented by its corresponding leaf in a tree. At each scale the resulting geometry is multiscale and calculated by a procedure that minimizes the Lagrangian cost function.

Implementation

The bandelet transform first computes the 2D wavelet transform of the input original image (Peyré & Mallat, Apr 2005). This transform is based on orthogonal or biorthogonal filter banks and results in four smaller images (children) containing low- and high-frequency components. By selecting a dyadic square and recursively splitting input wavelet image four new sub-squares are created. Further on geometric flow parameterization is performed in each of these sub-squares in every possible direction. Let us assume that each of these squares has a width of k pixels then the number of potential directions d is a little less than $2k^2$. The sampling location is then projected along potential direction and afterwards sorting the resulting 1D points is performed from left to right direction. These points define 1D discrete signal f_d (Le Pennec & Mallat, Apr 2005) which is later on transformed with 1D discrete wavelet transform. For a given user defined threshold T, the bandelet transform has to find the best available direction, which in fact produces the less approximation error. Best geometry is obtained by choosing best direction d that minimizes the Lagrangian

$$\mathscr{L}(f_d, R) = \|f_d - f_{dR}\|^2 + \lambda T^2 (R_G + R_B) \quad (1)$$

where f_{dR} is the recovered signal from quantized coefficients acquired by inverse 1D wavelet transform, R_G is the number of bits needed to code geometric parameter d, R_B is the number of bits needed to code the quantized coefficients and $\lambda = 3/28$ (Le Pennec & Mallat, Apr 2005).

When there are gathered all approximations over each individual dyadic square, the quadtree can be constructed. The algorithm starts with the smallest squares that represent a leaf in quadtree and initialize the cumulative Lagrangian of the sub-tree. Within these dyadic squares, a best bandelet approximation is obtained by minimizing a Lagrangian cost function (Le Pennec & Mallat, Dec 2005). Fig. 2 shows an example of denoising obtained with the bandelet transform including dyadic squares that indicate a progress of dyadic levels. This image is represented by indexing a dyadic level used in bandelet transform, where white indicates the first level and black the last level achieved.

a) b) c)

Fig. 2. An example of image denoising using a bandelet transforms. a) Original image, b) Denoised image using a bandelet transforms, and c) Dyadic squares tree

2.2 Contourlets

Contourlet transform (Do & Vetterli, 2005) is also classified as a second generation wavelet transform for which a Fourier transform is not needed anymore. Main advantage of second generation wavelet transform over the first generation is a true discrete 2D transformation, which is able to capture geometry of an image, but the first generation wavelet transform does not perform very well on edge regions. This transformation therefore results in adaptive multi-resolution and directional image expansion using contour segments.

Best performance of wavelets is achieved in 1D case which is for example only one row of a 2D picture. Because pictures are not simply stacks of rows, discontinuities evolve along smooth regions. 2D wavelet transform thus captures edge points, but on the other hand the throughput on smooth regions is not quite as good anymore. Moreover wavelet transform can only capture a fraction of image directionality, which is clearly seen in Fig. 3 where wavelet transform needs a lot more subdivisions and information then a contourlet transform.

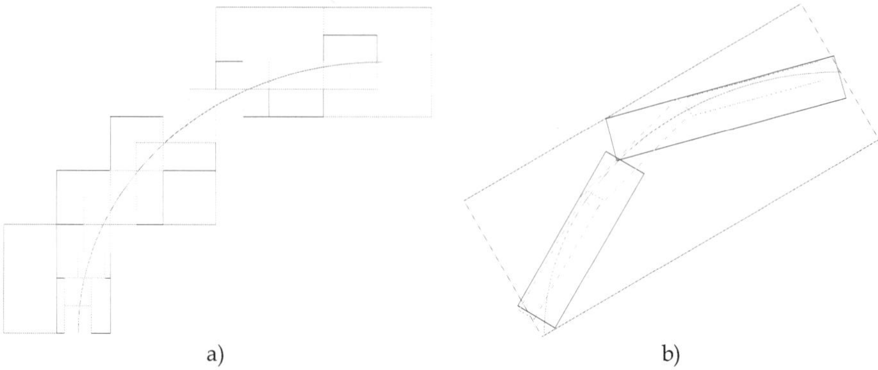

Fig. 3. a) Subdivision comparison between wavelet, and b) Contourlet transform

In order to capture as much as possible directional information a new type of filter bank has to be constructed. Thus a 2D directional filter bank (Bamberger & Smith, 1992) is used in Contourlet transform. Directional filter bank is represented by *k*-binary tree, which decomposes original image into 2^k subbands as represented in Fig. 4. The algorithm based on contourlet transform uses a simpler version of directional filter bank, where the first part is constructed from two-channel quincunx filter bank (Vetterli, 1984), while the second part is sampling and reordering operator. With this composition a frequency partition is achieved and also a perfect reconstruction is obtained. As shown in Fig. 6 one can obtain different 2D spectrum decompositions with appropriate combinations of aforementioned building blocks. Thus a *k*-level binary tree directional filter bank can be viewed as 2^k parallel channel filter bank with equivalent filters and its sampling matrices as shown in Fig. 5 (Do & Vetterli, 2005). In Fig. 5 *D* denotes an equivalent directional filter.

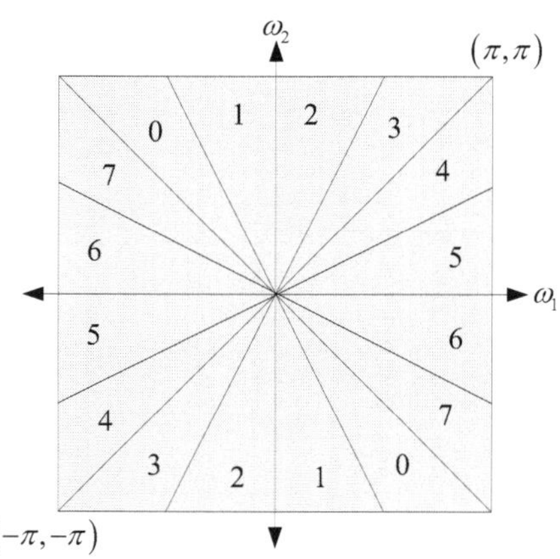

Fig. 4. Frequency partitioning where $k = 3$ and there are $2^3 = 8$ real wedge-shaped frequency bands. Subbands 0-3 correspond to the mostly horizontal directions, while subbands 4-7 correspond to mostly vertical directions

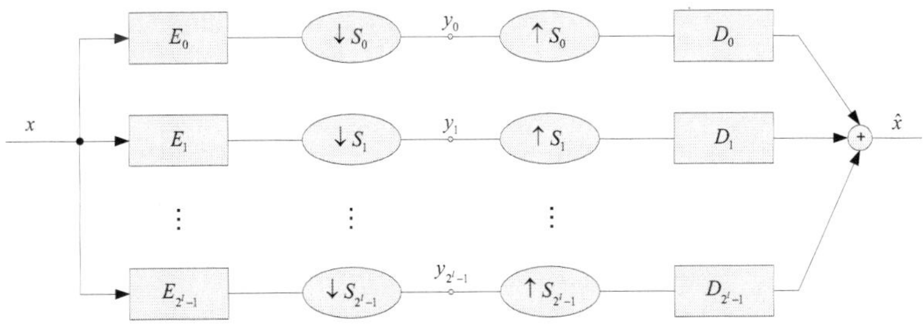

Fig. 5. The multichannel view of a k-level tree-structured directional filter bank

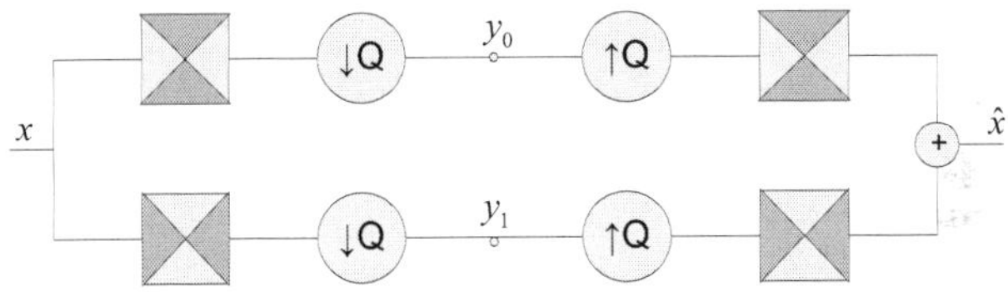

Fig. 6. 2D partition of spectrum using quincunx filter banks with fan filters. Darker shades represent the ideal frequency supports of each filter. Denotion Q represents a quincunx sampling matrix

These directional filter banks have a flaw mainly because they are designed to capture directions, which is mainly done in high frequency spectrum of the input image and thus low frequencies are obstructed. As Fig. 5 shows frequency partition a low frequencies can easily penetrate into several different directional subbands and therefore corrupt the transformation subbands. It is therefore wise to combine multiscale decomposition with directional decomposition with the help of Laplacian pyramid as a low frequency filter. Laplacian pyramid throughput is a bandpass image which is then led to directional filter bank where a directionality of the image is captured. This scheme can be further applied on a coarser image and thus an iterative scheme can be achieved. It can be concluded that applying iterative contourlet scheme derives to directional subbands in presence of multiple different scales, which is depicted in Fig. 7.

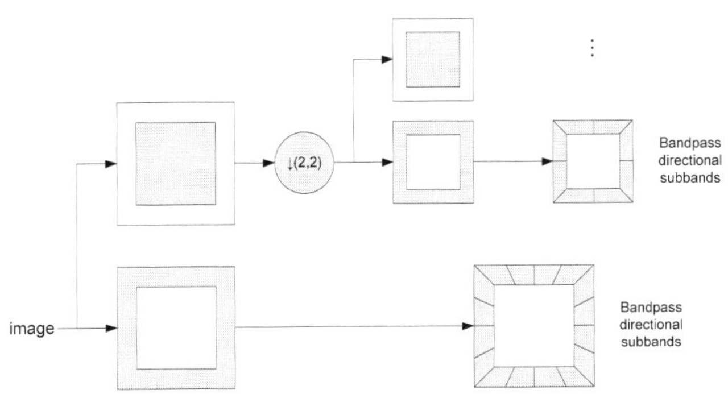

Fig. 7. Construction of contourlet filter bank

3. Bayesian inference incorporated into second generation wavelet transform

The first level of Bayesian inference is given by

$$p(x|y,\theta)=\frac{p(y|x,\theta)p(x|\theta)}{p(y|\theta)} \tag{2}$$

where y represents a noisy image, x represents a noise-reduced image, the θ's are the model parameters, $p(y\,|\,x,\ \theta)$ denotes the conditional pdf called **likelihood**, $p(x\,|\,\theta)$ denotes **prior** pdf, and $p(y\,|\,\theta)$ represents **evidence** pdf. In Eq. (2), the evidence pdf does not play a role in the maximization over x, and therefore, the MAP estimator can be written by

$$\hat{x}(y)=\arg\max_{x} p(y|x,\theta)p(x|\theta) \tag{3}$$

where the likelihood and prior pdfs should be defined. The MAP estimator is an optimal estimator and minimizes the given cost function. The speckle noise in SAR images is modeled as multiplicative noise, i.e. $y = x \cdot z$, where z represents pure speckle noise. A multiplicative speckle noise can also be modeled using an additive signal-dependent model, as proposed in (Argenti & Alparone, 2002) $y = x \cdot z = x + x(z - 1) = x + n$, where n is a non-stationary signal-dependent additive noise equal to $x(z - 1)$.

Models describing texture parameters are widely used in SAR image despeckling (Walessa & Datcu, 2000). Let us model the image as generalized Gauss-Markov random fields (GGMRF) given by

$$p(x_s|\theta)=\frac{\nu\eta(\nu,\sigma_x)}{2\Gamma(1/\nu)}\exp\left(-\left[\eta(\nu,\sigma_x)\left|x_s-\sum_{r\in\zeta_s}\theta_r\left(x_{s+r}+x_{s-r}\right)\right|\right]^{\nu}\right) \tag{4}$$

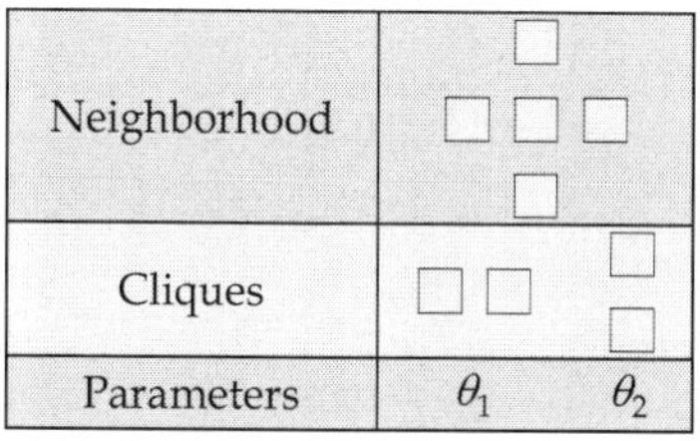

Fig. 8. First order cliques

Let σ_x and θ_s define the GGMRF with a neighborhood set ζ_s. The MRF model characterizes the spatial statistical dependence of 2D data by a symmetric set called neighboring set. The expression $\Sigma\theta_r(x_{s+r} + x_{s-r})$ in Eq. (4) represents the sum of all the distinct cliques of neighboring pixel at a specific subband level. A clique is defined as a subset of sites neighboring the observed pixel, where every pair of sites is neighbors of each other. In this double site, cliques are used. A sum is performed over horizontal and vertical neighboring pixels, for the first model order of the MRF. The neighbor set for a first model order is defined as $\zeta = \{(0, 1), (0, -1), (1, 0), (-1, 0)\}$, and can be seen in Fig. 8. Moreover, the neighbor set for a second model order is defined as $\zeta = \{(0, 1), (0, -1), (1, 0), (-1, 0), (1, 1), (-1, -1), (1, -1), (-1, 1)\}$. The MRF model is defined for the symmetric neighbor set; therefore, if $r \in \zeta_s$, then $-r \notin \zeta_s$, and ζ is defined as $\zeta = (r: r \in \zeta_s) \cup (-r: r \in \zeta_s)$. The parameter ν in (4) represents the shape parameter of the GGMRF, $\Gamma(\cdot)$ represents the Gamma function, and η is given by

$$\eta(\nu,\sigma_x) = \sigma_x^{-1}\sqrt{\frac{\Gamma(3/\nu)}{\Gamma(1/\nu)}} \tag{5}$$

A likelihood pdf is given by a Gaussian distribution

$$p(y_s|x_s) = \frac{1}{\sqrt{2\pi\sigma_n^2}}\exp\left(-\frac{(y_s - x_s)^2}{2\sigma_n^2}\right) \tag{6}$$

where σ_n^2 is a noise variance.

The noise variance σ_n^2 can be estimated using the results presented in (Argenti & Alparone, 2002), and is given by

$$\sigma_n^2 = \psi_l \mu_x^2 C_F^2 \left(1 + C_x^2\right) \tag{7}$$

where $\mu_x = E[x]$, and $E[x]$ denotes a mathematical expectation. C_x^2 is given by

$$C_x^2 = \frac{C_{Wy}^2 - \psi_l C_F^2}{\psi_l\left(1 + C_F^2\right)} \tag{8}$$

The normalized standard deviation of the noisy wavelet coefficient is given by $C_{Wy} = \sigma_{Wy}/\mu_y$, where σ_{Wy} is a standard deviation calculated within the wavelet domain, and μ_y is the mean value calculated in the spatial domain. C_F denotes the normalized standard deviation of the speckle noise. The parameter ψ_l is defined as a product of the coefficients from high-pass (g_k) and low-pass (h_k) filter used at the l-th level of the wavelet decomposition. If the wavelet coefficients of a diagonal detail are of interest, then the parameter ψ_l is given by

$$\psi_l = \left(\sum_k h_k^2\right)^2 \left(\sum_k g_k^2\right)^{2(l-1)} \tag{9}$$

Moreover, if the wavelet coefficients in the horizontal and vertical details are of interest, then the parameter ψ_l is given by

$$\psi_l = \left(\sum_k h_k^2\right)\left(\sum_k g_k^2\right)^{2l-1} \tag{10}$$

Since the random variable z of the speckle noise is normalized (i.e. $E[z] = 1$), the parameter C_F for intensity images is given by

$$C_F = 1/\sqrt{L} \tag{11}$$

while for the amplitude images the parameter C_F is given by

$$C_F = \sqrt{(4/\pi - 1)/L} \tag{12}$$

The parameter L represents the number of looks of the original SAR image. However, its value is unknown, thus an approximation has to be done, which is $L = \mu^2/\sigma^2$. The noise variance is then given by

$$\sigma_n^2 = \frac{C_F^2\left(\psi_1 \mu_y^2 + \sigma_{Wy}^2\right)}{1 + C_F^2} \tag{13}$$

where μ_y = E[y]. Noise-reduced variance can be computed using the results presented in the paper (Argenti & Alparone, 2002). Thus, noise-reduced the variance is given by

$$\sigma_x^2 = \psi_1 \mu_x^2 C_x^2 \tag{14}$$

Where μ_x^2 is the mean value calculated within the wavelet domain over a predefined window size.

The MAP estimate using the GGMRF primarily defined in (4) and the likelihood defined in (6) is given by

$$-v\eta(v,\sigma_x)\left[\eta(v,\sigma_x)\left|x_s - \sum_{r\in\zeta_s}\theta_r\left(x_{s+r} + x_{s-r}\right)\right|\right]^{v-1} + \frac{y_s - x_s}{\sigma_n^2} = 0 \tag{15}$$

The evidence maximization algorithm is used in order to find the best model's parameters (v, θ). The analytical solution for the integral over the posterior $p(y \mid x)p(x \mid \theta)$ does not exists; therefore, the evidence is approximated. The multidimensional pdf is approximated by the multivariate Gaussian distribution with Hessian matrix $\boldsymbol{H}$ centered on the maximum of the a posteriori distribution (Walessa & Datcu, 2000), (Sivia, 1996). The integral over a posterior pdf consists of mutually independent random variables; therefore, a conditional pdf can be rewritten as a product of their components

$$\begin{aligned} p(y|\theta) &= \int p(y|x)p(x|\theta)dx \\ p(y|\theta) &\approx \int \prod_{i=1}^{N} p(y_i|\hat{x}_i)p(\hat{x}_i|\theta)\exp\left(-\frac{1}{2}\Delta x^T H \Delta x\right)dx \\ p(y|\theta) &\approx \frac{(2\pi)^{N/2}}{\sqrt{|H|}}\prod_{i=1}^{N} p(y_i|x_i)p(x_i|\theta) \end{aligned} \tag{16}$$

where $\Delta x = x - \hat{x}$ and Hessian matrix $\boldsymbol{H}$ is a square matrix of the second-order partial derivatives of a univariate function

$$H = -\nabla\nabla\sum_{i=1}^{N}\log\left(p(y_i|x_i)p(x_i|\theta)\right) \tag{17}$$

The MAP estimate is computed using a numerical method. The texture parameters θ of the GGMRF model are estimated using the Minimum Mean Square Error (MMSE) estimation technique, and therefore given by a linear model as

$$\theta = \left(GG^T\right)^{-1}\left(G^T X\right) \tag{18}$$

where X are the observed coefficients inside the window of a size $N \times N$, and matrix G consists of neighboring coefficients attributed around each individual observed coefficient x_s inside a window of a size $N \times N$. The organization of a neighborhood for the bandelet and contourlet domain is shown in Fig. 9 and Fig. 10, respectively. Those figures show the parent-child relationships for the bandelet and contourlet transform. Each parameter θ weights the clique on different subbands.

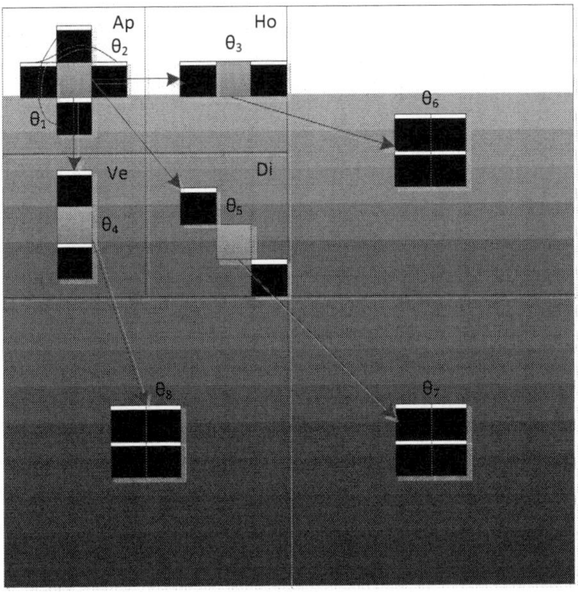

Fig. 9. Neighborhood cliques' organization for bandelet transforms

A logarithmic form can be introduced to simplify Eq. (16) as

$$\log p(y|x) \approx \sum_{i=1}^{N} \frac{1}{2}\left(\log(2\pi) - \log(h_{ii})\right) + \log p(y_i|\hat{x}_i) + \log p(\hat{x}_i|\theta) \tag{19}$$

where h_{ii} are the diagonal elements of the Hessian matrix $\boldsymbol{H}$, which has dimensions of $N \times N$, and N represents the dimension of moving window. Another approximation is then made

$$|H| \approx \prod_{i=1}^{N} h_{ii} \tag{20}$$

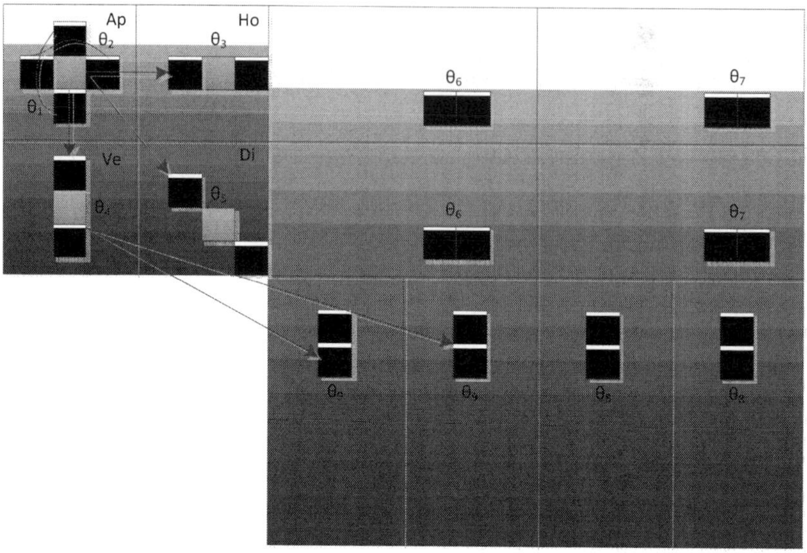

Fig. 10. Neighborhood cliques' organization for contourlet transforms

This approximation is possible, because all off-main diagonal elements represent covariances, and these are sparsely set matrixes that are close to zero, therefore those elements can be neglected. This assumption is in accordance with the statistical independence in Eq. (16). Only main-diagonal elements are needed for the Hessian matrix ***H***, which are defined by

$$h_{ii} = \sum_{i=1}^{N} -v(v-1)\eta(v,\sigma_x)^2 \left(\eta(v,\sigma_x) \left| \hat{x}_i - \sum_{i\in\zeta} \theta_j \left(x_i^j + x_i^{j'} \right) \right| \right)^{v-2} - \sum_{i=1}^{N} \frac{\hat{x}_i}{\sigma_n^2} \quad (21)$$

4. Outline of the proposed algorithm

1. The proposed despeckling algorithm transforms SAR images using bandelet (Le Pennec & Mallat, Apr 2005) or contourlet (da Cunha et al., 2006) transform. The number of decompositions depends on the size of the image. The number of levels l is chosen in such a way that the size of the approximation subband is larger than or equal to 64 × 64 pixels (minimum size).
2. The model parameters ν and θ are estimated inside a window with a size of $N \times N$ pixels. In all experiments, a window with 7 × 7 pixels was used.
3. The noise and signal variances are estimated using (13) and (14), respectively.
4. The parameter θ is estimated using the MMSE defined in (18).
5. The shape parameter ν is changed within the interval [0.5 … 2.5] with a step size of 0.1.
6. The noise-reduced coefficients are estimated using the MAP estimate (15) for each value ν. Each time, the texture parameters θ are estimated using the MAP estimate obtained in the previous step.

7. The MAP estimate is used for the evidence estimation (21).
8. The best MAP estimate $\hat{x}$ is accepted where the evidence has maximum value.
9. The algorithm proceeds to the next pixel.

5. Experimental results

5.1 Synthetic SAR images

The synthetic SAR image, shown in Fig. 11, is composed of four different areas and with added four-look multiplicative speckle noise. The SAR image size shown in Fig. 11 is 512 × 512 pixels; therefore three levels of decomposition are used for bandelet transform. First let us show the difference between the pure bandelet and contourlet, and the MBD method.

Fig. 11. a) Original speckled image, b) Despeckled image obtained with the original bandelet denoising scheme, c) Despeckled image obtained with the original contourlet denoising scheme, and d) Despeckled image obtained with the MBD denoising technique

The bandelet transform is composed of a larger sliding window with a size of 16 × 16 (i.e. moving window per window), meanwhile inside a larger window, a smaller one with the size of 4 × 4 pixels moves on pixel basis. Those two sliding windows are used for searching the best decomposition inside the dyadic wavelet transform (Le Pennec & Mallat, Apr 2005). The contourlet transform is constructed using eight directions at the first level of decomposition. The last two levels are chosen to be dyadic, but this is not a requirement. The despeckled images obtained using the bandelet and contourlet transform are shown in Fig. 11 b) and c), respectively. Moreover, the despeckled image obtained using the MBD (Walessa & Datcu, 2000) is shown in Fig. 11 d).

And now with the MAP incorporated into the bandelet and contourlet transform.

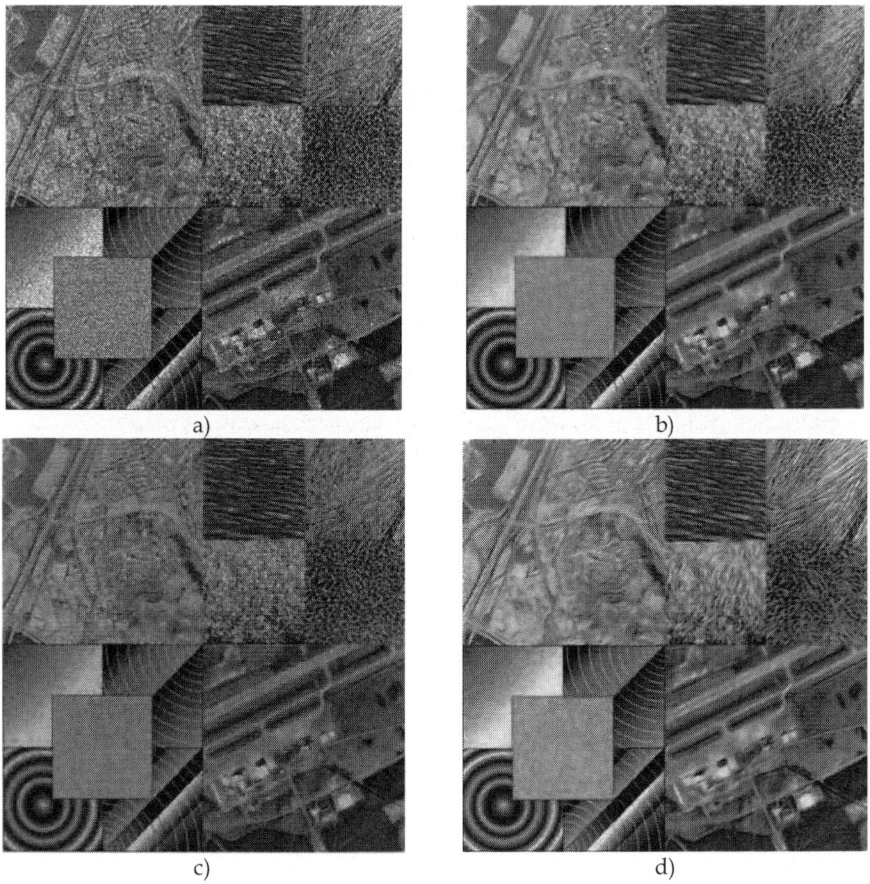

Fig. 12. a) Original speckled image, b) Despeckled image obtained with the bandeleted denoising scheme, c) Despeckled image obtained with the contourlet denoising scheme, and d) Despeckled image obtained with the MBD denoising technique

μ = 127.94	*Bandelet*	*Contourlet*	*MBD*
MSE	331	447	463
Mean	127.64	127.4	126.49
ENL ($\hat{x}$)	506	510	539
ENL (y/ $\hat{x}$)	3.14	3.2	3.18
Mean (y/ $\hat{x}$)	1.047	1.048	0.94

Table 1. Filter evaluation for synthetic test images

In Table 1, the objective measurements are presented for the denoising of image shown in Fig. 12. Objective measurements include the mean-square error (MSE), the equivalent number of looks (ENL), the mean value of the despeckled image, the ENL of speckle noise (ENL(y/ $\hat{x}$)), and the mean value of speckle noise y/ $\hat{x}$. The ENL of the image is given by μ^2/σ^2. The best MSE results are from bandelet transform in combination with Bayesian inference, thus having better results than those obtained from the contourlet transforms. A drawback of the contourlet transform is that it produces contours in the reconstructed image, which affects a MSE value. All wavelet-based methods well preserve the mean of the despeckled images. On the other hand, the MBD method well estimates the speckle noise, but it overblurs the reconstructed image, yielding a worse MSE value.

Figs. 13 a)-c) show the ratio images between the original and the reconstructed mosaic images obtained with bandelet, contourlet, and MDB. From these ratio images we can conclude that edges are well preserved, and that the speckle noise in the homogeneous areas is well estimated (i.e. removed) using the MBD method and second generation wavelets, as reported in Table 1.

a) b) c)

Fig. 13. Ratio images y/ $\hat{x}$. a) Ratio image obtained with the bandelet-based despeckling, b) Ratio image obtained with the countourlet-based despeckling, and c) Ratio image obtained with the MBD method

The efficiency of the texture separation regarding the proposed method is demonstrated on four Brodatz textures, which are presented in a single mosaic composition and shown in Fig. 14. The textures are corrupted with a four-look speckle noise. The estimated parameter θ_2 obtained from bandelet and contourlet transforms is shown in Fig. 14 b) and c), respectively. The estimated texture parameters θ are classified into four classes using the K-means algorithm, and the classification results are shown in Fig. 14 d) and e), respectively. The best texture separation is obtained using a contourlet transform. The unsupervised classification of the texture parameters has an accuracy rate of 82 % and 89 %, for texture parameters obtained from the bandelet and contourlet transforms, respectively. Fig. 14 f) shows the classification of the texture parameter θ obtained with the MBD method. This method cannot well estimate classes on the right side of the image shown in Fig. 14 f).

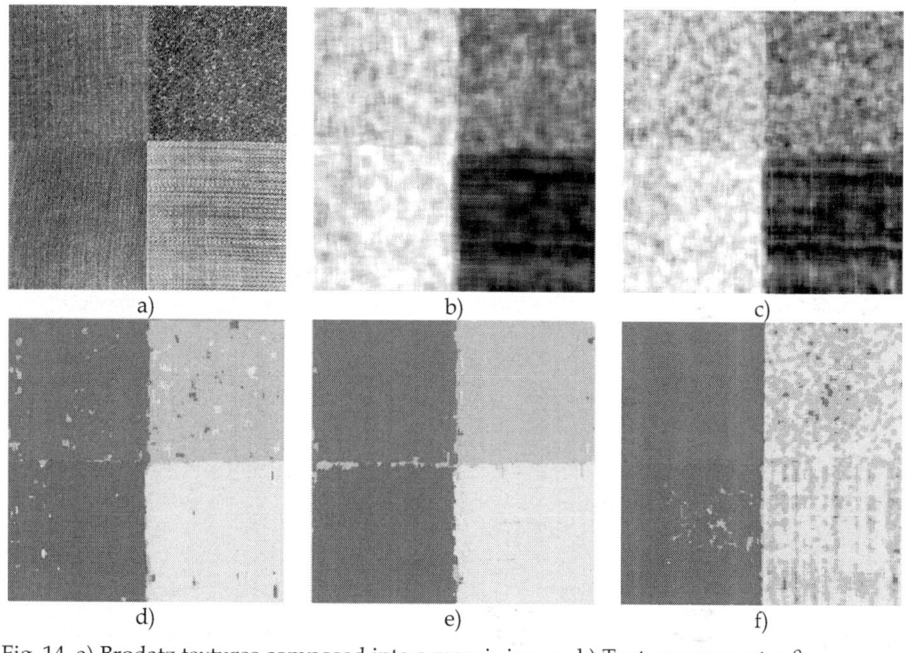

Fig. 14. a) Brodatz textures composed into a mosaic image, b) Texture parameter θ_2 obtained with the bandelet transform, c) Texture parameter θ_2 obtained with the contourlet transform, d) Classified parameter θ obtained with the bandelet transform using the K-means unsupervised classification into four classes, e) Classified parameter θ obtained with the contourlet transform using the K-means unsupervised classification into four classes, and f) Classified parameter θ obtained with the MBD method and K-means unsupervised classification into four classes

5.2 Real SAR images

The real SAR images are a sample images taken by TerraSAR-X satellite. The amplitude part of a single-look complex (SLC) SAR image is shown in Fig. 15 with a size of 2048×2048 pixels and ENL equal to 1.1. Four levels of dyadic decomposition are used for the bandelet decomposition. Five levels of contourlet transform are used, where the last two decompositions are dyadic and all other levels are contourlet directional subbunds consisted of eight directional subbands. The Daubechies symmetric four-filter bank (Daubechies, 1992) is used for the construction of bandelet and contourlet transforms.

a)

b)

c)

d)

Fig. 15. a) Original TerraSAR-X image © DLR (2007), b) Despeckled image obtained with the bandelet transform, c) Despeckled image obtained with the contourlet transforms, and d) Despeckled image obtained with the MBD method

Fig. 15 a)-d) shows the original SLC SAR image and the despeckled images obtained using the bandelet- and contourlet-based despeckling techniques, and the MBD despeckling method. Their ratio images are shown in Fig. 16 a)-c). The quality of the reconstructed images using the bandelet and contourlet transforms is nearly the same. However, the despeckling method based on bandelet transform has left out some speckle noise in the homogeneous regions. On the other hand, the homogeneous regions are well despeckled in the reconstructed image based on the contourlet transform, but undesired artifacts emerge in places around strong scatter returns in shape of lines, that are a consequence of contourlet subbands decomposition. This artifact is clearly visible in Fig. 16 b). Figs. 17 a)-c) show how strong scatterers are despeckled within the bandelet, contourlet, and dyadic wavelet domain.

a) b) c)

Fig. 16. Ratio images $y/\hat{x}$ for SAR images. a) Ratio image obtained with the bandelet transform, b) Ratio image obtained with contourlet transform, and c) Ratio image obtained with the MBD method

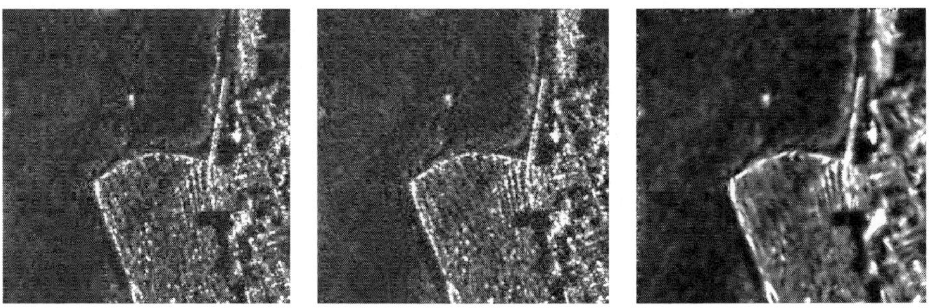

a) b) c)

Fig. 17. Despeckling of strong scatterers using a) bandelet transform, b) contourlet transform, and c) MBD method

The despeckling within the bandelet and dyadic wavelet domain are able to remove speckles around the strong scatterers, while the contourlet transform produces artifacts in this configuration. Higher image values are difficult to despeckle, because of the nature of the contourlet transform. Therefore, the noise is still present in those areas of the reconstructed image. However, the bandelet transform is overall computationally more demanding than contourlet transform (around 5.6 times), yet the despeckling of each contourlet subband takes about 4.5 times longer than with bandelet transform. Therefore, these methods are also computationally comparable.

To extract texture information from the denoised TerraSAR-X images we have used General Gauss-Markov Random Fields (GGMRF) as a prior pdf (Gleich & Datcu, 2007). As a prior pdf a first order model was used with cliques defined as Gauss-Markov Random Fields and shown in Figs. 9 and 10. Cliques were used to estimate central pixels for both transforms created in a 7 × 7 window which is moving throughout the whole picture. This was applied on transform's first approximation and its corresponding subbands. The texture parameters are iteratively estimated until second order Bayesian inference is increasing, which is used for finding the best model (Gleich & Datcu, 2007). The results of this method can be seen in Fig. 18, where the classification parameters for *K*-means algorithm were 5 classes and 7 iterations.

a) b) c)

Fig. 18. Comparison on information extraction. A) Original TerraSAR-X© image, b) Classified image on bandelet transform subbands, and c) Classified image on contourlet transform subbands

Texture parameters θ obtained during the despeckling procedure of the SAR image shown in Fig. 15 with bandelet, contourlet, and MBD method are shown in Fig. 19 b)-d). The algorithm used for classification into four different classes is the *K*-means algorithm. Fig. 19 a) is an indication of *K*-means algorithm applied to original image scene, where no textures can be identified as no processing was applied. The texture parameters obtained with both proposed algorithms clearly separate between homogeneous and heterogeneous areas. The contourlet transform compared to bandelet transform better separates the homogeneous and heterogeneous areas. From images it can be concluded, that contourlet transform is able to separate more heterogeneous areas from homogeneous ones. As a comparison, the MBD method can also distinct between homogeneous and heterogeneous areas as well as separate different textures in the scene, as shown in Fig. 19 d).

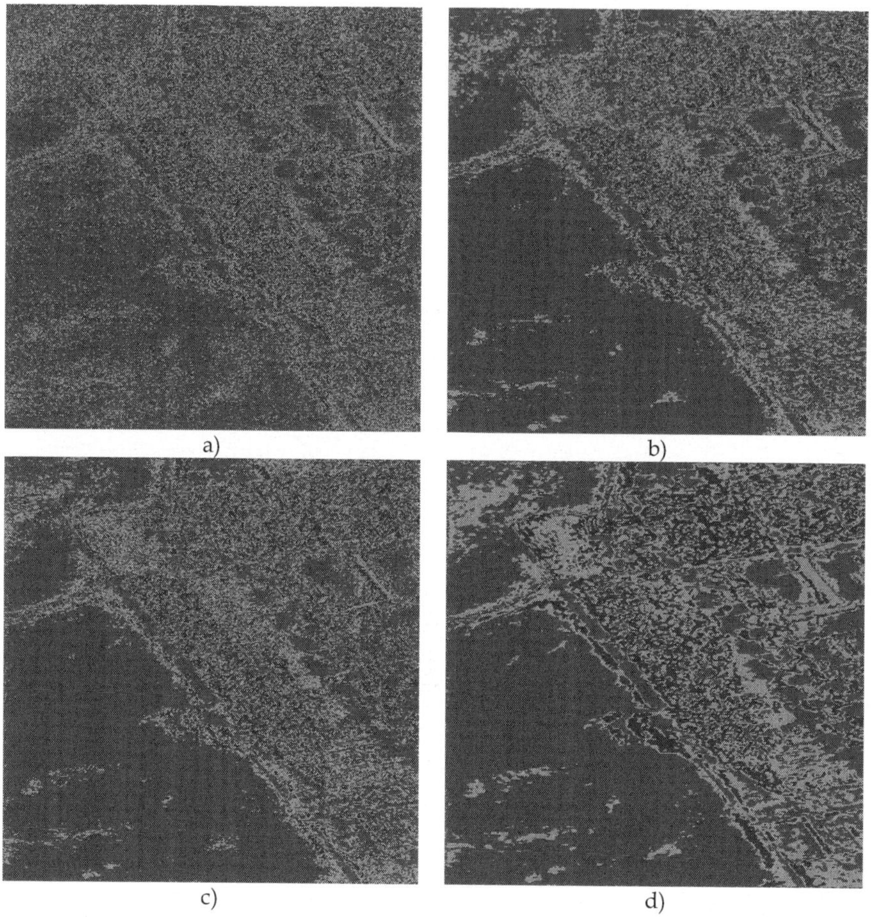

Fig. 19. Classification of texture parameter θ using the K-means algorithm and the a) original, b) bandelet, c) contourlet, and d) MBD-based algorithm

6. Conclusion

This book chapter has presented the proposed methods for despeckling a synthetic and real SAR images using second-generation wavelets. The Bayesian approach in incorporated into second generation wavelets using the wavelet domain. The prior and likelihood pdfs are modeled using GGMRF and Gaussian distribution. The second order Bayesian inference is used to better estimate model parameters and to find the best values possible. The evidence has been simplified and approximated using the Hessian approach. The experimental results have shown that the despeckling of real SAR images using second-generation wavelets is comparable with the dyadic wavelet-based despeckling algorithm (Gleich & Datcu, 2006). Moreover, information extracted using the contourlet domain gives good results using synthetic as well as real SAR data. Unfortunately, the contourlet-based despeckling introduces lines, which are consequences of cutting low-frequency components in the subband decomposition, which can be corrected by introducing a new filter or by post-processing step.

7. References

Argenti, F., and Alparone L. (2002). Speckle Removal From SAR Images in the Undecimated Wavelet Domain. *IEEE Tran. Geoscience and Remote Sensing,* Vol. 40, No. 11, (November 2002), pp. 2363-2374

Bamberger, R. H., and Smith, M. J. T. (1992). A filter bank for the directional decomposition of images: Theory and design. *IEEE Trans. Signal Proc.,* Vol. 40, No. 4, (April 1992), pp. 882-893

Chuna, A. L., Zhou, J. and Do, M. N. (2006). The Nonsubsampled Contourlet Transform: Theory, Design, and Application. *IEEE Tran. Image Processing,* Vol. 15, No. 10, (October 2006), pp. 3089-3101

Cui, J., and Wong W. (2006). Adaptive Chirplet Transform and Visual Evoked Potentials. *IEEE Tran. on Biomedical Engineering,* Vol. 53, No. 7, (July 2006), pp. 1378-1384

da Cunha, A. L., Zhou, J., and Do, M. N. (2006). The Nonsubsampled Contourlet Transform: Theory, Design, and Applications. *IEEE Transactions on Image Processing,* Vol. 15, No. 10, (October 2006), pp. 3089-3101

Dai, M., Cheng, P., Chan, A. K., and Loguinov D. (2004). Bayesian Wavelet Shrinkage with Edge Detection for SAR Image Despeckling. *IEEE Tran. Geoscience and Remote Sensing,* Vol. 42, No. 8, (August 2004), pp. 1642-1648

Daubechies, I. (June 1, 1992). *Ten Lectures on Wavelets* (1st edition), SIAM: Society for Industrial and Applied Mathematics, 978-0898712742, Philadelphia, Pennsylvania

Do, M. N. and Vetterli, M. (2005). The Contourlet transform: an efficient directional multiresolution image representation. *IEEE Trans. Image Process.,* Vol. 14, No. 12, (December 2005), pp. 2091-2106

Foucher, S., Benie, G. B., and Boucher, J. M. (2001). Multiscale MAP filtering of SAR Images. *IEEE Tran. Image Processing,* Vol. 10, No. 1, (January 2001), pp. 49-60

Frost, V. S., Stiles J. A., Shanmugan K. S., and Holtzman J. C. (1982). A model for radar images and its application to adaptive digital filtering of multiplicative noise. *IEEE Trans. Pattern Anal. Mach. Intell.,* Vol. 4, No. 2, (February 1982), pp. 157-166

Gleich, D., and Datcu, M. (2006). Gauss-Markov Model for SAR image Despeckling. *IEEE Signal Processing Letters.,* Vol. 13, No. 6, (June 2006), pp. 365-368

Gleich, D., and Datcu, M. (2007). Wavelet-Based Despeckling of SAR Images Using Gauss–Markov Random Fields. *IEEE Transactions on Geoscience and Remote Sensing,* Vol. 45, No. 12, (December 2007), pp. 4127–4143

Kuan, D. T., Sawchuk A. A., Strand T. C., and Chavel P. (1985). Adaptive noise smoothing filter for images with signal-dependent noise. *IEEE Trans. Pattern Anal. Mach. Intell.,* Vol. 7, No. 2, (February 1985), pp. 165-177

Le Pennec, E., and Mallat, S. (2001). Bandelet Image Approximation and Compression. In Proc. Int. Conf. Image Processing, ISBN: 0-7803-6725-1, Thessaloniki, Greece, October 2001

Le Pennec, E., and Mallat, S. (2005). Bandelet Image Approximation and Compression. *SIAM Journ. of Multiscale Modeling and Simulation,* Vol. 4, No. 3, (December 2005), pp. 992-1039

Le Pennec, E., and Mallat, S. (2005). Sparse geometric image representations with bandelets. *IEEE Transaction on Image Processing,* Vol. 14, No. 4, (April 2005), pp. 423–438

Lee, J. S. (1980). Digital image enhancement and noise filtering by use of local statistics. *IEEE Trans. Pattern Anal. Machine Intell.,* Vol. 2, No. 2, (March 1980), pp. 165-168

Li, Y., He, M. and Fang, X. (2006). A New Adaptive Algorithm for Despeckling of SAR images Based on Contourlet Transform. *IEEE Conference on Signal Processing,* ISBN 0-7803-9736-3, Guilin, China, November 2006

Peyré, G., and Mallat, S. (2005). Surface compression with geometric bandelets. *ACM Transactions on Graphics,* Vol. 24, No. 3, (July 2005), pp. 601-608

Sivia, D. S. (September 26, 1996). *Data Analysis: A Bayesian Tutorial* (1st edition), Oxford University Press, 978-0198518891, USA

Sveinsson, J. R., Semar Z., and Benediktsson, J. A. (2008). Speckle Reduction of SAR Images in the Bandelet Domain. *IEEE International Conference on Geoscience and Remote Sensing*, ISBN: 978-1-4244-2807-6, Boston, MA, July 2008

Vetterli, M. (1984). Multi-dimensional subband coding: some theory and algorithms. *Signal Processing,* Vol. 6, No. 2, (April 1984), pp. 97-112

Walessa, M., and Datcu M. (2000). Model-Based Despeckling and Information Extraction form SAR images. *IEEE Tran. Geoscience and Remote Sensing,* Vol. 38, No. 5, (September 2000), pp. 2258-2269

Wikipedia. (18 January 2011). TerraSAR-X, In: *Wikipedia,* October 6 2011, Available from: http://en.wikipedia.org/wiki/TerraSAR-X

Yang, S., Liu, F., Wand, M., and Jiao, L. (2007). Multiscale bandelet image compression. *International Symposium on Intelligent Signal Processing and Communication Systems,* ISBN 978-1-4244-1447-5, Xiamen, November 2007

17

The Wavelet Transform for Image Processing Applications

Bouden Toufik[1] and Nibouche Mokhtar[2]
[1]*Automatic Department, Laboratory of Non Destructive Testing, Jijel University*
[2]*Bristol Robotic Laboratory, Department of Electrical and Computer Engineering, University of the West of England*
[1]*Algeria*
[2]*UK*

1. Introduction

In recent years, the wavelet transform emerged in the field of image/signal processing as an alternative to the well-known Fourier Transform (FT) and its related transforms, namely, the Discrete Cosine Transform (DCT) and the Discrete Sine Transform (DST). In the Fourier theory, a signal (an image is considered as a finite 2-D signal) is expressed as a sum, theoretically infinite, of sines and cosines, making the FT suitable for infinite and periodic signal analysis. For several years, the FT dominated the field of signal processing, however, if it succeeded well in providing the frequency information contained in the analysed signal; it failed to give any information about the occurrence time. This shortcoming, but not the only one, motivated the scientists to scrutinise the transform horizon for a "messiah" transform. The first step in this long research journey was to cut the signal of interest in several parts and then to analyse each part separately. The idea at a first glance seemed to be very promising since it allowed the extraction of time information and the localisation of different frequency components. This approach is known as the Short-Time Fourier Transform (STFT). The fundamental question, which arises here, is how to cut the signal? The best solution to this dilemma was of course to find a fully scalable modulated window in which no signal cutting is needed anymore. This goal was achieved successfully by the use of the wavelet transform.

Formally, the wavelet transform is defined by many authors as a mathematical technique in which a particular signal is analysed (or synthesised) in the time domain by using different versions of a dilated (or contracted) and translated (or shifted) basis function called the wavelet prototype or the mother wavelet. However, in reality, the wavelet transform found its essence and emerged from different disciplines and was not, as stated by Mallat, totally new to mathematicians working in harmonic analysis, or to computer vision researchers studying multiscale image processing (Mallat, 1989).

At the beginning of the 20th century, Haar, a German mathematician introduced the first wavelet transform named after him (almost a century after the introduction of the FT, by the French J. Fourier). The Haar wavelet basis function has compact support and integer coefficients. Later, the Haar basis was used in physics to study Brownian motion (Graps,

1995). Since then, different works have been carried out either in the development of the theory related to the wavelet, or towards its application in different fields. In the field of signal processing, the great achievements reached in different studies by Mallat, Meyer and Daubechies have allowed the emergence of a wide range of wavelet-based applications. In fact, inspired by the work developed by Mallat on the relationships between the Quadrature Mirror Filters (QMF), pyramid algorithms and orthonormal wavelet bases (Mallat, 1989), Meyer constructed the first non-trivial wavelets (Meyer, 1989). However, the most important work was carried out by Ingrid Daubechies. Based on Mallat's work, Daubechies succeeded to construct a set of wavelet orthonormal basis functions, which have become the cornerstone of many applications (Daubechies, 1988). Few years later, the same author, in collaboration with others (Cody, 1994), presented a set of wavelet biorthogonal basis function, which later found their use in different applications, especially in image coding. Recently, JPEG2000, a biorthogonal wavelet-based compression has been adopted as the new compression standard (Ebrahimi et al., 2002).

2. Continuous Wavelet Transform

Different ways to introduce the wavelet transform can be envisaged (Starck et al., 1998). However, the traditional method to achieve this goal remains the use of the Fourier theory (more precisely, STFT). The Fourier theory uses sine and cosine as basis functions to analyse a particular signal. Due to the infinite expansion of the basis functions, the FT is more appropriate for signals of the same nature, which generally are assumed to be periodic. Hence, the Fourier theory is purely a frequency domain approach, which means that a particular signal f(t) can be represented by the frequency spectrum F(w), as follows:

$$F(\omega) = \int_{-\infty}^{+\infty} f(t) e^{-j\omega t} dt \tag{1}$$

The original signal can be recovered, under certain conditions, by the inverse Fourier Transform as follows:

$$f(t) = \frac{1}{2\pi} \int_{-\infty}^{+\infty} F(\omega) e^{j\omega t} d\omega \tag{2}$$

Obviously, discrete-time versions of both direct and inverse forms of the Fourier transform are possible.

Due to the non-locality and the time-independence of the basis functions in the Fourier analysis, as represented by the exponential factor of equation (1), the FT can only suit signals with "time-independent" statistical properties. In other words, the FT can only provide global information of a signal and fails in dealing with local patterns like discontinuities or sharp spikes (Graps, 1995). However, in many applications, the signal of concern is both time and frequency dependent, and as such, the Fourier theory is "incapable" of providing a global and complete analysis. The shortcomings of the Fourier transform, in addition to its failure to deal with non-periodic signals led to the adoption by the scientific community of a windowed version of this transform known as the STFT. The STFT transform of a signal f(t) is defined around a time θ through the usage of a sliding window w (centred at time θ) and a frequency ω as (Wickerhauser, 1994; Graps, 1995; Burrus et al., 1998; David, 2002 & Oppenheim & Schafer, 2010):

$$STFT(\theta, w) = \int_{-\infty}^{+\infty} f(t)w(t-\theta)e^{-jwt}dt \tag{3}$$

As it is apparent from equation (3), even if the integral limits are infinite, the analysis is always limited to a portion of the signal, bounded by the limits [-θ, θ] of the sliding window. The time-frequency plane of a fixed window STFT transform is illustrated in Figure 1.

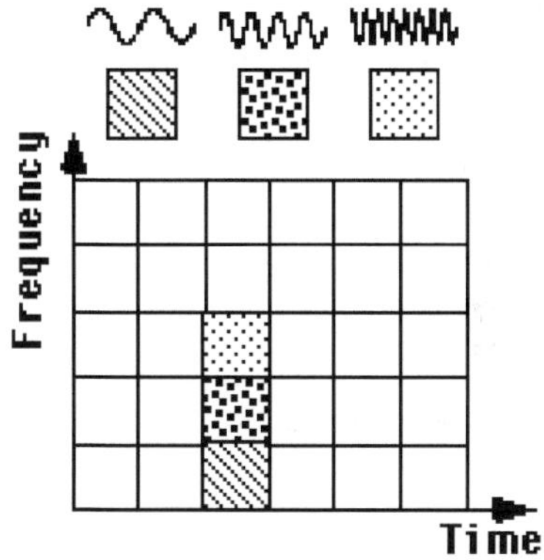

Fig. 1. Fourier time-frequency plane (Graps, 1995)

Although, this approach (using STFT transform) succeeds well in giving both time and frequency information about a portion of the signal, however, as its predecessor, it has a major drawback. The fact is that the choice of the window size is crucial. As stated by Starck and al (Starck et al., 1998): " The smaller the window size, the better the time-resolution. However, the smaller the window size also, the more the number of discrete frequencies which can be represented in the frequency domain will be reduced, and therefore the more weakened will be the discrimination potential among frequencies". This problem is closely linked to the Heisenberg's uncertainty principle, which states that a signal (e.g. a very short portion of the signal) cannot be represented as a point in the time-frequency domain.

This shortcoming brings us to rise the fundamental question: how to size then the sliding window? Not surprisingly, the answer to this question leads us by means of certain transformations to the wavelet transform. In fact, by considering the convolution of the sliding window with the time-dependant exponential e^{-jwt} within the integral of equation (3):

$$K_{\theta,\omega}(t) = w(t-\theta)e^{-jwt} \tag{4}$$

And replacing the frequency ω by a scaling factor a, and the window bound θ by a shifting factor b, leads us to the first step leading to the Continuous Wavelet Transform (CWT), as represented in equation (5):

$$K_{a,b}(t) = \frac{1}{\sqrt{a}}\psi^*(\frac{t-b}{a}) \qquad a \in R^+, b \in R \tag{5}$$

The combination of equation (5) with equation (3), leads to the CWT as defined by Morlet and Grossman (Grossman & Morlet, 1984).

$$W(a,b) = \frac{1}{\sqrt{a}} \int_{-\infty}^{+\infty} f(t) \psi^* (\frac{t-b}{a})\, dt \tag{6}$$

Where f(t) belongs to the square integrable functions space, $L^2(R)$. In the same way, the inverse CWT can be defined as (Grossman & Morlet, 1984):

$$f(t) = \frac{1}{C_\psi} \int_0^{+\infty} \int_{-\infty}^{+\infty} \frac{1}{\sqrt{a}} W(a,b) \psi(\frac{t-b}{a}) \frac{da\,db}{a^2} \tag{7}$$

The C_ψ factor is needed for reconstruction purposes. In fact, the reconstruction is only possible if this factor is defined. This requirement is known as the admissibility condition. In a more general way, $\psi(t)$ is replaced by $\chi(t)$, allowing a variety of choices, which can enhance certain features for some particular applications (Starck et al., 1998; Stromme, 1999 & Hankerson et al., 2005). However, the CWT in the form defined by equation (6) is highly redundant, which makes its direct implementation of minor interest. The time-frequency plane of a wavelet transformation is illustrated in Figure 2. The differences with the STFT transform are visually clear.

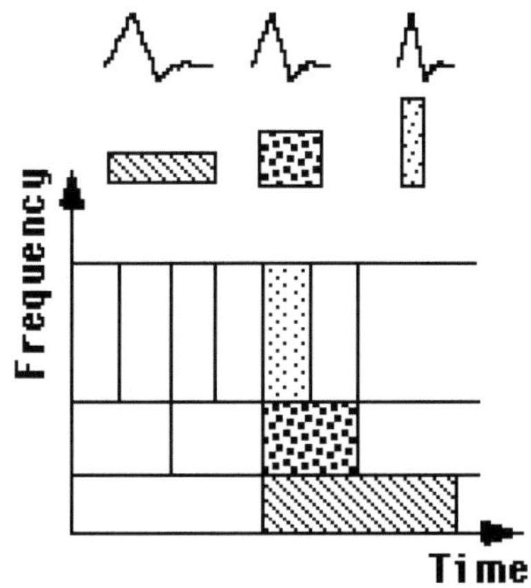

Fig. 2. Wavelet time-frequency plane ((Graps, 1995) with minor modifications)

At this stage and after this brief introduction, it is natural to ask the question: therefore what are wavelet Transforms?

Although wavelet transforms are defined as a mathematical tool or technique, there is no consensus within the scientific community on a particular definition. This "embarrassment" has been stated by Sweldens as (Sweldens, 1996): "Giving that the wavelet field keeps growing, the definition of a wavelet continuously changes. Therefore it is impossible to rigorously define a wavelet". According to the same author, to call a particular function a wavelet system, it has to fulfil the three following properties:

- Wavelets are building blocks for general functions: They are used to represent signals and more generally functions. In other words, a function is represented in the wavelet space by mean of infinite series of wavelets.
- Wavelets have space – frequency localisation: Which means that most of the energy of a wavelet is confined in a finite interval and that the transform contains only frequencies from a certain frequency band.
- Wavelets support fast and efficient transform algorithms: This requirement is needed when implementing the transform. Often wavelet transforms need O(n) operations, which means that the number of multiplications and additions follows linearly the length of the signal. This is a direct implication of the compactness property of the transform. However, more general wavelet transforms require O(nlog(n)) operations (e.g. undecimated wavelet).

To refine the wavelet definition, the three following characteristics have been added by Sweldens and Daubechies (Sweldens, 1996 & Daubechies, 1992, 1993) as reported in (Burrus et al., 1998):

- Oneness of the generating function: Refers to the ability of generating a wavelet system from a single scaling function or wavelet function just by scaling and translating.
- Multiresolution ability: This concept, which has first been introduced by Mallat, states the ability of the transform to represent a signal or function at different level, by different weighted sums, derived from the original one.
- Ability of generating lower level coefficients from the higher level coefficients. This can be achieved through the use of tree-like structured chain of filters called Filter Banks.

3. Multiresolution

The multiresolution concept has been introduced first by Mallat (Mallat, 1989). It defines clearly the relationships between the QMF, pyramid algorithms and orthonormal wavelet bases through basically, the definition of a set of nested subspaces and a so-called scaling function. The strength of multiresolution lies in its ability to decompose a signal in finer and finer details. Most importantly, it allows the description of a signal in terms of time-frequency or time-scale analysis.

3.1 Nested subspaces

The basic requirement for multiresolution analysis is the existence of a set of approximation subspaces of $L^2(R)$ (square integrable function space) with different resolutions, as represented schematically for the three intermediate subspaces in Figure 3 and stated by equation (8):

$$V_{-\infty} \ldots \subset V_{-1} \subset V_0 \subset V_1 \subset \ldots V_{\infty} = L^2(R) \tag{8}$$

In such a way that, if $f(t) \in V_j$ then $f(2t) \in V_{j+1}$. Which means that the subspace containing high resolution will automatically contains those of lower resolution. In a more general case, if $f(t) \in V_0$, then $f(2^k t) \in V_k$. This implication is known as the scale invariance property.

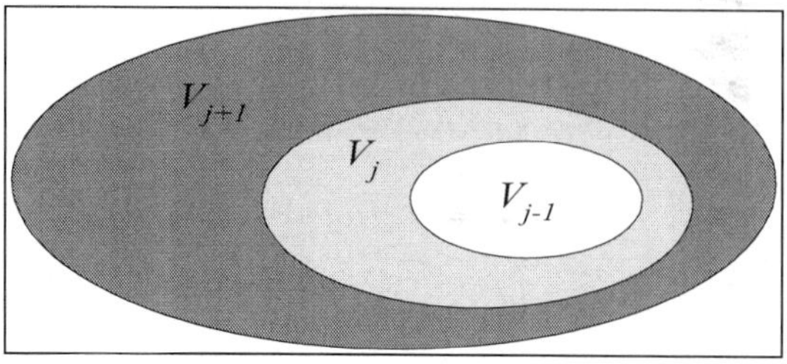

Fig. 3. Nested subspaces

3.2 Scaling function

The existence of a so-called scaling function $\phi(t)$ is primordial in order to benefit from the multiresolution concept. In this context, let us define the scaling function first and then define the wavelet function through it (Burrus et al., 1998). Let the scaling function be defined by the following equation:

$$\varphi_k(t) = \varphi(t-k) \qquad k \in Z \qquad \varphi \in L^2(R) \tag{9}$$

Which forms with its translates an orthonormal (The orthogonality is not necessary, since a non orthogonal basis (with the shift property) can always be orthogonalised (Sweldens, 1995)) basis of the space V_0:

$$V_0 = \underset{k}{\text{span}}\{\varphi_k(t)\} \tag{10}$$

This means that any function belonging to this space ($f(t) \in V_0$) can be expressed as a linear combination of a set of so-called expansion coefficients, with the scaling function and its consecutive translates (since $\varphi_k(t)$ are the basis functions):

$$f(t) = \sum_k c_k \varphi_k(t) = \sum_k c(k)\varphi(t-k) \tag{11}$$

Where the expansion coefficients c_k (or $c(k)$) are calculated using the inner product:

$$c_k = \langle f(t), \varphi_k(t) \rangle \tag{12}$$

By simply scaling and translating, a two-dimensional scaling function is generated from the original scaling function defined in equation (9):

$$\varphi_{j,k}(t) = \frac{1}{\sqrt{a}}\varphi\left(\frac{t-b}{a}\right) \tag{13}$$

Where a and b are, the scaling and the shifting factors as defined in equation (5), respectively. To ease the implementation of a wavelet system, the translation and the scaling factor have been adopted to be a factor of two. In fact (Graps, 1995):

$$a = 2^{-j} \quad , \quad b = 2^{-j}.k \tag{14}$$

These values are adopted for the remaining of the chapter. Thus equation (13) can be rewritten as:

$$\varphi_{j,k}(t) = 2^{j/2}\,\varphi(2^j t - k) \tag{15}$$

Identically, the two-dimensional scaling function forms with its translates an orthonormal space over k:

$$V_j = \operatorname*{span}_k\{\varphi_{j,k}(t)\} \qquad k \in Z \quad \text{and} \quad j \in Z \tag{16}$$

And as such any function $f(t)$ of this space can be expressed as:

$$f(t) = \sum_k c(k)\,\varphi(2^j t + k) \tag{17}$$

As a consequence, if $\varphi(t) \in V_0$, then since $V_0 \subset V_1$, $\varphi(t)$ can be expressed as a linear combination of the scaling function $\varphi(2t)$ spanning the space V_1:

$$\varphi(t) = \sum_k h(k)\sqrt{2}\,\varphi(2t - k) \tag{18}$$

Where the coefficients h(k) are the scaling function coefficients. The value $\sqrt{2}$ ensures that the norm of the scaling function is always equal to the unity. This equation is fundamental to the multiresolution theory and is called the multiresolution analysis equation.

4. Wavelet function

What has been done so far to define the scaling function, its translates and the corresponding spanned spaces, can also be applied in the same way to the so-called wavelet function. Let us suppose for this purpose that the subspace $V_0 \subset V_1$ has an orthogonal complement W_0, such as V_1 can be represented as a combination of V_0 and W_0 as follows:

$$V_1 = V_0 \oplus W_0 \tag{19}$$

Where the complementary space W_0 is spanned also by an orthonormal basis:

$$\psi_k(t) = \psi(t - k) \qquad k \in Z \qquad\qquad \psi \in L^2(R) \tag{20}$$

The function $\psi(t)$ is known as the mother wavelet, the wavelet prototype or the wavelet function. The same properties, which apply to the scaling function, are also applicable to the wavelet function. In other words, a function $f(t) \in W_0$ can be expressed as:

$$f(t) = \sum_k d_k \psi_k(t) = \sum_k d(k)\psi(t-k) \tag{21}$$

Where, the expansion coefficients d_k (or $d(k)$) are calculated using the inner product:

$$d_k = \langle f(t), \psi_k(t) \rangle \tag{22}$$

Likewise, since $W_0 \subset V_1$, $\psi(t)$ can also be expressed in terms of the scaling function $\varphi(2t)$ of the higher space V_1:

$$\psi(t) = \sum_k g(k)\sqrt{2}\,\varphi(2t-k) \tag{23}$$

Where g(k) are the wavelet coefficients. This leads to a dyadic decomposition as represented by the grid of Figure 5. The equation (19) can be generalised to an arbitrary number of subspaces, such as, V_2 is represented in terms of V_1 and W_1, V_3 in terms of V_2 and W_2, and so on. The whole decomposition process is illustrated in Figure 4.

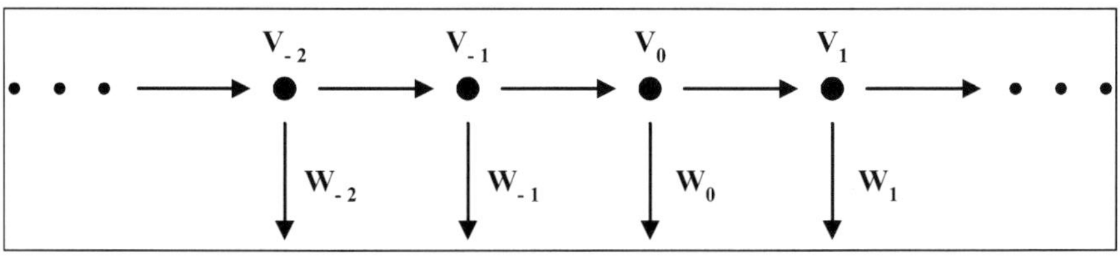

Fig. 4. Space decomposition

More generally, a subspace V_j is spanned by W_{j-1} and V_{j-1}. Thus, the $L^2(R)$ space can be decomposed as follows:

$$L^2(R) = V_j \oplus W_j \oplus W_{j+1} \oplus W_{j+2} \oplus \ldots W_0 \oplus W_1 \ldots \tag{24}$$

The index j represents the depth or the level of decomposition, which is arbitrary in this case. As for the scaling function, a two-dimensional scaled and translated wavelet function is defined as:

$$\psi_{j,k}(t) = 2^{j/2}\psi(2^j t - k) \tag{25}$$

In such way that:

$$W_j = \operatorname*{span}_k \{\psi_{ji,k}(t)\} \tag{26}$$

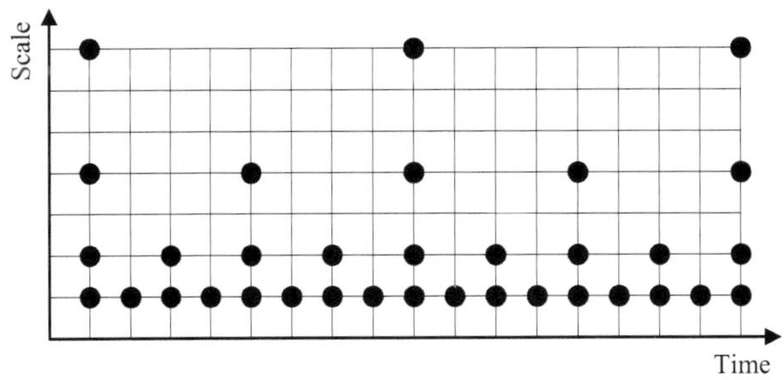

Fig. 5. Dyadic wavelet transform space representation

5. Series expansions and Discrete Wavelet Transforms

According to equation (24), a function $f(t)$ belonging to the $L^2(R)$ space can be expanded in series in terms of the scaling function spanning the space V_j and the wavelet functions spanning the spaces $W_j, W_{j+1}, W_{j+2}, \ldots, W_0, W_1 \ldots$ as follows:

$$f(t) = \sum_k c_j(k)\varphi_{j,k}(t) + \sum_{n=j}^{+\infty}\sum_{k=-\infty}^{+\infty} d_n(k)\psi_{n.k}(t) \qquad (27)$$

Where $\varphi_{j,k}(t)$ is defined by equation (15) and $\psi_{n.k}(t)$ is defined by equation (25). In this case, the index j, which is arbitrary, represents the coarsest scale, while the remaining are the high resolution details. Equation (27) represents the wavelet expansion series of the function $f(t)$, which plays a major role when deriving a more practical form of the wavelet transform.

The coefficients in the wavelet expansion series $c_j(k)$ and $d_n(k)$ (or $c(j,k)$ and $d(n,k)$) are the so-called discerete wavelet transform of the function $f(t)$. Since the basis functions are orthonormal, they can be calculated using equations (12 and 22), respectively. We will see later in this chapter that the orthonormality condition can be relaxed allowing the implementation of another important basis, namely, the biorthogonal basis.

6. Filter banks and wavelet implementations

In general, wavelet transform-based applications involve discrete coefficients instead of scaling and/or wavelet functions. For practical and computational reasons, discrete time filter banks are required. Such structures decompose a signal into a coarse representation along with added details. To achieve this representation, the relationship between the expansion coefficients at lower and higher scale levels need to be defined. This can be easily done by using a scaled and shifted version of equation (18) along with simple transformations as reported in (Burrus et al., 1998). This relation is defined by:

$$c_j(k) = \sum_n h(n-2k)c_{j+1}(n) \qquad (28)$$

And

$$d_j(k) = \sum_n g(n-2k)c_{j+1}(n) \quad (29)$$

Where $n \in Z$ and $k \in Z$. The computation of such equations is achieved through the use of the well-established digital filtering theory. In particular, for finite length signals (which is the case for digital images), the use of a Finite Impulse Response filter (FIR) is the most appropriate choice. However, since equations (28 and 29) compute one output for each two consecutive inputs, a modification needs to be made. The basic operation required here, is derived from the multirate signal processing theory (Fliege, 1994; Hankerson et al., 2005; Cunha et al., 2006; Lu & Do, 2007; Nguyen & Oraintara, 2008 & Brislawn, 2010). It simply consists of using a down-sampler or decimator by a factor of two. In practice, it consists of applying a pair of FIR filters; each followed by a decimator as illustrated by Figure 6:

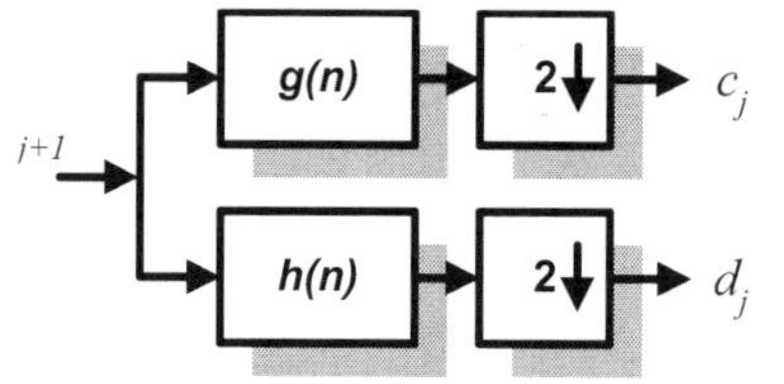

Fig. 6. Analysis Filter Bank

The filter bank is defined as a combination of a low pass filter and high pass filter, both followed by a factor of two decimation (Strang & Nguyen, 1996). Thus, the decomposition is reduced to two basic operations from the digital signal processing theory: a filtering and a down sampling.

The structure in Figure 6 is generally used to implement Mallat's algorithm. To allow further level of decomposition, identical stages are cascaded leading to a multiresolution analysis. This analysis scheme is known as the Subband Coding structure (Burrus et al., 1998) and is illustrated in the following figure.

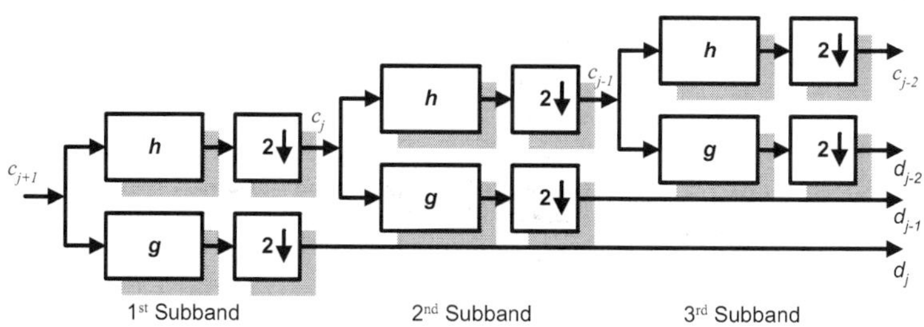

Fig. 7. Three-Stage analysis Subband Coding

At each stage, the spectrum frequency of the analysed signal is halved by a factor of two. This leads to a logarithmic set of bandwidths as illustrated by Figure 8.

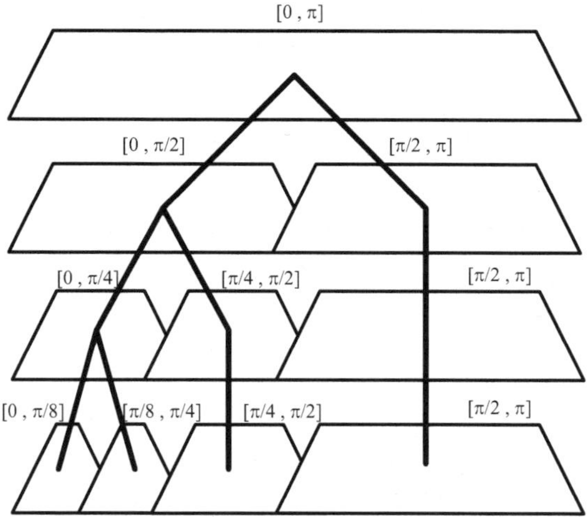

Fig. 8. Frequency Spectrum of a three-stage Subband Structure

To recover the original signal from the previously analysed one, a reversed version of the analysis filter bank of Figure 6 is required. This can be achieved by using two basic operations: a filtering and an up sampling or interpolating process. In multirate digital signal processing, appending a zero sample between two consecutive samples performs the up sampling. Thus, for each input sample, we get two output samples. A three-stage synthesis subband coding is illustrated in Figure 9.

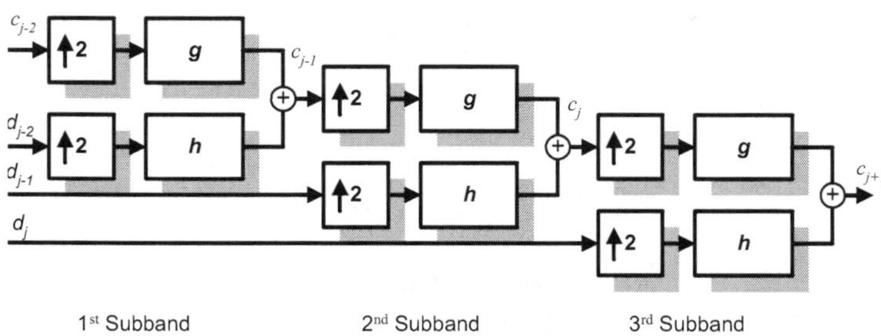

Fig. 9. Three-Stage synthesis Subband Coding

7. Algorithms for Wavelet Transform computation

This section is concerned with a review of variety of algorithms dedicated to implement wavelet transforms. We focus on both 1-Dimensional and 2-Dimensional systems.

7.1 Burt's Pyramid

Dedicated initially to lossless image coding, the pyramid algorithm was first introduced by Burt (Burt & Adelson, 1983). Basically, it decomposes a signal in a low-resolution signal along with some higher resolution signals through a repetition of reduction and expansion processes. At each level, the reduced and expanded signal is compared with the original signal and the difference is stored. In the same time, the reduced signal is repeatedly decomposed by further using the reducer block in the chain. The analysis/synthesis process is shown in Figure 10.

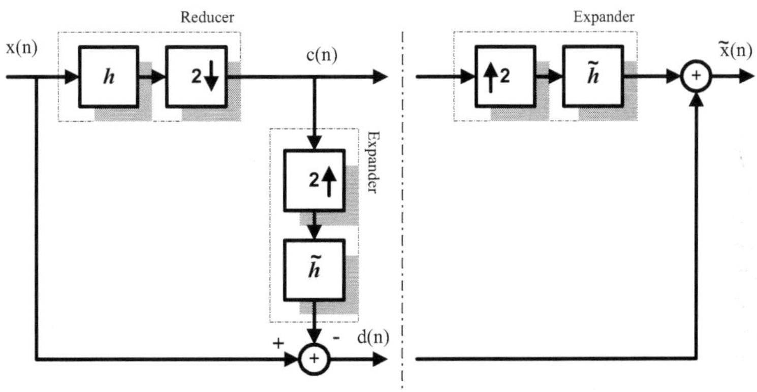

Fig. 10. Pyramidal analysis and synthesis

The reduction block performs the two basic operations of a low pass filtering and decimating by a factor of 2. The expansion block up samples the signal first, then filters it through the use of a synthesis low pass filter. To reconstruct the original signal, the difference signal at each level is added to a previously expanded signal. Repeatedly, the resulting signal is expanded and added to the corresponding difference signal.

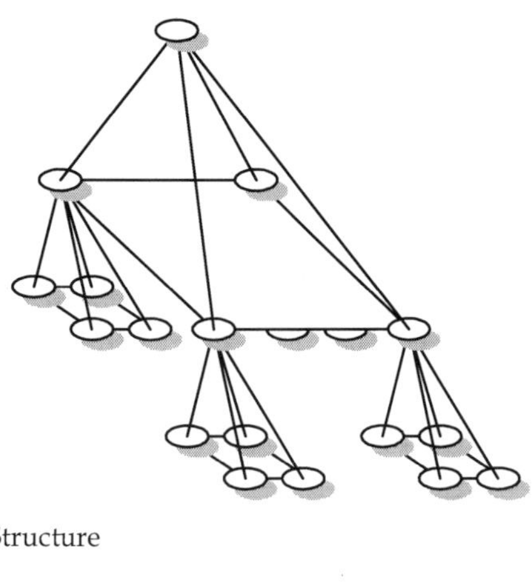

Fig. 11. 2-D Pyramidal Structure

The decomposition and the reconstruction processes for a 2-D signal, as in image processing, is achieved through the use of a 2-D filtering process. In this case, only 1/4 of the original signal is obtained at the output of the reducer (the decimation is performed twice). This scheme can be represented by the pyramidal structure of Figure 11.

This type of decomposition makes this algorithm suitable for a progressive image transmission scheme.

7.2 Mallat's Pyramidal algorithm

Mallat's pyramid is a direct consequence of the multiresolution concept developed by the same author and presented in section 6. Up to date, it is the most widely used approach - both in software and hardware - for implementing the wavelet transform (Masud, 1999). Since the one-dimensional decomposition and reconstruction schemes have been already introduced in section 6, we will focus in this section on two-dimensional schemes, which are more suitable for image analysis and synthesis. The two-dimensional decomposition approach is based on the property of separation of the functions into arbitrary x and y directions. The first step is identical to the one-dimensional approach, however, instead of keeping the low-level resolution and processing the high level resolution, both are processed using two identical filter bank after a transposition of the incoming data. Thus, the image is scanned in both horizontal and vertical directions. This result in an average image (or subimage) and three detail images generated by the following 2-D scaling function $\varphi(x,y)=\varphi(x)\varphi(y)$ and the vertical, the horizontal and the diagonal wavelet functions: $\psi_1(x,y)=\varphi(x)\psi(y)$, $\psi_2(x,y)=\psi(x)\varphi(y)$ and $\psi_3(x,y)=\psi(x)\psi(y)$, respectively. To recover the original image, the inverse process is applied. Figure 12 illustrates the analysis and synthesis stages built using three filter banks each.

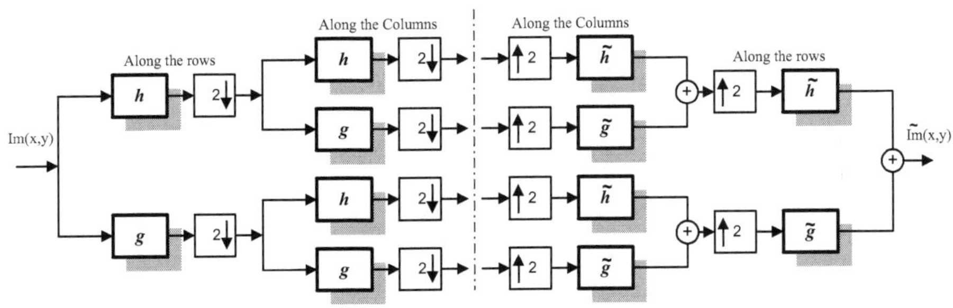

Fig. 12. Two-dimensional Mallat's analysis and synthesis tree

In this case, the frequency band is halved at each stage by a factor of four as represented by Figure 13.

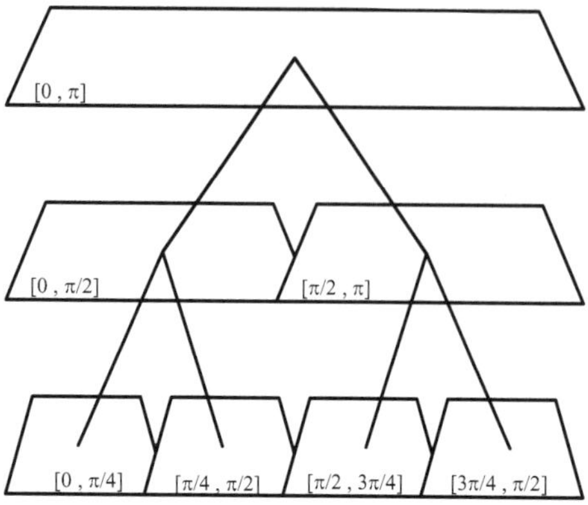

Fig. 13. Frequency Bands of Mallat's 2-D Analysis Algorithm

7.3 Feauveau's non-dyadic structure

Based on Adelson's work (Adelson et al., 1987), this approach has been introduced by Feauveau (Feauveau, 1990). This decomposition is also known as Quincux. It differs from Mallat's two-dimensional approach by the fact that only the decimated output from the low pass filter is transposed and then processed through a "similar" filter bank. The result is a low resolution average image along with two different detail images from two different resolution levels. The fact is that the decomposition is not dyadic and the initial resolution of a factor of 2 is replaced by a $\sqrt{2}$ factor leading to an asymmetrical support. Figure 14 shows an analysis and synthesis stage of a Quincux structure.

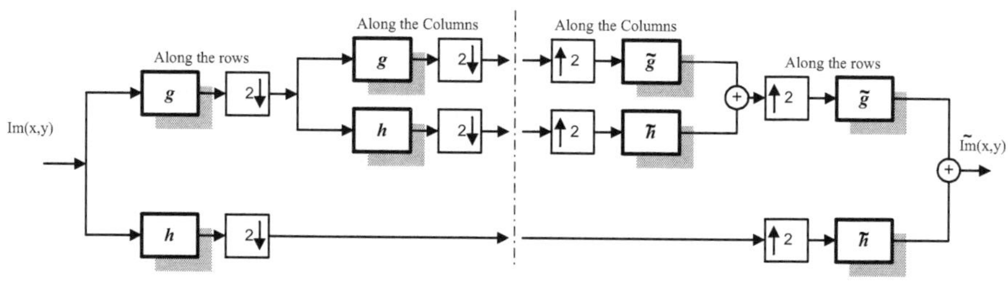

Fig. 14. Feauveau's analysis and synthesis tree

Due to the removal of the filter bank at the output of the high pass filter - as reported in (Starck et al., 1998) only a wavelet image is involved at each stage. Recently, this approach has been used in an image compression scheme and found to give often better overall performances than other approaches (Stromme, 1999; Ebrahimi et al, 2002; Smith, 2003; Hankerson et al., 2005; Xiong & Ramchandran, 2005; Nai-Xiang et al., 2006; Raviraj & Sanavullah, 2007 & Oppenheim & Schafer, 2010). The frequency bands of a Quincux analysis is shown in Figure 15.

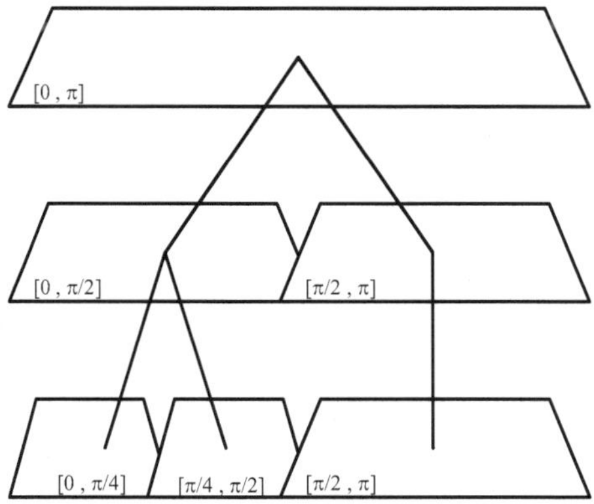

Fig. 15. Frequency bands of Feauveau's Quincux decomposition

7.4 Swelden's lifting scheme

Unlike the three previous methodologies, the lifting scheme follows another philosophy. The fact is that the Fourier theory is not involved anymore and the construction of any wavelet system lies only in the spatial domain. If the explanation of the theory relies on the works of Sweldens (Sweldens, 1995, 1996 & Valens, 2004) the lifting approach has links with many other schemes (Burrus et al., 1998; Do & Vetterli, 2003, 2005; Cunha et al., 2006; Lu & Do, 2007; Nguyen & Oraintara, 2008 & Brislawn, 2010). The lifting-based wavelet transform can be seen as a succession of three operations: split, predict and update. In the first operation, data is the split into even and odds parts (known also as the lazy wavelet transform). Then, differences or details are calculated through the usage of a predictor. Finally, to compute the average, the even part is updated using the details previously calculated. Figure 16 shows an analysis and synthesis lifting-based wavelet transform.

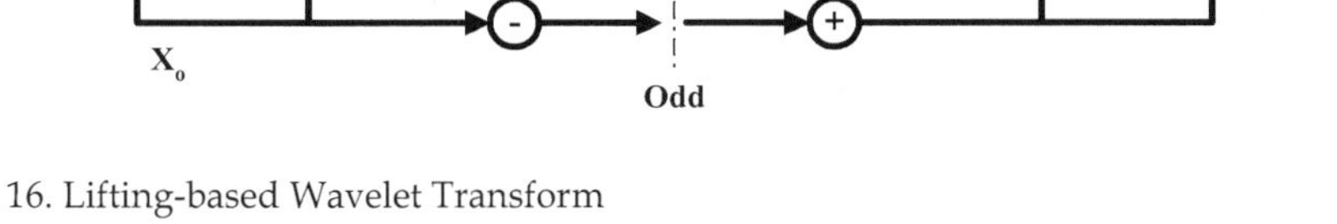

Fig. 16. Lifting-based Wavelet Transform

The reconstruction operation does exactly the same, but using the reverse process. The data is first predicted, then updated and finally merged. Figure 17 illustrates split and merge operations using the polyphase property (Fliege, 1994).

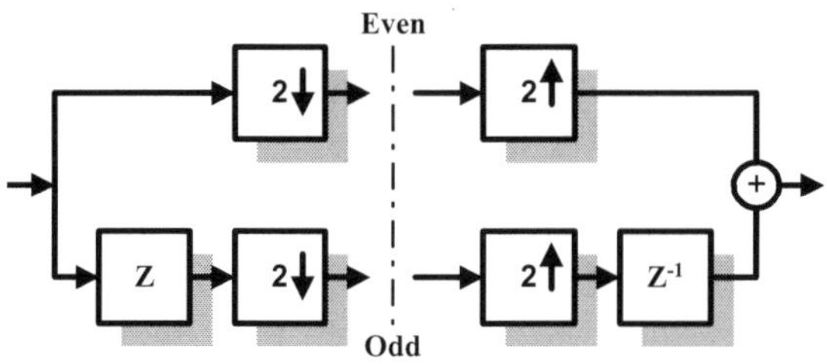

(a) (b)

Fig. 17. Lazy Wavelet Transform: (a) Split, (b) Merge

8. The Wavelet Transform revisited

In many practical problems, both the orthonormal basis (Daubechies, 1988, 1992, 1993) and the biorthogonal basis (Cody, 1994) can be used. The two bases (or families) present similarities and differences. Another scheme, called wavelet packet, which involves either orthonormal basis or biorthogonal basis is also possible (Wickerhauser, 1994). The following briefly describes the main features of orthonormal and biorthogonal bases together with extension to the wavelet packet scheme. It is worth mentioning that other schemes like undecimated wavelet, adaptive wavelets and multiwavelets exist and are beyond the scope of this brief overview.

8.1 Orthonormal basis

The orthonormal basis emerged from the work initiated by Mallat and Daubechies (Mallat, 1989 & Daubechies, 1988, 1993). The orthonormality property is somewhat seen as the discrete version of the orthogonality property (Masud, 1999). However, the basis functions are further normalised. These concepts have been mentioned when the multiresolution feature and the scaling function have been introduced. The admissibility and the orthogonality conditions ensure the existence and the orthogonality feature of the scaling function, defined by equation (18). This is achieved if:

$$\sum_n h(n) = \sqrt{2} \tag{30}$$

And

$$\sum_n h(n)h(n+2k) = \delta(k) \tag{31}$$

Furthermore, using the two equations above alongside with equation (23), which defines the wavelet function, the orthogonality of the scaling function and the wavelet function at the same scale can be derived. This can be achieved only if the following equality is verified:

$$g(n) = (-1)^n h(1-n) \tag{32}$$

The orthogonality between the wavelet coefficients and the scaling coefficients is then only a simple implication:

$$\sum_{n} h(n)g(n) = 0 \tag{33}$$

The scaling coefficients, which satisfy equation (33), are called Quadrature Mirror Filters (QMF).

To achieve perfect reconstruction, the analysed signal has to be identical to the synthesised one. In other words, $c_j(n) = \tilde{c}_j(n)$, where $c_j(n)$ and $\tilde{c}_j(n)$ are the input and the output of a two-band filter (or filter bank) as shown in Figure 18, respectively.

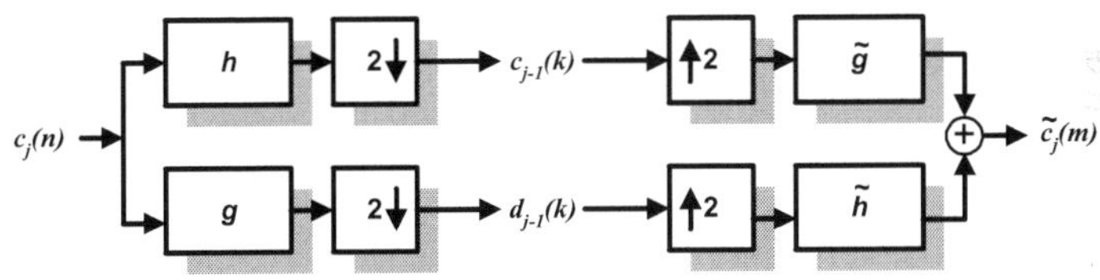

Fig. 18. Two-band analysis and synthesis filter bank

8.2 Biorthogonal basis

Biorthogonal wavelet basis can be seen as a generalisation of the orthogonal wavelet basis where some imposed restrictions on the latter have been relaxed. Unlike the case of orthogonal basis, the scaling and the wavelet functions need be neither of the same length, nor even numbered. Hence, the quadrature mirror property is not applicable and is replaced with a dual property. For the perfect reconstruction equation to hold, the scaling and the wavelet coefficients have to fulfil the following equations:

$$\tilde{g}(n) = (-1)^n h(1-n) \tag{34}$$

$$g(n) = (-1)^n \tilde{h}(1-n) \tag{35}$$

It is clear that when the analysis and the synthesis filters are similar, the system becomes orthogonal. The "orthogonality" condition in this case is defined by:

$$\sum_{n} \tilde{h}(n)h(n+2k) = \delta(k) \tag{36}$$

Previously, in orthogonal basis, only the analysis scaling coefficients (or wavelet coefficients) along with their shifted versions were used. In biorthogonal case, the analysing scaling coefficients are kept unchanged, while their shifted versions are replaced by the shifted versions of the synthesis dual filter. In other words, the analysis filter is orthogonal to its synthesis dual filter. The biorthogonal denomination comes from this feature.

At the expense of the energy partitioning property stated by Perseval's equality, which is a direct consequence of the lack of orthogonality, a greater flexibility can be achieved by using the basis and dual basis (Burrus et al., 1998). One of the most "important" features in the biorthogonal basis is the linear phase property, which leads to the filter coefficients (when implementing a wavelet system) being symmetric. In addition, the difference of length between dual filters must be even, leading either to odd or even length of the low pass and the high pass filters. In general, biorthogonal wavelet systems present the following features (Daubechies, 1992):

- The coefficients of the filters are either real numbers or integers;
- The filters in this family present either even or odd orders;
- The low pass and the high pass filters used in the filter bank have not the same length;
- The low pass filter is always symmetric;
- The high pass filter is either symmetric or antisymmetric.

8.3 Wavelet packets

In contrast to the "traditional" Mallat's decomposition, which leads to narrow frequency bandwidths (low frequencies) and wide frequency bandwidths (high frequencies), the wavelet packet approach emerged first as a way of adjusting high frequency resolutions. Hence, the Mallat's decomposition scheme is applied to both parts of a filter bank leading to the split of frequencies in progressive finer resolutions. The generic structure of wavelet packet decomposition is shown in Figure 19 and the frequency bandwidths illustrated by Figure 20. In this scheme, the number of filters increases by a factor of $(2^{i} - 2^{j})$ at each successive subband, where i and j represent two consecutive resolutions and $i - j = 1$.

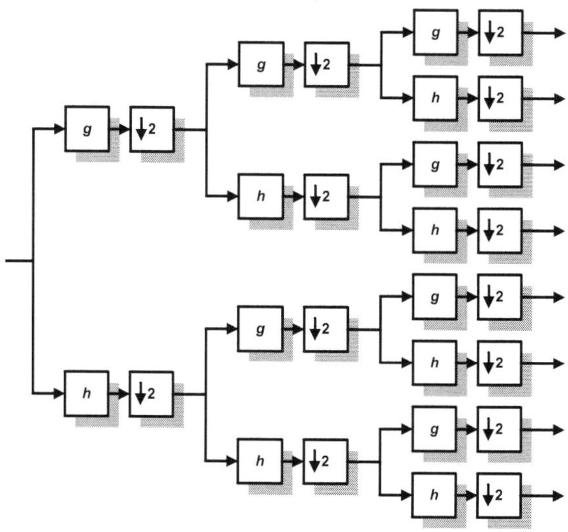

Fig. 19. Three-stage Wavelet Packet Decomposition

In comparison to classical wavelet approach, the wavelet packet scheme presents the following features (Daubechies, 1992):

- Possibility of using different wavelet from a level to another. This strategy has been used in (Masud, 1999) to implement a two-level orthonormal wavelet packet and a three-level biorthogonal wavelet packet.
- Possibility of choosing a particular wavelet packet decomposition from the general generic structure of Figure 19. Thus, one can choose either to preserve the orthonormality feature of the decomposition (Wickerhauser, 1994), or highlight the peculiarities of the signal (Masud, 1999). A binary search for the best decomposition tree is also possible (Burrus et al., 1998).

However, there is a cost to be paid. In this case, the computational complexity of a wavelet packet structure is O(nlog(n)) in contrast to the O(n) of the classical wavelet transform.

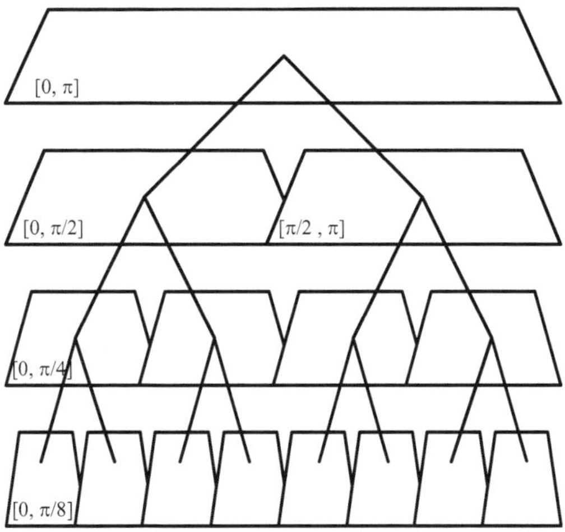

Fig. 20. Two-band analysis and synthesis filter bank

9. Wavelet-based applications

Recently, The wavelet transform is being increasingly used, not only in the field of image and signal processing applications but also in many other different areas, ranging from mathematics, physics, astronomy to statistics and economics. In image processing based applications, image compression, image denoising and image watermarking are at the cutting edge, and as such, a brief description of these wavelet-based applications is given in the following subsections (Strang & Nguyen, 1996; Burrus et al., 1998; Stromme, 1999; Ebrahimi et al, 2002; Nibouche et al., 2000, 2001a, 2001b, 2001c, 2001d, 2002, 2003; Smith, 2003; Do & Vetterli, 2003, 2005; Hankerson et al., 2005; Nai-Xiang Yap-Peng, 2005; Xiong & Ramchandran, 2005; Chappelier & Guillemot, 2006; Cunha et al., 2006; Nai-Xiang et al., 2006; Raviraj & Sanavullah, 2007; Hernandez-Guzmane et al., 2008; Firoiu et al., 2009; Mallat, 2009; Brislawn, 2010; Oppenheim & Schafer, 2010; Ruikar & Doye, 2010 & Chen & Qian, 2011).

9.1 Image compression

Even though the wavelet transforms have been widely used in image coding since the late 80s, they only gained their notoriety in the field by the adoption of the first wavelet-based compression standard scheme, known as the FBI fingerprint compression standard Bradley, et al., 1993). Recently, what did Sweldens state in (Sweldens, 1996) as a need of standardising a wavelet-based compression scheme under the header "problems not sufficiently explored with wavelets", has seen the day, by the adoption of the JPEG2000 new compression standard (Ebrahimi et al., 2002). The block diagram of the JPEG2000 standard does not really differ from the JPEG standard one. The discrete wavelet transform, which replaces the DCT, is applied first to the source image. The transformed coefficients are then quantised. Finally, the output coefficients from the quantiser are encoded (using either Huffman coding or arithmetic coding techniques) to generate the compressed image (Smith, 2003; Do & Vetterli, 2005; Hankerson et al., 2005; Xiong & Ramchandran, 2005; Chappelier & Guillemot, 2006; Nai-Xiang et al., 2006; Raviraj & Sanavullah, 2007; Mallat, 2009; Oppenheim & Schafer, 2010). To recover the original image the inverse process is applied. Figure 21 shows the basic JPEG2000 Encoding Scheme (Ebrahimi et al., 2002).

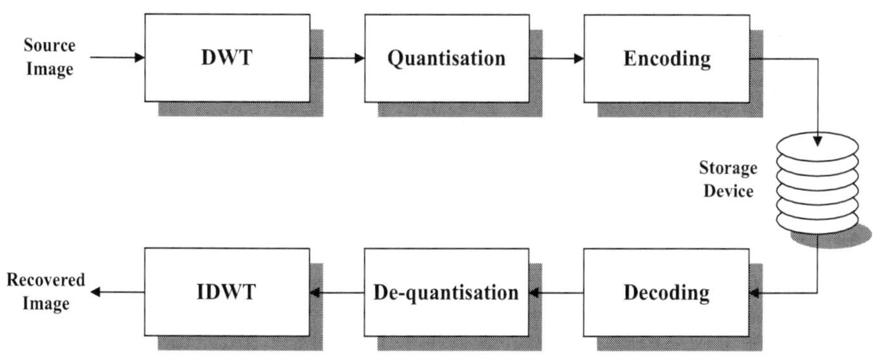

Fig. 21. Wavelet-based encoding scheme

9.2 Image denoising

Image manipulation, includes a wide range of operations like digitising, copying, transmitting, displaying ... etc. Unfortunately, such manipulations generally degrade the image quality by spanning many types of noise. Hence, to recover the original structure of the image, the undesired added noise needs to be localised and then removed. In image processing, noise removal is achieved through the usage of filtering-based denoising techniques (Nai-Xiang & Yap-Peng, 2005; Chappelier & Guillemot, 2006; Firoiu et al., 2009; Mallat, 2009; Nafornita et al., 2009; Ruikar & Doye, 2010; Oppenheim & Schafer, 2010 & Chen & Qian, 2011). Traditionally, image denoising or image enhancement is performed using either linear filtering or non-linear filtering. Linear filtering is achieved either by using spatial techniques, as low pass filtering, or frequency techniques, as the Fast Fourier Transform (FFT). On the other hand, statistical and morphological filters are typical examples of non-linear filtering. However, the filtering techniques lead in some cases to baneful effects when applied indiscriminately to an image. In fact, if it is not the whole image that is blurred, some of its important features (e.g. edges) are.

A solution to overcome this problem has been introduced by Denoho and Johnstone (Donoho & Johnstone, 1994). Instead of exploiting either linear or non-linear filtering, their technique consists of using the DWT followed by a thresholding operation. This method exploits the energy compaction ability of the wavelet transform to separate the image from the added noise. The role of the threshold is to eliminate the noise present in the image. Finally, the enhanced "denoised" image is recovered by applying the inverse DWT. This method is also known as the wavelet shrinkage denoising, and is classified as a nonlinear processing technique due to the thresholding operation involved in the process as illustrated in Figure 22.

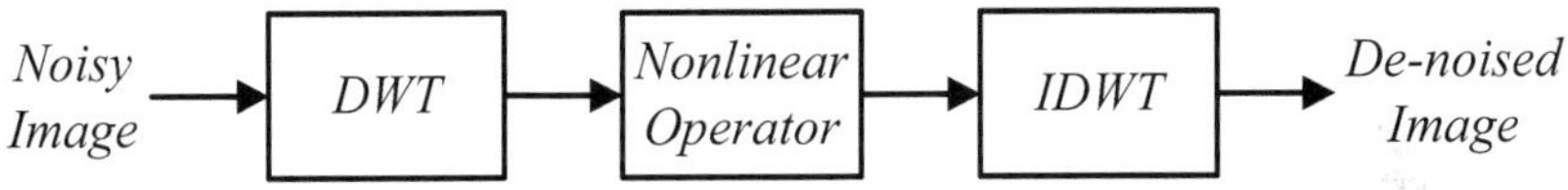

Fig. 22. Wavelet-based denoising system

Another method, which achieves better performances when compared to the previous one, consists of using an undecimated version of the DWT (Donoho & Johnstone, 1995) This choice is motivated by the fact that originally, the DWT is not a shift-invariant transform, and as such, visual artifacts can be spanned by the transform. This like-noise is more apparent around discontinuities in the image. However, in this particular case the inverse transform is not unique. As a solution, it is appropriate to take the average of the possible reconstruction. The computational complexity of this approach is O(nlog(n)).

9.3 Image watermarking

Image watermarking emerged in the mid 90s as a discipline, among the wide range of multidisciplinary field of data hiding, as a methodology of protecting digital images from any piracy act. It consists of embedding a watermark (a trace) within a digital image before using or publishing it. The efficiency of a watermarking method lies generally in its ability to fulfil three requirements: robustness, security and invisibility.

Watermarking techniques can be classified into two categories; spatial domain methods and transform-based methods. The wavelet-based watermarking technique falls into the latter. In (Kundur & Dimitrios, 1997, 1998 & Hernandez-Guzman et al., 2008) both the original image and the watermark are first transformed to the wavelet domain, then the resulting image pyramids are fused according to certain rules, which take into account the characteristics of the Human Visual System (HVS). The wavelet in this case facilitates a simultaneous spatial localisation and frequency spread of the watermark within the source image. It has been shown that the method is robust under compression, additive noise and filtering (Kundur & Dimitrios, 1997, 1998)

To the best of our knowledge, there is no general baseline framework for a wavelet-based watermarking system. However, in most cases, the multiresolution feature of the transform is exploited to achieve robust image watermarking implementations (Kundur & Dimitrios, 1997, 1998; Tsekeridou & Pitas, 2000; Wu et al., 2000 & Hernandez-Guzman et al., 2008).

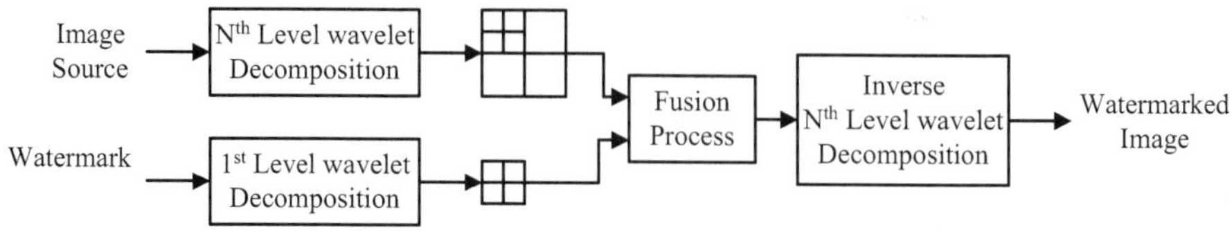

Fig. 23. Wavelet-based watermarking system

10. FPGA implementation

Quick time-to-market, low cost and high performance are typically the treble that digital system designers wish to achieve when developing new products. Although, each goal taken individually is possible, the set of three is generally beyond the capabilities of traditional design and implementation approaches (Villasenor et al., 1995; Villasenor & Mangione-Smith, 1997; Barr, 1998; Ritter & Molitor, 2000; Chrysafis & Ortega, 2000; Lafruit et al., 2000; Russel & Wayne, 2001; Ebrahimi et al., 2002; Nibouche, et al., 2000, 2001a, 2001b, 2001c, 2001d, 2002, 2003; Katona et al., 2006; Angelopoulou et al., 2008 & Lande et al., 2010). Versatile hardware such as general purpose processors (GPP), for example, can perform a wide range of operations and tasks, but fails to reach the system speed of a more specialised hardware. On the contrary, an oriented application-specific hardware, such as Application Specific Integrated Circuits (ASICs), can perform a restricted set of operations/tasks more quickly, however, at the cost of losing in generality. Hence, reconfigurable computing, generally in the form of Field Programmable Gate Arrays (FPGAs), appears to be the promising land for hardware designers. This is old/new paradigm allies the flexibility of software while preserving the hardware performances. This leads to a good trade-off between speed and generality. Unlike the case of custom hardware in the form of ASICs, which cannot be reused for a slightly different problem to the one they were designed for, configurable hardware based FPGAs allows modifications at almost any stage of the design process. In fact, configurable hardware is easily upgraded (due to its inherent nature) to suit any changes of a primal design. Used in a desktop, reconfigurable hardware can be tailored to speed up or accelerate applications, which require a system speed superior to that offered by general purpose processors. The hardware here needs to adapt itself to continual changes in response to end users needs. Obviously, the reconfigurable capabilities of such hardware will not eliminate the need for general-purpose microprocessors running on today's Personal Computers (PCs). In fact, *"FPGAs will never replace microprocessors for general-purpose computing tasks"*, as stated by Villasenor J. and Mangione-Smith W. in (Villasenor & Mangione-Smith, 1997).

The idea of reconfigurable computing was introduced first at the late 60s at the University of California at Los Angeles (UCLA) (Villasenor & Mangione-Smith, 1997 & Barr, 1998). However, the real emergence of this new paradigm for hardware computation was piloted by the commercialisation of the first SRAM-based FPGA by Xilinx Corporation in 1986 (Russel & Wayne, 2001). The first configurable devices from both Xilinx Corporation and Altera Corporation, composed typically of a fine grained structure, allowed a system speed in the range of 2MHz - 5MHz and a chip area of less than a 100 of logic blocks (Russel & Wayne, 2001). The efforts deployed by academicians and industrials since then brought to light new developments but also new challenges. In fact, the reconfigurable hardware field has dramatically maturated either by the developments in the microelectronic technology, which led to the emergence of a new range of devices providing a system gate beyond a million (e.g. Xilinx Virtex family) or by the continual emergence of a wide range of FPGA based system.

In general, FPGA devices are organised as 2D arrays of configurable logic blocks or logic elements. The parallel nature of FPGA devices make them very good targets for application that require parallel processing such as in image and video processing. In such applications, these FPGA devices are used either as co-processors or accelerators (real time applications). It is not the aim of this section to survey the field of wavelet based FPGA implementation but rather to highlight some implementation of the DWT for application in the field of image/video processing (in line with section 9).

Due to its high computational complexity, real time video compression has always been a very challenging topic for digital system designers. The implementation of such systems on FPGAs does not fail to the rule. In probably one of the earliest works in the field, Villasenor et al. in (Villasenor et al., 1995) investigated wavelet transforms based video compression algorithms for use in low-power wireless communications. Using this previous work as a basis, the same authors have further described two implementations using a single FPGA (Schoner et al., 1995). In the first approach, the proposed video compression scheme is directed towards low-complexity implementations using a single in system reprogrammable FPGA. The optimisation of the algorithm to fit the system results in an efficient implementation, however, the system is limited to only a single compression algorithm. In the second approach, to allow more flexibility, the FPGA chip is combined with an external special purpose Video Signal Processor (VSP). The FPGA/VSP combination allows the implementation of four common compression algorithms and their execution in real time. The proposed design schemes were both implemented on a Xilinx FPGA. The first design runs at 20 frames per seconds (fps) when processing a 256x256 frames with a spacial precision of 8-bits. It includes a wavelet transform, a simplified quantiser and a run-length encoder. The second scheme is capable of implementing a DCT, a 2-D FIR, a Vector Quantisation scheme (VQ) and the wavelet transform using a single generic equation. It delivers different performances: 13.3 fps for 7x7 mask 2-D filter, 55 fps for an 8x8 block DCT, 7.4 fps for a 4x4 VQ (at 1/2 bit per pixel) and 35.7 fps for a single wavelet stage.

Partitionning images prior to computation is a well known technique in the field of image processing. It has been widely used in DCT-based image compression schemes. In the last decade, this technique has been adopted in the wavelet-based JPEG2000 new compression standard (Ebrahimi et al., 2002). In (Ritter & Molitor, 2000), a biorthogonal Cohen-daubechies-Fauveau (CDF) 5/3 wavelet pair followed by Embedded Zerotree Encoding (EZT) technique is used in a lossy and a lossless compression schemes, respectively. Since the 5/3 pair is an integer-to-integer wavelet, a lifting scheme based architecture is used for the implementation. In the lossless compression scheme, the image is partitioned into a set of 32x32 tiles before processing. The system is then implemented onto an FPGA prototyping board. The system achieved an operating speed of 20MHz. In the second scheme, in order to avoid excessive increase of the internal memory, a rearrangement of the filtered and decimated outputs is proposed (interlocked external memory access. Because of its integer nature (integer to integer), as well as, for its adoption in the JPEG 2000 standard, the biorthogonal 5/3 wavelet is the focus of many studies. Since the wavelet transform algorithms are inherently multi levels, requiring complex computation schedule in hardware, a comparison of different computation schedule algorithms is presented in (Angelopoulou et al., 2008). The most widely used schedule algorithms such as the row column based algorithm (Mallat, 1989), the line based algorithm (Chrysafis & Ortega, 2000) and the block based algorithm (Lafruit et al., 2000) are implemented in FPGA using the lifting scheme and 2D DWT architecture. The 2D DWT FPGA implementation is fully parameterised. Based on the lifting scheme, Lande et al. in (Lande et al., 2010) introduce a robust invisible watermarking method to be used with still images. The scheme is incorporated in the JPEG 2000 lossless algorithm, featuring an integer to integer biorthogonal 5/3 CDF wavelet filters. The proposed algorithm targets the consumer electronics market. The objectives of the proposed FPGA implementation of this wavelet based watermarking scheme include low power usage, real time performance, robustness and ease of integration.

Denoising still images and video sequences is another field of predilection of the wavelet transform (see section 9). Katona et al. (Katona et al., 2006) suggest a real time wavelet based video denoising system and its implementation in FPGA. The method adopts a parallel approach to implement an advanced wavelet domain noise filtering algorithm, which uses a non-decimated wavelet transform. The approach relies on the wavelet "a trous" algorithm and the Daubechies minimum phase wavelet (Daub4). The proposed implementation is decentralised and distributed over two FPGAs. As a proof of concept, digitised television signals are adopted as real time video sources.

11. Conclusion

Since the late 80s, the wavelet transform has been widely used in different scientific applications including signal and image processing. This ongoing growing success, which has been characterised by the adoption of some wavelet-based schemes, is due to features inherent to the transform, such as time-scale localisation and multiresolution capabilities. In this chapter, the basic concepts of the wavelet transform have been introduced. First, the historical development of the wavelet transform and its advent to the field of signal and image processing were reviewed. Then, its features and the mathematical foundations behind it were reviewed. To ease the understanding of the wavelet theory, the related notations and terms, such as the scaling function, multiresolution, filter bank and others were described and then briefly explained.

Depending on the application at hand, different algorithms for implementing the wavelet transform have been developed. Four of these algorithms, namely, Burt's pyramid, Mallat algorithm, Feauveau's scheme and the lifting scheme were briefly described. Finally, some wavelet based image processing applications were also given.

12. References

Adelson, E. H.; Simoncelli E. & Hingorani, R. (1987). Orthogonal pyramid transforms for image coding, *SPIE Visual Communication and Image Processing II,* Vol. 845, pp. 50-58

Angelopoulou, M. E.; Cheung, P. Y. K ; Masselos, K. & Andreopoulos, Y. (2008). Implementation and comparison of the 5/3 lifting 2D discrete wavelet transform computation schedule on FPGAs, *Journal of signal processing systems,* Vol. 51, pp. 3 - 21

Barr, M. (1998). A Reconfigurable Computing Primer, *Multimedia Systems Design,* pp. 44-47

Bradley, J.; Brislawn, C. & Hopper, T. (1993). *The FBI Wavelet/Scalar Quantization Standard for Gray-scale Fingerprint Image Compression,* Tech. Report LA-UR-93-1659, Los Alamos Nat'l Lab, Los Alamos

Brislawn, C. M. (April 2010). Group Lifting Structures for Multirate Filter Banks II: Linear Phase Filter Banks, *IEEE Transactions on Signal Processing,* Vol. 58, No. 4, pp. 2078 - 2087, ISSN 1053-587X

Burt, P. J. & Adelson, A. E. (1983). The Laplacian pyramid as a compact image code, *IEEE Transactions on Communications,* Vol. 31, No. 4, (Apr 1983), pp. 532-540, ISSN 0090-6778

Burrus, C. S.; Gopinath, R. A. & Guo, H. (1998). *Introduction to Wavelets and Wavelet Transforms: A primer,* Prentice Hall

Chappelier, V. & Guillemot, C. (2006). Oriented Wavelet Transform for Image Compression and *Denoising, IEEE Transactions on Image Processing,* Vol. 15, No. 10, pp. 2892-2903, ISSN 1057-7149

Chen, G. & Qian, S. (2011). Denoising of Hyperspectral Imagery Using Principal Component Analysis and Wavelet Shrinkage, *Geoscience and Remote Sensing, IEEE Transactions,* Vol. 49, No. 3, pp. 973 - 980, ISSN 0196-2892

Chrysafis, C. & Ortega, A. (2000). Line based reduced memory wavelet image compression, *IEEE Transactions on Image Processing,* Vol. 9, No. 3, pp. 378-389, 010-1024, ISSN 1057-7149

Cunha, A. L.; Zhou, J. & Do, M. N. (October 2006). The nonsubsampled contourlet transform: Theory, design, and applications, *IEEE Transactions on Image Processing,* Vol. 15, No. 10, pp. 3089–3101, ISSN: 1057-7149

Cohen, A.; Daubechies, I. & Feauveau, J. (1992). Biorthogonal bases of compactly supported wavelets, *Communications on Pure and Applied Mathematics,* Vol. 45, No. 5, pp. 485-560

Cody, M. A. (1994). The Wavelet Packet Transform, *Dr. Dobb's Journal,* Vol. 19, Apr. 1994

Daubechies, I. (1988). Orthonormal bases of compactly supported wavelets, *Communications on Pure and Applied Mathematics,* Vol. 41, pp. 909-996

Daubechies, I. (1992). Ten lectures on Wavelets, *SIAM,* Philadelphia

Daubechies, I. (Mar. 1993). Orthonormal bases of compactly supported wavelets II, variations on a theme, *SIAM Journal of Mathematical Analysis,* Vol. 24, No. 2, pp. 499-519

David F. W. (2002). *Wavelet Analysis,* Birkhauser, ISBN-0-8176-3962-4

Do, M. N. & Vetterli, M. (January 2003). The finite ridgelet transform for image representation. *IEEE Transactions on Image Processing,* Vol. 12, No. 1, pp. 6–28, ISSN 1057-7149

Do, M. N. & Vetterli, M. (December 2005). The contourlet transform: An efficient directionalmultiresolution image representation. *Transactions on Image Processing,* Vol. 14, No. 12, pp. 2091-2106, ISSN 1057-7149

Donoho, D. L. & Johnstone, I. M. (1994). Ideal Spatial Adaptation via Wavelet Shrinkag, *Biometrika,* Vol. 81, No. 3, pp. 425-455, Online ISSN 1464-3510 - Print ISSN 0006-3444

Donoho, D. L. & Johnstone, I. M. (Dec. 1995). Adaptation to Unknown Smoothness Via Wavelet Shrinkage, *Journal of American Statistical Association*, Vol. 90, No. 432, pp. 1200-1224, ISSN 01621459

Ebrahimi, T.; Christopoulos, C. & Lee, D. L. (Eds) (Jan. 2002). JPEG2000, *Special Issue of Signal Processing: Image Communication*, Vol. 17, No. 1, Elsevier Science

Feauveau, J. C. (1990). *Analyse multiresolution par ondelettes non-orthogonales et bancs de filtres numeriques.* PhD Thesis, Universite Paris Sud, France

Firoiu, I.; Nafornita, C.; Boucher, J. M. & Isar, A. (2009). Image Denoising Using a New Implementation of the Hyperanalytic Wavelet Transform, *IEEE Transactions on Instrumentation and Measurement*, Vol. 58, No. 8, pp. 2410 – 2416, ISSN 0018-9456

Fliege, N. J. (1994). *Multirate Digital Signal Processing: Multirate Systems, Filter Banks, Wavelets*, John Wiley & Sons, ISBN: 0471939765, Inc. New York, NY, USA

Grossman, A. & Morlet, J. (1984). Decomposition of hardy functions into square integrable wavelets of constant shape, *SIAM Journal of Mathematical Analysis*, Vol. 15, No. 4, pp. 723-736, ISSN 00361410

Graps, A. L. (1995). An introduction to Wavelets, *IEEE Computational Science and Engineering*, Vol. 2, No. 2, pp. 50-61, ISSN: 1070-9924

Hankerson, D. C.; Harris, G. & Johnson, P. (2005). *Introduction to Information Theory and Data Compression*, Taylor & Francis e-Library, ISBN 1-58488-313-8

Hernandez-Guzman, V. ; Cruz-Ramos, C. ; Nakano-Miyatake M. & Perez-Meana, H. (2008). Watermarking Algorithm based on the DWT, *Latin America Transactions, IEEE (Revista IEEE America Latina)*, Vol. 4, No. 4, pp. 257-267, ISSN 1548-0992

Katona, M.; Pizurica, A.; Teslic, N.; Kovacevic, V. & Philips, W. (2006). A Real time wavelet domain video denoising implementation in FPGA, *EURASIP Journal of Embedded Systems, Hindawi Publishing*, Vol. 2006, No. 1, pp. 1-12, ISSN 1687-3955, EISSN 1687-3963

Kundur D. & Dimitrios H. (1997). A robust digital image watermarking method using wavelet-based fusion (1997), *ICIP (1)'1997, Proc. of IEEE Int. Conf. on Acoustics, Speech and Sig. Proc., vol. 5, pp. 544-547 Seattle,Washington (1997-5)*

Kundur D. & Dimitrios H. (1998). Digital watermarking using multiresolution wavelet decomposition, *In Proceedings of IEEE ICAPSSP '98*, Vol. 5, pp. 2969 – 2972, Seattle, WA, USA, May 1998

Lafruit, G.; Nachtergaele, L.; Vanhoof, B. & Catthoor, F. (2000). The Local Wavelet Transform: a Memory Efficient, High Speed Architecture Optimised to Region Oriented Zero Tree Coder, *Integrated Computer Aided Engineering Journal*, Vol. 7, No. 2, pp. 89-103, ISSN:1069-2509

Lande, P. U. ; Talbar, S. N. & Shinde, G. N. (2010). FPGA Prototype of Robust Image Watermarking For JPEG 2000 With Dual Detection, *Int. Journal of Computer Science and Security*, Vol. 4, No. 2, pp 226-236, ISSN 1985-1553

Lu, Y. & Do, M. N. (April 2007). Multidimensional Directional Filter Banks and Surfacelets, *In Image Processing, IEEE Transactions*, Vol. 16, No. 4, pp. 918-931, ISSN: 1057-7149

Mallat, S. (July 1989). A theory for multiresolution signal decomposition: the wavelet representation, *IEEE Transactions on Pattern Recognition and Machine Intelligence*, Vol. 11, No. 7, pp. 674-693, ISSN 0162-8828

Mallat, S. (2009). *A Wavelet Tour of Signal Processing, Third Ed…(Hardcover)*,Copyrighted Material, Elsevier Inc. ISBN 13: 978-0-12-374370-1

A theory for multiresolution signal decomposition: the wavelet representation, *IEEE Transactions on Pattern Recognition and Machine Intelligence,* Vol. 11, No. 7, pp. 674-693, ISSN 0162-8828

Masud, S. (1999). *VLSI system for Discrete Wavelet Transforms,* PhD thesis, Department of Electrical Engineering, The Queen's University of Belfast, Ireland

Meyer, Y. (1987). Wavelet with compact support. *Zygmund Lectures,* University Chicago 1987

Nai-Xiang L. & Yap-Peng T. (2005). Color image denoising using wavelets and minimum cut analysis, *Signal Processing Letters IEEE,* Vol. 12, No. 11, pp. 741-744, ISSN 1070-9908

Nai-Xiang, L.; Vitali, Z. & Yap-Peng T. (2006). Error inhomogeneity of wavelet image compression, *IEEE,* pp. 1597-1600, ISSN 1522-4880

Nguyen, T. T. & Oraintara, S. (Oct. 2008). The Shiftable Complex Directional Pyramid—Part I: Theoretical Aspects, *IEEE Transactions on Signal Processing,* Vol. 56, No. 10, pp. 4651-4660, ISSN 1053-587X

Nibouche, M.; Bouridane, A.; Nibouche, O.; Crookes, D. & Boussekta, S. (2000). Design and FPGA implementation of orthonormal discrete wavelet transforms, *The 7th IEEE International Conference, Electronics, Circuits and Systems, ICECS 2000,* Vol. 1, pp. 312-315, ISBN 0-7803-6542-9

Nibouche, M.; Bouridane, A.; Crookes, D. & Nibouche, O. (2001a). An FPGA-based wavelet transforms coprocessor, *International Conference on Image Processing, Proceedings 2001,* Vol. 3, pp. 194-197, ISBN: 0-7803-6725-1

Nibouche, M.; Bouridane, A.; Nibouche, O. & Crookes, D. (2001b). Rapid prototyping of orthonormal wavelet transforms on FPGAs, *Circuits and Systems, 2001. ISCAS 2001. The 2001 IEEE International Symposium, Vol. 2,* pp. 577-580, ISBN 0-7803-6685-9

Nibouche, M.; Bouridane, A.; Nibouche, O. & Belatreche, A. (2001c). Design and FPGA implementation of orthonormal inverse discrete wavelet transforms, *Wireless Communications, 2001. (SPAWC '01). 2001 IEEE Third Workshop on Signal Processing Advances,* pp. 365-359, ISBN 0-7803-6720-0

Nibouche, M.; Bouridane, A. & Nibouche, O. (2001d). A framework for a wavelet-based high level environment, *Electronics, Circuits and Systems, 2001. ICECS 2001. The 8th IEEE International Conference,* Vol. 1, pp. 429-432, ISBN 0-7803-7057-0

Nibouche, M. & Nibouche, O. (2002). Design and implementation of a wavelet block for signal processing applications, *Electronics, Circuits and Systems, 2002. 9th International Conference,* Vol.3, pp. 867-870, ISBN 0-7803-7596-3

Nibouche, M.; Nibouche, O. & Bouridane, A. (Dec. 2003). Design and implementation of a wavelet based system, *Electronics, Circuits and Systems, 2003. ICECS 2003. Proceedings of the 2003 10th IEEE International Conference,* Vol. 2, pp. 463-466, ISBN 0-7803-8163-7

Oppenheim, A. V. & Schafer, R. W. (2010). *Discrete-Time Signal Processing,* Prentice Hall, Upper Saddle River, NJ, third edition, ISBN-13 978-0613-198842-2/ISBN-10 0-13-198842-5

Raviraj, P. & Sanavullah, M. Y. (Apr-Jun 2007). The modified 2D-Haar Wavelet Transformation in image compression, *Middle East Journal of Scientific Research,* Vol. 2 , No .2, pp. 73-78, ISSN 1990-9233

Ritter, J. & Molitor, P. (2000). A Partitioned Wavelet-based Approach for Image Compression using FPGAs, *Proceedings of the IEEE Custom Integrated Circuits Conference (CICC),* pp. 547-550, Orlando, Florida, USA, May 2000

Ruikar, S. & Doye, D. D. (2010). Image denoising using wavelet transform. *IEE Mechanical and Electrical Technology (ICMET), 2010 2nd International Conference*, pp. 509-515, ISBN 978-1-4244-8100-2

Russel T. & Wayne B. (2001). Reconfigurable Computing for Digital Signal Processing: A Survey, *Journal of VLSI Signal Processing systems,* Vol. 28, pp 7-27, ISSN 0922-5773

Schoner, B.; Villasenor, J.; Molloy, S. & Jain, R. (1995). Techniques for FPGA Implementation of Video Compression Systems, *Proceedings of the Third International ACM Symposium on FPGA '95.*, pp. 154-159, ISBN: 0-7695-2550-4

Smith, S. (2003). *Digital Signal Processing : A practical guide for engineers and scientists*, Elsevier, ISBN 0-75067444-X, USA

Starck, J. L.; Murtagh, F. & Bijaoui, A. (1998). Image Processing and Data Analysis: The multiscale approach, *Cambridge University Press,* 1998, First published 1998, Reprinted 2000, ISBN 0521 59084 1- ISBN 0521 59914 8, U. K.

Strang G. & Nguyen T. (1996). Wavelets and Filter Banks, *Wellesley-Cambridge Press,* ISBN 09614088-7-1, USA

Stromme, O. (1999). *On the applicability of wavelet transforms to image and video compression,* PhD thesis, Department of Computer Science, the University of StrathClyde

Sweldens, W. (1996). Wavelets: what next?, *Proceedings of the IEEE,* vol. 84, No. 4, pp. 680-685, ISSN 0018-9219

Sweldens, W. (1995). The Lifting Scheme: A new philosophy in biorthogonal wavelet constructions, *Wavelet Applications in Signal and Image Processing III,* pp. 68-79, Proc. SPIE 2569

Tsekeridou, S. & Pitas, I. (2000). Wavelet-based Self-similar Watermarking for Still Images, *IEEE International Symposium on Circuits and Systems,* Geneva, Switzerland, Print ISBN 0-7803-5482-6

Valens, C. (2004). A Really Friendly Guide To Wavelets, Latest version: V02122004, available from http://perso.wanadoo.fr/polyvalens/clemens/

Villasenor, J; Jones, C. & Schoner, B. (1995). Algorithms and System Prototype for Low-Power, Low-bit-rate Wireless Video Coding, *IEEE Transactions on Circuits and Systems for Video Technology,* Vol.5, No. 6, pp 565-567, ISSN 1051-8215

Villasenor, J. and Mangione-Smith, W. (1997). Configurable Computing, *Scientific American,* June 1997

Wickerhauser, M. D. (1994). *Adapted Wavelet Analysis from Theory to Software,* First Edition, ISBN 1568810415/1-56881-041-5, A. K. Peters Ltd, Natick, Massachusetts, U.S.A

Wu, X.; Zhu, W.; Xiong Z. & Zhang Y. (2000). Object-based Multiresolution Watermarking of Images and Video, *IEEE International Symposium on Circuits and Systems,* vol. 1, pp. 545–550, Geneva, Switzerland

18

Wavelet Based Image Compression Techniques

Pooneh Bagheri Zadeh[1], Akbar Sheikh Akbari[2] and Tom Buggy[2]
[1]Staffordshire University,
[2]Glasgow Caledonian University
UK

1. Introduction

With advances in multimedia technologies, demand for transmission and storage of voluminous multimedia data has dramatically increased and, as a consequence, data compression is now essential in reducing the amount of data prior storage or transmission. Compression techniques aim to minimise the number of bits required to represent image data while maintaining an acceptable visual quality. Image compression is achieved by exploiting the spatial and perceptual redundancies present in image data. Image compression techniques are classified into two categories, lossless and lossy. Lossless techniques refer to those that allow recovery of the original input data from its compressed representation without any loss of information, i.e. after decoding, an identical copy of the original data can be restored. Lossy techniques offer higher compression ratios but it is impossible to recover the original data from its compressed data, as some of the input information is lost during the lossy compression. These techniques are designed to minimise the amount of distortion introduced into the image data at certain compression ratios. Compression is usually achieved by transforming the image data into another domain, e.g. frequency or wavelet domains, and then quantizing and losslessy encoding the transformed coefficients (Ghanbari, 1999; Peng & Kieffer, 2004; Wang et al., 2001). In recent years much research has been undertaken to develop efficient image compression techniques. This research has led to the development of two standard image compression techniques called: JPEG and JPEG2000 (JPEG, 1994; JPEG 2000, 2000), and many non-standard image compression algorithms (Said & Pearlman, 1996; Scargall & Dlay, 2000; Shapiro, 1993).

Statistical parameters of image data have been used in a number of image compression techniques (Chang & Chen, 1993; Lu et al., 2000; Lu et al., 2002; Saryazdi and Jafari, 2002). These techniques offer promising visual quality at low bit rates. However, the application of statistical parameters of the transformed data in image compression techniques has been less reported in the literature. Therefore, the statistical parameters of the transformed image data and their application in developing novel compression algorithms are further investigated in this chapter.

The performance of image compression techniques can also be significantly improved by embedding the properties of the Human Visual System (HVS) in their compression algorithms (Bradley, 1999; Nadenau et al., 2003). Due to the space-frequency localization properties of wavelet transforms, wavelet based image codecs are most suitable for embedding the HVS model in their coding algorithm (Bradley, 1999). The HVS model can be embedded either in the quantization stage (Aili et al., 2006; HSontsch & Karam, 2000; Nadenau et al., 2003), or at the bit allocation stage (Antonini et al., 1992; Sheikh Akbari & Soraghan, 2003; Thornton et al., 2002; Voukelatos & Soraghan, 1997) of the wavelet based encoders. In this chapter, HVS coefficients for wavelet high frequency subbands are calculated and their application in improving the coding performance of the statistical encoder is investigated.

2. Fundamental of compression

The main goal of all image compression techniques is to minimize the number of bits required to represent a digital image, while preserving an acceptable level of image quality. Image data are amendable to compression due to the spatial redundancies they exhibit and also because they contain information that, from a perceptual point of view, can be considered irrelevant. Many standard and non-standard image compression techniques have been developed to compress digital images. These techniques exploit some or all of these image properties to improve the quality of the decoded images at higher compression ratios. Some of these image coding schemes are tabulated in Table 1.

Image compression techniques can be classified into two main groups, named: lossless and lossy compression techniques. In lossless compression process, the original data and the reconstructed data must be identical for each and every data sample. Lossless compression is demanded in different applications such as: medical imagery, i.e. cardiography, to avoid the loss of data and errors introduced into the imagery. Also, it is applied to the case that is not possible to determine the acceptable loss of data.

In most image processing applications, there is no need for the reconstructed data to be identical in value with its original. Therefore, some amount of loss is permitted in the reconstructed data. This kind of compression techniques, which results in an imperfect reconstruction, is called lossy compression. By using lossy compression, it is possible to represent the image with some loss using fewer bits in comparison to a lossless compression.

3. Characteristics of the Human Visual System

Research has shown that embedding the Human Visual System (HVS) model into compression algorithms yields significant improvement in the visual quality of the reconstructed images (Aili et al., 2006; Antonini et al., 1992; Bradley, 1999; HSontsch & Karam, 2000; Nadenau et al., 2003; Sheikh Akbari & Soraghan, 2003; Thornton et al., 2002; Voukelatos & Soraghan, 1997). It has been shown in (Bradley, 1999; Nadenau et al., 2003) that the performance of image compression techniques can be significantly improved by exploiting the limitations of the HVS for compression purposes. To achieve this aim, the HVS-model can be embedded in the compression algorithm to optimise the perceived visual quality.

<table>
<tr><td colspan="2">Standard image coding techniques</td><td>Non standard image coding techniques</td></tr>
<tr><td>DCT-base</td><td>Wavelet-base</td><td rowspan="2">Differential Pulse code Modulation (DPCM)
Vector Quantization (VQ)
Zero-Tree Coding
Fractal
Neural Networks
Trellis Coding</td></tr>
<tr><td>JPEG (1980)</td><td>JPEG2000 (2000)</td></tr>
</table>

Table 1. Standard and non-standard image compression techniques.

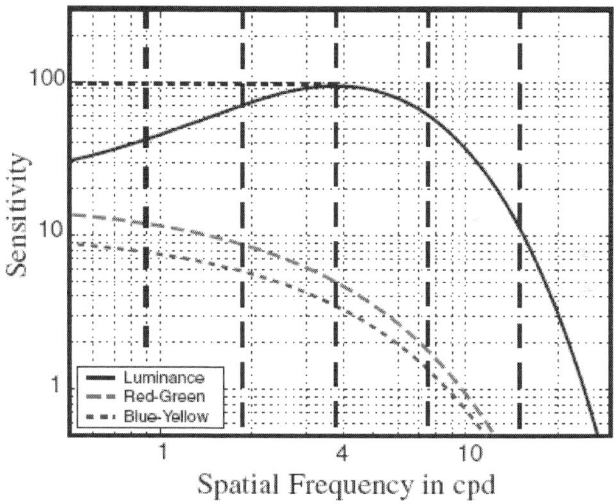

Fig. 1. The CSF curves for the luminance and chrominance channels of the HVS (Nadenau et al., 2003).

Due to the complexity of the human visual processing system, assessments of the performance of HVS-models are based on psychophysical observations. Physiologists have performed many psycho-visual experiments with the goal of understanding how the HVS works. One of the limitations of the HVS, which was found experimentally, is the lower sensitivity of the HVS for patterns with high spatial-frequencies. Exploiting this property of the HVS model, and embedding it into compression algorithms, can significantly improve the visual quality of compressed images. Natural images are composed of small details and shaped regions. Therefore, it is necessary to describe the contrast sensitivity as a function of spatial frequency. This phenomenon has been known as the Contrast Sensitivity Function (CSF) (Nadenau et al, 2003; Tan et al, 2004). Figure 1 shows the CSF curves for the luminance and chrominance channels of the HVS. From Figure 1, it can be seen that the HVS is more sensitive to the luminance component than the chrominance components. The sensitivity of the HVS in terms of luminance is greatest around the mid-frequencies, in the region of 4 cycles per optical degree (cpd). It rapidly reduces at higher spatial frequencies, and slightly decreases at lower frequencies. The HVS, in terms of chrominance components behaves like a low pass-filter; therefore there is no decrease in its sensitivity at low frequencies.

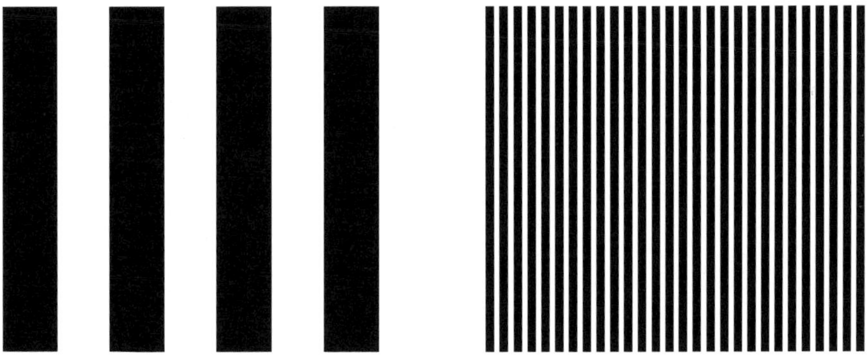

Fig. 2. A low frequency pattern (left) and a high frequency pattern (right), the high frequency pattern appear less intense.

To give a sense of the sensitivity of HVS to different frequencies, two black and white patterns are shown in Figure 2, a low frequency pattern on the left and a high frequency pattern on the right. In both patterns, the black and white have the same brightness, but the black and white colours of the right hand pattern appears less intense than the pattern in the left side. This can be explained by the fact that the HVS is less sensitive to high frequency components.

3.1 Human Visual System in compression techniques

Wavelet-based image coding schemes have proven to be ideally suited for embedding complete HVS models, due to the space-frequency localization properties of the wavelet decompositions (Bradley, 1999). The HVS model has been embedded either at the quantization stage (Aili et al., 2006; HSontsch & Karam, 2000; Nadenau et al., 2003), or at the bit allocation stage (Antonini et al., 1992; Sheikh Akbari & Soraghan, 2003; Thornton et al., 2002; Voukelatos & Soraghan, 1997) of the codec, which yields significant improvement in the visual quality of the reconstructed images. Antonini et al. (Antonini et al., 1992) developed a wavelet-based image compression scheme using Vector Quantization (VQ) and the property of the HVS. This algorithm performs a Discrete Wavelet Transform (DWT) on the input image and then the resulting coefficients in different subbands are vector quantized. The bit allocation among different subbands is based on a weighted Mean

Squared Error (MSE) distortion criterion, where the weights are determined based on the property of the HVS introduced in (Campbell & Robson, 1968). (Voukelatos & Soraghan, 1998) introduced another wavelet based image compression technique using VQ and the properties of the HVS. They first calculated the value of the Contrast Sensitivity Function (CSF) for the central spatial frequency of each subband. These values were then used to scale the threshold value for each subband, which were used in vector selection prior to the VQ process. A weighted MSE distortion criterion using perceptual weights is also employed to allocate bits among different subbands. Voukelatos and Soraghan reported significant improvement over existing block-based image compression techniques at very low bitrates. Thornton et al (Thornton et al., 2002) extended the Voukelatos and Soraghan's algorithm (Voukelatos & Soraghan, 1998) to video for very low bitrate transmission. Thornton et al. incorporated the properties of the HVS to code the intra-frames and reported significant improvement in objective visual quality of the decompressed video sequences. Sheikh Akbari and Soraghan (Sheikh Akbari & Soraghan, 2003) developed another wavelet based video compression scheme using the VQ scheme and the properties of the HVS. They calculated the value of the CSF for the central spatial frequency of each subband of the Quarter Common Intermediate (QCIF) image size. These values were then used to scale the threshold value for each subband, which were used in vector selection prior to the VQ process and also in the bit allocation among different subbands.

The JPEG 2000 standard image codec supports two types of visual frequency weighting: Fixed Visual Weighting (FVW) and Visual Progressive Coding or Visual Progressive Weighting (VPW). In FVW, only one set of CSF weights is chosen and applied in accordance with the viewing conditions, and in the VPW, different sets of CSF weights are used at the various stages of the embedded coding. This is because during a progressive transmission stage, the image is viewed at various distances. For example, at low bitrates, the image is viewed from a relatively large distance, while as more bits are received, the quality of the reconstructed image is increased, which implies that the viewer looks at the image from a closer distance (Skodras et al, 2001). Nadenau et al. incorporated the characteristic of the HVS into a wavelet-based image compression algorithm using a noise-shape filtering stage prior to the quantization stage (Nadenau et al., 2003). They filtered the transformed coefficients using a "HVS filter" for each subband. This algorithm improves the compression ratio up to 30% over the JPEG2000 baseline for a number of test images. A new image compression method based on the HVS was proposed by Aili et al. (Aili et al., 2006). In this codec, the input image is first decomposed using a wavelet transform, and then the transformed coefficients in different subbands are weighted by the peak of the contrast sensitivity function (CSF) curve in the wavelet domain. Finally the weighted wavelet coefficients were coded using the Set Partitioning in Heretical Tree (SPIHT) algorithm. This technique showed significantly higher visual and almost the same objective quality to that of the conventional SPIHT technique.

3.2 Calculation of perceptual weights

In this section, the perceptual weights that regulate the quantization steps in different image compression techniques are specifically calculated for a Quarter Common Intermediate Format (QCIF) image size. The derivation of the weighting factors is based on the results of subjective experimental data that was presented in (Van Dyck & Rajala, 1994).

3.2.1 Calculation of spatial frequencies

The perceptual coding model is designed for a QCIF image size, thus this corresponds to a physical dimension of 1.8×2.2 inches on the workstation monitor, i.e. videophone display. Therefore, the pixel resolution r, which is measured in pixels per inch, in both the horizontal and vertical dimensions, will be 80 pixels/inch. Let us assume the viewing distance v, which is measured in metres, be 0.30 metres. This distance is a good approximation of the natural viewing distance of a human using a videophone device. The sampling frequency, f_s in pixels per degree, can be then calculated using Equation 1 (Nadenau et al., 2003):

$$f_S = \frac{2\, v \tan(0.5^\circ)\, r}{0.0254} \tag{1}$$

The signal is critically down-sampled at Nyquist rate to 0.5 cycle/pixel. Hence the maximum frequency represented in the signal is:

$$f_{\max} = 0.5\, f_S \tag{2}$$

Thus the maximum frequency represented in the QCIF image size with the thirty centimetre distance will be 8.246 cycles/degree. The centre radial frequency for each subband is determined by the Euclidean distance of its centre from the origin where subbands are in a square of length 8.246 and the base-band is in the origin. Figure 3 shows the centre radial frequencies for each sub-band of a three level wavelet decomposition.

3.2.2 Mean detection threshold

The mean detection threshold is the smallest change in a colour that is noticeable by a human observer and is used to calculate the perceptual weighting factors. It is a function of spatial frequency, orientation, luminance and background colour. The initial data presented in (Van Dyck & Rajala, 1994) was measured in the xyY colour space, where x and y are the C.I.E. chromaticity coordinates and Y is the luminance. Table 2 gives the set of thresholds for various frequencies and orientations measured along the luminance, Red-Green and Blue-Yellow directions when the luminance value Y_0 is 5 cd / m^2 and background colour is white. The chromaticity coordinates for white are: $(x_0, y_0) = (0.33, 0.35)$. For transition along the Red-Green and Blue-Yellow direction each mean detection threshold gives two chromaticity coordinates corresponding to the maximum and minimum of the sinusoidal variation as shown in equations 3 and 4, respectively.

$$x_i = x_0 \pm \Delta x \,.\, t \tag{3}$$

$$y_i = y_0 \pm \Delta y \,.\, t \tag{4}$$

where t is the mean detection threshold, Δx and Δy are the step sizes for the changes in the x and y direction. The values used for Δx and Δy for all three directions are given in Table 3.

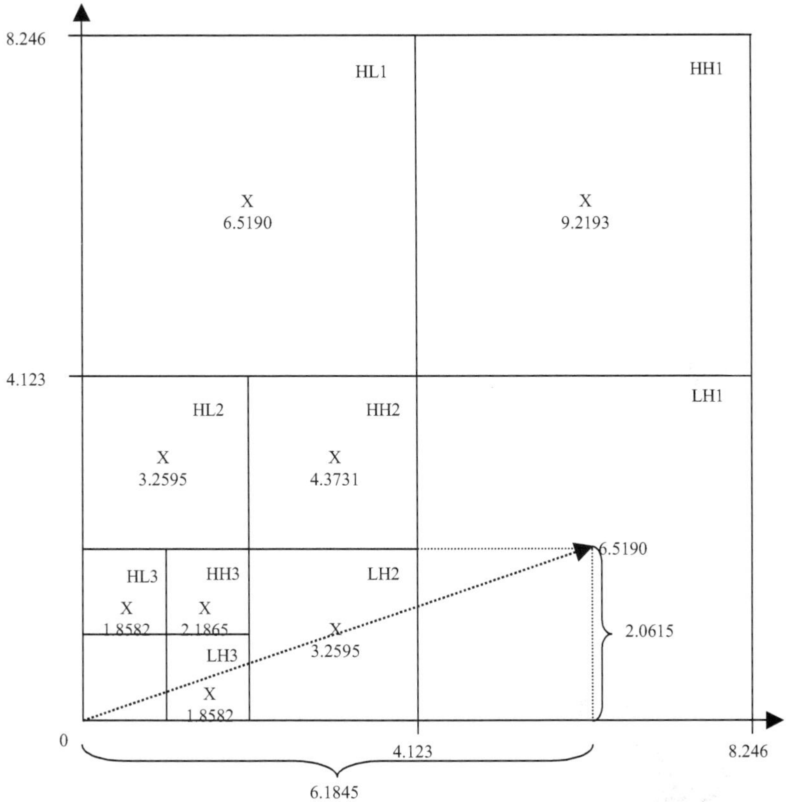

Fig. 3. Subband centre spatial frequencies in cycles/degree.

3.2.3 Perceptual weight factors

The perceptual weight for each subband is the reciprocal of its mean detection threshold. Hence, the mean detection thresholds for the YIQ space need to be calculated before the perceptual weights can be determined. The mean detection thresholds in the xyY space for the centre frequencies of the subbands shown in Figure 3 are first calculated by linearly interpolating the values in Table 2. In wavelet decomposition, the diagonal subbands (HH) do not discriminate between left and right, so an average of the two values is employed. The resulting thresholds in the *xy*Y space for the centre of the high frequency subbands are listed in Table 4. By using equations 3 and 4, two chromaticity coordinates $\left(x_i \ , \ y_i \ , \ Y_0\right)$, where $i = 1 \ , \ 2$ for each subband can be calculated. These two chromaticity coordinates are in the xyY space. Therefore they are converted from the xyY space to the C.I.E. XYZ space using the equations in 5: (Ghanbari, 1999).

Spatial Direction	Colour Direction	Spatial frequency cycles/deg				
		1.0	2.0	5.0	10.0	20.0
Horizontal (LH)	Luminance	6.750	6.330	7.250	13.500	65.083
	R-G	4.750	4.750	7.617	17.417	77.417
	B-Y	6.000	6.833	32.667	70.167	150.000
Vertical (HL)	Luminance	6.833	6.250	6.833	22.500	77.800
	R-G	5.583	7.083	9.250	23.000	90.375
	B-Y	6.667	9.417	31.833	65.700	150.000
Left Diagonal (HH)	Luminance	7.667	6.917	11.167	37.083	49.000
	R-G	7.917	7.167	16.083	37.500	100.750
	B-Y	12.417	18.500	45.500	86.500	150.000
Right Diagonal (HH)	Luminance	8.083	7.583	9.167	42.583	85.750
	R-G	7.750	6.333	13.833	35.417	103.500
	B-Y	13.750	19.750	47.750	83.000	114.000

Table 2. Mean detection thresholds in xyY space (Van Dyck 1994).

Direction	ΔY	Δx	Δy
Luminance	0.0124	0.0	0.0
R-G	0.0	0.000655	-0.000357
B-Y	0.0	0.000283	0.000689

Table 3. Step size for changes in each direction (Van Dyck 1994).

SUBBAND	Mean Detection Threshold		
	Luminance	R-G	B-Y
LH1	8.731	9.939	41.554
HL1	10.546	12.508	39.859
HH1	32.436	48.890	75.188
LH2	6.664	5.793	16.236
HL2	6.462	7.871	17.576
HH2	9.556	13.242	40.877
LH3	6.520	4.750	6.454
HL3	6.514	6.402	8.168
HH3	7.431	7.261	20.839

Table 4. Mean detection thresholds in xyY space for subbands.

$$\begin{aligned} X_i &= x_i \ Y_0 \ / \ y_i \\ Z_i &= \left(1 - x_i - y_i\right) Y_0 \ / \ y_i \\ & \\ \mathit{for} \ i &= 1 \ , \ 2 \end{aligned} \tag{5}$$

For the luminance direction each mean detection threshold also provides two XYZ values that are calculated using the equations in 6:

$$\begin{aligned} X_i &= X_0 \pm \Delta Y.\frac{X_0}{Y_0}.t \\ Y_i &= Y_0 \pm \Delta Y.t \\ Z_i &= Z_0 \pm \Delta Y.\frac{Z_0}{Y_0}.t \end{aligned} \tag{6}$$

where ΔY is given in Table 3, t is the mean detection threshold and $i = 1,2$. The vector$\left(X_0 \ , \ Y_0 \ , \ Z_0\right)$ contains the coordinates of the white point, computed from equation 6. The resulting values are then transformed into the YIQ space. The Red-Green line lies approximately in the I-direction and the Blue-Yellow line lies mostly in the Q direction. The linear transformations in equations 7 and 8 are used to give two points for each direction in the YIQ space.

$$\begin{bmatrix} R \\ G \\ B \end{bmatrix} = \begin{bmatrix} 1.910 & -0.533 & -0.288 \\ -0.985 & 2.000 & -0.028 \\ 0.058 & -0.118 & 0.896 \end{bmatrix} . \begin{bmatrix} X \\ Y \\ Z \end{bmatrix} \tag{7}$$

$$\begin{bmatrix} Y \\ I \\ Q \end{bmatrix} = \begin{bmatrix} 0.299 & 0.587 & 0.114 \\ 0.596 & -0.274 & -0.322 \\ 0.211 & -0.523 & 0.312 \end{bmatrix} . \begin{bmatrix} R \\ G \\ B \end{bmatrix} \tag{8}$$

The YIQ mean detection threshold for each direction is the inverse Euclidean distance between these two points. The computed weighting factors for each subband of QCIF video, based on the properties of the HVS, are shown in Table 5. These values represent the perceptual weights that can be used to regulate the quantization step-size in the pixel quantization of the high frequency subbands' coefficients of the Multiresolution based image/video codecs.

4. Statistical parameters in image compression

Statistical parameters of the image data have been used in a number of image compression techniques (Chang & Chen, 1993; Lu et al., 2000; Lu et al., 2002; Saryazdi & Jafari, 2002) and have demonstrated promising improvement in the quality of decompressed images, especially at medium to high compression ratios. A vector quantization based image compression algorithm was proposed by Chang and Chen (Chang & Chen, 1993). It first generates a number of sub-codebooks from the super-codebook, and then employs the statistical parameters of the upper and left neighbour vectors to decide which codebook is to be used for vector quantization. This coding scheme has been extended by Lu et al. (Lu et al., 2000) who generated two master-codebooks, one for the codewords whose variances are larger than a threshold, and another one for the remainder codewords. Lu et al. exploited the current vector's statistical parameter to decide which of these two master codebooks to use for vector quantization, and then Chang and Chen's algorithm was applied to perform vector quantization. Lu et al. (Lu et al., 2002) successfully developed other gradient-based vector quantization schemes and reported further improvement at low bit rates. In the Lu et al. proposed algorithms, one master codebook is first generated and codewords are then sorted in ascending order of their gradient values. In the first algorithm, Chang and Chen's (Chang and Chen, 1993) technique is used to perform vector quantization, with the difference that gradient parameters instead of statistical parameters are used to decide which codebook is to be used for vector quantization. In the second algorithm, the number of codebooks was increased, which resulted in further bit reduction. Another statistically-based image compression scheme was reported by (Saryazdi and Jafari, 2002). In this algorithm, the input image is divided to a number of blocks. The statistical parameters are then used to classify each block into uniform and non-uniform blocks. The uniform blocks are coded by their minimum values. The non-uniform blocks are coded by their minimum and residual values, where the residual values are vector quantized. They reported promising visual quality at high compression ratios.

SUBBAND	Y-DOMAIN	I-DOMAIN	Q-DOMAIN
LH1	4.3807	2.0482	1.0502
HL1	3.4573	1.6159	1.0992
HH1	1.2372	0.6978	0.6065
LH2	5.9673	3.6449	2.6340
HL2	6.1708	2.7149	2.4728
HH2	4.1934	1.6384	1.1331
LH3	6.1796	4.5685	7.1443
HL3	6.1984	3.3243	5.5495
HH3	5.3931	2.9888	2.2339

Table 5. Perceptual weight factors for the YIQ colour domain.

4.1 Distribution of wavelet transform coefficients

Wavelet transform is one of the most popular transform that has been used in many image-coding schemes. As each statistical distribution function has its own parameters, knowledge of the statistical behaviour of the wavelet transformed coefficients in each subband of an image, can play an important role in designing an efficient compression algorithm. Study of many non-artificial images has shown that distribution of the wavelet-transformed coefficients in high frequency subbands of natural images follow a Gaussian distribution (Altunbasak & Kamaci, 2004; Kilic & Yilmaz, 2003; Eude et al., 1994; Valade & Nicolas, 2004; Yovanof & Liu, 1996). In the following, the Gaussian distribution and its statistical parameters are first reviewed. Then, a review of the study on the distribution of the wavelet transform-coefficients of images is given. A one dimensional Gaussian distribution function $f_g(x)$ is defined as follow:

$$f_g(x) = \frac{1}{\sqrt{2\pi\sigma^2}} e^{\frac{-(x-\mu)^2}{2\sigma^2}} \tag{9}$$

where μ is the mean value of $f_g(x)$ and is calculated using Equation 10:

$$\mu = \int_{-\infty}^{+\infty} x\, f_g(x)\, dx \tag{10}$$

and σ is known as the standard deviation, which determines the width the of the distribution. The square of the standard deviation, σ^2, is called the variance and is determined as follows:

$$\sigma^2 = \int_{-\infty}^{+\infty} x^2\, f_g(x)\, dx \tag{11}$$

where the mean value, μ , and variance, σ^2, of discrete data, are calculated using Equations 12 and 13, respectively.

$$\mu = \frac{1}{n} \cdot \sum_{i=1}^{n} x_i \tag{12}$$

$$\sigma^2 = \frac{1}{n} \cdot \sum_{i=1}^{n} (x_i - \mu)^2 \tag{13}$$

where n is the number of the discrete data, and x_i is the data. Every Gaussian distribution function is defined by two parameters: the mean value, which defines the central location of the distribution, and the variance, which defines the width of the distribution. Four Gaussian distribution functions, with different mean values and variances, are shown in Figure 4.

Study of the distribution of wavelet transform coefficients in each subband has shown that the distribution of the coefficients in the detail subbands of the wavelet-transformed data of natural images is approximately Gaussian (coefficients in the baseband are excluded) [Valade and Nicolas, 2004][Kilic and Yilmaz, 2003]. Distributions of the wavelet coefficients of an image, after applying a three level 2D-wavelet transform, are shown in Figure 5. From Figure 5, it can be seen that except for the lowest frequency coefficients, the distribution of the coefficients in high frequency subbands is approximately Gaussian.

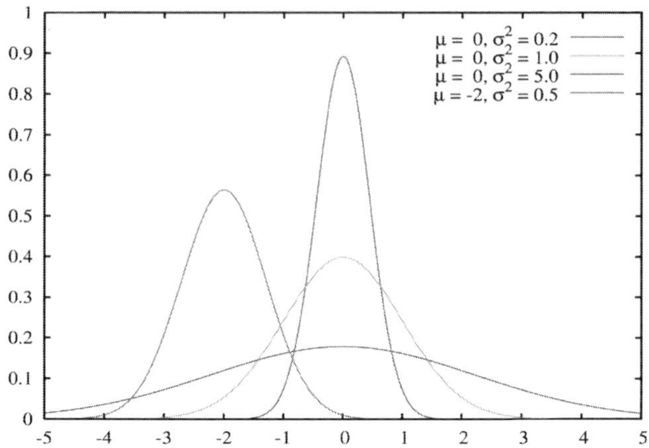

Fig. 4. Gaussian distribution functions (http://en.wikipedia.org/wiki/Normal - distribution).

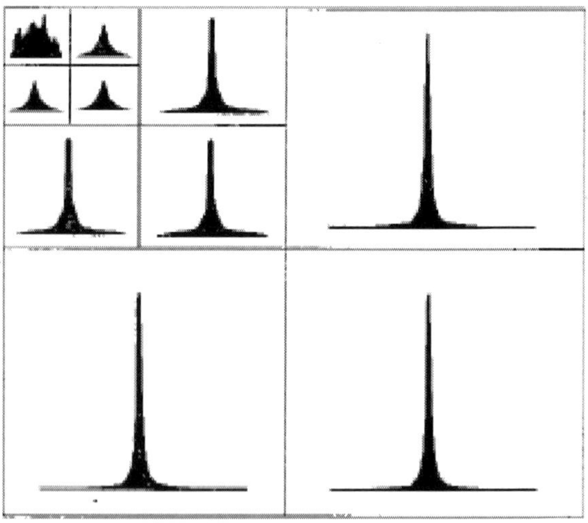

Fig. 5. Histogram of three level wavelet transform of an image (Kilic & Yilmaz, 2003).

In summary, it can be concluded that distribution of the wavelet coefficients in high frequency subbands of natural images can be well approximated by a Gaussian distribution. Therefore, effective use of statistical parameters of the transformed image data (mean values and variances of a Gaussian distribution function) is key in estimation of the transformed data and yielding compression.

4.2 Statistical encoder

In section 4.1 the Gaussian distribution function and its statistical parameters were reviewed. It was shown that every Gaussian distribution function is defined by two parameters: the mean value, which defines the central location of the distribution, and the variance, which defines the width of the distribution. It was also noted that the distribution of the coefficients in each detail subband of the wavelet-transformed data of the natural images is approximately Gaussian has led to the development of a Statistical Encoding (SE) algorithm. The SE algorithm assumes that the coefficients in the 2D input matrix partly follows the Gaussian distribution. Therefore it estimates those parts through a novel hierarchical estimation algorithm, which codes in a lossy manner those parts with their mean values. The SE algorithm applies a threshold value on the variance of the input data to determine if it is possible to estimate them with the mean value of a single Gaussian distribution function or if it needs further dividing into four sub-matrices. This hierarchal algorithm is iterated on the resulting sub-matrices until the distribution of the coefficients in all sub-matrices fulfils the above criteria. Finally, the SE algorithm takes the Gaussian mean values of the resulting sub-matrices as the estimation value for those sub-matrices. The SE algorithm generates a quadtree-like binary map along with the mean values to keep a record of the location of the sub-matrices, which are estimated with their mean values.

A block diagram of the SE algorithm is shown in Figure 6. A two dimensional matrix of size N×N, which for simplification is called U, along with a threshold value, which represents the level of compression, are input to the SE technique. The SE algorithm performs the following process to compress the input matrix U: The SE algorithm first defines two empty vectors called mv (mean value vector) and q (quadtree-like vector). It then calculates the variance (var) and the mean value (m) of the matrix U and compares the resulted variance value with the threshold value. If the variance is less than the threshold value, the matrix is coded by its mean value (m) and one bit binary data equal to 0, which are placed in the mv and q vectors, respectively. If the variance is greater than the threshold, one bit binary data equal to one is placed at the q vector and the size of the matrix is checked. If the size of the matrix is 2×2, the four coefficients of the matrix are scanned and placed in the mv vector and encoding process is finished by sending the mean value vector mv and the quadtree-like vector q. If the size of the matrix is greater than 2×2, the matrix U is divided into four equal non-overlapping blocks. These four blocks are then processed from left to right, as shown in Figure 6. For simplify, only the continuation of the coding process of the first block, U1, is discussed. This process is repeated exactly on the three other blocks. Processing of the first block U1 is described as follows: The variance (var1) and the mean value (m1) of the sub-matrix U1 are first calculated and then the resulting variance value is compared with the input threshold value. If it is less than the threshold value, the calculated mean value (m1) is concatenated to the mean value vector mv and one bit binary data equal to 0 is appended to the quadtree-like vector q. The encoding process of this sub-block is terminated at this stage. Otherwise, the size of the sub-block is checked. If it is 2×2, one bit binary data equal to 1 is appended to the current quadtree-like vector q and the four coefficients of the sub-block are scanned and concatenated to the mv vector and encoding process is ended for this sub-block. If its size is larger than 2×2, one bit binary data equal to 1 is concatenated to the current quadtree-like vector q and the sub-block U1 is then divided into four equal non-overlapping blocks. These four new sub-blocks are named successor sub-blocks and are processed from left to right in the same way that their four ancestor sub-blocks were encoded. The above process is continued until whole successor blocks are encoded. When the encoding process is finished two vectors **mv** and **q** represent the compressed data of the input matrix U.

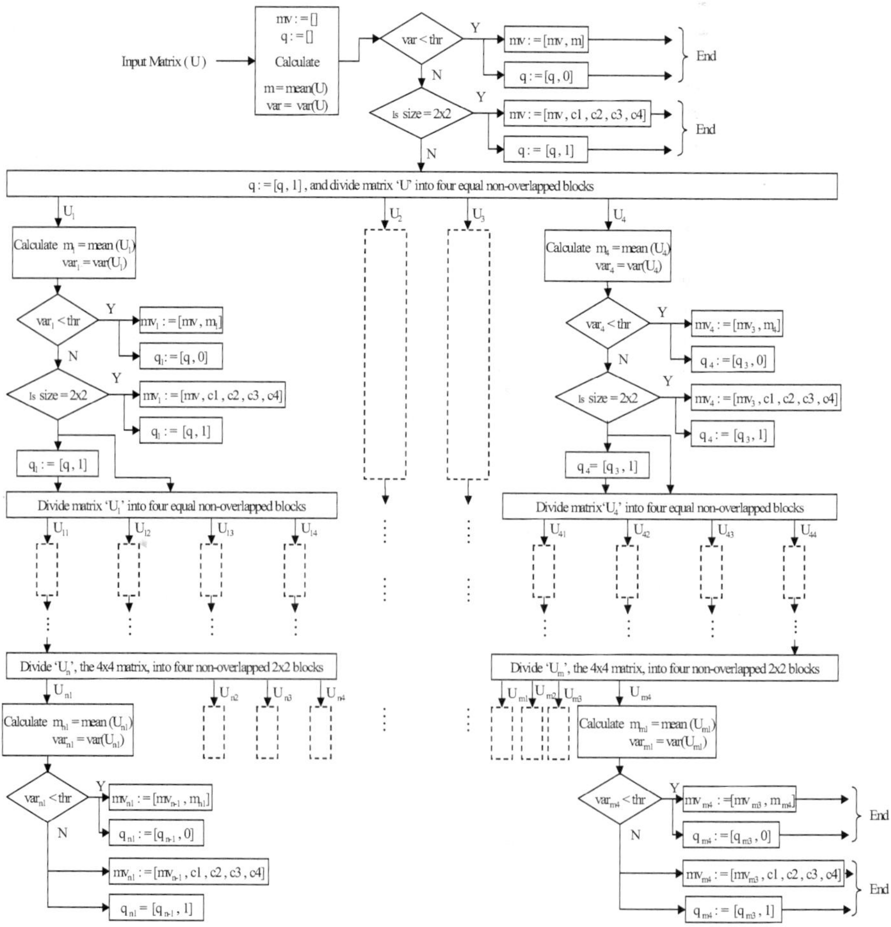

Fig. 6. Block diagram of the Statistical Encoder.

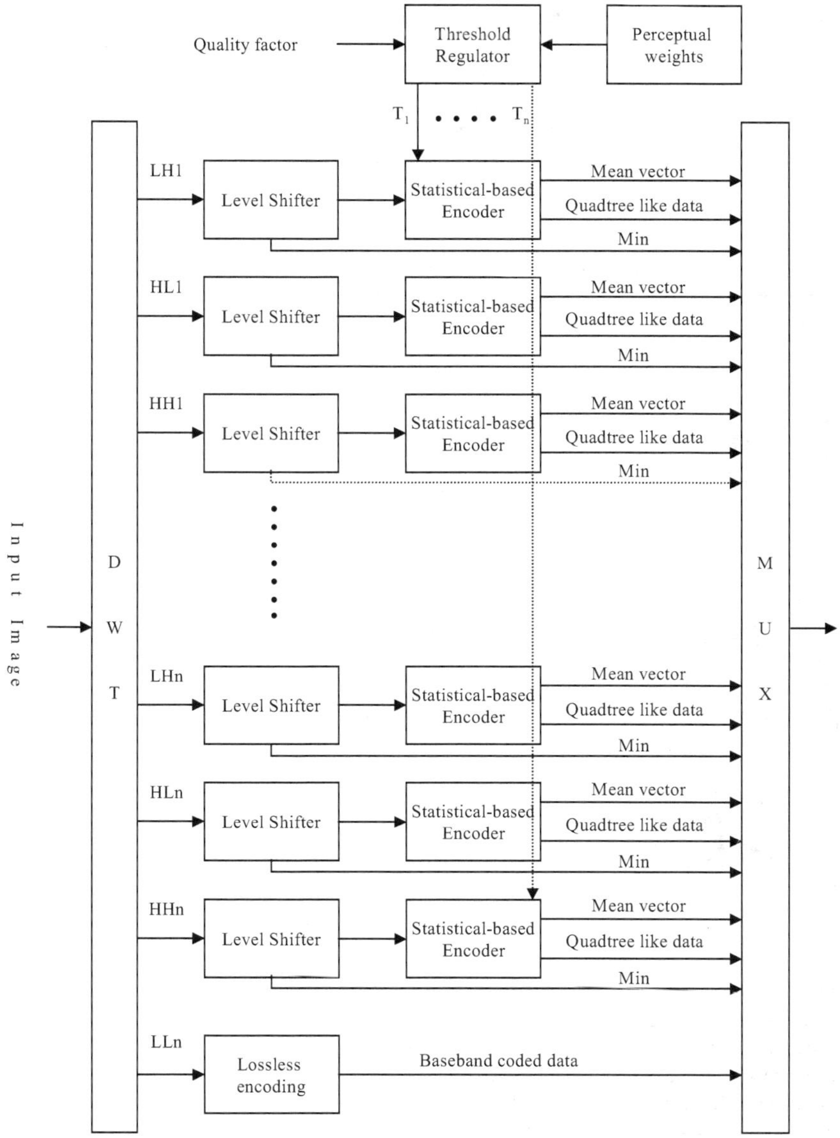

Fig. 7. The multi-resolution and statistical based image encoder.

4.3 Statistical and wavelet based image codec

A block diagram of the Multi-resolution and Statistical Based (MSB) image-coding algorithm is shown in Figure 7. A gray scale image is input to the image encoder. The MSB encoder then applies a 2D lifting based Discrete Wavelet Transform (DWT) to the input image data and decomposes them into a number of subbands. The DWT concentrates most of the image energy into the baseband. Hence, the baseband is losslessly coded using a Differential Pulse Code Modulation (DPCM) algorithm, which will be explained at the end of this section, to preserve visually important information in the baseband. Coefficients in each detail subband are coded using the procedure that is illustrated in Figure 7 as follows: (i) The coefficients in each detail subband are first level shifted to have a minimum value (Min) of zero; (ii) The resulting level shifted coefficients are then coded using the SE algorithm. The SE algorithm takes the level shifted coefficients of a detail subband and a threshold value, which is specifically designed for that subband, and performs the encoding process (The procedures for generating threshold values for different subbands are explained in Section 4.2.1); (iii) The output of each SE encoder is a mean value vector (mv), which carries the mean values, and a quadtree-like vector (q), which carries the quadtree-like data; (iv) Finally the multiplexor combines all the resulting data together and generates the compressed output bitstream.

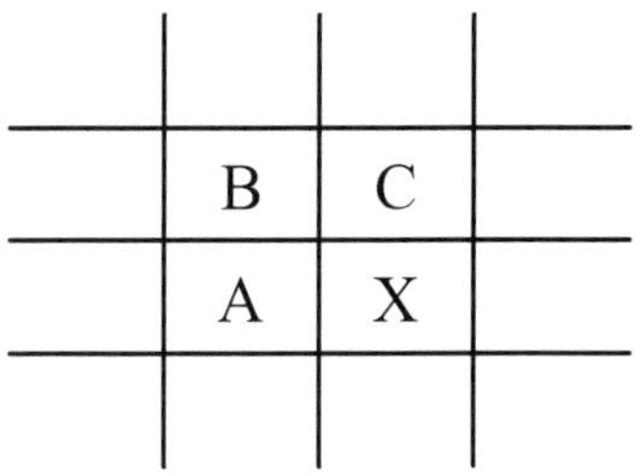

Fig. 8. Three-sample prediction neighbourhoods for DPCM method.

In the DPCM method pixel X with the value of x, is predicted from its three neighbouring pixels, called: A, B and C, with the values of a, b and c respectively, as shown in Figure 8. The prediction value of pixel X, called Px, is calculated using Equation 14:

$$P_x = b + \frac{a - c}{2} \tag{14}$$

The predicted value of pixel X is then subtracted from the actual value of pixel X to generate an error value, and all the resulting error values are finally losslessly coded.

4.3.1 Threshold generation

In this research work, perceptual weights are employed to regulate the threshold values for different subbands. Hence, the threshold value for each detail subband is generated using a uniform quality factor divided by the perceptual weight of the centre of that subband, where the uniform quality factor can take any positive value. There is a direct relationship between the uniform quality factor and the resulting compression ratios. In Section 3.2 an algorithm for calculating the perceptual weights for detail subbands of a wavelet transformed image data was given. The proposed algorithm is used to calculate the perceptual weights for the centre of each detail subband of an image of size 512×512 and a viewing distance of 40 centimetres, which are shown in Table 6.

DWT Level	Subband	Y-Domain	I-Domain	Q-Domain
	LH	3.0230	1.3251	0.7258
ONE	HL	2.0443	1.0275	0.7681
	HH	0.8713	0.4273	0.4697
	LH	5.4726	2.9355	1.6570
TWO	HL	5.5166	2.3270	1.6560
	HH	2.4531	1.0992	0.8321
	LH	6.1930	4.2479	4.9906
THREE	HL	6.3060	2.9823	4.0070
	HH	4.8143	2.2390	1.6068

Table 6. Perceptual weights for the YIQ colour domain (512×512 image size and a viewing distance of 40 cm).

4.3.2 Results

In order to evaluate the performance of the proposed MSB codec two sets of experiments were performed. In the first sets of experiments the performance of the MSB codec using perceptual weights is compared to that of MSB without using perceptual weights to regulate the threshold values for different subbands, which are presented in Sub-section 4.3.2.1 In the second sets of experiments, the MSB codec using perceptual weights is compared to those of JPEG and JPEG2000 standard image codecs, where the results are illustrated in Sub-section 4.3.2.2.

4.3.2.1 Results for the codec with and without using perceptual weights

The performance of the MSB image codec was investigated on three greyscale test images (with resolution of 8-bits per pixel) and size of 512×512 pixels: 'Lena', 'Elaine', and 'House'. These test images cover all range of spatial frequencies from very low frequency smooth areas, to textures with middle frequencies, and very high frequency sharp edges. In order to evaluate the effect of the perceptual weights on the performance of the proposed codec, 'Lena', 'Elaine', and 'House' test images were compressed using the proposed codec with and without using perceptual weights to regulate the uniform threshold value for different subbands. A three level Daubechies 9/7 wavelet transform was used to decompose the input image into ten subbands for this experiment. The PSNR criterion was used to evaluate the quality of the reconstructed images. The PSNR measurements for the test images at different compression ratios using the MSB codec with and without perceptual weights are given in Figure 9(a) to 9(c) respectively. From these Figures, it is clear that the MSB codec using perceptual weights gives significantly higher performance to that of the MSB codec without perceptual weights. However, it is well known that the PSNR is an unreliable metric for measuring the visual quality of the decompressed images (Kaia et al., 2005). Hence, to illustrate the true visual quality obtained using the MSB codec with and without perceptual weights, the reconstructed 'Lena', 'Elaine', and 'House' images at compression ratio of 16 using the proposed codec are shown in Figure 10(I) to 10(III), respectively. From theses figures, it can be seen that the reconstructed images, when perceptual weights are used in the encoding process, have significantly higher visual quality with less blurred edges and better surface details. From Figure 10(I) and 10(II), which show decoded 'Lena' and 'Elaine' test images, it is obvious that the images using the MSB codec using perceptual weights have a noticeably higher quality to those decoded using the MSB codec without employing perceptual weights. It can also be seen that the decoded test images using the MSB codec with perceptual weights have clearer facial details with less blurring in the faces. From Figure 10(III) it is clear that the reconstructed 'House' test image using MSB with HVS have significantly higher visual quality with lower blurred edges and clearer surface details.

4.3.2.2 Results of the MSB, JPEG and JPEG2000 codecs

In this section, the performance of the MSB codec with perceptual weights is compared to JPEG and JPEG2000 (JPEG2000, 2005) standard image coding techniques. The MSB, JPEG and JPEG2000 were used to compress "Lena', 'Elaine', and 'House' test images at different compression ratios. The PSNR measurements for the encoded images using the MSB, JPEG, and JPEG2000 image codecs at different compression ratios are shown in Figures 11(a) to 11(c), respectively. From these figures it can be seen that the MSB codec gives superior performance to JPEG and JPEG2000 at low compression ratios. From Figure 11(a) and 11(b), it can be observed that the proposed codec offers higher PSNR in coding 'Lena' and 'Elaine' test images to those of JPEG and JPEG2000 at compression ratios lower than 5. From Figure 11(c), it is clear that the MSB codec outperforms JPEG and JPEG2000 in coding 'House' test images at compression ratios of up to 4. However, it is well known that the PSNR often does not reflect the visual quality of the decoded images, thus a perceptual quality evaluation seems to be necessary. To demonstrate the visual quality achieved using the MSB, JPEG and JPEG2000 coding techniques at different compression ratios, the decoded 'Lena' and 'Elaine' test images at compression ratios 5 and 40 using these techniques are shown in Figures 12 and 13, respectively.

From Figures 12(a), it can be seen that the visual quality of the decoded Lena test image at a compression ratio of 5 using MSB codec is high. It is also clear that the quality of the decoded Lena test image using MSB codec is slightly higher than that of JPEG and almost the same as that of JPEG2000. The Elaine test image contains significant high frequency details and is more difficult to code. From Figure 12(b), which illustrates the decoded Elaine test images at compression ratio of 5, the high visual quality of all the decoded images is obvious. From Figures 13(a), which illustrates the decoded Lena test images at a compression ratio of 40, the severe blocking artefact of the decoded image using JPEG is quite obvious, where the MSB decoded image contains some blurring around the mouth and ringing artefacts around edges in the image. In terms of overall visual quality, the MSB decoded Lena test image has superior visual quality to that of JPEG. It is also clear that the quality of the MSB decoded image is slightly inferior to that of JPEG2000. From Figures 13(b), which illustrates the decoded Elaine test images at a compression ratio of 40, it is obvious that: a) the decoded JPEG image exhibits severe blocking artefacts; b) the MSB decoded image has higher visual quality but suffers from blurring in the background of the image and ringing artefacts in its sharp edges and c) the JPEG2000 decoded image has high visual quality but slight blurring and ringing artefacts can be seen in some regions of the background and sharp edges of the image. It is clear that the JPEG2000 decoded images have slightly higher visual quality than MSB decoded images.

The results presented here demonstrate that the MSB codec outperforms JPEG and JPEG2000 image codecs, subjectively and objectively, at low compression ratios (up to compression ratio of 5). The results also show that at middle-range compression ratios JPEG decoded images somewhat suffer from blocking artefacts, while the visual quality of the MSB decoded images is significantly higher.

The results at high compression ratios (around 40) indicate that a) the JPEG decoded images severely suffer from blocking artefacts, so much so that there is no point in using JPEG to code images at high compression ratios; b) the MSB decoded images have significantly higher visual quality than that of JPEG, while they slightly suffer from patchy blur in regions with soft texture and ringing noise at sharp edges; c) decoded MSB images have significantly lower PSNR in comparison to that of JPEG2000 but their visual quality is slightly inferior to that of JPEG2000.

5. Conclusion

In this Chapter first a novel statistical encoding algorithm was presented. The proposed SE algorithm assumes that the distribution of the coefficients in the input matrix is partly Gaussian and uses a hierarchal encoding algorithm to estimate the coefficients in the input matrix with the Gaussian mean values of multiple distributions; then a multi-resolution and statistical based image-coding scheme was developed. It applies a 2D wavelet transform on the input image data to decompose it into its frequency subbands. The baseband is losslessly coded to preserve the visually important image data. The coefficients in each detail subband were first dc level shifted to have a minimum value of zero and then coded using the SE algorithm. The SE algorithm takes the dc level shifted coefficients of a detail subband and a threshold value, which is generated for that subband. The encoding process is then performed. Perceptual weights were calculated for the centre of each detail subband and used to regulate the threshold value for that subband.

Experimental results showed that the proposed coding scheme provides significantly higher subjective and objective quality when perceptual weights are used to regulate the threshold values. The results also indicated that the proposed codec outperforms JPEG and JPEG2000 coding schemes subjectively and objectively at low compression ratios. Results showed that the proposed coding scheme outperforms JPEG subjectively at higher compression ratios. It offers comparable visual quality to that of JPEG2000 at high compression ratios.

a) Lena

b) Elaine

c) House

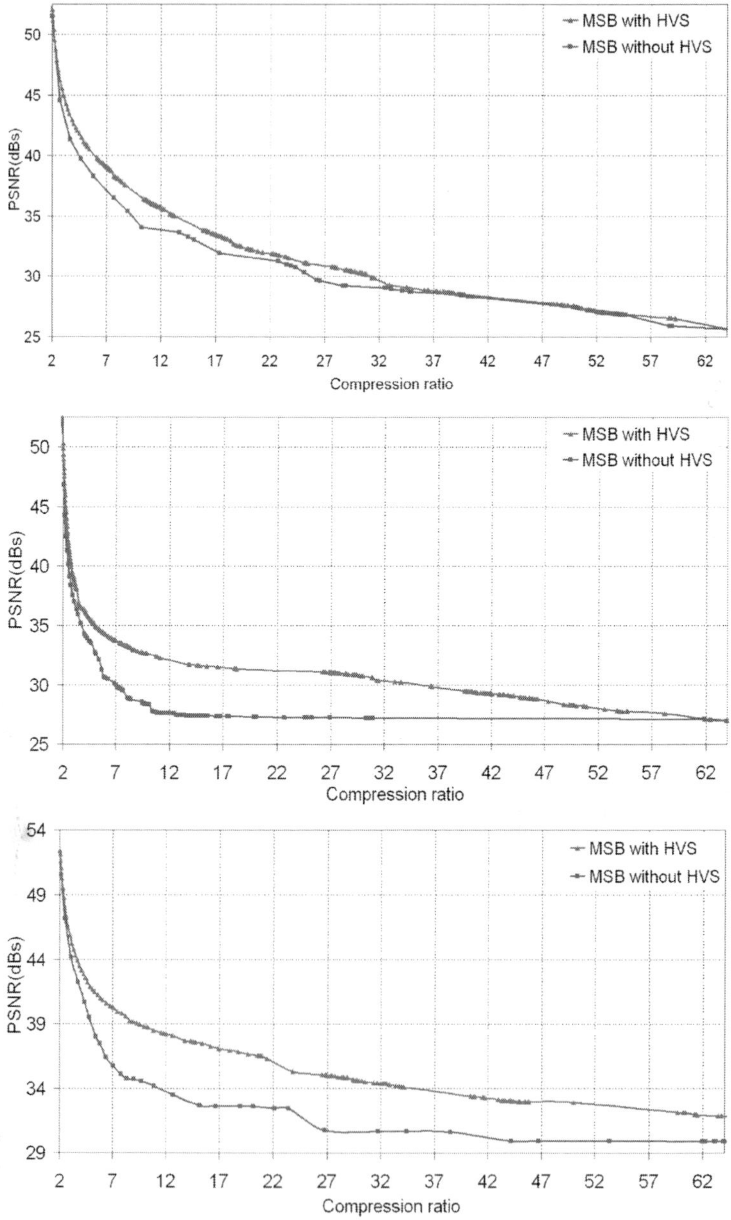

Fig. 9. PSNR measurements for a) 'Lena', b) 'Elaine' and c) 'House' test images at different compression ratios using MSB codec with and without employing perceptual weights.

I) Lena

II) Elaine

III) House

a) MSB with HVS

b) MSB without HVS

Fig. 10. Reconstructed I) 'Lena', II) 'Elaine' and II) 'House' test images at compression ratio of 16 using the MSB codec a) with HVS and b) without HVS.

a) Lena

b) Elaine

c) House

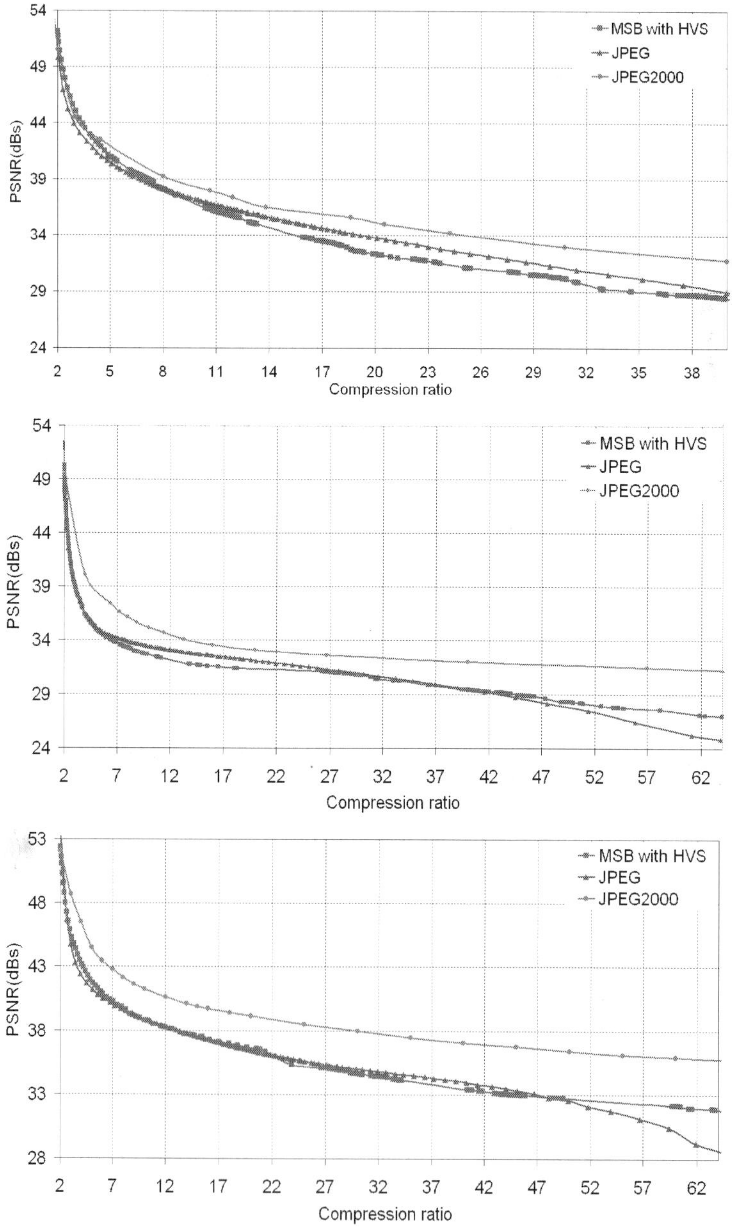

Fig. 11. PSNR measurements for a) 'Lena', b) 'Elaine' and c) 'House' test images at different compression ratios using MSB, JPEG and JPEG2000 codecs.

I) MSB

II) JPEG

III) JPEG 2000

a) Lena

b) Elaine

Fig. 12. Reconstructed a) 'Lena' and b) 'Elaine' test images at compression ratio of 5 using I) MSB codec, II) JPEG and III) JPEG2000.

I) MSB

II) JPEG

III) JPEG 2000

a) Lena b) Elaine

Fig. 13. Reconstructed a) 'Lena' and b) 'Elaine' test images at compression ratio of 40 using I) MSB codec, II) JPEG and III) JPEG2000.

6. References

(Aili et al., 2006) W. Aili, Z. Ye and G. Yanfeng, "SAR Image Compression Using HVS Model", International Conference on Radar 2006, pp. 1-4, Oct. 2006.

(Altunbasak & Kamaci, 2004) Y. Altunbasak and N. Kamaci, "An Analysis Of The DCT Coefficient Distribution with The H.264 Video Coder", *ICASSP2004*, pp.178-180, 2004.

(Antonini et al., 1992) M. Antonini, M Barlaud, P. Mathieu and I. Daubechies, "Image coding using the wavelet transform," *IEEE Transaction on Image Processing,* Vol. 1, No. 2, pp. 205-220, April 1992.

(Bradley, 1999) A. P. Bradley, A wavelet visible difference predictor, *IEEE Transaction on Image Processing*, vol.8, no. 5, 1999.

(Campbell & Robson, 1968) F.W. Campbell and J. G. Robson, "Application of Fourier Analysis to the Visibility of Gratings", *Journal of Physiologic*, vol. 197, pp. 551–566, 1968.

(Eude et al., 1994) T. Eude, H. Cherifi and R. Grisel, "Statistical distribution of DCT coefficients and their application to an adaptive compression algorithm", *IEEE International Conference TENCON1994*, pp. 427-430, 1994.

(Ghanbari, 1999) M. Ghanbari, "Video coding an introduction to standard codecs," *Published by: The Institution of Electrical Engineering, London, UK,* 1999.

(Chang & Chen, 1993) R. F. Chang and W. T. Chen, "Image Coding Using Variable-Rate Side -Match Finite-State Vector Quantization," *IEEE Transaction on Image Processing*, vol. 2, no. 1, January 1993.

(HSontsch & Karam, 2000) I. Höntsch and L. Karam, "Locally adaptive perceptual image coding," *IEEE Transaction on Image Processing*, vol. 9, no. 9, pp. 1472–1483, September 2000.

(JPEG, 1994) Information Technology-JPEG-Digital Compression and Coding of Continuous-Cone Still Image-Part 1: Requirement and Guidelines, 1994. ISO/IEC 10918-1 and ITU-T Recommendation T.81.

(JPEG2000, 2000) JPEG 2000 Part I Final Committee Draft Version 1.0, ISO/IEC JTC1/SC29/WG1 N1646R, Mar. 2000.

(Kilic & Yilmaz, 2003) I. Kilic and R. Yilmaz, "A Video Compression Technique Using Zerotree Wavelet and Hierarchical Finite State Vector Quantization" Proceedings of the 3rd International Symposium on Image and Signal Processing and Analysis2003 (ISPA2003), pp. 311-316, 2003.

(Lu et al., 2000)] Z. M. Lu, J. S. Pan and S. H. Sun, "Image Coding Based On Classified Side-Match Vector Quantization," *IEICE Transaction Information System*, E83-D, no. 12, December 2000.

(Lu et al., 2002) Z. M. Lu, B. Yang and S. H. Sun, "Image Compression Algorithms Based On Side-Match Vector Quantization With Gradient-Based Classifiers," *IEICE Transaction Information System*, E85-D, no. 9, September 2002.

(Nadenau et al., 2003) M. J. Nadenau, J. Reichel and M. Kunt, "Wavelet-Based Colour Image Compression: Exploiting the Contrast Sensitivity Function", *IEEE Transaction on Image Processing*, vol. 12, no. 1, pp. 58-70, January 2003.

(Ostermann et al., 2004) J. Ostermann, J. Bormans, P. List, D. Marpe, M. Narroschke, F. Pereira, T. Stockhammer, and T. Wedi, "Video coding with H.264/AVC: Tools, Performance, and Complexity," *IEEE Circuits and System Magazine,* Vol. 4, No. 1, pp. 7-28, First Quarter 2004.

(Peng & Kieffer, 2004) K. Peng and J. C. Kieffer, "Embedded Image Compression Based on Wavelet Pixel Classification and Sorting," *IEEE Transaction on Image Processing*, vol. 13, no. 8, pp. 1011-1017, August 2004.

(Said & Pearlman, 1996) A. Said and W. Pearman, "A new, Fast, and Efficient Image Codec Based on Set Partitioning in Hieratical Trees", *IEEE Transaction on Circuits and Systems for Video Technology*, Vol. 6, no. 3, pp. 243-250, June1996.

(Saryazdi & Jafari, 2002) S. Saryazdi and M. Jafari, "A High Performance Image Coding Using Uniform Morphological Sampling, Residues Classifying, and Vector Quantization," *EurAsia-ICT 2002*, Shiraz, Iran, October 2002.

(Scargall & Dlay, 2000) L. D. Scargall and S. S. Dlay, "New methodology for adaptive vector quantization", *IEE Proceedings on Vision, Image and Signal Processing*, Vol. 147, No. 6, December 2000.

(Shapiro, 1993) J.M Shapiro, "Embedded image coding using zerotrees of wavelet coefficients", *IEEE Transactions on Acoustics, Speech, and Signal Processing*, vol. 41, Issue 12, pp. 3445 - 3462, 1993.

(Sheikh Akbari & Soraghan, 2003) A. Sheikh Akbari and J.J. Soraghan, "Adaptive Joint Subband Vector Quantization Codec For Handheld Videophone Applications", *International Journal of IEE Electronic Letters*, VOL. 39. NO.14, pp. 1044 - 1046, 2003.

(Skodras et al, 2001) A. Skodras, Ch. Christopoulos, and T. Ebrahimi, "The JPEG 2000 Still Image Compression Standard," *IEEE Signal Processing Magazine*, vol. 18, no.5, September 2001.

(Tan et al, 2004) D. M. Tan, H. R. Wu, and Z. Yu, "Perceptual Coding of Digital Monochrome Images," *IEEE Signal Processing Letters*, Vol. 11, no. 2, pp. 239-242, February 2004.

(Thornton et al., 2002) L. Thornton, J. Soraghan, R. Kutil, M. Chakraborty, "Unequally protected SPIHT video codec for low bit rate transmission over highly error-prone mobile channels," *Elsevier Science: Signal Processing: Image Communication*, vol. 17, pp. 327–335, 2002.

(Valade & Nicolas, 2004) C. Valade, J. M. Nicolas, "Homomorphic wavelet transform and new subband statistics models for SAR image compression" IEEE International Proceedings on Geoscience and Remote Sensing Symposium, IGARSS 2004, Vol.1, 2004.

(Van Dyck & Rajala, 1994) R.E. Van Dyck, and S. A. Rajala, "Subband/VQ Coding of Colour Images with Perceptually Optimal Bit Allocation", *IEEE Trans. on Circuits and Systems for Video Technology*, vol. 4, no. 1, February 1994.

(Voukelatos & Soraghan, 1997) S. P. Voukelatos and J. J. Soraghan, "Very Low Bit Rate Color Video Coding Using Adaptive Subband Vector Quantization with Dynamic Bit Allocation", *IEEE Transaction on Circuits and Systems for Video Technology*, vol. 7, no. 2, pp. 424-428, April 1997.

(Voukelatos & Soraghan, 1998) S. P. Voukelatos and J. J. Soraghan, "A multiresolution adaptive VQ based still image codec with application to progressive image transmission", *EURASIP Signal Processing: Image Communication*, vol. 13, no. 2, pp. 135-143, 1998.

(Wang et al., 2001) J. Wang, W. Zhang and S. YU, "Wavelet coding method using small block DCT," *Electronic Letters*, Vol. 37, No. 10, pp.627-629, May 2001.

(Yovanof & Liu, 1996) Yovanof and S. Liu, "Statistical analysis of the DCT coefficients and their quantization error", Thirtieth Asilomar Conference on Signals, Systems and Computers, pp. 601-605, 1996.

Image Denoising Based on Wavelet Analysis for Satellite Imagery*

Parthasarathy Subashini and Marimuthu Krishnaveni
Department of Computer Science,
Avinashilingam University for Women,
Coimbatore, Tamil Nadu,
India

1. Introduction

Digital images are prone to a variety of types of noise. Noise is the result of errors in the image acquisition process that result in pixel values that do not reflect the true intensities of the real scene (Gagnon & Smaili, 1996). There are several ways that noise can be introduced into an image, depending on how the image is created. For example if the image is scanned from a photograph made on film, the film grain is a source of noise. Noise can also be the result of damage to the film, or be introduced by the scanner itself. If the image is acquired directly in a digital format, the mechanism for gathering the data (such as a CCD detector) can introduce noise. Electronic transmission of image data can introduce noise. Noise is considered to be any measurement that is not part of the phenomena of interest. Noise can be categorized as Image data independent noise and image data dependent noise.

Wavelets are mathematical functions that cut up data into different frequency components, and then study each component with a resolution matched to its scale (Durand & Froment,1992). They have advantages over traditional Fourier methods in analyzing physical situations where the signal contains discontinuities and sharp spikes. Wavelets were developed independently in the fields of mathematics, quantum physics, electrical engineering, and seismic geology. Interchanges between these fields during the last ten years have led to many new wavelet applications such as image compression, turbulence, human vision, radar, and earthquake prediction.

Synthetic aperture radar is a radar technology that is used from satellite or airplane (Lee,Jukervish 1994). It produces high resolution images of earth's surface by using special signal processing techniques. Synthetic aperture radar has important role in gathering information about earth's surface because it can operate under all kinds of weather condition (whether it is cloudy, hazy or dark).However acquisition of SAR images face certain problems. SAR images contain speckle noise which is based on multiplicative noise or rayleigh noise. Speckle noise is the result of two phenomenon, first phenomenon is the coherent summation of the backscattered signals and other is the random interference of electromagnetic signals. Speckle noise degrades the appearance and quality of SAR images (Brunique,1997). Ultimately it reduces the performances of important techniques of image processing such as detection, segmentation, enhancement and classification. That is why speckle noise should be removed before applying any image processing techniques. There are three main objectives of any speckle filtering. First is to remove noise in uniform regions. Second is to preserve and enhance edges and image features and third is to provide a good visual appearance. Unfortunately 100% speckle reduction is not possible. Therefore, tradeoff has to be made among these requirements. Speckle reduction usually consists of three stages. First stage is to transform the noisy image to a new space (frequency domain). Second stage is the manipulation of coefficients. Third is to transform the resultant coefficients back to the original space (spatial domain).Currently many statistical filters are available for speckle reduction, such as, Mean, Kuan, Frost and Lee filter etc. Results show that statistical filters are good in speckle reduction but they also lose important feature details. Additionally prior knowledge about noise statistics is a prerequisite for statistical filters. In recent years, there has been active research on wavelet based speckle reduction because wavelet provides multi resolution decomposition and analysis of image (Durand & Froment,1992).. In wavelet sub bands noise is present in small coefficients and important feature details are present in large coefficients. If small coefficients are removed, we will get noise free image. Previously most of the researchers use discrete wavelet transformation for reduction of speckle. Draw back of discrete wavelet transformation is that it is not translation invariant. That means it will lose lots of important coefficients during translation from original signal to sub bands(Nabil ,2009). In order to solve this problem and to save the coefficients, derivated form of discrete wavelet transformation is used called undecimated wavelet transformation. Basic idea is that it does not lose any coefficients, all coefficients remain intact. That is why it is also called redundant wavelet transformation. It requires more storage space and need more time for computation. Whether discrete or undecimated wavelet is used, biggest problem is the selection of optimal thresholding .Some researchers use wavelet based hard or soft thresholding. Other thresholding techniques were also used such as VisuShrink, SureShrink and neighshrink.

1.1 Aim and objectives of the chapter

Image denoising has a significant role in image pre processing. As the application areas of image denoising are more, there is a big demand for efficient denoising algorithms. In this chapter, a method that involves Wavelet with shrinkage concepts is proposed and applied it to denoise images corrupted with speckle noise. The intention behind this method is to reduce the convergence time of conventional filter and thereby increase its performance. The proposed method produces excellent results and comparison is made with two wavelet shrinkage and case study is carried over for ice classification based in SAR imagery.

To this the objectives are:

1. to analysis various wavelet concepts in image processing
2. to generalize from current research thus, reaching a coherent view of the role of Wavelet in image denoising ;

3. to propose wavelet concept for describing the denoising of images using shrinkage methods
4. to produce a case study to support the denoising approach within the goal-driven concept.

Wavelet based methods are always a good choice for image denoising and has been discussed widely in literatures for the past two decades .Wavelet shrinkage permits a more efficient noise removal while preserving high frequencies based on the disbalancing of the energy of such representation. The technique denoises image in the orthogonal wavelet domain, where each coefficient is thresholded by comparing against a threshold; if the coefficient is smaller than the threshold, it is set to zero, otherwise it is kept or modified.

This chapter does not attempt to investigate in deep the theoretical properties of the proposed model in general settings. The primary goal is to demonstrate that how the performance of wavelet shrinkage based denoising methods can be applied by using the best wavelet family. In the following paragraphs, Section 2 reviews the existing works on wavelet concepts in image processing, Section 3 describes the state-of-the-art of image denoising, Section 4 explains the various shrinkage methods of wavelet, Section 5 explains about the solution for denoising in SAR imagery using wavelet Section 6 ends up with a case study and, finally, Section 7 discuss future works in the area of wavelet.

2. Review based on wavelet concepts in image processing

The main issue discussed in this section is to identify the nature of the dependence between the pixels in the original image and to estimate noise in signal. For astronomical images of sparsely distributed stars an independence assumption may be reasonable, while for many other kinds of images (including astronomical images of galaxies) such an assumption is inappropriate (Lopez & Cumplido 2004). If independence is a reasonable assumption then the CLEAN, maximum entropy, and maximally sparse methods are appropriate and the choice largely depends on the desired balance between accuracy and speed. For example, the CLEAN method is fast but can make mistakes for images containing clustered stars. For images that are expected to be relatively smooth then the Wiener filter and iterative methods are appropriate. If the images are known to satisfy some additional constraints (for example, the intensities are often known to be non-negative for physical reasons) or if the blurring function is space varying then the iterative methods such as Richardson-Lucy or constrained least squares are appropriate. Otherwise it is better to use the Wiener filter because it is fast and approximately includes the iterative methods as special cases. The wavelet methods tend to give a good compromise for images containing such a mixture of discontinuities and texture. Below are the research work in which wavelet concepts and methods are applied to image processing applications.

2.1 Motion estimation

Magarey developed a motion estimation algorithm based on a complex discrete wavelet transform. The transform used short 4-tap complex filters but did not possess the PR property. The filter shapes were very close to those used in the DT-CWT suggesting that the conclusions would also be valid for the DT-CWT. The task is to try and estimate the displacement field between successive frames of an image sequence. The fundamental property of wavelets that makes this possible is that translations of an image result in phase changes for the wavelet coefficients. By measuring the phase changes it is possible to infer the motion of the image. A major obstacle in motion estimation is that the reliability of motion estimates depends on image content. For example, it is easy to detect the motion of a single dot in an image, but it is much harder to detect the motion of a white piece of paper on a white background. Magarey developed a method for incorporating the varying degrees of confidence in the different estimates. In tests on synthetic sequences the optimised CDWT-based algorithm showed superior accuracy under simple perturbations such as additive noise and intensity scaling between frames. In addition, the efficiency of the CDWT structure minimises the usual disadvantage of phase-based schemes- their computational complexity. Detailed analysis showed that the number of floating point operations required is comparable to or even less than that of standard intensity-based hierarchical algorithms.

2.2 Classification

Efficient texture representation is important for content based retrieval of image data(Lopez &Cumplido 2004). The idea is to compute a small set of texture-describing features for each image in a database in order to allow a search of the database for images containing a certain texture. The DT-CWT has been found to be useful for classification by number of authors.Each uses the DT-CWT in different ways to compute texture features for an entire image:

1. De Rivaz and Kingsbury compute features given by the logarithm of the energy in each subband.
2. Hill, Bull, and Canagarajah compute the energies of the subbands at each scale. However, in order to produce rotationally invariant texture features, they use features based on either the Fourier transform or the auto-correlation of the 6 energies at each scale.
3. Hatipoglu, Mitra, and Kingsbury use features of the mean and standard deviations of complex wavelet subbands. However, instead of using the DT-CWT based on a fixed tree structure, they use an adaptive decomposition that continues to decompose subbands with energy greater than a given threshold (Nabil, 2009).

2.3 Denoising

In many signal or image processing applications, the input data is corrupted by some noise which need to be removed or at least reduced. Wavelet denoising techniques work by adjusting the wavelet coefficients of the signal in such a way that the noise is reduced while the signal is preserved (Sivakumar,2007). There are many different methods for adjusting the coefficients but the basic principle is to keep large coefficients while reducing small coefficients. This adjustment is known as thresholding the coefficients.One rationale for this approach is that often real signals can be represented by a few large wavelet coefficients, while (for standard orthogonal wavelet transforms) white noise signals are represented by white noise of the same variance in the wavelet coefficients. Therefore the reconstruction of the signal from just the large coefficients will tend to contain most of the signal energy but little of the noise energy. An alternative rationale comes from considering the signal as being piecewise stationary. For each piece the optimum denoising method is a Wiener filter whose frequency response depends on the local power spectrum of the signal. When the signal power is high, the power is kept mostly; when the signal power is low, the signal is attenuated. The size of each wavelet coefficient can be interpreted as an estimate of the power in some time-frequency bin and set the small ones to zero in order to approximate adaptive Wiener filtering. The first wavelet transform proposed for denoising was the standard orthogonal transform. However, orthogonal wavelet transforms (DWT) produce results that substantially vary even for small translations in the input and so a second transform was proposed, the nondecimated wavelet transform (NDWT) , which produced shift invariant results by effectively averaging the results of a DWT-based method over all possible positions for the origin. Experiments on test signals show that the NDWT is superior to the DWT. The main disadvantage of the NDWT is that even an efficient implementation takes longer to compute than the DWT, by a factor of the three times the number of levels used in the decomposition.Kingsbury has proposed the use of the DT-CWT for denoising because this transform not only reduces the amount of shift-variance but also may achieve better compaction of signal energy due to its increased directionality. In other words, at a given scale an object edge in an image may produce significant energy in 1 of the 3 standard wavelet subbands, but only 1 of the 6 complex wavelet subbands.

2.4 Compression and matching

Compression algorithms with wavelet-based transformations were selected in competition with compression using fractal transformations. FBI's standard has similarities with the JPEG2000 standard, and especially with an extension to the JPEG2000 standard. Further decomposition of the LH-, HL- and HH-bands like this may improve compression somewhat, since the effect of the filter bank application may be thought of as an "approximative orthonormalization process". The extension to the JPEG2000 standard also opens up for this type of more general subband decompositions. In FBI's standard different wavelets can be used, with the coefficients of the corresponding filter banks signalled in the code-stream. The only constraint on the filters is that there should be no more than 32 nonzero coefficients. This is much longer than lossy compression in JPEG2000 (9 nonzero coefficients).

2.5 Segmentation

Texture is an important characteristic for analyzing many types of images, including natural scenes and medical images. With the unique property of spatial-frequency localization, wavelet functions provide an ideal representation for texture analysis. Experimental evidence on human and mammalian vision support the notion of spatial-frequency analysis that maximizes a simultaneous localization of energy in both spatial and frequency domain.These psychophysical and physiological findings lead to several research works on texture-based segmentation methods based on multi-scale analysis. One important feature of wavelet transform is its ability to provide a representation of the image data in a multi-resolution fashion. Such hierarchical decomposition of the image information provides the possibility of analyzing the coarse resolution first, and then sequentially refine the segmentation result at more detailed scales. In general, such practice provides additional robustness to noise and local maxima (Mallat,1989).

3. Preliminary investigation of image denoising

Noise reduction is the process of removing noise from image. Noise reduction techniques are conceptually very similar regardless of the signal being processed, however a priori knowledge of the characteristics of an expected signal can mean the implementations of techniques vary greatly depending on the type of signal. Noise can be random or white noise with no coherence or coherent noise introduced by the device mechanism or processing algorithms. In photographic film and magnetic tape, noise (both visible and audible) is introduced due to the grain structure of the medium. In photographic film, the size of the grains in the film determines the film's sensitivity, more sensitive film having larger sized grains. In magnetic tape, the larger the grains of the magnetic particles (usually ferric oxide or magnetite), the more prone the medium is to noise. To compensate for this, larger areas of film or magnetic tape may be used to lower the noise to an acceptable level.

3.1 Noise study

Estimating the noise level from a single image seems like an impossible task: the image should be recognized whether local image variations are due to color, texture, or lighting variations from the image itself, or due to the noise. It might seem that accurate estimation of the noise level would require a very sophisticated prior model for images. Capturing a pinhole image (large depth-of-field) is important to many computer vision applications, such as 3D reconstruction, motion analysis, and video surveillance. For a dynamic scene, capturing pinhole images however is difficult: we have often to make a tradeoff between depth-of-field and motion blur. For example, if a large aperture and short exposure to avoid motion blur, the resulting images will have small depth-of-field; otherwise, if we use a small aperture and long exposure, the depth-of-field will be large, but at the expense of motion blur.

3.2 Potential disadvantages of noise filters in images

Many types of distortions limit the quality of digital images during image acquisition, formation, storage and transmission. Often, images are corrupted by impulse noise. The intensity of impulse noise has the tendency of being either relatively high or low thereby causing loss of image details. It is important to eliminate noise in images before using them for other image processing techniques like edge detection, segmentation, registration etc. Several filtering methods have been proposed in the past to address impulse noise removal(Wang &Hang 1999). One of the more famous filters for gray scale images is the standard median filter which rank orders the pixel intensities within a filtering window and replaces the center pixel with the median value. Extending the idea of a scalar median filter to color images is not straightforward due to the lack of a natural concept of ranking among the vectors. Color distortion may occur when the scalar median filter is applied separately to every single component of the color vectors. A method called Vector Median Filter (VMF) which considers all the three color components and rank orders the vectors. Various modifications of the standard VMF have been introduced like Directional Median Filter and Central Weighted Vector Median Filter. The biggest drawback of the conventional vector median approaches is that they apply median operation to each pixel, irrespective of it being corrupted or not. An intuitive solution to overcome this disadvantage is to first detect the corrupt pixels and then to apply filtering on those pixels alone (Trygve &Hakon 1999). One of the main problems with impulse noise detection is that it is difficult to differentiate between an edge and an impulse noise. In the intensity space, both these stand as peaks in their neighborhood. The difference between the center pixel with the minimum and maximum gray value in the filtering window is taken and if greater than a certain threshold, the center pixel is considered as noise. The disadvantage of this method is that the false positive rate is very high and most of the edges also get detected as noise. Coherent processing of synthetic aperture radar (SAR) data makes images susceptible to speckles (Lee,Jukervish 1994). Basically, the speckles are signal-dependent and, therefore, act like multiplicative noise. This report develops a statistical technique to define a noise model, and then successfully applies a local statistics noise filtering algorithm to a set of actual SEASAT SAR images. The smoothed images permit observers to resolve fine detail with an enhanced edge effect. Several SEASAT SAR images are used for demonstration.

The standard algorithm shows very good performance removing the additive noise. In SAR images, on the contrary, the noise is multiplicative. In particular three procedures are there to obtain the speckle noise reduction:

1. Use of a logarithmic transformation in order to translate the noise from multiplicative to additive.
2. Use of repeated applications of filtering algorithm.
3. Use of non-symmetric membership functions optimized by using a genetic algorithm.

Regarding the first point, the logarithmic transformation allowed to apply the standard fuzzy filtering algorithm obtaining a significant removal of the multiplicative noise.

The repeated application of the filtering algorithm permits to reduce the speckle noise granularity without degradation of the sharpness. This is very important for the subsequent recognition of the pattern present in the image.

3.3 Wavelet denoising in images

The fundamental objective in image enhancement is to improve or accentuate subsequent processing tasks such as detection or recognition (Chang,2000,2006). Classical image enhancement techniques consider the use of spatial-invariant operators either in the spatial or in the fourier domain. Examples of techniques in the spatial domain are related with the histogram modification by a predetermined transformation as in histogram equalization and stretching. These methods are global in the sense that the pixels are modified in the entire image. However, it is often necessary to perform the enhancement process over small patches of the image. Examples of such techniques include local histogram stretching (in overlapping or non-overlapping windows), smoothing and sharpening . In the fourier domain, most methods are based in supressing low spatial frequencies relative to high spatial frequencies as in homomorphic filtering. Local image enhancement can also be performed by means of a multiscale image representation.Fourier transform based spectral analysis is the dominant analytical tool for frequency domain analysis. However, fourier transform cannot provide information of the spectrum changes with respect to time. Fourier transform assumes the signal as stationary, but PD signal is always non-stationary. To overcome this deficiency, a modified method-short time fourier transform allows representing the signal in both time and frequency domain through time windowing functions (Akansu et al., 1992). The window length determines a constant time and frequency resolution. Thus, a shorter time windowing is used in order to capture the transient behavior of a signal by sacrificing the frequency resolution.

A continuous-time wavelet transform of f(t) is defined as:

$$CWT_{\upsilon}f(a,b) = W_f(b,a) = |a|^{-1/2} \int_{-\alpha}^{\alpha} f(t)\psi^*(\frac{t-b}{a})dt \tag{1}$$

Here a,bεR , $a \neq 0$ since they are dilating and translating coefficients respectively. The asterisk denotes a complex conjugate. This multiplication of $|a|^{1/2}$ is for energy normalization purposes so that the transforms signal will have the same energy at every scale. The analysis function $\psi(t)$, the so called mother wavelet, is scaled by a, so a wavelet analysis is often called a time scale analysis rather than a time frequency analysis. The wavelet transform decomposes the signal into different scales with different levels of resolution by dilating a single prototype function, the mother wavelet. Furthermore, a mother wavelet has to satisfy that it has a zero net area, which suggest that the transformation kernel of the wavelet transform is a compactly support function (localized in time), thereby offering the potential to capture the PD spikes which normally occur in a short period of time. The general wavelet denoising procedure is as follows:

- Apply wavelet transform to the noisy signal to produce the noisy wavelet coefficients to the level which it can properly distinguish the PD occurrence.
- Select appropriate threshold limit at each level and threshold method (hard or soft thresholding) to best remove the noises.
- Inverse wavelet transform of the thresholded wavelet coefficients to obtain a denoised signal.

4. Denoising using shrinkage methods

Conservative methods based on wavelet transforms have been emerged for removing Gaussian random noise from images. This local preprocessing speckle reduction technique is necessary prior to the processing of SAR images. Wavelet Shrinkage or thresholding as denoising method is the best identified method here. It is well known that increasing the redundancy of wavelet transforms can significantly improve the denoising performances. Thus a thresholding process which passes the coarsest approximation sub-band and attenuates the rest of the sub-bands should decrease the amount of residual noise in the overall signal after the denoising process (Achim et al.,2003). One dimensional dyadic discrete time wavelet transform is a transform similar to the discrete Fourier transform in that the input is a signal containing N numbers, say, and the output is a series of M numbers that describe the time-frequency content of the signal. The Fourier transform uses each output number to describe the content of the signal at one particular frequency, averaged over all time. In contrast, the outputs of the wavelet transform are localised in both time and frequency. The wavelet transform is based upon the building block shown in figure 1. This block is crucial for both understanding and implementing the wavelet transform.

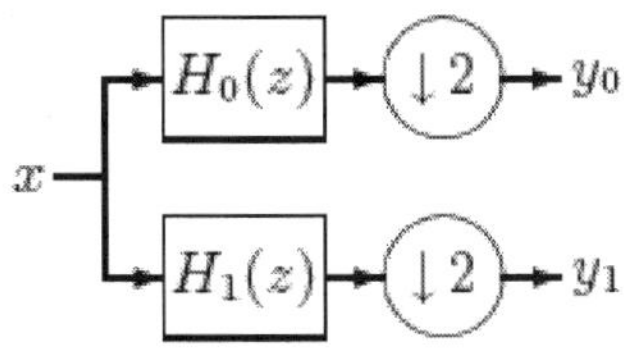

Fig. 1. Building block for wavelet transform

This diagram is to be understood as representing the following sequence of operations

1. Filter an input signal (whose value at time n is x (n)) with the filter whose Z-transform is $H_0(z)$.
2. Downsample the filter output by 2 to give output coefficients y_0 (n).
3. Filter the input signal x(n) with the filter whose Z-transform in $H_1(z)$.
4. Downsample the filter output by 2 to give output co-efficients $y_1(n)$

The two main confines in image accuracy are categorized as blur and noise. Blur is intrinsic to image acquisition systems, as digital images have a finite number of samples and must respect the sampling conditions. The second main image perturbation is noise. Image denoising is used to remove the additive noise while retaining as much as possible the important signal features. Currently a reasonable amount of research is done on wavelet thresholding and threshold selection for signal de-noising, because wavelet provides an appropriate basis for separating noisy signal from the image signal. Two shrinkage methods are used over here to calculate new pixel values in a local neighborhood. Shrinkage is a well known and appealing denoising technique. The use of shrinkage is known to be optimal for Gaussian white noise, provided that the sparsity on the signal's representation is enforced using a unitary transform. Here a new approach to image denoising, based on the image-domain minimization of an estimate of the mean squared error-Stein's unbiased risk estimate (SURE) is proposed and equation (3.1) specifies the same. Surelet method directly parameterizes the denoising process as a sum of elementary nonlinear processes with unknown weights. Unlike most existing denoising algorithms, using the SURE makes it needless to hypothesize a statistical model for the noiseless image. A key of it is, although the (nonlinear) processing is performed in a transformed domain-typically, an undecimated discrete wavelet transform, but nonorthonormal transformsis also addressed and this minimization is performed in the image domain.

$$sure(t;x) = d - 2.\#\{i : |x_i| \le t\} + \sum_{i=1}^{d}(|x_i| \Lambda t)^2 \tag{2}$$

where d is the number of elements in the noisy data vector and x_i is the wavelet coefficients. This procedure is smoothness-adaptive, meaning that it is suitable for denoising a wide range of functions from those that have many jumps to those that are essentially smooth.

It have high characteristics as it out performs Neigh shrink method. Comparison is done over these two methods to prove the elevated need of Surelet shrinkage for the denoising the SAR images. The experimental results are projected in graph format which shows that the Surelet shrinkage minimizes the objective function the fastest, while being as cheap as neighshrink method. Measuring the amount of noise equation (3) is done by its standard deviation , $\sigma(n)$, one can define the signal to noise ratio (SNR) as

$$SNR = \frac{\sigma(\mu)}{\sigma(n)}, \tag{3}$$

Where $\sigma(\mu)$ in equation (3) denotes the empirical standard deviation of $\mu(i)$,

$$\sigma(\mu) = \left(\frac{1}{|I|} \sum_i (u(i) - \overline{\mu})^2 \right)^{1/2} \tag{4}$$

And $\bar{\mu} = \frac{1}{|I|} \sum_{i \varepsilon I} \mu(i)$ is the average grey level value. The standard deviation of the noise can also be obtained as an empirical measurement or formally computed when the noise model and parameters are known. This parameter measures the degree of filtering applied to the image It also demonstrates the PSNR rises faster using the proposed method than the former. Hence the resulted denoised image is conceded to the next segment for the transformation to be applied and it is also proved to improve detection process.

4.1 Wavelet shrinkage - Description and short history

Wavelet shrinkage is a quite recent denoising method compared to classical methods like the Wiener filter or convolution filters and is applied very successfully to various denoising problems (Liu &Raja, 1996).. A very interesting thing about wavelet shrinkage is that it can be motivated from very different fields of mathematics, namely partial differential equations, the calculus of variations, harmonic analysis or statistics.

A heuristic way to wavelet shrinkage goes as follows. A signal f is considered which is distributed by additive white noise: $g = f + \varepsilon$ .Since the discrete wavelet transform is linear and orthogonal, the wavelet transform of g has the form $g_\gamma = (f_\gamma) + (\varepsilon_\gamma)$ where the coefficients ε_γ of the noise are given white noise. Usually the signal f results in a few number of large wavelet coefficients and most of the coefficients are zero or nearly zero (Chen &Bui 2003). The noise on the other hand leads to a large number of small coefficients on all scales. Thus, the small coefficients g_γ mostly contain noise. Hence, it seems to be a good idea to set all the coefficients which are small to zero. But what shall happen to the large coefficients? The two most popular ones are hard and soft shrinkage. By application of hard shrinkage one leaves the large coefficients unchanged and sets the coefficients below a certain threshold to zero. Mathematically speaking one applies the function

$$S_\lambda(x) = \begin{cases} x, |x| > \lambda \\ 0, |x| \le \lambda \end{cases} \tag{5}$$

to the wavelet coefficients. Another famous way is soft shrinkage where the magnitude of all coefficients is reduced by the threshold in which one applies the function

$$S_\lambda(x) = \begin{cases} x - \lambda, x \geq \lambda \\ 0, |x| \leq \lambda \\ x + \lambda, x \leq -\lambda \end{cases} \quad (6)$$

to the coefficients. Beside these two possibilities there are many others (semi-soft shrinkage, firm shrinkage,....) and as long as the shrinkage function preserves the sign $(sign(S_\lambda(x)) = sign(x))$ and shrinks the magnitude ,one can expect a denoising effect.

The interesting thing about wavelet shrinkage is, that it appears in very different fields of mathematics in a natural way. Four places where shrinkage appears naturally are :

1. As the subgradient descent along the absolute value.
2. As the function which maps an initial value onto the minimizer of a variational functional.
3. As the function "identity minus projection onto a convex set" which is also motivated by variational analysis.
4. As the maximum a posteriori estimator for an additively disturbed signal, where the signal and the noise are distributed in a certain way.

4.2 Applying shrinkage methods

The effect of wavelet shrinkage is illustrated in this section. An image of an eye is taken which is a closeup on a man's eye. It is a suitable image for illustrative purposes because it provides very different regions: small and sharp details like the eyelashes, texture-like parts of different contrast like the eyebrows or the skin below the eye, smooth parts like the eyeball or the skin above the eye and sharp edges like the edge of the lower lid. The image has a resolution of 256 times 256 pixels, 256 gray levels For calculations the gray levels have been scaled to the interval [0, 1].

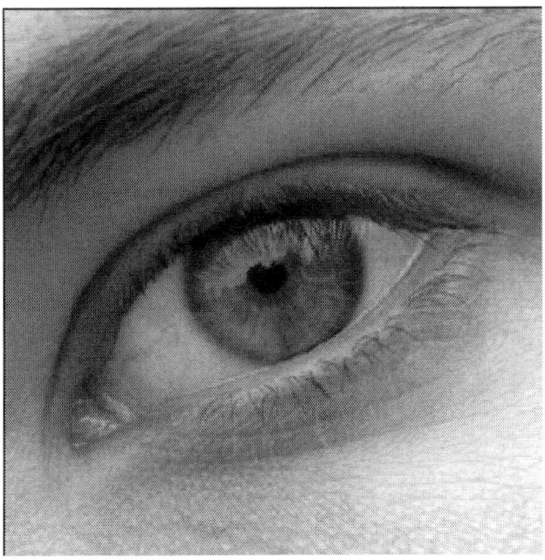

Fig. 2. The image eye.

4.3 Discrete wavelet shrinkage

This is the place where shrinkage methods have their origin and where they are used the most.

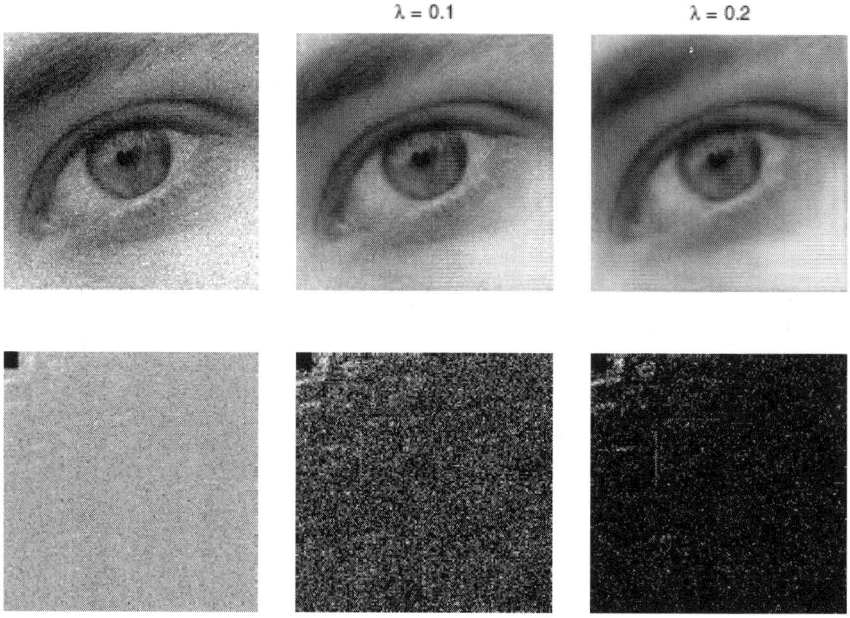

Fig. 3. Illustration of discrete wavelet shrinkage. The wavelet used here is the coiflet. Top row, from left right: the noisy image, wavelet shrinkage for different values of λ. The second row shows the discrete wavelet transform of the upper row.

Consider an orthogonal periodic wavelet base $\{\psi_\gamma)_{\gamma\varepsilon\tau}$ of $L^2(I)$

Define the orthogonal mapping as

$$W : L^2(I) \to l^2(1 \cup \Gamma) \text{ via } f \to (\langle f \mid 1 \rangle, (f_\gamma)_{\gamma\varepsilon\Gamma}) \tag{7}$$

The mapping W is invertible and isometrical.

Define $\Phi onl^2(1 \cup \Gamma)$ by $\Phi(a) = \|a\|_{l^1(1\cup\Gamma)}$ and the functional need is $\Psi : L^2(I) \to \bar{R}$ defined by

$$\Psi(f) = \Phi(Wf) = \begin{cases} |\langle f \mid 1 \rangle| + \|(f_\gamma)_{\gamma\varepsilon\Gamma}\|_{l^1(\Gamma)} \\ \infty \end{cases} \tag{8}$$

The result obtained that the discrete wavelet shrinkage

$$\mu(t) = S_t(\langle f \mid 1 \rangle) + \sum_{\gamma \varepsilon \Gamma} S_t(f_\gamma)\psi_\gamma \tag{9}$$

is a solution of the descent equation

$$\partial_t \mu + \partial \Psi(\mu) \ni 0, \mu(0) = f \tag{10}$$

4.4 Continuous wavelet shrinkage

The wavelet transform is an isometry and explained as

$$L^2(R) \to rangeL_\psi \subset L^2(R^2, dadb / a^2) \tag{11}$$

But the range of the wavelet transform is a proper subspace of the space $L^2(R^2, dadb / a^2)$. In particular range L_ψ is not invariant under shrinkage.

Unfortunately, a subgradient descent in such a subspace is in general not a subgradient descent in the original Hilbert space and vice versa.

Soft Shrinkage : The well known soft shrinkage function $S_\lambda(x) = (|x| - \lambda) + signx$ gives

$$g(|x| = (1 - \frac{(|x| - \sqrt{2\lambda})_+}{|x|} \tag{12}$$

which is a diffusivity. It is decreasing and according to the above proposition it hols g(0)=1 and g(x) $\to$ 0 for $x \to \infty$

Hard Shrinkage: The Hard shrinkage function (or hard thresholding)

$S_\lambda(x) = x(1 - \chi_{[-\lambda\lambda]}(x))$ leads to

$$g(|x|) = \begin{cases} 1 for |x| \leq \sqrt{2\lambda} \\ 0 else \end{cases} \tag{13}$$

This is a "piecewise linear diffusion" where diffusion is forbidden if the derivative has absolute value larger that $\sqrt{2\lambda}$ .With regard to wavelet shrinkage denoising, the theoretical justifications and arguments in its favor remain highly compelling. The procedure does not require any assumptions about the nature of the signal, permits discontinuities and spatial variation in the signal, and exploits the spatially adaptive multiresolution features essential to the wavelet transform. Furthermore, the procedure exploits the fact that the wavelet transform maps white noise in the signal domain to white noise in the transform domain. Thus, while signal energy becomes more concentrated into fewer coeffcients in the transform domain, noise energy does not. It is this important principle that enables the separation of signal from noise. Wavelet shrinkage denoising has been theoretically proven to be nearly optimal from the following perspectives: spatial adaptation, estimation when local smoothness is unknown, and estimation when global smoothness is unknown. This section presents an extensive study for wavelet denoising methods and shows that many of them are leading to the idea of shrinkage in a general sense.

5. Finding a solution for denoising in sar imagery using wavelet

The wavelet transform is a mathematical tool widely used in image processing. Some applications of the transform to remote sensing images have been investigated in the literature. It was found useful for texture analysis , image compression and noise reduction . The transform allows representation of a signal onto an orthonormal basis. Each term of the basis represents the signal at a given scale. In order to decompose the signal onto the basis, the algorithm developed is applied to the signal. It consists of iterations of one-dimensional high-pass and low-pass filtering steps. The algorithm creates a pyramid of low-resolution approximations as well as a wavelet pyramid in which the details a stored as wavelet coefficients. This representation is called wavelet representation(Jiang et al., 2000).. One way of image analysis, is to choose the wavelet for speckle in SAR images which is always problematic(Ali,2007). Often, it is impenitent to reduce noise-before trying to extract scene features. Many filters have been developed to improve image quality by conserving the intrinsic scene features and textures. Interpretation of SAR images by human is possible in the presence of speckle. The wavelet transform, as the mammal visual system, provides and allows for a multiscale analysis of images. This section presents how the wavelet transform can be used for extraction of linear features such as edges and thin stripes. It will also show how speckle can be relaxed by taking into account the speckle contribution to wavelet coefficients.

5.1 Noise in SAR imagery

A proportionality relation exists between Speckle noise and the wavelet coefficients . Since Speckle is approached as a multiplicative noise, this contribution will be larger for higher reflectivity regions. It is also known that speckle in SAR images is spatially correlated. That is to say the noise is colored. Therefore its behavior in the Fourier domain is such that there is a peak of a given width around the zero frequency. This is readily observed as a wavelet coefficient variance plateau when decomposing a correlated noise model on a wavelet basis. As decomposition gets to scales larger than the correlation length, the contribution from speckle decreases linearly.

5.2 Using Wavelet for SAR speckle denoising

- The main advantage of wavelet analysis is that it allows the use of long time intervals where more precise low frequency information is wanted, and shorter intervals where high frequency information is sought.
- Wavelet analysis is therefore capable of revealing aspects of data that other image analysis techniques miss, such as trends, breakdown points, and discontinuities in higher derivatives and self-similarity.
- Wavelets are also capable of compressing or de-noising a image without appreciable degradation of the original image.

5.3 Wavelet transform

The *wavelet transform* can be used to analyze time series that contain nonstationary power at many different frequencies. Assume that one has a time series, *xn*, with equal time spacing d*t* and n = 0 ... N - 1. Also assume that one has a *wavelet function*, $\psi_n = (n)$, that depends on a nondimensional "time" parameter h. To be "admissible" as a wavelet, this function must have zero mean and be localized in both time and frequency space. An example is the Morlet wavelet, consisting of a plane wave modulated by a Gaussian:

$$\psi_o(\eta) = \pi^{-1/4} e^{i\omega_0 n} e^{-n^{2/2}} \tag{14}$$

where w0 is the nondimensional frequency, here taken to be 6 to satisfy the admissibility condition . The term "wavelet function" is used generically to refer to either orthogonal or nonorthogonal wavelets. The term "wavelet basis" refers only to an orthogonal set of functions. The use of an orthogonal basis implies the use of the *discrete wavelet transform,* while a nonorthogonal wavelet function can be used with either the discrete or the continuous wavelet transform (Grossman et al.,1989). The continuous wavelet transform of a discrete sequence xn is defined as the convolution of xn with a scaled and translated version of $\psi_n = (n)$:

$$W_n(s) = \sum_{n'=0}^{N-1} x_{n'} \psi^* \left[\frac{(n' - n)\delta t}{s} \right] \tag{15}$$

where the (*) indicates the complex conjugate. By varying the *wavelet scale s* and translating along the *localized time index n,* one can construct a picture showing both the amplitude of any features versus the scale and how this amplitude varies with time. The subscript 0 on y has been dropped to indicate that this y has also been normalized (see next section). Although it is possible to calculate the wavelet transform using (2), it is considerably faster to do the calculations in Fourier space. To approximate the continuous wavelet transform, the convolution (2) should be done N times for each scale, where N is the number of points in the time series (Kaiser 1994). (The choice of doing all N convolutions is arbitrary, and one could choose a smaller number, say by skipping every other point in n.) By choosing N points, the convolution theorem allows us do all N convolutions simultaneously in Fourier space using a discrete Fourier transform (DFT). The DFT of xn is

$$\hat{x}_k = \frac{1}{N} \sum_{n=0}^{N-1} x_n e^{12\pi kn/N} \tag{16}$$

where $k = 0 \ldots N - 1$ is the frequency index. In the continuous limit, the Fourier transform of a function y(t/s) is given by y\$ (sw). By the convolution theorem, the wavelet transform is the inverse Fourier transform of the product:

$$W_n(s) = \sum_{k=0}^{N=1} \hat{x}_k \hat{\psi}^* (s\omega_k) e^{i\omega_k \eta \delta t} \tag{17}$$

where the angular frequency is defined as

$$\begin{aligned} \omega_k &= \left\{ \frac{2\pi k}{N\delta t} : k \le \frac{N}{2} \right\} \\ \omega_k &= \left\{ -\frac{2\pi k}{N\delta t} : k \le \frac{N}{2} \right\} \end{aligned} \tag{18}$$

Using (4) and a standard Fourier transform routine, one can calculate the continuous wavelet transform (for a given s) at all n simultaneously and efficiently.

5.4 Normalization

To ensure that the wavelet transforms at each scale s are directly comparable to each other and to the transforms of other time series, the wavelet function at each scale s is normalized to have unit energy:

$$\hat{\psi}(s\omega_k) = \left(\frac{2\pi s}{\delta t}\right)^{1/2} \hat{\psi}_0(s\omega_k) \tag{19}$$

Using these normalizations, at each scale s one has

$$\sum_{k=0}^{N-1} \left|\hat{\psi}(s\omega_k)\right|^2 = N \tag{20}$$

where N is the number of points. Thus, the wavelet transform is weighted only by the amplitude of the Fourier coefficients $x\$k$ and not by the wavelet function. If one is using the convolution formula (2), the normalization is

$$\psi\left[\frac{(n' - n)\delta t}{s}\right] = \left(\frac{\delta t}{s}\right)^{1/2} \psi_0\left[\frac{\left(n' - n\right)\delta t}{s}\right] \tag{21}$$

where $\psi_n = (n)$ is normalized to have unit energy.

5.5 Wavelet functions

One criticism of wavelet analysis is the arbitrary choice of the wavelet function, $\psi_n = (n)$. (It should be noted that the same arbitrary choice is made in using one of the more traditional transforms such as the Fourier, Bessel, Legendre, etc.) In choosing the wavelet function, there are several factors which should be considered

1. *Orthogonal or nonorthogonal.* In orthogonal wavelet analysis, the number of convolutions at each scale is proportional to the width of the wavelet basis at that scale. This produces a wavelet spectrum that contains discrete "blocks" of wavelet power and is useful for signal processing as it gives the most compact representation of the signal. Unfortunately for time series analysis, an a periodic shift in the time series produces a different wavelet spectrum. Conversely, a nonorthogonal analysis (such as used in this study) is highly redundant at large scales, where the wavelet spectrum at adjacent times is highly correlated. The nonorthogonal transform is useful for time series analysis, where smooth, continuous variations in wavelet amplitude are expected.
2. *Complex or real.* A complex wavelet function will return information about both amplitude and phase and is better adapted for capturing oscillatory behavior. A real wavelet function returns only a single component and can be used to isolate peaks or discontinuities.
3. *Width.* For concreteness, the width of a wavelet function is defined here as the *e*-folding time of the wavelet amplitude. The resolution of a wavelet function is determined by

the balance between the width in real space and the width in Fourier space. A narrow (in time) function will have good time resolution but poor frequency resolution, while a broad function will have poor time resolution, yet good frequency resolution.

4. *Shape.* The wavelet function should reflect the type of features present in the time series. For time series with sharp jumps or steps, one would choose a boxcar-like function such as the Harr, while for smoothly varying time series one would choose a smooth function such as a damped cosine. If one is primarily interested in wavelet power spectra,then the choice of wavelet function is not critical, and one function will give the same *qualitative* results as another.

5.6 Wavelet bases

Many wavelet families with various characteristics are known. Some wavelet families are especially useful for specific application. Most wavelets are based on FIR filters although research work is also done for wavelets constructed by IIR filters. The orthogonal and biorthogonal wavelets are the two basic categories of wavelets.

Type	Filter	Symmetry	Orthogonality	Fast algorithm
Haar	FIR	Symmetric	Orthogonal	Yes
Daubechies	*FIR*	*Asymmetric*	*Orthogonal*	*Yes*
Symlets	FIR	Near symmetric	Orthogonal	Yes
Coiflets	*FIR*	*Near symmetric*	*Orthogonal*	*Yes*
Spline	*FIR*	*Symmetric*	*Biorthogonal*	*Yes*
Morlet	IIR	Symmetric	No	No
Mexican Hat	IIR	Symmetric	No	No
Meyer	IIR	Symmetric	Orthogonal	No
Butterworth	*IIR*	*Asymmetric*	*Orthogonal*	*Yes*

Table 1. Main properties of wavelet families

Table 1 summarizes the main properties of most well-known wavelets. The primary consideration in the use of wavelets for surface profile analysis is the amplitude and phase transmission characteristics of the wavelet basis. A combination of good amplitude and linear phase transmission is always desired to achieve minimum distortion of surface features. Among the listed wavelets in Table 1, Haar wavelet is the oldest and simplest wavelet that is not continuous. The Symlet and Coiflet wavelet come from Daubechie wavelet, but are more symmetric (Daubechies,1989,1992). Both the scaling function and wavelet of Meyer are defined in frequency domain. Although the scaling function and wavelet of Meyer are symmetric, no fast algorithm is available for its wavelet transform.The Morlet and Mexican wavelets only have wavelet functions and the corresponding scaling functions don't exist Four wavelets in three categories are selected for study here. They are orthogonal Daubechies wavelets and

Butterworth wavelets with nonlinear phase, orthogonal Coiflets wavelets with near linear phase, and biorthogonal Spline wavelets with linear phase (Daubechies, 1989, 1992). All of them are associated with FIR filters except Butterworth wavelets.

5.7 Wavelet families in SAR images

- Haar wavelet is the simplest of the wavelet transforms.
- This transform cross-multiplies a function against the Haar wavelet with various shifts and stretches, like the Fourier transform cross-multiplies a function against a sine wave with two phases and many stretches.
- Daubechies wavelets are a family of orthogonal wavelets defining a discrete wavelet transform and characterized by a maximal number of vanishing moments for some given support.
- Meyer's wavelet construction is fundamentally a solvent method for solving the two-scale equation.
- Symlet wavelet is only nearly symmetric, and is not exactly symmetrical.
- Coiflets are discrete wavelets designed by Ingrid Daubechies, to have scaling functions with vanishing moments.
- biorthogonal wavelet is a wavelet where the associated wavelet transform is invertible but not necessarily orthogonal.
- Reverse biorthogonal is a spline wavelet filters.

5.8 Performance evaluation

5.8.1 Subjective evaluation

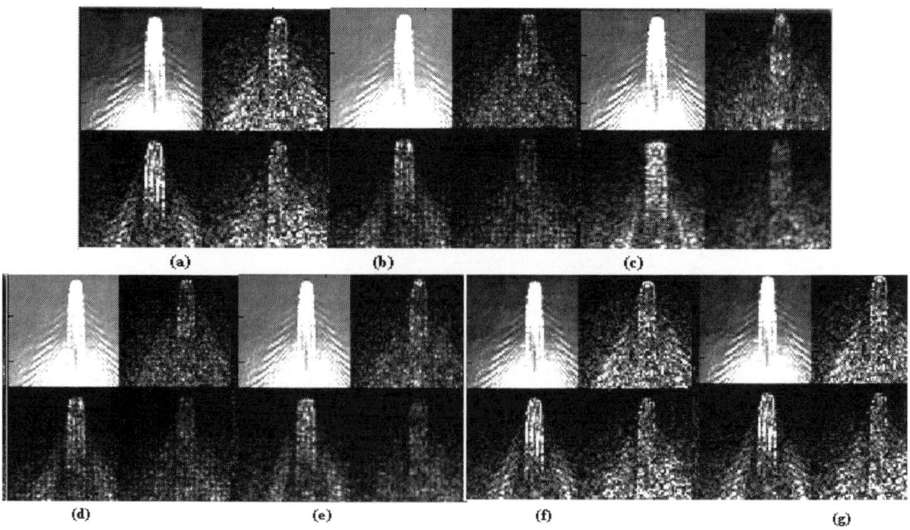

Fig. 4. (a) Haar wavelet (b) Daubechies wavelet (c) Meyer Wavelet (d) Symlet wavelet (e) Coiflets wavelet (f) Bi orthogonal wavelet (g) Reverse Bi orthogonal

5.8.2 Objective evaluation

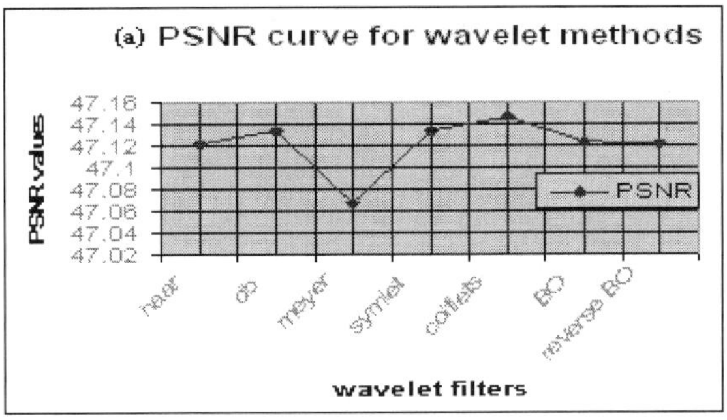

Fig. 5. Peak to Signal noise ratio for wavelet methods

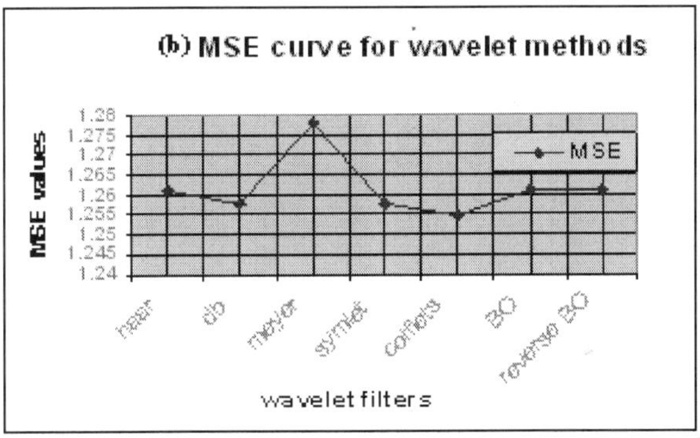

Fig. 6. Mean square error rate for wavelet methods

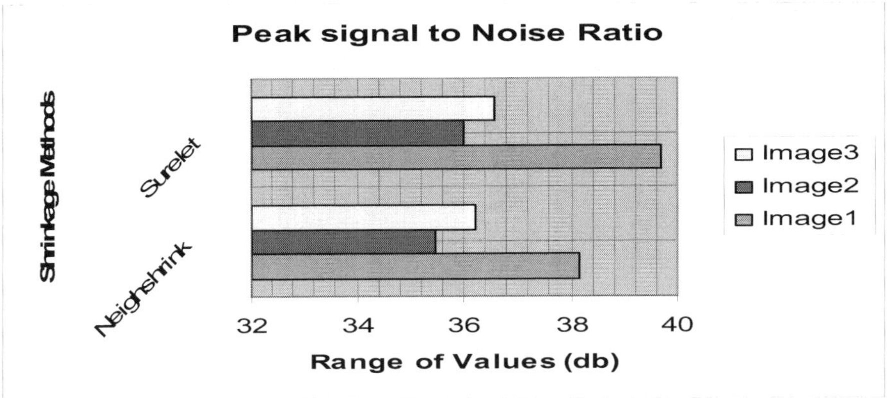

Fig. 7. PSNR values for shrinkage method based on coiflet Wavelet family

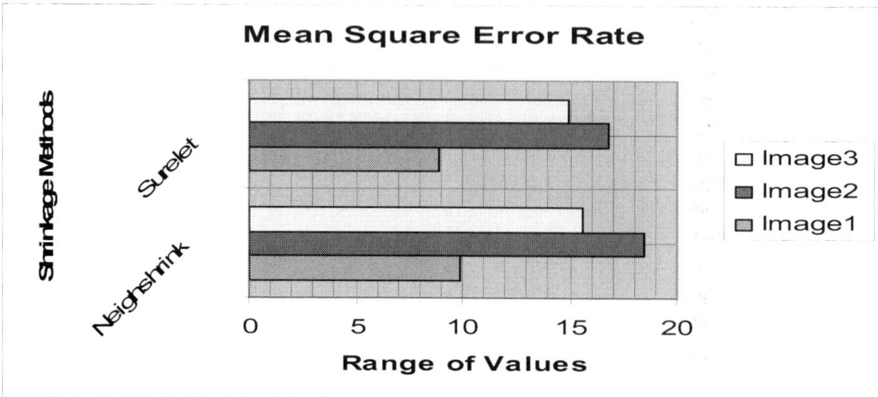

Fig. 8. MSE values for shrinkage method based on coiflet Wavelet family

The wavelet transform is computed separately for different segments of the time-domain signal at different frequencies. Discrete wavelet transform (DWT), which transforms a discrete time signal to a discrete wavelet representation. The reconstruction of image is far better in wavelet by analysis and it is implemented with the given SAR image. Some of the parameters taken for analysis of wavelet on SAR images are

Mean Square error rate - MSE is called **squared error loss**.

MSE of an estimator is one of many ways to quantify the amount by which an estimator differs from the true value of the quantity being estimated.

PSNR -This ratio is often used as a quality measurement between the original and a compressed image. The higher the PSNR, the better the quality of the compressed or reconstructed image.

The *Mean Square Error (MSE)* and the *Peak Signal to Noise Ratio (PSNR)* are the two error metrics used to compare image quality. The MSE represents the cumulative squared error between the compressed and the original image, whereas PSNR represents a measure of the peak error. The lower the value of MSE, the lower the error.

From the above got results the coiflets of wavelet denoising method out performs the rest of the wavelet families. This study presented an analysis and comparison of the wavelet families using for image denoising considering PSNR and visual quality of image as quality measure. The effects of bio orthogonal , Reverse bio orthogonal, Daubechies, coiflets and symlets wavelet families on the test images have been examined. The PSNR and visual image quality for wavelet functions of each family is also presented. The PSNR is taken as the objective measure for performance analysis of wavelets using for images denosinig. Here it is analyzed -the results for a wide range of wavelets families and found that the wavelet coifilets provides best performance for SAR images.The computational time required for the Bio orthogonal and reverse bio orthogonal wavelet families is more in comparison to other wavelet families is more in comparison to other wavelet families. The performance of wavelet function depends not only size of the image but also on the content and resolution of the images. Finally, it is concluded that the selection of wavelet for image denoising depends on size, contents and resolution of the images for desired image quality.

6. Wavelet analysis for ice classification in SAR imagery

Automation in river ice image classification assists the ice experts in extracting geophysical information from the increasing volume of images. Rivers and streams are the key elements in the terrestrial re-distribution of water. An ice cover has significant impact on rivers such as modifies ecosystem, affects microclimate, cause flooding, restrict navigation, impact hydropower generation. The regions that are affected by ice are fishing industry, coastal zone and lake water levels and navigation.

6.1 Importance of ice covers

- Impacts both global/regional energy and water cycles.
- High reflectance, thermal insulation, storage of water extent (areal coverage), depth, water equivalent (water content), wet/dry state.
- Snowfall/solid precipitation .Indicator of climate variability and change
- Input/validation of models - NWP, hydrological, climate
- Environmental monitoring/prediction - flood forecasting, severe weather(blowing snow), soil moisture/drought, forest fire risk, wildlife
- Socio-economic - hydropower production/management, agriculture, tourism

6.2 SAR basics

Satellite-based Synthetic Aperture Radar (SAR) provides a powerful vessel surveillance capability in front of time consuming traditional methods. SAR images are larger in volume. SAR images typically consist of 32 bit complex pixels with large dimensions. The entropy of SAR images is higher than optical images (Sery et al., 1996).. SAR images carry information in low frequency bands as well as high frequency bands. SAR images have larger dynamic range than optical images. SAR sea images are highly heterogeneous and this fact affects to the viability of the approach. The major advantages of SAR are (i)Sensitive to texture (ii) Good for vegetation studies (iii) Ocean waves, winds, currents(iv) Seismic Activity and Moisture content.

6.3 SAR image denoising using Wavelet

This is the first and lowest level operation to be done on images. The input and the output are both intensity images. The main idea with the preprocessing is to suppress information in the image that is not relevant for its purpose or the following analysis of the image (Subashini &Krishnaveni, 2010). The pre-processing techniques use the fact that neighboring pixels have essentially the same brightness. There are many different pre-processing methods developed for different purposes.Interesting areas of pre-processing for this work is image filtering for noise suppression. Two shrinkage methods are used over here to calculate new pixel values in a local neighborhood. Shrinkage is a well known and appealing denoising technique. On the experiment evaluation, Daubechies wavelet family of orthogonal wavelets is concluded as the appropriate family for shrinkage method as it is defined as a discrete wavelet transform and characterized by a maximal number of vanishing moments for some given support.

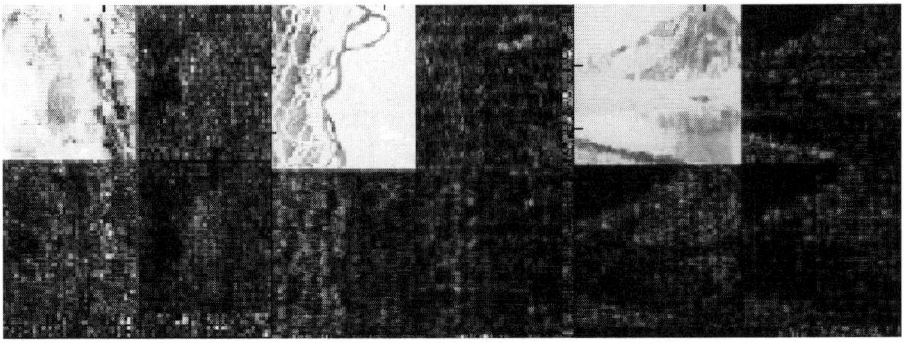

Fig. 9. Daubechies wavelet based on level 2 decomposition

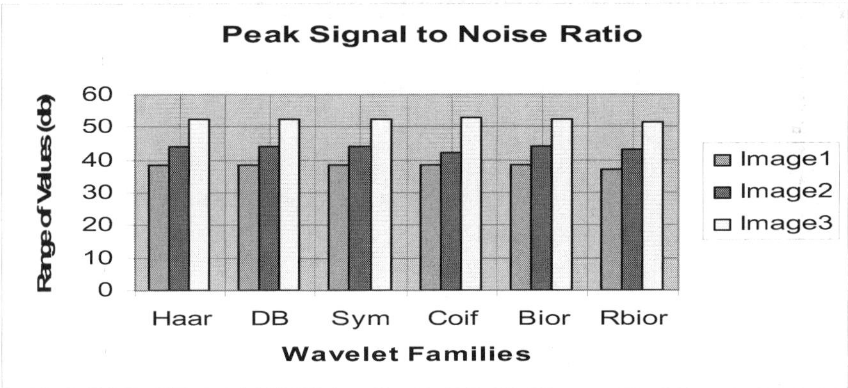

Fig. 10. Peak to Signal noise ratio for wavelet methods

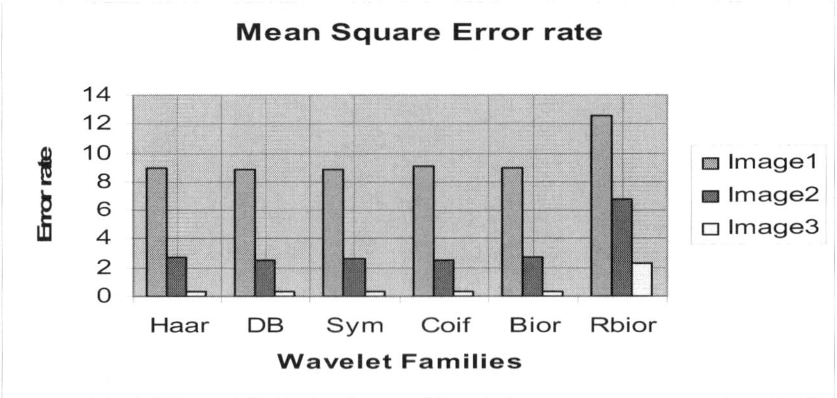

Fig. 11. Mean square error rate for wavelet methods

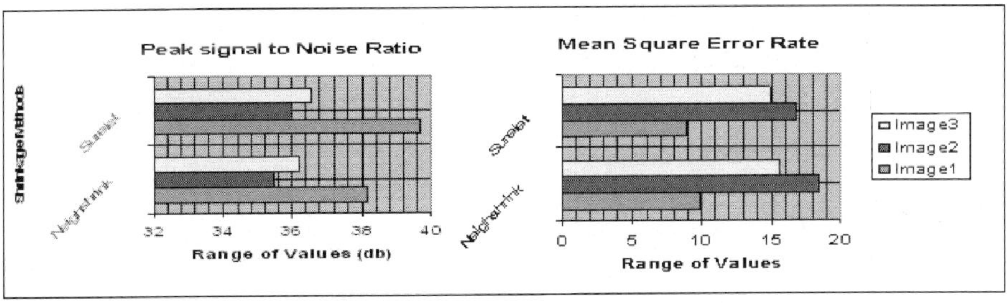

Fig. 12. PSNR and MSE values for shrinkage method based on DB Wavelet Family

Figure 10, 11 shows the evaluation of wavelet families to find the best and Daubechies wavelet is been concluded for wavelet shrinkage denoising. Figure 12 represents the objective evaluation of the shrinkage methods and finally surelet shrinkage is been concluded as the optimal method for denoising. Here an attempt is made to find a superior methodology for denoising than the conventional fixed-form neighborhoods. This approach also determines optimal results by using finest threshold instead of using the suboptimal universal threshold in all bands. It exhibits an excellent performance for ice detection and the experimental result also signifies the same by producing both higher PSNRs and enhanced visual eminence than the former and conventional methods. In future, research will be carried out to reduce the computational load of the proposed image classification algorithm and shorten the execution time of the projected approach.

7. Conclusion and further development

Recently, there has been considerable interest in using the wavelet transform as a powerful tool for recovering SAR images from noisy data. The main reason for the choice of multiscale bases of decompositions is that the statistics of many natural signals, when decomposed in such bases are significantly simplified. When multiplicative contamination is concerned, multiscale methods involve a preprocessing step consisting of a logarithmic transform to separate the noise from the original image. However, thresholding methods have two main drawbacks: i) the choice of the threshold, arguably the most important design parameter, is made in an *ad hoc* manner; and ii) the specific distributions of the signal and noise may not be well matched at different scales. To address these disadvantages, Bayesian theory can be introduced , which outperform classical linear processors and simple thresholding estimators in removing noise from visual images.

Denoising should not be confused with smoothing. Smoothing removes high frequencies and retains low frequencies whereas denoising attempts to remove whatever noise is present and retain whatever signal is present regardless of the spectral content of the noisy signal.Wavelet shrinkage denoising is denoising by shrinking (i.e., nonlinear soft thresholding) coefficients in the wavelet transform domain. It consists of three steps: 1) a linear forward wavelet transform, 2) a nonlinear shrinkage denoising, and 3) a linear inverse wavelet transform. Because of the nonlinear shrinking of coefficients in the transform domain, this procedure is distinct from those denoising methods that are entirely linear. Moreover, it is considered as a nonparametric method. Thus, it is distinct from parametric methods, including both linear and nonlinear regression, in which parameters must be estimated for a particular model that must be assumed a priori. If the common sense approach to practical problem solving is adopted, then the practitioner should exploit any and all *a priori* information available for his particular problem, and use an appropriate denoising procedure as determined by the most relevant outcome measure. Determining the most appropriate procedure necessarily involves experiments to compare the performance of a wavelet shrinkage denoising method with any other methods under consideration. In addition, issues of computational complexity must be considered. Complexity of algorithms may be measured according to CPU computing time and flops, or the number and kind of algorithm steps and their impact on firmware or hardware requirements. Here a new statistical representation for the wavelet decomposition coefficients of SAR images is introduced and it is found that shrinkage is to be more effective than traditional methods both in terms of speckle reduction and signal detail preservation. The SAR images evaluated all are coded in eight-bit. The motivation is that as wavelet transform is good at energy compaction, the small coefficients are more likely due to noise and large coefficient due to important signal features . The proposed technique is based upon the analysis of wavelet transform which uses a soft thresholding method for thresholding the small coefficients without affecting the significant features of the image. In the chapter, image denoising is studied using various wavelets for different images at various levels of decomposition and comparison are done between the families and wavelet shrinkage techniques. It is unlikely that one particular wavelet shrinkage denoising procedure will be suitable, no less optimal, for all practical problems. However, it is likely that there will be many practical problems, for which after appropriate experimentation, wavelet-based denoising with either hard or soft thresholding proves to be the most effective procedure. Estimation of the power spectrum by wavelet-based denoising of the log-periodogram may prove to be one such important application with great promise for further development.

8. References

A. Gupta, S. D. Joshi, and S. Prasad. (2005).A new approach for estimation of statistically matched wavelet. IEEE Transac- tions on Signal Processing, 53:1778–1793, May 2005.

Achim, A,P.Tsakalides and A. Bezerianos.(2003)." SAR Image Denoising via Bayesian Wavelet Shrinkage Based on "Heavy –Tailed Modeling In : IEEE Trans Geosci Remote Sensing,41 (8):1773-1784.DOI:10.11.09/TGRS.2003 813488 INSPEC:7733902.

Akansu, A. N., and Haddad, R. A. (1992). Multiresolution Signal Decomposition, Transforms, Subbands, and Wavelets, Academic Press, Inc., London, UK, 1992.

Ali, S.M., M.Y Javed and N.S.Khattak.(2007)."Wavelet based despeckling of synthetic aperture radar images using adaptive and mean filters .Int J.Computer Sci Eng.,1 (2) :108-112

Dabuchies, I.(1992). "Ten Lectures on Wavelets, Notes from the 1990 CBMS-NSF Conference on Wavelets and Applications at Lowell, MA, SIAM, Philadelphia, PA, 1992.

Daubechies, I., (1989) "Orthonormal Bases of Compactly Supported Wavelets II. Variations on a Theme," Technical Memo., #11217-891116-17, AT&T Bell Labs., Murray Hill, and preprint, 1989.

F. Sery, A. Lopes, D. Ducrot, R. Fjørtoft, E. Cubero-Castan, and P. Marthon,.(1996). "Multisource classification of SAR images with the use of segmentation, polarimetry, texture and multitemporal data," in Proc. EurOpto Image and Signal Processing for Remote Sensing, Vol. SPIE 2955, Taormina, Italy, Sept. 1996, pp. 186-197.

G. Chang, B. Yu, and M. Vetterli. .(2000).Adaptive wavelet thresholding for image denoising and compression. IEEE Transactions on Image Processing, 9:1532–1546, September 2000.

G. Y. Chen and T. D. Bui.(2003). "Multi-wavelet De-noising using Neighboring Coefficients," IEEE Signal Processing Letters, vol.10, no.7, pp.211-214, 2003.

Grossmann, A., Kronland-Martinet, R., and Morlet, J.(1989)."Reading and Understanding Continuous Wavelet Transform, in Wavelets, Combes, J. M., Grossmann, A., and Tchamitchian, Ph., eds., Springer-Verlag, Berlin, 2-20, 1989.

J. Bruniquel and A. Lopes.(1997). "Multivariate speckle reduction in SAR imagery," Int. Journal of Remote Sensing, Vol. 18, No. 3, pp. 603-627, Feb. 1997.

J. S. Lee and I. Jurkevich .(1994). "Speckle filtering of synthetic aperture radar images: A review," Remote Sensing Reviews, Vol. 8, pp. 313-340, 1994.

L. Gagnon and F.D. Smaili.(1996) 'Speckle Noise Reduction of Airborne SAR Images with Symmetric Daubechies Wavelets', SPIE Proc. #2759, pp. 1424, 1996

Liu, X. and Raja J. (1996). "The Application of Wavelet Filter Bank in Surface Metrology", SPIE Vol. 2825, Aug. 1996.

Lopez S, Cumplido R(2004) "A Hybrid Approach for Target Detection Using CFAR Algorithm and Image Processing" Fifth Mexican International Conference on Computer Science. 2004.

M. Unser. (1995). "Texture Classification and Segmentation Using Wavelet Frames", IEEE Trans. on Image Processing, Vol. 4, No. 11, Pg No :1549-1560.

P.Subashini, Krishnaveni.M .(2010). "An optimum threshold based segmentation for ice detection in SAR images using Gabor filter' - Proceedings of International Conference on Computing, ICC 2010, New Delhi, Dec 27th - 28th.

R. Sivakumar..(2007). Denoising of Computer Tomography Images using Curvelet Transform. ARPN Journal of Engineering and Applied Sciences. February.

S. Durand and J. Froment.(2003). Reconstruction of wavelet coeffients using total variation minimiza tion, SIAM Journal on Scienti¯c computing, 24(5), pp. 1754-1767, 2003.

S. G. Mallat,(1989) "Multifrequency channel decompositions of images and wavelet odels", IEEE Trans. Acoust. Speech Signal Process, 37(12):2091-2110, 1989.

S.G. Chang, Y. Bin and M. Vetterli.(2006). 'Adaptive wavelet thresholding for image denoising and compression', IEEE Trans. On Image Processing, vol. 9, no.9, pp. 1532- 1546, Sep 2006

T. Nabil, Mathematics Department, Faculty of Sciences, King Khalid University, P.O. Box 9004, Abha 16321, Kingdom of Saudi Arabia .(2009). "SAR Image Filtering in Wavelet Domain by Subband Depended Shrink", The Permanent address: Basic science Department Faculty of Computers and Informatics, Suez Canal University, Ismailia, Egypt e-mail:t_3bdelsadek@yahoo.com, Int. J. Open Problems Comp. Math., Vol. 2, No. 1, March 2009

Trygve Randen, and John Hakon Husoy. (1999). " Filtering for Texture Classification: A Comparative Study" , IEEE Transaction on Pattern Analysis and Machine Intelligence, vol. 21, no. 4, pp. 291-310.

X.Q.Jiang, L.Blunt, K.J.Stout (2000) "Development of a lifting wavelet representation for surface characterization", Proc. R. Soc. Lond. A (2000) 456, 2283-2313.

Z. Wang and D. Hang. (1999) " Progressive Switching Median Filter for the Removal of Impulse Noise from Highly Corrupted Images," IEEE Trans. on Circuits and Systems-II: Analog and Digital Signal processing, vol. 46, no. 1, pp. 78-80 Jan. 1999.

20

Image Watermarking in Higher-Order Gradient Domain

Ehsan N. Arya, Z. Jane Wang and Rabab K. Ward
The University of British Columbia, Vancouver, Canada

1. Introduction

With the widespread use of Internet and digital multimedia technologies, the interest in copyright protection of digital content has been rapidly increased. Digital watermarking has emerged as a possible solution for intellectual property rights protection. Watermarking has also proven to be a promising tool in many applications such as broadcast monitoring, fingerprinting, authentication and device control. In digital watermarking, additional information, called the *watermark*, is *imperceptibly* embedded into the original digital content.

Different applications pose different requirements on watermarking. For example, fragile watermarking is required in content authentication applications, while in applications such as copyright control the watermark should be robust to attacks[1]. In each application, the watermarking method makes a trade-off between the perceptual invisibility, robustness, security, data capacity and availability of side information. For instance, to increase the robustness of a watermark, the watermark strength needs to be increased, which in turn may make the watermark more visible. The invisibility requirement of watermarking limits the maximum amount of watermark bits (watermarking capacity) that can be embedded into a digital signal.

In the last two decades, a lot of work has been done in the field of image watermarking. The reader may refer to (Cox, 2008) for a survey of watermarking methods. Watermarking approaches can generally be classified into two categories (Wu & Liu, 2003): *spread spectrum* (SS) based watermarking (Cox et al., 1997; Podilchuk & Zeng, 1998) and *quantization* based watermarking (Chen & Wornell, 2001; Kundur & Hatzinakos, 2001; Moulin & Koetter, 2005). Below, these two approaches are discussed with some detail.

1.1 Spread spectrum watermarking

In general, any watermarking system that spreads the host signal over a wide frequency band can be called *spread spectrum* watermarking (Barni, 2003). In most SS type methods, a pseudo-random noise-like watermark is added (or multiplied) to the host feature sequence (Cox et al., 1997). While SS watermarking methods are robust to many types of attacks, they suffer from the host interference problem (Cox et al., 1999). This is because the host signal itself acts as a source of interference when extracting the watermark, and this may reduce the detector's performance.

[1] The attacks are defined as the processes that may impair the detection of the watermark.

The first approach to alleviate this problem is through designing better embedders at the encoder side. For example, the improved SS (ISS) method proposed in (Malvar & Florencio, 2003) exploits the information about the projection of the signal on the watermark. This knowledge is then used in the embedding process to compensate the signal interference.

Another approach to improve the performance of SS watermarking methods is to use the statistics of the host signal in the watermark detection (Zhong & Huang, 2006). Based on the distribution of the coefficients in the watermark domain, different types of optimum and locally optimum decoders have been proposed (Akhaee et al., 2010; Barni et al., 2003; Cheng & Huang, 2001; Hernandez et al., 2000; Kalantari et al., 2010).

1.2 Quantization-based watermarking

To overcome the host-interference problem, the quantization (random-binning-like) watermarking methods have been proposed. Chen and Wornell (Chen & Wornell, 2001) introduced *quantization index modulation* (QIM) as a computationally efficient class of data-hiding codes which uses the host signal state information to embed the watermark. In the QIM-based watermarking methods, a set of features extracted from the host signal are quantized so that each watermark bit is represented by a quantized feature value[2]. It has been shown that the QIM methods yield larger watermarking capacity than SS methods (Barni et al., 2003). The high capacity of these methods makes them more appropriate for data hiding applications.

Researchers have proposed different quantization-based watermarking methods. Gonzalez and Balado proposed quantized projection method that combines QIM and SS (Perez-Gonzlez & Balado, 2002). Chen and Lin (Chen & Lin, 2003) embedded the watermark by modulating the mean of a set of wavelet coefficients. Wang and Lin embedded the watermark by quantizing the super trees in the wavelet domain (Wang & Lin, 2004). Bao and Ma proposed a watermarking method by quantizing the singular values of the wavelet coefficients (Bao & Ma, 2005). Kalantari and Ahadi proposed a logarithmic quantization index modulation (LQIM) (Kalantari & Ahadi, 2010) that leads to more robust and less perceptible watermarks than the conventional QIM. Recently, a QIM-based method, that employs quad-tree decomposition to find the visually significant image regions, has also been proposed (Phadikar et al., 2011).

Since QIM methods do not suffer from the host-interference problem, their robustness to additive Gaussian noise is higher than that of SS methods. However, they are very sensitive to amplitude scaling attacks. Even small changes in the image brightness can significantly increase the bit error rate (BER) (Li & Cox, 2007). During the last few years, many improved techniques have been proposed to deal with this issue. These methods can be classified into the following main categories (Perez-Gonzalez et al., 2005):

- The first type of methods embed a pilot sequence in the signal (Eggers, Baeuml & Girod, 2002; Shterev & Lagendijk, 2005; 2006). Since the sequence is known to the decoder, it can be used to estimate any change in the signal amplitude.
- The second type of methods rely on designing amplitude-scale invariant codes, such as Trellis codes (Miller et al., 2004), orthogonal dirty paper codes (Abrardo & Barni, 2004) and order-preserving lattice codes (Bradley, 2004).

[2] The QIM method is discussed with more detail in subsection 2.5

- The third type of methods estimate the scaling factor based on the structure of the received data (Eggers, Bäuml & Girod, 2002; Lagendijk & Shterev, 2004; Shterev & Lagendijk, 2006).
- The fourth type of methods embed the watermark in the gain-invariant domains (Ourique et al., 2005; Perez-Gonzalez et al., 2005).

Among these methods, watermarking in a gain-invariant domain seems to be the best solution (Perez-Gonzalez et al., 2005).

1.3 The outline

The aim of this chapter is to describe how to insert robust, imperceptible and high-capacity watermark bits using a gain-invariant domain. Towards that goal we describe the *gradient direction watermarking* (GDWM) method (N. Arya et al., 2011). In this method, the watermark bits could be inserted into the angles of vectors of a higher-order gradient of the image, using the *angle quantization index modulation* (AQIM) method (Ourique et al., 2005). The AQIM has the advantages of QIM watermarking, but it also renders the watermark robustness to amplitude scaling attacks. In the GDWM method, the imperceptibility requirement is fulfilled by the following three mechanisms:

- By embedding the watermark in the significant (i.e. large) gradient vectors, the watermark becomes less perceptible. This is due to the observation that the human visual system (HVS) is less sensitive to distortions around the significant edges (i.e. represented by the significant gradient vectors) than to distortions in smooth areas (Barni et al., 2001).
- It is well known from comparing the additive with the multiplicative SS watermarking methods, that a disturbance proportional to the signal strength is more difficult to perceive (Langelaar et al., 2000). Therefore, by showing that a gradient change introduced by AQIM is proportional to the gradient magnitude, we can conclude that this method yields a less perceptible watermark.

  Assume that the angle of the gradient vector is altered by $\Delta\theta$. As the gradient vector g equals to $r\exp(i\theta)$, it is easy to obtain the absolute gradient change $|\Delta g|$ due to the angle change $\Delta\theta$:

  $$|\Delta g| = |r\exp(i(\theta+\Delta\theta)) - r\exp(i\theta)| \approx r|\sin(\frac{\Delta\theta}{2})| \tag{1}$$

  where r denotes the gradient magnitude. It can be seen that the value of $|\Delta g|$ is proportional to r (i.e. $d \propto r$) and therefore AQIM results in a less perceptible watermark.
- The change in the higher order gradient vectors is less perceptible than the change in the first order gradients.

To increase the watermark capacity, the watermark bits are embedded in gradient vectors extracted from the multiscale wavelet coefficients of the image. This is accomplished by using a multiscale wavelet transform. For example, to embed a 256-bit watermark, 128, 64 and 64 bits can be embedded in the gradient fields obtained from scales 3, 4 and 5 of the wavelet transform of the image.

The rest of this chapter is organized as follows: a brief overview of the discrete wavelet transform (DWT), multi-scale gradient estimation, quantization index modulation (QIM) and angle quantization watermarking is given in Section 2. The watermark embedding scheme, called *gradient direction watermarking (GDWM)* (N. Arya et al., 2011), is described in Section 3. In this scheme, the image is first mapped to the wavelet domain from which the gradient fields are obtained. The gradient field at each wavelet scale is then partitioned into blocks. The watermark bits are embedded by changing the angles of the significant gradient vectors in each block using the AQIM method. The resultant (watermarked) wavelet coefficients of the image are computed. Finally the watermarked coefficients are inversely mapped to obtain the watermarked image. The decoding steps are discussed in Section 4, where the watermark bits are decoded following the reverse encoding steps, and the summary is given in Section 6.

2. Preliminaries

2.1 Notation

In this chapter, bold lower case letters, e.g. $\boldsymbol{x}$, and bold capital letters, e.g. $\boldsymbol{X}$, denote vectors (or discrete signals) and matrices, respectively. The vector or matrix elements are denoted by lower case letters with an index, e.g. x_i or x_{ij}. The vector at pixel (i, j) in the discrete vector field is represented as $\boldsymbol{f}_{i,j}$.

2.2 Continuous wavelet transform (CWT)

Wavelet transform decomposes a signal into shifted and scaled versions of a mother wavelet. The *continuous wavelet transform (CWT)* (Mallat, 1997) of a 1-dimensional continuous signal x is defined by

$$W_{s,u}x = \langle x, \psi_{s,u} \rangle = \frac{1}{\sqrt{s}} \int_{-\infty}^{\infty} x(t) \psi \left(\frac{t-u}{s} \right) dt \tag{2}$$

where ψ represents a *bandpass* wavelet function, called the *mother wavelet*, $\langle . \rangle$ denotes the inner product and the parameters s and u denote the *scale* and *translation (shift)*, respectively.

Similarly, the 2-dimensional *continuous wavelet transform (2D CWT)* of a continuous image $x(t_1, t_2)$ can be defined as

$$W_{s,u_1,u_2}x = \langle x, \psi_{s,u_1,u_2} \rangle = \frac{1}{\sqrt{s}} \int_{-\infty}^{\infty} \int_{-\infty}^{\infty} x(t_1, t_2) \psi \left(\frac{t_1 - u_1, t_2 - u_2}{s} \right) dt_1 \, dt_2 \tag{3}$$

where u_1 and u_2 denote the *horizontal* and *vertical* shifts, respectively.

2.3 Discrete Wavelet Transform (DWT)

Since the continuous wavelet transform is highly redundant, it is more efficient to sample the continuous shift-scale plane $u - s$, to obtain the *discrete wavelet transform* (DWT). In the dyadic DWT (i.e. $W_{j,n}x$), the scale and translation components, s and u, are respectively sampled at intervals of $\{2^j\}_{j \in \mathbb{Z}}$ and $\{n2^j\}_{n \in \mathbb{Z}}$, where j and n denote the discrete scale and translation parameters, respectively, and $\mathbb{Z}$ denotes the set of integer numbers.

The multiscale discrete wavelet transform represents a continuous signal $x(t)$ (or a discrete signal) in terms of bandpass filters $\psi_{j,n}(t)$ and shifted versions of a scaled lowpass filter $\phi(t)$ (called the *scaling function* (Mallat, 1997)) as

$$x(t) = \sum_{n \in \mathbb{Z}} a_J[n] \phi_{J,n}(t) + \sum_{j=1}^{J} \sum_{n \in \mathbb{Z}} d_j[n] \psi_{j,n}(t) \tag{4}$$

where $a_J[n]$ and $d_j[n]$ are called *approximation* and *detail wavelet coefficients* at scales J and j, respectively. In Eq. (4), the wavelets $\psi_{j,n}(t)$ and $\phi_{J,n}(t)$ can be expressed as

$$\psi_{j,n}(t) = 2^{-j/2}\psi\left(2^{-j}t - n\right), \quad \phi_{J,n}(t) = 2^{-J/2}\phi\left(2^{-J}t - n\right) \tag{5}$$

For an *orthogonal* DWT The approximation and detail coefficients $a_J[n]$ and $d_j[n]$, are obtained by projecting $x(t)$ onto $\phi_{j,n}(t)$ and $\psi_{j,n}(t)$ as

$$a_J[n] = \langle x, \phi_{J,n}\rangle, \quad d_j[n] = \left\langle x, \psi_{j,n}\right\rangle. \tag{6}$$

DWT can also be extended to 2-dimensional images by decomposing the continuous image $x(t_1, t_2)$ using 2-dimensional scaling functions $\phi_{J,n_1,n_2}(t_1, t_2)$ and bandpass wavelets $\psi^k_{j,n_1,n_2}(t_1, t_2)$, such that

$$x(t_1, t_2) = \sum_{n_1,n_2\in\mathbb{Z}} a_J[n_1, n_2]\phi_{J,n_1,n_2}(t_1, t_2) + \sum_{k=1}^{3}\sum_{j=1}^{J}\sum_{n_1,n_2\in\mathbb{Z}} d^k_j[n_1, n_2]\psi^k_{j,n_1,n_2}(t_1, t_2), \tag{7}$$

As can be seen, at each scale j, the 2D DWT decomposes an image into 3 highpass subbands HL, LH and HH (denoted by superscript $k = 1,2,3$) and one lowpass subband LL. The approximation and detail wavelet coefficients in an orthogonal 2-dimensional DWT (2D DWT) can be obtained as

$$a_j[n_1, n_2] = \left\langle x, \phi_{j,n_1,n_2}\right\rangle, \quad d^k_j[n_1, n_2] = \left\langle x, \psi^k_{j,n_1,n_2}\right\rangle, \quad 1 \le k \le 3 \tag{8}$$

The 2-dimensional (2D) wavelets ϕ_{J,n_1,n_2} and ψ^k_{j,n_1,n_2} are usually obtained from tensor products of 1-dimensional (1D) orthogonal wavelets as

$$\begin{aligned}
\phi_{J,n_1,n_2}(t_1, t_2) &= \phi_{J,n_1}(t_1)\phi_{J,n_2}(t_2),\\
\psi^1_{j,n_1,n_2}(t_1, t_2) &= \psi_{j,n_1}(t_1)\phi_{J,n_2}(t_2),\\
\psi^2_{j,n_1,n_2}(t_1, t_2) &= \phi_{J,n_1}(t_1)\psi_{j,n_2}(t_2),\\
\psi^3_{j,n_1,n_2}(t_1, t_2) &= \psi_{j,n_1}(t_1)\psi_{j,n_2}(t_2).
\end{aligned} \tag{9}$$

where $\psi^1_{j,n_1,n_2}(t_1, t_2)$, $\psi^2_{j,n_1,n_2}(t_1, t_2)$ and $\psi^3_{j,n_1,n_2}(t_1, t_2)$ are respectively the *horizontal*, *vertical* and *diagonal* continuous-time 2D wavelets that are shifted to the point (n_1, n_2).

Eqs. (3)-(9) can also be written in the discrete domain. For example, the 2-dimensional discrete time Haar wavelet transform uses the 1D discrete-time Haar lowpass vector $\boldsymbol{\varphi}_{1,0} = [+1, +1]^T$ and bandpass vector $\boldsymbol{\psi}_{1,0} = [-1, +1]^T$ to calculate the 2D discrete-time wavelets $\boldsymbol{\Psi}^1$, $\boldsymbol{\Psi}^2$ and $\boldsymbol{\Psi}^3$, as

$$\begin{aligned}
\boldsymbol{\Psi}^1 &= \boldsymbol{\psi}^T_{1,0} \otimes \boldsymbol{\varphi}_{1,0} = \begin{pmatrix} -1 & +1 \\ -1 & +1 \end{pmatrix},\\
\boldsymbol{\Psi}^2 &= \boldsymbol{\varphi}^T_{1,0} \otimes \boldsymbol{\psi}_{1,0} = \begin{pmatrix} +1 & +1 \\ -1 & -1 \end{pmatrix},\\
\boldsymbol{\Psi}^3 &= \boldsymbol{\psi}^T_{1,0} \otimes \boldsymbol{\psi}_{1,0} = \begin{pmatrix} -1 & +1 \\ +1 & -1 \end{pmatrix}.
\end{aligned} \tag{10}$$

where $\otimes$ and superscript T denote the *tensor product* and *matrix transpose*, respectively.

2.4 Multiscale gradient estimation Using 2D CWT

In this subsection, the relationship between the p-th order gradient vector of a continuous image and the 2-D wavelet coefficients is obtained.

Let us assume that the unshifted (i.e. $u_1 = u_2 = 0$) *horizontal* and *vertical* wavelets $\psi^1(t_1, t_2)$ and $\psi^2(t_1, t_2)$ have p vanishing moments, i.e.

$$\int_{-\infty}^{+\infty} t_1^k \, \psi^1(t_1, t_2)\, dt_1 = 0 \;\text{ and }\; \int_{-\infty}^{+\infty} t_2^k \, \psi^2(t_1, t_2)\, dt_2 = 0 \quad \text{for} \quad 0 \le k \le p. \tag{11}$$

It was shown in (Mallat & Hwang, 1992) that $\psi^1(t_1, t_2)$ and $\psi^2(t_1, t_2)$ with p vanishing moments can be written as

$$\psi^1(t_1, t_2) = (-1)^p \frac{\partial^p \rho(t_1, t_2)}{\partial t_1^p}, \quad \psi^2(t_1, t_2) = (-1)^p \frac{\partial^p \rho(t_1, t_2)}{\partial t_2^p} \tag{12}$$

where $\rho(t_1, t_2)$ is a smoothing function whose double integral is nonzero. Let $\psi_s^1(t_1, t_2)$ and $\psi_s^2(t_1, t_2)$ denote the scaled versions of $\psi^1(t_1, t_2)$ and $\psi^2(t_1, t_2)$, respectively, given as

$$\psi_s^1(t_1, t_2) = \frac{1}{s^2}\psi^1\left(\frac{t_1}{s}, \frac{t_2}{s}\right), \quad \psi_s^2(t_1, t_2) = \frac{1}{s^2}\psi^2\left(\frac{t_1}{s}, \frac{t_2}{s}\right) \tag{13}$$

where s denotes the continuous wavelet scale . Using Eqs. (12) and (13), it is easy to show that the horizontal and vertical wavelet components of the 2-D image $x(t_1, t_2)$ can be obtained as

$$\begin{aligned} W_s^1 x &= x(t_1, t_2) * \psi_s^1(t_1, t_2) = (-s)^p \frac{\partial^p (x(t_1, t_2) * \rho_s(t_1, t_2))}{\partial t_1^p} \\ W_s^2 x &= x(t_1, t_2) * \psi_s^2(t_1, t_2) = (-s)^p \frac{\partial^p (x(t_1, t_2) * \rho_s(t_1, t_2))}{\partial t_2^p} \end{aligned} \tag{14}$$

where $*$ denotes the *convolution operator*, and

$$\rho_s(t_1, t_2) = \frac{1}{s^2}\rho\left(\frac{t_1}{s}, \frac{t_2}{s}\right) \;\text{ and }\; W_s^1 x = \{W_{s,u_1,u_2}^1 x \mid \forall (u_1, u_2) \in \mathbb{R}^2\}. \tag{15}$$

where $W_{s,u_1,u_2}^1 x$ denotes the horizontal wavelet coefficient of x at scale s and point (u_1, u_2).

Eq. (14) shows that the vector of wavelet coefficients $W_{s,u_1,u_2}x = [W_{s,u_1,u_2}^1 x, W_{s,u_1,u_2}^2 x]^T$ can be interpreted as the pth-order gradient vector of $x * \rho_s$ at point (u_1, u_2).

2.5 Quantization Index Modulation (QIM)

To embed a watermark bit b in vector x, the QIM method quantizes x using the quantizer $\mathcal{Q}_0(.)$ when $b = 0$ and $\mathcal{Q}_1(.)$ when $b = 1$. The possible values of the quantizers $\mathcal{Q}_0(.)$ and $\mathcal{Q}_1(.)$ belong to the lattices Λ_0 and Λ_1, respectively:

$$\begin{aligned} \Lambda_0 &= 2\Delta\mathbb{Z}^2 \\ \Lambda_1 &= 2\Delta\mathbb{Z}^2 + \Delta[1, 1]^T \end{aligned} \tag{16}$$

where Δ and $\mathbb{Z}^2$ denote the *quantization step size* and the 2D set of integer values, respectively. for For the two-dimensional (2-D) QIM, the lattices Λ_0 and Λ_1 are shown in Fig. 1. The

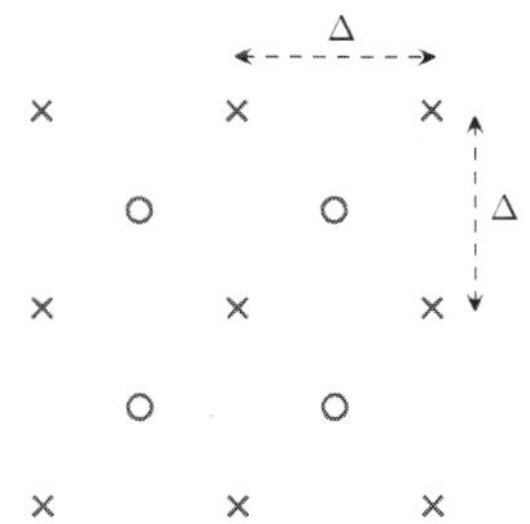

Fig. 1. Illustration of the 2-D uniform quantization index modulation (QIM). Lattices Λ_0 and Λ_1 in Eq. (16) are marked by $\times$ and $\circ$, respectively.

watermarked vector x^w is then obtained as the closest lattice point in Λ_0 to x when $b = 0$, or as the closest one in Λ_1 when $b = 1$. This can be expressed as

$$x^w = \begin{cases} \mathcal{Q}_0(x) \text{ if } b = 0 \\ \mathcal{Q}_1(x) \text{ if } b = 1 \end{cases} \tag{17}$$

At the decoder side, the value of the watermark bit $\hat{b}$ is extracted from the received vector x' by finding whether the nearest lattice point to the point x^w belongs to Λ_0 or Λ_1, i.e.

$$\hat{b} = \mathcal{B}(x') = \arg \min_{b \in \{0,1\}} \|x' - \mathcal{Q}_b(x')\|. \tag{18}$$

2.6 Angle quantization watermarking

As mentioned in subsection 1.2, the QIM method is fragile to amplitude scaling attacks. To address this concern, *angle quantization watermarking* embeds the watermark bit in the angle of the 2-dimensional vector. In angle quantization watermarking, the angle θ of vector x is assigned to a binary number 0 or 1.

In this section, we only describe the *uniform* angle quantization, in which the quantization circle is divided into a number of equiangular sectors in the range $(-\pi, \pi]$, as shown in Fig. 2. Two angle quantization watermarking methods are now described:

2.6.1 Angle Quantization Based Watermarking Method (AQWM)

The first method we consider is the angular version of the method proposed in (Kundur & Hatzinakos, 1999). The *quantization function*, denoted by $Q(\theta)$, maps a real angle θ to a binary number as follows:

$$Q(\theta) = \begin{cases} 0 \text{ if } \lfloor \theta/\Delta \rfloor \text{ is even} \\ 1 \text{ if } \lfloor \theta/\Delta \rfloor \text{ is odd} \end{cases} \tag{19}$$

where the positive real number Δ represents the *angular quantization step size* and $\lfloor . \rfloor$ denotes the floor function. To embed a watermark bit $b = 0$ or 1 into an angle $\theta \in [-\pi, \pi]$, the following rules are used:

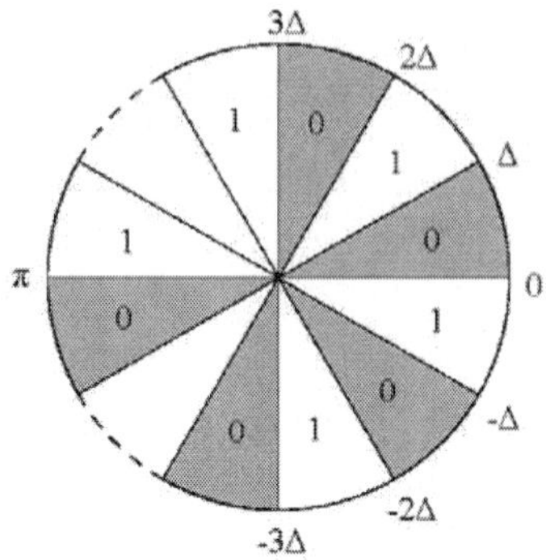

Fig. 2. The angle quantization circle with a fixed quantization step Δ.

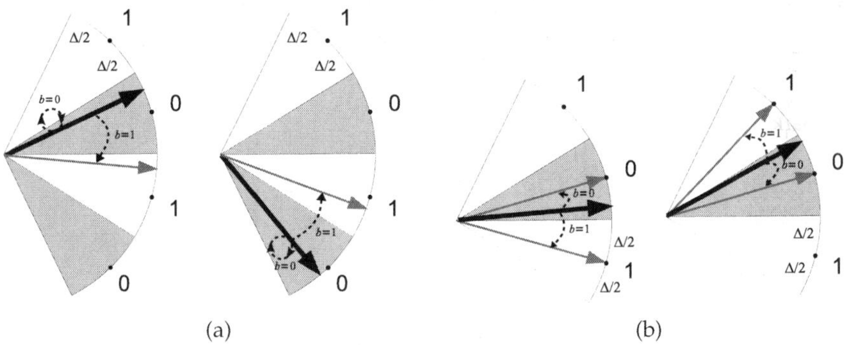

Fig. 3. Illustration of different angle quantization watermarking methods: (a) AQWM and (b) AQIM. Vectors before and after watermarking are represented by "thick black" and "thin gray" arrows, respectively.

- If $Q(\theta) = b$, then θ is not changed.
- If $Q(\theta) \neq b$, then θ is decreased by Δ if $\theta > 0$, and increased by Δ if $\theta \leq 0$.

These rules are illustrated in Fig. 3(a) and can be formulated as:

$$\theta^w = \begin{cases} \theta & \text{if } Q(\theta) = b \\ \theta - \Delta & \text{if } Q(\theta) \neq b \text{ and } \theta > 0 \\ \theta + \Delta & \text{if } Q(\theta) \neq b \text{ and } \theta \leq 0 \end{cases} \tag{20}$$

where θ^w denotes the watermarked angle.

2.6.2 Angle Quantization Index Modulation (AQIM)

One drawback associated with AQWM is that if $Q(\theta) \neq b$, the angle is not necessarily modified toward the *nearest sector* having bit b. In other words, AQWM may change the angle more than required and this could lead to a perceptible watermark. Another drawback of AQWM is its low robustness to small angle perturbations. If the watermarked angle θ^w is

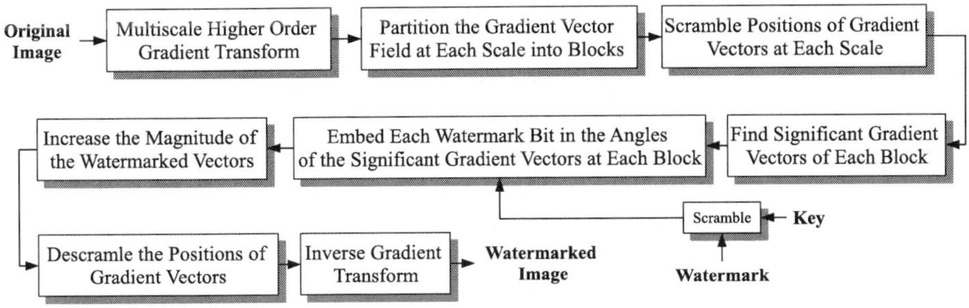

Fig. 4. The block diagram of the watermark embedding scheme.

close to sector boundaries, even a small amount of noise could be enough to make the angle pass the boundary and thus generate an error when the watermark bit is decoded.

To overcome these two drawbacks, the angle quantization index modulation (AQIM) method forms a possible alternative. AQIM (Ourique et al., 2005) is an extension of the QIM (Chen & Wornell, 2001) method, where the following rules are used to embed a watermark bit b into an angle θ:

- If $Q(\theta) = b$, then θ takes the value of the angle at the center of the sector it lies in.
- If $Q(\theta) \neq b$, then θ takes the value of the angle at the center of one of the two adjacent sectors, whichever is closer to θ.

These rules are shown in Fig. 3(b).

3. The gradient watermark embedding method

The block diagram of the gradient watermark embedding strategy (N. Arya et al., 2011) is shown in Fig. 4. The embedding steps are summarized as follows:

Step 1 To embed the watermark in the gradient of the image, first a domain that represents the gradient must be obtained. As shown in Eq. (14), the horizontal and vertical wavelet coefficients could be used to calculate the horizontal and vertical gradients of the image. Thus, based on the selected gradient order (e.g. 2nd, 3rd, 4th or 5th-order gradient), the image is transformed to the wavelet domain using the corresponding wavelet (e.g. Symlet2, Symlet3, Symlet4 or Symlet5). Thus, Symlet2 is used to obtain the 2nd-order gradient, Symlet3 to obtain the 3rd-order gradient and so on. The gradient field at a certain wavelet scale is then obtained using the the wavelet coefficients at the same scale. For example, (for gradient order 3) the gradient fields of image Lena at scales 3, 4 and 5 are obtained from the wavelet coefficients (obtained using Symlet3) at corresponding scales 3, 4 and 5, as shown in Fig. 5. The wavelet-based gradient estimation is described in subsection 3.1.

Step 2 To embed the bits of the watermark, the gradient field at each scale is partitioned into blocks (see Fig. 6(a)). The number of blocks depends on the number of bits to be embedded. Thus, bits can be embedded in the gradient fields corresponding to more than one scale.

Step 3 The positions of the gradient vectors are uniformly scrambled at each scale, as illustrated in Fig. 6(b). The watermark bits are inserted into the significant gradient

(a) Original image (b) Gradient fields at scales 3, 4 and 5.

Fig. 5. Image Lena and its representations in the gradient domain. The Symlet3 wavelet is used to obtain the gradient vectors.

vectors of each block. Significant gradient vectors are the gradient vectors with large magnitudes. Embedding the watermark bits in the significant vectors makes it robust to many attacks. As some blocks do not contain significant gradients, and as a watermark bit is inserted into each block, scrambling the locations of the significant gradient vectors is used. The scrambling used should guarantee that statistically each block contains at least one significant gradient vector. More details about the scrambling method are given in subsection 3.2.

Step 4 The significant gradient vectors of each block are calculated.

Step 5 For security reasons, the binary watermark message is scrambled using a secret key.

Step 6 In each block, one bit of the watermark is embedded in the angle of the most significant gradient vectors, using angle quantization index modulation (AQIM) (see Fig. 6(c)). It is preferred however to embed the same bit using 2 (or even more) gradient vectors. The number of the most significant gradient vectors as the bit is embedded in is denoted by BR. The AQIM method in the gradient domain is discussed in subsection 3.3.

Step 7 The correct detectability of the watermarked gradient vectors is enhanced by increasing their magnitudes relative to the nonsignificant (unwatermarked) vectors, as illustrated in Fig. 6(d). More explanations are given in subsection 3.4.

Step 8 The watermarked gradient fields at each scale are descrambled, using the descrambling method associated with the scrambling method in step 3 (cf. Fig. 6(e)). The descrambling method is explained in subsection 3.2.

Step 9 The watermarked wavelet coefficients are obtained from the watermarked gradient vectors.

Step 10 Finally, the watermarked image is obtained using the inverse wavelet transform on the watermarked wavelet coefficients.

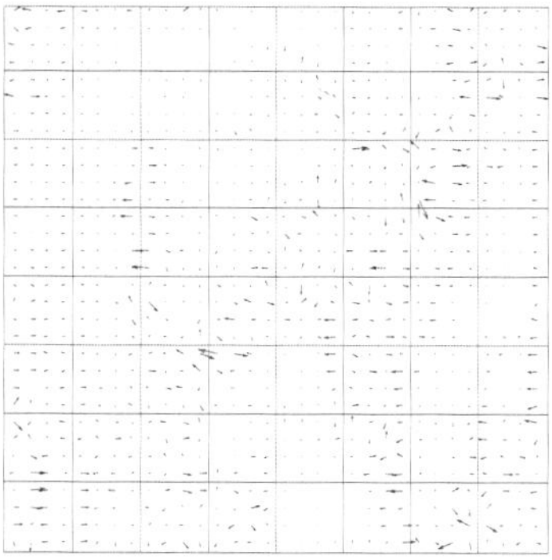

(a) Partitioned gradient field at scale 4.

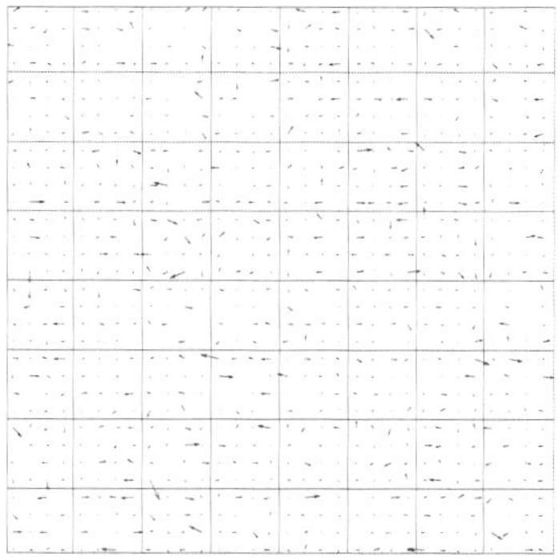

(b) Scrambled gradient field

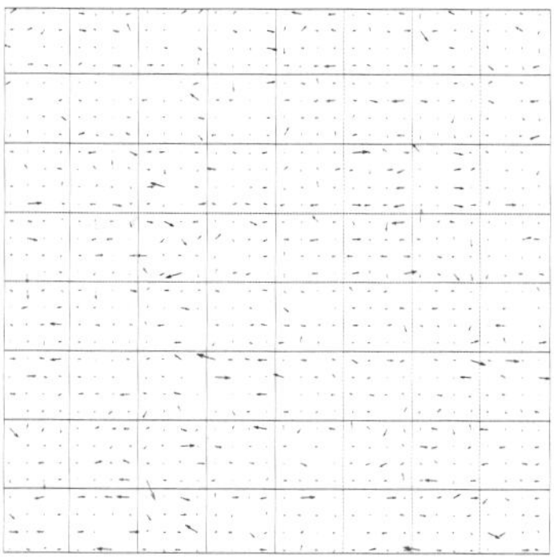

(c) Watermarked scrambled gradient field

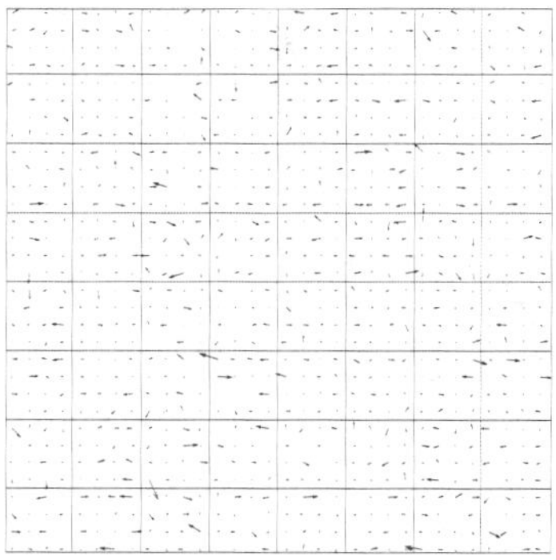

(d) Enhanced watermarked gradient field

(e) Descrambled watermarked gradient field

(f) Watermarked image of Lena

Fig. 6. Illustration of different steps during embedding a pseudo-random binary watermark of size 8×8 into image Lena. A 64-bit watermark is inserted into the gradient field obtained using Symlet3 at scale 4.

3.1 Higher-order multiscale gradient transform

To obtain the gradient vector $g_j[m] = g_{h_j}[m] + i\, g_{v_j}[m]$ at pixel $\boldsymbol{m} = (m_1, m_2)$ and wavelet scale j, the horizontal and vertical wavelet coefficients $d_j^1[\boldsymbol{m}]$ and $d_j^2[\boldsymbol{m}]$ are used:

$$\begin{pmatrix} g_{h_j}[\boldsymbol{m}] \\ g_{v_j}[\boldsymbol{m}] \end{pmatrix} = \boldsymbol{A}_j \begin{pmatrix} d_j^1[\boldsymbol{m}] \\ d_j^2[\boldsymbol{m}] \end{pmatrix} \tag{21}$$

and using Eq. (14) matrix $\boldsymbol{A}_j$ is obtained as

$$\boldsymbol{A}_j = \begin{pmatrix} 1 & 0 \\ 0 & 1 \end{pmatrix} \tag{22}$$

Based on the type of the gradient operator used to calculate the gradient vectors, other versions of matrix $\boldsymbol{A}_j$ can also be used (N. Arya et al., 2011). In this chapter, the identity matrix is used to obtain the higher-order gradient vectors at each scale. This means that the horizontal and vertical wavelet coefficients are the same as the gradient vector components.

3.2 Scrambling and descrambling the gradient fields

As mentioned before, to embed the watermark bits, the gradient fields of the image are obtained. The straightforward way to embed the watermark bits is to partition the gradient fields into non-overlapping blocks and each watermark bit is then embedded into each block. The bit is inserted into the BR most significant gradient vectors of the block, since embedding the watermark in the significant vectors makes it robust to attacks. However in natural images, the spatial distribution of the significant gradient vectors in the gradient fields is non-uniform (as some parts of the image may have all or most of the significant gradient vectors, while other parts may have no significant gradient vectors). If a bit is embedded into a block with no significant gradient vectors, then the robustness of the watermark bit to noise and other attacks is reduced. Therefore the straightforward uniform embedding may reduce the robustness of the watermark bits in the image areas with no significant gradient vectors.

To solve this problem, the locations of all gradient vectors are uniformly scrambled, so that each block contains at least one significant gradient vector. As shown in Fig. 6(c), the positions of the gradient vectors at each scale are uniformly scrambled over the gradient field. At each block, the watermark bits are inserted into the angles of significant gradient vectors, using AQIM method. The gradient vectors are then descrambled so they are located back at their original positions.

3.2.1 Scrambling method

The scrambling method should be a geometric transform that would ideally result in a uniform distribution of the locations of the significant gradient vectors. Different geometric image scrambling methods have been proposed. These include the Fibonacci transformation (Zou et al., 2004), Arnold Cat transformation (Ming & Xi-jian, 2006) and Gray Code transformation (Zou & Ward, 2003). It has been shown in (Xue Yang & Jia, 2010) that most of the geometric transforms are special cases of the *affine modular transformation* (Zou et al., 2005). Therefore, the affine modular transform is employed, due to its generality.

In a gradient field of size $M \times M$, let the coordinate vectors of each vector in the original and scrambled gradient fields be denoted by $[m_1, m_2]^T$ and $[m'_1, m'_2]^T$, respectively. The *affine modular mapping* from $[m_1, m_2]^T$ to $[m'_1, m'_2]^T$ is defined as

$$\begin{pmatrix} m'_1 \\ m'_2 \end{pmatrix} = \left[\begin{pmatrix} a & b \\ c & d \end{pmatrix} \begin{pmatrix} m_1 \\ m_2 \end{pmatrix} + \begin{pmatrix} e \\ f \end{pmatrix} \right] \mathrm{mod}(M) \tag{23}$$

where a, b, c, d, e and f are scrambling parameters. If the absolute value of the determinant of the matrix $S = [a, b; c, d]$ equals to 1 (i.e. $det(S) = |ad - bc| = 1$), the transform is area preserving and one-to-one mapping. For a given positive integer M, the *necessary* and *sufficient* condition for the *periodicity* of the affine modular transform is that $det(S)$ and M are primal to each other (Zou et al., 2005).

3.2.2 Descrambling method

By using the periodicity property of the affine modular transform, the original image can be recovered from the scrambled image. Let the smallest period of this map be denoted by t_M. If the scrambled image is constructed by applying this transformation t times, the descrambled image can be exactly recovered after consecutively applying the same transformation $t_M - t$ times (Xue Yang & Jia, 2010). To reduce the number of parameters needed in embedding and to make it an area preserving transform, the elements of the mapping matrix S are assigned the values $a = 1$, $b = p$, $c = q$ and $d = 1 + pq$. The mapping matrix S is then given by

$$S = \begin{pmatrix} 1 & p \\ q & 1 + pq \end{pmatrix}. \tag{24}$$

3.3 AQIM in the gradient domain

As mentioned before, to insert the watermark bits, the angles of the significant gradient vectors are changed. The amount of change $\Delta\theta$ in the angle is obtained by Eq. (**??**). To rotate a gradient vector by $\Delta\theta = \theta^w - \theta$, the *rotation matrix* $\boldsymbol{R}_{\Delta\theta}$ (of size 2×2) is used:

$$\boldsymbol{R}_{\Delta\theta} = \begin{pmatrix} \cos(\Delta\theta) & -\sin(\Delta\theta) \\ \sin(\Delta\theta) & \cos(\Delta\theta) \end{pmatrix}. \tag{25}$$

Thus, the watermarked gradient is obtained as

$$g_j^w[m] = \boldsymbol{R}_{\Delta\theta} g_j[m] \tag{26}$$

3.4 Enhancing the detectability of the watermarked gradient vectors

Attacks may change the watermark bits in one of the following ways:

- The attack may result in a change in the angle of a significant gradient vector, such that the extracted bit is different from the embedded one.
- The attack may result in a reduction in the magnitude of a significant gradient vector, such that the decoder can no longer identify it as a significant vector. In this case, a watermark bit is extracted from a gradient vector that was not amongst the BR most significant vectors.

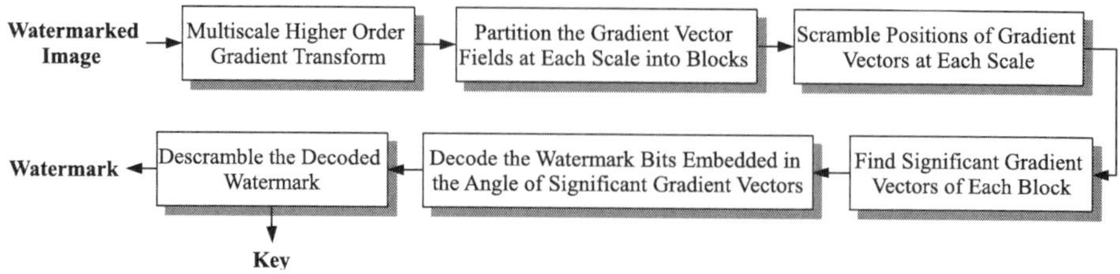

Fig. 7. The block diagram of the watermark decoding scheme.

In the first case, to increase the watermark robustness, a larger angle quantization step size Δ is preferred. Note that the maximum step size is constrained by the imperceptibility constraint on the embedded watermark. In the second case, one solution is to enhance the detectability of the watermarked gradient vectors by increasing the magnitude r of such a vector.

Let us denote the magnitude of the gradient vector g_j by r. To increase the magnitude of each watermarked vector, dr can be calculated by:

$$dr = \frac{\alpha}{r} e^{-(r - r_{LIS})} \tag{27}$$

where α is a constant that adjusts the overall gradient magnitude change in the image and r_{LIS} is the magnitude of the *largest insignificant* gradient vector in each block.

4. The watermark decoding method

The block diagram of the watermark decoding method is shown in Fig. 7. The decoding steps are as follows:

Step 1 Step 1 of watermark embedding process is repeated. That is the watermarked image is mapped to the gradient domain using the multiscale gradient transform, discussed in subsection 3.1.

Step 2 As in step 2 of the watermark embedding, the gradient field at each scale is partitioned into blocks. The blocks should be of the same size as those used in the embedding process.

Step 3 The positions of the gradient vectors are uniformly scrambled with the same method and parameters used in step 3 of the the embedding process.

Step 4 The significant gradient vectors of each block are detected.

Step 5 The bits of the BR most significant gradient vectors of each block are decoded, using the AQIM decoder, as discussed in subsection 2.6. If all the BR decoded bits have the same value (e.g. $\hat{b}$), the decoded watermark bit will also be the same bit (i.e. $\hat{b}$). In the case, the bits have different values, they are assigned weights based on the following rules:

- A watermark bit extracted from a large gradient vector is given more weight than a bit extracted from a small gradient vector.
- A watermark bit extracted from an angle close to the center of a sector, is given more weight than a bit extracted from an angle close to a sector boundary.

Based on these two rules, each watermark bit is weighted by

$$a_k = r^{\gamma} . \left[\frac{\Delta}{2} - \left| |\theta| - \left(\Delta \lfloor \frac{|\theta|}{\Delta} \rfloor + \Delta/2 \right) \right| \right], \quad k = 1, \ldots, BR \tag{28}$$

Image	Δ_3 (rad)	Δ_4 (rad)	Δ_5 (rad)	α	PSNR (dB)
Lena	$\pi/10$	$\pi/22$	$\pi/24$	0.05	42 dB
Barbara	$\pi/12$	$\pi/20$	$\pi/26$	0.5	42 dB
Baboon	$\pi/12$	$\pi/16$	$\pi/18$	0.60	42 dB
Peppers	$\pi/12$	$\pi/22$	$\pi/26$	0.25	42 dB

Table 1. Values of the quantization step size Δ, the gradient magnitude enhancement coefficient α, and the PSNR of the watermarked image.

where BR denotes the number of watermarked significant gradient vectors in each block, γ is a constant that represents the importance of magnitude weighting vs. angle weighting. Based on the weights determined by Eq. (28), the watermark bit in each block after decoding is given the value

$$\hat{b} = \begin{cases} 1 \text{ if } b^w \geq 0.5 \\ 0 \text{ Otherwise} \end{cases} \quad (29)$$

where b^w is defined as

$$b^w = \frac{\sum_{k=1}^{BR} a_k \mathcal{B}(\theta_k)}{\sum_{k=1}^{BR} a_k} \quad (30)$$

where the function $\mathcal{B}(\theta)$ is as defined in Eq. (18).

Step 6 Since the extracted watermark is the scrambled version of the original message, it should be descrambled using the same key used in the embedding process.

5. Example

Different pseudo-random binary watermarks of size 256 are embedded in the grayscale images *Lena, Barbara, Baboon* and *Peppers*. All the images are of size 512 × 512. To obtain the 2nd, 3rd, 4th and 5th order gradients, Symlet2, Symlet3, Symlet4 and Symlet5 wavelets are used, respectively. The Symlet wavelets are chosen because of their near-symmetrical shapes. Irrespective of the order of the gradient used, for a 256-bit watermark, 128, 64 and 64 bits are embedded in the gradient fields at scales 3, 4 and 5 using the block sizes 4 × 8, 4 × 4 and 2 × 2, respectively.

The parameters (p, q) for images Pappers, Baboon, Barbara and Lena are set to $(3, 4)$, $(1, 1)$, $(2, 3)$ and $(2, 1)$, respectively. The value of the parameter γ in Eq. (28) is set to 4. Each bit is embedded in the 2 most significant (largest) gradient vectors of each block, i.e. BR=2. The angular quantization step size Δ and the gradient magnitude enhancement coefficient α, given in Eq. (27), are obtained separately for each image and gradient transform. Table **??** shows the optimum values of Δ for each image. To evaluate the robustness of the scheme, each watermarked image is distorted by different types of attacks. After the attacks, each watermark is extracted and is compared with the original watermark to estimate the *bit error rate* (BER). The overall BER is obtained by averaging over 100 runs with 100 different pseudo-random binary watermarks.

The BER (%) results of the *gradient direction watermarking* (GDWM) method, under amplitude scaling, Gaussian filtering, median filtering and JPEG compression is shown in Table **??**. It can be seen that GDWM is robust to amplitude scaling attack, no matter which gradient transform

Image	Wavelet	Amplitude Scaling (scale=2)	Gaussian Filter 7 × 7	Gaussian Filter 9 × 9	Median Filter 3 × 3	Median Filter 5 × 5	JPEG (Q) 10	JPEG (Q) 20
Lena	Sym2	0	1.19	4.99	0.66	5.23	8.17	0.45
Lena	Sym3	0	0	3.23	0.33	4.61	7.79	0.48
Lena	Sym4	0	6.36	15.78	0.51	9.42	16.95	4.20
Lena	Sym5	0	**0**	**0.95**	**0**	**2.83**	**6.67**	**0.32**
Barbara	Sym2	0	0.64	2.20	0	3.46	7.57	0.49
Barbara	Sym3	0	0.59	1.74	**0**	2.57	7.35	**0.28**
Barbara	Sym4	0	3.10	11.84	1.57	16.50	19.20	5.55
Barbara	Sym5	0	**0.09**	**1.22**	0.41	**2.41**	**6.62**	0.32
Baboon	Sym2	0	0.94	5.95	2.27	14.81	**6.92**	0.16
Baboon	Sym3	0	1.23	**4.65**	1.91	18.33	7.59	**0.13**
Baboon	Sym4	0	4.40	16.26	7.29	28.16	18.83	5.99
Baboon	Sym5	0	**0.18**	5.70	**0.98**	**14.80**	8.15	0.15
Peppers	Sym2	0	0.93	5.66	0.51	4.43	7.72	0.79
Peppers	Sym3	0	2.28	6.59	**0.01**	3.81	7.69	**0.36**
Peppers	Sym4	0	24.97	37.16	1.07	10.95	21.13	5.91
Peppers	Sym5	0	**0.92**	**3.25**	0.22	**2.81**	**7.50**	0.48

Table 2. The BER (%) results of GDWM under different types of attacks.

is used. For the Gaussian filtering, median filtering and JPEG compression attacks, Symlet5 (i.e. the 5th-order gradient of the image) gives the best results.

Fig. 8 presents the image Lena watermarked with the GDWM method, using Symlet2, Symlet3, Symlet4 and Symlet5 wavelets. To compare the original and watermarked images, the SSIM metric is employed due to its compatibility with the human visual system (Wang et al., 2004). As shown in Fig. 8, the GDWM method yields imperceptible watermarks at PSNR=42 dB. Based on visual inspection, Symlet4 (i.e. the gradient of order 4) gives the most imperceptible watermark. However, the best SSIM value is obtained by Symlet5 (i.e. the gradient of order 5).

Table 3 compares the BER results of the GDWM method with the method in (Wang et al., 2002) under median filtering, JPEG compression, AWGN and salt & pepper noise attacks. As in (Wang et al., 2002), the watermark length in both methods is 256 bits and the PSNR of all the watermarked test images is 42 dB. Symlet5 wavelet is used to implement the GDWM method.

Image	Method	Median Filter 3×3	JPEG $Q = 11$	AWGN $\sigma = 10$	S&P $p = 0.01$
Lena	Wang	30.80	29.80	1.45	2.45
Lena	GDWM	**0**	**5.54**	**0.29**	**1.67**
Barbara	Wang	24.95	16.45	1.45	2.25
Barbara	GDWM	**0.41**	**4.73**	**0.16**	**2.12**
Baboon	Wang	31.65	16.95	1.30	1.95
Baboon	GDWM	**0.98**	**4.61**	**0.11**	**1.60**
Peppers	Wang	29.35	26.10	1.25	**2.00**
Peppers	GDWM	**0.22**	**5.67**	**0.40**	2.60

Table 3. The BER comparisons between the GDWM and Wang's method (Wang et al., 2002) under different types of attacks (Message length=256 bits, PSNR=42 dB)

(a) Symlet2, SSIM=0.9944 (b) Symlet3, SSIM=0.9935

(c) Symlet4, SSIM=0.9958 (d) Symlet5, SSIM=0.9963

Fig. 8. Test image Lena watermarked using different gradient transforms in the GDWM method. In each case, a 256-bit watermark is embedded with PSNR=42dB.

The results clearly demonstrate that the GDWM method consistently outperforms the Wang's method under all considered attacks.

In Table 4 the GDWM is compared with the non-blind method proposed in (Akhaee et al., 2010). In both methods, a 128-bit pseudo-random binary message is embedded in the images Baboon and Barbara with PSNRs 39.53 dB and 36.63 dB, respectively. To embed 128 bits, 64, 32 and 32 bits are inserted in the gradient fields at scales 3, 4 and 5, respectively. Symlet5 wavelet is used to obtain the 5th-order gradient fields. It can be seen that the GDWM method outperforms Akhaee's method (Akhaee et al., 2010) under the spatial scaling, JPEG compression and AWGN noise attacks. However, GDWM is slightly less robust under the salt & pepper noise attacks.

Image	Method	Scaling ($s = 0.8$)	JPEG ($Q = 20$)	AWGN ($\sigma = 20$)	S&P ($p = 0.05$)
Barbara	Akhaee	2.34	0.40	0.10	**1.48**
Barbara	GDWM	**0**	**0**	**0**	1.61
Baboon	Akhaee	3.20	1.80	0.30	**2.89**
Baboon	GDWM	**0**	**0.22**	**0.16**	4.31

Table 4. The BER comparison between the GDWM method and Akhaee's method (Akhaee et al., 2010) under different types of attacks (Message length=128 bits)

6. Conclusion

This chapter describes a gradient-based image watermarking method, called gradient direction watermarking (GDWM). In this method, the watermark bits are embedded in the angles of the gradient vectors of the image. The gradient vectors correspond to a higher-order gradient of the image. The gradient fields are obtained from the wavelet coefficients of the image at different scales. To embed the watermark bit in the gradient angle, the angle quantization index modulation (AQIM) method is used. AQIM makes the watermark both imperceptible and robust to amplitude scaling attack.

The GDWM method is tested on different real images. The experimental results show that implementing the GDWM method in the 5th-order gradient domain (obtained using using Symlet5 wavelet) yields both robust and imperceptible watermarks. It is also shown that the GDWM outperforms other watermarking methods and it is robust to a wide range of attacks.

7. References

Abrardo, A. & Barni, M. (2004). Orthogonal dirty paper coding for informed data hiding, *Security, Steganography, and Watermarking of Multimedia Contents VI* 5306(1): 274–285.

Akhaee, M., Sahraeian, S. & Marvasti, F. (2010). Contourlet-based image watermarking using optimum detector in a noisy environment, *IEEE Trans. on Image Proces.* 19(4): 967 –980.

Bao, P. & Ma, X. (2005). Image adaptive watermarking using wavelet domain singular value decomposition, *IEEE Trans. on Circ. and Sys. for Video Tech.* 15(1): 96 – 102.

Barni, M. (2003). What is the future for watermarking? (part ii), *Signal Processing Magazine, IEEE* 20(6): 53 – 59.

Barni, M., Bartolini, F., De Rosa, A. & Piva, A. (2003). Optimum decoding and detection of multiplicative watermarks, *IEEE Trans. on Signal Proces.* 51(4): 1118 – 1123.

Barni, M., Bartolini, F. & Piva, A. (2001). Improved wavelet-based watermarking through pixel-wise masking, *IEEE Trans. on Image Proces.* 10(5): 783 –791.

Bradley, B. A. (2004). Improvement to cdf grounded lattice codes, *Security, Steganography, and Watermarking of Multimedia Contents VI* 5306(1): 212–223.

Chen, B. & Wornell, G. (2001). Quantization index modulation: a class of provably good methods for digital watermarking and information embedding, *IEEE Trans. on Information Theory* 47(4): 1423 –1443.

Chen, L.-H. & Lin, J.-J. (2003). Mean quantization based image watermarking, *Image and Vision Computing* 21(8): 717 – 727.

Cheng, Q. & Huang, T. (2001). An additive approach to transform-domain information hiding and optimum detection structure, *IEEE Trans. on Multimedia* 3(3): 273 –284.

Cox, I. (2008). *Digital watermarking and steganography*, The Morgan Kaufmann series in multimedia information and systems, Morgan Kaufmann Publishers.

Cox, I., Kilian, J., Leighton, F. & Shamoon, T. (1997). Secure spread spectrum watermarking for multimedia, *IEEE Trans. on Image Proces.* 6(12): 1673 –1687.

Cox, I., Miller, M. & McKellips, A. (1999). Watermarking as communications with side information, *Proceedings of the IEEE* 87(7): 1127 –1141.

Eggers, J. J., Baeuml, R. & Girod, B. (2002). Estimation of amplitude modifications before scs watermark detection, *Security and Watermarking of Multimedia Contents IV* 4675(1): 387–398.

Eggers, J. J., Bäuml, R. & Girod, B. (2002). Estimation Of Amplitude Modifications before SCS Watermark Detection, *Proceedings of SPIE Security and Watermarking of Multimedia Contents IV* 4675: 387–398.

Hernandez, J., Amado, M. & Perez-Gonzalez, F. (2000). Dct-domain watermarking techniques for still images: detector performance analysis and a new structure, *Image Processing, IEEE Transactions on* 9(1): 55 –68.

Kalantari, N. & Ahadi, S. (2010). A logarithmic quantization index modulation for perceptually better data hiding, *IEEE Trans. on Image Proces.* 19(6): 1504 –1517.

Kalantari, N., Ahadi, S. & Vafadust, M. (2010). A robust image watermarking in the ridgelet domain using universally optimum decoder, *IEEE Trans. on Circ. and Sys. for Video Tech.* 20(3): 396 –406.

Kundur, D. & Hatzinakos, D. (1999). Digital watermarking for telltale tamper proofing and authentication, *Proc. of the IEEE* 87(7): 1167 –1180.

Kundur, D. & Hatzinakos, D. (2001). Diversity and attack characterization for improved robust watermarking, *IEEE Trans. on Signal Proces.* 49(10): 2383 –2396.

Lagendijk, R. & Shterev, I. (2004). Estimation of attacker's scale and noise variance for qim-dc watermark embedding, 1: 55–58.

Langelaar, G., Setyawan, I. & Lagendijk, R. (2000). Watermarking digital image and video data. a state-of-the-art overview, *IEEE Signal Proces. Mag.* 17(5): 20 –46.

Li, Q. & Cox, I. (2007). Using perceptual models to improve fidelity and provide resistance to valumetric scaling for quantization index modulation watermarking, *IEEE Transactions on Information Forensics and Security* 2(2): 127 –139.

Mallat, S. (1997). *A Wavelet Tour of Signal Proces.*, AP Professional, London.

Mallat, S. & Hwang, W. (1992). Singularity detection and processing with wavelets, *Information Theory, IEEE Transactions on* 38(2): 617 –643.

Malvar, H. & Florencio, D. (2003). Improved spread spectrum: a new modulation technique for robust watermarking, *IEEE Transactions on Signal Processing* 51(4): 898 – 905.

Miller, M., Doerr, G. & Cox, I. (2004). Applying informed coding and embedding to design a robust high-capacity watermark, *IEEE Trans. on Image Proces.* 13(6): 792 –807.

Ming, C. & Xi-jian, P. (2006). Image steganography based on arnold transform, *Computer appl. research* 1: 235–237.

Moulin, P. & Koetter, R. (2005). Data-hiding codes, *Proc. of the IEEE* 93(12): 2083 –2126.

N. Arya, E., Wang, Z. & Ward, R. (2011). Robust image watermarking based on multiscale gradient direction quantization, *Information Forensics and Security, IEEE Transactions on* (99): 1.

Ourique, F., Licks, V., Jordan, R. & Perez-Gonzalez, F. (2005). Angle qim: a novel watermark embedding scheme robust against amplitude scaling distortions, *Proc. IEEE Int. Conf. on Acoust., Speech, and Signal Proces. (ICASSP '05)* 2: ii/797 – ii/800 Vol. 2.

Perez-Gonzalez, F., Mosquera, C., Barni, M. & Abrardo, A. (2005). Rational dither modulation: a high-rate data-hiding method invariant to gain attacks, *IEEE Trans. on Signal Proces.* 53(10): 3960 – 3975.

Perez-Gonzlez, F. & Balado, F. (2002). Quantized projection data hiding, *Proc. of Int. Conf. on Image Proces.* 2: 889–892.

Phadikar, A., Maity, S. P. & Verma, B. (2011). Region based QIM digital watermarking scheme for image database in DCT domain, *Computers & Electrical Engineering* In Press.

Podilchuk, C. & Zeng, W. (1998). Image-adaptive watermarking using visual models, *IEEE Journal on Sel. Areas in Comm.* 16(4): 525 –539.

Shterev, I. D. & Lagendijk, R. L. (2005). Maximum likelihood amplitude scale estimation for quantization-based watermarking in the presence of dither, *Security, Steganography, and Watermarking of Multimedia Contents VII* 5681(1): 516–527.

Shterev, I. & Lagendijk, R. (2006). Amplitude scale estimation for quantization-based watermarking, *Signal Processing, IEEE Transactions on* 54(11): 4146 –4155.

Wang, S.-H. & Lin, Y.-P. (2004). Wavelet tree quantization for copyright protection watermarking, *IEEE Trans. on Image Proces.* 13(2): 154 –165.

Wang, Y., Doherty, J. & Van Dyck, R. (2002). A wavelet-based watermarking algorithm for ownership verification of digital images, *IEEE Trans. on Image Proces.* 11(2): 77 –88.

Wang, Z., Bovik, A., Sheikh, H. & Simoncelli, E. (2004). Image quality assessment: from error visibility to structural similarity, *IEEE Transactions on Image Processing* 13(4): 600 –612.

Wu, M. & Liu, B. (2003). Data hiding in image and video .i. fundamental issues and solutions, *IEEE Trans. on Image Proces.* 12(6): 685 – 695.

Xue Yang, Xiaoyang Yu, Q. Z. & Jia, J. (2010). Image encryption algorithm based on universal modular transformation, *Inf. Tech. Journal* 9(4): 680–685.

Zhong, J. & Huang, S. (2006). An enhanced multiplicative spread spectrum watermarking scheme, *IEEE Transactions on Circuits and Systems for Video Technology* 16(12): 1491 –1506.

Zou, J., Tie, X., Ward, R. & Qi, D. (2005). Some novel image scrambling methods based on affine modular matrix transformation, *Journal of Info. and Compt. Sci.* 2(1): 223–227.

Zou, J. & Ward, R. (2003). Introducing two new image scrambling methods, *IEEE Pacific Rim Conf. on Comm., Comp. and signal Proces.* 2: 708 – 711 vol.2.

Zou, J., Ward, R. & Qi, D. (2004). A new digital image scrambling method based on fibonacci numbers, *Proc. of Int. Symp. on Cir. and Sys.* 3: 965–968.

21

Signal and Image Denoising Using Wavelet Transform

Burhan Ergen
Fırat University
Turkey

1. Introduction

The wavelet transform (WT) a powerful tool of signal and image processing that have been successfully used in many scientific fields such as signal processing, image compression, computer graphics, and pattern recognition (Daubechies 1990; Lewis and Knowles 1992; Do and Vetterli 2002; Meyer, Averbuch et al. 2002; Heric and Zazula 2007). On contrary the traditional Fourier Transform, the WT is particularly suitable for the applications of non-stationary signals which may instantaneous vary in time (Daubechies 1990; Mallat and Zhang 1993; Akay and Mello 1998). It is crucial to analyze the time-frequency characteristics of the signals which classified as non-stationary or transient signals in order to understand the exact features of such signals (Rioul and Vetterli 1991; Ergen, Tatar et al. 2010). For this reason, firstly, researchers has concentrated on continuous wavelet transform (CWT) that gives more reliable and detailed time-scale representation rather than the classical short time Fourier transform (STFT) giving a time-frequency representation (Jiang 1998; Qian and Chen 1999).

The CWT technique expands the signal onto basis functions created by expanding, shrinking and shifting a single prototype function, which named as mother wavelet, specially selected for the signal under considerations. This transformation decomposes the signal into different scales with different levels of resolution. Since a scale parameter shrinking or expanding the mother wavelet in CWT, the result of the transform is time-scale representation. The scale parameter is indirectly related to frequency, when considered the center frequency of mother wavelet.

A mother wavelet has satisfy that it has a zero mean value, which require that the transformation kernel of the wavelet transform compactly supports localization in time, thereby offering the potential to capture the spikes occurring instantly in a short period of time (Mallat 1989; Rioul and Vetterli 1991; Akay and Mello 1998).

A wavelet expansion is representation of a signal in terms of an orthogonal collection of real-valued generated by applying suitable transformation to the original selected wavelet. The properties and advantages of a family of wavelets depend upon the mother wavelet features. The expansion is formed by two dimensional expansion of a signal and thus provides a time-frequency localization of the input signal. This implies that most of the energy of the signal will be captured a few coefficient. The basis functions in a wavelet transform are produced from the mother wavelet by scaling and translation operations. When the scaling is chosen as power of two, this kind of wavelet transform is called dyadic-orthonormal wavelet transform, which makes a way for discrete wavelet transform (Zou and Tewfik 1993; Blu 1998) . If the chosen mother wavelet has orthonormal properties, there is no redundancy in the discrete wavelet transforms. In addition, this provides the multiresolution algorithm decomposing a signal into scales with different time and frequency resolution (Mallat 1989; Daubechies 1990).

The fundamental concept involved in mutiresolution is to find average features and details of the signal via scalar products with scaling signals and wavelets. The spikes in signal are typically of high frequency and it is possible discriminate the spikes with other noises through the decomposition of multiresolution into different levels. The differences between mother wavelet functions (e.g. Haar, Daubechies, Symlets, Coiflets, Biorthogonal and etc.) consist in how these scaling signals and the wavelets are defined (Zou and Tewfik 1993; Blu 1998; Ergen, Tatar et al. 2010).

The continuous wavelet transform is computed by changing the scale of the mother wavelet, shifting the scaled wavelet in time, multiplying by the signal, and integrating over all times. When the signal to be analyzed and wavelet function are discredited, the CWT can be realized on computer and the computation time can be significantly reduced if the redundant samples removed respect to sampling theorem. This is not a true discrete wavelet transform. The fundamentals of discrete wavelet transform goes back to sub-band coding theorem (Fischer 1992; Vetterli and Kova evi 1995; Vetterli and Kovacevic 1995). The sub-band coding encodes each part of the signal after separating into different bands of frequencies. Some studies have made use of wavelet transform as a filter bank in order to separate the signal.

After discovering the signal decomposition of a signal into frequency bands using discrete wavelet transform, the DWT has found many application area, from signal analysis to signal compression (Chang and Kuo 1993; Qu, Adam et al. 2003; He and Scordilis 2008).

The one of the first application of the DWT is the denoising process, which aims to remove the small part of the signal assumed as noise (Lang, Guo et al. 1996; Simoncelli and Adelson 1996; Jansen 2001). All kind of the signal obtained from the physical environment has contains more or less disturbing noise. Therefore, wavelet denoising procedure has applied many one or two dimensional signal after particularly soft or hard thresholding methods had proposed (Donoho and Johnstone 1994; Donoho 1995). Such signals some time are one-dimensional simple power or control signals (Sen, Zhengxiang et al. 2002; Giaouris, Finch et al. 2008) as well as more complex medical images (Wink and Roerdink 2004; Pizurica, Wink et al. 2006). Especially, wavelet denoising has found an application field about image processing recently (Nasri and Nezamabadi-pour 2009; Chen, Bui et al. 2010; Jovanov, Pi urica et al. 2010).

2. Noise consideration

A signal or an image is unfortunately corrupted by various factors which effects as noise during acquisition or transmission. These noisy effects decrease the performance of visual and computerized analysis. It is clear that the removing of the noise from the signal facilitate the processing. The denoising process can be described as to remove the noise while retaining and not distorting the quality of processed signal or image (Chen and Bui 2003; Portilla, Strela et al. 2003; Buades, Coll et al. 2006). The traditional way of denoising to remove the noise from a signal or an image is to use a low or band pass filter with cut off frequencies. However the traditional filtering techniques are able to remove a relevant of the noise, they are incapable if the noise in the band of the signal to be analyzed. Therefore, many denoising techniques are proposed to overcome this problem.

The algorithms and processing techniques used for signals can be also used for images because an image can be considered as a two dimensional signal. Therefore, the digital signal processing techniques for a one dimensional signal can be adapted to process two dimensional signals or images.

Because the origin and nonstationarity of the noise infecting in the signal, it is difficult to model it. Nevertheless, if the noise assumed as stationary, an empirically recorded signal that is corrupted by additive noise can be represented as;

$$y(i) = x(i) + \sigma\varepsilon(i)\,,\ i = 0,1,...,n-1 \qquad (1)$$

Where $y(i)$ noisy signal, $x(i)$ is noise free actual signal and $\varepsilon(i)$ are independently normal random variables and σ represents the intensity of the noise in $y(i)$. The noise is usually modeled as stationary independent zero-mean white Gaussian variables (Moulin and Liu 1999; Alfaouri and Daqrouq 2008).

When this model is used, the objective of noise removal is to reconstruct the original signal $x(i)$ from a finite set of $y(i)$ values without assuming a particular structure for the signal. The usual approach to noise removal models noise as high frequency signal added to an original signal. These high frequencies can be bringing out using traditional Fourier transform, ultimately removing them by adequate filtering. This noise removal technique conceptually clear and efficient since depends only calculating DFT (Discrete Fourier Transform)(Wachowiak, Rash et al. 2000).

However, there is some issue that must be under consideration. The most prominent having same frequency as the noise has important information in the original signal. Filtering out these frequency components will cause noticeable loss of information of the desired signal when considered the frequency representation of the original signal. It is clear that a method is required in order to conserve the prominent part of the signal having relatively high frequencies as the noise has. The wavelet based noise removal techniques have provided this conservation of the prominent part.

3. Discrete Wavelet Transform (DWT) and Wavelet Packet Decomposition

The wavelet transform has become an essential tool for many applications. However, the wavelet transform has been presented a method representing a time-frequency method, continuous wavelets transform (CWT), and the wavelet transform generally has used for the decomposition of the signal into high and low frequency components. The wavelet coefficient represents a measure of similarity in the frequency content between a signal and a chosen wavelet function. These coefficients are computed as a convolution of the signal and the scaled wavelet function, which can be interpreted as a dilated band-pass filter because of its band-pass like spectrum (Valens ; Rioul and Vetterli 1991) .

In practice, the wavelet transform is implemented with a perfect reconstruction filter bank using orthogonal wavelet family. The idea is to decompose the signal into sub-signals corresponding to different frequency contents. In the decomposition step, a signal is decomposed on to a set of orthonormal wavelet function that constitutes a wavelet basis (Misiti, Misiti et al.). The most common wavelets providing the ortogonality properties are daubechies, symlets, coiflets and discrete meyer in order to provide reconstruction using the fast algorithms (Beylkin, Coifman et al. 1991; Cohen, Daubechies et al. 1993).

The use of wavelet transform as filter bank called as DWT (Discrete Wavelet Transform). The DWT of a signal produces a non-redundant restoration, which provides better spatial and spectral localization of signal formation, compared with other multi-scale representation such as Gaussian and Laplacian pyramid. The result of the DWT is a multilevel decomposition, in which the signal is decomposed in *'approximation'* and *'detail'* coefficients at each level (Mallat 1989). This is made through a process that is equivalent to low-pass and high passes filtering, respectively.

As stated previous section, the wavelet transform is firstly introduced for the time-frequency analysis of transient continuous signals, and then extended to the theory of multi-resolution wavelet transform using FIR filter approximation. This managed using the dyadic form of CWT. In dyadic form, the scaling function is chosen as power of two. And then, the discrete wavelets $\psi_{m,n}(t) = 2^{-m/2}\psi(2^{-m}t - n)$ used in multi-resolution analysis constituting an orthonormal basis for $L^2(\Re)$ (Vetterli and Herley 1992; Donoho and Johnstone 1994).

If a signal, $x(t)$, decomposed into low and high frequency components, that they are respectively named as approximation coefficients and detail coefficients, $x(t)$ reconstructed as;

$$x(t) = \sum_{m=1}^{L}\left[\sum_{k=-\infty}^{\infty} D_m(k)\psi_{m,k}(t) + \sum_{k=-\infty}^{\infty} A_l(k)\phi_{l,k}(t)\right] \tag{2}$$

Where $\psi_{m,k}(t)$ is discrete analysis wavelet, and $\phi_{l,k}(t)$ is discrete scaling, $D_m(k)$ is the detailed signal at scale 2^m, and $A_l(k)$ is the approximated signal at scale 2^l. $D_m(k)$ and $A_l(k)$ is obtained using the scaling and wavelet filters (Mallat 1999).

$$\begin{aligned} h(n) &= 2^{-1/2}\langle\phi(t), \phi(2t-n)\rangle \\ g(n) &= 2^{-1/2}\langle\psi(t), \phi(2t-n)\rangle \\ &= (-1)^{n} h(1-n) \end{aligned} \tag{3}$$

The wavelet coefficient can be computed by means of a pyramid transfer algorithm. The algorithms refer to a FIR filter bank with low-pass filter **h**, high-pass filter **g**, and down sampling by a factor 2 at each stage of the filter bank. Fig. 1 shows the tree structure of DWT decomposition for three levels. DWT decomposition leads to a tree structure as shown in Fig. 1, where approximation and detail coefficients are presented.

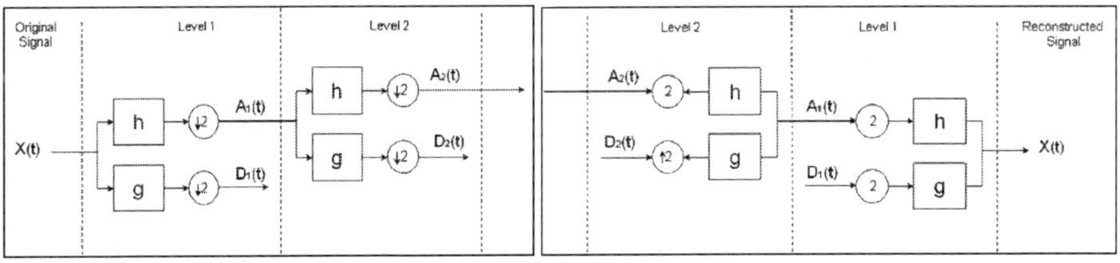

(a) (b)

Fig. 1. The DWT decomposition and reconstruction steps of a 1D signal for level of 2; a. Decomposition, b. Reconstruction

In this figure, ↓2 and ↑2 refers to down sampling and up sampling, respectively. This decomposition sometimes called as sub-band coding. The low pass filter produces the approximation of the signal, and the high pass filers represent the details or its high frequency components. The decomposition successively can be applied on the low frequency components, approximation coefficients, in DWT.

Whereas the successive decomposition is applied on the approximation coefficients only as in the DWT, the decomposition may be applied on both sub part of the signal, approximation coefficients and detail coefficients. If the decomposition is applied on the both sides, approximation and details, this kind of decomposition called as wavelet packet transform or wavelet packet tree decomposition. Fig. 2 represents wavelet packet decomposition and reconstruction.

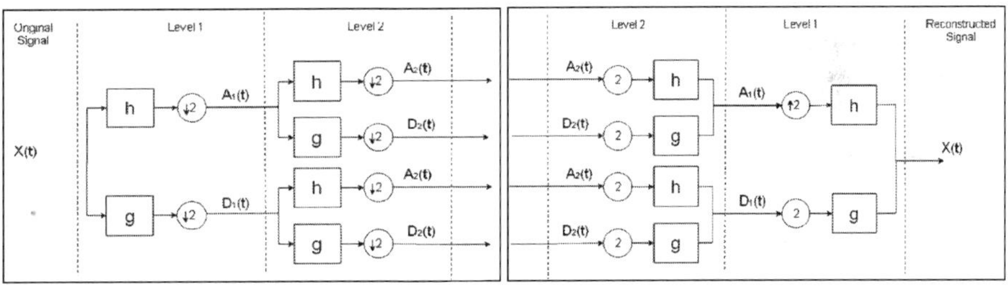

(a) (b)

Fig. 2. The wavelet packet decomposition and reconstruction steps of a 1D signal for level of 2; a. Decomposition, b. Reconstruction

In 2D case, the image signal is considered as rows and columns as if they are one dimentional signals. In DWT, firstly the each rows of the image is filtered, then the each columns are filtered as in 1D case. Figure 3 demonstare the decompositon of an image for one level. As in signal decomposition, after each filtering, the subsampling is realized. The result of this process gives four images; approximation, horizantal details, vertical details and diagonal details. Because of subsampling after each filtering, the result subimages of the original image has the quarter size of the original image.

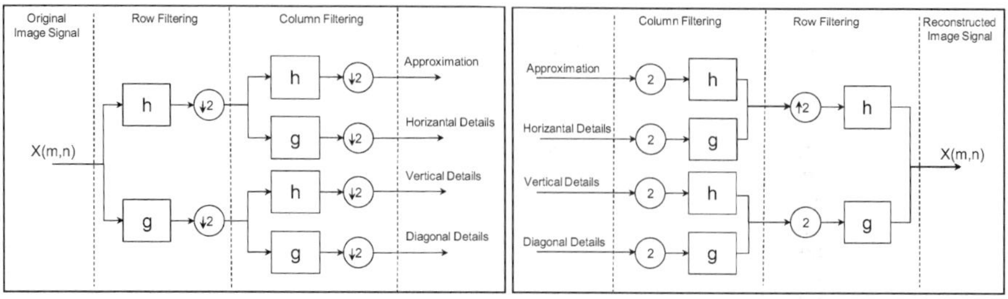

(a) (b)

Fig. 3. The DWT decomposition and reconstruction steps of a 2D image signal for level of 2; a.Decomposition, b. Reconstruction

4. Thresholding and threshold estimation techniques

The simpler way to remove noise or to reconstruct the original signal from a contaminated signal, in case of 1D or 2D, using the wavelet coefficients which are the result of decomposition in wavelet transform, is to eliminate the small coefficient associated to the noise. After updating the coefficients by removing the small coefficients assuming as noise, the original signal can be obtained by the reconstruction algorithm using the noise free coefficients. Because it is usually considered that the noise has high frequency coefficients, the elimination of the small coefficient generally applied on the detail coefficients after the decomposition. Indeed, the main idea of the wavelet denoising to obtain the ideal components of the signal from the noisy signal requires the estimation of the noise level. The estimated noise level is used in order to threshold the small coefficient assumed as noise.

The procedure of the signal denoising based on DWT is consist of three steps; decomposition of the signal, thresholding and reconstruction of the signal. Several methods use this idea proposed and implements it in different ways. When attempting to decrease the influence of noise wavelets coefficient, it is possible to do this in particular ways, also the need of information of the underlying signal leads to different statistical treatments of the available information.

In the linear penalization method every wavelet coefficient is affected by a linear shrinkage particular associated to the resolution level of the coefficient. It can be said that linear thresholding is appropriate only for homogeny signals with important levels of regularity. The wavelet thresholding or shrinkage methods are usually more suitable. Since the work of Donoho and Johnstone (Donoho and Johnstone 1994), there has been a lot of research on the way of defining the threshold levels and their type. Donoho and Johnstone proposed a nonlinear strategy for thresholding. In their approaches, the thresholding can be applied by implementing either hard or soft thresholding method, which also called as shrinkage.

In the hard thresholding, the wavelet coefficient below a give value are stetted to zero, while in soft thresholding the wavelet coefficient are reduced be a quantity to the thresh value. The threshold value is the estimation of the noise level, which is generally calculated from the standard deviation of the detail coefficient (Donoho 1995). Fig. 4 indicates the two types of thresholding, which can be expressed analytically as;

$$Hard\ threshold: \begin{cases} y = x & if\ |x| > \lambda \\ y = 0 & if\ |x| < \lambda \end{cases} \tag{4}$$

$$Soft\ threshold: \{y = sign(x)(|x| - \lambda)\} \tag{5}$$

Where x is the input signal, y is the signal after threshold and λ is the threshold value, which is critical as the estimator leading to destruction, reduction, or increase in the value of a wavelet coefficient.

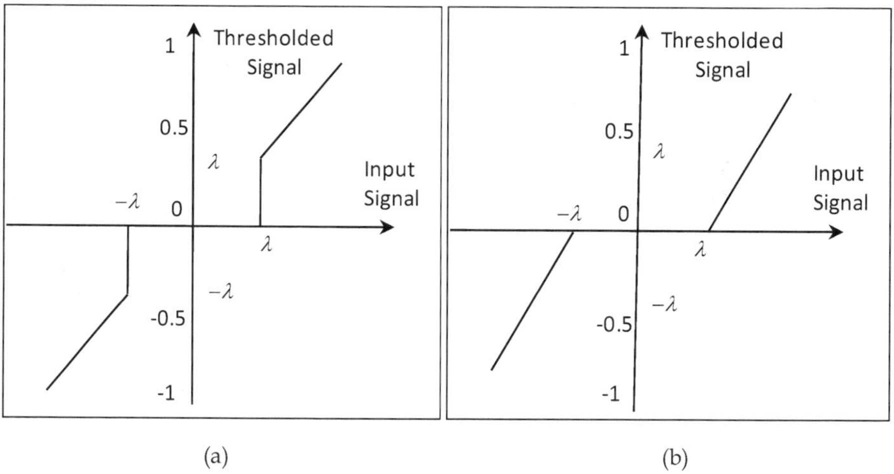

Fig. 4. Threshold types; a. Hard, b. Soft.

Hard thresholding method does not affect on the detail coefficients that grater the threshold level, whereas the soft thresholding method to these coefficients. There are several considerations about the properties and limitation of these two strategies. However the hard thresholding may be unstable and sensitive even to small changes in the signal, the soft thresholding can create unnecessary bias when the true coefficients are large. Although more sophisticated methods has been proposed to overcome the drawbacks of the described nonlinear methods, it is still the most efficient and reliable methods are still the hard and soft thresholding techniques (Donoho 1995).

One important point in thresholding methods is to find the appropriate value for the threshold. Actually, many approaches have been proposed for calculating the threshold value. But, all the approaches require the estimation of noise level. However the standard deviation of the data values may be use as an estimator, Donoho proposed a good estimator σ for the wavelet denoising given as;

$$\sigma = \frac{median(d_{L-1,k})}{0.6745}, \quad k = 0,1,...,2^{L-1} - 1 \tag{6}$$

where L denotes the number of decomposition levels. As mentioned above, this median selection made on the detail coefficient of the analyzed signal.

The most known threshold selection algorithms are minimax, universal and rigorous sure threshold estimation techniques (Donoho and Johnstone 1994; Donoho and Johnstone 1998).

The *minimax* threshold value λ_M proposed by Donoho consists an optimal threshold that derived from minimizing the constant term in an upper bound of the risk involved in the estimation. The proposed threshold depends of the available data and also takes into account the noise level contaminating the signal. The optimal threshold is defined as;

$$\lambda_M = \sigma \lambda_n^* \tag{7}$$

where λ_n^* is defined as the value of λ and satisfying as;

$$\lambda_n^* = \inf_\lambda \sup_d \left\{ \frac{R_\lambda(d)}{n^{-1} + R_{oracle}(d)} \right\} \tag{8}$$

where $R_\lambda(d) = E(\delta_\lambda(d) - d)^2$ and $R_{oracle}(d)$ named as oracle used to account for the risk associated to the modification of the value of a given wavelet coefficient. Two oracles are considered, the diagonal liner projection (DLP) and the diagonal linear shrinker (DLS)(Donoho and Johnstone 1994). The ideal risks for these oracles are given by

$$R_{oracle}^{DLP}(d) = \min(d^2, 1) \tag{9}$$

$$R_{oracle}^{DLS}(d) = \frac{d^2}{d^2 + 1} \tag{10}$$

The minimax method is used in statistics to design estimator. The minimax estimator is realizes the minimum of the maximum mean square error, over a given set of functions. Another proposed threshold estimator by Donoho is the *universal* threshold, or global threshold, as an alternative to the minimax threshold, however it uses a fixed threshold form given as;

$$\lambda_U = \sigma \sqrt{2\log(n)} \tag{11}$$

Where n denotes the length of the analyzed signal and σ is given by Eq. (6). The advantage of this thresholding appears in software implementation due to easy to remember and coding. Additionally, this threshold estimator ensures that every sample in the wavelet transform in which the underlying function is exactly zero will be estimated as zero.

Again another common estimator is Rigorous Sure (rigresure) threshold proposed by Donoho. This threshold describes a scheme which uses a threshold λ at each resolution level l of the wavelet coeffient. The Rigorous Sure, also known as *SureShrink*, uses the Stein's Unbiased Risk Estimate criterion to obtain unbiased estimate. The threshold is given as follows;

$$\lambda_S = \arg\min_{0<\lambda<\lambda_U} Sure\left(\lambda, \frac{S(a,b)}{\sigma} \right) \tag{12}$$

Where Sure is defined as

$$Sure(\lambda, X) = n - 2 \cdot \Theta\{i : |X_i \le \lambda|\} + [\min(|X_i|, \lambda]^2 \tag{13}$$

Where the operator $\Theta(\cdot)$ returns the cardinality of the set $\{i : |X_i \le \lambda|\}$, it is found that Sure is an un biased estimate of the $l^2 - risk$.

5. Denoising application examples

5.1 Comparison assessments

The best way to test the effect of noise on a signal is to add a Gaussian white noise, in which case its values independently and identically distributed (i.i.d) Gaussian real values. After the denoising process, the performance can be measure by comparing the denoised signal and the original signal. However, many methods have been proposed to measure the performance of denoising algorithms, the signal to noise ratio (SNR) and peak signal to noise ratio (PSNR) has generally accepted to measure the quality of signal and images, respectively. For one dimensional signal, measuring the performance of the denoising method by calculation of the residual SNR given as;

$$SNR = 10\log_{10}\left(\sum_{n=0}^{N-1} x^2(n) \Big/ \sum_{n=0}^{N-1} \left(\overline{x}(n) - x^r(n])\right)^2 \right) \tag{14}$$

where $x(n)$ is the original signal, $x_r(n)$ is the denoised signal and $\overline{x}(n)$ refers to the mean value of $x(n)$.

In order to measure the quality of image, it is generally used PSNR, which given as;

$$PSNR = 10\log_{10}\left(L \Big/ \sum_{n=0}^{N-1} \sum_{m=0}^{M-1} \left(\overline{x}(n,m) - x^r(n,m)\right)^2 \right) \tag{15}$$

where L denotes the quantized gray level of the images, $x(n)$ is original images, $\overline{x}(n,m)$ is the mean value of $x(n)$, and $x^r(n,m)$ refers to reconstructed image. In order to get visible alteration on signal, the power of noise should be chosen adequately. Indeed, SNR is usually the most important measure rather than the power of noise, when taking into consideration that the power of the signal to denoise can be varied. When the SNR is chosen above 3dB, it is generally enough to get the visible corruption.

5.2 Phonocardiogram denoising

The records of the acoustical vibrations produced by heart, acquired through microphones from human chest, called phonocardiogram (PCG), consist of the heart sounds and the murmurs. This records of acoustic signals are unfortunately disturbed by various factors which effecting as noise. These effects decrease the performance of visual and computerized analysis (Akay, Semmlow et al. 1990; Ergen, Tatar et al. 2010).

The respiration sounds by lung mechanical actions, patient movement, and improper contacts of microphone to the skin, and external noises from the environments are added as noise signal into PCG records. The traditional method to remove the noise from a PCG signal is to use a low or band pass filter with cut off frequencies. However the filtering techniques are able to remove a relevant of the noise, they are incapable if the noise in the band of the signal to be analyzed.

The frequency components of a normal PCG signals can be rise up 200Hz, and the energy of the most significant components concentrates around the frequency band 100-150Hz (Ergen, Tatar et al. 2010). The frequency bands of the signal are very important when we use the denoising technique using DWT approaches. Because the DWT approaches decomposes the signal into frequency bands to eliminate the small detail components assumed as noise, the decomposition level reflects directly on the frequency components that cause the smoothed version of the signal.

As stated previous section, the most reasonable way to determine the effectiveness of denoising method is to compare an original signal and the denoised signal obtained from its noise added form. Therefore, here, we will use the noise added signal to examine the effectiveness of wavelet denoising method through the comparison between the original signal and the denoised signal (or reconstructed) signal. Figure 5.a shows a PCG during cardiac period and its noise added form.

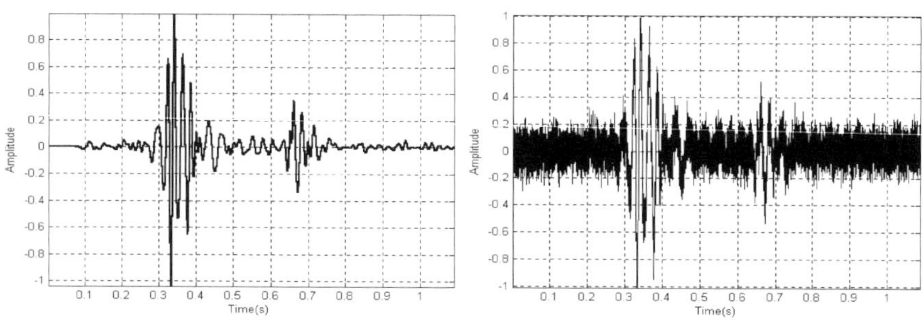

(a) (b)

Fig. 5. Wavelet denoising of a PCG signal, a) Original signal, b) Noisy signal

The result of the DWT is a multilevel decomposition, in which the signal is decomposed in 'approximation' and 'detail' coefficients at each level. This is made through a process that is equivalent to low-pass and high passes filtering, respectively. DWT decomposition leads to a tree structure as shown in Fig. 6, where approximation and detail coefficients are presented.

The approximation coefficients and the detail coefficients of the noisy signal for the decomposition level of one and two are given Figure 7. In Fig. 7c and Fig. 7d are the results of the decomposition of the approximation coefficient at level one, which represented in Fig. 8a.

As an example of denoising process for PCG signal, the denoised signal and the difference between the original signal and the denoised signal are given in Fig. 7, respectively. *'symlet8'*, *'rigresure'* and *'soft thresholding'* parameters are used in the denoising process. When we compared even the original the original signal and the denoised signal visually, the wavelet denoising process has a quite success.

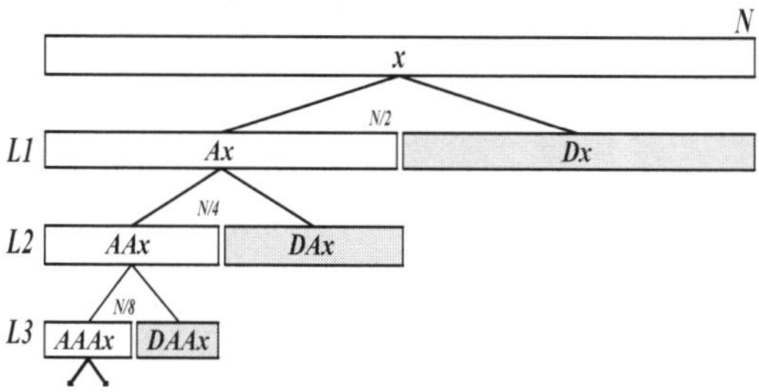

Fig. 6. The approximation and the detailed coefficients in the tree structure of the DWT.

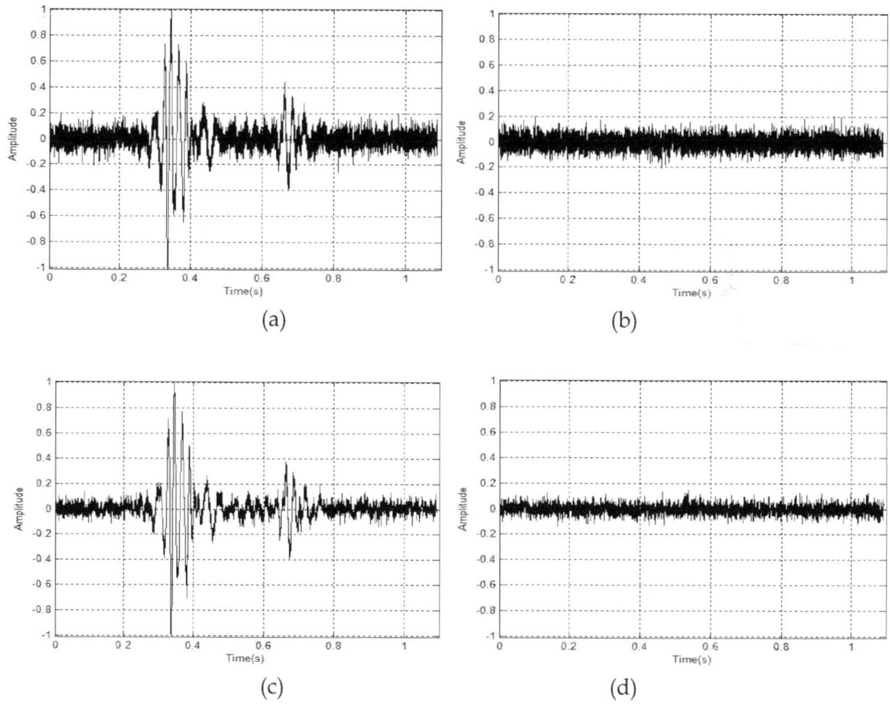

Fig. 7. Decomposition of the noisy signal,
a) Approximation coefficients at level one, b) Detail coefficients at level one,
c) Approximation coefficients at level two, b) Detail coefficients at level two.

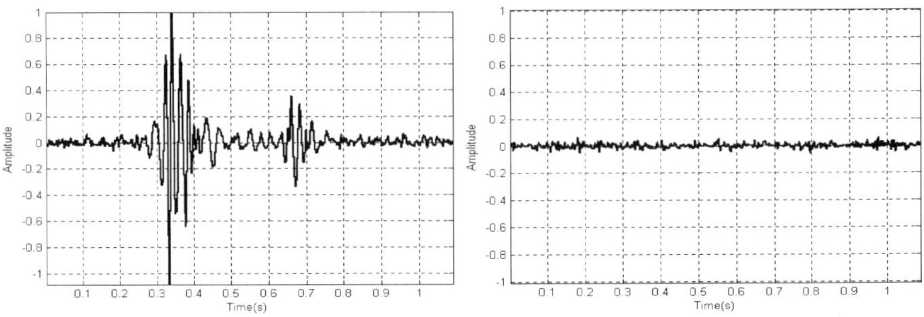

(a) (b)

Fig. 8. Denoised signal, a) Denoised signal, d) Difference between the original and the denoised signal.

Also, the effected components in DWT decomposition are related to not only decomposition level but also sampling frequency. The decomposition level influences the frequency bands by dividing the sampling frequency respect the power of two. When we choose the decomposition level is as five, the interested frequencies are about 300Hz while the sampling frequency is 11.5KHz.

Therefore, the most important factor determining the SNR level is the level of the decomposition. Table 1 presents the SNR results respect to the decomposition level by using *symlet8* and *rigresure* estimation for hard and soft thresholding as denoising parameter. For the both tresholding techniques, it is seen that the highest SNR value obtained when the decomposition level is five. If the decomposition level is chosen too high, the thresholding will effect on the main frequencies of the original signal. Thus, the SNR has lower values for the level higher than five.

Level	Hard	Soft
1	8.1209	7.8843
2	11.1471	10.9218
3	14.3251	14.0031
4	17.2973	16.9275
5	20.1305	19.4396
6	13.2248	13.2472
7	12.1531	9.8726
8	10.8010	8.3255
9	10.4986	8.1632
10	10.4912	8.1593

Table 1. SNR level respect to the depth of decomposition.

The other parameters to obtain best SNR level are the kind of the wavelet and the thresholding rule. Table 2 presents the SNR levels using different wavelet when the decomposition level is five. In table 2, there is no significant difference in SNR in terms of wavelet types.

Wavelet Type	Hard	Soft
Daubechies2	16.5378	16.5057
Daubechies3	18.9391	18.8353
Daubechies4	19.8138	19.8002
Daubechies5	19.8747	19.7425
Symlet2	16.3487	16.4181
Symlet3	18.5401	18.7874
Symlet4	19.5732	19.8002
Symlet5	19.4795	19.5458
Coiflet1	16.7746	16.7658
Coiflet2	19.4866	19.4501
Coiflet 3	19.7812	19.6252
Discrete Meyer	19.9018	19.7154

Table 2. SNR values respect to wavelet types (Rigrsure, level=5)

Nevertheless, it is attracting that the mother wavelets having high oscillation number produces better SNR results. For instance, the symlet wavelet having eight oscillations in its mother wavelet produces better SNR level than the lower ones. In this case, it can be say that the choice of the very lower oscillation frequency to avoid the computational complexity of the wavelet causes the lower SNR results.

When the performance of the noise estimation techniques is considered in the respect of the decomposition level and the initial SNR level, the estimation techniques show the same performance for the level five respects to the initial SNR level. For the comparison, the initial SNR level before denoising is increased from 1dB to 30dB, and the result SNR level after denoising is calculated. Fig. 9 presents a comparison of the four noise estimation methods for level five and level six when *'symlet8'* used.

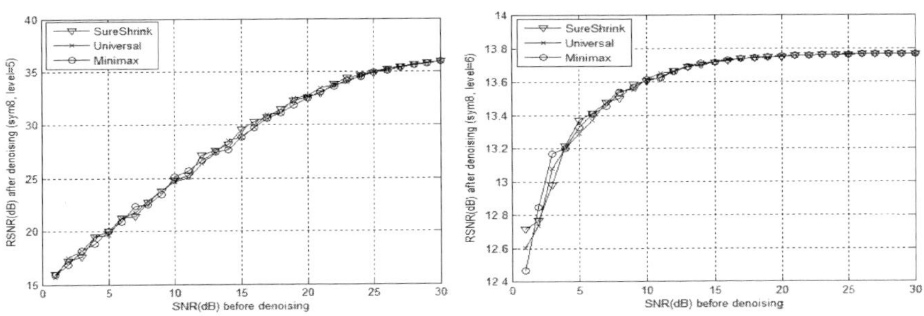

(a) (b)

Fig. 9. The SNR values after denoising before denoising for level 5 and 8.

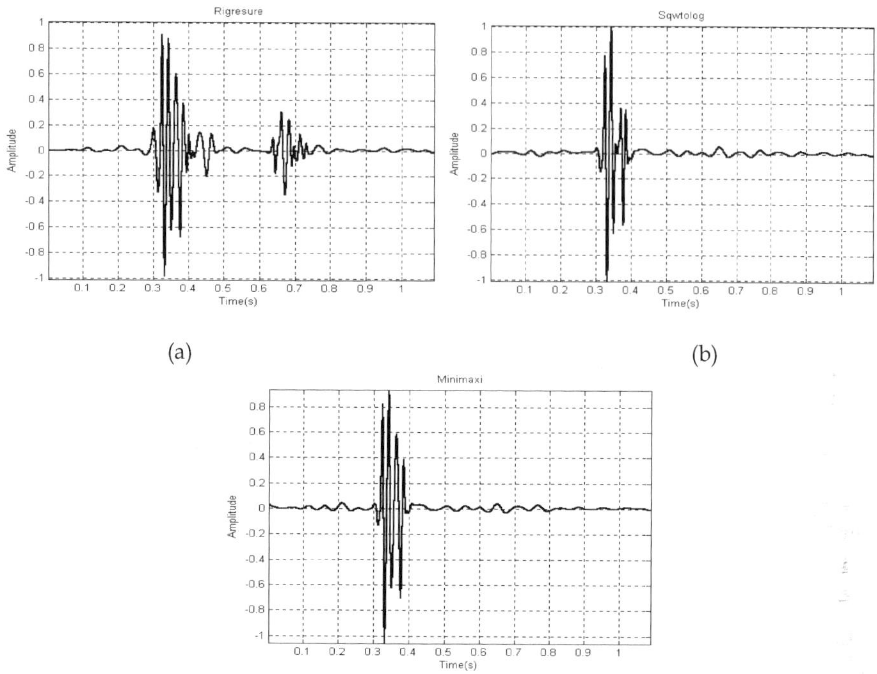

(c)

Fig. 10. The denoised signal using three different threshold rules at level eight.

We have observed no distinguishing evidence among the noise level estimation methods until level six. After this level, rigresure method has produced better SNR values. And it is observed that rigresure preserve the second heart sound in PCG signals while the other methods destroying. This situation is clearly seen in Fig. 10. The signal part related to second heart sound taking place at around 0.7s in Fig.10a is not able to seen in Fig. 10b and Fig. 10c. This shows that the rigresure preserve the main characteristic of the signal. Therefore, we can conclude that the rigresure is the better noise estimation method.

A level-dependent scaling of the thresholds was used to remove Gaussian white noise from the signal. Although it could not found evidence that a single wavelet was the best suited for denoising PCG signal, some wavelets used in this study were slightly better than the others. We conclude that reasonable decomposition level is absolutely depending on the sampling frequency and the frequency band of the signal. Just in this study, the decomposition level of 5 produced reasonable results because the frequency band of a normal PCG signal is around 150-200Hz and the sampling frequency is 11.5KHz. Since the noise level method is one of the important parameter in wavelet denoising, it is examined for different levels. We have not seen any noteworthy differences in the methods from level 1 to level 6. After this level, rigresure method has showed superiority to the other methods in terms of SNR level. Consequently, it is determined that the wavelet type is not very important if the oscillation number is not very low, the decomposition level is absolutely depends on the frequency band of the PCG signal and its sampling frequency, and rigresure method is best of the noise estimation techniques.

5.3 Image denoising

All digital images contain some degree of noise due to the corruption in its acquisition and transmission by various effects. Particularly, medical image are likely disturbed by a complex type of addition noise depending on the devices which are used to capture or store them. No medical imaging devices are noise free. The most commonly used medical images are received from MRI (Magnetic Resonance Imaging) and CT (Computed Tomography) equipments. Usually, the addition noise into medical image reduces the visual quality that complicates diagnosis and treatment.

Because the wavelet transform has an ability to capture the energy of a signal in few energy transform values, the wavelet denoising technique is very effective as stated previous parts. As stated previous sections, when an image is decomposed using wavelet transform, the four sub-images are produced, approximation, horizontal details, vertical details and diagonal details. Fig. 11 represents a sample medical image which belongs to a patient having cranial trauma and its four subimages when decomposed for one level using DWT. This image has acquired from a BT device. A noise added MRI image and its denoised form using wavelet denoising procedure is given Fig. 12. The added noise has Gaussian distribution, and symlet6, decomposition level of two, hard thresholding are chosen as wavelet denoising parameters.

Fig. 11. Decomposition of a sample medical image; original, approximation, horizontal details, vertical details, and diagonal details in left to right.

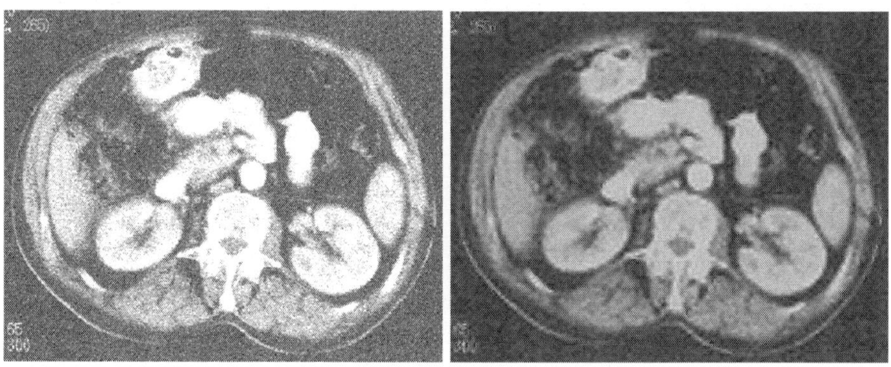

Fig. 12. A noisy image having PSNR 62dB and its denoised version.

Quantitatively assessing the performance in practical image application is complicated issue because the ideal image is normally unknown. Therefore the rational approach is to use known images for the tests, as in other image processing applications, in order to test the performance of the wavelet denoising methods like one dimensional signal denoising. Figure 13 represents the medical test images to be used.

Here, we use again a classical comparison receipt based on noise simulation. The comparison can be realized on the result reconstructed image and the original image after adding Gaussian white noise with known power to the original signal. Then it will be computed the best image recovered from the noisy one for each method. Firstly, we should determine the effective decomposition level because the most important factor in wavelet denoising is decomposition level. For this purpose, a noise added image will be used to obtain how the performance is changing respect to the decomposition level. The recovering process is made on the test image given in Fig 11, on which a Gaussian noise added to be PSNR is 62dB. The noisy image and a sample recovered or denoised is given Fig. 12a and Fig. 12b, respectively. The PSNR values after denosing process is given Table 3. In this denoising process, the symlet6 and universal thresholding is chosen as mother wavelet and noise level estimator.

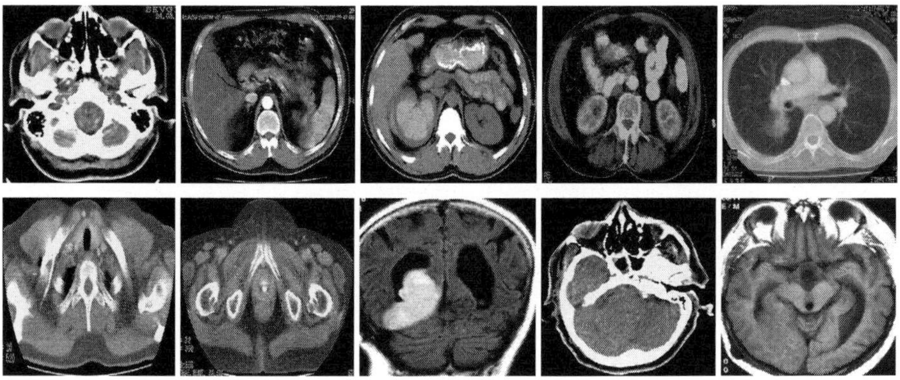

Fig. 12. Medical test images.

Level	PSNR
1	68.1196
2	69.3269
3	70.5006
4	70.7768
5	68.6232
6	68.8183
7	68.7272
8	69.8037
9	66.8912
10	66.3877

Table 3. PSNR values respect to decomposition level after DWT denoising.

The best PSNR is obtained at the decomposition level of two. As can be seen in Table 3, the result PSNR value is decreasing if the decomposition level getting higher. The wavelet transform concern the main component of the original signal when the decomposition level is increased. If the higher decomposition level is used, the thresholding can eliminate some coefficients of the original signal, as in 1D signal denoising process. Therefore, to increase the decomposition level too high will decrease the PSNR after an optimal level and also increase the complexity of decomposition. In further part of the study, the decomposition level is chosen as two because the performance of the DWT denoising obtained at this level. Another question about the performance of the wavelet denoising is if it is dependent on the content or the distribution of the coefficient of the image. We can answer the question by applying the denoising algorithm on different images. Table 4 represents the PSNR values respect to the number of the test images given in Fig. 9 after the denoising process.

Number	Noisy Image	Denoised Image (level1)	Denoised Image (level2)	Denoised Image (level3)	Denoised Image (level4)
1	62.0974	68.1252	73.2903	72.9250	70.3792
2	62.1251	67.3979	69.3305	68.4441	67.3593
3	62.1140	67.9648	71.7193	70.4829	68.8435
4	62.0942	67.9819	72.2531	72.4830	70.8092
5	62.0974	67.0273	69.5873	69.9803	69.2444
6	62.1023	67.8774	71.7282	71.4382	70.0891
7	62.1138	67.6268	70.6594	70.8403	69.8362
8	62.0995	68.1391	73.7535	74.2233	71.6437
9	62.1224	67.9712	71.3191	69.4574	67.9060
10	62.1070	67.9048	71.0798	69.1241	67.4048
Mean Standard Deviation	62.1069 0,176	67.8016 0.3521	71.4721 1.4230	70.9399 1.8322	69.3515 1.4656

Table 4. PSNR's respect to image number, mean and standart deviation.

6. Conclusion

The wavelet denoising techniques offers high quality and flexibility for the noise problem of signals and image. The performances of denoising methods for several variations including thresholding rules and the type of wavelet were examined in the examples in order to put forward the suitable denoising results of the methods. The comparisons have made for the three threshold estimation methods, wavelet types and the threshold types. The examinations have showed that most important factor in wavelet denoising is what the decomposition level is rather than the wavelet type, threshold type or the estimation of threshold value.

However, someone has not seen any noteworthy differences in the methods from level one to level six, after this level, rigresure method has showed a better performance than the other methods in terms of SNR level. Consequently, it is determined that the wavelet type is not very important if the oscillation number is not very low, the decomposition level is absolutely depends on the frequency band of the signal to be analyzed and its sampling frequency.

7. References

Akay, M. and C. Mello (1998). Wavelets for biomedical signal processing, IEEE.

Akay, M., J. Semmlow, et al. (1990). "Detection of coronary occlusions using autoregressive modeling of diastolic heart sounds." Biomedical Engineering, IEEE Transactions on 37(4): 366-373.

Alfaouri, M. and K. Daqrouq (2008). "ECG signal denoising by wavelet transform thresholding." American Journal of Applied Sciences 5(3): 276-281.

Beylkin, G., R. Coifman, et al. (1991). "Fast wavelet transforms and numerical algorithms I." Communications on pure and applied mathematics 44(2): 141-183.

Blu, T. (1998). "A new design algorithm for two-band orthonormal rational filter banks and orthonormal rational wavelets." Signal Processing, IEEE Transactions on 46(6): 1494-1504.

Buades, A., B. Coll, et al. (2006). "A review of image denoising algorithms, with a new one." Multiscale Modeling and Simulation 4(2): 490-530.

Chang, T. and C. C. J. Kuo (1993). "Texture analysis and classification with tree-structured wavelet transform." Image Processing, IEEE Transactions on 2(4): 429-441.

Chen, G. and T. Bui (2003). "Multiwavelets denoising using neighboring coefficients." Signal Processing Letters, IEEE 10(7): 211-214.

Chen, G., T. Bui, et al. (2010). "Denoising of three dimensional data cube using bivariate wavelet shrinking." Image Analysis and Recognition: 45-51.

Cohen, A., I. Daubechies, et al. (1993). "Wavelets on the interval and fast wavelet transforms." Applied and Computational Harmonic Analysis 1(1): 54-81.

Daubechies, I. (1990). "The wavelet transform, time-frequency localization and signal analysis." Information Theory, IEEE Transactions on 36(5): 961-1005.

Do, M. and M. Vetterli (2002). Texture similarity measurement using Kullback-Leibler distance on wavelet subbands, IEEE.

Donoho, D. L. (1995). "Denoising by soft-thresholding." IEEE Trans. Inform. Theory 41(3): 613-627.

Donoho, D. L. and I. M. Johnstone (1994). "Ideal spatial adaptation via wavelet shrinkage." Biometrika 81(3): 425-455.

Donoho, D. L. and I. M. Johnstone (1998). "Minimax estimation via wavelet shrinkage." Annals of statistics: 879-921.

Donoho, D. L. and J. M. Johnstone (1994). "Ideal spatial adaptation by wavelet shrinkage." Biometrika 81(3): 425.

Ergen, B., Y. Tatar, et al. (2010). "Time-frequency analysis of phonocardiogram signals using wavelet transform: a comparative study." Computer Methods in Biomechanics and Biomedical Engineering 99999(1): 1-1.

Fischer, T. R. (1992). "On the rate-distortion efficiency of subband coding." Information Theory, IEEE Transactions on 38(2): 426-428.

Giaouris, D., J. W. Finch, et al. (2008). "Wavelet denoising for electric drives." Industrial Electronics, IEEE Transactions on 55(2): 543-550.

He, X. and M. S. Scordilis (2008). "Psychoacoustic music analysis based on the discrete wavelet packet transform." Research Letters in Signal Processing 2008: 1-5.

Heric, D. and D. Zazula (2007). "Combined edge detection using wavelet transform and signal registration." Image and Vision Computing 25(5): 652-662.

Jansen, M. (2001). Noise reduction by wavelet thresholding, Springer USA.

Jiang, Q. (1998). "Orthogonal multiwavelets with optimum time-frequency resolution." Signal Processing, IEEE Transactions on 46(4): 830-844.

Jovanov, L., A. Pi urica, et al. (2010). "Fuzzy logic-based approach to wavelet denoising of 3D images produced by time-of-flight cameras." Optics Express 18(22): 22651-22676.

Lang, M., H. Guo, et al. (1996). "Noise reduction using an undecimated discrete wavelet transform." Signal Processing Letters, IEEE 3(1): 10-12.

Lewis, A. S. and G. Knowles (1992). "Image compression using the 2-D wavelet transform." Image Processing, IEEE Transactions on 1(2): 244-250.

Mallat, S. and Z. Zhang (1993). "Matching pursuits with time-frequency dictionaries." IEEE Transactions on signal processing 41(12): 3397-3415.

Mallat, S. G. (1989). "A theory for multiresolution signal decomposition: The wavelet representation." Pattern Analysis and Machine Intelligence, IEEE Transactions on 11(7): 674-693.

Mallat, S. G. (1999). A wavelet tour of signal processing, Academic Pr.

Meyer, F., A. Averbuch, et al. (2002). "Fast adaptive wavelet packet image compression." Image Processing, IEEE Transactions on 9(5): 792-800.

Misiti, M., Y. Misiti, et al. "Wavelet Toolbox(tm) 4." Matlab User's Guide, Mathworks.

Moulin, P. and J. Liu (1999). "Analysis of multiresolution image denoising schemes using generalized Gaussian and complexity priors." Information Theory, IEEE Transactions on 45(3): 909-919.

Nasri, M. and H. Nezamabadi-pour (2009). "Image denoising in the wavelet domain using a new adaptive thresholding function." Neurocomputing 72(4-6): 1012-1025.

Pizurica, A., A. M. Wink, et al. (2006). "A review of wavelet denoising in MRI and ultrasound brain imaging." Current Medical Imaging Reviews 2(2): 247-260.

Portilla, J., V. Strela, et al. (2003). "Image denoising using scale mixtures of Gaussians in the wavelet domain." Image Processing, IEEE Transactions on 12(11): 1338-1351.

Qian, S. and D. Chen (1999). "Joint time-frequency analysis." Signal Processing Magazine, IEEE 16(2): 52-67.

Qu, Y., B. Adam, et al. (2003). "Data reduction using a discrete wavelet transform in discriminant analysis of very high dimensionality data." Biometrics 59(1): 143-151.

Rioul, O. and M. Vetterli (1991). "Wavelets and signal processing." Signal Processing Magazine, IEEE 8(4): 14-38.

Sen, O., S. Zhengxiang, et al. (2002). "Application of wavelet soft-threshold de-noising technique to power quality detection [J]." Automation of Electric Power Systems 19.

Simoncelli, E. P. and E. H. Adelson (1996). Noise removal via Bayesian wavelet coring, IEEE.

Valens, C. "A Really Friendly Guide to Wavelets. 1999." URL: http://perso. orange. fr /polyvalens/ clemens/ wavelets/ wavelets. html [Last accessed: 13 December 2007].

Vetterli, M. and C. Herley (1992). "Wavelets and filter banks: Theory and design." Signal Processing, IEEE Transactions on 40(9): 2207-2232.

Vetterli, M. and J. Kova evi (1995). Wavelets and subband coding, Citeseer.

Vetterli, M. and J. Kovacevic (1995). Wavelets and Subband Coding. Englewood Clis, NJ: Prentice-Hall.

Wachowiak, M. P., G. S. Rash, et al. (2000). "Wavelet-based noise removal for biomechanical signals: A comparative study." Biomedical Engineering, IEEE Transactions on 47(3): 360-368.

Wink, A. M. and J. B. T. M. Roerdink (2004). "Denoising functional MR images: a comparison of wavelet denoising and Gaussian smoothing." Medical Imaging, IEEE Transactions on 23(3): 374-387.

Zou, H. and A. H. Tewfik (1993). "Parametrization of compactly supported orthonormal wavelets." Signal Processing, IEEE Transactions on 41(3): 1428-1431.

22

A DFT-DWT Domain Invisible Blind Watermarking Techniques for Copyright Protection of Digital Images

Munesh Chandra
DIT School of Engineering, Greater Noida India

1. Introduction

The great success of Internet and digital multimedia technology have made the fast communication of digital data, easy editing in any part of the digital content, capability to copy a digital content without any loss in quality of the content and many other advantages.

The great explosion in this technology has also brought some problems beside its advantages. The great facility in copying a digital content rapidly, perfectly and without limitations on the number of copies has resulted the problem of copyright protection. Digital watermarking is proposed as a solution to prove the ownership of digital data. A watermark, a secret imperceptible signal, is embedded into the original data in such a way that it remains present as long as the perceptible quality of the content is at an acceptable level. The owner of the original data proves his/her ownership by extracting the watermark from the watermarked content in case of multiple ownership claims

In general, any watermarking scheme (algorithm) consists of three parts.

- The watermark.
- The encoder (insertion algorithm).
- The decoder and comparator (verification or extraction or detection algorithm).

Each owner has a unique watermark or an owner can also put different watermarks in different objects the marking algorithm incorporates the watermark into the object. The verification algorithm authenticates the object determining both the owner and the integrity of the object [1].

1.1 Embedding process

Let us denote an image by I, a signature by $S = s_1, s_2, \ldots$ and the watermarked image by I'. E is an encoder function, it takes an image I and a signature S, and it generates new image which is called watermarked image I', mathematically,

$$E(I, S) = I' \quad (1)$$

It should be noted that the signature S may be dependent on image *I*. In such cases, the encoding process described by (1) still holds. The figure 1 illustrates the encoding process [1].

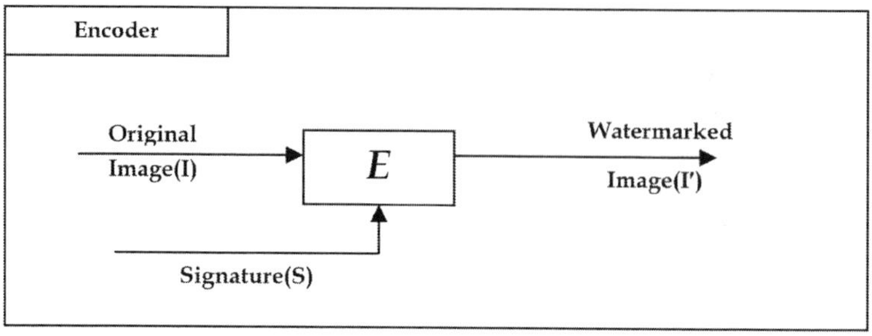

Fig. 1. Encoder

1.2 Extraction process

A decoder function *D* takes an image *J* (*J* can be a watermarked or un-watermarked. image, and possibly corrupted) whose ownership is to be determined and recovers a signature S′ from the image [1].

In this process an additional image *I* can also be included which is often the original and un-watermarked version of J. This is due to the fact that some encoding schemes may make use of the original images in the watermarking process to provide extra robustness against intentional and unintentional corruption of pixels. Mathematically,

$$D\,(J,\,I) = S' \tag{2}$$

In proposed algorithm, original image is not used while extracting watermark from watermarked image and we provide robustness by using some keys.

The extracted signature S' will then be compared with the owner signature sequence by a comparator function C_δ and a binary output decision generated. It is 1 if there is match and 0 otherwise, which can be represented as follows.

$$C_3(S',\,S) = \begin{Bmatrix} 1.\ c \le \delta \\ 0.\ \text{Otherwise} \end{Bmatrix} \tag{3}$$

Where *C* is the correlator, x= c_3(S,S′). *C* is the correlation of two signatures and δ is certain threshold. Without loss of generality, watermarking scheme can be treated as a three-tupple (*E, D,* C_δ). Following figure 2 & figure 3 demonstrate the decoder and the comparator respectively.

A watermark must be detectable or extractable to be useful. Depending on the way the watermark is inserted and depending on the nature of the watermarking algorithm, the method used can involve very distinct approaches. In some watermarking schemes, a watermark can be extracted in its exact form, a procedure we call watermark extraction. In

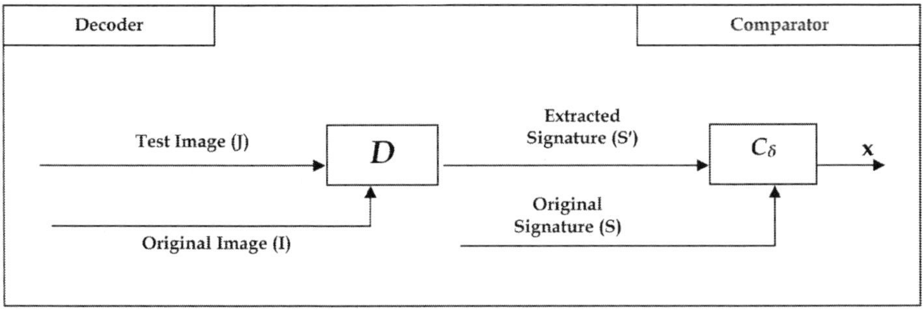

Fig. 2. Decoder

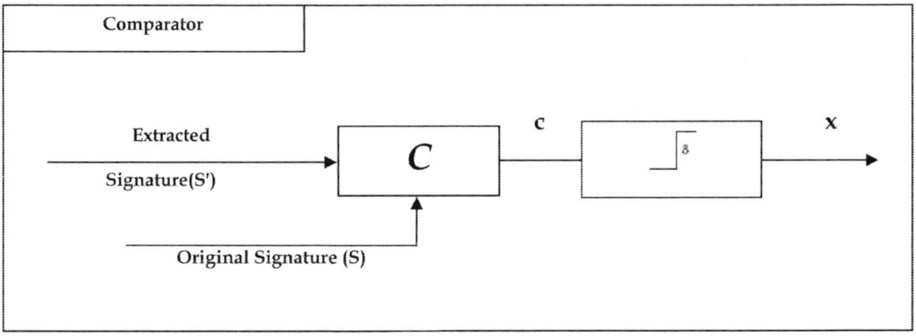

Fig. 3. Comparator

other cases, we can detect only whether a specific given watermarking signal is present in an image, a procedure we call watermark detection. It should be noted that watermark extraction can prove ownership whereas watermark detection can only verify ownership.

The proposed technique extract watermark to prove ownership.

The quality of extracted watermark can also be measured by: *PSNR* (Peak Signal-to-Noise Ratio) and *AR* (Accuracy rate)

PSNR is provided only to give us a rough approximation of the quality of the watermark.

$$\mathrm{PSNR} = 10\log_{10}\left(\frac{255^{Z}}{\mathrm{MSE}}\right)\mathrm{dB} \tag{4}$$

Where *MSE* is mean square error of an image with H × W pixels is defined as:

$$\mathrm{MSE} = \frac{1}{\mathrm{HXW}}\sum_{i=1}^{H}\sum_{j=1}^{W}\left(a_{ij} - \bar{a}_{ij}\right)^{2} \tag{5}$$

Where a_{ij} is the original pixel value and $\bar{a}_{ij}$ is the processed pixel value.

Besides, we utilized the accuracy rate *AR* to evaluate the robustness of a copyright protection scheme for a specific attack. The formula for *AR* is shown below:

$$\mathrm{AR} = \frac{\mathrm{CP}}{\mathrm{NP}} \tag{6}$$

Where *NP* is the number of pixels of the watermark image and *CP* is the number of correct pixels in the extracted watermark image.

1.3 Classification of watermarking techniques

Watermarking techniques can be divided into four categories according to the type of document to be watermarked as follows [1]: Text Watermarking, Image Watermarking, Audio Watermarking and Video Watermarking.

In the case of images from implementation point of view, watermarks can be applied in spatial domain and in frequency domain. In Spatial domain, pixels of one and two randomly selected subsets of an image are modified based on perceptual analysis of the original image. In Frequency domain, values of certain frequencies are altered from their original.

According to human perception, digital watermarks can be divided into three categories as follows [2]: Visible, Invisible-robust and Invisible-Fragile. Visible watermark is where the secondary translucent overlaid into the primary content and appears visible on a careful inspection. Invisible-Robust watermark is embedded is such a way changes made to the pixel value are perceptually unnoticed. Invisible –Fragile watermark is embedded in such a way that any manipulation of the content would alter or destroy the watermark. Sometimes another watermarking called dual watermarking is used. Dual watermark is a combination of a visible and an invisible watermark [1]. In this type of watermark an invisible watermark is used as a back up for the visible watermark as clear from the following diagram.

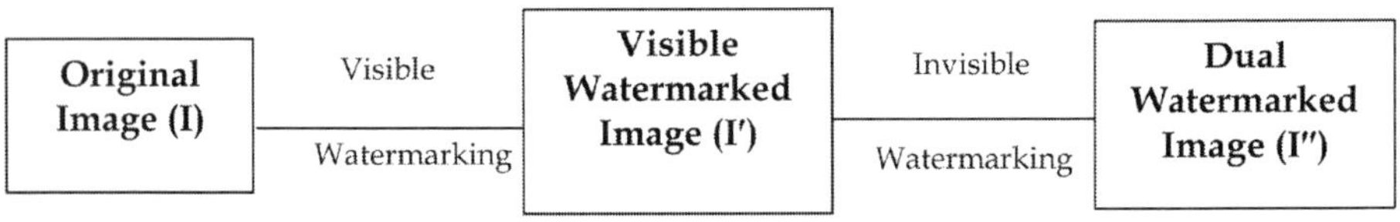

Fig. 4. Schematic representation of dual watermarking

From application point of view, digital watermarking could also be [2]: source based and destination based. In source based a unique watermark identifying the owner is introduced to all the copies of particular content being distributed. Destination based is where each distributed copy gets a unique watermark identifying the particular buyer. Different types of watermarks are shown in the figure. 5.

Current digital image watermarking techniques can be grouped into two major classes: spatial-domain and frequency-domain watermarking techniques [3]. Compared to spatial domain techniques [4], frequency-domain watermarking techniques proved to be more effective with respect to achieving the imperceptibility and robustness requirements of digital watermarking algorithms [5].

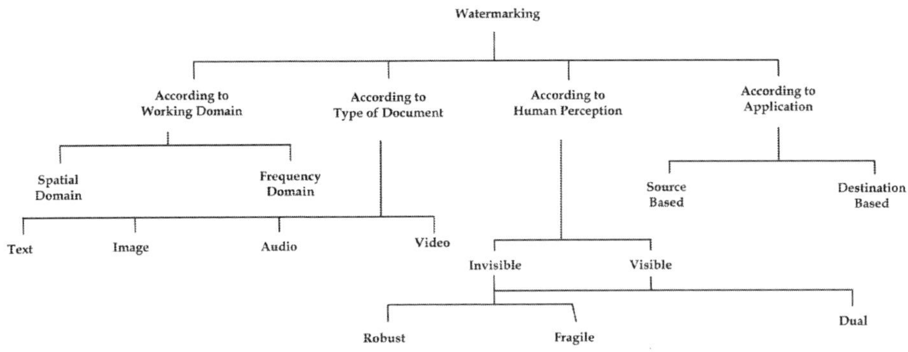

Fig. 5. Types of watermarking techniques

Commonly used frequency-domain transforms include the Discrete Wavelet Transform (DWT), the Discrete Cosine Transform (DCT) and Discrete Fourier Transform (DFT). The host signal is transformed into a different domain and the watermark is embedded in selective coefficients. Here we have described DFT and DWT domain techniques.

1.3.1 Discrete Fourier transform

The Discrete Fourier Transformation (DFT) controls the frequency of the host signal. Energy of watermarking message can be distributed averagly in space domain after the signal is implemented DFT. It enables the schemes further to embed the watermark with the magnitude of its coefficients.

Given a two-dimensional signal f(x, y), the DFT is defined

$$F(u,v)=\frac{1}{MN}\sum_{x=0}^{M-1}\sum_{y=0}^{N-1}f(x,y)e^{(-j2\pi(ux/M+vy/N))} \tag{7}$$

For u = 0, 1, 2..., M-1, v = 0, 1, 2 ,., N-1 and $j=\sqrt{-1}$

The inverse DFT (IDFT) is given by:

$$F(x,y)=\sum_{u=0}^{M-1}\sum_{v=0}^{N-1}F(u,v)e^{(j2\pi(ux/M+vy/N))} \tag{8}$$

where, (M, N) are the dimensions of the image.

The DFT is useful for watermarking purposes because it helps in selecting the adequate parts of the image for embedding, in order to achieve the highest invisibility and robustness.

1.3.2 The wavelets transform

Wavelet transform decomposes an image into a set of band limited components which can be reassembled to reconstruct the original image without error. The DWT (Discrete Wavelet Transform) divide the input image into four non-overlapping multi-resolution sub-bands

LL1, LH1, HL1 and HH1. The process can then be repeated to computes multiple "scale" wavelet decomposition, as in the 2 scale wavelet transform shown in Fig. 6.

One of the many advantages over the wavelet transform is that it is believed to more accurately model aspects of the HVS as compared to the FFT or DCT. This allows us to use higher energy watermarks in regions that the HVS is known to be less sensitive, such as the middle frequency bands (LH, HL) and high resolution band (HH). But watermark embedded in high resolution band can be easily be distorted by geometric transformation, compression and various signal processing operations.

Embedding watermarks in middle frequency regions allow us to increase the robustness of our watermark, at little to no additional impact on image quality [6].

<table>
<tr><td>LL_2</td><td>HL_2</td><td rowspan="2">HL_1</td></tr>
<tr><td>LH_2</td><td>HH_2</td></tr>
<tr><td colspan="2">LH_1</td><td>HH_1</td></tr>
</table>

Fig. 6. Scale 2 Dimensional DWT

1.4 Watermarking applications

Although the main motivation behind the digital watermarking is the copyright protection, its applications are not that restricted. There is a wide application area of digital watermarking, including broadcast monitoring, fingerprinting, authentication and covet communication [7, 8, 9, 10].

By embedding watermarks into commercial advertisements, the advertisements can be monitored whether the advertisements are broadcasted at the correct instants by means of an automated system [7, 8]. The system receives the broadcast and searches these watermarks identifying where and when the advertisement is broadcasted. The same process can also be used for video and sound clips. Musicians and actors may request to ensure that they receive accurate royalties for broadcasts of their performances.

Fingerprinting is a novel approach to trace the source of illegal copies [7, 8]. The owner of the digital data may embed different watermarks in the copies of digital content customized for each recipient. In this manner, the owner can identify the customer by extracting the watermark in the case the data is supplied to third parties. The digital watermarking can also be used for authentication [7, 8]. The authentication is the detection of whether the content of the digital content has changed. As a solution, a fragile watermark embedded to the digital content indicates whether the data has been altered. If any tampering has occurred in the content, the same change will also occur on the watermark. It can also provide information about the part of the content that has been altered.

Covert communication is another possible application of digital watermarking [7,8]. The watermark, secret message, can be embedded imperceptibly to the digital image or video to communicate information from the sender to the intended receiver while maintaining low probability of intercept by other unintended receivers.

There are also non-secure applications of digital watermarking. It can be used for indexing of videos, movies and news items where markers and comments can be inserted by search engines [8]. Another non-secure application of watermarking is detection and concealment of image/video transmission errors [11]. For block based coded images, a summarizing data of every block is extracted and hidden to another block by data hiding. At the decoder side, this data is used to detect and conceal the block errors.

1.5 Watermarking requirements

The efficiency of a digital watermarking process is evaluated according to the properties of perceptual transparency, robustness, computational cost, bit rate of data embedding process, false positive rate, recovery of data with or without access to the original signal, the speed of embedding and retrieval process, the ability of the embedding and retrieval module to integrate into standard encoding and decoding process etc. 7, 8, 9, 12, 13].

Depending on the application, the properties, which are used mainly in the evaluation process, varies.

The main requirements for copyright protection are imperceptibility and robustness to intended or non-intended any signal operations and capacity.

The owner of the original data wants to prove his/her ownership in case the original data is copied, edited and used without permission of the owner. In the watermarking research world, this problem has been analyzed in a more detailed manner [13, 14, 15, 16, 17, 18].

The imperceptibility refers to the perceptual similarity between the original and watermarked data. The owner of the original data mostly does not tolerate any kind of degradations in his/her original data. Therefore, the original and watermarked data should be perceptually the same. Robustness to a signal processing operation refers to the ability to detect the watermark, after the watermarked data has passed through that signal processing operation.

The robustness of a watermarking scheme can vary from one operation to another. Although it is possible for a watermarking scheme to be robust to any signal compression operations, it may not be robust to geometric distortions such as cropping, rotation, translation etc. The signal processing operations, for which the watermarking scheme should be robust, changes from application to application as well. While, for the broadcast monitoring application, only the robustness to the transmission of the data in a channel is sufficient, this is not the case for copyright protection application of digital watermarking. For such a case, it is totally unknown through which signal processing operations the watermarked data will pass. Hence, the watermarking scheme should be robust to any possible signal processing operations, as long as the quality of the watermarked data preserved.

The capacity requirement of the watermarking scheme refers to be able to verify and distinguish between different watermarks with a low probability of error as the number of differently watermarked versions of an image increases [17]. While the robustness of the watermarking method increases, the capacity also increases where the imperceptibility decreases. There is a trade off between these requirements and this trade off should be taken into account while the watermarking method is being proposed.

2. Proposed techniques

We have proposed a blind invisible watermarking technique for copyright protection of the colored images.

In blind techniques, during the extraction process original image is not required. Watermarking systems which involve marking imperceptible alteration on the cover data to convey the hidden information, is called invisible watermarking. Here 512*512 grayscale image of 'peppers' is taken as host image and 32*32 binary image is taken as watermark image.

Then implement second level wavelet transform on host image using wavelet function 'haar' and extracted middle level components (HL_2, LH_2) for embedding watermark. Middle level components are selected for embedding watermark as much of the signal energy lies at low-frequencies sub-band which contains the most important visual parts of the image and high frequency components of the image are usually removed through compression and noise attacks.

We have divided the HL_2 and LH_2 bands in to 4x4 blocks and applied DFT in these blocks and used to two highly uncorrelated pseudo random sequences (treated as key: key1) to embed watermarking message according to template matrix. We reshaped watermark image of 32x32 into a row vector of size 1024, called watermark message.

A template matrix is such a matrix whose size is 4x4 and elements are 0 and 1. Watermarking message is embedded into image blocks only in the position where the template matrix's element is 1. Through amounts of experiments, we found when the template matrix is set to $[1,1,1,1;1,0,0,1;0,0,0,1;0,0,0,1]^T$,imperceptibility and robustness of the algorithm can get better balance. Here template matrix is used as a key2.

We have embedded watermark according to the (9) given below.

$$I_w(x, y) = I(x, y) + k * W(x, y) \tag{9}$$

In (9), k denotes a gain factor, and I_W the resulting watermarked image, I the cover image and W the watermark to be embedded. Increasing k increases the robustness of the watermark at the expense of the quality of the watermarked image.

The algorithm for the proposed method is given below:

The watermark embedding steps are as follows:

- Implement second level wavelet transform on host Image H using wavelet function 'Haar' and Extract middle frequency components (LH_2, HL_2).
- Divide the HL_2, LH_2 components in several blocks of size 4x4 and DFT is applied to these blocks.
- Perform search to find highly uncorrelated pseudo random (PN) sequences (seq_zero and seq_one) and use these as a key1.
- Defines the template matrix of an 4x4.
- Set gain factor K and embed the watermark to the cover image under the following rule:
- If wa(i,j) ==0 then

If template(m,n)==1 then
I(m,n)=I(m,n) + K*seq_zero(m,n)
End
Else
if template(m,n)==1 then
I(m,n)=I(m,n)+K*seq_one(m,n)
End
End
Where $1 \leq i \leq M$, $1 \leq j \leq N$, and $1 \leq m,n \leq 4$
Here I denotes to 4x4 DFT blocks.

- Apply IFFT to each image block and use the result as the middle frequency component of DWT to recover the component which has been embedded watermarking messages.
- Replace the component of the host image by the watermarked component.
- Display watermarked image.

The watermark extraction steps of this technique are as follows:

- Implement Wavelet transform on Host image using wavelet function 'Haar' and Extract middle frequency components (LH_2, HL_2).
- Divide the HL_2, LH_2 components in several blocks of size 4x4 and DFT is applied to these blocks.
- Use same highly uncorrelated PN sequences (key1) and the template matrix of 4x4 (key2) to select elements that are embedded watermarking message to make up sequence.
- Calculate the correlation separately between sequence and seq_zero and between sequence and seq_one. The result is stored in corr_zero and corr_one respectively.
- Detect the watermark according the following rule:
  If corr_zero(i) > corr_one(i) then
  watermark_detected(i)=0;
  Else
  watermark_detected(i)=1
  End
  - Reshape the recovered message.
  - Display recovered message.
  - Calculate the quality of recovered image by using PSNR function according to the (4).
  - Calculate the Accuracy rate of recovered image by using AR function as per the (6).

3. Experimental results

In this section, we show some experimental results to demonstrate the effectiveness and success of our digital watermarking techniques. The standard 512 × 512 grayscale image "pepper" is used as host image, as shown in Fig. 7. The 32 × 32-pixels binary image is used as the watermark image, as shown in Fig. 8.

We applied the peak-signal to noise rate (PSNR) given in (4) to measure the image quality of an attacked image and accuracy rate AR given in (5) to evaluate the robustness of a copyright protection scheme for a specific attack.

Fig. 7. Original image of pepper

Fig. 8. Watermark image

3.1 Experimental result and analysis

The experimental results are represented in the following, respectively for watermarked image and extracted watermark image as shown in Fig. 9 (i), and Fig. 9 (ii), while taking the different values of gain factor *K*. And various observations for experiment are depicted in Table I.

K=10

K=20

K=30

K=50

Fig. 9. (i) Watermarked image, (ii) Extracted watermark image

Exhaustive testing against signal processing operation, Geometric distortion , collusion still has to be performed.

Gain Factor(K)	Execution Time	AR	PSNR
K=10	176.6796	89.4532	60.3456
K=20	175.6307	93.0640	55.2389
K=30	173.3867	91.3765	54.7829
K=40	175.3912	93.5621	54.6047

Table 1.

4. Conclusion

The need for digital watermarking on electronic distribution of copyright material is becoming more prevalent. In this paper an overview of the digital watermarking techniques are given and a blind invisible watermarking technique for grayscale images based on DWT and DFT is presented. The algorithm use 512*512 gray images as a host image and 32*32 binary image as watermarked image.

Firstly, two level wavelet decomposition is implemented on the host image. Then, the middle frequency components are extracted and divided in to several blocks of size 4*4 and DFT is implemented on them. Finally, two pseudo random sequences are created and embedded to blocks which have implemented DFT according to whether the corresponding position is 0 or 1 in the watermark matrix which has been implemented.

The original image is not required while extracting the watermark Instead, correlations among each block and two sequences are respectively calculated. Watermark is recovered on foundation of the relative magnitude of correlation between the corresponding block and one sequence or the other. The idea of applying two transform is based on the fact that combined transforms could compensate for the drawbacks of each other, resulting in effective watermarking.

5. References

[1] S.P. Mohanty, et al., "A Dual Watermarking Technique for Images", Proc.7th ACM International Multimedia Conference, ACM-MM'99, Part 2, pp 49-51, Orlando, USA, Oct. 1999

[2] Yusnita Yusof and Othman O. Khalifa , "Digital Watermarking For Digital Images Using Wavelet Transform", Proc 2007 IEEE conference, pp 665-669

[3] Potdar, V., S. Han and E. Chang, 2005. "A Survey of Digital Image Watermarking Techniques", in Proc. of the IEEE International Conference on Industrial Informatics, pp: 709-716, Perth, Australia.

[4] Chan, C. and L. Cheng, 2004. "Hiding Data in Images by Simple LSB Substitution", Pattern Recognition, 37(3):469-474.

[5] Wang, R., C. Lin and J. Lin, " Copyright protection of digital images by means of frequency domain watermarking," Proc. of the SPIE Conference On Mathematics of Data/Image Coding, Compression, and Encryption, USA.

[6] G. Langelaar, I. Setyawan, R.L. Lagendijk, "Watermarking Digital Image and Video Data", in IEEE Signal Processing Magazine, Vol 17, pp 20-43, September 2000.

[7] Ingemar J.Cox, Matt L. Miller and Jeffrey A. Bloom, "Watermarking Applications and their properties", Int. Conf. On Information Technology'2000, Las Vegas, 2000.

[8] Gerhard C. Langelaar, Iwan Setyawan, and Reginald L. Lagendijk, "Watermarking Digital Image and Video Data", IEEE Signal Processing Magazine, September 2000.

[9] Maurice Mass, Ton Kalker, Jean-Paul M.G Linnartz, Joop Talstra, Geert F. G. Depovere, and Jaap Haitsma, " Digital Watermarking for DVD Video Copy Protection", IEEE Signal Processing Magazine, September 2000.

[10] Fabien A.P. Petitcolas, " Watermarking Schemes Evaulation", IEEE Signal Processing Magazine, September 2000

[11] Technical Report, submitted to The Scientific and Technical Research Council of Turkey (Tübitak) under project EEEAG 101E007, April 2002

[12] Jean François Delaigle, " Protection of Intellectual Property of Images by perceptual Watermarking", Ph.D Thesis submitted for the degree of Doctor of Applied Sciences, Universite Catholique de Louvain, Belgique.

[13] Ingemar J. Cox, Joe Kilian, Tom Leighton, and Talal Shamoon, "Secure Spread Spectrum Watermarking for Multimedia", IEEE Trans. on Image Processing, 6, 12, 1673-1687, (1997).

[14] Mitchell D. Swanson, Mei Kobayashi, and Ahmed H. Tewfik, "Multimedia Data-Embedding and Watermarking Technologies", Proceedings of the IEEE., Vol. 86, No. 6, June 1998.

[15] Mitchell D. Swanson, Bin Zhu, and Ahmed H. Tewfik, "Transparent Robust Image Watermarking", 1996 SPIE Conf. on Visual Communications and Image Proc.

[16] Christine I. Podilchuk and Wenjun Zeng, " Image-Adaptive Watermarking Using Visual Models", IEEE Journal of Selected Areas in Communications, Vol.16, No.4, May 1998.

[17] Raymond B. Wolfgang, Christine I. Podilchuk and Edward J. Delp, "Perceptual Watermarks for Image and Video", Proceedings of the IEEE, Vol. 87, No. 7, July 1998.

[18] Sergio D. Servetto, Christine I. Podilchuk, Kannan Ramchandran, "Capacity Issues in Digital Image Watermarking", In the Proceedings of the IEEE International Conference on Image Processing (ICIP), Chicago, IL, October 1998.

23

The Wavelet Transform as a Classification Criterion Applied to Improve Compression of Hyperspectral Images

Daniel Acevedo and Ana Ruedin
Departamento de Computación
Facultad de Ciencias Exactas y Naturales
Universidad de Buenos Aires
Argentina

1. Introduction

Satellites continually feeding images to their base, pose a challenge as to the design of compression techniques to store these huge data volumes. We aim at lossless compression of hyperspectral images having around 200 bands, such as AVIRIS images. These images consist of several images (or bands) obtained by filtering radiation from the earth at different wavelengths. Compression is generally achieved through reduction of spatial as well as spectral correlations.

Most of the hyperspectral compressors are prediction–based. Since spectral correlation is usually high (much more higher than spatial correlation) pixels are predicted with other pixels in an adjacent band (rather than other pixels surrounding the one to be predicted). SLSQ (Rizzo et al., 2005), a low-complexity method designed for hyperspectral image compression, performs a simple prediction for each pixel, by taking a constant times the same pixel in the previous band. The constant is calculated by least squares over 4 previously encoded neighboring pixels. SLSQ–OPT version of SLSQ performs one band look–ahead to determine if the whole band is better compressed this way or with intraband prediction, while in the SLSQ–HEU version this decision is taken by an offline heuristic. CCAP (Wang et al., 2005) predicts a pixel with the conditional expected value of a pixel given the context. The expected value is calculated over coded pixels having matching (highly correlated) contexts. Slyz and Zhang (Slyz & Zhang, 2005) propose 2 compressors (BH and LM) for hyperspectral images. BH predicts a block as a scalar times the same block in the previous band. Coding contexts are defined by the quantized average error. LM predicts a pixel by choosing among different intraband predictions the one that works best for several pixels at the same position in previous bands.

Mielikainen and Toivanen proposed C-DPCM (Mielikainen & Toivanen, 2003), a method that classifies the pixels at the same location and through all the bands, with vector quantization. Interband prediction is performed using the pixels at the same position in 20 previous bands. Weights, calculated for each class/ band, are sent into the code, as well as the 2D template with the classes. Aiazzi et al. (Aiazzi et al., 1999) classify the prediction context of every pixel using fuzzy clustering, and then calculate the weights for each class. For compression of hyperspectral images (Aiazzi et al., 2007) they divide each band into small blocks (16×16), they calculate weights for interband prediction over each pixel in a block, and then make a fuzzy clustering of the weights obtained for all the blocks. For each pixel a membership degree is computed according to the efficiency of the weights (from different clusters) on a causal context of the pixel. The final prediction for a pixel is obtained by a combination of linear predictions involving weights from different clusters, pondered by the degrees of membership of the pixel to each cluster. It is worth mentioning that wavelet-based compressors such as JPEG2000 (Taubman & Marcellin, 2002) have been successfully used for lossy compression of multiband images, either hyperspectral (Blanes & Serra-Sagrista, 2010; Fowler & Rucker, 2007) or general earth data (Kulkarni et al., 2006).

In this work we will improve the well-known algorithm which was developed for hyperspectral images: LAIS-LUT. This algorithm makes predictions of each pixel using other pixels in the same band. Which pixel is used for prediction is determined by inspecting in the previously encoded band. This algorithm uses two possible candidates for prediction. We will introduce the wavelet transform as a tool for classification in order to make better decisions about which of these two possible candidates acts as a more appropriate prediction. First, LAIS-LUT will be introduced, as well as the LUT algorithm on which it is based. Then we show how the wavelet transform is used to improve it. Finally, we give some results and conclusions of our method, called Enhanced LAIS-LUT.

2. Look-up table based algorithms

2.1 LUT algorithm

The Look Up Table algorithm (Mielikainen, 2006) is a fast compression technique based on predicting a pixel with another pixel from the same band. The previous band is inspected in order to determine which pixel in the same band is used for prediction. As an example, suppose pixel $I_{x,y}^{(z)}$ in band z wants to be predicted. Then we seek on band $z-1$ the pixel with the same intensity as $I_{x,y}^{(z-1)}$ which is nearest to it in a causal neighborhood. Let $I_{x',y'}^{(z-1)}$ be that pixel. Then, the prediction for pixel $I_{x,y}^{(z)}$ will be $I_{x',y'}^{(z)}$. If no match is found, pixel $I_{x,y}^{(z-1)}$ is the one selected for prediction. In order to speed things up, a look up table data structure is used for searching the pixel on the previous band. With this data structure the algorithm is efficiently implemented as shown in Fig 1 for consecutive bands z and $z-1$. Then, the difference $I^{(z)} - P^{(z)}$ between the band and its prediction is entropy coded and this process is repeated for $z = 2, \ldots, 224$.

In Fig. 2 entropy values are ploted for each band of the Jasper Ridge image. In dashed line, entropies of the pixels of the image are ploted. 6 steps of the 2D S+P wavelet transform were computed and the entropy of the coefficients is plotted in dotted line for each band. Finally it is shown in gray line the entropy of the prediction differences for the LUT algorithm. It is remarkable how high is the compression achieved with this simple algorithm, which is only based on indexing and updating a table. It is entirely based on the premise of high correlation between bands and designed in order to take advantage of this fact.

Data: Bands $I^{(z)}$, $I^{(z-1)}$ and table initialized as $\text{LUTable}(i) = i$
Result: Prediction for band z: $P^{(z)}$
for *every pixel* $I^{(z)}_{x,y}$ **do**
  $P^{(z)}_{x,y} \leftarrow \text{LUTable}(I^{(z-1)}_{x,y})$;
  $\text{LUTable}(I^{(z-1)}_{x,y}) \leftarrow I^{(z)}_{x,y}$;
end

Fig. 1. Look-up Table algorithm.

Original	Wavelet S+P	LUT prediction
8.6656	6.6587	4.9504

Table 1. Average entropies for first scene of Jasper Ridge.

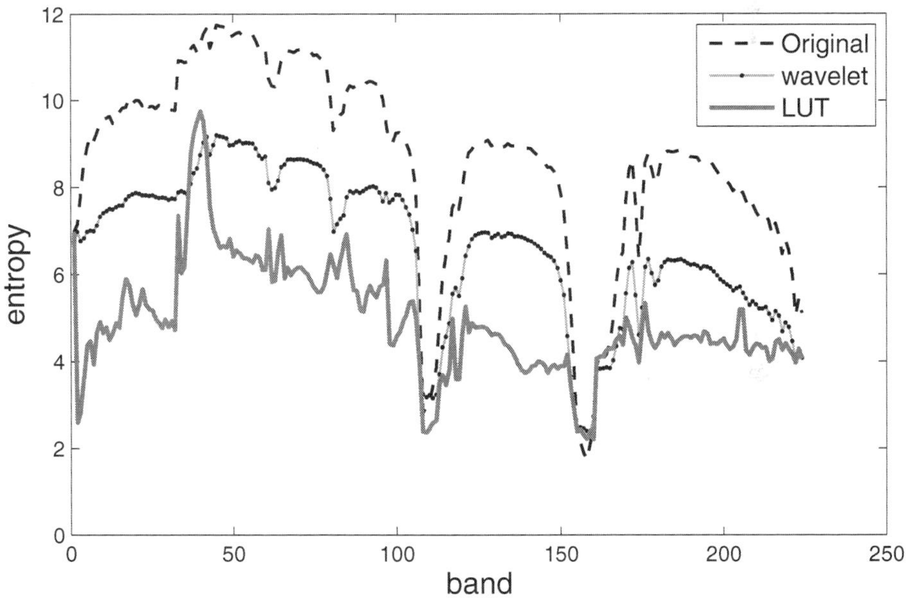

Fig. 2. Entropy values for every band of the Jasper Ridge image computed over the original image (dashed), over the prediction differences for the LUT method (gray), and over the 2D S+P wavelet transform (dotted). See averaged values in Table 1.

2.2 LAIS-LUT

An improvement over the LUT algorithm has been presented in (Huang & Sriraja, 2006). It was named LAIS-LUT after Locally Averaged Interband Scaling LUT and it behaves more accurately in presence of outliers. This modification adds an extra LUT table and the predictor is selected from one of the two LUTs. Using a scaling factor α which is precomputed on a causal neighbourhood, an estimate $\tilde{P}^{(z)}_{x,y}$ is calculated for a current pixel $I^{(z)}_{x,y}$ as $\tilde{P}^{(z)}_{x,y} = \alpha I^{(z-1)}_{x,y}$, where

$$\alpha = \frac{1}{3}\left(\frac{I^{(z)}_{i-1,j}}{I^{(z-1)}_{i-1,j}} + \frac{I^{(z)}_{i,j-1}}{I^{(z-1)}_{i,j-1}} + \frac{I^{(z)}_{i-1,j-1}}{I^{(z-1)}_{i-1,j-1}}\right) \tag{1}$$

Since two values are now possible candidates for prediction (one for each LUT), the one that is closer to $\tilde{P}^{(z)}_{x,y}$ is selected as the final prediction (Fig. 3 shows LAIS-LUT algorithm). When prediction $P^{(z)}$ for band z is estimated, the prediction error $I^{(z)} - P^{(z)}$ is entropy coded. This is repeated for $z = 2, \ldots, 224$. Notice that when the tables are not initialized, $P^{(z)}_{x,y}$ is selected for prediction, and, the value of the first LUT is used for prediction only when this table is initialized.

Data: Bands $I^{(z)}$, $I^{(z-1)}$, tables LUTable_1 and LUTable_2 are not initialized
Result: Prediction for band z: $P^{(z)}$
for *every pixel* $I^{(z)}_{x,y}$ **do**
  if *both tables are not initialized on entry (x,y)* **then**
    $P^{(z)}_{x,y} \leftarrow \alpha I^{(z-1)}_{x,y}$;
  else if *only* LUTable_1 *is initialized in (x,y)* **then**
    $P^{(z)}_{x,y} \leftarrow \text{LUTable}_1(I^{(z-1)}_{x,y})$;
  else
    $P^{(z)}_{x,y} \leftarrow$ closer value of $\{\text{LUTable}_1(I^{(z-1)}_{x,y}), \text{LUTable}_2(I^{(z-1)}_{x,y})\}$ to $\alpha I^{(z-1)}_{x,y}$;
  end
  $\text{LUTable}_2(I^{(z-1)}_{x,y}) \leftarrow \text{LUTable}_1(I^{(z-1)}_{x,y})$;
  $\text{LUTable}_1(I^{(z-1)}_{x,y}) \leftarrow I^{(z)}_{x,y}$;
end

Fig. 3. LAIS-LUT algorithm.

2.3 LAIS-QLUT

Mielikainen and Toivanen proposed a modification to the LAIS-LUT method in order to shrink Lookup tables (Mielikainen & Toivanen, 2008). For that, the value used for indexing into the LUTs is quantized and smaller LUTs can be used (i.e., the value x used as an index in the LUT is replaced by $\lfloor x/q \rfloor$ for some quantization step q, being $\lfloor \cdot \rfloor : \mathbb{R} \rightarrow \mathbb{Z}$ a function that maps a real number to a close integer). In the previous section, LAIS-LUT found exact matches in the previous band in order to obtain the predictor in the current band. For LAIS-QLUT, this search is no more exact and the predictor's selection in the current band is based on 'similarities' in the previous band. The best quantization step is obtained by an exhaustive search on each band (LAIS-QLUT-OPT version) or determined offline for each band by training on a set of images (LAIS-QLUT-HEU version). We decided not to add classes to the context over LAIS-QLUT, since a combination of the two would result in a prohibitive increase in complexity.

3. The wavelet transform as a tool for classification

In order to improve compression bitrates, the scaling factor in LAIS-LUT will be estimated more accurately. For that, a classification stage will be added to the algorithm. The scaling factor is computed as an average of quotients of collocated pixels in consecutive bands according to Equation 1. These pixels belong to a close neighbor of the pixel to be predicted (either on the current band, or on the previous band). Once classes are established for each pixel, not all the pixels in the close causal neighbor will be used for estimating the scaling factor α. Instead, we may use only those pixels that belong to the same class of the pixel to be predicted so as to obtain a more accurate estimation. This will enhance the LAIS-LUT algorithm, by allowing a better decision on which of the two look up tables yields a better prediction.

In order to establish classes we will make use of the wavelet transform. Since hyperspectral images have a considerable number of bands, the wavelet transform can be applied in the spectral direction. AVIRIS images have 224 bands. Considering each pixel as a vector in $\mathbb{Z}^{224}$, each of them may be 1D-wavelet transformed. And with the information of the wavelet transform of each 'pixel' classes can be determined. First, the wavelet transforms used in this work are introduced.

3.1 The wavelet transform

The wavelet transform allows the representation of a signal in multiresolution spaces. In the wavelet representation, the transformed signal can be viewed as an approximation of the original signal plus a sum of details at different levels of resolution. Each of these details and approximations are associated to function basis which have good time-frequency localization (Mallat, 1999). In images –a simple extension of the 1-dimensional case–, decorrelation is achieved obtaining a sparse representation. Two different types have been considered in this work: orthogonal wavelets and lifting-based wavelets.

For the classical orthogonal wavelet, consider a 1D signal $\mathbf{x} = [x_n]_{n=0,\dots,N-1}$ of length N (even). For a step of the wavelet, $\mathbf{x}$ is transformed into approximation coefficients $\mathbf{s} = [s_n]_{n=0,\dots,\frac{N}{2}-1}$ and detail coefficients $\mathbf{d} = [s_n]_{n=0,\dots,\frac{N}{2}-1}$, where $\mathbf{s}$ is the result of convolving $\mathbf{x}$ with a lowpass filter followed by a decimation. The same process happens to $\mathbf{d}$, but a high pass filter is used instead. For more steps, the wavelet transform is applied recursively over the approximation coefficients $\mathbf{s}$. The original signal can be recovered if the inverse process is carried out in order (upsampling followed by the convolution with the corresponding reversed filter –see Fig. 4). Depending on the filter, wavelets with different properties can be obtained. In this work we use the Daubechies 4 wavelet (Daubechies, 1992) whose lowpass filter is $[h_3, h_2, h_1, h_0] = \frac{1}{4\sqrt{2}}[3+e, 1-e, 3-e, 1+e]$ with $e = \sqrt{3}$, and high pass filter $g' = [-h_0, h_1, -h_2, h_3]$. The Symmlet wavelet, with 8 vanishing moments (and filter of length 16), was also used in this work.

Another way of constructing different wavelets is by the lifting scheme (Daubechies & Sweldens, 1998). They are built in the spatial domain. The basic idea is to split the signal into two components, for instance, odd samples ($\mathbf{x}_{\text{odd}} = x_{2k+1}$) and even samples ($\mathbf{x}_{\text{even}} = x_{2k}$). Then, detail coefficients are obtained by using one component to predict the other: $\mathbf{d} = \mathbf{x}_{\text{odd}} - P(\mathbf{x}_{\text{even}})$. Better predictions will yield more zeros, and therefore more decorrelation is

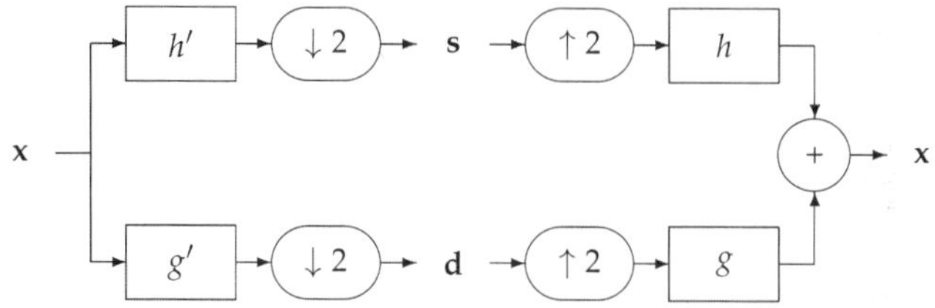

Fig. 4. Orthogonal wavelet analysis via convolutions and decimations followed by the synthesis via upsampling and convolution. Highpass filter g is obtained from lowpass filter h as $g_k = (-1)^k h_{1-k}$, and g' indicates the g filter reversed.

achieved. In order to obtain the approximation part of the transformed signal, the unpredicted component is softened with an 'update' of the detail previously obtained: $\mathbf{s} = \mathbf{x}_{\text{even}} + U(\mathbf{d})$. See Fig. 5 for an illustration of this scheme. With the lifting scheme it is possible to construct wavelets that map integers into integers (Calderbank et al., 1998) by the use of a rounding operator at the prediction or update stage. For this work the $(2, 2)$ and S+P wavelets have been considered (see Table 2).

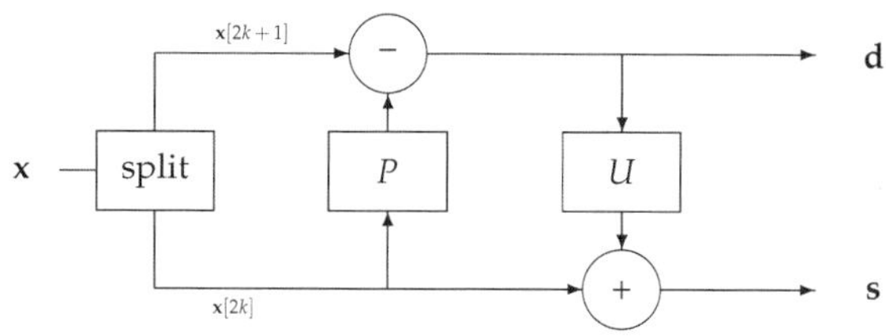

Fig. 5. Lifting scheme analysis for a 1-D signal $\mathbf{x}$.

Wavelet	Formula
(2,2)	$d_n = x_{2n+1} - \left\lfloor \frac{1}{2}(x_{2n} + x_{2n+2}) + \frac{1}{2} \right\rfloor$ $s_n = x_{2n} + \left\lfloor \frac{1}{4}(d_{n-1} + d_n) + \frac{1}{2} \right\rfloor$
S+P	$d_n^{(1)} = x_{2n+1} - x_{2n}$ $s_n = x_{2n} + \left\lfloor \frac{d_n^{(1)}}{2} \right\rfloor$ $d_n = d_n^{(1)} + \left\lfloor \frac{2}{8}(s_{n-1} - s_n) + \frac{3}{8}(s_n - s_{n+1}) + \frac{2}{8} d_{n+1}^{(1)} + \frac{1}{2} \right\rfloor$

Table 2. Wavelet transforms that maps integers into integers.

4. Classification of hyperspectral images

Using images captured by the scanner system called AVIRIS (Airborne Visible/Infrared Imaging Spectrometer) developed by JPL (Jet Propulsion Laboratory; see http://aviris.jpl.nasa.gov), we aim at determining classes for pixels. These images have 224 bands, each corresponding to a response in a certain range of the electromagnetic spectrum. Each pixel represents 20 meters and is allocated in a 2 byte signed integer. AVIRIS images usually have 614 columns and every 512 rows, the image is partitioned into 'scenes', and each scene is stored in a different file.

Considering each pixel $I_{x,y}$ as a vector in $\mathbb{Z}^{224}$ where each component belongs to a different band, different behaviours depending on what type of soil is being considered can be observed. Figure 6 shows the first scene of the Jasper Ridge image with four pixels belonging to different classes, marked with symbols '$\oplus$', '$\circ$', '$\heartsuit$' and '$\diamondsuit$'. The spectral vectors associated to the same 4 positions are plotted in Figure 7; where the characteristic signal -called the spectral signature- of the type of soil can be observed.

Fig. 6. Band 50 of Jasper Rigde image.

In order to classify the image, for every pixel, a 1-D wavelet transform is applied along the spectral direction. The entropy of each transformed spectral vector is computed, giving an image C where $C_{x,y} := H(W(I_{x,y}))$, being $W(\cdot)$ a 1-D wavelet transform function and $H(\cdot)$ the entropy function weighted by wavelet subband. Since AVIRIS images have 224 bands, 5 steps of the wavelet transform are applied to each pixel. So we have 5 detail subbands and 1 approximation subband. Since decimation is performed after each step, these subbands are different in size. Therefore, the total entropy of the 1-D wavelet transform is computed as the

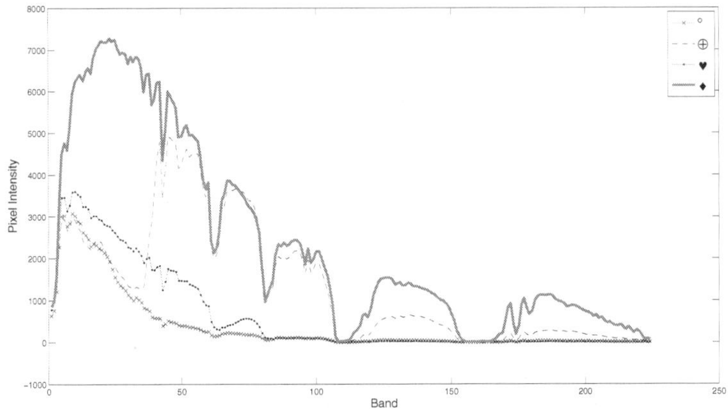

Fig. 7. Spectral signatures of different classes: values of selected pixels in Fig. 6 throughout the bands.

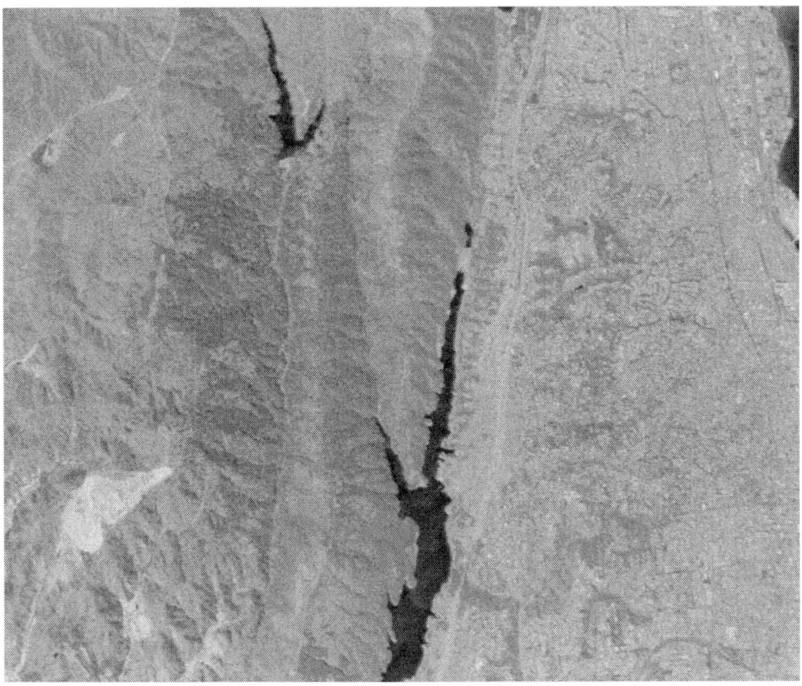

Fig. 8. Entropy of the wavelet transform of every pixel. Darker pixels indicate lower entropy values.

Image	Enhanced LAIS-LUT				LAIS-LUT	LUT
	Daubechies 4	Symmlet 8	S+P	(2,2)		
Low Altitude	3.17875	3.17546	3.17793	3.17797		
Jasper Ridge	3.43895	3.43855	3.43914	3.43833	3.42	3.23
Cuprite	3.71393	3.71394	3.71390	3.71390	3.58	3.44
Lunar Lake	3.58201	3.58198	3.58198	3.58201	3.53	3.4

Table 3. Compression ratios for Enhanced LAIS-LUT (with classes for estimating the scaling factor) and classical LAIS-LUT and LUT algorithms.

sum of the entropies of each subband, weighted by the size of the subband relative to the size of the whole transform.

In Figure 8 a grayscale image of the entropies is displayed. This image may be further split into classes with an unsupervised classifier. In this work, mean-shift (Comaniciu & Meer, 2002) was used.

5. Results

Results of compressing AVIRIS images with LAIS-LUT and the enhanced version (in which the scaling factor is calculated with pixels belonging to the same class, considering a causal neighbor of 4×4 pixels around the one to be predicted) is shown in Table 3.

The name of the wavelet in the table indicates the wavelet used to transform each pixel (and all the bands) followed by the entropy estimation and mean shift classification. Compression ratio results for LAIS-LUT and LUT algorithms were obtained from (Mielikainen & Toivanen, 2008). It can be observed that the enhanced version of LAIS-LUT using Daubechies 4 for classification outperforms the other methods.

We may conclude that the scaling factor α plays an important role in the compression performance of LAIS-LUT algorithm. When introduced, it was intended to decrease the deterioration produced by outliers in the original LUT algorithm. We have also been able to make use of the information in the wavelet domain and apply it to develop an efficient classifier. Since hyperspectral images have many bands because of their high spectral resolution, the information of the signal that each pixel represents (in all bands) was well captured by the wavelet transform and was fed into a powerful classifier such as mean-shift, giving good compression results.

6. References

Aiazzi, B., Alba, P., Alparone, L. & Baronti, S. (1999). Lossless compression of multi/hyperspectral imagery based on a 3-D fuzzy prediction, *IEEE Trans. Geos. Remote Sensing* 37(5): 2287–2294.

Aiazzi, B., Alparone, L., Baronti, S. & Lastri, C. (2007). Crisp and fuzzy adaptive spectral predictions for lossless and near-lossless compression of hyperspectral imagery, *IEEE Geos. Remote Sensing Letters* 4(4): 532–536.

Blanes, I. & Serra-Sagrista, J. (2010). Cost and scalability improvements to the karhunen-loêve transform for remote-sensing image coding, *Geoscience and Remote Sensing, IEEE Transactions on* 48(7): 2854 –2863.

Calderbank, A. R., Daubechies, I., Sweldens, W. & Yeo, B. (1998). Wavelet transforms that map integer to integers, *Applied and Computational Harmonics Analysis* 5(3): 332–369.

Comaniciu, D. & Meer, P. (2002). Mean shift: a robust approach toward feature space analysis, *IEEE Transactions on Pattern Analysis and Machine Intelligence* 24(5): 603–619.

Daubechies, I. (1992). *Ten lectures on wavelets*, Soc. Indus. Appl. Math.

Daubechies, I. & Sweldens, W. (1998). Factoring wavelet and subband transforms into lifting steps, *The Journal of Fourier Analysis and Applications* 4: 247–269.

Fowler, J. E. & Rucker, J. T. (2007). 3d wavelet-based compression of hyperspectral imagery, *in* C.-I. Chang (ed.), *Hyperspectral Data Exploitation: Theory and Applications*, John Wiley & Sons, Inc., pp. 379–407.

Huang, B. & Sriraja, Y. (2006). Lossless compression of hyperspectral imagery via lookup tables with predictor selection, *SPIE* 6365.

Kulkarni, P., Bilgin, A., Marcellin, M., Dagher, J., Kasner, J., Flohr, T. & Rountree, J. (2006). Compression of earth science data with jpeg2000, *in* G. Motta, F. Rizzo & J. A. Storer (eds), *Hyperspectral Data Compression*, Springer US, pp. 347–378.

Mallat, S. (1999). *A Wavelet Tour of Signal Processing*, Academic Press.

Mielikainen, J. (2006). Lossless compression of hyperspectral images using lookup tables, *IEEE SPL* 13(3): 157–160.

Mielikainen, J. & Toivanen, P. (2003). Clustered DPCM for the lossless compression of hyperspectral images, *IEEE Trans. Geos. Remote Sensing* 41(12): 2943–2946.

Mielikainen, J. & Toivanen, P. (2008). Lossless compression of hyperspectral images using a quantized index to look-up tables, *IEEE Geos. Remote Sensing Letters* 5(3).

Rizzo, F., Carpentieri, B., Motta, G. & Storer, J. A. (2005). Low complexity lossless compression of hyperspectral imagery via linear prediction, *IEEE Signal Processing Letters* 12(2): 138–141.

Slyz, M. & Zhang, L. (2005). A block-based inter-band lossless hyperspectral image compressor, *IEEE Proc. Data Compression Conf.* .

Taubman, D. & Marcellin, M. (2002). *JPEG2000: Image compression fundamentals, standards and practice*, Kluwer Academic Publishers, Boston.

Wang, H., Babacan, D. & Sayood, K. (2005). Lossless hyperspectral image compression using context-based conditional averages, *IEEE Proc. Data Compression Conference* .

Part 5

Applications in Engineering

24

Robust Lossless Data Hiding by Feature-Based Bit Embedding Algorithm

Ching-Yu Yang
Department of Computer Science and Information Engineering
National Penghu University of Science and Technology
Taiwan

1. Introduction

Recently, data hiding, or information hiding, plays an important role in data assurance. Generally speaking, data hiding techniques can be classified into steganography and digital watermarking (Cox et al., 2008; Shih, 2008). The marked images generated by the steganographic methods (Gu & Gao, 2009; Liu & Shih, 2008; Qu et al., 2010; Wang et al., 2010; Zhou et al., 2010; Fan et al., 2011) were prone to catch damage (by manipulations) and resulted in a failure extraction of the message. However, based on the spatial domain, the steganographic methods often provide a large payload with a good perceived quality. Major applications of the techniques can be found in private data saving, image tagging and authentication, and covert communications. On the other hand, the robustness performance with a limited payload is a key feature of digital watermarking approaches (Lai et al., 2009; Al-Qaheri et al., 2010; Lin & Shiu, 2010; Yamamoto & Iwakiri, 2010; Yang et al., 2010; Martinez-Noriega et al., 2011). Most of the robust watermarking approaches which based on the transform domain such as discrete cosine transform (DCT), integer wavelet transform (IWT), and discrete Fourier transform (DFT) can be tolerant of common image processing operations. Their usages can be found in owner identification, proof of ownership, and copy control. Note that conventional data hiding techniques were irreversible, namely, the host media can not be recovered after data extraction. To preserve or protect the originality of the valuable (or priceless) host media, for example, military or medical images, and law enforcement, the reversible data hiding schemes, also known as lossless data hiding schemes were suggested to achieve the goal. For some applications, it requires to completely recover the host media if the marked images remain intact, and to extract the hidden message when the marked images were intentionally (or unintentionally) manipulated by the third parties. But, most of reversible data hiding schemes (Tian, 2003; Alattar, 2004; Hsio et al., 2009; Hu et al., 2009; Tai et al., 2009; Wu et al., 2009; Lee et al., 2010; Xiao & Shih, 2010; Yang & Tsai, 2010; Yang et al., 2010, 2011) were fragile in the sense that the hidden message can be unsuccessfully extract even if a slight alteration to the marked images, not to mention the recovery of the host media. Several authors (Zou et al., 2006; Ni et al., 2008; Zeng et al., 2010) therefore proposed robust reversible data hiding algorithms to overcome the issue.

Zou et al. (Zou et al., 2006) presented a semi-fragile lossless watermarking scheme based on integer wavelet transform (IWT). To obtain a good perceptual quality, they only embed data bits into the low-high (LH) and high-low (HL) of the IWT coefficients. During bit embedding, the IWT blocks remain intact if an input bit is 0, otherwise, the proposed embedding process were applied to the blocks. Simulations showed that the hidden message was robust against lossy compression to a certain degree. Ni et al. (Ni et al., 2008) presented a robust lossless data hiding technique based on the patchwork theory, the distribution features of pixel groups, error codes, and the permutation scheme. The marked images generated by the technique contained no salt-and-pepper noise with a limited payload size. In addition, the marked images were robust against to JPEG/JPEG2000 compression. Zeng et al. (Zeng et al., 2010) adjusted the mathematical difference values of a block and designed a robust lossless data hiding scheme. A cover image was first divided into a number of blocks and the arithmetic difference of each block was calculated. Data bits were then embedded into the blocks by shifting the arithmetic difference values. Due to the separation of the bit-0-zone and the bit-1-zone, as well as the particularity of mathematical difference, a major merit of the method was tolerant of JPEG compression to some extent. Compared with Ni et al.'s work (Ni et al., 2008), the performance of Zeng et al.'s scheme (Zeng et al., 2010) was significantly improved.

Currently there are a few robust lossless data hiding techniques published in the literature. Since the payload provided by the above techniques (Zou et al., 2006; Ni et al., 2008; Zeng et al., 2010) was not good enough, we therefore propose the FBBE algorithm so that to introduce an effective robust lossless data hiding method. Moreover, to provide a high-capacity version of lossless data hiding scheme that based on IWT domain, we use a smart allocation of the coefficients in an IWT block to achieve the goal. The scheme not only provides a high payload but also generates a good perceived quality.

This chapter is organized as follows. In section 2, a robust lossless data hiding via the feature-based bit embedding (FBBE) algorithm is introduced followed by a high-performance lossless data hiding scheme. Section 3 provides both test results and performance comparisons. We conclude this chapter in section 4.

2. Proposed method

Based on the integer wavelet transform (IWT), we propose two lossless data hiding methods, namely, a robust version and a high-capacity one. First, a robust lossless data hiding via the feature-based bit embedding (FBBE) algorithm is specified. Instead of embedding data bits directly into the IWT coefficient blocks, we use the FBBE algorithm to encode a block so that it can carry data bits and can be successfully identified later at the receiver. Then, a high-performance lossless data hiding scheme is presented to provide a large hiding storage by adjusting the location of each IWT coefficient in the host block. More specifically, the FBBE algorithm can be used to generate a robust lossless data hiding method. Whereas, the proposed smart adjustment of the IWT coefficients can be used to generate a high-performance lossless data hiding scheme.

2.1 FBBE algorithm

To achieve a robust lossless data hiding method, we embed a secret message into transform domain via the FBBE algorithm. An input image was first decomposed to the IWT domain. The IWT coefficients can be acquired by using the following two formulas:

$$d_{1,k} = s_{0,2k+1} - s_{0,2k} \tag{1}$$

and

$$s_{1,k} = s_{0,2k} + \left\lfloor \frac{d_{1,k}}{2} \right\rfloor, \tag{2}$$

where $s_{j,k}$ and $d_{j,k}$ are the kth low-frequency and high-frequency wavelet coefficients at the jth level, respectively (Calderbank et al., 1998). The $\lfloor x \rfloor$ is a floor function. Then, data bits were embedded into the blocks which derived from the LH and HL sub-bands of the IWT coefficients, respectively. The FBBE algorithm consists of four parts, namely, Up-U (UU) sampling, Down-U (DU) sampling, Up-Down (UD) sampling, and Left-Right (LR) sampling. Each sampling is allowed to carry a single data bit. For each host block, the above four samplings is conducted according to the sequence of UU, DU, UD, and LR samplings. The details are specified in the following sections.

2.1.1 Bit embedding

Let $C_j = \{c_{jk}\}_{k=0}^{n^2-1}$ be the jth block of size $n \times n$ taken from the LH (or HL) sub-bands of IWT domain. Also let $C_j = \{\hat{C} \cup \tilde{C} \cup C' \cup C''\}$ with $\hat{C} = \{\hat{c}_i \mid i = 0,3,5,6\}$, $\tilde{C} = \{\tilde{c}_u \mid u = 9,10,12,15\}$, $C' = \{c'_v \mid v = 1,2,13,14\}$, and $C'' = \{c''_w \mid w = 4,7,8,11\}$ be the UU, DU, UD, and LR samplings coefficients, respectively, as shown in Fig. 1 if n=4. In addition, let

$$C_{jp} = \{\hat{c}_i \mid \beta \le \hat{c}_i < 2\beta\} \tag{3}$$

and

$$C_{jm} = \{\hat{c}_i \mid -2\beta \le \hat{c}_i < -\beta\} \tag{4}$$

be the two focal groups being used to 'carry' data bits. The β used here is a robustness parameter.

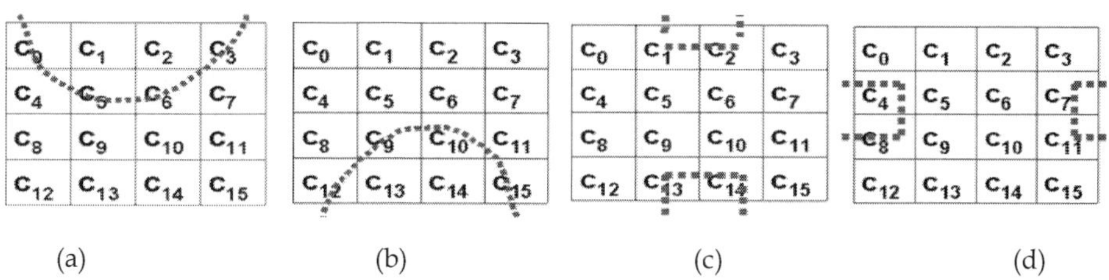

Fig. 1. A 4×4 IWT coefficients block. (a) UU, (b) DU, (c) UD, and (b) LR sampling coefficients.

The main steps of UU (or DU, UD, LR) samplings are specified as follows:

Step 1. Input a block C_j not processing yet.

Step 2. If an input bit ϕ=0 and $|C_{jp}|>|C_{jm}|$ then do nothing, which means a bit 0 can be carried by the UU (or DU, UD, LR) sampling coefficients without alteration of their value, and go to Step 8.

Step 3. If ϕ=0 and $|C_{jp}|=|C_{jm}|$ then add β to the coefficients c_{jk} in C_j with $0 \le c_{jk} < \beta$, respectively, mark a flag to the shifted coefficient, and go to Step 8.

Step 4. If ϕ=0 and $|C_{jp}|<|C_{jm}|$ then add β to the coefficients in C_{jm}, respectively, mark a flag to the shifted coefficient, and go to Step 8.

Step 5. If ϕ=1 and $|C_{jp}|<|C_{jm}|$ then do nothing, which means the UU (or DU, UD, LR) samplings coefficients carry a bit 1, and go to Step 8.

Step 6. If ϕ=1 and $|C_{jp}|=|C_{jm}|$ then subtract β from the coefficients c_{jk} in C_j with $-\beta \le c_{jk} < 0$, respectively, mark a flag to the shifted coefficient, and go to Step 8.

Step 7. If ϕ=1 and $|C_{jp}|>|C_{jm}|$ then subtract β from the coefficients in C_{jp}, respectively, mark a flag to the shifted coefficient.

Step 8. Repeat Step 1 until all IWT coefficients blocks have been processed.

Notice that the coefficients $\hat{c}_i$ which belong to either C_{jp} or C_{jm} have to be changed to $\tilde{c}_u$, c'_v, or c''_w, respectively, when the DU, UD, or LR samplings was employed. From the above procedures we can see that each block can carry at most four data bits. This resulted in a total payload of $\lfloor M/2n \rfloor \times \lfloor N/2n \rfloor \times 2 \times 4 \le \frac{2MN}{n^2}$ bits provided by the proposed method, where M and N is the size of a host image.

2.1.2 Bit extraction

Let $D_j = \{d_{jk}\}_{k=0}^{n^2-1}$ be the jth hidden block of size $n{\times}n$ taken from the LH (or HL) sub-bands of IWT domain derived from a marked image, and $D_j = \{\hat{D} \cup \tilde{D} \cup D' \cup D''\}$ with $\hat{D} = \{\hat{d}_i \mid i = 0,3,5,6\}$, $\tilde{D} = \{\tilde{d}_u \mid u = 9,10,12,15\}$, $D' = \{d'_v \mid v = 1,2,13,14\}$, and $D'' = \{d''_w \mid w = 4,7,8,11\}$. Also let

$$D_{jp} = \{\hat{d}_i (\text{or } \tilde{d}_u, d'_v, d''_w) \mid \beta \le \hat{d}_i (\text{or } \tilde{d}_u, d'_v, d''_w) < 2\beta\} \tag{5}$$

and

$$D_{jm} = \{\hat{d}_i (\text{or } \tilde{d}_u, d'_v, d''_w) \mid -2\beta \le \hat{d}_i (\text{or } \tilde{d}_u, d'_v, d''_w) < -\beta\} \tag{6}$$

be the two subsets of D_j. The procedure of bits extraction for the UU (or DU, UD, LR) sampling can be summarized in the following steps.

Step 1. Input a hidden block D_j not processing yet.

Step 2. If $|D_{jp}|>|D_{jm}|$ then a bit 0 can be identified. Subtract β from either the coefficients d_{jk} in D_j with $-\beta \le d_{jk} < 0$ or the coefficients $\hat{\mathrm{d}}_\mathrm{i}(\text{or } \tilde{\mathrm{d}}_\mathrm{u}, \mathrm{d}'_\mathrm{v}, \mathrm{d}''_\mathrm{w})$ in D_{jp} when the corresponding flag was set at 1, and go to Step 6.

Step 3. If $|D_{jp}|<|D_{jm}|$ then a bit 1 can be extracted. Add β to either d_{jk} in D_j with $0 \le d_{jk} < \beta$ or the coefficients $\hat{\mathrm{d}}_\mathrm{i}(\text{or } \tilde{\mathrm{d}}_\mathrm{u}, \mathrm{d}'_\mathrm{v}, \mathrm{d}''_\mathrm{w})$ in D_{jm} when the corresponding flag was set at 1, go to Step 6.

Step 4. If $|D_{jp}|=|D_{jm}|$ and the flag of the coefficients d_{jk} in D_j with $-\beta \le d_{jk} < 0$ was set at 1, a bit 0 can be identified, and go to Step 6.

Step 5. If $|D_{jp}|=|D_{jm}|$ and the flag of the coefficients d_{jk} in D_j with $0 \le d_{jk} < \beta$ was set at 1, a bit 1 can be identified.

Step 6. Repeat Step 1 until all hidden bits have been extracted.

The number of bits for the overhead information which used to signify whether or not a coefficient of the block undergone adjustment is $\left\lfloor \frac{M}{2} \Big/ n \right\rfloor \times \left\lfloor \frac{N}{2} \Big/ n \right\rfloor \times n^2 \times 2 \le \frac{MN}{2}$.

2.2 High-performance lossless data hiding scheme

To provide a high-capacity with a good perceived quality, the proposed scheme, which based on the adjustment of the locations of the coefficients in a host block, embeds a secret message into the three high sub-bands of IWT domain. The details are described in the following subsections.

2.2.1 Data embedment

Let $C_j = \{\mathrm{c_{jk}}\}_{k=0}^{n^2-1}$ be the jth block of size $n \times n$ taken from the LH (or HL, HH) sub-band of IWT domain. Also let $C_{jp} = \{\mathrm{c_p} \mid \beta \le \mathrm{c_p} < 2\beta\}$ and $C_{jm} = \{\mathrm{c_m} \mid -2\beta \le \mathrm{c_m} < -\beta\}$ be two subsets of C_j. The main steps of bit embedding are specified as follows:

Step 1. Input a block C_j not processing yet.

Step 2. If $|C_{jp}| \ne \varnothing$ then subtract β from each coefficient of C_{jp} and mark a flag to the modified coefficient.

Step 3. If $|C_{jm}| \ne \varnothing$ then add β to each coefficient of C_{jm} and mark a flag to the modified coefficient.

Step 4. After adjustment, for a coefficient $c_i \in C_j$ with $0 \le c_i < \beta$ (or $-\beta \le c_i < 0$), multiply c_i by 2 to obtain $\hat{c}_i$, and add an input bit to $\hat{c}_i$.

Step 5. Repeat to Step 1 until all blocks have been processed.

The purpose of steps 3 and 4 are tried to further dig out hiding space from the selected coefficients. The schema of the adjustment of the coefficients values for the above two steps can be illustrated in Fig. 2.

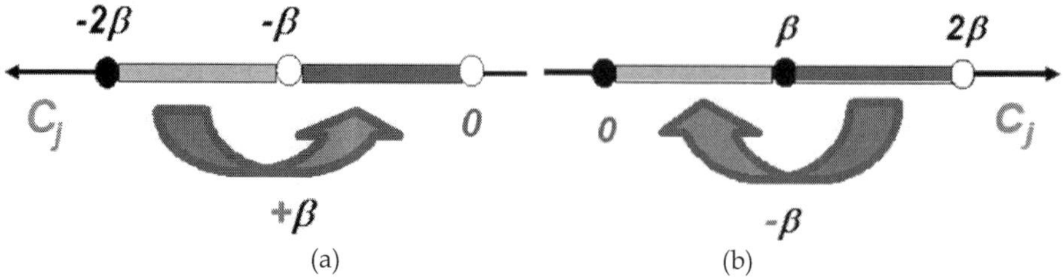

Fig. 2. The schema of the coefficients adjustment. (a) The positive part and (b) the negative part.

To increase payload size, multiple bits can be hidden in each IWT coefficient. In this case, the above steps 2-4 are rewritten as follows:

Step 2a. For a coefficient $c_t \in C_j$ with $-\beta < c_t < \beta$, multiply c_t by 2^k to obtain $\hat{c}_t$, and mark a flag to the modified coefficient.

Step 3a. For each $\hat{c}_t$, add data bits ϕ to $\hat{c}_t$ if $\hat{c}_t \geq 0$, otherwise, subtract ϕ from $\hat{c}_t$.

The parameter k is an integer. To maintain a good resulting perceived quality, the value of k is no more than 2. From the above procedure we can see that the number of bits used for recording the indices of the modified coefficients is $\lfloor M/2n \rfloor \times \lfloor N/2n \rfloor \times n^2 \times 3 < 3MN/4$.

2.2.2 Data extraction

To extract the hidden message, the overhead information can be losslessly compressed by using either the run-length coding algorithm or JBIG2. The resulting bit stream can then sent by an out-of-band transmission to the receiver. Without loss of generality, let D_j be the jth hidden block of size $n \times n$ taken from the LH (or HL, HH) sub-band of IWT domain which derived from a marked image, and $\hat{D}_j = \{\hat{d}_j \mid -2\beta \leq \hat{d}_j < 2\beta\}$ with $\hat{D}_j \subseteq D_j$. The procedure of bits extraction can be summarized in the following steps.

Step 1. Input a block D_j not processing yet.

Step 2. A data bit can be extracted by performing modulus-2 to $\hat{d}_j$.

Step 3. The IWT coefficients $\tilde{d}_j$ which hid data bit can be restored by performing either $\tilde{d}_j = \lfloor \hat{d}_j / 2 \rfloor$ if $\hat{d}_j \geq 0$ or $\tilde{d}_j = \left| (\hat{d}_j / 2) - 0.5 \right|$ if $\hat{d}_j < 0$.

Step 4. The original IWT coefficients can be recovered by adding (or subtracting) β to (or from) $\tilde{d}_j$ if $\tilde{d}_j \geq 0$ (or $\tilde{d}_j < 0$) while the flag of $\tilde{d}_j$ was marked.

Step 5. Repeat to Step 1 until all data bits have been extracted.

Note that $\lfloor x \rfloor$ and $\lceil x \rceil$ in step 3 denote the floor and ceiling functions, respectively. To perform multiple bits extraction for each coefficient, the above steps 2-4 are rewritten as follows:

Step 2b. A data bit can be extracted by performing modulus-2^k to d'_j with $-2^k\beta \le d'_j < 2^k\beta$.

Step 3b. The IWT coefficients $\tilde{d}_j$ which hid data bits can be restored by performing $\tilde{d}_j = \lfloor \hat{d}_j / 2^k \rfloor$ if the flag of $\tilde{d}_j$ was marked.

Step 4b. The original IWT coefficients can be recovered by adding (or subtracting) $(2^k - 1)\beta$ to (or from) $\tilde{d}_j$ if $\tilde{d}_j \ge 0$ (or $\tilde{d}_j < 0$).

To specify the idea of data embedding, two examples were presented in Figs. 3-4. The figures illustrate the cases of full-bit ($n{\times}n$ bits) and partial-bit hidden, respectively. The k used here is 1. The control parameter β is set to be 4. A host IWT-block was shown in Fig. 3(a). Figure 3(b) illustrates a shifted block, which obtained by according to the steps 2-3 of Sec. 2.2.1. Note that each of the shifted coefficients was marked by a rectangle. According to the step 4 of Sec. 2.2.1, we can see that all of the coefficients in the shifted block can be used to hide bits. Namely, a full-bit (or 16-bit) can be embedded in Fig. 3(b). Figure 3 (c) shows the hidden block. The mean square error (MSE) computed from Figs. 3(a) and 3(c) is 7.667. Another example of hiding partial-bit (or 12-bit) in an IWT-block was shown in Fig. 4(a). A shifted block was shown in Fig. 4(b). Notice as well there are 4 coefficients (in bold type) containing null bits. The resulting hidden block was depicted in Fig. 4(c). In this case, the MSE for the hidden block is 6.444. To recover the original block, a similar reverse process (with a bitmap) can be performed to Figs. 3(c) and 4(c), respectively.

(a)

-5	-8	-3	-2
3	-7	-7	-2
6	-3	-8	-5
5	0	-6	-8

(b)

-1	-4	-3	-2
3	-3	-3	-2
2	-3	-4	-1
1	0	-2	-4

(c)

-2	-7	-5	-4
6	-5	-6	-4
4	-5	-8	-1
3	1	-4	-8

Fig. 3. Example of 16-bit embedding with a bit-stream of 0110 0100 0101 1100. (a) The original IWT-block, (b) shifted block, and (c) hidden block.

(a)

8	17	0	11
0	1	-15	2
-5	1	-6	-7
6	5	1	4

(b)

8	**17**	0	**11**
0	1	**-15**	2
-1	1	-2	-3
2	1	1	0

(c)

8	17	0	11
1	3	-15	4
-2	3	-3	-6
4	2	3	1

Fig. 4. Example of 12-bit embedding with a bit-stream of 0110 0110 0011. (a) The IWT-block, (b) shifted block, and (c) hidden block.

2.2.3 Overflow/underflow issues

An overflow/underflow can be occurred during bit embedding if a pixel value of the host image is a little either less than 255 or larger than 0. To overcome the overflow/underflow issues, a pixel-shifting approach can be performed in the spatial domain before data embedment. Namely, if a pixel value p in a host image satisfied either $p < \phi_1$ or $p > \phi_2$, p can be adjusted to a new value by adding to ϕ_1 or subtracting from ϕ_2. Both ϕ_1 and ϕ_2 are two predetermined threshold values.

3. Experimental results

Several greyscale images of size 512×512 were used as host images. A quarter of the host image *Lena* was used as the test data. To provide a variety of embedding rate, the value of the control parameter β is not fixed. Simulations generated by the proposed FBBE algorithm were first shown in the following subsection. Subsequently, a high-performance hiding scheme was examined.

3.1 Simulations of the FBBE algorithm

Figure 5 depicts the relationship between peak signal-to-noise ratio (PSNR) and robustness parameter β that generated by the proposed FBBE algorithm. The size of the block was 4×4. The figure indicated that the optimal PSNR value of 57.45 dB is achieved with β=1.

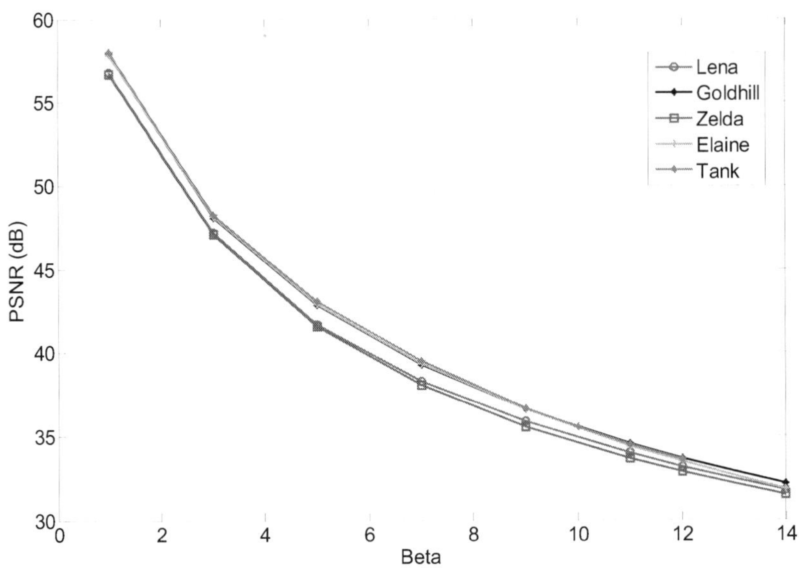

Fig. 5. The relationship between PSNR and β.

The PSNR value is approximately linear decreased as β increased. Actually, the larger the value of β, the more robust performance can be obtained by the proposed method. The PSNR is defined by

$$PSNR = 10 \times \log_{10} \frac{255^2}{MSE}, \tag{7}$$

where $MSE = \frac{1}{MN} \sum_{i=1}^{N} \sum_{j=1}^{M} (\hat{x}(i,j) - x(i,j))^2$. Here $x(i,j)$ and $\hat{x}(i,j)$ denote the pixel values of the original image and the marked image. Figure 6 shows the marked images generated by the proposed method with β=12. Their average PSNR value was 33.35 dB with an embedding rate of 0.125 bits per pixel (bpp). It can be seen that the perceptual quality was acceptable.

Fig. 6. The marked images generated by the proposed FBBE algorithm. (a) Lena, (b) Goldhill, (c) Zelda, (d) Elaine, and (e) Tank.

For comparison, two graceful schemes, namely, Ni et al.'s algorithm (Ni et al., 2008) and Zeng et al.'s approach (Zeng et al., 2010) are compared with our method. Table 1 indicates the performance comparison of these methods on three test images. From Fig. 5 and Table 1 we can see that the proposed method with β =5 (or β of which value being less than 6) provides the largest payload among these methods while the PSNR for the proposed method is superior to that for the other two techniques. Moreover, Table 1 shows that the average hiding capacity provided by the proposed method is two times that achieved by Zeng et al.'s approach (Zeng et al., 2010), and five times larger than that achieved by Ni et al.'s algorithm (Ni et al., 2008).

Methods	Images			
	Lena	*Zelda*	*Goldhill*	Average
Ni et al.'s algorithm	6,336/ 40.19	4,480/ 40.47	6,336/ 40.18	5,717/ 40.28
Zeng et al.'s approach	16,384/ 38.07	16,384/ 38.09	16,384/ 38.10	16,384/ 38.09
Proposed Method	32,768/ 41.71	32,768/ 41.56	32,768/ 42.84	32,768/ 42.04

Table 1. Hiding performance (Payload/ PSNR) comparison between various methods.

To demonstrate the robustness performance of the proposed method, examples of extracted watermarks after various manipulations of the image are given in Table 2. A logo of size 63×63 with 8 bits/pixel 2 colours was used as the test watermark, as shown in Fig. 7. The bit correct ratio (BCR) is also included. The BCR is defined by

$$BCR = \left(\sum_{i=0}^{ab-1} \overline{w_i \oplus \widetilde{w}_i} \Big/ a \times b \right) \times 100\%, \tag{8}$$

Fig. 7. The test watermark.

where w_i and $\widetilde{w}_i$ represent the values of the original watermark and the extracted watermark respectively, as well as the size of a watermark is $a \times b$. Note that a majority-vote decision was employed during bits extraction. Although the BCR for those watermarks, which extracted from the images that gone through attacks such as JPEG2000, JPEG, equalized, interleaved, and inversion are not high, they are identifiable. Although the BCR for the watermark extracted from an image which manipulated by inversion attack is only 1.99%, it is recognizable. Furthermore, Fig. 8 shows the BCR performance of the survived watermarks under a variety of degree of Uniform/Gaussian noise additions attacks. From the figure we can see that the proposed method is more robust against Uniform than Gaussian noise additions attacks. Similarly, Fig. 9 indicates the proposed method has the better performance in resisting JPEG200 than JPEG attacks. Figure 10 shows that the proposed method is nearly free from brightness attacks. Finally, Fig. 11 indicates that the extracted watermarks are tolerant of colour quantization attack even if the number of level of pixel-value in a marked image is reduced to 8.

Attacks	Survived Watermarks	Attacks	Survived watermarks
Cropping (50%) BCR =87.88 %		Brightness (+90%) BCR = 87.45%	
JPEG2000 (CR*=8.33) BCR=71.89%		Brightness (-100%) BCR = 89.65%	
JPEG (CR=5.54) BCR=75.36%		Contrast (40%) BCR = 87.48%	
Uniform noise (5%) BCR = 78.94%		Contrast (-15%) BCR = 78.18%	
Gaussian noise (4%) BCR = 74.38%		Posterized (8-level) BCR = 85.26%	
Edge sharpening BCR = 98.92%		Equalized BCR = 80.78%	
Mean filtering (3×3) BCR = 98.34%		Interleaved (Odd) BCR = 54.14%	

Attacks	Survived Watermarks	Attacks	Survived watermarks
Median filtering (3×3) BCR = 98.76%		Interleaved (Even) BCR = 53.87%	
Quantization[†] BCR = 95.67%		Inversion BCR = 1.99%	

*CR stands for compression ratio, which is defined as the ratio of the size of a host image to that of a compressed image.
†The last four bits of the pixel in the marked image were truncated.

Table 2. Examples of watermarks extracted from image *Lena*. (β=12)

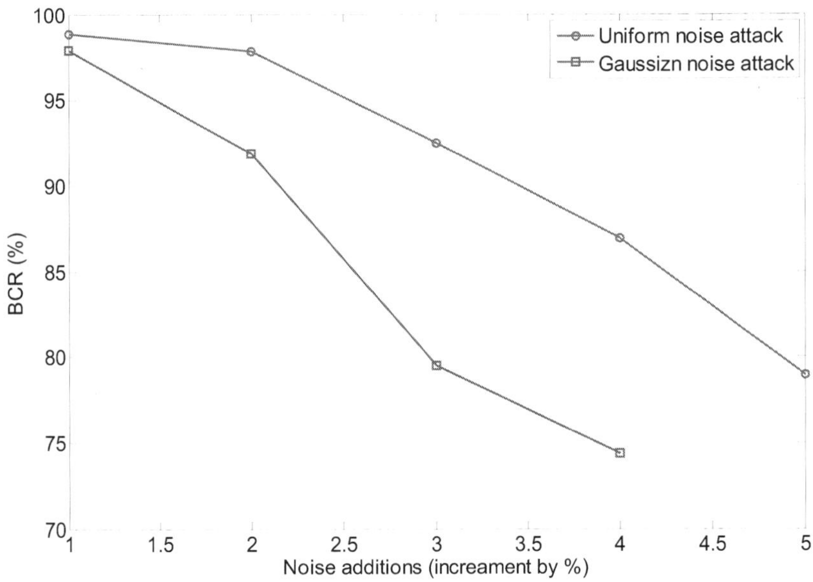

Fig. 8. The BCR for the proposed method under Uniform/Gaussian noise additions attacks, respectively.

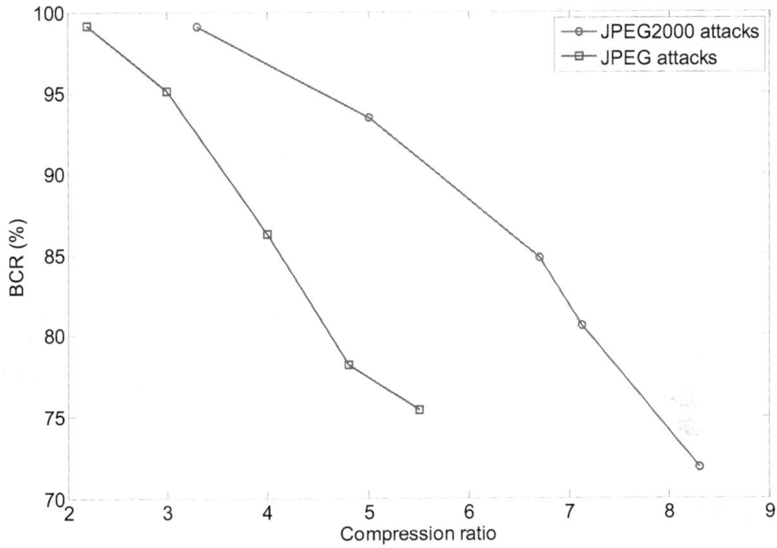

Fig. 9. The BCR for the proposed method under JPEG2000/JPEG attacks, respectively.

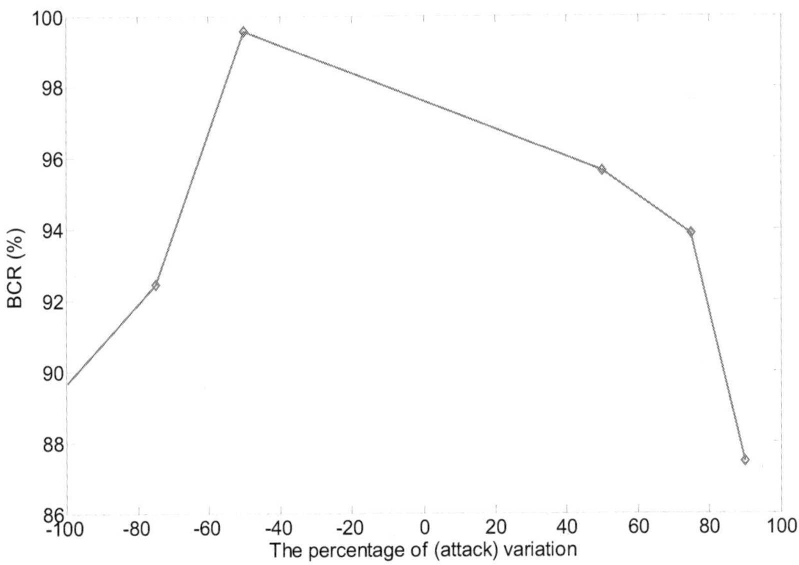

Fig. 10. The BCR for the proposed method under Brightness attacks.

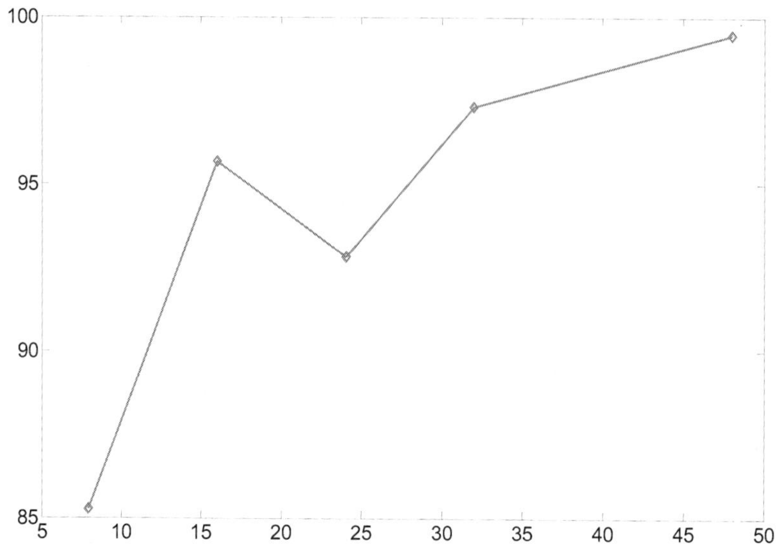

Fig. 11. The BCR for the proposed method under (color) quantization attacks.

3.2 Simulations of high-performance hiding scheme

The trade-off between PSNR and payload for the proposed scheme was depicted in Figure 12. The figure indicated that the average PSNR achieved by the proposed scheme was approximately 55 dB at a bit rate of 0.236 bpp. Whereas, the optimal PSNR value of 37.76 dB can be achieved in image *Zelda* with bit rate of 0.747 bpp. In addition, the relationship between payload (or embedding rate) and robustness parameter β was drawn in Fig. 13. From the figure we can see that the larger the value of β, the higher the bit rate was achieved.

For comparison, three outstanding approaches: Wu et al.'s scheme (Wu et al. 2009), Lee et al.'s algorithm (Lee et al., 2010), and Yang & Tsai's technique (Yang & Tsai, 2010) were compared with our method. Performance comparison between these methods was given in Table 3. It is obvious that the proposed method provides the largest payload among these methods while the PSNR for the proposed method is superior to that for the other three algorithms. Moreover, Table 3 implies that the hiding capacity provided by the proposed method is approximately two times that achieved by the Wu *et al.*'s scheme (Wu et al. 2009), and is two times that achieved by Lee et al.'s algorithm (Lee et al., 2010). Moreover, Table 4 revealed the superiority of our scheme when the PSNR value around 43 dB. The average embedding rate for the proposed scheme was two times larger than that for the Wu et al.'s technique (Wu et al. 2009).

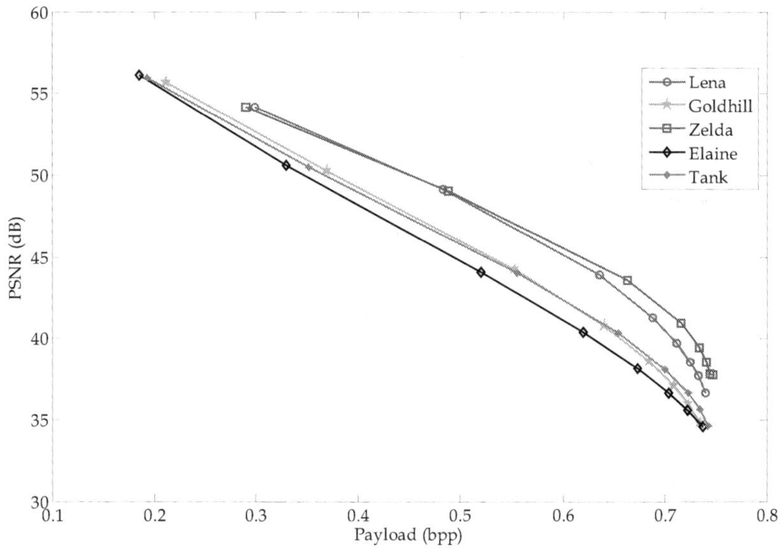

Fig. 12. The trade-off between payload and PSNR for the proposed scheme.

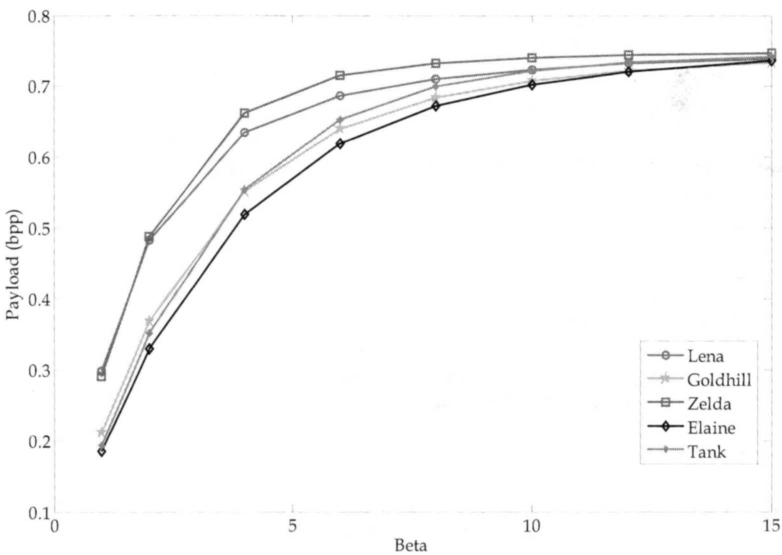

Fig. 13. The relationship between payload and β.

Methods	Images				
	Lena	*Zelda*	*Goldhill*	*Peppers*	Average
Wu et al.'s scheme	0.20/ 47.55	0.19/ 47.75	0.15/ 48.25	0.37/ 48.25	0.23/ 47.95
Lee et al.'s algorithm	0.23/ 48.25	0.18/ 48.25	-	0.17/ 48.25	0.20/ 48.25
Yang & Tsai's technique	0.38/ 48.81	-	0.26/ 48.81	0.33/ 48.81	0.33/ 48.81
Proposed method	0.48/ 49.14	0.49/ 49.02	0.40/ 50.27	0.43/ 49.37	0.45/ 49.45

Table 3. Embedding rate and PSNR performance comparison between various methods when PSNR value was approximately 48 dB.

Methods	Images				
	Lena	*Zelda*	*Goldhill*	*Pepper*	Average
Wu et al.'s scheme	0.24/ 43.60	0.40/ 43.60	0.28/ 43.60	0.23/ 43.60	0.29/ 43.60
Lee et al.'s algorithm	0.53/ 43.15	0.42/ 43.15	-	0.41/ 43.15	0.46/ 43.15
Yang & Tsai's technique	0.62/ 43.84	-	0.45/ 43.84	0.55/ 43.84	0.54/ 43.84
Proposed method	0.64/ 43.94	0.66/ 43.56	0.55/ 44.24	0.60/ 43.75	0.61/ 43.87

Table 4. Embedding rate and PSNR performance comparison between various methods when PSNR value was approximately 43 dB.

4. Conclusion

In this chapter, we first propose a robust lossless data hiding via the feature-based bit embedding (FBBE) algorithm based on integer wavelet transform (IWT). Data bits can be effectively carried by the IWT blocks via the FBBE algorithm and the hidden message can be successfully identified later at the receiver. Moreover, the FBBE algorithm can completely recover the host media if the marked image remains intact, and extract (most part of) the hidden message if manipulations were intentionally (or unintentionally) altered to the marked images. In addition, we employ a smart arrangement of the IWT coefficients so as to provide a high-capacity lossless data hiding scheme. Simulations validate that the marked images generated by the proposed FBBE algorithm are robust to a variety of attacks such as JPEG2000, JPEG, cropping, noise additions, (colour) quantization, bits truncation, brightness/contrast, mean/median filtering, and inversion. Furthermore, the payload and PSNR provided by the proposed two methods outperform those provided by existing schemes.

The proposed two methods can be extended to color images by embedding data bits in the RGB system separately. In addition, to further enlarge the hiding storage of the FBBE algorithm, an extra one (or two) data bits could be hidden in each IWT coefficients block during data embedment. However, a tradeoff between PSNR and payload size may be a problem with this algorithm. These issues will be discussed in detail in future work. Furthermore, to reduce memory space and transmission delay, the decreasing of the overhead bits will be our future study.

5. References

Alattar, A. M. (2004). Reversible watermark using the difference expansion of a generalized integer transform. *IEEE T. Image Processing*, Vol. 13, No. 8, pp. 1147-1156.

Al-Qaheri, H.; Mustafi, A. & Banerjee, S. (2010). Digital Watermarking using Ant Colony Optimization in Fractional Fourier Domain. *Journal of Information Hiding and Multimedia Signal Processing*, Vol. 1, No. 3, pp. 179-189.

Calderbank, A.R.; Daubechies, I.; Sweldens, W. & Yeo, B.L. (1998). Wavelet transforms that map integers to integers. *Applied & Computational Harmonics Analysis*, Vol. 5, No. 3, pp.332-369.

Cox, I.J.; Miller, M.L.; Bloom, J.A.; Fridrich, J. & Kalker T. (Ed(s.)) (2008). *Digital Watermarking and Steganography*, 2nd Ed., Morgan Kaufmann., MA.

Fan, L.; Gao, T. & Yang Q. (2011). A novel watermarking scheme for copyright protection based on adaptive joint image feature and visual secret sharing. *International Journal of Innovative Computing, Information and Control*, Vol. 7, No. 7(A), pp. 3679-3694.

Gu, Q. & Gao, T. (2009). A novel reversible watermarking algorithm based on wavelet lifting scheme. *ICIC Express Letters*, Vol. 3, No. 3 (A), pp. 397-402.

Hu, Y., Lee; H. K. & Li, J. (2009). DE-based reversible data hiding with improved overflow location map. *IEEE T. Circuits and Systems for Video Technology*. Vol. 19, No. 2, pp. 250-260.

Hsiao, J. Y.; Chan, K.F. & Chang, J.M. (2009). Block-based reversible data embedding. *Signal Processing*, Vol. 89, pp. 556-569.

Lai, C.C.; Huang, H.C. & Tsai, C.C. (2010). A digital watermarking scheme based on singular value decomposition and micro-genetic algorithm. *International Journal of Innovative Computing Information and Control*, Vol. 5, No. 7, pp. 1867-1873.

Lee, C.F.; Chen, H.L. & Tso, H.K. (2010). Embedding capacity raising in reversible data hiding based on prediction of different expansion. *The Journal of Systems and Software*, Vol. 83, pp. 1864-1872.

Lin, C.C. & Shiu, P.F. (2010). High capacity data hiding scheme for DCT-based images. *Journal of Information Hiding and Multimedia Signal Processing*, Vol. 1, No. 3, pp. 220-240.

Liu, J. C. & Shih, M. H. (2008). Generalization of pixel-value differencing staganography for data hiding in images. *Fundamenta Informaticate*, Vol. 83, pp. 319-335.

Martinez-Noriega, R.; Nakano, M.; Kurkoski, B. & Yamaguchi, K. (2011). High Payload Audio Watermarking: toward Channel Characterization of MP3 Compression. *Journal of Information Hiding and Multimedia Signal Processing*, Vol. 2, No. 2, pp. 91-107.

Ni, Z.; Shi, Y.Q.; Ansari, N.; Su, W.; Sun, Q. & Lin, X. (2008). Robust lossless image data hiding designed for semi-fragile image authentication," *IEEE T. Circuits and Systems for Video Technology*, Vol. 18, No. 4, pp. 497-509, 2008.

Qu, Z.G.; Chen, X.B.; Zhou, X.J.; Niu, X.X. & Yang, Y.X. (2010). Novel quantum steganography with large payload. *Optics Communications*, Vol. 283, No. 23, pp. 4782-4786.

Shih, F.Y. (2008). *Digital watermarking and steganography: fundamentals and techniques*. CRC Press, FL.

Tai, W.L.; Yeh, C.M. & Chang, C.C. (2009). Reversible data hiding based on histogram modification of pixel differences. *IEEE T. Circuits and Systems for Video Technology*, Vol. 19, No. 6, pp. 906-910.

Tian, J. (2003). Reversible data embedding using a difference expansion. *IEEE T. Circuits and Systems for Video Technology*, Vol. 13, No. 8, pp. 890-896.

Wang, S., Yang, B. & Niu, X. (2010). A secure steganography method based on genetic algorithm. *Journal of Information Hiding and Multimedia Signal Processing*, Vo1. 1, No. 1.

Wu, H.C.; Lee, C.C.; Tsai, C.S.; Chu, Y.P. & Chen, H.R. (2009). A high capacity reversible data hiding scheme with edge prediction and difference expansion. *The Journal of Systems and Software*, Vol. 82, pp. 1966-1973

Xiao, D. & Shih, F.Y. (2010). A reversible image authentication scheme based on chaotic fragile watermark. *International Journal of Innovative Computing, Information and Control*, Vol. 6 No. 10, pp. 4731-4742.

Yamamoto, K. & Iwakiri M. (2010). Real-time audio watermarking based on characteristics of PCM in digital instrument. *Journal of Information Hiding and Multimedia Signal Processing*, Vol. 1, No. 2, pp. 59-71.

Yang, C.H. & Tsai, M.H. (2010). Improving histogram-based reversible data hiding by interleaving predictors. *IET Image Processing*, Vol. 4, No. 4, pp. 223-234.

Yang, C.Y.; Hu, W.C. & Lin, C.H. (2010). Reversible data hiding by coefficient-bias algorithm. *Journal of Information Hiding and Multimedia Signal Processing*, Vol. 1, No. 2, pp. 91-100.

Yang, C.Y.; Hu, W.C.; Hwang, W.Y. & Cheng, Y.F. (2010). A simple digital watermarking by the adaptive bit-labeling scheme. *Int. Journal of Innovative Computing, Information and Control, Vol. 6, No. 3*, pp. 1401-1410.

Yang, C.Y.; Lin, C.H. & Hu, W.C. (2011). Block-based reversible data hiding," *ICIC Express Letters*, Vol. 5, No. 7, pp. 2251-2256.

Zeng, X.T.; Ping, L.D. & Pan, X.Z. (2010). A lossless robust data hiding scheme. *Pattern Recognition*, Vol. 43, pp. 1656-1667.

Zhou, S.; Zhang, Q. & Wei, X. (2010). An image encryption algorithm based on dual DNA sequences for image hiding. *ICIC Express Letters*, Vol. 4, No. 4, pp. 1393-1398.

Zou, D.; Shi, Y.Q.; Ni, Z. & Su, W.A. (2006). A semi-fragile lossless digital watermarking scheme based on integer wavelet transform. *IEEE T. Circuits and Systems for Video Technology*, Vol. 16, No. 10, pp. 1294-1300.

25

Time-Varying Discrete-Time Wavelet Transforms

Guangyu Wang, Qianbin Chen and Zufan Zhang
Chongqing Key Lab of Mobile Communications, Chongqing University of Posts and Telecommunications (CQUPT)
China

1. Introduction

Discrete-time wavelet transform (DWT) is found to be better than other transforms in the time-varying system analysis, e.g. for time-varying parametric modelling [16], time-varying systems identification [17], time-varying parameter estimation [18] and time domain signal analysis [19]. In the literature the common method to analyze the time-varying system using discrete-time wavelet transform is to model the time-varying system with a time-invariant system firstly, because a general analysis of time-varying discrete-time wavelet transform (TV-DWT) is still missing. To analyze the time-varying system directly using the time-varying discrete-time wavelet transform, we need the theory for the time-varying discrete-time wavelet transform.

The theory of time-invariant discrete-time wavelet transform (DWT) are quite complete [1,2,3]. For time-varying discrete-time wavelet transform, in literature there are some papers related with this topic by studying the changes of two different filter banks [10,11,12]. In [10] the authors analyzed the time-varying wavelet transform through changing the two-band filter banks used in the tree-structured implementation of DWTs with an simple example. In [11] the time-varying wavelet packets built with time-varying cosine-modulated filter banks were investigated. Similar with [10], in [12] the authors studied time-varying wavelet packets more theoretically with changing the two orthogonal two-band filter banks used in tree-structure of DWTs. Generally, in the existed theory of time-varying discrete-time wavelet transform it lacks a basic definition and description of the time-varying discrete-time wavelet transform. A basic analysis of time-varying discrete-time wavelet transform is also missing. The author has studied TV-DWT since some years and has published a series of papers about this topic. In this Chapter we summarize the author's main research results.

In our method the time-varying discrete-time wavelet transform is studied using a time-varying octave-band filter bank with tree structure. With this implementation the analysis of the time-varying discrete-time wavelet transform is equal to the analysis of the time-varying discrete-time octave-band filter bank. Then, the time-varying filter bank theory can be used in TV-DWT analysis. In this chapter we provide some theorems for the time-varying discrete-time wavelet transform with proofs.

2. Formulation of time-varying discrete-time wavelet transforms

From the point of view of digital signal processing, the time-varying discrete-time wavelet transform can be implemented by a time-varying octave-band filter bank with tree structure. Fig. 1 shows the most general time-varying discrete-time wavelet transform implemented with a time-varying octave-band filter bank, where the lowpass and highpass filter $H_l(z,m)$, $H_u(z,m)$, the stage number of the split-merge $J(m)$, all are varying with time index m. In other words, both the frequency characteristic and the time-frequency tiling of the discrete-time wavelet transform are varying with time. Fig. 2 shows the time-varying nonuniform filter bank implementation. With this implementation the analysis of the time-varying discrete-time wavelet transform is equal to the analysis of the time-varying discrete-time octave-band filter bank.

Note that we define the time-varying discrete-time wavelet transform varying with index m which is equivalent to the output index at the last stage of octave-band filter banks. The time indices of the other output are related to m by

$$m_j = 2^{J(m)-i-j} \cdot m, \quad 0 \le j \le J(m) - 2. \tag{1}$$

In the literature there are some papers related with this topic by studying changes between two time-invariant filter banks [10,11,12]. In particular, in [10] the authors have discussed the transition behavior during the change between two time-invariant discrete-time wavelet transforms. Different from the existed publications, in this chapter we analyze the general time-varying discrete-time wavelet transform in detail based on the octave-band filter bank and the nonuniform filter bank implementation.

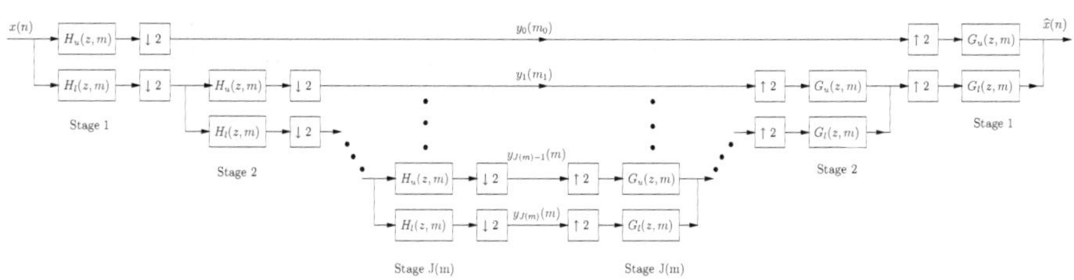

Fig. 1. Time-varying discrete-time wavelet transform implemented with time-varying octave-band filter banks.

3. Implementation with time-varying octave-band filter Banks

To make the analysis simple, in the following analysis we suppose that the stage number J does not change with time and is a constant. Then we get a J-stage time-varying octave-band filter bank. Just as depicted in Fig. 1, a J-stage octave-band time-varying filter bank consists of J stages of two-channel time-varying filter bank. In the analysis side, the input signal $x(n)$ is first split by the two-channel time-varying filter bank at the first stage, then the lowpass output is spilt again by the same two-band time-varying filter bank at the second stage.

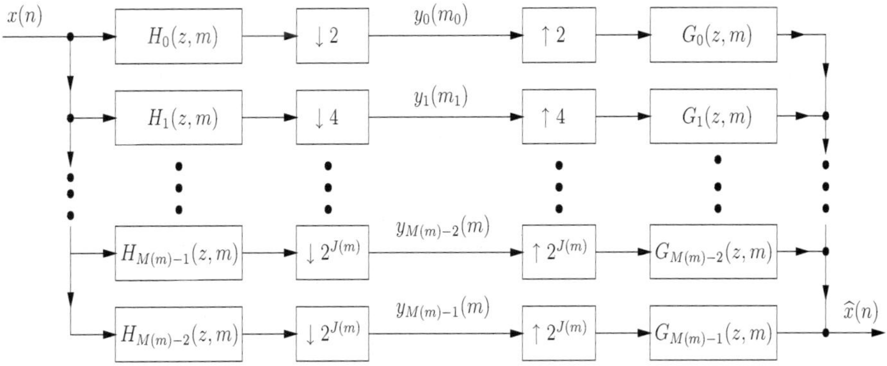

Fig. 2. Time-varying nonuniform filter bank implementation, where $M(m) = 2^{J(m)}$.

The process is ongoing until J-stage. In the synthesis side, the signal is merged to generate the reconstructed signal $\widehat{x}(n)$. From the theorem of time-invariant discrete-time wavelet transform [2], we know that if the individual two-channel filter bank, or each split-merge pair is perfectly reconstructed, the octave-band filter bank is as well. Such statement is also valid for the time-varying octave-band filter bank. Therefore, we have following theorem.

Theorem 1: A time-varying discrete-time wavelet transform implemented with a time-varying octave-band filter bank is a biorthogonal time-varying transform if each two-channel time-varying filter bank is perfectly reconstructed.

We cannot use the method used in the time-invariant case to prove the above theorem because the system is time-varying. To prove theorem 1, we define analysis and synthesis matrices of the j-stage two-channel time-varying filter bank shown in Fig. 3 as

$$\mathbf{T}_{ma}^{(j)} = \begin{bmatrix} & \vdots & \vdots & \vdots & \vdots & \vdots & \vdots & \\ \cdots & \mathbf{h}_0(m_j) & \mathbf{h}_1(m_j) & \cdots & \mathbf{h}_{N(j)-1}(m_j) & \mathbf{h}_{N(j)}(m_j) & \mathbf{h}_{N(j)+1}(m_j) & \cdots \\ \cdots & \mathbf{0} & \mathbf{h}_0(m_j) & \cdots & \mathbf{h}_{N(j)-2}(m_j) & \mathbf{h}_{N(j)-1}(m_j) & \mathbf{h}_{N(j)}(m_j) & \cdots \\ \cdots & \vdots & \vdots & \ddots & \vdots & \vdots & \vdots & \cdots \\ \cdots & \mathbf{0} & \mathbf{0} & \cdots & \mathbf{h}_0(m_j) & \mathbf{h}_1(m_j) & \mathbf{h}_2(m_j) & \cdots \\ \cdots & \mathbf{0} & \mathbf{0} & \cdots & \mathbf{0} & \mathbf{h}_0(m_j+1) & \mathbf{h}_1(m_j+1) & \cdots \\ & \vdots & \vdots & \vdots & \vdots & \vdots & \vdots & \end{bmatrix} \quad (2)$$

$$\mathbf{T}_{ms}^{(j)} = \begin{bmatrix} & \vdots & \vdots & \vdots & \vdots & \vdots & \\ \cdots & \mathbf{g}_0(m_j) & \mathbf{0} & \cdots & \mathbf{0} & \mathbf{0} & \cdots \\ \cdots & \mathbf{g}_1(m_j) & \mathbf{g}_0(m_j) & \cdots & \mathbf{0} & \mathbf{0} & \cdots \\ \cdots & \vdots & \vdots & \ddots & \vdots & \vdots & \cdots \\ \cdots & \mathbf{g}_{N(j)-1}(m_j) & \mathbf{g}_{N(j)-2}(m_j) & \cdots & \mathbf{g}_0(m_j) & \mathbf{0} & \cdots \\ \cdots & \mathbf{g}_{N(j)}(m_j) & \mathbf{g}_{N(j)-1}(m_j) & \cdots & \mathbf{g}_1(m_j) & \mathbf{g}_0(m_j+1) & \cdots \\ \cdots & \mathbf{g}_{N(j)+1}(m_j) & \mathbf{g}_{N(j)}(m_j) & \cdots & \mathbf{g}_2(m_j) & \mathbf{g}_1(m_j+1) & \cdots \\ & \vdots & \vdots & \vdots & & & \end{bmatrix}, \tag{3}$$

where

$$N(j) = 2^{J-j}, \quad j = 1, 2, \cdots,, \tag{4}$$

and

$$\mathbf{h}_i(m_j) = \begin{bmatrix} h_u(L-2i-1, m_j) & h_u(L-2i-2, m_j) \\ h_l(L-2i-1, m_j) & h_l(L-2i-2, m_j) \end{bmatrix}, \tag{5}$$

$$\mathbf{g}_i(m_j) = \begin{bmatrix} g_u(2i, m_j) & g_l(2i, m_j) \\ g_u(2i+1, m_j) & g_l(2i+1, m_j) \end{bmatrix}, \tag{6}$$

where L is the filter length.

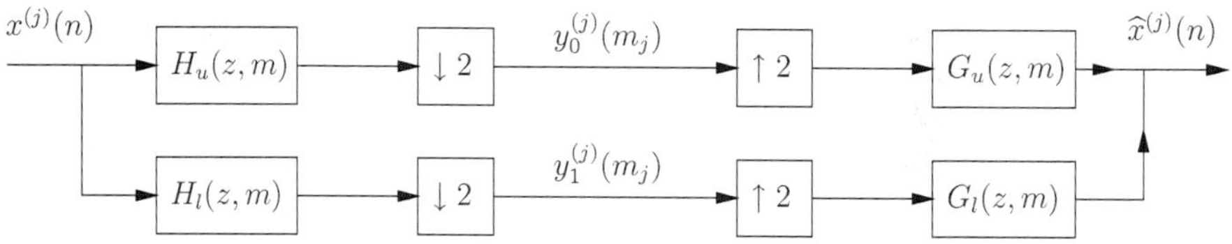

Fig. 3. The j-th stage two-channel time-varying filter bank.

Furthermore, we define two special matrices $\mathbf{\Lambda}_0$ and $\mathbf{\Lambda}_1$

$$\mathbf{\Lambda}_0 = \begin{bmatrix} & \vdots & \vdots & \vdots & \vdots & \vdots & \\ \cdots & 1 & 0 & 0 & 0 & 0 & \cdots \\ \cdots & 0 & 0 & 1 & 0 & 0 & \cdots \\ & \vdots & \vdots & \vdots & \vdots & \vdots & \end{bmatrix} \tag{7}$$

$$\mathbf{\Lambda}_1 = \begin{bmatrix} & \vdots & \vdots & \vdots & \vdots & \vdots & \\ \cdots & 0 & 1 & 0 & 0 & 0 & \cdots \\ \cdots & 0 & 0 & 0 & 1 & 0 & \cdots \\ & \vdots & \vdots & \vdots & \vdots & \vdots & \end{bmatrix}, \tag{8}$$

to extract the lowpass and highpass output like

$$\mathbf{y}_0^{(j)} = \mathbf{\Lambda}_0 \mathbf{y}^{(j)}, \tag{9}$$

$$\mathbf{y}_1^{(j)} = \mathbf{\Lambda}_1 \mathbf{y}^{(j)}, \tag{10}$$

where

$$\mathbf{y}^{(j)} = \left[\cdots y_0^{(j)}(-1)\, y_1^{(j)}(-1)\, y_0^{(j)}(0)\, y_1^{(j)}(0)\, y_0^{(j)}(1)\, y_1^{(j)}(1) \cdots \right]^T, \tag{11}$$

$$\mathbf{y}_0^{(j)} = \left[\cdots y_0^{(j)}(-1)\, y_0^{(j)}(0)\, y_0^{(j)}(1) \cdots \right]^T, \tag{12}$$

$$\mathbf{y}_1^{(j)} = \left[\cdots y_1^{(j)}(-1)\, y_1^{(j)}(0)\, y_1^{(j)}(1) \cdots \right]^T. \tag{13}$$

Based on the above matrix definitions we can describe the filter bank at the j-th stage showed in Fig. 3 as

$$\widehat{\mathbf{x}}^{(j)} = \mathbf{T}_{ms}^{(j)}\, \mathbf{T}_{ma}^{(j)}\, \mathbf{x}^{(j)}. \tag{14}$$

After adding the (j+1)-th stage with a biorthogonal time-varying two-channel filter bank shown in Fig. 4, we have

$$\begin{aligned}
\widehat{\mathbf{x}}^{(j)} &= \mathbf{T}_{ms}^{(j)}\, \mathbf{y}^{(j)} \\
&= \mathbf{T}_{ms}^{(j)} \left\{ \mathbf{\Lambda}_0^T \mathbf{y}_0^{(j)} + \mathbf{\Lambda}_1^T \mathbf{y}_1^{(j)} \right\} \\
&= \mathbf{T}_{ms}^{(j)} \left\{ \mathbf{\Lambda}_0^T \mathbf{\Lambda}_0 \mathbf{T}_{ma}^{(j)} \mathbf{x}^{(j)} + \mathbf{\Lambda}_1^T\, \mathbf{T}_{ms}^{(j+1)}\, \mathbf{T}_{ma}^{(j+1)}\, \mathbf{\Lambda}_1 \mathbf{T}_{ma}^{(j)} \mathbf{x}^{(j)} \right\}.
\end{aligned} \tag{15}$$

Because we suppose that the added two-channel filter bank is biorthogonal, we have

$$\mathbf{T}_{ms}^{(j+1)}\, \mathbf{T}_{ma}^{(j+1)} = \mathbf{I}, \tag{16}$$

$$\mathbf{\Lambda}_0^T \mathbf{\Lambda}_0 + \mathbf{\Lambda}_1^T \mathbf{\Lambda}_1 = \mathbf{I}. \tag{17}$$

Then, we can rewrite (15) as

$$\begin{aligned}
\widehat{\mathbf{x}}^{(j)} &= \mathbf{T}_{ms}^{(j)} \left\{ \mathbf{\Lambda}_0^T \mathbf{\Lambda}_0 + \mathbf{\Lambda}_1^T \mathbf{\Lambda}_1 \right\} \mathbf{T}_{ma}^{(j)}\, \mathbf{x}^{(j)} \\
&= \mathbf{T}_{ms}^{(j)}\, \mathbf{T}_{ma}^{(j)}\, \mathbf{x}^{(j)} \\
&= \mathbf{x}^{(j)}
\end{aligned} \tag{18}$$

which means that the time-varying octave-band filter bank is still perfectly reconstructed after adding next stage of time-varying biorthogonal two-channel filter bank. In other words, theorem 1 is correct.

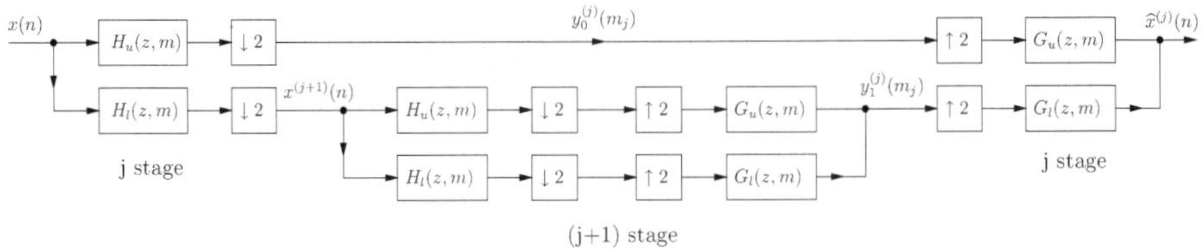

Fig. 4. Adding the $(j+1)$-th stage.

4. Implementation with time-varying nonuniform filter banks

Fig. 2 shows another implementation of a time-varying wavelet transform with $(J(m)+1)$-channel time-varying nonuniform filter bank. To make the analysis easy we suppose that $J(m)$ does not change with time and is equal to constant J. For analysis of the $(J+1)$-channel time-varying nonuniform filter bank we first reconstruct the nonuniform filter bank to a time-varying uniform filter bank through adding following filters between $H_i(z,m)$ and $H_{i+1}(z,m)$ $(0 \leq j\, J-1)$

$$H_{i,k}(z,m) = z^{-k\cdot 2^{i+1}} H_i(z,m), \;\; 1 \leq k \leq 2^{J-i-1} - 1. \tag{19}$$

After adding additional filters in the nonuniform filter bank in Fig. 2 the filter bank becomes M-channel time-varying uniform filter filter bank. The number of channel M is calculated by

$$\begin{aligned} M &= \sum_{i=0}^{J-2} (2^{J-i-1} - 1) + (J+1) \\ &= 2^{J-1} \sum_{i=0}^{J-2} 2^{-i} + 2 \\ &= 2^J (1 - 2 \cdot 2^{-J}) + 2 \\ &= 2^J. \end{aligned} \tag{20}$$

For the time-varying system in Fig. 5 we have following theorem.

Theorem 2: A time-varying discrete-time wavelet transform implemented with a time-varying nonuniform filter bank is biorthogonal if each two-channel time-varying filter bank in its tree-structured implementation is perfectly reconstructed.

To prove theorem 2, we need to describe the filter $H_i(z,m)$ in Fig. 5 based on the tree structure in Fig. 1. In the time-invariant discrete-time wavelet transform the description of such filters can be simply got using the convolution role in the transform-domain. However, in the time-varying case, we cannot describe $H_i(z,m)$ as product of functions in the previous stages, like $H_0(z,m)H_1(z^2,m)$, because the system is time-varying and the convolution role does not exist. Referencing to definitions of $\mathbf{T}_{ma}^{(j)}$ and $\mathbf{T}_{ms}^{(j)}$ in (2) and (3), we find that the analysis output

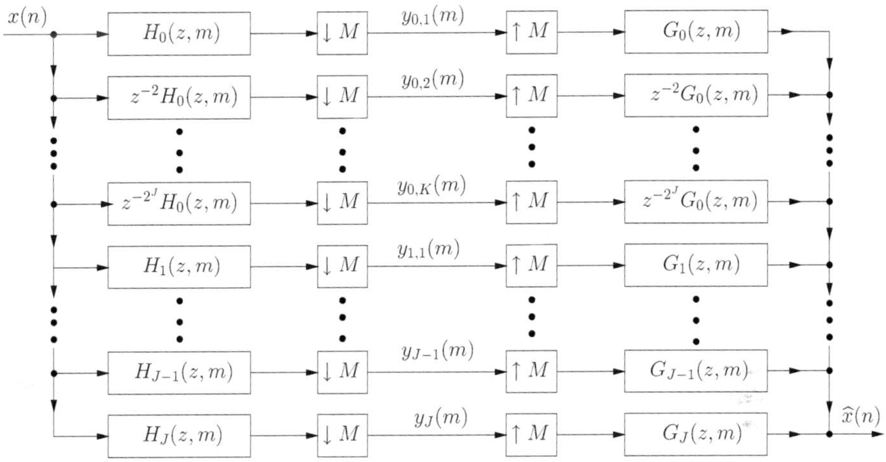

Fig. 5. The equivalent M-channel time-varying uniform filter bank.

$\mathbf{y}_0(m_0)$ can be expressed as

$$\mathbf{y}_0 = \mathbf{\Lambda}_0 \, \mathbf{T}_{ma}^{(1)} \, \mathbf{x}, \tag{21}$$

where

$$\mathbf{y}_0 = [\, \cdots \mathbf{y}_0(-1) \, \mathbf{y}_0(0) \, \mathbf{y}_0(1) \cdots]^T, \tag{22}$$

$$\mathbf{y}_0(m) = [\, y_{0,1}(m) \, y_{0,2}(m) \, \cdots y_{0,K}(m) \,]^T, \tag{23}$$

and $K = 2^{2^J-1} - 1$. In general, we have

$$\mathbf{y}_{j-1} = \underbrace{\mathbf{\Lambda}_0 \, \mathbf{T}_{ma}^{(j)} \, \mathbf{\Lambda}_1 \, \mathbf{T}_{ma}^{(j-1)} \, \cdots \, \mathbf{\Lambda}_1 \, \mathbf{T}_{ma}^{(1)}}_{\mathbf{H}_{j-1}} \, \mathbf{x}, \tag{24}$$

where $1 \le j \le J-1$, and

$$\mathbf{y}_{J-1} = \mathbf{\Lambda}_0 \, \mathbf{T}_{ma}^{(J)} \, \mathbf{\Lambda}_1 \, \mathbf{T}_{ma}^{(J-1)} \, \cdots \, \mathbf{\Lambda}_1 \, \mathbf{T}_{ma}^{(1)} \, \mathbf{x} = \mathbf{H}_{J-1} \, \mathbf{x}, \tag{25}$$

$$\mathbf{y}_{J} = \mathbf{\Lambda}_1 \, \mathbf{T}_{ma}^{(J)} \, \mathbf{\Lambda}_1 \, \mathbf{T}_{ma}^{(J-1)} \, \cdots \, \mathbf{\Lambda}_1 \, \mathbf{T}_{ma}^{(1)} \, \mathbf{x} = \mathbf{H}_{J} \, \mathbf{x}, \tag{26}$$

where

$$\mathbf{y}_{j-1} = \left[\, \cdots \mathbf{y}_{j-1}(-1) \, \mathbf{y}_{j-1}(0) \, \mathbf{y}_{j-1}(1) \cdots \right]^T, \tag{27}$$

$$\mathbf{y}_{j-1}(m) = \left[\, y_{j-1,1}(m) \, y_{j-1,2}(m) \, \cdots y_{j-1,K}(m) \,\right]^T, \tag{28}$$

for $K = 2^{2^J - j} - 1$ and $1 \leq j \leq J - 2$, and

$$\mathbf{y}_{J-1} = \left[\cdots\ y_{J-1}(-1)\ y_{J-1}(0)\ y_{J-1}(1) \cdots\right]^T, \tag{29}$$

$$\mathbf{y}_J = \left[\cdots\ y_J(-1)\ y_J(0)\ y_J(1) \cdots\right]^T. \tag{30}$$

At synthesis side, we have similar definitions as

$$\widehat{\mathbf{x}}_{j-1} = \underbrace{\mathbf{T}_{ms}^{(1)}\ \mathbf{\Lambda}_1^T\ \mathbf{T}_{ms}^{(2)}\ \cdots\ \mathbf{\Lambda}_1^T\ \mathbf{T}_{ms}^{(j)}\ \mathbf{\Lambda}_0^T}_{\mathbf{G}_{j-1}}\ \mathbf{y}_{j-1}, \tag{31}$$

$$\widehat{\mathbf{x}}_{J-1} = \mathbf{T}_{ms}^{(1)}\ \mathbf{\Lambda}_1^T\ \mathbf{T}_{ms}^{(2)}\ \cdots\ \mathbf{\Lambda}_1^T\ \mathbf{T}_{ms}^{(J)}\ \mathbf{\Lambda}_0^T\ \mathbf{y}_{J-1} = \mathbf{G}_{J-1}\ \mathbf{y}_{J-1}, \tag{32}$$

$$\widehat{\mathbf{x}}_J = \mathbf{T}_{ms}^{(1)}\ \mathbf{\Lambda}_1^T\ \mathbf{T}_{ms}^{(2)}\ \cdots\ \mathbf{\Lambda}_1^T\ \mathbf{T}_{ms}^{(J)}\ \mathbf{\Lambda}_1^T\ \mathbf{y}_J = \mathbf{G}_J\ \mathbf{y}_J, \tag{33}$$

Now, based on the definition in (23), we can build the analysis output vector for th time-varying filter bank in Fig. 5 as

$$\mathbf{y} = \left[\cdots\ \mathbf{y}_0(-1)\ \cdots \mathbf{y}_J(-1)\ \mathbf{y}_0(0)\ \cdots \mathbf{y}_J(0)\ \mathbf{y}_0(1)\ \cdots\right]^T. \tag{34}$$

Suppose that $\mathbf{T}_{ma}$ and $\mathbf{T}_{ms}$ are the analysis and synthesis matrices for the time-varying filter bank in Fig. 5. Referencing (34), $\mathbf{T}_{ma}$ is constructed by interleaving the rows from $\mathbf{T}_{ma}^{(1)}$ to $\mathbf{T}_{ma}^{(J)}$ with same time index m, $\mathbf{T}_{ms}$ is built with similar way, but interleaving the columns. Then, the production $\mathbf{T}_{ma}^{(1)}\mathbf{T}_{ma}^{(J)}$ can be expressed by

$$\mathbf{T}_{ms}\ \mathbf{T}_{ma} = \sum_{j=0}^{J} \mathbf{G}_j\ \mathbf{H}_j. \tag{35}$$

Substituting $\mathbf{H}_i$ and $\mathbf{G}_i$ defined in (24)-(26) and (31)-(33) into (35), and using properties in (16) and (17), we get

$$\mathbf{T}_{ms}\ \mathbf{T}_{ma} = \mathbf{I}, \tag{36}$$

which means that the time-varying nonuniform filter bank in Fig. 2 is perfectly reconstructed.

Finally, we give another property related with filter coefficients of the time-varying filter bank in Fig. 2. Suppose that $h_i(n,m)$ and $g_i(n,m)$ represent the analysis and synthesis filter coefficients in Fig. 2, then we have following equation

$$< g_i(n - kM, m + r),\ h_j(n - lM, m + s) >= \delta(k - l)\ \delta(i - j)\ \delta(r - s), \tag{37}$$

where $M = 2^J$. The proof of equation (37) can be simply got by using the PR condition in (36).

5. Conclusion

In the theory of discrete-time signal expansion, the wavelet transform is very important. In this chapter, we defined the general discrete time-varying dyadic wavelet transform and analyzed its properties in detail. Some theorems describing properties of time-varying discrete-time wavelet transforms were presented. The conditions for a biorthogonal time-varying discrete-time wavelet transform were given. The theory and algorithms presented in this chapter can be used in design of time-varying discrete-time signal expansion in practice.

6. Acknowledgments

This work is supported by the National Natural Science Foundation of China (No. 61071195) and Sino-Finland Cooperation Project (No. 1018).

7. References

[1] H.S. Malvar, *Signal Processing with Lapped Transforms.* Boston, MA: Artech House, 1992.

[2] M. Vetterli and J. Kovacevic, *Wavelets and Subband Coding,* Englewood Cliffs, NJ: Prentice Hall, 1995.

[3] Alfred Mertins, *Signal Analysis, Wavelets, Filter Banks, Time-Frequency Transforms and Application* England: John Wiley & Sons, 1999.

[4] V. DeBrunner, W. Lou, and J. Thripuraneni, "Multiple Transform Algorithms for Time-Varying Signal Representation," *IEEE Trans. Circuits and Systems-II: Analog and Digital Signal Processing,* vol. 44, No. 8, pp. 663-667, Aug. 1997.

[5] M. Morhac and V. Matousek, "New Adaptive Cosine-Walsh Transform and its Application to Nuclear Data Compression,"*IEEE Trans. Signal Processing,* vol. 48, No. 9, pp. 2663-2696, September 2000.

[6] N. Prelcic, A. Pena, "An Adaptive Tiling of the Time-Frequency Plane with Application to Multiresolution-Based Perceptive Audio Coding," *Signal Processing,* vol. 81, pp. 301-319, Feb. 2001.

[7] P. Srinivasan and L. Jamieson, "High-Quality Audio Compression Using an Adaptive Wavelet Packet Decomposition and Psychoacoustic Modeling," *IEEE Trans. Signal Processing,* vol. 46, No. 4, pp. 1085-1093, April 1998.

[8] ISO/IEC JTCI/SC29, "Information technology-coding of moving pictures and associated audio for digital storage media at up to about 1.5 Mbit/s-IS 11172-3 (audio)," 1992.

[9] C. Guillemot, P. Rault, and P. Onno, "Time-invariant and time-varying multirate filter banks: application to image coding ," *Annales des Telecommunications-Annals of Telecommunications,* vol. 53, No.5-6, pp.192-218, May-Jun 1998.

[10] I. Sodagar, K. Nayebi, and T.P Barnwell,III, "Time-varying filter banks and wavelets," *IEEE Trans. Signal Processing,* vol. 42, No. 11, pp. 2983-2996, Nov. 1994.

[11] R.L. de Queiroz, K.R. Rao, "Time-varying lapped transform and wavelet packets," *IEEE Trans. Signal Processing,* vol. 41, No. 12, pp. 3293-3305, Dec. 1993.

[12] C. Herley, M. Vetterli, "Orthogonal Time-Varying Filter Banks and Wavelet Packets," *IEEE Trans. Signal Processing,* vol. 42, No.10, pp. 2650-2663, Oct. 1994.

[13] G. Wang and U. Heute, "Time-varying MMSE modulated lapped transform and its applications to transform coding for speech and audio signals," *Signal Processing,* vol. 82, No. 9, pp. 1283-1304, Sept. 2002.

[14] G. Wang, "The most general time-varying filter bank and time-varying lapped transforms," *IEEE Trans. on Signal Proccesing*, vol. 54, No. 10, pp. 3775-3789, Oct. 2006.

[15] G. Wang, "Analysis of M-channel time-varying filter banks," *Digital Signal Processing,* vol. 18, No. 2, pp. 127-147, May 2008.

[16] H. Wei, S.Billings and J. Liu, "Time-varying parametric modelling and time-dependent spectral characterisation with applications to EEG signals using multiwavelets", *International Journal of Modelling, Identification and Control*, vol. 9, No. 3, pp. 215-224,2010.

[17] X. Xu, Z.Y. Shi and Q. You, "Identification of linear time-varying systems using a wavelet-based state-space method", *Mechanical Systems and Signal Processing*,doi:10.1016/j.ymssp.2011.07.005.

[18] Z. Lua, O. Gueganb, "Estimation of Time-Varying Long Memory Parameter Using Wavelet Method", *Communications in Statistics - Simulation and Computation,* vol. 40, No. 4, pp. 596-613, March 2011.

[19] M. Gokhale1 and D. Khanduja, "Time Domain Signal Analysis Using Wavelet Packet Decomposition Approach", *Int. J. Communications, Network and System Sciences,* doi:10.4236/ijcns.2010.33041.

[20] Guangyu Wang, Zufan Zhang, and Qianbin Chen, "Analysis and Properties of Time-Varying Modified DFT Filter Banks," *EURASIP Journal on Advances in Signal Processing,* vol. 2010, Article ID 342865, 15 pages, 2010. doi:10.1155/2010/342865.

[21] G. Wang, Q. Chen and Z. Ren, "Modelling of time-varying discrete-time systems", *IET Signal Processing,* vol. 5, No. 1, pp104-112, Feb. 2011.

26

Optimized Scalable Wavelet-Based Codec Designs for Semi-Regular 3D Meshes

Shahid M. Satti, Leon Denis, Ruxandra Florea, Jan Cornelis, Peter Schelkens and Adrian Munteanu
Department of Electronics and Informatics (ETRO)
Vrije Universiteit Brussel-IBBT, Brussels, Belgium

1. Introduction

3D graphics applications make use of polygonal 3D meshes for object's shape representation. The recent introduction of high-performance laser scanners and fast microcomputer systems gave rise to high-definition graphics applications. In such applications, objects with complex textures are represented using dense 3D meshes which consist of hundreds of thousands of vertices. Due to their enormous data size, such highly-detailed 3D meshes are rather intricate to store, costly to transmit via bandwidth-limited transmission media, and hard to display on end-user terminals with diverse display capabilities. Scalable compression, wherein the source representation can be adapted to the users' requests, available bandwidth and computational capabilities, is thus of paramount importance in order to make efficient use of the available resources to process, store and transmit high-resolution meshes.

State-of-the-art scalable mesh compression systems can be divided into two main categories. A first category includes codecs that directly compress the irregular topology meshes in the spatial domain. In such codecs, the connectivity information is encoded losslessly while mesh simplification methods such as vertex coalescing (Rossignac & Borrel, 1993), edge decimation (Soucy & Laurendeau, 1996) and edge collapsing (Ronfard & Rossignac, 1996) are employed to encode geometry. These mesh simplification methods progressively remove those mesh vertices which yield the smallest distortion. In order to enable the reconstruction of the original mesh at various levels of detail (LODs), the discarded vertices are encoded in the compressed bit-stream. Mesh compression systems belonging to this category include Progressive Meshes (Li & Kuo, 1998), (Pajarola & Rossignac, 2000) and Topological Surgery (Taubin et al., 1998). These techniques generally exhibit two major drawbacks: first, due to the highly irregular topology of the input mesh, a large source rate is needed for lossless encoding of connectivity. Secondly, encoding the removed vertices in the compressed bit-stream is quite costly for high-resolution meshes. Therefore, such schemes are not useful for complex meshes containing a large number of vertices. An alternative that solves the problem of the large source rates needed to encode the connectivity information, described above, is remeshing, which can be used to convert the original irregular mesh into a mesh consisting of regular elements, such as B-spline (Eck & Hoppe, 1996) or subdivision connectivity patches (Eck et al., 1995). The regular mesh lends itself better to compression, and hence compared to the irregular mesh a much lower rate is needed to losslessly encode its connectivity information. Furthermore, multiresolution techniques alleviate the second problem of having to encode all the original vertices, because only detail information has to be encoded in order to create multiple LODs (or multiple resolution levels). Remeshing together with subdivision-based multiresolution (Lounsbery et al., 1997) are the two major components of the second category of codecs which use space-frequency dilation methods such as wavelet transforms to decorrelate the input mesh data (Khodakovsky et al., 2000), (Denis et al., 2010b). The generated wavelet coefficients are compressed using tree-based bit-plane coding methods (Shapiro, 1993), (Munteanu et al., 1999b) to achieve high compression efficiency. Multiresolution mesh compression techniques provide substantial compression gains compared to their competing schemes, and in this chapter we will confine our discussion to these techniques only.

In the recent past, several multiresolution scalable mesh compression schemes have been proposed. The majority of these schemes use coding techniques which were specifically developed for image compression. However, in general, image and mesh data exhibit different statistical characteristics as the images are consisting of pixels (with intensities) while mesh data involve geometry, i.e., the positions of vertices in a 3D space. Thus, one must be cautious when extrapolating image compression techniques towards mesh geometry encoding.

In this book chapter, we propose a constructive design methodology for multiresolution-scalable mesh compression systems. The input mesh is assumed to possess subdivision connectivity (Lounsbery et al., 1997), i.e., the connectivity in the mesh is built through subdivision[1]. A 3D mesh with subdivision connectivity is also referred to as a semi-regular mesh. With respect to *design*, we address two major aspects of scalable wavelet-based mesh compression systems, namely, the optimality of embedded quantization in scalable mesh coding and the type of coefficient dependencies that can assure the best compression performance. In this context, thorough analyses investigating the aforementioned aspects are carried out to establish the most appropriate design choices. Later on, the derived design choices are integrated as components of the scalable mesh coding system to achieve state-of-the-art compression performance.

The remainder of the book chapter is organized as follows: in Section 2, a brief overview of multiresolution analysis of the mesh geometry is given. Section 3 presents a model-based theoretical investigation of optimal embedded quantization in wavelet-based mesh coding. An information theoretic analysis of the statistical dependencies among wavelet coefficients and the conclusions regarding the best exploitable statistical dependency are detailed in Section 4. Section 5 gives an overview of the state-of-the-art mesh compression systems.

2. Multiresolution analysis of semi-regular meshes

A 3D mesh $M = \{\mathbf{c}, \mathbf{p}\}$ is generally represented as a set of two components, a vertex list $\mathbf{c}$ and a polygon list $\mathbf{p}$. $\mathbf{c}$ is a matrix whose *i*th row c_i contains the x, y and z position of the *i*th vertex, i.e., $c_i = \left[c_{i,x}, c_{i,y}, c_{i,z}\right]$. $\mathbf{p}$ is a list of polygons made up of edges where each edge is a line connecting two vertices. In computer graphics, 3D meshes are constructed

[1] In general, an initial remeshing step (Eck et al., 1995) is required to convert the original irregular mesh into a mesh with the required connectivity.

using different polygonal shapes, e.g., triangles, rectangles etc. However, in this chapter, we will confine our discussion to the triangular meshes only.

In the following, a brief theoretical overview of semi-regular multiresolution analysis is presented. Later on, two practical transforms, namely the lifting-based wavelet transform and the spatially adapted wavelet transform are detailed.

2.1 Theory

2.1.1 Subdivision surfaces

Subdivision is a process of iteratively refining a control polyhedron M^0 into fine geometry polyhedra such that the refined polyhedra $M^1, M^2, M^3...$ converge to a limit surface M^∞. In general, subdivision schemes consist of *splitting* and *averaging* steps. In the *splitting* step, each triangular face is split into four sub-triangles by adding new vertices. This way, an intermediate polyhedron $\bar{M}^j$ is created for any level j. The *averaging* step is used to determine the position of each vertex in M^j from its local neighborhood of vertices in $\bar{M}^j$, $j = 1,2,...,J$.

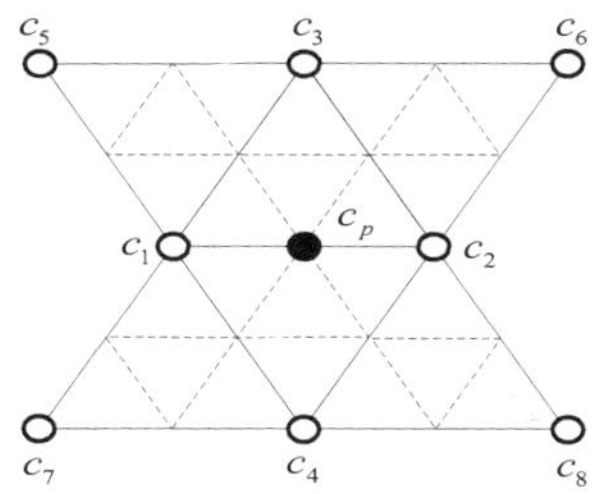

Fig. 1. Butterfly subdivision stencil.

$\mathbf{P}^j \in \mathbb{R}^{N_{j-1} \times N_j}$ and $\mathbf{Q}^j \in \mathbb{R}^{N_{j-1} \times N_{j-1}}$ (where N_j denotes the number of vertices of M^j) are the splitting and averaging matrix at level j. The subdivision process, expressed in matrix form, can be written as:

$$\mathrm{c}^{j+1} = \mathrm{Q}^j \cdot \mathrm{P}^j \cdot \mathrm{c}^j, \; j = 0,1,2,...,J-1 .$$

A commonly used subdivision is Butterfly subdivision (Dyn et al., 1990). The subdivision stencil for Butterfly is shown in Fig. 1, where the position of a newly introduced vertex p is computed as, $c_p = \sum_{i=1}^{8} a_i c_i$ whereby a_i's denote the Butterfly weights (Dyn et al., 1990). Loop (Loop et al., 2009) and Catmull-Clark (Catmull & Clark, 1978) are among the other commonly used subdivision schemes for 3D meshes.

2.1.2 Multiresolution analysis

Lounsbery (Lounsbery et al., 1997) first invented the multiresolution analysis for arbitrary topology semi-regular surfaces using subdivision. He proved that refinable bases exist when a coarse mesh M^0 is refined through subdivision, i.e.,

$$\boldsymbol{\phi}^j(\mathbf{x}) = \boldsymbol{\phi}^{j+1}(\mathbf{x}) \cdot \mathbf{P}^j \text{, for } \mathbf{x} \in M^0 \text{ and } 0 \le j < J. \tag{1}$$

$\boldsymbol{\phi}^j(\mathbf{x})$ in the above equation denotes the row vector of scaling functions ϕ_i^j. Given these refinable scaling functions, scalar-valued function spaces associated with the coarsest geometry M^0 are defined as (Lounsbery et al., 1997):

$$V^j(M^0) := \text{Span}(\boldsymbol{\phi}^j(\mathbf{x})) \text{, for } 0 \le j < J. \tag{2}$$

Eq (1) implies that these spaces are indeed nested, i.e.,

$$V^0(M^0) \subset V^1(M^0) \subset V^2(M^0) \subset \dots, \tag{3}$$

The wavelet space $W^j(M^0)$ is defined as a space which is the orthogonal complement of $V^j(M^0)$ in $V^{j+1}(M^0)$. Hence, $W^j(M^0)$ and $V^j(M^0)$ together can represent any scalar-valued piecewise function in the space $V^{j+1}(M^0)$. If $\psi^j(\mathrm{x})$ is a row vector containing refinable bases functions of $W^j(M^0)$, the following stands (Lounsbery et al., 1997):

$$\psi^j(\mathbf{x}) = \boldsymbol{\phi}^{j+1}(\mathbf{x}) \cdot \mathbf{Q}^j \text{, for } \mathbf{x} \in M^0 \text{ and } 0 \le j < J. \tag{4}$$

Combining (1) with (4) yields

$$(\boldsymbol{\phi}^j(\mathbf{x}), \psi^j(\mathbf{x})) = \boldsymbol{\phi}^{j+1}(\mathbf{x}) \cdot (\mathbf{P}^j, \mathbf{Q}^j), \text{ or } (\boldsymbol{\phi}^j(\mathbf{x}), \psi^j(\mathbf{x})) \cdot (\mathbf{P}^j, \mathbf{Q}^j)^{-1} = \boldsymbol{\phi}^{j+1}(\mathbf{x}). \tag{5}$$

A set of scaling functions $\boldsymbol{\phi}^{j+1}(\mathbf{x})$ can then be used to decompose a surface S^{j+1} in $V^{j+1}(M^0)$, i.e.,

$$S^{j+1} = \sum_i c_i^{j+1} \phi_i^{j+1} = \boldsymbol{\phi}^{j+1}(\mathbf{x}) \cdot \mathbf{c}^{j+1}, \tag{6}$$

where c_i^{j+1} is the ith vertex in M^{j+1}. Since the analysis filters are uniquely determined by the relationship

$$\left(\mathbf{P}^j \middle| \mathbf{Q}^j \right)^{-1} = \begin{pmatrix} \mathbf{A}^j \\ \mathbf{B}^j \end{pmatrix}, \tag{7}$$

by combining Eq (5) and Eq (6) and making the above substitution for $\left(\mathbf{P}^j \middle| \mathbf{Q}^j \right)^{-1}$, we obtain:

$$S^{j+1} = \boldsymbol{\phi}^j(\mathbf{x}) \cdot \mathbf{A}^j \cdot \mathbf{c}^{j+1} + \psi^j(\mathbf{x}) \cdot \mathbf{B}^j \cdot \mathbf{c}^{j+1}. \tag{8}$$

From Eq (8), Eq (9) one derives the forward wavelet transform, given by:

$$\mathbf{c}^j = \mathbf{A}^j \cdot \mathbf{c}^{j+1}, \quad \mathbf{d}^j = \mathbf{B}^j \cdot \mathbf{c}^{j+1}, \quad \forall j: 0 \le j < J, \tag{9}$$

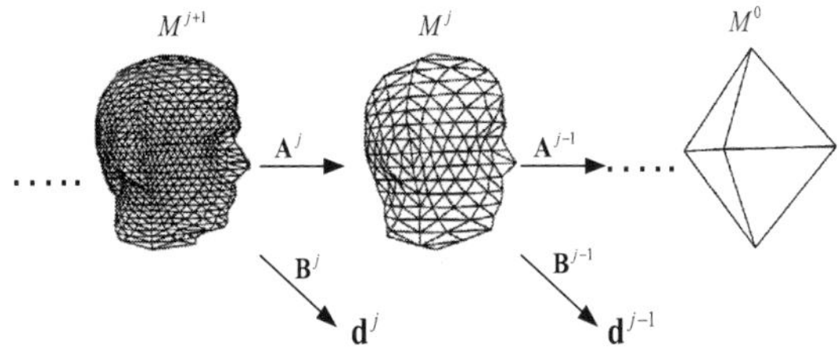

Fig. 2. Pictorial representation of the forward wavelet decomposition, (Lounsbery et al., 1997).

where $\mathbf{d}^j$ is a matrix containing the wavelet coefficients for the jth level of the transform. In general, after the transform, a fair amount of correlation still exist between x, y and z wavelet component. Local frame representation (Khodakovsky et al., 2000) of wavelet coefficients is often used to make wavelet components much more independent. After the local frame transformation, each wavelet coefficient consists of a *normal* and two *tangential* components. $\mathbf{A}^j$s and $\mathbf{B}^j$s are matrices representing the low and the high-pass filters, respectively, also referred to as analysis filter pairs.

A similar reasoning as for Eq (9) can be used to formulate the inverse wavelet transform, expressed by:

$$\mathbf{c}^{j+1} = \mathbf{P}^j \cdot \mathbf{c}^j + \mathbf{Q}^j \cdot \mathbf{d}^j \text{, for } \forall j: 0 \le j < J. \tag{10}$$

Hence, $\mathbf{P}^j$s and $\mathbf{Q}^j$s jointly form the synthesis part of the decomposition for the lossless reconstruction of the input semi-regular mesh M^J. Note that the computation of the $\mathbf{A}^j$s and $\mathbf{B}^j$s involves the inversion of a large matrix, which makes the forward transform more complex than the inverse transform.

2.2 Lifting-based wavelet transform

As explained earlier, the filter bank implementation of multiresolution analysis is quite complex in the sense that the computation of analysis filters involve the computationally intensive inversion of large subdivision matrices. In this context, the lifting-based wavelet implementation (Schröder & Sweldens, 1995) provides a low complexity construction of multiresolution methods. In lifting-based multiresolution analysis, each scaling function ϕ_i^j of the jth level exists so that $\{\phi_i^j \mid i \in M^j\}$ is a Riesz basis of $V^j\left(M^0\right)$ (Schröder & Sweldens, 1995). The refinement relation for the scaling functions is then:

$$\phi_i^j = \sum_l p_{i,l}^j \cdot \phi_i^{j+1}, \tag{11}$$

where l is the set which defines all linear combination of scaling functions and $p_{i,l}^j$ forms the entries of a matrix similar to $\mathbf{P}^j$. A similar refinement relation as Eq (11) is also defined for wavelet functions, i.e., each wavelet function ψ_k^j exists so that $\{\psi_k^j \mid k \in K^j\}$ is a Riesz basis of $W^j\left(M^0\right)$:

$$\psi_k^{\,j} = \sum_l q_{k,l}^j \cdot \phi_k^{\,j+1}. \tag{12}$$

K^j and M^j are disjoint sets and they jointly form the scaling function index set of the next higher level, i.e., $M^{j+1} = M^j \oplus K^j$. The lifting-based forward decomposition is expressed by the following relations (Schröder & Sweldens, 1995):

$$\begin{aligned}
&\forall i \in M^j: \quad c_i^{\,j} = c_i^{\,j+1} \Rightarrow \text{subsample} \\
&\forall k \in K^j: \quad d_k^{\,j} = c_k^{\,j+1} - \sum_{i \in M^j} a_i . c_i^{\,j} \Rightarrow \text{prediction} \\
&\forall k \in K^j: \begin{cases} c_1^j = c_1^j + \tilde{a}_1 \cdot d_k^{\,j} \\ c_2^j = c_2^j + \tilde{a}_2 \cdot d_k^{\,j} \end{cases} \Rightarrow \text{update}
\end{aligned} \tag{13}$$

In the forward transform, the first step is to produce a lower-resolution mesh M^j starting from a higher-resolution version M^{j+1}. The wavelet coefficient $d_k^{\,j}$ is the *prediction error* when a high-resolution vertex $c_k^{\,j+1}$ is predicted based on its low-resolution neighborhood in M^j. After the prediction, an *update* step is used to modify the low resolution mesh M^j. The *update* step is carried out on a pair $\{c_1, c_2\}$ of low-resolution vertices joined by a parent edge (Schröder & Sweldens, 1995) using the update weights $\{\tilde{a}_1, \tilde{a}_2\}$. In general, the prediction and update weights only depend on the connectivity with respect to the vertex to be predicted. However, specific multiresolution analyses for which the weights depend on the specific resolution level and the underlying geometry can be also constructed (more details are given in Section 2.3).

The inverse transform can be formulated by following the forward-transform steps in the reverse order, i.e.:

$$\begin{aligned}
&\forall k \in K^j: \begin{cases} c_1^j = c_1^j - \tilde{a}_1 \cdot d_k^{\,j} \\ c_2^j = c_2^j - \tilde{a}_2 \cdot d_k^{\,j} \end{cases} \Rightarrow \text{inverse update} \\
&\forall k \in K^j: \quad c_k^{\,j+1} = d_k^{\,j} + \sum_{i \in M^j} a_i \cdot c_i^{\,j} \Rightarrow \text{inverse predict} \\
&\forall i \in M^j: \quad c_i^{\,j+1} = c_i^{\,j} \Rightarrow \text{inverse subsample}
\end{aligned} \tag{14}$$

2.3 Spatially Adaptive Wavelet Transform (SAWT)

As mentioned earlier, lifting-based transforms generally employ fixed prediction weights, independent of the spatial position and geometry around the vertex to be predicted. A simple observation reveals that a better prediction can result from adapting the prediction to the underlying geometry of the mesh. This argument is explained with a simple example: Fig. 3, referring to the position variable of the vertices, shows a scenario where the vertex to be predicted c_p lies on the straight line joining the vertex pair $\{c_1, c_2\}$, while the remaining six coarser vertices $\{c_i\}_{i=3}^8$ lie on two different planes. In this situation, a prediction function for c_p involving all eight coarser vertices will not be optimal and a better prediction could result by using c_1 and c_2 only. This is logical since c_p lies on the edge formed by the vertex pair $\{c_1, c_2\}$ and is geometrically more correlated to vertices $\{c_1, c_2\}$. Thus, an efficient prediction can be achieved if the prediction process is adapted to the local mesh geometry. Efficient prediction results in smaller energy of wavelet coefficients and hence an improved compression performance of the mesh coding system. To reverse the prediction operation, the decoder needs to know the weights used by the encoder for the prediction of each vertex c_p. Since additional rate (compared to classical Butterfly) needs to be spent for coding the prediction weights, the total compression efficiency in the geometry adaptive case is a compromise between the bitrate saved due to the efficient prediction and the extra bitrate needed for signaling the prediction weights.

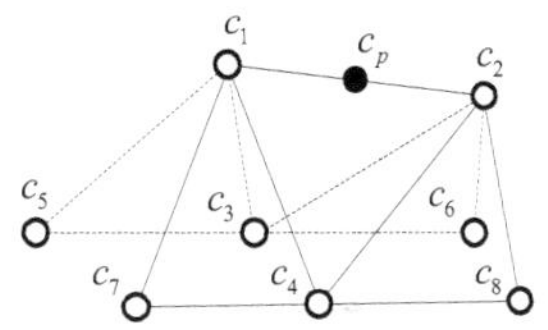

Fig. 3. Butterfly footprint on an edge.

In the following, a finite set of prediction filters is proposed in the context of spatially-adaptive wavelet transforms (SAWT) (Denis et al., 2010a). The idea is to use one filter out of this set which best suits the geometry around the vertex to be predicted and which results in the smallest prediction error. A careful application of such an adaptive approach will provide an average rate gain if the reduction in the bitrate due to better prediction dominates the extra bitrate needed to signal the filter type to the decoder.

In a first step, the input semi-regular mesh is segmented into regions as follows. Let $B(r,s)$ denote the bounding box of the input semi-regular mesh, where $r=(x_B,y_B,z_B)$ and $s=(s_x,s_y,s_z)$ represent the coordinates of the top-left corner and the size vector, respectively. Considering the bounding box as the root cell, each cell on a certain tree level is recursively split into eight equally sized sub-cells to create the next level of the octree. This recursive splitting continues until the number of vertices in the highest-level cells are smaller than a user-defined threshold α. This way, the semi-regular mesh is divided into regions of approximately the same size - see Fig. 4.

For each region k, the wavelet analysis is performed by selecting one of the six candidates filters given below:

$$f_1=\tfrac{1}{2}(c_1+c_2)+\tfrac{1}{8}(c_3+c_4)-\tfrac{1}{16}(c_5+c_6+c_7+c_8)\Rightarrow(\text{Butterfly})$$
$$f_2=\tfrac{1}{2}(c_1+c_2)+\tfrac{1}{4}(c_3+c_4)-\tfrac{1}{8}(c_5+c_6+c_7+c_8)\Rightarrow(\text{Modified Butterfly})$$
$$f_3=\tfrac{3}{8}(c_1+c_2)+\tfrac{1}{8}(c_3+c_4)\Rightarrow(\text{Loop})$$
$$f_4=\tfrac{1}{2}(c_1+c_2)\Rightarrow(\text{edge})$$
$$f_5=\tfrac{1}{2}(c_3+c_4)\Rightarrow(\text{anti edge})$$
$$f_6=\tfrac{1}{4}(c_1+c_2+c_3+c_4)\Rightarrow(\text{Hybrid of } f_4 \text{ and } f_5)$$

Note that the above set of filters is defined using a mixture of Butterfly, Loop and midpoint subdivision schemes.

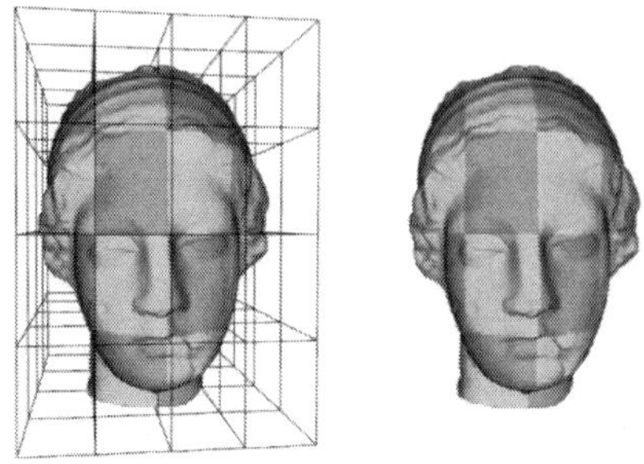

Fig. 4. Mesh partitioning for $\alpha = 400$. The red and green patches indicate different regions for which different prediction filters will be selected.

Similar to (Chang & Girod, 2006), a filter candidate for a particular region k in M^J, is chosen in an optimal distortion-rate (D-R) manner. More specifically, a predictor for each region k is selected such that the following Lagrangian cost function is minimized:

$$\Lambda_{M^J,k} = \arg\min_{l \in \{1,2,..,6\}} \left\{ E_k\left[\left(c_p - \tilde{c}_{p,f_l} \right)^2 \right] + \lambda \cdot R_k(f_l) \right\} \tag{15}$$

where $R_k(f_l)$ denotes the rate necessary for encoding the filter index l used for prediction in the region k.

3. Scalable quantization of wavelet coefficients

In scalable mesh compression, the wavelet coefficients in the subbands are quantized using a generic family of embedded deadzone scalar quantizers (EDSQ) (Taubman & Marcelin, 2001), in which every wavelet coefficient X is quantized to:

$$q_{\xi,n} = \begin{cases} sign(X) \cdot \left\lfloor \frac{|X|}{\Delta_n} + \xi_n \right\rfloor & if \ \frac{|X|}{\Delta_n} + \xi_n > 0 \\ 0 & otherwise \end{cases} \tag{16}$$

where $n \in \mathbb{Z}_+$ denotes the quantization level. ξ_n and Δ_n denote the deadzone control parameter and the step size for any $n \geq 0$, respectively, with $\xi_n = \xi_0 / 2^n$ and $\Delta_n = 2^n \Delta_0$, where ξ_0 and Δ_0 are the parameters for the highest rate quantizer $(n = 0)$. Note that $\xi_0 = 0$ corresponds to the well-known SAQ (Shapiro, 1993) in which the deadzone size is twice the step size Δ_n for any n.

3.1 Wavelet coefficient histogram

In general, the observed histogram H_k^j of the kth, $k \in \{x, y, z\}$, coordinate component of the jth wavelet subband is symmetric around its center of mass which is often zero or very close to zero. Moreover, the histogram is peaky around the mean and the frequency of occurrence decays as the magnitude of the coefficient's component increases. Fig. 5 depicts the observed histograms of the d^{J-3} subband of *Rabbit* (*non-normal* mesh) and *Dino* (*normal* mesh) obtained using the classical Butterly transform. It is observed experimentally that, in general, $\sigma^2(H_k^{j+1}) < \sigma^2(H_k^j)$ for $1 \le j < J$.

In the literature, the observed histogram of any component of a wavelet subband is generally modeled using a zero mean generalized Gaussian (GG) distribution (Mallat, 1989), expressed by:

$$\forall x \in \mathbb{R} \quad f_{GG}(x,\sigma,\alpha) = \frac{\alpha \upsilon^{1/\alpha}}{2\Gamma(1/\alpha)} e^{-\upsilon|x|^{\alpha}}, \tag{17}$$

where α, $\alpha \in (0,2]$, is the shape control parameter. $\upsilon > 0$ is the scaling factor and $\upsilon^{1/\alpha} = \sqrt{\Gamma(3/\alpha)/\sigma^2\Gamma(1/\alpha)}$, where Γ is the Gamma function. Note that, for $\alpha = 1$, Eq (17) transforms into a zero-mean Laplacian probability density function (PDF) given by:

$$\forall x \in \mathbb{R} \quad f_L(x,\sigma) = \frac{1}{\sigma\sqrt{2}} e^{-\frac{\sqrt{2}}{\sigma}|x|} = \frac{\lambda}{2} e^{-\lambda|x|} \text{ where } \lambda = \frac{\sqrt{2}}{\sigma}, \tag{18}$$

and for $\alpha = 2$ Eq (17) corresponds to a zero-mean Gaussian PDF.

Although GG distributions closely approximate the observed histogram of wavelet coefficients, only approximate rate and distortion expressions for a uniformly quantized GG random variable are known (Fraysse et al,. 2008). The extension of these expressions to embedded quantization is not evident as the rate and distortion functions for such distributions are not easily tractable and can only be computed numerically. Moreover, computing these quantities gets very cumbersome due to the slow numerical integration of expressions involving a GG probability function, especially for $\alpha << 1$.

3.2 Proposed Laplacian mixture model

In order to avoid the aforementioned drawbacks of GG distributions, we propose a simple Laplacian mixture (LM) model which not only gives an easy closed-form derivation of the distortion and rate quantities but also better approximates the observed histogram of wavelet coefficients in the majority of cases. The proposed LM is a linear combination of two Laplacian PDFs, i.e.,

$$\forall x \in \mathbb{R} \quad f_{LM}(x) = \beta \cdot f_L(x,\sigma_1) + (1-\beta) \cdot f_L(x,\sigma_2). \tag{19}$$

Note that $f_{LM}(x)$ indeed defines a probability function, as $\int_{-\infty}^{\infty} f_{LM}(x)dx = 1$.

The LM model is fitted over the observed data using the expectation maximization (EM) algorithm (Dempster et al., 1977) in order to determine the parameters σ_1, σ_2 and β. The E-step in the EM process calculates two responsibility factors

$$r_1(i) = \frac{\beta \cdot f_L(x_i,\sigma_1)}{\beta \cdot f_L(x_i,\sigma_1) + (1-\beta) \cdot f_L(x_i,\sigma_2)}, \quad r_2(i) = \frac{(1-\beta) \cdot f_L(x_i,\sigma_2)}{\beta \cdot f_L(x_i,\sigma_1) + (1-\beta) \cdot f_L(x_i,\sigma_2)},$$

of each observation $x_i, 1 \le i \le N$ and the M-step updates the parameters to be estimated, as:

$$\sigma_m = \sqrt{2}\frac{\sum_{i=1}^{N} r_m(i).|x_i|}{\sum_{i=1}^{N} r_m(i)}, \quad m = 1,2, \text{ and } \beta = \frac{1}{N}\sum_{i=1}^{N} r_1(i).$$

The E- and M- steps are executed in tandem till the algorithm achieves minimum *Kullback-Leibler* (KL) distance between the observed and model histograms. A better convergence rate is achieved by the initialization condition $\sigma_1^2 = 0.5\sigma_E^2$, $\sigma_2^2 = 2\sigma_E^2$ and $\beta = 0.9$, where σ_E^2 is the estimated data variance. Histogram fitting for GG distributions is done using the brute-force method where parameters σ_1, σ_2 and β are exhaustively computed for a minimum KL distance.

3.3 Distortion-Rate (D-R) function

Closed-form expressions for the output distortion D_L and the output rate R_L of a Laplacian source quantized using an n level EDSQ are derived in the Appendix. In this section, we derive the D-R function for our proposed LM model. Since the distortion is a linear function of the source PDF, the output distortion D_{LM} of the LM PDF for any quantization level n can be written as:

$$D_{LM}\left(Q_{\delta_n,\Delta_n}\right) = \beta \cdot D_L\left(Q_{\delta_n,\Delta_n}\right) + (1-\beta)\cdot D_L\left(Q_{\delta_n,\Delta_n}\right), \text{ with } \delta_n = 1 - \xi_n. \tag{20}$$

This does not hold for the output rate R_{LM} since the entropy involves the non-linear $\log(.)$ function. Instead, R_{LM} can be computed as an infinite sum:

$$P_0 = 2\int_0^{\delta_n\Delta_n} f_{LM}(x)dx,\ P_k = \int_{(k-1+\delta_n)\Delta_n}^{(k+\delta_n)\Delta_n} f_{LM}(x)dx,\ k = 1,2,3\ldots, \text{ and } R_{LM}(Q_{\delta_n,\Delta_n}) = -\sum_{k=-\infty}^{\infty} P_k \log_2 P_k$$

,

where P_k denotes the probability mass of the kth quantization cell ($k = 0$ corresponds to the deadzone cell). Since the LM model is symmetric around its mean, $P_k = P_{-k}$. Note that the probability mass function (PMF) can be computed exactly due to the possibility of analytical integration of $f_{LM}(x)$. For the GG distribution, however, only numerical integration is possible.

3.4 Model validation

This section demonstrates that the proposed LM model is able to approximate the observed histogram and the observed D-R function of 3D wavelet coefficients more accurately compared to the commonly utilized GG distributions. For comparison purpose, results for the single Laplacian $f_{LM}(\beta = 0)$ case are also reported.

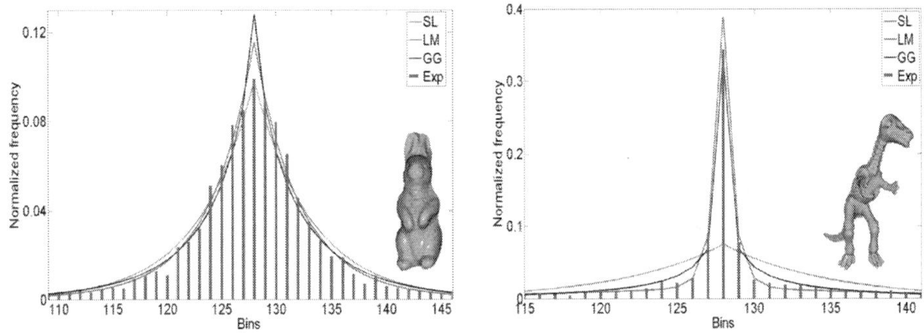

Fig. 5. Probability function fitting over the observed histogram (Exp) for $\mathbf{d}^{J-3}$ *-normal component* for Rabbit (left) and Dino (right). SL is used as the abbreviation of single Laplacian PDF.

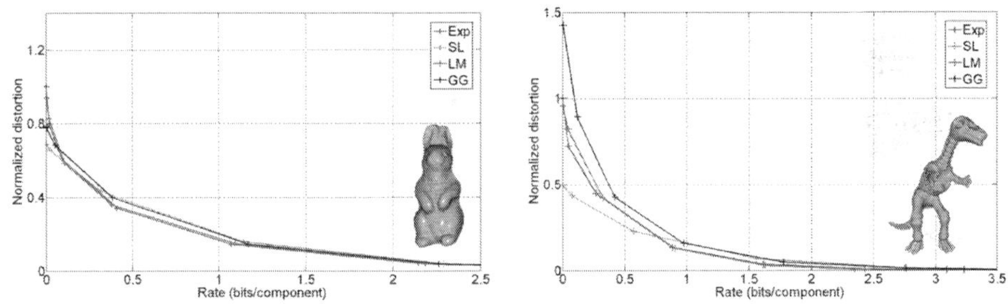

Fig. 6. Modeled and observed D-R functions for the histograms of Fig. 5. Rate is taken as bits per spatial coordinate component.

Fig. 5 illustrates that the proposed mixture model provides a better fitting probability function for the observed histogram compared to the Laplacian and GG distributions. This is especially true for the middle range positive and negative coefficients values - see Fig. 5. For the Rabbit mesh, LM gives only slightly better fitting than the other two models. However, for Dino, the LM can clearly model the fast decay of the observed histogram more accurately than the GG. The Laplacian PDF in this case only gives a very coarse approximation of the observed histogram.

Mesh Type	Mesh (Filter)	SL			LM			GG		
		Nor	*Tan 1*	*Tan 2*	*Nor*	*Tan 1*	*Tan 2*	*Nor*	*Tan1*	*Tan 2*
Non-Normal	*Venus(U-BF)*	0.097 (6.3)	0.114 (10.3)	0.103 (8.9)	0.075 (1.3)	0.100 (3.3)	0.091 (2.8)	0.086 (4.7)	0.102 (5.0)	0.089 (4.7)
	Venus(L-BF)	0.137 (11.4)	0.137 (10.1)	0.104 (6.0)	0.090 (2.0)	0.108 (2.9)	0.080 (1.9)	0.112 (8.1)	0.121 (5.4)	0.092 (4.1)
	Venus(Loop)	0.113 (9.4)	0.102 (7.3)	0.091 (6.7)	0.085 (3.3)	0.090 (1.8)	0.069 (1.7)	0.098 (7.1)	0.092 (3.9)	0.081 (5.0)
	Rabbit(U-BF)	0.170 (8.6)	0.171 (10.4)	0.172 (10.2)	0.134 (1.4)	0.136 (2.0)	0.132 (1.8)	0.150 (5.7)	0.143 (5.2)	0.147 (6.2)
	Rabbit(L-BF)	0.208 (12.0)	0.188 (10.7)	0.177 (8.4)	0.143 (2.5)	0.140 (1.5)	0.138 (1.8)	0.160 (6.7)	0.152 (5.1)	0.153 (5.3)
	Rabbit(Loop)	0.167 (11.2)	0.207 (11.2)	0.173 (8.3)	0.115 (2.4)	0.156 (1.8)	0.135 (2.3)	0.136 (7.9)	0.177 (7.6)	0.152 (5.2)
Normal	*Dino(U-BF)*	0.527 (16.2)	0.656 (34.3)	0.971 (42.7)	0.145 (5.6)	0.147 (7.8)	0.154 (9.4)	0.165 (7.5)	0.132 (23.4)	0.141 (30.3)
	Skull(U-BF)	1.108 (37.2)	1.473 (44.9)	1.877 (50.4)	0.120 (3.9)	0.138 (7.9)	0.157 (20.5)	0.145 (12.8)	0.141 (15.4)	0.141 (19.9)
	Skrewdriver(U-BF)	0.5294 (33.0)	0.6477 (42.4)	0.6377 (41.9)	0.309 (14.4)	0.251 (17.0)	0.263 (20.0)	0.315 (25.0)	0.262 (34.8)	0.249 (35.2)

Table 1. *KL* (%*ME*, the modeling error as defined in Eq (19)) for the *normal* (*NOR*) and the two *tangential* components (*TAN1, TAN2*) averaged over the five subbands. *U-BF* (Unlifted Butterfly), *L-BF* (Lifted Butterfly).

Fig. 6 plots the observed and model D-R curves for the same subband as the one used in Fig. 5. For Rabbit, the LM D-R almost completely overlaps the observed D-R curve. In both cases, the D-R function of the proposed LM model follows the experimental D-R curve more closely than the other two models.

In Table 1, the average *KL* divergence results for the Laplacian, GG and LM models for two non-normal (Venus, Rabbit) and three normal (Dino, Skull, Skredriver) meshes are shown. Each of the three coordinate components is considered separately. For each trial of Table 1, average is taken over five highest resolution subbands. For the large majority of cases, the LM model gives better fitting of the observed histogram than the competing GG model. Note that the Laplacian model gives always the worst fitting results. Also, the LM model gives equally good fitting for both *normal* (*Nor*) and *tangential* (*Tan 1* and *Tan 2*) components. Superior histogram fitting results of our proposed model are also observed for the SAWT of Section 2.3. These results are not reported here due to lack of space.

In Table 1, the percentage modeling error $ME(\%)$ relative to the *KL* divergence is shown in parenthesis of each table entry. The $ME(\%)$ is defined in order to gauge the D-R accuracy of the proposed mixture model with respect to other two models. $ME(\%)$ is defined as:

$$ME(\%)=\frac{\int_{R\in\Re}\left|D_M(R)-D_E(R)\right|}{\int_{R\in\Re}\max_R\left\{D_M(R),D_E(R)\right\}}\times 100\,. \tag{21}$$

Mesh Type	Mesh (Filter)	SL			LM			GG		
		$J-1$	$J-2$	$J-3$	$J-1$	$J-2$	$J-3$	$J-1$	$J-2$	$J-3$
Non-Normal	*Venus(U-BF)*	0.044 (13.6)	0.038 (8.4)	0.039 (3.5)	0.014 (2.9)	0.008 (0.85)	0.025 (1.5)	0.027 (9.5)	0.024 (5.6)	0.033 (2.8)
	Venus(L-BF)	0.050 (13.8)	0.070 (13.9)	0.076 (7.6)	0.010 (2.1)	0.010 (1.5)	0.027 (1.7)	0.029 (9.9)	0.041 (10.1)	0.049 (4.1)
	Venus(Loop)	0.051 (13.8)	0.054 (11.0)	0.038 (4.0)	0.016 (2.4)	0.009 (1.6)	0.023 (0.80)	0.036 (11.0)	0.031 (6.8)	0.032 (2.7)
	Rabbit(U-BF)	0.064 (14.0)	0.062 (11.4)	0.082 (8.1)	0.008 (1.5)	0.011 (1.0)	0.035 (1.3)	0.029 (8.6)	0.032 (6.8)	0.054 (4.9)
	Rabbit(L-BF)	0.069 (14.2)	0.093 (13.9)	0.111 (11.2)	0.007 (1.5)	0.011 (1.1)	0.035 (1.8)	0.029 (8.6)	0.040 (8.6)	0.058 (5.9)
	Rabbit(Loop)	0.082 (16.4)	0.088 (14.7)	0.085 (9.0)	0.011 (2.0)	0.013 (1.9)	0.034 (2.0)	0.042 (11.5)	0.038 (8.7)	0.058 (5.4)
Normal	*Dino(U-BF)*	1.208 (56.7)	0.873 (46.7)	0.623 (34.7)	0.029 (13.7)	0.074 (12.8)	0.049 (4.6)	0.031 (41.3)	0.042 (32.9)	0.058 (20.4)
	Skull(U-BF)	2.039 (65.7)	1.981 (49.9)	1.832 (32.4)	0.054 (34.2)	0.040 (7.6)	0.076 (5.1)	0.036 (40.2)	0.068 (15.1)	0.066 (8.3)
	Skrewdriver(U-BF)	0.536 (67.0)	0.696 (61.6)	0.483 (39.7)	0.067 (53.2)	0.074 (18.2)	0.065 (7.3)	0.035 (64.0)	0.064 (54.3)	0.101 (25.4)

Table 2. *KL* (%*ME*) for three resolution subbands averaged over the three coordinate components.

From Table 1, it is evident that on average the proposed LM model performs better than the GG and Laplacian models also in the *ME* sense. Better *ME* results are also obtained for SAWT (not reported here). Hence, the proposed LM model along with the derived D-R function is a better choice for modeling both the histogram and the D-R curve of mesh wavelet coefficients compared to the contemporary models. One notices that, a best histogram fitting in KL sense may not always yield the lowest ME.

Table 2 reports the model validation results for different resolution subbands. For each trial the average is taken across the three spatial coordinate components. It is observed that the GG model performs slightly better for the low-resolution subbands of some meshes. The observed histograms in such cases are more Gaussian-alike, i.e., they have a round top. In general, the LM model faces difficulty in approximating such a round-top histogram due to the peaky nature of each of its Laplacian components; the GG fits well such histograms, as it corresponds to a Gaussian distribution for $\alpha = 2$. Nevertheless, the results show that, on average, the LM model outperforms the Laplacian and the GG models in *KL* as well as in *ME* sense.

3.5 Optimal embedded quantization

In this section, conclusions regarding the optimal EDSQ to be used in scalable wavelet-based coding of meshes are drawn. Let z denote the ratio between the deadzone size for n = 0 (see Eq. (16)) and the step size for $n \geq 0$ of a general EDSQ. The total average signal-to-noise ratio (*SNR*) difference which is utilized to measure the performance gap of different embedded quantizers is defined as:

$$\Delta\overline{SNR} = \frac{1}{N}\sum_{\Re}\left(\underset{z=1}{SNR(R)} - \underset{z>1}{SNR(R)} \right),$$

which is computed over a rate range $\Re$ for N rate points, where *SNR*(*R*) denotes the discrete *SNR*-rate function. The $SNR = 10\log_{10}(\sigma^2/D)$ is computed in dBs, where D is the total distortion in the transform domain. The difference in *SNR* is computed relative to the uniform embedded quantizer (UEQ), i.e., $z=1$. $\Delta\overline{SNR}$ for five embedded deadzone quantizers is plotted in Fig. 7. over a wide range of standard deviation ratios σ_2/σ_1. In Fig. 7., the commonly observed proportion $\beta = 0.9$ is considered, as mentioned in Section 3.2.

We determined experimentally that at lower standard deviation ratios, $\Delta\overline{SNR}$ is positive and the UEQ is optimal for $\sigma_2/\sigma_1 < 120$. For $120 < \sigma_2/\sigma_1 < 290$, the quantizer with $z = 1.5$ performs better compared to all other quantizers. Similarly, $z=2$ (i.e. the SAQ) performs the best in the range $290 < \sigma_2/\sigma_1 < 600$, while $z = 2.5$ performs the best for $600 < \sigma_2/\sigma_1$. In general, small standard deviation ratios correspond to α close to 1, observed in non-normal meshes, while higher ratios correspond to $\alpha \ll 1$, observed in normal meshes. These results show that one cannot determine a single embedded quantizer that provides the best performance for *all* 3D meshes. However, an optimal quantizer per wavelet coordinate can be determined based on the corresponding σ_2/σ_1 extracted from the model.

Overall, for $\sigma_2/\sigma_1 < 120$, the difference between SAQ and the UEQ is significant, and hence UEQ is the optimal choice. For $\sigma_2/\sigma_1 \geq 120$, SAQ is not always the optimum, but lies not far from the optimum.

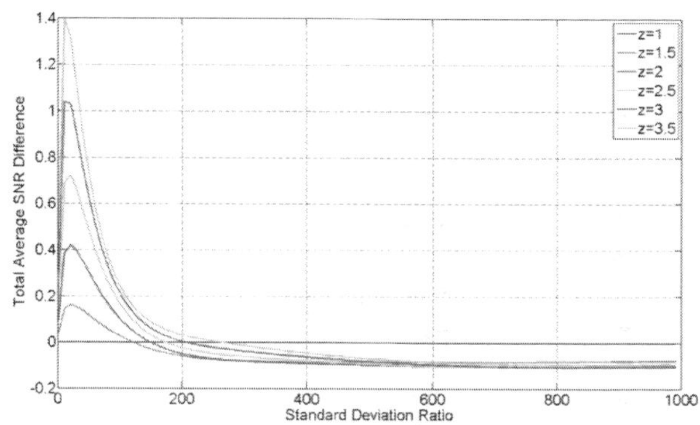

Fig. 7. *SNR* difference for five EDSQs with respect to UEQ.

Given the fact that SAQ is closely linked to bit-plane coding and that it can be implemented using simple binary arithmetic, one concludes that SAQ is not an optimal, but an acceptable solution in scalable coding of meshes.

4. Analysis of wavelet coefficient dependencies

Similar to images, parent-children and neighboring wavelet coefficient dependencies exist in wavelet decomposed mesh structure. In Fig. 8 (middle, right), the positions of the wavelet coefficients at different levels of the transform are shown with the help of white and dark circles. In particular, wavelet coefficients have a one-to-one correspondence with the edges of the coarser mesh. For each wavelet coefficient there are rings of neighboring coefficients which lie in the same wavelet subband - see Fig. 8 (right). Also, a set of four wavelet coefficients have a parent coefficient at the next coarser resolution - see Fig. 8 (middle, right).

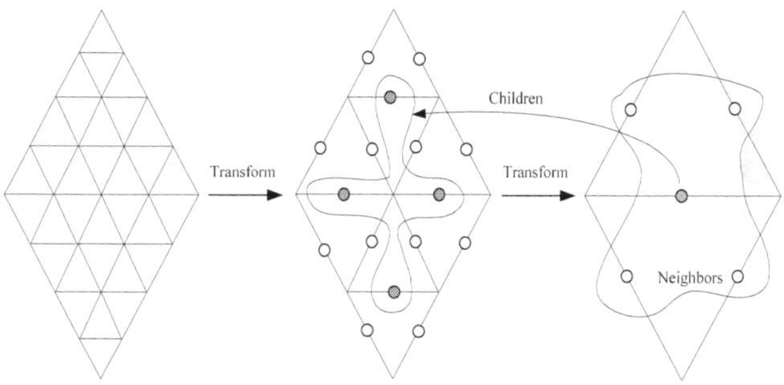

Fig. 8. Parent-children and neighboring wavelet coefficients: actual mesh (left); coarser meshes after one (middle), and after two wavelet decomposition levels (right).

Statistical intraband dependencies exist between neighboring coefficients of each resolution level. The main reason for the existence of these dependencies is the smoothness of the surface. Wavelet coding paradigms that exploit the intraband dependencies between the wavelet coefficients are known as intraband wavelet codecs such as block-based coding techniques (Munteanu et al., 1999a), quadtree coding approaches (Munteanu et al., 1999b), and the EBCOT codec employed in the JPEG-2000 scalable image coding standard (Taubman, 2000).

Statistical dependencies also exist between the parent and descendants (children) due to the natural decay of the coefficients' magnitude for increasing frequencies. In other words, if a parent coefficient magnitude is below a certain threshold, then there is a high probability that the magnitude of its descendants will be also below this threshold. This corresponds to the so-called zerotree-model, firstly introduced by Shapiro in (Shapiro, 1993). The wavelet coding paradigms that exploit the parent-children dependencies are known as interband wavelet codecs.

Finally, there is a third category of coding paradigms, exploiting both the interband and intraband statistical dependencies between the wavelet coefficients. They are generally known as composite codecs, EZBC (Hsiang & Woods, 2000) and the ECECOW approach of (Wu, 1997) are typical examples of codecs in this category.

In the following, an information theoretical analysis of the aforementioned coefficient dependencies is presented. Our aim is to single out the type of dependencies which can ensure best compression performance in the context of wavelet-based mesh compression.

4.1 Mutual information analysis

The mutual information is the reduction in the entropy of one random variable due to the knowledge of the other random variable.

$$I(X;Y) = h(X) - h(X/Y) \ , \tag{22}$$

It is known that $I(X,Y) = I(Y,X)$. In the wavelet domain, we define the following mutual information quantities:

$I(X;P_X)$: denotes the mutual information between a wavelet coefficient X and its parent coefficient P_X.

$I(X;\mathbf{n}_X)$: denotes the mutual information between a wavelet coefficient X and its neighboring wavelet coefficients $\mathbf{n}_X = [n_{1,X}, n_{2,X}, \dots n_{N,X}]$.

$I(X;P_X;\mathbf{n}_X)$: denotes the composite mutual information.

From the basics of information theory (Cover & Thomas, 1991), we know that:

$$I(X;P_X;\mathbf{n}_X) \ge I(X;\mathbf{n}_X) \quad \text{and} \quad I(X;P_X;\mathbf{n}_X) \ge I(X;P_X). \tag{23}$$

For the estimation of $I(X;\mathbf{n}_X)$, we need to estimate the joint PDF $p(x,\boldsymbol{n}_x)$ which can have high dimensionality depending on the number of considered neighbors. Since the amount of data needed to accurately estimate a PDF increases exponentially with its dimensionality, it is difficult to reliably estimate a high-dimensional PDF. To alleviate this problem, the reduction in dimensionality as proposed in (Liu & Moulin, 2000) is used here. We summarize the neighborhood of X through a so-called summarizing function $T = g(\mathbf{n}_X)$. This function maps the neighboring wavelet coefficients to a single value. We note that such a many-to-one summarizing function cannot increase the mutual information, i.e.,

$$I(X;\mathbf{n}_X) \ge I(X;T) \ . \tag{24}$$

Equality in the above equation holds if $\mathbf{n}_X \to T \to X$ forms a Markov chain. The summarizing function used in our analysis is:

$$T = f(\mathbf{n}_X) = \sum_{i=1}^{N} \left(n_{i,X}\right)^2. \tag{25}$$

Due to this summarizing function, it is sufficient to compute the joint PDF $p(x,t)$, t is a realization of the random variable T, instead of $p(x,\boldsymbol{n}_x)$, for the estimation of the intraband mutual information $I(X;\mathbf{n}_X)$.

In our analysis, the mutual information for the defined quantities is estimated using the adaptive partitioning method (Darbellay & Vajda, 1999) instead of the traditional histogram method. This is because the histogram method highly depends on the bin size and for a small bin size there may not be sufficient number of observations in some bins to make a correct estimate. The adaptive partitioning method (Darbellay & Vajda, 1999) on the other hand, ensures that there are always sufficient numbers of observations in each bin, and provides reliable estimates of the mutual information.

		Butterfly			Loop		
Mesh Type	MESH	INTRABAND	INTERBAND	COMPOSITE	INTRABAND	INTERBAND	COMPOSITE
Non-Normal	Venus	0.3727	0.1902	0.6886	0.8320	0.5591	1.5847
	Bunny	0.3960	0.1992	0.6844	0.8033	0.5628	1.5427
	Horse	0.5615	0.2869	0.9873	1.0482	0.6943	1.9684
	Rabbit	0.4048	0.2017	0.7089	0.8996	0.6450	1.7425
	Feline	0.8277	0.2134	1.0696	1.1471	0.6285	2.0287
Normal	Venus	0.3052	0.2130	0.5741	-	-	-
	Skull	0.3381	0.2922	0.7001	-	-	-
	Dino	0.3043	0.2804	0.6672	-	-	-

Table 3. Average mutual information in bits for several non-normal and normal meshes.

Table 3 shows the average mutual information results for interband, intraband and composite dependencies for various mesh models. Since in mesh coding three different components need to be coded for each vertex position in space, the average mutual information $I_{avg} = (I_X + I_Y + I_Z)/3$ is reported instead of the mutual information for the three components individually. It is observed from Table 3 that for both normal and non-normal meshes mutual information of interband models is the least, independent of the wavelet transform employed. On the other hand mutual information for intraband models is significantly higher than for the interband models. Finally, composite models which gather the characteristics of both interband and intraband models exhibit even higher mutual information than interband or intraband models alone. Mathematically we can summarize our numerical findings as:

$$I(X;P_X) \ll I(X;\mathbf{n}_X) \ll I(X;P_X;\mathbf{n}_X) \cdot \tag{26}$$

Experimental results for the mutual information based estimation of interband, intraband and composite dependencies seem to indicate that exploiting the composite dependencies should be preferred. Additionally, it is important to point out that favoring intraband over zerotree-based interband models brings along the additional benefit of resolution scalability. Specifically, by following an intraband codec design, only those wavelet subbands that are needed in order to reconstruct a target mesh resolution-level need to be encoded, while the others can be discarded. This does not hold in case of interband and composite codec designs, due to the tree-structures that span all the wavelet decomposition levels. Since composite models cannot be discarded altogether due to their highest mutual information property, a careful implementation of a composite mesh coding system needs to be carried out into order to get the benefit of both the higher compression efficiency and the resolution scalable decoding at the same time.

Finally, it is important to point out that the differences in terms of mutual information do not give any indication about the final performance differences between interband, intraband and composite coding systems. Hence, an actual development and comparison of such coding systems is needed in order to experimentally validate the conclusions of this information-theoretic analysis of wavelet-based mesh coding designs, which is presented next.

5. Scalable mesh compression overview

In this section, we give a brief overview of the scalable mesh compression systems. Based on the design choices established earlier, we designed intraband and composite mesh coding systems which provide state-of-the-art compression performance, together with resolution as well as quality scalability of the compressed mesh.

5.1 Progressive Geometry Compression (PGC)

The first scalable wavelet-based geometry compression technique is the progressive geometry compression (PGC) codec proposed by Khodakovsky et al. in (Khodakovsky et al., 2000). PGC makes use of the well-know zero-tree coding (Shapiro, 1993) of wavelet coefficient's bitplanes in order to encode the decomposed mesh structure. Significant improvements in the compression performance against the contemporary scalable as well as non-scalable mesh coding systems were reported in (Khodakovsky et al., 2000). However, a major drawback of PGC schemes is their inability to provide resolution scalability. This is caused by the zero-tree structure which, for a given bitplane, spans all the wavelet decomposition levels. For a detailed understanding of the PGC system we refer to (Khodakovsky et al., 2000).

5.2 Scalable Intraband Mesh Compresion (SIM)

Despite of the great success of zerotree-based coding techniques in image coding, the choice of an interband codec design is not necessarily the best option in the context of scalable mesh coding. This was illustrated in Section 4 where different types of dependencies among wavelet coefficients were studied. Based on this analysis, we opt for an intraband dependency model in our codec design. As mentioned before, favoring intraband models over interband models brings along the additional benefit of resolution scalability. Specifically, by following an intraband codec design, only those wavelet subbands that are needed in order to reconstruct a target mesh resolution-level need to be encoded, while the others can be discarded.

In the designed scalable intraband mesh (SIM) compression system (Denis et al., 2010b) each resolution subband is encoded independently of the others. Similar to (Shapiro, 1993), SAQ is applied to each resolution subband to determine the significance of the wavelet coefficients with respect to a series of monotonically decreasing thresholds. Based on the significance outcome, a tree node is split into eight equal volume nodes. The resulting octree nodes may contain an unequal number of wavelet coefficients. In general, the number of coefficients in all nodes of a same tree-depth is roughly the same. This way, an octree is constructed for each resolution subband, wherein the depth of the tree (number of levels in the octree) is equal to the number of bitplanes of the subband. All magnitude bitplanes are sequentially coded using the non-significance, the significance and the refinement coding passes. For a detailed presentation of the SIM codec the interested reader is referred to (Denis et al., 2010b).

Using the octree-based bitplane coding, separate symbol streams are first generated for all bitplanes of each resolution subband. Depending on the type of scalability, i.e., resolution or quality scalability, the encoded symbol streams are entropy coded using a predefined progression order of bitplanes. For quality scalability, bitplanes of certain significance, from all resolution subbands, are first encoded before encoding the bitplanes of lower significance. However, in resolution scalability mode, all bitplanes of a lower resolution subband are progressively encoded before encoding the next higher resolution subband.

We compared the SIM codec with the PGC codec for both normal and non-normal 3D meshes. The decoded meshes are compared against the original semi-regular input meshes using the peak signal-to-noise ratio (PSNR) as the distortion metric, which is defined as:

$$PSNR = 20 \cdot \log_{10}\left(\frac{peak}{RMS}\right)(\text{dBs}),$$

where *peak* and *RMS* denote the size of the bounding box and the root mean squared error calculated on the distances between the decoded vertex positions with respect to the original ones, respectively.

Fig. 9 depicts PSNR versus bitrate (bits per semi-regular vertex) plots, evaluated for the semi-regular non-normal Venus and Bunny meshes using the Butterly transform. The results demonstrate that for both meshes, SIM yields superior performance when compared to PGC.

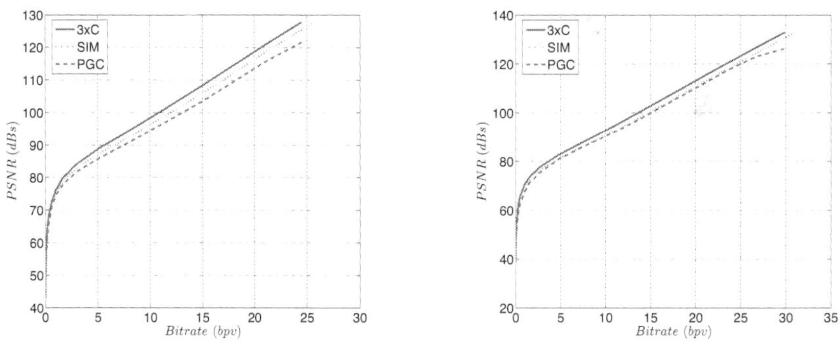

(a) (b)

Fig. 9. PSNR versus bitrate for non-normal mesh models in the quality scalability mode: (a) Venus, (b) Bunny . The lifted Butterly transform is employed for all three codecs.

The averaged gain in PSNR when compressing the Venus and Bunny meshes goes up to 2.22 dB and 2.35 dB, respectively. One may also notice the increasing performance difference with increasing bitrates; this indicates that the SIM coder tends to code the high frequency information more efficiently. For the spatially adaptive wavelet transform (SAWT) the compression results are reported in (Denis et al., 2010a).

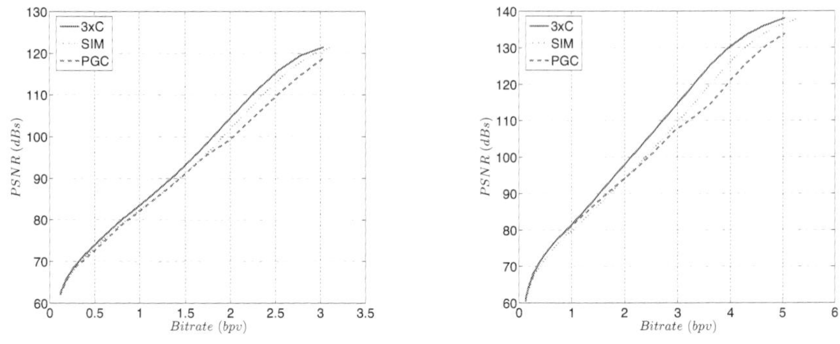

(a) (b)

Fig. 10. PSNR versus bitrate for normal mesh models in the quality scalability mode: (a) Skull, (b) Dino. The un-lifted Butterly transform is employed for all three codecs.

Fig. 10 shows compression performance plots for two normal meshes, Skull and Dino. One notices that at low bitrates, PGC tends to compress better. However, the ability of SIM to capture and code more efficiently the high-frequency components is noticeable at high bitrates and leads to an improved performance when compared to PGC.

5.3 Composite Context-conditioned Compression (3xC)

The mutual information analysis presented earlier showed that the composite dependencies between the wavelet coefficients are by far the strongest. However, one may notice that, employing composite models may hinder, similar to interband models, the possibility of providing resolution scalability. Thus one must be careful in exploiting the parent-children dependencies within composite models. A careful observation reveals that exploiting parent-children dependencies in a causal fashion (Denis et al., 2010b) does not limit resolution scalable decoding of the compressed mesh. Following this observation, we proposed a scalable composite mesh compression system in (Denis et al., 2009), (Denis et al., 2010b). The bitplane coding modules of the SIM codec and the 3xC codec are identical. The two designs differ at the entropy coding level. In particular, for 3xC, parent coefficient based context-conditioning is employed in the entropy coding module. For context-conditioning, significant, non-significant as well as sign information is entropy coded using the designed context tables. The refinement information is encoded without context-conditioning; this is because including the parental information when entropy coding the refinement symbols does not improve compression performance. For a detailed presentation of the 3xC codec the interested reader is referred to (Denis et al., 2009).

Fig. 9 also depicts the PSNR curves computed for the non-normal Venus and Bunny meshes using our implementation of the un-lifted butterfly based 3xC mesh compression system. The figure clearly demonstrates that, when dealing with non-normal meshes, 3xC systematically yields superior performance compared to PGC as well as SIM.

In the case of normal meshes (Fig. 10) our coder employs the same transform as PGC. Both codecs perform the same at very low bitrates. However, overall, 3xC yields the best compression performance. 3xC gives approximately equivalent results when compared with the intraband SIM codec for normal meshes. This is because the context-conditioning is only possible for the normal component of vector valued wavelet coefficients. Overall, it is clear that the proposed 3xC codec produces similar, and in almost all cases, superior performance compared to PGC and SIM codecs.

5.4 Visual comparison: PGC vs 3xC

Visual comparisons of Bunny and Skull meshes, compressed and reconstructed using 3xC at different bits per vertex (bpv), are presented in Fig. 11 and Fig. 12, respectively. The colored regions highlight the distortions introduced by lossy compression. For low-to-medium bitrates, the pure red color indicates areas where the distance between the original and decoded vertex is larger than 0.1% of the diagonal of the bounding box of the semi-regular mesh. For high bitrates, the distortion is visualized with respect to 0.02% of the diagonal. The mesh is shaded greener as the distortion lowers, with pure green indicating no distortion.

When visually comparing the compressed Bunny and Skull meshes produced by 3xC and PGC, it is very clear that 3xC yields superior performance for all bitrates. Taking the result at 0.050 bpv as an example, we observe that many areas which are shaded red for PGC are green for 3xC. At high rates, the differences between the mesh geometries may not be visually significant, yet the colors reveal that 3xC is able to approximate the original mesh much more accurately compared to the PGC system.

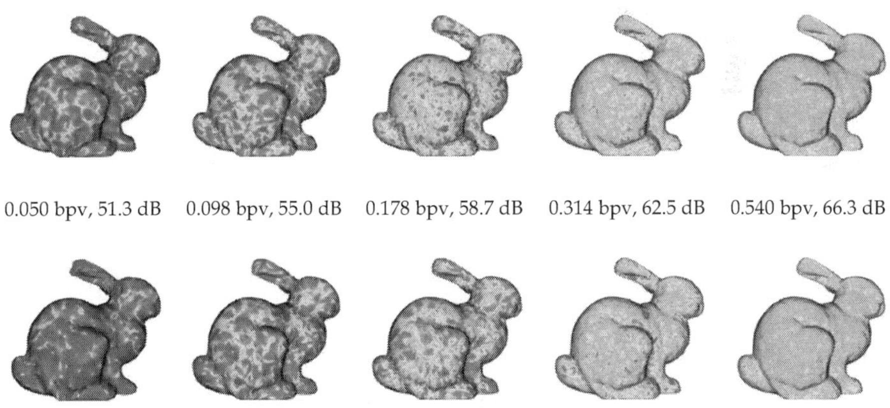

Fig. 11. Visual comparison of non-normal Bunny mesh using (top row) the 3xC codec and (bottom row) the PGC codec. The red color intensity reflects the distortion with respect to the uncompressed semi-regular mesh. The rate for the base mesh (i.e., M^0 - see section 2.1.2) is not included in the reported rate values.

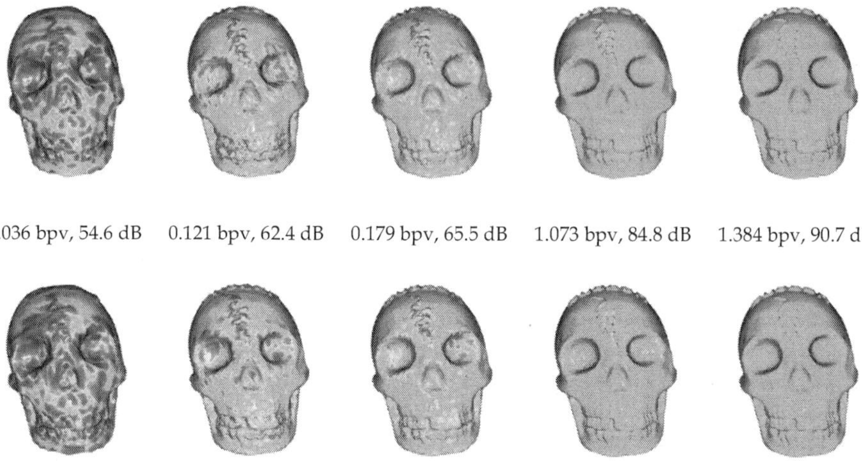

0.036 bpv, 54.6 dB 0.121 bpv, 62.4 dB 0.179 bpv, 65.5 dB 1.073 bpv, 84.8 dB 1.384 bpv, 90.7 dB

0.036 bpv, 53.9 dB 0.121 bpv, 61.9 dB 0.179 bpv, 65.2 dB 1.073 bpv, 83.4 dB 1.384 bpv, 88.9 dB

Fig. 12. Visual comparison of normal Skull mesh using (top row) the 3xC codec and (bottom row) the PGC codec. The red color intensity reflects the distortion with respect to the uncompressed semi-regular mesh. The rate for the base mesh is not included in the reported rate values.

The visual comparisons of the normal mesh Skull at different bpv are shown in Fig. 12. Though, at first glance it may appear that both codecs perform very similar, small differences are noticeable when investigating the meshes more closely. When examining the comparison at 0.036 bpv, we notice that the PGC codec preserves more details in Skull's teeth. The green shade for 3xC at rate 0.179 bpv, however, seems more pure compared to PGC for which it is rather yellowish green. We also observe that no red regions are present for 3xC at rate 1.073 bpv, whereas some are visible for PGC at the same rate.

6. Conclusions

In this book chapter, we propose a constructive methodology for the design of scalable wavelet-based mesh compression systems. Our design strategy differs from conventional designs which simply opt for reusing methods from wavelet-based image coding for the design of mesh coding systems. In particular, our methods are motivated by an information-theoretic analysis of the statistical dependencies between wavelet coefficients which shows that, intraband dependencies are systematically stronger than interband ones for both normal and non-normal meshes, and that composite models are the best. We also investigate the optimality of successive approximation quantization, commonly used in scalable compression, in the context of wavelet-based mesh compression. Using a Laplacian mixture model, it is shown that successive approximation quantization is an acceptable, but in general not an optimal solution. Anchored in these results, novel intraband and composite coding systems are presented which improve the state-of-the-art in scalable mesh compression, both in terms of scalability and compression efficiency.

7. Appendix

The output distortion D_L of a Laplacian PDF, quantized using an n level EDSQ and reconstructed using midpoint reconstruction, can be written as:

$$D_L(Q_{\xi_n,\Delta_n}) = \underbrace{\lambda\int_0^{(1-\xi_n)\Delta_n} x^2 e^{-\lambda x}\,dx}_{D_{DZ}} + \underbrace{\lambda\sum_{k=1}^{\infty}\int_{(k-\xi_n)\Delta_n}^{(k+1-\xi_n)\Delta_n}\left(x-(k+0.5-\xi_n)\Delta_n\right)^2 e^{-\lambda x}\,dx}_{D_{REST}},$$

where D_{DZ} and D_{REST} denote the distortion contributions of the deadzone and the other quantization cells, respectively. By proper substitution and letting

$$\sum_{k=1}^{\infty} e^{-\lambda\Delta_n k} = \frac{e^{-\lambda\Delta_n}}{1-e^{-\lambda\Delta_n}}, \text{ as } e^{-\lambda\Delta_n} \le 1, \tag{27}$$

the following closed-form expression for the distortion is obtained:

$$D_L(Q_{\delta_n,\Delta_n}) = \frac{2}{\lambda^2} + e^{-\lambda\Delta_n\delta_n}\left\{\left(\frac{1}{4}-\delta_n^2\right)\Delta_n^2 - \left(2\delta_n + \coth\left(\frac{\lambda\Delta_n}{2}\right)\right)\frac{\Delta_n}{\lambda}\right\}, \tag{28}$$

where $\delta_n = 1-\xi_n$.

Similarly, the output rate R_L of a Laplacian PDF, quantized using an n level EDSQ can be written as:

$$R_L(Q_{\xi_n,\Delta_n}) = \underbrace{-2\left(\frac{\lambda}{2}\int_0^{(1-\xi_n)\Delta_n} e^{-\lambda x}\,dx\right)\log_2 2\left(\frac{\lambda}{2}\int_0^{(1-\xi_n)\Delta_n} e^{-\lambda x}\,dx\right)}_{R_{DZ}}\ldots$$

$$\ldots\underbrace{-2\sum_{k=1}^{\infty}\left(\frac{\lambda}{2}\int_{(k-\xi_n)\Delta_n}^{(k+1-\xi_n)\Delta_n} e^{-\lambda x}\,dx\right)\log_2\left(\frac{\lambda}{2}\int_{(k-\xi_n)\Delta_n}^{(k+1-\xi_n)\Delta_n} e^{-\lambda x}\,dx\right)}_{R_{REST}}.$$

Again making use of the summation reduction identity of (27) along with the identity

$$\sum_{k=1}^{\infty} e^{-\lambda\Delta_n k}\log_2\left(e^{-\lambda\Delta_n k}\right) = \log_2\left(e^{-\lambda\Delta_n}\right)\sum_{k=1}^{\infty} k\left(e^{-\lambda\Delta_n}\right)^k = \frac{\log_2\left(e^{-\lambda\Delta_n}\right)e^{-\lambda\Delta_n}}{\left(1-e^{-\lambda\Delta_n}\right)^2},$$

the expression for the rate can be reduced to the following closed-form:

$$R_L(Q_{\delta_n,\Delta_n}) = c_\delta \log_2\left(\frac{2d_{\delta_n}}{d_1 c_1^{1/d_1} e^{\lambda\Delta_n(1-\delta_n)} d_{\delta_n}^{1/c_{\delta_n}}}\right), \tag{29}$$

where $c_{\delta_n} = e^{-\lambda\Delta_n\delta_n}$ (hence $c_1 = e^{-\lambda\Delta_n}$) and $d_{\delta_n} = 1 - c_{\delta_n}$ (hence $d_1 = 1 - c_1$).

8. Acknowledgements

The authors would like to thank Cyberware, Headus, The Scripps Research Institute, Washington University, and Stanford University for providing 3D models. The authors are particularly grateful to Igor Guskov for providing them with the normal meshes, and to Andrei Khodakovsky and Peter Schröder for providing the PGC software.

This research was supported by the Agency for Innovation by Science and Technology (IWT) - Flanders (OptiMMa project) and the Fund for Scientific Research - Flanders (postdoctoral mandate Peter Schelkens and project G014610N).

9. References

Catmull, E. & Clark, J. (1978). Recursively Generated B-Spline Surfaces on Arbitrary Topological Surfaces. *Computer-Aided Design*. Vol. 10, No. 6, (November 1978), pp. 350-355, ISBN 1-58113-052-X.

Chang, C.-L. & Girod, B. (2006). Direction-Adaptive Discrete Wavelet Transform Via Directional Lifting and Bandeletization. Proc. *IEEE International Conference on Image Processing*, pp. 1149-1152, Atlanta, GA, USA.

Cover, T. M. & Thomas, J. A. (1991). *Elements of Information Theory*. Wiley-Interscience, ISBN 0-471-24195-4, New York, USA.

Darbellay, G. A. & Vajda, I. (1999). Estimation of the Information by an Adaptive Partitioning of the Observation Space. *IEEE Transactions on Information Theory*. Vol. 45, No. 4, (May 1999), pp. 1315-1321, ISSN 0018-9448.

Dempster, A. P., Laird, N. M. & Rubin, D. B. (1977). Maximum Likelihood from Incomplete Data Via the Em Algorithm. *Journal of The Royal Statistical Society, Series B*. Vol. 39, No. 1, (May 1977), pp. 1-38.

Denis, L., Ruxandra, F., Munteanu, A. & Schelkens, P. (2010a). Spatially Adaptive Bases in Wavelet-Based Coding of Semi-Regular Meshes. *Proceedings of the SPIE*, pp. 772310-772310-8, Brussels, Belgium.

Denis, L., Satti, S. M., Munteanu, A., Cornelis, J. & Schekens, P. (2010b). Scalable Intraband and Composite Coding of Semi-Regular Meshes. *IEEE Transactions on Multimedia*. Vol. 12, No. 8, (December 2010), pp. 773-789, ISSN 1520-9210.

Denis, L., Satti, S. M., Munteanu, A., Cornelis, J. & Schelkens, P. (2009). Context-Conditioned Composite Coding of 3D Meshes Based on Wavelets on Surfaces. *IEEE International Conference on Image Processing*, pp. 3509-3512, ISSN 1522-4880, Cairo, Egypt, November 2009.

Dyn, N., Levin, D. & Gregory, J. A. (1990). A Butterfly Subdivision Scheme for Surface Interpolation with Tension Control. *ACM Transactions on Graphics*. Vol. 9, No. 2, (April 1990), pp. 160-169, ISSN 0730-0301.

Eck, M., Derose, T., Duchamp, T., Hoppe, H., Lounsbery, M. & Stuetzle, W. (1995). Multiresolution Analysis of Arbitrary Meshes. *ACM SIGGRAPH, Proceedings of the 22rd Annual Conference on Computer Graphics and Interactive Techniques*, pp. 173-182 ISBN 0-89791-701-4, Los Angeles, California, USA, August 6-11, 1995.

Eck, M. & Hoppe, H. (1996). Automatic Reconstruction of B-Spline Surfaces of Arbitrary Topological Type. *ACM SIGGRAPH, Proceedings of the 23rd Annual Conference on Computer Graphics and Interactive Techniques*, pp. 325–334, ISBN 0-89791-746-4.

Fraysse, A., Pesquet-Popescu, J. C. (2008) Rate-distortion Results on Generalized Gaussian Distributions, *IEEE International Conference on Acoustic, Speech Signal Processing*, pp. 3753-3756, Las Vegas, NV, USA, March 30-April 04, 2008.

Hsiang, S.-T. & Woods, J. W. (2000). Embedded Image Coding Using Zeroblocks of Subband/Wavelet Coefficients and Context Modeling. *IEEE International Symposium on Circuits and Systems*, pp. 662-665, Geneva, CH, May 28-31.

Khodakovsky, A., Schröder, P. & Sweldens, W. (2000). Progressive Geometry Compression. *ACM SIGGRAPH, 27th International Conference on Computer Graphics and Interactive Techniques*, pp. 271-278, ISBN 1-58113-208-5, New Orleans, Lousiana, USA, July 23-28, 2000.

Li, J. & Kuo, C. C. J. (1998). Progressive Coding of 3-D Graphic Models. *Proceedings of the IEEE* Vol. 86, No. 6, pp. 1052-1063, ISSN 0018-9219.

Liu, J. & Moulin, P. (2000). Analysis of Interscale and Intrascale Dependencies between Image Wavelet Coefficients. *International Conference on Image Processing*, pp. 669-671, Vancouver, Canada, September 11-13, 2000.

Loop, C., Schaefer, S., Ni, T. & Castaño, I. (2009). Approximating Subdivision Surfaces with Gregory Patches for Hardware Tessellation. *ACM Transactions on Graphic, SIGGRAPH Asia*. Vol. 28, No. 5, (December 2009), pp. 151:1 - 151:9, ISSN 0730-0301.

Lounsbery, M., Derose, T. D. & Warren, J. (1997). Multiresolution Analysis for Surfaces of Arbitrary Topological Type. *ACM Transactions on Graphics*. Vol. 16, No. 1, (January 1997), pp. 34-73.

Mallat, S. G. (1989). A Theory for Multiresolution Signal Decomposition: The Wavelet Representation. *IEEE Transactions on Pattern Analysis and Machine Intelligence*. Vol. 11, No. 7, (July 1989), pp. 674-693, ISSN 0162-8828.

Munteanu, A., Cornelis, J. & Cristea, P. (1999a). Wavelet-Based Lossless Compression of Coronary Angiographic Images. *IEEE Transactions on Medical Imaging*. Vol. 18, No. 3, (March 1999), pp. 272-281.

Munteanu, A., Cornelis, J., Van der Auwera, G. & Cristea, P. (1999b). Wavelet Image Compression - the Quadtree Coding Approach. *IEEE Transactions on Information Technology in Biomedicine*. Vol. 3, No. 3, (September 1999), pp. 176-185, ISSN 1089-7771.

Pajarola, R. & Rossignac, J. (2000). Compressed Progressive Meshes. *IEEE Transactions on Visualization and Computer Graphics*. Vol. 6, No. 1, (January-March 2000), pp. 79-93, ISSN 1077-2626.

Ronfard, R. & Rossignac, J. (1996). Full-Range Approximation of Triangulated Polyhedra. *Proceeding of Eurographics, Computer Graphics Forum*. Vol. 15, No. 3, (August 1996), pp. 67-76, ISSN 0167-7055.

Rossignac, J. & Borrel, P. (1993). *Multi-Resolution 3d Approximation for Rendering Complex Scenes*. Springer-Verlag, ISBN 0387565299.

Schröder, P. & Sweldens, W. (1995). Spherical Wavelets: Efficiently Representing Functions on the Sphere. *ACM SIGGRAPH, Proceedings of 22nd Annual Conference on Computer Graphics and Interactive Techniques*, pp. 161-172, ISBN 0-89791-701-4, Los Angeles, California, USA, August 6-11.

Shapiro, J. M. (1993). Embedded Image Coding Using Zerotrees of Wavelet Coefficients. *IEEE Transactions on Signal Processing*. Vol. 41, No. 12, (1993), pp. 3445-3462.

Soucy, M. & Laurendeau, D. (1996). Multiresolution Surface Modeling Based on Hierarchical Triangulation. *Computer Vision and Image Understanding*. Vol. 63, No. 1, (January 1996), pp. 1-14, ISSN 10773142.

Taubin, G., Guéziec, A., Horn, W., William, A. & Lazarus, F. (1998). Progressive Forest Split Compression. *ACM SIGGRAPH, Proceedings of 25th International Conference on Computer Graphics and Interactive Techniques*, pp. 123-132, ISBN 0-89791-999-8, Orlando, Florida, USA, July 19-24, 1998.

Taubman, D. (2000). High Performance Scalable Image Compression with EBCOT. *IEEE Transactions on Image Processing*. Vol. 9, No. 7, (July 2000), pp. 1158-1170, ISSN 1057-7149.

Taubman, D. & Marcelin, M. (2001). *Jpeg2000: Image Compression Fundamentals, Standards and Practice*. Springer, ISBN 978-0792375197.

Wu, X. (1997). High-Order Context Modeling and Embedded Conditional Entropy Coding of Wavelet Coefficients for Image Compression. *31st Asilomar Conference on Signals, Systems and Computers*, pp. 1378-1382, Pacific Grove, CA, November 2-5, 1997.

Application of Wavelet Analysis for the Understanding of Vortex-Induced Vibration

Tomoki Ikoma, Koichi Masuda and Hisaaki Maeda
Department of Oceanic Architecture and Engineering, College of Science and Technology (CST), Nihon University Japan

1. Introduction

1.1 Marine riser

Oceans are quite important fields for us because many resources lurk there which are oil and gas under seabed, mineral resources, water heat energy and so on. Development of submarine oil has been major in the North Sea and in the Gulf of Mexico. Today, submarine oil has been developed at ultra-deep water fields of offshore of Brazil and West Africa, which does deep over 1000m. Deepest field developed is more than 3000m in water depth of Brazilian seas. Riser system is necessary to develop and to production submarine oil. The riser is a tubing structure which is for drilling and production. Diameter of a drilling riser is greater than 50cm and that of a production riser is about 20cm. The riser is thin rope-like tube in oceans. Therefore, the tubing behaves elastically by marine currents and ocean waves and so on.

These motion behaviors are called as Vortex-Induced Vibration (VIV). VIV of the riser is a complex phenomenon, which is dominated by the natural frequency of the riser system and behavior of vortex shedding around the rider. VIV is very important for structural design of the riser system and the platform of the drilling and the production of submarine oil and so on.

There are many studies of VIV of the riser and the drilling or the production system including the riser system in the ocean engineering field with numerical approaches, theoretical approaches and model experimental approaches. Behaviors of time variation of VIV obtained from numerical calculations or model experiments using model risers in a water tank include a complicated mechanism so it is not easy to understand them, because the time variation is not steady but transient and chaos. Therefore, we need to understand VIV phenomenon in not only time characteristics but also frequency characteristics.

For understanding frequency characteristics, we often use a power spectrum with the FFT analysis or others. However, a power spectrum does not inform us time variation of VIV characteristics. Then, the wavelet analysis can be applied to the VIV analysis because we can simultaneously understand the characteristics in time domain and frequency domain.

1.2 Application of wavelet analysis for study of marine riser

The authors have investigated VIV characteristics of a circular cylinder with forced oscillation tests in still water (Ikoma & Masuda et al., 2006, 2007). As these results, VIV behaviors have been classified to the four power spectrum pattern. However an actual orbit of the model cylinder was different even if the spectrum pattern was same. Therefore detail of VIV characteristics and behaviors cannot be understood from only a power spectrum with the FFT analysis of a time history of vibrations. In addition, a vibration phenomenon of a marine riser etc. is a non-steady problem in practice so that fluid velocity in the ocean and oscillation of an upper structure such like a production platform are an unsteady phenomenon. Therefore vibration characteristics such like VIV varies to time table.

The Hilbert transform was applied to analysis of cylinder vibration with VIV (Khalak & Wiliamson, 1999). In there, it is described that phase deviation occurs in region entering into VIV lock-in. The Hilbert transform was useful in order to analysis of marine riser vibrations and examined frequency characteristics which vary to time table.

The wavelet transform is applied to analysis of vibration problems with VIV of a rigid circular cylinder which cross-flow vibration is allowed due to vortex shedding in this study. The wavelet analysis is possible to do the time-frequency analysis as same as the Hilbert transform analysis. Objectives of this study are: 1) to examine possibility of application of the wavelet transform to VIV analysis and 2) to discuss VIV characteristics from results of the wavelet analysis. In 2010, the wavelet analysis and the Hilbert transform were also applied to the estimation of riser behaviors (Shi et al., 2010).

This chapter introduces application of the wavelet analysis in the ocean engineering field using results of VIV characteristics. From the model experiment, relationship between the orbit pattern of vibration of the model cylinder and a contour pattern of the wavelet is considered. As a result, effectiveness of the wavelet analysis in order to understand VIV detail is given.

2. Model experiment

2.1 Method of experiment

Model experiments using a single circular cylinder or two arranged circular cylinders in tandem are carried out at a wave tank that has 27 m in length, 7 m in width and 1 m in water depth in the campus of Funabashi at CST of Nihon University. We cannot generate current so that forced oscillation tests in still water are carried.

An experimental method and concepts follow our own past model testing (Ikoma & Masuda et al., 2006, 2007). In this study, a single cylinder or double cylinders in tandem arrangement to inline direction are used.

Test models of a cylinder are made of acryl resin which is rigid. However the cylinder system is not fixed because elastic vibration is allowed in only cross-flow direction by attaching a flat spring on top of the cylinder. The flat spring does not allow inline movement of the cylinder. Inline movement is due to only forced oscillation by the oscillator. VIV occurs such like rolling motion around x axis which center is the flat spring.

Number of degrees of freedom is two in sway motion and roll motion. The sway in this experiment is horizontal displacement of center of gravity in y direction and rolling is rotation around x axis in a coordinate system of Fig. 1. Freedom of surge corresponding to x axis motion is allowed and decided due to forced oscillation by experimental operators.

2.2 Experimental setup system

The cylinder is suspended under a load cell through the flat spring. Most of the cylinder is submerged in still water. Side views of the experimental setup system, which corresponds to the z-x plane, are illustrated in Fig. 2. The direction of forced oscillations is right and left in Fig. 2.

A load cell for measuring the total load in inline direction, which including the inertia force of a cylinder and hydrodynamic forces on a cylinder, is attached under the forced oscillation device. A Doppler current meter is installed at the straightly back of the cylinder, the current meter which moves together with the cylinder due to the forced oscillation. The current meter can measure fluid velocity of three directions in x, y and z axis. We measure the vertical bending moment with a flat spring on which strain gages are set.

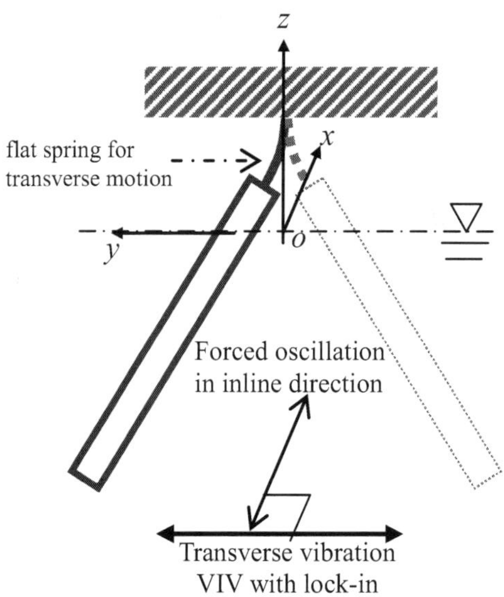

Fig. 1. Idealization of VIV in experiment

In the experiment, 1) inline displacement of forced oscillation with a potentiometer, 2) the total inline load with the load cell, 3) the bending moment with the flat spring and 4) fluid velocity at the back of the cylinder with the Doppler current meter are measured. The fluid velocity is measured at midship depth of the submerged cylinder. The VIV is evaluated by using the vertical bending moment and cross-flow displacement predicted from the bending moment.

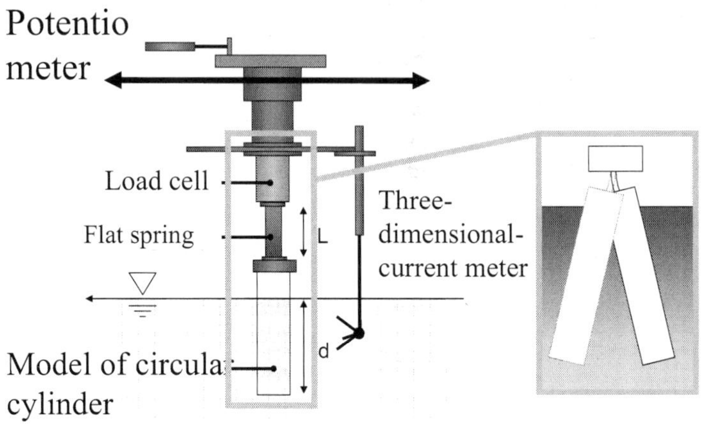

a) in case of one cylinder

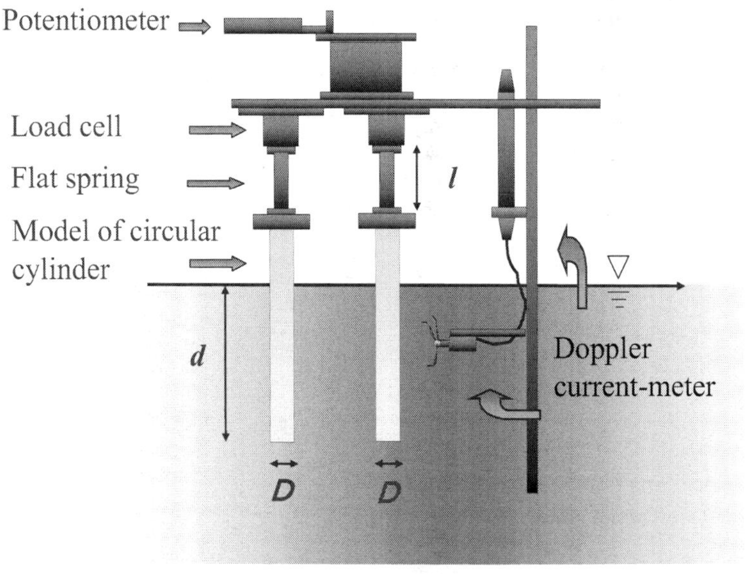

b) in case of two cylinders

Fig. 2. Side views of experimental setup system

Photo 1. Side view of experimental setup system

2.3 Experimental conditions

Detail of the cylinder models is described in the paper (Ikoma et al., 2007). Length of the flat spring is expressed as "l" in Table 1. Natural periods T_n of cross-flow vibration of a suspended cylinder were obtained with the plucked decay test in still water.

Water depth is set to 1.0 m. The amplitude of forced oscillation is 7.2 cm, the Keulegan-Carpenter (K_C) number accordingly corresponds to 5.7 and 9.0 in the experiments.

In case of double cylinders, the cylinders are straightly suspended, and then the distance l_d between the center to center of both the cylinders is varied such as Table 2. The distance ratio s is defined as follows,

$$s = \frac{l_d}{D}. \tag{1}$$

The front cylinder and the back cylinder are defined as Fig. 3.

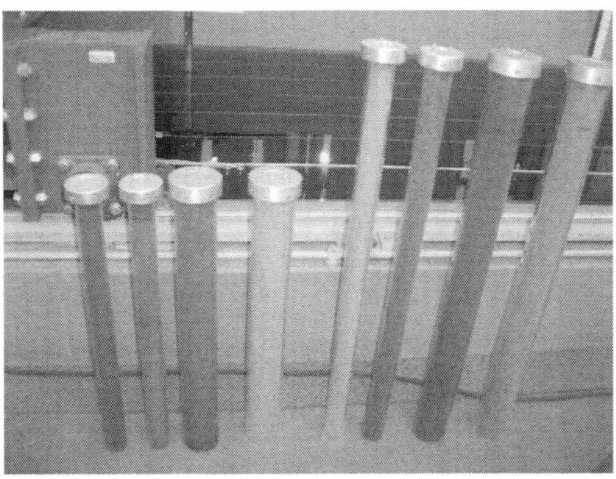

Photo 2. Experimental models filled with sand

case	diameter D	draft d	l	filled with water: measured natural period in water Tn	filled with water: period of forced oscillation in case of St=0.2, Ts	filled with sand: measured natural period in water Tn	filled with sand: period of forced oscillation in case of St=0.2, Ts
1	8cm	30cm	10cm	0.86s	0.95s	0.93s	1.05s
2	8cm	80cm	13cm	3.28s	3.70s	2.72s	3.10s
3	5cm	30cm	10cm	0.54s	1.15s	0.57s	1.05s
4	5cm	80cm	13cm	2.15s	3.90s	2.08s	3.75s
5	5cm	80cm	10cm	1.86s	3.35s	1.85s	3.35s
6	5cm	60cm	10cm	1.21s	2.20s	1.28s	2.30s
7	8cm	60cm	10cm	1.91s	2.15s	1.79s	2.00s
8	8cm	60cm	4cm	1.18s	1.35s	1.20s	1.35s
9	8cm	80cm	4cm	1.91s	2.15s	1.83s	2.10s
10	5cm	80cm	4cm	1.20s	2.20s	1.23s	2.25s

a) for single cylinder

model	diameter D	draft d	l	measured natural period in water T_n	period of forced oscillation in case of St=0.2, T_s
1	5cm	60cm	10cm	1.28 s	2.00 s
2	5cm	80cm	10cm	1.85 s	3.35 s
3	8cm	60cm	10cm	1.79 s	2.00 s
4	8cm	80cm	10cm	2.52 s	2.85 s

b) for double cylinders

Table 1. Principal particulars of cylinder model setting

D	5 cm					8 cm	
l_d cm	10	13	15	18	20	16	20
S	2.0	2.5	3.0	3.5	4.0	2.0	2.5

Table 2. Variation of distance ratio of straight cylinders

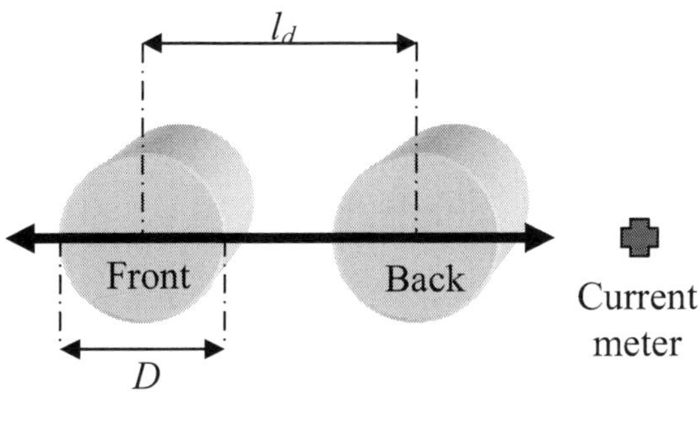

Fig. 3. Distance ratio between two cylinders

2.4 Definitions of nominal period and nominal frequency

The K-C number and the period of T_s are defined as same as them (Ikoma et al., 2007) as follows,

$$K_C = \frac{U_O T}{D}, \tag{2}$$

where U_O is the maximum velocity of forced oscillation, T stands for the period of the forced oscillation. The forced oscillation is simple harmonic motion in this study, hence eqn. (2) can be rewritten as follows,

$$K_C = 2\pi \frac{a}{D}, \tag{3}$$

in which a is amplitude of the forced oscillation in inline direction.

The range of periods of the forced oscillation is from about 0.4 seconds to 4.6 seconds, the Reynolds (R_e) numbers accordingly correspond to about 5.0e+3 to 6.0e+5 if the maximum velocity U_O of the forced oscillations are applied to the calculation.

The natural frequency of transverse vibration varies due to the length of a flat spring. The experimental conditions of each case are shown in Table 1. 'S_t' in Table 1 is the Strouhal number and is defined in this study as follows,

$$S_t = \frac{f_s D}{U_O}, \tag{4}$$

in which f_s is the frequency of vortex shedding. The Strouhal number has been well known as about 0.2 in range of R_e>1.0e+3. In this paper, the Strouhal number is approximately fixed to,

$$S_t \approx 0.2\,. \tag{5}$$

'T_s' in Table 1 corresponds to the period of the forced oscillation which corresponds to about 5.0 in the nominal reduced velocity. The lock-in phenomenon of VIV is therefore expected in each experimental case when the model is in forced inline oscillations with the period of T_S. 'T_s' is calculated with following equations,

$$\frac{f_s D}{U_O} = 0.2\,, \tag{6}$$

$$f_s = 0.2\frac{U_O}{D}\,, \tag{7}$$

$$T_s = \frac{1}{f_s}\,. \tag{8}$$

Therefore, the frequency of vortex shedding f_s is not an actual frequency, but is a nominal frequency in this study.

3. Wavelet analysis

The wavelet analysis is the time-frequency analysis for time histories such like the Hilbert transform. The wavelet transform is defined as follows,

$$W_T(b,a) = \frac{1}{\sqrt{|a|}}\int_{-\infty}^{\infty} f(t)\cdot\psi\left(\frac{t-b}{a}\right)dt\,, \tag{9}$$

where $f(t)$ is a time history, a stands for a dilation parameter and b stands for a location parameter. "$\psi(t)$" is the mother wavelet function. The Gabor's mother wavelet is applied such as follows in this study,

$$\psi(t) = \frac{1}{\sqrt{2\pi\sigma^2}}\exp\left[-\frac{t^2}{2\sigma^2}\right]\cdot e^{i\omega_0 t}\,, \tag{10}$$

where σ is a damping parameter of the mother wavelet function and ω_0 is a principle angular frequency. Half of the natural angular frequency of each model is applied in this study.

When the damping parameter σ becomes smaller, the mother function be attenuated soon. And then, resolution of frequency is high although resolution of time gets worse. It is a merit to select the Gabor's wavelet because the dilation parameter a, which corresponds to a scaling parameter, is individual to the resolution parameter σ. The parameters are consequently individual each other so that the tuning of the parameters in order to draw the wavelet contour is not difficult.

In this study, b is set at 0.4 seconds, a is carried out from 0.0 to 3.0 with resolution of 0.2 and σ is 1.0.

A sampling frequency of the experimental recording has been 500 Hz, which corresponds to 2.0e-3 seconds in the sampling time. '0.4 seconds' of b in the time sifting for the wavelet analysis corresponds to 200 sampling data skipping. In addition, the shortest natural period of cross-flow vibration in the experimental models in Tables 1a) and 1b) is 0.86 seconds. If the bi-harmonic vibration in VIV in this case occurs, the vibration period is 0.43 seconds. The resolution would be thereby enough 0.4 seconds. Using b=0.4, variation pattern of the wavelet would be able to be reproduced. The step of a is now 0.2. The parameter a corresponds to a resolution of the frequency component. The cross-flow vibration appears relatively simply from the FFT analysis so that the resolution of 0.2 may be reasonable.

4. Orbit patterns and power spectrum patterns

In case of a single cylinder experiment (Ikoma & Masuda et al., 2006, 2007), the four patterns of the power spectrum of VIV have been found such like Fig. 4. In addition, there was an adequate correlation between the orbit pattern and the spectrum pattern in the paper (Ikoma et al., 2007). However both the power spectrum patterns of the orbit patterns of the type U and the type 8 correspond to the pattern 4 which is bi-harmonic type. Therefore detail of VIV behavior cannot be understood from a result with the FFT analysis of VIV.

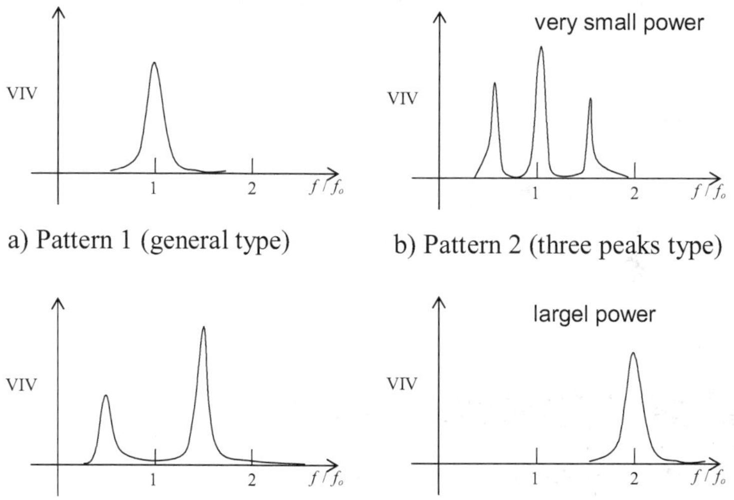

a) Pattern 1 (general type) b) Pattern 2 (three peaks type)

c) Pattren 3 (two peaks type) d) Pattern 4 (bi-harmonic type)

Fig. 4. Classifications of power spectrum patterns of VIV [1]

5. Results and discussion

5.1 Orbit patterns

From the experiment using the single cylinder, orbit patterns can be classified to six patterns such as Fig. 5. The net type is specified to $N1$ and $N2$. It can be considered that response of the type U and the type 8 corresponds to VIV lock-in.

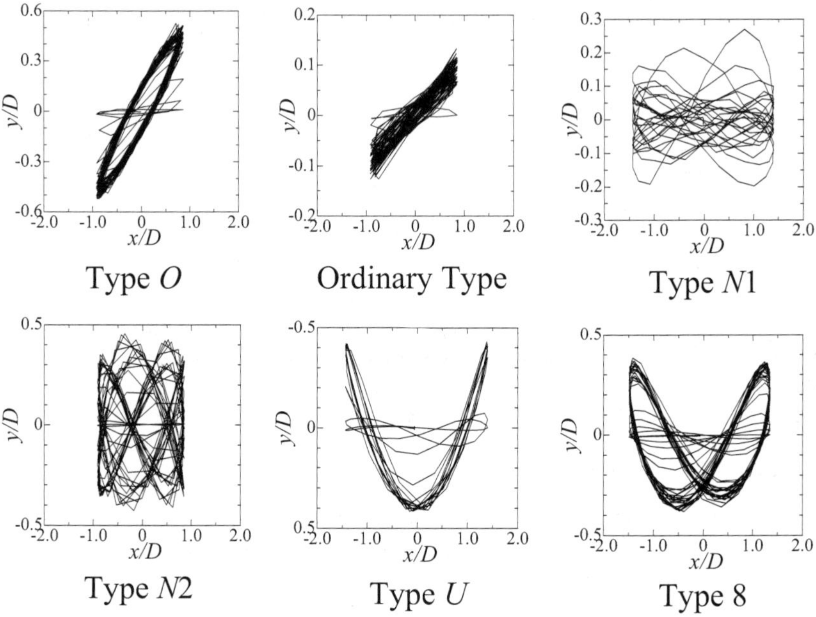

Fig. 5. Classifications of orbit patterns of VIV

5.2 Wavelet characteristics of single cylinder

In case of a single cylinder, wavelet patterns are made a general classification to five. These patterns are not decided due to experimental cases such as Table 1-a). Results of wavelet analysis in case of the case 8 show in Figs. 6, where "T" in subtitles stands for period of the forced oscillation. A vertical axis is the dilation parameter a and horizontal axis is time of VIV response. These results are the vertical bending moment which corresponds to cross-flow vibration.

In Figs. 6, a) corresponds to the orbit pattern of Type *O*. In Wavelet contours from a) to c), response frequency is confirmed in wide band of a which is vertical axis. In case of Type *U*, there is no striped pattern from 0.0 to 1.0 in a.

Such this tendency can be also confirmed in case of Type 8. In the case 8, Type 8 doesn't occur so that a wavelet pattern corresponding to Type 8 is explained by using the case 3.

From Figs. 6-e) and 7-b) which results correspond to Type *U*, in range from 2.0 to 3.0 in a, we can confirm a clear striped pattern. However, the striped pattern is broken around a=1.0 when the orbit gets Type 8.

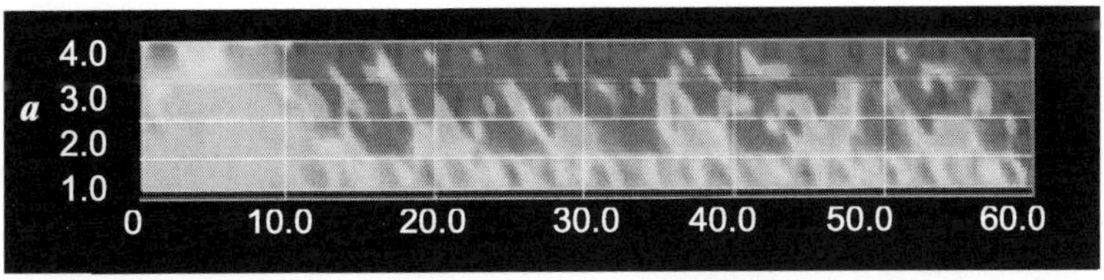

a) T=1.15 s, orbit corresponding to Type *O*

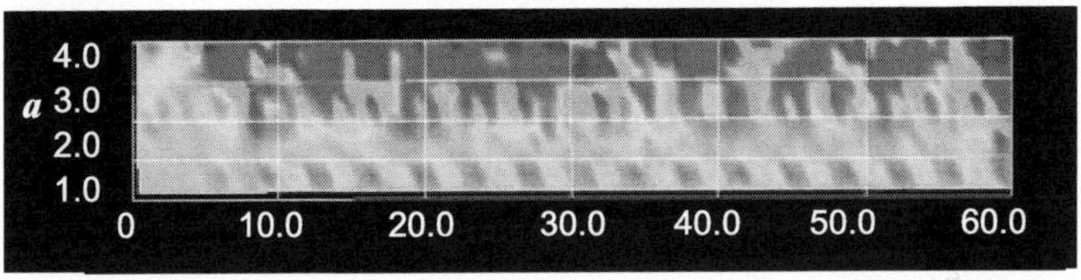

b) T=1.25 s, orbit corresponding to Ordinary Type

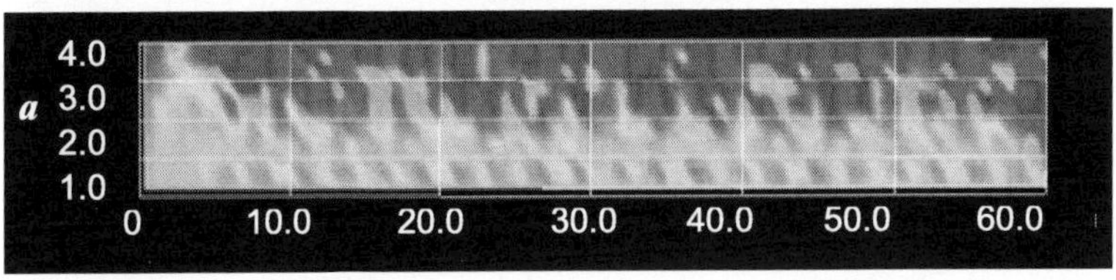

c) T=1.55 s, orbit corresponding to Type *Net* 1

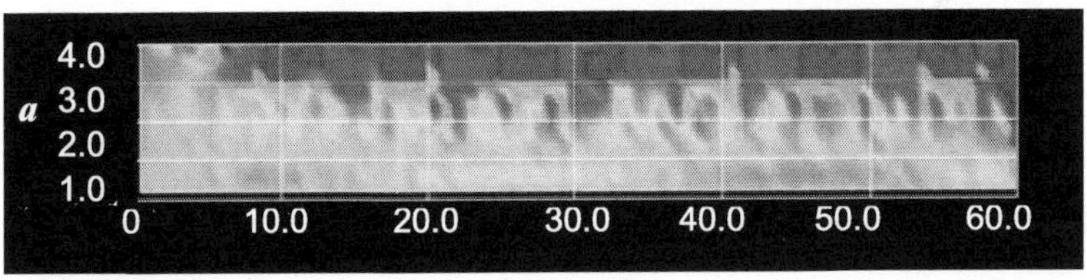

d) T=2.00 s, orbit corresponding to Type *Net* 2

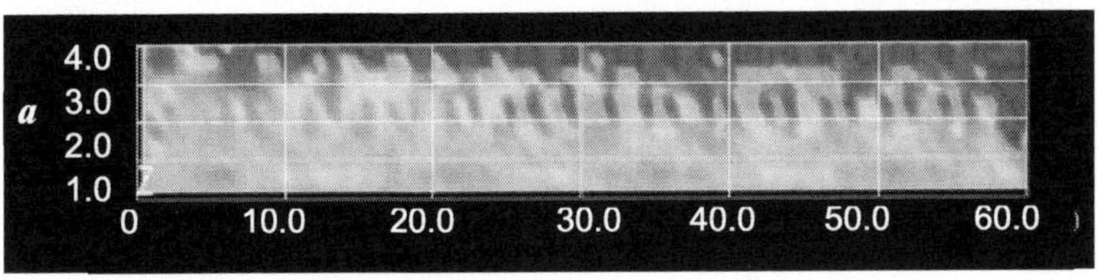

e) T=2.30 s, orbit corresponding to Type *U*

Fig. 6. Patterns of wavelet analysis of Case 8

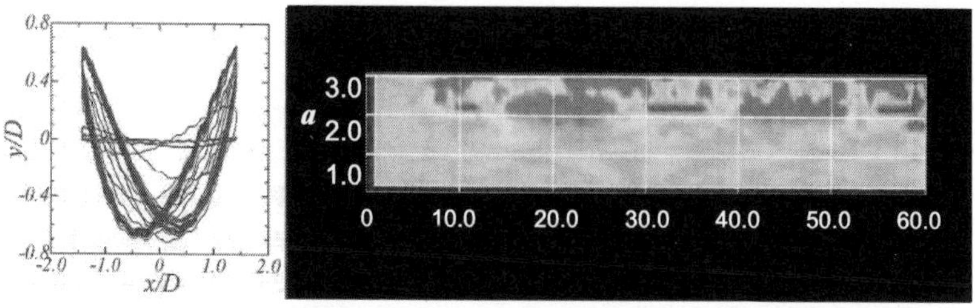

a) T=1.00 s, orbit corresponding to Type 8

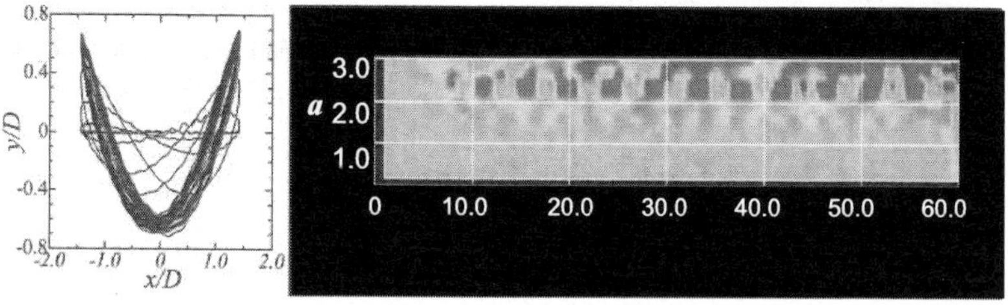

b) T=1.05 s, orbit corresponding to Type *U*

Fig. 7. Patterns of wavelet analysis of Case 3

5.3 Wavelet characteristics of double cylinders in tandem

Results of the vertical bending moment corresponding to VIV with the wavelet analysis are discussed using the results in case of the model 1 in Table 1-b). Correspondence between the orbit and the wavelet pattern was similar to cases of the single cylinder. When the distance ratio increased, VIV behavior resembled the single cases. Therefore the results in case of the distance ratio s=2.0 are described here.

Figures 8 to 13 show results of the wavelet analysis, the orbit and a power spectrum of the vertical bending moment. Representations of "front" and "back" in the figures mean follows. The cylinder set on a side of starting direction of the forced oscillation corresponds "front" such as Fig. 3. "f" is a frequency Hz and "f_0" is also a frequency Hz of the forced oscillation on the horizontal axis of the power spectra.

In Figs. 8, the behavior of vibration of both the cylinder is quite different. VIV is not induced strongly. VIV lock-in is confirmed in Figs. 9 to 12. However the behavior of the vibration is different each case from the orbit, even then a shape of the power spectrum of Figs. 9 to 12 are same very much. VIV occurs as bi-harmonic vibration to the frequency of the forced oscillation. The third harmonic vibration can be found on the power spectrum in Figs. 12-a). When the character of "8" is broken and becomes flat, a response component which is higher than the bi-harmonic frequency emerges.

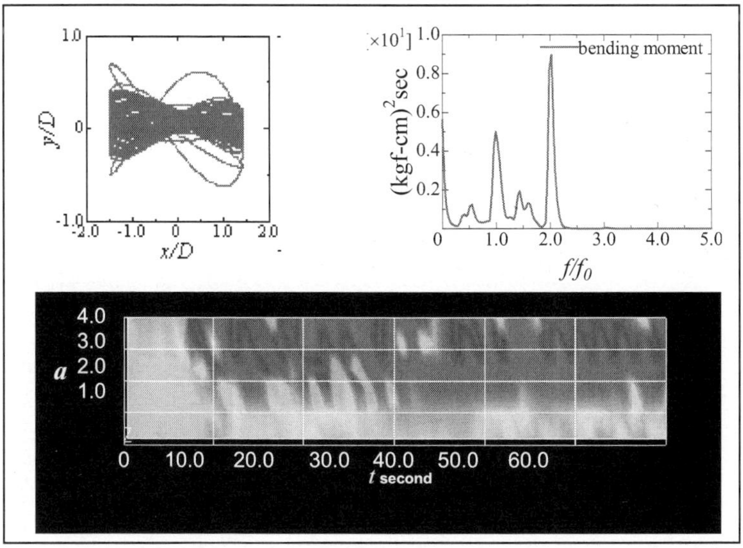

a) on front cylinder

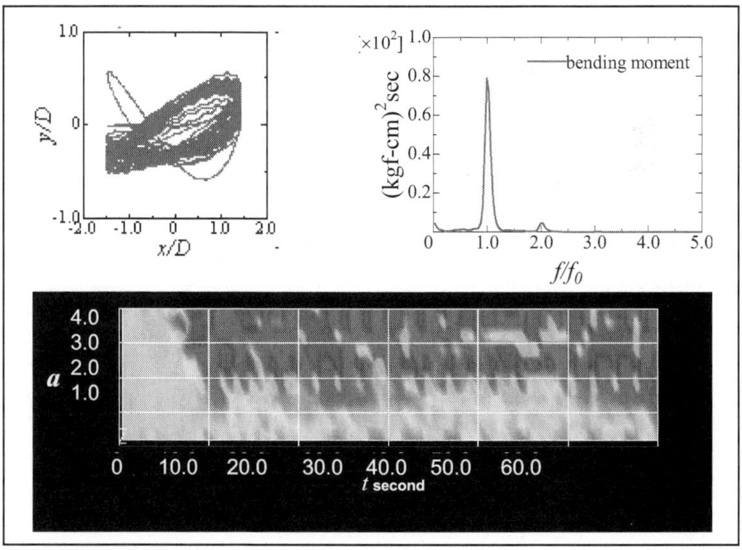

b) on back cylinder

Fig. 8. Comparisons of orbit, power spectrum and wavelet pattern of vertical bending moment in case of s=2 and T=1.2 s

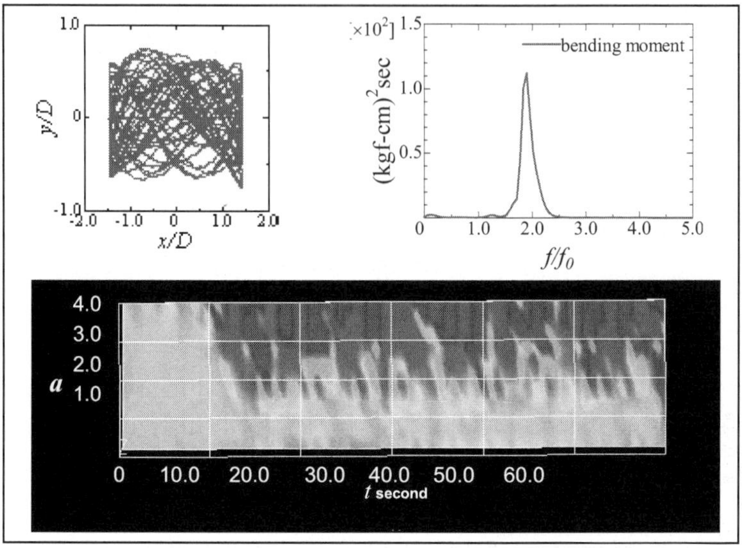

a) on front cylinder

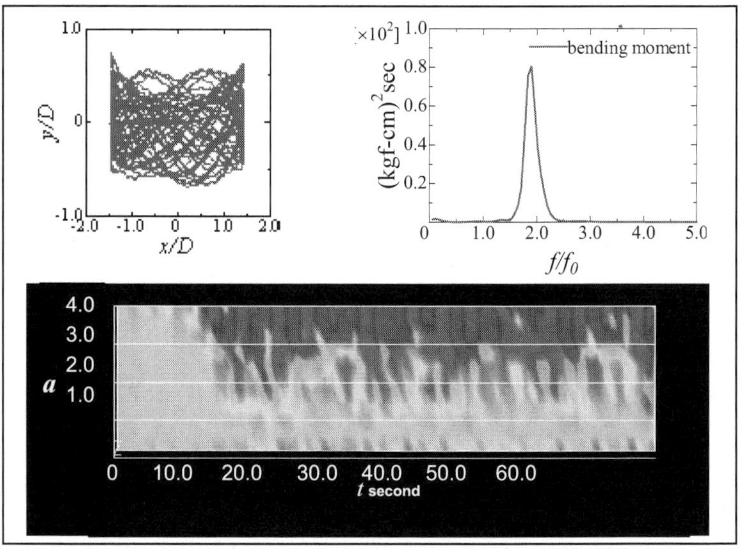

b) on back cylinder

Fig. 9. Comparisons of orbit, power spectrum and wavelet pattern of vertical bending moment in case of s=2 and T=2.0 s

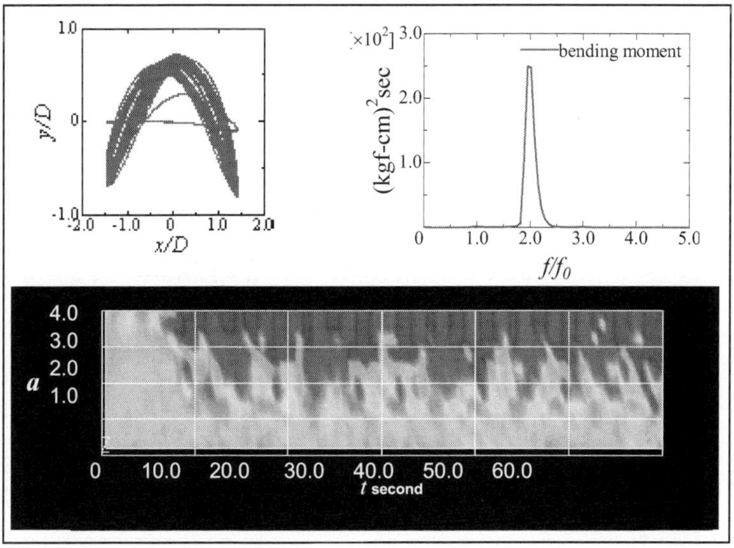

a) on front cylinder

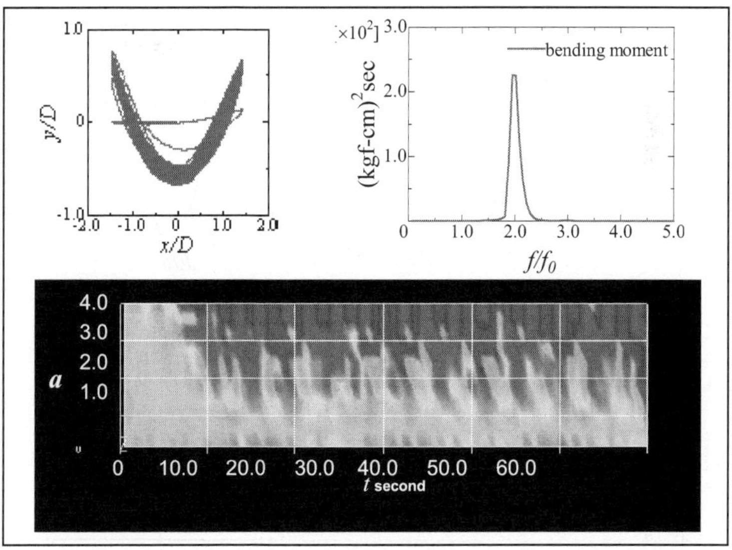

b) on back cylinder

Fig. 10. Comparisons of orbit, power spectrum and wavelet pattern of vertical bending moment in case of s=2 and T=2.2 s

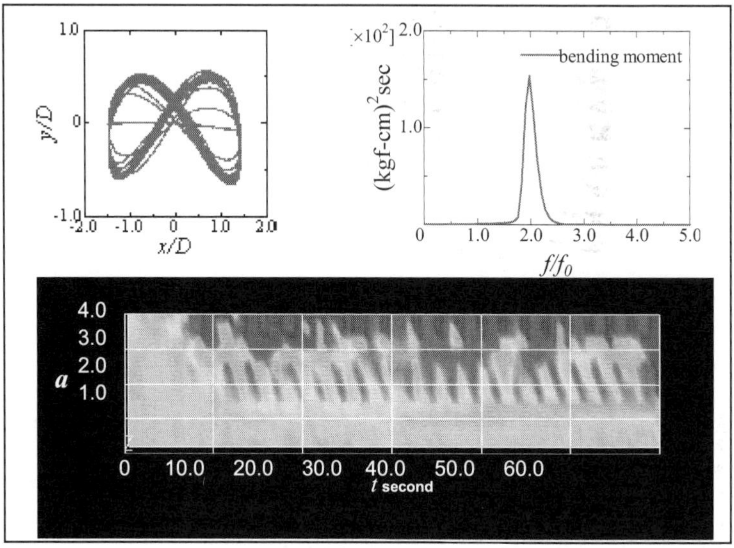

a) on front cylinder

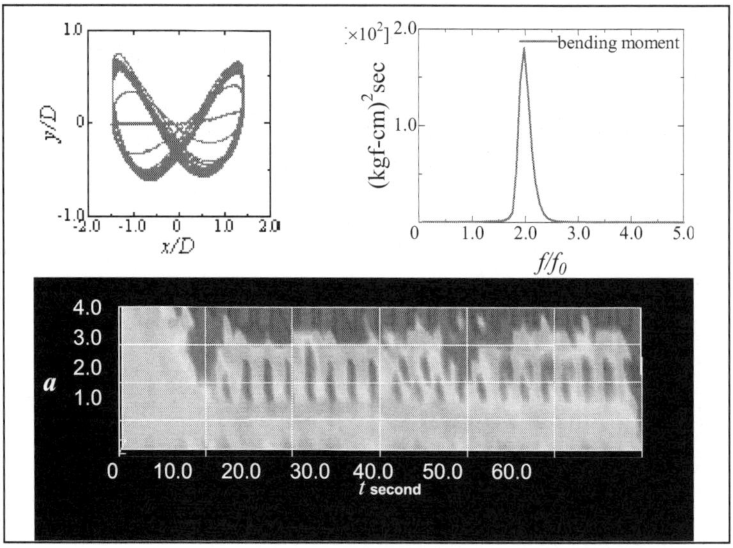

b) on back cylinder

Fig. 11. Comparisons of orbit, power spectrum and wavelet pattern of vertical bending moment in case of s=2 and T=2.4 s

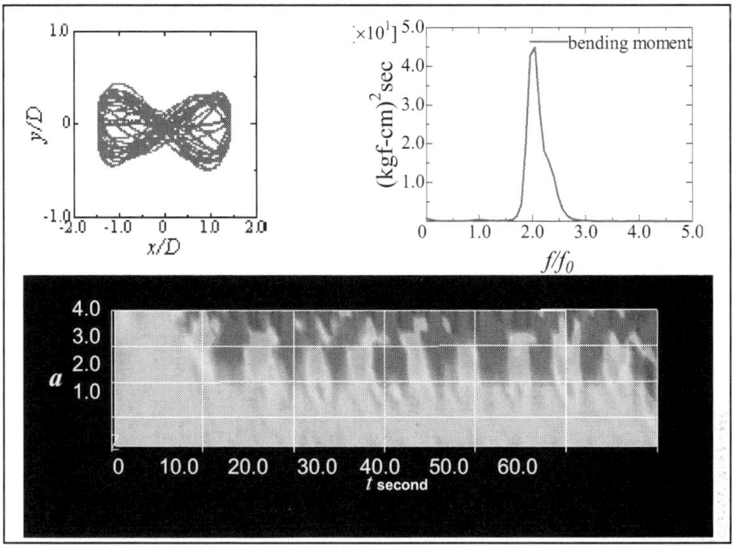

a) on front cylinder

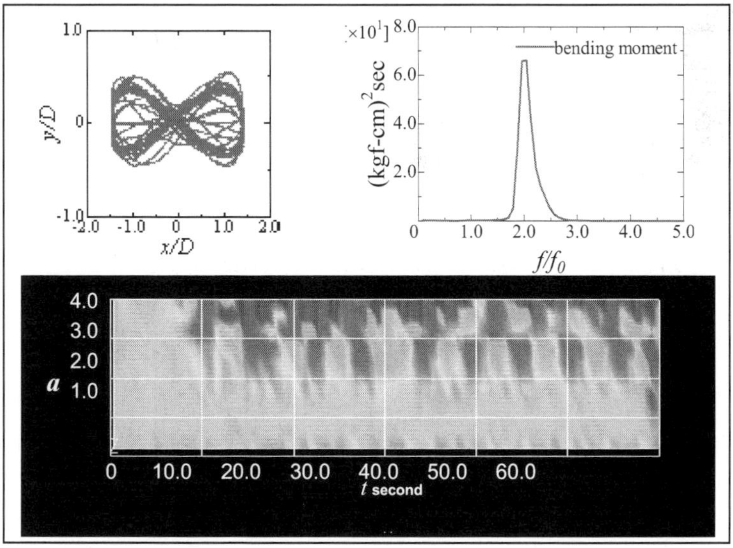

b) on back cylinder

Fig. 12. Comparisons of orbit, power spectrum and wavelet pattern of vertical bending moment in case of s=2 and T=2.8 s

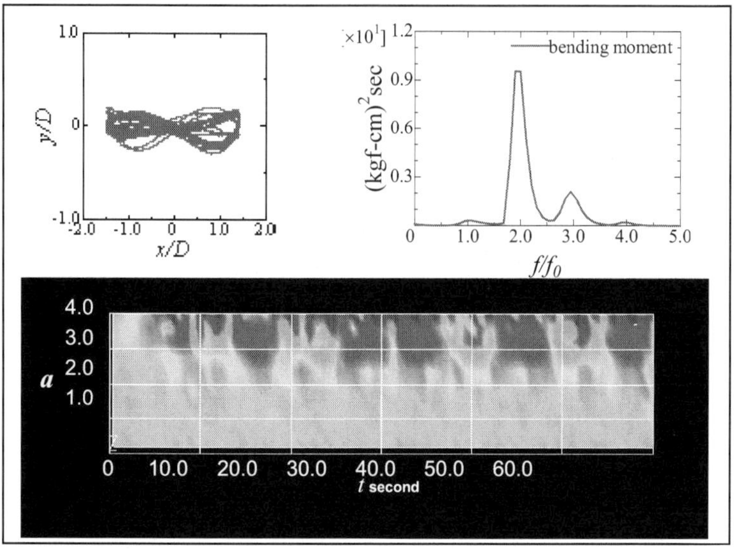

a) on front cylinder

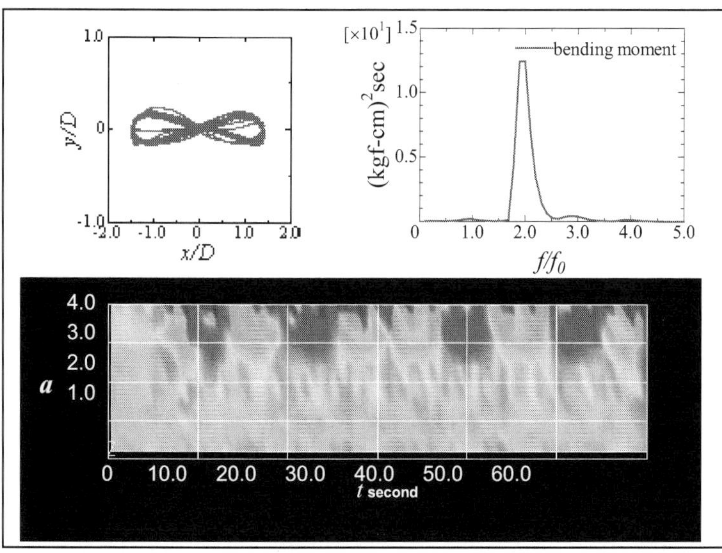

b) on back cylinder

Fig. 13. Comparisons of orbit, power spectrum and wavelet pattern of vertical bending moment in case of s=2 and T=3.45 s

Above discussions can be explained from results of the orbits and the power spectra. However all of the wavelet patterns, comparing with results of each period of the forced oscillation, are clearly different. In particular, difference of the VIV behavior cannot be understood from only the power spectra drawing the bi-harmonic vibration such as Figs. 12 to 15. We can found the unique striped pattern on the wavelet contours. At first we notice that the striped pattern gets blurred when the orbit is more complex. When the stripe becomes clearer, in range from 1.5 to 2.5 in a, the orbit varies from the *Net* type to the 8 type through the *U* type. From the wavelet pattern, we can know vibration behavior of the cylinder including cross-flow and in-line vibration. In Figs. 16, it can seem that not only the third order but also the fourth order vibration component appear. At around 2.5 in a, the wavelet stripes of Fig. 16 get blurrier than that of Fig. 15. From these, it can be considered that a result with the wavelet analysis is higher resolution or more sensitive than that with the FFT analysis to frequency components. Therefore detail of vibration behaviors of cylindrical structures with VIV can be investigated by using the wavelet transform analysis.

6. Conclusion

In this paper, the wavelet transform was applied to the analysis of time histories of vibration of circular cylinders with the vortex induced vibration. From the results, the summary is as follows:

- The orbit pattern of the cylinder roughly corresponds to the unique pattern of the wavelet contour. Therefore the vibration behavior can be known from time history data of arbitral vibration with the wavelet analysis. However calibration is necessary.
- Results with the wavelet analysis are more sensitive than that with the FFT analysis to frequency resolution.
- When VIV lock-in occurs, the pattern of the wavelet contour becomes to clear stripes.
- The Gabor's mother wavelet function is useful for analysis of VIV. In addition, the wavelet transform analysis is effective in order to investigate VIV detail.

7. References

Ikoma, T.; Masuda, K.; Maeda, H. & Hanazawa, S. (2007) *Behaviors of Drag and Inertia Coefficients of Circular Cylinders under Vortex-induced Vibrations with Forced Oscillation Tests in Still Water*, Proceedings of OMAE'07, CD-ROM OMAE2007-29473, ASME

Khalak, A. & Williamson C.H.K. (1999) *Motions, Forces and Mode Transitions in Vortex-induced vibration at low mass-damping*, Journal of Fluids and Structures, Vol.13, pp.813-851

Masuda, K.; Ikoma, T.; Kondo, N. & Maeda, H. (2006) *Forced Oscillation Experiments for VIV of Circular Cylinders and Behaviors of VIV and Lock-in Phenomenon*, Proceedings of OMAE'06, CD-ROM OMAE2006-92073, ASME

Shi, C.; Manuel, L.; Tognarelli, M.A. & Botros, T. (2010) *On the Vortex-Induced Vibration Response of a Model Riser and Lacatin of Sensors for Fatigue Damage Prediction*, Proceedings of OMAE'10, CD-ROM OMAE2010-20991, ASME

Williamson, C.H.K. & Roshko, A. (1988) *Vortex formation in the wake of an oscillating cylinder,* Journal of Fluids and Structures 2, pp.355-381

Application of Wavelets Transform in Rotorcraft UAV's Integrated Navigation System

Lei Dai[1,2], Juntong Qi[1], Chong Wu[1,2] and Jianda Han[1]
[1]*State Key Laboratory of Robotics, Shenyang Institute of Automation, Chinese Academy of Sciences*
[2]*Graduate School of Chinese Academy of Sciences*
People's Republic of China

1. Introduction

Rotorcraft UAV (RUAV) has similar mechanical structure with helicopter. It can be operated in different flight modes which the fixed-wing UAV is unable to achieve, such as vertical take-off/landing, hovering, lateral flight, pirouette, and bank-to-turn. For these advantages, RUAV can be used in many fields where human intervention is considered difficult or dangerous (Napolitano et al., 1998). So it can perform the tasks such as regional surveillance, aerial mapping, communications relay, power-line inspection, aerial photography and precision load dropping, etc. RUAV has many advantages, such as small in size, low cost, simple operation and convenient transportation. Therefore, RUAV has broad application prospects, high demands, and advantages that the fixed-wing unmanned aircrafts and unmanned airship can not replace.

Integrated navigation system can give the movement information of the carrier, thus every UAV has an integrated navigation system. Because of the limitations of weight, volume, power supply and cost, there is no redundant navigation system in RUAV. RUAV does not have the emergency landing properties of fixed-wing aircrafts or airships in case of failures. Therefore, a failure in any part of a RUAV can be catastrophic. If the failure is not detected, identified and accommodated, the RUAV may crash. The use of wavelet transforms the situation of accurately localizing the characteristics of a signal both in the time and frequency domains, the occurring instants of abnormal status of a sensor in the output signal can be identified by the multi-scale representation of the signal (Dabechies, 1988; Isermann, 1984; Zhang, 2000). Once the instants are detected, the distribution differences of the signal energy on all decomposed wavelet scales of the signal before and after the instants are used to claim and classify the sensor faults.

In low cost and small size integrated navigation system, MEMS (Micro Electronic Mechanical System) inertial sensors are used widely. But MEMS inertial sensors, especially MEMS gyroscopes have large noise. It affects the calculation accuracy of angle rotation matrix, and will further affect calculation accuracy of other navigation data such as position, velocity, and angular velocity. In order to improve the calculation precision of position and angle, digital filter is required to reduce the noise of gyroscope. Commonly, we used

Kalman filters to decreasing the random noise. And we need to build the mathematic model of sensors' errors. The MEMS gyroscope has random drift characteristics of weak nonlinear, non-stationary, slow time-varying. And it is sensitive to external environments such as vibration and temperature. The result of Kalman filter is often imprecision and even divergence, because of inaccurate drift error model of MEMS gyroscope. Wavelet transform has the characteristics of multi-resolution and time-frequency localization, and we do not need to build the mathematic model of sensor errors. So it is ideal for signal processing and analysis of MEMS gyroscope.

However, Synthetic data simulated by means of a computer using real flight data from ServoHeli-20 and ServoHeli-40 RUAV, which is designed and implemented by Shenyang Institute of Automation, have verified the effectiveness of the proposed method.

The following part of this paper is organized as follows. In Section 2, the fault detection approach based on the wavelet transform is established. The RUAV verification platform is introduced in Section 3. The integrated navigation system and the characteristic of inertial sensor are discussed in Section 4. Real RUAV flight fault detection experiments in manual mode are described and discussed in Section 5, and conclusions are given in Section 6.

2. The RUAV platform

During years of research, we have developed two RUAV platforms. The ServoHeli-20 RUAV platform was designed to be a common experimental platform for control and fault-tolerant related study before 2009 (Qi, et al., 2006). The hardware components were selected with considerations of weight, availability and performance. After that, we miniaturized the hardware and used 40Kg industry helicopter. And we developed ServoHeli-40 RUAV platform. This RUAV platform can be used for control and navigation algorithm verification and experimental payload platform.

2.1 ServoHeli-20 platform

As the basic aircraft of the RUAV system, we chose the small-scaled model helicopter which is available in the market. Such a choice is easy for us to exchange the accessories and reduce the cost (Qi, et al., 2010).

2.1.1 Modified RC helicopter

ServoHeli-20 aerial vehicle is a high quality helicopter which is changed by us using a RC model helicopter operating with a remote controller. The modified system allows the payload of more than 5 kilograms, which is sufficient to carry the whole airborne avionics box and the communication units. The fuselage of the helicopter is constructed with sturdy ABS composite body and the main rotor blades are replaced by heavy-duty carbon fibre reinforced ones to accommodate extra payloads. The vehicle is powered by a 90-class glow plug engine which generates 3.0hp at about 15000 rpm, and practical angular rate ranging from 2,000 to 16,000 rpm. The full length of the fuselage is 1260mm and the full width of it is 160mm. The total height of the helicopter is 410mm, the main rotor is 1600mm and the tail rotor is 260mm.

The overall rotorcraft UAV control system comprises: the aerial vehicle platform, the onboard avionics control system, and the ground monitoring station. The UAV helicopter itself is able to operate with the independent control computer system and onboard sensors.

2.1.2 Navigation sensors

In order to navigate following a desired trajectory while stabilizing the vehicle, the information of helicopter's position, velocity, acceleration, attitude, and the angular rates should be known to the guidance and control system. The ServoHeli-20 RUAV system is equipped with sensors including IMU (Inertial Measure Unit), GPS and digital compass, to obtain above accurate information about the motion of the helicopter in association with environment.

Sensor	PARAMETERS
IMU400 IMU	Angular Rate Range: $\pm 100^{\circ}/\sec$ Acceleration Range: $\pm 4g$ Digital Output Format: RS-232 Update Rate: > 100 Hz Size: 76.2 × 95.3 × 81.3 mm Weight: <640g
Crescent GPS	Position Accuracy (CEP): 1.5m Digital Output Format: RS-232 Update Rate: 10 Hz Size: 71.1 × 49.6 × 1.2 mm Weight: 20g
HMR3000 Compass	Pitch, Roll Angular Range: $\pm 40^{\circ}$ Digital Output Format: RS-232 Update Rate: 20 Hz Size: 15 × 42 × 8.8 mm Weight: 92g

Table 1. Sensors parameters

The picture of sensors in the avionics box is shown in Fig. 1, and their primary parameters are shown in Table I.

2.1.3 Processor and control system

The flight computer installed in avionics box is a typical industrial embedded computer system, so-called PC-104 in the whole system is kept as compact and light-weight as possible. The PC-104 has the ISA or PCI bus which features a $108.2\text{cm} \times 115.06\text{cm}$ footprint circuit board. Our flight computer system consists of a main CPU board and some other peripheral boards such as DC-DC power supply board, 8-channel serial communication device and PWM generation board. The main CPU board has a Celeron processor at 400MHz with 256MB SDRAM, fully compatible with the real-time operation system such as QNX. Hard drive or other equivalent mass-storage device for booting and running an operation system and storing useful sensor data is needed to the flight computer.

To our flight control system, a real-time operation system (RTOS) is required for the onboard computer system. After carefully consideration and comparison, QNX Neutrino RTOS is selected as the operation system, which is ideal for embedded real-time applications. It can be scaled to very small size and provide multitasking threads, priority-driven pre-emptive scheduling, and fast context-switching–all essential ingredients of an embedded real-time system. The applied program can be coded and debugged in the remote windows-host computers and can be executed in the airborne computer system independently, which provides great convenience during the flight experiments without modifying the program in onboard computer.

2.1.4 Implementation

Designing the avionics box and packing the box appropriately under the fuselage of the helicopter are two main tasks to implement of the RUAV system.

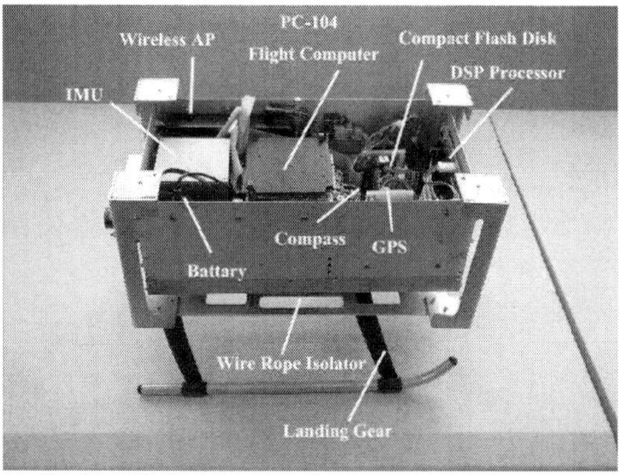

Fig. 1. The avionics control system

In the actual flight environment, the weight and the size of the avionics box are strict limited. Our airborne control box, which is shown in Figure 1, is a compact aluminum alloy package mounted on the landing gear. The center of gravity of the box lies on the IMU device where is not the geometry center of the system that ensure the navigation data form IMU accurate. The digital compass and the IMU are installed on the same line, which are taken as the horizontal center of the gravity of the avionics system to locate and the other components.

The original landing gear of the model helicopter is plastic, in which is no enough room to install the designed avionics system in the fuselage of the helicopter. While, we re-design a landing gear with aluminum alloy and make a larger room under the fuselage of the model helicopter for the control box. To avoid the disciplinary vibration about 20Hz caused by characteristic of the helicopter, ENIDINE® aviation wire rope isolators which are mounted between the avionics box and the changed landing gear are chosen. They are comprised of stainless steel stranded cable, threaded through aluminum alloy retaining bars, crimped and mounted for effective vibration isolation. The assembled RUAV system with the necessary components is shown in Figure 2.

Fig. 2. Implemented ServoHeli-20 RUAV

The full duplex wireless-LAN equipments are installed in the ground station and the airborne system to exchange data between them including receiving commands from the ground system and reporting the operating status or possible damages to the ground station. The architecture of the RUAV control system is presented in Figure 3.

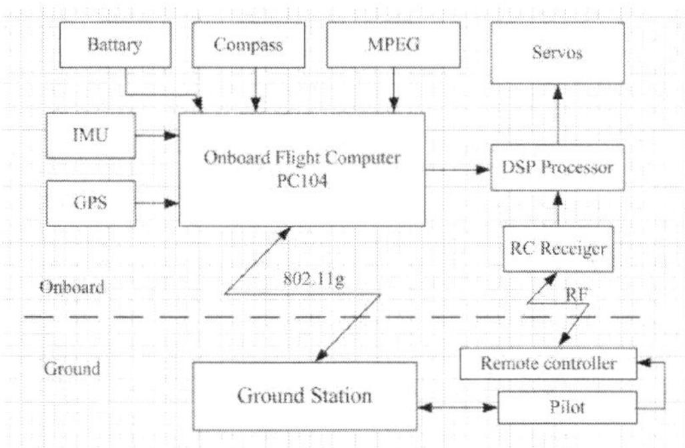

Fig. 3. Architecture of the RUAV control system

2.2 ServoHeli-40 platform

ServoHeli-40 RUAV platform is a flexible platform. It can carry 15Kg payloads to do aerophotography or experiment. It is also easy for us to replace the accessories and the cost is affordable.

2.2.1 ServoHeli-40 helicopter

ServoHeli-40 aerial vehicle is a high reliability helicopter. It uses traditional helicopter configuration of single-rotor with tail rotor. The power is come from 8hp twin-cylinder two-stroke air-cooled gasoline engine. The fuselage of the helicopter is constructed with aluminium. The bearings and the other parts are standard industry parts. So it is easy to buy and repair. ServoHeli-40's maximum takeoff weight is 40Kg, and its maximum payload is 15 kg. It can carry different kinds of instruments to do experiment. The rotor diameter is

2150 mm. The total height of the helicopter is 770mm, the full width of it is 720mm, and the total length is 2680mm. The maximum airspeed is 100 km/h, and it can cruise 1 hour at 36 km/h speed.

2.2.2 Navigation system

In the design of the navigation system, we followed some principles. First, the system must be compact and easy to equip on the airframe. Second, the system should use low-cost sensor to reduce the RUAV system's cost. Third, the system should be designed as light as possible to save fuel and increase the payload. Precision navigation information of flight state is needed to realize the autonomous control of the RUAV. Generally, navigation information must include positions, velocities, accelerations, attitude, heading and angular velocities in 3-axis. The architecture of the navigation system is shown in Figure 4 (Wu, et al., 2010).

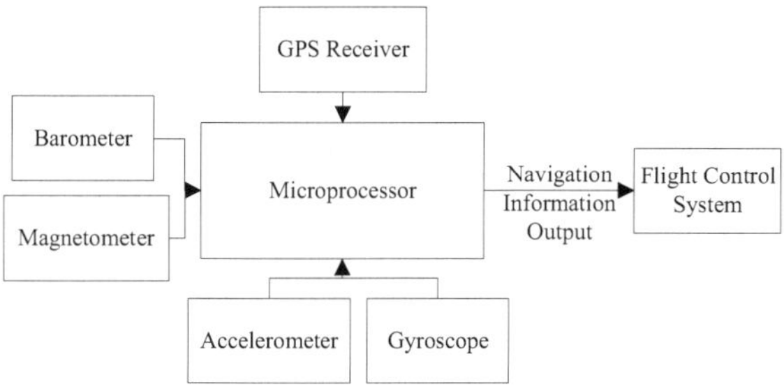

Fig. 4. Hardware Architecture of Navigation System

We use GPS receiver to give position and velocity. But the altitude given by GPS generally has a fluctuation of 5m, and it is not accurate enough to control the RUAV. So a barometer is needed to give a more accurate measurement of the relative altitude. Even though the barometer is more accurate in relative altitude, it is susceptible to weather condition and may vary significantly in different weather. Because the altitude given by GPS is much more unsusceptible to weather, a combination of GPS altitude and barometer altitude will give more accurate and stable altitude information.

Attitudes' accuracy is the key point for the stability of the RUAV since the position control of the RUAV is coupled with the attitude. We use IMU to measure the acceleration and angle velocity. By referring to a low-cost attitude design described in literature (Gao et al., 2006), we determine the attitude in pitch and roll by accelerometers and gyroscopes. A simple calculation of acceleration may be suitable for the RUAV in hovering and other mode with low maneuverability in low acceleration, but in high maneuverability mode with high acceleration, the measurement will deviate a great deal because the measurement of accelerometers include not only gravity acceleration but also absolute acceleration. So a feedback from velocity is added to decrease the influence of absolute acceleration.

The yaw of RUAV will be calculated by the magnetic field measured by the magnetometer. Due to the deviation of magnetic field of the earth in different places, a revision of magnetic field would be necessary to get the real yaw.

Compared with previous generation, this navigation system uses independent processor. We choose LPC3250 as the calculation and acquisition processor. A two-stage EKF is implemented to estimate the flight state. Further research in navigation theory can be conducted by using this system.

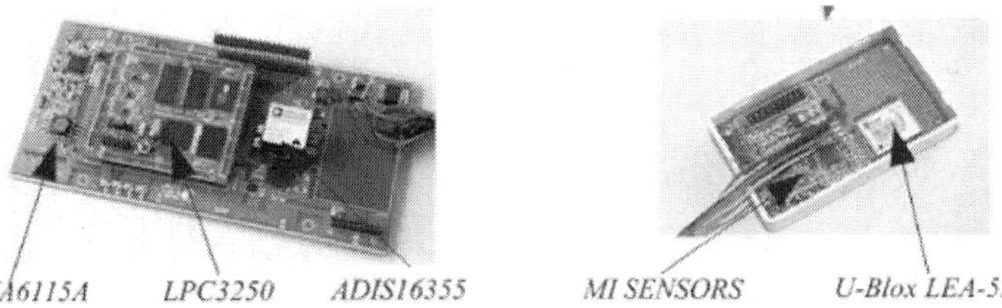

Fig. 5. The navigation system

The IMU, GPS, barometer, magnetometer and processor are integrated in a compact circuit, as shown in Figure 5. The primary parameters of compacted navigation system are shown in Table2.

Sensor	PARAMETERS
ADIS16355 *IMU*	Angular Rate Range: $\pm 300^\circ/\sec$ Acceleration Range: $\pm 18g$ Digital Output Format: SPI Update Rate: 50 Hz Size: 23 × 23 ×23mm
U-Blox LEA-5H *GPS*	Position Accuracy (CEP): 3m Digital Output Format: Uart Update Rate: 4Hz Size: 17 × 22.4 × 3mm
SmartSens *Magneto-inductive* *Compass*	Pitch, Roll Angular Range: $\pm 40^\circ$ Analog Output Update Rate: 20 Hz
MPXA6115A *Barometer*	Sensor range: 15 to 115 kPa Analog Output Update Rate: 50 Hz Size: 7.5 × 10 ×10mm

Table 2. Sensors Parameters

2.2.3 Flight control system

The fight control processor uses the same processor as the navigation system, so we can share the code of the operating system and reduce the debug time. The LPC3250 with an ARM926EJ-S CPU Core implementation uses Harvard architecture with a 5-stage pipeline and operates at CPU frequencies up to 266 Hz. The Vector Floating Point (VFP) coprocessor makes the micro controller suitable for advanced navigation and control algorithm, and processing speed and interface versatility is guaranteed. The industry standard operation temperature from -40℃ to 80℃ extends the usage of RUAV in various environments. The LPC3250 includes a USB 2.0 Full Speed interface, seven UARTs, two I²C interfaces, two SPI/SSP ports, and two I2S interfaces; Such a great number interfaces of LPC3250 makes it very suitable for navigation and control system with a plenty of sensors in standard interface. We designed interface circuit to drive the actuator and log the flight data.

To decrease the developing work in programming, while increasing the system stability, a μC/OS-II embedded system is installed to organize the software development. This small sized embedded system is quite convenient to install; the hard-real-time architecture also makes it suitable for a time critical avionics system in RUAV. We divided the work of software into 5 parts. First, the OS Kernel is to maintain the whole system and arrange the task schedule. Second, the algorithms implements navigation and control theory. Third, the device interface process is to handle the task for sensor data acquire and drive the actuator. Fourth, the user interface carries out the job to display and receive necessary information to the user. Fifth, the log interface is to log the flight data for our experiment. To make sure that the algorithms can be calculated in time, a hardware timer is used instead of the software timer provided by operator system. With a proper design of the software architecture, the system's stability is maintained and the flexibility is also provided for other algorithm implementations.

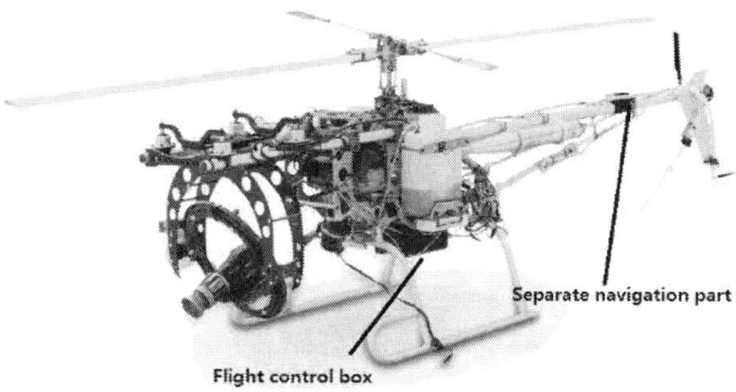

Fig. 6. Implemented ServoHeli-40 RUAV

2.2.4 System realization

The GPS receiver and magnetometer are in a separate part and the others are in the main navigation part. The flight control system and main navigation system are assembled in an anti-jamming aluminum box, and called flight control box. Such a separation is with the consideration that the GPS and magnetometers are susceptible to the install position because they may be influenced if it is covered by the airborne or near some magnetic material. The flight control box is mounted under fuselage of the RUAV. The separate part can be equipped in a proper place on the airframe. To avoid the disciplinary vibration about 20-22.5Hz caused by revolving of main rotor, ENIDINE aviation wire rope isolators are also used. They are comprised of stainless steel stranded cable, threaded through aluminum alloy retaining bars, crimped and mounted for effective vibration isolation. The assembled RUAV system with the necessary components is shown in Figure 6.

To increase the control distance and reliability, the half duplex industry radios are installed in the ground station and the airborne system to exchange data. The data includes commands, operating status and possible damages, which is received and reported to the ground station. The flight data can be logged in SD card, we can analysis the data after flight test. The architecture of the RUAV control system is presented in Figure 7.

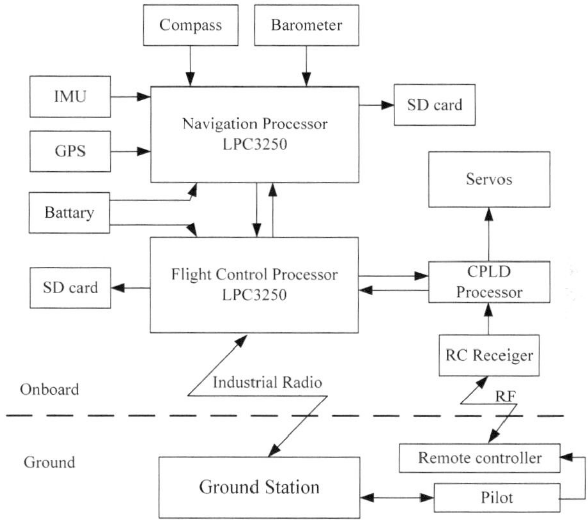

Fig. 7. Architecture of the RUAV control system

3. Wavelet-based fault detection

Without loss of generality, assume that the vehicle's sensor output $y(t)$ is described as (Zhang & Yan, 2001):

$$y(t) = f[x(t)] + n(t) \tag{1}$$

Where $n(t)$ is a noise signal and the measured $x(t)$ changes with a k-degree polynomial function $f[x(t)]$ which describes the measured process changes. Stone-Weierstrass Theorem states that any continuous function on a compact set can be approximated to any degree of accuracy by a polynomial function (Rudin, 1976). Therefore, using a polynomial function to represent any function $f[x(t)]$ will not lose the generality. Let $\psi(t)$ be a wavelet function and $\psi_s(t) = (1/s)\psi(t/s)$ be the dilation of $\psi(t)$ by the scale factor s. The wavelet transform of $y(t)$ can be written as:

$$WT_f(s,\tau) = y(t) * \psi_s(t) = f[x(t) + n(t)] * \psi_s(t) \tag{2}$$

Where $*$ denotes the convolution and $WT_f(s,\tau)$ represents the wavelet transform. A wavelet $\psi(t)$ is said to have m vanishing moments if and only for all positive integers $k<m$, the following equation is satisfied:

$$\int_{-\infty}^{+\infty} t^k \psi_s(t)dt = 0 \tag{3}$$

Now, let us call a smoothing function, any real function $\theta(t)$ such that $\theta(t) = O(1/1(1+t^2))$ and whose integral is nonzero. A smoothing function can be viewed as the impulse response of a low-pass filter. Let $f[x(t)]$ and $\theta_s(t) = (1/s)\theta(t/s)$ be a real function in $L^2(R)$. The abrupt changes of the sensor data at scale s are defined as local sharp variation points $f[x(t)]$ smoothed by $\theta_s(t)$. The method of detecting these sharp variation points with a wavelet transform is explained as follows.

Let $\psi^1(t)$ and $\psi^2(t)$ be the two wavelets defined by:

$$\psi^1(t) = \frac{d\theta(t)}{dt} \tag{4}$$

$$\psi^2(t) = \frac{d\theta^2(t)}{dt^2} \tag{5}$$

The wavelet transform defined with respect to each of these wavelets are given by:

$$W^1(t) = f * \psi_s^1(t) = f * (s\frac{d\theta_s}{dt})(t) = s\frac{d}{dt}(f * \theta_s)(t) \tag{6}$$

$$W^1(t) = f * \psi_s^1(t) = f * (s\frac{d\theta_s}{dt})(t) = s\frac{d}{dt}(f * \theta_s)(t) \tag{7}$$

The wavelet transforms of $W^1 f(s,t)$ and $W^2 f(s,t)$ is proportional respectively to the first and second derivatives of $f[x(t)]$ smoothed by $\theta_s(t)$. As a result, the local maxima of $|W^1 f(s,t)|$ indicate the locations of sharp variation points and singularities of $f[x(t)] * \theta_s(t)$ (Mallat & Hwang, 1992).

From (4) to (7), it can be concluded that the wavelet transform of the signal (1) only includes some sharp variation points induced by sensor faults and random noise. Once a sharp variation point is claimed, and alarm will be triggered for a failure of the sensor.

4. Fault detection experiment

4.1 Fault detection system design

The sensors of the navigation system with different mechanism also have different performance. We cannot get the ideal fault detection results using the traditional fault detection techniques.

In order to accompany the short control period and the highly update rate, we use the parallel wavelet analyzer, which is shown as figure 8.

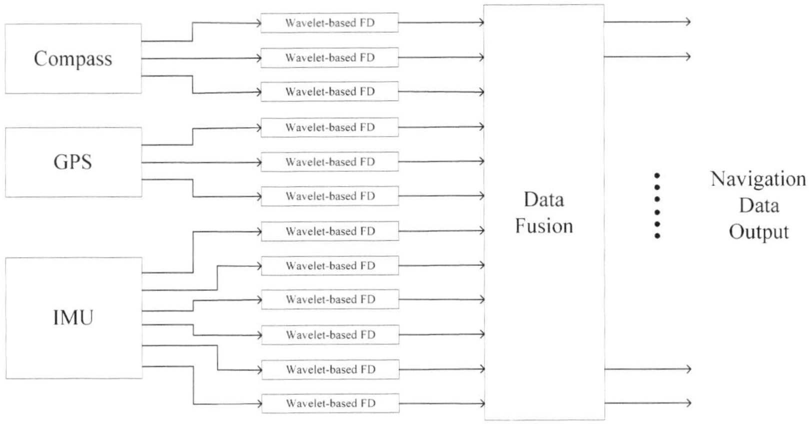

Fig. 8. Architecture of wavelet-based sensor system

Table 1 shows us that there are three sensors in the RUAV sensor system which have three channel separately. We design 12 wavelet analyzers for 12 channels of all sensors. The sensors data will directly send to the data fusion system when the data are in the normal states. However, if the sensors data is abnormal in one or some channels as a result of the failure of specific sensors, the alarms will send to the flight computer while the data link will be cut off. Then the navigation system will continue to compute with degraded sensors data.

4.2 Experimental results and discussion

The proposed wavelet-based fault detection system tested using the ServoHeli-20 RUAV system in manual mode.

Fig. 9. ServoHeli-20 fault detection experiment

The use of the mathematical model makes it easier to test the wavelet-based fault detection system, but the characteristic of the datasets may not reflect the real flight environment and the actual actuator failures. On the other hand, real autonomous flight experiments with an injected sensor failure can be potentially dangerous for the helicopter because it can take the RUAV out of control and RUAV may crash. Thus, we planned to inject the sensor failure while the absence of the security problems of the RUAV with its manual mode. As is shown in the figure 9, the pilot controls the helicopter using radio controller. The onboard computer online detects the fault with wavelet-based algorithm (Qi & Han, 2007).

To demonstrate the effectiveness of the fault detection scheme, the failure scenario of abrupt bias and spike in compass roll channel is assumed.

A "db2" ("db" is define in Matlab) wavelet with a vanishing moment 2 is applied to these abrupt faults of sensor. Figure 10 and 11 show their wavelet transforms in scale-D1 to scale-S3 including the original data signals. In figure 10, scale-D1 to scale-D3 denote the details of the wavelet transform of the signals on scales 1 to 3, respectively, while the scale-S3 represents the approximation of them on scale 3.

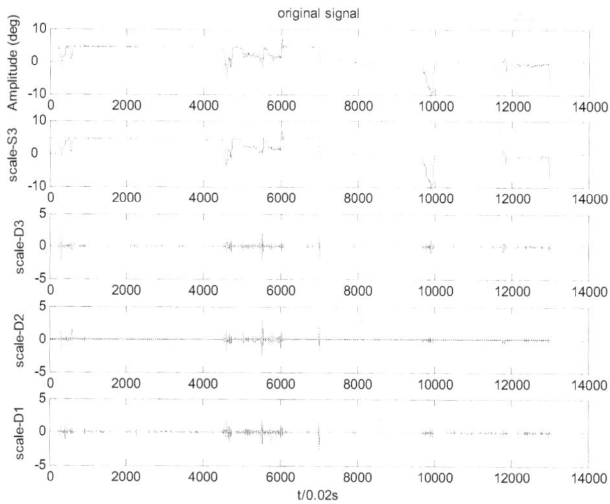

Fig. 10. Bias failure and its wavelet transform(t=0.02s)

4.2.1 Failure of bias

In figure 10, an example sensor failure experiment is presented. At the point of 7000, the compass roll channel gets bias of 5 degree.

The local maxima of the first derivative are sharp variation points of $f[x(t)]*\theta_s(t)$. For abrupt failure detection, we are only interested in the local maxima of $|W^1 f(s,t)|$. When detecting the local maxima of $|W^1 f(s,t)|$, we call also keep the value of the wavelet transform at the corresponding location.

As is shown in the figure 11, discontinuity point of signal is displayed obviously, it is allocated very accurately in time-domain, and fault point of bias signal is contained in signal abruption. Using the $|W^1 f(s,t)|$ criterion, the fault detection system can detect locations of the bias fault at 7000 that we can see the local maximum value of module indicates the signal singularity accurately.

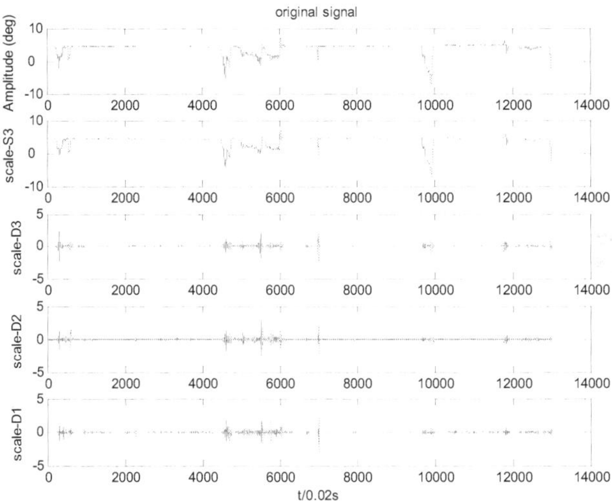

Fig. 11. Spike failure and its wavelet transform(t=0.02s)

4.2.2 Failure of spike

We also made a spike failure injection to RUAV system in manual mode to test the performance of the wavelet-based fault detection system. At the point of 7000, the compass roll channel gets spike which the signal return to zero.

Similar to the bias failure experiment, the location of fault agree with the maximum values of the wavelet transform on different scales.

From the results, it can be conclude that the proposed method is effective for detection the abrupt faults of the RUAV sensor system. Fault point could be also being described accurately at some certain resolution. Local characteristics of wavelet are represented well in time and frequency-domains.

5. Wavelet for gyroscope de-noising

5.1 MEMS gyroscope signal analysis

With the development of microelectronics technology, low cost MEMS gyroscopes begin to be used widely. It makes the great development of integrated navigation system, especially in UAV system. Compared with high costs gyroscope, the MEMS gyroscope devices have some drawbacks, such as large bias stability, big temperature noise, high noise density. And all these disadvantages lead to that the long-term accuracy of navigation system is very low. While random vibration due to main rotor of RUAV, have an impact on gyroscopes measurements. Simple passive vibration damping measures cannot be completely filtering the vibration. And the measurement error is unacceptable (Ma et al., 2007). In order to eliminate noise of MEMS gyroscope, error analysis of signals need to be done. This is very important to improve the performance of integrated navigation system and increase the stability of the RUAV system.

According to the frequency spectrum characteristics of MEMS gyroscope, its errors can be divided into long-term errors and short-term errors. Long-term errors include bias stability, scale non-linearity, angular random walk, bias variation over temperature, rate noise density, and so on. These errors can be predicted by the mathematic model and adjusted. According to the error mechanism of MEMS gyroscope, an ARMA model is established. Then, using parameter identification, the parameter of the ARMA model is identified. So the long-term errors can be compensated. The short-term errors include random interference noise, measurement noise, and so on. It is a tricky problem to deal with errors. Usually, we use digital filters to compensate the error. These conventional denoising methods include Low-Pass filter, Kalman filter, and wavelet filter. Under the principle of linear least mean squares error, angular velocity estimation is recursively calculated by Kalman filtering in literature (Shi & Zhang, 2000). Although the approach is successfully used in reducing gyroscope noise on the stationary platforms, it is based on the assumption that the signal is corrupted by Gaussian noise and model is exactitude. Unfortunately, for imprecise model and colored noise, this method may yield worse results. Low-Pass filter passes low-frequency signals but reduces the amplitude of signals with frequencies higher than the cutoff frequency. And greater accuracy in approximation requires a longer delay. It can be realized by cheap hardware, while its low quality, however, is not very satisfactory. Wavelet transforms have excellent multi-resolution analysis feature and do not need model. So it is suitable for non-stationary signals processing. And wavelet transforms have been successfully applied to the denoising of signals or images in recent years. This method has achieved good results in gyroscope signal denoising process (Imola et al., 2001; Qu et al., 2009).

5.2 Wavelet for denoising

Wavelet transform is method of time-frequency localization analysis. Its window size (area) is fixed, but the shape can be changed. Wavelet transform developed the short - time Fourier transform of localized. It has a high frequency resolution and lower time resolution in low frequency part of the signal. And in high frequency part of the signal, it has a high time resolution and lower frequency resolution. Wavelet transform method has the character of frequency analysis, and it can indicate the occurred time. It is very suitable for noise reduction of MEMS gyroscopes.

The discrete wavelet function $\psi_{j,k}(t)$ in Discrete Wavelet transform (DWT) can be expressed as :

$$\psi_{j,k}(t) = s_0^{-j/2}\psi\left(\frac{t - ks_0^j\tau_0}{s_0^j}\right) = s_0^{-j/2}\psi\left(s_0^{-j}t - k\tau_0\right) \tag{8}$$

The discrete wavelet translate factor can be expressed as :

$$C_{j,k} = \int_{-\infty}^{\infty} f(t)\psi^{*}{}_{j,k}(t)dt = \langle f, \psi_{j,k} \rangle \tag{9}$$

The reconstruction function of Discrete Wavelet transform can be expressed as :

$$f(t) = C\sum_{-\infty}^{\infty}\sum_{-\infty}^{\infty} C_{j,k}\psi_{j,k}(t) \tag{10}$$

Where s denotes the scale factor, τ denotes the translate factor. The $f(t)$ represents the signal function.

The purpose of wavelet transform for denoising is to extract useful signal and remove the interference signal in the output signal. In other words, the useful signal and noise signal are separated by the method of wavelet transform. There are 4 common methods of wavelet denoising (Burrus et al., 1998; Guo et al., 2003):

1. Thresholding Denoising Method. It is also called wavelet shrinkage. The basic idea of this method can be described as: The wavelet coefficients have different characters in particular wavelet scales. According to this characteristic of the signal and noise, the noise signals are converted by wavelet transform in certain wavelet scales. According to a certain threshold processing strategies for treatment of wavelet coefficients, the coefficients, which are greater than the threshold, are kept (hard thresholding method) or shrunk (soft thresholding method). The coefficients, which are less than the threshold, are considered to be noise and set to zero directly. Then based on these wavelet coefficients, the original signal is reconstructed using inverse wavelet transform. And this method requires the assumption that the noise signal is Gaussian white noise.
2. Wavelet Decomposition and Reconstruction Method. It is also known as the Mallet method. It decomposes the signal with noise in scale into different frequency bands, sets the bands with noise to zero and reconstructs the signal using wavelet method. This method will remove the noise signals with the useful signals. So it may distort the reconstructed signal.
3. Modulus Maximum Method. In different wavelet scale, this method uses the variation features of wavelet transform modulus' maxima value to denoising the signal. The extreme points, whose amplitude decrease with scale increasing in signal, are removed. The extreme points, whose amplitude increase with scale increasing in signal, are retained. Using alternating projection method, the original signal is reconstructed from de-noised diagram of maxima modulus. And the noise signal is de-noised.
4. Translation Invariant Method. It is a method improved from the basis of the Thresholding Denoising method. The noise signals are taken n times cycles shift by this method. And the translated signals are de-noised using thresholding denoising method. In the end, de-noised signal are equilibrated. This method has a smaller mean square error and improves signal-to-noise ratio.

5.3 Thresholding denoising method

Through the above analysis, the modulus maximum method and translation invariant method have large calculation amounts. And this will affect the real-time calculation of integrated navigation system. So considering the speed of calculation and the ease of implementation, thresholding denoising method is used in our navigation system.

The step of thresholding denoising method is as follows (Song et al., 2009; Su & Zhou, 2009):

1. Selecting the Wavelet function. Then the signal with noise $y_i, i = 0,1,...,N-1$ is discrete using wavelet transformation. A group of wavelet transform coefficients $d_{j,k}$ is got. The subscript j is the wavelet scale.
2. Thresholding the wavelet transforms coefficients $d_{j,k}$. The hard threshold, soft threshold or other threshold method can be used to deal with the coefficients. After the computation, a new wavelet transforms coefficients $\hat{d}_{j,k}$ is got.

The hard threshold estimation is defined as follows:

$$\hat{d}_{j,k} = \begin{cases} d_{j,k}, & |d_{j,k}| \geq \lambda_j \\ 0, & |d_{j,k}| < \lambda_j \end{cases} \tag{11}$$

The soft threshold estimation is defined as follows:

$$\hat{d}_{j,k} = \begin{cases} \operatorname{sgn}(d_{j,k})(|d_{j,k}| - \lambda_j), & |d_{j,k}| \geq \lambda_j \\ 0, & |d_{j,k}| < \lambda_j \end{cases} \tag{12}$$

Where λ_j is the threshold constant.

3. Wavelet reconstruction. Using the inverse of discrete wavelet transform formulas, we can get the de-noised signal $\hat{y}_i$.

6. Gyroscope denoising simulation and analysis

In this section, several control experiments are taken on gyroscope signal denoising using wavelet methods. The experiment uses the real flight data recorded by the flight control system of ServoHeli-40. The flight data is recorded at the 100Hz rate, and each point represents 10ms. It is sufficient to describe the motion of ServoHeli-40 RUAV both in time domain and in frequency domain.

In this simulation experiment, the length of the data is 14,950 points. And it means the data continued about 2.5 minutes. During this period of time, the RUAV did the following actions: standing still, engine ignition, speed idle, hovering , and trajectory tracking. In these flying modes, the data of gyroscope have different amplitude characters. This reflects the vibration differences in different flying modes. The original signal of ServoHeli-40's Y axis gyroscope is shown in the figure 12.

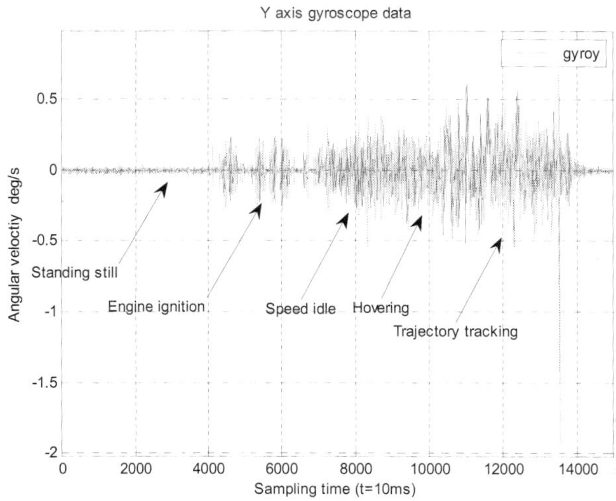

Fig. 12. The original signal of ServoHeli-40's Y axis gyroscope

In order to find a appropriate wavelet functions and decomposition levels, the simulation compared the thresholding denoising method using harr, db2, db4, db6, sym2, sym4, coif2, bior1.5 and bior5.5 wavelet functions. The decomposition levels are respectively 2, 5 and 8. The standard deviation of de-noised signal's residuals is calculated to compare the wavelet denoising results. The results are shown in Table 3. And the standard deviation of the original data is 0.06606.

Level \ wavelet	haar	db2	db4	db6	sym2	sym4	coif2	bior1.5	bior5.5
2	0.01841	0.1378	0.01323	0.01285	0.01378	0.01329	0.01288	0.01906	0.01271
5	0.04229	0.05397	0.05467	0.05489	0.05397	0.05561	0.05558	0.05514	0.05572
8	0.06552	0.06537	0.06576	0.0658	0.06573	0.06578	0.06582	0.06573	0.06583

Table 3. Standard deviation of de-noised signal's residuals

In Table 3, when decomposition level increases to more than 5 layers, improvement in de-noised signal's residuals is unobvious. When the de-noised signal's residuals approach to 0.06606, the de-noised signal is close to straight line. And the computation cost is increased as layers increasing. So decomposition level of 5 is a good choice.

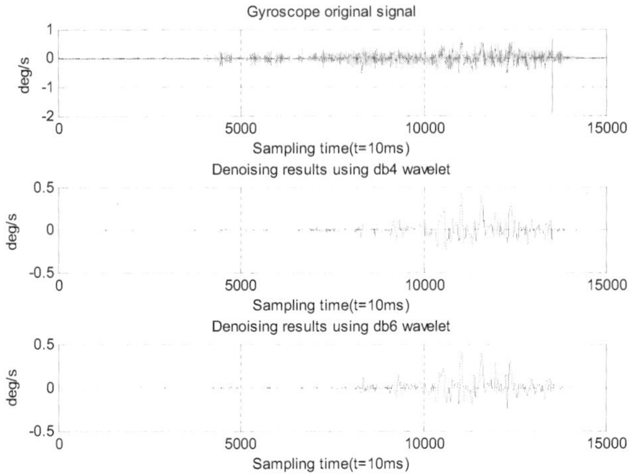

Fig. 13. Contrast of denoised signal and original signal

According to the simulation results, db4, db6 and bior5.5 may be good choice for wavelet functions, because the curve of these de-noised signal are smoother than the others. But bior5.5 have lager computation cost, it is not suitable for real time computation. In Figure 13, the de-noised signals of db4, db6 are compared with the original signal. The denoising result, got from db6 wavelet function, is smoother than the result of db4. And the de-noised signal of db6 is closer to the real angular moment of RUAV than the original signal.

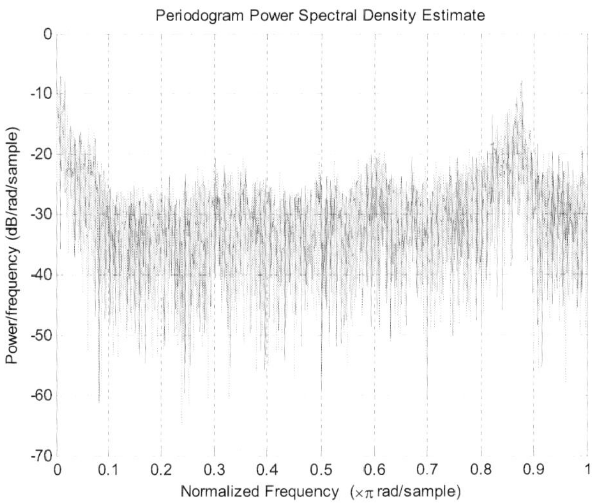

Fig. 14. The periodogram power spectral density estimate of original signal

The periodogram power spectral density estimate of original gyroscope signal is shown in Figure 14. The normalized frequency is 50Hz in this diagram. At 0.87(about 37Hz), the signal has a gain of -10db. In ServoHeli-40 RUAV system, there is a 16.7-45Hz vibration band. This vibration is caused by the rotation of main rotor, engine and tail rotor. 37Hz signal is in this noise band, and it is need to be eliminated.

For the characters of the control system, actuator system, and airframe of helicopter, the motion response of ServoHeli-40 is no more than 3Hz. The vibration frequency larger than 3Hz is out of the control of flight control system. Using the denoising result of db6 wavelet function, the spectrum energy density is analyzed. The periodogram power spectral density estimate of de-noised signal is shown in Figure 15. In this diagram, the noise signal more than 2.5Hz are eliminated by the algorithm. The wavelet filter can just remove high frequency noise. The denoising results reflected the actual movement of the aircraft. This method is suitable for denoising the noise of gyroscope.

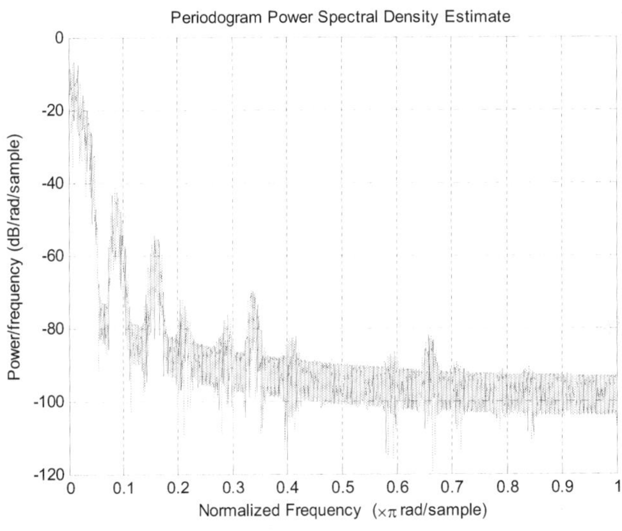

Fig. 15. The periodogram power spectral density estimate of denoised signal using db6 wavelet function

7. Conclusion

In this chapter, wavelet-based algorithm is applied to fault diagnosis and gyroscope noise reduction. Its advantage is that it does not require a prior model of a sensor. The proposed wavelet-based algorithm for fault detection of the RUAV sensor system gives us a multi-scale analysis approach to identify the feature of flight data failures, which are not readily identified by traditional approaches. The results presented in this chapter have shown that the method based on wavelet transform is a promising alternative to other approaches to the fault detection system for RUAV system. With the wavelet-based scheme, the RUAV sensor fault detection system can detect the failure locations of abrupt signal effectively. In order to overcome the drawbacks of the low-pass filter, the thresholding denoising method base on wavelet transformation is used to reduce the short-term measured noise of the MEMS gyroscope. The article compared different wavelet functions and level of decompositions, and found the effective filter parameters. Using db6 wavelet function at level 5, the de-noised signal is suitable for integrated navigation system and flight control system. This will improve the calculation precision of angle rotation matrix, and the high frequency noise will be decrease.

In the Further, further flight tests are needed to verify the actual performance of wavelet-based denoising method and wavelet-based fault detection in ServoHeli-40's integrated navigation system.

8. Acknowledgments

This work was partially supported by the National Natural Science Foundation of China, "A novel method about the flight control for flying-robot, based on the characteristics of human's brain decision" (No.61005086). And the authors gratefully acknowledge the contribution of Shenyang Institute of Automation, Chinese Academy of Sciences and reviewers' comments.

9. References

Burrus C. Sidney, Gopinath Ramesh A, Guo Haitao. (1998). *Introduction to Wavelets and Wavelet Transforms: A Primer.* Prentice Hall, Inc, 0134896009, New Jersey.

Daubechies Ingrid. (1988). Orthonormal bases of compactly supported wavelets. *Communications on Pure Applied Mathematics,* Vol.41, No.7, (October 1988), pp.(909–996), 10.1002/cpa.3160410705.

Gao Tongyue, Gong Zhenbang, Luo Jun, Ding wei, Feng wei. (2006). An Attitude Determination System For A Small Unmanned Helicopter Using Low-Cost Sensors. *Proceedings of the 2006 IEEE International Conference on Robotics and Biomimetics, 1-4244-0570-X,* Kuming China, December 2006.

Guo Jiang-chang, Teng Jian-fu, Zhang Ya-qi. (2003). The denosing of gyro signals by bi-orthogonal wavelet transform. *IEEE Canadian Conference on Electrical and Computer Engineering,* 0-7803-7781-8, Montreal, Canadian, May 2003.

Imola. K. Fodor, Chandrika Kamath, Rika Kamath. (2001). Denoising through wavelet shrinkage: An empirical study. *J. Electron. Imaging,* Vol. 12, No.1,(2003), pp. (151 - 160), 10.1117/1.1525793.

Isermann Rolf. (1984). Process fault detection based on modeling and estimation methods—A survey. *Automatica,* Vol.20, No.4, (1984), pp. (387–404), 10.1016/0005-1098(84)90098-0

Ma Jianjun, Zheng Zhiqiang, Wu Mei-ping. (2007). Spectral analysis and denoising of MIMU raw measurement. *Optics and Precision Engineering*, Vol.15, No.2, (February 2007), pp. (261-266), 10042924X(2007) 0220261206.

Mallat S, Hwang W L. (1992). Singularity detection and processing with wavelets. *IEEE Transactions on Information Theory*, Vol.38, No.2, (March 1992), pp. (617–643). 0018-9448

Napolitano M R, Windon D A, Casanova J L, Innocenti M, Silvestri G. (1998). Kalman filters and neural-network schemes for sensor validation in flight control systems. *IEEE Transactions on Control System Technology*, Vol.6, No.5, (September 1998), pp.(596–611), 1063-6536.

Qi Juntong, Han Jianda. (2007). Application of Wavelets Transform to Fault Detection in Rotorcraft uav sensor failure. *Journal of Bionic Engineering,* Vol.4, No.4, (December 2007) pp.265-270, 10.1016/S1672-6529(07)60040-7.

Qi Juntong, Song Dalei, Dai lei, Han Jianda. (2010). The ServoHeli-20 rotorcraft UAV project. *International Journal of Intelligent Systems Technologies and Applications*, Vol.8, No.1-4, (2010) pp.(57-69), 10.1504/IJISTA.2010.030190.

Qi Juntong, Zhao Xinggang, Jiang Zhe, Han Jianda. (2006). Design and implement of a rotorcraft UAV testbed. *IEEE International Conference on Robotics and Biomimetics*, 1-4244-0571-8/06, Kunming, China, December 2006.

Qu Guofu, Zhao Fan, Liu Guizhong, Liu Hongzhao. (2009). Adaptive MEMS Gyroscope Denoising Method Based on the à Trous WaveletTransform. *The Ninth International Conference on Electronic Measurement & Instruments*, 978-1-4244-3864-8/09, Beijing, China, February 2009.

Rudin W. (1976). *Principles of Mathematical Analysis* (Third), McGraw-Hill, 007054235X, New York.

Shi Yu, Zhang Xianda. (2000). Kalman-filtering-based angular velocity estimation using infrared attitude information of spacecraft. *Optics and Precision Engineering*, Vol.39, No.2, (February 2000), pp. (551-557), 10.1117/1.602394.

Song Lijun, Qin Yongyuan,Yang Pengxiang. (2009). Application of Wavelet Threshold Denosing on MEMS Gyro. *Journal of test and measurement technology*, Vol.23, No.1, (April, 2008), pp.(33-36), 1671-7449(2009)01-0033-04.

Su Li, Zhou Xue-mei. (2009). Application of improved wavelet thresholding method for de-nosing gyro signal. *Journal of Chinese Inertial Technology*, Vol.17, No.2, (April 2009), pp.(231-235), 1005-6734(2009)02-0231-05.

Wu Chong, Song Dalei, Dai Lei, Qi Juntong, Han Jianda,Wang Yuechao. (2010). Design and Implementation of a Compact RUAV Navigation System. *IEEE International Conference on Robotics and Biomimetics, 978-1-4244-9319-7,* Tianjing, China, July 2010.

Zhang Jianqiu, Ma Jun, Yan Yong. (2000). Assessing blockage of the sensing line in a differential-pressure flow sensor by using the wavelet transform of its output. *Measurement Science and Technology*, Vol.11, No.3, (March 2000), pp.(178–184),10.1088/0957-0233/11/3/302.

Zhang Jianqiu, Yan Yong. (2001). A wavelet-based approach to abrupt fault detection and diagnosis of sensors. *IEEE Transaction on Instrumentation and Measurement*, Vol. 50, No.5, (October 2001), pp.(1389–1396), 0018-9456.